P9-DFZ-737

WORLD *of* SOCIOLOGY

WORLD *of* SOCIOLOGY

Joseph M. Palmisano, *Editor*

Volume 1
A-M

GALE GROUP

Detroit
New York
San Francisco
London
Boston
Woodbridge, CT

GALE GROUP STAFF

Joseph M. Palmisano, *Editor*
Laura L. Brandau and Jennifer M. York, *Assistant Editors*

William H. Harmer and Rebecca Parks, *Contributing Editors*
Brian J. Koski, *Contributing Associate Editor*
Shelly Dickey, *Managing Editor*

Maria Franklin, *Permissions Manager*
Margaret A. Chamberlain, *Permissions Specialist*
Debra Freitas, *Permissions Associate*

Mary Beth Trimper, *Composition Manager*
Evi Seoud, *Production Manager*
Stacy L. Melson, *Buyer*

Kenn Zorn, *Product Design Manager*
Michael Logusz, *Graphic Artist*

Barbara Yarrow, *Imaging and Multimedia Content Manager*
Robyn V. Young, *Imaging and Multimedia Content Project Manager*
Randy Bassett, *Image Database Supervisor*
Pamela A. Reed, *Photography Coordinator*

Susan Kelsch, *Indexing Manager*
Lynne Maday, *Indexing Specialist*

Mark Springer, *Technical Training Specialist*

Theresa Rocklin, *Technical Support Systems Director*
Andrea Lopeman, *Programmer Analyst*

Library of Congress Cataloging-in-Publication Data

World of sociology/Joseph M. Palmisano, editor
      p.cm.
   Includes bibliographical references and indexes.
   ISBN 0-7876-4965-1 (set) - ISBN 0-7876-5070-6 (vol. 1) - ISBN 0-7876-5071-4 (vol. 2)
   1. Sociology-Encyclopedias. I. Palmisano, Joseph M.

HM585.W67 2000
301'.03-dc21   00-048399

Printed in the United States of America
10 9 8 7 6 5 4 3 2 1

CONTENTS

INTRODUCTION

Welcome to the *World of Sociology*. The 1,000 individual entries in this two–volume ready–reference source explain in concise, detailed, and jargon–free language some of the most important topics, theories, discoveries, concepts, and organizations in sociology. Brief biographical profiles of the people who have made a significant and lasting impact on the field of sociology and society in general are also included. More than 230 photographs, statistical charts, and graphs aid the reader in understanding the topics and people covered in the reference work.

World of Sociology has been designed and written with students and non–experts in mind. In so doing, we have compiled a vast array of straightforward, alphabetically arranged entries that will be useful to students who need accessible and concise information for school–related work, as well as to others who want reliable and informative introductions to the numerous aspects of the discipline of sociology.

It becomes increasingly important for all people to have a practical, theoretical, and historical understanding of sociology because it reflects real world issues—from aging, bioethics, and crime to terrorism, voting behavior, and women's studies. We hope that the entries contained in the *World of Sociology* will help you understand some of these and other important issues and how they affect you and the world in which you live.

How to Use This Book

This first edition of the *World of Sociology* has been designed with ready reference in mind.

- **Entries are arranged alphabetically**, rather than chronologically or by subdiscipline.
- **Boldfaced terms** direct readers to related entries.
- **Cross–references** at the end of entries alert readers to related entries that may not have been specifically mentioned in the body of the text.
- A **Sources Consulted** section lists many worthwhile print and electronic materials encountered in the compilation of this volume. It is offered to readers who want additional information on the topics, theories, discoveries, concepts, organizations, and people covered in this reference source.
- The **Historical Chronology** includes over two hundred significant events in the social sciences and related fields spanning from 1640 through 2000.
- A **Nationality Index** assists those readers seeking biographical profiles by national heritage.
- A **General Index** guides readers to all topics, theories, discoveries, concepts, organizations, and people mentioned in the book. Page numbers appearing in boldface indicate major treatment of entries. Italicized page numbers refer to photos, statistical charts, or graphs found throughout the *World of Sociology*.

ACKNOWLEDGMENTS

Advisory Board

In compiling this edition, we have been fortunate in being able to call upon the following people, our panel of advisors who contributed to the accuracy of the information in this premiere edition of the *World of Sociology*. To them we would like to express sincere appreciation:

Eric D. Albright
Head of Public Services
Duke Medical Center Library, Duke University
Durham, North Carolina

Bette J. Dickerson
President
Association of Black Sociologists
Professor of Sociology
American University
Washington, D.C.

Tom Horne
Selection Librarian
Seattle Public Library
Seattle, Washington

Carla B. Howery
Deputy Executive Officer
American Sociological Association, Committee on the
   Status of Women in Sociology
Washington, D.C.

Muqtedar Khan
Primary Contact
Association of Muslim Social Scientists
Professor of Political Science
Washington College
Herndon, Virginia

Harry D. Perlstadt
Primary Contact

Commission of Applied Clinical Sociology
Professor of Sociology
Michigan State University
Lansing, Michigan

Joseph H. Strauss
Executive Director
Western Social Science Association
Professor of American Indian Studies
University of Arizona
Tucson, Arizona

Contributors

Maureen Aitken, Matthew Archibald, Geraldine Azzata, Gianpaolo Baiocchi, Virginia Battista, Kari Bethel, Rose Blue, Stephanie A. Bohon, David Boyns, Rebecca Brooks, Lilian Brown, Kimberly Burton, M. Jean Campo, Neal Caren, C Lyn Carr, Bob Carrothers, Ruth Chananie, James Ciment, Corey Colyer, Amy Cooper, Heith Copes, Danielle Currier, Akosua Darkwah, Gretchen Dehart, Jeffery Dennis, Catherine Dybiec Holm, T. D. Eddins, Carla D. Edwards, Chris Fairclouth, Tina Fetner, Lydia Fink-Cox, Lara Foley, Joah Francoeur, Ellis Godard, Richard Goe, Chad Goldberg, Teresa Gowan, Jill Griffin, Terrence Hill, Laura Holland, Shirley Hollis, Kathleen Hunt, Arthur Jipson, Jodi T. Johnson, Andrew Jolivette, Steven Jones, Kent Kerley, Nikki Khanna, Paul Lachelier, Steph Lambert, Lawrence Lanahan, Jason LaTouche, Leslie Lockart, Martha Loustaunau, Maureen McClarnon, Matthew McKeever, Melodie Monahan, Gillian Murphy, Sally Myers, Corinne Naden, Pat Nation, Stephanie Nawyn, Mya Nelson, Carolette Norwood, Patricia Onorato, Erica Owens, Jean-Pierre Reed, Monica Robbers, Pamela Rohland, Melanie Sberna, Lisa L. Sharp, Elizabeth Shostak, Catherine Siebel, Karrie Snyder, Donald Stewart, Tammy Reedy Strother, Andrea Trombley, Judy Van Wyk, Dane Walker, Susan Marnell Weaver, Laura West, Esther I. Wilder, Jonathan R. Wivagg, Aaron Young, Nicole Youngman.

A

ABNORMAL

When used in the sociological arena, the term *abnormal* means anything deviating from the usual or typical pattern of behavior or social form within a **society** or **group**, especially where such behavior can also be viewed as maladjustment, maladaptation, or **dysfunction**.

However, any sociological use of the term faces the problem of determining "normality." For example, French sociologist Émile Durkheim made the assumption that the average social form at a particular level of social development was also the functional form. However, while conceptions of functional normality and abnormality may be relatively evident in relation to biological organisms, the utility of these concepts in **sociology** has been widely questioned. With the partial exception of Durkheim and functionalist sociology, sociologists have usually conceptualized individual and social variability and deviation from established patterns of behavior in ways other than in terms of "normality" and "abnormality."

ABOLITION

Slavery has existed throughout nearly all of recorded history. Calls for its end, or abolition, did not begin in earnest until the eighteenth century. In early Greek and Roman civilizations, slavery was an accepted way of life. Holy Wars between Muslims and Christians in the Middle Ages added to the slave population. When Spanish explorers reached South America in the fifteenth century, they enslaved the natives and put them to work in the fields and mines, where they died in alarming numbers from harsh treatment and exposure to European diseases. Thus came the need for importing slaves from the Old World to work in the New World. In 1619, the first African slaves in North America arrived at the English colony of Jamestown, Virginia. As the slave population grew, so did cries for abolition. With the Enlightenment, an intellectual movement in Eu-

rope, societies were formed to end the slave trade. This was known as the Abolitionist Movement (1783–1888) in western Europe and the Americas.

The Abolitionist Movement in the United States and other parts of the world took different routes. By the Middle Ages, the slavery of serfs, a captive **labor force** for the gentry, was already on the way out in Europe. In 1833, Britain abolished slavery and set up a system to provide training for ex-slaves and compensation for the former slave owners. But it was not until 1838 that slaves in the West Indies and South Africa were freed and not until 1843 that slavery was declared illegal in British India. As part of its revolutionary reforms in 1848, France abolished slavery in its territories, as did Denmark. Russia in 1861 and Romania in 1864 became the last European countries to emancipate the serfs. During the last half of the nineteenth century, slavery was virtually abolished in South America. Spain had freed most of its slaves on the mainland by the 1850s, then in Puerto Rico in 1873 and Cuba in 1886. The Dutch freed their slaves in 1863. The last country in South America to abolish slavery was Brazil, in 1888.

Abolition in the United States, however, was in a sense more difficult because it was far more a domestic than a colonial issue. The economic and social **structure** of the South depended on slaves. Cotton was king, and cotton needed cheap labor. There is no labor cheaper than slavery.

The Abolitionist Movement in the United States met with fierce resistance. One of the first groups to call for slavery's end was the Quakers, a religious group with a long history of fighting for **peace** and **justice**. The great abolitionist, William Lloyd Garrison (1805–1879), was a relentless crusader. His newspaper *The Liberator* became America's most uncompromising antislavery journal. Although a pacifist, when civil war was imminent, Garrison backed the policies of Abraham Lincoln.

As the nation struggled with pro- and antiabolitionist forces, certain factors made war inevitable. The compromises of 1820 and 1850 only prolonged the argument over slavery in the new states and territories. The Fugitive Slave Law of

Among these twelve members of the Pennsylvania Abolition Society was William Lloyd Garrison (bottom right) *(The Library of Congress)*.

1850, which mandated that runaways be returned to their owners, brought out such ruthless behavior by slave hunters that even fence-sitters in the North began to revolt. And in 1852, a highly emotional response to an antislavery novel by Harriet Beecher Stowe, *Uncle Tom's Cabin*, threw many doubters into the abolitionist camp.

After Abraham Lincoln was elected in 1860, 11 southern states seceded. The result was four years of civil war (1861–1865) and a Union victory. With passage of the Thirteenth Amendment to the Constitution (1865), slavery was abolished forever in the United States.

Legally, slavery no longer exists. Mauritania in Africa became the last country in the world to abolish it in 1980, although people are still thought to be held there in servitude. Since Bosnia declared independence from Yugoslavian 1991, fighting has continued among Serbs, Muslims, and Croats. Serbs continually have been charged with holding refugees in forced labor camps as part of "ethnic cleansing." The organization known as Amnesty International maintains that slavery exists in poor rural areas of the Andes Mountains of South America where governments cannot or are unwilling to intervene.

See also Slavery and Involuntary Servitude

ABSOLUTISM

Absolutism is the political practice of unlimited power and absolute sovereignty, especially as held by a monarch. The control is total; the checks and balances that apply to most democratic systems are nonexistent. Louis XIV, who ruled France from 1643 to 1715, gave perhaps the most direct description of absolutism when he said, *"L'etat c'est moi"* ("I am the state").

Throughout recorded history, absolutism has existed in various forms, often for long periods of time. The ancient Babylonian and Assyrian civilizations were governed by principles of absolutism, as was ancient Egypt until about the middle of the fifth dynasty (c. 2450 BC). The pharaoh, or head of state, held the position of absolute ruler. Life or death, feast or famine rested solely on the whim, pleasure, or displeasure of the monarch. Gradually, however, the pharaoh's control in Egypt began to shift until it became more that of a head of a small, elite ruling group, still totally awesome in power but not completely absolute. In contrast, political **authority** in the ancient civilizations of Greece and Rome was held by dictators whose complete control was often mitigated by powerful forces within the governing **structure**.

Beginning about the Middle Ages, new nation-states could survive only with political control over the strong authority of feudal lords and the church. Control took the form of absolute power, which the monarch as head of the state exercised. By the eighteenth century, the absolute monarch prevailed in much of western Europe. In addition to Louis XIV, the Tudors in the person of Henry VIII, ruler of England 1509-1547, and James I of the House of Stuart, who took the throne on the death of Elizabeth I in 1603, epitomized this new type of political **organization**. In defense of absolute rule came the simple justification of "the divine right of kings." If kings derived their authority from God, they were justified in their rule, no matter how tyrannical or how harsh the punishment of their people. At first, this power coincided with the spiritual control held by the leader of the Roman Catholic Church. In time, however, monarchs assumed control over the church as well as the state. Further justification for absolutism was the assertion that a nation's order and security relied on complete obedience to one strong leader.

Revolutions in America and France challenged the idea of absolutism in the eighteenth century. These occurred long after a Puritan revolution in England had diluted the power of the monarch. As constitutional government in various forms spread throughout the world in the nineteenth century, absolutism was replaced even in nations, such as Russia and Japan, where it had been deeply entrenched.

The twentieth century witnessed a new brand of absolutism with the emergence of the totalitarian concept of fascism in Germany under Adolf Hitler and in Italy under Benito Mussolini. The word, fascism, itself is derived from the Italian *fascismo*, which comes from the Latin *fasces*, a bundle of rods with an ax, which was the sign of authority in ancient Rome. The Fascist party in Italy and the National Socialist (Nazi) movement in Germany differed in that Hitler was far more intent on attaining racial and national power and security. Yet, both systems were committed to the doctrine of total, absolute authority by the state and submission of individual will to the so-called unified will of the people. Theoretically, that unified will is expressed by the leader, such as Hitler, who speaks for the state and who is the state. Totalitarianism seeks to dominate all aspects of human life, whereas absolutism in its ancient form sought control mainly over **government** and politics.

In the twenty-first century, the theory of absolutism is related to the power system known as authoritarianism. Under this rule, one person or a group of persons acting as a unit assumes all powers of the state. In practice if not in theory in modern **society**, authoritarianism operates much like absolutism. Examples of modern authoritarian rule include Fidel Castro, who took over leadership of the Caribbean island of Cuba in 1959, and the late religious leader Ayatollah Khomeini, who, in 1979, was named both political and religious leader of Iran for life.

ACCOUNTABILITY

The term "accountability" implies the ability to take responsibility for an action or an intention. The idea of such responsibility and the opinions surrounding it have existed probably since humans gathered together for survival. Responsibility is alluded to in the Bible; Luke 12:48 reads, "For unto whomsoever much is given, of him shall be much required," which was paraphrased slightly by John F. Kennedy in a 1961 speech when he said, "For of those to whom much is given, much is required." John D. Rockefeller, Jr. spoke about it, too:"every right implies a responsibility, every opportunity, an obligation."

The British philosopher **Jeremy Bentham** (1748–1832) brought a pragmatic interpretation of accountability to socio logical literature. Bentham believed that all humans were accountable for providing equal happiness to all. Bentham, who took his ideas beyond theorizing, was active in reforming aspects of **government**, law, the educational system, and religions. Bentham wrote *An Introduction to the Principles of Morals and Legislation,* published in 1789.

French philosopher **Jean-Paul Sartre** (1905–1980) wrote extensively on responsibility and believed that freedom and responsibility were naturally connected. Sartre stated that many people denied their own freedom and thus evaded personal responsibility. The existentialist movement, prevalent in the nineteenth and twentieth centuries and associated with Sartre, pondered the effect of such freedom in people's everyday lives. Sartre's companion, the French feminist Simone de Beauvoir (1908–1986), also wrote about responsibility and accountability. De Beauvoir believed that while humans are born free, they generally live in a state of ambiguity and must assume responsibility for their lives as well as independence.

The issue of accountability and responsibility arose in surprising ways toward the end of the twentieth century. An editorial in *Reason* (June 1998) puzzled over the fact that after a school shooting in Jonesboro, Arkansas, the governor blamed **society** as a whole for the **crime** rather than laying blame solely on the perpetrators. The author, Brian Doherty, claimed that such socially injurious behavior would be more readily resolved by tracing accountability to those who committed the injurious act. Beyond taking responsibility for wrongs committed, the issue of accountability also has a positive side, such as when societal leaders advise young adults to assume responsibility for making contributions to society. For example, a Florida college dean urged her students in a graduation speech to be accountable to leaving something behind in life that the next generation can use.

ACHIEVED STATUS

Achieved status is any of a range of social positions within a **group** or **society** that is attained through effort or achievement. Generally, an achieved status is any status in which individuals must have accomplished some acts or goals in order to legitimately claim those particular positions. Examples of achieved statuses include personal relationships (friend, spouse), **professions** and occupations (doctor, retail manager), and hobbies and recreational activities (stamp collector, sports fan). In his 1936 work *The Study of Man*, Ralph Linton was the first to highlight the importance of delineating the difference between positions gained through effort and those conveyed by extraneous forces.

Achieved status is consistently paired with **ascribed status** (statuses or social positions that are conferred by society with no consideration of the individual's abilities or characteristics such as sex, **race**, or kinship).Ascribed and achieved status are typically viewed as opposite poles of a spectrum ranging from positions based solely on individual achievement (achieved) to positions which completely ignore personal accomplishments (ascribed). Actually these concepts tend to work more in a system of direct opposition than as points along a continuum. Often an individual's ascribed status impedes progress toward a goal, making achievement more difficult, or altering the expectations and requirements for achievement. For example, becoming a construction worker may be more difficult for a woman because the expectations and stereotypic **norms** accompanying the female gender generally opposed to construction work. The perceived inability of women to meet the requirements for this type of labor will reduce the chances that any woman will be given the opportunity to compete for this position.

Some positions such as social class can be argued to be both ascribed and achieved at various points in individuals' lives. Although individuals' socio-economic standings are often the direct result of achieved statuses, the social classes into which they are born remain beyond their control, potentially allowing for this status to fit the definition for either. Moreover, achieved statuses tend to be more highly valued in **American society** due to the emphasis on individuality and personal accomplishment. This emphasis on achievement often results in the downplaying and ignoring of the potential effects of ascribed status on achievement potential thereby providing an inaccurate picture of those who fail to attain desired positions.

ACQUIRED IMMUNE DEFICIENCY SYNDROME

Also known as AIDS, Acquired Immune Deficiency Syndrome is caused by an infection of the human immunodeficiency virus (HIV) and belongs to a family of similar viruses called *retroviruses*. HIV is transmitted through direct contact with an infected person's bodily fluids. These fluids are: blood, semen, breast milk, urine, and (for about 1% of HIV positive

New U.S. AIDS cases decreasing

AIDS cases diagnosed per year in the United States, to 1997

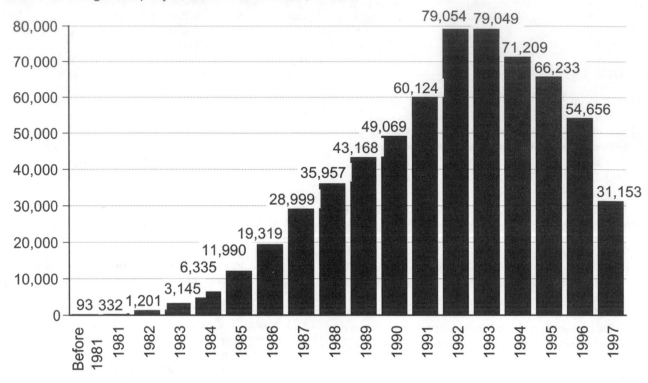

Source: "HIV/AIDS Surveillance Report, Vol 9, No. 2," Centers for Disease Control, 1998

individuals) a trace of the virus in saliva. They reverse the normal production order within the cells that they infect, a process called *reverse transcription*. The origin of AIDS is not clear. Recently, it has come to light that more than one virus is responsible for the ascendancy of the AIDS pandemic, but HIV is responsible for the most cases.

According to the World Health Organization (WHO), by late 1997 about 31 million people worldwide were infected with HIV, the vast majority of whom live in developing nations of whom live in developing nations. WHO predicts that this number will reach forty million or more in the year 2000, with ninety percent of this total living in developing countries in Africa, Asia, Latin America, and the Caribbean. Furthermore, it was projected that by the end of the twentieth century, at least two million people worldwide would die each year of AIDS.

Nearly seventy percent of the world's HIV-infected people live in Africa. The demographic impact of AIDS is most immediate and serious in two geographic areas: Central-Austral African and West Africa, specifically in the country of Côte d'Ivoire. In both regions, falling **life expectancy** and increasing **infant and child mortality** have already been observed.

Given the high proportion of the population already infected —up to thirty percent of young adults in some urban areas— and the high mortality resulting from the **disease**, a further impact over the next two decades is inevitable in these areas.

In some sub-Saharan African nations, such as South Africa, the number of HIV-infected persons is doubling every five to twelve months, and AIDS is currently the leading cause of adult death in several of these countries. In Uganda, one of the nations most devastated by AIDS, almost every family has been touched by this dreaded disease.

According to WHO, the rate of HIV infections is higher for women than men in most African nations. In several large cities in Africa, one out of three pregnant women are HIV infected. A large percentage of these women are monogamous but nevertheless have been infected by husbands who according to long-lived African tradition, are not. According to one expert on African cultural traditions, African women "who are conditioned to their husbands having other women, are not in a position to negotiate safe sex, with the result that they develop reproductive tract infections which, in turn, increase their risk of contracting HIV." In one recent study almost four thousand men and women in Nigeria were interviewed regarding their attitudes about male **sexual behavior**. The majority of the respondents, both males and females, indicated that men are naturally nonmonogamous irrespective of their marital **status**. The widespread nature of these cultural beliefs in African nations is just one of many factors that hinder efforts to slow the HIV/AIDS pandemic in this hardest-hit area of the world.

Africa is not alone in suffering the ravages of the HIV/AIDS pandemic. The contingent of Asia now ranks second to Africa in the number of cases of HIV/AIDS, and many world health experts fear that in the near future Asia may surpass Africa, led by countries such as India and Thailand, where HIV/AIDS is fast becoming endemic in the population. HIV/AIDS is also rapidly expanding in Latin America. As in Africa, HIV is primarily transmitted by heterosexual activity in both Asia and Latin America, and women are often the hardest hit by this deadly epidemic.

Thailand is a country that has seen the epidemic sweep through its population with unprecedented speed since the first case of AIDS was reported in 1984. An estimated 700,000 to 1 million Thai citizens are HIV infected. One of the primary reasons why the HIV epidemic is raging in Thailand is that a commercial sex industry flourishes in this country, where it is something of a cultural tradition for men to use the services of a prostitute. One recent study found that fifty percent of married men and forty-three percent of single men had visited a female prostitute sometime in their lives, and that thirteen percent of married men had done so with the previous year. This is an especially troubling finding in light of other research indicating that over fifty percent of Thailand's female sex workers are HIV infected.

The infection on infants at birth or shortly thereafter is fast emerging as an especially tragic consequence of the global HIV/AIDS pandemic. WHO estimates that well over a million children worldwide are infected with HIV, the majority is sub-Saharan Africa. Babies often acquire HIV from their mothers through breast-feeding. As awareness of this mode of transmission increases, another dimension might be added to the horror of Africa's HIV/AIDS tragedy. Clearly, many African children, who live in conditions of **poverty**, would suffer from lack of proper nourishment if they could no longer be breast-fed.

One additional horrific aspect of Africa's struggle with HIV/AIDS is beginning to emerge. A recent report from the United Nations Program on HIV/AIDS estimated that there will be more than ten million African children orphaned by the disease by the beginning of the twenty-first century.

In the United States, almost 645,000 cumulative cases of AIDS had been reported by January 1998, and almost 400,000 had died of the disease since it was first diagnosed in 1981. An estimated 650,000 to more than 1 million people in the United States are currently infected with HIV. To date, about 31 million people worldwide are HIV infected.

The number of new AIDS cases reported annually in the United States grew rapidly through the early 1980s, increasing by about eighty-five percent per year, reaching a peak growth rate in the middle of the decade. The rate of new AIDS diagnoses slowed in the late 1980s, and this more moderate rate has continued into the 1990s. As reflected in the table ''New U.S. AIDS Cases Decreasing,'' a steady decline in reported AIDS cases from 1994 through 1997 is consistent with the belief that the AIDS epidemic in the United States has leveled off. Yet, even in light of these numbers, it appears that a second-wave of the AIDS epidemic in the United States may be gaining momentum outside the traditional exposure categories, population groups, and geographic areas hit hardest by the first wave. An escalation of AIDS in young age categories and those due to heterosexual contact represent relatively recent trends suggesting that HIV infection is an endemic problem that will affect future generations.

ADAPTATION

Adaptation is the process through which social systems respond to their environment. In physical terms, all cultures develop strategies to survive within their particular habitats. Traditional Inuit societies, for example, adapted to an environment that is extremely cold and had almost no vegetation. They sew fur clothing; make sea kayaks from animal skins; use snow, sod, or skins for shelter; hunt with bows and arrows and harpoons; and travel over ice-covered terrain by dogsled. The San, an African culture, adapt to an extremely arid climate by living as nomadic hunters and gatherers. They live in portable lightweight huts, keep few possessions, hunt with poison-tipped arrows or snares, and make carrying bags from animal skins.

The role of adaptation in cultural and institutional change was of particular interest to neoevolutionary theorists, including anthropologists Leslie A. White and Julian H. Steward. Their work focused on issues of general human evolution, as well as on ways in which different cultures adapted to similar environments. Sociologist **Talcott Parsons**, however, articulated what is considered the most complex **theory** of how adaptation is used by organizations (including **family** groups, corporations, and **nation-states**). He considered adaptation to be one of four functional prerequisites necessary for the survival of any social system. He theorized that social evolutionary breakthroughs, such as **language** and writing, monetary systems, legal structures, markets, **bureaucracy**, and stratification, enhanced a society's ''general adaptive capacity,'' and that the development of a specialized economy satisfied the need for adaptation in industrialized societies.

ADDAMS, (LAURA) JANE (1860-1935)
American social reformer and feminist

(Laura) Jane Addams (1860–1935), a social reformer, internationalist, and feminist, was the first American woman to win the Nobel prize for peace. Best known as the founder of Chicago's **Hull House**, one of the first social settlements in North America, she was widely recognized for her numerous books and articles, social activism, and international efforts for world peace.

Addams was born in Cedarville, Illinois, on September 6, 1860, the eighth of nine children of Sarah and John Huy Ad-

Jane Addams *(The Library of Congress)*

dams. When she was only two, her mother died in childbirth. Her father, a prosperous businessman and Illinois state senator, was a friend of President Abraham Lincoln and a widely respected leader in the community.

In 1881 Addams graduated from Rockford College (then Rockford Women's Seminary), the valedictorian of a class of 17. Over the next six years, while intermittently studying medicine, she traveled and studied in Europe, battled an illness characterized by chronic exhaustion, and underwent surgery for a congenital spinal defect.

Confronted with the limited **career** opportunities available to women in the late nineteenth century, Addams searched for a way to be of service to society. In 1888, at age 27, during a second tour of Europe, she and a college friend, Ellen Gates Starr, visited a pioneering settlement house called Toynbee Hall in a desperately poor area of London. This visit crystallized in their minds the idea of opening a similar facility in one of Chicago's most underprivileged working-class neighborhoods.

The two friends returned home to a city that Lincoln Steffens, a famous writer of the period, described as "loud, lawless, unlovely, ill-smelling, new; an overgrown gawk of a

village, the teeming tough among cities." In 1889, Addams acquired a large, vacant mansion built by Charles Hull in 1856 at the corner of Halsted and Polk Streets. She and Ellen Starr moved in and opened the doors of Hull House on September 18, 1889.

The settlement house was an immediate success. By the end of its second year, Hull House was host to two thousand people every week and was soon famous throughout the country. Journalists, educators, and researchers came to observe its operations, well-to-do young women gave their time and effort, and well-known social workers and reformers lived at the settlement and assisted in its activities.

Hull House eventually included 13 buildings and a playground as well as a camp near Lake Geneva, Wisconsin. Facilities included a day nursery, a gymnasium, a community kitchen, and a boarding club for working women. Among the services provided were the city's first kindergarten and day care center. Hull House also offered college-level courses in various subjects; training in art, music, and crafts; and the nation's first little theater group, the Hull House players. An **employment** bureau, an art gallery, and libraries and social clubs for men, women, and children were among other services and cultural opportunities offered to the largely immigrant population of the neighborhood.

As her reputation increased, Addams expanded her vision to focus on many crucial social issues of the time. Local activities at Hull House gave way to national activities on behalf of the underprivileged. In 1906 she became the first woman president of the National Conference of Charities and Corrections. She led investigations on midwifery, narcotics consumption, milk supplies, and sanitary conditions. In 1910 she received the first honorary degree ever awarded to a woman by Yale University.

In 1914, at the onset of World War I (1914–1918), Addams worked for peace, refusing to endorse American participation in the war. For her opposition, she was expelled from the Daughters of the American Revolution and widely attacked in the press. She devoted herself to providing relief supplies of food to the women and children of the enemy nations. In 1915 she accepted the chairmanship of the Women's Peace Party and, four months later, was named president of the International Congress of Women. That organization later became the Women's International Peace League for Peace and Freedom, of which Addams remained president until her death.

In 1931, with Nicholas Murray Butler, Addams was named a co-winner of the Nobel prize for peace. Hospitalized for heart problems at the time of the award ceremony, she was unable to deliver the Nobel lecture in Oslo. She died in 1935 of cancer; appropriately, her funeral service took place in the courtyard of Hull House.

ADOLESCENCE

Adolescence can be defined as the transitional period between childhood and **adulthood** that is marked by numerous physical changes along with psychological, intellectual, and emotional developments. Traditionally, the stage of adolescence, commonly defined as between 12 and 19 years old, with wide allowance for individual variants to the typical timetable, has been characterized as a time of turbulence, rebellion, and instability. Changes in social, emotional, and physical development, often occurring concurrently, can be complex and confusing and consequently bring on a crisis of **identity** and self-esteem that are manifested in forms ranging from moodiness to delinquency. However, recent scholars have questioned the validity of the crisis **paradigm** and have offered new theories of adolescent development that describe the period in a more positive light.

Except for the physical changes that take place in conjunction with the ability to reproduce, all other stages of adolescent development are socially defined. The transition into adulthood is primarily a result of taking on the roles and responsibilities associated with adult life. Historically, in agrarian societies, adolescence is a brief, sometimes barely recognizable, period between childhood and adulthood and is closely associated with the arrival of puberty. The adult roles of **employment** for men and childbearing for women are assumed during the second decade of life. In industrial societies, employment is postponed by educational needs, thus extending the adolescent period. Although the physical marks of adulthood are acquired (e.g., ability to reproduce, facial hair for boys, breast development for girls), adolescents are denied access to adult roles, such as full-time employment, marriage, and independence.

Numerous physical developments, **role** changes, and identity issues are commonly associated with the teen years. First, puberty brings marked physical changes to both boys and girls. Girls begin menstruation and develop breasts and pubic hair. Boys grow facial and pubic hair. Their voices get lower and their muscle structure develops. Second, peer relations become more important and influential than parent relations. Peer pressure is often seen as a powerful negative **influence** that provokes antisocial behavior such as drinking and drug use. Third, the time of adolescence is a period of noticeable cognitive and social learning. Not only do teens learn more, they process the information differently using new intellectual abilities such as abstract thinking, propositional logic, and deductive reasoning. These new skills lead to improved cognitive development and to a better understanding of social roles and expectations, namely, **moral development**. Finally, in Western society, adolescents are expected to take on more economic responsibility, which can materialize as working part-time or deciding future careers and necessary educational paths.

The paradigm of adolescence as a period of crisis was introduced early in the twentieth century by G. Stanley Hall. Social changes brought on by technological advancements and industrialization had, for the first time in history, created a large **group** of post-puberty youth who had not yet entered adult roles and relationships. Namely, adolescence as a significant and extended life stage came into existence. Hall's initial assessment of adolescence as marked by strife, conflict, and inner turmoil became so widely accepted that it practically de-

Major changes occur during adolescence that can produce such concerns as peer pressure and dating or sex issues *(Field Mark Publications)*.

fined the term. Until the last two decades of the twentieth century, this paradigm dominated the study of adolescence and the differences among scholars revolved around various approaches and theories as a means to explain the onset of the adolescent crisis.

Three approaches have been used to account for the changes and developments associated with the adolescent years: psychoanalytical, mechanistic, and organismic. Each paradigm is distinct in the importance it places on internal and external factors and its formulation of the role and function of changes in adolescents. The psychoanalytical approach is commonly associated with the psychosexual assessment of **Sigmund Freud** who believed that inner urges and impulses, sexual in nature, drive human behavior, and life's struggle is to overcome and control those desires. Freud saw adolescence as a time of great sexual awakening and, consequently, great inner strife. Thus, the adolescent's goal is to disengage from childhood caretakers and develop an independent personality.

Unlike Freud's psychosexual theory of inner conflict, the mechanistic paradigm places primary importance on external, social factors as the triggers for adolescent developments. Exemplified by the social learning theory of Albert Bandura, mechanistic theory developed out of the **behaviorism** approach of John Watson and B. F. Skinner. Conducting research during the 1960s, Bandura was an early critic of the traditional approach to adolescent studies. He saw social influences as the primary determining factor in adolescent behavior and condemned social scientists for overstating the importance of biological changes. Because environmental factors precipitate change throughout the lifespan, adolescence is viewed as part of the ongoing process of a lifetime of change and development.

Rather than focusing on what happens to an adolescent as the determinant of a behavior, the organismic theorists explore how adolescents interpret events. In a combination of inner and outer influence, adolescents internally process external factors which in turn account for development, change, and behavior. Proponents of the organismic paradigm also tend to distinguish patterns or **stages of development** through the life **cycle** that are constant and repeated, although the timing and duration can be widely divergent. There are several major organismic theories, including psychosocial, represented by Erik Erikson, and cognitive, represented by **Jean Piaget** and **Lawrence Kohlberg**. Both theories share an understanding that development occurs in stages that are passed through by all individuals. Erikson, like Freud, viewed adolescence as a period of developing emotional maturity and believed that the teen years were crucial in the development of an individual's identity. Unlike Freud, however, Erikson acknowledged both emotional and social factors in identity development. Piaget, and his follower Kohlberg, understood development as an intellectual, rather than emotional, activity. As individuals pass through life stages, not only do they learn more, they learn qualitatively differently. Whereas a child may not steal candy for fear of punishment, an adult may not steal because of the moral implications and social expectations. Thus, adolescence is a period of intellectual development that results in new cognitive abilities that prepare the adolescent for adulthood.

The traditional understanding of adolescent has not gone without criticism. Research conducted by J.C. Coleman and L. Hendry, which resulted in the publication of *The Nature of Adolescence* (1990), suggests that emotional turmoil and rebellious behavior are not inherent to the adolescent period. In fact, such crises are neither a normal nor a healthy part of growing up as they have been previously characterized. The occurrence of dysfunctional behavior, such as emotional problems, eating disorders, and depression, was found only in a minority of teenagers. According to Coleman, although their relevance tends to be exaggerated by social scientists, major changes do occur during the teen years that can produce concern, such as parental relations, peer pressure, and dating or sex issues. However, the adolescent usually addresses each concern at different times. Because these stressful life changes are staggered, it is possible for a teen to move successfully through these stressful changes. Adolescents develop difficulties in coping when they must deal with two or more concerns simultaneously. This shift of paradigms points to a new path for the study of adolescence that focuses more carefully upon the social expectations placed on teens along with the cultural definitions of childhood, adolescence, and adulthood.

ADOPTION

Adoption refers to a legal act that creates a relationship between a parent and child. Roman law originally recognized adoption, but it did not become law in the United States until the mid-1800s. By the early 1990s, adoption was law in all of the states as well as Great Britain. The law was developed to create a legal bond between a child and an adult other than the child's biological parent. Establishing this bond usually requires the consent of the adopting adult as well as that of the child, given that the child is beyond a certain age.

Adoption confers certain rights and responsibilities for both parties; adoptive parents assume the rights and duties of biological parents while adopted children assume those of biological children. Natural parents who agree to release a biological child for adoption relinquish their rights and duties concerning the adopted child. In parts of the United States, however, an adopted child may still legally inherit assets from a biological parent. As a legal process, adoption is usually established in court under a judge.

Issues concerning adoption made a sociological impact on the United States during the twentieth century. For example, in 1999 Oregon passed legislation making it possible for adoptees (of 21 years or older) to be provided with the their biological parents' identity. Previously, despite the desire to contact their biological parents, adoptees did not have legal access to the information. Such legislation may affect negatively those biological parents who do not want to be contacted by the child they gave up for adoption.

Increased awareness of **human rights** for gays and lesbians in the late twentieth century resulted in more public attempts by same-sex couples to adopt children. Toward the end of the twentieth century gay couples in the United States could adopt through private, international, or social service channels, but these couples risked societal disapproval and expensive social service adoptions.

During the twentieth century, international upheaval (including poverty, famine, and **war**) caused many babies from struggling countries to be available for adoption into families from wealthier countries, such as the United States. For example, economic collapse in Russia resulted in 113,000 children in 1997 and in 1998 becoming available for adoption. However, desperate economic conditions in distressed countries gave adoption facilitators the opportunity to charge extremely high prices of those wishing to adopt.

ADORNO, THEODOR W. (1903-1969)
German philosopher

German philosopher Theodor W. Adorno (1903–1969) moved freely across academic disciplines exploring contemporary European **culture** and the predicament of modern man. A leading member of the influential intellectual movement known as the Frankfurt school, he was born in Frankfurt-am-Main, Germany, on September 11, 1903, the only son of an upper middle-class family. His father, Oskar Wiesengrund, was an assimilated Jewish merchant; his musically gifted mother, Maria Calvalli-Adorno, of Italian-Catholic descent. He adopted his mother's patronomic Adorno in the late 1930s.

An economically secure, artistically rich home encouraged Adorno's talents in both music and humanities. Adorno was encouraged by his mother to study piano, his mastery of which sustained his interest in music's philosophical and technical aspects. Enrolled at the Frankfurt University, Adorno was interested in **philosophy**, **psychology**, **sociology**, and music, and he wrote a dissertation on Husserl's **phenomenology**. Impressed by *Wozzeck*, Alban Berg's opera, Adorno began a serious study of music. Two years in Vienna taught Adorno about contemporary music and led him even to attempt musical composition. Adorno analyzed published on the work of Schoenberg.

Returning to Frankfurt in 1925 Adorno wrote two *Habilitationsschrift,* the second of which (on Søren Kierkegaard) qualified him for university appointment. The chief contention of his *Habilitationsschrift* was that Kierkegaard, having rejected Georg Hegel's grandiose systematization of philosophy, retreated into pure subjectivity.

Adorno informally joined the Institute for Social Research, established in 1923 as an affiliated body of the Frankfurt school. Marxist in outlook, the Institute researchers were concerned with intellectual work rather than direct political action.

Adorno began teaching philosophy at his alma mater in 1931, but Hitler's seizure of power disrupted Adorno's academic career and eventually forced him into exile. Adorno went to Oxford, England (1934–1937) and then to the United States. He returned to Germany in 1949 to resume teaching at Frankfurt University. Jewish suffering and the crimes of the Third Reich became his major concerns.

Adorno wrote for the Institute's official journal: "The Social Condition of Music" in the first issue (1932); "Jazz" (1936); and the more important "Fetish Character of Music and the Regression of the Listeners" (1936). In the last, Adorno observed that the commercially oriented music industry manipulates listeners' musical tastes. Helpless listeners are seduced into accepting arbitrary cuts and interruptions in radio broadcasting. He maintained that such cuts are made for commercial gains at the expense of the music's integrity and in disregard of listeners' intelligence. This article details his arguments against the culture industry which were developed more fully in his later writings.

In the United States (1937–1949) Adorno worked on a number of projects which the members of the Institute for Social Research conducted individually or collectively. At Princeton, he played a leading role in a large collaborative project which resulted in the publication of the influential *Authoritarian Personality.* Toward the end of the war Adorno and Horkheimer wrote *Dialectic of Enlightenment* published in Amsterdam (1947). Defining enlightenment as demythologizing, the authors traced the process of taming nature in Western civilization. The argument here is that in the name of enlightenment a technological civilization which sets humans apart from nature has been developed causing dehumanization and regimentation in modern **society**. They asserted that **civilization** is an instrument for controlling nature and people rather than enhancing human dignity and originality. In the book's 1969 edition, shortly before Adorno's death, the authors declared that the enlightenment led to **positivism** and to identification of intelligence with what is hostile to spirit (Geistfeindschaft).

After World War II many Frankfurt school members remained in the United States or in Great Britain, but Horkheimer and Adorno returned to Germany. Adorno returned to Germany in 1949 although he spent a year in the United States in 1952. Adorno wrote many articles and books and trained a new generation of German scholars. The true extent of his originality cannot be determined until the projected twenty-three volumes of his complete works are available.

In 1951 he published *Minima Moralia: Reflections from Damaged Life* consisting of articles he wrote during the war.

During the late twentieth century, international upheaval caused many children from Eastern Europe to be available for adoption *(AP/Wide World Photos, Inc.).*

The most personal of his writings, these short essays were written in an aphoristic style reminiscent of Schopenhauer and Nietzsche.

Negative Dialectics (1966), is a sustained polemic against the dream of philosophers from Aristotle to Hegel to construct philosophical systems enclosing coherently arranged propositions and proofs. One terse statement in the book is "Bluntly put, closed systems are bound to fail." As this statement indicates, Adorno's aim in this book was to vindicate the vitality and intractability of reason.

Prisms, (1967) another major work, contains essays on a wide range of topics from **Thorstein Veblen** to Franz Kafka. However, the main theme in the book is the gradual decomposition of culture under the impact of instrumental reason. In this book and in *Aesthetic Theory,* his last major work unfinished at the time of his death in 1969 but edited and published posthumously, Adorno advanced the thesis that the integrity of creative works lies in the autonomous acts of artists who are at once submerged in and triumphant over social forces.

A persistent critic of positivism in philosophy and sociology and a bitter foe of commercialism and dehumanization

In recent times, adult education has reflected an era of rapidly evolving technology *(Corbis Corporation [Bellevue])*.

promoted by the culture industry, Adorno championed individual dignity and creativity in an age increasingly menaced by what he regarded as mindless **standardization** and abject conformity. At a time when many academic philosophers were weary of dealing with questions for fear of violating the canon of rigorous philosophical reasoning, Adorno boldly asserted that the function of philosophy is to make sense out of the totality of human experience. Adorno, who was hailed as one of the ideological godfathers of the New Left Movement in the 1960s because of his indictment of both **capitalism** and **communism**, was criticized and humiliated by his former followers for his opposition to violent social activism.

ADULT EDUCATION

Adult education in one form or another has been part of the American ideal since the colonies were first settled. One aspect of the philosophical rejection of European class systems was the idea that individuals should be given the opportunity to improve themselves. Another important part of the loosely organized system that developed involved citizenship classes for the new immigrants who started arriving in huge numbers in the 1830s.

With President Lyndon Johnson's Great Society plan of 1964, the federal government began to operate a truly organized educational system for adults. The Adult Basic Education (ABE) program of that year began a cooperative effort of the federal and state governments to provide basic education opportunities for adults who had not finished school. The program was run by local school districts using federal grant money provided by the Department of Health, Education, and Welfare (HEW). In 1981 English as a Second Language became a key part of the curriculum.

In 1998 the Workforce Investment Act (WIA) replaced ABE, and the focus shifted from general education to a partnership between education and the local business community. This change was meant to emphasize job training in an era of rapidly evolving technology. Even the skills of relatively well-educated people were in danger of becoming quickly obsolete in the new marketplace—a syndrome that the WIA sought to prevent.

ADULTHOOD

The transition into adulthood does not occur within the context of a single event but rather takes place over a period of time and is marked by both formal and informal rites of passage. The timing of this transition tends to be ambiguous because the transitional markers vary by social and economic conditions, are numerous and often informal, and are experienced at different ages. Nonetheless, certain patterns in the movement from **adolescence** into adulthood can be identified and categorized.

The trend in advanced industrial societies has been for an increasingly delayed entrance into adulthood. In medieval times, individuals moved rapidly from infancy into the adult world as soon as they became able to work alongside their elders. With the introduction of formal education, a new stage of childhood was added. With the shift from agriculture to industry, adult **status** was delayed again as a period of apprenticeship was added. At the beginning of the twentieth century, formal schooling had been sufficiently extended so that the adolescent phase was introduced. By the end of the twentieth century, the growing need for extended **higher education** created an even later induction into adulthood, sometimes called postadolescence or emerging adulthood, prolonging a full transition as far as an individual's late twenties.

The transition into adulthood is marked by various rites of passage, both formal and informal. Formal identifications of achieving adult status include completion of formal education, economic independence, moving out of the parents' home, voting, full-time **employment**, and **marriage**. These easily identifiable markers are approved by **society** as appropriate steps toward adulthood. However, social, economic, and educational factors affect the age at which these roles are assumed. The poor segments of the population may find it difficult to achieve such milestones as employment, economic independence, and completed education. Informal rites of passage are often taken on by adolescents in an attempt to claim adult status well before the time society is willing to bestow it upon them. These behaviors include drug and alcohol use, smoking, and sexual activity and teenage pregnancy. Although they are viewed negatively by society, adolescents and those who feel powerless to achieve more formal milestones use informal status markers as a means to identify their place in the adult world.

A traditional twentieth-century understanding of adult development is best explained by Yale psychologist Daniel Levinson in his book *The Seasons of a Man's Life* (1978). Levinson conducted extensive interviews with forty men, ages 35 to 45, and as a result concluded that there is an underlying identifiable "life structure." This life **structure** is shaped primarily by the social and physical environment related to **family** and work, but it can also be influenced by such factors as religion, **race**, and economic conditions. According to Levinson, men go through a series of stages as they grow older. Pre-adulthood spans the ages from birth to 22 and includes early adult transition. Early adulthood lasts from age 22 to 40 and is marked by family and **career** developments. Middle adulthood begins at age 40 and ends at age 60. During these years, men must deal with unfulfilled life expectations and ultimately focus on cultivating their skills and assets. Late adulthood, a time of reflection and **leisure**, extends from age 60 until death. In a subsequent study, Levinson interviewed women and found similar patterns although women's stages tended to be more closely linked to the family life **cycle**.

This understanding of life stages came into question in the 1990s with the emergence of a new generation of people in their twenties who defied the traditional transitional time frames. Although this age group only recently came under scholarly study, it received extensive attention by the media and the public. This group received the nickname ''Generation X'' from the novel by the same name (1991), which depicts three young people in their mid- to late twenties who refuse to participate in the expected **role** transitions into adulthood, such as marriage and career development. The book sparked a national interest in a generation marked as pessimistic about the future and reluctant to claim adult status.

The demographic changes in the last thirty years of the twentieth century support the theory of delayed passage into adulthood. In 1970 the median age of marriage was 21 for women and 23 for men. By 1996, the ages had risen to 25 for women and 27 for men. Age at the time of having a baby followed a similar pattern. Also, the number of people extending education beyond high school rose sharply from 48 percent in 1970 to 60 percent in 1993. Jefrey Jensen Arnett suggested in *Youth and Society* that a new stage in life development between adolescence and adulthood must be recognized: ''The late teens and early 20s are no longer a period in which the typical pattern is to enter and settle into long-term adult roles. On the contrary, it is a period of life characterized for many young people by a high degree of change, experimentation, and instability.''

Robert Thompson, a popular **culture** expert and professor at Syracuse University, suggested that because the transition into adulthood has become so long that many people in their late twenties may experience what he termed an ''early-life crisis.'' He told the *Boston Herald*: ''The midlife crisis for people in their 40s and 50s was based on a **model** that made sense in the '40s and '50s. Established in a job, married with children and a mortgage, by the time a person reached his 40s and 50s, this life became old and sometimes stale. These new younger crises now are not so much based upon regret over roads not traveled, but more from a position of delayed identity crisis.''

However and whenever the transition into adulthood is identified, it is clear that the period between adolescence and adulthood are highly formative years, marked by many events that go a long way toward shaping an individual's character and role **identity** in adulthood. Although adulthood itself is not a stagnant stage, the process by which the stage is claimed and

The novel ''Generation X'' depicted an American youth refusing to conform to expected societal roles *(St. Martin's Press, Inc.).*

achieved is of inextricable importance to self- and social identity.

See also Fatherhood; Motherhood

AFFECT CONTROL THEORY

Affect control theory is a cybernetic theory of **identity** and identity processes. This theory links motivation, emotion, and consequences of social action to an identity held by an individual, the setting in which the action takes place, and the expected behavior of someone holding a given identity in the situation under consideration. The theory, developed by David Heise in the early 1980s, used a structural symbolic interactionist framework in attempting to demonstrate how an individual's identity was affected by adequate performance within the **role** and the predicted emotional response that accompanies appropriate and inappropriate behavior. These emotional responses are then interpreted as signals by the individual to gauge performance in the role-identity and to establish or confirm fundamental beliefs about the self and others.

According to affect control theory, a situation is labeled with culturally infused meanings, referred to as fundamental sentiments, which assist the individual in defining the situation. Heise highlighted three fundamental sentiments: evaluation (positive versus negative), potency (powerful versus powerless), and activity (lively versus quiet). These dimensions parallel the three dimensions of affective response and correspond to the social dimensions of **status**, power, and expressivity. These responses are tied to appropriate behaviors in a given situation. For example, "the husband hugs his wife" is an appropriate and expected behavior by people in a spousal relationship, and this behavior would be met with positive emotional reactions. However, "the husband is unfaithful to his wife" is an inappropriate cultural behavior and would cause negative emotional responses. The difference between the situational meanings and the expected fundamental sentiments is known as deflection. In the first scenario, deflection is low, as the man is behaving in ways expected of a husband. Because deflection is low, the man's claim to the identity of husband is supported. In the second scenario, the marital infidelity of the man is not culturally supported as appropriate behavior, the emotional reaction to the action will likely be negative, and deflection will be high. As a result, the evaluation of the husband will be downgraded appropriately, depending on the amount of deflection.

According to affect control theory, people will construct events to minimize deflection and appear to be appropriately enacting the role in question. Because emotions are powerful motivating forces, behavior can be, and often is, altered to elicit positive emotional responses. The husband who has cheated on his wife should feel bad about his actions and will likely take action to restore positive feelings within the role. This action could involve attempts to justify the action ("she cheated on me first"), attempts to restore the previously held identity of "good husband", or cessation of the identity (through divorce or annulment). In this way, either the behavior within the identity is transformed in order to be viewed as culturally appropriate, or the identity is considered irreparably damaged and abandoned. The latter option is rather severe and may not always be possible.

The strength of affect control theory lies in its ability to construct the normative emotional experience of a situation and demonstrate the impact of the experience on an individual. However, it does not differentiate between experienced and expressed emotion, nor does it offer an explanation for when feeling **norms** may play a role in altering these experiences. In other words, Heise's theory stresses the emotions that should be shown in order to maintain a certain identity but offers no insight as to when impressions may be managed or manipulated in order to display an affective response that is not truly being felt by the individual.

AFFIRMATIVE ACTION

The legal and political effort to increase the number of minorities and women in the public sectors of the United States began during the Civil Rights Movement of the 1960s. The term *affirmative action* was first used in an executive order given by President John F. Kennedy in 1961, which established the President's Committee on Equal Employment Opportunity. At its inception, the concept of affirmative action covered general issues of fairness in federal employment, such as widespread advertising of positions and opportunities. The scope of affirmative action began to increase with the passage of the Civil Rights Act of 1964, which outlawed discrimination based on **race**, color, national origin, and sex in **government** programs, public facilities, and **employment**.

By 1971 affirmative action had evolved into a full federal program, and its definition was entered into the *Code of Federal Regulations* as Revised Order No. 4, which stated in part: "An affirmative action program is a set of specific and result-oriented procedures to which a contractor commits itself to apply every good effort. The objective of those procedures plus such effort is equal employment opportunity." Thus all entities that received federal funding were accountable for affirmative action policies, including all contractors, universities, colleges, and hospitals.

By the mid-1970s, affirmative action had spread throughout the United States as state and local governments enacted either formal or informal affirmative action programs. Many large private companies, in an effort to diversify their workforces, created their own versions of affirmative action initiatives. Also, most major colleges and universities enacted affirmative action admissions standards in an attempt to create diversity on campus.

With the proliferation of affirmative action came increasing controversy and numerous legal challenges. In 1978, Allan Bakke sued the University of California (*University of California Regents v. Bakke*) because he had been denied admission to the university's medical school in Davis, whereas a black student with lower test scores had been accepted. The Supreme Court agreed with Bakke, and the medical school abandoned its policy of designating 16 of 100 new admissions for minority students. Although the court ruled against strict quotas, it did leave room to allow race as a consideration for employment and admission.

In the 1990s affirmative action became an increasingly hot political issue as many established affirmative action programs came under fire. In June 1995 the Supreme Court heard the case *Adarand Constructors v. Pena.* The Court's ruling struck down a federal law requiring that ten percent of federal money spent on highway projects must be awarded to businesses owned by socially or economically disadvantaged individuals.

In 1994, in the case *Hopwood v. Texas,* four white students filed suit against the University of Texas Law School. They contended they were victims of **discrimination** because they were denied admission, even though other black and Hispanic students with lower test scores had been accepted. U.S. District Judge Sam Sparks ruled that the students should be allowed to reapply, but he refused to rule on the school's admission policy. The case was heard again in March 1996 by the Fifth U.S. Circuit Court of Appeals, which ruled with the students, and the admission policy was struck down, thereby overturning the *Bakke* decision that allowed for race to be a consideration for admission.

The University of California came under public scrutiny in 1995 when California governor Pete Wilson (R) led an effort to abolish the University's affirmative action policies. In July 1995 the California Board of Regents did just that, removing any consideration of race, religion, sex, color, ethnicity, or national origin for purposes of admission, employment, or scholarships. Despite vigorous protests from students and affirmative action supporters, the Board of Regents confirmed its decision in February 1996, and the new policy became effective in 1998.

In November 1996, just months after the Board of Regents' decision, Californians went to the polls and passed the California Civil Rights Initiative (CCRI) by 54 percent to 46 percent. Widely known as Proposition 209, the CCRI closely follows the wording of the 1964 Civil Rights Bill: ''The state shall not discriminate against, or grant preferential treatment to, any individual or group on the basis of race, sex, color, **ethnicity**, or national origin in the operation of public employment, public education, or public contracting.'' Despite protests and several court appeals, the CCRI went into effect in August 1997.

The passage of the initiative, along with the Board of Regents' decision, sparked a nationwide debate over affirmative action, and it created an avalanche of parallel actions in other states. In 1996, Colorado, New Jersey, Louisiana, and Georgia all saw either legal or political action that severely limited the scope of affirmative action policies. During the late 1990s, public school districts across the nation were presented with numerous cases of reverse discrimination based on race-based admissions policies.

With the courts continuing to rule that the need for diversity is not compelling enough to justify affirmative action policies, supporters went on the offensive. In 1999, a suit was filed against the University of California at Berkeley, charging that the school's admission policy was discriminatory because it placed significant importance on high school honors and advanced placement classes. Because many minorities attend schools that do not offer these courses, they are at a disadvantage in the admission process. Another civil rights suit was filed against the California county of Contra Costa, claiming that contracts were continuously awarded to the same businesses, and minority-owned businesses were not given the right to free and fair competition.

At the beginning of the twenty-first century, the success or failure of affirmative action has yet to be worked out completely. Supporters vow to continue their work to create a **society** that makes amends for the nation's egregious history of racism. Opponents contend that affirmative action is an attempt to end discrimination by discriminating. In a nation of ever-increasing diversity, it is clear that the debate will continue.

See also Discrimination

AFFLUENT SOCIETY

The term *affluent society* was coined by economist John Kenneth Galbraith in *The Affluent Society* (1958). Economists subsequently used the term to describe the **culture** of the United States in the late 1950s and 1960s. In post-World War II America, the working class experienced unprecedented eco-

Governor Pete Wilson led an effort to abolish the University of California's affirmative action program in 1995 *(Archive Photos, Inc.)*.

nomic security so that many were able to seek and obtain middle-class **status**. According to Galbraith's theory, the result of this broader-based affluence was increased **privatization** of needs and a growing demand for consumer goods at the expense of public welfare.

The mass market of middle-class consumers arose, and with it came a change in **values** and attitudes. Consumption became the foundation of American culture, with personal ownership a determining factor in status. Now, not only the wealthy could expect to own a car and buy a house, but also the factory worker. However, private affluence did not, according to the theory, translate into public prosperity. Galbraith noted in a 1999 interview with *Dollars and Sense:* ''We had expensive radio and television and poor schools, clean houses and filthy streets, weak public services combined with deep concern for what the government spent. Public outlays were a bad and burdensome thing; affluent private expenditure was an economically constructive force.''

Historically, the understanding of increased middle-class wealth as a determining factor in the economic and **political culture** of a **society** can be identified in the study of Marxist theory. **Karl Marx** believed that the working class would ultimately tire of the burden of **capitalism** and eventually revolt against its oppression. However, because many workers were able to achieve, or at least to have hopes of achieving, middle-class status, they did not move against the capitalist system. According to Marx, this phenomenon, termed *embourgeoisement*, undermined the working-class identity and unity, thus thwarting its role as an agency of social and political change.

The issues of affluence and embourgeoisement became much more widely addressed in North America after World War II. Along with Galbraith, liberal economists, including S. M. Lipset and Clark Kerr, formulated theories regarding wealth distribution. Although their theses varied, the basic causal structure of each was founded on an understanding of how the working-class identity changed with economic stability and buying power. The birth of suburban life, a growing market for skilled labor, and increased mobility, all led to the disintegration of closely formed, inner-city, working-class neighborhoods. The collective nature of these communities was replaced by a privatization of concerns and focus. Thus, the working class sought the affluence previously only afforded to the much smaller middle class and wealthy. In turn, the ideals of commonality were abandoned in favor of individual respectability and social status.

The theories of embourgeoisement lost much of their credibility in the United States in the 1970s when government spending increased in an effort to provide better public services. However, the issue arose again during the 1980s and 1990s when **public opinion** and political action reflected a growing shift away from government-funded programs and support. Forty years after writing *The Affluent Society,* Galbraith continued to assert his basic theory: ''... there is still persistent and powerful pressure for restraint on public outlay. In consequence, we are now more than ever affluent in our private consumption.''

AFRICAN AMERICAN STUDIES

African American Studies is an academic discipline that focuses on the cultural, political, economic, religious, and social development of black Americans. First established in American universities in the late 1960s, African American Studies Departments were, in part, the product of student protests and the social climate created by the Civil Rights movement and the Black Power movement.

The Civil Rights struggle of the 1960s, with its censure of segregation and racist practices, gave rise to intergroup confrontation and persistent demands for equality. In 1960, the Student Nonviolent Coordinating Committee (SNCC) propelled thousands of African American students into action to dismantle segregation and organize southern blacks for political action. Later in the 1960s, students protested the Vietnam War and criticized universities for their unfair practices and involvement in pro-war activities.

The **Black Power movement** incited African Americans to seek freedom by any means necessary. The term ''Black Power,'' attributed to Stokely Carmichael, leader of SNCC, suggested black unity, acknowledged a common heritage, and implied strong communities supported by black-led organizations.

A cauldron of political movements propelled college students to demand that African American Studies Departments be established. In 1966, students at San Francisco State College presented a list of demands to school officials calling for a Department of Black Studies. This group established a student-funded series on black arts and **culture**. Although the university did not oppose the series, it was apprehensive about the push for a Black Studies Department.

By 1968, with the Black Studies Department still not fully implemented, students closed down the school with a strike, which created chaos, police conflict, and political upheaval among university officials. Finally, the university capitulated and San Francisco State became the first institution to establish a Black Studies curriculum and department in the fall of 1968. Dr. Nathan Hare, one of the founders of the Black Studies movement, who wrote extensively on the need for and the relevance of the discipline, had been appointed director of the department months before. By 1969, institutions such as Harvard, Yale and Columbia adopted Black Studies programs, as did historically black colleges and universities such as Fisk, Howard, and Tuskegee University.

The founders of the Black Studies movement had several objectives. First, they set out to study African Americans, what their experience had been and what it was becoming. Along with courses and granting degrees in Black Studies, the programs tackled issues of fair treatment for campus students. Many programs sought special entrance requirement programs and financial aid for African American students to ensure that their enrollment and retention rates increased. Proponents of African American Studies were concerned, as well, with training more scholars who would analyze, write about, and research African American life. These intellectuals would help develop and advance black communities. In this way, the programs intended to reach beyond campus life to members of the African American community.

According to Maulana Karenga, Black Studies is an interdisciplinary social science, divided into seven basic subject areas: religion, history, politics, social organizations, **psychology**, economics, and creative production. Karenga proposes that application of these areas is essential for solving the problems African Americans face.

African American Studies is, like **sociology** and other social sciences, concerned with the relationships of groups, struggles, and various social and cultural phenomena. The discipline intersects with sociology in its concern with issues such as economic opportunities, **race** and class relations, and intergroup conflict. African American Studies, however, is a particular social science which focuses on the unique experiences of American blacks. African American Studies includes the history of U.S. slavery and its effects on the culture and lives of blacks. Migration patterns of African Americans from southern to northern **cities** between the 1880s and the middle of the twentieth century is another topic within this interdisciplinary course of study. Many African American Studies Departments offer a broad selection of courses, which encompass studies in Classical African Civilizations and Ancient Egypt and other civilizations. The study of these civilizations increased greatly during the 1970s and 1980s. African languages, most notably Swahili, are common course offerings in university African American Studies Departments.

In the 1980s, Molefi Assante published *Afrocentricity*, a major contribution to the field of African American Studies. Assante advocated afrocentricity, an attitude that sees the world from the perspective of Africans or those of African descent. The afrocentric school of thought has garnered much debate and critique from scholars who claim that it places too much emphasis on Africa and dismisses important viewpoints. As a sector of African American studies, however, afrocentricity has helped to define African American Studies for some, and for the discipline as a whole, it has extended the dialogue among scholars about what African American Studies is and how it should evolve.

AFRICAN STUDIES

African Studies is the systematic examination of the people, history, culture, and institutions of Africa. During the colonial period, roughly between 1880 and 1960, European nations colonized much of tropical Africa and to some extent learned about the land they had called the "dark continent." Prior to this time, however, Africa was unknown to much of the world. Americans, who had seldom traveled to Africa, began to do so in the 1950s. African Studies programs were first instituted in American and European universities during the 1950s, as well. Before this period, traditionally black colleges and universities were the primary providers of courses on African life and **culture**, as part of their black history curriculum.

African Studies typically encompass regions below the Sahara desert. Egypt and the Northern Islamic states are considered within the study of the Middle East or Mediterranean, even though they are located on the African continent. Sub-Saharan African Studies is further divided into four regions: East Africa (Kenya, Somalia, and Tanzania), West Africa (Nigeria, Ghana, and Senegal), Central Africa (Zaire, Congo, and Central African Republic) and southern Africa (South Africa and Zimbabwe).

Perceptions of Africa and its people have often been filtered through the biases and beliefs held by western Europeans. The belief in European superiority and dominance fed myths, and this egocentrism distorted "knowledge." For example, beginning in the 1700s, European maps inflated the size of Europe and depicted the African continent as roughly the size of North America. In actuality, Africa is nearly four times the size of North America, and one-fifth of the earth's total land mass. Although typically thought of as a land of jungles, tropical rain forests comprise a very small fraction of the land. Snow-capped mountains, dry plains, and vast lakes are significant parts of the landscape, as well.

Although the land itself is vast, the continent contains only ten percent of the world's population. These people are diverse in terms of physical appearance, **language**, and culture. It is estimated that over 1400 indigenous languages are spoken in Africa. Although scholars tend to agree that the notion of **race** is neither an exact, nor absolute classification, the concept can be useful to explore migration patterns and describe physical types in a particular region. People with Negroid features are the dominant group in sub-Saharan Africa. There are numerous other "racial" groups that inhabit the continent. Among these groups are the Ethiopian/Somali, Indian, Khoisan, Oriental, Pygmy, and Caucasian. White-skinned minorities who have enforced systems to deny access to power for darker skinned people have influenced the relationships between these groups.

European control of Africa is thought to have been a 400-year process, beginning in the 1400s and culminating in the late 1800s. Various factors, including European weapons, long distance ships, **capitalism**, as well as political and economic crises in various African nations, contributed to African vulnerability to European domination. In 1884 and 1885, at the Berlin Conference, European nations divided much of the Af-

rican continent among themselves. The only African nations to retain sovereign rule during this time were Liberia and Abyssinia, which now constitute the nation of Ethiopia. These colonial divisions were made in the interest of European powers without consideration of existing African cultural or national ties. Thereafter, the people of Africa continued to be exploited and culturally dominated.

The African slave trade exported millions, primarily from West Africa to the Americas between the seventeenth and nineteenth centuries. Communities and ways of life were disrupted, heinous acts of violence were committed, and nations were robbed of generations of people who would have otherwise contributed to the growth of their native lands.

A variegated African diaspora resulted from this forced migration of Africans, illustrated by the Portuguese, Dutch, French and English spoken by persons of African descent across the globe. Many dialects have developed that retain Africanisms or evince African influence, as well. The patois spoken by the Gullah people of the Sea Islands, off the coast of Georgia and South Carolina, provide one example, as does the patois spoken by many blacks in Jamaica.

African racial **identity** is particularly complex in this context of alienation and acculturation. Creative production has been influenced by the cultures that Africans encountered in far away lands. Indigenous African art, music, and dance are studied and have influence on other cultures of the world. The study of African **family** structures and religions also present unique challenges for European scholars. Although **Islam**, **Christianity**, and **Judaism** have, for centuries, gained large numbers of converts, native religions, which embrace pantheism, are part of the complicated religious fabric of Africa.

Much recent study of African political systems has been devoted to South African **apartheid**. A system of extreme racial stratification in place for over forty years, apartheid was a dramatic model of group domination of Africans by white colonizers. The end of the colonial era, characterized by African nations gaining freedom from European powers on a large scale, provided many African states with the opportunity to reinvent their political systems and their lives. Some have chosen **socialism**; others have aligned themselves with capitalist powers. Others still struggle to find economic and social systems that suit their **values**, aspirations, and social realities.

AGE OF ENLIGHTENMENT

The Age of Enlightenment refers to a period in the eighteenth century when thinkers in Europe, England, and the United States fostered an emphasis on rational thought and reason. The period grew out of a trend that questioned previous modes of thought and social organization. Certain social conditions also laid the groundwork for the Age of Enlightenment. For example, French rule during the 1700s had been oppressive. Economically, France struggled under this period of governance, particularly when several French finance ministers made decisions that contributed to the country's economic instability. The French **bourgeoisie**, frustrated with the political situation and independent enough financially to act, assisted in laying the groundwork for the Age of Enlightenment. Eventually, the influence of the Age of Enlightenment contributed to the French Revolution.

Specifically, thinkers of the Age of Enlightenment questioned previously-held paradigms. For example, they questioned a reliance on metaphysical knowledge as in the seventeenth-century **philosophy** of Descartes and sought practical ways to apply reason. The concept of reason took on an expanded role; reason came to be used as a tool of reform or as a necessary way to assert authority. Thus, the expanded understanding of reason led to its application in a variety of fields. Previous categories of thought and knowledge, such as natural science, astronomy, philosophy, politics, and education, were examined with new criteria. The movement was away from ignorance and toward new social, scientific, and philosophical ideas—all through the use of reason.

Many thinkers advocated the use of reason as a new way to understand phenomena. They developed interpretations and applications of their own. Philosophers of the Age of Enlightenment wrote and talked about this new **paradigm** and spread an understanding of it to the general public. Influential French thinkers who shaped the movement included Voltaire (1694-1778), Montesquieu (1689-1755), Holbach (1723-1789), and Diderot (1719-1784). These men used reason and logic to rethink physical phenomena; they wrote on science, politics, and other subjects. Despite having unique approaches, these men shared the common hope of freeing humans from ignorance and superstition and leading people to a reasoned, practical, and logical understanding of the world. Philosophers of the Age of Enlightenment were not limited to France; other influential thinkers who shaped this movement included the British Joseph Addison and Sir Richard Steele; the Americans **Thomas Paine**, Thomas Jefferson, and Benjamin Franklin; and the German **Immanuel Kant**, who emphasized the importance of the individual.

The Age of Enlightenment signaled a major attempt to move away from despotic **leadership** and to replace it with—in some cases—democracy. Influential philosophers envisioned that reforms would foster a freer populace, who would depend on their own reason rather than tyrannical rule. Such people, according to these philosophers, could bring about change, such as increased equality, improved education, and shared wealth for all. These reforms would be made possible through changed social institutions that now operated according to tenets of reason. Modern sociologists regard the movement as placing too much emphasis on human **progress** and as lacking a grounding in empirical research. Nonetheless, the movement's significance is that it represented a distinct shift from traditional to modern thought, and it thus influenced the shape of modern social organizations.

AGGRESSION

Aggression is forceful or hostile, often destructive behavior. It may be appropriate as when used in self-defense or inappro-

priate as when used to harm oneself. The term "aggression" is sometimes used to refer to harmful actions, while the term "assertiveness" is used when the behavior has no harmful intent. In addition to military aggression, when one nation or group takes up arms against another, human aggression in its most violent form manifests itself in physical or verbal attacks against another person.

Various theories are offered to explain aggressive behavior in animals and humans. According to the ethological/instinctive theory, aggression is an instinct to protect the species, such as a mother bear threatening an intruder that comes too close to her cub. Aggression also promotes survival of the fittest.

Austrian zoologist Konrad Lorenz is the father of modern ethology, the study of animal behavior through comparative zoological methods. In his book *On Aggression* (1963), he argues that fighting, or aggressive behavior, in lower animals aids their survival. By showing aggression, animals maintain their own **territory** and dispense with competitors. Lorenz believes that aggression in humans is also inborn but that hostile tendencies can be ritualized into acceptable social patterns of behavior. Critics of this aggression theory point out the minor role that Lorenz attributes to principles of learning.

Another theory, frustration-aggression, also called the psychoanalytic theory, states that aggressive behavior occurs when humans or animals become frustrated. When frustration exists, due to an action denied or a goal not reached, aggression follows. Although the aggression is generally directed at the source of the frustration, it may in fact be indirect or misplaced, aimed at whatever is in the way. Critics of this theory say it is too narrow. Aggressive behavior can occur without frustration; it can be learned just like any other response. In addition, even when frustration does occur, it can result in other responses.

A third theory is that aggression is learned. If in the past, aggressive behavior in a certain situation led to positive results, individuals are likely to use that same behavior if like conditions recur. When initial aggressive acts are reinforced, aggression becomes an acquired trait. This theory acknowledges that a person's potential aggressive behavior is probably the result of many factors—genetics, hormones, physical characteristics, and the central nervous system.

A major influence on learned aggression, however, is familial, subcultural, and symbolic modeling. In familial modeling, children who have been abused or watch abuse in the home are likely to become abusers as adults. In some instances, children or teenagers may be taught to use aggressive behavior and rewarded for it by other **family** members. In subcultural modeling, youngsters learn aggression by watching aggressive actions of peers. If those actions are rewarded in some way, youngsters will acquire the same behaviors. Symbolic modeling occurs by watching **television** or movies and by reading comic books. In all these learned behaviors, the key factor is that the aggression, from whatever model, is rewarded.

Some social scientists believe that predicting aggressive behavior is one way to stop it. Children who are cruel to ani-

People living longer
Life expectancy for men and women, 1950-2075

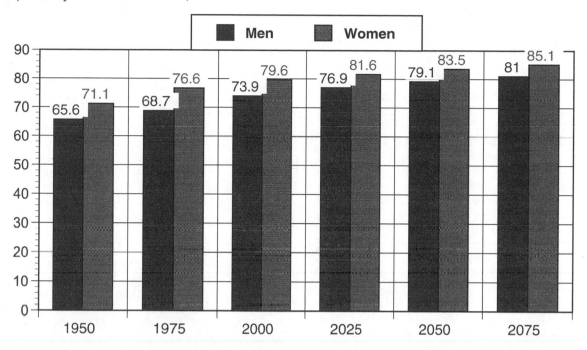

NOTE: Numbers 2000 and onwards are estimates based on intermediate cost assumptions

Source: "The 2000 Annual Report of the Board of Trustees of the Federal Old-Age and Survivors Insurance and Disability Trust Funds"

mals or who set fires may be on the path to destructive aggression. In general, however, efforts to predict overt aggression in any one individual or any one group of adults have been unsatisfactory. Others look for ways to control violent tendencies. Training in relaxation, self-control, and **communication** skills helps. In self-control training, individuals are taught to make verbal statements that help them to respond to frustration or other stimuli in a less aggressive manner. In communication skills training, individuals learn how to negotiate with others to resolve conflicts without resorting to violence. Sometimes, the use of rewards and nonphysical punishment has proved effective in countering hostile outbreaks in certain individuals. It is important to remember, however, that aggressive behavior very often remains as part of an individual's makeup simply because it pays. If the sought-after incentive is obtained, the aggression has been rewarded.

AGING

Unlike scientists who study medicine and biology whose views are restricted to more specific areas, sociologists consider the process of aging from a broader perspective. Obviously the medically related physical and biological aspects are inher-

ent, essential parts of the aging process, but by the very nature of **sociology** as a science the sociologist considers the social processes as well. Of particular interest to sociologists is the fact that in most instances, the physical and biological changes that occur as part of the aging process lead to observable and measurable changes in the aging person's general behavior, including the **role** performed in **society**. As part of those changes in the social role, the person's perceptions, concept of self, and approach to daily living may change as part of this complex and comprehensive process.

Of particular concern to sociologists is the fact that all changes related to the aging process will in the twenty-first century have a more significant impact on society than ever before. Increasingly larger numbers of older people will comprise a great proportion of society as a whole in most western societies. This increase in the aged population is due largely to improved conditions of nutrition, sanitation, housing, and **health care**.

For example, U.S. Census Bureau figures reveal that in 1993 overall life expectancy in the United States was 75.5 years, an increase in the average life span of over fifty percent since 1900 when American **life expectancy** was 47.3 years. Similarly, in 1940 the American population classified as elderly (persons 65 years of age and older) comprised about seven percent or nine million people. But by 1993 the number of elderly had nearly doubled, increasing to about 13 percent of the population, or roughly 33 million people. Demographers, those who study numerical and statistical changes in population trends, estimate that by the year 2050 roughly 21.8 percent of all Americans will be classified as elderly, that number comprising more than one-fifth of the total population.

Thus, greater understanding of the impact of these numbers is extremely important for future stability and successful continuation of American society. The population currently approaching elderly **status** is the most educated and affluent elderly **cohort** in the history of the world. These elderly Americans are accustomed to a very high **standard of living** and, because of their large numbers and increasingly visible political activism, they are likely to exercise their political clout to **influence** legislation that will assure their needs are met and their standard of living is maintained. In fact, the single political action **group** with the largest membership in the United States is the American Association of Retired Persons (AARP).

By 1995 the AARP, which was founded only in 1958, had grown to more than 33 million members. Maintaining a full time staff in excess of 1,800, the AARP occupies an eight story building in Washington, D.C., from which its executive officers oversee the expenditure of a budget in excess of $430 million. The fact that a significant portion of the AARP budget is directed at influencing legislation that favors the elderly is not lost on members of Congress. Lawmakers, aware of the growing numbers of elderly, as well as their social unity attained through membership in an **organization** such as AARP, pay close attention to their social needs and to legislation in which the growing elderly population has a vested interest.

From the sociological perspective, the multiple processes in which this group is engaged provide enormous opportunity for study and research. The elderly have multiple roles of social **interaction** and social impact. Too affluent and politically active to accept secondary status, this population may redefine the way in which families interact within their own units as well as within society as a whole.

AGRARIAN SOCIETY

Any social organization based primarily on the production of agriculture and its associated crafts is known as an agrarian **society**. Examples are the preindustrial civilizations of China, Europe, and India. In more recent times, the antebellum South in the United States was a society based economically and culturally on the production of agriculture, chiefly cotton and tobacco crops.

Some historians say that the period when human **civilization** began to change from that of hunter/gatherer to food producer occurred about 9000-7000 BCE. In China, the Yellow River Valley is said to be the birthplace of that country's early agriculture-based society. There are records of a Chinese irrigation system in use as early as 2200 BCE, and the Tukiang Dam was built about 200 BCE. By the second century CE, food production was so important to China that too many

poor growing seasons were enough to topple more than one dynasty. The Chinese were rotating crops for better production by the sixth century, and with arable land becoming less and less available as the population grew, numerous revolutions took place over how best to utilize farmland. Today, only about ten percent of China's total land area is devoted to agriculture. Although by the late twentieth century, China was making great leaps into a largely industrial society, about eighty percent of the population still lived in the countryside. Until the 1980s, most of these people made their living directly from farming.

In Europe, crop farming flourished in Roman times, and most farmers worked with hand tools that are similar to today's implements. Agriculture was also practiced in Britain and Gaul both before and during the Roman era. Farming in the Western world falls into two divisions. The first is the development period, lasting until about the thirteenth century. Plows were improved, and open-field systems, strips of land separated by furrows, came into use. Expansion of farmland took place during this period all over the European continent. However, beginning about the fourteenth century, disasters in the form of wars, climatic changes, and pestilence sent the agricultural systems of Europe into recession, which would take some two centuries for recovery. New farm machines aided the comeback as did a planting system that involved rotating crops on the same land for better yields.

Rice played an important role in the settlement of the Indian subcontinent. The success of the Indus Valley civilization, about 1750 BCE, must be due in part to an abundant food production system, although few archaeological records confirm this. By the seventh century BCE, farm settlements had spread to the Ganges Delta. A Greek envoy visiting the court of the Mauryan Empire about 300 BCE wrote of vast Indian fertile plains and a system of irrigation. When Western powers began to arrive in India about the year 1600, an ocean-going trade based on agricultural goods was developing. Today, rice is still India's most important crop, and along with fishing and forestry, farming provides work for about two-thirds of the population. However, the agricultural system is still largely at the mercy of weather changes, and cultivated land is poorly and unevenly distributed.

Indirectly, an agrarian society was one of the main causes of the American Civil War. The southern U.S. states were far less industrialized than those in the North. The South had fertile soil, long growing seasons, and mild climate. These factors combined to form a society that was economically and culturally bound to the land. Cotton was king, and by the mid-nineteenth century, it accounted for half of all U.S. exports. But farming was done largely by hand. It needed lots of labor, cheap enough to make it profitable. Hence, the South felt itself tied to slavery, the main subject of dispute which gave rise to the Civil War.

In eighteenth-century England, the **Industrial Revolution** brought on the decline of agrarian society, a decline that spread throughout Europe and the world. New machines, the factory system, and developments in transportation and **communication** combined to end dependence solely on land. In addition, better methods of farming, producing more and better crops in less space, and less dependence on farmland as a source of wealth contributed to the end of agrarian society.

AGRICULTURAL INNOVATION

Agricultural innovation is the process of implementing new ideas or methods into farm practice. Sociologists who study this process generally find that new ideas are resisted in rural areas. Ways of carrying out agricultural practices are often well established over generations, and it takes an imaginative mindshift, in some cases, for those involved to be willing to try a new method.

Agricultural innovation includes changes in crop types, machinery, fertilizers, and animal husbandry methods. In *Human Problems in Technological Change,* (1952), Edward Spicer claimed that much research on agricultural innovation had a pro-innovation **bias**, and care must be taken since "changing people's customs is an even more delicate responsibility than surgery." Joseph Schumpeter's *Capitalism, Socialism, and Democracy* (1950) applied an economic context to agricultural innovations, suggesting that each innovation introduced a new production function and, therefore, a new set of economic possibilities.

Agricultural innovations are accepted depending on how well they match regional **norms** and **values**. Some innovations lend themselves to a trial period; some cost more than others or may bring more prestige. With regard to change acceptance, sociologists focus on diffusion, the process by which the innovation is adopted among rural communities. Everett Rogers wrote in *The Diffusion of Innovations* (1983) that **communication** is crucial to diffusion, and it may come either through impersonal paths (such as the media) or through social networks. The diffusion process ends with either adoption or rejection. To reach a conclusion about the innovation, Rogers posited that a person goes through a process of forming an **attitude**, making a decision, and taking action.

Rogers' research also created a framework that labelled people in their different reactions to innovation. He called the first two to three percent of those who adopted an innovation the "innovators." The next 10 to 15 percent who adopted an innovation were designated "early adopters." According to Rogers, this group consisted of responsible local leaders; they were well educated, had larger farms than their neighbors, and were open to progressive business practices. Rogers' other classifications included the "early majority" (the next 30-35 percent who are deliberate in their opinions), the "late majority" (the next 30-35 percent who are cautious yet open to innovation when facing social or economic pressures), and the "laggards" (the last 15 percent and the last to adopt an innovation who are he characterized as traditional). Rogers and others admitted that these classifications did not always apply. However, research by David Gartrell and John Gartrell (*Social Status and Agricultural Innovation: A Meta-Analysis* [1985]) as well as Scott Lewis, et al. (*Upper-Middle-Class Conservatism in Agricultural Communities: A Meta-Analysis* [1989]) again demonstrated a **correlation** between social **status** and the ability to accept innovation.

While it has played a big part in innovation study, diffusion research has received some criticism. One limit to the effectiveness of such research is the fact that the research is generally biased toward innovation. This slant is especially noticeable if the research is funded by a company with a vested interest in seeing a particular agricultural innovation become adopted. James Hightower addressed this bias, particularly as it applied to research funded at land grant universities, in his book *Hard Tomatoes, Hard Times: The Failure of America's Land Grant College Complex,*(1972). Hightower described a project launched by agricultural scientists in California which introduced hard tomatoes that could be easily picked with newly introduced mechanized pickers. As a result of these innovations, many people lost jobs and consumers got less desirable tomatoes. Regardless of its inherent biases, adoption-diffusion research offers a way to ascertain whether technological advances in agricultural innovation might be effective.

In a *Forbes* article (November 8, 1993), agricultural economist Dennis Avery claimed that agricultural innovation made it possible to feed growing third-world countries in the early 1990s. Avery cited such advances as high yield farming. Another advance is the development of hybrid, disease-resistant crops. Crops have also been developed with shorter growing seasons, making possible double or triple successive plantings per year. Avery also mentioned conservation tillage methods, which are implemented to decrease soil erosion.

AID TO FAMILIES WITH DEPENDENT CHILDREN (AFDC)

Aid to Families with Dependent Children (AFDC) was welfare program, administered by the Department of Health and Human Services, designed to provide financial assistance to needy families with children under age eighteen. The program was sanctioned under Title IV of the Social Security Act of 1935 and its later amendments. Although administered at the federal level, individual states determined eligibility requirements. Among these requirements was the restriction that welfare funds be used to benefit only children in the family. Employment **status** and income levels of adults living in the home were other requirement factors considered for eligibility. By 1991 AFDC had become the costliest **government** welfare program in the United States. Effective July 1, 1997, the Temporary Assistance for Needy Families (TANF) Program, created by the Welfare Reform Law of 1996, replaced the Aid to Families with Dependent Children program.

ALCOHOLISM

An estimated 14 million Americans (approximately 7.5 percent of the population) struggle with alcoholism. Over 7,000 seek help for their dependence on any given day, either through inpatient or outpatient care, making alcohol the most prevalent addiction in American society. The financial cost to

Temporary Assistance for Needy Families (TANF)—Families and Recipients: 1980 to 1999

[In thousands (3,642 represents 3,642,000). Average monthly families and recipients, except as noted. Prior to TANF, the cash assistance program to families was called Aid to Families With Dependent Children (1980-96). Under the new welfare law (Personal Responsibility and Work Opportunity Reconciliation Act of 1996), the program became TANF. Includes Puerto Rico Guam, and Virgin Islands]

Year	Families	Recipients	Year	Families	Recipients
1980	3,642	10,597	1990	3,974	11,460
1981	3,871	11,160	1991	4,374	12,592
1982	3,569	10,431	1992	4,768	13,625
1983	3,651	10,659	1993	4,981	14,143
1984	3,725	10,866	1994	5,046	14,226
1985	3,692	10,813	1995	4,876	13,652
1986	3,748	10,997	1996	4,553	12,649
1987	3,784	11,065	1997	3,946	10,936
1988	3,748	10,920	1998	3,179	8,770
1989	3,771	10,934	1999 (March)	2,668	7,335

Source: U.S. Administration for Children and Families, "Temporary Assistance for Needy Families (TANF): 1936-1999;" <http://www.acf.dhhs.gov/news/stats/3697.htm>; (accessed: 20 September 1999).

the economy totals more than an estimated $148 billion dollars annually in care, recovery, **crime**, and lost productivity. Resulting social and personal problems, such as **divorce**, child abuse, **suicide** and homicide, are also significantly high.

The definition of alcoholism has been an issue of considerable debate, and as the understanding of alcoholism has changed, so have the terms used to describe it. Repeated, uncontrolled drunkenness has been referred to as a sickness for hundreds of years. Roman philosopher Seneca called it a form of insanity. The term "alcoholism" was coined by Swedish physician Magnus Huss in his 1849 article "Alcoholismus Chronicus," and the condition was first defined as a **disease** in the mid-twentieth century. Although also branded a genetic disorder, a psychological problem, or a result of social or personal dysfunction, alcoholism as a disease became the most widely accepted understanding of alcohol dependence.

Alcoholism, understood as a disease, is viewed as an illness which the alcoholic is not personally responsible for having contracted. The National Council on Alcoholism and Drug Dependence defines alcoholism as "a primary, chronic disease with genetic, psychosocial, and environmental factors influencing its development and manifestations." As such, alcoholism is a medical disorder that produces the symptoms of alcoholic behavior. The illness is further understood to be incurable but controllable by total abstinence. This view is supported by the American Medical Association, the National Institute on Alcohol Abuse and Alcoholism, and Alcoholics Anonymous, the world's largest self-help program for alcoholics. Also, according to a 1987 Gallup Poll, 87 percent of Americans considered alcoholism a disease. Supporters of this interpretation also point to recent scientific research that may link alcoholism to genetic makeup.

Although widely supported by many alcohol experts and researchers, this definition became more controversial by the end of the twentieth century. Many behavioral scientists and

sociologists rejected the idea of alcoholism as a disease. The concept supported by these social scientists concentrates on the behavior of excessive drinking itself. Thus alcoholism identifies the pattern of frequent, abusive drinking and the resulting personal and social dysfunctions. Excessive drinking is not a symptom of an underlying illness, but the actual focus of the explanation. This understanding gained support in the 1990s when the World Health Organization abandoned the concept of alcoholism as a disease in favor of a broader understanding that more clearly incorporated social and cultural issues.

Intoxication occurs when alcohol is consumed at a faster rate than the body can process, thus circulating it through the blood stream and depressing the central nervous system. Alcohol is not stored or passed through the body, but rather it is metabolized in the liver at a fixed rate of .25 and .33 ounces (7.1-9.4 grams) per hour, depending on the individual. Thus if consumption surpasses the liver's ability to process it, signs of intoxication begin to appear. With a blood-alcohol content (BAC) of .05 percent, the drinker's concentration, visual function, and reaction time are affected. Legal intoxication is defined by most states between .08 and .10 percent BAC. Between a BAC of .14 and .17, all physical and mental abilities become impaired, including difficulty maintaining balance while walking or standing. At the level of .40 to .60 percent and above, the BAC becomes dangerously high, with the possibility of alcohol-induced coma and death.

Chronic abuse of alcohol can result in numerous medical conditions, including cirrhosis of the liver, heart disease, high blood pressure, diseases of the digestive system, malnutrition, and cancer of the larynx, esophagus, and liver. In men, sexual dysfunction can also occur because alcohol inhibits the body's production of testosterone, with impotence and testicular atrophy as possible results. Women who abuse alcohol while pregnant place their unborn children at risk for fetal al-

Many sociologists view alcoholism as a pattern of frequent, abusive drinking that results in personal and social dysfunctions (AP/Wide World Photos, Inc.).

cohol syndrome and a range of other physical, developmental, and psychological conditions. Prolonged heavy drinking can lead to two organic brain disorders: alcoholic dementia, a condition in which the alcoholic loses general intellectual functions, and Wernicke-Korsakoff's syndrome, a condition in which the alcoholic loses physical coordination and suffers from incoherence and mental confusion.

The treatment of alcoholism is varied but usually includes professional advice, self-help support, and sometimes medical treatment. Chronic alcohol abusers may experience severe withdrawal symptoms with sudden abstinence. Characterized by tremors, vomiting, and convulsions, withdrawal from alcohol can be difficult and dangerous, and include delirium tremens, a final phase of withdrawal that brings on insomnia, hallucinations, and maniacal behavior. Many alcoholics need a controlled setting to move successfully through the detoxification process. Often alcoholics need the assistance of several treatment programs to achieve sobriety. The major approaches to treatment include behavior therapy, motivational

therapy, and Alcoholics Anonymous or another self-help program. Anticraving and aversive medications may also be used to supplement behavioral modification. Also, pharmacological treatment may be used to relieve accompanying psychiatric conditions, such as depression and anxiety.

Alcohol abuse in American society comes with a expensive price tag. A large share of the economic burden caused by alcohol consumption, in the form of crime, alcohol-related accidents, and numerous **social services**, is borne by taxpayers. Due to alcohol's ability to block inhibitions and promote aggressive behavior, as many as seventy percent of violent attacks and murders were committed or experienced by people under the influence of alcohol. According to a study by E. Glucksman, 47 out of 100 alcoholics die from the effects of alcohol: 18 by homicide, 17 by accident, 11 from suicide, and 7 from natural causes. Alcohol abuse has also been linked to **juvenile delinquency** and family violence.

The inability of many alcoholics to maintain productive work habits and positive relationships leads to dysfunction in both the personal and social arenas of the alcoholic's life. As alcoholism progresses, it can be marked by increased tolerance and thus increased consumption, blackouts, and violent behavior. As a result, alcoholism brings on increasingly severe problems for not only the alcoholic, but also **family**, friends, coworkers, and society-at-large.

ALEXANDER, JEFFREY CHARLES
(1947-)
American sociologist and educator

Jeffrey Charles Alexander, a longtime faculty member at the University of California, Los Angeles (UCLA), was born in Milwaukee on May 30, 1947, to Frederick Charles Alexander and Esther Lea (Schlossman) Alexander. He received a B.A. from Harvard College in 1969 and a Ph.D. from the University of California, Berkeley (UCB) in 1978. Alexander's academic career has included appointments at UCLA as an assistant professor (1976-81), as a full professor (1981-), and as chair of UCLA's sociology department (1989-92). Additionally, he has been a visiting faculty member or fellow at numerous institutions, including the Institute for Advanced Studies at Princeton University (fellow, 1985-86), the University of Bordeaux, France (visiting professor, 1994), and the Center for the Advanced Study in the Behavioral Sciences at Stanford University (fellow, 1998-99). Additionally, Alexander has held elected positions in various associations, including the American Sociological Association and the International Sociological Association, for which he is the co-chair of the Research Committee on Sociological Theory.

Alexander has specialized in the areas of social theory, cultural sociology, and civil society. His many publications include: *Theoretical Logic in Sociology,* vols. 1-4 (1982-83); *Neofunctionalism* (1985); *Sociological Theory Since World War II* (1987); *Action and Its Environments: Towards a New Synthesis* (1988); *Culture and Society: Contemporary Debates* (1990); *Rethinking Progress: Movements, Forces, and Ideas at the End of the Twentieth Century* (1990); *Relativism, Reduction, and the Problem of Reason* (1995); *Neofunctionalism and After* (1998); and *Diversity and Its Discontents* (co-edited with Neil J. Smelzer, 1999). He also has served on the editorial boards of several professional publications.

In describing his work in cultural sociology, Alexander has said that he takes a ''post-Durkheimian'' approach. He has attempted to move in new theoretical directions, linking sociology with literature, **political science**, and **philosophy**. *Diversity and Its Discontents,* for example, examined the American ''culture wars'' of the late twentieth century, which accompanied changes in family structure, immigration patterns, sexual expression, and urban lifestyles. Alexander and various contributors concluded that cultural conflict always has been a part of American life, often more extreme than in recent years, and that there are many unappreciated but strong forces encouraging cohesion in American life.

ALIENATION

The idea of alienation has been studied by philosophers since the times of ancient Greece, though the concept was the object of particular focus during the 1960s. Alienation refers to an individual's feeling of disconnection or not belonging. It has been studied in a general societal context, as well as specific contexts—such as individuals' relationships to their workplace.

The modern sociological use of the concept of alienation developed mainly from the work of **Karl Marx**. In his *Economic and Philosophic Manuscripts,* written in 1844 and published in 1932, Marx discussed the concept of alienation, including the meaning given the word by the philosopher Hegel. Marx proposed that the term could be considered in three contexts: philosophical, psychological, and sociological. According to Marx, the manifestation of alienation in an individual was the result of that individual's relationship to **society**. Marx stated that the sociological implications of alienation were particularly important, since in his opinion, workers in capitalistic societies are alienated by a social **structure** that requires them to work for others. In such cases, Marx argued, workers were alienated since they could not grow as persons. Such workers were unable to realize their potential fully, according to Marx.

Marx's concept of alienation became better known in the 1950s, after *Economic and Philosophic Manuscripts* became better known in sociological circles. Many sociologists and Marxist writers were influenced by Marx's thoughts on alienation, including Fromm and Marcuse, who argued that alienation was tied to needs which **capitalism** artificially creates. Moving away from a strictly Marxist interpretation, social psychologist M. Seeman attempted to use the concept of alienation in a broader sense. Seeman proposed that alienation manifested in the following five ways: lack of power, loss of meaning, lack of **norms**, isolation, and estrangement. In *Alienation and Freedom,* R. Blauner suggested that increased industrialization and mass production induced feelings of alienation among workers. Marxist writers found fault with Blauner's tenets, claiming that Blauner lacked supporting data or that available data was biased.

By the 1960s, the term alienation was used widely to describe aspects of society in the United States. Increasingly popular was the perception that large organizations of many kinds (including the **government**, political parties, labor unions, and businesses) were unresponsive, detached, and untrustworthy in meeting the public's needs. Many societal groups adopted the term to describe their feelings of dissatisfaction. These included workers, rebellious youth, and minorities. The widespread use of the concept led to ongoing debates, as well as opinion polls that attempted to measure the actual level of alienation. Additionally, sociologists attempted to discover the causes and implications of alienation. Seymour Lipset and Earl Raab suggested that the lack of power and meaning which results from alienation might occur in a person who disregards societal norms. Such disregard of norms could lead to violence or large scale protests, trends that concerned sociologists. Sociologists also discovered that alienated individuals were less likely to effect change through traditional political processes.

The prevalence of alienation in U.S. society did not go away after the tumultuous 1960s and 1970s. New research, along with potentially troubling societal trends, caused alienation to be considered in light of new problems. In 1996, Frank Sulloway, in *Born to Rebel,* a book based on his study of thousands of people, suggested that birth order might predispose persons toward feelings of alienation. The author claimed that last born or later born children were more likely to rebel against the status quo and first born children were more likely to defend it. Robert Bly claimed that Americans' dependence on technology, **television**, and affluence had created a society of alienated, passive-aggressive individuals. Psychologist Mary Pipher claimed that electronic communities, such as those found on the Internet, are changing social **interaction** and contributing to alienation. In *Tikkun,* sociologist Svi Shapiro applied tenets of alienation in order to explain the rash of murders among schoolchildren in the 1990s. He suggested that prevalent commercialism in the United States, which encourages what he called "competitive individualism," causes people (even children) to become alienated and place less value on other people's lives.

ALTHUSSER, LOUIS (1918-1990)

French philosopher

Aligned with the French Communist Party, philosopher Louis Althusser (1918–1990) strove to explain contemporary developments by reinterpreting the doctrines of **Karl Marx** and **Friedrich Engels**.

Louis Althusser was born at Birmandreis, Algeria (then a colony of France), October 16, 1918. He was briefly imprisoned in concentration camps in World War II. In 1948 he took his degree in **philosophy** from the Ecole Normale Supérieure in Paris and taught there for the next 32 years. In 1980 he strangled his wife and lived most of the next ten years, until his death in 1990, confined to mental asylums.

Prior to and through World War II, 1939–1945, Althusser was involved in the Roman Catholic youth movement and advocated some of the church's more conservative teachings. During the Nazi occupation of France his thinking underwent a radical transformation, as he along with many others embraced Marxist ideologies. During this time he found himself involved with the French Resistance and attracted to one of its more prominent activists, Helene Legotier, eight years his senior and a member of the French Communist Party (PCF). In 1948, Althusser also joined the party. After the war Legotier continued her activism, while Althusser spent most of his time in academia. His lectures and writings became very influential and he was seen by many to be the party's most outstanding intellectual.

Althusser attempted to reconcile the views of French *structuralism* with those of Marxism by denying the primary role of the individual subject in the face of historically unfolding social structures. His most important works are *For Marx* (1965), *Lenin and Philosophy* (1969), and his contributions to a book of essays called *Reading Capital,* all of which were popular with student revolutionaries during the decade of social upheaval in the 1960s.

Author Robert Bly claims that America's dependence on technology has created a society of alienated individuals *(Courtesy of Chris Felver).*

While many Marxists were looking for a more "humane" alternative to the **totalitarianism** unfolding in the Soviet Union and a way to resolve the split caused by the Chinese revolution, Althusser, taking the opposite tack, proposed a purely scientific approach, one he ascribed to the maturing Marx himself in *For Marx,* (1970). In *Reading Capital* and in *Lenin and Philosophy and Other Essays* (1971) he aimed at an objective account of how the total **society** works from its technological top down, generating the classes that run and do the work of a society. In the latter collection he described how such a **structure** operates through the languages we speak in common. These, he said, tend to instill in people their sense of reality and of themselves and their social roles, all in the interest of perpetuating the order of the given society: this is the thought-controlling use of **language** called "ideology."

Althusser sketched the underlying fabric of a society with the help of French structuralist theory. This led to the development of a comprehensive and intricate Marxist **model** for society as a whole, although access to the model is made difficult by Althusser's style and terminology.

In the structuralist view society cannot be understood through the subjective experience of individuals seen as in some way differentiated from the unfolding processes in which

Louis Althusser *(Corbis Corporation [Bellevue])*

they are enmeshed. A society functions as a single organism in a manner determined by its technology and its modes of production. Every individual action is solely determined by its role in relation to that technology. Althusser's critique was partly in reaction to prevailing individualistic philosophies, as well as the increasingly embarrassing historical degenerations of the Marxist system under Stalin. Critics of Altusser's thinking largely objected to the extreme austerity of a system which denies the primacy of the subjective experience, insisting that a system which so entirely subordinates the individual to the "total" structure can never hope to sustain itself in any realm other than the theoretical.

The Chinese experience reminded Marxists that contradictions were the essence of their world view; unity is achieved only through the play of opposites, and all wholes contain and even consist of the struggles internal to them. As an organism breaks down food to build up nourishment, the state takes life to protect itself. Later disciples of Althusser would point out that both language and personality reveal inherent tensions in the makeup of the self. These as oppositions can be counted on to result in change and progress as they are products of the internalization of "idealistic" structures in the society as a whole. Marxists who preferred to see change as brought on from "the bottom up" (the oppressed, the working class) criticized Althusser for this scheme of resistance from

"the inside out" (the repressed inside any group, body, or system: in the economic system, workers). Others found this to be one of his most fruitful new turns of thought.

Althusser long suffered as a manic depressive, Legotier acting as his nurse. In 1976 they were married, but in November of 1980 the philosopher strangled his wife to death and was committed to a Paris hospital for the insane. He spent the last ten years of his life in and out of various institutions. During this time he continued to write essays, attempting to explain his homicidal action in the light of a wider social analysis. A posthumous autobiography of collected memoirs *The Future Lasts Forever* was published in 1992.

ALTRUISM

Altruism refers to selfless action which aids other people without regard to personal cost or benefit. The good of others is the end of the moral action. The term itself was coined in the nineteenth century by **Auguste Comte** (1798–1757), French philosopher and founder of **positivism**, a system of thought proposed as a basis for modern political **organization**. Altruism is generally cited as the opposite of egoism, which bases good on the pursuit of self-interest.

Human action abounds with tales of seemingly altruistic behavior. A man dashes off the street into a burning building to rescue someone he does not know. A woman shares her last $10 with a homeless person on a city street. A young boy jumps into a rising creek to save a drowning dog. What can account for such behaviors?

Two factors that may be part of some altruistic actions are reciprocity and social exchange. All major **world religions** teach reciprocity, the Golden Rule in one form or another. We learn this **concept** as children, and as adults, we may feel guilty if we do not apply the teaching. Guilt may well be a large factor in many altruistic actions. Social exchange implies that one good deed will get back another. We may do something good for someone with the unstated belief that at some time and place, someone will do good for us.

Does true altruism exist? Some philosophers argue that it does not. How is it possible to know if what appears as altruistic behavior actually can be accounted for by self-directed motives? The answer seems to be that there is no proof, only plausible interpretations.

Whether based on hidden self-directed forces or true altruism, what makes one person act in an altruistic way when another does not? One way to study this question is by examining the bystander effect, or bystander intervention. Such an examination often begins with the killing of Kitty Genovese in a quiet New York City neighborhood on a predawn March morning in 1964. While walking to her apartment building, she was stabbed three times over a 30-minute period. Not one of the 38 neighbors who heard and/or watched the brutal murder came to her aid, not even to the extent of phoning the police.

Why did no one help? The so-called bystander effect suggests that people are less likely to become involved if someone else is around rather than if they are alone. There is a tendency when several people are involved to "let someone else do it." Some of those who heard the Genovese murder may have assumed that someone else was calling for help. Using that theory, presumably, if only one neighbor had witnessed the murder, he or she would have sought aid.

The bystander effect also comes into play when certain conditions are present. A person is less likely to exhibit altruistic behavior in a crucial situation when (1) the person in trouble seems to be intoxicated, (2) the victim is of a different ethnic group than the bystander, (3) the situation is confusing to the bystander, (4) those involved in the fight seem to be related, or (5) the bystander views the situation as bringing personal immediate harm to him- or herself.

Altruistic behavior carried to the extreme is termed "altruistic suicide" by some sociologists. In this self-destructive action, a person gives up his or her life for the good of the group. According to Émile Durkheim in his *Suicide,* this happens only when the individual "has no interests of his own." Examples include Japan's Kamikaze pilots in World War II, monks who set themselves on fire to protest the war in Vietnam, or various individuals who have starved themselves to death for a country or a cause.

In one sense, it may be said that altruism, whenever exhibited, is simply following social **norms**. In most societies, children are shaped by certain ways of thinking and modes of behavior. Their adult actions may result from how well they have accepted these cultural patterns and the degree to which they are threatened or motivated by carrying them out.

AMALGAMATION

Amalgamation (also called the melting pot) refers to intermarriage of different racial and ethnic groups to create new blends of identities and a new **culture**. In equation form, it is sometimes described as cultures A + B + C = Culture D. Amalgamation is the final step in structural assimilation. New immigrants to the United States generally achieve structural assimilation in three steps. The first step is economic assimilation (economic opportunity), then spatial assimilation (integrated neighborhoods), and then social assimilation (ranging from club membership to intermarriage). Amalgamation refers to the later stage, indicating adaption on the part of the dominant culture as well as the other assimilated cultures.

The triple melting pot thesis also represents a form of amalgamation or intermarriage, separated by three dominant **religious orientations**. It describes amalgamation of different nationalities while maintaining religious boundaries for Catholics, Jews, and Protestants. For example, amalgamation takes place when Italian Catholics marry Irish Catholics, when German Jews marry Polish Jews or when German Protestants marry English Protestants. Research by Richard Alba reveals intermarriage outside one's culture is most frequent after the third or fourth generation.

The products of amalgamation are apparent in the cultures of many countries. For example, amalgamations of African, European, Native, and Asian ancestry exist in many countries in the Caribbean, Latin America, and South America. New cultures are determined by the mix of settlers. For example, Uruguay has a heavily Italian influence, while Argentina has a heavily German one. Brazil has four distinct amalgamated cultures.

Another example of amalgamation is in the United States. It is described as a melting pot which generally means a blend of Western European cultures. Early European settlers formed a dominant culture with **language**, religions, and customs derived from German, Welsh, English, Irish and Scots. In some areas the French also occupied a prominent place in this mix. Eastern European and Italian were later incorporated into the U.S. melting pot as well.

AMERICAN FAMILIES

American families have diverse origins, backgrounds, and experiences. Consequently, there is no such thing as a "typical" American **family**. The numerous forms that American families take throughout history have depended upon many social, economic, and political factors. A discussion of American family structures must include various historical forces that have shaped American family life.

The historical experiences of Native American families have been shaped by social, economic, and political forces in vital ways. Because the social organization of Native American family life has historically differed from one tribe to another, it is impossible to condense the family experiences of diverse North American indigenous tribes into one large category. However, the arrival of Europeans on North American soil affected all forms of indigenous tribal family life. Through **war** and **genocide**, families were broken up and whole tribes were obliterated. Ways of life sufficient for the social and economic survival of tribal families were violently disrupted by European action.

The colonial families of early America were also significantly shaped by social, economic, and political forces. **Marriage** was an important element of family life, and **divorce** rates were extremely low. The fact that divorce was uncommon during colonial times does not necessarily indicate the prevalence of intact families, however. Spousal desertion occurred more frequently, and widowhood was a factor in single-parent households. Although colonial households were significantly larger than contemporary families, not all residents were necessarily related to one another. Non-family member residents often served economic functions. For instance, some families employed servants, while others housed apprentices and employees. Furthermore, many families took in boarders to supplement **household** income.

Many analyses of "the colonial family" exclude the familial experiences of people of color from this era of American history. Narrow focus upon the family structures of white Americans has obscured the African American experience. While maintenance of slave family life was extremely difficult, historical records have shown that, even though legal marriage was not an option, slaves did perform their own mar-

Most U.S. households have historically been family households, and most of these have included married couples *(AP/Wide World Photos, Inc.)*.

riage rituals. Even when nuclear families were disrupted, slaves often found ways to preserve **ritual** marital bonds. Furthermore, extended family ties and fictive kin relationships were highly prevalent among African American slaves and free blacks during the era of slavery.

The industrialization of America transformed many people's social, economic, and political roles. Mills and factories created jobs outside the home. The shift from self-sustaining agrarian lifestyle to industrial wage labor reshaped the American family **structure** in various ways. Prior to the Industrial Revolution, family members worked together as an economic unit in the home or on the family farm, with families producing much of what they consumed. With the development of the commercial economy, the workplace was located away from the family unit, which created a sharp distinction between work and family life. Increasingly, women's roles were defined by activities assumed to be noneconomic, in the form of nurturing and caring for family members. Men were viewed as having primary responsibility for the economic welfare of their families. No longer an economically interdependent unit, families were transformed such that women and children became economically dependent on the primary wage earner.

Women only began to enter the wage-earning workforce in significant numbers when World War II drew many men out of the workforce to fight in the military. Although many women were displaced from these jobs once the men returned from the war, it was the start of a growing acceptance of women in the workforce.

The period directly following World War II is often referred to as the golden age of family life because of the lower rates of divorce, lower ages at marriage, and higher rates of childbearing, spurred on by the greater economic prosperity. Since that period, social factors have increased the average age of marriage, which was 23 years of age for women and almost 26 years for men as of 1986. Examination of non-Hispanic whites, blacks, and Hispanic whites shows that age at first marriage has climbed more rapidly for blacks than for non-Hispanic whites, with blacks now marrying later than non-Hispanic whites. In contrast, Hispanics marry at younger ages than do other groups.

Factors promoting later age at marriage in recent decades include greater societal acceptance of singlehood and **cohabitation** as well as greater emphasis on educational attainment. The size of the unmarried population is increasing, due primarily to later ages at marriage and increases in divorce. In 1980, 5.4 percent of men and 5 percent of women ages 55 to 64 had never married, and among blacks the percentage was even higher (7.9 percent and 6.4 percent, respectively). Due to the continuing stigmatization of **homosexuality**, it is difficult to ascertain the numbers of single persons who are gay and lesbian. Researchers have estimated that 4 percent of men and 2 percent of women are exclusively homosexual. Though homosexual marriages are not legally recognized, many gay and lesbian couples form lasting unions.

The same factors that contribute to a delay in marriage, also contribute to recent trends in childbearing, which sees women waiting longer to have a first child and spacing children farther apart than women in the 1960s, as they focus on educational and economic achievements. This trend is not evident with black couples, however, who generally have children within twelve to seventeen months of marriage. Compared to the total population, black couples are likely to have more children on average and to have a child present at the time of marriage.

Divorce rates have been rising in the United States since the Civil War. Over the past century, the proportion of adults currently divorced rose from one in three hundred to one in thirteen women and one in eighteen men. Divorce rates rose more sharply after every major war during the twentieth century, with a 100 percent increase between 1963 and 1975. By the early 1970s, the chance of eventual divorce reached almost fifty percent, which was still true at the end of the century. Most persons who divorce eventually remarry, which has resulted in "blended" families becoming increasingly common. These can consist of couples who have previously been married to different partners, the children born in those previous marriages, and the children born to the current marital partners. In 1980, 41 percent of all marriages involved one previously married partner, up from 30 percent only ten years before.

As defined by the U.S. Census Bureau, "family households" are those containing persons who are related to the household head. "Nonfamily households" consist of one or more unrelated persons. Historically, most American households have been family households, and most of these have included married couples. In 1910, 80 percent of all households included married couples. By 1980, this percentage had declined to 61 percent. A breakdown of all U.S. households in 1980 shows that 31 percent were married couples with no children under age eighteen; 7 percent were single parents with children under age eighteen; 6 percent were family households that did not include a married couple or any children of the householder; and 26 percent were "nonfamily." Of the nonfamily households, 86 percent consisted of individuals who were living alone.

Breakdowns of family structure by **race** and **ethnicity** show that Americans of Korean, Filipino, Vietnamese, and Mexican heritage are most likely to live in family households (for each group, about 84 percent live in family households). African Americans and non-Hispanic whites are somewhat less likely to live in family households. Also, compared to

In a controversial ruling, AIM member Leonard Peltier was sentenced to life imprisonment for the murder of two government agents *(Corbis Corporation [Bellevue])*.

other racial and ethnic groups, Puerto Ricans are most likely to live in a household consisting of a mother and one or more children (with 23 percent living in this type of household), followed by African Americans, Native Americans, and Hawaiians.

The historical examination of American families illustrates the national and ethnic diversity that characterizes U.S. family life. Current familial trends that have tended to cut across national and ethnic lines are crucial to the analysis of American family life as well. It is therefore impossible to speak of any one type of "American family." Diversity is perhaps the broadest characterization that applies to American families.

AMERICAN INDIAN MOVEMENT (AIM)

The American Indian Movement (AIM) synthesized a long history of Indian resistance. AIM was conceived in 1968 during discussions between inmates in the Stillwater State Penitentiary. Clyde Bellecourt, Edward Benton-Banai, and Dennis Banks began to discuss their vision for helping Indian people to find pride in Native American tradition. Clyde Bellecourt left prison in 1968 and founded the first AIM chapter in Minneapolis, in response to the needs of Native Americans trying to live in an urban American setting. Initially, the group patrolled the streets of Minneapolis/St. Paul and monitored police brutality against Indians. The movement quickly became political, however, focusing on regaining the land that had been taken from Native American tribes. As AIM's activism grew, so did its membership and within four years of its founding, active members were in every state.

Between 1971 and 1972, AIM members participated in what was called the "Trail of Broken Treaties" which took place in many locations across the country, where AIM members visited reservations and government offices in an effort to recover Indian land and make their grievances against the U.S. government known. Federal law provided that military land previously owned by the government should revert to its previous owner when abandoned. AIM members determined that they would make claims on land through this law, starting in the west and moving on to the east coast. Their first action in this movement was taking of Alcatraz Island in November, 1969. Protestors were not removed until June, 1971. After many events across the country, the Trail of Broken Treaties culminated in a November, 1972, confrontation with government officials and the sacking of the **Bureau of Indian Affairs** (BIA) office in Washington, D.C.

The incident for which AIM is most well known, the 1973 conflict at Wounded Knee, began when approximately two hundred AIM supporters and leaders gathered in the village of Wounded Knee, the site of the December, 1890 Massacre. This group took over the trading post, museum, gas station, and several churches on February 27, 1973. Seeking to voice the concerns of the Oglala Sioux of the Pine Ridge Reservation, they outlined a list of goals for the tribal government. Federal agents moved in immediately, and the AIM members traded gunfire with forces sporadically throughout the occupation. A series of tense negotiations followed, culminating in an agreement that provided for the evacuation of Wounded Knee on May 8, 1973, and led to the arrest of over 110 American Indians. Over four hundred people were arrested during the conflict. Conflicts with federal agents and reservation police squads continued for years after this incident and resulted in the deaths of both federal agents and many Native Americans.

In another controversial case, Leonard Peltier was convicted of the murder of two government agents after a confrontation on the Oglala reservation between AIM members and federal agents. Two other AIM members were acquitted, but Peltier was sentenced to two consecutive life sentences; yet many believe Peltier to be innocent of the crime. During Peltier's time in prison, much public outcry has called for further investigation.

AIM has received criticism on many fronts. Because of the movement's political nature, AIM members, and often Native Americans in general, have been labeled as agitators, both within the Indian **community** and outside it. Members are often seen as excessively violent and public in the way that they promote the Indian cause. Claims have been made that they maintain a racist approach and that their anti-establishment positions have created dissent between elders and younger members. Nonetheless, AIM has also been seen as a way to help the Indian people and has provided Indians with recogni-

tion and an **identity**. AIM has provided an outlet for the pride in traditional values that its founders had hoped for and has enabled the Native American community to openly defy its oppressors. The American Indian Movement has served as an organization of empowerment and a significant force for change in the American Indian community.

AMERICAN SOCIETY

American Society, in the words of **Alexis de Tocqueville** "opened a thousand new roads to fortune and gave any obscure adventurer the chance of wealth and power." This comment, made in his prescient 1835 book *Democracy in America* captured both the reality and the mystique of the young United States. Those "roads to fortune" led, soon after, to manifest destiny and the conquering of the west; a flood of immigrants from Europe, then Asia, and, eventually, all parts of the globe; and the domination of America, politically and culturally by the end of the twentieth century. This school of thought continues to rule American society.

The land that would become the United States was settled by Europeans from absolute monarchies, but these settlers had a strong sense of individual liberty and resented any attempt to limit their movements or financial opportunity. Despite the dangers of Indian attack, **disease**, and harsh weather, they continued to press westward seeking new opportunities.

When the British were ousted in the Revolution, the new **government** immediately sought to expand as far and as fast as possible and encouraged its citizens to fill the continent. At the same time they attempted to isolate themselves from world affairs; the American continent was enough to occupy their energies and though there was still a natural connection to England, the United States remained neutral in European concerns. The Monroe Doctrine of 1823 succinctly announced this policy as well as the United States' intention to control its own hemisphere. Immigration and the Civil War brought a new relationship between America and the world, but the prevailing sentiment was toward isolationism until World War II. Since then, however, the United States has become a globalist nation and is deeply involved in international politics and economics. The average U. S. citizen, though, remained less interested in the rest of the world than the world is in the United States.

America's **progress** to world power has been a steady and unqualified success, but internally there have been troubling contradictions between the ideals outlined in the Declaration of Independence and the struggle for equality of women, Native Americans, African Americans, and immigrant groups. While defining the standard of freedom for the world, in the Bill of Rights, the country has generally lagged behind in extending those freedoms to all of its citizens. To some extent, this trend can be traced to the strong libertarian tendencies and rugged **individualism** which Americans have historically embraced.

There is a suspicion of government interference in daily affairs that tends to favor the status quo. The sweeping social programs of twentieth century Europe have not been as widely accepted in the United States. Despite a history of dynamic innovation in business and industry, America has been culturally conservative and generally favors a society ruled by the markets. Free markets, it is thought, are the most democratic way for all people to have their chance at success. Even if opportunity is demonstrably unequal, the system still works as a whole and will eventually encompass everyone. While some changes in the system may be widely supported, gradual change from within is preferred to government intervention.

The political and economic stability of the United States would seem to support this way of thinking. Large scale radical activism in the 1960s and 1970s helped bring about long overdue improvements in civil rights for minorities and women, but the country soon returned to its historical conservatism. The belief that anyone who works hard enough can succeed in America remains a powerful axiom. Excessive taxation and government subsidies could undermine that ideal.

The **values** of individual Americans differ depending on gender, race, wealth, and other factors, and yet the nation as a whole has maintained a fairly consistent self-image even as its make-up has drastically changed. Except for extreme cases, such as war and **crime**, Americans still generally value the rights of the individual over the interests of the state in a way that sets them apart from the rest of the world. Some may see this as a negative quality—an unwillingness to share the wealth, so to speak—but this mindset also limits the possibility of a totalitarian regime attaining power. Action is also favored over philosophy, and work over **leisure**. Americans are working longer hours, despite their increasing wealth while Europeans are working less and demanding long vacations.

At the end of the twentieth century, the world seems to be moving toward a macrocosm of American society. The success, politically and economically, of the United States—not to mention the dominance of the pop culture—has greatly altered the cultures of other nations. **Capitalism** and **democracy** are flourishing, but so too are crass commercialism and an impatience with history and tradition. Such a trend may serve the marketplace at the expense of the rich diversity of the world that immigration brought into America.

AMERICAN SOCIOLOGICAL ASSOCIATION (ASA)

The American Sociological Association (ASA) is the most prestigious national membership **organization** in the United States dedicated to advancing sociology as a scientific discipline and profession. Founded in 1905, the non-profit ASA has more than 13,000 members, including sociologists who are faculty, researchers, social science practitioners, and students. About twenty percent of the membership works in **government**, business, or non-profit agencies.

The ASA holds annual meetings at which sociologists keep abreast of the latest research in the discipline. Faculty and students present and discuss their work in a variety of settings. The most common presentation formats include lectures,

round table discussions during which several papers are discussed, and panel discussions. These five-day conferences meet in a different city and region late each summer and are attended by thousands of sociologists. The annual meetings usually follow a theme which guides some of the larger sessions. For example, in August, 2000, the meeting theme was "Oppression, Domination, and Liberation: Challenges for the Twenty-first Century."

The ASA publishes eight journals, each pertaining to a different branch of sociological thought and practice: *American Sociological Review*, *Social Psychology Quarterly*, *Contemporary Sociology*, *Sociological Methodology*, *Journal of Health and Social Behavior*, *Sociological Theory*, *Sociology of Education*, and *Teaching Sociology*. Published bi-monthly or quarterly, the journals contain peer-reviewed articles, book reviews, and critical discussions of contemporary work. Here, sociologists record ideas, progress, and innovation in the understanding of social behavior and thought. These journals provide a living classroom for the wide field of **sociology**. The ASA also publishes the monthly newsletter *Footnotes*, as well as some section journals and newsletters, books (including the well-regarded Rose series), monographs, reference guides, directories, a variety of teaching resources and other academic materials.

Membership in the ASA is divided into more than forty sections which promote specialty areas within the field. Examples of some specialty areas are: Aging and the Life Course, **Collective Behavior** and Social Movements, Environment and Technology, **Methodology**, Rational Choice, Sex and Gender, Sociology of Law, **Theory**, and Undergraduate Education. Sections publish newsletters to keep members informed of research and grant opportunities, and other information. Some sections also publish a journal, and some maintain web sites. Sections are headed by elected coordinators who facilitate section meetings during conferences and other section activities. Members may belong to as many sections as relate to their interests. Sections distribute annual awards to honor members' contributions to the field through articles, books, dissertations, and career achievements.

The ASA also communicates employment, funding, and research opportunities to its members. The newsletter *Footnotes* regularly publishes details of opportunities for which members might apply, and these listings also appear on the ASA's website (www.asanet.org). Other listings in *Footnotes* include calls for papers for upcoming conferences, notable accomplishments of members, book reviews, and publication announcements.

In 1999, the ASA established a Student Forum to facilitate students' integration into the field and into the ASA itself. As another service to student members and to increase student involvement in all aspects of the ASA, the Association dispenses competitive travel awards for students to travel to its annual meeting.

The ASA also provides sociologists with a Code of Ethics regarding professional responsibilities and conduct. These principles promote the highest standards of professional competence and integrity; professional, scientific and social responsibility; and respect for dignity, diversity and people's rights. The ASA also sponsors a Committee on Professional Ethics.

ANALYSIS OF VARIANCE AND COVARIANCE (ANOVA AND ANCOVA)

Analysis of variance (ANOVA) and analysis of covariance (ANCOVA) are statistical methods for comparing the means of several groups. ANOVA allows the researcher to **model** and analyze the relationship between a quantitative response **variable** and a qualitative explanatory variable. ANCOVA enables the analysis of models which include both quantitative and qualitative explanatory variables, in which the researcher can control for at least one variable.

ANOVA is essentially a comparison of the amount of variance around the mean that is observed within each **group**, the between-group estimate of variance, to the amount of variance that is observed within each group, the within-group estimate of variance. ANOVA uses the test statistic F to test the **null hypothesis** that the means of all the groups are equal against the alternative hypothesis that the means are not equal. The F statistic is based on the **ratio** of the between-group estimate of variance to the within-group estimate of variance.

For example, we might be interested in knowing how much of the variability in standardized test scores is within states versus between states. In our example we would be testing the null hypothesis that the variance in test scores is within states against the alternative hypothesis that the means vary between states. The F test will show us the **probability** that the null hypothesis is true.

The between estimate of variance is calculated by dividing the between group sum of squares (BSS) by its **degrees of freedom**. The BSS equals the sum of the squares of the difference between the **mean** of each group and the overall mean, with each squared difference weighted by the sample size of the group. For g groups each with n cases, $BSS = n_1(Y_1-Y)^2 +... + n_g(Y_g -Y)^2$. The BSS has $(g-1)$ degrees of freedom. The between estimate of variance is determined by $BSS/(g-1)$.

The within-group estimate of variance is equal to the within-group sum of squares (WSS) divided by the degrees of freedom. The WSS is the pooled sums of squares for each of the g groups $(Yg-Y)^2$ and its degrees of freedom is equal to the total number of cases in all groups N minus the number of groups g or $(N-g)$. The within estimate of variance is equivalent to $WSS/(N-g)$.

The F statistic equals $[BSS/(g-1)] / [WSS/(N-g)]$. When F is larger than 1, then the estimate of variance is large and the group means are not all equal. The larger the F statistic, the smaller the p-value, and the lesser probability that the null hypothesis is true. The p-value associated with F and its degrees of freedom is obtained from a standard t-distribution table or from statistical analysis software, which reports the value in ANOVA or **regression** analysis. If the mean of even a single group is dissimilar to the others, then there is less evi-dence in favor of the null hypothesis that the means of all of the groups are equal.

In more complicated models of ANOVA we may add **interaction** variables to the model. These variables allow the possibility that the explanatory variables are related to each other as well as to the response variable. This step allows us to compare the means of a quantitative response variable across categories of a qualitative variable while controlling for another variable.

We make the following assumptions when we use ANOVA: The distribution of the response variable is normal in each of the populations we are comparing; the standard deviations of the population distributions are normal, and the samples were selected randomly and independently.

ANCOVA combines elements of regression analysis and ANOVA to enable the comparison of multiple group means for combinations of quantitative and qualitative response variables, while controlling for at least one variable. This analysis enables the researcher to compare group means as if the groups were equal in terms for which the variable was controlled. For example, we might want to compare the incomes of groups 1 and 2, controlling for the groups' different levels of education. Our **theory** might be that if we control for education, groups 1 and 2 have the same incomes. ANCOVA allows this type of comparison. The computational details of this analysis are quite complicated. Both ANOVA and AN-COVA are best performed using statistical analysis software.

ANARCHY

Anarchy is an absence or lack of **authority**. It is drawn from the Greek words *av* (pronounced ''an''), meaning absence or lack of, and *apxn* (pronounced ''arkhe''), meaning authority, **government**, or ruler. Despite the popular usage as a synonym, anarchy is not a state of chaos. Anarchism is a school of political and philosophical thought whose central tenet is that all authority is neither wanted nor needed. The anarchist movement aspires to construct a **social order** without political, economic, or social hierarchies. Hierarchy is the organizational arrangement that actualizes authority. Because the state is the ''highest'' level of coercive power, anarchists are definitively anti-state.

Anarchist philosophies share several core positions. They oppose both government and **capitalism** and advocate a new social order based on voluntary cooperation. Anarchists view profit as usury or exploitation and exploitative associations, which are viewed as the natural outcome of capitalist systems, as not freely entered.

The term ''libertarian socialism'' was used prior to the creation of the term ''anarchism.'' Eighteenth-century Mexican radicals advocated libertarian **socialism**. **William Godwin** (1756-1836) is considered anarchism's founding father with his groundbreaking work *Political Justice*. Pierre Proudhon (1809-1865) extended Godwin's theory of anarchy to include mutual aid and the rejection of private **property** with his work *What is Property?*. Anarchism developed into a full theory with the contributions of both Mikhail Bakunin (1814-1876) and Peter Kropotkin (1842-1921).

With the coming of the twentieth century, the anarchist movement was peaking, and the definition of anarchism became solidified. The 1886 imprisonment and subsequent execution of a group of anarchists known as the ''Haymarket Eight'' in Chicago sparked a wave of anarchism in the United States. Voltairine de Cleyre, Lucy Parsons, and Emma Goldman joined the anarchist movement as a direct result of these executions. Parsons' husband had been one of the Chicago Eight. Goldman further broadened the meaning of anarchism and introduced many influential ideas of anarchist **feminism**.

Emma Goldman's companion, Alexander Berkman, played a major part in defining anarchism with his book *ABC of Anarchism*. Berkman wrote, ''Anarchism means you should be free; that no one should enslave you, boss you, rob you, or impose upon you.''

ANCESTOR WORSHIP

Ancestor worship is the religious or **cult** practice of honoring dead spirits who are regarded as ancestors. Though not universal, ancestor worship was widespread among ancient cultures in Asia and Europe and continues to be prevalent among preliterate societies in Asia, Africa, and the Pacific, as well as in India, China, and Japan. Ancestor cults occur in societies structured around the importance of kinship and inheritance. They are not suited to societies based on the nuclear **family**.

The worship of ancestors is associated with the belief that actual or mythical deceased ancestors remain actively involved in human social life. These ancestors may be friendly, or they may be wrathful beings whose displeasure with the living can be assuaged through rituals of respect and worship. The living may ask ancestors' help in ensuring the continuation of the family line, guaranteeing a good harvest, protecting against illness, or interceding with the gods. In some societies, such as the *manes* or *parentes* cults of ancient Rome, all the dead of a particular family group were worshiped communally. More often, societies either practiced the worship of individual ancestors or combined individual worship with communal worship, as in the Roman emperor cult or the Japanese worship of imperial houshold members.

Where individual ancestors are worshiped, hierarchies are observed. Ordinary members of a group are worshiped only by their immediate relatives, if at all. Important personages, however, receive elaborate and prolonged worship in which the entire group may participate. The founder of a family line or an individual who attained great status, for example, receives extensive worship through many generations.

The rites and ceremonies observed in ancestor worship are similar to those associated with other kinds of spirits or gods. These include acts of reverence such as **prayer** and offerings, sacrifices, adherence to moral behavior, and ceremonial activities that may include dance, music, or performance. However, some spiritual rites occur exclusively in the worship of ancestors. These include annual commemorative ceremonies and the tending of graves, altars, or other symbols associated with the ancestor.

Ancestor worship may be a means of reinforcing a society's ideas concerning kinship and inheritance. It may also

Villagers of Ambatondrazaka, Madagascar dance beside a shrouded corpse during Famadihana, a traditional rite of ancestor worship *(AP/ Wide World Photos, Inc.).*

serve as a means of legitimating authority and sanctioning social **conformity**, or of strengthening a group's coherence in segmented societies.

ANDROCENTRISM

Androcentrism is defined as a male-centered view or approach. In this male-centered view, men are used as the normative standard by which women are judged. Androcentrism, by the nature of its definition, offers a partial or limited view of the world. Using this partial, or androcentric, view causes studies of history and **culture** to be distorted. These distortions are apparent in many history textbooks that illustrate men as the **group** who created history in conjunction with only a few women. Through the androcentric viewpoint, we see that males are the favored group. Many religions including Christianity, the dominant U.S. religion, have roots in the androcentric idea that women are subordinate to men. Early **personality theories** in **psychology** also display androcentric tenets. Androcentrism is common and pervasive in many cultures, religions, and societies.

Charlotte Perkins Gilman (1860-1935) was one of the first sociologists to advance the idea that our culture is androcentric. In her *The Man-Made World, or Our Androcentric Culture* (1911), Gilman asserted that **society** needs to consider the differences between men and women. Gilman stated that society as a whole is modeled after masculine experiences and interests, and society accepts this androcentrism without question. She asserts that men and women should be judged according to human rather than male standards. Gilman and other feminist leaders have worked to increase awareness of the androcentric perspective.

Androcentrism is also a concern for many research groups. Feminist researchers note that many sociological studies contain male biases within the sample groups. Many studies completed in the field of **sociology** have focused on male subjects even when women needed to be included to make the study valid. Feminist groups have recognized this discrepancy and have begun replicating such studies using both men and women. Feminist groups are particularly exploring attitudes and behaviors of women, something previously missing in the sociological literature. These new studies give a more inclusive reading of human behavior.

See also Patriarchy

ANOMIE

The term, "anomie," emanates from the Greek word *anomia*, meaning lawlessness. The term appeared later in the sixteenth century to describe lack of religious affiliation. In sociology, anomie was first used by Émile Durkheim (1858–1917), who proposed that anomie is an **abnormal** state of social pathology or social illness, where lawlessness and lack of **norms** prevail. Durkheim wrote of anomie as a social phenomenon in *The Division Of Labor in Society* (1893) and as an individual phenomenon in *Suicide* (1897). Robert Merton (b. 1910) later used anomie to explain crime and **deviance** (1938). Subsequently, anomie became synonymous with the modern term strain, and was used predominantly in theories of **crime** and delinquency by sociologists such as Albert Cohen, Richard Cloward, Lloyd Ohlin, Robert Dubin, Robert Agnew and Richard Rosenfeld and Steven Messner.

In *The Division of Labor*, Durkheim wrote that societies possess many different structures or institutions, which all have boundaries. Boundaries are the laws of a **society**. Although constantly evolving, all laws were originally derived from religion. Laws maintain a state of equilibrium or balance in society. If the balance is disturbed, institutions and people are thrown into a state of lawlessness or anomie.

The evolution of laws mirrors the evolution of society. Primitive societies are characterized by mechanical solidarity or repressive legal systems based on religious tenets. Punishment is a ritualistic way of affirming the common values of the **community**. Primitive societies eventually evolve into more complex societies characterized by organic solidarity. The boundaries or laws found in organic societies are restitutive based. Restitutive law is based on the many social contracts that exist between parties and is akin to civil sanctions. When a society is in transition between mechanically and organically based solidarity, repressive sanctions have no **legitimacy** because there is no longer a moral consensus, and restitutive sanctions have not yet been developed. Social chaos or anomie thrives during this period. People become socially isolated or alienated as a direct result of anomie.

Durkheim also identified several types of anomie that occur in organic societies. First is the anomic **division of labor** which occurs when the population of a society has multiplied and spread over a large area. Individuals cannot grasp "the big picture" of society as a whole, and with increased specialization, individuals are no longer bound together by their work. Individuals become increasingly alienated. A second type of anomie in organic societies, the forced division of labor, oc-

curs when specialization becomes a tool of certain social groups, for example, social elites. Instead of individual worth, factors of birth, class, and connection determine where an individual fits into the division of labor. People who are passed over because of their low social status experience **alienation**.

In *Suicide*, Durkheim writes that the loss of cohesion in society and an absence of suitable morals by which to orient oneself can result in individual anomie. Durkheim cites **divorce** as one situation where individual anomie can occur. Overnight, the constraints on the individual's life become completely different, and the person may not be able to cope with the new social constraints. The fault does not lie with the individual, Durkheim suggests, but with social structures. It is from this definition of individual anomie that modern anomie **theory** was created by Merton.

Referred to as "anomie theory," and alternatively as "classic strain" theory, Merton's theory purports to explain some forms of crime, deviance and drug use. The theory interprets these actions as either irrational, nonrational, or rational responses to anomie. Like Durkheim, Merton sees social disorder as the cause of strain. However, the two theorists disagree on the causes of social disorder: Merton cites social **competition**; Durkheim blames sudden social change.

According to Merton, the system of order breaks down and anomie occurs when "there is an acute disjunction between the cultural norms and goals, and the socially structured capacities of members of the **group** to act in accordance with them" (1968: 216). In this case, society's members subscribe to a certain set of cultural goals, but not everyone has the means necessary to achieve these goals. People who do not have means experience anomie or strain. The means-ends disjuncture is evident in the pursuit of the American Dream, a commonly recognized group of goals based on material success, such as owning a big house, fancy cars, and vacation homes.

In response to strain produced by disjuncture between ends and means, Merton posited that people could adopt any of five responses or adaptations: conformity, innovation, ritualism, retreatism, and rebellion. This theory of anomie has probably played the most important role in the development of modern-day delinquency theory.

ANTHONY, SUSAN BROWNELL (1820-1906)
American women's rights activist, abolitionist, and woman's suffrage leader

Susan Brownell Anthony (1820–1906) was an early leader of the American woman's suffrage movement and pioneered in seeking other equalities for women. An active abolitionist, she campaigned for emancipation of the slaves.

Susan B. Anthony was born on February 15, 1820, in Adams, Massachusetts, one of seven children. Her family had settled in Rhode Island in 1634. She attended Quaker schools and began teaching at the age of 15 for $1.50 a week plus board. When the family moved to Rochester, New York, in

1845, her brilliant father, Daniel Anthony, the dominant influence in her life, worked with important abolitionists. Frederick Douglass, William Lloyd Garrison, Wendell Phillips, and other guests at the Anthony farm helped form her strong views on the abolition of slavery.

Though her family attended the first Woman's Rights Convention held in Seneca Falls and Rochester, New York, in 1848, Anthony did not take up the cause of woman's rights until 1851, when male hostility to her temperance efforts convinced her that women must win the right to speak in public and to vote before anything else could be accomplished. Her lifelong friendship and partnership with **Elizabeth Cady Stanton** also began in 1851, as did her temporary doffing of corsets in favor of the revolutionary "bloomer" costume—which was women's first major dress reform in the movement. Anthony attended her first woman's-rights convention in 1852; from then until the end of the Civil War she campaigned from door to door, in legislatures, and in meetings for the two causes of **abolition** of slavery and of woman's rights. The New York State Married Woman's Property and Guardianship Law in 1860 was her first major legislative victory.

With the outbreak of the Civil War in 1861, woman's rights took second place. Anthony organized the Women's National Loyal League, which mobilized the crucial petitions to force passage of the Thirteenth Amendment to the Constitution to abolish slavery. In 1865 she began her battle in the content of the Fourteenth and Fifteenth Amendments, hoping to gain the franchise for women as well as for African American males. But her former male allies in the abolitionist struggle brushed her aside, saying the time was not yet ripe for woman's suffrage. Saddened but not deterred by this defeat, Anthony worked solely for woman's suffrage from this time to the end of her life, organizing the National Woman Suffrage Association with Stanton. The association's New York weekly *The Revolution* was created in 1868 to promote women's causes. After its bankruptcy in 1870, Anthony lectured throughout the nation for six years to pay its $10,000 debt.

In the 1872 presidential race Susan Anthony and 15 Rochester comrades became the first women ever to vote in a national election. That they were promptly arrested for their boldness did not dismay her, as she sought to test women's legal right to vote under the Fourteenth Amendment by carrying the case to the U.S. Supreme Court. Her case was singled out for prosecution, and trial was set for 1873 in Rochester. Free on bail of $1,000, Anthony stumped the country with a carefully prepared legal argument, "Is It a Crime for a U.S. Citizen to Vote?" She lost her case, following some dubious legal maneuvering by the judge, but was unfortunately barred from appealing to the Supreme Court when her sentence was not made binding.

Susan Anthony spent the rest of her life working for the federal suffrage amendment—a strenuous effort that took her not only to Congress but to political conventions, labor meetings, and lyceums in every section of the country. Mindful of the nearly total omission of women from historical literature, in 1877 she forced herself to sit down with her colleagues to begin the monumental and invaluable *History of Woman Suf-*

Susan B. Anthony *(National Archives and Records Administration)*

frage in five volumes. She later worked with her biographer, Ida Husted Harper, on two of the three volumes of *The Life and Work of Susan B. Anthony,* which were drawn largely from her continuous scrapbooks (1838–1900), now in the Library of Congress, and her diaries and letters.

Up to just one month before her death in 1906, Anthony was still active: she attended her last suffrage convention and her eighty-sixth birthday celebration in Washington. She closed her last public speech with the words, "Failure is impossible." When she died in her Rochester home on March 13, only four states had granted the vote to women. Fourteen years later the suffrage amendment, the nineteenth, was added to the Constitution.

ANTICIPATORY SOCIALIZATION

Anticipatory socialization is preparation for specific roles necessary to take on new statuses in **society**. Young children attend nursery school in preparation for roles as elementary students. During this time they learn to sit in their seats, pay attention to a teacher, follow instructions, interact with other students in appropriate manners. They also learn about appropriate dress, times to talk, and lunchroom **rules**. People in vocational training or pre-professional training learn expectations for the new **status**. As part of this process they might lose their idealized expectations and learn to adopt the **values** of others in the profession. Engagement is anticipatory socialization for **marriage**. During this period the engaged persons officially stop dating others and discusses expectations for day to day life as a married couple. They might live together as part of this preparation.

Anticipatory socialization is also part of the socialization for occupations and perpetuates **social stratification**. Traditionally physicians have one of the highest rates of occupational inheritance. Sons of doctors are most likely to become doctors. They learn the attitudes, values, **norms**, and ex-

South African leader Nelson Mandela stands alongside former President F. W. de Klerk celebrating the end of apartheid rule.

pectations as they mature. Similarly, children of blue-collar workers learn the traits that enable their parents to maintain jobs. Emphasis on respect for authority, punctuality, and following instructions at home makes it easy for children of workers to fill positions in factories and mines. As the job structure changes in the United States and educational opportunities become more available, many schools are taking on the role of teaching children to evaluate their options and orient themselves in chosen directions. Schools, therefore, can also serve as agents of anticipatory socialization.

APARTHEID

Apartheid, an Afrikaans word literally meaning "apartness," refers to the policy of racial segregation and its concomitant economic and political discrimination that was adopted by the South African **government** for a half century. Coined in the late 1930s by the South African Bureau for Racial Affairs (SABRA), apartheid reflected the social, yet non-legal, practices of South Africans. In the 1940s, the Afrikaner National Party used it as their political slogan. When they won the election in 1948, apartheid was written into law.

Apartheid rested on the sociological and theological assumption that the most fundamental category for dividing humanity is **race**. The Population Registration Act of 1950 made it obligatory for all South Africans to be divided into distinct racial groups: Asians (Indians and Pakistanis), Bantu (all black Africans), Colored (all those of mixed race) and White. Each race, or in the case of blacks each ethnolinguistic **group**, was believed to share its own peculiar **culture** and destiny that was best fulfilled if the racial groups lived apart from each other. This position explains why apartheid's apologists sometimes referred euphemistically to apartheid as "separate development" or "co-operative coexistence". To ensure that each race adequately fulfilled its destiny, members of each race were expected to live together in autonomous states. In reality, though, blacks were given only ten homelands of their own.

Irrespective of one's actual residence, the Bantu Homelands Citizenship Act of 1970 made all black South Africans citizens of one of these ten homelands. Four of these were granted independence as republics. Though blacks made up about seventy-five percent of the South African population, these ten homelands constituted only thirteen percent of South Africa's total land mass. Most blacks did not live in the homelands because these homelands did not have the resources that would make them viable economic centers and provide their citizens with livelihoods. Besides, the survival of the South African economy, which existed outside of the homelands, depended on the black population. While only blacks were given autonomous states, the Group Areas Act of 1950 delimited urban areas into residential and business sections for each race. Members of other races were prohibited from owning **property**, operating businesses, or living in areas not designated for members of their race. To ensure that individuals did not encroach on areas meant for members of other races, "pass" laws were strictly enforced. These "pass" laws required non-whites to carry documentation that authorized their presence in areas otherwise reserved for whites. Segregation was not limited to housing or **employment** situations. Public and educational facilities were also segregated. In addition, separate educational standards were developed for the white and non-white population. Education was only free and compulsory for white children between the ages of seven and sixteen. Interracial marriages were also prohibited.

Apartheid was opposed on both national and international fronts. South Africans showed their opposition through demonstrations and strikes despite the massacres and brutality that accompanied their protest attempts. One early protest occurred in the black township of Sharpeville in 1960. On March 21, some twenty thousand Africans met to demonstrate against the "pass" laws. The South African government responded by declaring a state of emergency. Another well-known attempt to highlight indignities of Apartheid was the Soweto riot of 1976, a protest against the enforcement of Afrikaans as a language requirement for black South African students, in which about 140 demonstrators were killed.

Opposition on the international front began as far back as 1961. Then, the Republic of South Africa was forced to withdraw from the Commonwealth because its racial policies conflicted with other Commonwealth nations. During the 1960s and 1970s, the anti-apartheid movement in various parts of the world called for boycotts of sporting and cultural links with South Africa. These calls for international sanctions were extended to the economic arena in the 1980s. In 1985, international bankers pulled out their loans to South Africa. That same year, the governments of the United Kingdom and United States imposed selective economic sanctions on the South African government.

Efforts of anti-apartheid protesters both in and outside South Africa began to pay off in the mid-1980s. Anti-miscegenation laws were repealed in 1985. In 1986, although blacks were still prohibited from living in white areas, the "pass" laws were abolished. Anti-apartheid demonstrations were legally permitted in October, 1989. On February 11,

1990, then president of South Africa, F. W. de Klerk released Nelson Mandela, a black anti-apartheid activist, who had been in prison at Robben Island for 27 years. In 1991, the majority of the laws that served as the basis for apartheid, including the Population Registration Act of 1950, were repealed. In March 1992, a referendum was held to determine whether the white population of South Africa supported the idea of ending apartheid. The majority of them endorsed its dissolution. In April 1994, the first free and fair democratic election in South Africa, open to all South Africans regardless of race, was held. Mandela became the first black president of South Africa and has since been succeeded by Thabo Mbeki. For their efforts to change the apartheid policies in a non-violent manner, both de Klerk and Mandela won the Nobel Peace Prize in 1995. In 1996 South Africa's experiment in restorative **justice** was organized. The commission's goal was to investigate **human rights** violations committed between 1960 and 1994 and to grant reparations to victims and amnesty to perpetrators. The 3500-page final report was presented to the President in 1998. Thus, the South African government worked to redress the negative impact of apartheid policies on the black majority.

See also Discrimination; Segregation and Desegregation

APPLIED RESEARCH

Applied research provides solution-focused results to a specific problem. Applied research projects thus have centralized research questions and topics which vary considerably. For example, one applied study may investigate production efficiency in a shoe company, while another may investigate the impact of a new environmental policy. The results of applied research are often used to influence **social policy** and ultimately provide remedies for social problems. Results of applied studies must therefore be practical and applicable to the social world. This purpose of practicality distinguishes applied research from pure research (sometimes referred to as basic research). Pure research—knowledge for its own sake—is used primarily for testing and advancing new theories. Research questions in pure research are less defined and results may not serve a particular practical purpose. Among early successful examples of applied research studies in **sociology** were the **Hull House** project, conducted by **Jane Addams** and Florence Kelley, and the establishment of the National Association for the Advancement of Colored People (NAACP) by W.E.B. DuBois.

In addition to purpose, applied research also differs from pure research in context. Pure research is most often conducted within academia, is characterized by scientific rigor, and is usually received by an audience of sociologists and others in the scientific community. In contrast, applied research is normally conducted by sociologists in a sponsored or paid environment, where topics, design methods, and scientific rigor may be constrained by employers or stakeholders, those parties who have influence in the decision-making process or are affected by the proposed program or policy. Time may also be a constraint in applied research: results are often needed quickly, limiting the **methodology** used. Further, results may not be fully disclosed, especially if results are at odds with sponsors' interests. A good illustration of these issues can be seen in the recent movie *The Insider* in which a researcher being paid by a tobacco company to investigate addiction risks of long-term tobacco smoking is constrained in his dissemination of results after damaging evidence is found. The researcher then struggles between obligations to the company and to scientific ethics.

While the pure researcher is usually interested in results that are statistically significant, the applied researcher must consider both statistical and practical significance. Consider an evaluation of an electronic monitoring program for parolees. To ascertain whether the monitoring program is successful, the applied researcher compares recidivism rates for parolees who completed the electronic monitoring program to recidivism rates for parolees who completed regular parole programs. A statistically significant result is found even if there are only seven more subsequent arrests among the regular parolees. For pure research, this finding is important. However, practically speaking, such a small difference will probably not justify continued funding for the program.

Different methods for conducting applied research include action research, social impact assessment research, **evaluation research**, needs assessment research, cost-benefit analysis, contingency evaluation, and actual cost evaluation. Action research tackles a current social issue from a particular political perspective and is aimed at redistributing power relationships by increasing awareness. Such research is not value neutral as the researchers usually hold strong views (e.g., feminist, radical, liberal, conservative, environmental, etc.) on the issue being studied. Social impact research involves assessing the probable effects of a proposed policy change. For example, a social impact study may examine the effects of tax cuts on public school funding. Because there can be many consequences of a proposed change to policy, this type of applied research is interdisciplinary: it may involve environmental science, economics, health, and **psychology**.

Evaluation research is conducted once a program or policy has been implemented to ascertain whether it was successful. There are two types of evaluation research. The first, *formation research*, is ongoing research of a program or policy designed to monitor its success or failure. The second, *summative research*, is conducted at the conclusion of a program or policy and assesses outcomes. Evaluators can be internal (sponsored by the implementing **organization**) or external. Both ethical and political issues can arise in evaluation research as programs or policies may actually be unsuccessful. Agencies needing evaluation research function in education, healthcare, criminal justice, private businesses, and government.

The first step in applied research is often a needs assessment where the researcher investigates the social problem or issue and defines what is needed to alleviate it. For example, a needs assessment of the number of homeless shelters required in a particular city may involve redefining homelessness, taking a **census** of the homeless, and interviewing a sample of homeless people to inquire about their needs. The second step often taken is a cost-benefits analysis which involves estimating all costs of a proposed project or policy and weighing these against proposed benefits. All costs are included and assigned a monetary value. Proposed benefits address the program or policy purpose and could include such factors as decreasing the crime rate, improving environmental conditions, or increasing resources for the homeless. Benefits are also assigned a monetary value in order for costs and benefits to be easily compared. Cost-benefit analysis which appears straightforward may lead to disagreement over benefit evaluation. For example, a city proposes to implement community policing. One element of the proposed policy is to increase the police officers on the street. One person may see a positive benefit because people may feel safer, but someone else may view the benefit negatively as more police do not necessarily decrease crime rate and they cost millions in tax dollars that have to be raised by cutting funding in other areas.

One way to assign monetary values to costs and benefits is *contingency evaluation* which asks people who will be affected by the proposed policy how much a benefit is worth to them. Thus, policy makers can get some sense of what the public believes. A second way to estimate costs is *actual cost evaluation* which involves totaling the monetary costs of a proposal. Because this method does not consider non-monetary costs, it is a conservative estimate. Sociologists with expertise in applied research are currently highly sought after in major U.S. cities given the rising public expectation of government accountability.

Applied Sociology

Applied sociology is the application of sociological theories, concepts, methods, and findings to problems identified in wider **society**. It is policy-oriented, action-directed, and intends to assist people and groups to think reflectively about what it is they do, or how it is that they can create more viable social and internal conditions.

The nature of applied sociology can be better understood by examining those characteristics that set it apart from basic sociology. Basic sociology is oriented toward those who have a concern for the advancement of sociological knowledge. The quality of such work is evaluated in accordance with agreed-upon standards of scientific merit. Applied sociology is oriented more toward those who are making decisions, developing or monitoring programs, or concerned about the **accountability** of those who are making decisions and developing programs. The quality of applied work is evaluated in accordance with a dual set of criteria: 1) how useful it is in informing decisions, revealing patterns, improving programs, and increasing accountability; and 2) whether its assumptions and methods are appropriately rigorous for the problems under investigation.

The boundaries of applied sociology may also be specified by enumerating the activities that play a central role in what it is that applied sociologists do. Thus, it has been sug-

gested that these activities include: mapping and social indicator research; modeling social phenomena; evaluating purposive action; and conceptualizing, studying, and facilitating the adaptability of alternative social forms.

The origins of applied sociology trace back to the publication of American sociologist Lester Frank Ward's *Dynamic Sociology: Or Applied Social Science* (1883), a text in which Ward laid the groundwork for differentiating between an understanding of causal processes and how to intervene in them to foster social **progress**. Today, applied sociology has entered into every arena of sociological endeavor.

Archetypes

From the Greek *archetypos*, meaning beginning pattern, an archetype is the original **model** or form from which something is made or develops. The term is generally attributed to the psychological theories of Swiss psychologist Carl Jung (1875–1961). According to Jung, human consciousness develops from an unconscious psyche that plays a pivotal role in human personality. This psyche functions with or without an individual's awareness. In addition to the **ego**, which is the awareness part of the conscious mind, there are two basic parts of the unconscious mind—the personal and the collective.

The contents of the personal unconscious come from lifetime experiences of the individual. They are the repressed thoughts, feelings, and memories unique to each person. The contents of the collective unconscious are inherited and, Jung believed, are shared by everyone. These contents, or archetypes, are instinctive, emotionally charged patterns or images with a universal character. They are basic ways of knowing and acting. They have always existed, although they are unconscious and lack clear content. The conscious experience supplies the material that brings these images to a realized form. These forms, or archetypes, erupt spontaneously in **dreams**, fantasies, myths, and delusions. Jung believed that the collective unconscious is the deepest layer of the unconscious mind. Therefore, his psychoanalytic **theory** is sometimes called depth psychology.

Jung developed his contested theory of archetypes while working at the Burgholzli mental hospital of the University of Zurich, Switzerland. He observed that some of the psychotic patients experienced the same religious and theological symbols. These relatively uneducated people could not have learned these symbols through any kind of formal study. Therefore, Jung concluded that such imagery did not come from lifetime experiences but from an eruption of unconscious material. From this theory came the idea of the archetype, which Jung further explored by closely examining his own fantasies and dreams. He also examined religious symbolism, believing that archetypes are of fundamental importance to that study.

The emotionally charged symbols of the collective unconscious express experiences and urges that are basic to humankind. Evolutionary history, said Jung, proves the existence of deep psychic predispositions with the power to excite human imagination and influence human actions. The ways in which humans respond to these inherited tendencies are unconscious, but they come to life in stirring images and ideas. These unconscious archetypes, which Jung also called primordial images, constantly emerge in dreams, insane delusions, childhood fantasies, religious lore, and even fairy tales.

Jung thought that archetypes are limited in number, although there are many forms, such as persons, numbers, shapes, and supernatural figures. There is the magna mater, or mother earth archetype, for example. Other archetypes include the hero, birth and death, the demon, the old wise man, and magic. The shadow archetype is immoral and **evil** and represents the human darker self. Examples are Satan, Dracula, and Darth Vader of the *Star Wars* films. Convinced of the **bisexuality** of men and women, Jung designated the anima as the feminine archetype of men and the animus as the masculine archetype of women. These archetypes, which may be positive or negative, not only influence the ways in which the genders regard and act toward each other, but also are the reason that each gender manifests certain characteristics of the other, such as passivity in the female and assertiveness in the male. Some archetypes appear as figures in dreams, becoming the source of such cultural symbols as gods and goddesses. Other archetypes do not appear in a personal form. Jung called these archetypes of transformation and many appear as patterns in folklore. Jung's theories of the collective unconscious and archetypes have been often criticized by other psychologists, who claim that his reasoning is too obscure and too rooted in mysticism. Yet, his thorough study of the range of human experience assures his place as a profound psychological theorist.

Besides the archetypes of Jung's psychology, the word may be used to indicate the original ancestor of a group of animals or plants. It also may indicate the universal image of a specific type. The college professor archetype might wear horn-rimmed glasses and a tweed jacket, whereas the housewife archetype would wear an apron.

ART AND SOCIETY

The study of the relationship between art and **society** is complex because broad ranges of subject matter and **methodology** are involved. Art includes literature, painting, and performance. It can be further divided into numerous, not necessarily disparate categories, such as popular, elite, folk, and mass culture. Then, too, sociological approaches differ in their understanding of art's impact on society and society's impact on art.

A sustained interest in the **sociology** of art did not develop in the United States until the 1970s. Since that time, sociology of art has matured both in Europe, which preceded the United States in the field, and in U.S. sociological research. One explanation for the late developing sociological study of the arts is the conflicting perspectives that often characterize the nature of the relationship between the arts and the social scientists. Artists tend to accentuate the uniqueness of their work. By contrast, sociologists tend to focus on the collective,

While artists accentuate the uniqueness of their work, sociologists tend to focus on the collective, interrelated nature of art, artists, and society *(AP/Wide World Photos, Inc.)*.

interrelated nature of art, artists, and society. For example, a poet may write from inner feelings and personal reflections on the nature of humanity. Yet a sociologist may attempt to understand the poet's poem in terms of social factors such as the age, sex, **culture**, or educational background of the poet. Given the difficulty in defining objective categories and developing statistical foundations, sociologists have avoided the study of art.

As a result, social research in the arts has grown slowly. A few social scientists began to research the arts during the 1950s; only a few publications on the subject existed until the mid–1960s. During this time, scholars of the arts began to accept the significance of social influences, and social scientists became more open to research that was not limited to strict empirical standards. Whether this somewhat uncomfortable fit of the arts and sociology led to a viable, productive sociology of the arts is a matter of debate.

According to Marcello Truzzi in his contribution ''Toward a General Sociology of the Folk, Popular, and Elite Arts'' in *Research in Sociology of Knowledge, Sciences and*

Art (1978), sociological study of the arts has been dominated by subjective categorization not existing in other areas of sociological study. "Throughout the general area known as sociology of art," Truzzi wrote, "the majority of work has unfortunately too often left objectivity behind and assumed a stance of indirect aesthetic criticism." According to Truzzi, sociologists of art often use poorly defined boundaries between "high" and "low" culture and impose vague, unsubstantiated meanings on these categories. He also argued that the art community, not the sociologist, dictates an artist's or artwork's standing in the culture, the placement of which is not questioned by the sociologist.

To avoid pitfalls, Truzzi suggested that sociology of art be based on the distinctions of focal areas and cultural levels. The three basic focal areas are (1) the producer of art product, (2) the art product itself, and (3) the audience of the art product. Cultural levels of folk, popular, and elite are redefined by Truzzi based on a socially defined continuum. Art is evaluated on such issues as simplicity or complexity of form, process of communication (mass media to elite audience), and perceived differentiation between artist and consumer (peer-produced to highly skilled specialist). Approaching art from this perspective, argued Truzzi, would allow art to be studied as a product of complex social processes that consequently lead to definitions that suggest art products are a result of social labeling that identifies certain products as art.

Sociological research into the arts generally focuses on either a general theory of sociology of the arts or theories of **socialization** based on art study groups. Theories of socialization focus on specific groups of artists or the art community to create **case studies**. A theoretical concept of art itself is secondary to the theoretical concept of socialization. By contrast, sociologists who attempt to define a sociology of the arts address the aesthetics as an all-encompassing subject and work to develop an overall theory of art and society. Much work in the field has had the less ambitious goal of using art as a basis for sociological study. Unfortunately, these studies do not contribute to an overall definition of the sociology of arts. At the same time, art is often broadly defined to include diverse aesthetic forms which contribute complexity to the process of formulating a general social theory of art.

ASCETICISM

Asceticism is the practice of denying worldly pleasures in order to attain a spiritual goal. The term comes from the Greek *askesis,* or training. In ancient Greece, athletes who wanted to achieve ideal physical fitness were expected to undergo rigorous physical discipline and testing and to abstain from normal physical pleasures. In time, asceticism became a central principle of ethics. Plato taught that the soul could not be free to seek knowledge unless bodily desires were rejected. Similarly, the Stoics adopted asceticism as a means to control the emotions and achieve transcendence over worldly appetites.

Various forms of ascetic practice can be found in almost all world religions. Ascetic acts are generally associated with concepts of sin and atonement, or with the realization of the world's transitory nature. Celibacy, abdication of worldly goods, and fasting are common among Hindu, Buddhist, and Christian ascetics, and fasting is obligatory in **Islam**. Some traditions also practice psychological asceticism by meditating on guilt, sin, death, and atonement, or advocate pain-producing acts such as self-laceration, flagellation, and castration. Asceticism is not generally found in **Judaism** but was practiced among the Essene sect which existed from the first century BCE through first century CE. Though ascetic practices were forbidden in Zoroastrianism, a religion founded in Persia in the seventh century BCE, the tradition was practiced by small numbers.

In addition to its religious significance, asceticism is an important part of rites and rituals in **traditional societies**. Among many American Indian tribes, for example, young men endure a period of fasting and physical self-denial before being accepted as adult members of the **community**. Asceticism is a similar part of puberty rites in native Australian **culture** and in many African cultures.

Though primarily associated with spirituality, asceticism has had a broader cultural influence. It was never embraced by the leaders of the Protestant Reformation but nevertheless became an important part of Calvinist thought and was thus associated with the **Protestant ethic**, which German sociologist **Max Weber** argued in *The Protestant Ethic and the Spirit of Capitalism* (1904-05), played a central role in the growth of modern **capitalism**. Asceticism has also been used to advance political goals, most notably in modern times by Indian leader **Mahatma Gandhi,** who advocated self-denial and endured extended fasts to inspire the Indian independence movement and help bring about the end of British colonialism on the subcontinent.

ASCRIBED STATUS

Each **society** has a stratified system of social hierarchy which means certain individuals occupy recognized social positions. For example, the wealthy hold a higher social position than the poor, and some minority groups may not fill the higher social positions but be clustered in the lower positions. Whatever the criteria for judging **status**, a social hierarchy exists in every society.

Ascribed status defines an individual's social position as decided by birth or some other involuntary way. Examples of ascribed status are a widower, a daughter, an Asian, or an adolescent. Individuals have little or no control over their ascribed status. Some ascribed statuses can prove to be unfavorable in certain cultures or societies. The hierarchical class system creates competition for social positions. Thus, even though, for example, individuals come from poor **family** backgrounds, they can move to a higher social class through personal achievements. Limits to acquired social position are linked to ascribed status. However, sometimes a self-made man or woman claims to have beaten the odds and broken free of social position dictated by ascribed status.

Some societies are organized by a caste systems. In this type of system, individuals exist in the social hierarchy as defined by ascribed status. The traditional caste system of India is one example. An individual born into a certain social class must stay in that class. Family background dictates choice of spouse, location for home, pursuit of occupation, and even political affiliation. In a system such as this, what people accomplish does not affect social rank. Another example of a caste system is **apartheid** in South Africa. In South Africa, prior to 1994, being born black secured a low rank in the social hierarchy. Black South Africans were denied the right to own property, received little schooling, and were forced to work menial jobs for little pay; as a result most lived in **poverty**. Whether a society maintains a class system or a cast system, ascribed status plays an integral part in the social position of individuals.

See also Caste and Class; Social Stratification

ASIAN AMERICAN STUDIES

Asian American studies is a broad label applied to research on those populations with ancestry in Asian countries, including the Pacific Islands. This all-inclusive label is a misnomer, however, because the various populations included in this label often have more differences than similarities. But until recently, Western researchers, politicians, and administrators have used this term for ease of grouping information. This area has been a focus of research since the early twentieth century. There have been five time periods of research: first, before World War II, when research focused on Chinese immigrants; second, during World War II, when most research focused on Japanese Americans; third, post-World War II, when there was an emphasis on **culture** and personality in general; fourth, the 1960s and 1970s, when research focused on the concept of **ethnicity** and the many differences between the various groups; and fifth, the current period which started in the 1980s and is characterized by its diversity and focus on previously-ignored populations.

The first period of research (late nineteenth and early twentieth century) began as a result of the mass immigration of Asians to the United States. There were two waves of immigration. The first was a result of poor economic and social conditions in Asian countries. Many of these immigrants were Chinese seeking a change from their rural economy. However, partly as a result of this influx and partly as a result of racism, in the 1920s the Chinese were the first group in history to be barred from becoming U.S. citizens because of their **race**. This bar was not lifted until 1965, when a new surge of Asian immigrants began to arrive in the United States. Early research focused on discrimination, **social distance**, and the high levels of isolation and low levels of assimilation among Asian immigrants.

The character of the second period of research was determined by the international relationships during World War II. Research focused on the social and political structures of Japan, which varied tremendously from those found in the United States—the Japanese had a focus on **community**, family, and group well-being that was contradictory to the strict **in-**dividualism found in the United States. The majority of this research dealt with the high level of **social cohesion** and the low level of individualism found in Japanese culture.

After World War II, the nature of research changed, and researchers began looking at the behavioral differences between Asian immigrants and other Americans. The focus, however, remained on the Japanese and their social structure. Much emphasis was put on culture and how it shapes individuals.

With the coming of the Civil Rights Movement in the United States, the nature of Asian American studies changed dramatically. A large number of Asian Americans became college-age during the 1960s and became increasingly vocal on college campuses. San Francisco State University and the University of California at Berkely became the starting points for student protests and demands for new programs in Asian American studies. There was a search for common **identity** among Asian Americans as well as a somewhat conflicting search for personalized ethnic identity within the different Asian American groups in the United States. Much research focused on the effects of oppression on ethnic minorities, research that could then be generalized to other minority populations such as women or African Americans. There was also a new interest in the experiences of the original Asian immigrants to the West and how their experiences had or had not affected American culture. It was during this time period that Asian American studies was established as a discipline in academia. This made clear how little information had been collected and created about the Asian American experience and how a large portion of it had focused on the Chinese and the Japanese, excluding Filipinos, Koreans, Vietnamese, and Indians.

The current research environment is diverse and active. By the late 1980s, many American and Asian-born researchers had begun researching numerous aspects of Asian culture and experience. One of the defining characteristics of this research has been to question traditional sociological questions and methods. These researchers claim that the historically white and androcentric bias of **sociology** has skewed both the subjects addressed and the statistics collected over the years. (This is similar to feminist theory and pedagogy.) Much current research addresses the issues of economy, culture, language, assimilation, Asians as a ''model minority,'' and the vast differences between the cultures in Asia (and thus differences in their experience in the United States).

There are two large problems remaining for those researching Asian Americans. The first is the lack of economic and **social statistics** on the many different groups of Asian Americans. There are various **government** agencies that gather information about these groups, but there is no clearinghouse for this information, and the many ways in which this information is collected often makes comparisons difficult if not impossible. The second problem is the lack of Asian-American Studies departments in the United States.

In response to these problems facing the study of Asian Americans, an Asian American contigency at Yale University founded the *Amerasia Journal* in 1970. After two issues, the publication was moved to the University of California at Los Angeles to be produced by the university's Asian Studies Center. The Center also published *Roots: An Asian American Reader* (1971), the first textbook in the field. Since that time, the body of research has grown immensely as the first generation of Asian American scholars have become tenured faculty and continue to publish books and articles at an ever-increasing rate. Consequently, the number of Asian American studies programs has grown, captivating on the success of the first programs at the San Francisco State University and the University of California at Berkeley. Additional programs first developed in other California universities, but Cornell University became the first Ivy League school to create a program in 1987. During the 1990s, the number of programs grew from 22 to 41. Programs have also expanded into new geographic regions represented by such schools as the University of Conneticut (1993), the University of Michigan (1994), Loyola University at Chicago (1995), New York University (1996), and Arizona State University (1998).

Despite such improvements, however, Asian American presence in academia does not adequately reflect their proportion of the American population. They are present in most West Coast colleges and universities, where there are large populations of Asian Americans, but they are rare on the East Coast (except in large urban areas with large populations of Asian Americans) and also in the Midwest and South (excluding Florida). Thus, they are not studied to the extent warranted by their presence in the United States. This means that they are still seen as "outsiders" in many areas of the country. This outsider status, combined with the lack of knowledge about their cultures leads to misunderstanding and social conflict between them and other racial and ethnic groups in the United States.

ASSOCIATION OF BLACK SOCIOLOGISTS

The Association of Black Sociologists (ABS) is a national organization originally founded in 1968 as the Caucus of Black Sociologists. Instituted by African American scholars, the **organization** established a forum for the dissemination of information among blacks in the field of **sociology**. Although membership is not limited by **race**, the organization encourages research, scholarship, and training on issues relevant to African Americans.

In 1976, the organization changed its name to the Association of Black Sociologists. Members sponsor annual conferences on issues relevant to African American life. By bestowing annual awards for excellence in scholarly work, the organization aids student research and career development.

The Association of Black Sociologists publishes the monthly ABS Newsletter, which includes information on the profession and current social issues. In addition, ABS publishes the quarterly journal *Race and Society*. The interdisciplinary journal includes related studies in anthropology, political science, economics and other social sciences. Also included are articles on Latinos, Native Americans, and Asian Americans.

ATTITUDE

Attitude is referred to as a learned and enduring tendency to perceive or act toward a person, product, idea, event, or situation in a particular way.

Among sociologists, there are a variety of definitions of attitude. While some sociologists suggest that holding an attitude leads to behaving in a certain way, others hold to the idea that an attitude may only exist mentally, since overt behavior can be constrained situationally. It is, therefore, useful to perceive an attitude as involving three distinct elements: a cognitive part—beliefs and ideas; an affective part—values and emotions; and a behavioral part—predisposition to act and actions.

An attitude fulfills one or more of four functions. First, an attitude serves an instrumental function: An individual develops a favorable attitude towards objects that aid or reward the individual and an unfavorable attitude towards objects that thwart or punish the individual. Second, an attitude often serves a knowledge function. It provides the person with a meaningful and structured environment. Third, an attitude expresses the individual's basic **values** and reinforces self-image. Fourth, an attitude protects the person from recognizing certain thoughts or feelings that threaten his or her self-image or adjustment.

A *stereotype* is one type of attitude. Originally, the term referred to a rigid and simplistic "picture in the head." Presently though, a **stereotype** is thought to be a belief about the characteristics of members of some specified social **group**. A stereotype may be positive or negative. Most stereotypes are resistant to change.

ATTRIBUTION THEORY

An attribution is an inference about why an event occurred (i.e., linking an event to its causes). American sociologist Kathleen Crittenden in her 1983 journal article "Sociological Aspects of Attribution, "which appeared in *Annual Review,* stated that "attribution is a process that begins with **social perception**, progresses through casual judgment and social inference, and ends with behavioral consequences." Even though attribution has been one of the most popular social psychological research topics of the past two decades, only a few theories of attribution exist.

The development of theories of attribution originated with German sociologist Fritz Heider's *The Psychology of Interpersonal Relations* (1958) in which he maintained that people strive to understand, predict, and control events in their everyday lives by forming theories about their social worlds, and new observations then serve to support, refute, or modify these theories. Although Heider did not develop an explicit theory of attribution, he did assert several principles that have guided all subsequent theorizing on this topic. Primary among these principles is the notion that people are inclined to attribute actions to stable or enduring causes rather than to transitory factors.

Beginning in the late 1960s, American sociologist Harold Kelley proposed a covariational model of attribution that addressed the question of whether a given behavior is caused by an actor or, alternatively, by an environmental stimulus with which the actor engages. According to this model, the attribution of cause is based on three types of information and their possible combinations: consensus (i.e., the similarity between the actor's behavior and the behavior of other people in similar circumstances), distinctiveness (i.e., the generality of the actor's behavior), and consistency (i.e., the actor's behavior toward this stimulus across time and modality).

American sociologist Edward E. Jones, along with Keith E. Davis in 1965 and later with Daniel McGillis in 1976, proposed the theory of correspondent inference, which addresses the attribution of personality traits to actors on the basis of their behavior and focuses on attributions about persons in greater depth than does Kelley's covariational model. The theory of correspondent inference focuses more narrowly on the actor but also yields more information about the actor in that it specifies what it is about the actor that caused the behavior. Jones and his co-authors predicted that two factors guide attributions: 1) the attributor's prior expectancies for behavior, specifically, expectancies based either on knowledge of earlier behaviors of the actor (target-based) or on the actor's social category memberships (category-based), and 2) the profile of effects that follow from the behavioral choices available to the actor.

In the mid-1970s, American sociologist Bernard Weiner and his colleagues began to apply attributional principles in the context of achievement situations. According to this model, people make inferences about an individual's success or failure on the basis of the actor's ability to do the task in question, how much effort is expended, how difficult the task is, and to what extent luck may have influenced the outcome. Other possible causal factors have since been added to this list. More important perhaps is Weiner's development of, first, a structure of causal dimensions in terms of which these causal factors can be described and, second, the implications of the dimensional standing of a given causal factor. The major causal dimensions are locus (internal or external to the actor), stability (stable or unstable), and controllability or **intentionality** of the factor. This model has been used extensively in educational research and has guided therapeutic educational efforts such as attribution retraining.

Although the proportion of published research that focuses on this topic declined somewhat during the 1980s, attribution remains one of the most popular fields of social psychological research today.

AUTHORITARIAN PERSONALITY

Authoritarian personality refers to someone that is prone to think in a stereotypical and narrow-minded way. Someone with an authoritarian personality does not believe in democratic or **group** decision-making. People with this personality type tend to be rigid, uncompromising, prejudiced, and intolerant of difference (particularly racial/ethnic, religious, and sexual); they value strength, have a strong dislike for weakness of any

kind, and tend to believe in strict discipline. This personality type can manifest itself in both political and personal arenas. One of the major characteristics of people with authoritarian personalities is a disdain for democratic ideals and practices.

Some researchers believe that attitudes and beliefs come from early childhood **socialization** and are a reflection of the culture's **norms**. Others believe that the innate structure of one's personality makes that person predisposed to reject democratic ideals. Much research has focused on the seemingly predisposed attraction of authoritarian personalities to Fascism, Nazism, and other similarly rigid political beliefs. The most well-known study on this topic is Theodor Adorno's 1950 *The Authoritarian Personality*. Other research was conducted by **Erich Fromm** and W. Reich. These authors contended there are several common characteristics of authoritarian personalities: hierarchical parent-child relationships characterized by a lack of **love** and affection; a polarized view of **society** and different social groups based on stereotypical attitudes about people; adherence to traditional morals and ways of doing things; and an uncompromising attitude about life. Others criticized this research and contended that the measurements are not reliable or valid. However, the findings in this research mirror modern research on general prejudice.

People with authoritarian personalities believe that their beliefs are ''right''. They believe in their right to control other people or in the authority of someone else to control them. They tend to be either controlling and self-righteous or passive and acquiescent to the demands of others. Those who are controlling tend to have the narcissistic belief that they are stronger, better, smarter, more organized, and in general superior to most of the people around them. In a cruel and selfish way, those people will often take advantage of others emotionally, psychologically, intellectually, financially, or physically. They can be people who rule through a **cult** of personality. Dictators and military leaders often have authoritarian personalities. Those with passive or acquiescent authoritarian personalities tend to be followers, such as cult members or Nazis.

AUTHORITY

Authority is defined as the power to enforce laws, exact obedience, command, determine, or judge. The concept of authority is closely related to power, the analysis of both being essential for studying political and legal systems. Authority can also refer to the ability to **influence** or persuade, based on knowledge. In this sense, a person with authority legitimates his or her information based on such characteristics as a history of integrity or a particular area of expertise.

Max Weber's account of authority has resulted in a wide influence of sociological theory. Weber delineated three types of authority: rational-legal, traditional, and charismatic. The first kind of authority, ration-legal, relies on a particular office or political **role** from which a certain individual derives his or her authority to give certain orders or participate in certain activities. Traditional authority is dependent upon the past. Persons respecting traditional authority do so because they have

Much sociological research has dealt with the attraction of authoritarian personalities to fascism, such as the following gained by Adolf Hitler *(AP/Wide World Photos, Inc.).*

done so for an extended period of time, the tradition of obedience to the leader becoming itself respected. Finally, charismatic authority relies on the abilities of its possessor. In this case, the person is considered to be a person worth obeying or following because he or she is perceived as having the appropriate qualities to lead.

Authority remains distinct from power even though a person needs power in order to exert his or her authority. The distinction relies on the two separate types of **legitimacy**. There is legitimacy by rule, as in a government that controls the political **organization** of a country or a teacher that has the power to reward and punish students. But there is also legitimacy by approval. In this case, the **government** also has the consent to rule by the people it administers and the teacher is respected as an authority by students. A person with the power to rule, therefore, will not always be able to exert this authority unless they also earn approval for **leadership**, generally one of the types discussed by Weber. Additionally, authority is distinct from power because authority can be the source of power for an individual.

Another realm of authority persists in academic and religious disciplines. An academic authority is one who has earned the respect of other members of the academic authority, usually in a certain area of expertise. The tests of this authority include publication in the recognized and authoritative texts in the field and the publication of books. Religious authority has been widely discussed throughout history. For example, the theologian Peter Abelard (1079–1142) concluded that authority by itself was not adequate to define the structure of religion. Instead, religious authority must be backed by reason and tied to the material world. Here, Abelard makes the distinction between the absolute authority (and also power) invested in a religious figure by his office in the **church** and the role of reason in his decision-making processes.

The topic of authority has remained relevant during contemporary times. According to Gerald F. Kreyche in *USA Today* (September 1993), Americans in the 1990s have confused authority with authoritarianism. Kreyche claimed that people with authority were no longer given the respect or trust that they might deserve. Instead, the general American public adopted the opinion that any person's viewpoint was as good as another's. Such people, asserted Kreyche, have argued against any form of authority which led to the demise of what Kreyche called moral authority or authority from those who perceived as leaders.

In a similar vein, Woody West of *Insight on the News* (18 November 1996) claimed that contemporary America at the end of the twentieth century lacked a standard for behavior, being overly concerned with individual rights. West cited David Gelernter *1939–The Lost World of the Fair*, who stated that ''power remains today authority has all but vanished.''

AUTONOMY

The original meaning of autonomy (from the Greek 'self' + 'law') implied self rule in a political context. Autonomy's extended meaning also applies to entities that are self—governing, including businesses, church membership, and religious groups. An autonomous **group** develops its own **rules** that govern its internal actions.

Autonomy may also refer to individual freedoms and liberties. **Immanuel Kant** developed an account of autonomy that he linked closely with **morality**. The autonomous person, according to Kant, had the ability to act freely, rationally, and morally. He distinguished autonomy from heteronomy, the concept that all moral imperatives are derived from the state or **society**. Heteronomy provides that a person passively accepts moral **values** given to him by an outside source. In contrast, autonomy entails that a person is free to accept a moral value and act in accordance with it. Contrary to a popular conception that autonomy implies that the actor not take part in any moral codes, for Kant, an autonomous agent makes the moral code his own with his completely free decision to act in such a way.

In contemporary views, autonomy has come to be considered not only the ability to act freely, but also the ability to make informed and self-determining decisions, in a sense, to make oneself. In a social context, understanding individuals as autonomous agents has implications for legal systems. For example, voluntary **euthanasia** should be allowed if we are to fully respect an individual's autonomy. However, this also relies on the 'informed consent' of the patient, in which the patient understands the implications of his action and freely makes the decision. Moreover, emphasis on individual autonomy correlates to an emphasis on education, as only well-informed citizens can make responsible decisions.

In contrast to Kant's radical understanding of autonomy, contemporary sociologists have taken a more balanced view. For example, Hollis defined the *autonomous man* in relation to the *plastic man*. The autonomous man is, as defined above, the free and rational **social actor**. The plastic man is determined by biology and social structures. According to Hollis, **sociological theory** must take both aspects of individuals into account when considering particular models. In essence, therefore, sociologists must recognize the impacts of individual actors on their society as well as societal influences on individuals that necessarily limits their complete freedom. This is a key issue as well for **rational choice theory**, which explains social life in terms of the consequences of the choices of social actors.

B

BAGEHOT, WALTER (1826-1877)
English journalist and economist

Holding a distinct place in Victorian society, Walter Bagehot wrote on a wide variety of subjects including economics, education, history, law, literature, politics, and religion. Although he was only 51 years old when he died, Bagehot produced a body of work that filled fifteen volumes. His writing style, described as fresh, witty, vivid, and akin to good conversation, earned him respect and admiration.

Bagehot was born in the small Somerset town of Langport on February 3, 1826, to Thomas Watson and Edith Stuckey Bagehot. His mother, a beautiful widow with three sons when she married Bagehot's father, was the niece of the founder of Langport bank, and his father, ten years her junior, was a partner in the bank. Initially, Bagehot had a happy childhood, marked by a good relationship with both his parents. Later, however, Walter, the youngest in the family, witnessed his mother's mental health deteriorate when his only full sibling died at age three, two of his half-brothers died, and his half-sister proved to be mentally handicapped. These tragedies caused bouts of madness in his mother that colored much of Bagehot's life as his mother remained dear to him until her death just seven years before his own. In contrast to his mother, Bagehot's father was a dependable, affectionate man. Well-read in the areas of history, **philosophy**, and politics, he carefully oversaw Bagehot's education and learning.

In 1839, when Bagehot was thirteen, his father sent him to Bristol College, where he excelled academically. In 1842, being denied entrance into both Oxford and Cambridge based on his father's Unitarian affiliation, Bagehot enrolled in University College in London. Once again he proved himself gifted, earning high honors in the classics and philosophy. During his time at University College, Bagehot established important friendships with Richard Holt Hutton, William Roscoe, and Timothy Smith Osler. He published his first article in the *Prospective Review* in 1847, followed by two more articles in 1848. In 1851, during a period in Paris when he was avoiding his call to the bar, Bagehot published seven witty, ironic letters in the Unitarian journal, the *Inquirer.*

Returning to London in 1852, Bagehot entered the family bank business. Continuing to write in his leisure, in 1855 he founded the *National Review* with his friend Hutton, and the two served as co-editors until it ceased publication in 1864. In 1857 he became acquainted with James Wilson, founder of *The Economist* and married Wilson's daughter, Eliza, in 1858. Although he published a distinguished collection of essays as *Estimates of Some Englishmen and Scotchmen* in 1858, Bagehot did not gain widespread recognition until the next year when he published an article on parliamentary reform in the *National Review.* When Wilson left England for a government position in India in 1859, he turned over the *National Review* to Bagehot and Hutton. When Wilson died in India the next year and Hutton moved on to become the editor of *Spectator,* Bagehot assumed sole control of *The Economist.*

As editor of *The Economist* until his death, Bagehot wrote two to three articles every week, sometimes more. His acclaim grew dramatically during this time, making Bagehot one of the most influential financial journalists of his time. He also published three major works during the last decade of his life: *The English Constitution* (1867), an examination of the changes to the constitution between the First and Second Reform Bills; *Physics and Politics* (1872), a study of societal growth based on **social Darwinism**; and *Lombard Street* (1873), an important economic study of the London money market. While working on his *Economic Studies,* Bagehot died at his father's Langport home on March 20, 1877. His death was heralded as a great loss for England.

Despite his wide acclaim among many of the world's elite, including Woodrow Wilson, Bagehot's books were not widely read. Ruth Dudley Edwards, editor of *The Best of Bagehot* (1993), offered several reasons why Bagehot managed to be both one of the Victorian Age's best-known and least-read authors. First, Edwards suggested that because of the difficult pronunciation of Bagehot (pronounced *ba'juht*),

Bankruptcy Cases, by State: 1995 to 1998

[In thousands (858.1 represents 858,100). For years ending June 30. Includes outlying areas, not shown separately. Covers only bankruptcy cases filed under the Bankruptcy Reform Act of 1978. **Bankruptcy:** legal recognition that a company or individual is insolvent and must restructure or liquidate. Petitions "filed" means the commencement of a proceeding through the presentation of a petition to the clerk of the court]

State	1995	1996	1997	1998	State	1995	1996	1997	1998
United States ..	858.1	1,042.1	1,317.0	1,411.4	Missouri	15.1	19.8	24.2	27.4
Alabama	24.3	29.3	33.3	33.8	Montana	2.1	2.5	3.2	3.7
Alaska	0.9	1.0	1.3	1.4	Nebraska	3.4	4.6	5.7	6.1
Arizona	14.8	18.0	23.2	24.7	Nevada	7.3	8.9	12.3	14.4
Arkansas	7.9	11.2	14.7	16.5	New Hampshire.	3.1	3.4	4.3	5.1
California	140.4	164.3	200.1	211.3	New Jersey	25.5	30.6	38.8	44.5
Colorado	13.1	14.9	17.9	18.9	New Mexico	3.7	5.2	6.8	7.9
Connecticut	8.5	10.2	12.7	13.5	New York	48.8	56.1	69.8	76.9
Delaware	1.4	1.9	2.4	2.7	North Carolina.	14.0	18.9	24.9	26.5
District of Columbia . .	1.4	1.6	2.2	2.8	North Dakota	1.2	1.5	1.9	2.1
Florida	43.4	51.9	67.4	76.4	Ohio	32.4	38.8	50.1	55.5
Georgia	42.1	50.9	59.9	62.6	Oklahoma	13.2	16.1	20.8	22.5
Hawaii	1.8	2.4	3.8	5.1	Oregon	13.2	15.1	17.9	17.9
Idaho.	3.7	4.8	6.2	7.5	Pennsylvania	22.0	28.2	38.3	45.2
Illinois	39.2	48.5	60.3	64.6	Rhode Island	3.0	3.8	5.1	5.4
Indiana	22.3	26.0	33.7	38.5	South Carolina	6.9	8.5	10.7	11.3
Iowa	5.9	7.6	9.6	9.7	South Dakota	1.3	1.7	2.1	2.3
Kansas	8.5	10.1	12.5	13.2	Tennessee	35.5	43.7	52.1	52.6
Kentucky	13.0	16.6	20.6	22.1	Texas	43.8	54.2	69.5	72.0
Louisiana	13.4	17.1	22.6	23.2	Utah	6.9	8.0	10.6	13.5
Maine	1.9	2.6	3.6	4.4	Vermont	0.9	1.2	1.7	1.9
Maryland	16.3	20.4	28.8	34.5	Virginia	25.5	31.7	40.7	43.4
Massachusetts	14.3	15.9	22.5	22.1	Washington	18.6	25.0	31.7	33.6
Michigan	22.7	28.0	36.1	41.2	West Virginia	3.8	4.9	7.6	8.8
Minnesota	14.1	16.3	19.9	19.5	Wisconsin.	11.8	14.4	17.9	19.6
Mississippi	10.6	13.3	18.2	19.1	Wyoming	1.2	1.5	2.0	2.1

Source: Administrative Office of the U.S. Courts, unpublished data.

people were reluctant to quote him. Second, Bagehot's association with the *Economist* did not offer any indication of his wit and charm. Third, because he wrote on such a wide range of topics and held a variety of social and profession positions, including banker, editor, essayist, and journalist, he was difficult to categorize. Fourth, his books' rather dry titles tended to dissuade the general public from attempting to read his work. Finally, the intellectual community tended to dismiss Bagehot as a serious thinker because his writing is entertaining and colloquial.

BANKRUPTCY AND CREDIT

Originally credit referred to the exchange of goods and service with the promise of future payment. Business credit serves to increase the power of business capital, while consumer credit, which is estimated to comprise more than thirty percent of all retail sales, allows a customer to make a purchase without an initial outlay of cash. Bankruptcy allows debtors to settle debts they are unable to pay. The process of bankruptcy is carried out in court, and the judicial system assists in distributing debtors' assets in order to satisfy outstanding debts. Bankruptcy law originated in the United States in 1898 and has been

amended several times since then. The most recent change occurred with the Bankruptcy Reform Act of 1978 which introduced new leniency into bankruptcy proceedings. The Chapter 11 option of bankruptcy proceedings allows courts to reorganize assets of a person or company filing for bankruptcy rather than requiring the filer to completely liquidate assets.

Leniency in more recent bankruptcy laws caused a surge in filings. Between 1980 and 1997, bankruptcies increased by over 500 percent. During 1998, over 1,442,000 businesses and individuals filed for bankruptcy. This action cost business and consumers over $40 billion. The rapidly accelerating trend in bankruptcies caused the U.S. Chamber of Commerce to push for bankruptcy law reform once again in 1999. The proposed reforms sought to make it harder for solvent companies to file Chapter 7 bankruptcy which allows total liquidation of all debt. Advocates for such reform argued that if unchecked, current bankruptcy trends would continue to escalate. But under current bankruptcy laws, companies sometimes use bankruptcy proceedings as a strategy to aid a merger or litigation, rather than as a means to reorganize or eliminate debts.

In the latter part of the twentieth century, personal credit debt trends in the United States had taken a unique turn of their own. By the late 1990s, over 35 percent of adults in the United States admitted that they were close to the credit limits on their personal credit cards. Of Americans, those between 25 and 34 years were most likely (43 percent) to be near the limits on their credit cards. Adults over 55 years were least likely to be plagued with over-extension on personal credit. In a *Forbes* article (24 March 1997), Peter Huber commented that the credit industry in the United States had evolved from emphasizing personal relationships to manufacturing credit out of huge financial databases. Additionally, credit regulation had relaxed in the late 1990s, and banks were able to charge high interest for personal credit. At the end of the century, credit had become an automated, anonymous, and profitable business for lenders.

BAR CHART

A bar chart is a graphic display of categories within one **variable** and can be used for both nominal and ordinal level variables. Nominal variables are those whose categories are different in name only and cannot be ranked according to some quality. Examples of this type of variable would be a dichotomous variable (those with yes/no responses, for instance) or state of residence (one state does not have more of a quantity of "stateness" but is simply distinguished by name). Ordinal variables are those whose categories have some inherent ranking or fall along a continuum. For example, categories for this variable might include responses of "agree strongly," "agree," "neither agree nor disagree," "disagree," and "disagree strongly." One might begin the ordering either with "agree strongly" or "disagree strongly," but the order after the initial choice is clear.

Bar charts represent information and reveal no more than a table of the values would, but because they communicate information more efficiently, they provide a sort of quick overview of **data**. Bar charts are interpreted in the same way as pie charts, and are preferred over pie charts if the data have more than four or five categories because they tend to appear less cluttered than pie charts.

Typically the names of categories of the variable are placed along the horizontal axis, and the frequencies of responses are placed along the vertical axis. The frequency of each category is indicated by a height corresponding to the frequency value. The bars on the chart all have a constant width and do not touch. The placement of the categories typically follows common conventions. For nominal data, the categories of the variable are usually ordered by frequency from highest to lowest. The common exception to this convention is the catch-all category, such as "Other," which is generally placed at the end of the graph, regardless of frequency. Ordinal data is typically ordered by the natural order of the categories.

By using multiple bars for each category, bar charts can also be used to show relative frequency of various respondents within a given category, such as gender, race, or political affiliation. For example, a researcher could subdivide categories of religious preference according to gender and plot the frequencies of women and men separately for each category of religious preference.

BEHAVIORISM

Behaviorism, an approach to psychological study based philosophically on logical-positivism that denies the relevance of consciousness in understanding behavior, explains human behavior entirely in terms of observable and measurable responses to environmental stimuli. It also assumes that all observable behavior patterns that result are the product of **conditioning** (positive and negative encouragement or reward and punishment). Emerging at the beginning of the twentieth century, behaviorism appeared as a response to the introspective approach, which dominated **psychology** at the time. While introspection focused on the workings of consciousness, which was most often studied through self-examination, behaviorism rejected the introspective premise that consciousness could be either observed or measured. A famous example of early behaviorist study was conducted by Russian **Ivan Pavlov**, who won the Nobel Prize in 1904 for his study of conditioning. Pavlov experimented with dogs by ringing a bell simultaneously with the smell or sight of food, which caused the dogs to salivate. Ultimately, the dogs were conditioned to salivate when the bell rang without the presence of food.

In *The War Between Mentalism and Behaviorism* (2000), William R. Uttal identified four major figures in the development of behaviorism: John B. Watson, E. C. Tolman, Charles L. Hull, and B. F. Skinner. In *Behaviorism* (1913), Watson, who is often referred to as the founder of the behaviorist movement, wrote, "Behaviorism... holds that the subject matter of human psychology *is the behavior of the human being.* Behaviorism claims that consciousness is neither a definite nor a usable concept. The behaviorist, who has been trained always as an experimentalist, holds, further, that belief in the existence of consciousness goes back to the ancient days of superstition and magic." Although he stopped short of denying the existence of the consciousness, Watson criticized attempts to study mental processes as pre-scientific, arguing that introspective study cannot be experimentally proven, tends to be vague, and is inherently subjective. Therefore, the introspective approach affords no basis for standardized methods or consistent theories of behavior. There are, in fact, according to Watson, as many introspective theories as there are introspective theorists.

Tolman's version of behaviorism, outlined in his 1932 book *Purposive Behavior in Animals and Men,* gave a wider berth to mentalism than did Watson's understanding. Tolman defined behaviorism as "Any type of psychology which, in contrast to mentalism, holds that 'mental events' in animals and human beings can, for the purposes of science, be characterized most successfully in terms wholly of the ways in which they function to produce actual or probable behavior." Unlike Watson, who saw observable behavior as the end result, Tolman reintroduced the role of the consciousness by suggesting that behavioral observation is simply the best avenue to revealing the underlying mental processes. Thus, he rejected introspection as a method but acknowledged the importance of the consciousness in human behavior.

Writing two decades after Tolman, Hull distinguished between scientific observation and scientific **theory**. Conceding that if scientists had the ability to dissect the mental functions of humans, such a method would be highly preferable. Arguing that such knowledge is unobtainable by direct study, he affirmed the place of the behaviorist approach as the empirical means to the theoretical ends. In other words, he focused on the development of basic laws of behavior, including inferred mental variables. His efforts led to inclusion of mathematical and statistical models.

B. F. Skinner, one of the most influential figures in contemporary psychology, introduced a radical version of behaviorism, which is referred to as "operant behaviorism." Unlike Pavlov's reflexive behaviorism's emphasis on involuntary reactions such as salivation in dogs, operant behaviorism focuses on the actor's voluntary response. The distinction lies between the passive conditioning of Pavlov's theory and Skinner's view that humans operate within an environment of external stimuli. He was clear, however, that although the behavior is perceived as voluntary, it is not uncaused. It results not from free will or conscious decision but from outside forces. Skinner, who like his predecessors never denied the existence of mental processes, took a radically negative view of their importance. Unlike Hull's search for the inferred meaning behind the behavior, Skinner was adamant that the behavior was the one and only meaningful aspect. Detailing his operant behaviorist approach in *About Behaviorism* (1973) as a follow-up to his vision of **utopia** based on behaviorism, *Walden Two* in 1948, Skinner helped behaviorism become a dominating influence in psychology, especially in the United States.

Practical applications of behaviorist theory in the application of stimuli-response conditioning within psychology took the form of aversion therapy, desensitization, and operant conditioning. Aversion therapy uses negative stimulation as punishment to reduce the tendency of an individual to act in a certain manner, for example, the administration of an electric shock each time an individual performs a specific behavior such as cursing. Desensitization is used most often to treat phobias; gradually exposing the patient to that which is feared, such as high places or spiders, the patient is conditioned to be less anxious. Operant conditioning uses the systematic application of rewards and punishments to discourage negative behaviors or reinforce positive behaviors. Behavioral therapy operates on the assumption that all behavior is a learned response to environmental influences; therefore, desirable behavior can be learned and undesirable behavior can be unlearned by systematic application of external stimuli.

Sociology has been predominately hostile toward the behaviorism on the basis of the approach's denial of the role and impact of **society** and its emphasis on the individual, rather than social aspects of human activity. According to its critics, including sociologist **George Herbert Mead**, behaviorism is limited because it can only address what people are doing, not what they are thinking or feeling. On the micro-level, in direct opposition to behaviorism is the sociological approach of **symbolic interactionism**, which focuses on the meaning behind human actions and interactions. At the macro-level, sociologists reject behaviorism because it ignores the influence of social systems and it is unable to account for meaningful social or cultural activity.

BELIEF SYSTEM

The philosophical meaning of the term "belief" implies an intellectual assent and commitment to some idea. A belief system is the collective beliefs of a particular **society** or **culture**. Belief systems include the knowledge and beliefs within a society, such as scientific and technological knowledge. The concept of belief system has most often been used to describe the patterns of religious beliefs and **values** that underlie thought in a society or culture.

Belief has been studied through time, but less so than the related concepts of faith and **probability**. Philosopher and mathematician René Descartes (1596–1650) felt that belief was determined by will. He contended that it was necessary to remove all presuppositions, or systematically doubt everything within one's general belief system, and rebuild a truly verifiable system of beliefs to have certain knowledge about man and the world. According to **David Hume** (1711–1756) accepting a particular system of beliefs was not subject to the rational inquiry of Descartes, but was instead the result of an emotional commitment to a body of knowledge. In a similar vein, C. S. Peirce (1839–1914) considered beliefs to be established by habitual action. If we see the ball fall to the floor every time that we drop it, we will believe that it will fall the next time we do so. A belief system for a given group of people is characterized by the beliefs accepted by the individuals within that group. Different communities and culture share different belief systems.

BELL, DANIEL (1919-)
American sociologist

Born in Brooklyn in 1919 to Jewish immigrant parents, Daniel Bell was raised in New York's Lower East Side. Bell's early childhood was difficult. His father died when he was six months old and Bell's mother worked long hours in a factory to support herself and her son. She was forced to put Bell in a day orphanage. Bell's childhood was spent in a world characterized by poverty and the hopes and frustrations of a Jewish immigrant population drawn largely from Eastern Europe. For a variety of historical and sociological reasons, this population maintained a clear and persistent association with socialist politics.

At the age of 13 the then Daniel Bolotsky joined the Young People's Socialist League, a youth organization of the Socialist Party. Particular components of this heightened political environment had a powerful effect on Bell's later views about leftist politics. Debates with the militant Young Communist League and the frustration of using non-violent means to advance the cause of American trade unionism in an age of union-busting made Bell sensitive to extremism on both the right and the left. It was the insights born of these experiences that later made Daniel Bell a prominent and astute observer of the American labor movement, first as a staff writer and editor of *The New Leader* and then as labor editor of *Fortune*.

Until he left *Fortune* in 1956, Bell wrote articles about the changing face of the American labor movement. He emphasized the declining role of ideology—specifically Marxism—in the movement. These articles became the working models for his controversial book *The End of Ideology* (1960). Bell's thesis in this book was that Marxism no longer evoked the passions of American intellectuals because it had become irrelevant to the American experience. Marxism emphasized righting the social and economic inequalities produced by **capitalism**. However, as Bell wrote, in America these inequalities were resolvable through existing political and administrative structures.

The development of these themes—the "exhaustion of the political left" and the irrelevance of **ideology** in American political thought—occupied Bell throughout his career as an American sociologist and policy analyst. They led him to construct his theory of the postindustrial **society**, which was a theory of **social change**. He identified the United States, Germany, and Japan as societies undergoing major structural changes. The most significant of these changes were the displacement of the traditional market economy, the growing preeminence of the public sector in sponsoring basic scientific research, and a new reliance on stochastic methods and abstract thinking in the planning process.

In *The Coming of the Post-Industrial Society* (1973), Bell characterized this society as an arena in which the working political, cultural, and economic principles were contradictory and in conflict. Politically, there was an emphasis on **democracy**. Culture was undergoing both de-institutionalization and radicalization. In economics, there was an emphasis on rationalism and efficiency. This view constituted Bell's non-Marxist **conflict theory** of social change and was the first significant challenge to Talcott Parson's structure-functionalist view of contemporary **American society**. Bell's theory calls for a new philosophy of **welfare state liberalism**. Bell called it the philosophy of the "public household."

The Coming of the Post-Industrial Society and the call for a new philosophy of the public **household** were the fruits of Bell's work as chairman of the Presidential Commission on the Year 2000 (1966–1968). He helped articulate an agenda of social welfare and political problems which challenged the basis of American liberalism. His publications earned him a reputation as something of a futurist. Also cementing his stature as a futurist was his 1976 book *The Cultural Contradictions of Capitalism*. In this work Bell presages such later predominant theories as the relationship of capitalism and culture as modes of production and consumption, post structuralism, deconstruction, and quite accurately as Bell puts it, "The underlying problem... (of the)... breakup in the very discourses—the languages, and the ability of a **language** to express an experience."

Bell's futurism was of a specific kind. His task was to ask the questions which Western society must answer if there is to be domestic **peace** and stability in the future. Implicit in Bell's asking was the admonition to move slowly; to eschew extremism. This grew out of Bell's early experiences in the American trade union movement and out of his own intellectual struggle to reconcile the "Hellenistic" world view of **Karl Marx** and John Dewey with the "Hebraism" of Rheinhold

Daniel Bell *(The Library of Congress)*

Niebuhr. "Hellenism" has faith in the inevitability of social progress through science and reason. The "Hebraic" world view emphasizes the limits of planning and reason in human affairs.

Bell also earned the reputation of being a neoconservative precisely because of his predisposition to move slowly and to be wary of extremism. He shared the neoconservative designation with such peers and colleagues as Daniel Patrick Moynihan, **Nathan Glazer**, and Irving Kristol. The applicability of such labels is always debatable. What was not debatable was Bell's place in the social sciences. He was a relevant and challenging sociologist whose critical analyses of contemporary economic theory and American capitalism defied simplistic categorization. His self evaluation served well. Bell claimed to be "a liberal in politics, a conservative in culture, and a socialist in economics."

Beginning in 1969, Bell served as Henry Ford Professor of Social Science at Harvard University and in the late 1980s as a Pitt Professor at Cambridge University, England. In 1988 he traveled to the former Soviet Union, a place very close to his heart, to give a series of lectures at various universities. Together with Irving Kristol Bell founded and edited *Public Interest,* a **social policy** journal.

BENDIX, REINHARD (1916-1991)
German sociologist and educator

Reinhard Bendix was born February 25, 1916, in Berlin, Germany, the son of attorney Ludwig Bendix and Else (Henschel) Bendix. In his native land, Bendix participated in the antifascist organization *Neu Beginnen.* Then, in 1938, he immigrated to the United States as a political refugee. He married Jane L. Walstrum on July 5, 1940. The couple had three children: Karen Moya, Erik Michael, and John Steven. He obtained a doctorate in **sociology** from the University of Chicago in 1943. Bendix began teaching at the University of California, Berkeley, in 1947, and he would remain affiliated with the university throughout his career. From 1968 to 1970, he directed the university's Education Abroad program. Throughout the course of his career, Bendix also accepted the positions as the Theodor Huss Professor as the Free University of Berlin (1694–5), visiting professor at St. Catherine's College, Oxford University (1965), fellow at Nuffield College, Oxford University (1971), and public lecturer. Bendix was also a member of several organizations. He was a member of the American Philosophical Society and the Pacific Sociological Society. Bendix also served as vice-president of the International Sociological Association and as president of the American Sociological Association and vice president of the International Sociological Association.

Bendix's writings often focus on **authority** and economic relations in Russia, Japan, and Western Europe. Among these books are: *Work and Authority in Industry,* which has been published in Spanish, German, Italian, and Japanese; *Class, Status and Power, Social Mobility in Industrial Society,* which has been published in Polish, Japanese, and Spanish; *Nation-Building and Citizenship, Embattled Reason, Max Weber: An Intellectual Portrait,* which has been published in German, Japanese, Hindi, Polish, and Italian; and *Scholarship and Partisanship.* His autobiography *From Berlin to Berkeley: German-Jewish Identities* was published a few years before his death from a heart attack, February 28, 1991, in Berkeley, California.

BENEDICT, RUTH FULTON (1887-1948)
American cultural anthropologist and professor

The American cultural anthropologist Ruth Fulton Benedict (1887–1948) originated the configurational approach to **culture**. Her work has provided a bridge between the humanities and anthropology, as well as background for all later culture-personality studies.

Ruth Fulton was born in New York City, the daughter of a surgeon. She entered Vassar College in 1905 and specialized in English literature. After graduation she taught English in a girls' secondary school. In 1914 she married the biochemist Stanley Benedict, and the next five years were spent waiting for the children who never came and experimenting with a variety of creative tasks, such as writing poetry (her pen name as a poet was Anne Singleton), studying dance, and exploring the lives of famous women of the past. In 1919 she began to study anthropology and received her doctorate from Columbia University in 1923.

Her first anthropological work was a study of the way in which the same themes, such as the "Vision Quest," were organized differently in different Native American cultures. During the next nine years she was editor of the *Journal of American Folk-Lore* and did a substantial amount of fieldwork among the Native Americans of the Southwest. In all of this early work she was impressed with the extraordinary diversity of human cultures, but she did not yet have any way of integrating this diversity.

In the summer of 1927, while doing fieldwork among the Pima, she developed her configurational theory of culture: each culture could be seen as "personality writ large"—a set of emphases derived from some of the innumerable potentialities of the human personality. *Patterns of Culture* (1934), her best-known book, develops this theme. This book contrasts the Native American cultures of the Southwest as Dionysian and Appolonian, borrowing terminology from Nietzsche; and Kwakiutl and Dobuan cultures as megalomaniac and paranoid, borrowing terms from psychiatry. This eclectic choice illustrated her open-ended approach to history and her lesser concern with universals. She is sometimes associated with a theory of cultural relativity which treats all **values** as relative; actually, however, she was deeply committed to the relevance of anthropology to man's control of his own evolution.

During the 1940s she devoted her energies to dispelling myths about race (*Race: Science and Politics,* 1940) and to a discussion of how warfare, now outmoded, could be superseded. During World War II she worked on studies of countries to which the United States had no access: Romania, the Netherlands, Thailand, and Japan. After the war she published *The Chrysanthemum and the Sword: Patterns of Japanese Culture* (1946), which was the best received of all the anthropological studies of national character. In 1947 she was elected president of the American Anthropological Association, and in 1948, belatedly, she was designated full professor of anthropology at Columbia University.

In 1947 Benedict inaugurated a great cross-cultural study, the Columbia University Research in Contemporary Cultures (France, Syria, China, Russia, Eastern European Jews, Czechoslovakia), in which 120 scholars from 14 disciplines and of 16 nationalities worked harmoniously together. In the summer of 1948 she visited Europe for the first time since 1926 and saw again at firsthand some of the cultures she had analyzed at a distance. She had gone to Europe against the advice of physicians, and she died a week after her return in September 1948, leaving a devoted group of younger collaborators to finish the work.

BENTHAM, JEREMY (1748-1832)
English philosopher

Jeremy Bentham is most well known as the founder of *utilitarianism*, a theory of **morality** that determines the rightness of acts by the consequences of those acts. Bentham's work in the areas of legal philosophy, penal reform and **criminology** sought to apply his philosophical principles to the English legal system and other social institutions. Bentham sought to codify the English **common law** and developed the Panopticon, a system for prison reform.

Jeremy Bentham was born on February 15, 1748, to Alicia Grove Whitehorne and Jeremiah Bentham, a London attorney. He began studying Latin at the age of three and attending Westminster School at seven. At twelve, he entered Queen's College, Oxford, and was awarded a bachelor's degree in 1764. He began to prepare for a career as a barrister by entering Lincoln's Inn and attending the Court of King's Bench beginning in 1763, was awarded a master's degree at Oxford in 1767, and was admitted to the bar in 1769. However, Bentham was more interested in the theoretical form of the legal system, and he never actually practiced law. His father died in 1792, leaving Bentham the family estate and rendering him an independently wealthy gentleman. With his wealth, Bentham centered himself in English intellectual life. A prominent author, he continued to produce works on social causes throughout his life and co-founded *The Westminster Review* with **James Mill** in 1824. Upon his death in 1832, Bentham willed his body to University College London, and instructed that his preserved skeleton be made into an effigy of himself, stuffed and dressed in his own clothes, and displayed.

Bentham, whose thought was influenced by French philosopher Claude-Adrien Helvétius, conceived of the principle of utilitarianism in order to define morality. **Utilitarianism** described utility as the ability to produce the greatest happiness for **society** in general and the principle was introduced in Bentham's work *A Fragment on Government*. Originally called the "principle of utility" and later renamed the "greatest happiness principle," this principle was carried on through the nineteenth century by Bentham's followers, the Philosophical Radicals. Bentham and his followers defined happiness in terms of good and pleasure and purported that pleasure could be measured through the "felicific calculus." In what could be seen as an early form of cost-benefit analysis, Bentham proposed that individuals cared only about their own greatest good, but that an individual should do what brought the greatest good for the greatest number. Immoral or unethical acts were those that were incompatible with the greatest happiness of society. Bentham sought to apply this principle to many of England's social systems of the day, including the **government**, legal, and education systems.

Also using the pseudonym Gamaliel Smith, Bentham wrote widely on the social issues of the day. Among his most well known works are the *Defence of Usury*, which considers taxation and the *Panopticon*. This series of works details a system of organization for prisons that provided for the maximum surveillance of inmates. Bentham's brother, Samuel, provided

Ruth Fulton Benedict *(The Library of Congress)*

the initial architectural design for the building, and this sparked the ideas of prison reform, which were to possess Bentham for more than twenty years. While he was recognized as a great critical thinker by his contemporaries, including **John Stuart Mill** and William Hazlitt, Bentham was often criticized as one whose ideas were difficult to follow. What is more, his ideas on morality and social reform have been hotly debated since the early 1900s, with critics claiming that Bentham's methods were cold and mechanistic and did not respect the individual's natural need for privacy. Though controversial, Bentham is recognized as having made significant contributions to many areas of social reform, including public health, universal suffrage, the electoral process, and public safety.

BERGER, PETER LUDWIG (1929-)
Austrian sociologist

Since the publication of his widely read *The Sacred Canopy* in 1966, sociologist Peter L. Berger has been known as one of the most interesting and often controversial writers on the sociological aspects of religion, economics, and modern society. Berger was born on March 17, 1929, in Vienna, Austria, the son of George William and Jelka (Loew) Berger. In 1946 he emigrated to the United States and in 1952 became a naturalized citizen. On September 28, 1959, he married Brigitte Kellner. They had two sons, Thomas Ulrich and Michael George. Berger received a Bachelor of Arts degree from Wagner College in 1949. He earned his Master of Arts and Doctor of Philosophy degrees from the New School for Social Research in 1950 and 1954, respectively.

In 1954, Berger began his career as a sociologist at the University of Georgia, Columbus. Over the next 25 years he held positions at numerous universities, including Evangelical Academy in Bad Boll, Germany, from 1955-1956, Women's College of the University of North Carolina (now University of North Carolina at Greensboro) from 1956-1958, Hartford Seminary Foundation in Hartford, Connecticut, from 1958-1963, New School for Social Research in New York City from 1963-1970, Rutgers University from 1970-1979, and Boston College from 1979-1981. In 1981 Berger became professor at the University of Boston.

Berger has written over a dozen books, all of which have focused primarily on the sociology of religion and sociological theories pertaining to economic development. In *The New York Times Book Review,* Eleanor Munro refers to Berger's *The Social Construction of Reality,* (with Thomas Luckmann) (1966), *The Sacred Canopy,* (1967), and *The Heretical Imperative* (1979) as "milestones in the study of the life of ideas in contemporary society." Later works of note include *The Capitalist Revolution: Fifty Propositions about Prosperity, Equality, and Liberty* (1986), *A Rumor of Angels: Modern Society and the Rediscovery of the Supernatural* (1990), and *Redeeming Laughter: The Comic Dimension of Human Experience* (1997).

Keenly interested in the role of religion in the public realm, Berger draws both praise and criticism for mixing a scientific approach with his religious beliefs. In *A Far Glory: The Quest for Faith in an Age of Credulity,* Berger argued, "If there is a true self, it can only be revealed as true in a transcendent frame reference." Believing that humanity is God's reflection in the world, Berger attempts to prove empirically that religion can provide true enlightenment beyond the simple, everyday experience.

Sharply critical of post-modern Christian institutions as being without substance, Berger, a Lutheran himself, insists that the world still yearns for a transcendental experience. In an interview with *Christian Century,* he explained, "I think what I and most other sociologists of religion wrote in the 1960s about **secularization** was a mistake. Our underlying argument was that secularization and modernity go hand in hand. With more modernization comes more secularization. It wasn't a crazy theory. There was some evidence for it. But I think it's basically wrong. Most of the world today is certainly not secular. It's very religious." While lauded by some for his determination to bring his faith along with his science, other critics dismiss Berger's Christian perspective as a fundamental betrayal of any plausible scientific method.

In 1985 Berger became the director of the Institute for the Study of Economic Culture (ISEC) at the University of Boston. This newly formed research center was created to systematically study the relation between economic development and sociological change on a global level. In a 1999 letter to "Friends of the ISEC," Berger explained the intent of the center's study at its inception. "There was indeed an underlying orientation to wit, to study the cultural foundations of capitalism free of the anti-capitalist ideology which at that time was still very prominent in academia." Following the work of Alexis de Tocqueville, Berger maintains that organizations that affect everyday life, which he calls intermediate or mediating institutions, such as schools, labor unions, and churches, make up the foundation of **democracy**. The subject of *The Capitalist Revolution,* Berger draws the conclusion that capitalism is the economic system that will cultivate the highest levels of civic virtue and liberty.

BERKELEY, GEORGE (1685-1753)
Irish philosopher

Philosopher George Berkeley was born at Dysert Castle, near Thomastown, Ireland, on March 12, 1685. He graduated from Trinity College, Dublin, with a Bachelor of Arts in 1704 and was elected a fellow of the college in 1707. Three years after taking holy orders, he traveled to London, where he became acquainted with such literary figures as Swift, Addison, and Pope. After spending several years traveling across Europe, Berkeley returned to Ireland in 1721, where he filled various academic posts, including Divinity Lecturer, Hebrew Lecturer, Proctor, Dean of Dromore, and in 1724, Dean of Derry.

Hoping to establish a college in the Bermuda Islands, Berkeley sailed for America in 1728, landing at Newport, Rhode Island. After waiting three years for funding that never materialized, Berkeley aborted his mission and returned to London in 1732. Two years later, in 1734, he was appointed Bishop of Cloyne. Berkeley resided in Cloyne until 1752 at which time he retired to Oxford to live the remainder of his life with his son, a senior student at Christ Church. Berkeley died on January 14, 1753.

Berkeley's first publication *An Essay Toward a New Theory of Vision* concerns the relation between the senses of sight and touch. "The objects of sight and touch," he writes, "make, if I may so say, two sets of ideas which are widely different from each other.... A man born blind, being made to see, would at first have no idea of distance by sight: the sun and stars, the remotest objects as well as the nearer, would all seem to be in his eye, or rather in his mind." Because the objects or ideas of sight and the objects of touch are distinct, any **correlation** between the two must be learned by observing a constant, albeit arbitrary, connectedness. What we see is what we can expect to touch.

The primary exposition of Berkeley's philosophy of **idealism**, for which he is best known, appears in *A Treatise Concerning the Principles of Human Knowledge* (1710) and *Three Dialogues between Hylas and Philonous* (1713). To refute Locke's acceptance of Descartes' dualism of spirit and matter, which he believed would lead to skepticism and atheism, Berkeley built on his previous writings regarding the primacy of the mind (i.e., sight) as the source of knowing, ultimately concluding that "no object exists apart from the mind, mind is therefore the deepest reality." Whereas Locke affirmed the physical presence of an object which is perceived by the mind, but whose existence does not depend on that perception, Berkeley starts with the mind, suggesting that nothing that is not perceived can exist.

Because a person can only be aware of the world insofar as the person has ideas about the world, Berkeley considered his argument to be in support of common sense. If ordinary objects are a "collection of ideas," then there can be no doubt that we perceive things as they are. The visible world is a compilation of ideas of the mind, which for Berkeley was an affirmation, not a rejection, of the existence of a real, cognizable world. He further validates the source of our perceptions by arguing that they cannot come from the material (as Locke would suggest) because inert object have no power to cause a perception. Rather, Berkeley asserts that only an intelligent mind could cause an idea to act on the mind, namely God, "who works all in all, and by whom all things consist."

Although Berkeley continued to modify and defend his philosophy of idealism throughout his life, after he became bishop in 1734 many of his writings centered on social and religious concerns and the need for reforms, outlined primarily in *The Querist* (1735). Later, he wrote about his fascination with tar-water as a universal medicine, including *Inquiries Concerning the Virtues of Tar-water* (1744). From his earliest days, he wrote scathing articles against the free-thinkers and materialists and bemoaned the disintegration of morals and spirituality in society. Arguably Ireland's greatest philosopher, in his book *George Berkeley: Idealism and the Man* (1996) biographer David Berman calls Berkeley's attempt to create a philosophy that reunited spirit and body "a magnificent achievement, possibly the last great and creative theological synthesis."

BERNSTEIN, EDUARD (1850-1932)
German political theorist

Eduard Bernstein, born in Berlin, Germany, on January 6, 1850, was one of the first socialists to attempt a revision of the tenets of Karl Marx. Called the "father of revisionism," Bernstein advocated a type of social democracy that included private enterprise as well as social reform. His father was a railroad engineer, and the family's financial resources were limited. At the age of sixteen, Bernstein became an apprentice in a bank, rising to bank clerk within a few years. Perhaps through the influence of his uncle, Aaron Bernstein, editor of a Berlin newspaper that supported the progressive working class, young Bernstein announced, in 1872, that he was joining the Social Democratic Party. In this, he shared the aspirations of many educated Germans of the time, who called for national unity and democracy. A genial man, Bernstein was drawn to the pacifist Social Democrats over the more authoritarian General German Workers' Association.

Bernstein became an active party member. When Germany was thrown into an economic crisis in 1873, lasting well

George Berkeley *(The Library of Congress)*

into the decade, his anticapitalism feelings became stronger. But when Chancellor Otto von Bismarck's antisocialist laws were adopted in Germany, Bernstein emigrated to Switzerland. Before long, he became editor of the official publication and rallying center of the underground Social Democrats. The paper found its way into Germany. As a result, in 1880, at Bismarck's urging, the Swiss government expelled Bernstein from their country.

Continuing the underground publication in London, Bernstein met and became a close friend of **Friedrich Engels**, German socialist and Marx's collaborator. He also became friendly with members of the Fabian Society, a socialist organization that rejected the revolutionary ideas of Marx and favored a gradual development into **socialism**. The ideas formulated in England laid the basis for Bernstein's theory of revisionism.

By the time Bernstein returned to Germany in 1901, his break with traditional Marxism had become clear. His revisionist position, including such changes as seizure of power by the proletariat and refusal to await the imminent collapse of **capitalism**, was published in a series of articles in *Die neue Zeit*, an official party publication, in 1898. The following year, after criticism by some groups within the Social Democratic Party, Bernstein wrote a defense of his position, *Evolutionary Socialism*, a classic statement of the revisionist position. In it, Bernstein stated that socialism was not a product of revolt

Eduard Bernstein *(AP/Wide World Photos, Inc.)*

against capitalism, but the end result of **liberalism**, which exists in all human dreams. He did not believe that the concentration of productive industry was taking place as fast as Marx predicted, that capitalism was on the verge of collapse, or that oppressive tactics could be attributed only to the **bourgeoisie**. He argued that the successful road to socialism lay in a steady advance, not a violent overthrow. Despite his arguments, revisionism was condemned by the Social Democratic Party in 1903. This rift in the party's wings existed until after World War II.

In 1902, Bernstein became a member of the Reichstag (parliament) and was reelected several times. Although a member of his party's right wing, during World War I, Bernstein sided with the Independent Socialists. He opposed violence between nations just as he opposed violence between classes. At the war's end, however, he returned to his party and voted against those who wanted to turn the November 1918 political revolution into a social revolution in Germany. A parliamentary republic, Bernstein felt, was the most successful path to **progress**. In 1919, he served as secretary of state for economy and finance.

Although social democracy became a popular reformist movement in Germany and he contributed to the party program, Bernstein was powerless to stop the onslaught of fascism. He regarded Nazi tactics as the work of unbalanced minds. Weeks after his death on December 18, 1932, the democratic state in which he so passionately believed fell to the dictatorship of Adolf Hitler.

Bernstein was never totally successful in seeing his theories become a working reality, but many of his ideas became part of the party's program in West Germany after World War II. Abandoning revolutionary theory, cutting across class lines, emphasizing action and reform were some of the ways in which the new Germany party incorporated the revisionist ideas of Eduard Bernstein.

BIAS

Bias is defined as conscious or unconscious actions executed by a researcher or a group of researchers that affect the outcome of the a study or research project. Bias can occur in research as a result of statistical mistakes. Some statistical mistakes include citing **correlation** as a cause, overgeneralizing, building in bias, faking **data**, and using data selectively.

A correlation is a relationship between two variables. When data show that variables are correlated, stating that one **variable** causes the other is incorrect. Overgeneralization can occur when a group of people are selected to be studied (for example, people over the age of 70) but the results are generalized to people of all ages. Building in bias can occur, for example, in the following way. In a soft drink taste test sponsored by Soda X, Soda X was served to tasters a few degrees cooler than Soda Y (the competitor). This temperature difference stands for the built in bias that could cause tasters to prefer Soda X. Faking data, one of the most disreputable forms of bias, consists in altering the results of a study or fabricating data. The last of the statistical biases is using data selectively. For instance, a toothpaste company conducts a study that measures how well their product cleans and shines teeth. The findings show that their product makes teeth 25% shinier, but does not clean teeth well, it actually causes people's teeth to decay. If this particular company goes on to reports the data on making teeth shinier but leaves out the negative finding, its presentation of research is biased.

Bias can also occur within the individual researcher. A researcher who believes that **homosexuality** is wrong may put bias into the results of a study on gay **marriage**. Along the same vein, a researcher from the United States who wishes to study aboriginal Australians may look at them with an ethnocentric eye. The reports of behavior may be slanted by the researcher's American viewpoint. It is virtually impossible to remove all bias from research because people by nature think subjectively and hold certain biases. Nonetheless, bias can be partially eradicated through education, careful data collecting, and reliable statistical techniques.

BIBLICAL SOCIOLOGY

Biblical sociology is the attempt to apply social scientific methodology to the study of biblical texts in order to draw conclusions regarding the social setting, social structures, and social relationships of the historical community in which the text is set. Although biblical scholars and sociologists often hold contrasting presuppositions and employ diverse social scientific methodologies, they are united in affirming the important **role** that the social construction of the biblical communities plays in the formation and interpretation of the texts themselves. Norman K. Gottwald, a leading figure in the social scientific criticism of the Old Testament, writes in "Social Matrix and Canonical Shape (*Theology Today,* October 1985), "Social scientific criticism, also known as sociological criticism or biblical sociology, starts from the premise that biblical writings are social products. They were written by people shaped by and interacting within institutional structures and symbolic codes operative in the primary sectors of communal life, such as economy, **family**, **government**, law, **war**, **ritual**, and religious belief."

During the mid-nineteenth century, the study of religion focused primarily on the individual aspects of religious belief. Exemplified in the work of E.B. Tylor and **William James**, this individualistic presupposition approached religious studies based on the psychological aspects of individual experience. By the late nineteenth century, Robertson Smith had published his *Lectures on the Religion of the Semites: The Fundamental Institutions* (1889), which related religion to **society** by examining the role of ritual within early society. However, the major breakthrough in the study of the social aspects of religion was instigated by French sociologist Émile Durkheim in *The Elementary Forms of the Religious Life* (1912). Durkheim posited that religion was entirely a product of the collective life. Maintaining a position of absolute **reductionism**, Durkheim discounted any transcendent or divine origin in religion. **Max Weber** and **Karl Marx** also formulated multidimensional, dynamic models of social construction that contributed to the eclectic endeavor of biblical sociology.

The rapid expansion of the academic fields of sociology, cultural and social anthropology, and social psychology during the mid-twentieth century provided for the entrance of the social sciences into biblical interpretation, joining the already well-established presence of **philosophy**, history, and ethics. An interest specifically in biblical sociology developed within the last several decades of the twentieth century, with most contributions being made by biblical scholars. John G. Gager's publication of *Kingdom and Community* (1975), along with efforts by the Society of Biblical Literature, energized the field of biblical sociology during the 1970s. However, the introduction of a social scientific approach to biblical studies was not met unchallenged.

As a cross-disciplinary endeavor, biblical sociology has been approached differently by biblical scholars and social scientists. This has caused several obstacles in the development of a comprehensive sociological analysis of biblical societies. First, as Anthony J. Blasi writes in *Making Charisma: The Social Construction of Paul's Public Image* (1991), "The interdisciplinary nature of the sociology of biblical era societies poses problems for those of us who pursue this genre of work as well as for the reader. Most scholars are specialists who have training in one field and a broader education that only superficially addresses the second." Second, due to what Gottwald terms "the myopia of academic overspecialization" in *The Tribes of Yahweh* (1979), there is little effort made at developing a comprehensive analysis of either Israelite or early Christian social history. Most scholars are trained and encouraged to give their research a narrow focus that does not encompass the diversity of social and historical aspects of any given biblical setting to offer an overarching perspective of the social nature of the biblical communities.

Finally, those who attempt to apply sociological frameworks to biblical studies often face a skeptical audience. The religious community, which views social scientific **methodology** as stripping the scriptures of their inherently sacred nature, often greets the sociological study of biblical texts with suspicion if not outright hostility. "The fear is," writes Robert A. Atkins, Jr. in *Egalitarian Community: Ethnography and Exegesis* (1991), "that this [sociological] explanation—in that it is used to group social phenomena like the early Christian community in the context of similar social phenomena displayed by other communities, religious and nonreligious—explains away the role of God and the unique message of the **church**. The fear is that sociological descriptions of religious phenomena, especially Christian phenomena, are reductionist."

In *The First Christians in Their Social Worlds: Social-Scientific Approaches to New Testament Interpretation* (1994), Philip F. Esler suggests that "the New Testament documents speak to us from particular social worlds and need to be investigated using disciplines developed specifically to comprehend the social dimensions of human experience. Without this, our understanding of the texts will be unnecessarily impaired." In contemporary biblical sociology, the significance of the social reality of both the Israelite and early Christian communities, insofar as social scientists and biblical scholars can reconstruct it, remains a matter of many opposing opinions and diverging perspectives.

BIOETHICS

Bioethics deals with the study of moral, legal, social, and ethical issues that involve the biological sciences. Of paramount interest is biological research, its implications and applications, especially those concerning the transfer of body parts from person to person or animal to person, genetic engineering, cloning, **euthanasia**, and forms of birth control. Ethical issues have long been a concern in medicine and biology, the doctor's Hippocratic oath being an example.

In the eighteenth century, English physician Thomas Percival laid the foundation for a code of ethics established by the American Medical Association (AMA) in 1846. It was also the basis of the Nuremberg Code for Research Ethics, used at

During 1945 and 1946, Nazi leaders went on trial at Nuremberg, Germany, for unethical biomedical experiments conducted on human beings *(AP/Wide World Photos, Inc.)*.

the Nuremberg, Germany, war crime trials following World War II, 1945-1946. Among other counts, Nazi leaders were charged with unethical human medical experiments. Concerns over such issues rose dramatically in the late twentieth century, however. The swift advance of medical technologies brought on new problems or intensified old ones. An article by Henry Beecher of Harvard Medical School in 1966 cited abuse of human subjects at several U.S. universities and medical centers. His claim that subjects were sometimes used in experiments without consent or informed knowledge began serious debate in and out of medical institutions. The Tuskegee Study (1932-1972) found that the U.S. Public Health Service, while investigating the progression of syphilis, had withheld data and effective treatment from black men in the study. In response, in 1977, Congress passed legislation requiring informed consent from all such study participants.

Through biomedical engineering, we can now detect many early difficulties in a developing fetus. Is abortion ethical if the child will not be perfect? Should we withdraw life-sustaining equipment in an elderly or brain-dead patient? What about storing human embryos? Is it ethical to clone a human being?

The first bioethics study institute, Hastings Center, Briarcliff Manor, New York, was opened in 1969. Since then, hundreds of bioethics organizations have been established worldwide. They all search for answers to these medical and moral issues.

Throughout much of the twentieth century, any new medical discovery that promised a longer life seemed beneficial. Concerns arose, however, when technology either prolonged life without regard for quality or prevented a peaceful death. The human being seemed to lose out in the race for better machines. An example is the history of artificial heart research. Today, the emphasis has shifted to heart transplants, although the search for the perfect artificial heart goes on. In the early years of artificial heart research, the **quality of life** of

many patients was seriously compromised. Monitoring the implanted device was very frightening to some; for others, it simply did not work as planned, the result being sudden, critical illness or death. Scientists began to ask whether this avenue of research was worthwhile considering the enormous amounts of money that would be required to build the perfect artificial heart. Is it ethical to channel vital time and energy into devising a life-saving device that only the very wealthy can afford?

New medical technology has even changed the way we view death. Once the absence of pulse or breathing meant the patient died. Today's respirators keep up the apparatus of breathing, but is the patient living as we generally define life? That raises the related question of whether it is ethical to prolong someone's life because we are able to do so.

Many questions face the new breed of researchers. As each advance in medical engineering aims to prolong human life, we are asking these people to become so-called moral pioneers. There is little doubt that heart-lung and artificial kidney devices have extended life, or that devices such as a pacemaker allow millions to function almost normally. There is also little doubt that other artificial organs will be engineered and other natural body organs replaced. As medical advances take giant steps forward, so does the field of bioethics. It has affected the way in which professionals and students regard each new discovery. They now routinely address moral issues along with health-care problems. Bioethics seeks to forge a bond between applications of medical research and implications regarding what these advances will or will not do for human life.

BIRTH AND DEATH RATES

Birth and death rates are the frequency of either occurrence in a given population. They are the major part of the data collection called vital rates, which concern any important happening that affects changes in the size and makeup of a **group** such as a nation, state, or **community**. The relative frequency of births and deaths effects changes in the population, which then can indicate the need for more or fewer schools, hospitals, and other facilities. When vital rates are calculated per 1,000 inhabitants as they usually are they are called crude rates. To reflect more subtle changes in a population, the rates are refined down from 1,000. Calculating birth and death rates, which in the United States is part of the work of the Department of Health and Human Services, can help to control the effects of population size in a given group. The difference between birth and death rates in a specified population is the rate of natural increase or the rate of decrease if there are more deaths than births.

To calculate the crude birth rate, the number of times a birth occurs in a given period, usually a year, is divided by the midyear population of the specific group for that year. The rate is expressed per 1,000 people in the population. The crude birth rate is the most common measure of fertility. Countries in North America, Europe, and Japan, for instance, have a crude birth rate of less than 18 births per 1,000 population. That number increases to about 40 per 1,000 in many African and Asian nations.

Births and Birth Rates, by Race, Sex, and Age: 1980 to 1997

[Births in thousands (3,612 represents 3,612,000). Births by race of child. Excludes births to nonresidents of the United States. For population bases used to derive these data, see text, this section, and Appendix III]

Item	1980	1985	1989	1990	1991	1992	1993	1994	1995	1996	1997
Live births [1]	3,612	3,761	4,041	4,158	4,111	4,065	4,000	3,953	3,900	3,891	3,895
White	2,936	3,038	3,192	3,290	3,241	3,202	3,126	3,121	2,753	3,093	3,085
Black	568	582	673	684	683	674	695	636	394	595	601
American Indian	29	34	39	39	39	39	39	38	26	38	38
Asian or Pacific Islander	74	105	133	142	145	150	153	158	135	166	170
Male	1,853	1,928	2,069	2,129	2,102	2,082	2,049	2,023	1,996	1,990	(NA)
Female	1,760	1,833	1,971	2,029	2,009	1,983	1,951	1,930	1,903	1,901	(NA)
Males per 100 females	105	105	105	105	105	105	105	105	105	105	(NA)
Age of mother:											
Under 20 years old	562	478	518	533	532	518	514	518	512	503	500
20 to 24 years old	1,226	1,141	1,078	1,094	1,090	1,070	1,038	1,001	966	945	946
25 to 29 years old	1,108	1,201	1,263	1,277	1,220	1,179	1,129	1,089	1,064	1,071	1,075
30 to 34 years old	550	696	842	886	885	895	901	906	905	898	888
35 to 39 years old	141	214	294	318	331	345	357	372	384	400	408
40 years old or more	24	29	46	50	54	58	61	66	70	75	78
Birth rate per 1,000 population	**15.9**	**15.8**	**16.4**	**16.7**	**16.3**	**15.9**	**15.5**	**15.2**	**14.8**	**14.7**	**14.6**
White	15.1	15.0	15.4	15.8	15.4	15.0	14.7	14.4	14.2	14.1	(NA)
Black	21.3	20.4	22.3	22.4	21.9	21.3	20.5	19.5	18.2	17.8	(NA)
American Indian	20.7	19.8	19.7	18.9	18.3	18.4	17.8	17.1	16.6	16.6	(NA)
Asian or Pacific Islander	19.9	18.7	18.7	19.0	18.2	18.0	17.7	17.5	17.3	17.0	(NA)
Male	16.8	16.7	17.2	17.6	17.1	16.7	(NA)	(NA)	(NA)	(NA)	(NA)
Female	15.1	15.0	15.6	15.9	15.6	15.2	(NA)	(NA)	(NA)	(NA)	(NA)
Plural birth ratio [2]	19.3	21.0	23.0	23.3	23.9	24.4	25.2	25.7	26.1	27.4	(NA)
White	18.5	20.4	22.5	22.9	23.4	24.0	24.9	25.5	26.0	27.5	(NA)
Black	24.1	25.3	26.9	27.0	27.8	28.2	28.7	29.4	28.8	29.8	(NA)
Fertility rate per 1,000 women [3]	**68.4**	**66.2**	**69.2**	**70.9**	**69.6**	**68.9**	**67.6**	**66.7**	**65.6**	**65.3**	**65.3**
White [3]	64.8	64.1	66.4	68.3	67.0	66.5	65.4	64.9	64.4	64.3	64.2
Black [3]	84.7	78.8	86.2	86.8	85.2	83.2	80.5	76.9	72.3	70.7	70.8
American Indian [3]	82.7	78.6	79.0	76.2	75.1	75.4	73.4	70.9	69.1	68.7	68.9
Asian or Pacific Islander [3]	73.2	68.4	68.2	69.6	67.6	67.2	66.7	66.8	66.4	65.9	66.5
Age of mother:											
10 to 14 years old	1.1	1.2	1.4	1.4	1.4	1.4	1.4	1.4	1.3	1.2	1.2
15 to 19 years old	53.0	51.0	57.3	59.9	62.1	60.7	59.6	58.9	56.8	54.4	52.9
20 to 24 years old	115.1	108.3	113.8	116.5	115.7	114.6	112.6	111.1	109.8	110.4	110.9
25 to 29 years old	112.9	111.0	117.6	120.2	118.2	117.4	115.5	113.9	111.2	113.1	114.3
30 to 34 years old	61.9	69.1	77.4	80.8	79.5	80.2	80.8	81.5	82.5	83.9	85.4
35 to 39 years old	19.8	24.0	29.9	31.7	32.0	32.5	32.9	33.7	34.3	35.3	36.0
40 to 44 years old	3.9	4.0	5.2	5.5	5.5	5.9	6.1	6.4	6.6	6.8	6.9
45 to 49 years old	0.2	0.2	0.2	0.2	0.2	0.3	0.3	0.3	0.3	0.3	0.3

NA Not available. [1] Includes other races not shown separately. [2] Number of multiple births per 1,000 live births. [3] Per 1,000 women, 15 to 44 years old in specified group. The rate for *age of mother 45 to 49 years old* computed by relating births to mothers 45 years old and over to women 45 to 49 years old.

Source: U.S. National Center for Health Statistics, *Vital Statistics of the United States,* annual; *National Vital Statistics Report (NVSR)* (formerly *Monthly Vital Statistics Report*); and unpublished data.

As in any data collection, raw statistics can be difficult to interpret. Knowing the number of live births in a given population tells little about the fertility rate. That can be determined only by knowing the number of childbearing-age women in the population as well as the overall birth rate.

Death rates are calculated as the number of deaths in a given year divided by the midyear population in that year times 1,000. The death rate in the United States, for example, for the year 1998 was 8.7; generally developed countries have death rates between 7 and 12. This rate contrasts with a death rate of more than 20 in some African countries. The lowest death rates overall, however, are found in some developing nations, those with very high fertility rates and declining mortality. Developing countries have a smaller proportion of people over age 65 than do developed lands. Therefore, those nations with a higher proportion of elderly people have higher crude death rates than those that do not, even though there is no difference in risk of dying at any age.

Of paramount interest to vital rates collectors is the infant mortality, or death, rate. This is generally calculated as the number of deaths under age 1 in a certain year divided by the number of live births in that year times 1,000. The infant mortality rate for the United States, for example, in 1998 was 7.2 compared to 6 for Japan. Many African and some Asian nations have much higher rates. Infant mortality rates differ according to gender as well; the rates for U.S. infants in 1997, for example, was 8.0 for males and 6.5 for females. Such gender differences continue into **adulthood**. The greatest disparity concerns those in their twenties; U.S. males between the ages of 20 and 24 are three times more likely to die than U.S. females of the same age, presumably because of auto accidents.

Crude birth and death rates are basic to **demography**, which is the scientific study of population. It originated with **John Graunt** (1620-1674), who studied death lists of Londoners. Later, Edmund Halley (1656-1742), who predicted the return of the comet named for him, further refined the idea of inferring length of life for group members by calculating the lifetimes of other group members. Thus began the calculation of the life table, which shows the approximate year of life left to a certain group of people after they have lived for a certain number of years. In the United States, for example, life expectancy in 1998 was 73.9 for males and 77.3 for females.

BISEXUALITY

Bisexuality refers to a sexual orientation that demarcates a sexual attraction to members of both sexes. It can be further viewed as an individual who is able to both enjoy and recognize a desire to engage in sexual behaviors with males and females. The term "bisexuality" only refers to a sexual orientation; it is properly used as a descriptive adjective rather than a noun that labels an entire **identity**. It is not just the choice of sexual behavior outside of a social context. Some people may occasionally engage in sexual activity with a member of the same sex, while being primarily heterosexual. People with a homosexual orientation frequently establish heterosexual relationships prior to recognizing a same-sex erotic attraction. In fact, it may take many years after recognizing an attraction to both sexes for individuals to consider themselves bisexual.

According to Alfred Kinsey, sexual orientations can be placed on a seven-point continuum that he devised. The number zero corresponds to exclusively heterosexual activities and erotic attraction, while a score of six indicates entirely homosexual behaviors and erotic appeal. A score of three on this sale would indicate an equally homosexual and heterosexual orientation, or perfect bisexuality. That is not to say that is the only score for a bisexual. Some aspects of bisexuality can be found on all points except the two extremes.

There are several varieties of bisexuality: real, transitory, transitional, and as a denial of **homosexuality**. Bisexuality may be a real orientation, meaning that some people are born being attracted to both sexes which continues through adulthood. Bisexual behavior may be transitory, meaning an indi-

vidual may be involved in bisexual behaviors while actually having a homosexual or heterosexual orientation. It may further function as a transition period occurring while an individual is shifting from a homosexual to heterosexual or a heterosexual to homosexual orientation. Lastly, bisexual behavior may also be an individual's attempt to deny an exclusively homosexual orientation, a response perhaps due to an effort to minimize the social stigma typically associated with homosexuality. This type of bisexuality is likely to be found within Asian American culture where fulfilling socially prescribed familial roles is highly valued. In current Western **culture**, a bisexual orientation is problematic given that many understand sexuality in terms of either heterosexual or homosexual orientation.

See also Heterosexuality; Homosexuality

BIVARIATE ANALYSIS

Bivariate analysis refers to the examination of the effect of one variable on another. This type of analysis is predictive, in that it estimates the extent to which change in one **variable** predicts change in another. Measures of association include eta, gamma, lambda, Pearson's r, Kendall's tau, Spearman's rho, and **chi square**, among others.

Two variables can be causally related or simply correlated. For illustration, in a graph where one variable's attributes are listed along the horizontal axis and the other variable's attributes along the vertical axis, we can plot each case with a dot that corresponds to each respondent's scores on each of the two variables. Then, a line (called the regression line) fitted to the dots represents the least distance from each dot to the line itself. If the line runs parallel to either the horizontal or vertical axes, then the two variables are not correlated. Following the **regression line**, when scores on one variable move up or down, there is virtually no change in the scores on the other variable. If, however, the line slopes in any direction, this indicates a **correlation** between the two variables. The closer the slope is to representing a 45-degree angle, in any direction, the more highly correlated the two variables are.

The regression line not only indicates the strength of a bivariate relationship but also the direction. If the regression line slopes from low scores to high scores along the horizontal (or X) axis, then there is a positive relationship between the two variables. When scores along the horizontal axis rise, scores along the vertical axis (or Y axis) rise as well. If the regression line runs at an opposite angle, then there is a negative relationship between the two variables. As scores along the horizontal axis rise, scores along the vertical axis decline.

If both variables are measured at the **ratio** or interval levels, then the direction of the relationship is important to know. For example, when household income rises, are families more or less likely to take longer vacations? However, if one of the two variables or both of them are measured at the nominal or ordinal level, then the direction of the relationship makes less sense, and it is necessary to look at the association among the two variables in a categorical format such as cross tabs. Different statistics are used to calculate a bivariate relationship depending on the levels at which the two variables are measured.

In order to predict causation between two variables in a bivariate analysis, three criteria must first be met. First, the two variables must be correlated with one another as illustrated above. Second, they must be logically time-ordered. In other words, the causal variable must precede the dependent variable. Third, there must not be some third variable causing the association among the independent and dependent variables. The relationship cannot be spurious. If all three criteria are met, then bivariate analysis measures the extent to which one variable causes change in the other.

BLACK POWER MOVEMENT

The Black Power Movement was a radical grass-roots response to the perceived failure of the Civil Rights Movement, led by Dr. Martin Luther King, Jr., to change social conditions that kept African Americans impoverished and disenfranchised a century after the **abolition** of slavery. Especially attractive to a younger generation impatient with the slow pace of earlier civil rights activism, the Black Power Movement rallied African Americans to reject white American values as inherently racist, and to focus on black self-defense, self-determination, racial pride, and political and economic power.

Student Nonviolent Coordinating Committee (SNCC) leader Stokely Carmichael (Kwame Toure) coined the term "Black Power" at a march in 1966 to protest the shooting of civil rights activist James Meredith. Racial integration, Carmichael argued, was a way of giving in to **values** that subtly perpetuated white supremacy. Emphasizing that African Americans who participated in peaceful demonstrations were met with brutality and arrests, he urged blacks to unite against the white establishment and to seize power for themselves. He articulated this belief further in his 1967 book, *Black Power: The Politics of Liberation in America*, coauthored with Charles V. Hamilton. In the book's preface, the authors warned that their framework for radical change "represents the last reasonable opportunity for this society to work out its racial problems short of prolonged destructive guerilla warfare."

This aggressive approach inspired many followers, who supported various elements and degrees of Black Power's message. Relatively moderate groups, such as SNCC and the Congress of Racial Equality (CORE), recognized the importance of emphasizing black solidarity and promoted ideals of black pride. For many African Americans, the Black Power Movement meant respecting and celebrating the achievements, values, **family** structures, aesthetic norms, and creative expression that made African American **culture** unique. Advocates of Black Power urged African Americans to recognize that "Black is Beautiful" and to insist on the validation of black achievements in literature, other arts, and all areas of endeavor, instead of accepting white concepts of worth. More militant, however, were organizations such as the Nation of Islam, which vehemently opposed integration, and the Black Pan-

According to Alfred Kinsey, sexual orientations can be placed on a seven-point continuum that he devised *(The Library of Congress)*.

thers, which embraced radical Marxist ideology in open hostility toward the white establishment, and engaged in armed confrontations with police. Among black leaders who espoused the more extreme elements of Black Power were Panther founders Huey Newton and Bobby Seale, activists Eldridge Cleaver and H. Rap Brown, and writers Le Roi Jones (Amiri Baraka) and James Baldwin.

The Black Power Movement profoundly affected **race** relations in the United States. Its uncompromising rhetoric and tactics drew support among radical whites and some liberals, but alienated others and added fuel to segregationist attitudes. In general, white Americans tended to see Black Power as a call to violent revolution and an articulation of black supremacist ideas. This perception was strengthened by escalating racial violence that plagued the country through the late 1960s and early 1970s; in Los Angeles, New York, Washington, Detroit, Newark, Omaha, Louisville, Cleveland, and other cities, African Americans abandoned peaceful protests and rioted to demand an end to oppression. This civil disorder led to some immediate social changes, including a small increase in black **employment**; more important, it forced the government to acknowledge the seriousness of race problems and the depths of black frustration and rage.

Tommie Smith (center) and John Carlos (right) give the "Black Power" salute at the 1968 Summer Olympics in Mexico City, Mexico (Corbis Corporation [Bellevue]).

Yet African Americans resented whites' efforts to blame urban violence on Black Power. They tended to see the movement as a call to unite against social injustice and pointed out that institutionalized racism, not Black Power, was the root cause of violence. Even so, African Americans generally rejected the most extreme Black Power agendas. Dr. King and other older civil rights leaders, while supporting ideals of racial pride and unity, saw the "Black Power" slogan as divisive and feared it would ultimately harm the civil rights cause. Women, too, were troubled by elements of Black Power in particular, what they decried as its blatant sexism.

Scholars continue to debate the relative importance of the Black Power Movement. Some consider it to have been an effective means of radical self-empowerment; others argue that it polarized the black community and weakened black leadership. By the late 1970s, the Black Power Movement had lost some of its more militant impetus and shifted from street confrontations and campus rallies to the pursuit of electoral power.

BLAU, PETER MICHAEL (1918-)
American sociologist and educator

Peter Michael Blau, a renowned author and professor, was born in Vienna in 1918, to Theodor I. Blau and Bertha Selka Blau. He left Austria in 1939 just prior to the outbreak of World War II and came to the United States, where he became a naturalized citizen in 1943. Blau received a bachelor of arts at Elmhurst College in 1942, and then served as an intelligence agent in the U.S. Army until the end of World War II. Afterward he returned to his studies, receiving a Ph.D. at Columbia University in 1952; he later was awarded a masters of arts from Cambridge University in 1966. Blau's first marriage to Zena Smith in 1948 produced one daughter, Pamela Lisa; he also had a daughter, Reva Theresa, with his second wife, Judith Rae Fritz, whom he married in 1968.

Blau's career in academia began as an instructor, first at Wayne State University (1949-51) and then at Cornell University (1951-53). In 1953 he was appointed as an assistant professor of sociology at the University of Chicago, where he rose to the rank of full professor and remained until 1970. While at this prestigious university, Blau began his work in the field of organizational theory, gaining a considerable reputation from his books, such as *The Dynamics of Bureaucracy* (1955) and *Formal Organizations: A Comparative Approach* (co-written with W. Richard Scott, 1962).

In *The Dynamics of Bureaucracy,* Blau challenged the prevailing literature that focused on organizational oligarchy and displacement from the original organizational goals. In his study of two **government** agencies, Blau concluded that a rigid **bureaucracy** does not necessarily emerge once an organization has achieved its original goals, or once these goals have become undesirable. Instead, he observed a process of "succession of goals" by which organizations adopt new goals.

While at the University of Chicago, Blau also launched his important work in the areas of **exchange theory** and occupational **structure**. His *Exchange and Power in Social Life* (1964) proposed a theory of "social exchange" under which social life and relationships are governed by reactions from other people. According to Blau's theory, "...reciprocated benefactions create social bonds among peers, whereas unreciprocated ones produce differentiation of status." *The American Occupational Structure* (1967), co-written with **Otis Dudley Duncan**, was an empirical study that won for Blau the American Sociology Association's Sorokin Award.

In 1970 Blau accepted an appointment as the Quetelet Professor of Sociology at Columbia University, where he remained through 1988. While at Columbia, he published numerous works that continued his exploration of organizational and social structure. These include: *The Structure of Organizations* (with R.A. Schoenherr, 1971); *The Organization of Academic Work* (1973); *On the Nature of Organizations* (1974); *Approaches to the Study of Social Structure* (editor, 1975); *Inequality and Heterogeneity* (1977); *Continuities in Structural Inquiry* (edited with R.K. Merton, 1981); and *Crosscutting Social Circles* (with J.E. Schwartz, 1984).

Blau left Columbia in 1988 to become the Robert Broughton Distinguished Professor of Sociology at the University of North Carolina, a position he still held in 2000. In 1994 he published the book that synthesized his long career in developing sociology theory, *Structural Contexts of Opportunities*. The American Association of University Presses described this book as one in which Blau, focusing on both the influences of population structures and interpersonal relationships, ''has brought together these concerns to form a wide ranging theory of population structures and their influence on social life—from opportunities in job choice and social mobility, to organizational participation and intergroup relations.''

During his distinguished career, Blau also became a member and officer of many professional associations, and received various prestigious awards. He has been a fellow of the American Academy of Arts and Sciences since 1975 and a member of the National Academy of Sciences since 1980. He served on the board of directors of the Social Sciences Research Council (1966-69) and as president of the American Sociological Association for a term (1973-74). In addition to the Sorokin Award, Blau also was a recipient of the Commonwealth Award (1981) and the Irwin Award (1986).

BLAUNER, ROBERT (1929-)
American sociologist and educator

Much of Robert Blauner's work on **race** relations, the lives of factory workers, and **men's studies**, is deeply rooted in his personal experience. He was born in Chicago on May 18, 1929, to Samuel Blauner, a lawyer and sometime poet, and Esther (Shapiro) Blauner. He graduated with a bachelor of arts from the University of Chicago in 1948, and went on to earn a master of arts from the University of California, Berkeley (UCB), two years later, and a doctorate from UCB in 1962. After receiving his Ph.D., Blauner immediately married Rena Katznelson, a child psychotherapist, and later married Karina Epperlein. He has two children, Marya and Jonathan.

Blauner's long career as an academic sociologist began at San Francisco State University as an assistant professor of sociology in 1961. The next year he went to the University of Chicago and became a faculty member at UCB in 1963. He stayed at UCB for the rest of his career and became a full professor in 1978. Before beginning his teaching career, however, Blauner also worked for five years as a factory laborer. This hands-on experience greatly influenced his first book *Alienation and Freedom: The Factory Worker and His Industry* (1964).

At UCB Blauner went on to publish two notable works on racial issues, *Racial Oppression in America* (1972) and *Black Lives, White Lives: Three Decades of Race Relations in America* (1989). *Black Lives, White Lives* is a collection of the personal stories of 16 blacks and 12 whites, beginning with interviews conducted by Blauner and his team during the often violent racial turmoil of 1968. He reinterviewed most of the participants in 1979, and again in 1986. By conducting these multiple interviews, Blauner was able to construct a contemporary image of the changing racial relations in America over three decades, without the distortion possible in oral histories collected many years after the actual events.

In 1997 Blauner edited an anthology that reflected his interest in men's studies, *Our Mothers' Spirits: Great Writers on the Death of Mothers and the Grief of Men*. In this work, authors such as John Updike reflect on their thoughts and feelings about the deaths of their mothers. Blauner believes that, regardless of a man's age, the death of a man's mother is a disorienting event, and it is ''momentous'' for a man even if his mother was elderly.

Blauner received grants from many prestigious foundations and organizations during his career, including the **Social Science Research Council**, the National Institute of Mental Health, the Ford Foundation, and the Rockefeller Foundation. He also became a frequent contributor to sociology journals and other periodicals such as *Psychiatry* and *Transaction*. During the 1999-2000 academic year Blauner was an emeritus professor at UCB. He retained an interest in race relations, gender and men's experience, interviewing and oral history, and age phenomena.

BLUMER, HERBERT (1900-1987)
American sociologist

Herbert Blumer was born in St. Louis, Missouri, in 1900. His father was a cabinet worker and his mother a homemaker. He attended the University of Missouri from 1918-22 and remained to teach from 1922-25. In 1928 he received his doctorate from the University of Chicago, where he came under the academic influence of **George Herbert Mead**, W. I. Thomas, and **Robert Park**. Upon graduation he accepted a teaching position at the University of Chicago, where he remained as a professor until 1952. He spent the last twenty years of his teaching career, from 1952-72, as the Chair of Sociology at the University of California at Berkeley. Blumer was active in professional football for seven years, was regarded highly as an arbitrator in labor negotiations, and reportedly had many connections to members of Chicago's **organized crime** scene.

Symbolic Interactionism: Perspective and Method, Blumer's most influential writing, was published in 1969 and outlined the main tenets of his **sociological theory** and **methodology**. His earlier work included *Movies and Conduct* (1933) and *Movies, Delinquency, and Crime* (1933). A collection of essays concerning social organization and industrialization formed from the perspective of social interactionism was published posthumously in 1990 as *Industrialization as an Agent of Social Change*.

Known as the founder of the **symbolic interactionism** concept, Blumer coined the phrase in 1937 in an article on the nature of social psychology published in *Man and Society*. In developing his theory of symbolic interactionism, Blumer drew heavily from several sources. He built on Mead's understanding of the individual as an acting entity and the importance of empirical observation as primary to methodology. He was also influenced by Thomas's idea that each situation must be defined, and John Dewey's understanding of the **interaction** between humans and the natural world.

In conflict with many of his contemporaries, Blumer believed that meaning was created, and re-created, through social interaction. He built symbolic interactionism on three main principles. First, human beings respond to things based on the meanings those things hold for them. Second, these meanings are formed from the interaction of the individual with others. And, third, the individual uses an interpretative process to assess, formulate, and modify these meanings each time the person encounters them in his or her environment.

According to Blumer, traditional methodology severely underestimated the importance of the meaning a person places on things when he or she comes into contact with them. Meaning for the individual was a dismissable factor because, for the traditionalists, meaning is innate to the object itself, so the individual need not interpret or create it but simply discover that which already exists. Although Blumer believed that an object had an independent empirical existence, he suggested that to ascertain the meaning most relevant to human behavior, it must be seen in the context of social interaction.

In stark contrast to the traditionalists, Blumer argued against innate meaning, asserting that meaning is assigned to the object through an interactive interpretative process. The individual first notes those things that have meaning toward which he or she is acting and then, using an internalized social process of interpretation, assigns meaning by a process of formulation, reconsideration, and revision. Thus, for Blumer, meaning has a dynamic nature given to it through this self-interacting process.

Using the premise of interaction as the foundation to the creation of meaning, Blumer created a structure of basic ideas that he referred to as ''root images.'' These images pointed to and depicted not only self-interaction but, subsequently, human groups and societies. Emphasizing the action of individuals as key, Blumer asserted that social interactionism allowed for the best, direct observation of human behavior and interaction because the sociologist must necessarily be involved in the exploratory study at the micro-level of individual phenomenon.

Blumer held numerous prestigious positions, including the presidency of both the Society for the Study of Social Problems in 1955 and the American Sociological Association in 1956. In 1934 he began editing the *Prentice Hall Sociology Series,* and he also edited the *American Journal of Sociology* from 1940-52. He was well known for his impassioned teaching of his theories along with those of Mead, whose classes he took over upon his mentor's death in the early 1930s.

BLUMSTEIN, PHILIP (1944-1991)
American sociologist

Philip Blumstein was born in New York City on October 2, 1944. He received his bachelor of arts degree in 1966 from Reed College. He earned both his master and his doctorate degrees in sociology from Vanderbilt University in 1967 and 1970, respectively. He began his career as a sociologist and teacher in 1969 as an assistant professor at the University of Washington, where he remained until his death in 1991. In 1975 he became an associate professor and the director of the

Center for the Studies of Social Psychology. He received a National Science Foundation research grant from 1977-79 and held several memberships in professional organizations, including the American Sociology Association and the International Academy for Sexual Research.

Nationally known for his research on human sexuality and relationships, Blumstein's most important book *American Couples: Money, Work, Sex* was written in conjunction with fellow sociologist Pepper Swartz. It was published in 1983 and reprinted in paperback in 1985. This major study of heterosexual—both married and cohabiting—and gay couples explored such issues as emotional intimacy, the balance of power in sexual relations and income production, work versus private time, infidelity, and why certain couples dissolve their relationships. The authors stated their purpose in the introduction: ''Our task here is take relationships as we find them: diverse, inconsistent, and changing. We take as our mandate, description of what is actually going on among different kinds of couples and analysis of how these different patterns work for the individuals who have created them.''

The study was conducted by sending extensive questionnaires to four cohabiting couple types: 7,397 heterosexual couples (both married and cohabiting), 1,875 gay male couples, and 1,723 lesbian couples. With an overall return rate of approximately 52 percent, over 6,000 couples were included in the study. Out of those, Blumstein and Swartz conducted personal interviews with over 300 couples (129 heterosexual, 98 gay males, and 93 lesbian couples). The resulting book contains three chapters that analyze the results of the survey on the main topics of **money**, work, and sex, followed by an epilogue that draws conclusions on why some relationships work and others fail. Blumstein and Swartz then include a section that discusses the personal situations of twenty couples (five from each cohabiting category) with whom they conducted personal interviews.

Because Blumstein and Swartz included three types of nontraditional couples, which are historically stigmatized by **society**, *American Couples* offers a unique and seldom-studied perspective of cohabiting couples. Eighteen months after the study was complete, a follow-up questionnaire was distributed. The findings showed that approximately five percent of married couples had divorced, and from 12 to 22 percent of the nontraditional couples had broken up. The reasons for the breakups tended to result from arguments about money, income level, and work. Also, relationships in which one partner was more ambitious or more dependent were at greater risk for dissolution. Increased interaction time decreased the likelihood of a breakup in all groups.

In the late 1980s, Blumstein paired with Peter Kollock to develop a model for personal relationships that would successfully account for the diverse nature of human interaction. They identified five key dimensions by which personal relationships could be categorized: (1) whether the relationship is based on kinship, (2) whether the relationship has a sexual-romantic aspect, (3) whether the relationship involves **cohabitation**, (4) whether the relationship is hierarchical or egalitarian, and (5) whether it is a same-sex or cross-sex relationship.

By using these five determining characteristics as a basis for categorization, Blumstein and Kollock suggested that personal relationships can be more easily compared and analyzed.

Blumstein also participated in various other studies of human relationships. His research with Judith A. Howard and Swartz resulted in two articles published in the *Journal of Personality and Social Psychology*. In 1986, the trio published "Sex, Power, and Influence Tactics in Intimate Relationships," a study of the relative power and influence distribution within both same-sex and cross-sex couples. "Social or Evolutionary Theories? Some Observations on Preference in Human Mate Selection," published in 1987, discussed the major dimensions of preferences, **sex differences** in preferences, and the actual characteristics of obtained partners. Blumstein also conducted a study with Kollock and Swartz on equity in relationships, which was published posthumously in 1994 as "The Judgment of Equity in Intimate Relationships" in *Social Psychology Quarterly*.

Boas, Franz Uri (1858-1942)
German anthropologist, linguist, and educator

Franz Boas, an anthropologist and linguist, helped to found modern cultural anthropology in the United States. He and his students influenced all areas of anthropology through the 1930's, revolutionizing fieldwork methodology, linguistics, and the analysis of local texts and enabling local researchers to document their own history. Boas' studies focused on empirical ethnographic study of the Native American cultures of the Pacific Northwest, particularly of the Kwakiutl.

Born in Minden, North Rhine-Westphalia, Germany, in 1858, Franz Boas studied mathematics at the University of Heidelberg and Bonn. In 1882, he received his Ph.D. from the University of Kiel. His initial course of study was geography, and he taught geography at the University of Berlin. In 1886, he traveled to Vancouver Island and studied Pacific Northwest Indian tribes. He then moved to New York and taught anthropology from 1888 until 1892 at Clark University in Worcester, Massachusetts. In 1893, he went to Chicago to work at the World's Columbian Exposition and the Field Museum of Natural History. In 1896, Boas became the first professor of anthropology in the United States, teaching at Columbia University. He also served as curator of anthropology for the American Museum of Natural History from 1896 until 1905. In 1897, Boas convinced Morris Jesup to fund the Jesup North Pacific Expedition, documenting the native cultures in the Pacific Northwest between 1897 and 1902. He worked on editing the reports of the expedition until 1930. Though Boas formally retired in 1936, he taught as professor emeritus at Columbia until his death in 1942.

A cultural relativist, Boas disdained generalized theories of anthropology in his work and focused on concrete scientific observation. An influential thinker in the area of racism, Boas decried the notion that heredity was the determinant of character and insisted that **culture** and variations within cultures were of primary concern in any anthropological study. He argued

Franz Boas *(The Library of Congress)*

that cultures should be studied as whole systems, made of many interrelated parts, and that cultures should be understood in their own terms. Many thinkers of the time were putting forth the notion that there were specific, identifiable differences between the races of man. Yet Boas found that these ideas were based on biased research, on the assumption that the higher achievement of certain races indicated greater **intelligence**. He discovered little evidence to support the theory and declared the assumption false. In particular, Boas argued that there was no proof of the inferiority of black Americans, and that negative characteristics that some black Americans showed were "the result of social conditions, rather than of hereditary traits." He argued this point in many of his significant works, such as *Race, Language, and Culture* (1940) and *The Mind of Primitive Man* (1911), and thus brought a new approach to modern anthropological study.

Boas was a prolific writer who published over six hundred monographs and articles. He published many different types of works, including field notes, Indian folklore, and linguistic studies of Northwestern Native American tribal languages. His work influenced several generations of anthropologists, including his own students Alfred L. Kroeber,

Melville Herskovits, and Ruth Benedict, and her student **Margaret Mead**.

BONACICH, EDNA (1940-)
American sociologist and educator

Edna Bonacich built her career around exploring the relationship between minorities and the economic system, especially in urban settings. She was born in the affluent suburb of Greenwich, Connecticut, on March 30, 1940, to Meyer Miller, a rabbi, and Shulamith (Wittenberg) Miller. Bonacich began her education at the University of Natal in Durban, South Africa, where she received a bachelor's degree in 1960. She later obtained both a master's of arts (1966) and doctorate (1969) from Harvard University. In 1964 she married fellow sociologist Phillip Bonacich, with whom she had two daughters, Emma and Jane.

In 1969 Bonacich became a faculty member at the University of California, Riverside (UCR), starting her academic career as an assistant professor of sociology. Her first published work was *Deadlock in School Desegregation: A Case Study of Inglewood, California* (co-authored with Robert F. Goodman, 1972). However, her attention soon turned to what became one of the cornerstones of her work: minorities and economics. In 1980, Bonacich and John Modell published *The Economic Basis of Ethnic Solidarity,* based on a study of Japanese immigrants to the West Coast. Bonacich and Modell found that most of this ethnic group had been impoverished upon coming to the United States around the turn of the twentieth century. However, the group's members soon became successful, operating more than 3,500 small businesses by 1909, as well as becoming owners of almost 42,000 farms by 1925.

Bonacich continued to study Asian immigrant communities on the West Coast. In 1991, she and Ivan H. Light published *Immigrant Entrepreneurs: Koreans in Los Angeles, 1965-1982.* Korean immigrants in general had earned a reputation for being extremely entrepreneurial, having established small businesses in many cities. Light and Bonacich focused on their role in Los Angeles, which contained the largest number of Koreans living outside of their native country. *Immigrant Entrepreneurs* explored both the reasons for Korean immigrants' high rate of business ownership and the growing Korean-black tensions in American cities.

In *The New Asian Immigration in Los Angeles and Global Restructuring* (1997), Bonacich (with co-editors Paul Ong and Lucie Cheng) once again looked at the Asian immigrant communities of Los Angeles. This collection of essays concluded that there is now a global interaction between the changing Pacific Rim economy, immigration patterns, and local immigrant communities.

In the mid-1990s Bonacich began to publicize the plight of workers in the apparel industry, first in *Global Production: The Apparel Industry in the Pacific Rim* (1994) and then in *Behind the Label: Inequality in the Los Angeles Apparel Industry* (2000), a study of the Los Angeles apparel industry co-authored with Richard Appelbaum. In 2000 Los Angeles remained the home of the largest apparel industry, still-growing despite the massive migration of American companies to foreign countries where labor costs are low. At a 1999 presentation sponsored by the Asian Pacific Coalition in Los Angeles, Bonacich explained that large American companies have been subcontracting to small factories, both in the United States and abroad, that have become the "sweatshops" of modern times. In the University of California, Los Angeles's *Daily Bruin,* in 1999 she said, "The beauty of the sweatshop system, from their point of view, is that they don't have to take any responsibility for any of it."

A full professor of sociology at UCR in 2000, Bonacich at that time was conducting research and teaching in the areas of racism; **class and race** inequality; race, class, and gender; the labor movement; and garment workers. She was working on a study of "racialized labor" (a comparison of slavery and sweatshops), as well as an examination of the labor movement's problems in dealing with a global economy.

BOURDIEU, PIERRE (1930-)
French sociologist

Rare among French cultural theorists of the post-World War II era, Pierre Bourdieu is an empiricist, who bases his complex and challenging theories about 'popular' aesthetics on extensive empirical research. During the 1960s and 1970s, Pierre Bourdieu conducted a series of studies on the way people consume the products of mass **culture**, focusing on attendance at art museums. In 1979, he published his findings in *Distinction: A Social Critique of the Judgement of Taste*, arguably his best-known and most influential work. In it, Bourdieu disagreed with the aesthetic theories growing out of the work of nineteenth-century philosopher **Immanuel Kant**, who believed that the value and quality of works of art could be judged by objective criteria. Instead, Bourdieu argued, cultural and aesthetic tastes were social constructs. The bourgeois pure aesthetic— valuing a detached approach to cultural and artistic products— was, he said, no better and no worse than popular aesthetics, with their emphasis on immediacy and pleasure.

Bourdieu was born in Denguin, France, in 1930. He graduated from the École Normale Superieure, with an agregre (diploma) in philosophy in 1954. For the next two years, he was a professor of philosophy at the Lycee de Moulins, Moulins. In 1956, he was conscripted into the army and served in Algeria, then a French colony fighting a war of national liberation. Bourdieu stayed on in Algeria after his conscription, serving as an assistant professor of sociology at the Faculte des Lettres in Algiers. During his sojourn in North Africa, he conducted anthropological fieldwork that led to "The Kabyle House or the World Reversed," eventually published in *The Logic of Practice* (1980).

After returning to France, he was an assistant professor of sociology at the Faculte des Lettres in Paris in 1960 and 1961 and for the next three years served as professor of sociology at the Faculte des Lettres in Lille. Since 1964, Bourdieu has worked as a professor of sociology at the prestigious École des Hautes Etudes in Paris. In addition, he has served as professor of sociology at the College de France, Paris, since 1981.

Over the course of his career and in his varied sociological writings, Bourdieu has emphasized class, both as a category that figures prominently in a person's life history and a critical determinant of the structures of society. Beginning in the 1960s, he examined the impact of class background on educational achievement and cultural consumption. Influenced by Marxist thinking in his early years, Bourdieu often uses economic analogies in his studies of culture and **society**. He has argued that cultural and artistic tastes can be understood as the working out, as it were, of aesthetic market forces.

He has also used these economic analogies to debunk the premises on which his own profession operates. Bourdieu has stirred up controversy by his argument that the acceptance and popularity of academic theories has as much to do with their proponents' social prominence and salesmanship as it does with the intrinsic value of the ideas themselves. Bourdieu is also the author of *Reproduction in Education, Culture and Society* (with Jean-Claude Passeron) and *The Field of Cultural Production*, published in 1970 and 1993, respectively.

BOURGEOISIE

Bourgeoisie is a word of French origin denoting the business or middle class of a **society**. The term was originally used in medieval France to refer to the residents of walled towns, who were artisans and craftspeople located socially between the rural landlords and the peasants. This class was instrumental in putting **feudalism** to rest in the sixteenth century and in pushing for democratic reform in the eighteenth century.

The bourgeoisie were highly conservative, eager to invest in land and business, keenly attuned to social hierarchies, disposed toward emulation of the nobility, and certain of their superiority to workers and peasants. Their separation from the peasantry went beyond the walls and gates of their towns to the **quality of life** within those walls; the streets were cobbled, the homes beautiful, food plentiful, and consumerism flourishing. The walls and gates were useful to the bourgeois in keeping out beggars, maintaining quarantine, and refusing aid to the hungry during failed crop seasons.

The mechanization that arrived with the onset of the Industrial Revolution created a schism among the artisans and craftspeople, separating each group into employers and employees. The former remained part of the bourgeoisie, while the latter became the working class, or proletariat. After the Industrial Revolution, the bourgeois class further refined its boundaries, distinguishing between the industrialists and bankers who made up the *high bourgeoisie*, and the artisans, shop owners and craftspeople, now demoted to the *petit bourgeoisie*.

Karl Marx and **Friedrich Engels** brought the term into the international lexicon with the publication of the *Communist Manifesto* (1848). Marx pitted the bourgeoisie, the capitalist class in control of the means of production, against the proletariat in the revolutionary class war that would ultimately lead to a communist society. Marx viewed the petit bourgeoisie as future members of the proletariat; although they worked for

themselves and sometimes had employees, their position was tenuous and their livelihoods subject to the whims of the high bourgeoisie. As a result, the petit bourgeoisie tended toward downward mobility.

Bourgeois entered into contemporary popular **culture** in the 1960s, when newly-enlightened, revolution-oriented students hurled the term at their parents as an epithet. This derogation retains its currency as an accusation of **materialism**, concern for appearances and **status**, and a lack of originality.

BOWLES, SAMUEL (1939-)
American economist

Samuel Bowles was born in 1939 in New Haven, Connecticut. He grew up in rural New England and lived in India with his parents in the early 1950s. In 1958 he ventured on a two-year tour of Russia as a musician—albeit not a very good one by his own account. He also spent three years in Nigeria, employed by the government of Northern Nigeria as a high school teacher. In 1960 he received a bachelor of arts degree from Yale University, during which time he became actively involved in the civil rights movement. In 1965 he earned his doctor of philosophy degree in economics from Harvard University.

Bowles's first book was published in 1969 as *Planning Educational Systems for Economic Growth,* a revised version of his doctoral thesis. In 1970 he published *Notes and Problems in Microeconomic Theory,* with D. Kendrick. Both publications were based on the dominant neoclassical understanding of economics of education and microeconomics. However, by the late 1960s, Bowles had already formed friendships with numerous leftist, radical economists such as Arthur MacEwan, Thomas Weisskopf, and Herbert Gintis. In 1968 he became a founding member of the Union for Radical Political Economics. As explained in the *Biographical Dictionary of Dissenting Economists,* Bowles and his contemporaries sought a new economic paradigm that "could illuminate rather than ignore or obfuscate our political concerns with racism, sexism, imperialism, injustice and the **alienation** of labour. Not surprisingly, Marxism was an important intellectual guidepost in this quest."

In 1971 Bowles was hired as an associate professor of economics at Harvard University. However, his time at Harvard as a faculty member was fairly tumultuous. Deeply involved in the protest against the United States' involvement in Vietnam and already collaborating with fellow radical economist Gintis, Bowles came into conflict at Harvard as a new professor when he refused to sign an oath of loyalty to the U.S. Constitution. He was fired, but successfully pursued legal action to overturn both the dismissal and the oath requirement. However, when he was denied tenure in 1973, Bowles left Harvard for the University of Massachusetts (UMass) at Amherst, where he was the chair of the Department of Economics by the year 2000.

The first published paper reflecting Bowles's Marxist approach to economics appeared as "Schooling and Inequality from Generation to Generation" in the May/June issue of *Journal of Political Economy.* With the publication of *Schooling of Capitalist America,* (1976) cowritten with Gintis, Bowles's rejection of orthodox economics was complete. In this work, Bowles and Gintis explored the relationship between capitalism and the educational system. In so doing, they coined the term "corresponding principle," suggesting that school systems tend to adopt a hierarchical structure that mirrors the **structure** found in the labor market of a capitalist economy. Using this principle, they critiqued liberal educational philosophy, coming to the conclusion that educational reform is incompatible with a capitalist society.

After publishing *Schooling in Capitalist America,)* Bowles collaborated with David Gordon and Weisskopf to study the stagnation of the U.S. economy of the late 1970s and the ensuing escalation of rightist political economic policy. The result was a series of papers calling for a left-social democratic policy. The papers were subsequently published in two volumes as *Beyond the Waste Land* (1983) and *After the Waste Land* (1991). Bowles also continued his work with Gintis, and in 1986 they published *Democracy and Capitalism.* In this work, they critiqued the theoretical, historical, and contemporary connections between **democracy** and **capitalism**.

During the remainder of the 1980s and in the 1990s, Bowles continued his study of capitalism from a Marxist perspective, concluding in such papers as "Contested Exchange" (1990) and "The Democratic Firm" (1992) that a capitalist economic system is both undemocratic and inefficient. His other projects include *Recasting Egalitarianism: New Rules for Markets, States, and Communities* (co-author, 1999), *Understanding Capitalism: Competition, Command, and Change* (co-author, 2000), and *Economic Institutions and Behavior: An Evolutionary Approach to Microeconomics,* scheduled for publication in 2001.

In 2000, Bowles taught courses at UMass in microeconomics and the theory of institutions. He was also a research associate of the Santa Fe Institute and co-chair of the research network on the effects of inequality on economic performance. He was appointed by South African President Nelson Mandela to serve as a member of South Africa's Commission on the Labour Market and assist in designing economic policies to overcome the effects of **apartheid**.

BRAVERMAN, HARRY (1920-1976)
American editor and writer

Harry Braverman was born on December 9, 1920, in Brooklyn, New York, to Jewish Polish parents, Morris and Sarah (Wolf) Braverman. His father, a shoe worker, tried to provide his son with a college education, but after one year at Brooklyn College, Braverman was forced to withdraw and find employment. He would not return to college until the 1960s, earning his bachelor of arts degree from the New School for Social Research in 1963. Nonetheless, the short time he did spend as a young college student greatly influenced him as the radical ideas of **socialism** and Marxism were spreading through New York's college campuses. Braverman found an ideological home with the Young People's Socialist League.

Merely 16 years old, Braverman went to work at the Brooklyn Naval Yards as a coppersmith apprentice. During his four years on the docks, Braverman also mastered steel-fabrication layout, refitting the asbestos-covered pipes of docked ships (an important factor in his early death at the age of 54). During this time, he met Miriam Ruth Gutman, and they married on December 25, 1941. They had one son, Thomas Raymond, and eventually separated in 1964.

Braverman was drafted in 1944 and spent two years in Cheyenne, Wyoming, working on locomotive pipes. From 1946-51, he and his wife lived in Youngstown, Ohio, where Braverman was employed in the steel industry. Braverman continued to be an outspoken supporter of socialist ideals, spending time in an intensive six-month course in Marxist study at the Socialist Workers Party's (SWP) Trotsky School. However, in 1953 he was expelled from the SWP after an internal power struggle in the organization.

In the 1950s, Braverman became involved in publishing, establishing the *American Socialist* as a co-editor with fellow socialist Bert Cochran. After five years, the publication folded, and in 1960 Braverman moved on to become an editor for Grove Press. He established himself as the publishing company's vice-president and general manager before leaving in 1967 to become the director of the socialist *Monthly Review Press,* where he remained until his death in 1976.

In 1974 Braverman published his landmark work *Labor and Monopoly Capital: The Degradation of Work in the Twentieth Century.* Never out of print, the work is a study of the labor process and, specifically, a critique of the segmentation of the labor market. Braverman builds his thesis on the Marxist understanding of the importance of labor in the definition of the human experience, asserting, "...work as purposive action, guided by intelligence, is the special product of humankind." However, according to Braverman, the capitalist system in the United States so dehumanizes work that it also dehumanizes the worker.

Focusing on the labor process, Braverman was interested in studying the manner in which management continuously works to control production, producing the most amount of goods through maximized worker efficiency for the greatest profit possible. The key to this control, according to Braverman, is the regulation of the **division of labor**. This division reduces work into minimized tasks that require the worker to produce through highly repetitive, unskilled activities that require no knowledge of or connection to the end product. The result is that the worker becomes alienated from the work.

Braverman dates the beginning of the fragmentation and degradation of work to the first part of the twentieth century, when the theory of scientific management was applied to the labor process. A job was divided into segments, and each segment was analyzed and measured so that optimum conditions could be established for the greatest productivity. Combined with the introduction of the assembly line, Braverman argues that it was at this time period that workers lost almost all control over their work and became mere extensions of the machines they operated, at a rate controlled by management.

As labor started to lose its meaning to the work, management responded with higher wages. Braverman notes this as an adjustment in workers' attitudes: "Conceding higher relative wages for a shrinking proportion of workers in order to guarantee uninterrupted production was to become, after the Second World War, a widespread feature of corporate labor policy, especially after it was adopted by the labor unions." However, according to Braverman, placating workers with higher pay does nothing to restore meaningfulness to the work. The only way workers can regain their full humanity is to regain control over the labor process itself.

BRITISH SOCIOLOGY

British **sociology** developed in the nineteenth century as a scientific extension of seventeenth- and eighteenth-century Enlightenment philosophy. The focus in British sociology is not on an overpowering social system or structure but on the nature of individual human beings and the effect of their actions on **society**. The ideas of British Enlightenment philosophers and nineteenth-century sociologists shaped fundamental social institutions and **culture** in both Britain and America.

The origins of British sociology stem from the Enlightenment and the social and historical context of seventeenth- and eighteenth-century Europe. Society was changing tremendously in Europe at this time. Exploration and commerce were bringing wealth to Europe, and people moved from the country into towns. Traditional forms of **government** and sovereignty were changing. The advancement of science and reason challenged the dominant role of religion. Surrounded by massive **social change** and newly enamored of reason, philosophers argued that by studying humans and the world in which they lived, they could modify themselves and that world toward perfection.

Philosophers did not limit their efforts to the physical world but used reason to pursue a secular ethic for society through an understanding of human nature and **morality**. Donald Levine argues that the writings of philosopher Thomas Hobbes in the seventeenth century regarding **human nature** provided the foundation for British sociology. Hobbes believed that human nature directed the social world and that human desires to gain power and avoid death were part of this nature.

Hobbes' belief that society could be explained in terms of the nature of the individuals who exist within it influenced British social thought for the next two centuries. Levine writes that later in the seventeenth century, the Earl of Shaftesbury stated that humans have a natural tendency to associate with other people. Philosophers **John Locke** and **Bernard Mandeville** also explained society in terms of the nature of individuals, arguing that selfish behavior could have positive consequences for society.

The idea that humans' pursuit of their own interests could benefit society led to the development of utilitarian theory in the eighteenth century by philosophers Frances Hutcheson, **David Hume**, and **Adam Smith**. Levine states that Hutcheson argued that the most moral actions were those that were the most utilitarian, or accomplished the greatest good

for the greatest amount of people, and that Hume argued that humans naturally revere the things that are most useful to society.

According to Levine, Smith contended that humans have a number of innate propensities that lead to actions that benefit all of society. The tendency to trade leads to markets, and the tendency to save leads to capital, both of which increase the wealth across society. The human tendencies to admire people in positions of **authority** and to respect **rules** lead to shared norms and stability for society. Smith argued that because humans' pursuit of their own interests ultimately benefits society, governments should not interfere in their pursuit of those interests.

The idea that society is shaped and stabilized by the nature of humans and their actions was still prevalent in the nineteenth century when social philosophy became more scientific and developed into the formal discipline of sociology. Using the model of physics, these sociologists attempted to scientifically discover the laws of the social world. Levine notes that their focus on the individual led the British to analyze society in an "atomic" manner, studying society in terms of the "elements," or individuals, that constitute it.

One of the first British examples of social science was the attempt by philosopher **Jeremy Bentham** in the early nineteenth century to create a mathematical model of human action. According to Levine, Bentham's model calculated the pain and pleasure resulting from an act for both the actor and all persons affected. This measurement indicated the utility of an act, or the extent to which it benefits the greatest amount of people.

John Stuart Mill, son of philosopher **James Mill** who founded the Utilitarian Society in Britain in 1823, followed Bentham's utilitarian method but expanded it to account for more than pain and pleasure. Levine noted that Mill also incorporated **utilitarianism** into the actual practice of social science, arguing that it should be used practically to increase the happiness of the individuals in society.

Herbert Spencer, a former engineer who became a sociologist in his forties during the late eighteenth century, contributed to sociology the concept of social evolution. George Ritzer maintains that Spencer believed that humans adapt to their circumstances and that humans were evolving from a military stage to an industrial stage. In the military stage, political institutions were repressive, and humans were egoistic and often at war. In the industrial stage, industry and commerce required **voluntary associations**, and humans became more altruistic, forming charitable societies and enacting laws to protect citizens.

Thomas Malthus, a nineteenth-century British political economist, had an approach similar to Spencer's. He evaluated the possible trajectory of society in terms of the actions of individuals. His focus, however, was on the impact on living conditions of overpopulation and overconsumption of natural resources.

These theories affected British and American society. The utilitarian belief that humans' pursuit of their own interests benefited society and Spencer's belief that society should

Buddha was a prince who achieved enlightenment after six years and spent the rest of his life devoted to spreading his teachings *(Field Mark Publications).*

be left to evolve influenced the development of the capitalist free market. British and American governments are founded on what many of these thinkers believed was an individual's right to pursue personal interests without interference. The American political system has checks and balances to ensure minimal interference in the activities of individuals.

According to George Ritzer, Phillip Abrams contended that the work of these thinkers also led to a tendency in British society, called amelioration, the attempt to solve **social problems** by reforming individuals. Whereas the French focused on the power of social institutions and consequently tried to overthrow the government in the French Revolution, the British focused on reforming individuals because the prevailing social thought did not espouse the primacy of social structures.

BUDDHISM

The religion of Buddhism originated in India during 525 BCE. Siddhartha Gautama, referred to as the Buddha, was a prince

who became disillusioned with his life of wealth. By the age of 29, Siddhartha Gautama had renounced his life of privilege to search for a solution to human suffering. Buddhist philosophy maintains that Siddhartha Gautama achieved enlightenment after six years and spent the rest of his life devoted to the dissemination of his teachings and the establishment of communities of nuns and monks (sangha).

All Buddhism is based on doctrine known as the "four noble truths": existence is suffering (dukhka); suffering has a cause which is craving and attachment (trishna); there is a cessation of suffering (nirvana); and there is a path to the cessation of suffering. The path to the cessation of suffering includes eight aspects: right views, right resolves, right speech, right action, right livelihood, right effort, right mindfulness, and right concentration. Other general Buddhist tenets include the concept of reality as process and relationship, rather than substance or material entity. Buddhism also teaches the concept of non-self, or the idea that all happenings are related and dependent on cause. The concepts of reincarnation and karma are a part of Buddhist doctrine; Buddhists believe that the practice of emptying one's self can free a person from an endless **cycle** of reincarnation.

When Siddhartha Gautama died in 483 BCE, his teachings were transferred by word of mouth until the first century BCE when the tenets of Indian Buddhism were first preserved in a written form. Various sects of Buddhism began to thrive. Today, the main sects of Buddhism include the Theravada (or Hinaayana, represented in Sri Lanka and southeast Asia), the Mahayana (prevalent in China, Mongolia, Korea, and Japan), and the Vajrayana (prevalent in Tibet and Japan). The earliest Buddhist texts include the *Pali Canon*, a set of rules for Buddhist monks. Buddhism later declined in India significantly by the thirteenth century, due to a revival in **Hinduism**. However, the *Pali Canon* was preserved in Sri Lanka and elaborated on by writers, including Buddhaghosa, who lived during the fifth century.

Buddhism continued to spread across the globe and eventually became one of the world's major religions. By the first century, Buddhist tenets were practiced in China, although the religion faced opposition from other Chinese paradigms such as **Confucianism** and Taoism, and it was resisted by the Chinese government as early as the ninth century. By the seventh century, Buddhism had taken hold in Tibet. Between the sixth and the twelfth centuries, Buddhist beliefs were adopted in various forms by many Japanese. During the twentieth century, Buddhist sects across the globe were primarily of the Theravada sect.

Because of Buddhism's long history, many writers, philosophers, and practitioners have studied and shaped the direction of Buddhism. Among the earliest of these was Nagarjuna (second century CE) who founded the school of Mahayana Buddhism. This school emphasized a middle of the road interpretation of phenomena, veering away both from nihilism and eternalism. Nagarjuna also claimed that as a Buddhist, he could refute perspectives of his opponents while maintaining a neutral perspective. In the sixth century, this philosophy was challenged when Bhavaviveka claimed that a Buddhist could refute arguments if he possessed a positive (rather than neutral) view of his own. Many twentieth century writers have produced work on Buddhism, including R. H. Robinson (*The Buddhist Religion,* third edition, 1982), K.S.S. Ch'en (*Buddhism in China,* 1964), and Jun Ishikawa (*The Bodhisattva,* 1990).

By 1990, over 300 million people in the world practiced Buddhism. The United States was home to an estimated 920,000 practitioners of Buddhism during the twentieth century. In the 1960s Buddhist practitioners in South Vietnam and other Asian countries took on an unusual political role to protest the oppressive political regimes. Monks performed untypical actions in these countries such as organizing protests and developing political manifestos. A Buddhist monk in 1962 Saigon set himself on fire to protest the regime then in power.

The growth of Buddhism in America has paralleled the rising popularity and recognition of the fourteenth Dalai Lama. Buddhists believe that the Dalai Lama is regularly reincarnated to represent an earthly incarnation of the deity of compassion and mercy. The current Dalai Lama is the spiritual leader and political leader of Tibet. He won a 1989 Nobel Peace Prize for his efforts to free Tibet from Chinese rule and to improve the state of **human rights** worldwide.

BUREAU OF INDIAN AFFAIRS

Established by Secretary of War John C. Calhoun in 1824 without authorization from Congress, the Bureau of Indian Affairs is responsible for maintaining the relationship between the United States and federally recognized Native American tribes. In 1832, Congress authorized a Commissioner of Indian Affairs, appointing Elbert Herring at a salary of $3,000 per year. In 1834, the Bureau was officially approved. All actions of the Bureau stem from these following long-held concepts. Indian tribes are separate sovereign nations to be dealt with on a government-to-government basis, and, as such, their internal affairs are their responsibility. The United States considers itself in a trust relationship with American tribes and Alaska natives, stemming from English law, which held that the Crown had the title to newly discovered lands but native people had the right of occupancy. Accordingly, the United States holds the title to land in trust for Native Americans. The Bureau of Indian Affairs is charged with the responsibility of managing these resources. Its record is blemished.

In 1849, the Bureau went from military to civilian control. Later that century, the United States set aside large tracts of land in the West for the use of specified tribes. The Bureau was organized into two groups of supervisors: superintendents, who were responsible for affairs in a large geographical area, and agents, who were concerned with one or more tribes. But agents of the Bureau were often lax or corrupt in carrying out their responsibilities. Cattlemen, farmers, and prospectors, hungry for land, clashed with Native Americans in savage wars and raised questions about the government's Indian policy. After World War II, the present system was established, with a three-tier structure that runs from the Bureau in Washington, D.C., to area offices down to agencies at the reservation level.

New conflicts emerged in 1973 when the Bureau was just one of many responsibilities under an assistant secretary in the Interior Department. With land and water resources more a concern than Indian affairs, the Bureau was frequently in dispute with other department agencies. But in 1977, with the appointment of Forrest Gerard of the Blackfeet tribe as the first Assistant Secretary for Indian Affairs, the Bureau had a voice in policy matters directly concerning Native Americans.

The latter half of the twentieth century was known as the "Self-determination Era" for Native Americans. Congress passed the Self-determination and Education Act in 1975, allowing tribes to gain more control in their local schools, once administered by the Bureau. Activists began the "Trail of Broken Treaties," moving from Alcatraz Island in San Francisco to Washington, D.C. They demanded the end to U.S. policies that dismantled tribes and attempted to assimilate the people into mainstream **society** or laws that allowed states to hear criminal and civil cases occurring on reservation lands.

By the 1990s, much of the Native American population had moved to urban areas. Many centers set up to govern their social, cultural, and community matters in the 1980s were forced to close because of federal program downsizing. One area in which Native Americans gained wide authority was in management of casinos, after the U.S. Supreme Court, in 1988, said the Cabazon tribe in southern California had the right to operate gaming casinos on their own land. With the passage of the Indian Gaming and Regulatory Act that same year, Indian gaming was allowed, providing that the tribes set up agreements with those states that surrounded their **territory** concerning rules and profits. From this act, some Native Americans have generated huge amounts of income. In addition, most casinos on reservation lands are not in urban areas and employ mainly their own workers or others from lower socioeconomic levels. Some of this money is channeled by the tribes into projects to strengthen their own communities.

The Bureau of Indian Affairs today is still concerned with issues of tribal sovereignty, as well as land claims and water and fishing rights. Of paramount interest is repatriation of tribal sacred remains, an issue which often come in conflict when U.S. business enterprises claim an area. An example is the Lakota tribe of South Dakota, which is fighting to preserve the state's Black Hills as their sacred site and wintering place. The Bureau is also concerned with matters of education. Native Americans still do not graduate in high numbers from U.S. colleges. Tribal colleges were established on reservations starting in 1978, with 29 such schools operating today. They include tribal history with college courses which prepare students for transfer to mainstream educational institutions.

BUREAUCRACY

The term *bureaucracy* refers to the administrative structure of an organization—usually a large one. French in origin and dating from the 1700s, bureaucracy initially implied efficiency and suggested a fixed hierarchical **organization**, within which people were promoted according to merit and salaries were fixed. An organization that contained a bureaucracy was characterized by clear **rules** and regulations. Bureaucracy was practiced in imperial Rome, China, and national monarchies. A key drive behind bureaucracy was the orchestration of individuals within the organization so that these individuals' actions ultimately contributed positively to the direction of the organization.

Although figures such as **Karl Marx** and **Alexis de Tocqueville** studied bureaucracies in such areas as the military, **Max Weber** (German sociologist, 1864-1920) ultimately shaped bureaucracy as an important sociological topic. Weber saw bureaucracy as a superior way of structuring administration in a business and suggested that it was particularly valuable to large, complex organizations. Much of his research was conducted at the end of the 1800s and beginning of the 1900s but not formally recognized until the 1940s. Weber studied bureaucracies in China, Egypt, Prussia, and France. Through his research he defined three aspects of bureaucracy—power, **authority**, and systems of administration—and their relationships to each other. Power was defined as the ability to ensure that people in a bureaucratic system followed given rules; authority referred to the ability or standing of those with the power, and systems of administration described the chain of command through which power and authority were effected.

Other characteristics which generally described bureaucracies included: behavior prescribed and controlled through the enforcement of rules, a hierarchy representing a chain of command, promotion based on competence, creation of continuous and full time **employment**, clearly defined job duties, and required documentation and record keeping. While other organizations not defined as bureaucracies might also incorporate rules, bureaucracy stood apart because of the types of rules implemented as well as the justification behind these rules.

Stanley Udy ("Bureaucracy and Rationality in Weber's Organizational Theory," *American Sociological Review,* [1959]) took a closer look at the concept of bureaucracy and proposed that different characteristics within bureaucracy might be studied in regards to their relationships with each other. Richard Hall ("The Concept of Bureaucracy: An Empirical Assessment," *American Journal of Sociology,* [1963]) took the concept further, suggesting that the features of bureaucratic organizations might operate independently of each other. Hall's work portrayed bureaucracy as a multifaceted rather than a unified phenomenon. Further research by D. S. Pugh, et al. ("Dimensions of Organizational Structure," *Administrative Science Quarterly,* [1968]) pursued this tangent and found that "organizations may be bureaucratic in a number of ways."

Increasingly complex growth in the administration of **government** caused bureaucracy to grow both in the public and private sector. In modern times, the perception of bureaucracy shifted to include being marred by inefficiency. The term became associated with duplication of effort, unresponsiveness, rigidity, and a narrow outlook on the part of organizations. The shift in perception of bureaucracy was due in part to the maladies that these large organizations faced and the effects they had on the people whom they served. The public complained increasingly of unresponsiveness, blaming it on the bureaucracy that existed in such social segments as education, **health care**, worker unions, and insurance services. Weber himself had recognized some of the potentially negative aspects of bureaucracy, including a monopoly of information and a organizational **culture** that perpetuated secrets, the difficulty of implementing change in a bureaucracy, and the trend for bureaucracies to be run as autocracies.

By the 1990s in the United States, the hope for reducing bureaucracy in government was familiar and well received. David Osborne (with Ted Gaebler) published *Reinventing Government* (1992), a look at streamlining the massive administration of U.S. governmental systems. The Clinton-Gore presidential campaign used some ideas in the book for their platform. When elected, Clinton created the National Performance Review (NPR), specifically conceived to restructure government for more efficiency. The NPR succeeded in streamlining clumsy personnel processes and purchasing processes in some governmental agencies. Additionally, U.S. government agencies submitted yearly goals and progress reports, beginning in 1997. Europe adopted similar initiatives, beginning in 1996. Several European countries focused specifically on decentralizing decision-making, instilling benchmarks to measure progress, and giving more authority to lower levels in an organization.

In *Banishing Bureaucracy* (1997), Osborne and Peter Plastrik maintain that contrary to popular **stereotype**, most employees of a bureaucracy want to work hard, but the system in place may prevent them from doing so. The authors suggested that regular performance and program reviews would help in eliminating bloat in bureaucracy. Other suggestions included involving employees rather than controlling them, modeling desired behavior, bringing in new blood, relinquishing the past, eliminating fear, valuing **communication**, and staying committed to the initiative in the long term.

Following the Asian economic crisis in the late 1990s, Japan's bureaucracy was the target of criticism. According to an article in the *Economist* (10 May 1997), bureaucrats (rather than politicians) had always held the policy making power in Japan. The economic crisis gave Japan's political parties an opportunity to call for reform in government, but an *Economist* journalist suggested that specific bureaucratic reforms should include replacing cabinet ministers based on competence rather than seniority. Peter Drucker (in *Foreign Affairs,* September-October 1998) suggested that criticism of the Japanese bureaucracy missed the point. Drucker suggested that bureaucracy was prevalent in most developed countries. The difference between Japan and America, according to Drucker, was that the ruling elite in America had political ties, but the ruling elite of Japan was a bureaucracy. On this view, Japan placed primacy on its social ideology, rather than allowing its economic situation to define its **society**. Therefore, one could gain more insight into Japan's economic problems of the late 1990s by understanding the importance Japanese place in their society than by focusing on the supposed ineffectiveness of the Japanese bureaucracy.

BURKE, EDMUND (1729-1797)

Northern Irish political writer and statesman

When in 1765 at the age of 36, he began his long career as a member of the British Parliament, Edmund Burke was already widely known for his intellectual ability as editor of the highly acclaimed journal the *Annual Register* and as the author of *A Philosophical Enquiry into the Origin of our Ideas of the Sublime and Beautiful*. An eloquent and thoughtful orator, his speeches soon earned him a place of prominence within Parliament and as the leading figure of the Rockingham Whigs. He undertook many controversial issues during his political career and in his writings, including state policies regarding the American colonies, Ireland, India, and the French Revolution. Honored by modern conservatives for his commitment to tradition, **morality**, and orderly **society**, Burke was also heralded by liberals for his dedication to tolerance, liberty, and reform.

Burke was born in Dublin, Ireland, on January 12, 1729, to Richard Burke, attorney of His Majesty's Court of Exchequer, and Mary Nagle Burke. As a child, Burke was sent to live in south Ireland with his mother's relatives in hopes of curing his asthma. At the age of 12, he and two of his brothers were sent to study in Ballitore under the tutelage of a Quaker schoolmaster. In 1744, the 16-year-old Burke entered Trinity College and pursued a variety of academic interests, including science, logic, history, and literature. After receiving his A.B. degree in 1748, he left Ireland to study law in London at Middle Temple, a course of action dictated more by his father's wishes than by his own desires. Consequently, in the mid-1750s, much to his father's dismay, Burke abandoned his legal studies to pursue his growing interest in writing. He married Jane Nugent, a doctor's daughter, on March 12, 1757, and they had two sons, Richard and Christopher (the latter died in early childhood).

Burke began his writing career with the publication of *A Vindication of Natural Society* (1756), a satirical criticism of deist Henry St. John, Viscount Bolingbroke, and *A Philosophical Enquiry into the Origin of Our Ideas of the Sublime and Beautiful* (1757), a well-received examination of aesthetic principles. The latter publication placed Burke well within the circle of influential writers, which included Sir Joshua Reynolds, David Garrick, and Elizabeth Montagu. This success led to an invitation to become the editor of the *Annual Register*, a journal of politics, science, history, and the arts. While he was the anonymous author of the history section for over a decade, Burke's growing interest in politics was reflected in his eloquent writing on such topics as the Seven Years' War in Europe, the increasing tensions in the American colonies, and the British efforts to colonize India.

In 1765 Burke became the secretary to George Montagu Dunk, Earl of Halifax, lord lieutenant of Ireland. His secretarial duties required him to travel to his native Ireland, where he was deeply affected by the discriminatory laws against Irish Catholics that restricted their ability to acquire wealth, own land, and participate in society. Burke recorded his concern for the state of his homeland in fragmentary papers, "Tracts on the Popery Laws," published posthumously. Burke, who had

Edmund Burke

been raised Protestant and married a Protestant, nonetheless had Catholic connections through his mother and relatives in Nagle. Throughout his political career, he would be falsely portrayed by his enemies as a devout Catholic who pledged his allegiance to the Pope.

In 1765 Burke accepted a position as secretary to Charles Watson Wentworth, Marquis of Rockingham. Just months later, Ralph, Lord Verney suggested that Burke assume a vacancy in the borough of Wendover. After easily winning the election, Burke became a deeply devoted member of the Rockingham Whigs, a position that would place him in the political minority for all but a short time during his political career. He continued to write on matters of political and civil **organization** and became the Rockingham Whig's primary and most important defender. Just days after his entry into the House of Commons, on April 19, 1774, Burke made his first speech to the assembly; his topic was the American colonies, an issue to which he would return often. Two of his most famous speeches were published in 1775 as the *Speech on American Taxation* and the *Speech on Conciliation with the Colonies*. Not necessarily supporting succession from British rule, Burke implored the British government to answer the crucial questions: "First, whether you ought to concede; and secondly, what your concession ought to be." He adamantly supported the colonists' claim to British citizenship and rejected their treatment as outcasts and rebels. After the American

Revolution began, Burke turned his attention to Ireland. He worked diligently to pass the Catholic Relief Bill, a measure that would ease the restrictions on Catholics' ability to inherit and own **property**. Upon the passage of the bill, mobs of Protestants rioted in protest; Burke, however, escaped harm.

Returning to an issue he first addressed as editor of the *Annual Register,* Burke took up the politically charged debate regarding England's presence in India. Focusing on the corrupt actions of the East India Company, a trading company that had held a royal charter in India since 1600, Burke worked throughout the early 1850s to bring action against the trading company and replace India's rule under parliamentary control. His efforts culminated in the impeachment trial of Warren Hastings, governor general of the East India Company. The long affair lasted seven years and included 148 sittings. Burke, as the main advocate for prosecution, postponed his intended retirement to see the matter to fruition although the stress affected on his health. On June 21, 1794, the day after the case was finally forwarded to the House of Lords for judgment, Burke offered his resignation from the House of Commons. A year later Hastings was acquitted of all charges.

In the midst of the Hastings affair, Burke also responded to the debate in England over the **legitimacy** of the French Revolution. Written in the personalized style of a letter, Burke offered his opposition to the revolt in *Reflections on the Revolution in France* (1790). Clearly, Burke was not nearly as interested in the outcome of the French resistance as he was the impact of French revolutionary ideas on England. Arguing against individual rights as society's primary goal, he stood firmly for the moral authority of political rule. Burke's position was not popular within his own Whig party, and he soon found himself out of favor. Nonetheless, he continued to publish his opinions on the matter, which engrossed him until his death on July 9, 1797. A consummate thinker and statesman, Burke continues to influence the understanding of political and civil society more than two hundred years after his death.

BUSING

On May 17, 1954, the U.S. Supreme Court unanimously decided that mandatory segregation of public school students based on **race** was unconstitutional. The ruling led to court-ordered busing in the attempt to racially and ethnically diversify schools. The busing of children across district lines to create more racially balanced schools proved to be a very controversial and divisive issue.

The landmark case, brought before the Supreme Court as *Brown v. Board of Education of Topeka, Kansas,* partly overturned the precedent set in 1896 by *Plessy v. Ferguson,* which provided for "separate but equal" public facilities. In the court's decision to end mandatory school segregation, Chief Justice Earl Warren stated: "We conclude that in the field of public education the doctrine of 'separate but equal' has no place. Separate educational facilities are inherently unequal."

Prior to the ruling, 17 Southern states and the District of Columbia enforced mandatory segregation. In four other states, segregation was permitted. Although mandatory segregation was not an issue in the northern states, district lines that were drawn along corresponding racially homogeneous neighborhoods effectively segregated many schools across the nation. Because of socioeconomic factors, black schools did not have the financial resources of most white schools, therefore, blacks were not afforded the same educational opportunities as their white counterparts.

Desegregation was bitterly opposed by many whites who protested, sometimes violently, the integration of black students into white schools. Desegregation moved slowly over the ten years following *Brown v. Board of Education,* but by the mid-1960s, the courts began taking a more direct role to ensure the integration of schools. Court rulings began to require direct, proactive policies, such as busing, racial quotas, and reevaluation of district lines as means of fostering racial integration.

Opposed by many affected states, the issue of the constitutionality of busing first reached the Supreme Court in 1971 as *Swann v. Charlotte-Mecklenburg Board of Education.* The court ruled unanimously that busing was a constitutional means of dismantling segregated school systems. The decision struck down a ruling by a U.S. appeals court that overturned U.S. Judge James B. McMillan's approval of an extensive cross-town busing plan for Charlotte, North Carolina, on the grounds that it was unreasonable and burdensome. The Supreme Court sided with McMillan, asserting that the Charlotte school board had failed to offer an alternative plan for integration.

The court did place some limits on its decision. It did not require racial balance or the elimination of all-black schools, and it made clear that busing was not proper if "the time or distance is so great as to risk either the health of the children or significantly impinge on the educational process." In 1974 the Supreme Court reaffirmed the limitations on busing with its 5 to 4 decision in the case *Milliken v. Bradley,* in which it ruled that busing could not be used to alleviate racial imbalance caused by demographics alone.

Busing came to the forefront of the nation's attention again in 1974 when U.S. District Court Judge W. Arthur Garrity, Jr., ruled that Boston deliberately maintained a segregated public school system and therefore must use every legal means to remedy the situation, including busing. The suit against Boston public schools, filed by black parents and the National Association for the Advancement of Colored People, maintained that the city's teachers and students were purposefully divided along racial lines through special attendance and grading patterns. Under the newly devised state plan, the number of black-majority schools would be reduced from 68 to 40, and 6,000 black and white students (out of 94,000) would be bused across district lines.

When Boston schools opened on September 12, 1974, there were protests and scattered violence, especially in the predominantly white area of South Boston. White parents staged a boycott at South Boston High School and fewer than 100 of the school's 1,500 students attended the first two days of classes. Violent protests continued through the week, with reports of buses carrying black students being pelted with rocks as they left school and a bus carrying white students being stoned as it passed through a black neighborhood. Police made 19 arrests before the protests subsided.

School busing did increase the racial diversity in public schools to some extent. The number of students attending integrated schools rose steadily through the 1970s and peaked in the late 1980s. In 1988, 43.5 percent of black students in the South attended integrated schools where white students were the majority. However, in the 1990s, numerous court decisions, along with changing demographics and **public opinion**, led to a massive scale-back of busing and a return to resegregated neighborhood schools. By 1996, the number of blacks attending predominantly white schools had fallen almost ten percent, and 35 percent of blacks were attending schools with a minority population of 90 to 100 percent.

The Supreme Court was instrumental in the abandonment of the busing experiment. In 1991 the court decided 5 to 3 in *Board of Education of Oklahoma City v. Dowell* that court-ordered busing could end if school districts had made good-faith attempts to eliminate discrimination. The ruling affirmed that busing was not justified in the cases where single-race schools result from demographics. Thus, in the 1990s many urban school systems abandoned busing programs, including Cleveland, Denver, Nashville, St. Louis, and Norfolk, Virginia. Although court-ordered busing had been rescinded by an appeals court decision in 1987, in 1999 the Boston school board voted to officially end its controversial busing policy by the year 2000. In the fall of 1999, a judge ruled against busing in Charlotte, the first city to implement it three decades earlier.

The dramatic decline of busing leaves open the question of its value and effectiveness. In a 1999 editorial "What Busing Leaves Unfinished," appearing in *America,* the anonymous author wrote: "There may be nothing left for busing to do, but there remains the massive unfinished business of furnishing the children of the urban poor, almost all of them black or Latino, with a quality education."

See also Segregation and Desegregation

C

CANADIAN STUDIES

Canadian studies is the academic discipline that addresses issues associated with Canadian **society** and **culture**. The field of Canadian studies originated during the 1960s. The *Journal of Canadian Studies* was founded in 1966 at Trent University, and three years later the first undergraduate Canadian Studies program was established at Mount Allison University. During the 1970s, Canadian studies expanded within Canada, through the support of the office of the Secretary of State, and internationally, though the support of the Department of External Affairs. By 2000, over 36 countries, including China, Japan, India, Russia, Sweden, the United Kingdom, and the United States, had established Canadian studies centers or programs. The reasons for the advent of the structured study of Canadian life are multiple. The need to define its independence, delineate itself from the United States, and understand its complex social makeup has led to the institution of Canadian studies at all major Canadian universities, along with a wide range of programs around the globe.

The birth of Canadian studies can be dated, at least in part, to the U.S. involvement in Vietnam. Within its borders, the debate raged over Canada's role in the conflict, with many Canadian intellectuals strongly opposed. Marked by its role as a sanctuary for U.S. men who resisted the draft, Canadian society was profoundly challenged to examine its own nationhood and separation from the United States. The proposition of free trade agreements with the United States also stirred the fire of **nationalism**, as many believed that continental free trade would place Canada squarely under the thumb of its powerful neighbor.

The nature of Canada's multicultural makeup has also provided incentive for the study of Canadian culture. Throughout its history, Canada, under the political control of its English-speaking population, has struggled with its relationship with those native to the land. By the mid-1860s, the federal parliament was controlling native Indian policies. Reservations were created, and a wide range of restrictions was placed

on native Indians. For example, the 1876 Indian Act outlined the numerous steps required for native Indians to become enfranchised and thus earn the rights to Canadian citizenship, a process spanning at least six years and completely at the discretion of the Indian agent. Aboriginal claims to rights, land, and self-determination developed in the 1970s and 1980s in response to this history of **discrimination**, and the relationship between the native populations and the dominant society currently remains polarized over numerous issues.

Another facet of the culturally diverse character of Canadian society is the strained relationship between its French-speaking and English-speaking populations. Although Francophones only account for twenty percent of the overall population, eighty percent of Quebec's population is French-speaking. This gives Quebec a distinct cultural identity that has resulted in the desire for separation and independence from Anglophone domination. Although unsuccessful in their attempts to disengaged themselves from the rest of Canada, Quebec's citizens have mounted a political drive that received international attention.

A final aspect to be considered is the remainder of Canada's ethnic populations. Large numbers of Asians, especially from China and Japan, immigrated to Canada in the late nineteenth century. Until after World War II, when racial discrimination began to be recognized, Asian Canadians, along with African Canadians, were considered undesirable and inassimilable. As a result, like native Indians, various restrictions were placed on ethnic minorities. Black children attended segregated school that were created by law or by local policy, Jewish Canadians wishing to attend a university were subject to quotas, and Asians were prohibited from holding certain jobs. Asians were excluded outright from entrance into the country, immigrants from India were required to fulfill impossible travel requirements, and blacks were repeatedly rejected on "medical grounds." By the 1930s, almost no persons of African or Asian descent were entering Canada.

The tides of racial discrimination began to turn after World War II. Numerous laws and policies based on racial identity were repealed. Passed in 1946, the Citizenship Act removed **race** as a factor in obtaining citizenship, although native Indians were not allotted the right to vote in federal elections until 1960. Along with native Indians, Asian and African minorities have continued to push for reforms in policy and law that would mend the wounds of past discrimination.

CAPITAL ACCUMULATION THEORY

The theory of capital accumulation refers to concepts in Marxist sociology and economics. A central concept of Marxist theory, outlined by Karl Marx in the three volumes of *Capital* (1973), is that commodities and capital appear to be independent things unto themselves in ways that obfuscate the social relationships that created them. Capital, therefore, in Marxist theory refers to more than the common-sense usage having to do with **money** available for investment. Rather, in Marxist theory, capital refers to a social relationship and specifically the social relationship between producers and owners of production embodied in it. While owners accumulate capital in the form of money or the apparatuses that make production possible, Marxists have pointed out that capital embodies relationship. A fundamental axiom of Marxist thinking is that this relationship is always contradictory and full of conflict; classes have fundamentally opposing interests which divide modern **society**. This cleavage stems from the fact that owners must constantly seek to accumulate capital and to do so must reduce the wages paid to employees whose goals include better wages. Marx himself analyzed the role of circulation of commodities, the composition of capital, the falling rate of profit within capitalist society, and the mandate of capitalists to accumulate.

Later Marxists, as Rosa Luxemburg, Ernest Mandel, Paul Baran and Sweezy, Harry Braverman, and others have taken up the analysis of the contradictions inherent in these opposing mandates and have all, to some extent, postulated periodic crises of **capitalism** as a result. Rosa Luxemburg, for instance, proposed that one of the outcomes of the constant need to accumulate would be periodic crises of underconsumption because market levels of demand would fall as a result of the impoverishment of the working class. One important mechanism for avoiding these crises is investment in the military sector of advanced societies. Baran and Sweezy's *Monopoly Capital* (1963) made a similar point, though emphasizing the importance of investing in foreign countries. Braverman examined the role of scientific management in the current era of capitalism as part of the control over the work process necessary to the accumulation of capital.

Sociologists have received inspiration from this analysis in a variety of ways. That periodic crises of capitalism force industrial nations to continue to seek foreign investment plays a role in the world-systems analysis of Immanuel Wallerstein. Sociologist Michael Burawoy, in his ethnographic investigation of the work process, explored why workers work so hard in industrial plants, challenging the assumption that they are duped by owners.

CAPITALISM

Capitalism, also known as a free market economy or a free enterprise economy, is an economic system (or, in Marxist terminology, a mode of production) characterized by three essential features. First, the factors of production are commercialized and the means of production are privately owned. Second, economic surplus in the form of profits is generally reinvested for further production rather than simply consumed or devoted to nonproductive ends. Third, production and investment decisions as well as income distribution are generally determined through the mechanism of markets. The term "capitalism" was introduced by socialist thinkers in the nineteenth century, originally with a critical connotation.

Marxist sociology sees capitalism as a social and economic formation following **feudalism** and preceding **socialism**. **Karl Marx** traced the origins of capitalism to the struggles of urban corporations and communes in late medieval Europe to free themselves from feudal arrangements, under which property was regarded as a trust. The result, according to Marx, was the emergence of what he called civil society, a sphere of social life in which economic activity could be pursued largely free of political and religious restrictions. These conditions made the accumulation of capital possible, according to Marx, and thus the technological innovations that led to the Industrial Revolution. According to Marxist accounts, capitalism is inherently unstable, for the exploitation of labor through the appropriation of surplus value gives rise to unavoidable class conflict and irresolvable crisis tendencies.

Where Marx saw capitalism as a distinctive historical formation, Max Weber defined it more broadly as pursuit of profit through exchange, which has, in Weber's words, "existed everywhere" in various forms. What makes modern capitalism distinctive, according to Weber, is its highly rationalized organization, which in turn was made possible by the separation of business from the **household** and the rise of rational bookkeeping. According to Weber, technological innovations and the legal and administrative structures of the modern national state also played a role in the development of this modern, rationalized form of capitalism. Ultimately, however, Weber traced its origins to the **Protestant ethic**. In his view, the Protestant ethic furthered the rationalization characteristic of modern capitalism and fostered capital accumulation by encouraging the acquisition of wealth while discouraging enjoyment of it. Thus for Weber, **rationalization** ultimately eroded the Protestant ethic that had done so much to foster it, thereby stripping economic acquisition of its earlier religious meaning and significance and rendering the modern capitalist economy an "iron cage."

Since its emergence, modern capitalism has undergone several profound transformations, including the shift from commerce to industry in the eighteenth century and the end of laissez-faire in the wake of the Great Depression and World War II. Sociologists typically distinguish between early or liberal capitalism and late or organized capitalism. In contrast to liberal capitalism, organized capitalism has been characterized by economic concentration and increased state intervention.

On the one hand, individual or **family** ownership of the means of production was supplanted by the joint stock company, national corporations, and eventually multinational corporations. The economic competition characteristic of liberal capitalism tended increasingly toward oligopoly or monopoly in at least some sectors of the economy. On the other hand, the state tended to supplement or in part replace the market in order to compensate for its dysfunctions. This tendency, in turn, gave rise to a large public sector within organized capitalism. On the whole, however, investment decisions continued to be determined by the expectation of private profits. As a result of both economic concentration and state intervention, the class structure of capitalism also underwent profound changes. Just as price competition gave way to price setting in the monopolistic sector of capitalist economies, wages were determined through collective bargaining agreements rather than individual contractual exchanges and further supplemented by the emergence of a "social wage" provided by the **welfare state**. As a result of these changes in class **structure**, class conflict was substantially reduced or at least made latent.

In recent decades, some sociologists have suggested that capitalist economies are undergoing yet another shift to a postindustrial, "disorganized," or post-Fordist form. Where organized capitalism involved economic concentration and mass production, advanced capitalist economies are increasingly characterized by flexible and decentralized forms of production. Where the interventionist welfare state was central to organized capitalism, economic globalization has weakened the regulatory power of the national state and strengthened the hand of increasingly independent multinational corporations. As a result of these trends, class structure is also undergoing transformation. Service employment as well as new computer- and information-based occupations have supplanted manufacturing in advanced capitalist societies, giving rise to new divisions between well-paid, skill-flexible workers, on the one hand, and marginal, low-paid, time-flexible workers, on the other hand. The largely routinized and institutionalized modes of class conflict characteristic of organized capitalism have given rise to new, institutionally unmediated, and highly fragmented social conflicts. However, the consequences and implications of these new forms of conflict remain to be seen.

See also Communism; Socialism

CAREER

A career in its most basic sense refers to the temporal progression of an individual through life or a distinct portion of life such as an educational career. A career can also be thought of more narrowly as an individual's progression through a specific occupational sequence such as a medical career or a teaching career. Sociologists have been particularly interested in the work careers of individuals. An early study of the bureaucratic career was done by sociological theorist **Max Weber**. Within a bureaucracy's hierarchy are a set pattern of positions distinguished by tasks, importance, status, and salary. In ideal bureaucratic careers, people enter the **bureaucracy** at a low

The opening of this McDonald's restaurant marked the emergence of capitalism in the communist state of China *(Susan D. Rock)*.

position in the hierarchy, and then as they attain **skill** and experience, they move up the bureaucratic ladder. However, a career can consist of both vertical and horizontal movements.

A career can be thought of as the record of an individual's vertical moves through positions within a work **organization**, such as an insurance company or a university, or through an occupation niche, such as medicine or law. For example, a lawyer may after gaining skill and expertise move up from being an associate to being a partner. The lawyer may move up within a single firm or may find a new job in a different firm in order to advance. Workers can also move down the career hierarchy by being demoted.

A career can also include horizontal movements. Individuals can move among positions at the same occupational level. Although the positions may be of the same rank and similar in terms of responsibility, prestige, and income, the actual duties may be very different in positions at a single level. For example, first and fifth grade teaching positions may be similar in terms of rank, social prestige, and compensation but will differ greatly in grade content. A teacher may switch from one grade to another not necessarily to increase **status**, but to increase personal job satisfaction.

Each position entails duties, specific compensation, and benefits. Moreover, changing positions within an occupational sequence influences worker identity. Howard Becker, a sociologist, theorized that career movements within work organizations and occupations heavily influence adult **identity**. As individuals move up or down the career tracks, they internalize both the image and responsibilities of new positions. Workers begin to look at themselves in terms of their newly acquired status. Thus, position within the career hierarchy is central to adult personality and identity.

Actually individual careers are not necessarily as rigid as the above discussion implies. Careers may be multidirectional, encompassing both horizontal and vertical movements. In addition, workers may have several occupations throughout their lives. Also, not all occupations have a clear hierarchy of positions and expected career trajectories. For example, a printer may be expected to complete a rigid apprenticeship, while a lucky actor may land a starring role on a television show without having experience.

Regarding research on work careers, sociologists often compare the career trajectories of different groups, for example men and women. The expected male career trajectory often does not occur for women. Sociologist Rosabeth Kanter studied the career paths of corporate men and women. She found that mobility within an occupation is dependent on more than open opportunity and access to necessary training. Her research revealed that men and women are not equally represented in the corporate world's upper echelons. While men and women may appear to have equal chances, Kanter found men are advantaged by being privy to informal networks such as sponsorship from male superiors. Kanter found that men, with the support of mentors, are better able to ascend the corporate ladder.

Sociologists have also used the career metaphor to study other areas, including criminal activities. Sociologists have long considered individual criminal careers by looking at how and why individuals begin criminal activity and how and why they desist from it. By using career analysis, sociologists have also considered how people maintain deviant lifestyles. Becker studied the deviant career progression of the marijuana smoker in *The Outsiders: Studies in the Sociology of Deviance*. Beginning a deviant career, an individual must commit a deviant act such as smoking marijuana. Some individuals may quit marijuana smoking after one or two tries and never fully enter into a deviant career or lifestyle. Sociologists are more interested in "the person who sustains a pattern of **deviance** over a long period of time, who makes deviance a way of life, who organizes his identity around a pattern of deviant behavior" (30). In order to become a marijuana smoker, according to Becker, the individual must learn the technique of smoking and learn to perceive and enjoy the effects of marijuana from more experienced users. The person must also be caught, perhaps by parents or the police, and publicly labeled as a deviant. The label leads the individual to become marginalized from conforming **society**, and the user begins to spend more time with fellow smokers. In the final stage of the deviant career the individual enters a deviant **subculture**; for the marijuana smoker this could mean associating exclusively with fellow smokers. Marijuana smoking becomes not only a frequent activity but also an organizing principle for the individual's daily life and identity.

CARLYLE, THOMAS (1795-1881)
Scottish essayist, historian, philosopher, and social critic

Thomas Carlyle was a significant social thinker in Victorian-era England. The Scottish author wrote in many different forms and styles, including satirical journalism, essay, history and fiction. He concerned himself primarily with the larger themes of order and **anarchy**, the social condition of Victorian England, his feelings against **democracy**, and the hero and leader.

Thomas Carlyle was born in the small farming village of Ecclefechan, Scotland, in 1795, to stone-mason James and Margaret Aitken Carlyle. He attended Edinburgh University from 1809 to 1814 but did not complete his degree. Originally studying science and mathematics, he rejected careers in teaching, law, the Church, and translation. Carlyle first earned a living as a tutor and schoolmaster but began his writing career in 1819. At that time, he moved to Edinburgh and began writing articles on science and literature for magazines and encyclopedias. He married Jane Carlyle in 1826. Like her husband, Jane became a member of the intellectual elite and was particularly involved in the question of women's rights.

In 1833 Carlyle published one of his most famous works *Sartor Resartus*, a semi-autobiographical work about a German professor who struggles with his **identity** and his relationship to **society**. In 1834, Carlyle moved to London and began writing *The French Revolution* (1837), one of his most celebrated historical works. In 1841, he wrote *On Heroes, Hero-Worship, and the Heroic in History* which put forth the idea that a strong and heroic leader was the main thrust behind social **progress**. In *Chartism* (1839), and *Past and Present* (1843), Carlyle wrote on anarchy, implying that anarchy will overtake society if the aristocracy does not fulfill its responsibility to the **government** and if society does not consider the social and ethical concerns of the time such as poverty, pollution, and population explosion. Carlyle's six volume work on Frederick the Great, written in the 1850's, showed his approval for a leader he considered heroic, though Frederick the Great clearly violated the rules of justice to promote his own view of society. When Carlyle's wife died in 1866, he effectively stopped writing for the public, but he did write his autobiographical work *Reminiscences*, which was published posthumously, in 1887.

Carlyle's ideas were controversial and his beliefs were a study in contradictions. He puzzled and intrigued his reading public throughout his writing career. His distinctive writing style, described as "Carlylese," is notoriously difficult to follow. Carlyle's reputation as a man of letters declined during the early to mid 1900s but has since been resurrected. His most famous works are not only significant social commentaries but are also stylistically revolutionary, rendering him one of the most important and artistic social critics of his time.

CASE STUDIES

A case study is an in-depth analysis of a unit—a person, group, institution, **community**, or culture—generally over an extended time period. Often the tool of social scientists and medical researchers, a case study may be used in various other fields, such as business or education. The method accumulates and analyzes several case histories in order to form general principles. This may involve extensive interviews with the major participants, or direct observations of how a community or **organization** operates and how its members interact. The case study does not rely on laboratory experiments or survey data. Its focus is on events as they occur naturally and on existing relationships. For example, a sociologist may believe that most daughters who grow up in the home of a batterer will tend to date and/or marry batterers when they are adults. To support this **theory**, the sociologist undertakes numerous case studies of girls whose fathers were batterers in order to analyze their feelings and eventual actions. If the studies confirm the sociologist's, a general principle about girls and abusive fathers may be formulated. However, all information generalized from case studies must be used with caution. Each person is unique and may react like no other.

Sociological case studies in the United States first developed at the University of Chicago, under the influence of Robert E. Park (1864-1944). He is especially noted for his work on ethnic minority groups as well as human ecology. Park used case studies to show his students how social structures and processes shape human lives and community organization. Over the years, social scientists modified and refined Park's approach. Case studies were used, for instance, to analyze different aspects of work conditions in order to understand workers' needs. Sociologist **Talcott Parsons** (1902-79) employed structural-functional case studies to show how social systems adapt themselves to changes in environmental circumstances. **Robert K. Merton** (1910) used the same approach in his study of society and social **adaptation**.

Swiss psychologist **Jean Piaget** (1896-1980) was a leader in the case study method. In 1921, he published his findings from his systematic observations of how children learn. Throughout his lifetime and in more than fifty books and monographs, Piaget continued to develop his theory that a child's mind evolves as it passes through a series of set stages to **adulthood**.

In the late 1990s, sociologists reevaluated the importance of the case study in developing theories of sociological significance. Sociologists focused on radical case studies, reality construction, and political/poetic concerns in the writing of these studies. Radical case studies are used to bring about the researcher's political and/or theoretical aims. A Marxist sociologist, for example, is concerned with how social classes are continued and how capitalism is justified. Radical case studies have been used in feminist sociology, particularly to show how the contributions of women in social relationships and institutions often go unacknowledged, or in the study of how general social processes help to shape the lives of individuals.

Case studies of reality construction show how the realities of social exchange are created and maintained, and how they change through the use of language. For instance, science has generally been treated as a process that adheres simply to the scientific method, leaving little room for matters of inter-

Thomas Carlyle *(The Library of Congress)*

pretation. But new case studies of the scientific discipline focus on the scientists' view of their own experiments and how that impacts socially on the facts that emerge. Other recent studies involve **ethnomethodology**, or conversation analysis, showing how, among other things, test results such as that which measures **intelligence** (IQ test) are shaped by how the test givers interact with the test takers.

Sociologists are questioning if merely conducting a case study is enough. Should they not only inform those concerned of the results, but also help the subjects to resolve some of the issues that might have been raised? Sociologists also raise issues of how to publish study results in as objective and authoritative a manner as possible.

CASTE AND CLASS

Caste and class are markers of **socioeconomic status**; the first is a formalized system of stratification, generally tied to religion, while the second is aligned closely with economic **status**. Both caste and class determine a large portion of any individual's experiences.

Indian **society** provides the best example of a caste system; Portuguese travelers in the sixteenth century used the word "*casta*," meaning "race" or "breed," to describe the social system in India. "*Jati*," the commonly used term within

Lower caste Hindus line a road in Bihar to protest their inability to take part in Indian general elections *(AP/Wide World Photos, Inc.).*

India, refers to the smallest endogamous social group. The caste system in India is quite rigorous, boasting 3,000 castes and 25,000 subcastes; memberships range between the hundreds and the millions. India's caste system originated in **Hinduism**, but other religious groups in India subscribe to similar systems.

Each of the 3,000 castes fall into one of four classes, or *varnas*; these categories are used both popularly and legally. Priests and scholars occupy the top strata as *Brahmans*; followed by the rulers and warriors of the *Kshatriyas*; the farmers, merchants and traders of the *Vaishyas*; and at the bottom of the **structure** are the slaves, servants, artisans, and laborers of the *Sudras*. Occupation is the primary determining variable for caste membership but poses a conundrum for those wishing to increase their status: caste, which is hereditary, determines which jobs are traditionally available to its members. **Marriage** must remain within the caste, as intermarriage results in a demotion for the higher-ranking individual; these penalties are more severe for women than for men.

At the heart of the divisions between castes is the level of ritual pollution occasioned by one's occupation, diet, and other customs. The principle of non-harm, or *ahimsa*, is a primary tenet of Hinduism; those who eat animals (especially cows), or slaughter them for other reasons, are defiled as a re-

sult of their activities. Any occupation involving death and decay is defiling, as is touching a person of a lower class or eating the wrong foods. Hindus participate in religious practices concerning diet and hygiene, both to rectify defilement and to increase individual purity; the goal of these exercises is to be born into a higher caste, and ultimately released from the cycle of reincarnation.

Social mobility in India has increased since the country gained independence from Britain in 1947. Castes at the top of the social structure improve themselves through Westernization; members of lower castes try to improve their station by emulating the practices of the superior castes and restricting the types of individuals with whom they may interact. Modernization and industrialization are altering the nature of India's caste system, relaxing some of the strictures against inter-caste **interaction**; the government guarantees equal treatment for all castes and runs some **social support** programs to improve the lives of the lowest castes.

Industrialization in the West replaced traditional feudal divisions of rank with economically-determined groups; in the nineteenth century, these groups became widely known as classes. Class theory grew alongside the fledgling discipline of **sociology**; **social stratification** was a popular topic among early social theorists, such as **John Locke**, **Thomas Hobbes**,

Jean-Jacques Rousseau, and Henri de Saint-Simon. Saint-Simon drew the connection between means of production and the form taken by government, while subsequent theorists conceptualized the working class as a political force; these ideas were crucial to the development of Karl Marx's class theories.

So great is Marx's impact on the topic of social stratification that the subject is rarely discussed without reference to his theories. Marxist thought distinguishes societies by their mode of production, defined by the shape of their technology and **division of labor**; in turn, the mode of production creates a unique class system in which those who control the means of production control the state and the workers, exploiting the working class for goods, services, and the production of capital. The owners of the means of production also create a society's dominant **culture**.

Marx positioned the capitalists, or the *bourgeoisie*, in an adversarial relationship with the working class, or *proletariat*. The capitalist society held the seeds of its own destruction; according to Marxist theory, the proletariat would tire of being exploited by the **bourgeoisie** and use its anger and frustration to incite a revolution, which would ultimately result in the founding of a classless, Communist society.

The twentieth-century proletariat proved itself to be relatively complacent and not inclined to revolt. The Communist governments that ruled Eastern Europe for the majority of the twentieth century fell in the late 1980s and early 1990s, and capitalist states were being established in their stead.

Modern social scientists view society as divided into three basic classes: upper, middle, and working/lower. The extremes of the middle class fuse with the classes above and below. A new class, the working poor, arose in the 1990s; the term refers to families or individuals who hold one or more jobs, yet have difficulty meeting their basic needs, such as food, shelter, and health insurance. The gap between the classes at the top and bottom of U.S. society is broadening, while the middle class is disappearing; a minority of the population owns the majority of the nation's wealth, in a parallel to the global trend that concentrates the world's wealth in the hands of a few nations. Traditionally, members of the upper class inherited their wealth, in the form of investments, **money**, and land. Industrialization increased opportunities for social mobility via the amassing of wealth; the newly wealthy became known as the *nouveau riche*, a class with less status than the "old rich." However, as a result of the Internet-driven stock market successes of the 1990s, the borders between types of wealth are blurring.

Socioeconomic status begins at birth to shape many sectors of an individual's life, such as health, education, **mental health** status, and **family** size and cohesion. All of these also affect a person's chances for social mobility; combined, these factors give the individual either a cumulative advantage or cumulative disadvantage from which to move up or down the social ladder.

See also Class and Race; Social Stratification

CAUSAL INFERENCE MODELS

Sociologists use causal inference models to explain the mechanisms that affect the social phenomenon under study. A typical study design may consist of a problem statement, in which the research question is identified and contextualized; a causal inference model, in which the relevant variables and the theoretical mechanisms by which the independent variables produce an effect on the dependent variable are introduced; discussions of **data**, sampling, **measurement**, analysis, interpretation and, finally, a conclusion. The causal model explains the logic that will be used to explore the research question and determines the study design. In other terms, the causal model consists of a falsifiable hypothesis that will be tested in the study.

The type of causal model used most often in the social sciences is the *causal inference model*. Much of what social scientists study can only be inferred from results of studies, and most hypotheses cannot be tested through **experimentation**. In the physical sciences researchers may expose subjects to both experimental and control conditions to study an effect. Such experimentation is rare in **sociology**. Further complicating a researcher's ambition to explain phenomena, it is assumed that **causality** can never be directly observed; it is always an interpretation of that which is observed. Causal statements are always inferential statements. Causal inference models represent a researcher's best guess towards explaining an effect.

John Stuart Mill laid out the basic groundwork for determining causality. Mill explained temporal ordering in causality: the cause must precede the effect. In order for A to have an effect on C, A must occur before C. Mill also produced a set of explicit procedures for identifying causes. Although somewhat methodologically limited by today's standards, Mill's logical procedures identified the necessary and sufficient conditions that are the crux of causality.

A causal model may be as simple as suggesting that levels of variable A (income, for example) tend to vary with levels of variable C (years of education). A somewhat more complicated causal mechanism might suggest that A operates on D which then operates on C. Variable D is called an **intervening variable**. Other more complicated systems in which multiple variables interact or act through complicated paths to produce an effect may be modeled.

Researchers must be careful to take into account and look for some effects that may be spurious, (i.e., variables X and Y seem to be related but are not). Both ice cream sales and violent crimes increase in the summer months, but ice cream does not cause violent crime, although summer heat may lead to higher levels of each variable. Another research pitfall to be aware of is that other variables may be producing an effect that the causal model does not take into account. Because most social science research is non-experimental, researchers must evaluate their causal inference models on logical assumptions about causality made from real-life observation and belief about the way the world works. Statistical analysis of the results can only begin to make sense if the logic of the causal model is sound.

Acts of censorship, such as book burnings, are generally enacted by governments and powerful organizations to prevent public consumption of opposing ideas *(Corbis Corporation [Bellevue]).*

CAUSALITY

Causality is the relationship between cause and effect. A causal relationship usually requires: the existence of a spatial and temporal contiguity between two events, the occurrence of one event before the other, and the unlikelihood that the second event could have occurred unless the other event occurred first. A causal relationship is also often thought to exist when a particular type of event always or almost always occurs in a particular way. Such a lawlike relationship, however, is not necessarily evidence of a direct causal relationship but may only show a **correlation**.

Causality usually involves both an immediate cause and some more underlying cause. For example, the immediate cause of the First World War was the assassination of Archduke Ferdinand; an underlying cause was nationalist tension exacerbated by the European arms race. To determine the relative importance of such multiple causes and to distinguish correlation from causality, sociologists have developed various analytical systems, including **multivariate analysis** and causal modeling. In addition, sociologists consider whether causality associated with purposive actions follows the same rules as does causality in physical science. Another question of interest is whether functional explanation is a type of causal analysis.

Many theorists consider concepts of causation to be flawed. Philosophers argue that causation does not easily fit with classical conceptions of logic because it identifies as causal some conditions that may not be necessary or sufficient to create the effect in question. And epistemologists point out that it is scientifically impossible to state conclusively that any given relationship is necessarily causal.

CENSORSHIP AND THE REGULATION OF EXPRESSION

Censorship, at its most basic level, is the suppression of speech. This suppression is generally enacted by governments and powerful organizations to prevent public consumption of opposing ideas, placing freedom of expression in jeopardy. Methods of censorship run the gamut from subtle to inhumane; perhaps individuals are not allowed on a meeting's agenda, as with female members of the Students for a Democratic Society in the 1960s, or a government throws writers who do not adhere to the party line into prisons and work camps, a common tactic in the former United Soviet Socialist Republic and in China from the days of Mao to the present. The disabling of challenges to a governing body's rule is only one form of institutional censorship; the suppression of materials deemed damaging to a community's morals is more common in democratic states. Such censorship is debated at all levels of society in the United States, in a tug-of-war between the country's founding principles and what some people find offensive.

The Pilgrims sailed for North America in the early part of the sixteenth century to escape the religious persecution they suffered at the hands of the English government. Freedom of speech thus became one of the founding principles of the United States of America; its importance to the spirit of the nation is underscored by the First Amendment to the Constitution. Influenced by the writings of **Thomas Paine** and championed by James Madison, the First Amendment, part of the Bill of Rights, guarantees freedom of speech, religion, petition, and assembly to the American people.

The determination of what constitutes speech is frequently at issue when censorship gets attention in the United States. An obvious manifestation of speech, freedom of the press, is explicitly referred to by the First Amendment. The twentieth century saw challenges to the First Amendment and its relationship to literature, film, music, the visual and performing arts, **pornography**, flag burning, and the financing of political campaigns as forms of speech. When challenged, the rights of individuals and groups to express themselves through these media generally are upheld by the courts.

The motive behind many contemporary attempts at censorship is the control of obscenity. Many writers now considered part of the literary canon found their works censored in both England and America; expatriate writers published their novels in Paris, leaving readers to pass around smuggled copies sent by friends living or traveling overseas. Writers and books banned in the twentieth century include: James Joyce, *Ulysses*; Vladimir Nabokov, *Lolita*; Henry Miller, *Tropic of Cancer*; J.D. Salinger, *Catcher in the Rye*; and several novels by D.H. Lawrence.

The Supreme Court, in *Roth v. United States* (1956), ruled that any work containing even a small amount of redeeming social value is not obscene and that explicit sexual content is not equivalent to obscenity. ''Obscene'' is defined as any work which deals with sexual issues in a way calculated to appeal to an audience's prurient interests; obscenity is also measured by ''contemporary community standards,'' a vague formulation valuable to potential censors. The Court refined the concept of redeeming social value in *Miller v. California* (1973), which produced the ''SLAPS'' test for obscenity: a work must be lacking in any serious literary, artistic, political, or social value to be considered obscene.

The content of visual and performing arts came under attack in the 1990s, both by members of Congress and conservative Christian organizations. First, an exhibit of photographs by the late Robert Mapplethorpe, mounted in Cincinnati in the spring of 1990, was shut down on grounds of obscenity. Mapplethorpe photographed flowers, rock stars, nude men, and sadomasochistic sexual acts; the offending images fell into the last two categories. Following protests by supporters of the arts and the First Amendment, and the issuance of a court order, the exhibit reopened to large, curious crowds, but with one concession: the curators placed the images deemed most offensive in a separate room. Later that year, four performance artists, denied grants from the National Endowment for the Arts (NEA) on grounds of obscenity took the NEA to court. As a result, Congress decided that, while artists have a right to free speech, they do not have a right to government funding of their endeavors, and mandated that the NEA abide by community standards when giving out grants.The beginning of the twenty-first century brings new forms of speech and new challenges to freedom of expression, as the government and private organizations try to regulate content on the electronic frontier of the **Internet**.

CENSUS

A census is a complete enumeration of some population. In sociology, the term is most commonly used to refer to a population census, which is a complete count of individuals within some politically defined area such as a country or a city. A census of individuals, however, could involve all students in a school district, all prisoners in a prison system, or all residents of nursing homes in a state. The term is also sometimes used to refer to complete counts of items at a higher level of generalization, for example, data that detail the attributes of all farms in a county, counties in a state, or countries of a continent.

A census is commonly contrasted to a survey, in which only a sample of individual members of a defined population is selected for study. Using data in sociological research from a complete census rather than a survey entails the issue of **statistical inference**. When evaluated, sample **data** findings infer characteristics about the population as a whole. Findings are found to be "statistically significant" if they are true for the population, given that the data represent only a sample of that population. When researchers use census data, **statistical significance** is not an issue because the data consist of the whole population. Thus, for example, observed differences between groups of people must be true, if all members of these groups are in the data.

The idea of a population census is quite old, and references to such political activities can be found in many ancient texts and at archeological sites. One example can be found in the New Testament. In Luke, the parents of Jesus, just before his birth, are reported as returning to Bethlehem due to the Roman emperor's order of a census. A more recent example, the Domesday Book, documents the effort made by William the Conqueror in 1086 to assess the state of the land and population of England in order to tax his new subjects more effi-

As mandated in the U. S. Constitution, a national census is conducted every ten years *(National Archives and Records Administration)*.

ciently. In most modern countries a population census is conducted at regular intervals for the same reasons that motivated William the Conqueror: to count the population and assess changes in various qualities such as the distribution of age, education, occupation, and income.

In the United States, as specified in the Constitution, a census is conducted every ten years, with the most recent occurring in 2000. The main purpose of the U.S. Census is to assess the distribution of the population across the country, so that political boundaries for members of the House of Representatives can be set. Over the years, however, additional items have been added to the Census to get more information on the current state of the U.S. population. Most households receive what is known as the "short form" **questionnaire**, which asks residents to fill out information on the name, relationship to the **household** head, sex, age, **race**, and **ethnicity** of each person living in that household. To gather additional information the Census Bureau also sends a longer form of the census questionnaire to approximately one in six households. In addition to asking for all the information requested on the short form, this questionnaire asks questions on marital status, care for grandchildren, educational level, nativity, income and work, previous residence, and housing status.

Most sociological analysis of U.S. Census data makes use of a five percent sample of individuals who filled out this long form questionnaire. This information is made available to researchers in the Public Use Micro-sample, or PUMS, data set. In addition the Census Bureau provides data organized geographically instead of by individuals for those who do research on the types of places people live. Examples of research in **sociology** that use data from the U.S. Census are analyses of income level or housing type, demographic studies of aging or the changes in ethnic and racial distributions, and studies of residential segregation. Often these data are combined with other **surveys**. For example, it is possible to combine individual surveys on **crime** with U.S. Census data on **cities** to understand how both individual and neighborhood characteristics affect who is likely to be victimized.

Recent problems with the U.S. Census, such as high costs and low response rates, have resulted in some political debates about ways to improve its accuracy. For example, the 1990 census cost 2.6 billion dollars to conduct, and it is estimated that more than eight million residents were not counted. One main feature that raises the cost of the census involves attempts to interview households whose residents are repeatedly unavailable. If a household does not return the survey initially mailed to it, the Census Bureau will send workers to that address in order to make sure people live there and then to attempt to **interview** them. These visits are the most expensive single aspect of the census. In order to both control costs and get a more accurate count of those who remained uncounted in the 1990 census, primarily urban minorities, the Census Bureau suggested that actual census counts be supplemented with sampling based on those households that were counted. This proposal argued that principals from statistical sampling could be used both to save money and more accurately count the population of the country. This idea proved controversial, and in the end it was struck down by the U.S. Supreme Court as unconstitutional.

See also United States Census Bureau

CENTERS FOR DISEASE CONTROL AND SOCIAL CHANGE

An agency of the U.S. Public Health Service (PHS), the Centers for Disease Control and Prevention (CDC) is charged with numerous health-related tasks. In its efforts to identify and contain communicable diseases, the CDC researches the origins of disease, collects **data** on occurrence of disease, and develops methods for preventing or controlling disease. It also is involved in a wide variety of social health issues, such as tobacco use, alcohol abuse, sexually transmitted diseases, work-related injuries and illness, violence in the home, and special minority health concerns. Through its education and training programs, the CDC seeks to inform the public of preventative health measures.

Originally established as the Communicable Disease Center, the CDC opened its first headquarters in 1946 in Atlanta, Georgia, where its central offices and laboratories remain to date. The CDC was charged with the task of coordinating with state and local agencies to combat malaria, typhus, and other communicable diseases. The following year the PHS added national disease relief to the CDC's responsibilities. Combining research with prevention and response efforts, the CDC expanded rapidly through the following decades. During the 1950s the CDC established the Epidemic Intelligence Service, the Polio Surveillance Unit, and the Influenza Surveillance Unit. CDC research developed a fluorescent antibody test for the rapid identification of bacteria and viruses, and by 1959 a fluorescent antibody test for rabies was introduced that proved to be the first completely accurate field test.

During the 1960s, the CDC took on smallpox, launching a smallpox eradication program aimed at eliminating smallpox

and controlling measles in 20 African nations. By the late 1970s smallpox was officially announced to be eradicated worldwide. Other initiatives during the decade included assuming the responsibility for publishing the *Morbidity and Mortality Weekly Report,* a weekly health update that reports on important health issues, mortality data, and disease information for every state. In 1967 the CDC established the Family Planning Evaluation Unit, which was created to provide technical assistance to **family planning** clinics and test the safety and effectiveness of contraceptive methods.

In 1970, the CDC was renamed the Center for Disease Control to reflect its extended scope and functions. The Birth Defects Monitoring Program, the National Nosocomial Infections Surveillance Unit, the National Institute for Occupational Safety and Health, and the Vessel Sanitation Program were all incorporated into the CDC during the decade. In its response to health-related emergencies, the CDC led public health teams to Zaire and the Sudan to address epidemics of ebola hemorrhagic fever, investigated the effects of the Three Mile Island nuclear accident, and, after discovering that hepatitis B was transmitted sexually, began trial studies on a vaccine.

In order to reflect a new **organizational structure**, in 1980 the CDC became known as the Centers for Disease Control. During this decade, the CDC focused on preventive health and the fast-paced spread of acquired immunodeficiency syndrome (AIDS). Reporting on the first cases of AIDS in 1981, the CDC organized a task force to respond to the growing AIDS crisis, creating an AIDS hotline in 1983. In 1985, the CDC co-sponsored the first International Conference on AIDS, and in 1988 the CDC AIDS task force mailed an informational piece, ''Understanding AIDS,'' to every household in the United States. In 1982 the CDC centered on the alcohol abuse as part of an effort to address diseases and injuries related to abuse of alcohol. The next year the Violence Epidemiology Branch was created to provide guidelines for the prevention of child abuse, homicide, and **suicide**.

As in the two previous decades, the CDC's official name changed again during the 1990s. Reflecting its continuing expansion, the CDC officially became the Centers for Disease Control and Prevention; however, the agency continued to use the acronym CDC. Consistently addressing social issues, the CDC conducted research on high-risk behavior by teenagers through a national youth risk behavior survey. Also, in 1994, the Office of Women's Health was created, and the *Surgeon General's Report on Report on Preventing Tobacco Use Among Young People* was released, which contained research data on tobacco use by teenagers and young adults, including brand preference and nicotine withdrawal symptoms. This report was followed by the 1998 publication of *Tobacco Use Among U.S. Racial/Ethnic Minority Groups.*

The CDC's organizational **structure** consists of six centers and one institute, along with four program offices. The six national centers focus on the areas of chronic disease prevention and **health promotion**, environmental health, health statistics, AIDS, **sexually transmitted diseases**, and tuberculosis prevention, infectious diseases, and injury prevention and control. The National Institute for Occupational Safety and Health provides guidelines for work-related safety, monitors occupational health issues, and devises preventative approaches.

CHAMPAGNE, DUANE (1951-)
American sociologist and educator

Champagne began life as one of seven sons in the rural setting of Belcourt, North Dakota, on the Turtle Mountain Reservation on May 18, 1951. Both of his parents were enrolled members of the Chippewa tribe. He attended school on the reservation from third grade through secondary school and, in 1969, graduated from Turtle Mountain Community High School. He stayed close to home during his undergraduate study, attending North Dakota State University in Fargo directly after high school. He received his bachelor of arts degree in mathematics and sociology in the summer of 1973.

Champagne did not take the traditional route from undergraduate work to graduate school. He opted instead for a tour of public service via Volunteer in Service to America (VISTA), the domestic counterpart of the peace corps. During his service, Champagne collected and analyzed **data** for the United Tribes Technical Training Center (now United Tribes Technical College) in Bismarck, North Dakota. Since the program required him to enroll in a graduate program, he began a master's program in sociology with a minor in mathematics at North Dakota State University in Fargo, receiving his degree in 1975. Although he was accepted to a number of schools for doctoral study, Champagne chose the sociology department at Harvard University. He arrived at the school in 1975, and received his Ph.D. in sociology in 1982. A fellowship from the Rockefeller Foundation allowed Champagne to conduct post-doctoral studies with the Tlingit in southeast Alaska, and with the Northern Cheyenne in Montana in 1982. He then accepted a year-long teaching position with the sociology department at the University of Wisconsin in Milwaukee in 1983.

In 1984, he relocated to the University of California-Los Angeles, where he began work as an associate professor of sociology. Champagne became involved with the university's *American Indian and Culture Research Journal*, which had begun publication in the 1970s. Champagne became the journal's main editor in 1986. Under his direction, the journal has grown in length and scope, and has attracted more diversified writers.

After heading the journal for three years, Champagne was named associate director of the UCLA American Indian Studies Center in 1990, and, in 1991, he became director of the center. As director, his main responsibility was to oversee the daily machinery of what he termed in an interview with Jennifer Gray Reddish as "organized research." Champagne explains, "We carry on various activities [at the American Indian Studies Center]. We have a library and a publications department, where we publish the *American Indian and Culture Research Journal*, and we publish books." The center caters to a "reservation audience" and many of the books address issues of culture preservation, economic development, and academia. Other publications include research aid manuals and books concerning the Child Welfare Act. Although UCLA does not have a formal undergraduate American Indian studies major, the center is closely involved with a master's program in that area. Champagne is quick to point out that the American

Indian Studies Center, though primarily a research institution, also supports Native UCLA students by creating "a less threatening environment to help them adjust." The center offers counseling services, meeting rooms and computer resources in order to offset the strain some American Indian students encounter while in a dominant **society** environment. In addition, the center encourages students to organize a pow-wow each year at the university, fostering fellowship and activity among American Indian students.

Outside of his work as the director of the center, Champagne is an author in his own right. Over thirty of his articles have appeared in scholarly journals and as chapters in books. He has published two books: *American Indian Societies: Some Strategies and Conditions of Political and Cultural Survival* and *Social Order and Political Change: Constitution Governments Among the Cherokee, the Choctaw, the Chickasaw, and the Creek*. He has also written chapters for various published books. He was the main editor of the *Native North American Almanac*, published in 1994, featuring biographies of noted Indian persons throughout the United States and Canada during various time periods in history.

Despite leading an active professional career, Champagne does take time out of his work schedule for his family and recreation. He and his wife Liana have lived in Los Angeles, California, with their three children: the oldest a daughter named Talya, followed by a son Gabriel and their youngest, a daughter, Demelza. Champagne's wide-range of hobbies include playing basketball and chess. Having concentrated on his chess game, he earned a master's title in both over-the-board and correspondence chess at the national level. Champagne is actively involved with the Los Angeles American Indian community having served as a member and past chair of the Los Angeles City/County American Indian Commission, trustee for the Southwest Museum, and other community committees and boards.

CHARISMA

In scholarly usage since the early twentieth century, the word "charisma" applied to magnetic leaders, whether they are political, secular, or religious, who exhibit awe-inspiring and almost magical powers of person and personality. In the United States, the term is frequently used to distinguish those in or seeking public office. Franklin D. Roosevelt, John F. Kennedy, and Ronald Reagan are often singled out as American presidents possessing charisma. It is not to be confused with the policies, politics, or aims of the leader, however. Charisma applies only to the person and to that **leadership** quality that attracts others in a sometimes almost mystical way. Nor is charisma recognized solely in political leaders. The great homerun hitter Babe Ruth had charisma if the legions of his fans are any testimony. So did movie stars Marilyn Monroe and John Wayne and singers Frank Sinatra and Judy Garland. We say that such people have "star quality." It is not necessary to like them or even to admire them in order to recognize this trait that sets them apart.

The term "charisma" was first attributed to German sociologist Max Weber (1864-1920), best known for his "Prot-

Legions of baseball fans were attracted to the charisma of baseball's home run "slugger" Babe Ruth *(The Library of Congress)*.

pose and belief made him charismatic to his followers. Cult figure Jim Jones was also a man with charisma. A self-proclaimed messiah, Jones led his followers to South America and in November 1978 into an ordered mass suicide in what came to be known as the Jonestown Massacre.

Are we born with charisma, or can it be learned? Is there a DNA gene for charisma? Most people think that charisma is an inborn, inexplicable trait, but some acknowledge that it might be developed. Charisma in the modern world has meanings quite different from the original interpretation. The word itself comes from the Greek, meaning "gift," as in the divine grace that is bestowed upon saints. In its original use, figures like Siddartha Gautama (Buddha), Jesus, and Muhammad would be called charismatic. But the modern use of the word is much broader. In some cases, it may be based mainly on physical attractiveness, and for some individuals it may be equivalent to sex appeal. Others feel that what people see as charisma is really a highly developed sense of self-confidence. Most people do not have this personality trait to such a fine degree. Therefore, this confident sense of self, combined with purpose and energy, an attractive physical presence, and the ability to express one's feelings and emotions may be interpreted by others as the fascinating power of a personality we call charismatic.

See also Cult of Personality

CHI SQUARE

Sociologists rely heavily upon statistics to aid in understanding social data. If a researcher wanted to know if men and women had different attitudes toward the president's policies on education, for example, that researcher could use several measures of association to determine if a relationship exists between gender and attitudes. The measure of association most commonly used by sociologists to examine relationships of this sort is the chi square (χ^2).

The popularity of chi square stems from the fact that it is powerful, easy to understand, and relatively quick to calculate. The basic idea is to determine if the values that are seen are close to the values that would be expected if there were no relationship between two factors. For example, if a poll were conducted regarding American attitudes toward affirmative action, and twenty-five percent of blacks opposed it, it would be expected that about twenty-five percent of whites would also oppose affirmative action, if **race** were not a significant predictor of attitudes. The chi square test can tell researchers whether race and attitudes toward affirmative action are related. The closer a calculated chi square value is to zero, the more likely it is that no relationship exists between the two variables. A drawback of chi square is that it cannot tell the researcher the direction of a relationship. In other words, using chi square cannot tell sociologists which racial group is more favorable toward **affirmative action**.

The term "chi square" actually refers to both the chi square test and the chi square test statistic. The chi square test is considered a descriptive statistic because it describes how

estant Ethic" thesis. Weber described charisma as a quality that sets certain individuals apart and bestows on them an almost supernatural power. The recognition of charisma is generally spontaneous and not based on rational feeling.

Weber characterized charisma as one of three kinds of existing authorities. Traditional and legal authorities are generally stable, but charisma, the third **authority**, is apt to be unstable and sometimes fleeting. Charismatic authority may appear in response to a revolutionary social situation, such as Fidel Castro in Cuba.

Charismatic leaders often arise out of severe social crises that stem from some type of national instability. The chaos that is produced stimulates people's natural reaction to such a leader. People are looking for someone to follow, and the individual with charisma is apt to win their attention over a less colorful figure with more stable, even more workable solutions. In the end, however, if the aims of the charismatic leader go unfulfilled - for instance, if Castro had not taken over Cuba - his appeal will likely diminish. Because charisma is so personal, even if the leader's aims are realized, a stable succession is unlikely. The next leader almost certainly will not have the original's power of attraction.

A charismatic leader generally draws admiration, but that is not necessarily so. Both Winston Churchill and Adolf Hitler, major figures of World War II, are acknowledged to have been charismatic leaders, although their aims were decidedly dissimilar. **Mohandas Gandhi**, India's religious leader and man of peace, was certainly charismatic. Yet, he was not a bold figure as compared to some political leaders. While Gandhi was quiet, small, and self-effacing, his steely sense of pur-

much one factor (attitudes toward affirmative action, for example) is dependent on the other (race). For this reason, the chi square test is sometimes referred to as the chi square test of independence. The chi square statistic is also considered an inferential statistic because it allows researchers to infer how certain they are that the two factors are dependent on each other. In other words, researchers can state if a relationship appears between race and attitudes toward affirmative action and the degree to which they are certain that a relationship exists.

THE CHICAGO SCHOOL

The Chicago School was the center of sociological thought in America between roughly 1890 to 1940. In the 1940s, Ivy League institutions Columbia and Harvard took a leading and guiding role in the discipline. The Chicago School, so named because of its location at the University of Chicago, was constituted by an interdisciplinary group of social researchers, reformists, and philosophers. It was the first program of **sociology** that was not dominated by a central figure but rather was composed of a several prominent members. The collective enterprise focused on scientific research and social amelioration, an underlying philosophical framework of **pragmatism** and an unquestioned goal of **social order** and reform. The most prominent members were Robert Park, W. I. Thomas, and Ernest Burgess, and in later years of the school, Herbert Blumer. Pragmatist philosophers John Dewey and **George Herbert Mead** provided important intellectual stimulation and conversation for its members.

Gradually, **Robert Park** became the figurehead of the Chicago school of sociology. Park developed the school's graduate program and focused the program on urban ecology. A newspaper reporter before pursuing graduate work in sociology Park grasped the importance of urban **social problems** and the need for sociologists to observe these first-hand.

A principal criticism of the Chicago sociological project was that it neglected **theory** in pursuit of **empiricism**. However, Park and Thomas had studied in Germany under many of that country's primary philosophers and social theorists, including **Georg Simmel**. However, while certainly not forgetting their theoretical and philosophical foundations, the Chicago sociologists stressed that for sociology to develop as an academic enterprise in the United States it would have to focus its attention on solving the social problems caused by **urbanization**, industrialization, and capitalist expansion. This goal led to an emphasis on the relationship of science and theory. By science, the members meant careful empirical observation, which took the form of ethnographies of urban Chicago life. Students in the department wrote dissertations on dance halls, thieves, race relations, and hobos. They were encouraged in their studies to "get the seats of their pants dirty," as Park once extorted. It was an **urban sociology** of the streets. In order to change life, devotees argued, one had to see life first-hand.

Even as the power of the University of Chicago's sociology department waned in the late 1940s and early 1950s, it continued to produce eminent sociologists such as **Erving Goff-**

An increase in the number of mothers employed outside the home has led to a greater demand for childcare services over the past several decades *(AP/Wide World Photos, Inc.)*.

man and Howard Becker. Not centralized in any department, these sociologists carried the tradition of the Chicago school to departments throughout the United States. Some have referred to this second generation of scholars as the Second Chicago school, scholars who felt a disdain for the development of refined theories and deep methodological rigor. That was left to sociologists spawned from the Ivy League schools. Instead, emphasis was placed on getting close to the social world and seeing it first-hand. Along with Blumer's theory of **Symbolic Interactionism**, the importance of qualitative, ethnographic observation remains, perhaps, the Chicago school's greatest contribution to the discipline.

CHILD CARE

Child care refers to the upbringing, daily responsibility, or welfare of children. In modern terms, it often means the daily care or supervision of a child by a non-parent, as in at a day-care center, while the parent is at work. The increase in American mothers employed outside the home has led to a dramatic growth in the need for child care over the past few decades. According to U.S. **government** statistics, eight out of ten employed mothers with children under six are likely to use some form of non-parental child care arrangement, whether in a home-based (a relative or paid child caregiver comes into the home) or center-based setting.

In the United States, child care has become a national issue, particularly with the recognition that proper care affects children's growth and development of a child. Several federally-sponsored programs, such as the Child Care Bureau and the National Child Care Information Center, both part of the U.S. Department of Health and Human Services' Administration for Children and Families, have been created to improve and promote the quality, affordability, and supply of child care options.

To protect the health, safety and welfare of children, many states have standards and requirements for child care centers and encourage parents to use licensed child care providers in home settings. State child care facility standards may include maximum group sizes, child-to-staff ratios, and minimum requirements for caregiver training. There may also be requisite health-related procedures and requirements for age-appropriate activities, nutrition, discipline, space, equipment, supplies, policies and records.

Still, care within the parent's home is not generally regulated by the government and not all child care facilities or providers are required to be licensed. Many state and local governments have child care resource and referral network systems to assist parents with their decisions.

CHILD SUPPORT

Not originating with the **divorce** boom of the 1970s, child support can be traced to the nineteenth century. Though divorce was rare before the 1800s, the nineteenth century witnessed a dramatic increase in single mothers. During this same time, the previously standard rule of granting custody to a child's father gave way to the new perception that mothers were the better caretakers of their children. By 1900, mothers were almost exclusively given custody of their children. Child labor laws were tightened and children were viewed less for their ability to contribute to the **household** income and more for their need to develop and be educated. Thus, children became consumers of household income. The increase in single **motherhood** and the resulting scarcity of means for supporting dependent children caused American courts to create a child support duty, holding that a father had a legal duty to support his children.

Traditionally, child support has been a matter of **family** law and, thus, is in state jurisdiction. Therefore, child support systems are varied, and the amount of support paid is determined by local courts. The degree to which laws are enforced also varies, and prior to legislation, fairly little was done to punish fathers who did not make regular payments. The first major federal child support legislation, passed in 1974, was the addition of part D to Title IV of the Social Security Act. It provided extensive support for the enforcement of child support payments. The act established the Child Support Enforcement program, created the federal Office of Child Support Enforcement, required states to establish state offices comparable to the OCSE and authorized federal funding for three-quarters of the states' expenditures on child support enforcement.

Further legislation passed, and in 1980, legislation made permanent the federal support that would fund offices to serve mothers of all children eligible for support, regardless of income or welfare **status**. By 1984 legislation required states to provide services universally. In 1988 the Family Support Act passed. Finally, the toughest legislation was the Personal Responsibility and Work Opportunity Reconciliation Act of 1996 (the PRWORA, often called the "Deadbeat Dads Act"),

which required states to set up comparable collection policies for child support, and required states to provide information from motor vehicle registrations and police records to other states so that nonresident parents who move across state lines and evade child support can be found. Many states and the federal government have made significant strides in reforming child support policy in order to secure support for children of single mothers.

See also Family Law

CHOMSKY, NOAM AVRAM (1928-)
American linguist, philosopher, and political commentator

Noam Avram Chomsky was born in Philadelphia on December 7, 1928. He studied at the University of Pennsylvania, receiving his Ph.D. in linguistics in 1955. After that year, he taught at the Massachusetts Institute of Technology, where he was the Institute Professor of Linguistics.

Chomsky received international acclaim for his work in linguistics, philosophy, and social/political theory. A prolific writer, he revolutionized linguistics with his theory of transformational-generative grammar. His work in **epistemology** and **philosophy** of mind was controversial; his social and political writings were consistently critical of American foreign and domestic policy.

In two seminal books on linguistic theory—*Syntactic Structures* (1957) and *Aspects of the Theory of Syntax* (1965)—Chomsky argued that the grammar of human language is a formal system consisting of abstract logical structures which are systematically rearranged by operations to generate all possible sentences of a language. Chomsky's theory is applicable to all components of linguistic description (phonology, morphology, syntax, semantics, and so forth). In phonology, for example, Chomsky argues that the sound system of a **language** consists of a set of abstract binary features (phonemic level) which are combined and recombined by means of phonological processes to produce the sounds which people actually say (phonetic level). In syntax, which has received the most attention by linguists, the theory specifies a set of abstract phrase-structure **rules** (deep structures) which undergo transformations to produce all possible sentences (surface structures).

Chomsky's assumption was that a grammar is finite, but that the sentences which people produce are theoretically infinite in length and number. Thus, a grammar must generate, from finite means, all and only the infinite set of grammatical sentences in a language. Chomsky has further argued that all languages have the same underlying, abstract structure—universal grammar.

Evidence for these claims is strong. The most commonly cited evidence is that children learn language rapidly, totally, and similarly by the age of five or six, irrespective of the **culture** into which they are born or the language which they learn. Chomsky thus claimed that children have innate linguistic competence, a reflection of universal grammar.

Chomsky broke from previous structuralist dominance of linguistics and revolutionized the field in several ways. First, he converted linguistics into a theoretical discipline. Second, he pluralized the word "grammar": he showed that there are many possible theories of language—grammars—and he argued that the purpose of scientific linguistics is to demonstrate which of all possible grammars is the most explanatory feasible. Third, he linked linguistics to mathematics, **psychology**, philosophy, and neuropsychology, thereby broadening the discipline immensely. Chomsky's later work in linguistics focused on spelling out the details of universal grammar. He was particularly concerned with the sorts of constraints that limit the power of transformations [see, for example, *Lectures on Government and Binding,* (1981)].

Critics of Chomsky generally argued that grammar is not a formal system, but a social tool. They raised as counter-evidence such things as language variation, social and cultural differences in language use, and what they claim to be the unprovability of the innateness hypothesis: that innateness is a theorist's intuition, not an empirical **fact**. In all fairness to Chomsky, he never ruled out variation or the functional aspect of language, but preferred instead to focus on the similarities across languages. His work, furthermore, generated considerable interest in both the neuropsychology and biology of language, which provided considerable evidence for innateness.

Chomsky demolished any connection between linguistics and behaviorist psychology with the scathing "Review of B. F. Skinner's *Verbal Behavior*" (1959), in which he argued that stimulus-response theory could in no way account for the creativity and speed of language learning. He then produced a series of books in favor of rationalism, the theory that a human is born with innate organizing principles and is not a *tabula rasa* (blank slate): *Cartesian Linguistics* (1966), *Language and Mind* (1972), *Reflections on Language* (1975), and *Rules and Representations* (1980).

Chomsky was also an ardent critic of American domestic and foreign policy. His libertarian socialist ideas can be found in such works as *American Power and the New Mandarins* (1969), *For Reasons of State* (1973), *The Political Economy of Human Rights* (1979), and *Towards a New Cold War* (1982). Chomsky's position was always that U.S. international aggression is rooted in the American industrial system, where capitalism, by its aggressive, dehumanizing, and dominating nature, spawns a corresponding militaristic policy. Historian Michael Beschloss, writing for the *Washington Post Book World* found in Chomsky's *American Power and the New Mandarins* a strong denunciation of the "system of values and decision-making that drove the United States to the jungles of Southeast Asia." Chomsky's strongest vitriol, however, was directed toward the so-called "New Mandarins"—the technocrats, bureaucrats, and university-trained scholars who defended America's right to dominate the globe. *Times Literary Supplement* contributor, Charles Townshend noted that Chomsky "[sees] a totalitarian mentality" arising out of the mainstream American belief in the fundamental righteousness and benevolence of the United States, the sanctity and nobility of its aims. Yet "the publicly tolerated spectrum of discussion"

Noam Chomsky *(Archive Photos, Inc.)*

of these aims is narrow. Chomsky transcended that narrow spectrum by offering examples to illuminate how American policies proved otherwise. Chomsky's political views, though, caused his historical/political scholarship to be taken less seriously than his work in linguistics. Steve Wasserman wrote in the *Los Angeles Times Book Review* that Chomsky had been "banished to the margins of political debate. His opinions have been deemed so kooky—and his personality so cranky—that his writings no longer appear in the forums... in which he was once so welcome."

In later years Chomsky continued his criticism of American foreign policy in works such as *The ABC's of U.S. Policy Toward Haiti* (1994), *Free Trade and Democracy* (1993), *Rent-A-Cops of the World: Noam Chomsky on the Gulf Crisis* (1991), and *The New World Order Debate* (1991). Appreciation, if not acceptance, attended Chomsky's later works. According to Christopher Lehmann-Haupt in the *New York Times*, Chomsky "continues to challenge our assumptions long after other critics have gone to bed. He has become the foremost gadfly of our national conscience." *New Statesman*

Essential to Christian religion is the belief that Jesus's crucifixion illustrates God's love for humankind and identifies Jesus as savior *(Corbis Corporation [Bellevue]).*

correspondent Francis Hope concluded of Chomsky's lingering suspicions of **government** motives: "Such men are dangerous; the lack of them is disasterous."

CHRISTIANITY

Christianity is the religion that was formed in Palestine by those who followed the teachings of Jesus of Nazareth, a Jew who was born about 7 B.C. and became a public figure after he turned thirty. The New Testament covers several aspects of his life, including his ministry, teachings (especially the Sermon on the Mount), miracles attributed to him, his death by crucifixion, and his resurrection. The underpinning of Christianity is the concept of a three-person God or Trinity (God, the father; God, Son [incarnated as Jesus]; and God, the Holy Spirit). Essential to Christian religion is the belief that Jesus' life, crucifixion, resurrection, and ascension illustrate God's love for humankind and identifies Jesus as Savior of the world. Another tenet is that those who believe in God (and accept

Jesus as the Christ [Messiah or anointed one], as God's divinely appointed Son) will attain salvation and eternal life. Christianity is also characterized by the use of sacraments; Christian worship usually takes place in an organized **church** under the leadership of trained clergy. However, Christianity has been organized differently and practiced various ways by different Christian religions.

The differences in Christian religions today have historical explanations. After Jesus' death, the apostle Paul established Christian groups that broke from Jewish tradition. These groups of Christians or followers of Christ spread across the Roman Empire and, perhaps as early as A.D. 200, resembled a cohesive organization with a doctrine, liturgy, and ministry. By the fourth century, the Catholic Church—the largest Christian organization in the world—had spread from Spain to India. The Roman state initially persecuted Christians, but the Christian religion was legalized by Constantine the Great (in A.D. 313). By A.D. 380, Christianity was declared the state religion, and the previous pagan religion was suppressed. During these times, the Christian church was relatively unified, although the Catholic church was threatened by disagreements over doctrine. To settle debate, a standard Christian creed was formed by bishops at the Ecumenical Council of Nicaea (in A.D. 325).

Over the next twelve hundred years, Christianity fractured twice, first to the east, then to the west. In the centuries following Constantine's fourth-century removal of the Roman Empire capital from Rome to Byzantium (renamed Constantinople, now Istanbul), the Church suffered a major schism which ultimately resulted in the establishment of Eastern Orthodoxy. In 1517, Martin Luther, a Roman Catholic priest, nailed his ninety-five Theses on the church doors in Wittenberg, Germany; thus, in his open criticism of the Church sale of indulgences and other thinly disguised revenue collection means, Luther initiated the Protestant Reformation. This complicated shift from the "universal" Catholic Church to local churches (primarily in northwest Europe and England), involved reshaping tenets long proclaimed by the Roman church.

Regarding the Catholic belief in priests as intermediaries, Luther believed that all baptized Christians really served as priests and, therefore, had the responsibility to minister to fellow humans. Luther also felt that the sacraments of the Catholic church were contrived; to him, the only sacrament was God's word. In the Lutheran church, God's word encompassed baptism, penance, and the Eucharist. Luther's opinions and independent action led to his excommunication and the eventual establishment of the Lutheran church.

In the 1900s Christian churches began to emphasize unity in what was called the Ecumenical Movement which established the World Council of Churches in 1948 and was later joined by Protestant and Orthodox churches. The World Council coordinated ecumenical missionary efforts to spread Christianity across the globe. Currently, Christianity is divided into three broad categories—Roman Catholic, Protestant, and Eastern Orthodox. Each category incorporates a number of divergent religions or sects. By the late twentieth century, social action had become an increasingly important element of Christianity. This focus drew some further from the Christian story and tradition that formed the basis for the Christian church. The Catholic church in particular was known for its social justice initiatives.

Bertrand Russell (British philosopher, 1872-1970), one of Christianity's many critics, believed God's existence a fallacy and considered the Christian church service—particularly the Catholic service—to be full of superstition. According to Russell, the Christian church was responsible for repressing intellect and creativity, while at the same time it extolled people who were involved in complex often destructive events. Russell claimed that the church erroneously emphasized the virtues of Jesus, without considering his faults.

At the beginning of the twenty-first century, Christianity experienced rapid growth in sub-Saharan Africa. In 1970, African Christians made up one in ten of the world's Christians; by the year 2000 African Christians were one in five. Internationally, the number of Christians in Africa was expected to be second only to Latin America. African Christian churches blend traditional spirituality and evangelical faith healing with traditional Christian tenets. Such churches focus on local problems, such as drought, and emphasize the possibility of wealth in this lifetime for members.

See also Church

CHURCH

Traditionally, the meaning of the word ''church'' is broad and includes the group of believers who have in common a belief in Jesus Christ. The term also includes followers of the Christian faith who are deceased. According to the doctrine of Christian religion, the church was founded by Christ, through his apostles. Some Christians recognize descriptive divisions within the church, including the militant church (living members), the suffering church (the dead of purgatory), and the triumphant church (the saints in heaven). The church has four descriptive aspects. It is said to be one (meaning that it is united), holy (meaning that it produces holy lives), catholic (meaning that its boundaries are universal), and apostolic (meaning that its continuity was established with the apostles of Christ's time).

Throughout history, various groups or religions have lent their unique interpretations to the concept of church. During the Reformation, for example, Martin Luther and his followers rejected the doctrine that stated that the church received its continuity through the apostles. This group believed that the **authority** of the church was passed only through the Scriptures. On the other hand, the Roman Catholic Church, the Eastern Orthodox Church, and the Church of England maintained their belief in apostolic succession. Such a tenet meant that apostles of the church had the authority to administer sacraments such as communion. The Protestant Church lent its own interpretation to the general meaning of church; Protestants believed that the church represented the concept of oneness because it was mystically present among all Christian faiths.

Churches, such as Notre Dame Cathedral in Paris, France, were erected to glorify Western-European interpretation of God *(Courtesy of Jeffrey D. Hill).*

Sociologists elaborated on the broader concept of church and analyzed it in more descriptive categories. Weber and Troeltsch, and later Howard Becker (1950) established a continuum that included the ideas of church (in a smaller sense), denomination, **sect**, and **cult**. An occasional fifth category included the Ecclesia, or a large, international **organization**. The Roman Catholic church is an example of Ecclesia. According to these sociologists, sects are dynamic, require high commitment, and can instill rapid political or religious change. Sects and cults, if they succeed, tend to be organized, hierarchical, and conservative.

Toward the end of the twentieth century, sociological data showed that almost half of the U.S. population regularly attended weekly church. The figures were lower for people of other nations: twenty-seven percent of Britain's populace attended church weekly; twenty-one percent in France; four percent in Sweden. More than half of Americans considered religion an important part of their lives, while church attendance in Northern Europe dropped drastically. Near the turn of the century, two-thirds of Americans belonged to a church, even though only seventeen percent of Americans belonged to a church in 1776.

Even though data suggested that Americans fostered a strong connection to church in the late twentieth century, Samuel L. Dorn (in the *Futurist*) warned that the Christian church would need to adapt to major sociological changes into the twenty-first century. Dorn predicted that ties between church and state would be completely severed in developed countries. He also claimed that the rapid population growth in Third World countries, such as those in Latin America and certain parts of Africa, would dramatically change the worldwide composition of Christians; by 2025, the percentage of white Christians would fall to thirty percent (from forty-five percent in 1989). Such trends would also mean that in the future missionaries of Christian religions would come increasingly from underdeveloped countries. Dorn suggested that the growing number of Christians in less developed countries would not favor a separation of church and state but would look to the church to improve economic circumstances. Additionally, a growing interest in mystical phenomena in the Western world might very well force the church during the twenty-first century to acknowledge and incorporate mystical elements.

The church has fostered much thought from writers and sociologists on its relationship to **society**. In a *National Catholic Reporter* article, Bernard Cooke suggested that the Catholic church was a reflection of contemporary societal trends. He claimed that women's struggle for equality within society was mirrored within Catholic church policy and that the church must remain open to dialogue. Robert E. Willoughby (in the *Humanist*) suggested that controversy within the church was absolutely essential and the key to freedom for the church; without freedom, a church ran the risk of becoming ineffective.

CIRCULATION OF ELITES

An elite is a privileged class of people that has the advantage of superior intellectual, social, or economic **status**. In **sociology**, the term "elite" generally refers to those with a privileged political status. The "circulation of elites," a term developed by **Vilfredo Pareto**, refers to a continues cycle of rule by elites, one political elite **group** replacing another. He asserted: "a political system in which the 'people' expresses its will (supposing it had one, which is arguable) without cliques, intrigues, lobbies, and factions, exists only as a pious wish of theorists. It is not observable in the past or present either in the West or anywhere else." Elitist rule, then is an endless **cycle**, untouchable by even the strongest democratic impulse.

Pareto described the circulation of elites as a rotation between two groups, the *lions* and the *foxes*. The lions are characterized by their fortuitous combinations and conservative attitudes. On the other hand, the foxes are more clever, but less worthy of trust. Pareto considered the alternation between these two elitist groups to supersede the possibility of any more democratic system.

CITIES

Cities are a fairly recent human invention, first developing about ten thousand years ago, as previously nomadic human populations increased and began to create permanent settlements. This new way of life allowed a more complex **division of labor** to develop; people had more specialized jobs and a greater choice of lifestyles. More complex and hierarchical power structures developed, with an accompanying increase in inequality among urban residents. The emergence of city life also changed the ways people relate to one another on a daily basis.

Sociology as a discipline began during the nineteenth century, a time of increasing **urbanization** and industrialization in Europe. Several classical theorists were concerned that city life was changing human relations for the worse. Ferdinand Tönnies distinguished between a form of social life he called *gemeinschaft*, which was characteristic of small, rural villages, and *gesellschaft*, which was characteristic of the modern city. *Gemeinschaft* referred to a "community" in which relations between members were close and intimate, bound by a common **language**, **values**, and way of life. *Gesellschaft*, however, referred to an "association," where city residents are individualistic and perhaps hostile to one another, uninterested in getting to know one another past superficial encounters. Similarly, Émile Durkheim contrasted rural and urban life in his theories of "mechanical solidarity" and "organic solidarity." The first, which describes rural life, refers to societies based on members who are very like one another, sharing customs and beliefs. The second, which describes urban life, refers to societies based on individual differences, where people have specialized ways of earning a living and thus are dependent on one another like the different parts of a single organism. Simmel also theorized that city living made people more rational, calculating, and efficient at the expense of meaningful human relationships. Weber emphasized the increased role of commerce and trade in urban life, a change from rural societies where people could be more self-sufficient.

However, these theorists have been criticized for taking too much of an "either/or" approach. While city life does create more anonymity among its residents, this can be liberating for those who find small town life, where everyone knows everyone else, to be stifling and restricting. Urban residents are frequently able to create support and friendship networks that are not necessarily based on physical proximity. Likewise, cities tend to be more tolerant of people of different races, ethnic groups, religions, sexual orientations, etc. This heterogeneity can create a multicultural environment that many people prefer over smaller towns where residents are very similar to one another. Urban residents have more freedom "to be themselves" without worrying about breaking the strict **norms** of a tightly-knit, small community.

Even so, the massive inequalities present in cities, particularly between ethnic or racial groups, can cause serious problems. Decentralization and the growth of suburbs in American cities have exacerbated the difficulties faced by more vulnerable urban populations. The emergence of mass transportation in the mid-nineteenth century made it possible for those who could afford it to move their homes farther away from the city center; residential and commercial districts became increasingly separated. Factories and other businesses often moved to suburban areas as well, following the residential shift. African Americans and immigrant communities have frequently been left behind in the inner city (sometimes called the "transition zone") when their employers closed down and left and they could not afford to move in search of new work opportunities.

These problems were worsened by the destruction of the once-extensive streetcar lines in most American cities in the 1930s and 1940s. National City Lines (NCL), an organization controlled by General Motors and other powerful corporations in the oil and transportation industry, acquired controlling interest in city streetcar lines across the country, closing them down and replacing them with diesel buses that increased pollution and decreased services. The U.S. Department of Justice found NCL guilty of "conspiracy to monopolize the local transportation field" in 1946, but its organizers faced only minimal fines. As the interstate highways were built with massive federal funding in the 1950s and 1960s, Americans were increasingly forced to rely on cars for transportation, while those who could not afford them continued to rely on buses. Local governments have bought what was left of many public transportation systems, but have had difficulty maintaining them due to lack of funding.

Municipal governments, strapped for funds and increasingly surrounded by wealthier suburbs, have created "growth machines" to improve their economies and increase their revenue. Politicians, entrepreneurs, civic groups, etc. work together to attract new business and industry to the city, in order to create jobs and encourage commerce, tourism, and residential redevelopment. This growth, however, often benefits the city's elites at the expense of low-income populations. New industries often hire people from outside the area rather than local residents, new shopping areas or hotels may be built by destroying preexisting neighborhoods, and "gentrified" residential districts renovated to attract wealthier residents back to the downtown area frequently displace earlier renters who can no longer afford to live there. Additionally, new businesses are often given massive tax breaks and other subsidies by local and state governments, limiting the amount of new revenue municipal governments actually receive from the development they encourage.

However, some redevelopment efforts, particularly those spurred by community groups, have been beneficial, encouraging people to remain in or return to urban neighborhoods. As suburbs sprawl and commutes lengthen, some workers have found moving back to the city an increasingly attractive prospect. An improved economy and decreasing **crime** rates have also helped city life look more attractive. It remains to be seen, however, if the needed investments in well-paying jobs, transportation, pollution reduction, education, and human services will materialize in a way that truly benefits all urban residents.

As suburbs sprawl and commutes lengthen, some workers have found moving back to the city an increasingly attractive prospect (Field Mark Publications).

CITIZEN RIGHTS

In contemporary political philosophy, the concept of rights has proven an attractive base from which to build political theory. Indeed, rights have been central to Western political debate since its inception. The foundational events of Western political history were essentially concerned with the rights of individuals verses the state. From the English Magna Carta adopted by the British crown in 1215 to the Bill of Rights attached to the United States Constitution in 1791, Western politics have been largely shaped by various declarations of rights. For example, Thomas Paine's well known work *The Rights of Man*, published in 1800, shaped several decades of political philosophy.

In modern **society** rights are understood as entitlements and privileges due an individual or group upon which there can

be no infringement. There can be rights *to* do something, for instance the right to choose where one lives. There can also be rights *from* something, for example the right protecting one from random imprisonment. The sociological study of rights has focused on the way in which rights are guaranteed by various communities. Normally, that community is the state. But a given state can only guarantee the rights of its own population, thus the notion of citizen rights. These are the rights that all members of a body politic can expect to receive. What **community** guarantees a particular right is an important question because it allows us to differentiate between, for instance, **human rights** and citizen rights. Citizens of the United States might be appalled at the treatment people receive in another country; they might rally against a violation of free speech. But the United States cannot enforce the Bill of Rights on behalf of citizens of another country because citizen rights only apply to members of the particular body politic that guarantees them.

Much current scholarship on citizen rights has grown out of a dialogue begun by British social theorist T. H. Marshall in *Citizenship and Social Class* published in 1950 and in his *Class, Citizenship, and Social Development* (1977). Marshall identified three types of rights to which citizens can lay claim. Civil Rights are understood as the expectation of equal protection under the law. These are necessary for the exercise of individual freedom and are often invoked to protect the individual against abuses of power by the state. For instance, prohibitions against unreasonable search and seizure are civil rights. Political rights, the second type identified by Marshall, guarantee participation in government and the political process. Voting rights for women and for African Americans are examples of political rights. Finally, social rights provide a minimum standard of social and economic security to all citizens. In modern society, social rights include universal education, the welfare system, and increasingly health care. In recent years, the expansion of social rights has engendered the most conflict. While Marshall's categories have proven influential among scholars, the public dialogue about rights generally does not make these distinctions. For instance, the Civil Rights Movement led by Martin Luther King, Jr. actually sought rights that would, in Marshall's scheme, be considered political and social rights as well as civil rights. Nevertheless, his view that citizenship included the legitimate claim to an ever-expanding body of rights has proven enormously influential.

While much attention has focused on the modern West's preoccupation with rights, recent scholarship has stressed the corresponding, but less popular, notion of citizen responsibility. For instance, Mary Ann Glendon's 1991 book *Rights Talk* and Amitai Etzioni's 1996 work *The New Golden Rule* attempt to rediscover the balance between individual citizen's rights and communal responsibility.

Civil Religion

For sociologists religion is a social **institution** that celebrates sacred phenomena. The sacred, as differentiated from the profane, refers to those aspects of human belief and experience that transcend the material and the scientific. Such phenomena remind individuals that they do not exist in isolation from a greater whole. Sociologically, religious rituals contribute to group cohesion and solidarity.

Beginning with Émile Durkhiem in the nineteenth century, some sociologists reason that secular symbols, rituals, and ceremonies displace sacred ones in modern societies. That is, figures like presidents and practices like voting provide the same sense of corporate belonging and meaning today as supernatural objects did in the past. In this sense civic figures become icons; they take on elements of the sacred. This perspective has gained legitimacy with the development of secularization theory. As religious institutions lose social **authority**, institutions in the secular sphere replace them. Yet, proponents of civil religion do not argue that traditional reli-

gion and civil religion are entirely incompatible. Rather, they coexist in a reciprocal relationship. The rites and contents of civil religion borrow heavily from traditional religious sources.

While not the first to establish this **concept**, Robert Bellah coined the phrase, civil religion, as a sociological term in the late 1960s. He based his study on the content of speeches presidents delivered at their inaugurations. In these speeches Bellah detected religious notions including references to a divine creator, salvation, and favored destiny of a chosen people. He pointed out the extent to which events and personalities of American history have been transformed into mythic icons with religious dimensions. For instance, he noted that Abraham Lincoln maintains the aura of a savior figure. Americans worship these icons through rituals and ceremonies that are institutionalized as holidays, traditions, and civic duties. For instance, on the fourth Thursday of every November, most Americans gather with their families for a Thanksgiving feast; regardless of the citizen's specific heritage, Thanksgiving is a ritual exercise in giving thanks for the shared American heritage. Similarly, the fourth of July brings parades and fireworks in celebration of national independence and Memorial Day is dedicated to people killed in military service. These icons and rituals serve to reinforce the legitimacy of a collective American heritage that transcends that of specific individuals. All are examples of civil religion.

Civilization

When discussing civilizations, sociologists use two prevalent definitions of the term. First, civilization is referred to as a well-established, complex **society**. Essential characteristics of a civilization include the emergence of towns and **cities**; an increasingly specialized **division of labor**; the development of trade, manufacture, and commerce; centers of local and national political and legal administration; systems of **communication**; literacy; and an elite **culture** of artistic and religious expression. Therefore, the historical worlds of the Aztecs and Incas, Imperial China, Ancient Greece, and the Roman Empire, to name a few, may all be regarded as examples of civilizations.

Second, civilization is considered to be a term that is almost commensurate with culture (i.e., codes of manners, dress, **language**, rituals, **norms** of behavior, and systems of belief), signaling the shared standards of political, economic, and social behavior among different societies, as in Western civilization.

In both cases, the material precondition for the emergence of civilization is an economy that has a productivity above subsistence level. It is this point that gives the term its value-positive connotation: *civilization* is usually contrasted favorably with the primitivism that has been to prevail when existence is dominated by the need to ensure simple survival. However, this view and its implications of moral advancement is not only considered arrogant, but also inaccurate, when one considers such events as the two world wars of the twentieth century, as well as the consuming work-related activities of peoples living in advanced industrial societies.

Two Navajos of the Coyote Clan grind corn to make bread *(AP/Wide World Photos, Inc.)*.

CLAN

The term clan refers to an established social **group**, originating in the descent of a common ancestor. The descent of a person in a clan is traced through the male line or the female line. A clan may include several family groups. Usually, clan members marry outside the clan, considering marriage within the clan as **incest**. In some societies, the word clan designates only groups that trace their origin through female lineage; in this case, the word "gens" describes a clan that traces lineage through the male and the word "sib" refers to both types of clans. A clan may also encompass several systems of lineage. Clans have existed throughout the world and often designate a totem (plant, animal, or **symbol**) that serves as protection. A group of clans is referred to as a "phratry." A well-known clan system exists in the Scottish Highland and also in the Balkans among the South Slavs, who called their clan system a "zadruga." The South Slav clan system was practiced in Serbia into the 1900s.

Clans provide a tribal **structure** in which assets may be shared among members and **rules** and conventions benefit everyone. According to James Fallows, *Washington Monthly* (March 1989), clan systems generally protect members, and individuals wanting to move away from the clan have difficulty leaving clan **identity** behind them. However, Fallows stressed that people in such groupings are generally happier being with their own "tribe," even though the United States "accepts individuals regardless of their 'tribal' background."

The Gypsy clan system transcends geographical boundaries. Rosa Tachyon Janus attempted to dispel some myths about Gypsy **society** in an October 1984 article in *UNESCO Courier*. Janus and her sister Catarhine Tachyon (author of *We Are Gypsies*) were born into the Gypsy heritage and made it a point in the 1960s to educate people about Gypsy society which, according to Janus, is actually a well organized social system of clans and rules designed to protect the Gypsy population. These included such conventions as obeying elders,

William Julius Wilson believed that race has been replaced by class as the cause of inequality among African Americans *(Courtesy of William Julius Wilson)*.

sharing earnings equally across a Gypsy camp, clearly delineated responsibilities for looking after children, and arranged marriages. Traditional customs included formal farewells by members of the camp when a member approached death, and birthing customs that excluded most members of the camp from visiting a mother during the two weeks after she had given birth. The latter tradition also helped preserve hygiene, since historically mainstream doctors would not treat gypsies.

See also Family; Group

CLASS AND RACE

Class (economic strata) and **race** (physiological type) are, in fact, intertwined concepts that have major social impact. The term class refers to a **group** of persons with a common economic, occupational, or social status. Race refers to several physiological categories which attempt to divide people by physical type. The interconnection of class and race has had profound ramifications on individual groups and their access to power.

With regard to African Americans in the United States, numerous views of race have been espoused. In the 1930s, for instance, scientific claims were made that the cranial capacity of blacks was smaller than that of whites, indicating a corresponding difference in **intelligence**. This type of research appeared to justify or validate discriminatory practices and beliefs. Many scholars now conceptualize race as a set of fluid biosocial categories. This school of thought believes that there is no absolute means for racially categorizing human beings, who are themselves racially diverse, and who produce offspring with a variety of physical appearances and genetic compositions.

The concept of race, therefore, is arguably a socially constructed notion influenced by the **values**, social practices, and political climate of a given society. A person considered black in the United States might be considered "colored" (or mixed) in another country or white in a third country. The "one drop rule" of race, prevalent in the American South during slavery and beyond, deemed a person black, regardless of appearance or cultural identification, if the person was known to have "one drop of black blood." Such a view expressed the prevailing belief in the inferiority of African Americans and the belief that whiteness could be tainted by blackness.

Theories of **caste and class** were common in the 1930s and 1940s, which compared the system of American racial order to the caste system in India. African American sociologists W.E.B. DuBois and **Oliver Cox** challenged this notion, using Marxist theories to help explain the connection between racism and the capitalist system. **Karl Marx** posited that economic **structure** determines the shape of **society**. He argued that systems of production provide the basis for class groups. Farmers, traders, and workers, for example, form separate classes in a farming system, since each group has a different relationship to crop production. Each group has its own concerns and level of control over the production process.

In order to understand race and class relations in the United States, Marxist sociologists closely examine **capitalism**. Under this system, a nonowning class must exist, whose labor assures owners of making a profit. When European capitalism expanded beyond Europe into an imperialistic system in colonies, whites dominated people of different races across the globe. African, Asian, and indigenous people across the world were subjected to violence, cultural domination, and racial hostility. Dark skin was viewed as a mark of inferiority and a less evolved **civilization**, while white skin was equated with purity, beauty, and advancement. Persons of color became providers of menial labor and often comprised the nonowning class. Thus, racial oppression benefited those imperialists who controlled the capitalist system because the oppressed populations provided cheap labor.

However, scholars influenced by the New Left of the 1960s believe that American race relations cannot be completely explained by class dynamics. This school of thought views race and racism as having a profound impact on social groups that is independent from class forces. In his 1979 book *The Declining Significance of Race*, William Julius Wilson contended that race has been replaced by class as the determining factor in the inequality of African Americans. Wilson based his contention on government intervention and the rise of service industry jobs, and the growth of the African American middle class.

Critics of Wilson assert that race is not less significant but that racism against the black middle class is perhaps, less significant. Critics also assert that the African American middle class is less well established and few blacks hold great economic power and wealth. Inequality persists, as the debates continue regarding how class and race determine access to power and resources. Clearly, the United States is still divided along racial and class lines, attributable to a complex web of change-resistant factors.

CLINICAL SOCIOLOGY

The emergence of clinical sociology as a recognized field of social science has been long and often arduous. The term "clinical sociology" itself has been given broad and varied definitions since it was formally entered into academic discussion by Chicago sociologist **Louis Wirth** in his 1931 *The American Journal of Sociology* article "Clinical Sociology." Although many variations exist, sociologists who work in the clinical setting agree on the dual approach of analysis and intervention. The Sociological Practice Association (SPA), formed in 1978 as the Clinical Sociology Association, defines the field as the "application of the sociological perspective to the analysis and design of intervention for positive change at any level of social organization, from the micro to the macro."

Although the roots of clinical sociology can be traced back as far as the first scientist-practitioners of the fourteenth century and later to the applied approaches of classical sociologists such as **Auguste Comte**, Émile Durkheim, and **Karl Marx**, the development of contemporary clinical sociology is best identified with the University of Chicago in the 1920s. "The Chicago School," as it was called, referred to the sociology professors at the University of Chicago who showed pressing interest in using sociological methods to solve social and **community** problems. They directed their students to work in the field, using the neighborhoods and settlement houses as their "sociological laboratories." Several child guidance centers also became training grounds for clinical sociologists.

Enthusiasm for the clinical approach dissolved by the end of World War II and was replaced by a renewed emphasis on empirical studies, development of **theory**, and academic employment of sociologists. Although scholarly journals published an occasional article dealing with the sociologist as clinician, for the most part, the subfield went unnoticed by the profession until the mid-1970s. With the creation of the SPA in 1978, clinical sociology once again gained recognition, although it was still often viewed with suspicion by many traditional sociologists.

The animosity between classic and clinical sociologists is centered on the issues of scientifically verifiable **data** and objectivity. As clinical sociologist Rodney L. Lowman explained in *Exploring Clinical Methods for Social Research* (1985): "Traditional researchers seek to reduce information about social systems to quantitative data that can be analyzed statistically. Clinicians recognize that numbers are only one way to express knowledge and make liberal use of alternative ways of reporting findings." Whereas traditional sociologists find fault with the "subjectivity" of this type of study, clinical sociologists claim higher ground in their attempt to go beyond study and theory to applied practice. Howard Rebach and John Bruhn, editors of the *Handbook of Clinical Sociology* (1991), claim that "sociology must go beyond the theoretical to provide knowledge applicable to real human problems. The application of theory addresses the scientific concern; application is the crucial test of theory."

Despite the struggle to receive recognized **validity** from mainstream sociology, clinical sociologists continue to affirm their rightful place in the field. The SPA began offering certification in clinical sociology in 1984, thus giving the profession a measure of control and credibility. According to Jan M. Fritz, in her 1991 article "The Contributions of Clinical Sociology in Health Care Settings" in the journal *Sociological Practice,* although the contributions of certified practitioners vary greatly depending on such factors as setting (individual, **group**, **organization**, community, national, international), area of concern, and experience, these clinicians have several common traits, including theoretical analysis, methodological sophistication, intervention skills, and a specialized body of knowledge.

First, clinical sociologists are expected to be thoroughly trained in theory and possess a working knowledge of multiple major theories. They understand theory and be able to translate the theories into practical use. Rebach and Bruhn offer insight into the practitioners' use of three traditional theories: structural functionalism, **conflict theory**, and symbolic interactionism. Functionalism views the social **structure** as a system comprised of numerous interrelated systems and sub-systems, which is controlled by the dynamic relation between stability and change within the system. The clinical sociologist can apply functionalist theory to emphasize the interconnectedness of social life, identify levels of conflict, and assess the function of behaviors and systems that are detrimental.

Unlike structural functionalism, conflict theory acknowledges conflict as a normal part of social systems, which are characterized by inequality among members and dominance of some. The dynamic relation in this theory is the struggle to obtain or preserve power and control. Using the conflict theory, intervention for the clinical sociologist focuses on conflict management, observation and assessment of systems of dominance and inequality with a specific social system, and recognition of both implicit and explicit means of control.

Applied primarily at the micro-level, **symbolic interactionism** focuses on the individual interpretation of self through **interaction** with others. Because one's understanding of the world is based on interaction with others, development of shared meaning is stressed as a means to create a viable social system. Thus the goal of intervention is to identify areas where shared meaning does not exist and help the actors find mutual understanding.

Second, certified clinical sociologists must be trained in methodology and be able to recognize and assess the various weaknesses and strengths of both qualitative and quantitative methods. Third, practitioners should possess intervention skills. Stressing interdisciplinary training and practical experience, according to Fritz, "The certified practitioner would get

beyond simply pointing out a few of the difficulties in the situation. The practitioner would provide analysis, suggest alternative ways of dealing with a situation and, and when possible, actually initiate or assist in the intervention." Finally, clinical sociologists are expected to develop a limited area of expertise, such as socioeconomic conditions, gender, or **ethnicity**. Within that field, clinicians should possess several skills that contribute to the success of their practice (health promotion, counseling, **social policy**, etc.).

As the role of clinical sociology continues to evolve, so does the evaluation of its place in the field of social science. Best established in the health care setting, clinical sociologists can also be found in such positions as organizational or community consultant, conflict mediator, counselor, and group facilitator or trainer. Comprised of so many differing practices and specialties, advocates for the expanded development of the field will be required to continue to appeal to both their peers and the academic community to build more comprehensive training programs aimed at the practice of clinical sociology.

COALITIONS

Coalitions are alliances formed between individuals or groups which tend to be temporary rather than permanent because the goals each member pursues through the alliance may differ dramatically or even be incompatible. Coalitions are rational, means-oriented alliances designed to increase the probability of success for any of its members by improving members' access to shared resources.

One conception in work by Mills and Borgatta defines coalitions according to verbal **interaction** in three-person discussion groups. From this micro-level perspective, individuals who engage in positive verbal interaction in order to complete a task are considered to have a coalition. More prominent theories are connected to game **theory** and strategic interaction, and also to various branches of macro sociology, including political and economic sociology. Some historical scholarship concerning coalitions tends to be primarily descriptive. However, the dominant sociological branch of coalition theory grew out of Simmel's work and focuses on triadic relationships. Sociologists Mills, Caplow, Vinacke, and Arkoff examined the formation of triadic relationships. Their theories are not descriptive but normative. That is, they determine how actors *should behave* to maximize payoff, not how actors *actually behave*. Their research focuses on outcomes of coalition formation rather than on interactions that lead to their formation, maintenance, and dissolution.

Relationships in groups of three members (triads) can take a discrete number of forms based on the types of relations between members. Several forms allow for coalition formation. Other triadic possibilities include negative relationships between all actors or positive relations between all actors. But coalitions are competitive: for any members to succeed, others must fail. Success and failure are measured in terms of the payoff. An individual increases his or her own payoff by reducing the payoff of others. When two individuals form a coalition, both individuals increase their own payoff by reducing the payoff to the third member of the triad who is excluded.

Theories of coalitions that are rooted in game theory focus on actors' choices to maximize the **ratio** of resources contributed to the coalition to the payoff received when the coalition is successful. The coalition structure is frequently considered to result from power relationships among the actors. Interestingly, Vinacke and Arkoff found that less powerful actors were frequently members of winning coalitions. Weaker members had fewer resources to contribute; therefore, their share of payoffs was lower, making them desirable partners. However, after several experimental iterations, the weak member's share of total payoffs was greater than that of other stronger members as a result of being chosen frequently as a partner.

COERCION

Coercion, perhaps the most readily recognizable form of power, is often defined as the exercise of physical force, or the threat thereof, to exert control over a person or **group**. Coercion is typically non-consensual, that is, it is exercised in order to get a person or group to do something they would not otherwise do. Coercion may indeed be the oldest form of power known to humankind.

However, in modern societies, even as coercion is still widely exercised by individuals, gangs, the police, military, and many others, some political scholars argue that coercion is declining in favor of more subtle, less physical, and/or more consensual forms of power. This point is perhaps nowhere more true than in the case of state power. **Max Weber** defined the state as that entity which monopolizes the legitimate use of force or coercion in a given territory. Yet despite the modern state's substantial internal (e.g., the police, prisons) and external (the military) instruments of coercion, it exercises arguably more far-reaching power through its extensive legal regulation, budget expenditure, and social welfare programs. Such state power derives far less through coercive force than through legal, financial, and administrative regulation, and many sociological scholars old and new have expressed concern about such power. For instance, as far back as the 1840s, the French scholar Alexis de Tocqueville in his classic work *Democracy in America* expressed serious concern about the emergent risk of ''soft despotism,'' whereby the modern democratic state would quietly, kindly, and gradually rob all or most citizens of their democratic freedoms rather than coerce a select few citizens as ''hard despots'' would. Today, echoing Tocqueville, scholars like Jürgen Habermas argue that modern welfare states paradoxically undermine the privacy and freedom of their citizens even as such states free their citizens to varying degrees, through social welfare programs, from the coercion of capitalist labor markets.

As the preceding sentence indicates, many sociologists argue that the modern capitalist economy is a major if not the most significant instrument of coercion, exceeding the coercive power of the state in its control over so many citizens' lives. Marxist economic sociologists particularly emphasize how capitalist economies are coercive by nature in as much as they require most people to sell their labor in order to meet their most basic needs for food, shelter, clothing, **health care**, etc. This obligation, these sociologists maintain, fundamentally contradicts the popular myth that workers in capitalist economies are under free contract, that is, free to exit one job and find another as they please. Furthermore, some economic sociologists study how capitalist employers may use additional means of coercion—such as intimidation, demotions, layoffs, and firing, or the threats thereof—to exert control over their employees.

COGNITIVE CONSISTENCY THEORIES

Theories of cognitive consistency pertain to congruity in people's attitudes. Underlying these theories is the assumption that people strive to maintain harmony or agreement among their beliefs, evaluations, and the behaviors which stem from the attitudes they hold because **attitude** consistency is a comfortable, desirable state. Conversely, discord among attitudes is unpleasant and brings about change aimed at restoring consistency. Based on this fundamental assumption are two theories of cognitive consistency: balance theory and the theory of cognitive dissonance.

Balance theory was developed by Fritz Heider in the mid–1940s. Heider considered three elements in attitude consistency: (1) the person [P] under consideration who holds some attitude, (2) some other person [O], and (3) an attitude object [X]. Balance theory contends that the person under consideration strives to maintain consistency among the attitudes connecting P, O, and X. For instance, the person, P, supports the death penalty (X), but his/her friend, O, does not. Because people's attitudes toward their friends are positive, P's attitudes toward both X and O are positive, while O's attitude toward X is negative. When the signs of these three attitudes are multiplied, the resulting sign is negative. Heider called such a result a minus state, which represents an imbalance among the attitudes.

Because balance among attitudes is the desired state, a minus state motivates people to reduce the imbalance and the **stress** it brings. Attitude change thus results from a state of imbalance. In the above instance, three changes are capable of bringing about a state of balance: (1) P could change his/her attitude toward the death penalty; (2) P can reject his/her friend; or (3) P can change O's attitude toward the death penalty. Balance theory predicts that the easiest of these options will be chosen to reduce the imbalance.

Therefore, balance theory involves the interrelationships among two people's attitudes toward each other and some attitude object. Developed by **Leon Festinger** in the mid–1950s, the theory of cognitive dissonance is similar to balance theory, but it incorporates behavior into the equation. Whereas balance theory only concerns the evaluative and cognitive components of attitudes and the agreement between them, cognitive dissonance theory involves the relationships between two or more attitudes and/or behaviors. Unlike with balance theory, other people's attitudes are irrelevant to the theory of cognitive dissonance. Instead, only one person's attitudes and behaviors, and the connections between them, are relevant. Hence, in comparison, balance theory is an interpersonal theory of cognitive consistency, as the congruity among the attitudes of two people is involved, while cognitive dissonance theory is intrapersonal and concerned solely with agreement among one individual's attitudes.

Despite this difference, the theory of cognitive dissonance is similar to balance theory in that the basic assumption of both is that agreement is a desirable state, and inconsistency is undesirable. The theory of cognitive dissonance holds that people try to maintain consistency or consonance between their attitudes and behaviors. In other words, people try to avoid inconsistency or dissonance, which produces stress, tension, and feelings of unease. Festinger named this internal state of tension and unease that comes about when individuals notice the dissonance from an inconsistency in their attitudes and behaviors.

For instance, individuals might hold the attitude that eating low-fat foods is desirable and important for one's health. However, when they find themselves eating fatty foods, their behavior contradicts their attitude. Because of this contradiction, individuals experience cognitive dissonance. Since inconsistency in one's attitudes and behaviors is an undesirable and uncomfortable state, individuals try to reduce the discomfort and restore consonance.

Restoring consistency can be achieved in a number of ways. First, individuals can change behaviors which contradict the attitudes. In the above instance, then, individuals might stop eating fatty foods. Second, the individual can change the perceived importance of the cognitive component of the attitude in question. This involves minimizing or trivializing the belief which is contradictory to the behavior, in an attempt to justify that behavior. For example, individuals might try to convince themselves, after eating fatty foods, that a low-fat diet is not that important in becoming and staying healthy. Finally, additional cognitions can be introduced in order to restore consistency between attitudes and behaviors. Thus, the individual might incorporate the belief that people need to include some fat in their diets to survive. Any of these actions will act to reduce cognitive dissonance and bring about cognitive consistency.

COHABITATION

Cohabitation generally refers to a man and woman living together, though not legally married. Previously known as "concubinage" and long considered taboo or sinful in many cultures, cohabitation has increasingly gained acceptance in Western society. According to the U.S. Census Bureau, more than half of all marriages now follow cohabitation, with the number of people living together without **marriage** in the United States having risen more than 80 percent between 1980 and 1991.

Despite a growing moral acceptance, the legal implications of cohabitation still cause dilemma in many countries.

Traditionally, **family** law has not been concerned with unions not sanctified by legal marriage, although some legal systems recognize a natural child by a father for purposes of support or inheritance. The family unit based on cohabitation or "concubinage" has been ignored or overlooked by the law because such unions are often fleeting or difficult to define, considered immoral, occur primarily among poorer or less educated classes (as in some Latin American countries), or are associated with an inferior status of the female (especially in African and Asian countries). In some jurisdictions, common-law marriages are recognized based on a man and woman's agreement to consider themselves married, or even based on their cohabitation.

COHORT

Cohort is a term generally used to describe a **group** of people who have experienced the same event during the same time period. The Class of 1999, for example, is a cohort of people who graduated from school in that year. Cohorts can also be used to describe objects. For example, when a car dealership advertises that its 2001 models are in, the dealership is referring to an automobile cohort. The most commonly used cohort is the birth cohort, usually defined as all persons in a **society** born during the same five or ten year period. American Baby Boomers and Generation X, for example, are birth cohorts. In fact, cohorts so often refer specifically to birth cohorts that sociologists often use the terms interchangeably.

Cohort analysis is used in **sociology** because it is assumed that people in the same cohort share a common experience. A cohort of college freshmen, for example, similarly experience adjustment to college life regardless of each person's age or previous life experiences. At the same time, cohorts should not be confused with *age groups*, because the two concepts serve distinct purposes. An age group of 20 to 29 year-olds will gain members over time as 19 year-olds turn 20, and it will lose members as 29 year-olds turn 30. A 20 to 24 year-old age cohort, on the other hand, will retain its members and simply be re-labeled as a 25 to 29 year-old age cohort after five years. For this reason, age cohorts are usually referred to by their birth year (1970–1974) rather than their age. Making this distinction is important because it can be expected that most people will share similar experiences at older ages. Everyone entering the 65 to 70 year-old age group, for example, will likely share the common experience of **aging** and making the transition to **retirement**. On the other hand, a cohort of people born from 1930 to 1935 (those in the 65 to 70 year-old age group in 2000) also shared the experience of living as a child during World War II. Having this shared experience may affect their **attitude** towards war or totalitarianism in a way that will not affect later 65 to 70 year-old age groups.

In addition to examining the effects of shared experiences, cohort analysis is important to sociologists because it can allow researchers to distinguish different types of societal change. For example, if a poll in 1960 showed that thirty percent of all Americans opposed school integration and a poll in

1990 showed only ten percent opposition, it could be concluded that Americans' attitudes toward school integration had changed. By analyzing the **data** by cohorts, however, sociologists can determine if individuals are becoming less opposed to integrated schools or if the oldest cohorts are simply dying and being replaced by younger cohorts who are less concerned about racial mixing in education.

Among the major areas of sociology, the cohort concept is most vital to the study of **demography**, since the calculation of various rates by cohort is useful in understanding population change. Cohort rates are essential tools in many **demographic methods**, and such calculations as life expectancy and birth rates could not be made without the cohort concept.

COLEMAN, JAMES SAMUEL (1926-1995)
American sociologist

A sociologist deeply concerned with education, James S. Coleman was born in Bedford, Indiana, on May 12, 1926, to James Fox and Maurine Lappin Coleman. He served in the U.S. Navy during World War II (1944–1946) and graduated from Purdue University, West Lafayette, Indiana (1949). Coleman became a chemical engineer with Eastman-Kodak, Rochester, New York, but was soon so fascinated with **social problems** that he went on to Columbia University in New York City. He earned a Ph.D. in 1955 while working as a research associate with the Bureau of Applied Social Research (1953–1955). During that time, he became interested in the work of Paul Lazarsfeld, the Austrian-born sociologist whose studies concerning mass media's **influence** on **society** have become classics.

After a year (1955–1956) as a fellow at the Center for Advanced Study of Behavioral Science, Palo Alto, California, Coleman joined the University of Chicago as assistant professor of sociology. In 1957, he first became involved with problems of schooling. Directed by the U.S. Office of Education, he and his colleagues began a detailed study of ten high schools in Illinois. Their four-year examination of academic and social aspects resulted in a research monograph *Social Climates in High Schools* (1961).

Coleman left Chicago in 1959 for Johns Hopkins University, Baltimore, Maryland, where he joined the department of social relations as associate and then full professor of sociology. After the 1964 Civil Rights Act, the U.S. commissioner of education selected Coleman and Ernest Q. Campbell of Vanderbilt University, Nashville, Tennessee, to organize a $1.5-million study concerning lost equal educational opportunities for minorities in American public schools. Over the next two years, they looked at schooling opportunities for blacks, native and Mexican Americans, poor whites, Puerto Ricans, and Asians. The study involved some 60,000 teachers and more than 600,000 students. Known as the Coleman report—more formally, Equality of Educational Opportunity—and published in 1966, the study drew many influential conclusions, among which are the following: segregation and poorer resources were not the determining factors in the academic performance of minorities; black students dropped out of

school at twice the rate of whites; and minority schools, no matter how improved, cannot overcome poor home environment. Coleman vetoed tracking students according to ability and urged development of attitudes such as "black pride." He pointed out that minority students placed in predominantly middle-class schools improved dramatically with no academic loss to the more privileged students. When the Norfolk, Virginia, schools set up new integration policies in 1970, they were guided by the Coleman report.

In 1973, Coleman and his wife, Louise Richey, were divorced. He is the father of three sons, Thomas, John, and James. That year, Coleman returned to Chicago and became senior study director at the National Opinion Research Center of the university. He continued to critique America's educational establishment. In a *Forbes* article in 1987, he urged not blaming the deteriorating school system "all on the teachers: the greatest culprits are parents and changes in family structure." He argued that Catholic schools do a far better job of educating than either public or nonreligious private schools in America because they "function much closer to the American ideal of the 'common school,' educating children from different backgrounds alike." He also rejected the practice, begun in the 1960s, of "course proliferation." Students were allowed to select so-called relevant classes, such as sci-fi or film making, in addition to regular studies. Coleman argued this might be fine for the A student in English but not so fine for the marginal learner.

James Coleman served as advisor to President Richard Nixon in 1970 concerning plans to give northern and southern school districts some $1.5 billion to lessen the harmful effects of school segregation. However, he was critical of Nixon for claiming the administration would act against *de jure* (by law) segregation and not *de facto* segregation (what actually exists). Coleman said that racial segregation had to be erased no matter what the cause because doing so is the most "consistent mechanism for improving the qualify of education of disadvantaged children."

Among Coleman's many publications are: *Adolescents and the Schools* (1965); *Multilevel Information Systems in Education* with Nancy Karweit, *Resources for Social Change* (1971), and *Youth: Transition from Adulthood* with others (1974). He died in Chicago on March 25, 1995.

COLLECTIVE ACTION

Collective action is the general term for activities performed by groups of people, encompassing such disparate events as an Easter parade and the Watts Riots. However, the term is most frequently used in a political sense, to refer to strikes, protest marches, demonstrations, wars, and similar activities involving large numbers of people. Collective action can be fleeting or sustained, spontaneous or planned, violent or peaceful, and performed inside or outside a system or **institution**. Cornell University Professor of Government Sidney Tarrow, a leading American scholar on political and **social movements**, distinguishes between action of the Easter Parade variety and that of riots by naming the latter an example of contentious collective action. Collective action undergirds all political and social movements; when actors outside of elite decision-making bodies challenge the status quo in these institutions by putting forth new claims, collective action becomes contentious.

Sustained interaction with elites and authorities, solidarity born of a common purpose, and the mounting of collective challenges are the four empirical properties of contentious collective action, as defined by Tarrow. Much like Karl Marx, Tarrow contends that contentious collective action is situated in a particular historical and political moment; individual movements and other expressions of contentious politics cannot be studied as a historical occurrences. The power of contentious collective action as an engine of social change is exemplified by the Civil Rights movement, the first and second waves of **feminism**, the fall of **Communism** in Eastern Europe, and the movements involving abortion rights, both pro-life and pro-choice.

COLLECTIVE BEHAVIOR

Collective behavior is a form of social behavior in which groups of people, in response to some **influence** or stimulus, act in spontaneous and unstructured ways. These actions usually violate dominant social **norms** of behavior and may be explosive, unstable, and/or unpredictable. Collective behavior may be best understood when contrasted to behavior that is relatively institutionalized. Voting, obeying a fire drill, or participating in a classroom lecture are all examples of behavior that is routine, stable, and predictable.

Sociologist Robert E. Park founded the field of collective behavior in the 1920s. Sociologist Ernest Burgess worked extensively with Park to develop the field. Although definitions of collective behavior often imply negative connotations, Park believed that such action played a role in social change. Earlier efforts to explain the unconventional behavior of crowds had a distinctively psychological approach which emphasized the crowd's irrationality and abnormality. Prior to Park's conception of collective behavior, European scholars began to write about "crowd psychology," "collective psychology," and "group psychology." An example of these earlier works is Gustave LeBon's *The Crowd: A Study of the Popular Mind* (1896). The study of collective behavior is a precursor to the study of **social movements**. Today, sociologists who study collective behavior are more interested in questions related to the characteristics and **interaction** of individuals who participate in collective behavior and social movements.

Forms of collective behavior vary from behavior that is less regulated to behavior that is more regulated. These include panics, crowds, fashions, rumors, **public opinion**, and social movements. A **panic** is a type of collective behavior in which people who are confronted with a potentially threatening situation, act irrationally and uncooperatively. Panic results in a chaos that increases the threat of danger. The term, "crowd," refers to a temporary gathering of individuals with a common purpose. Large crowds may create concern for **social control** agents but not all crowds are unruly. Fashion refers to a collective, short-term preference for a particular style of appearance or behavior. Sociologist **Georg Simmel** noted that fashions are an avenue for the conflicting needs of individuals to be unique and to fit in with a **group**. The term, "rumor," refers to unconfirmed information that is informally passed from one individual or group to another. The original information may be either true or false, but, as the information is spread, it usually becomes distorted. The term, "public opinion," refers to the collective ideas and attitudes held by a population. Since it is impossible to question all individuals in a **society**, researchers select a representative sample of opinions and generalize to the entire population. The term, "social movement," refers to groups that are organized to prevent or promote social change. Social movements are more purposeful than collective behavior, so they are studied differently. Social movements are the result of the highly structured efforts of individuals and organizations and are more enduring than other forms of collective behavior.

Some theories developed to explain collective behavior are: contagion theory, **convergence** theory, emergent-norm theory and value-added theory. Contagion theory, developed by French social psychologist Gustave LeBon, emphasized the emotional and irrational aspects of crowd behavior. Contagion theorists suggested that the contagious excitement generated by a crowd of individuals caught up in a mob or riot led to a herd mentality. In such situations, it was believed that the normal restraints of society were put aside and individuals acted more like irrational animals and felt a sense of release from their usual social constraints. Convergence theory departs from the view that collective behavior is irrational. Convergence theorists argue that individuals who hold the same views or attributes may come together (i.e. converge) in collective behavior where they express their concerns in a rational way. Emergent-norm theory, representing an expansion of **symbolic interactionism**, was developed by sociologists Turner and Killian (1993). Emergent-norm theory views collective behavior participants as rational, although their actions may appear irrational. According to the emergent-norm theory, norms emerge as behavior unfolds. Crowd members may propose a course of action. The norms that emerge as a result of the proposed action represent the collective identity of the crowd. Individuals are believed to evaluate the crowd's actions and motivations and make a rational choice for or against participation.

Value-added theory, developed by sociologist **Neil Smelser** in the 1960s, accounts for the structural factors that generate collective behavior. Smelser argued that six preconditions must be met before collective behavior takes place. Each condition necessarily precedes the next. The six preconditions are structural conduciveness, structural strain, **generalized belief**, precipitating factors, mobilization for action, and failure of social control. Structural conduciveness refers to the idea that society must be structured in such a way to permit collective behavior. Structural strain is some strain (e.g. event) that causes a population segment to experience discontent and motivates them to **collective action**. A generalized belief refers to the development of a shared idea about the source of the problem and an appropriate collective response to alleviate the problem. Precipitating factors are events that prompt a response of collective behavior. Mobilization for action occurs when the participants collectively engage in some action. Finally, the failure of social control refers to the inability of agents of control to prevent the collective behavior event. The 1992 Los Angeles riots are often used as an example of Smelser's six pre-conditions. Examples include: structural conduciveness, (the right of a segregated population to assembly freely), structural strain (the Rodney King verdict that was perceived to symbolize the police brutality and racism experienced by the black population), generalized belief (the belief that the poor conditions of the rioting population were the consequences of racism), precipitating factors (the announcement of a "not guilty" verdict in the trial of four white police officers accused of beating Rodney King), mobilization for action (the onslaught of rioting and vandalism), and failure of social control (the inability of the police and national guard to control the situation).

COLLECTIVE CONSCIENCE

In the *Division of Labor in Society* (1893), Émile Durkheim looked for social facts that were correlated with social solidarity. He asked, what produces **social solidarity** when societies move from simple to complex societies (i.e., traditional agricultural societies to modern complex industrial societies)? Durkheim argued, when they are simple, societies are segmented into isolated and relatively small groups, within which members share common traditions and experiences (i.e., **values**, beliefs, **norms**, and so on) so that consciences of individuals bear a high degree of resemblance. This collective conscience comes to regulate the thoughts and actions of society's members. Durkheim calls the type of solidarity produced by a dominating collective conscience mechanical solidarity.

However, with the increase in the **division of labor, society** becomes more complex. For example, more **role** specialization exists, groups in society are more diverse and interdependent, and members are relatively heterogeneous in terms of shared common traditions and experiences. A new form of solidarity occurs, which Durkheim termed organic solidarity. Societies that exhibit organic solidarity become cohesive because the various parts are dependent on each other for the continuing existence of the system. Modern social institutions or social structures such as the **family**, **government**, the economy, religion, become functionally interdependent. In this case, Durkheim argued that social order comes from the way modern structures in society are organized. Moreover, with institutional differentiation and specialization, the collective conscience becomes more diversified in order to encompass all human experiences. Therefore, the collective conscience becomes less specific in order to provide norms, beliefs, and values broad enough to apply to everyone's different life situation, creating social bonds and a stable coherent **social order**.

COLLINS, PATRICIA HILL (1948-)
American writer

Perhaps best known for award-winning *Black Feminist Thought: Knowledge, Consciousness, and the Politics of Empowerment*, Patricia Hill Collins outlined American Black **feminism** expressed in music, fiction, poetry, and oral history. Collins saw three themes: oppressions are interconnected; black women create alternative worldviews for self-definition and self-determination; and black women have often internalized imposed restricting definitions of who they are—especially racialized concepts of beauty, skin color, and physique. Collins points to areas that have been overlooked: racialized **gender roles** within **family** and work, politics, violence—in the home, on the job, and in the street—and **homophobia**.

Collins draws on black women's experiences and voices to explain concepts that have been obscured institutionally, philosophically, and ideologically. Collins's interdisciplinary **methodology** employs a "both/and" analytical approach to **domination** and subordination. Collins rejects oppositional thought because "either/or thinking categorizes people, things, and ideas in terms of their differences from one another" which requires objectification and subordination.

Because racism, sexism, classism, and homophobia are interrelated, it is not effective to simply address one form of oppression or another. However, identifying a "political economy of domination" does not mean that oppressions are interchangeable or analogous. Rather, forms of domination overlap, have what Collins calls "points of convergence" as well as areas of difference or divergence. Collins also rejects the notion that one person is either oppressing or oppressed, completely subjugating or colonizing. An individual can be oppressed (because of **race**, gender, and/or sexuality, for example), and have access to privileges because of race, gender, and/or sexuality. For example, a black woman who is heterosexual faces various forms of domination, but, as a heterosexual, she also has access to privileges. Collins emphasizes complex ways in which simultaneity operates which either/or oppositional thinking obscures and elides. Thus, Collins advocates a both/and approach to thinking about domination, **identity**, and **epistemology**.

Rejecting traditional theories of knowing, Collins sees **positivism** as inadequate: "Positivist approaches aim to create scientific descriptions of reality by producing objective generalizations." However the "result of this entire process is often the separation of information from meaning." Meaning and information can become separated because the researcher (knower) is supposed to separate emotion and reason, wisdom and knowledge. The researcher must objectify and decontextualize her/him self. **Relativism** is also unsatisfactory approach to evaluating and developing truth claims and knowledge because no one group's ideas are more valid than another's. Collins rejects relativism and positivism because both approaches "minimized the importance of specific location in influencing a group's knowledge claims, the power of inequities among groups that produce subjugated knowledges, and the strengths and limitations of partial perspective."

Because Collins wants to take into consideration the *positions* of the knower, standpoint epistemology would seem to be the answer. However, she identifies several problems with it. Many standpoint theorists have argued that the oppressed's outsider or marginal **status** *necessarily* provides them with fewer obstructions to finding the truth. This approach advocates the idea that there is one version of the truth and also implies a "biological prerequisite" for access to subjugated knowledge. Collins argues that since race and gender are questionable biological categories (not fixed, distinct, or immutable), to solidify them as such is neither feminist nor Afrocentric.

Collins's both/and epistemological approach is evident in her discussion of who can develop and create black feminist thought. Afrocentric feminist thought is rooted in a black women's standpoint, an "outsider-within" point of view of distinct economic and material work experiences (such as in domestic service, in which employees both do and do not have contact with employers' world).

Because she rejects biological prerequisites as a basis for certain kinds of knowledge, Collins suggests that not only black women can further black feminist thought. Thus, she advocates both standpoint and non-standpoint approaches by discussing Bell Hooks's idea that to advocate an Afrocentric feminism does not require one to *be* black and female. Such an approach still necessitates that black women's experiences be "at the center of any serious efforts to develop Black feminist thought."

In other words, we should develop transformational analysis in an interconnected both/and manner in order to be more effective. Some critics have argued that Collins's approach is contradictory or undeveloped. However, Collins does not necessarily view apparent contradiction as a source of strength, creativity, and possibility. She does not intend to solve our troubles: instead, she wants to trouble or problematize the ways in which Afrocentrism and feminism have traditionally been practiced and conceived. According to Collins, several key concepts in Black feminist thought embrace a both/and approach: a wisdom-knowledge and a thought-activism continuum; a self-community connection; an ethic of care that requires a "dialogue of reason and emotion"; and an ethic of personal responsibility and **accountability**.

The concept of dialogue, or call and response, is central. To evaluate and validate the viability of any truth claim or idea, one must think about a larger **community** (as a self in context, a relational self). Collins uses the analogy of black women's quilting aesthetic as a way to illustrate the idea of an ethically bound self-in-context. African American women's quilts derive symmetry by using contrast and diversity rather than symmetry, causing "individual uniqueness in a community setting." Dialogue requires others to respond and participate. Living these ideas, Collins worked in the community schools movement in Boston, was active in the Girl Scouts, and has debated about *Black Feminist Thought* with inmates at an Ohio prison. Dialogue is also apparent in her method and writing style. She uses diverse interdisciplinary sources, and she avoids jargon.

Collins asserts the both/and analysis and an ethics of care could transform the ways in which we think about knowl-

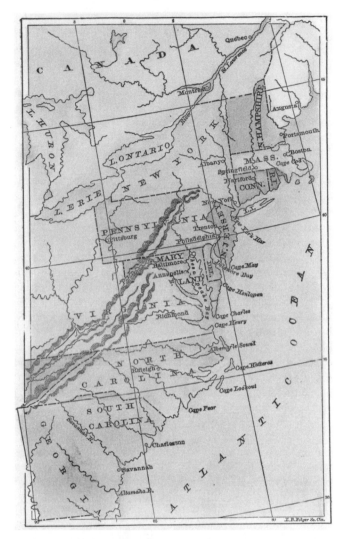

Colonization of the Western Hemisphere was widely perceived as a solution for European social and economic problems of the 18th century.

edge claims. Her work has made Afrocentric and feminist thought more accountable, broader in scope, and more radical. She forces her readers to think differently and to reexamine the way in which truth and knowledge are produced, reproduced, and validated—or eradicated and obscured.

COLONIALISM

Colonialism is the economic, political, and cultural exploitation of a country by a foreign power. From the perspective of historian, D. K. Fieldhouse, colonialism must be understood in relation to three other concepts: imperialism, colonization, and neo-colonization. **Imperialism** evolves first, then colonialism or colonization, which inevitably leads to neo-colonization. Colonialism is the quest by Europeans to establish Western European **culture** and lifestyle in non-European territories. This Eurocentric action is sometimes referred to as settlement. The phrase, settlement, romantically camouflages the brutality of the colonial motivation and process. More importantly, it fails to acknowledge the political and economic activities that emerge on behalf of the colonizing country and its settlers. Restricting the phrase to European colonization after 1450 eliminates consideration of other colonial activities, such as the Moors occupation in Spain; Japanese conquest in southeast Asia and the south pacific; the Ottoman Empire in North, East, and West Africa, the Middle East and east Europe; and the expansions of the USSR.

For subjugated people, colonialism is "cultural imperialism," often equated with rape, the rape of the land for it's natural resources and the rape of a people of it's culture, traditions, and **values**. According to Frantz Fanon the distinguished Francaphone author of *The Wretched of the Earth*, "Colonialism tended not only to deprive a society of its freedom and its wealth, but of its very character, leaving its people intellectually and morally disoriented." The naïve notion that European colonialism primarily intended to civilize native people was nothing more than a self-serving hypocrisy. For Europeans, being civilized meant being Christian. Aimé Césaire, Francaphone author of *Discourse on Colonization* asserted "that the chief culprit in this domain is Christian pedantry, which laid down the dishonest equations, Christianity = **Civilization**, paganism = savagery, from which there could not but ensue abominable colonials and racist consequence, whose victims were to be Indians, the yellow people, and the Negroes."

In Immanuel Wallerstien's modern world systems framework, colonization is a necessary process in global economic system. In this global world system there exist core and periphery regions. Core countries are imperial states that economically and politically dominate periphery states or colonies. All resources extracted from the land directly benefit the core region and the colonial setters. Any capital gain is reinvested in the core country, serving the interest of the colonial (meterpoli) not the development of the colony. Under colonialism, a dependent state is totally controlled by the imperial power. Its governmental, social, legal, educational, cultural and religious life is molded by alien hands.The motives for colonialism have evolved over time. For Europe and other non-European colonial powers motives for colonization include opening new markets for force-trade, pillaging foreign natural resource, developing military strategies and sometimes establishing metropolis pride. Moreover, in the case of Europe, colonization was widely considered a solution for internal social and economic problems such as overpopulation, bad economy due to failed crops and internal politics, famine, **disease**, and the civil unrest.

Western colonialism is commonly understood to have two distinct waves. The first colonial wave occurred between 1450 1820 and was initiated by Portugal and Spain. This wave may be characterized as "colonization by extermination." The colonial routine here involved mass genocide of native inhabitants for new Western European settlement. This kind of colonization took place in the United States, Australia, New Zealand, and most South and Central American countries. In most of these territories, the native population today makes up less than three percent of the total population. The second wave of colonialism occured mostly during the latter half of the nineteenth century between 1860 and 1947. In 1884-85 western European powers (France, Germany, the UK, Belgium, and Portugal) met at the Berlin conference to divide foreign territories among themselves. So, for instance, prior to the middle 1800s most of Africa, particularly the interior, and Southeast Asia was untouched by the West. Significantly, the second wave occurred during industrialization after most first-wave colonies had been given their independence and after slavery had been abolished in most European colonized countries. An agricultural economy requires a large and inexpensive **labor force**. This kind of economy perfectly corresponds with a **society** that is dependent on slave labor. As the economy changed, the need for slave labor gave way to the need for natural resources. Securing natural resources was an important motive behind the second wave colonization.

While England and France initiated the second wave of Western colonization, the United States, Germany, Belgium, Netherlands, and Russia also participated. This colonial wave maybe characterized as "colonization by duel exploitation" and "colonization by departmental representation." In dual exploitation, the natives were robbed of both their native tongue and native religious practices. This kind of colonization took place in mostly in Africa and parts of Southeast Asia. Today, the native populations in these territories make up nearly ninety percent of the total population. "Colonization by departmental representation" refers mostly to the West Indies. Like first wave colonization, these territories maintained African slaves and the native populations were either absorbed or exterminated. Today, these countries contain a majority populations of slave descendants and have officially recognized colonial language and religion as apart of their national identities. Perhaps the most alarming feature of colonization in these territories is that some colonies are still maintained today mostly by France; only now they are conveniently referred to as having departmental representation as in Guadeloupe and Martinique.

COMMON LAW

Common law, also known as unwritten law or Anglo-American law, is the system of law originating in England around the twelfth century B.C. by judges who made decisions based on **custom** or precedent rather than civil laws or statutes. Common law continued to evolve in England and its colonies through the nineteenth century. At the time of the American Revolution, the United States was following a separate form of common law, dismissing several British practices and developing a distinctly American system. Common law has varied by state, although Louisiana's system, based on a French civil-law model, is unique. Common law has the least authority in the U.S. legal system, preceded by state statutory law, state constitutions, acts of Congress and foreign treaties, and the Constitution. Although common law remains influential today, legislator-instituted statutory law in state and federal systems has increasingly replaced it.

COMMUNICATION

The term "communication" refers to the conveyance of information, including such things as thoughts and messages. Communication takes place using visual signs and sounds such as **language**. When communication became a written phenomenon, **society** was able to preserve thoughts and words. Writing also provided an alternative when spoken communication was not possible.

Communication increased as book publishing and journalism grew and as a result of the telegraph, radio, **television**, and telephone. With advances in technology, instantaneous international communication became possible. By 1962 the first live television broadcast was shown simultaneously in Japan, Europe, the United States, and South America. During the twentieth century, communications via mass media have influenced social, political, economic, and educational aspects of society. By the end of the twentieth century, world mass communication included instantaneous transmission via computer. Such improvements are important to **sociology** because as the means of communication cross geographic and cultural barriers, the concept of communities must also be extended. Global communication, for example, has made possible the concept of a global **community**.

In Asimov's 1994 *Chronology of Science and Discovery*, he remarked that the Sumerians may have been the first society to develop written communications around 3500 BC. Symbols were produced by using a stylus to make wedge-like marks in clay. Each **symbol** represented a word, and the small literate proportion of the population, needed to understand and memorize each symbol. The Egyptians further developed a written language, with symbols that came to be called "hieroglyphics," or "priestly language," since Greeks later discovered the symbols in Egyptian temples, preserved on thin papyrus sheets. Asimov speculated that writing is more permanent than the spoken work as a form of communication. Written language communicates not only to the present, but also to the thinkers of the future. It allows a community to develop over time by more effectively building upon the achievements of the past. According to Asimov, societies that used the written word, such as the Sumerians, are historic and societies prior to the Sumerians, and prior to the advent of written communication, are considered prehistoric.

COMMUNISM

Communism, in its simplest definition, refers to any **ideology** based on a social system in which all major resources are held in common and the means of production are controlled by, and for the benefit of, the community, thus creating a classless **society** in which all members contribute and all members' needs are met. **Karl Marx** was the most influential proponent of communist theory, publishing the *Communist Manifesto* with Friedrich Engels in 1848. However, the basic concepts of communism had existed well before Marx, evidenced by forms of communal thought found in Plato's *Republic* and in early Christian communities.

V. I. Lenin triumphantly led the Bolsheviks during the Russian Revolution and created the Communist Party *(Archive Photos, Inc.).*

With the rise of **capitalism** and the onset of the Industrial Revolution in the early nineteenth century, communist ideology began to be put forth as a means to address the plight of the poor working class, who often lived in abysmal conditions. Such people as utopian socialists **Robert Owen** and Charles Fourier, anarchist P. J. Proudhon, and revolutionary Auguste Blanqui supported communistic ideology. At this time, small utopian communities based on notions of communal ownership and mutual cooperation appeared, but usually failed.

The definition of communism was refined into a clearer concept of structured society by Marx, and subsequently communism became closely associated with Marxist philosophy. Drawing from German philosophers Hegel and Feuerbach and early economists **Adam Smith** and **Thomas Malthus**, Marx presented his understanding of the course of history and **progress** most clearly and concisely in the *Communist Manifesto*. By expanding on utopian socialism's romantic vision of **community** life based on fellowship and harmony, he created a concept of a historically possible communist community. Marx, in collaboration with Engles, published the *Communist Manifesto* in London as a declaration of the intent and purpose of the Communist League, a secret organization of emigrant German artisans and intellectuals.

Marx details his understanding of modern society, claiming class struggle as the predominant event in historical action and envisioning a viable utopian society based on the violent overthrow of capitalism. According to Marx, capitalism was fraught with problems and contradictions. The natural outcome of this economic system dictated that the capitalists, or **bourgeoisie**, add to their wealth while the number of poor working class, or proletariat, living in squalor continue to increase. As **quality of life** for the working class deteriorates, the historical scene will be set for the violent downfall of capitalism. Marx believed that the conflict created by capitalism was, in fact, a prerequisite for a socialist, classless society, thus he believed that the workers' revolution would begin in the highly industrialized nations of Western Europe.

According to Marxist ideology, the socialist society would progress in two stages. The first stage, which he referred to as **socialism** or the ''rule of the proletariat,'' would bring many improvements to the quality of life. He predicted such improvements as the introduction of universal suffrage, election of state officials from the working class, education accessible to everyone, and an end to the rights of inheritance. However, during this transitional stage, some elements of capitalism would remain. As socialism progressed, it would eventually evolve into communism, or the ''realm of freedom.'' In this higher form, society would be so radically transformed that such things as money, prices, wages, profits, insurance, and lawsuits would be no longer necessary. Work would not be burdensome and alienating, but a creative and free activity. As Marx stated: ''From each according to his ability; to each according to his need.''

The modern Communist political movement began in Russia in 1903 when the Russian Social Democratic Labor Party split into opposing factions, the Bolsheviks and the Mensheviks. In 1917 the Bolsheviks, led by V. I. Lenin, won the Russian Revolution and in 1918 created the Communist Party. Lenin's ideology differed from Marxist communism on three major points. First, Lenin introduced the idea of a ''vanguard party.'' Believing that Marx was overly optimistic on the working class's ability to develop the necessary skills to make communism work, Lenin suggested that a group of intellectuals was needed to protect and educate the working class. Second, Lenin rejected the idea that communism can only be viable in highly industrialized capitalist countries. Given the fact that Russia was at the time a largely undeveloped country, with a great number of illiterate poor, Lenin suggested that the vanguard party would be capable of leading the nation through the transition into communism. Finally, Lenin concurred with Marx's assertion that communism would come in two stages. However, whereas Marx viewed the first stage as a brief interlude, Lenin asserted that the lower stage would require an expansive time across history before the higher state of communism would be achieved.

Upon Lenin's death, Joseph Stalin ruled Communist Russia, creating a totalitarian state that forced into action all the human resources available to bring economic and military advancement to the nation. Hardly resembling the utopian ideal set forth by Marx, the political rhetoric of the Communist Party continued to define its mission in Marxist terms. After World War II, Stalin developed numerous satellite communist states in Eastern Europe, and the realm of communism greatly

expanded. In 1949, China created its own indigenous version of communist rule under Mao Zedong. Communism in various forms also spread into Southeast Asia, Latin America, and Africa. Tensions regarding communism between Russia and the United States led to the Cold War and the conflicts in Korea and Vietnam.

By the early 1980s, Communist states were numerous around the world. Russia had achieved some of its goals, becoming the second largest industrial and military power in the world. However, a surge in **nationalism** within its republics combined with resentment over harsh rule, scarce food, and poor living conditions led the Communist Party into crisis. In 1991, the Soviet Communist Party collapsed, and the country was dissolved. The political climate in Eastern Europe was also changing rapidly. The number of Communist governments across Europe and around the world was greatly reduced by the end of 1991, and traditional Communist dictatorships existed only in China, Cuba, Laos, North Korea, and Vietnam.

Despite Communism's fall from power in the 1990s, Communist parties still play an important role in the politics of many former communist countries. In those countries that still claim to abide by Marxist ideology, their differing interpretations of doctrine and form of rule make them far from homogeneous. Also, around the world, numerous communist movements continue to espouse variations of Marx's and Lenin's theory of the class struggle.

See also Capitalism; Socialism

COMMUNITARIANISM

Communitarianism is both a theoretical perspective and a social movement within the discipline of **sociology**. At the root of communitarian theory is a concern for the perceived rampant **individualism** of North American society and the corresponding loss of **community** life brought about by historical forces such as industrialization, **urbanization**, and the Enlightenment.

Although the perspective has been officially recognized only since the early 1990s, much of communitarian thought is not new. Classical sociologists such as Ferdinand Tönnies and Émile Durkheim in the late 1800s were concerned with the social changes engendered by the rise of industrialization and urbanization. They suggested that shifts from agrarian to industrial economies and from rural to urban residences would cause the bonds of community and **family** to be substantially weakened. They also expressed concern over the impact of Enlightenment thought. According to Enlightenment philosophy, individuals should be free to pursue their own self-interests without the shackles of community and family bonds.

A more recent figure in the development of contemporary communitarianism is sociologist Robert A. Nisbet. Writing primarily from the 1950s to the 1970s, Nisbet lamented the loss of traditional elements of community life in works such as *The Quest for Community*, *Tradition and Revolt*, and *The Twilight of Authority*. Nisbet observed that the French and American Industrial Revolutions and Enlightenment thought served to undermine the **influence** of community, familial, social, and religious groups (what he termed ''intermediate social structures'') and focused attention instead on individual achievement and success.

Nisbet argued that with the loss of community came a growing reliance on **government** to fulfill basic human needs such as kinship, loyalty, belonging, and association. Nisbet believed that individuals are searching for attachment and security in political and commercial organizations that were once provided by family, neighborhood, and **church** groups. The price of individuality, therefore, is the loss of shared experience and membership in community groups.

The person most associated with contemporary communitarianism is sociologist Amitai Etzioni. His major explications of communitarian theory include *The Moral Dimension*, *The Spirit of Community*, and *The New Golden Rule*. Etzioni is considered by most to be the founder of communitarianism as an intellectual area of study from the mid-1980s to the present. Other major contributors include sociologists such as William Galston, Robert Bellah, and Mary Ann Glendon. Contemporary communitarians argue for a new moral and social order based on shared **values** that unite individuals in communities and not on rigid, religious absolutes. They argue for ''responsive communities'' based on traditional values such as strong kinship ties and **social cohesion**, along with newer values of non-discrimination, adherence to the law, and tolerance.

Like Nisbet, Etzioni argues that the dramatic shift toward industrialization and urbanization led to the weakening of community social bonds. Etzioni asserts that these processes led individuals to develop excessive independence and **autonomy** at the expense of social bonds based on family and community. Etzioni's main concern is balancing the tension associated with the forces of individuality and community. In *The Spirit of Community*, Etzioni argues that there is a tendency among individuals to argue for rights, while shunning responsibilities. Etzioni contends, however, that there must be a proper mixing of rights and responsibilities. For example, he notes that although individuals claim a trial by jury in a criminal proceeding as a basic right, few individuals are willing to serve on a jury. Likewise, Etzioni notes a need for both order and autonomy. Without a proper amount of order, **anarchy** prevails. Without a proper amount of autonomy, authoritarianism becomes the norm. Etzioni and contemporary communitarians continue to be optimistic that despite the excessive individualism and concern for individual rights characteristic of contemporary **society**, a vision of a responsive community based on a balanced sense of rights and responsibilities and order and autonomy remains attainable. They believe that communities centered around contemporary values may still be vibrant and important socializing factors in the lives of individuals.

Although often criticized for being politically conservative, communitarians resist this charge. In fact, they suggest that much of their work is consistent with sociological **conflict theory** in that they locate the causes of excessive individualism and other current social problems in economic shifts and the spread of global **capitalism**. Currently, the position of communitarianism in theoretical sociology is not prominent, but many of its ideas are becoming more influential, especially in political **discourse**.

COMMUNITY

The term ''community'' refers to a diverse range of social phenomena. In a critical analysis of the concept, Joseph Gusfield defined two usages. First, it refers to a physical **territory**, or geographical area, where human beings reside and/or work. Second, it refers to the quality or character of human relationships that bind persons to each other to form a **group**. Many sociological studies combine these, while others use a different definition altogether.

The concept of community can be traced to Ferdinand Tönnies' influential book *Gemeinschaft und Gesellschaft,* (*Community and Society*) first published in 1887. Tönnies was concerned with the issue of **social cohesion**; that is, ''...the sentiments and motives which draw people to each other, keep them together, and induce them to joint action....which resulting therefrom, make possible and sustain a common existence.'' For Tönnies, the basis of social cohesion was termed the *collective will* (analogous to group norms), which sets behavioral expectations and governs social relationships among individuals forming a group. Tönnies contended that the basis of social cohesion was undergoing a transition from Gemeinschaft (community) to Gesellschaft (**society**).

Tönnies believed that community was the traditional basis of social cohesion characterized by what he termed the natural will. Simply put, social relationships guided predominantly by the natural will were characterized by emotional attachment, sentiment, intimacy, and shared characteristics such as kinship or religious beliefs. In contrast, society as viewed by Tönnies was the emergent basis of social cohesion characterized by the rational will. Social relationships guided predominantly by the rational will were characterized by indifference, rational calculation, competition, and self-interest. Tönnies thought that with the development and advance of **capitalism**, social relationships based on community were becoming subordinate to the rational will as the primary basis of social cohesion. In sum, this dimension of Tönnies' work expresses the view of community as a particular quality of social relationships among members of a group involving emotional attachment, intimacy, and sentiment. Later theorists equated social relationships in community with Charles Horton Cooley's concept of a **primary group** or Mark Granovetter's concept of strong interpersonal ties within a group of social actors.

Tönnies also discussed ideal prototypes of social forms that were ''Gemeinschaft-like'' or ''Gesellschaft-like.'' Regarding social organizations and corporate bodies, he stated that the ideal Gemeinschaft prototype is an agrarian village, whereas the ideal Gesellschaft prototype is a city. Thus, he set the precedent for viewing community as a location, or geographic area and also advanced the notion that communities must be small in size with members living in close geographic proximity. As a result, community is frequently equated with a village, town, city, neighborhood, or suburb, all of which are defined by geo-political boundaries. One important tradition in community research is the community study which selects a particular town, village, neighborhood, or suburb as a site for case study. A combination of **research methods** is then used to analyze social life within the community. Typically, these methods include field research and **ethnography**.

Through the twentieth century, alternative social theories have applied the concept of community. Important theories include human ecology, social systems theory, **symbolic interactionism**, and Marxist theory. In human ecology and social systems theory community is a structured system of social units that perform interdependent functions in order to meet the living needs of a human population. At a broad level, the definition has a territorial dimension. With the human ecological definition, in particular, **cities**, and even larger metropolitan areas, could be considered communities.

In symbolic interactionism community is viewed as a process where individual persons socially construct identities as members of a group with which they share common characteristics and have specific rights and obligations. In Marxist theory community is a geo-political territory. The focus is on how the territory serves as a site for capital accumulation, either through growth and construction of the built environment, the growth of industries or businesses in general, or through the control and exploitation of labor that resides and works in the area.

Over the last several decades, the theory and methods of social network analysis have been applied to the concept of community. Here, community is defined as a network of strong, primary relationships among a set of social actors. A point of debate is whether close geographic proximity is necessary for the formation and maintenance of communal relationships. Barry Wellman proposed the concept, "liberated community," in which communal relationships are established and maintained over a broader geographic space as a result of modern communications and transportation technology. This notion parallels the development of the **Internet**.

COMMUNITY ACTION

Community action refers to social activities undertaken to achieve specific goals that will benefit a community. While this definition appears straightforward, substantial debate concerns what constitutes community action and under what conditions a community is likely to act. Using a definition of community as a geographic **territory** (e.g. town, village), Willis Sutton, Jr., and Jiri Kolaja argued that whether a particular social activity is a community action depends on the degree to which the activity is related to the locality; the persons carrying out the activity identify with the locality; and local people participate in the activity. However, a number of questions surrounding the process of community action have been raised: Must all members of the community participate in the activity or just a select few? Should the goals of the action be determined democratically? Should they be determined by a select few community members? Should the action benefit all members of the community equally? Does the action qualify if it benefits a few members while imposing costs on others?

A focus in sociological **discourse** concerning community action is that in contemporary **society**, communities (de-

fined as a local geographic territory) lack solidarity and decreasingly engage in **collective action**. As a result, what passes for community action often involves small groups that act on the basis of common interests rather than a solidaristic whole that acts on the basis of shared common territory and concern. Charles Tilly outlined three conditions under which communities may be mobilized to engage in community action on the basis of sharing a common territory: (1) communities are homogenous with respect to the main divisions of power at a regional or national level; (2) the cost of **communication** rises rapidly as a function of distance; and (3) control over land (as compared with other factors of production) is valuable but uncertain.

COMMUNITY BASED ORGANIZATION

An **organization** is a **group** of persons that assembles with a particular goal or purpose in mind. A **community** based organization has its basis within a community, or a locale where people live. Contemporary community based organizations are varied and serve unique purposes. An article in *Parks and Recreation* (October 1991) described a community based program developed jointly by the state of New York and the New York State Division for Youth. The program worked with New York communities to rehabilitate juvenile offenders in parks and recreation settings.

Community based organizing has also been used to address issues such as local drug and alcohol abuse. In 1985, concerned citizens from Portland and Vancouver, Oregon met to develop a program that addressed **alcoholism** trends in the elderly population. The community based program included prevention, intervention, detoxification, treatment, and ongoing care. Citizens wrote and received funding for a grant for a resource center; they also established inpatient programs at local hospitals and worked with community nursing homes to provide care for elderly recovering alcoholics. Internationally, community based organizing has produced rehabilitation programs that help people with disabilities, their families, and their communities. Such a program in Zimbabwe assisted over one thousand people in a two year period and created fifteen self-help projects for affected people in the communities served.

In addition to rehabilitation or treatment, community based organizations can form with the goal of community renovation or rehabilitation. The San Francisco Garden Project was started by a citizen in the 1980s who successfully combined prison inmate rehabilitation with horticulture. Inmates learned gardening techniques and were paid to work on transforming abandoned or deteriorated areas of the **cities** into vegetable gardens. Another example of community based organization in New Orleans revitalized poor neighborhoods. The project, titled "At Home in New Orleans," rehabilitated fifty homes during 1998 and made them available to first home buyers.

COMPARABLE WORTH

Jobs which are considered women's and men's vary substantially across various cultures and economic systems. In fact, the construction of difference tends to value men over women, at least in industrial or capitalist societies, and this value creates a gendered segregation in pay. Comparable worth is used as a basis for claiming an employer has discriminated between wages in male- and female-dominated positions by using separate criteria in determining these wages.

Despite women's increasing participation in the labor market and the increasing enforcement of bans against gender **discrimination**, women still tend to work in predominately female occupations for lower wages than men. This gendered wage gap persists despite evidence that it is narrowing. This disturbing wage differential emphasizes the fact that predominately female occupations are not equivalent in **status** or in advancement opportunities to male-dominated occupations.

Comparable worth has been put forth as a method by which pay equity may be achieved between females and males. It rests on the assumption that it may have the potential to eliminate the wage gap attributable to the undervaluation of women's work. The strategy of comparable worth seeks to achieve gender pay equity by assigning points to separate aspects of jobs, adding up these points, and ensuring that the points correlate with wages. Possible candidates for points are education, training, skills, responsibility, dangerousness, and dirtiness. Evaluation is in the form of worth points for each component of the job.

Comparable worth is a possible remedy that would enforce pay equity under the Equal Pay Act of 1963. This remedy generally assumes that by increasing pay for workers in female-dominated occupations, the earnings gap will be reduced. The idea is to recognize female-dominated occupations for their value to the labor market and duly compensate women as comparable to men in male-dominated occupations. The primary approach is to use existing job evaluation plans and compare the relative worth of jobs in order to achieve pay equity. As a result, the courts have had to deal with whether an employer violates Title VII by failing to give equal pay to employees who perform jobs of comparable value to the employer where that results in lower pay to those jobs that are predominately held by women. In 1985 the case of *AFSCME v. Washington* the court ruled that the comparable worth approach would not be used to establish a violation of Title VII. As a result of this decision confidence in comparable worth as a remedy for pay inequity diminished.

Not simply a technocratic reform, comparable worth has also been a grass-roots movement of low-paid, pink-collar women acting on their own behalf. The movement suggests not only a solution to the gender wage-gap but also advances a respect and valuation for the work that women do. Comparable worth has been a step in affirming of the value of women's work and in questioning the market's value determination process. In sum, then, comparable worth argues that sex-based discrimination exists if employees in job classifications occupied primarily by women are paid less than employees in job classifications filled primarily by men, if the jobs are of equal value to the employer, regardless of similarity.

Comparable worth strategies have been criticized as ineffective. The approach is difficult to use as a standard applicable across industries. Women and men tend to predominate in different industries, thus making comparable worth as a wage equity mechanism difficult if not impossible to implement. In addition, employers do not use one method to evaluate job components of knowledge, **skill**, mental effort, **accountability**, and working conditions necessary for comparable worth strategies to be effective. Comparable worth has also been criticized for accepting the market driven wages with some adjustment rather than setting precedent for a new wage structure. As such, comparable worth may ignore certain problems that are causally related to the sex-based wage gap. Therefore, jobs that are considered dangerous or dirty are more highly rewarded than jobs that are adverse in their working conditions due to **routinization** and high levels of supervision, such as those females tend to occupy. Furthermore, the work done by assistants is rarely regarded as highly or rewarded as much, under the current market driven wage structure, and this job category has a concentration of women in it.

COMPARATIVE METHOD

Comparative method is an element of all scientific research. Comparisons are introduced into research design to see if findings are replicated in similar cases. The more difference between cases, the better the researcher can test the scope of the theory and the degree to which it is broadly generalizable. Even where only one case is examined, a comparison is usually implicit. For example, if the aim of the researcher is to test an established theory in a new substantive field, then there will be an implicit comparison between the new case and the original case or cases through which the theory was developed. The researcher will, therefore, choose cases which show the most potential for challenging or refining the theory.

In **sociology**, comparative method has come to mean research which emphasizes the comparison of cases rather than the comparison of variables. While the variable-oriented method is suitable to those using statistical analysis, those wishing to study cases holistically are often frustrated within this framework. For example, it is difficult for those undertaking international or historical comparisons to produce the regularity of **measurement** across cases necessary to establish **reliability** and **validity**. Similarly, those using ethnography or **interview** methods generally find that the simplifications necessary for variable-oriented manipulations do violence to the complexity and subtlety of their **data**. The comparative method, in contrast, frees the researcher to concentrate on the specific causal patterns within the cases rather than searching for the perfect (abstracted) causal **model**.

Sociologists using comparative method use a framework based on the work of **John Stuart Mill**. In *A System of Logic* (1843), Mill explained various tools for the development of sound inductive generalizations. Of these methods, the two most commonly used in sociology are the method of agreement and the indirect method of difference.

In the method of agreement, researchers progress through various cases with the same outcome, looking for similarities. They carefully try to isolate the condition (or combination of conditions) present in every case. The condition which remains constant across all cases is gradually established as the primary cause of the outcome. While most sociologists use the method of agreement at points in their research, the method is scientifically weak, as Mill himself recognized. It is impossible to establish that the condition truly caused the outcome. The biggest problem is that there may be some other condition that researchers have not taken into account which is also present in all the cases and is, in fact, the true cause.

Mill's other method, the indirect method of difference, strengthens the method of agreement by adding a second stage of analysis. After establishing that condition *A* is always present with outcome *C*, researchers look at cases where outcome *C* is absent and check to see whether condition *A* is also absent. If *A* and *C* are always either both present or both absent, then causality is established. The second stage of analysis also enables researchers to rule out other possible causes. For example, if conditions *A* and *B* are both present whenever outcome *C* is present, but condition *B* is present when outcome *C* is absent, then condition *B* can be ruled out as a cause.

Charles Ragin, whose book *The Comparative Method* (1987) is the definitive contemporary work on the subject, showed that both of Mill's methods are unreliable in a case where the outcome can be caused by more than one different condition. For example, if outcome *C* can be caused by either condition *A* or condition *B*, yet neither was present in all cases, the method of agreement would fail to recognize either condition as a cause.

Ragin argued that the problems with Mill's methods can be resolved using Boolean analysis, a non-numerical system of algebra developed by a nineteenth-century British logician, George Boole. First, researchers should build truth tables to express the conditions of each case, where each condition is marked either present or absent. The next step is to lay out all the possible combinations which lead to the outcome. Finally, they use an algorithm to reduce these combinations to the only ones which are strictly necessary for the outcome to occur. The resulting model can account for multiple conjunctural causality, where there may be more than one common road to the outcome, and the outcome may be based on various different conjunctions of the same causes.

COMPARATIVE-HISTORICAL SOCIOLOGY

Some prominent practitioners claim that no such specific field of comparative-historical sociology exists. They do not deny the existence of the many influential works that fall under this category, nor do they deny that the term comparative-historical describes their own work. Rather, they claim that no specific field of comparative-historical sociology can exist because all **sociology**, by its very nature, is historical and comparative. For instance, in his influential book *Historical Sociology*, Philip Abrams argued that the distinctions between the disciplines of history and sociology are primarily matters of institutional arrangement rather than substantive difference. Historians,

Abrams argued, produce narratives of particular (*ideographic*) events, while sociologists tend towards general (*nomothetic*) models of social phenomena. Although the usefulness of this distinction has been questioned by both historians who feel it limits their work and sociologists who feel it relegates them to the sidelines of inquiry, for Abrams, the difference is one of emphasis; all good sociology is necessarily historical. No methodological distinctions separate the disciplines. Similarly, comparative analysis lies at the heart of the sociological enterprise. In *Rules of Sociological Method* (1895) Émile Durkheim held that all sociology is comparative because representing the phenomena under study as either typical or unique implies comparison. His well known work *Suicide*, for instance, compares the rates of **suicide** across national lines, religious affiliation, and several other characteristics. Likewise his *Elementary Forms of Religious Life* (1912) compares Aboriginal religious traditions to construct a general **model** of religious development. If we consider Durkheim and Abrams as representative examples of the field, sociology appears to be both historical and comparative in nature.

A substantial enormously influential body of work self-consciously embraces a framework we can call comparative-historical sociology. Indeed, many prominent recent books are identified with the comparative-historical method. For instance, Theda Skocpol's 1979 work *States and Social Revolutions* and Michael Mann's *The Sources of Social Power* (1986) are both identified as comparative-historical sociology. This field of inquiry has been shaped less by methodological technique than by the contributions of various scholars like Skocpol and Mann who are identified as comparative-historical sociologists. These scholars have examined various historical phenomena and looked at them across multiple units of analysis. For instance, Skocpol examined three different social revolutions in an effort to find both the continuities and discontinuities between them. While most of the work identified as comparative-historical sociology concerns matters of political or economic development, other areas of interest such as sexuality or slavery have been addressed as well.

In spite of the influence these works have had, the method is not without detractors. Numerous criticisms have been offered against not only specific comparative-historical works but against the framework as a whole. These critiques fall into two categories. First, several scholars have raised concerns about the evidence used by comparative-historical practitioners. The argument here is that sociologists often rely on the secondary literature produced by historians as if they were objective renderings of the past. Instead of doing the primary research themselves, comparative-historical sociologists are accused of letting their colleagues in the history department do the footwork and then relying on the historical accounts that best fit with the argument they want to make about a general model. Thus, critics say, historical-comparative sociology is really a sort of **secondary analysis** of historical scholarship more than history itself. While admitting the legitimacy of this danger, Theda Skocpol argued that it would be nearly fatal to comparative-historical work if practitioners were expected to redo the original studies before doing comparative work. In her 1984 book *Vision and Method in Historical Sociology*, she offered a cogent defense of the discipline while at the same time encouraging comparative-historical sociologists to move beyond dependence on an overly narrow body of historical studies. Another argument, also against the type of resources comparative-historical sociologists use, is that the extant vestiges of the past used by researchers often do not directly address the issues in which sociologists are interested. For instance, questions about the subjective experiences of people from the past are difficult to get at on the basis of historical relics. Sources such as court or census records simply do not address motives or the meanings people attached to particular experiences, and yet these are precisely what some comparative-historical sociology claims to be about. In response to this charge a body of literature has emerged that examines diaries, letters, and other forms of more personal communication more than official, historical records.

The second criticism aimed at comparative-historical sociology is that it often suffers from a lack of explanatory power. Edgar Kiser and Michael Hechter in particular have argued that the field suffers from under-specified causal relationships which, they claim, results from too quickly rejecting the role of general theory in sociology. General theory is intended to supply the causal linkages between phenomena. Kiser and Hechter, themselves advocates of **rational choice theory**, argue that without a general theory to guide their research, comparative-historical sociologists can only tell us what happened, not why it happened. For the most part, sociologists that engage in comparative-historical research have resisted the adoption of general theories for a number of reasons. First, adopting general theories implies that the researcher accepts a model of how and why things happen before the research work even begins. Second, to adopt a particular general theory is to invite a host of criticism based not on the work itself, but on the general theory embraced by the comparative-historical researcher. Nonetheless, since this method of inquiry seems well suited for some emerging topics of interest to sociologists, such as globalization and the emergence of **post-industrial society**, it is safe to say that comparative-historical sociology will continue to gain adherents among the next generation of scholars.

COMPETITION

Competition is broadly defined as attempts by individuals or groups to gain an end, often some kind of resource, under the restrictive condition that not all parties will have access or complete access to that end. To accomplish these ends, the mechanism of competition may be direct or indirect, and it may be or may not be socially or normatively regulated (Jary and Jary 1991). Competition is most closely associated with the rise of modern capitalism and the nation state. Competitive markets are institutionalized to the extent that almost all modern political economies depend on them, even those in formerly socialist countries.

Competition was the leitmotif of Adam Smith's *Wealth of Nations*. In this treatise, Smith proposed that free and open competition, called "laissez-faire capitalism," is a more desirable way of organizing an economy than mercantile **capitalism**. The core premise is that the invisible hand of the market will reduce inefficiency that accrues to public regulation of exchange under a mercantilist regime. Consequently, unregulated competition should produce greater material wealth than otherwise and reduce **social inequality**. Liberal political doctrines support this competitive ideal. In contrast, many nineteenth-century social scientists, such as Karl Marx and **John Stuart Mill**, found that **liberalism** did not produce social equilibrium as expected but instead contributed to material inequality. Evidence was supplied by fierce antagonism between classes, civil strife, and **war** between states. Even when it did not produce outright class hostility, the rise of capitalism, with its atomistic, self-interested individual, was not viewed by all as an unmitigated good. For example, the latter part of the twentieth century witnessed a recurrent debate between those who favor liberal doctrines and those who believe its premises should be modified or rejected in favor of communitarian ideals.

The notion of competition pervades sociological literature. Competition may refer to any number of variations on the concept of differential access to resources. Its study ranges from the methodological individualist premises of **rational choice theory** to the literature on stratification. An even superficial review of competition in the empirical research includes but is not limited to studies in stratification, **criminology**, urban **ecology**, organizational ecology, political economy, **economic sociology**, social psychology, **demography**, and the sociology of religion. Opposing concepts are **altruism**, cooperation, and mutualism.

See also Capitalism

COMPLEX ORGANIZATIONS

Complex organizations are historically grounded, socially constructed systems that store, organize, and allocate two types of resources: capital forms, such as land, **money**, labor power, and machinery, and administrative forms, such as **ideology**, information, and codes of behavior or **rules**. Depending on the perspective from which they are viewed, numerous defining characteristics can be assigned to complex organizations, including the existence of formal structures that delineate specific roles and levels of **authority**, presence of **collective action** toward a common purpose, and constructed boundaries that delineated members from nonmembers. In addition, organizations originate at a definable time and are governed by formal rules that define relations between various parts and individuals.

In *The Theory of Organizations* (1970), David Silverman identified three main assumptions presupposed in the evaluation of organizations as systems. First, every **organization** is a set of interdependent parts, with each part both contributing to and receiving from the organization. According to Silverman, the process by which these parts interact should be the main area of study. Second, organizations satisfy a series of needs that are required for survival. Goal attainment is a

•

necessary feature of organizational systems, even if some parts of the organization are unaware or unconcerned about the overall goals. Needs attainment also accounts for informal goals that may not be clearly stated or defined. Third, organizations have the ability to act as a unified system. In other words, some actions taken by an organization can be attributed to the organization as a whole and cannot be reduced to a specific, individual action from within.

Complex organizations are products of the **Industrial Revolution** and the need for more explicit control over production, technology, and wealth. Although some organizations, such as families, churches, and armies, exist within all societies, complex organizations possess certain characteristics that distinguish them from more informal organizations. With the rapid advances in technology, rational calculation of individual behavior was developed as a means to monitor production and coerce individual productivity. According to Michael I. Reed in his book *The Sociology of Organizations* (1992), the development of bureaucratic organizations "seemed to provide the right combination of cognitive instrumentality, moral anonymity and technical effectiveness that secured the necessary prerequisites for the successful transition from a **social order** based on **custom** and tradition to one founded on rational calculation and control." Because they are necessarily tied to a specific time, place, and purpose, an innumerable variety of organizational forms can be found. Complex organizations have drawn the attention of social scientists, resulting in several theoretical approaches to understanding the role and impact of organizations on **society**.

Organization theory developed along two different avenues of interest. The Industrial Revolution, which created the need for large-scale organizations to manage the increased complexity of production brought on by the specialization of duties and mass production, led to the **scientific management** approach. Advocated by Frederick William Taylor and later developed by **Max Weber** as a theory of **bureaucracy**, scientific management focused on the structural formation of organizations. In other words, scientific management theorists were primarily interested in the characteristics of specific offices and duties within the organization, along with powers associated with these positions and their implied and explicit relationship to the stated goals of the organization. The second early approach to the study of organizations focused on the social processes within organizations. Rather than assessing **interaction** based on the formal hierarchical **structure**, social process theorists concentrated on the informal relationships and their effects on hindering or promoting organizational goals.

Two models can be used to categorize most contemporary approaches to the study of organizations: systematic and associative. Systematic conceptualization, which uses macro-level models, focuses on the organization as a system that functions based on **role** assignment. Assessing the structure of formal relations, divisions of labor, and organizational activity as a means to achieve certain ends, the systematic model addresses organizations as basically stable, self-sustaining units of shared activity. Systematic models include institutional, functionalist, and ecological perspectives. The associative approach, which focuses at the micro-level, studies an organization's participants who, to ensure the organization's survival, must constantly ascribe to shared goals. Within this interpretative framework, organizations are often described as marketplaces of incentives, bundles of transactions, or arenas of class conflict.

Organizational theory can also be categorized by the degree to which theorists account for external influences as closed systems, partially opened systems, and open systems. Employing the perspective of closed-system analysis, organizations are considered unaffected by extra-organizational factors (e.g., social background, life problems, and interests of individuals within the organization). This approach is most often used by theorists interested in studying such organizational dimensions as workgroup relations and the psychological variables within internal interactions. Although closed-system theories are criticized for the assumption that outside forces can be ignored, this approach can be useful in the examination of the dynamics of **group** relations. Partially opened system theory acknowledges that external factors affect organizational functioning but gives priority to the importance of internal relations and accounts for extra-organizational factors only in the end result of the study to address complexities unaccounted for by internal factors.

Whereas closed system and partially open system theories are founded on positivist assumptions that behavior is determined and the source of study, open system theories develop from an interactionist perspective that places emphasis on the meaning and intended purpose of particular actions. Acknowledging the interdependence of organizations as a series of systems and subsystems, open system theorists emphasize the impact of environmental factors on the dynamics of organizational functioning.

The sheer number of existing complex organizations attests to the important roles organizations play in modern society. In the United States alone, over five million businesses with at least one employee are in operation. That figure increases again when the vast array of governmental, nonprofit, and voluntary organizations are counted. Most organizations are small, although the few large business organizations control a vast amount of the resources. For example, only thirty of the fourteen thousand banks in the United States, or one-fifth of one percent, control about half of all U.S. banking assets. As a general rule, smaller and newer organizations are more likely to succumb to environmental pressures and dissolve. Large organizations, which wield more power and control more resources, are better prepared to fend off threats to their existence. Sociological study on complex organizations has ranged from issues of differentiation and integration, diversification, executive-level changes, organizational mortality, and corporate structure.

COMPLIANCE AND CONFORMITY

Compliance and **conformity** are styles of social **influence**. Compliance relies on use of power and mediation of rewards and punishment to influence the target of the action while conformity emphasizes **group** membership and maintenance of group standards. Compliance is the intended result of attempts by a source (those attempting to exercise influence) to change of behavior, attitudes, or opinions of a target (those being influenced). This influence is effective when the behavior of the target changes to meet the requirements or demands of the source. It should be noted that the influence is not always intended to alter both physical and psychological manifestations in the target. Often the compliance may be behavior modification in which attitudinal change is not required to achieve the goal. In such cases compliance is the true goal of the **interaction**.

A common mode of inducing compliance is through the use of threats and promises toward a target. Threats and promises take on similar formats with the major difference being what serves as motivation for the target to comply to the wishes of the source. Threats take a general form in which the source informs the target that if the goals set by the source are not met then some sanction will be taken against the target. An example of a threat would be the parent telling the child that if the child's chores are not completed by dinner time (goal set by the source), then the child will be grounded for a period of time (**sanction** taken against the target for the goal not being reached). Promises follow a similar format only instead of a sanction being threatened for failure to reach a goal, the source provides an incentive or reward that will be given if the goal is met by the target. Using the previous example, the parent may tell the child that if all of the child's chores are completed by dinner (goal set by the source), then the child will get ice cream for dessert (reward for reaching the goal). Threats and promises can be problematic, however, as their effectiveness are greatly affected by the magnitude of the threat or promise and the perceived ability of the source to follow through with the reward or punishment.

On a more structural level, Amatai Etzioni identified three types of compliance through which organizations can encourage members to achieve the goals set by the group and remain loyal to the cause. Organizations have the ability to employ coercive power based on physical threats, remunerative or utilitarian power based on the promise of rewards controlled by the organization, or through normative or identitive power which plays upon prestige and emotions to assure compliance.

Conformity is the use of social influence by a group or organization in the attempt to encourage individuals to adhere to the **norms** and standards set by the group. The pressure exerted by the group is typically related to forcing the target to help achieve the group goals. Attempts to force a target to conform typically involve either the use of normative or informational influence.

Normative influence involves members of the group conforming to the wishes of the majority so that they may reap the rewards associated with achieving the group goals or avoid the punishments that would come with failing to fulfill that expectation. Normative influence usually involves some sort of surveillance, either by peers or figures of **authority**, among the

group to assure that all members are meeting the norms. Informational influence focuses on the ability of the group to define reality for its members. In this style of conformity, group members accept as factual any information provided them by others members of the group. In this way, social reality, and especially any ambiguous situation, is defined for the individual by the group and the member's behavior is controlled. Perhaps the most well-known study of conformity, Solomon Asch's study of the conformity **paradigm** illustrated both of these methods of conformity. Asch arranged an experiment in conformity where a subject would be faced with a decision to give the correct answer to an obvious question (in reference to the approximate distance of a line) or to give the obviously incorrect answer that each of the other subjects had given before. In two-thirds of the cases the subject conformed to the group and gave the obviously wrong answer thereby demonstrating the influence of a group on individual behavior.

See also Influence

COMPUTER APPLICATIONS IN SOCIOLOGY

The subject matter of **sociology** lends itself to observation with the naked eye and **measurement** via the operationalizations of concepts. As such, sociologists have routinely relied upon paper and ink more than other technology and upon the application of ideas rather than of apparatuses. However, computer use has connected with sociology, directly or indirectly, also. Computer applications in sociology have matured and expanded.

By engaging with computers, sociologists have also engaged the sociology of computing, including examinations of the adoption and use of computer technologies (Rob Kling). Their investigations have ranged from the stratification of computer access and use to the cultural and structural impact of connectivity and have considered changes in the business environment (Michael Morton), the social impact of new software on secretarial pools (Suzanne Iacano), the organizational power shifts threatened by new and unregulated means of communication (Lee Sproull and Sara Keisler), new mechanisms of control introduced by computers (Gary T. Marx), and ethical dilemmas faced by computerization (Ena Wagner). But sociological investigations of computer applications have not been markedly self-referential.

Early computer applications in sociology were somewhat marginal and limited to mechanisms for political polling and the mathematics of observed relationships. But the maturation of applications in sociology matches patterns observable elsewhere, including businesses, other organizations, and other disciplines. In sociology as elsewhere, increased use has come hand-in-hand with more specialized uses.

With the increasing power and availability of computers and as they spread into businesses throughout the 1970s, sociologists began making more sophisticated uses of them, particularly for advanced statistical calculations and estimations.

With the blossoming of the personal computer revolution, beginning in the 1980s, and its spread to non-business organizations from foundations to families, sociology began to engage computers in the same breadth found in **society** at large.

In the late 1970s, some sociologists (and some doing work used by sociologists) used some tools (such as statistical software) used by businesses. By the 1980s, they were adopting customizable spreadsheets for a range of tasks including data analysis, departmental management, and grading. Soon after, they began to use desktop publishing, including both word processors and more complex tools such as software for publications and slides, for the production of reports, papers, presentations, and classroom needs.

Gradually, more specialized uses developed, such as CATI (computer-assisted telephone interviewing, which integrates **data** collection and data entry in an ideally seamless interaction) and CAT (computer-assisted teaching, primarily for statistical and computing skills). At the frontier of computer applications in sociology, modeling has expanded from statistical relationships to geographic information systems (GIS) displays and are now engaging modeling of social life itself, including attempts at artificial life and artificial intelligence.

In many instances, sociologists (like society at large) have benefited from computer applications developed in the military. The first computer, ENIAC, was developed to calculate missile trajectories. Many statistical and modeling tools began in the military and in conjunction with military funding. In 1969, the **Internet** began through a Department of Defense project. Decades later, in the 1990s, sociologists began adopting the related communication services that were just then reaching critical mass. As elsewhere, this adoption was slow and initially limited in location (such as by sociologists at technical universities) and social networks (such as among those employing advanced mathematics or those already using computers for other means). But media attention to expanded usage and the marketing of new powerful features attracted the attention of sociologists as it did many others.

Entry to the Internet and the explosion of network connectivity gave sociologists what it gave other individuals and organizations: a new and expanded means of both exchanging and acquiring ideas. Sociologists now engage in a multitude of email-based discussion groups, Usenet newsgroups, Web pages, and more, and uses of the Internet are likely to expand as new services and features become available and widely used. Sociologists share data, ideas, and job openings online. Sociologists are also prominent in efforts to bring college courses online, ranging from supplementary discussion locales to a means of delivering lectures, tests, and other interactions. In some sense, and to some degree, this movement online constitutes a change in the way sociology occurs.

Increasingly, sociologists study cyberspace itself and uses of it, including discussions of power, conflict, and cooperation, and changes in the meaning of gender (Camille Paglia) and self (Sherry Turkle). By early 2000, attention had even begun to flow in a new direction, as Internet-related and based businesses began promoting online communities as a marketing tool and competitive advantage. This development invites sociologists to affect and design computer applications in business. The Internet is thus becoming, and is likely to ultimately become, a central modus, locus, and focus for sociological investigation: a way of practicing sociology, a place to engage in that practice, and an item of attention for that practice.

COMTE, AUGUSTE (1798-1857)
French philosopher

Born in Montpellier, Auguste Comte abandoned the devout Catholicism and royalism of his family while in his teens. He entered the École Polytechnique in 1814 and proved himself a brilliant mathematician and scientist. Comte was expelled in 1816 for participating in a student rebellion. Remaining in Paris, he managed to do immense research in mathematics, science, economics, history, and **philosophy**.

At 19, Comte met Henri de Rouvroy, Comte de Saint-Simon, and as a "spiritually adopted son," he became secretary and collaborator to the older man until 1824. The relationship between Saint-Simon and Comte grew increasingly strained for both theoretical and personal reasons and finally degenerated into an acrimonious break over disputed authorship. Saint-Simon was an intuitive thinker interested in immediate, albeit utopian, social reform. Comte was a scientific thinker, in the sense of systematically reviewing all available data, with a conviction that only after science was reorganized in its totality could men hope to resolve their **social problems**.

In 1924, Comte began a common-law marriage with Caroline Massin when she was threatened with arrest because of prostitution, and he later referred to this disastrous 18-year union as "the only error of my life." During this period, Comte supported himself as a tutor. In 1826, he proposed to offer a series of 72 lectures on his philosophy to a subscription list of distinguished intellectuals. After the third lecture, Comte suffered a complete breakdown, replete with psychotic episodes. At his mothers's insistence, he was remarried in a religious ceremony and signed the contract "Brutus Napoleon Comte." Despite periodic hospitalization for mental illness during the following 15 years, Comte was able to discipline himself to produce his major work, the six-volume *Course of Positive Philosophy* (1830–1842).

Positivism is a term usually understood as a particular was of thinking. For Comte, additionally, the **methodology** is a product of a systematic reclassification of the sciences and a general conception of the development of man in history: the law of three stages. Comte, like the **Marquis de Condorcet** whom he acknowledged as a predecessor and G. W. F. Hegel whom he met in Paris, was convinced that no **data** can be adequately understood except in the historical context. Phenomena are intelligible only in terms of their origin, function, and significance in the relative course of human history.

But, unlike Hegel, Comte held that there is no *Geist*, or spirit, above and beyond history which objectifies itself through the vagaries of time. Comte represents a radical **relativism**: "Everything is relative; there is the only absolute thing." Positivism absolutizes relativity as a principle which makes all previous ideas and systems a result of historical conditions. The only unity that the system of positivism affords in its pronounce anti-metaphysical **bias** is the inherent order of human thought. Thus, the law of the three stages, which he discovered as early as 1820, attempts to show that the history of the human mind and the development of the sciences follow a determinant pattern which parallels the growth of social and political institutions. According to Comte, the system of positivism is grounded on the natural and historical law that "by the very nature of the human mind, every branch of our knowledge is necessarily obliged to pass successively in its course through three different theoretical states: the theological or fictitious state; the metaphysical or abstract state; finally, the scientific or positive state."

These stages represent different and opposed types of human conception. The most primitive is theological thinking, which rests on the "empathetic fallacy" of reading subjective experience into the operations of nature. The theological perspective develops dialectically through fetishism, polytheism, and **monotheism** as events are understood as animated by their own will, that of several deities, or the decree of one supreme being. Politically, the theological state provides stability under kings imbued with divine rights and supported by military power. As **civilization** progresses, the metaphysical stage begins as a criticism of these conceptions in the name of a new order. Supernatural entities are gradually transformed into abstract forces just as political rights are codified into systems of law. In the final stage of positive science, the search for absolute knowledge is abandoned in favor of a modest but precise inquiry into the relative laws of nature. The absolutist and feudal social orders are replaced gradually by increasing social progress achieved through the application of scientific knowledge.

From this survey of the development of humanity, Comte was able to generalize a specific positive methodology. Like René Descartes, Comte acknowledged a unity of the sciences. It was, however, not that of a univocal method of thinking but the successive development of man's ability to deal with the complexities of experience. Each science possesses a specific mode of inquiry. Mathematics and astronomy were sciences that men developed early because of their simplicity, generality, and abstractness. But observation and the framing of hypotheses had to be expanded through the method of experimentation in order to deal with the physical sciences of physics, chemistry, and biology. A **comparative method** is required also to study the natural sciences, man, and social institutions. Thus, even the history of science and methodology supports the law of the three stages by revealing a hierarchy of sciences and methodological direction from general to particular and simple to complex. **Sociology** studies the particular societies in a complex way since man is both the subject and the object of this discipline. One can consider social groups from the standpoint of "social statics," which comprises the element of cohesion and order such as family and institutions, or form the perspective of "social dynamics," which analyzes the stage of continuous development that a given **society** has achieved.

In 1842, Comte's marriage had dissolved, and he was supported by contributions from various intellectuals. In 1844,

Auguste Comte *(The Library of Congress)*

he met Clothhilde de Vaux, and they fell deeply in love. Although the affair was never consummated because Madame de Vaux died in the next year, this intense love influences Comte in his later work toward a new religion of humanity. He proposed replacing priests with a new class of scientists and industrialists and offered a catechism based on the cult of reason and humanity, and a new calendar replete with positivist saints. While this line of thought was implicit in the aim of sociology to synthesize order and **progress** in the service of humanity, the farcical elements of Comet's mysticism has damaged his philosophical reputation. He died in obscurity in 1857.

CONCENTRIC ZONE THEORY

In the early part of the twentieth century, the United States experienced rapid growth in many **cities** because of the rise in industrialization and in immigration. Ernest Burgess, a sociologist at the University of Chicago, noted that many cities experienced similar patterns of growth. Namely, American cities expand outward in a series of concentric circles that are differentiated by their primary land uses. His theory, first published in *The City* in 1925, eventually became known as the concentric zone theory.

The concentric zone theory distinguishes five zones of urban land use. Zone I contains the "loop," the central business district, an area of major commercial activity. Zone II, commonly called the "zone in transition," immediately surrounds the central business district. It is in the process of being taken over by commercial interests but includes areas where the poor and immigrants reside. Here people may expect to find the highest rates of **crime**, vice, and mental illness. The zone of transition is followed by Zone III, the zone of working-class homes. Traditionally, Zone III is the place to which working-class families moved in order to escape the deteriorating zone in transition. Middle-class residents live clustered in Zone IV, designated the residential zone. This zone contains high-priced residential housing, both in apartments and in districts of exclusive individual homes. The outermost zone, Zone V, the commuters' zone, may stretch far into suburban and rural areas and is not necessarily part of the urban **community**.

This pattern of zones emerges because of **competition** for real estate. Land values are highest where transportation networks are clustered and businesses located. Over time, business activity expands, invading surrounding zones. This process is called succession. Areas adjacent to the business loop are in the process of being taken over for commercial use. These areas are not desirable places to live, and residences are often run-down and are thus occupied by the poor. Burgess did not assert that the concentric zone model would fit all cities perfectly. Instead, he meant for the theory to be used as a model for studying cities. While the concentric zone theory was popular in the early to middle part of the twentiety century, its prominence declined later.

CONCEPT

A concept is a name for some observed or unobserved phenomenon. It is a perception labeled and animated by **language**. We call a chair, "a chair". That is the general distinction for the thing that we use to sit in. It is a vague distinction in that there are many different kinds of chairs. Certainly an office chair and a beanbag chair generate two distinctly different perceptions of the same concept. Nonetheless, both an office chair and a beanbag chair are within the agreed upon and acceptable range of perceptions for the concept for those who speak the English language.

The definition of any given concept can be altered by historical and cultural changes. Take for instance, the concept, "family". The 1950s ushered in the definition of the **family** as a dual parent, heterosexual **household** in which children were reared. Today, families cannot be so easily defined. The range of variation is much more encompassing when we refer to the family today. Families can consist of any number of people, in a wide variety of relationships. Several aspects of the concept of family have changed over time including the family's composition, purpose, and its functions. Every aspect of its definition has been altered over time. In other words, the concept of the family has changed.

Sociologists examine concepts—their components, definitions, creation, and linkages among them. As a concept changes, there is less social agreement about its definition,

which generates confusion. Before sociologists can describe a concept or study the effects of any given concept on another, they must define it as accurately as possible. This process is known as conceptualization.

CONDITIONING

The Russian physiologist Ivan Pavlov developed the principles of classical conditioning. In his Nobel Prize-winning research on the digestive processes, he placed meat powder in the mouths of his research animals and recorded their levels of salivation. At one point, he noticed that some of his research animals began to salivate in the absence of food. He reasoned that the presence of the animal caretakers led the animals to anticipate the meat powder, so they began to salivate even without the food.

When classical conditioning occurs, an animal or person initially responds to a naturally occurring stimulus with a natural response (e.g., the food leads to salivation). Then the food is systematically paired with a previously neutral stimulus (e.g., a bell), one that does not lead to any particular response. With repeated pairings, the natural response occurs when the neutral stimulus appears.

Pavlovian (i.e., classical) conditioning influenced social scientists greatly, even though Pavlov himself was skeptical of the work others performed. In the United States, John Watson, the first widely known behaviorist, used the principles of classical conditioning in his research. For example, in a widely cited study, Watson tried to develop a classically conditioned phobia in an infant.

Although classical conditioning became the dominant Russian model for the study of behaviorism, another form of conditioning took hold in the United States. This version, which became known as operant or instrumental conditioning, initially developed from the ideas of the psychologist Edward Thorndike. Thorndike began his psychological research by studying learning in chickens, then in cats. Based on the problem solving of these animals, he developed the Law of Effect, which in simple form states that a behavior that has a positive outcome is likely to be repeated. Similarly, his Law of Exercise states that the more a response occurs in a given situation, the more strongly it is linked with that situation, and the more likely it is to be repeated in the future.

Operant conditioning was popularized by the psychologist B.F. Skinner. His research and writings influenced not only social scientists but also the general public. Operant conditioning differs from classical conditioning in that, whereas classical conditioning relies on an organism's response to some stimulus in the environment, operant conditioning relies on the organism's initiating an action that is followed by some consequence.

For example, when a hungry person puts money into a vending machine, he or she is rewarded with some product. In social scientist's terms, the behavior is reinforced; in everyday language, the person is satisfied with the outcome. As a result, the next time the person is hungry, he or she is likely to repeat the behavior of putting money into the machine. On the other hand, if the machine malfunctions and the person gets no food, that individual is less likely to repeat the behavior in the future. This refers to punishment.

Any time a behavior leads to a positive outcome that is likely to be repeated, it is said that behavior has been reinforced. When the behavior leads to a negative outcome, social scientists refer to punishment. Two types of reinforcement and punishment have been described: positive and negative.

Positive reinforcement is generally regarded as synonymous with reward: when a behavior appears, something positive results. This leads to a greater likelihood that the behavior will recur. Negative reinforcement involves the termination of an unpleasant situation. Thus, if a person has a headache, taking some kind of pain reliever leads to a satisfying outcome. In the future, when the person has a headache, he or she is likely to take that pain reliever again. In positive and negative reinforcement, some behavior is likely to recur either because something positive results or something unpleasant stops.

Just as reinforcement comes in two versions, punishment takes two forms. Social scientists have identified positive punishment as the presentation of an unpleasant result when an undesired behavior occurs. On the other hand, when something positive is removed, this is called negative punishment. In both forms of punishment, an undesired behavior results in a negative consequence. As a result, the undesired behavior is less likely to recur in the future.

Many people mistakenly equate negative reinforcement with punishment because the word "negative" conjures up the idea of punishment. In reality, a situation involving negative reinforcement involves the removal of a negative stimulus, leading to a more satisfying situation. A situation involving punishment always leads to an unwanted outcome.

Beginning with Watson and Skinner, social science circles in the United States adopted a behavioral framework in which researchers began to study people and animals through conditioning. From the 1920s through the 1960s, many social scientists performed conditioning experiments with animals with the idea that what was true for animals would also be true for humans. Social scientists assumed that the principles of conditioning were universal. Although many of the principles of learning and conditioning developed in animal research pertain to human learning and conditioning, social scientists now realize that each species has its own behavioral characteristics. Consequently, although the principles of conditioning may generalize from animals to humans, researchers must consider the differences across species as well.

CONDORCET, MARQUIS DE (1743-1794)
French mathematician, politician, and philosopher

Marie Jean Antoine Nicolas Caritat, Marquis de Condorcet, was born on September 17, 1743, in Ribemont, Picardy, in southern France. His family had an ancient and noble heritage tied to the principality of Orange, and most of his male ances-

tors had pursued either military or ecclesiastical careers. His father died when Condorcet was four years old, and his mother, twice widowed, reacted by smothering her son in a blanket of protection. Dedicating him to the Virgin to protect him from the "Evil Eye," his mother dressed Condorcet as a girl until he was eight years old. Ending his informal education conducted by his mother at the age of 11, Condorcet was sent to his uncle, the Bishop of Lisieux, who arranged for a Jesuit tutor for Condorcet. In 1758, Condorcet enrolled in the University of Paris and studied **philosophy** and mathematics at the College of Navarre.

Upon graduation in 1760, Condorcet, as a young nobleman, was expected to embark on a military career. Instead, he proclaimed his intent to study mathematics. This shocked his family, who was violently opposed to the idea. Mathematics, as a branch of science, glorified the individual and progress, ideas which threatened the claims of hereditary power. Despite his family's resistance, Condorcet returned to Paris where he lived a quiet life of study, often reading mathematics for ten hours a day. In 1769, at the age of 26, Condorcet was elected as a junior academician to the Academy of Sciences. Subsequently, he was named Secretary of the Academy of Sciences and became Permanent Secretary in 1777, a position he held the remainder of his life.

In his association with the Academy of Sciences, Condorcet encountered highly regarded mathematician and philosopher Jean d'Alembert, who became a powerful friend and advocate. Condorcet also developed a close friendship with Turgot, a statesman and reformer, who drew Condorcet into the arena of politics, economics, and reforms. When Turgot became Minister of Finance in 1774, he appointed Condorcet as Inspector-General of the Mint. He also appointed Condorcet, along with d'Alembert, to the Commission of Three, which oversaw an extensive expansion of inland navigation via new canals.

Working within Turgot's circle of advisors, Condorcet was instrumental in the development of Turgot's reform plan. Unfortunately, Turgot was removed from office in 1776, before the work was presented to Louis XVI. Turgot's fall from power left Condorcet in despair. Critical of Turgot's replacement whose misguided financial policies pushed France toward revolution, Condorcet published his objections in two letters: *Letter of a Laborer in Picardy* and *Memoir on the Corn Trade*. Enraging his rivals, Condorcet resigned his government position. Believing that extending the common good was the highest calling, Condorcet wrote to Voltaire, a Turgot supporter: "It is cold comfort to labor for nothing but glory after flattering oneself for a time that one was working for the public good."

Over the next six years Condorcet attempted to formulate a comprehensive understanding of the social sciences. Elected to the influential French Academy in 1782, he introduced his social theory in his reception speech. Further developed in his 1785 paper *Essay on the Application of Mathematics to the Theory of Decision-Making,* Condorcet argued that the advancement of both moral and political sciences was bound by the same laws as the physical sciences. In other words, **progress** of **morality**, **society**, and nature all operated under the same law; therefore, just as nature progresses based on rational laws, so do all aspects of life.

In 1786, Condorcet married Sophie de Grouchy. The French Revolution broke out three years later, and in 1791 Condorcet was elected to the Legislative Assembly, serving first as Secretary and then as president. He helped draft both the proclamation that declared France to be a republic and the moderate (also known as Gerondist) version of the new constitution. However, the Jacobin leader, Robespierre, managed to block its passage and influence the development of a new constitution, which was hastily drafted by a revised committee. Outraged at the many defects in the document, Condorcet published the highly critical letter *Advice to the French on the New Constitution*. Although published anonymously, his authorship was discovered, and on July 8, 1793, Condorcet was denounced and charged with treason.

Avoiding arrest by hiding out in a sympathizer's home, Condorcet knew his time was limited. Working hastily, Condorcet began to work out his understanding of the progress of human thought, outlined as *Sketch for a Historical Picture of the Progress of the Human Mind*. Within his final work, Condorcet advocates the possibility for the infinite perfectibility of the human race in all areas, including physical, mental, and moral development. Predicting the end to the major flaws of **civilization**, Condorcet believed that gradual, yet inevitable, progress would lead to the extinction of such evils as gender inequality, religious bigotry, **disease**, **war**, slavery, economic injustice, and the separation of societies based on exclusive languages.

In March 1794, Condorcet received a warning that he had been discovered, and soldiers were on their way to arrest him. Wishing to protect his kind hostess who had risked her life to hide him, Condorcet disguised his appearance and fled to the countryside. After several days of wandering without food or shelter, Condorcet entered a village tavern. He drew suspicion when, exhausted and muddled, he requested an omelet with a dozen eggs. When he could not produce the required identification papers, the police were called. Condorcet, who was so weak he had to be placed in a cart, was arrested and taken to jail. He was found dead in his cell two days later, on March 29, 1794. His *Sketch* was published posthumously in 1795.

CONFLICT THEORY

Conflict theory is one of the major sociological paradigms, or an overall framework or **model** for understanding the social world. First, the conflict paradigm holds that conflict is a common and ongoing feature of **society**. In fact, conflict is the most basic feature of social life. Second, society is made up of various social groups who hold conflicting **values** and interests. This circumstance leads to a third proposition of conflict theory, which states that societal conflict occurs between dominant and subordinate social groups that are in **competition** with one another over resources. These resources consist primarily of economic resources and social power.

The conflict perspective, developed during the late eighteenth and nineteenth centuries, is primarily associated with two German thinkers, **Karl Marx** and Max Weber. Although Marx was not a self-proclaimed sociologist, his ideas have provided the basis for much of historical and contemporary sociological thought. Marx asserted that there are two subgroups or classes in society that are in ruthless competition for scarce and valued resources. According to Marx, such competition takes place primarily within the economic domain. The capitalist class or *bourgeoisie* owns and controls the means of production, while also overseeing the distribution of goods and services in society. The working class or *proletariat* provides the labor necessary to produce such goods and services.

Marxian ideology posits that the ongoing conflict between the dominant capitalist class and the subordinate working class exists as the cornerstone of capitalist society. Such conflict is thus a normal state of affairs within the context of **capitalism**. In any capitalist society the primary goal of the bourgeoisie is the accumulation of capital or wealth. In order to achieve this goal, capitalists must actively exploit the labor of the workers or the proletariat, for that labor creates the products from which capitalists make money. In order to turn a profit capitalists must pay workers less than what they actually bring in from the sale of their products. Because subordinated workers are opposed to their own exploitation, the capitalist exploitation of workers provides the primary site for conflict in a capitalist society.

Max Weber also asserted that society is primarily an arena of conflict and struggle over scarce resources. Like Marx, Weber contended that this conflict occurs between dominant and subordinate groups. Weber did not, however, limit society to two classes or confine social conflict to the economic realm. Weber argued that there are many *status groups* in society, which possess varying degrees of social power. Although certain status group members do derive social power from the accumulation of wealth and capital, power can also be derived in the context of other social arenas, such as politics, **ethnicity**, gender, and religion.

From Weber's perspective then, society does not simply consist of one dominant group and one subordinate group. While conflict is indeed a characteristic of the capitalist-worker dyad, conflict also characterizes various other social relationships. Therefore, individuals may be dominant in one social group while subordinate in another. A capitalist may be dominant within a capitalist economy, but as an Independent party member he is subordinate in a political system dominated by Republicans and Democrats. A congresswoman may be a dominant member of her state government; however, as an African American woman she is subordinate within a society marked by racial and gender inequality.

The thinking and writings of Karl Marx and Max Weber, often characterized as the bedrock of conflict **sociology**, have influenced the social theorizing of many contemporary sociologists as well. The work of contemporary Immanuel Wallerstein and his *world-systems theory* are referred to as a neo-Marxian sociology. Wallerstein employed a conflict perspective in his examination of capitalists and workers throughout the world, also exploring how the relationship between these competing groups shapes the world economy. Theda Skocpol's theory of social revolutions has been dubbed neo-Weberian sociology. Skocpol used a conflict perspective to illustrate the ways in which political conflict and struggle influenced the rise of various national revolutions throughout history. The works of these and various other contemporary sociologists have made conflict theory perhaps the most dominant sociological perspective in the field today.

CONFORMITY

Conformity refers to actions or behaviors which fit with current customs, rules, or styles in a **society**. Groups are characterized by the **norms** to which their members conform. Often, such behavior is induced by **group** pressure and individuals feel a need to conform to such expectations. Conformity has been the topic of a significant amount of sociological research. The degree of an individual's conformity to a group has been determined to rely upon variables such as the prestige of the group to which they belong, the degree to which their decisions might be considered ambiguous, and the group's size.

Additionally, two types of conformity have been distinguished. First, a person may conform through internalization. In this case, the norms subscribed to by the group have become his own. His opinions are the group's opinions. On the other hand, a person may also conform through compliance. That is, he outwardly acts in accordance with the norms of the group, but does not accept the opinions of the group.

There are also reasons a person could decide not to conform to a group. For example, the ''Peculiar People'' were founded in London by John Banyard in 1838. They so named themselves as a contrast to the biblical ''chosen people'' of Israel. The ''Peculiar People'' chose not to conform to certain societal institutions, such as medical treatment. This group, which included many dissenting Protestant sects, refused medical treatment on religious grounds. It should be noted, however, that in choosing not conform to the general trends of society by forming an alternate group, the members, in effect, established a new set of norms with which to conform.

Historically, thinkers have spoken out against conformity. In an 1841 essay, ''Self-Reliance'' Ralph Waldo Emerson insisted that ''whoso would be a man, must be a nonconformist.'' He called the integrity of the individual mind ''sacred'' and urged others to worry about what concerned themselves, not others. Conformity to Emerson deadened personal character and made it hard to truly know the real person.

See also Influence

CONFUCIANISM

Confucianism is a moral **ideology** or social tradition fathered by the Chinese philosopher Confucius and his disciples in the sixth and fifth centuries B.C. It is concerned with the principles

Confucius

of civil conduct, common sense, and proper social relationships. Not only has Confucianism influenced the Chinese perspective toward life, it is the foundation on which Chinese politics and institutions are based. Confucian teachings have been followed for more than two thousand years, spreading beyond China to Korea, Japan, and Vietnam, and capturing the interest of Westerners as well.

While frequently classed with the major religions of the world, Confucianism is not an organized religion, never having existed with a **church** or priesthood. Confucius never claimed divinity and although the Chinese have honored Confucius as a great sage, they do not worship him as a god. In fact, attempts to deify Confucius have failed because of his philosophy's secular nature.

The main Confucian ethic is *ren*, which can be translated as "love" or "kindness." Ren is considered a supreme virtue, exemplifying human character at its finest. Ren may be best expressed in the Confucian golden rule, "Do not do to others what you do not want done to yourself." Righteousness, integrity, good behavior, and devoutness are other important Confucian virtues. According to Confucianism, a person who possesses all of these qualities becomes "perfect." Politically, Confucius endorsed a **government** in which the rulers are honorable and benevolent and the citizens are obedient and respectful. Confucian teachings imply that a ruler should demonstrate moral perfection in order to set a good example for the people. The principles of Confucianism are contained in the nine ancient Chinese works by Confucius and his disciples. These writings can be divided into two groups: the Five Classics and the Four Books.

CONSERVATISM

Generally, conservative thinking is suspicious of change and seeks to maintain tradition, law and order, and respect for **authority**. Conservatism is critical of the idea that human beings and human societies can be perfected, and it accepts inequality, either as desirable or as inevitable. Conservative people tend to expect organized religion to be a central component and guiding force of social life and are concerned that **society** should encourage individuals to adopt morals and virtues that will lead them to act in ways that benefit the existing **social order**.

However, more specific definitions of conservative have changed greatly over the past few centuries. What **Anthony Giddens** termed "Old Conservatism" was a defense of the *ancien regime*—European monarchies, the Catholic Church, and the medieval feudal system—in the face of the French Revolution and the Enlightenment. It supported the traditional and existing hierarchy and aristocracy, stressed God's authority,and insisted that obligations to church, state, and **family** should be placed above individual rights. The Old Conservatism was also a reaction to modern changes, which stressed rationalism, industrialization, and secularism. Most importantly, conservatism was hostile to **capitalism**, which as a new economic system was creating rapid changes in the social **structure** and **culture** of Europe. This form of conservatism died out as capitalism became the dominant economic structure of the Western world.

While contemporary conservatives are concerned with maintaining traditions and slowing the pace of change, they have completely reversed the attitude of their forebears regarding capitalism. They now believe that market economies are essential to freedom and **democracy**; therefore, **government** intervention in economic matters ought to be avoided. For American conservatives, according to Wilson Carey McWilliams, "capitalism and the market are pillars of established authority," and the state should not be allowed to redistribute income from the wealthy to the poor. Such efforts at "social engineering," they argue, will only lead to negative "unforeseen consequences" that will worsen, not better, a society's overall **standard of living**. Rather than government intervention, conservatives stress the importance of individual responsibility: the poor should be encouraged to live moral lives according to society's **norms** and work their way up the social ladder. Charity work should be carried out through churches and other private organizations. The state's only role should be to maintain law and order and to protect business interests at home and abroad. This belief in the importance of free markets and minimal government is sometimes referred to as neoliberalism, since **liberalism** originally meant supporting capitalism and individual rights and the social changes inherent to them. Giddens, McWilliams, and others suggest that neoliberalism contains an inherent contradiction: the social norms and traditions it desires to protect are also highly subject to change in a market economy. For instance, the economic, social, and cultural changes that have led to more women working outside the home in recent decades have also led to changes in the family structures and previously established **gender roles** that conservatives wish to preserve.

Another branch of conservatism, known variously as the Religious Right, the Christian Right, or the New Right, became prominent in the United States in the mid–1970s. Consisting predominantly of Protestant fundamentalists, the Religious Right argues that the United States is a Christian nation that has abandoned its godly mission to create a society based upon Biblical mandates. The Religious Right generally focuses more on cultural than economic issues and in recent decades has been particularly concerned with society's changing gender roles and with the ongoing **secularization** of American public life. Specifically, the Religious Right has sought to recriminalize abortion, reinstate compulsory **prayer** in public schools, promote the teaching of "creation science" rather than evolution, and deny the extension of civil rights protections to homosexuals.

While there is often some overlap between neoliberals and the Religious Right, cultural and economic conservatism do not always go together. In fact, these two forms of conservatism are often at odds. For instance, there has been much debate within the Republican Party regarding its current anti-abortion position. Some party members feel that just as the government should not regulate the nation's economic system, it should not regulate personal reproductive decisions. Those who are culturally liberal (in the sense of being accepting of different lifestyles and open to change) and economically conservative usually prefer the term libertarian, believing that government interference should be kept to a minimum in both public/economic and private life.

CONSPICUOUS CONSUMPTION

According to the study of economics, consumption refers to the use of goods and services by consumers. The concept of consumption does not take into account the production of these goods. Consumption takes place both in the public and private sectors. The difference between consumption and conspicuous consumption (a term coined by **Thorstein Veblen**, American social critic and economist, 1857-1929) is that the latter is for appearances rather than utility. According to Veblen, the **leisure** class (and others) used conspicuous consumption to demonstrate their social **status**. Veblen also studied the ability of advertising to motivate people toward certain purchases, even though competing products might be essentially the same. Others who studied conspicuous consumption include Fred Hirsh and Bourdieu.

Consumption trends in the United States were significant in the 1990s. In 1997, private consumption in the United States totaled $5.5 trillion, and exceeded any other country on the globe. Internationally, consumption was far from evenly spread across all countries. According to a UN Human Development Report of 1998, the wealthiest twenty percent of people in the world consumed eighty-six percent of all goods and services in the world. In contrast, the twenty percent of the world's population that comprised the globe's poorest people only consumed 1.3 percent of worldwide goods and services. Consumption patterns clearly varied according to economic standing; the richest twenty percent of people in the world, for example, bought nine times as much meat as the poorest twenty percent of people in the world.

According to a *Business Week* article (24 April 2000), American consumer trends at the beginning of the twenty-first century showed no sign of abating. According to Robert Dugger of the Tudor Investment Corporation (in testimony to the U.S. Trade Deficit Commission), the scene was set to encourage U.S. consumerism during the Cold War. At that time, the U.S. government de-emphasized personal saving and gave people incentives to increase consumption, such as tax breaks on consumer credit interest. After the Cold War, the behavioral patterns and the policy that supported them remained the same, even though consumerism now supported commercial rather than patriotic objectives.

U.S. teenagers at the end of the twentieth century also spent more than any previous generation. By 1999 U.S. teenagers spent $141 billion per year, mostly for clothes, computers, music, and food. It was estimated that teens in the United States spent an average of $100 per week, though some of these purchases included **family** groceries. Teenagers as a group were expected to increase from 27 million in 1999 to 30 million in 2010, according to the U.S. census. Conditions at the end of the twentieth century were ripe for spending in this age group, as many teens had part time jobs.

CONSTRUCTIVISM

Constructivism, a loosely organized movement of thought, is critical of the assertion that absolute truths and ahistorical knowledge exist. Instead, it maintains the belief that knowledge is socially constructed by human agents and cannot be understood independently of historical or cultural context. It also questions taken-for-granted assumptions about how the practice of science works and attempts to denaturalize scientific knowledge. Constructivism's development overlapped with

labeling theory, **symbolic interactionism**, and ethnomethodology, and it shares with these lines of thought an emphasis on attaching labels and meanings, as well as the importance of social location to knowledge. It is often contrasted with **positivism**, which assumes a social reality that is independent of human agents. The term is sometimes used interchangeably with constructionism, **relativism**, deconstructionism, or other related concepts that infer a social reality created (at least in part) by human agents.

Most of the work in the social sciences up to the 1960s operated on the assumption that scientific laws and mathematical truths were in the world to be discovered. Once discovered, they were free from the influence of history and cultural context (this way of thinking is epitomized in the work of Karl Mannheim). The contribution of **Thomas Kuhn** in the 1960s, particularly his book *Structure of Scientific Revolutions* (1962), challenge the dominant conception of knowledge as ahistorical and acontextual. With the publication of Peter Berger's and Thomas Luckmann's book *The Social Construction of Reality* (1966), this new way of looking critically at knowledge was given its name.

Studies in the 1970s and early 1980s used constructivism to explore scientific practices. Most notable of these is the work of Bruno Latour, who demonstrated that activities in the laboratory are not so dissimilar from other human activities. Latour argued that this showed that the knowledge claims of scientists were similar to knowledge claims by nonscientists.

Constructivism has been criticized for being so relativistic as to make the very notion of knowledge meaningless. Some critics claim that if all knowledge is constructed, constructivism itself as a form of knowledge cannot claim legitimacy. Although there are some postmodern constructivists who might argue that no real knowledge exists, most constructivists do not embrace relativism and do not see their work as negating itself.

CONSUMER CULTURE

A consumer refers to a person who acquires goods or services for direct use or ownership. A consumer **culture** is dominated by consumption. During the last half of the twentieth century, societal trends indicated that the United States was increasingly becoming a consumer culture, and that other countries were starting to imitate the trend. **Max Weber** (1864–1920) had warned of this change, referring to a consumer culture as "an iron cage."

According to data cited in an *E* magazine article (March-April 1996), American consumption increased 45 percent per capita between the 1970s and the 1990s. These consumption patterns are reflected globally; eighty percent of the resources in the world are consumed by twenty percent of the global population. According to the Natural Resources Defense Council, a U.S. environmental advocacy group, the American consumer culture contributes to the fact that Americans use an inordinate amount of resources and produce an inordinate amount of waste compared to the rest of the world.

The American consumer culture appeared to be a model to emulate for other countries in the late twentieth century.

Consumption trends showed that the advent of imported **television** in countries, such as formerly communist East Germany, caused the desire for consumer goods to increase. East Germans purchased 200,000 used cars from the West during the first half of 1990. Because of the ease with which television can spread information about consumer goods, the world population consumed as many goods between 1950 and 1996 as did all previous generations in total. A 1996 article in *American Demographics* noted that the advent of television throughout the world has created a universal **language** and awareness based on marketing and brand names.

Economist Friedrich Schmidt-Bleek noted that environmental degradation is directly related to increased consumption and that worldwide materials consumption needed to be reduced by fifty percent to prevent further environmental damage. The consumer culture in the United States alone is also supported by the advertising industry, which spends more per capita in advertising dollars ($468) than any other country in the world.

A poll released in the 1990s (Merck Family Fund survey) found that although consumption patterns in the United States continued to increase, quality of life for consumers had decreased by over 50 percent. According to the poll, over one fourth of Americans had done something concrete to try and increase their satisfaction with life and reduce reliance on the consumer culture paradigm. People voluntarily attempted to simplify their lives in a number of ways such as buying less or reducing income in order to have more time to devote to other aspects of life. This movement has been referred to as ''voluntary simplicity.'' For example, Anna Quindlen, a well known columnist, willingly left her work to write books and be home with her children.

CONTAGION THEORY

Contagion may be defined as the spread of a behavior through social proximity. The exact nature of proximity has been a point of frequent discussion, with researchers arguing in turn for the importance of contact, communication and **competition** as being the defining element determining actual social proximity. When contagion theory is employed in the context of diffusion of innovation, it refers to a condition in which actors who are similar or identical in social structural positions use one another to manage the uncertainty of innovation. The transfer of a behavior from one actor to another is known as contagion. In this case innovation is facilitated by proximity within a social structure.

Some prominent work by Coleman, Katz, and Menzel based on contagion theory examined the diffusion of technological innovation among medical professionals. Other accounts of contagion have been offered in studies of social networks and in the fields epidemiology and anthropology. Early work on contagion theory in **sociology** explored what was known as ''hysterical contagion'' whereby a physiological reaction by a single victim to some agent would be repeated by others. As the behavior spread, the initial theory

identifying the cause of the reaction would break down until all possibilities were exhausted and the contagion had run its course of ''victims''. Thus contagious behavior was understood to be an attention-gaining device, yet there was some disagreement on whether the motives were generally conscious or unconscious. **Stress** was also understood to be a contributing factor in the adoption of the physiological reaction. The **panic** is similar to hysterical contagion, and both are usually characterized by a breakdown of the rational process. Contagion is believed to allow attractive possibilities for action in response to strain that were previously unavailable because of social constraints.

CONTENT ANALYSIS

Content analysis allows a researcher to reveal the content, that is, the messages and meanings, in different modes of **communication**, such as magazines, books, newspapers, videos, speeches, websites, movies, and poems. This type of research is unobtrusive given that the researcher is studying existing media and is not working with live subjects. Large amounts of information can be examined, allowing the analysis to span extensive time periods. The researcher quantifies content analysis by coding all of the information. A recent sociological example of content analysis *By Invitation Only,* conducted by David Croteau and William Hoynes (1994), investigated class, **race**, gender patterns, and political affiliations of guests who appeared on the television show *Nightline* over a 40-month period. The authors dissected transcripts of the show and concluded that *Nightline* was dominated by people from certain social groups. Although controversial, this study brought the utility of content analysis into the spotlight.

In beginning a content analysis, the researcher must decide on the research questions and the key variables of the study. For example, he or she may be interested in finding out how much violence children are exposed to in particular leisure activities. The researcher must then decide the medium to be examined, for example, the three mostly widely read children's comic books. Then the time period of study and the number of comics must be decided upon. The researcher may decide to examine a number of pages from three biweekly comics over a two-year period. Assuming the comics all had ten pages, this would yield a sampling frame of 720 pages. At this point the researcher can identify the units of analysis or the individual units to be analyzed. In this example, pages of a comic book would be the units of analysis. If a study were examining **family** income, families would be the units of analysis. Once a sampling frame is established, the researcher can then procure a sample. **Probability** sampling can easily be used in content analysis: simple random sampling, systematic sampling, stratified random sample and cluster sampling are all sampling methods than can be employed.

The most important part of content analysis is developing the coding schema. The first step in this process is to operationalize the variables and determine the attributes of each **variable**. For example, the attributes of violence for the above example may be pictures and dialogue of hitting, punching, biting, threats, and the presence of weapons. The researcher searches for attributes of each variable in the chosen pages and codes them accordingly. There are two types of coding. The first is *manifest coding* which is the coding of information that is actually visible. For example, the researcher decides to code the number of times characters actually hit or punch each other. The second type of coding is *latent coding* which involves a subjective interpretation of the underlying meaning in a medium. For example, the conversations between characters in a comic may suggest violence. Violence cannot actually be observed, but it is insinuated. Another example might be whether a newspaper takes a supportive stance toward a particular politician. Again, the paper's position is not likely to be spelled out but can be ascertained by reading between the lines.

To aid recording of **data** in content analysis, the researcher develops a recording sheet that is essentially a table containing all the specified attributes of variables. The researcher can then write in checks and frequencies. All coding schema should be pretested to ensure they will adequately address the research questions.

Manifest coding has the advantage of being high in **reliability**, as the next researcher will count the same frequency of violent depictions, but may be lacking **validity**. Latent coding, on the other hand, may increase validity because the researcher can be more flexible with operationalizing variables so that the **measurement** of variables is more accurate. However, because interpretation is subjective, one researcher may interpret a statement as an indicator or violence, while another researcher may not. Thus, reliability is compromised. To keep the loss of reliability and validity to a minimum, Earl Babbie (1992) suggested using both types of coding wherever possible. Overall, content analysis, like many other forms of secondary analysis, may fall short on validity simply because the existing information may not meet the research questions exactly.

The main advantages of content analysis are that it is cost effective, quick, and a large amount of information can be examined. The researcher does not have to spend exorbitant amounts of time interviewing or observing subjects. Further, content analysis is an effective way to study historical social processes. Social issues can be traced through time with relative ease. The main disadvantage of content analysis is its validity and reliability limitations.

CONTENT VALIDITY

Content **validity** is one of several types of validity that assess the accuracy of a **measurement** instrument. Specifically, content validity assesses the elements of the measurement instrument to make sure that the items included are relevant, comprehensive, and representative.

The content that comprises a measurement instrument must relate to the variable(s) specified by the researcher. For the instrument to have content validity, each item contained in the instrument must specifically measure its intended conceptualized **variable**. Content validity is threatened when a measurement indicator actually assesses something other than the variable in question, even if it is closely associated with that variable. For example, an instrument attempting to measure the variable **alienation** might include indicators that more rightfully assess frustration or depression. The inclusion of these factors as indicators of alienation would weaken content validity.

While measurement items that do not assess the intended variable must be modified or deleted, other measurement items may need to be added. Maximizing content validity requires that a measurement instrument include all facets of the variable identified by the researcher. For example, a measurement instrument designed to assess mathematical ability must include items measuring abilities in geometry and algebra, as well as arithmetic. An instrument claiming to measure mathematical ability that only included items assessing ability in arithmetic would lack content validity.

Though measurement items should be comprehensive to maximize content validity, it is rarely possible to include an exhaustive list. Therefore, it is important that the items included in a measurement instrument be representative of the various identified facets of the variable. All of the various dimensions of a variable should be assessed to ensure content validity. However, content validity also requires that these dimensions be equally represented by the items included on the measurement instrument. Referring to the example used above, an instrument assessing mathematical ability should include indicators that assess abilities in geometry, algebra, and arithmetic and indicators for these dimensions that proportionately reflect their relative importance in mathematical ability.

The most cursory assessment of content validity is **face validity**. Face validity is assessed and confirmed by the researcher and through the use of non-specialists who review the instrument to make sure the instrument addresses the variable in question. Face validity can identify problems with content validity but is not sufficient to assure content validity. To assure that the selected items of a measurement instrument comprehensively and representatively assess the range of meaning for each variable, researchers often use the consensus of a panel of acknowledged experts. Because research often measures concepts that do not have a universally agreed upon definition, soliciting a variety of knowledgeable perspectives and opinions is the best way to achieve high content validity.

CONTEST AND SPONSORED MOBILITY

Social mobility research examines the class or **status** position of people relative to that of their parents. Individuals are said to be upwardly mobile if they achieve a higher social status than their parents and downwardly mobile if they end up in a lower social status. One topic of mobility research is the social mechanisms through which individuals achieve their final social status, and a distinction is often made between contest mobility and sponsored mobility. A system of contest mobility is one where individuals begin on relatively equal grounds and rise to the top (or sink to the bottom) of the status hierarchy through their own achievements. Such a social system resembles a relatively equal "contest" where outcomes are determined solely by effort and individual attributes such as **intelligence**. In principle, most modern industrial societies promote this type of social system. In contrast, a system of sponsored mobility is one where individuals are placed in certain positions based on their social background or perceived individual characteristics and from which they are relatively more or less likely to advance. Social status is thus at least partially attributable, if not entirely so, to initial placement and not to individual performance. In this type of social system elite status is more like a social club, in which new members are selected, or "sponsored," by current ones. This type of social system will lead to less overall inter-generational mobility than a system of contest mobility.

This distinction is commonly applied in research regarding the educational system. In many countries those students who are identified as more promising or who come from privileged backgrounds are placed in rigorous educational programs with greater opportunity for advancement, while others are placed in simpler, more basic instructional education or vocational programs. The result of such sponsored mobility is that the final level of education achieved by students is due not only to how hard they work or how smart they are but also to which track they were placed in when they began their education. In contrast, countries with systems of contest mobility place all students in similar educational settings at the beginning of their schooling and only later assign them to lower or higher tracks based on their performance in these earlier years. In practice most modern educational systems combine elements of contest and sponsored mobility.

See also Social Mobility

CONTROL GROUP

In a classic experimental design, subjects are divided into two groups, a control group and an **experimental group**. These two groups are necessary in order to determine what effects on the **dependent variable** are due explicitly to the **independent variable** and what effects are due merely to spontaneous happenings that cannot be controlled by the researcher(s). The purpose of the control group is to serve as the baseline for all measurements. Since many other factors, in addition to the experimental stimulus, may affect subjects in an experimental group, the only way to take these possible changes into account is to have an identical group for comparison. The control group and the experimental group are assumed to be identical along all dimensions that could be relevant to the research.

If an experiment is being conducted on the effect of watching pornography on perceptions of women's equality, it might be important that the groups are similar in terms of number of males versus females. It might also be important for the groups to be similar in terms of average level of education, social class, religion, and previous exposure to pornography. The

control group is the group of subjects who are not exposed to the experimental stimulus, the independent **variable**, in this case pornographic images. For this reason, the control group is considered the comparison group. After being exposed to the experimental stimulus, the subjects in the experimental group are compared to the subjects in the control group. Any differences between the two groups become attributed to the experimental stimulus. Without the control group, experimenters could not be certain of the relationships among variables in the study.

CONVERGENCE

Convergence theory argues societies develop in such a manner that leads to common and uniform political, social, and cultural changes so that societal differences decrease over time. The notion that generally similar conditions appear in numerous, otherwise distinct, societies was advocated by such influential eighteenth- and nineteenth-century thinkers as de Tocqueville, Tönnies, Marx, Spencer, Weber, and Durkheim. Since the **Industrial Revolution**, convergence theories have consistently linked economic development with social structure. According to this specific application of convergence theory, the process of industrialization requires certain social characteristics to function properly. Accordingly, as societies become industrialized, they necessarily take on similar forms and functions.

According to Tony J. Watson in *Sociology, Work and Industry* (1995), associated with the twentieth-century **concept** of industrial society "is the idea that industrial growth creates certain problems for any society and that there is only a limited range of alternative ways in which any **society** can respond to those problems. Any society which is industrializing is thus bound to conform more or less to a certain pattern as it follows the imperatives and indeed the logic of industrialism." The general pattern prescribed by industrialization includes an increased social and technical division of labor; an extension of distance between the home and the workplace; the creation of a mobile, urban workforce; and the institution of a rational, systematic organization of economic matters.

During the 1950s and 1960s, widespread optimism regarding the potential for industrialized societies dominated American social thought. As a result, convergence theory became closely tied to theories of modernization. Namely, convergence theorists suggested that developing countries would progress toward industrial development on the same path followed by Western nations. In *Stages of Development* (1960) Walt Rostow offered a classic theory of modernization, proposing that all nations will pass through specific stages of development on the way to modernization. Clark Kerr offered a thesis of the "logic of industrialism" in his book *Industrialism and Industrial Man* (1960) as an alternative to the Marxist perspective on industrial society. Detailing the numerous common characteristics that emerge within industrial societies, Kerr suggested that these similar traits will appear regardless of differing political systems.

During the 1970s, convergence theory came under sharp attack. Numerous critiques emerged that questioned the **validi-**

ty of using convergence as an approach to social research. First, convergence theory was criticized as being deterministic and ethnocentric in its assumption that the Western model of civilization was superior to all other social structures. Second, there is uncertainty in the necessary form that industrialization must take. Must all components be present or can there be variations within a basic structure of industrialization? Third, convergence theorists link **social change** with technological advancement, making the former completely dependent on the latter, a suggestion that many sociologists found difficult to justify. Fourth, some argue that convergence theory is based more on **capitalism** than on industrialization, thereby skewing the perspective. Fifth, popular during the optimism of the 1960s, convergence theory lost some of its strength in light of the emergence of industrial decline, **unemployment**, and inflation. Finally, convergence theorists do not adequately account for a world economy in which some less-developed countries are structurally dependent on wealthier nations.

By the end of the 1970s few sociologists claimed to support an unmodified version of industrial convergence analysis. In *World Modernization: The Limits of Convergence* (1979), Wilbert E. Moore wrote, "Exaggeration of the commonalities among premodernized societies and neglect of the different historical paths to the present among societies that have been subject to varying external influences and local initiatives would be partially forgivable under two assumptions: (1) that all are headed for the same destination despite different starting-points and intermediate routs; and (2) that success is assured despite various obstacles such as meager resources, ethnic diversity and conflict, inept political organization, or a condition of 'neo-colonial dependency' imposed by powerful and prosperous countries." He continued to assess the assumptions underlying traditional **modernization theory** as naively suggesting that a "teleological orientation toward a more advanced 'stage' somehow inheres in all social systems but without conscious direction or decision." Even Kerr stepped back from his previously staunch support of convergence theory in the publication of *Industrialism and Industrial Man Reconsidered* (1975), defending his original writing, "But the term, pluralistic industrialism, as we conceived it, suggested also that there will never be total convergence because of the clash between 'uniformities' growing out of the local of industrialism and the 'diversities' springing from political, social, and cultural differences."

Like many trends in social theory, the traditional convergence approach was enthusiastically pursued for a certain time before losing popularity in the face of mounting critical assessment, finally being mostly ignored. Although this has been the fundamental case with convergence theory, there have been attempts to revive the approach, albeit on a less grandiose scale, within the last several decades. Alex Inkeles' work during the 1980s represents the most comprehensive reformulation of convergence theory. Suggesting in *Convergence and Divergence in Industrial Societies* (1981) that traditional convergence theories failed to adequately account for the varying components of social systems, Inkeles proposed five social elements that must be considered in order to

explain convergence: modes of production and use of resources, institutional forms and types, structures of social relationships, systems of popular **values** and beliefs, and types of political and economic control.

Picking up on Inkeles' reformation, other social scientists have used the model to address numerous social systems and structures in which convergence appears to take place. Along with a continued interest in industrial and workplace similarities, convergence theory has also been used in recent sociological research to study social theories such as demographic transitions, family patterns, education, and the emergence of the **welfare state**. Because all macrosociological perspectives address large structures and commonly use comparative analysis, it is not surprising that some form of convergence theory remains as an analytical framework for social formation.

COOLEY, CHARLES HORTON (1864-1929)
American psychologist, sociologist, and educator

The American social psychologist, sociologist, and educator Charles Horton Cooley (1864–1929) showed that personality emerges from social influences and that the individual and the **group** are complementary aspects of human association.

Charles Horton Cooley was born in Ann Arbor, Michigan, on August 17, 1864, the son of a well-known jurist, Thomas M. Cooley. After graduating from the University of Michigan (1887), Charles studied mechanical engineering and then economics. In 1889 he entered government work, first with the Civil Service Commission and then with the Census Bureau. He taught political science and economics (1892–1904) and then sociology (1904–1929) at the University of Michigan.

Cooley's first major work *The Theory of Transportation* (1894) was in economic theory. This book was notable for its conclusion that towns and **cities** tend to be located at the confluence of transportation routes—the so-called break in transportation. Cooley soon shifted to broader analyses of the interplay of individual and social processes. In *Human Nature and the Social Order* (1902) he foreshadowed George Herbert Mead's discussion of the symbolic ground of the self by detailing the way in which social responses affect the emergence of normal social participation. Cooley greatly extended this conception of the "looking-glass self" in his next book *Social Organization* (1909), in which he sketched a comprehensive approach to **society** and its major processes.

The first sixty pages of *Social Organization* were a sociological antidote to **Sigmund Freud**. In that much-quoted segment Cooley formulated the crucial role of primary groups (**family**, play groups, and so on) as the source of one's morals, sentiments, and ideals. But the impact of the **primary group** is so great that individuals cling to primary ideals in more complex associations and even create new primary groupings within formal organizations. Cooley viewed society as a constant experiment in enlarging social experience and in coordinating variety. He therefore analyzed the operation of such complex social forms as formal institutions and social class systems and the subtle controls of **public opinion**. He concluded that class differences reflect different contributions to society, as well as the phenomena of aggrandizement and exploitation.

Cooley's last major work *Social Process* (1918) emphasized the nonrational, tentative nature of social organization and the significance of social **competition**. He interpreted modern difficulties as the clash of primary group **values** (**love**, ambition, loyalty) and institutional values (impersonal ideologies such as **progress** or Protestantism). As societies try to cope with their difficulties, they adjust these two kinds of values to one another as best they can.

COOPER, ANNA JULIA (1858-)
American educator and writer

When Anna Julia Cooper died at the age of 105 in 1964, she left behind accomplishments remarkable for anyone, let alone a woman of color at a time when social taboos, laws, and even attitudes of fellow African American activists were obstacles to achievement. Cooper declared herself ''the voice of the South,'' speaking for black women, recently freed from legalized slavery when her best-known book was published in 1892. Scholars consider *A Voice from the South by a Black Woman of the South* the first work by an African-American feminist.

Most sources cite Cooper's birth year as August 10, 1858. Her mother, Hannah Stanley Haywood, was a slave; Cooper's father was probably her mother's owner, George Washington Haywood. Cooper was six or seven when the Civil War ended. She attended St. Augustine's Normal School and Collegiate Institute, created by Episcopal funds to provide education for newly freed blacks.

By the age of eight, Cooper showed such academic proficiency that she was made a pupil-teacher. She also helped her mother learn to read. But in her journals, Cooper detailed the struggles she encountered when she became interested in mathematics and sciences, subjects considered suitable only for male minds. Cooper graduated to the teacher level at St. Augustine's and converted to the Episcopal denomination under which it was run. In 1877, she married George C. Cooper, a candidate for the ministry at the school and former slave. She gave up her teaching career, since married women were barred from the profession, but her husband died just two years later and she never remarried.

In 1881, Cooper, who knew Greek, Latin, and higher math, was admitted to Oberlin College, one of the first co-educational and integrated secondary educational facilities in the United States. She received her B.A. degree in 1884 and M.A. in mathematics in 1888. Then she taught at Wilberforce University. In 1889, she was began teaching Latin and math at Washington High School in the nation's capitol (later renamed the M Street High School and then Dunbar High School).

For the next forty years, Copper taught at the school. Washington High prepared students for a college education and offered some business courses as well, but during the 1890s a racist sentiment developed that African Americans should restrict themselves to vocational education or the trades, and not pursue college degrees. Booker T. Washington, founder of Alabama's Tuskegee Institute, espoused the view that blacks should first build economic independence, then agitate for equality. Cooper argued that gifted African Americans should be given equal access to higher learning.

In her *A Voice from the South by a Black Woman of the South*, first published in 1892, Cooper wrote about intellectual abilities and the benefit of holding a degree. She was an ardent champion of education for African American women. Elsewhere Cooper wrote that ''the race is young and full of elasticity and hopefulness... its achievements are before it.''

Feminist and African American historians have deemed *A Voice from the South* the wellspring of modern black feminist thought. Even legislated equal rights for white women in America were still nothing but a hope at the time of its publication, and the idea that African American women should and could demand to be heard and their concerns be addressed was revolutionary.

Cooper spoke before the World's Congress of Representative Women in Chicago in 1893, touching on these topics before a largely white audience. She spoke of the African American women she met over the years who had sacrificed in order that their children could obtain an education and cited progress in school openings and in literacy rate increases since 1865. Cooper declared, ''I speak for the colored women of the South,'' (the title of her speech).

In 1901, Cooper became principal of M Street High School, the second woman in the District's public school system to reach this post. Yet an education bill in Congress presented a special curriculum for African American schools, and the efforts of Cooper and other educators eventually buried it. At M Street, she instituted a rigorous curriculum and saw success when some students won admittance to Ivy League schools like Harvard, and formed a scholarship fund to aid college-bound students. The local school board was particularly set against Cooper and her lofty goals for students; they tried to curtail her activities and when she disobeyed their injunctions, they fired her in 1906. Her biographer, Leona Gabel, wrote there was ''pressure from Tuskegee to drop her.''

Cooper was rehired in 1910 as a teacher. During the interim she took a teaching post in Missouri and spent time at Oberlin pursuing a doctorate degree. She studied French history and literature and from 1911 to 1914 spent summers in Paris at the Guilde Internationale. In 1914 at 56, she gained admittance to Columbia University in hopes of earning a Ph.D. there, and spent three years working part-time toward it; she continued to teach at M Street, give lectures, and write, and even more remarkably, she was a foster parent to five children of a relative. Her thesis on an eleventh-century epic of French history was published in France in 1925. She was admitted to the Sorbonne and completed her doctoral work by correspondence. Her dissertation, also published in France in 1925, explores democratic ideals that shaped the French Revolution of 1789 and the new Republic's hypocritical policies toward its slave colony in Haiti. At 65 Cooper finally received her doctorate from the Sorbonne, conferred in a special ceremony at Howard University.

Retired from teaching around 1929 or 1930 and in her seventies, Cooper became president of the Frelingshuysen Group of Schools for Employed Colored Persons, a privately funded institution for adult-education opportunities that existed until 1961. At times classes were even held in her home on T Street. She retired from Frelingshuysen in 1942 but continued to write on slavery, education, and other topics. She also wrote a 1951 work on the family of a friend of hers, *The Grimke Family*.

Born a slave, Cooper lived until the dawn of the Civil Rights Movement. She died a year after the Reverend Martin Luther King, Jr.'s famous march on the capitol. Her papers are collected at the Moorland-Spingarn Research Center of Howard University. Cooper was the subject of *The Voice of Anna Julia Cooper*, published in 1998.

COOPER, ANTHONY ASHLEY (1671-1713)

English philosopher

The moral philosopher Anthony Ashley Cooper, Third Earl of Shaftesbury (1671–1713), made his chief contributions in the fields of moral philosophy and esthetics. On February 26, 1671, Anthony Ashley Cooper was born in London. His grandfather gave the responsibility for the boy's education to John Locke. Locke hired a tutor, Mrs. Elizabeth Birch, for young Anthony, and her efforts met with such success that before his twelfth birthday he could easily read both Latin and Greek. Following the death of his grandfather in 1683, his parents enrolled him in Winchester College. Here, however, he was insulted and abused, perhaps because of his grandfather's activities as a Whig. After three years at Winchester, he persuaded his father to allow him to travel abroad. Together with two friends and tutors he spent three years on the Continent (1686–1689) before returning to England.

Cooper's health was poor, and the climate of London served to aggravate his asthma. In 1689 he was offered a seat in Parliament, but he did not accept at this time because of his desire to devote himself exclusively to his studies. In 1695 he was elected to Parliament as a Whig. As a member, he argued relentlessly for liberty and for the legal rights of the accused. His poor health forced him to resign his seat in 1698, and he then spent several months in Holland. After the death of his father in 1699, he assumed the title and the responsibilities of the Third Earl of Shaftesbury. King William II offered him the post of secretary of state, but Shaftesbury declined the offer because of his health. The only official position he held was that of vice admiral of Dorsetshire. Shaftesbury married Jane Ewer, whom he hardly knew, in 1709. They had one son, who became the Fourth Earl of Shaftesbury.

Shaftesbury devoted his life almost exclusively to his studies and to his writing after Queen Anne assumed the throne in 1702. Although his health was poor, Shaftesbury was diligent about his studies. Shaftesbury's writings were, for the most part, occasional pieces rather than systematic treatises. His essays include "An Inquiry Concerning Virtue or Merit" (1699), "A Letter Concerning Enthusiasm" (1708), "Sensus Communis, an Essay on the Freedom of Wit and Humour" (1709), "The Moralists, a Philosophical Rhapsody" (1709), and "Soliloquy, or Advice to an Author" (1710). These essays were republished in a three-volume collection as *Characteristics of Men, Manners, Opinions, Times* (1711). For this collection Shaftesbury wrote an introduction entitled "Miscellaneous Reflections on the Preceding Treatises." Seeking a more congenial climate, Shaftesbury left England in 1711. He finally settled in Naples, Italy, where he died on February 4, 1713.

In his moral philosophy Shaftesbury asserted that men by nature are not inherently selfish and can, even without the aid of religion, lead virtuous lives. He found true **morality** in a balance between egoism and **altruism**. This balance becomes possible because a harmony exists between **society** and the individual that makes the general welfare identical with individual well-being. Man is innately equipped with spontaneous instincts to develop and promote this harmony.

CORPORATE ORGANIZATIONS

Also called *corporations,* corporate organizations are units in which offices or individuals have distinct and interdependent functions and responsibilities. Generally, a central office that has the authority to issue orders organizes and directs the lower-level offices. Unlike organizations where assets are owned by a specific person, a corporate organization is owned collectively. The corporation, as a body, is distinct in three ways: it has legal rights and privileges, such as the right to sue, make contracts and purchase and receive **property**; the corporation exists in perpetuity; and finally, the responsibility of the owners of the corporation is limited.

A corporate **organization** is a social invention, formed to answer the needs of various communities. Most commonly present in business and other economic institutions, but also appears in religious institutions and political parties. The corporate organization has its roots in medieval times, when problems arose concerning **church** land and property ownership. Issues of ownership are equally important today. Many corporate organizations are held jointly by stockholders, who own the tangible property of the organization and have a say in the organization's legal practices. This ownership does not necessarily imply extensive control.

Sociologists study the control and **authority** within corporations. Researchers of control often focus on three main areas: the control of employees, the allocation of control between managers and owners, and **social control** of corporations. **Max Weber** explained corporate organizations in relation to questions of authority, rather than ownership. Weber considered corporate groups as defined by the different roles that individuals play within each **group**. Each **role** within a corporate group is distinguished by its authority or its requirement to submit to others' **rules**.

The corporate organization has become an integral part of society and a characteristic of the U.S. economic system *(Corbis Corporation [Bellevue])*.

Control of employees shifted drastically with the Industrial Revolution, when employees ceased to work for an individual and were supervised by an overseers. A move to **bureaucracy** and professional management by the end of the 1920s reduced the importance of the artisan or craftsman within an organization. Workers did less skilled work, and the pace was controlled by the machines producing the product or by the managers. While a bureaucratic structure often seems to improve efficiency, adopting bureaucracy can also be seen as a political move in which owners, seeking to eliminate risk and uncertainty, take control and eliminate worker **influence**. In spite of their lack of control, workers often find ways to serve their own needs in any position.

Contemporary research on managerial control shows it to be more dispersed than one might think. Some sociologists suggest that the corporation's managers hold more power than the widely dispersed control of the stockholders and the concentrated power of the owner while other studies have shown both that managers have little power and that much of a corporation's power resides in a smaller tier of the corporation's managers and board, with interests that go beyond the boundaries of the corporation and even the industry.

Because they are so prevalent, corporate organizations have caused problems and conflict. They have been the focus of unethical risk-taking and, occasionally, of **crime**. Because corporation resources are often greater than those of any indi-

vidual, corporate organizations may sometimes work outside the law. Corporate organizations are encouraged to consider themselves responsible to the public and, therefore, to seek ways to promote the common good, such as raising funds for **community** programs, promoting volunteerism among employees, or encouraging donations to public causes. But the interests and **norms** of organizations are diverse, and tremendous difference exists between corporate **values** public responsibility.

Through the 1980s corporate organizations became large, bureaucratic systems. Then, in the 1990s, many large corporate organizations began to contract. Corporations grow and then shrink, depending on societal changes such as availability of resources and large-scale changes in the fabric of society (population ecology). In spite of this flux, the corporate organization has become an integral part of **society** and a characteristic of the American economic system.

CORRELATION

Correlation statistics are summary statistics that describe the way two or more variables are related. This information is particularly useful in the social sciences as researchers frequently need to know how one variable may affect another; for example, knowing how alcohol abuse and domestic violence affect each other can influence treatment approaches to domestic offenders. In this example, we would expect an increase in alcohol abuse to be associated with an increase in domestic violence. The correlation statistic summarizing the relationship between these variables would, therefore, be positive; when one **variable** increases, so does the other. A negative correlation occurs when an increase in one variable is associated with a decrease in the other. For example, an increase in education may lead to a decrease in domestic violence.

Establishing a correlation between two variables confirms that there is a mathematical association between them and is the first element required to prove **causality**. Finding a correlation does not mean that the researcher can conclude *X* causes *Y*, or alcohol abuse causes domestic violence. This mistake is often made. In addition to an association, several other steps are involved in proving causality. First, there must be temporal priority: one variable must come before the other in time. Second, spurious or alternative variables must be accounted for. In the above example, income, occupation, and education may all be possible spurious variables affecting levels of domestic violence. Accounting for spurious variables is usually the most difficult step in determining casualty. George Bohrnstedt and David Knoke (1994) cited the classic Dutch study where the number of children was statistically associated with the number of storks nesting in chimneys. The comical assumption that storks nesting cause children to be born could be drawn in error if a researcher was to use correlation as the sole basis for determining causality.

The most commonly used correlation statistics are Pearson's product moment correlation (*Pearson's r*) and Spearman's rank-order correlation (*Spearman's rho*). Pearson's r is used when the **data** are measured at the interval or scale level. The data must also be normally distributed, and a linear relationship should exist between the variables considered. Pearson's r is a coefficient that ranges from -1 to +1. A coefficient of one indicates a perfect association and is likely to be found only when a variable is correlated with itself, or when two variables are so closely related they may be measuring the same thing. Interpreting a correlation coefficient involves commenting on the direction of the association—whether it is positive or negative—and describing the strength of the association (weak, moderate and strong). In the social sciences, a weak correlation is usually indicated by a value of less than 0.3, a moderate correlation is between 0.4 and 0.6, and a strong correlation is a value of 0.7 or greater. Interpretation can also include a discussion of **statistical significance**.

Strong correlations must be closely examined so that the nature of the relationship between the variables can be correctly ascertained. For example, the variables delinquency and delinquent dispositions may be highly correlated with each other. Delinquency may be measured as a frequency of the number of delinquent acts a person has committed, while delinquent dispositions may be measured as a scale indicating whether a person views certain delinquent acts as bad or not. Given the way the two variables are measured, both variables may really be measuring delinquency. Those people who do not view delinquent acts as bad are far more likely to have committed them than those who do view delinquent acts as bad.

Spearman's rho is calculated when one variable is measured at the ordinal level and the other(s) is measured at least at the ordinal level. It may also be used when the sample size is small. The statistic is interpreted in the same way as Pearson's r. *Kendall's tau* and *Goodman and Kruskal's gamma* can be used in place of Spearman's. Both of these nonparametric measures of association are interpreted in the same way as Pearson's r.

The coefficient of determination is easily calculated from correlation coefficients by taking the square of the coefficient. Thus a Pearson's r value of 0.6 yields a coefficient of determination of 0.36 indicating that 36 percent of the variance of the **dependent variable** is explained by its association with the **independent variable**. This amount also indicates that 64 percent of the variance in the dependent variable is not explained by its association with the independent variable leaving the researcher to ponder which important independent variables have been left out of the equation.

Correlation coefficients are also used as indicators of reliability. For example, Pearson's r can be used to estimate test-retest reliability and inter-rater **reliability**. Correlations also form the basis for estimation in **regression** analysis. Among more advanced types of correlation are multiple correlation, partial correlation, and **path analysis**.

COSER, LEWIS ALFRED (1913-)
American sociologist

Born into a Jewish bourgeois family on November 27, 1913, in Berlin, Germany, Lewis Coser soon rebelled against the upper-middle-class life provided to him by his parents, Martin (a banker) and Margarete (Fehlow) Coser. As a teenager, he joined the socialist movement, and although he was not an exceptional student and disliked school, he read voluminously on his own. When Hitler came to power in Germany, Coser fled to Paris, where he worked odd jobs to sustain a meager existence. He became active in the socialist movement, joining several radical groups, including a Trotskyist organization called "The Spark." In 1936, he was finally able to secure better employment, becoming a statistician for an American brokerage firm. He also enrolled at the Sorbonne as a student of comparative literature but later changed his focus to sociology.

Coser's studies were interrupted by World War II as he was detained by the French police and sent to a concentration camp. Upon his release, he managed to obtain one of the last American entry visas issued to Germany refugees before the war began, and in 1941, he boarded a ship headed for New York City. Upon his arrival, he was employed in numerous jobs, including government agencies associated with the war effort. At the same time, he began publishing articles in journals, such as *Partisan Review, Politics,* and *The Nation.* He wrote for numerous left-wing publications using the pen names Louis Clair for Socialist Party articles and Europicus for Workers' Party submissions. In 1942, he married Rose Laub; they had two children, Ellen and Steven.

In 1948, after a brief period as a graduate student at Columbia University, Coser accepted a teaching position at the University of Chicago as an instructor of social science. In the same year, he became a naturalized U. S. citizen. In 1950, he returned to Columbia University once again to pursue his studies, earning his doctorate in 1954. He was hired by Brandeis University in Waltham, Massachusetts, in 1951, first as a lecturer and later as a professor of sociology. He remained at Brandeis, which was considered a haven for liberals, until 1968.

Published in 1956, Coser's first book *The Functions of Social Conflict* was an outgrowth of his doctoral dissertation. The book reflects Coser's eclectic approach to sociology. He adhered closely, but not completely, to several sociological approaches. He was drawn to functional analysis and deeply influenced by Parsons' *The Structure of Social Action,* but he found it lacked an adequate accounting of social conflict. Thus *The Functions of Social Conflict* was Coser's attempt to apply two dissimilar schools of thought to sociological study, as he stated in the conclusion to Chapter 9: "Whether social conflict is beneficial to internal **adaptation** or not depends on the type of issues over which it is fought as well as on the type of social **structure** within which it occurs."

Although he tried to remain value-neutral in his sociological studies and writings, Coser did not hesitate to write critically about the political and moral state of **society**. As a reaction to the intolerance of McCarthyism in the 1950s, he and friend Irving Howe created the radical anti-establishment journal *Dissent,* which remains in publication. He wrote in his autobiographical contribution to *Sociological Lives* (1988): "Throughout all these years, I have cultivated a kind of dual vision, a dual set of premises of pure sociological analysis and impure social and moral partisanship. It has not always been easy to maintain such a dual vision, and critics may well have been right when they have attempted to show that too often I have strayed into confounding those two realms.... In any case, I have never been uncomfortable with being, to use the terminology of Chairman Mao, both pink and expert.''

After almost twenty years at Brandeis, Coser became a distinguished professor of sociology at the State University of New York at Stony Brook (SUNY) in 1969, where he remained until 1987. In 1987 he was awarded the position of Distinguished Professor Emeritus of Sociology at SUNY and became an adjunct professor of sociology at Boston College. During this time, he continued to publish books, including *The American Communist Party: A Critical History* (1957), *Men of Ideas* (1965), *Sociology Through Literature* (1972), *Greedy Institutions* (1974), *Refugee Scholars in America* (1984), and *A Handful of Thistles* (1988). He has also been associated with numerous other publications as either an editor or contributor.

COUNTERCULTURE

A number of subcultures have belief systems that run counter to, or opposite mainstream social beliefs. These subcultures are known as countercultures. The term, ''counterculture,'' appeared in the 1960s as a response to the numerous alternative groups, such as the hippy movement, radical student groups, and civil rights activists. However, the notion of countercultures as groups who are at odds with dominant social views has existed for centuries as many religious groups, even Christians, were initially thought of as countercultures. Unlike subcultures whose value systems may be different from the dominant culture, but not at odds with them, countercultures are often ''at war'' with greater **society**. Two examples highlight these differences. The Amish set themselves apart from greater society by dress, religion, and lifestyle. While their value system is different, the Amish do not oppose the dominant culture within whose existing social framework they live. Members of the Ku Klux Klan, on the other hand, have **values** and beliefs that do run counter to those of society; for example, their belief in white supremacy runs counter to racial equality. Because countercultures are a division of subcultures, all countercultures are subcultures, but not all subcultures are countercultures.

Members of countercultures may seek to change the existing social structure or they may withdraw from society and immerse themselves in an alternative lifestyle. Some countercultures do both. Theodore Roszak (1969) wrote about both responses using countercultures of the 1960s. Examples of countercultures intent on changing the social **structure** are the Black Panthers, the National Association for the Advancement of Colored People (NAACP), and Vietnam war resistors. Countercultures are not necessarily negative, and the label may be socially constructed. The dominant **culture** may not have moral value systems, but because a smaller **group** practices opposing behavior, that group is labeled a counterculture.

Because some countercultures challenge the existing social structure, members are often viewed by greater society as

The term "counterculture" became prevalent during the 1960s and defined numerous alternative groups, such as the hippie movement, radical student groups, and civil rights activists *(Corbis Corporation [Bellevue])*.

a threat to **social order** and are subjected to **discrimination** and harassment. Members of the Unification Church, better known as the Moonies, led by Korean evangelist Sun Myung Moon, subscribe to exaggerations of philosophies found in the dominant culture, yet the group is still viewed as a threat. The Moonies have a conservative political **ideology**, believe in making large amounts of money and using that money to buy political power and **influence**. They have successfully influenced big business and even established *The Washington Times*, a nationally recognized conservative newspaper. This exaggerated capitalism has led to prominent Unification Church members being prosecuted for tax evasion, and politicians with Moonie affiliations being criticized. Other perceived Moonie practices run counter to those found in the dominant culture: mass weddings of couples who barely know each other, alleged kidnapping of young people, brainwashing, and confining people against their will in Moonie compounds. An example of a counterculture that worked for **social change** and withdrew from society to live an alternative lifestyle were the Branch

Since the time of Aristotle, political thinkers have recognized the need for a separate court system or judicial branch of government (Corbis Corporation [Bellevue]).

Davidians, who lived in Waco, Texas, under the leadership of David Koresh.

A unique countercultural gathering took place in upstate New York in 1968. This festival, near the town of Woodstock, was atypical in that the group of approximately 500,000 was comprised of young people who had withdrawn from society and were living alternative lifestyles, leftist activists who were intent on changing the social order, and inquisitive onlookers. The gathering at Woodstock was repeated in 1999, but with much less of a countercultural influence. There are numerous countercultures found in modern society that range from religious groups and sects, to groups deeply immersed in drug use (for example, so-called crack heads), and youth who follow certain popular music artists (for example, followers of Marilyn Manson).

See also Culture; Subculture

COURT SYSTEMS

Since the time of Aristotle, political thinkers have recognized the need for a separate court system, or judicial branch of **government**. Its major function in any nation, past and present, is to keep domestic **peace**. Beyond that, there is much diversity. In countries with a federal government system, such as the United States, there are generally two distinct classes of courts: those that hear national matters and those that preside over local disputes. France has a unitary form of government and operates under an integrated court system. Great Britain's court system is also generally unified. Iran, a republic under Islamic law, has a supreme court, supreme judicial council, and lower courts. In Japan, as in the United States and many European nations, the judiciary is completely independent of the executive and legislature branches of government.

In the United States, with its federal government and written constitution, the court—or judicial—system functions with 51 separate systems, 50 for the individual states and one for the federal government. They are similar but not identical.

Most judicial work is carried out in the state courts. Basic types of courts in this system are: criminal and civil, general and limited jurisdiction, and trial and appellate. *Criminal* courts handle cases involving those people accused of crimes. These courts decide guilt or innocence and fix sentence or punishment. *Civil* courts deal with so-called private matters, such as between two people or companies disputing the terms of a contract. Rather than punishment, the objective is to provide a remedy to the dispute, as in money damages arising from an automobile accident. Civil court claims do not usually stem from criminal acts. *General jurisdiction* courts handle both criminal and civil suits, a common practice in both the United States and Great Britain. They are also known as *superior* courts. Courts of *limited jurisdiction* are specialized, for example, dealing only with child **crime** or abuse (juvenile courts), settling of estates (probate courts), or motor vehicle disputes (traffic courts). They are sometimes called *inferior* courts because they generally deal with minor matters. All of the above are trial courts, or so-called courts of the first instance. Above these are *appellate* courts, which review the work of the trial courts and correct any errors that may have occurred in the trials.

Federal courts can hear cases based only on federal law, which the U.S. Constitution limits to areas within **authority** of the federal government, such as interstate commerce or foreign relations. The federal system divides the nation into 90-plus areas, each with a U.S. district court hearing both civil and criminal cases. Over these trial courts are 11 U.S. courts of appeal. Each of these courts can hear appeals only from district courts in its territory. They are neither superior nor inferior to state courts but operate on a parallel level.

The apex of the American judicial system is the U.S. Supreme Court, which hears cases from both state and federal courts involving questions that arise under the Constitution or federal statutes and treaties. The Supreme Court operates with one chief justice and eight associate judges. It hears only those appeals deemed to be of major national significance, amounting to about 125 cases a year.

In nations with written constitutions recognizing "judicial supremacy," courts have the power to decide the validity of a law and thereby determine it to be void. The classic example is the U.S. Supreme Court and its decision in *Marbury vs. Madison* (1803), the first case in which the high court declared a congressional act unconstitutional. Secretary of State James Madison, directed by President Thomas Jefferson, refused a congressional commission to William Marbury, who had been appointed by outgoing President John Adams "at the midnight hour," just before leaving office, under a judiciary act passed by Congress. Marbury requested the Court to deliver a "writ of mandamus" forcing Madison to honor the appointment. The Court denied the request, ruling that it lacked jurisdiction in the matter because the congressional act of 1789, which authorized such a writ, was unconstitutional and, therefore, invalid. Said the Court, in conflict between Constitution and congressional law, the Constitution always takes precedence. In American constitutional law, *Marbury vs. Madison* is the classic expression of judicial review. Supreme Court judges, and all federal judges on district and appeals courts, serve for life. They are chosen by the president of the United States with the advice and consent of the Senate.

COURTSHIP

Trends and rules in courtship have mirrored those of American society for the last century. In the twentieth century, dating replaced calling as the primary form of courting. A courting **interaction** between a man and a woman switched from the private interaction within the woman's home to a private interaction between the couple in a public situation. In a calling situation the woman was always in control, but when dating became the primary form of courting, the man gained control due to the financial positions of the sexes at the time.

In the nineteenth century and into the beginning of the twentieth century, the courtship system centered around "calling." Calling was the practice of the man going to the woman's home to sit with her in her family's parlor while the **family**, after the first call, left them alone. The method of calling made the woman the controlling gender. She determined the days that she was available for calling, whom she would ask to call, and when she would return calls.

In the early twentieth century, the practice of calling was replaced by the practice of dating. Dating began in 1910, and by 1924 it had replaced calling as the accepted form of courtship. Until this time, dating was a practice that was primarily done by the rebellious upper-class women and lower-class women who lived in over-crowded homes and had to find other ways to spend time courting with a man. The invention of the automobile in the thirties gave young people a much more private way to spend time together.

Dating at first revolved around a practice referred to as "dating and rating" which meant that a woman's popularity was based on the quality of men whom she dated and how many men she danced with in an evening. This system, in which the man introduced the woman to his friends so that they would ask her to dance, was meant to make the woman feel attractive.

Due to the scarcity of men caused by World War II, the forties and fifties saw a new trend in dating called "going steady." In this system, a woman would go on a date and dance with the same man all evening. Going steady was, in a sense, similar to the dating and rating system because adolescents usually had many steadies before they found the persons whom they would like to marry.

The sixties and seventies brought the "sexual revolution" which changed the rules of dating again. This revolution added other factors to the dating equation: sex and **cohabitation**. With the scientific development of female contraception and the legalization of abortion, sex became a major part of dating, and cohabitation stemmed from that because couples could have sex before **marriage** with much less of a threat of pregnancy or censure. After this revolution, couples did not have to wait until marriage for sex, so people began to wait until later in life to marry and have children.

In the 1980s and 1990s through the early twenty-first century, due to the rise of college-educated women and gen-der-equality within the workplace, young people often do not start to think about marriage until they are out of college and into well-established careers. It is not uncommon for couples to decide not to marry until they are well into their thirties. In this culture, belief in female independence leads many women to aspire to having careers and salaries rather than staying at home and raising a family and thus being financially dependent on their spouses.

COVARIATION

Covariates are independent variables that describe the dependent variable. Covariation occurs when levels of a quantitative **variable** vary across categories defined by both quantitative and qualitative response variables. Special statistical techniques are required to analyze group means that vary in this manner.

A researcher who is interested in the effect of education on height might find that height (quantitative) varies by both age (quantitative) and gender (qualitative)—adults are taller than children and men are taller than women. The partial results that describe height might include several categories of female children, female adults, male children and male adults. In this example, age and gender are covariates. The differences in height among the various categories defined by age and gender is covariation.

Covariation is analyzed using a technique called AN-COVA, or analysis of covariance. This technique enables the researcher to compare group means as if the groups were equal in terms of the variable controlled for. In the example above, the researcher might want to control for the effects of gender and age to examine how height changes in response to education levels. The computational details of ANCOVA are complicated, and this type of regression analysis is best performed using statistical analysis software.

COX, OLIVER CROMWELL (1901-1974)
Carribbean sociologist

Born August 25, 1901, in Trinidad, British West Indies, Oliver Cromwell Cox was the son of William Raphael and Virginia (Austin) Cox. Despite a crippling childhood bout with poliomyelitis, he became one of the most influential African American scholars of the twentieth century. In 1928 he received a Bachelor of Library Science degree from Northwestern University. Continuing his education, he earned his master's and doctorate from the University of Chicago in 1932 and 1938, respectively.

Cox began his teaching career in 1938 as a professor of economics at Wiley College in Marshall, Texas. In 1944 he accepted a position as a professor of sociology at the Tuskegee Institute in Alabama, where he remained for five years. In 1949 he began teaching sociology at Lincoln University in Jefferson City, Missouri, which would remain his academic home until his death in 1974. During his career, he was a member of the American Economic Association, American Sociological Association (fellow), and the Mid-west Sociological Association.

Cox's first, and perhaps most influential, book *Caste, Class, and Race* (1948) earned the George Washington Carver Award for that year. The book's publication had a significant impact on the study of **race** and class for several decades following. Cox first argues that racism is a fundamental and direct product of the rise of **capitalism**, and then he makes the seemingly contradictory suggestion that the advancement of capitalism actually reduces racism. Receiving mixed reviews from other radical scholars, Cox nonetheless set the phenomenon of racism clearly in the context of class consciousness, a concept that dominated racial **discrimination** studies well into the 1970s and early 1980s. Cox continued to focus his writing on the impact of capitalism on race relations, publishing four more major works during his career: *Foundations of Capitalism* (1959), *Capitalism and American Leadership* (1962), *Capitalism as a System* (1964), and *Race Relations: Elements and Social Dynamics* (posthumously, 1976).

Laying out his basic theory of capitalism and racism in *Caste, Class, and Race,* Cox postulates that the exploitation that occurred prior to capitalism was based on cultural, rather than racial, identity. He cites historical examples such as the Hellenic Greeks, who separated themselves from the ''barbarians,'' or those who did not share the Greek **culture** and language. However, the barbarians were encouraged to adopt the Greek culture regardless of racial identity. He also uses the examples of the Roman Empire, in which not race but rather citizenship was the criterion for superiority, and he points to the spread of Roman Catholicism as a means to curb racial prejudice, as the doctrine defined humanity in terms of Christian and non-Christian.

Before capitalism, no rationalized **ideology** existed for the subjugation of one race based on a belief of human inferiority. However, when Spain and Portugal started to colonize the world at the end of the fifteenth century, fueled by a capitalistic spirit of profit-making, there became an explicit need to justify the exploitation of workers (i.e., slavery) so that it could be condoned by **society**. In 1550, Spaniard Gaines de Sepulveda put forth the theory that certain races were innately inferior and, thus, assimilation was not conducive to a healthy society. As this ideology spread, the exploitation of people based on race alone received the justification it needed. Now, according to Cox, the capitalists had a massive workforce at their disposal, and the viable social theory to support their oppressive tactics. Accordingly, the new world of capitalist America was built on this social paradigm that allowed the importation of black slave labor.

Although capitalism in its early stages depended upon racial exploitation, Cox theorizes that as capitalism matures, it actually reduces racial prejudice. He makes this argument based on his Marxist understanding of class struggle as the primary dynamic in human history. Racism is simply one aspect of the relationship between the bourgeois, or capitalists, and the proletariat, or working class. In this paradigm, race relationships are primarily based on issues of labor and profit, not skin color. Therefore, following Marxist philosophy, as capitalism advances and its burden on the working class increases, all workers will unite to gain political and economic power from the bourgeois. As members of the proletariat, workers of differing racial identities will profit from the advances made to create a more democratic workplace. Ultimately Cox argues that although advanced capitalism relieves some racial discrimination, only a true socialist revolution could end it.

CREDENTIALISM

In his term ''social closure,'' **Max Weber** (1864-1920) recognized a system in which certain groups with a common set of interests attempt to realize their interests and maximize their benefits by controlling and restricting access to the resources necessary for these benefits. If a group can restrict others' access to resources and opportunities, then the group can secure a privileged position in the social **structure** relative to that of others. In other words, a group assumes a place of superiority by guaranteeing a place of inferiority for others.

Credentials are key in forming the boundaries at which social closure occurs. It is at the point of these credentials that people attempt to maintain and usurp power. Those with credentials emphasize their legitimacy for creating boundaries between the deserving and non-deserving of privilege and status. Those without credentials are given the burden of acquiring such credentials. Credentialism represents both an **ideology** and a process. The ideology is an understanding that those who hold certain qualifications possess the expertise and attributes necessary for and worthy of social ascent. The process is the conferring of class advantage and social **status** through acquiring academic or professional certification. These academic and professional qualifications are legitimated by a system of power.

This vying for power through acquisition of credentials feeds a constant inflation of credentialism. The more people who achieve a certain credential, the less powerful this credential is for maintaining a boundary and perpetuating social closure. A college degree is much less valuable now that master's degrees, doctorates, and even post-doctorate degrees set people apart. A master's and doctorate will become less valuable as a growing number of people earn them. All the while, those with just a high school diploma are excluded more and more from status and rewards based on academic credentials. Such a system, as with **meritocracy**, assumes **equality of opportunity** in the pursuit of credentials such that only those with expertise succeed and only those without expertise fail. Unfortunately, such an ideology ignores that the very system in which individuals are expected to compete for credentials, formal education in this case, is structured in such a way that systematically reproduces a qualified class on the basis of advantages and disadvantages due to ascribed characteristics rather than achieved characteristics.

CRIME

Crime is defined by **society** and relative to the society defining it. Traditionally, crime is considered an offence, a violation of public rules or laws. Crime is defined within each society by specific criminal laws on the national, state, and local levels. Actions that are offensive to an individual or group of people, but do not violate laws are not crimes. Punishment or other sanctions result from the violation of these laws, and the social system for monitoring and enforcing public **rules** or laws is put into action. The social system generally consists of an administrative authority that formally deals with crime and a force of representative officers to enforce the laws and act on behalf of society. Being guilty of a criminal act usually involves some form of conscious evil intent or recklessness. In unintentional cases, such as crimes committed by children or the insane, the criminal is not usually punished in the same manner as in intentional crime.

In order to be statistically counted, crime must be reported to and recorded by the police, the investigator, or the representative officers. It must be processed through the appropriate administrative system, and it then may become a part of the society's criminal statistics. Criminal statistics, however, are not entirely representative of a society's crime, since some crime is hidden and either unreported or unrecorded. Crime may also be unofficial and, therefore, not be considered crime. For example, industrial pollution breaks rules and laws, but it is not recorded as crime.

Often the definition of crime and its causes are shaped by perceptions of **morality** and responsibility, by social **norms**, and by religious precepts. In the past, crime was often closely related to morality and was, therefore, also connected to religious teaching. However, contemporary **sociology** tends to view crime as relative, not absolute. Émile Durkheim purported that laws changed as social **structure** changed, and historical shifts in social relations could be described and studied by looking at changes in legal code. Durkheim also proposed that, because no known society was free of crime, and because crime served to unite a **community** around its own perception of morality and against the criminal, a certain level of crime was functional within society. Sociologists also link crime to political classes or the vested interests of particular groups, holding that acts are either criminalized or legalized depending on the balance of power between groups. For example, strikes may be seen as criminal or legal, depending on the relative power of the employers and employees and their representatives.

Theories of crime and criminal activity are numerous and varied, but the reasons behind crime remain elusive. Theories suggest many possible causes. The theory of ''routine activities'' suggests that property crime depends on criminal motive and opportunities to perpetrate crime. It also contends that crime is influenced by the degree to which others act as guardians over neighborhoods and other people. This particular theory relates an increase in crime rate to an increase in crime opportunity and a decrease in guardianship. Research also shows that income inequality correlates to property crime as well as to the theory of routine activities.

See also Criminology

CRIME STATISTICS

In the United States, criminologists and criminal **justice** personnel rely on three primary sources of **data**: police reports, victimization surveys, and self-report studies. The most widely used source of police reports data in the United States is the Uniform Crime Report (UCR). The UCR was created in the 1930s to make uniform definitions of crimes, thereby allowing for the comparison of crime rates in different areas. Local **law enforcement** agencies compute and send data to the Federal Bureau of Investigation (FBI), following guidelines set out by the UCR. The UCR separates crimes into two parts. Part I crimes include murder and non-negligent manslaughter, forcible rape, robbery, aggravated assault, burglary, larceny-theft, motor vehicle theft, and arson. Part II crimes include simple assault, forgery and counterfeiting, fraud, embezzlement, vandalism, **prostitution**, **drug abuse** violations, gambling, vagrancy, and several other crimes.

The accuracy of crime statistics as charted by the UCR suffers from a number of limitations. First, the UCR must rely on the arrest patterns of police who use a great deal of discretion in their decisions to arrest. Second, the UCR relies on victims' cooperation. If the victim does not report the crime, the police often have no way of knowing that it occurred. Third, white-collar crimes, computer crimes, and organized crimes do not appear in the records. Fourth, the method of counting crime underestimates the crime rate for many crimes because in situations where numerous crimes are committed simultaneously, only the most severe crime is counted. The final limitation is that the crime rate as shown by the UCR is dramatically affected by administrative and bureaucratic changes within police departments.

The second type of official crime data comes from victimization studies. Typically, victimization studies examine representative samples of citizens in an attempt to discover what crimes people have experienced in a given period. By far the largest and most well-known victimization study is the National Crime Victimization Survey (NCVS) conducted by the Bureau of Justice Statistics. The NCVS was designed to discover more information about the amount of crime that goes unreported, what is known as the ''dark figure'' of crime. The NCVS began in 1972 and has been conducted every year since. The NCVS is based on a representative sample of approximately 45,000 U.S. households. Each member of the sample (approximately 98,000 people age 12 and over) is asked if they were the victim of a rape or sexual assault, robbery, assault, robbery or assault leading to personal injury, personal theft, burglary, household larceny, or motor vehicle theft during the past year.

Although the NCVS has added significantly to our understanding of crime, it, too, is limited in a number of ways. First, it underestimates the actual rate of crime because it relies on the ability of victims to vocalize their victimizations. Many crimes are of little significance to victims and are easily forgotten, or respondents may not feel comfortable telling the interviewer about their victimization because they are embarrassed or still traumatized. Second, the NCVS is limited in the types of crimes about which it inquires. It asks only about specific UCR Part I offenses and does not cover crimes such as commercial burglaries and shoplifting. Finally, it does not include information about offenders.

Self-report **surveys** are the third major source of crime data. Instead of using police records or asking victims of crime about criminal incidents, self-report studies ask offenders themselves about their participation in delinquent and criminal activities. Self-report studies are not official data sources and, therefore, lack a specific set of offenses investigated and design method. Currently, self-report surveys are the dominant method for studying why crime occurs. This method allows researchers to collect detailed information about individual offenders.

While self-report surveys have a number of advantages over official sources of data, they are not without limitations. Similar to victimization studies, respondents may have a difficult time recalling their past actions. Also, the sample sizes of self-report surveys frequently are small. Small sample sizes make it difficult to determine the geographic distribution of crime because they are not large enough to allow for detailed breakdown by geographic areas. A third limitation of self-report studies is that they make it difficult to obtain accurate information on crimes that occur infrequently, such as violent assaults. While all three sources of data have limitations, they all provide valuable sources of information and allow researchers to identify trends in criminal activity over time.

CRIMINAL AND DELINQUENT SUBCULTURES

Criminal and delinquent subcultures are generally assumed to be groups of individuals who do not conform to social **rules** about appropriate conduct. Sociologists recognize that what is defined as criminal and delinquent depends upon the **culture** and social **structure** of the area under study. For example, Rastafarians tend to value and emphasize economic communalism, solidarity within the **group**, and rejection of the economic values of the culture that surrounds it. In addition, Rastafarians adhere to beliefs and visible markers of their **identity**, such as their clothing, hairstyle, and linguistic usages, that set them apart from the larger **society**. Rastafarians are considered deviant and criminal when compared to the larger culture and can, therefore, be sanctioned as deviants and criminals. However, if we examine Rastafarians from another angle, they are very much conformists to another normative system. Thus, criminal and delinquent subcultures are groups of individuals whose behavior runs counter to those of the larger society and are often sanctioned as such. The delinquent or criminal within the **subculture** is a social individual who partakes in activities that are inconsistent with culturally permissible modes of conduct.

Explanations of criminal and delinquent subcultures originated in the Chicago school of **sociology** beginning in the early 1920s with Clifford Shaw and Henry McKay. During the 1920s, social awareness of high rates of urban delinquency, **poverty**, and vice led many groups to attempt social reform through common sense explanations of these events. Many explanations revolved around the moral decay of particular groups, specifically immigrant groups. Social scientists were dissatisfied with this perspective and began their own investigation.

Shaw and McKay began to examine the geographic distribution of delinquent groups within the Chicago area and found that delinquency was highly concentrated in some city areas. Furthermore, Shaw and McKay found connections between the distributions of delinquency and social conditions in those areas. They determined that physical deterioration and population loss, economic segregation, racial/ethnic segregation, and other **social problems** were specific to the zones with high delinquency. Therefore, Shaw and McKay postulated that social disorganization was the primary causal mechanism behind delinquent subcultures. In other words, a low level of **social control** over individuals within a given area was directly related to prevailing high levels of delinquency and crime.

In 1938, following the studies by Shaw and McKay, **Robert K. Merton** introduced a **theory** to explain why criminal and delinquent subcultures exist. According to Merton, culturally defined goals or aspirations are provided by social structure. In addition, culturally prescribed methods for attaining those goals or aspirations also result from the social structure. Merton believed that social groups coupled these desired ends with permissible procedures for attaining them. The delinquent and criminal behavior resulted most often when the culturally prescribed goals were internalized but the culturally prescribed means were not. For Merton, this form of behavior was called innovation. Moreover, Merton argued that American values were more concerned with the goals and successes than with the prescribed methods. The discrepancy between means and ends perpetuated by the class system led to a strain on certain groups of individuals who then took advantage of illegitimate means to acquire culturally defined goals. The heart of Merton's theory is that criminal and delinquent subcultures exist when a discrepancy exists between the culturally prescribed goals and means, leading to nonconformist behaviors labeled delinquent or criminal by the social structure in place.

Other theorists have focused on structural level variables to explain nonconforming behaviors. In 1955, Albert K. Cohen followed the path set by Merton in emphasizing the structural sources of strain that lead to deviance within certain groups. Cohen applied this perspective to a specific delinquent subculture, the lower-class adolescent male. Cohen argued that strain was produced in lower-class groups when an inability to gain **status** and acceptance in conventional society exists. The delinquent subculture is then a reaction to this strain. Richard Cloward and Lloyd Ohlin drew on Cohen's subcultural theory to propose a differential opportunity theory of delinquency designed to account for delinquent subculture activities. Cloward and Ohlin argued that delinquent subcultures existed when illegitimate opportunities were available to members and they were in an environment where the skills and abilities to be deviant could be learned. In sum, criminal and delinquent subcultures are argued to arise in response to environmental challenges, particularly in conditions of subordination or deprivation. Once they exist, the shared values, **norms**, beliefs, and use of material culture are passed on through a learning process.

CRIMINAL SANCTIONS

Across human history societies develop **rules** differentiating appropriate from inappropriate behavior. When these rules become institutionalized in formal law they are called criminal statutes. These laws specify which behaviors are inappropriate and designate the consequences that should follow. Consequences involving some form of punishment are called criminal sanctions. The ultimate purpose for these sanctions, across societies and history, has been to maintain social and civic order. However, vastly different sanctions are applied to similar crimes in particular contexts. Sociologists study criminal sanctions to explore the corporate **values** of different societies. Through examination of sanctions sociologists can gauge the relative importance a **society** places on particular forms of behavior.

In contemporary societies criminal sanctions are largely based on two moral philosophies. These philosophies are elaborations on natural law theory. In the Middle Ages (roughly 1000 AD–1600 AD) philosophers and theologians presumed that God's natural law created order, balance, and harmony. Crimes were viewed as transgressions against God's preordained order and elicited harsh penalties. In the seventeenth century, the enlightenment brought secular philosophy and a move from theology. The natural law assumptions of balance and order continued, but they were now based on philosophical rather than theological systems. Sanctions became more moderate; punishments were to be proportional to the **crime**. Thus harsh penalties such as death were reserved for particularly heinous crimes.

The first moral philosophy of criminal sanctions argues that proportional punishments are necessary when offenders violate criminal laws. Punishment restores the natural state of balance. Society has a duty to ensure order. Crime, from this perspective, is understood to be a violation against society and punishment reestablishes order and expresses social outrage. The sociological term for this action is retribution. Societies punish criminal offenses out of a sense of duty.

The other philosophical orientation to criminal sanctions treats punishment as a means to achieving greater good. This perspective, known as utilitarianism, asserts that right action creates the greatest happiness for the largest number of people. Criminal sanctions, from this perspective, serve one of three goals. First, sanctions are used as a means to rehabilitate criminal offenders. Through the **sanction** the offender is to be transformed into a law-abiding citizen. Second, sanctions are used as a means to deter offenders, or those who may imitate them,

from committing further crime. By experiencing the swift and certain discomfort that follows crime, offenders will refrain from future crimes. Last, sanctions are used to incapacitate those dangerous members of society who otherwise will continue to commit crimes, which will create unhappiness in the larger society.

In most contemporary societies criminal sanctions, anchored by the philosophies described above, fall along a continuum. At the least punitive end, sanctions involve repayment or restitution for wrongdoing. Here the offender is ordered to make amends to the victimized party, either through work equity or monetary payment. Typically, when the crime is a violation against the public or a municipality, restitution will be made through fines and public service. Intermediate sanctions allow offenders to remain in the **community** while simultaneously being placed under state supervision. Intermediate sanctions range from the use of probation, weekend (or other short term) jail sentences, house arrest, and various forms of electronic monitoring. Under intermediate sanctions offenders must agree to certain conditions and if those conditions are violated a higher sanction is imposed. At the far end of the continuum sanctions rely on incarceration. Here offenders are denied liberty for specified period of time. We could add to this continuum the penalty of death, which is still imposed in some countries, including the United States. However nearly every other industrial **democracy** eliminated the death penalty in the twentieth century.

Contemporary criminal sanctions are informed by both philosophical traditions. In some circumstances, such as when young people commit crime, the utilitarian model of rehabilitation guides sanction. But in other instances, such as when the crime is particularly heinous, sanctions follow from the retributive philosophy. Sociologists look for patterns in the ways that these philosophies are applied to particular types of crime and particular types of criminals in order to draw conclusions about the society.

CRIMINALIZATION OF DEVIANCE

Many criminologists attempt to explain why some people break the law while others do not. Conflict criminologists, such as Austin Turk, Richard Quinney, and Steven Spitzer, believe that the more important question is why the conduct of some is defined as criminal and that of others is not. They contend that to obtain an adequate understanding of criminal behavior one must understand the process of criminalizing **deviance**. The criminalization process can be defined as the process by which certain behaviors, actions, or substances are defined as illegal. The criminalization process is contingent on a variety of forces and circumstances relating to the relative threat that some behaviors pose for those who would seek to repress them and the relative power of those individuals to impose a criminal label.

To understand the criminalization process we must assume that the social order is based on the conflict between those who have power (authorities) and those who do not (subjects). Conflicts between these two groups arise over a wide range of social **norms**. Law is one mechanism for the resolution of conflict. If differences between groups do not reflect important value differences, conflict will be minimal and law will likely not be used. The use and creation of law is likely to be undertaken when the interest of one group is threatened by another. The greater the perceived threat, the more likely the action is to be criminalized.

Regardless of how threatened a group may feel, however, the chances that they will be successful in criminalizing the behavior of another is dependent on the relative power of the group experiencing the threat to the power of the group who is thought to be producing the threat. In general, the greater the power differences between the two, the greater the **probability** the authorities will be successful at criminalizing the behavior of the subjects. Those groups that have power rarely see their actions criminalized. For instance, corporations possess a great deal of political power in U.S. **society** and are able to prevent much of their behavior from being criminalized. Those that do not have power frequently see their actions come under **criminal sanctions**. Juveniles have significantly less power than adults, and consequently, much of their behavior has been criminalized. In short, the probability that a group's behavior will be criminalized is the product of the interaction between perceived threat and relative power.

This process can be exemplified by examining the criminalization of opium in the late 1800s. In the 1800s thousands of Chinese men came to the United States to help build the railroads. They brought opium with them, a drug that was then legal. After the railroads were completed, these Chinese men were thrown into the job market. They were willing to work cheaply and for long hours, posing a threat to white workers. In 1875, many West Coast cities, such as San Francisco, began to pass ordinances prohibiting opium dens. These laws were not aimed at opium but at the Chinese men who posed a threat to the economic security of the white working class. The political nature of the criminalization of opium is further supported by a Congressional Act that prohibited the importation of heroin by the Chinese but not by white Americans.

Conflict criminologists contend that the study of **crime** should encompass more than explanations of why people participate in illegal behavior. It should also study the political process by which behavior is defined as harmful and subsequently criminalized. While criminologists may or may not agree with crime definitions, they do agree that drawing attention to the political nature of those definitions is important.

CRIMINOLOGY

Criminology, an emphasis of **sociology** studying **crime** and delinquency as phenomena of the social world, has three foci: lawmaking, lawbreaking, and reactions regarding the breaking of laws. The study of lawmaking examines whether the basis of legal definitions is one of consensus or conflict. The consensus model argues that members of **society** agree on which behaviors are unacceptable. As a result, laws are simply a formal

codification, through legislation and court rulings, of prevailing notions of right and wrong. In contrast, the conflict model views society as composed of groups whose competing **values** and interests (i.e., politics, class, religion, **race**, gender, and so on) cause them to have different definitions of what behaviors are unacceptable. Groups with the most power in society have the ability to enact into law their definitions of right and wrong. Thus, law is a tool of the powerful to maintain their advantageous position over others.

The study of lawbreaking concerns why some individuals are more likely to commit crime. Attempts to answer this question, albeit with very different responses, have led to the majority of theories in criminology (e.g., Akers 2000, Barak 1998, Einstadter and Henry 1995). However, according to Barkan (1997), sociological criminology has three major subdivisions: social structure, social process, and critical theories. Social structural perspectives explain crime in terms of factors outside the individual that are part of the broader social environment or social forces. These perspectives include social disorganization, strain, and subcultural theories. Social disorganization theory stresses that characteristics of neighborhoods such as low-income housing, poverty, transience, and heterogeneous groups lead to a decrease in common social norms. As a result, a breakdown occurs in various social institutions (i.e., family, schools) and social bonds (i.e., long-term residents) that typically control behavior. All of these factors typify areas with high levels of social disorganization allowing crime and delinquency to flourish. Strain theorists argue that society has certain culturally approved goals (i.e., economic success) and culturally approved means of obtaining these goals (i.e., hard work, education, and thrift). Strain results when an individual accepts the goals, but the means are unavailable. In order to reduce feelings of strain, an individual may resort to reaching goals through illegitimate means. Subcultural theorists agree with the idea that society has certain goals and means but argue that individuals experience **status** frustration; that is, the status of respectability is unattainable by mainstream standards. However, membership in a subculture provides alternative **norms** and values through which individuals can achieve status and success.

In contrast, social process theories argue that crime is a result of social-psychological processes that arise from social **interaction**. Both learning and **social control** theories fall in the category of social process perspectives. Learning theory maintains that criminal behavior involves the same types of processes much like learning any other behavior. This learning also occurs through a process of association with others who communicate definitions favorable to law violation (i.e., motives, drives, rationalizations, and techniques). The most influential associations are those that are frequent in contact, intense or intimate, long in duration, and take priority over others, that is, occurring earlier in life such as in childhood rather than in adulthood. In contrast to other theories of crime causation, social control theorists ask why individuals do not commit crime. From this perspective, it is the lack of values and beliefs that usually restrain criminal tendencies. This state occurs when there is a disruption in an individual's bonds to society in terms of attachment, commitment, involvement, and belief, reducing their personal stake in **conformity**.

Critical theories on crime do not look at why individuals commit crime but ask how and why dominant or powerful members of society produce definitions of crimes and criminals and how these affect criminal behavior. Labeling, conflict and radical, and feminist theories are all critical in nature. According to labeling theorists, who or what is criminal depends on the negative meaning or label others in society attach to an act. Labeling theorists stress how two factors, moral entrepreneurs and social status and power, influence the labeling of acts as criminal. Moral entrepreneurs, such as police, legislators, and social reformers, are powerful groups in society that construct the moral meanings (i.e., notions of right and wrong) of acts. Whereas the actions of relatively low-status, powerless groups are more likely to be the target of negative labels. In addition, criminal labels, such as thief, prostitute, and murderer, may actually intensify an individual's commitment to a criminal identity and contribute to further criminality. This effect occurs because attaching a negative label or stigma to an individual limits conventional opportunities and individuals tend to align their behavior with stigmatizing labels. Conflict theories, also known as pluralist or interest group theories, stress that lawmaking, lawbreaking, and reactions toward breaking laws are a reflection of how the most powerful groups in society control all three processes to keep their dominant position. Radical theorists, however, maintain that all conflicts between groups are a consequence of economic inequality. Specifically, crime is the result of the exploitation of the working class by capitalists. In this instance, crimes of the working class may be the result of either a revolution against the capitalists or a response to the suffering brought about by economic inequality (i.e., stealing to eliminate poverty). From the feminist perspective, traditional criminological theories (discussion of theories thus far) are gender blind, that is, they are written by males to explain male criminality. In addition, testing the **validity** of these theories utilizes male populations. Thus, gender (i.e., female criminality, gender differences in criminal behavior, and the victimization of women) is central to feminist explanations of crime. The four major feminist approaches are: liberal, radical, Marxist, and socialist. Feminist theory (e.g., Muraskin and Alleman 1993) posits that criminogenic factors in society are the result of gender **discrimination**, **patriarchy**, **capitalism** and class relations, and class and patriarchy, respectively.

Finally, analyses of reactions toward breaking laws or techniques of crime control stem directly from assumptions regarding causes of criminal behavior. Adler, Mueller, and Laufer (1998), for example, stated that social structural theorists may emphasize organizing existing social structures to develop social stability in otherwise disorganized communities and design programs that either give lower-class people a means for reaching their goals or move individuals from delinquent subcultures into mainstream society. Learning theorists would favor exposing youths to definitions favorable to conventional behavior, whereas social control theorists would focus on strengthening an individual's bonds to society through improving the social institutions that encourage conventional behavior such as the **family**, schools, and the work-

place. According to Einstadter and Henry (1995) labeling theorists would advocate limiting reactions to criminal behavior to decriminalization, diversion, decarceration, and the philosophies of restitution and reparation. In contrast, conflict and radical theorists call for a total restructuring of society in order to correct existing power imbalances. Feminist solutions range from integrating women into male-dominate society to revising a system that they contend allows male control over women's lives.

CRITICAL SCHOOL

The critical school of **sociology** can ultimately be traced back to Karl Marx's call in 1843 for a "ruthless criticism of everything existing." The criticism that Marx had in mind, however, was to differ from the utopian variety that he attacked in the *Manifesto of the Communist Party* in three important respects. First, rather than criticize social institutions on the basis of tradition or transcendent **values**, Marx envisioned a criticism grounded in reason. Second, this criticism aimed to discover the emancipatory potential already present within existing social reality. In Marx's formulation, as Axel Honneth noted, "the potential for reason embodied in the productive forces is released... in social conflicts." Third, as Marx's own critique of **political economy** reveals, the criticism he envisioned was aimed at social-scientific knowledge as well as **society** itself.

This project of rational social criticism was continued and developed further by **Theodor Adorno**, Walter Benjamin, **Erich Fromm**, **Max Horkheimer**, Herbert Marcuse, and others associated with the Frankfurt Institute for Social Research, founded in 1922. While the work of these thinkers, collectively known as the Frankfurt School, was rooted in the Marxist tradition, these individuals also sought to incorporate and radicalize Freudian **psychoanalysis** and Max Weber's theory of **rationalization**. Their work hardly constitutes a monolithic and unified viewpoint. However, several common or overlapping elements and themes can be identified. Like Marx, their criticism was aimed at social-scientific knowledge as well as society itself. On the one hand, the Frankfurt School rejected positivist attempts to found a social science modeled on the physical and natural sciences and free of questions of value and moral judgment. Instead, they proposed an interdisciplinary social science that integrated empirical research with philosophical concerns. On the other hand, the Frankfurt School sought to understand how profound social changes since Marx's day systematically blocked and suppressed the social conflicts through which emancipation was to be realized. In particular, emphasis was placed on the shift from markets to bureaucratic planning, changes in the **structure** of the bourgeois nuclear family that gave rise to the "authoritarian personality," and new forms of domination embodied in mass media and mass **culture**. In later years, this critical understanding of society became more and more pessimistic as key members of the Frankfurt School increasingly stressed the historical unfolding and spread of instrumental **rationality**.

Although the Frankfurt Institute for Social Research was eventually disbanded in 1969, the project of developing a critical school of sociology has continued, most notably in the work of Jürgen Habermas. Habermas's work continues to develop many of the concerns of Marxism and the early Frankfurt School. However, with Habermas, an important break occurs within the critical school of sociology. Where Marx and the Frankfurt School took labor as their point of departure, Habermas shifted the focus to intersubjectivity, interaction, and **language**. This allowed him to distinguish between communicative and other forms of rationality, which he saw as crucial for reconstructing Weber's overly pessimistic view of rationalization. Rather than attributing the pathological aspects of modernity to rationalization per se, Habermas contended that they should instead be seen as the result of a one-sided and uneven rationalization process in which the development of instrumental and strategic rationality overtakes the development of communicative rationality. It is in this context that he spoke of modernity as an "unfinished project."

Habermas's work has been extremely influential, not only in sociology, but also in **philosophy** and in a variety of other disciplines as well. However, some have argued that communicative rationality provides too narrow of a basis for a critical diagnosis of our times. According to Axel Honneth, for example, Habermas lost sight of those social pathologies that have nothing to do with the developmental level of rationality, pathologies that can be better grasped with the concept of recognition. These debates demonstrate that, just as the critical school of sociology did not come to an end with the disbanding of the Frankfurt Institute for Social Research, neither did it come to any kind of culmination or completion with Habermas. On the contrary, the critical school of sociology remains active, vibrant, and subject to further innovation.

CRITICAL SOCIAL SCIENCE

Critical social science generally refers to social scientific production within specific critical traditions as **Marxist sociology** or **feminism** or to work that takes a specific political position. More specifically, sociological work can be thought of as critical in at least one of the two ways. It can be work that is critical of existing social relations and inequalities and that is aimed at changing those relations in some way, or it can be work that is critical of the traditional methods of **sociology** as quantitative surveys. What is distinctive about critical social science from critical social thought more generally is that despite its critical stance toward unreflexive uses of scientific methods, it has often been carried out in mainstream academic departments by scholars who have wished to retain the claim at science.

In the United States, critical social science is most often considered a post-World War II phenomenon. Though early unacknowledged scholars like W. E. B. Du Bois carried out work that is now claimed by critical social scientists, the explicit claim of work that was both critical and scientific dates from this time and is associated with Vance Packard and **C. Wright Mills**. Mills, who defined a critical position against the grand theory of functionalism and the abstract **empiricism** of opinion **surveys**, linked a critical method to a critical position against unjust institutions of American society. Mills, who in 1957 wrote *The Power Elite*, presented a particularly poignant critique of the functioning of American **democracy**: interlocking elites wielded power by the control of economic, political, and military institutions. These elites, who shared similar backgrounds, were a relatively small group of persons with similar goals and who were able to manipulate supposedly democratic processes. Other important critical scholars at the time were those associated with the Frankfurt school, **Theodor Adorno** and **Herbert Marcuse**. They wrote on the **culture** industry and the pacifying functions of mass culture. Scholars more explicitly influenced by Marxist positions also developed work that was critical of U.S. foreign policy and **imperialism**. Paul Baran's 1953 *Political Economy of Growth* was developed in critical dialogue with **modernization theory**, which espouses that factors endogenous to Third World nations, as the supposed lack of modern culture and **values**, account for the lack of development. Baran and those who followed him argued that it was U.S. involvement, in the form of military intervention and investment, that maintained those nations in the state of stunted development. The following generation of scholars within the **sociology of development**, grouped under dependency theory continued to challenge to modernization theory and to prevailing economic wisdom in the 1960s. It also represented the search for a solution to the continued lack of industrialization in post-colonial nations in the post-World War II period against the backdrop of the Cold War. Whereas modernization theory advocated greater sustained involvement of industrialized nations in the form of investment and cultural exchange, dependency theorists generally looked for alternative models of development, as present in the apparent successes of socialist experiments as those in Cuba and in Tanzania.

A resurgence of interest in Marxist works in the 1970s took place in such critical journals as *Socialist Revolution*, *New Left Review*, and *The Insurgent Sociologist*. One important development was a **critical theory** of the state. Whereas mainstream scholarship until the 1960s tended to view the functioning of the state within industrial democracies like the United States as the expression of the interests of competing groups within the polity, Marxist scholars pointed to the ways in which the state tended to reflect the interests of elites and to reproduce the conditions necessary for the accumulation of capital.

Feminist scholarship in the social sciences also contributed to the development of a critical social science, especially since the 1960s. Feminist standpoint theory calls into question sociological work done by privileged sociologists among underprivileged subjects. **Standpoint theory** calls into question the standpoint of the observer and posits that all social knowledge is partial and situated. Largely taking up the critique that social scientific work is influenced by the standpoint of the authors, scholars have also begun to explore the nature of sociological inquiry into **race** relations. Critical race theory is one of the most important areas of renewal in sociology today.

CRITICAL THEORY

Critical Theory has its origins in the Frankfurt school, a group of German intellectuals whose main preoccupation was the critique of social domination as it existed in various modern domains such as in the nature of scientific work, modern institutionalized conditions, and **culture**. They are especially known for their analysis of culture as it pertains to individual subjectivity. Influenced by Marxist theory, representative figures such as Max Horkheimer, Theodor Adorno, and **Herbert Marcuse** actively worked to develop a theoretical account of the socio-cultural, an area that was neglected by orthodox Marxism with its mechanistic and determinist interpretations of economic and political life. Instead, they embraced Hegel's dialectics, an approach that considered objective and subjective conditions and the way they are related to each other and vary in social life according to historical contexts. This type of approach sought to understand each social phenomenon as related to other parts and to the totality of social relations. The relationship between the subjective matters of individual consciousness and culture and the objective economic structure figured prominently into their analysis.

According to Horkheimer critical theory has its roots in both German idealism and **philosophy**. Critical theory pertains to men's everyday lives, contributing to the effort of creating a better world. Although the work of critical theory substantially interacts with the special sciences, its aim is not the mere appropriation of knowledge. Instead, Horkeimer claims that the goal of critical theory is to emancipate man from his servitude to science and transform the culture in which we live to better reflect man's needs.

A major concern for the school is understanding how the promise of the Enlightenment is to deliver a better social world has been distorted in modern times. This distortion they argue is mainly connected to the fact that **society** has entered a phase of repressive **rationality** (i.e., "technocratic thinking") as an extension of economic capitalist exploitative principles, in which seeking the most effective way of accomplishing a goal supersedes human concerns for social justice, **peace**, and happiness. Objective processes have consumed the subjective quality of life. As knowledge becomes more instrumental, its critical dimension decreases. Positivistic science, a major agent in the "legitimation" and expansion of instrumentalist logic, has thus reified the social world into natural processes. Harmful or detrimental socio-economic conditions are not questioned but rather taken for granted. The "common" culture in society is not seen as dominating, and it is welcomed. Knowledge as it is culturally understood and consumed is thus a facade for existing power relations. The actual process of individual self-consciousness has assumed an instrumentalist technocratic nature, and reason, the ability to make assessments in terms of human **values** and **justice**, has been distorted.

Liberation comes from thus questioning the course of the Enlightenment as it presents itself in modern society. Liberation is likely to be found in understanding how culture dominates. Culture, scientific knowledge, knowledge production, and the industry of culture thus become the focus of investigation which purports to understand the structural roots of oppression. Given that "social freedom is inseparable from enlightened thought" (Horkheimer and Adorno 1993), a critical posture means a questioning of things normally taken for granted.

The focus of critical theory, therefore, is *criticism*. According to Horkheimer (1972): "By criticism, we mean that intellectual, and eventually practical, effort which is not satisfied to accept the prevailing ideas, actions, and social conditions unthinkingly and from mere habit." Through criticism, the proponents of critical theory hope to overcome what they believe to be the negative effects of the Enlightenment and seek knowledge of things that recognizes not only their scientific (objective) aspects, but also their true essences. They aim to incorporate subjective realities into the very concept of knowledge and disarm the predominance of objectivity.

Succeeding at this aim requires the synthesis of objectivity and subjectivity in analysis by establishing a connection between the subject (who engages in subjectivity) and both nature and social reality. The "remembrance of nature in the subject, in whose fulfillment the unacknowledged truth of all culture lies hidden, enlightenment is universally opposed to domination" (Horkheimer and Adorno). To withhold such a connection would imply a lack of understanding of and respect for the human experience.

CROSS-CULTURAL ANALYSIS

Cross-cultural analysis involves the study of cultures and societies around the world. While cross-cultural research is typically conducted on a cross-national basis, it is also possible to conduct cross-cultural research within a single **society**. Because certain nations are home to numerous cultural groups, the study of diverse racial, ethnic, religious, or other social groups located within one particular society may be legitimately defined as cross-cultural analysis.

Cross-cultural research can be divided into two levels of social analysis. Macro-level cross-cultural analysis is identified as historical-comparative research. These studies tend to examine cross-national variation in large-scale social structures around the world. Micro-level cross-cultural analyses are most commonly conducted through the use of ethnographic field methods. Ethnographic research typically explores smaller-scale patterns of **interaction** within groups. Ethnography is also useful in the examination of individual and **group** interaction with larger social institutions.

Historical-comparative research has traditionally been the most prevalent form of cross-cultural analysis employed within the field of **sociology**. Although ethnographic studies have been historically more prevalent within anthropological research, the use of **ethnography** has become increasingly more common among sociologists in recent years. While anthropological ethnographic research has traditionally involved in-depth cross-cultural participant observation, sociologists have been more likely to employ intensive interviewing and survey methods in their cross-cultural ethnographic analyses.

Cross-cultural analysis allows social scientists to reveal the variety and diversity of cultural forms present in various societies. However, perhaps the most useful feature of cross-cultural research is its capacity to uncover cross-societal and cross-national cultural regularities. One of the primary objectives of sociological analysis involves the discovery of patterned social relationships within and between social groups. Therefore, cross-cultural analysis is particularly useful in that it moves beyond the examination of social patterns within individual cultures or societies to reveal broad, generalizable patterned relationships that are common to most, if not all cultural groups.

Cross-cultural research is also frequently employed in the testing and development of social theory. The findings of cross-cultural research are often used in support of existing social theories, providing additional evidence for the explanatory potential of such theories. However, the results of cross-cultural analysis have also been employed to refute elements of existing social theory. In these instances, empirical contradictions, which appear to counter broad-based theoretical assumptions about the nature of social interaction, have necessitated the reevaluation of existing social theories. Furthermore, in cases where cross-cultural findings have appeared to reveal social patterns unrelated to any existing currents of social theory, further analysis and replication of such findings have led to the construction of new theories of social interaction.

Because so much sociological research has conventionally focused upon patterned social relationships within individual societies, the propositions and theories developed within the field of sociology have typically been limited in their worldwide explanatory potential. This is particularly true within the context of American sociology. However, cross-cultural analysis is becoming much more prevalent within sociological analysis. The continued application of cross-cultural research will allow sociologists to develop an increasingly more inclusive and more complete picture of human social interaction.

CROSS-SECTIONAL RESEARCH

Cross-sectional research is a statistical method of analysis in which individual units of study are analyzed at a specified moment in time (the moment of **data** collection) in order to gather data about people in different life stages or in different circumstances. Cross-sectional analysis is an ideal method for determining specific population characteristics and cross analyzing these items. For example, the answers to a series of attitudinal questions could be compared by sex, age, **race**, place of residence, family composition, etc. This type of data is also known as the "snapshot" approach because, unlike a longitudinal approach, it cannot provide information on changing circumstances or developmental processes. The advantages of cross-sectional analysis are predominantly logistic: it is quicker, less expensive, reduces the loss of respondents that naturally occur over time, and is not dependent upon changing resources.

The 1965 Watts Riot was one of the most violent social rebellions in U.S. history *(Corbis Corporation [Bellevue]).*

However, using this approach prevents researchers from examining change over time, an impact felt by both quantitative and qualitative research.

There are two types of cross sectional research. The first, more traditional type is the unweighted method, which involves a truly random sample of the population. The second type is the weighted method, in which a specific subgroup (often a demographic distinction) is oversampled to achieve more data for that group. For example, minorities are often oversampled in an effort to achieve a wider variety of data based on racial or ethnic differences.

CROWDS AND RIOTS

When people gather together *en masse*, the outcome of that event can range as widely as the type of occurrence that drew them together. Reasons for social gatherings can be as far ranging as watching a sporting event or overthrowing the **government** by force. The study of the behavior of people within a collectivity has appeared under the category of social phenomenon called *collective behavior.*

Not every mass gathering is a *crowd* and not all **collective behavior** occurs with the crowd. In terms of the sociological study of collective behavior, a crowd is a mass gathering engaged in collective behavior, especially when that behavior is disruptive or non-normative. Some types of **group** or crowd activities, such as attending and cheering at a sporting event, are marked by highly conventional, socially-accepted behaviors. These events tend to be scheduled recurrent events that are sponsored by an official authority. These three things—conventional behaviors, calendaring, and official sponsorship—set apart the everyday crowd from the crowd associated with collective behavior.

Collective behavior can occur among individuals who are not in close physical contact, but who share common beliefs and engage in some form of common behavior. Examples of this type of diffuse collective behavior includes fads and crazes. Social scientists have long been concerned with the precipitating factors that motivate collective behavior, the processes that create these gatherings, and the results thereof—whether cheering or rioting. Gustave LeBon, a nineteenth century social theorist, explored the **psychology** of crowds in *The Crowd*, published in 1895. LeBon wrote that crowds are maladapted to reasoning and powerfully destructive forces that cause the loss of individual characteristics and motivations within the mass of the crowd.

One aspect of crowds that has interested sociologists is the tendency for individuals to behave differently within the crowd than they might behave individually, resulting in crowd behavior that is unlike the behavior of the individuals who make up the crowd. The close physical contact within the crowd has been associated with a loss of inhibitions among individuals. The resulting behavior, where the individual is protected and influenced by the group, may be explosive and unpredictable. Early theories, such as those of LeBon, now largely rejected by sociologists, suggest that crowd behavior is the result of *contagion,* whereby individuals are irrational, easily influenced by the behavior of others and unable to resist going along with the actions of the crowd.

Crowd behavior is now more commonly approached from a standpoint of rationality, whereby even non-normative behaviors are viewed as a rational response to strain. Crowds are frequently important aspects in the study of social movements and mass phenomena. Some typical "elementary forms" of patterned crowd behaviors have been identified by Clark McPhail and Ronald Wohlstein. These include a range of verbal and nonverbal behaviors such as assemblage, milling, common focus of attention, collective vocalization, convergent movement, and dispersal.

One special type of crowd behavior, the *riot,* is marked by property destruction and confrontation with authorities. In the context of protest or demonstration, sociological theories have suggested that the riot behavior that may occur in response to particular types of strain, especially when those engaged in the riot are subjected to constant deprivation, repression, and marginalization. Sociological theories downplay the idea that riots are irrational behaviors and that the causes are not identifiable or can be solely attributed to agitators.

Cult

A cult is typically the smallest in **group** membership and most ideologically radical of the religious **organization** styles outlined by Howard Becker in the 1960s. Cults are often secretive, isolated, and individual-based, and tend to focus their beliefs on the teachings of a charismatic leader. The ideologies of cultic religions are far removed from the traditional religious bases of **society**. This allows for cults to serve as conduits for the introduction of a new religion or a radical transformation of an established faith.

Cults tend to be similar in size to religious organizations classified as sects, a trait that occasionally causes misclassifi-

cation of the groups. The difference between cults and sects originates in their primary doctrines. Sects are renovations of a previously existing faith, often attempts to return to a religious doctrine which members of the **sect** feel have been abandoned by the established group (i.e., Amish rejection of the "worldliness" of the Mennonites). Conversely, cults wish to abandon previous religious traditions altogether. Cult doctrines are innovations of faith that attempt to completely separate their group from past religious practices, and often from society as well. Many cults require members to sever all past relationships in the traditional world so that they can begin life anew in the group. Cult religions may use this isolation to ensure that the members remain devoted to the faith and connected only to the other members of the cult, as a method of control.

Recently the term "cult" has been used less as a classification term and more as a means of defining small, radical, religious groups in a negative light. The labeling of a minor religious organization as a "cult" can serve to discredit the group as dangerous and unlawful, even though the group may not be a cult in the traditional meaning of the term. However, due to recent behavior of some religious cults, the term is now often associated with any religious organization considered threatening to the mainstream of society.

Recent high-profile cults include the Branch Davidians of Waco, Texas, and Heaven's Gate of San Diego, California. The Davidians followed the teaching of their leader David Koresh, whom they believed to be a messianic figure. The Heaven's Gate group held the belief that a spaceship was arriving in the tail of the Hale-Bopp comet to remove them from this planet and transport them to a heaven-like nirvana elsewhere in the galaxy. Both groups met violent, well-publicized ends, further lending credence to the belief that cults serve only as a haven to those with deviant beliefs. It should be noted however, that many religious factions portrayed as cults in their infancy have gained prominence and acceptance in society, including **Christianity** and The Church of Latter Day Saints.

See also Counterculture; Subculture

Cult of Personality

Cult of personality refers to a social or political phenomenon in which individuals have great power over others, based solely on personality. Those who lead by a cult of personality usually do not have any legal, political, or intellectual **authority** in the beginning of their **leadership**. They rely on **charisma**, gaining their power through personal characteristics that appeal to people who follow them. It is a system of **government** by awe not a system of government by law.

In a system dominated by a cult of personality, no democratic or group decision-making or collective leadership occur. This linear hierarchy gives one person all the authority and control. There is one Great Leader (a Messiah-type) upon whom the others rely and whom the others follow. Without checks and balances on decisions or power, this person often leads a life of excess. The desires and needs of the leader come before **group** priorities. This person usually claims credit for all accomplishments or victories, even if these are a group accomplishment.

Those who lead by a cult of personality tend to be paranoid and guard their authority with severe, often militaristic measures. In a cult of personality, criticism of the leader is not allowed and opposition is punished severely. This rigidity enforces complete adherence to the leader's demands and wishes, without which the system will not work and the leader's authority will be undermined. Those who live under or adhere to a cult of personality often have little hope. They tend to be people looking to be led or people looking for a solution to social or political turmoil. Because these people tend not to be autonomous or self-motivated, the Personality gains power easily. Some who have ruled by a cult of personality are: Hitler, Stalin, Mao Tse-Tung, and Evita Peron. Fascism and Nazism are political systems based on a cult of personality.

CULTURAL CAPITAL

The concept "cultural capital" as originally developed by **Pierre Bourdieu**, concerns the method with which the educational system echoes the **values** of cultural expression and linguistic proficiencies that are characteristic of the socially and economically dominant class in a given **society**. It is a form of **human capital**. Thus those mannerisms and tastes that are held as valuable by the socially and economically dominant class are also deemed essential by the schools. Students who bring this cultural capital into the educational system are likely to be successful in meeting criteria set by the schools. Bourdieu argues that schools require these competencies while failing to adequately instruct those who are from working-class backgrounds in those same competencies. The consequence is that the school system supports and validates the privileges of children of the affluent and influential class. In other words, while appearing to be a neutral gauge, educational assessment actually legitimates inequality by transforming socio-cultural abilities into hierarchies of achievement. These hierarchies then appear to be the outcome of natural ability. On the other hand, the educational institutions may conversely be viewed as imparting this form of capital on to students, thereby minimizing the inequality of opportunities for those not previously possessing this capital. The opportunity to acquire these abilities is deemed a necessary condition for an open class society.

CULTURAL INTEGRATION

Cultural integration, also known as acculturation, refers to those processes through which a **culture** becomes a whole entity. It is the development of shared ways of seeing and acting and the degree to which people have common frames of reference in a given **society**. It means bringing together people from diverse backgrounds to develop common experiences and views of life. It is based in the interdependence of beliefs,

Joseph Stalin's reign as Soviet leader was characterized by such cult of personality traits as paranoia and the use of terror to crush his enemies *(Corbis Corporation [Bellevue])*.

values, customs, **norms**, and behavior. Clearly, cultural integration is a matter of degree because there are always heterogeneous segments in a society. Cultural integration is not analogous to homogenization; it does not mean there is no variety in a given culture or that people act in exactly the same ways or believe exactly the same things. Instead, it implies that there is an interconnectedness and exchange between the different segments of a society.

An assumption of cultural integration is that a dominant culture already exists, a culture into which other cultures must assimilate completely or partially. This progression can mean that the beliefs, actions, or customs of some cultures are lost or buried in the larger culture or that the larger society adopts beliefs or customs from various and diverse cultures. Historically, personal interactions created and allowed for cultural integration (shared frames of reference). Different and diverse groups met and interacted and came to common understandings on how to act and what to believe. But in a technology-based world, cultural integration is helped by education and the media. These are social institutions in which we all partici-

A modern example of cultural lag is represented by the first mammal to be successfully cloned from an adult cell *(Archive Photos, Inc.).*

pate, with which we are all familiar, and by which we are all affected. But they do not require personal **interaction**. Just because many people watch or read the same media or receive the same information in school does not mean they share the same social network. But they are being taught the same messages about what to believe, how to act, and what to want in their given society. Certain factors impede cultural integration: some groups' resistance to assimilation; lack of a coherent or effective **communication** system to reach all people in a given society; the over-specialization of certain kinds of knowledge; or a high degree of diversity or variance between cultures that does not allow for overall cohesiveness or agreement on cultural components.

CULTURAL LAG

The concept of cultural lag, introduced by William Ogburn, is an aspect of a larger theory of technology developed in the early 1920s. Cultural lag refers to the maladjustment that occurs when the material **culture** of a society develops at a more rapid rate than the non-material culture. The consequence of

this uneven development is a dispute regarding the purpose, moral and ethical connotations of, and use for the material developments. Cultural lag is used to explain instances of **social change** and social disorganization and is also prevalent in research in substantive areas such as urban sociology and technology.

Ogburn established the ideas of a material culture and non-material culture in his work *Social Change* (1922). Material culture consisted of all physical and technological aspects of a **society** (raw materials, food, buildings, computers); while non-material culture consisted of customs, philosophies, and beliefs (religion, **democracy**, **free will**). Ogburn believed that non-material culture was more resistant to change than material culture. These differing rates of change may cause material developments to face legal or ethical challenges due to the slower progression of the non-material culture. This delay in response from the non-material culture is the cultural lag.

A modern example of cultural lag is the recent scientific advances in cloning. Some biologists claim the technology currently exists to clone a human being (material culture). However, the ability to complete this process successfully raises questions about **morality**, purpose, and usefulness (non-material culture). The extent to which any question regarding the use of the cloning technology has yet to be adequately addressed indicates a lag of the non-material culture behind the material on this issue.

CULTURAL MATERIALISM

Cultural **materialism** describes an approach to sociological research. Specifically, it attempts to explain human social and cultural systems through material and behavioral processes. According to the theory of cultural materialism, all **culture** and **society** is determined and dominated by production and reproduction. According to the theory, structures in society such as **government**, religion, and law continue to exist since they support production and reproduction.

Cultural anthropologist **Marvin Harris** (1927–) first developed the idea and the term cultural materialism is his work *The Rise of Anthropological Theory* (1968). Harris developed the core idea of the theory from Julian Steward's work on cultural ecology, a theory that described the social **adaptation** of humans as they interacted with their environment. However, Steward viewed the environment as having a more passive role than did Harris. Harris also considered culture as a system, while cultural ecology treated it as a set of traits.

The theory of cultural materialism was also influenced by the work of Karl Marx and B. F. Skinner. Marxism and cultural materialism share the belief that material parameters form constraints in social systems; the two theories differ in that cultural materialism does not work toward the goal of eliminating capitalism. Cultural materialism and the work of Skinner share a common emphasis on human behavior.

The theory interprets all socio-cultural systems as having three parts: a superstructure (which includes behavioral and mental aspects), a structure (which includes the domestic and political economies), and an infrastructure (which encompasses the processes of production and reproduction). According to the theory, the infrastructure determines the **structure**, and the structure determines the superstructure. In his work, Harris claimed that the collapse of the communist regime in Eastern Europe and the former Soviet Union was caused by a collapse in infrastructure that caused the other parts of the system (of cultural materialism) to fail.

Cultural materialism became widely known in the field of **sociology** during the 1970s. The theory caused a rift between cultural anthropologists; some insisted that anthropology should be modeled on the humanities. Others (including cultural anthropologists) wanted anthropology to be based on natural science.

CULTURAL PLURALISM

Cultural pluralism is defined as the maintenance of several different ethnic groups within the **structure** of a larger **society**. There is generally some shared political or economic system at work that keeps these different groups bound. To achieve cultural pluralism, distinct minority groups must exist within the larger group with some degree of harmony and acceptance. In societies such as these, each ethnic or cultural group keeps its own language and customs. Cultural pluralism has been expressed in terms of a relationship between the majority and the minority within a **culture**. Pluralism allows ethnic minority groups to exist without facing **prejudice** and discrimination. Many societies are not pluralistic and in these societies, people of different cultures exist together, but prejudice and **discrimination** does occur.

To understand cultural pluralism, it is important to understand the concept of assimilation. Assimilation occurs when people of diverse cultures within a society give up their native cultures and embrace the new culture of the larger society. In this process, new customs and languages are learned and practiced. The result is a society that holds a single culture. In societies where ethnic groups assimilate, there is less tolerance for groups that differ from the larger society.

Culture is also important to understand when discussing cultural pluralism. Culture consists of **language**, symbols, beliefs, **norms**, **values** and material culture (architecture, art) of a particular group. Food, dress, religious rites, customs, and languages vary greatly from culture to culture. What is acceptable in one culture may be unacceptable in other cultures. For example, the Chinese eat dog meat while Americans do not. Chinese loathe cow's milk, but Americans drink it. Customs and religious beliefs may clash in the larger society and in order to maintain a pluralistic society, the conflict must be accepted on some level in the larger society.

Many countries throughout the world have achieved a state of cultural pluralism. The United States has a pluralistic society in theory but not always in practice. There is still great pressure on ethnic groups to assimilate. Intolerance for diversity poses problems in the society and takes many forms,

CULTURAL RELATIVISM

Cultural relativism is an intellectual doctrine asserting that concepts are culturally constructed and can only be evaluated within their social context. This doctrine incorporates both intellectual standards of true or false (cognitive relativism) and ethical standards of right or wrong (moral relativism). Thus, ideas and behavior that an American researcher may consider repugnant, such as genital mutilation or infanticide, must be understood through the society's values, **norms** and processes of **socialization**.

The idea of cultural relativism derives from the ideas of linguistic philosophers **Edward Sapir** and Benjamin Whorf who maintained that any reality based upon the construction of **language** cannot exist independently; rather, it is molded by cultural and linguistic categories. Cultural relativism implicitly acknowledges the existence of ethnocentrism and its presence in cultural studies; thus, it influences ethnographic research, which then becomes a process of understanding of the meanings upon which a culture's social reality is based.

Two problems occur with cultural relativism. First, the position of cultural relativism is self-contradictory as it simultaneously asserts an absolute position and claims that no absolute statements can be made. Second, this theory disregards the fact that societies share basic **values** and that human needs do not vary cross-culturally.

CULTURAL STUDIES

Cultural studies is a mode of inquiry that examines the ways in which power and inequality shape cultural symbols, symbolic codes, and the cultural assignment of meaning to elements of a social system. While sociologists have long concerned themselves with the study of **culture**, historically approaching the topic from a variety of theoretical perspectives, the development of cultural studies as a separate and somewhat bounded theoretical perspective is traced to mid-twentieth century Europe. The works of such theorists as Raymond Williams, Michel Foucault, and **Pierre Bourdieu** are central to the cultural studies movement. Because cultural studies research remains a truly interdisciplinary endeavor, however, the perspective continues to lack a distinct core of internal organization. Still, despite the eclectic features of cultural studies research, the majority of social scientists employing the cultural studies perspective remain committed to one clearly defined political objective: bringing an end to world relations of **domination** and exploitation.

A variety of disciplines have contributed to the accumulation of cultural studies research, including anthropology, **sociology**, **political science**, linguistic studies, literary criticism, critical **race** studies, and feminist and women's studies. The diversity of cultural studies analyses is thus directly related to the diversity of topics traditionally examined in these different disciplines. Anthropologists, who view culture as an essential aspect of human existence, explore how power and domination shape the construction of cultural classificatory systems and other cultural forms. Sociologists, particularly those who specialize in cultural sociology, examine the ways in which power informs the organization and functioning of social structures in **society**. Many sociologists have also analyzed the ways in which various cultural products such as art, music, theater, and literature reflect the interests and experiences of the dominant cultural group. Political science has produced cultural studies analyses that investigate the role of power and domination in the cultural construction of political discourse, social policies, and political theories.

Linguistic analysts have explored the ways in which dominant group members contribute to the production of **language**, essentially constructing and shaping the very words used to describe elements of a culture. Furthermore, the structure and content of public **discourse** has been a central area of inquiry within linguistic analysis as well. The field of literary criticism has produced cultural analyses that examine the role of literature in producing and reproducing relational representations of power and domination. For instance, literary critics have analyzed various literary works historically lauded as ''authentic'' or ''high-culture literature,'' exploring the ways in which content, plot structure, and language reflect the interests of powerful cultural group members.

Critical race studies and **women's studies** have produced a much research examining the ways in which symbolic cultural codes and systems of classification have been shaped by powerful, dominant interests in various societies throughout the world. The symbolic system of racial classification was without question constructed explicitly within the context of dominance and subordination. Furthermore, discourse and **ideology** derived from classificatory race and gender systems have been historically constructed in the context of dominant/subordinate racialized and gendered relations.

It is evident that the diversity of cultural phenomena explored in the context of cultural studies makes it difficult to provide any one concise interpretation of this perspective. Moreover, many cultural studies theorists resist narrow categorization. While cultural studies is frequently classified as one of many individual disciplines within the social sciences, some theorists have described this field more in terms of a ''scientific direction of inquiry'' than a single discipline. It is precisely the interdisciplinary character of cultural studies that has allowed this area of study to defy the restrictive categorization of disciplinary boundaries. Furthermore, although cultural studies theorists have sought some measure of identification within the social sciences, the universal egalitarian objectives of the cultural studies project reveal the accessibility of this perspective to all scholarly approaches.

CULTURAL UNIVERSALS

People must solve certain basic tasks such as maintaining group organization and resolving conflict within their social milieu. Cultural universals are patterns for resolving issues that are common to all cultures, and each society develops institutions to deal with issues such as the **division of labor**, the incest **taboo**, **marriage**, the **family**, rites of passage in **adolescence**, and visionary thinking.

The family is an **institution** which regulates human **sexual behavior** and maintains kinship ties. Traditions and rituals develop around the institution of the family such as puberty rites, marriageability, and the necessity of women for the success of family life. It also provides a space in which offspring can grow.

The arrangement of these institutions will vary from **society** to society. Marriage might be exclusive in one **culture** and allow multiple partners in another, but the institution of the family serves a similar purpose. Likewise kinship patterns may be traced through the mother (matrilineal) or the father (partrilineal). The family institution may extend its duties to a series of tasks such as educating the offspring, providing economically, and controlling socially, or it may leave education to other institutions.

Cultural **norms**, **values**, and beliefs are factors that all people find necessary for cultural survival, and that survival depends on the transmission of these beliefs through the generations. All people adorn themselves in some fashion using either jewelry or make-up. Often customs prohibit certain behaviors thus unifying social members. Usually a taboo against a certain type of food unites a group, as among Semitic people pork is taboo and among Hindus meat-eating is sacrilegious.

All cultures participate in festivities that include celebration through music and dancing. There are artistic cultural outlets for creative productions in every culture. Generally there are superstitions amongst **community** members. Another similarity, which is common to all cultures, is the idea of hospitality. Of course, the methods and means of hospitality vary greatly, but all share the belief that the guests' comfort is essential to the reputation of the family, community, and sometimes even the overarching society.

Differences in how divergent societies interpret cultural universals may change through the process of globalization. The media provide mass communication and entertainment while the economic community ensures interdependence. A **standardization** of culture might lead to cultural leveling and diffusion with little room for cultural dissent.

CULTURE

Culture, for sociologists, refers to interconnected collective symbols, practices, and meanings specific to a **society** or to a **group** of persons within a society. The growing study of culture within **sociology** covers diverse topics, for example, art and literature, everyday culture and practices, subcultures and deviant cultures, the cultural meanings of politics and political activity, the cultural meanings of gender and **race**, and the cultural meanings of places, among others. The study of culture is connected to **Functionalism** and to Marxist-influenced cultural studies.

Studies in sociology through the early 1960s tended to approach culture in terms of its integrative function. After Talcott Parsons' multiple influential works on **social order** and social systems, culture provided the basis of social cohesion and harmony. The emphasis in these early studies was on culture as a source of **norms** (societal) and **values** (internal) that guaranteed social consensus. Scholarship within **the Chicago school**, for instance, sometimes looked to cultural features of immigrant groups to explain their lack of integration within mainstream society. These scholars posited that immigrant groups had cultural traditions that were out of step with mainstream American culture and that this was an impediment to their full integration. Weber's thesis that **rationalization** was a prerequisite and an outcome of modernization provided inspiration as well. Scholars developed schemes to differentiate between traditional and modern cultural features and treated North American culture as the **ideal type** of modern culture, as embodying universalistic, meritocratic, and democratic values. Gunar Myrdal questioned, however, in his study *The American Dilemma* whether American society did in fact live up to these ideals. The idea that culture could prevent the full integration of groups into mainstream society was further developed by Oscar Lewis (1963), who studied how slum-dwellers in Third World **cities** maintained value-systems, a "culture of poverty" that were not conducive to integration into modern social relations. Similarly, scholars asked about proper values and norms for **democracy**. Almond and Verba (1963) studied **political culture** in five nations to see if attitudes and beliefs were impediments or preconditions to democratic development.

A second influential strand in sociology of culture came from Britain in the mid-1970s, which tended to treat culture as an expression of ideology and the interests of ruling classes. The research of the Birmingham school of **cultural studies** by Stuart Hall, Raymond Williams, and others, have been particularly influential for sociologists. Marxist thinkers, like Antonio Gramsci, **Louis Althusser**, and the scholars of the Frankfurt school, were particularly important in the formation of the ideas of the cultural studies group. These Marxist thinkers emphasized the role that culture could play in guaranteeing the reproduction of **capitalism** and the way it could prevent the formation of a critical consciousness. Frankfurt school scholars Horkheimer and Adorno were particularly pessimistic about "mass culture", for example popular movies and jazz. The culture industry in this way tended to prevent the formation of critical perspectives. Sociologists have also studied the ways in which subaltern persons find ways to resist these influences. Sociologists influenced by the cultural studies group have included John Fiske, Jay McLeod, and Rick Fantasia. An important further strand of thinking about culture is expressed by Ernesto Laclau and Chantal Mouffe's transformation of Marxist ideas. Their position abandoned the idea of "objective capitalist interests" behind **ideology** and argued that discourses themselves structured political positions and interests.

Sociologists have also worked with conceptions of culture that do not rely on a notion of ideology in which culture reflects the prior interests of a pre-determined group, and they have developed notions in which culture itself embodies power relations. **Michel Foucault**, for instance, whose writings on discipline and power have been influential in recent years, described a relationship between power and knowledge in which

knowledge reflects a strategy of discipline. His studies on medical and criminological texts argued that the very strategies implicit in those sciences exercised power over persons; the constant need to separate, individuate, and test persons produced a kind of power over persons. **Pierre Bourdieu** wrote about the way culture and cultural objects embody certain values and function as a kind of currency to which persons have unequal access. He wrote, for example, in *Distinction* (1984), that the ability or inability to speak confidently about works of art or about matters of taste creates hierarchies among persons. A number of sociologists have followed Foucault or Bourdieu and include among others Michele Lamont, Nikolas Rose, Loic Wacquant.

Another important strand of the sociology of culture that departs from conceptions of ideology or integration is the study of democracy and civic life. Scholars have asked about the actual lived experience of persons who participate in Democracy. One important influence is Jürgen Habermas, who described the public sphere of democratic and rational deliberation as providing a potentially emancipatory activity in which citizens debate common problems. Sociologists like Margaret Somers, Michael Schudson, Nina Eliasoph, and others, have asked a number of questions about public spheres in civic life. Another influential strand in the study of democracy comes from the team of researchers headed by Robert Bellah who published *Habits of the Heart* in 1989. Bellah and his co-authors asked about the "state of democracy" in the United States and concluded that an individually-oriented culture was eroding the bases for collective life and civic engagement. In a similar vein, Robert Putnam's (1993) *Making Democracy Work* compares the South and North of Italy and concludes that the South lacks the proper cultural conditions for an active democratic life.

CULTURE OF POVERTY

Oscar Lewis (1914-1971) coined the phrase "culture of poverty" in the early 1960s as an explanation for the **cycle** of **poverty** experienced by certain groups in the United States over several generations. The thesis of the culture of poverty is based on the fatalistic **belief system** formed by those in the lowest economic regions of **society**. According to Lewis, the impoverished of society have typically lived in poverty their entire lives, as have the generations that preceded them. Due to the lack of success in traditional avenues of society, the impoverished stop attempting to gain acceptance using the middle-class standards of society and instead become resigned to their poverty. By accepting that there is little chance for upward mobility, the poor instead focus on the positive aspects of their poverty (i.e., freedom from responsibility) and reject the achievement-based lifestyle of middle-class society.

The culture of poverty thesis resulted from Lewis's ethnographic work *The Children of the Sanchez*, which tracked the experiences of Puerto Rican and Mexican families in the United States. Lewis believed the lifestyle surrounding low **socioeconomic status** was a primary cause of long-term poverty.

Lewis argued that the attitudes, beliefs, and behavior supported by this emergent culture are passed along from one generation to the next. This cycle creates a heritage of destitution.

Lewis's conclusions were the focus of great debate within the sociological community. Many believed the culture of poverty thesis blamed those in poverty for their situation, while downplaying the structural causes (i.e., lack of education, lack of **employment**, stigmatization of the poor) that also contribute to long-term poverty. Subsequent research tends to dispute Lewis's findings. Studies on the attitudes of those in poverty consistently show that most of these individuals have not become fatalistic in their beliefs, nor have they ceased attempting to improve their standing within society. Demographic research has indicated that those at or near the standard for poverty are constantly changing. Therefore Lewis's theory that several generations of the poor pass along a culture based on constant poverty is undermined by evidence of upward mobility. Despite these findings, the culture of poverty has remained a viable theory. Critics suggest this theory is maintained by the individualistic nature of American culture—a nature that tends to blame the individual for society's problems.

CULTURE SHOCK

Culture shock is a psychological and/or physical state of distress that sometimes occurs when a person enters a different culture. Culture shock takes place when the change is great and sudden. This state of "shock" occurs when surroundings are unfamiliar, the **language** is foreign, and customs are different perhaps alien. Culture shock tends to occur when the change in extreme. All types of people are susceptible to culture shock, travelers, researchers, and immigrants alike. Whatever the reason for experiencing the sudden change, people feel common effects from it.

To understand culture shock, one must also understand the components of culture. Culture consists of a society's language, symbols (stop signs, wedding bands), beliefs, **norms**, **values** and material culture (architecture, art). When individuals enter a **society** which differs drastically from own, the new culture shocks them. In this new situation, familiar hand gestures are of no use, signs are not readable, local belief and value systems are sometimes shocking, and sights, sounds, food and smells are all strange. Immersion in such a situation is the cause of culture shock. Buying fruit in a market may lead individuals to question what is appropriate or inappropriate technique.

Symptoms of culture shock range from homesickness to actual physical illness. Culture shock has several different stages. The first stage is the "honeymoon" stage where the individual may be excited about the prospects of being in a new culture. The second stage begins with feelings of anger and dissatisfaction stemming from inabilities to communicate effectively or difficulty in completing tasks. In the next stage, the individual becomes accustomed to the customs and language differences. At this point, the individual becomes more

adapted to the environment. The final stage, sometimes referred to as "re-entry shock," occurs when the person re-enters the home culture. Returning home can adjustment, too.

CUSTOM

A custom is a social practice, a way of doing things or a way of thinking about something in a particular **society** or **culture**. The term is usually used in anthropology, while the concept is usually called a norm in sociology. Customs are common practices, beliefs, or rituals shared by members of a social **group**, and provide one way of distinguishing cultures from each other. They are not natural, innate behavior, but are learned and are passed down from generation to generation (generational transmission). Customs are the different ways people fulfill their biological needs (food, shelter, sex, clothing). They are also the different ways people express their beliefs and morals, and they are often the basis of the laws in a given society.

Once adopted by a society or group of people, many customs last for a long time, partly because people learn to do something a particular way, do not know any other way to do it, and assume the way they do it is the best, and partly because many people do not like change. Those customs that change quickly are called fashion or fads. Some fashions and fads do become custom over a long period of time (e.g., eating with a fork and knife was a fashion in Europe in the 1500s, but it is now a custom in all Western societies).

When someone violates a custom, that person is subjected to a sanction, a social punishment. When a highly valued custom (called a more) is violated, the **sanction** can be severe (being put in jail). When a less-valued custom (called a folkway) is violated, the sanction can be mild (having someone shake his head in disapproval).

Cultural differences in customs are seen in the use of food and clothing. The United States produces and consumes large quantities of beef, but in Buddhist countries, eating beef is sacrilegious. In the United States, people do not eat insects, but in many African countries, they are a necessity, even a delicacy. In terms of clothing, in some Islamic countries women must be totally covered in public, while in the United States people wear bikinis on public beaches and in several European countries people can be nude on certain beaches.

CYBERNETICS

The term "cybernetics" was coined as early as 1945 by Norbert Weiner, who outlined the study in his work *Cybernetics or Control and Communication in the Animal and Machine*. Weiner's concept focused on the common processes at work in all systems. Thus, Cybernetics can be described as an area of natural science concerned with the self-maintenance and self-control of mechanical, biological, and social systems. This maintenance and control are established through a feedback loop where the system adjusts to changes in the environment, which are communicated to it in order to maintain a steady state and allow the system to function and survive. The feedback process also provides **data** about the information within such systems. Stimulated by advances in computing in the 1940s, the use of cybernetics as an analogy was popular through the 1960s. It fell out of favor when sociologists reacted against functionalist thinking and scientism.

Though Weiner's book is seen as flawed by modern critics, his concepts were influential, and the name "cybernetics" sparked the imaginations of many. The name is based on the Greek word "kubernetes," which means "helmsman." Similar terms were found in the mid-1800s writings of the physicist Andre-Maric Ampere, a Polish writer named Trentowski, and also in one of Plato's dialogues. After the popularity of the word was established, the term began to be referred to in compound words such as "cyborg" or "cybernation." The advent of the Internet sealed the term's popular use because anything having to do with computers can be described with the prefix "cyber."

CYCLE

A cycle refers to a repeated social process. In such a process, a series of events is followed by a similar series of events once the original cycle is complete. Many social processes follow a cyclical pattern, such as the life cycle. History may also repeat itself in a cyclical pattern. The sociological concept referred to as the "circulation of elites" is an example of a cycle, in which power is observed to shift from one **group** of privileged people to another.

Cycles, or cyclical processes, may be hampered by a negative feedback loop. When this happens, the original cycle is reversed. An example of a negative feedback loop occurs in economic systems when producers use current pricing methods to anticipate future supply needs. Theoretically this results in an overproduction of goods that are assumed will make a profit. The cycle reverses itself as the economic system attempts to reestablish a new equilibrium. An example of a negative feedback loop in a social situation could occur with the administration of vaccinations. Theoretically, as vaccines against a particular disease are increased, that **disease** should decrease. As the disease decreases, vaccines could again decrease. This could lead to the reappearance of the disease, which would cause an increase again in the administration of vaccines.

Norbert Wiener coined the term "cybernetics" as early as 1945 *(The Library of Congress).*

D

DAHRENDORF, LORD RALF GUSTAV (1929-)

English educator and author

The son of Gustav and Lina Witt Dahrendorf, Ralf Gustav Dahrendorf was born in Hamburg, Germany, May 1, 1929, became a British citizen in 1988, and was knighted in 1993. A noted social and political thinker and writer, he is regarded as an important contributor to human understanding of the modern world. Dahrendorf, who has received 24 honorary degrees from various universities, earned a Ph.D. from the University of Hamburg in 1952, with postgraduate studies at the London School of Economics, 1952–1954.

Dahrendorf taught at the University of Saarbrücken in the then Federal Republic of Germany before becoming a fellow at the Center for Advanced Study in the Behavioral Sciences, Palo Alto, California, 1957–1958. He returned to the University of Hamburg, where he was a professor of sociology, 1958-60, moving to the University of Tubingen for the next six years. From 1966-69, he taught at the University of Konstanz. For the next few years, Dahrendorf turned to politics. He served as a member of the parliament in the government of the Federal Republic of Germany and as parliamentary secretary of state in the German Foreign Office, 1969–1970. He was a member of the European Economic Community in Brussels, Belgium, 1970-1974, and director of the London School of Economics, 1974–1984. He returned to Konstanz for three years as a professor of social sciences, and from 1987–1997, Dahrendorf served as warden, St. Antony's College in Oxford, England.

Besides being a Decorated Knight commander, order of the British Empire, Dahrendorf has received awards from the governments of then West Germany, Austria, Belgium, Luxembourg, and Senegal. He is a Fellow in the Anglo Germany Society, a member of the British Academy, Royal Society of the Arts, Royal College of Surgeons, the American Philosophical Society, and others

Dahrendorf is the author of numerous publications, his early works all in German. Acknowledged as an original and experienced social and political writer, he has received praise for such works as *The Modern Social Conflict*, 1989. It is a survey of social and political conflict in Western societies from the eighteenth century. It details where Western democracies stand today, how they got there, and what must happen for their political and social freedom to continue. Another praised publication is his 1996 book *LSE: A History of the London School of Economics and Political Science, 1895-1995,* which covers the story of crises, philanthropists, foreign foundations, negotiated settlements, and the University of London. Other works include: *Reflections on the Revolution in Europe*, 1990, an attempt to make sense of communism's collapse in Europe; *On Britain*, 1982; *The New Liberty*, 1975; and *Class and Class Conflict in Industrial Society*, 1959, first published in German.

DARWIN, CHARLES ROBERT (1809-1882)

English biologist

The English naturalist Charles Robert Darwin (1809–1882) discovered that natural selection was the agent for the transmutation of organisms during evolution, as did Alfred Russel Wallace independently. Darwin presented his theory in *Origin of Species*.

The concept of evolution by descent dates at least from classical Greek philosophers. In the eighteenth century Carl Linnaeus postulated limited mutability of species by descent. But most naturalists were concerned with identifying species, the stability of which was considered essential for their work. Natural theology regarded the perfection of **adaptation** between **structure** and mode of life in organisms as evidence for a predetermined divine plan.

Charles Lyell wrote his *Principles of Geology* (1830–1833), which Darwin on his *Beagle* circumnavigation

Ralf Dahrendorf *(Hulton Picture Library)*

turned on October 2, 1836. During the voyage Darwin spent 535 days at sea and roughly 1200 on land. Adequate identification of strata could be done on the spot, but sufficiently accurate identification of living organisms required systematists accessible only in London and Paris.

During the trip Darwin discovered the relevance of Lyell's uniformitarian views to the structure of St. Jago (Cape Verde Islands). He found, for example, that small locally living forms closely resembled large terrestrial fossil mammals embedded between marine shell layers and that the local sea was populated with living occupants of similar shells. He also observed the overlapping distribution on the continuous Patagonian plain of two closely related but distinct species of ostrich. He observed the differences between species of birds and animals on the Galápagos Islands.

Darwin's *Journal of Researches* was published in 1839. With the help of a government grant toward the cost of the illustrations, the *Zoology of the Voyage of the Beagle* was published, in five quarto volumes, from 1839 to 1843. Two themes run through his valuable and mostly neglected notes: distribution in space and time and observations of behavior as an aid to species diagnosis. Darwin abandoned the idea of fixity of species in 1837 while writing his *Journal*. A second edition, in 1845, had a stronger tinge of transmutation, but there was still no public avowal. This delightful volume is his most popular and accessible work.

Darwin's Transmutation (Species) Notebooks (1837–1839) have been reconstructed. The notion of "selection owing to struggle" derived from his reading of Malthus in 1838. The breadth of interest and profusion of hypotheses characteristic of Darwin, who could carry several topics in his mind at the same time, inform the whole. From this medley of facts allegedly assembled on Baconian principles all his later works derive.

After the 1846 publication of his geological observations of South America, he started a paper on his "first Cirripede," a shell-boring aberrant barnacle, no bigger than a pin's head, he had found at Chonos Island in 1835. This was watched while living, then dissected, and drawn while the *Beagle* sheltered from a week of severe storms. The working out of the relationship to other barnacles forced him to study all barnacles, a task that occupied him until 1854 and resulted in two volumes on living forms and two on fossil forms.

In 1855 Darwin began to study the practices of poultry and pigeon fanciers and worldwide domesticated breeds, conducted experiments on plant and animal variation and its hereditary transmission, and worried about the problem of plant and animal transport across land and water barriers, for he was persuaded of the importance of isolation for speciation. Darwin's "principle of divergence" recognizes that the dominant species must make more effective use of the territory it invades than a competing species and accordingly it becomes adapted to more diversified environments.

On June 14, 1858, Darwin received Alfred Russel Wallace's essay containing the theory of evolution by natural selection—the same theory Darwin was working on. Wallace had intuited the theory without doing research. A joint paper by Wallace and Darwin was presented at a meeting of the Linnaean Society.

found extremely useful. Fossils in South America and apparent anomalies of animal distribution triggered the task for Darwin of assembling a vast range of material. Reading Thomas Malthus's *Essay on the Principle of Population* in 1838 allowed Darwin to complete his evolutionary conceptual scheme.

Recent study of Darwin's unpublished manuscripts and entire works reveal a continuity of purpose and integrity of effort to establish the high probability of the genetic relationship through descent in all forms of life. Darwin work created a **paradigm** shift of consummate importance to the history of science and ideas.

Darwin was born on February 12, 1809, at Shrewsbury, the fifth child of the eminent medical doctor Robert Darwin and Susannah Wedgwood Darwin, daughter of the famous potter Josiah Wedgwood. In 1825 Darwin went to Edinburgh University to study medicine, but he found anatomy and *materia medica* dull and surgery unendurable. In 1828 he entered Christ's College, Cambridge, with the idea of taking Anglican orders. He attended Henslow's course in botany, started his famous beetle collection, and read widely, especially Paley's *Natural Theology* (1802). He graduated with a divinity degree in 1831. He married Emma Wedgwood, his first cousin, in 1839; they had ten children, four of whom became scientists.

Darwin became the naturalist on H. M. S. *Beagle* for a five-year voyage to survey the coast of Patagonia and Tierra del Fuego and complete observations of longitude by circumnavigation. The *Beagle* left on December 27, 1831, and re-

In 1859, Darwin published *On the Origin of Species by Means of Natural Selection, or the Preservation of Favoured Races in the Struggle for Life.* Spencer's phrase "survival of the fittest" was misleading because the essence of Darwin's theory is that, unlike natural theology, adaptation must not be too perfect and rigid. Darwin's book secured worldwide attention and aroused impassioned controversy.

Darwin published on many topics, plants becoming an increasing preoccupation. Papers he published in 1864 were collected into *The Movements and Habits of Climbing Plants* (1875), and these ideas were further generalized on uniformitarian lines and published as *The Power of Movement in Plants* (1880). Darwin's last work was *The Formation of Vegetable Mould through the Action of Worms, with Observations on Their Habits* (1881). He died on April 19, 1882, and was buried in Westminster Abbey.

DATA

Data are recorded observations, which are often complied into what is known as a *dataset.* A single observation of data is called *datum.* Data are often collected through direct observation, interviews, or **surveys** and are usually recorded in textual or numeric form. Data may be the simple record of colors of cars in a parking lot or the esoteric capture of observed spatial distances that strangers employ in crowded areas. Regardless of the observation recorded, a key parameter of data is that they measure the same specified characteristic in each observation.

In order to understand and interpret data it is critical to know at what level of analysis the observations were recorded and what research design was used. Generally, data are recorded at one of two levels; individual or aggregate. Individual data would be the record of a person's age or sex, whereas aggregate, or group data, would record observations at such levels as household, corporation, city, or nation. In addition to the different units of analysis in which data can be recorded, different research designs often produce different styles of data such as cross-sectional data, time-series data, longitudinal data, or pooled data.

DAVIS, KINGSLEY (1908-1997)
American sociologist and demographer

Davis coined the terms, zero population growth and population explosion. The lifelong interest of sociologist Kingsley Davis was the comparative study of population **structure** and change. Davis was born in Tuxedo, Texas, August 20, 1908, and educated at the University of Texas (A.B. 1930, M.A. 1932) and Harvard University (Ph.D. 1936). He taught at Smith College, Northampton, Massachusetts (1934–1936), Clark University, Worcester (1936–1937), Penn State University, University Park (1937–1942), and Princeton University (1942–1949). In 1945, he edited *World Population in Transition,* an important analytical tool, and in 1948, he published his first major work

Charles Darwin *(The Library of Congress)*

Human Society, a classic textbook that detailed his interest in the family structure. From this came an offer to teach in the Bureau of Applied Social Research, Columbia University, New York City (1949–1955). In 1955, Davis went to the University of California, Berkeley, and in 1977, he was named Distinguished Professor of Sociology, University of Southern California, Los Angeles. He died in Stanford, California, February 27, 1997.

Davis took the temperature of the American family for half a century. Overall, he held a generally gloomy view, feeling that **marriage** was weakened by the ease of contraception, **divorce**, and gender equality. "Interchangeable" marriage partners and voluntary marriage bonds caused a profound, permanent change in the marriage institution, Davis said, a change he felt was for the worse. He also saw the demise of industrial societies, which do not replace themselves in number or quality, whereas nonindustrial societies produce some 92 percent of the world's population.

Kingsley Davis gained prominence for his theories of demographic transition and zero population growth. In 1957, he predicted that the world population figure would climb to six billion by the year 2000. He was remarkably close; the target was reached in October 1999.

DAWKINS, RICHARD CLINTON
(1941-)
English evolutionary biologist

Richard Dawkins was born in Nairobi, Kenya, on March 26, 1941. He immigrated to England in 1949 with his parents, Clinton John, a farmer, and Jean Mary Vyvyan (Ladner). Earning his undergraduate degree at Balliol College, Oxford University in 1962, he remained to study under Niko Tinbergen, an eminent Danish biology and Nobel Prize winner for biology. After receiving his doctorate in 1966, Dawkins accepted a position as an assistant professor of zoology at the University of California at Berkeley, where he taught until 1969. In 1970 he returned to Oxford as a lecturer in zoology and a fellow of New College, becoming a reader in zoology in 1990. In 1995 he was awarded the newly endowed position as the Charles Simonyi Chair of Public Understanding of Science, where he remains currently. Divorced twice previously, Dawkins married actress and artist Lalla Ward in 1992.

Building on the ideas of Tinbergen, the first modern ethologist, Dawkins studied of the nature of animal behavior. As did his mentor, Dawkins studied differences in animal instinct and learned behavior, cooperation and competition, and **group** and individual behavior. However, as early as 1965, Dawkins' focus shifted and expanded into evolutionary biology. Applying ethological theories of behavior, he hit on the unique concept that the gene, not the individual, species, or **society**, was the prime unit of evolution. Humans and animals alike were merely carriers to house the genes.

Dawkins applied his theory of evolution, which was formed on an expanded theory of Darwinism, to the group level to include a system of cultural transmission that accounted for the behavior and development of societies. He coined the term ''mimeme,'' which was later shortened to ''meme,'' to describe the basic unit of this social evolutionary process. As a writer for *Wired Magazine* explained: ''Memes are to cultural inheritance what genes are to biological heredity....Ideas—like genes—could compete and cooperate, mutate and conserve. They, too, are operated on by natural selection.'' Thus human evolution is the combined result of the co-evolution of genes and memes.

In 1976 Dawkins became a well-known figure in both popular **culture** and academic society when he debuted these ideas in his first publication *The Selfish Gene.* An international bestseller, the book was translated into numerous languages and reprinted in a second edition in 1989. Along with gaining notoriety for his new ideas on evolution, Dawkins also received widespread attention for his blunt assessment of religion. A staunch atheist, he compared religion, especially **Christianity**, to a parasitic virus that infects the mind and defined it as a childish and meaningless response to life that holds no truth.

In his second book *The Extended Phenotype* published in 1982, Dawkins expanded his theory of **replication**, first introduced in *The Selfish Gene.* He argued that the most significant unit in the transmission of survival traits is that which can be replicated. The replicating codes of both the gene and the meme are essential to evolution. Not only does an individual species evolve, but so do the methods and tools its members use to manipulate their environment. For example, the evolutionary process must account for both the bird and the nest that it builds to assist its reproducing (replicating) process. Phenotype is the physical expression of the genes; thus Dawkins' theory of extended phenotype points to a construction that accounts for evolutionary changes in both the individual and the physical environment.

Dawkins continued to develop his neo-Darwinian theory in his next books. *The Blind Watchmaker: Why the Evidence of Evolution Reveals a Universe Without Design* (1986) earned the author both the Royal Society of Literature Award and the *Los Angeles Times* literary prize. He followed this by publishing three more bestsellers: *River Out of Eden* (1995), *Climbing Mount Improbable* (1996), and *Unweaving the Rainbow* (1998).

In *Out of the River Eden,* Dawkins' basic understanding of existence implies that the events of the universe are the result of natural forces and genetic replication; there is no reason guiding the happenings of life; all is chance and there is no **justice** in the world. He concludes: ''The universe we observe has precisely the properties we should expect if there is, at bottom, no design, no purpose, no **evil**, and no good, nothing but blind, pitiless indifference.'' However, Dawkins is by no means a nihilist. He told *Skeptic* magazine, ''I can easily imagine saying that in a Darwinian world, the fittest, by definition, are the ones that survive and the attributes that you need to survive in Darwinian sense are the attributes that I don't want to see in the world.''

DEATH AND DYING

Sociologists refer to activities that observe or commemorate significant changes in our lives as rites of passage. Examples of three commonly observed and significant rites of passage are birth, **marriage**, and death. In many cultures, the rite of passage involving death is the most ritualized and highly observed. So important is death as a social process, Émile Durkheim chose one form of death, **suicide**, for the first scientifically organized sociological study in 1897. As part of his study *Le Suicide*, Durkheim established a clear sociologically-based theory for explaining of some social processes surrounding death. Durkheim felt, as do many sociologists today, that a person's resistance to the processes of dying and death relate directly to the individual's acceptance and practice of social **norms**. Being part of a strong family structure, deep involvement in religious practices, and success in business are all social norms Durkheim determined give people strong reasons to continue living as long as possible. He concluded that failure to identify with such norms, a condition he called *anomie,* results in an individual being more likely to commit suicide or have a lifestyle that might hasten the onset of death.

While the social processes leading up to and surrounding the actual event of death are important, the processes in which a society's members engage in the course of dying are equally so. Once considered an important function of a dying person's family, the **role** of care giver for the dying person has over the past one hundred and fifty years passed to institutions. Today hospitals continue in this function, but have gradually shifted their emphasis to healing. As part of that shift, physicians now commonly choose to delegate the procedures related to death. Instead of doctors, hospital employees including nurses, chaplains, and staff social workers are frequently called upon to relate the news of death to surviving family members. And the news of death is delivered commonly in terms intended to soften the impact.

Typically, deaths of important people are marked by highly visible social events, including organized public mourning, sometimes including parades and highly publicized public religious services that are intended to help fill the void created by the loss. Through such elaborate rituals, the society's weakness or vulnerability is camouflaged by visible evidence of orderly and controlling bureaucratic structure which outlives its individual members. In fact, **Max Weber** wrote extensively about the reality and dangers of bureaucracies whose powers and controls may outlive the leaders who created them.

Most deaths are of private individuals whose surviving family members must deal with the processes of dying and death. Instead, these people must turn to privately operated agencies for assistance. Religious services in observance of the death are commonly conducted by a **church**, synagogue, or other center of worship of which the deceased was a member. Typically, assistance in the actual burial process is sought from a commercially operated funeral home. And family and friends participate at some level in both processes. While not trained as a sociologist, Jessica Mitford wrote analyzed these private and social processes in her 1963 book *The American Way of Death,* exploring how the American funeral industry helps people deny the existence of the death rather than accept it as the normal culmination of the process of living. Openly critical of the funeral home industry, *The American Way of Death* attacked what Mitford believed were predatory economic practices engaged in at a time when family members were least able to make rational decisions. The book analyzes profit motive, a point fundamental to the sociological theory of Karl Marx.

Today, nearly fifty years later, many Americans continue to engage in the expensive processes Mitford criticized. The fear of death drives individuals to agree to medical procedures that commonly extend life only a matter of weeks at great cost significant suffering. When death finally occurs, families are encouraged to engage in funeral practices aimed at shielding them from the reality of the death. The encouragement of such practices is viewed by sociologists as being based in part on economic motives. The providers of services to the terminally ill, as well as the funeral industry, benefit greatly from the socially accepted behaviors that encourage such practices. From a sociological perspective, individuals on whom the practices are focused tend to respond to the providers of the death-related services based on their involvement in and desire to perpetuate the social norms around which they have structured their lives.

DECISION-MAKING THEORY AND RESEARCH

Decision Sciences and econometrics use statistical models as a basis for decision-making. Social sciences, however, focus on the organizational structure, resources, environment, situation, **leadership** style, and group dynamics. Three styles of decision-making are democratic, authoritarian, and laissez-faire. Research reveals that democratic leaders who are good consensus builders are the most effective. However, when leaders have high or low amounts of **social control**, they need to be authoritarian to accomplish tasks. Examples would be a military situation (high control) or a crowd (low control). Laissez-faire leaders are thought to be too uninvolved and process (rather than outcome) oriented. They do not provide enough **structure** to accomplish tasks.

Rational Choice Theory is derived from neoclassical economics. Participants try to achieve goals that are consistent with their **values**. Two constraints complicate this process: limited access to necessary resources to accomplish goals considering the opportunity costs (alternative goals more readily attainable with the resources available) and constraint by social institutions (norms imposed by religious, political, and schools). Two other factors are: aggregation mechanism (how complex the cooperative effort must be) and adequate information.

The **exchange theory** formulated by **George Homans** focuses on decisions as a product of maximizing rewards and minimizing costs. Behaviors that have been rewarded in the past are likely to be repeated, while behaviors that have not been successful in the past are not likely to be repeated. Other factors considered are: *the value proposition* (how valued the result is), *deprivation-satiation proposition* (how satiation affects appreciation of reward), *aggression-approval propositions* (how thwarted **aggression** is more important than the original reward), *rationality* (how the value of the result needs to be multiplied by the **probability** of attaining it).

The exchange theory formulated by **Peter Blau** is based on personal exchange giving rise to differentiation of **status** and power which leads to legitimization and organization, which become in turn the basis for opposition and change. Decisions are based on four values: *in-group solidarity*, universalistic (value of things); values that *legitimize authority* (give power); and *values of opposition* (need for change beyond **adaptation** of the system).

Game theory is based on rational strategies to maximize gains and minimize loses. One considers known contingencies. One application of game theory is the *Prisoner's Dilemma.* If two inmates are arrested and neither confesses or both confess then each gets ten years. If one inmate accuses the other and the other does not deny, then the accused gets twenty years while the accuser is free.

Cohen, Marsh, and Olsen developed the Garbage Can Theory of decision-making. They contend that within an organization, leaders have answers that they apply to problems. Preexisting answers are the garbage cans, and the leaders drop problems into whichever can they see as appropriate given

Children orphaned by the Angolan civil war—a conflict in which warring factions received military support from both the United States and the Soviet Union *(Corbis Corporation [Bellevue]).*

time, circumstances, and importance. The three most common approaches to making a decision are *flight* (avoid the issue), *oversight* (minimal attention to problems), and *resolution* (spending time and energy to solve problems). Other factors are how major are the problems, what options exist for a solution, what energy needs to be exerted by the decision-maker, and how difficult is the decision.

Ellen Chaffee stated that decision-making can be *linear* (in accordance with strategic planning), *adaptive* (responsive to environment and opportunities), and *interpretive* (parallel to corporate culture and symbolic management). Estella Bensimon sees decision-making in organizations as stemming from the administrators' approach and organizational culture. These can be *bureaucratic*, *symbolic* with focus on organizational culture, *collegial*, or *political* with emphasis on power and coalition building.

Many factors affect **group** decisions. Size is a factor. If two people have equal power, the **interaction** stops if one leaves. With three or more individuals then **coalitions** can **influence** group decisions. Risky shift phenomenon refers to the greater tendency of groups to make risky decisions than individuals would advocate if polled separately. Groupthink is the tendency of groups to push for consensus and **conformity** while they ignore outside forces or information. Dissent or critical questioning within the group is viewed as disloyal. An example of Groupthink is the decision to launch the Challenger despite questions about the effect of the solid rocket booster fuel on the seals. Michel's **Iron Law of Oligarchy** explores the concentration of power in the hands of a few even in organizations committed to **democracy**.

DECOLONIZATION

Decolonization is the process of achieving emancipation from a colonial system. As western colonization occurred in two waves, so did decolonization. First-wave colonies, like the United States and most Central and South American countries,

seized their independence during the eighteenth and nineteenth centuries. However, the term, decolonization, most commonly refers to second-wave colonies. After nearly a century of occupation, political independence was won primarily, but not entirely, during the middle half of the twentieth century. For example, Egypt and Ireland won their independence during the early part of 1920s. The morally repugnant political reign of Western European (primarily England and France, but also Germany, Italy, Dutch, Belgium, and Russia), American, and Japanese imperial states at last expired; however, it did not occur peacefully. Many native inhabitants sacrificed their blood and their lives for liberation as did soldiers of imperial states for the maintenance of their colonial status. The decolonial process is perhaps the most remarkable phenomenon to occur during post World War II and the Cold War periods.

The campaign for decolonization was fiercely taken on by subjected people and critics of **colonialism** such as Leopold Sedar Senghor, Amie Ceasaire, Jean-Paul Sartre. Perhaps the most notable attack was the literary movement of Francaphone writers called *Le mouvement negre*. One such famed artist was **Frantz Fanon**, author of *Black Skin, White Mask* and *The Wretched of the Earth*. Discussing decolonization at length and writing at the time of decolonial battles, Fanon contended that ''the need for this change exists in its crude state, impetuous and compelling, in the consciousness and in the lives of men and women who are colonized. But the possibility of this change is equally experienced in the form of a terrifying future in the consciousness of another 'species' of men and women: the colonizer.'' He continued, ''Decolonization is the meeting of two forces, opposed to each other by their very nature, which in fact owe their originality to that sort of substantification which results from and is nourished by the situation of the colonies.'' In social science Fanon finds a home along side other critical thinkers such a **Karl Marx** who also believed that revolution is the only means of ending colonial repression. For Marxists, decolonization, at least at the time, was as Marx had predicted; it was the revolution of the proletariat struggle against it oppressor. However, post-colonization would prove to be a grave disappointment, not only to Marxists who cheered for complete emancipation but to the colonies themselves which found that post-colonialism offered an economic reality similar to colonialism.

Additionally, the Cold War has important implications for Marxist prophecies and the maintenance of imperialist **capitalism** as world system. Immediately following the battle for independence, newly independent former colonies had to determine their economic fate. The question under consideration was would the newly independent state turn to **socialism** or capitalistic-democracy. Socialist states like Cuba and the USSR had been extremely instrumental in aiding native inhabitants in the wars for national liberation from western European imperialist states. Although, the Cold War was said to be exclusively between the United States and the USSR, newly independent colonies were very much a part of this process. Angola, a south-west African nation, is good example. During the wars of liberation warring natives in Angola received support in the form financial aid and weapons from both the USSR and the United States; the USSR supported the Popular Movement for the Liberation of Angola (MPLA), while the United States and Apartheid-South Africa supported the Union for the Total Liberation of Angola (UNITA). The question simply was if the newly independent colonies turned to socialism (as many did) what outcome would this have for capitalism as a world-system? Ex-colonies provided a significant and sizable market to imperialist states, but more importantly they supply virtually all the natural resources needed for imperial industries. The fate of the capitalist world system would partially be determined by the economic future of ex-colonies. After the collapse of the USSR in the early 1990s, socialism ceased being a potential threat to global capitalism.

DEDUCTIVE LOGIC

Conducting deductive research involves generating a hypothesis from an established **theory**, then testing one or more hypotheses using **data**. For example, **labeling theory** is often used to explain why some juveniles persist in delinquency and others do not, a phenomenon known as recidivism. In short, the theory's axioms are, first, that **deviance** that goes unreported, or undetected, is not likely to lead to recidivism. Such deviance is called "primary deviance", and it occurs when a juvenile commits a delinquent act and then is not identified with the act. The theory's second axiom is that once a juvenile is identified as deviant, then it becomes more difficult for him/her to desist from deviance, because labeling causes the juvenile to identify with that **role**. The juvenile's subsequent deviance is then called "secondary deviance" and is much more damaging to the juvenile.

To test this theory deductively, a researcher might generate the hypothesis that, "juvenile delinquents who are arrested and proceed through the juvenile justice system are more likely to recidivate than those whose delinquency goes unnoticed by justice officials." In this example, identification of offending is operationalized as contact with juvenile justice officials. In this manner, the researcher moves toward more specific reasoning, reasoning if further specified by operationalizing delinquency and identifying and operationalizing other factors that may lead to recidivism.

Data would be collected, possibly in the form of a general survey of juveniles ages 12 to 18. Questions could address whether, and if so, how often the respondents have committed various delinquent acts. Then, information would be gathered about each respondent's experiences that resulted from each act of delinquency: whether he/she was caught, and what happened as a result. Then, the researcher would statistically compare whether recidivism was more likely to occur for juveniles who experienced **secondary deviance**, as opposed to those who only experienced **primary deviance**.

If support for the theory is discovered, then the theory's applicability is restricted by the particular sample of juveniles used in the study, the conceptualization and **operationalization** of the variables, and the methods used to test the hypothesis. The theory could then be retested under different circum-

Studies have found that, due to their architectural design, some housing projects have significantly higher rates of crime *(Corbis Corporation [Bellevue])*.

stances in subsequent deductive studies. At this point, information generated from specific deductive conclusions could be generated using inductive logic to construct a larger theory.

DEFENSIBLE SPACE

Defensible space is based on the assumption that architectural design dramatically influences the rate of **crime**. In his analysis of low- and middle-income housing projects, Oscar Newman found that some housing projects had significantly higher rates of crime. For instance, he found that housing projects that consisted of buildings with seven or more stories had higher crime rates than demographically similar projects with six or fewer stories. He concluded that certain architectural designs enable inhabitants to successfully control or supervise their environment.

Oscar Newman described four features of the physical design of housing projects that facilitate inhabitants' ability to control their environment. First, physical design should create feelings of territoriality and a sense of proprietary interest in the area's protection. When people feel that an area is theirs they are more likely to take care of it and watch over it. It is possible to design housing projects that foster these feelings. Second, physical design should be able to provide surveillance opportunities for residents. Increased surveillance acts as a significant crime deterrent. Surveillance can also make residents feel an area is secure, causing them to use the area more, further increasing the sense of security.

A third feature of defensible space is that the physical design of projects should not foster feelings of distinctiveness or isolation and the corresponding stigma attached to them. When projects are architecturally distinctive, they may become stigmatized making them tempting targets for potential offenders. The fourth feature is the housing project's location to areas or streets that are considered safe. By positioning a housing unit's public zones and entries so that they face areas that are considered safe, it is possible to increase the safety of residential areas. Areas that are considered safe are public streets and pathways with high vehicular and pedestrian traffic.

It is now standard for all new housing projects to be designed with the principles of defensible space in mind. Schools and other large institutions are also being built or modified to provide more defensible space. In addition, the concepts put forth in defensible space have laid the foundation for situational crime prevention, which now an important value in **criminology**.

DEFERENCE

Deference, a concept of **legitimacy**, comes out of the Weberian tradition in the social sciences. Deference is most often used to characterize submissive behavior toward another on the part of a subordinate actor or group. Such behavior conforms to certain expectations pertaining to conduct within unequal power relationships. Deference requires following a certain set of behaviors, however, such behavior does not necessitate the existence of deferential attitudes on the part of the subordinate actor. Properties and personality traits such as kindness, humor, and being likeable are not deference-relevant qualities.

As with other concepts of legitimacy, deference implies certain dynamics on both sides of the power relationship. On the one hand is the superior actors or group. From their elevated position, relative to others, these individuals manage their superior position, constantly defining it and evaluating it, while attempting to maintain it. At the same time, those in a subordinate position are also evaluating the relationship, attempting to interpret and manipulate it.

Edward Shils devoted much time to this concept of deference. Deference, for Shils, is simply an acknowledgement of a person's worth. He felt that all social interactions involved a disparity in power and, therefore, an element of deference from one person or party toward the other. Contrary to popular use of the term to characterize only submissive behavior toward a superior, Shils broadened the scope. He theorized that

acts of deference could involve either appreciation which would refer to positive and/or high deference (e.g., flattering) or derogation which would refer to negative or low deference (e.g., interrupting). Hence, the actions of a superior toward a subordinate and the actions of a subordinate to a superior are both classes of deferential behavior in this conception. For example, in the military, people engage in several formal deferential behaviors, such as saluting. One officer saluting another and the other officer not having to salute are both instances of deference.

Several characteristics affect an evaluation of who is deserving of deference, in what direction they are deserving (positive or negative), and to what degree they deserve it. These characteristics, labeled by Shils as "deference-entitlements," can include wealth, income, occupation, lifestyle, educational level, political power, **ethnicity**, or simply just having kinship or close personal ties to those with deference-entitlements. While these deference-entitlements are objective characteristics, the subjective evaluations of these objective characteristics determine their value as entitlements. Based on these deference-entitlements, individuals will determine if they should grant deference to others and if they should expect deference to be expressed toward themselves. When people interact they make simultaneous assessments of one's own and the other's deference-entitlements in order to guide their behavior. One's "deference-position" is where one stands in terms to whom they defer and who in turn shows deference. A deference-position can also be thought of as one's **status**, but status is only relative given who is involved in an **interaction**, while a deference-position is maintained even outside any interaction. Deference-positions imply some level of stability and continuity because a deference-position is relatively pervasive unless replaced with another position due to some transition in deference-entitlements. Essentially the deference-position is the classification of an individual in a hierarchy. Deference, on the other hand, signifies a set of behaviors toward others based on their position in this hierarchy, their deference-position. Deference actions can encapsulate different combinations of tone of speech, demeanor, frequency and mode of contradiction, and turn-taking in conversation, as well as many other behaviors that also get combined with non-deferential components when in sustained interaction.

Deference-positions form a hierarchy, and one can conceive of society as made up several levels of deference strata. The determination of deference-position is interesting because placing others into a hierarchy has to be accomplished with only very fragmentary evidence regarding the objective entitlements. Therefore, conclusions about an individual's deference-position are often vague and approximate. Certain entitlements grant or exclude membership in specific strata. However, given that circles of social interaction are largely with those similar to ourselves, members of any particular deference stratum may be relatively oblivious or simply indifferent as to what characteristics form the foundations of other deference strata. Instead, individuals will be more concerned with the entitlement requirements for their deference stratum and where the boundaries are of the strata around them so as to concentrate on either avoiding expulsion or attempting to gain admission to these neighboring strata.

DEFINITION OF THE SITUATION

The *definition of the situation* is a theoretical notion that was developed during the early 1900s by social psychologist W. I. Thomas. Also referred to as the *Thomas Theorem*, the definition of the situation posits that individuals act or behave in accordance with the subjective meanings they assign to elements of the social world. According to Thomas, successive definitions of the situation shape life experiences, personalities, and social reality itself.

The definition of the situation further assumes that different individuals may define their social environments in disparate ways, even when exposed to identical social stimuli. People are not necessarily free, however, to create subjective definitions ''out of thin air.'' Individuals are born into a social world that operates in the context of previously constructed definitions of the situation. The sum total of existing definitions of the situation forms a normative system that both influences social action and constrains subsequent definitions of the situation.

Thomas's most notable elaboration of the definition of the situation states that if individuals define situations as real, then those situations are real in their consequences. In other words, individuals not only behave in relation to the objective features of a situation but also in the context of meanings they subjectively assign to that situation. Furthermore, because subjective meanings frequently overshadow the objective features of a social situation, social behavior is often based almost entirely upon one's own definition of the situation. Therefore, the Thomas Theorem holds that regardless of whether something objectively exists within the social world, individuals' or groups' definitions of the situation may support the belief that it does. Such a belief may then function to shape subsequent social action.

For example, if members of a particular **society** believe in witches, whether witches actually exist as an objective feature of the social world is of little consequence. If certain individuals believe that witches do exist, and subsequently behave in the context of that belief by killing those whom they define as witches, death becomes a very real consequence of their definition of the situation. In the United States the maltreatment of stereotypically-defined groups such as women and people of color occurs in much the same way. Therefore, definitions of the situation shape social reality by organizing the experiences of all members of the social world, including not only those individuals defining the situation but also those who are defined.

DEGREES OF FREEDOM

The phrase, ''degrees of freedom'' symbolized by d_f or υ, refers to the number of **values** in a **data** set that are free to vary. The concept is derived from the restrictions placed on deviations from the mean when calculating the variance of a distribution. To illustrate possible restrictions on data, suppose we are to select any six numbers—there are no restrictions upon which numbers we choose or the order in which they can be chosen. This distribution has six degrees of freedom as all six numbers are free to vary. If we then say that the numbers must add to less than twenty, one restriction is being placed upon the distribution since it will not matter what values we choose for the first five, but the sixth value will have to result in the distribution summing to less than twenty. The degrees of freedom in this case become $N-1$ (where N refers to the sample size).

Different statistical procedures impose restrictions on data so that not all values are free to vary. When calculating the variance, for instance, one step involves adding the deviations from the **mean** which will always equal zero if calculated correctly. Therefore, if we have deviation values of -3, -6, -9, 4 and 5, the sixth value is not free to vary, it must be 9 so that the sum of the deviations equals zero. In this case, because five of the six data points are free to vary, the number of degrees of freedom is N-1, or 5. The more restrictions placed on the data by the statistical procedure, the larger the number of degrees of freedom that are forfeited. Tests that compare two samples, for example, the t-tests of independent samples have degrees of freedom equal to $N_1 + N_2 - 2$, since the samples lose one degree of freedom each. In the calculation of other statistics such as one mean t-tests, chi-square one-sample **median** test, the degrees of freedom are N-1. Calculation of such statistics as ANOVA, other chi-square tests, and the sum of squared deviations (SSE) stipulate varying degrees of freedom.

DEINSTITUTIONALIZATION

During the 1950s a larger proportion of the U.S. population was institutionalized for mental illness than ever before. People who showed signs of being disturbed were brought into psychiatric hospitals for extended inpatient care, especially if they were not living under the **authority** of their parents. Yet the psychiatric profession was becoming uncomfortable with long-term inpatient care as the standard solution for patients with episodic mental illness. From the late 1950s onwards, many who had been living in asylums and psychiatric hospitals were released. From over 500,000 inmates in state hospitals in 1955, by 1990 there were under 100,000.

Deinstitutionalization passed through several phases. During the 1960s, many patients were discharged under the supervision of the new Community Mental Health Centers. Those less able to care for themselves were transferred to the psychiatric wards of general hospitals, **nursing homes**, or other forms of sheltered housing. Following the establishment of **Medicaid** in 1965, states were eager to move patients from state-funded psychiatric hospitals into these other forms of care, where their costs were then covered by the federal government. The discharge of patients was accelerated by the development of new drugs such as Thorazine and Lithium which muted the symptoms of schizophrenia and severe depression.

During the cultural revolution of the 1960s, social conventions and mechanisms of enforcement (such as religious, educational and psychiatric institutions) were reexamined as

The U.S. Capitol building in Washington, D.C., serves as one of the most well-known symbols of Western democracy *(Corbis Corporation [Bellevue]).*

mechanisms of **social control**. Within this context, actions previously understood as symptoms of mental illness were tolerated, even admired as freedom of expression. Influential intellectuals, notably **Erich Fromm, Michel Foucault, Erving Goffman**, Thomas Szasz, and R. D. Laing, patients' rights advocates, and civil liberties lawyers brought public attention to the authoritarian and often abusive regimes within many mental hospitals. As a result, by the end of the 1970s, both federal and state laws forbade the institutionalization of people with mental illness who showed no signs of being dangerous to themselves or to others, and state hospitals gradually discharged many remaining patients who had nowhere to go.

Deinstitutionalization is often cited as important cause of the rise of **homelessness** in the 1980s and 1990s. This argument has been supported by a great variety of service providers to the homeless, who consistently report that at least a third of their clients show signs of serious mental illness. Rather than being liberated from coercive institutions, as the patients rights advocates had hoped, a significant minority of the chronically mentally ill are now housed in homeless shelters with worse conditions and fewer resources than the old state hospitals.

DEMOCRACY

Democracy in sociological usage refers most broadly to a regime of popular rule and is generally contrasted with authoritarian systems or regimes. Unlike political science, **sociology** never developed a particular sub-area exclusively focused on the study of democracy. Rather, the study of democracy has been taken up most often in **political sociology**, which focuses on conditions conducive to democracy but also in the **sociology of development**, which focuses on the relationship between economic growth and democracy and in the sociology of culture, which studies the cultural features of democratic life.

Two founding figures have remained influential in studies of Democracy: **Max Weber** and Karl Marx. For Weber, the **rationalization** of **society**, which was both a prerequisite and an outcome of modernization, would require the withering away of types of **authority** based on charismatic rule and force. Rational, modern bureaucracies would guarantee democratic and legitimate rule. Marxist influence resulted in, on the other hand, a general skepticism about the possibility of a genuine democracy within capitalist society. Marx's own writings on fundamental cleavages in capitalist society translated to a series of studies that probed the ways in which political systems reflect the interests of some classes over others.

An early debate concerned the nature of North American democracy. Robert Dahl, who studied political processes in New Haven in the 1950s, espoused the view that democracy in North America represented the organized interests of plural pressure groups in his book *Who Rules* (1963). **C. Wright Mills**, who in 1957 wrote *The Power Elite*, presented the opposing view: interlocking elites wielded power by the control of economic, political, and military institutions. These elites, who shared similar backgrounds, were a relatively small group of persons with similar goals who were able to manipulate supposedly democratic processes.

Much work within sociology on democracy was at this point largely influenced by **modernization theory** and **functionalism**. Scholars, like Hoselitz (1960), developed schemes that differentiated the ideal characteristics of traditional and modern societies. Modern societies were differentiated, democratic, universalistic, and meritocratic. **Traditional societies** were undifferentiated, authoritarian, particularistic, and based rewards on ascriptive characteristics. Studies explored the conditions under which societies achieved these characteristics. An important focus was on attitudes and **values**. Almond and Verba's early study of political **culture** in five nations explored attitudes and beliefs to see if they were impediments or preconditions to democratic development. Seymor Martin Lipset's work throughout the 1960s sought to understand the preconditions for democracy. In *The First New Nation*, Lipset offered a comparison of the history of the United States with that of European countries and argued that American history had fostered a set of values about achievement and equalitarianism that made for a stable democracy. He found remnants of **elitism** in both France and Germany, which made them, in this view, unstable democracies. **Reinhard Bendix** developed similar arguments in his famous book *Nation-Building and Citizenship* (1964).

Within the sociology of development scholars asked about the relationship between economic development and democratic systems. A number of dependency theorists in the 1970s proposed that the relationship was, in fact, negative for Third World countries. Capitalist economic development was likely to lead to authoritarian regimes in developing countries, as scholars like Guillermo O'Donnel argued.

A third strand of sociological thought on democracy is concerned with the features of civic life. Largely within the sociology of culture scholars have explored the actual lived experience of persons who participate in democracy. One important influence was Jürgen Habermas, whose 1969 *The Structural Transformation of the Public Sphere* is probably the single most cited book in the area since its English translation in 1989. The "public sphere" described democratic deliberation as a potentially emancipatory activity and referred to those spaces of rational deliberation where citizens debate common problems. Margaret Somers, Michael Schudson, Nina Eliasoph, and others have asked a number of questions about public spheres in civic life. Another influential approach in the study of democracy came from the team of researchers headed by Robert Bellah that published *Habits of the Heart* in 1989. Bellah and his co-authors studied the "state of democracy" in the United States, and concluded that an individually-oriented culture was eroding the bases for collective life and civic engagement. In a similar vein, Robert Putnam's (1993) *Making Democracy Work* compares the South and North of Italy and concludes that the South lacks the proper cultural conditions for an active democratic life. Putnam's recent work argued that Americans are becoming more self-centered, and community life has less vitality. Paul Lichterman argued based on studies of civic groups that the culture of self-improvement that Bellah and his colleagues decry can serve the function of civic engagement.

DEMOGRAPHIC METHODS

Demography can be divided into two areas: formal demography and population studies. Formal demography deals with the scientific and mathematical study of population. Population studies examine all factors related to population change and is particularly focused on social forces behind fertility, mortality, and migration. Consequently, formal demography develops and refines demographic methods, while population studies use demographic methods as a tool to aid in explaining the impact of social and natural forces on population change.

Although some demographic methods, such as the life table, date back to the seventeenth century, most **adaptation** of mathematics to demography occurred in the 1900s. The work commonly considered to be a benchmark in demographic methods, Shryock and Siegel's *The Methods and Materials of Demography,* was published in 1971. Because the area is new, the basic knowledge assumed to be the domain of formal demographers continues to change rapidly as additional mathematical techniques are adapted for studying population. Thus, only a few modern textbooks on demographic techniques exist, and even the most recent are soon outdated, since they omit many calculations commonly used in research reported in leading demographic journals.

While several mathematical techniques fall within the rubric of demographic methods, no purely demographic methods exist. That is, each demographic method was developed in another area of science and has been adapted by demographers to study population. Even the oldest demographic method—the life table—was developed in the field of actuarial science, to which the famous astronomer, Edmund Halley, was a major contributor. Today, most demographic methods can as accurately be termed *statistical techniques*, although some statistical techniques are not considered demographic methods.

What distinguishes demographic methods from all other statistical formulations is that they comprise a series of techniques used specifically for examining population change. Demographic methods can be used to describe past events or current trends. They can also be used to estimate population growth. Most commonly, demographic methods are used to measure fertility, mortality, and migration; however, demographic methods also examine **marriage**, divorce, cohabitation, and related factors. The most basic demographic methods are population change rates in births, deaths, marriages, divorces, and migrations. Other commonly reported statistics gained through more complex demographic methods cover life expectancies, life spans, and population projections. The most complex demographic methods include parametric failure time models, age-period-cohort analyses, and multiple increment-decrement life tables.

Just as demographers have adapted methods of analysis from a variety of fields, other sociologists are now adopting demographic methods to their own analyses. For example, hazard models allow researchers to determine the probability of an event's occurrence based on characteristics of other individuals to whom the event has already happened. While hazard modeling is now a relatively common research tool used by criminologists, social psychologists, and family sociologists, it is based on life table analysis—a demographic method.

DEMOGRAPHIC TRANSITION

Demographic transition is the historical process by which countries move from high **birth and death rates** (pre-transition) to low birth and death rates (post-transition). It has three key stages: (1) high birth and death rates; (2) declining death rates followed by declining birth rates; and (3) low birth and death rates. The second, transitional stage is one of rapid population growth, since the decline in death rates occurs before the decline in birth rates.

The demographic transition model began as a classification of nations grouped according to their rates of population growth. Demographer Warren Thompson used **data** from a number of countries for the 1908-1927 period, and he identified three groups of nations. Group A included those countries that had moved from having very high rates of *natural increase* (births minus deaths) to very low rates. Much of northern and western Europe was included in Group A, as were many overseas nations settled by European immigrants. Group B consisted of countries in which both death rates and birth rates had fallen, but where death rates were declining as rapidly or more rapidly than the birth rates. The countries of southern and eastern Europe were included in Group B. Finally, Group C included those countries where neither birth nor death rates had declined from their preindustrial levels. Thompson estimated that Group C accounted for 70 to 75% of the world's population, including most of the peoples of Asia, Africa, and South America.

Research scientist Frank W. Notestein and sociology professor Kingsley Davis developed the classic formulation of

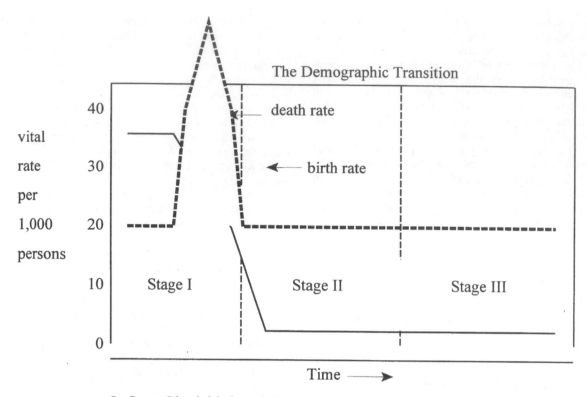

The Demographic Transition

In Stage I both birth and death rates are high, but the latter fluctuates due to famines and epidemics. Stage II is characterized by declining mortality followed by declining fertility. In Stage III both fertility and mortality have reached low levels and fertility is more prone to fluctuation.

This demographic transition model reflects the process by which countries move from high birth and death rates to low birth and death rates *(Courtesy of Esther I. Wilder).*

the demographic transition. In 1945, Notestein described three stages of population growth which parallel the groups that Thompson identified: high growth potential (Group C), transitional growth (Group B), and incipient decline (Group A). That same year, Kingsley Davis coined the term "demographic transition" in his seminal piece, "The World Demographic Transition." Both Notestein and Davis described the social and economic factors that were responsible for the demographic transition—the movement from high growth potential (high birth and death rates) to incipient decline (low birth and death rates).

The classic demographic transition model is linked to the gradual processes of socioeconomic modernization, industrialization, and **urbanization**. In pre-transition societies (Stage I), life is precarious and death rates are high. Premodern societies are, therefore, organized in ways that have strong pressures to reproduce. A variety of social institutions and **norms**, such as traditional gender roles, develop in response to the high economic value of children and the need to offset high mortality rates. As industrialization proceeds (Stage II), food supplies become more reliable, standards of living improve, and death rates decline. Fertility remains high at first, however,

due to established social norms and entrenched economic conditions. Stage II, the transitional stage, is therefore characterized by high rates of population growth. Eventually (Stage III) fertility declines in response to falling death rates, changing roles for children and women, changes in family structure, technological advancements (including contraception), and the rise of **individualism** and secularization. Some authors have argued that the notion of homeostasis (balance) underlies the framework of the demographic transition because there is a movement towards equilibrium in vital rates.

Since the original formulation of the demographic transition, demographers have focused considerable attention on certain fertility patterns that seem inconsistent with the model. For example, Ansley Coale, a professor of economics and public affairs, noted that the demographic transition has been unable to account for (a) large differences in the fertility of pretransition societies; (b) differences in **marriage** rates in premodern societies; (c) differences in marital fertility in pretransition populations; and (d) variations in fertility in industrialized societies. Moreover, mortality decline does not always precede fertility decline. European evidence suggests that fertility decline was not necessarily tied to specific levels of economic development but was closely linked to linguistic and cultural boundaries.

In response to these criticisms, demographic transition theory has been reformulated to more fully account for the role of cultural and ideational factors as likely causes of fertility decline. While efforts to modify demographic transition theory have provided insight into the diverse causes of the transition (socioeconomic, institutional, cultural, etc.), none has been able to pinpoint the threshold at which the transition occurs, even though this was one of the main criticisms of the classic formulation of the theory. In spite of ongoing revisions, the demographic transition model provides a graphic metaphor with strong predictive value, and few demographers would argue with its basic foundations. As demographer Paul Demeny notes, "In traditional societies fertility and mortality are high. In modern societies fertility and mortality are low. In between there is demographic transition."

DEMOGRAPHY

The term "demography" is derived from the Greek root *demos*, which means "the people," and *graphy*, which refers to writing or describing. The French political economist Achille Guillard is credited with coining the term demography (in French, *démographie*) in his *Éléments de Statistique Humaine, ou Démographie Comparée* (*Elements of Human Statistics, or Comparative Demography*), published in 1855.

In their classic 1959 definition, sociologists Philip M. Hauser and Otis Dudley Duncan described demography as "the study of the size, territorial distribution, and composition of population, changes therein, and the components of such changes." Demography, the scientific study of population, includes both formal demography and population studies. Formal demography (sometimes called "pure demography") focuses on the collection and statistical analysis of **data** on fertility (births), mortality (deaths), nuptuality (marriages), and migration. It is highly mathematical and is generally considered the "core" of the discipline. The field of population studies is more broadly defined. It deals with the causes and consequences of social and economic change and with the interaction of demographic processes, social relationships, and the natural environment.

Those who study demography, demographers, investigate issues ranging from the biosocial aspects of fertility and mortality to immigrant and ethnic variation in socioeconomic well-being. Consequently, demographers are drawn from a number of academic fields including anthropology, biology, ecology, economics, geography, **political science, psychology, sociology**, and public health. Sociology professor J. Mayone Stycos called demography an "interdiscipline" because it draws heavily on a wide range of subjects, although he acknowledged that demography does have a distinctive body of interrelated concepts, techniques, journals, and professional associations. Only a few U.S. universities (such as the University of California/Berkeley) maintain separate departments of demography, however. American demographers are more

often trained within departments of sociology, and some demographers see a special relationship between demography and sociology.

Demography may be counted among both the oldest and the newest disciplines. A concern with the components of population growth and change dates back to ancient times. Most early writings on population emphasized the relationships between population size and political and economic processes. For example, Plato and Aristotle attempted to determine the optimal population size for an efficient city-state. During the Middle Ages, Ibn Khaldun, a fourteenth-century social philosopher, developed a population theory putting forward the notion that societies pass through stages of development which are reflected in population growth.

More recent, scientific, study of population can be traced to the work of **John Graunt**, who is sometimes referred to as "the father of demography." Graunt, a Londoner, conducted the first known statistical analysis of demographic data (city and **church** records of burials and christenings). In 1662 he published *Natural and Political Observations Made Upon the Bills of Mortality*, which included systematic observations derived from data on the population in and around London. Through the seventeenth and eighteenth centuries, a growing number of scholars examined population-related issues. Their writings have been variously referred to as political arithmetic (John Graunt, William Petty), **political economy (Thomas Malthus)**, and human statistics (sometimes just "statistics"). Shortly after Graunt published his work, Sir William Petty (1690), a political economist, wrote *Political Arithmetik*, said to be the forerunner of the broader discipline of statistics. In the late eighteenth and early nineteenth centuries, Thomas Malthus, a clergyman, published several versions of his "Essay on the Principle of Population," in which he asserted the natural tendency for population growth to outstrip subsistence. Malthus is therefore widely associated with the pessimistic view of population growth.

Demography, as a unique discipline with its own professional organizations, meetings and journals, is a recent phenomenon. Scientific journals on population were not introduced until the 1930s and 1940s. The earliest of these were *Population Index* (1933), *Population* (1945), and *Population Studies* (1946). The Population Association of America (PAA) began in 1930 at New York University as an offshoot of the American National Committee of the International Union for the Scientific Study of Population (IUSSP), founded in 1927. The journal *Demography* was launched in 1964, about the same time that computers were gaining widespread popularity among population researchers.

The domain of population research evolves in response to public concern with population growth and the increasing recognition that population-related issues are important to individuals, families, governments, private organizations and **society** in general. In the post World War II era, demographers tried to understand the high fertility and rapid population growth that they found in both developed and developing countries. After the decline of fertility in the Western countries, however, concerns about high fertility were more often associated with less developed nations and with particular population groups, teenagers and unmarried persons, for example. Demographers today draw attention to women's issues, **aging**, family structure, social and behavioral determinants of health, anthropological demography, and AIDS. Many researchers examine environmental consequences of demographic behavior, including pollution and global warming. While some scholars argue that population growth results in widespread hunger and environmental devastation (Paul Ehrlich, Lester Ward), others maintain that population is the "ultimate resource" and that population growth facilitates economic development (Julian Simon). Over the years, demographic research has become increasingly empirical and sophisticated due to advances in statistical and analytic techniques. At the same time, the biomedical model is the framework increasingly used to train demographic specialists.

Demographic analysis is an essential component of social and economic planning and development. Consequently, demographers are employed in universities, private consulting firms, government agencies, and non-governmental organizations. They often take a leading role as researchers and administrators in census bureaus, labor bureaus, social welfare organizations, urban planning agencies, and international organizations such as the Agency for International Development, the Population Council, and the World Health Organization. Because of their strong statistical and analytic skills, population specialists are increasingly sought by market research and investment planning firms.

DEPENDENCY THEORY

Dependency theory explain the distorted capitalist development of countries in Latin America, Africa, and Asia. Drawing largely upon Marxist concepts and writings on the economic history of these regions, dependency theory has developed an account of Third World nations' underdevelopment as a result of continued contact and dependency on First World nations for industrial products, capital, and expertise. Some important antecedents of dependency theory include Hobson's theory of **imperialism**, the ideas of V. I. Lenin and Nikholai Bukharin, and the writings of leftist economists in the 1950s, like Paul Baran's 1953 *Political Economy of Growth*. Dependency theory was developed in critical dialogue with modernization theory, which espouses that factors endogenous to Third World nations, like the supposed lack of modern **culture** and **values**, account for the lack of development. Dependency theory represented a direct challenge to **modernization theory** and to prevailing economic wisdom in the 1960s. It also represented the search for a solution to the continued lack of industrialization in post-colonial nations during the Cold War. Whereas modernization theory advocated greater sustained involvement of industrialized nations in the form of investment and cultural exchange, dependency theorists generally looked for alternative models of development, as present in the apparent successes of socialist experiments like those in Cuba and in Tanzania.

Main exponents of dependency theory were developed in the nations in question, most notably in Latin America, with Cardoso and Faletto's *Capitalism and Underdevelopment* (1979) being the most sophisticated and subtle analysis, drawing upon political and economic factors to account for dependent development. Dependency theory is the immediate precursor to World-Systems theory.

Dependency scholars argued that because of the external ties of Third World nations that made them dependent on industrialized nations for capital, advanced technology, and expertise, these nations would remain in a state of underdevelopment or stunted economic and social growth. This level of development would be marked by **poverty**, continued dependence on international finance, and an export-oriented economy based on cash crops or basic manufactured goods. Also local elites tied to international capital, as large land-owners, benefited from this process and wielded strong influence over local government to facilitate it. Largely associated with scholars like Andre Gunther Frank, Theotonio dos Santos, and Samir Amin, dependency theory also posited negative impacts of dependent industrialization, for example, inequality between workers in foreign-owned industries and those in traditional sectors of the economy. Dependency scholars also pointed to other kinds of impacts like an uneven urban system that facilitated exports to the industrialized world.

Dependency theory varied in its predictions about the future of these nations. Some more extreme versions (Gunther Frank, 1967) predicted that Third World nations would never develop any substantial industrialization, while others (Amin, 1981) pointed to highly uneven patterns of industrialization. Other scholars drew on the Sociology of the State to account for the role of the dependent state in furthering these relationships while blocking effective movements for structural change from below. Finally, some scholars, like Walter Rodney, linked dependent relationships between First and Third World nations to patterns of racial exploitation and **domination**.

Dependency theory has long been criticized for having a static model of the relationships between countries and for being inattentive to local outcomes. Scholars have begun to point to countries like Brazil and Mexico that exhibit characteristics of both the industrialized world and the underdeveloped world. Also, several scholars have pointed to the success of East Asian industrialization as a way to call into question some assumptions of dependency theory. These scholars, like Peter Evans (1994), have pointed to the role of the state in creating conditions for successful development. It was argued that the role of a strong state in countries like Korea and Taiwan fostered development by creating incentives for local industry. The difficulties faced by regimes that underwent developmental experiments influenced by dependency theory, as Walter Manley's *Jamaica* (1976-1980), have also helped call into question the theory's prescriptions.

Dependency theory has been replaced by other research agendas in field. Recent changes in the world economy, as the rise of Export-Processing Zones and the mobility of capital, have called into question the usefulness dependency theory. **World-systems theory**, first advanced by **Immanuel Wallerstein** (1974), is more attentive to the impacts of globalization on all countries. This kind of analysis points to the interrelationship of, for example, changes in industry throughout the global economic system. Analyses of global patterns, as migration between industrializing and industrial nations, and of local solutions to development problems, through local credit arrangements for instance, have also tended to replace dependency theory work.

DEPENDENT VARIABLE

The dependent variable depends on some other **variable** in a research study. At the beginning of a study, a researcher poses hypotheses speculating how two or more variables are related to each other. The dependent variable is a response to some treatment or causal variable and is therefore effected by the study. For example, a **research hypothesis** states that the more alcoholic drinks a person has at one time, the more likely he or she is to engage in out-of-character behavior. In this case, out-of-character behavior depends on the number of alcoholic drinks the person has consumed and is thus the dependent variable.

The dependent variable is mathematically represented by Y. It can also be thought of as the outcome of a study since it is not manipulated by the researcher in any way. In the above example, assume the study is conducted as an experiment. Out-of-character behavior is simply being observed, while the amount of alcohol consumed is manipulated by the researcher. Some subjects may consume one or two drinks, while others may consume nine drinks. Only independent variables can be manipulated this way.

During the initial stages of a study, it is often difficult to determine which variables are independent and which are dependent. Independent variables come first in the relationship. For example, in a study of education level and salary, it is expected that education level determines salary or salary depends on education. Either way, education comes first in the relationship. This time order or temporal priority is the first step in establishing causality. If it is difficult to determine which variable comes first in the relationship, the researcher can also ask whether one variable has an impact or effect on the other. The impact variable is the **independent variable**, while the effected variable is the dependent variable. Using the same example, education is expected to have an impact on salary.

Simple studies, having one independent variable and one dependent variable, are rare in **sociology** since the study of people and the social world is complex. Sociologists are more likely to investigate the impact of a large set of independent variables on a single dependent variable or the impact of large sets of independent variables on multiple dependent variables. Being able to distinguish dependent variables from independent variables is crucial.

DESCRIPTIVE STATISTICS

Descriptive statistics are techniques used for describing, graphing, organizing and summarizing quantitative **data**. They describe something, either visually or statistically, about individual variables or the association among two or more variables. For instance, a social researcher may want to know how many people in his/her study are male or female, what the average age of the respondents is, or what the **median** income is. Researchers often need to know how closely their data represent the population from which it is drawn so that they can assess the data's representativeness.

Descriptive information gives researchers a general picture of their data, as opposed to an explanation for why certain variables may be associated with each other. Descriptive statistics are often contrasted with inferential statistics, which are used to make inferences, or to explain factors, about the population. Data can be summarized at the univariate level with visual pictures, such as graphs, histograms, and pie charts. Statistical techniques used to describe individual variables include frequencies, the **mean**, median, mode, cumulative percent, percentile, standard deviation, variance, and interquartile range. Data can also be summarized at the bivariate level. Measures of association between two variables include calculations of eta, gamma, lambda, Pearson's r, Kendall's tau, Spearman's rho, and chi^2, among others. Bivariate relationships can also be illustrated in visual graphs that describe the association between two variables.

The **regression** line in regression analysis is both a graphic depiction of the way in which two or more variables are associated and a statistical description of the relationship. To illustrate a **regression line**, one variable's attributes are listed along the horizontal axis and the other variable's attributes along the vertical axis. Each case is then plotted with a dot that corresponds to each respondent's scores on each of the two variables. Then, a line (called a regression line) is fitted to the dots that represents the least squared distance from each dot to the line itself. The regression line describes the strength of the relationship among the variables and the direction of the relationship. If the regression line slopes upward from low scores to high scores along the horizontal (or X) axis, then there is a positive relationship between the two variables. When scores along the horizontal axis rise, scores along the vertical axis (or Y axis) rise as well. If the regression line runs at an opposite angle, then a negative relationship exists between the variables. As scores along the horizontal axis rise, scores along the vertical axis decline. Describing multivariate relationships is also possible using regression analysis. Several regression lines are fitted to the data representing associations between and among different variables in the **model** simultaneously. Thus, in **multivariate analysis**, the relationships among three or more variables are described.

DETERMINISM

Determinism is a concept used in **sociological theory** to refer to the importance of social **structure**, rather than human agents, in producing particular outcomes. Deterministic theories use structures as an explanation for social circumstances and tend to downplay the importance of individual characteristics or the ability of individuals to affect social structures.

The discussion over the extent to which social structure determines human behavior is usually referred to as the agency-structure debate. Early theorists (such as **Karl Marx** and Émile Durkheim) tended towards determinism, seeing social structure as the most important causal agent in human behavior. More modern theorists coming out of symbolic interactionist and ethnomethodological schools stress the importance of human agency over social structure. In these schools of thought determinism is often used as a pejorative label to criticize theories that depend heavily upon structural explanations. For example, Marxist theory is often criticized as being economically deterministic in its explanations for human behavior, and theories of human behavior that use biology or evolution to explain human action are often criticized as being biologically deterministic.

Some social theorists have attempted to go beyond the dualism of the agency-structure debate by recognizing the relationship of human agency to the creation and maintenance of social structure. In their book *The Social Construction of Reality* (1969), **Peter Berger** and Thomas Luckmann argued that people give meanings to aspects of their social world which get institutionalized, producing social structure. People act upon these social structures as if they are real, thus making them real. They then pass down these social structures to their children through socialization, which results in social structures being continual and resistant to change. Therefore, structure may constrain human activity but it is also a product of human activity; the process is **dialectic** rather than deterministic. Pierre Bourdieu also attempted to describe the symbiotic relationship of agency and structure using a constructivist approach. His theory of the reproduction of **culture** emphasizes the intertwining of **structure and agency**, transcending the binary argument over whether structure determines agency or vice versa.

DEVIANCE

The term deviance is derived from "deviate" and is used by sociologists to describe behavior that violates social **norms**. Deviance appeared as a consequence of Howard Becker's *Outsiders*, (1963) a book that examined deviance as a socially constructed phenomenon among marijuana smokers and dance musicians. Becker defined deviance as the failure to obey group rules and added: "[it] is not the quality of the act the person commits, but rather a consequence of the application by others of rules and sanctions to an 'offender'." (1963: p. 9).

Deviant behavior is not necessarily a violation of legal codes; the term was designed to include the study of criminal behavior and also incorporate the study of social norm violations. Consider, for example, a person who is homeless. By nature of his or her social **status**, he or she is not committing a legal infraction but can be viewed as deviant because greater **society** does not condone living on the street. Other groups such as the mentally ill, homosexuals, the chronically obese, people with AIDS and the disabled can also be targetted as "deviant" because their lifestyles or conditions may exclude them from dominant **culture** activities. On the other hand, a person who assaults and robs another person at knife-point is both breaking the law and violating social norms. It is important to note that modern criminal deviance can be extended to include white collar deviance, criminal actions committed by corporations, government, or other social elites within the parameters of their occupations.

Deviance is socially constructed. Becker wrote: "social groups create deviance by making the rules whose infraction constitutes deviance, and by applying those rules to particular people and labeling them as outsiders" (1963: 9). This social construction of deviance was also presented by Émile Durkheim in *The Division of Labor* (1893/1933), which addressed the social construction of **crime**. Society defines what acts are criminal and because of this, society will always have crime. What is criminal today, may not be criminal tomorrow, but we will find new actions to define as criminal. Becker advocated that if society labels people as deviant because of their actions or believed actions, they will inevitably become deviant. This is the notion behind **labeling theory**. Self-concept develops according to how individuals are perceived, an idea reiterated in the work of **George Herbert Mead**, Irving Goffman, and other symbolic interactionists. Thus, if people are perceived as deviant, they may continue to violate social norms. This subsequent deviant behavior, termed **secondary deviance**, is a direct result of being labeled deviant (see Edwin Lemert, 1951). William Chambliss (1973) provided real-life support for this theory by studying two groups of high- school-age boys with different social class backgrounds. The middle-class group, The Saints, were expected to be norm-abiding boys and were treated as such by school personnel, their families, and the authorities, even when they violated social norms. The lower-class group, The Roughnecks, were treated as troublesome, problem students at school, at home, and by the authorities, even when they were norm and law abiding. Over time, the behavior of the Roughnecks began to conform to expectations. Of the six "deviant" group members, two ended up serving prison sentences for unrelated murders and only two attended college.

According to functionalists, deviance can be beneficial for a society by reminding members of what behaviors are acceptable and unacceptable. The punishment of deviance—if the deviant act is also a criminal offense—promotes social cohesion. People are bound together by their consensus of morals. Further, deviance can aid **social change** because if enough people act "deviantly" the behavior will no longer be thought of as deviant. For example, women wearing bathing suits to the beach were at one point considered deviant. Today, woman at the beach in the heat of summer covered from head to toe would be viewed as deviant.

What is deviant to some groups in society is not deviant in others. Loud, raucous behavior and drinking at NASCAR events may be seen by social elites as deviant, while among NASCAR fans, it is seen as normal. Further, what is deviant in one society may even be celebrated in others, for example, the smoking of marijuana in the United States and the Netherlands.

DIALECTIC

The term, dialectic, was first used by Georg Wilhelm Friedrich Hegel to describe the development of changing historical periods and social revolutions. He conceptualized dialectic as a process of opposite forces in conflict, in which an initial state eventually turns into its opposite. **Karl Marx** built on Hegel's idea of dialectic to argue that the transitions from one economic system to the next culminated from a build up of tensions, resulting in revolution and change. Hence, Marx's theory of economic change is referred to as dialectical materialism or historical **materialism**. **Friedrich Engels** extended Marx's use of dialectic to encompass a general theory of **social change**.

A dialectic process involves three stages: thesis, antithesis, and synthesis. In the first stage, a particular idea or set of ideas (thesis) exists that is commonly accepted by most people. In the second stage, a new idea or set of ideas that is contrary to the first (an antithesis) is introduced. The introduction of the antithesis causes conflict as the thesis and antithesis are debated. In the final stage, the thesis and antithesis are synthesized to produce a new idea or set of ideas (the synthesis) that then becomes the commonly accepted thesis.

The theory of dialectic can be applied to any process of social change, such as cultural systems, scientific paradigms, or historical periods, that go through the three stage process of thesis, antithesis, and synthesis. A dialectic process is contrary to the idea of progressive change, in which new and better ideas replace older ideas. A dialectic is a process of conflict and resolution, but it does not imply improvement over time. It is a useful concept for describing how old ideas are replaced with new ones and how human history progresses.

DIFFUSION THEORIES

Diffusion is concerned with the transmission of cultural aspects or practices from one **society** to another. This occurs through the contact of the two groups. Diffusion can occur either through direct contact or indirectly through a third party.

Diffusion theory emerged during the eighteenth and nineteenth centuries, and it was developed in reaction to **evolutionary theory**. While they vary substantially, both theories place the beginnings of human **culture** at the apex of their research agendas. Some diffusionists have asserted that human cultures are comprised of borrowed bits of other cultures, the best portions of which spreading outward from the center. By this logic, one could recreate this development by assuming that the most widespread cultural practices would also be the oldest. The most widespread practices simply would have had the longest amount of time to disseminate.

By contrast, other diffusion theories endeavored to show that all human culture originated from a single location and extended outward from there by diffusion. As an example, anthropologists like Elliot Smith (1871—1937) and W. Perry (1887—1949) believed that Egypt was the source of all human culture because the Mayan temples and Egyptian pyramids were very much alike to one another.

For the most part anthropology has shied away from the study of the evolution of cultural traits. Most social researchers

While recognized as legal and socially acceptable in some societies, the smoking of marijuana is viewed as deviant in other societies *(Corbis Corporation [Bellevue])*.

instead tend toward the notion that traits in separate regions developed independently of one another. Scholars currently lean more in the direction of criticizing diffusion theories for extracting cultural aspects from their context. A prominent belief currently in the social science community is that a cultural trait or phenomenon cannot be accurately examined outside of its context. To illustrate, despite similarities between Egyptian and Mayan temples, these structures serve very different functions within their given societies. However, that is not to say that diffusion theory is now defunct. A few anthropologists are still investigating some of the original interests of diffusion theory.

See also Evolutionary Theory

DISABILITY

In the United States, the term disability is legally defined in the Rehabilitation Act (PL 93-112; 29 U.S.C. 794) Amendments of 1974 and the Americans with Disabilities Act (PL

Since the 1970s, U.S. advocates for the disabled have won passage of numerous laws at the federal, state, and local levels of government (*AP/Wide World Photos, Inc.*).

101-336; 42 U.S.C. 12101) of 1990 as a physical or mental impairment that substantially limits one or more of the major life activities of an individual. Disabilities may be caused by congenital, traumatic, pathological, or other factors, and vary widely in severity. They may be temporary or permanent, correctable or irreversible. Physical disabilities include blindness, deafness, deformity, muscular and nervous disorders, paralysis, and loss of limbs. Paralysis is frequently caused by injuries to the spinal cord, with the extent of paralysis depending on the portion of the spine that is injured. Congenital disabilities include spina bifida, cystic fibrosis, and muscular dystrophy. Other causes of disabilities include cerebral hemorrhage, arthritis and other bone diseases, amputation, severe pulmonary or cardiac **disease**, nerve diseases, and the natural process of **aging**. Mental impairments are of two types: mental illness and mental retardation. Approximately 35 million people in the United States are disabled.

Professionals including physicians, physical and occupational therapists, social workers, and psychologists assist disabled persons in the rehabilitation process, helping them function at the highest possible physical, vocational, and social levels. Specialists in rehabilitation medicine, sometimes referred to as physiatrists, diagnose patients and plan individual treatment programs for the management of pain and disabili-

ties resulting from musculoskeletal injuries. People with hearing or vision loss require special education, including instruction in lip reading, sign language, or Braille. Physical rehabilitation for individuals with musculoskeletal disabilities includes passive exercise of affected limbs and active exercise for parts of the body that are not affected. Occupational training, including counseling, helps persons whose disabilities make it necessary for them to find new jobs or careers. Rehabilitation also involves the services of speech pathologists, recreational therapists, home planning consultants, orthotists and prosthetists, driver educators, and dieticians.

Recent technological advances—especially those involving computer-aided devices—have aided immeasurably in mainstreaming the disabled into many areas of **society**. These include voice-recognition aids for the paralyzed; optical character-recognition devices for the blind; sip-and-puff air tubes that enable quadriplegics to type and control wheelchair movements with their mouths; and computerized electronic grids that translate eye movements into speech. In addition to access, mobility for the disabled has become an area of concern. The American Automobile Association (AAA) estimates that there are 500,000 licensed drivers in the United States with significant physical impairments and another 1.5 million with lesser disabilities. AAA auto clubs throughout the country are working to improve the mobility of disabled drivers and travelers through improved driver education for those with impairments and improved facilities for the handicapped traveler, including motorist rest areas on the highway.

Public attitudes toward the disabled have changed. Since the 1970s, advocates for the disabled have won passage of numerous laws on the federal, state, and local levels aimed at making education, **employment**, and public accommodation more accessible through the elimination of physical barriers to access, as well as **affirmative action** in the hiring and professional advancement of disabled people. Whereas many people with disabilities were formerly confined to their homes or to institutions, the current trend is geared toward reintegrating disabled persons into the **community** in ways that enable them the greatest possible amount of independence in both their living arrangements and their jobs. Wheelchair access at building entrances, curbs, and public restrooms has been greatly expanded and mandated by law. Braille signs are standard in public areas such as elevators.

Two major pieces of federal legislation have protected the rights of the disabled: a 1975 law guaranteeing disabled children a right to public education in the least restrictive setting possible and the 1990 Americans with Disabilities Act (ADA), which extends comprehensive civil rights protection in employment and access to public areas. Title I of the ADA, which prohibits **discrimination** by private employers on the basis of disability, is intended to ensure that the same performance standards and job requirements are applied to disabled persons as to persons who are not. In cases where functional limitations may interfere with job performance, employers are required to take any necessary steps to accommodate reasonably the needs of a disabled person, including adjustments to the work environment or to the way in which the job is customarily performed. The ADA also contains provisions ensuring nondiscrimination in state and local **government** services (Title II) and nondiscrimination in public accommodations and commercial facilities (Title III).

DISASTER RELIEF ORGANIZATIONS

A wide variety of disaster relief organizations have appeared worldwide over the last one hundred years and especially since World War II. Greatly increasing the availability of information, the development of the electronic media has fostered an ever-increasing awareness of the needs and sufferings of others, and in so doing, has set the stage for the formulation of humanitarian responses. Traditionally, disasters have been defined as either natural, such as hurricanes and earthquakes, or man-made, such as wars and industrial accidents. However, in the discussion of relief organizations, disasters can be further classified as 1) sudden elemental, which are caused by unpredictable climatic and geological events; 2) foreseeable, such as famines and **epidemics**; 3) deliberate, which focus on war and civil conflict; and 4) accidental, which result from technological mistakes. A fifth category has recently been added to the terminology of relief workers: chronic disaster, such as extended military conflicts, on-going **poverty** and famine, and sustained environmental emergencies.

Disaster relief organizations exist at three institutional levels. The relief agencies associated with the United Nations (UN), called international governmental organizations (IGOs), function at the global level. Beneath IGOs exist individual **government** or inter-government programs, and finally, a myriad of non-governmental organizations (NGOs). Since the UN was chartered in 1945, a substantial number of disaster relief agencies have been established. The Office of the UN Disaster Relief Coordinator (UNDRO) acts as a clearinghouse for assistance to the afflicted area by coordinating both IGOs and NGOs in an effort to provide the most streamlined and effective relief. UNDRO also has a leading role in the study, prevention, control, and prediction of natural disasters.

By no means an exhaustive list of UN agencies that contribute to disaster relief, the four most important UN relief services, based on size and influence, are the United Nations Children's Fund (Unicef), the World Health Organization (WHO), the World Food Program (WFP), and the Office of the UN High Commission for Refugees (UNHCR). Unicef, which relies more heavily on private donations that other UN relief agencies, provides non-food assistance to mothers and children, such as shelter, drinking water, and immunizations programs. The WHO contributes technical advice on medical and health issue through its Emergency Planning and Response department. The WFP's International Emergency Food Reserve dedicates much of its resources to feeding disaster victims. Finally, UNHCR provides refugees with a wide range of assistance programs.

Most Western countries have established disaster response systems. The largest nation-based international disaster relief organization is the United States Agency for Internation-

The Red Cross, which is seen here bringing supplies to Ethiopia, is one of the most internationally-recognized disaster relief organizations *(Corbis Corporation [Bellevue])*.

al Development (USAID). One of USAID's most effective endeavors in disaster relief is in developing early warning systems to prevent famines in Africa. The Swiss Disaster Relief Unit uses a reserve force to service disaster areas. It provides a volunteer corps of over 1,200 men and women who, with the consent of their employers, devote two to four months in volunteer disaster relief service in areas worldwide. In 1992 the Commission of the European Communities reorganized its response system by creating the European Office for Emergency Humanitarian Aid.

All developed countries have internal disaster preparedness and disaster relief plans as well. In the United States, the Federal Emergency Management Agency (FEMA) is responsible for all aspects of intra-country disasters. According to its web site (http://www.fema.gov), FEMA "is an independent agency of the federal government, reporting to the President. Since its founding in 1979, FEMA's mission has been clear: to reduce loss of life and **property** and protect our nation's critical infrastructure from all types of hazards through a comprehensive, risk-based, emergency management program of mitigation, preparedness, response and recovery." FEMA works with state and local governments along with coordinated efforts by NGOs to address relief issues across the nation.

The largest source of humanitarian assistance outside the domain of governments is the Red Cross and Red Crescent Movement. Instrumental from the international to the local level, the Red Cross offers a wide array of disaster relief assistance, including fixed and mobile feeding stations, shelter, first aid, blood, food, clothing, and medical supplies. The International Committee of the Red Cross focuses on emergencies that result from human conflict, and the Federation of Red Cross and Red Crescent Societies serves a broader mission that includes response to natural disasters.

Too numerous to name, NGOs range widely in structure, purpose, and effectiveness. All major religious organizations have established disaster response charities under their wings. Others organizations are non-religious, but may coordinate with religion-based agencies, and yet others are religiously interdenominational in structure. Many NGOs, such as Oxfam, Save the Children, and Christian Aid, incorporate the concept of development along with relief. Aimed at generating self-reliance, development programs help deter certain foreseeable disasters, such as famine. Less glamorous in nature and longer in duration, development assistance usually receives little media attention and efforts are often only known by those who are well informed.

As publicity of disaster relief needs has increased, so has the number of organizations involved in disaster assistance. As a result, the questions of coordination and **accountability** have arisen. The UN has come under sharp criticism regarding its inability to effectively coordinate relief efforts and provide aid efficiently. NGOs are constantly monitored for ethical practices and responsible finances. Other problems that have arisen in the *ad hoc* creation of a global disaster relief structure include the complex political nature of many areas in crisis, the legitimacy of the government through which aid may be funneled, and the role of the media's influence in drawing attention to some disasters while virtually ignoring other, especially chronic, disasters. As national borders continue to shift and areas of the world previously unreachable for political reasons begin to open to relief workers and the media, disaster relief organizations will need to continue to address the matters of priority, coordination, and effectiveness.

DISCOURSE

Discourse refers to meaning produced by the interplay of text (written or spoken **language**) and the social factors surrounding its production. This idea is an extension of the work of linguist Ferdinand de Saussure, who identified the difference between what a word signifies, or defines, and the value of a word in use: "The value of just any term is accordingly determined by its environment; it is impossible to fix even the value of the word signifying 'sun' without first considering its surroundings: in some languages it is not possible to say 'sit in the *sun*.'"

According to theorists who have developed this concept, most notably Michel Foucault and H.P. Grice, meaning of language is only fully realized through the context in which it is used. Although words have specific meanings or definitions, meaning is not wholly contained in these definitions. All linguistic statements are subject to evaluation by their audiences. A statement must be deemed understandable, appropriate, and believable for it to be accepted by its audience. Because of this constraint, discourse is framed by the group or **organization** to which speakers belong. All groups have a system of shared meanings and expectations, and the use of language within the **group** must take into account these factors. These shared meanings form the sociological basis of discursive formation, according to Jean K. Chalaby: "Different texts share common philological properties because they are produced by a specific *field of discursive production*." For example, talk about motherhood might seem straightforward. However, the form and content of this talk will vary depending upon whether the

speaker is a medical student addressing an obstetrician, a lawyer trying to win a child custody suit for a female client, or an adult child returned home to visit his/her mother at Thanksgiving. In each case the same topic takes on a different meaning through the use of a different (i.e., medical, legal, or familial) discourse.

In turn, the discourse used contributes to the construction of shared reality by members of a group; what is continually spoken of and accepted as true is understood to be "real," while the process of developing the discourse itself is forgotten. This process of construction is explained fully in *The Social Construction of Reality* by sociologists Peter L. Berger and Thomas Luckmann. Because discourse helps define what is understood as real and valid, many social theorists have noted that discourse is inherently political and is often used as a tool of **domination** or oppression of less powerful groups and their ideas.

DISCRIMINATION

Discrimination is differential or unequal treatment of a particular group. Groups are usually distinguished or divided along religious, ethnic, and racial lines. Many other groups, such as the elderly, women, and homosexuals, however, can be discriminated against as well. Discrimination can be viewed as a continuum or a scale. At one end lies less severe forms of discrimination (verbal assault, denial of resources), and at the other end, more severe forms of discrimination are located (physical **aggression**, **genocide**). All other forms of discrimination lie at some point on this continuum.

Discrimination occurs on institutional and individual levels. Institutional discrimination is committed, collectively, by one the dominant group against another group. The discriminating group may deny services to the group being discriminated against in the following areas: **money** lending, hiring and job promotion, housing, medical care, and schooling.

Institution discrimination can sometimes take place unconsciously. One example of institutional discrimination takes the form of inferior schooling. Schools in inner city areas do not have the funding that schools in affluent areas do because funding is based on **property** taxes. As a result, inner city schools may be run down and lack necessary supplies and an adequate, certified staff. Students who graduate from these inferior schools do not have the same reading and math skills that students from other schools do because of the lack of books and qualified teachers. Thus they are less academically prepared for college, and they are less able to compete in the job market. The students who attend these schools are primarily racial and ethnic minorities. These racial and ethnic groups are facing institutional discrimination by not receiving the same schooling as those at wealthier schools.

While institutional discrimination and individual discrimination can take place along racial, ethnic, and religious lines, individual discrimination can take place based on arbitrary distinctions between groups. Clothing, accent, or even type of car driven can contribute to discriminatory practices.

Individual discrimination is defined as one person discriminating against another individual. A white shop owner who will not give an African American a job because of his/her **race** and a group of teenage girls who will not befriend a girl from a lower social class are examples.

Discrimination can be described as a set of events which stems from prejudices that are part of a **cycle**. At the beginning of the cycle, a group is discriminated against for an arbitrary reason (race, religion, gender, sexual orientation, age, income level). As a result, that group misses out on opportunities awarded to other groups that conform to or meet the dominant group image. Opportunities can include jobs, promotions, and college education. After missing opportunities, this group is viewed as unable to complete such tasks (get a good job, get promoted, get a college education), and thus they are viewed as inferior because they are unable to achieve these goals. The cycle then repeats itself. Laws in the United States try to ensure that discrimination does not occur in the form of lost job opportunities, housing, and education, but even laws have been discriminatory. However, discrimination still occurs in our **society** and in other societies in many ways.

DISEASE

Disease refers to a specific bodily state, or condition, outside the general, culturally-defined norm of health. This **abnormal** state was once thought to be caused by imbalances within the individual which occurred when self-protective abilities were disturbed or as divine punishment for wrongs committed. In the early 1800s, disease was basically attributed to *miasma*, meaning damaging emanations from the environment.

Modern biomedicine diagnoses or identifies disease through signs (x-rays, blood pressure, magnetic resonance imaging, etc.), and symptoms (aches and pains, loss of function, etc.). The problem is then treated, managed, or cured by physicians. This concept of disease grew out of the development of the *germ theory* in the latter 1800s by bacteriological researchers Louis Pasteur, Robert Koch, and others. The consequent progress in the field of medicine was thus grounded in precise scientific laboratory procedures and **methodology**. It was focused upon the idea that every disease was caused by a particular microorganism, and if that microorganism could be isolated and contained or removed, the disease could be contained or cured.

Since the advent of the germ theory, Western medicine has emphasized classifying diseases, diagnosing and treating patients, and finding cures. With this trend, it became the physician's task to find the *lesion* or physiological origin of disease within the body in order to treat and hence to legitimize the concept of disease.

The traditional criteria for disease have included the patient's subjective feelings of malaise, the physician's finding of a bodily **dysfunction**, and the fact that the patient's symptoms conform to a recognizable clinical pattern. Sociologically, however, disease is much more complex. Disease, an adverse physical state involving a physiological dysfunction,

Discrimination is defined as differential or unequal treatment of a particular group, such as the former use of separate bathroom facilities in the segregated South *(Corbis Corporation [Bellevue])*.

is differentiated from illness, (a subjective perception of having a disease), or sickness (a social state, defined by others). Medical sociologist David Mechanic noted that disease is closely connected with illness behavior and all three dimensions are interrelated.

Sociologically, the concept of disease is also connected to or originates in the political and economic realities of the social **structure** in which it exists. Both causes and cures for disease then become much more than a matter of physiological dysfunction or a medical label and require consideration of social, political, and economic forces that may affect a person's health and well-being.

DISENCHANTMENT OF THE WORLD

The Disenchantment of the World is a concept first conceived by Max Weber in the early 1900s in his essay *Science as a Vocation*. Weber wanted to show that our modern times were moving away from the mystic, sublime, and transcendental **values** (enchantment), to the rational or scientific explanations of the social world (disenchantment).

Weber also wished to characterize the cultural and intellectual transformations taking place between the sixteenth and eighteenth centuries. Essentially, the disenchantment of the world referred to the movement away from attributing human events and phenomena (such as illness) to religious or magical causes and origins, and toward giving rational, scientific explanations for such happenings. It has also been generally understood to mean the elimination of magic from human action and behavior.

Weber contended that the process of **rationalization** was manifested in all aspects of social life, from the personal to the

Modern biomedical diagnoses developed from the research conducted by Louis Pasteur *(The Library of Congress).*

DIVISION OF LABOR

A division of labor implies a set of individuals coordinating in such a way that each is responsible for a separate function that contributes to a whole. Each individual's activity is different from and also integrated with others. A division of labor involves both differentiation and specialization. Adam Smith (1723-1790) was the first to articulate the division of labor in his writings on **political economy**. Smith described several functions of the division of labor. One function is increasing wealth-creating capacity. Wealth is accrued through a division of labor because individuals are encouraged to specialize in tasks or trades,thereby maximizing their productivity. Simultaneously, the inherent differentiation in a division of labor encourages a rational exchange of goods and services.

Focusing extensively on the division of labor, Émile Durkheim (1858-1917) saw **society** as becoming increasing differentiated and specialized. In this way, society could be likened to a living organism because as organisms evolve their functions become more specialized. Assuming the increasing division of labor to be a natural consequence in society's development, Durkheim was interested in the moral effects of such a process. Increasing differentiation and specialization loosens the restraints of **social control**, erodes social trust, and allows egoism and individual desires to grow rampant. At the heart of many well known concepts developed by **Karl Marx** (1818-1883) (e.g., alienation, false consciousness) is an understanding of the division of labor, how it works and the effects it has. While some theorists take a functional approach to the division of labor and herald it as the mark of a truly efficient society, Marx recognized the inequality imbedded within the economic division of labor. Marx's conception asserts a fundamental division of class power between the owners and non-owners of the means of production.

The labor market is only one context in which the division of labor characterizes fundamental processes in action. Divisions can occur in terms of social and religious functions. The division of labor between men and women in societies usually extends to all of these functions. Adam Smith may have developed the term in the context of political economy, but patriarchy is an ancient form of forced and exploitive labor division. The sexual division of labor refers to the specialized roles that men and women take on, those of male wage earner and female housewife. **Talcott Parsons** (1902-1979) termed these to be "instrumental" and "expressive" roles respectively. While the tasks attributed to men and women in this particular division of labor are most likely specific to Western industrialized societies, most other societies also divide tasks on the basis of sex. Initially, research represented these differences as complementary in that men work outside the home, earn a wage, and support the **family** while women engage in the unpaid domestic labor involved in managing the **household** and caring for children. A feminist perspective defines such differentiation and specialization between men and women as exploitive and oppressive. This view is validated by works that explore women's increased movement into the workforce yet their persistently greater responsibility for

organizational. There was a withdrawal from the more spiritual, affective approaches to social relations, to approaches based on the motivation of means-end calculations. Magical explanations were replaced with the more rational and scientific explanations for human behavior and social phenomena.

Progressing intellectualization and rationalization, according to Weber, do not indicate greater knowledge and understanding of one's living conditions. We all generally know what we must know in order to survive. However, if we wished, we could increase our knowledge at any time. "Hence, it [scientific progress] means that principally there are no mysterious incalculable forces that come into play, but rather that one can, in principle, master all things by calculation. This means that the world is disenchanted." Intellectualization, says Weber, now allows us to use technical means and calculations for the same purposes that magical means and mysterious powers once served.

This concept has been adopted by others but has created some heated historical debate. A problem occurred, for example, in defining terms such as *magic* as well as determining the position of religion. It can also be argued that humankind has not abandoned all forms of enchantment as explanation, since there is wide variation in regard to culture and social context.

household and children. Women's maintenance of most house-hold and childcare responsibility despite their hours in the workplace beyond the home is most commonly referred to as the "second shift," a term coined by Arlie Hochschild. One specific form of this sex-based division of labor is the domestic division of labor in which specific roles, duties, and tasks are allocated to females while others are allocated to males. When household labor is performed by men, it is often sex-typed (lawn mowing, repairs, garage maintenance, etc.) and much less time intensive than those tasks performed by women. While a focus on division of labor among individual tasks is prevalent, a division of labor can also take place at other levels, such as between sectors of the economy and between occupations.

DIVORCE

From ancient times, there have been regulations on **marriage** and divorce. Jewish law allowed a man to leave his wife, for example, and Greeks and Romans recognized divorce. These early divorces were not regulated by law, however, but by social and religious **norms**. During the Protestant Reformation, divorce was presented as a concern of the **government**, and a variety of grounds for divorce developed. When a couple presented their case to a magistrate one spouse had to prove that the other was at fault in order to be granted a divorce. This at-fault divorce still exists today.

Divorce law in the early United States was enforced at the state level, and although it varied greatly from state to state, at-fault divorce cases became the norm. By the end of the nineteenth century, people seeking a divorce flocked to those states where one could easily be obtained. By the late 1930s, states with strict divorce laws had trouble regulating and enforcing the law. For example, demonstrating evidence of cruelty came to include mental cruelty. At this time, divorces brought to court were almost always granted. Divorce procedures became institutionalized in the 1940s, when ninety percent of divorce cases went uncontested. The women's movement of the 1960s criticized marriage and divorce, and by the late 1960s, marital breakdown or dissatisfaction were considered grounds for divorce.

At this time, states began to change divorce law and a pattern of divorce upon demand of one spouse became standard. In other words, no-fault divorce was possible. Grounds for divorce also changed, and today include reasons such as incompatibility, desertion, gross neglect, marital breakdown, cruelty, insanity, adultery, and **alcoholism** or drug addiction. A divorce is much easier to obtain because of these legal changes, although even couples in no-fault divorce cases often fall under scrutiny.

Until about 1985, divorce was very costly and socially embarrassing. Now filing for a divorce has less of a stigma than it did and is overall an easier process. An increase in divorce rates, therefore, does not just reflect short-lived marriages, but these other factors as well. Furthermore, because the divorce process if easier, marriages that ended in abandon-ment or legal separation in the past now end in divorce. In other words, an increase in divorces does not mean that more marriages are failing. It means that more marriages are ending in divorce than by other means.

Despite the drama of adultery, in reality, very few marriages end due to infidelity. Instead, divorce occurs when one spouse does not consider their partner to be a suitable friend, confidant, or helpmate. Women are often frustrated with their husbands as parents and helpers, too. Most divorces occur between two and five years after marriage and traditionally have been sought by women. This does not exclude a mutual agreement to divorce or husbands who ask their wives to petition for divorce and accept the blame as an act of chivalry.

The divorce rate differs among racial, socioeconomic, and age groups. African-Americans have a much higher divorce rate than any other racial group. Couples with **higher education** have a lower divorce rate, except for women with graduate degrees, who divorce at an unusually high rate, perhaps due to financial independence. As for age, women who marry before 18 and men who marry before they are 20 are almost four times as likely to divorce than those who marry in their twenties. Despite these figures, however, the number of teenage divorces are a very small part of the rising divorce rate.

Although a divorce may be less embarrassing than it was decades ago, it is still not an easy process socially or emotionally. In fact, going through divorce is similar to grieving, and individuals find themselves at a loss for control. The partners that they counted on helping them through crises are also lost, causing more distress.

One of the social difficulties divorced persons encounter is the disapproval of **family** and friends. Men especially fear this disapproval, but both men and women feel shamed by divorce, even if the spouse is blamed for the break-up. Indeed, the overall disapproval of divorce by loved ones can turn into disapproval of the individual, causing guilt. The divorce process creates a sense of failure, which can also negatively affect self-esteem. Self-esteem and self-worth lessens even more for women who become financially dependent on family and friends following divorce.

Much of the difficulties of divorce concern the relationship between ex-spouses, especially when children are involved. Joint custody is stressful and seems unfair to both sides. Efforts to "win over" a child can prove devastating to the parent-child relationship. Children grieve, too, for the missing parent. For years following divorce, and even into subsequent marriages, people remain focused on the aftermath of their first marriage and cannot move on. Hostility between divorced couples is common, and the patterns of power struggles continue after divorce. Divorced persons do not always completely sever emotional, romantic, or even sexual ties with their first spouse, making it difficult to accept the end of a marriage.

The **stress** of divorce is apparent. Divorced individuals grieve for their lost partners and lifestyle. Their social life changes, parenting changes, finances alter, and the home and family they envisioned grows into something entirely different. As the divorce rate increases, **society** must be ready for all that divorce carries with it: shame, low self-esteem, new family types, confusion, and grief.

DOMHOFF, GEORGE WILLIAM
(1936-)
American psychologist and sociologist

G. William Domhoff was born in Youngstown, Ohio, on August 6, 1936, the son of George William and Helen S. (Cornet) Domhoff. He married Judy Boman, a nursery school teacher, on August 28, 1961. They had four children: Lynne, Lori, William P., and James Joel. Domhoff received a Bachelor of Arts degree from Duke University in 1958 and a Master of Arts degree from Kent State University in 1959. He finished his postgraduate studies at the University of Miami at Coral Gables, Florida, earning his doctorate in 1962.

From 1962 to 1965, Domhoff was an assistant professor of psychology at Los Angeles State College. In 1965, he accepted a position as an assistant professor at the University of California, Cowell College, Santa Cruz, where he remains currently. He became an associate professor of psychology in 1969 and a professor of psychology and sociology in 1975.

Domhoff presented his understanding of politics and power in the United States in 1967 with the publication of his first book *Who Rules America?* that stirred controversy and attracted significant academic attention. Domhoff theorized that the United States has a structure of upper classes, the "power elite," that exercises its influence to control, or rule, the country. Outlining areas in which power positions are filled by members of this socially identifiable elite, especially in the corporate world, Domhoff concluded that "the income, wealth, and institutional leadership of... 'the American business aristocracy' are more than sufficient to earn it the designation 'governing class.'"

The elite wields power, suggested Domhoff, by influencing government policy-making through their support of foundations, think tanks, commissions, and institutes at prestigious universities. In a press release issued by the University of California/Santa Cruz, Domhoff noted that the connection between elite **status** and political power may not be obvious, but neither can it be hidden. "Americans as a group are reluctant to acknowledge the existence of the **power elite**, but the rich are in fact a very cohesive group that attends the same schools, goes to the same clubs, vacations at the same summer resorts, and shares a view of the world."

In the 1970s Domhoff continued his work on **political sociology**, publishing *The Higher Circles* (1970), *Fat Cats and Democrats* (1972), and *The Bohemian Grove and Other Retreats* (1974). *Who Really Rules?* (1978) is a reexamination of Richard Dahl's classic 1961 study on New Haven society *Who Governs?*. Also in 1978 Domhoff responded to critics of *Who Rules America?* by publishing *The Powers That Be*.

According to Domhoff, the United States' history of wealth and income inequality has been consistently overlooked by the public and academics. Using Marxian language,

he argues that the issues of class consciousness and class conflict are routinely overshadowed by a naive pluralist understanding of political decision-making. Although he acknowledges that the pluralists correctly assert that the democratic system allows everyone access to the political process, he points out that the access is disproportionately weighted to favor the upper class. In order to gain a clear understanding of the impact of wealth and income in the United States, he maintains that the criteria must change from "process" to "outcome." He wrote that the "predominant emphasis in American ideology is on the 'process' by which things are done—democracy in government, equality of opportunity in education, fairness before the law—and not on 'outcomes'.... Who benefits, the very essence of the power struggle, is hardly considered." Nonetheless, Domhoff conceded to the predominant sociological paradigm and offered four general processes as proof of the existence of the power elite in areas of special interest, policy formation, candidate selection, and **ideology**.

More recent writings in political sociology, such as *Who Rules America Now? A View for the '80s* (1983) and *Diversity in the Power Elite: Have Women and Minorities Reached the Top?* (1998), have been intermingled with Domhoff's study of dreams. In 1985 he published *The Mystique of Dreams,* in which he refuted the widely held belief that the Senoi people of Malaysia control **dreams** and have extraordinary **mental health**. In *Finding Meaning in Dreams: A Quantitative Approach* (1996), Domhoff uses an objective, quantitative **methodology** to score dreams based on a variety of factors including the frequency of recurring themes and elements of victimization and **aggression**. The results are compared to set standards to make predictions. "My work on power has had a greater impact and is much better known," Domhoff asserted in a press release for the University of California at Santa Cruz, "but in the long run, I'll bet my dream research stands just as tall."

DOMINATION

The term "domination" refers to the power that one person has over another or over a **group**. In a broader, sociological sense, domination refers to the **leadership** within a given **organization** and **society** and the probability that the leadership will be obeyed. According to **Max Weber**, domination differs from the concept of power, which describes a situation where a person attempts command others despite their resistance.

Weber's work on domination included differentiating between domination "by virtue of authority" and economic domination. The latter could constrain an individual, regardless of motivation. Weber argued that domination was facilitated by economic power (such as a class system), social power (which emphasized prestige and **status**), and political power (represented by political parties). According to Weber, any of these factors could lead to the other two. His work differed from that of **Karl Marx**, who claimed that domination in society was promoted mainly by unequal distributions in economic power. Property ownership was key to understanding

Naomi Epel, who wrote a book about famous authors and their dreams, poses in front of a painting of dreams at The Association for the Study of Dreams Symposium *(AP/Wide World Photos, Inc.)*.

domination from Marx's point of view; he believed that those who owned **property** or controlled the means of production in society dominated those who did not. Both Marx's and Weber's work on domination are different interpretations of the conflict perspective, which posits that **coercion** and the use of force bring about domination and ultimately, order in society.

DREAMS

Dreams, the mental activity engaged in during sleep, take place during the REM (rapid eye movement) sleep. Stimuli during dreams include images and thoughts and are visual in nature. Humans tend to dream less as they get older. An infant may spend up to half of its sleep time in the REM phase, but a teenager may only spend one to two hours per night dreaming. The body undergoes physiological changes during dreaming including increased heart rate and breathing rate. When humans become sleep deprived and lack REM sleep, irritability increases, and physical coordination decreases. Some people feel that dreams may provide a link to the supernatural or another world not so easily accessed during waking hours.

Sigmund Freud was one of the first to study dreams as a psychological phenomena and to suggest that they provide

insight into the unconscious. Freud defined the content of the dream (that which the individual remembers) as separate from the meaning of the dream. According to Freud, the meaning of a dream is an expression of the dreamer's desires. Freud's book *The Interpretation of Dreams* (1900) summarized his theory about dreams. Freud believed that dreams always have significance. He also suggested that much of the wish fulfillment of dreams is driven by unsatisfied sexual urges that originate in childhood. However, Freud's work on dreams allowed that everyone's subconscious provides different material and that "only the context could furnish the correct meaning" of a dream **symbol**. Therefore, Freud's work does not support the use of dream symbols that have one meaning for all. More important, he maintained that dreams provide a look into the subconscious and can reveal truths that are too difficult for the dreamer to face while awake. Such a phenomenon, argued Freud, could greatly facilitate psychoanalysis and treatment.

Carl Gustav Jung speculated further about dreams, suggesting that they provide the dreamer with a way to express neglected aspects of the dreamer's personality. Jung also believed that dreams can anticipate happenings in the future and that they give insight into the dreamer's unconscious mind. Others who studied dreaming believed that dreams originate from memories in various parts of the brain.

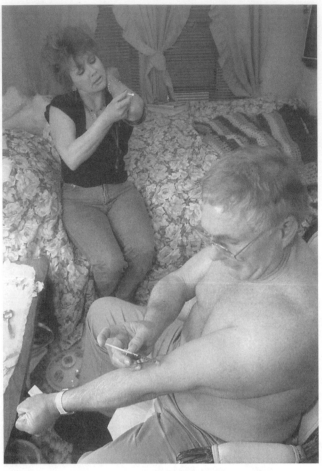

Heroin is one of the most addictive illegal substances commonly associated with drug abuse *(AP/Wide World Photos, Inc.)*.

Different types of dreaming processes are recognized. A nightmare is a significantly frightening dream. Daydreaming is done while awake and involves fantasies that the person constructs. Lucid dreaming refers to dreaming (while asleep) that the individual is able to direct.

DRUG ABUSE

Drugs are defined as any substance other than food that upon ingestion alters the body's structure and functioning. This broad definition includes a variety of substances that are not typically abused by members of sociey or considered harmful in any recognized way. Many sociologists contend that cultural and social **norms** determine which substances are considered drugs associated with abuse, making drug usage a social phenomenon. What is considered a drug varies between cultures and changes over time. However, the definition of drug abuse remains relatively constant. Regardless of which substance is ingested, the excessive and inappropriate use of a substance resulting in physical, psychological, or social harm is called drug abuse.

Alcohol, nicotine, cocaine, heroin, amphetamines, barbiturates, and marijuana, are just a few of the legal and illegal substances commonly associated with drug abuse in the United States. These substances are not typically used for medicinal or nutritional purposes. They are physically and psychologically addictive mind-altering drugs. Drug use becomes drug abuse when the user develops an addiction. Drug addiction is the development of a physiological dependence and an increased tolerance for habit-forming substances such as narcotics. Individuals can form a physiological and psychological dependence on the drug, meaning the body needs periodic dosages in order to function normally. A high tolerance for drugs can cause drug abusers to overdose because they hazardously increase the dosage in an attempt to achieve the same effect they once got from lower doses.

Most Americans report that drug abuse is the number one problem in the United States, despite the steady decline in the reported use of illegal drugs over the past thirty years. According to the National Household Survey on Drug Abuse (1998), illicit drug abuse was at its highest in 1979 when approximately fourteen percent of Americans over the age of twelve reported using illegal drugs in 1979. The number of reported drug users declined significantly in the 1980s and fell to less than five percent in 1997. The use of alcohol and other drugs is decreasing, and legal substances such as nicotine are becoming impermissible in public settings. This downward trend has been attributed to the active ''Just Say No'' and ''War on Drugs'' campaigns initiated in the 1980s. Yet, it may also result from the visible impact drug abuse has on social institutions, including the **family**, schools, and the criminal justice system.

Drug abuse is a social problem, as opposed to an individual problem, because drugs affect social beings and the entire **society**. Drugs cause problems for individuals, families, communities, and institutions. The abuse of legal substances, like alcohol and tobacco, and the use of illegal substances, such as marijuana or cocaine, can be costly for society. The over-consumption of alcohol is a leading cause of automobile accidents and is highly correlated with **family violence**. Some illegal drug abusers commit crimes in order to support their drug habit leading to an increase in the rate of violent and nonviolent **crime** in drug ridden communities. Drug abuse can affect a variety of social institutions by contributing to work place absenteeism, work-related accidents, and poor work performance. Last, excessive use of drugs can cause illness and death costing society billions of dollars in **health care** and lowered productivity.

Sociologists, like Thomas J. Sullivan (1997), theorize that individuals use drugs for several reasons. One popular explanation is that individuals acquire their **attitude** towards drugs from their social surroundings. Young people may learn that drinking alcohol is acceptable, but smoking marijuana is unacceptable from the images they see on **television** or from their interactions with peers, parents, and teachers. Therefore, an applicable solution to drug abuse involves using the media and mentoring relationships to alter messages individuals receive about drugs.

Another solution to drug-related problems may be changing the social and economic circumstances that lead people to abuse drugs. Some medical sociologists and conflict theorists contend that drug abuse is a means of self-medicating the wounds caused by economic and social oppression, emotional depression, or other stressful circumstances. Solutions may involve providing accessible treatment and rehabilitation programs for drug abusers and drug offenders.

Finally, the solutions originating from a more structural perspective address the strain drug abuse places on society. The applicable solution according to structural or strain theorists is to change societal responses to drug abuse. Solutions to drug-related problems include legalization of certain drugs such as marijuana, criminalization of the sale of narcotics, and the **medicalization** of alcohol abuse.

DU BOIS, WILLIAM EDWARD BURGHARDT (1868-1963)
American scholar, activist, writer, and editor

William Edward Burghardt Du Bois (1868–1963), African American scholar, protest leader, and an advocate of pan-Africanism, was born on February 23, 1868, in Great Barrington, Massachusetts, where he grew up. During his youth he did some newspaper reporting. In 1884, he graduated as valedictorian from high school. He got his bachelor of arts from Fisk University in 1888, having spent summers teaching in African American schools in Nashville's rural areas. In 1888 he entered Harvard University as a junior, took a bachelor of arts *cum laude* in 1890, and was one of six commencement speakers. From 1892 to 1894 he pursued graduate studies in history and economics at the University of Berlin. He served for two years as professor of Greek and Latin at Wilberforce University. In 1891 Du Bois earned his master of arts and in 1895 his doctorate in history from Harvard. In 1896 he married Nina Gomer, and they had two children.

In 1896–1897, Du Bois became assistant instructor in sociology at the University of Pennsylvania where he conducted the pioneering sociological study of an urban **community**, published as *The Philadelphia Negro: A Social Study* (1899). His dissertation on slavery and this second work assured Du Bois's place among America's leading scholars. Du Bois's life and work were geared toward gaining equal treatment for black people in a world dominated by whites and toward presenting evidence to refute myths of racial inferiority.

In 1905 Du Bois was a founder and general secretary of the Niagara movement, an African American protest group of scholars and professionals. Du Bois founded and edited the *Moon* (1906) and the *Horizon* (1907–1910) as organs for the Niagara movement. In 1909 Du Bois was among the founders of the National Association for the Advancement of Colored People (NAACP) and from 1910 to 1934 served it as director of publicity and research, a member of the board of directors, and editor of the *Crisis,* its monthly magazine.

In the *Crisis* Du Bois directed a constant stream of agitation at white Americans. Always publishing young African American writers, the Crisis served as a source of inspiration for African Americans. Racial protest during the decade fol-

W.E.B. Dubois *(Fisk University Library)*

lowing World War I focused on securing antilynching legislation. During this period the NAACP was the leading protest organization and Du Bois its leading figure.

In 1934 Du Bois left the leadership of the NAACP to begin advocacy of an African American nationalist strategy: African American controlled institutions, schools, and economic cooperatives. This approach opposed the NAACP's commitment to integration. However, he returned to the NAACP from 1944 to 1948, during which time he helped place grievances of African Americans before the United Nations, served as a consultant to the UN founding convention (1945) and wrote the famous "An Appeal to the World" (1947).

Du Bois was a member of the Socialist Party from 1910 to 1912 and always considered himself a socialist. In 1948 he was cochairman of the Council on African Affairs; in 1949 he attended the New York, Paris, and Moscow peace congresses; in 1950 he served as chairman of the Peace Information Center and ran for the U.S. Senate on the American Labor party ticket in New York. Du Bois traveled widely throughout Russia and China in 1958–1959 and in 1961 joined the Communist Party of the United States. He also took up residence in Ghana, Africa, in 1961. In 1900 Du Bois attended the First Pan African

Conference held in London, was elected a vice president, and wrote the "Address to the Nations of the World." In 1911 he attended the First Universal Races Congress in London along with black intellectuals from Africa and the West Indies.

Du Bois organized a series of pan-African congresses around the world, in 1919, 1921, 1923, and 1927. The delegations comprised intellectuals from Africa, the West Indies, and the United States. Though resolutions condemning colonialism and calling for alleviation of the oppression of Africans were passed, little concrete action was taken. The Fifth Congress (1945, Manchester, England) elected Du Bois as chairman, but the power was clearly in the hands of younger activists. Du Bois's final pan-African gesture was to take up citizenship in Ghana in 1961 at the request of President Kwame Nkrumah and to begin work as director of the *Encyclopedia Africana*.

Du Bois's most lasting contribution is his writing. He wrote 21 books and published over 100 essays. From 1897 to 1910 Du Bois served as professor of economics and history at Atlanta University, where he organized conferences titled the Atlanta University Studies of the Negro Problem and edited or coedited 16 of the annual publications, on such topics as *The Negro in Business* (1899), *The Negro Artisan* (1902), *The Negro Church* (1903), *Economic Cooperation among Negro Americans* (1907), and *The Negro American Family* (1908). He wrote *The Souls of Black Folk: Essays and Sketches* (1903), an outstanding collection of essays, and *John Brown* (1909), a sympathetic biography.

Du Bois also wrote two novels, a book of essays and poetry, and two histories of black people. From 1934 to 1944 Du Bois was chairman of the department of sociology at Atlanta University. In 1940 he founded *Phylon,* a social science quarterly. *Black Reconstruction in America, 1860–1880* (1935), perhaps his most significant historical work, details the role of African Americans in American society, during the Reconstruction period.

Black Folk, Then and Now (1939) is an elaboration of the history of black people in Africa and the New World. *Color and Democracy: Colonies and Peace* (1945) is a brief call for the granting of independence to Africans, and *The World and Africa: An Inquiry into the Part Which Africa Has Played in World History* (1947) anticipates many later scholarly conclusions regarding African history and **culture**.

Du Bois received honorary degrees, was a fellow and life member of the American Association for the Advancement of Science, and a member of the National Institute of Arts and Letters. Du Bois died in Ghana on August 27, 1963, on the eve of the civil rights march in Washington, D.C.

Dual Labor Market

Dual labor market theory was coined to explain the occupation and wage differentials between men and women. The theory was developed in response to the **human capital** theory, which suggested that income reflected an individual's education, on-the-job training, and work experience. Dual labor market theory offers a structural explanation for income differentials be-

tween men and women. The theory refers to the idea that the private sector of the economy is divided into two non-competing sectors: a primary and a secondary sector. Jobs in the primary labor market tend to be high paying, unionized, and skilled jobs that offer training, a formal mechanism for promotions, stable **career** prospects, and benefits such as health and dental insurance. Jobs in the secondary labor market, on the other hand, are menial, unskilled, non-unionized jobs that offer neither benefits nor opportunities for career advancement. Most individuals employed in the primary labor market are native born white men, while minorities, immigrants, and women often work in the secondary labor market. Some theorists argue that this division of the labor market exists to ensure that employers can offset the costs of maintaining the highly paid and often more skilled labor force by employing secondary sector workers to whom they can delegate the less central and yet crucial work activities of the company.

See also Comparable Worth

Dualism

The concept of "dualism" originated with René Descartes, a French philosopher, who theorized a dualistic existence of material bodies, on the one hand, and souls or minds defined by thought, on the other; he established the classic dualism of mind and matter. A dualism is an irreducible distinction between two categories in a classification scheme. Dualistic assumptions can be found in many areas of study. In **psychology**, there is the assumption that the mind and the body function completely independently, without any interchange. In theology, the world can be conceived of as a place where good and evil exist as mutually exclusive and antagonistic forces. With respect to sociology, dualities exist in both the way **sociology** is studied and what sociology studies.

A simple way to classify is to set up a system in which two categories are presented as diametrically oppose. An example of this can be found in the study of gender. Historically **femininity** and **masculinity** have been treated as a duality. Femininity is defined in contrast to masculinity and visa versa. Masculinity can be defined as what femininity is not. Research over the decades has transformed from this basic dualistic understanding of gender as two isolated extremes to a continuum, with the possibility for overlap and intersection.

Dualities also characterize the nature of sociology itself. Pierre Bourdieu explored dualities within sociology in his 1992 book *An Invitation to Reflexive Sociology*. For instance, subjectivity and objectivity are treated as a duality in sociology. Others include the split between the individual and sociology, **theory** and research, **structure** and agency, and micro- and macro-analysis. Bourdieu referred to these sets of concepts as "false antinomies" in that they are false distinctions that impair the sociological endeavor and need to be resolved to arrive at the truth of human practice.

DUNCAN, OTIS DUDLEY (1921-)
American sociologist

Otis Dudley Duncan was born on December 2, 1921, in Nocona, Texas, the son of Otis Durant and Ola (Johnson) Duncan. He attended Oklahoma Agricultural and Mechanical College (now Oklahoma State University) from 1938-1940 and Louisiana State University in 1941, where he received his bachelor's degree. In 1942 he earned a master's degree from the University of Minnesota. He spent 1943 studying at the University of Iowa before moving to the University of Chicago, where he was awarded his doctorate in 1949. On January 16, 1954, he married Beverly Davis, a writer with whom he collaborated on numerous studies.

Duncan's career as an expert in **social statistics** began in 1948 as an assistant professor of sociology at Pennsylvania State College (now University). From 1950-1951, he taught at the University of Wisconsin at Madison. He served as an assistant professor of sociology at the University of Chicago from 1951-1956, as an associate professor of human ecology from 1957-1960, and as a professor of human ecology from 1960-1962. Leaving the University of Chicago, Duncan taught sociology at the University of Michigan at Ann Arbor from 1962-1973 and at the University of Arizona at Tucson from 1973-1983. Duncan ended his academic career at the University of California at Santa Barbara, retiring in 1987 at which time he was awarded the title of professor emeritus.

In conjunction with his teaching, Duncan held numerous positions related to population and demographical issues. He served as advisor to the U.S. Department of Health, Education, and Welfare; the Department of Commerce; the U.S. Census Bureau; the **Social Science Research Council**; and the Institute of Social Research. He also acted as the associate director of Chicago Community Inventory (1951-1956), Population Research and Training Center (1953-1956), and Population Studies Center (1962-1967; director, 1967-1968). Duncan received various awards for his research, including the Samuel A. Stouffer Award given by the American Sociological Association in 1977 for contributions to the advancement of sociological research and the Commonwealth Award in 1980 for distinguished service in the field of sociology.

In 1961 Duncan published "A Socioeconomic Index for All Occupations" in *Occupations and Social Status*. Upon its introduction, Duncan's Sociological Index (SEI) was considered a revolutionary theory that altered the **methodology** of occupational studies. Unlike traditional paradigms made up of hierarchically layered occupations, Duncan's SEI placed all occupations on a continuous scale. Using the constructs of prestige associated with an occupation, along with educational and income levels, the SEI accounted for the complex and often overlapping relations between occupations and status attainment.

Of his many written works on population, demographics, and urban sociology, Duncan's *The American Occupational Structure,* co-authored with Peter M. Blau in 1967, is considered his most influential contribution to social statistical research. With Duncan focusing on the statistical methodology and Blau focusing on social **structure** and theory, the authors outlined the 1962 U.S. occupational system. Duncan and Blau wrote: "Processes of social mobility from one generation to the next and from career beginnings to occupational destinations are considered to reflect the dynamics of the occupational structure. By analyzing the patterns of these occupational movements, the conditions that affect them, and some of their consequences, we attempt to explain part of the dynamics of the stratification system in the United States." Duncan defines the process of stratification as "all that is involved in the intergenerational transmission of **status** and the impact thereof on status achievement and the securing of rewards." By accounting for all major relationships to various social structures (**family**, school, work) across the life span, Blau and Duncan create a conceptual basis for measuring **status attainment** within social strata. Blau and Duncan's work in *The American Occupational Structure* served as a baseline study used by other researchers as model.

In a joint effort with David L. Featherman and his wife Beverly Duncan, Duncan continued his examination of the process of status attainment in *Socioeconomic Background and Achievement* (1972). In this work, Duncan looked specifically at the cognitive and motivational links between family history and educational level by examining career achievement based on such variables as timing of first job, relocation, and **marriage** relationship. Duncan also wrote several works on social **measurement** and structural analysis for a series released by the Russell Sage Foundation, including *Notes on Social Measurement* (1984) in which Duncan offers a historical and critical assessment of the social measurement.

DURKHEIM, ÉMILE (1858-1917)
French philosopher, sociologist, and professor

The French philosopher and sociologist Émile Durkheim (1858–1917) was one of the founders of twentieth-century **sociology**. Durkheim was born at Épinal, Lorraine, on April 15, 1858. Following a long family tradition, he began as a young man to prepare himself for the rabbinate. While still in secondary school, however, he discovered his vocation for teaching and left Épinal for Paris to prepare for the École Normale, which he entered in 1879. Although Durkheim found the literary nature of instruction there a great disappointment, he was lastingly inspired by two of his teachers: the classicist Numa Denis Fustel de Coulanges and the philosopher Émile Boutroux. From Fustel he learned the importance of religion in the formation of social institutions and discovered that the sacred could be studied rationally and objectively. From Boutroux he learned that atomism, the reduction of phenomena to their smallest constituent parts, was a fallacious methodological procedure and that each science must explain phenomena in terms of its own specific principles. These ideas eventually formed the philosophical foundations of Durkheim's sociological method.

From 1882 to 1885 Durkheim taught **philosophy** in several provincial lycées. A leave of absence in 1885-1886 al-

Émile Durkheim

functions are united by their complementary roles. For Durkheim these were both conceptual and historical distinctions. Primitive societies and European society in earlier periods were mechanical solidarities; modern European society was organic. In analyzing the nature of contractual relationships, however, Durkheim came to realize that organic solidarity could be maintained only if certain aspects of mechanical solidarity remained, only if the members of society held certain beliefs and sentiments in common. Without such collective beliefs, he argued, no contractual relationship based purely on self-interest could have any force.

At the end of the nineteenth century, social **theory** was dominated by methodological **individualism**, the belief that all social phenomena should be reduced to individual psychological or biological phenomena in order to be explained. Durkheim therefore had to explain and justify his emphasis on collective beliefs, on ''collective consciousness'' and ''collective representations.'' This he did theoretically in *The Rules of Sociological Method* (1895) and empirically in *Suicide* (1897). In the first, he argued that the social environment was a reality and therefore an object of study in its own right. ''Sociological method,'' he wrote, ''rests wholly on the basic principle that social facts must be studied as things; that is, as realities external to the individual.'' The central methodological problem was therefore the nature of these realities and their relationship to the individuals who compose society.

In *Suicide* Durkheim demonstrated his sociological method by applying it to a phenomenon that appeared quintessentially individual. How does society cause individuals to commit **suicide**? To answer this question, he analyzed statistical **data** on suicide rates, comparing them to religious beliefs, age, sex, marital **status**, and economic changes, and then sought to explain the systematic differences he had discovered. The suicide rate, he argued, depends upon the social context. More frequently than others, those who are ill-integrated into social groups and those whose individuality has disappeared in the social **group** will kill themselves. Likewise, when social values break down, when men find themselves without **norms**, in a state of ''anomie'' as Durkheim called it, suicide increases.

From what source do collective beliefs draw their force? In *The Elementary Forms of Religious Life* (1912) Durkheim argued that the binding character of the social bond, indeed the very categories of the human mind, are to be found in religion. Behind religion, however, is society itself, for religion is communal participation and its authority is the **authority** of society intensified by being endowed with sacredness. It is the transcendent image of the collective consciousness.

During his lifetime Durkheim was severely criticized for claiming that social facts were irreducible, that they had a reality of their own. His ideas, however, are now accepted as the common foundations for empirical work in sociology. His concept of the collective consciousness, renamed ''culture,'' has become part of the theoretical foundations of modern **ethnography**. His voice was one of the most powerful in breaking the hold of Enlightenment ideas of individualism on modern social sciences. Durkheim died in Paris on November 15, 1917.

lowed him to study under the psychologist Wilhelm Wundt in Germany. In 1887 he was named lecturer in education and sociology at the University of Bordeaux, a position raised to a professorship in 1896, the first professorship of sociology in France.

On his return from Germany, Durkheim had begun to prepare review articles for the *Revue philosophique* on current work in sociology. In 1896, realizing that the task was too much for a single person to do adequately, he founded the *Année sociologique*. His purpose, he announced, was to bring the social sciences together, to promote specialization within the field of sociology, and to make evident that sociology was a collective, not a personal, enterprise. In 1902 Durkheim was named to a professorship in sociology and education at the Sorbonne. He remained there for the rest of his career.

The Division of Labor, Durkheim's doctoral thesis, appeared in 1893. The theme of the book was how individuals achieve the prerequisite of all social existence: consensus. Durkheim began by distinguishing two types of ''solidarities,'' mechanical and organic. In the first, individuals differ little from each other; they harbor the same emotions, hold the same values, and believe the same religion. **Society** draws its coherence from this similarity. In the second, coherence is achieved by differentiation. Free individuals pursuing different

DYAD AND TRIAD

Dyads and triads are forms of social interactions involving either two or three members, respectively. Each form of **interaction** possesses a unique set of characteristics which differentiate one **group** form from the other, regardless of whether the members are people, organizations (either formal or informal), or nations. The concepts of dyads and triads were first articulated by **Georg Simmel** (1858–1918), who considered many issues involving micro-level interactions and believed that group **structure** was an important part of group interaction. **Group size** is one component of structure.

As a group with two members, dyads are the smallest possible social groups. Dyads do not achieve meaning beyond the two parties involved. Simmel believed that dyads possess two distinct qualities. First, they are the most intimate and intense of all groups; all interaction within the group exists solely between these two members. Second, dyads require the constant, active participation of both members. If one member loses interest in the group and ceases to participate, the dyad no longer exists. As a result, a dyad is the most informal and unstable of all social groups. There is no independent group structure within a dyad, and each member retains a high level of individuality. Common examples of dyads include romantic partnerships, close friendships, bilateral agreements, and corporate mergers.

Another group structure considered by Simmel, the triad, is a group composed of three members. Since only three people are in this group, it remains intimate and intense. However, the intensity is less than that of the dyad because interactions do not necessarily involve all members of the group on an equal level within each interaction.

Triads can either initially form as such (for example, three members of an **organization** working together on a committee) or can be created from the dissolution of a larger group (one member moves away or simply leaves a four-member group) or from adding an additional outside member to a dyad (a couple has a child). The addition of a third party to a dyad radically alters the dynamics of the group. The larger size of the triad makes it more complex than the dyad. Whereas the dyad consists of a single relationship (that between Person A and Person B), triads consist of three possible relationships (Person A and Person B, Person A and Person C, and Person B and Person C). As a result, members of a triad retain much less of their individuality than members of a dyad, and the group develops a more formal social structure. One member often assumes the **role** of leader within the group, and other specialized roles begin to develop. Because of this, Simmel considered the triad to be an inherently stronger structure than a dyad. Unlike a dyad, if one member of the triad loses interest and no longer participates, the group does not cease to exist as a group but instead is transformed into a dyad.

While more stable than dyads, Simmel pointed out that triads are still inherently more unstable than larger groups. The structure of the group and the resultant hierarchy can create conflict within the group as members desire higher **status** roles for themselves. In addition, with the presence of three members, the possibility exists that two of the members will form a coalition against the third. Likewise, various combinations of the three members can form **coalitions** to achieve different goals, resulting in a more complex system of interactions. The resulting imbalance of power within the group may effectively leave the third member out of the decision-making process or feeling as if she or he has less say in the group and may ultimately lead to conflicts within the group, or even the breakdown of the group itself.

The third member, however, is not without power within this group. This member can take on the role of arbitrator or mediator and work as a peacemaker to resolve disagreements between the other two. She or he can also work for her or his own interests and use those disagreements to foster further conflict between the other two members, and possibly even gain control of the group. The third member can also turn the other two members against each other in **competition** over her or himself. Thus Simmel's concepts of dyads and triads are the simplest and most basic types of groups and offer insights into different forms of group structures.

DYSFUNCTION

As a sociological concept "dysfunction" was most popular in the postwar years, when **sociological theory** was dominated by structural functionalism. Within the structural functionalist framework developed by Talcott Parsons, institutions and activities were studied as elements of a larger social organism. More attention was paid to mechanisms increasing social cohesion, or homeostasis, which was implicitly judged to be both necessary and desirable. **Robert K. Merton** recognized some problems with the homeostatic version of **functionalism** and gave more emphasis to dysfunctions, social phenomena which challenge the existing order in some way. Nevertheless, his modifications failed to save structural functionalism from its rapid demise in the years following the student revolts of the late sixties.

From the late 1960s onwards, new generations of sociological theorists tended to reject functionalism and Parsonian **systems theory** and drawing on Marxist **political economy**, Antonio Gramsci's concept of **hegemony**, feminist theory and French **discourse** analysis (see **Michel Foucault**). They now studied institutions as unstable products of power struggles rather than measuring them according to how smoothly they functioned. Functionality, the generation of the seventies argued, should not be valorized. While certain institutions might increase the cohesion of an authoritarian or repressive social order, sociologists should not treat such cohesion as stable or desirable but instead should examine techniques of **persuasion**, forms of resistance, and potential alternatives. The term "dysfunction" was thus replaced by concepts such as resistance and **subculture**.

An important area where postwar functionalism collapsed in the face of more politicized analysis was the sociology of **gender roles**. During the earlier period, problems such as female depression, withdrawal from the world outside the house, or marital conflict initiated by wives was theorized as inadequate **role** adjustment, that is, the inability of the woman to maintain a functional female role within the **family** system. During the 1970s, feminist sociologists successfully challenged this interpretation, demonstrating that women's problems within the family stemmed from their unequal power and status. Problems such as depression and withdrawal were, therefore, not signs of dysfunctional deviation but quite the reverse. Women were suffering from their excessive compliance with a rigid and unrewarding gender script.

During the last twenty years of the twentieth century, the concept of dysfunction has become an important element of Anglophone popular culture, spreading from **psychology** into the 12-step movement, the array of contemporary self-help literature, and popular television and radio talk shows. The contemporary meanings of the concept are, however, very distant from postwar structural functionalism. References to dysfunction or, more popularly, to dysfunctional families or individuals, represent a therapeutic model of human relations, one which generally takes a strongly individualistic or family-centered view of **social problems**. Drug and alcohol addiction, violence, abuse of children, and authoritarian or rebellious behavior are interpreted by the therapeutic model as breakdowns in the proper functioning of the individual or family unit, caused by childhood trauma or abandonment.

Sociologists have in general been skeptical of the therapeutic model, as its extremely micro level of analysis comes into conflict with sociology's mission to analyze and describe the social construction of individual practices and beliefs. In *A Disease of One's Own* John Steadman Rice argued that the co-dependency movement, an influential branch of the 12-step movement, has used the concept of dysfunctionality to reject all sorts of social **conditioning** which they call cultural repression. In this case, the language of dysfunction represents the rejection of social construction not as analysis but as a real-life process, in the belief that it is possible to live unconstrained by social **rules**.

Many sociologists have criticized the therapeutic model itself as an increasingly important form of **social control** in contemporary industrial societies. Following Talcott Parsons' concept of the sick role, sociologists of medicalization have described how various behaviors have lost earlier connotations of sin or possession by spirits and are now understood as medical conditions. Many understand this progression as a product of the **rationalization** of society described by **Max Weber**. Over the last three centuries **suicide**, madness, addiction, gambling, **homosexuality**, infertility, hyperactivity, impotence, and educational failure have all become medicalized. Within this long trajectory, the popularity of the concept of dysfunctionality represents a new step, the medicalization of interpersonal relations.

E

ECOLOGICAL FALLACY

An ecological fallacy, also referred to as an ecological inference, is an error in reasoning that involves collecting **data** at a **group** or aggregate level and then using it to make inferences and draw conclusions about the individuals who belong to the group. The error in this reasoning is the assumption that the sum of individual parts is equal to the synergistic product created by the whole. To avoid committing an ecological fallacy, one should note that relationships observed at the macro level are not necessarily present at the micro level. As such, individual level correlations may be stronger, weaker, or even completely opposite to those found at aggregate levels.

For example, a researcher determines that a particular basketball team has a per game average of 14 successful free throws. From this data, the researcher then erroneously concludes that player number 36 and player number 21 each have a per game average of 14 successful free throws. However, in actuality, player number 36 is a star shooter whose performance pushed the overall team average up to 14 while player number 21 consistently missed free-throws thus bringing down the aggregate team average. In this instance, the researcher has committed an ecological fallacy by assuming that the characteristics of the group can be interpreted with the same meaning for each individual belonging to the group.

ECOLOGY

The term, ecology, was created in 1866 by Ernst Haekel, a German scientist who was a leading proponent of Darwin's theory of evolution. He defined it as "the science of relations between organisms and their environments," drawing the word from the Greek term *oikos*, meaning "household." Fritjof Capra suggested that ecology can be described as "the study of relationships that interlink all members of the Earth Household," and David Oates defined it as "how nature man-

ages its household." Thus, ecology focuses on whole *ecosystems,* which are interdependent communities of plants, animals, and microorganisms in a given environment. These systems can be studied at different levels, since smaller units of the environment are "nested" within larger units; for instance, the ecology of a bay or river exists within the larger ecology of an entire watershed. Ecologists seek to understand how organisms are interconnected and how they work together to ensure the survival of the whole system in which they are embedded. They are also interested in how species adapt to environmental changes and how they exchange matter and energy within their habitat. Ecology describes the world differently from physical sciences like physics; an object that burns or freezes merely "changes state" for physicists but for ecologists that object might be considered entirely destroyed.

Not only a scientific field of study, ecology also has a normative dimension; that is, it includes ethics and **values** concerning human relations within societies and with the rest of nature. Andrew Brennan called this dimension "metaphysical ecology," "a method of approaching problems... that applies to far more than living systems." John Barry wrote that ecology is "a form of social and moral theory" that "promises a unified science of nature and society." This worldview became more popular in the United States and Europe in the 1970s, partly through the publication of books such as Rachel Carson's *Silent Spring,* Paul Erlich's *The Population Bomb,* and Barry Commoner's *The Closing Circle.* Commoner developed what he called "four laws of ecology": "everything is connected to everything else"; "everything must go somewhere"; "nature knows best"; and "there is no such thing as a free lunch." These ideas had serious implications for issues of pollution control, energy consumption, resource, and wildlife conservation, etc. The language used by scientific ecologists was thus linked to concerns about environmental damage, as ecologists argued that failing to understand and work within nature's **ecosystems** would have dire consequences for human societies and for the planet as a whole. John Hannigan wrote, "Ecology, then, was transformed from a scientific model for

Activists have argued to put an end to "environmental racism," which disproportionately exposes minorities to toxic waste and other hazardous pollutants *(Stock Market)*.

ECONOMIC DETERMINISM

Economic **determinism** is a current of social thought that explains all social phenomena in relation to a society's material economic conditions. This perspective was central to the ideas advanced by German thinker Karl Marx during the mid-nineteenth century. Marx developed the *base-superstructure model* as a conceptual tool to illustrate the relationship between economic conditions and all other social conditions. This base-superstructure model provides the key to understanding the theoretical substance of economic determinism.

According to Marx, the *base* provides the underlying economic foundation of **society**. This economic base is made up of two distinct but interrelated components, the *forces of production* and the *relations of production*. The forces of production are those elements of society that are necessary for the economic production of goods and services. The most important elements in the forces of production are the natural environment and existing levels of technology in society. The natural environment contains the raw materials that are vital to economic production, including such things as wood, water, metals, and land. Existing technology determines the ways in which elements from the natural environment may be utilized most efficiently.

The relations of production are composed of the social relationships forged by those who play some active role in economic production. According to Marx, these relations are primarily based upon the ownership and control of a society's productive forces. Relations of production in earlier more egalitarian societies were characterized by communal ownership of the forces of production. In later societies, the development of private **property** stratified the relations of production. Marx asserted that **privatization** resulted in two classes, those individuals who owned the forces of production and those individuals whose labor fueled the productive forces. Taken together, the forces of production and the relations of production of a particular society are referred to as that society's mode of production.

According to Marx, the economic base, which is made up of the interrelation between the forces and relations of production, is responsible for, or determines, all that is not economic in a society. Marx referred to these non-economic elements of society as part of the superstructure. The superstructure includes such societal elements as the **family**, religion, politics, art, music, and consciousness. Because Marx placed particular emphasis upon politics and consciousness, the superstructure is often referred to as the "political and ideological superstructure."

Thus, economic determinism is the theoretical term most often used to describe the relationship between the base and the superstructure. Marx argued that the economic base determines the superstructure. The social construction or formation of every element of the superstructure is dependent upon the mode of production. Many American neo-Marxian sociologists have employed economic determinism in their analyses of various elements of the superstructure in capitalist America. For example, it has been argued that the contempo-

understanding plant and animal communities to a kind of 'organizational weapon' which could be used to systematize, expand, and morally reinvigorate the environmental message.''

There are several branches of this philosophical, values-oriented ecology. Arne Naess first distinguished between "shallow ecology" and "deep ecology" in the early 1970s. "Shallow ecology" is human-centered (anthropomorphic), envisioning humans as outside of and above the natural world. Plants, animals, landscapes, resources, etc., are therefore valued according to how useful they are for humans. "Deep ecology," however, sees intrinsic worth in all living things, and considers humans no more or less valuable than any other part of nature. Humans are considered a part of the "web of life" like any other species and thus do not have the right to pursue their own needs or interests at the expense of other parts of the natural world. Social and political ecologists and ecofeminists believe that environmental destruction is a result of flawed social structures and cultural systems and are critical of industrialism, capitalism, and the oppression of minorities, **indigenous peoples**, and women. These ecological activists have argued for the inclusion of the "folk knowledge" of local or indigenous peoples into scientific understandings of how ecosystems work and for an end to "environmental racism" that disproportionately exposes minorities to toxic waste and other pollution. They believe that the human domination and exploitation of nature is deeply connected to the domination of some humans by others who are more powerful.

Scientific ecologists often have mixed feelings about "metaphysical" ecologists. While many scientists care about environmental issues, they may also be uneasy with mingling "facts" and "values," for fear of being labeled "too political" or "unscientific." But other scientists seek to actively combine the two. Fritjof Capra, for instance, hopes to promote "ecological literacy"—a focus on partnership, cooperation, interdependence, recycling, and diversity—as a means of reversing environmental destruction and improving human societies.

rary structures of various families, educational institutions, and political institutions are intricately tied to the functioning of America's capitalist mode of production.

The economic deterministic perspective contends that specific family forms within a given society are determined by the economic conditions of that society. One common family form present in contemporary American society is characterized by small nuclear families residing some considerable distance from **extended family** members. Sociologists who employ perspectives of economic determinism would assert that current shifts in the American economy often require adults with families to move away from their home towns in order to obtain lucrative **employment**. As such, economic conditions are a major determinant of this particular family form.

The economic deterministic perspective may also be employed in the examination of educational institutions in capitalist societies. Various sociologists have argued that the **structure** of the public school system in America prepares students to become efficient workers. Requiring students to follow fixed rules and regulations, meting out punishments for unexplained absences and tardiness, and imposing strict deadlines for school work provide effective forms of anticipatory socialization for future workers.

A number of sociologists also assert that the organization of American political institutions is largely determined by the capitalist economic base. In the context of economic determinism it is argued that federal laws that afford generous tax breaks and other economic incentives to large corporations are clearly influenced by the capitalist economy. Furthermore, politicians who receive the bulk of their campaign funding from generous corporate sources are unlikely to vote against capitalist interests.

ECONOMIC INSTITUTIONS

Human beings depend upon systems that deliver goods and services for our continued survival. Humans could not continue to exist without continuous sources of food, water, shelter, clothing, and social **interaction**. All human societies, regardless of differences in **culture** require systematic arrangements that provide necessary material and sociological resources. Throughout the lifecycle—from birth until death—people are involved within different organizations that meet, shape, and constrain their needs. Our lives are constantly formed by the outcomes of organizational decisions.

An **institution** is a stable, yet changeable, form of social organization developed over time to meet some social **need** or desire. Economic institutions are but one form of social institutions. Other forms include, but are not limited to: religious, political, educational, military, medical, and family. Each type of social institution satisfies important concerns for a society. Although they change over time, economic institutions set the principal material conditions of life. In the mid-nineteenth century, the typical American worker was a farmer. The life style and labor of that worker was very different than the work of the mid-twentieth century factory worker. Today workers are

more likely to be based in service and information rather than manufacturing or agriculture. Future workers may engage in styles and types of work very different than contemporary conditions permit.

Economic organizations have coordinated productive activity throughout human history. Productive activity becomes more structured and dominant as economic systems have become more complex. With the emergence of private property, economic production engaged in for immediate results or physical survival becomes reconfigured as work for wages as capitalist forms of economy become increasingly dominant. Activity becomes valued in terms of usefulness and efficiency to the larger **political economy**. Useful activity has come to mean that which is directed to the producing, maintaining, and even reshaping of the inanimate or social world consistent with the current economic system. This process shapes our social interactions with one another.

Because an economy is a system for the creation, distribution, and maintenance of goods and services, it creates formal **rules**, hierarchies, and practices that organize productive or work-related livelihood. In modern economies, few areas of human endeavor are more central to human existence than the work that we perform. Not only do most of us spend the majority of our time preparing for work and then working, but the very meaning of our existences and identities are interconnected with the work we do. When we meet new people, we ask them "what do you do?"—a question that seeks to place an individual within the framework of the society's economic system. The work performed by others is as important in determining the parameters of our lives as is our own work. The way we live is dependent on the labor of millions of other workers around the world. The food that we consume, the clothes that we wear, the items that we purchase are created in a system of increasingly networked global production.

Thus, economic institutions are the complete set of **values**, beliefs, norms, practices, roles, and policies associated with economic organizations that shape productive activity at the personal and social level. Economic organizations are concerned with process and **structure**. Process is the attempt to create order and predictability among social actors. Structure is the sum of interlocked predictable actions that occur within an organization. The structure is the design of social relations within an **organization** or set of organizations that results in desired; people behave as expected and specified.

Economic institutions are the confluence of formality over productive activity. In order to stabilize an economic system, societies create ever increasing interdependent economic systems. Several organizations constitute a field of activity, such as the oil companies form the oil industry. All fields set the basic expectations for human behavior that occurs within them. And fields are shaped by the political economy; in other words, the actions of **government**, other economic organizations, individual workers, and consumers set the basic parameters for economic activity. However, few individuals are able to shape the economic system directly. The political economy stands in both a mutually influencing symbiotic relationship to the organizations, groups, and individuals who comprise the system.

Our personal and social lives are influenced, directed, and molded by economic institutions regardless of whether they are currently stable or changing. The study of economic institutions and their consequences on social life is among sociology's most important contributions to the understanding of the social world.

ECONOMIC SOCIOLOGY

Economic sociology is concerned with the relationship between the economic and non-economic characteristics of social life. Closely tied to the histories of both economics and sociology, socioeconomics can be interpreted differently, depending on the balance between economic theory and social theory. First, to define economic sociology as the study of economic phenomena from a sociological perspective, including the **structure** of the economic system, implies that socioeconomics stands as an alternative to pure economics. Second, some socioeconomists limit their research to an area of economic activity that involves social behavior, such as the influence of cultural **values** on the economy. This definition compliments economic theory, working on issues left unaddressed by economists. Third, economic sociology can be understood as the study of social structures within the economy. As defined in this matter, all economic study that addresses the issue of social **organization** is considered to be social economics. Although all three types of economic sociology exist, the first definition, which gives priority to **sociological theory**, has been the most often used throughout the century-long history of economic sociology.

From its inception, economic sociology has undergone four distinct phases of development. The first phase of socioeconomics, from the late eighteenth to the late nineteenth century, can be considered the precursor to modern economic sociology. During this time economics was classified as political economics. Economists were trained across the range of the social sciences and easily incorporated social, psychological, and philosophical elements into their economy theories. Economic study was considered to be a broad ranging field that necessarily addressed all areas of human **interaction**. In the decade before the twentieth century, **John Stuart Mill** suggested, "A person is not likely to be a good economist who is nothing else. Social phenomena acting and reacting on one another, they cannot rightly be understood apart."

The movement away from "political economics" toward "economics" began in the 1880s and lasted until the 1930s. During this period, the field of economics made a radical break from other social sciences, in particular history and by association, sociology. In Germany, a divisive battle within the field of economics erupted during the 1880s. German economics, which had a long-lasting tradition of historical economics, was led by Gustav von Schmoller, a professor at the University of Berlin, who adhered to the superiority of the historical study of economic life. His opponent, Carl Menger, a professor in Vienna, challenged Schmoller's economics. Developing his understanding in line with the British economics

that stressed general abstractions, Menger argued that historical analysis was outdated and the primary task of economics was theoretical in nature.

During this bitter argument over method, called the *Methodenstreit,* the field of economics in Germany became divided between those who were overtly historical and those who were overtly theoretical. While the overtly historical believed all economic study should be based on information from past economic experience, the overtly theoretical believed that economics should be constructed from abstractions and theorems developed independent of historical experience. **Max Weber**, who believed that economics should be both theoretically based and historically grounded, was deeply concerned over this development. In an attempt to dissolve the polarization of the field, he proposed a synthesis, which he called *Sozialökonomik,* or *socio-economics.* Weber believed that economics needed both theory and history to be complete. To this end, he developed a model of social economics based on "ideal types." According to Weber, historical facts should be set against and compared to these theory-based "ideal types."

Weber was joined in his efforts to develop a broad-based sociology of economics by Sombart and Schumpeter. Although their efforts ultimately failed to reunite the field of economics and ultimately history was disengaged from economic study, they each produced important works on economic sociology. One of Weber's many important contributions was *Economy and Society.* In his chapter "Sociological Categories of Economic Action," Weber develops a theoretical foundation of social economics by outlining various categories needed for a sociological analysis of economics, including "the concept of economic action" and "market economies and planned economies." Sombart published *Der Moderne Kapitalismus,* and Schumpeter wrote *Capitalism, Socialism, and Democracy.* George Simmel also published an important analysis of **money**, *The Philosophy of Money.*

Approximately during this same time, an independent effort to establish a socioeconomic approach occurred in France, led by Émile Durkheim, Marcel Mauss, and François Simiand. They were united in a belief that economic theory incorrectly ignores the primary importance of social aspects; therefore, economics should be replaced by a sociology of economics. The two most influential works produced were Durkheim's *The Division of Labor in Society* and Mauss's *The Gift.*

The third phase of economic sociology began in the 1930s and lasted through the 1960s. During this time, economists generally disregarded all social sciences and depended heavily on mathematics to formulate economic theories. For their part, sociologists removed themselves from all but peripheral economic issues. In his essay "The Battle of Methods," published in *Socio-Economics* (1991), Richard M. Swedberg referred to this period as characterized by "mutual ignorance and distortion" on the part of both economics and sociology. No new developments occurred in the field of economic sociology as it was generally ignored by both disciplines. In the 1950s **Talcott Parsons** and **Neil Smelser** did offer an isolated attempt at combining the fields, which was published as *Economy and Society.*

Ecosystems, such as this marsh and wetland strip, are central to nature's habitat *(Field Mark Publications)*.

Economic sociology was reborn in the fourth, and current, phase during the last three decades of the twentieth century. Spurred on by numerous interrelated events, such as the social upheaval of the 1960s and the re-emergence of Marxism during the 1970s, a new interest in the socioeconomic approach has appeared. Economic theorists have become increasingly interested in a broad range of issues previously only addressed by the social sciences, such as the family, the law, and the political system. Called "economic imperialism" based on the overarching position of economics as the foundation for study, this new approach has ignited a response by the sociological community, thus reawakening the development of economic sociology. As in the past, this rebirth, sometimes called sociology of economic life, is once again fueled by the debate regarding the places of economic theory and sociological theory within the field of social economics.

ECOSYSTEMS

The term "ecosystem" was coined in 1935 by British plant ecologist Arthur Tansley. An ecosystem is an interdependent, sustainable community in a particular environment, consisting of plants, animals, and microorganisms as well as abiotic (nonliving) materials such as solar energy, carbon, nitrogen, and water. Ecosystem networks are organizationally closed with respect to the flow of matter but open to flows of resources and energy within them. Nutrients flow through the system in a cyclical manner through food chains: organisms called autotrophs transform inorganic material into organic compounds and heterotrophs then eat these compounds, or other heterotrophs. All these nutrients are recycled: what is waste for one organism is food for another. Ecosystems are also characterized by a considerable flexibility that allows the system to bring itself back into balance after some part of it has been disturbed, if the disturbance is within the system's tolerance limits. This stability and flexibility is due largely to the diverse variety of organisms that an ecosystem contains. Each species adapts to a particular niche, so that different species cooperate rather than compete with one another to promote the survival of the whole. Different kinds of birds, for instance, may feed at different levels of the same tree and thus do not compete with one another for nutrients. Older ecosystems generally demonstrate more of this coevolution, or mutual **adaptation**, than younger ones.

Ecosytems are central to the science of **ecology** because they provide a basic **unit of analysis** where individual species cannot be truly separated from the environmental network in which they are embedded—that is, the parts are inseparable from the whole. This focus on interdependence and relationships rather than **individualism** and **competition** has led to new ways of looking at human communities as well. Social scientists are starting to pay more attention to both the social networks and ecosystems in which humans are embedded. Additionally, ecology suggests that human communities would do well to model themselves more like ecosystems, with focus on recycling, reasonable resource consumption, respect for diversity, and cooperation as ways to work towards social justice and end environmental destruction.

EDGE CITIES

Edge cities are the last phase of the roughly circular pattern of urban population movement which characterized the twentieth century. This phenomenon saw extreme population movement into **cities** in the first half of the century and a movement out of the cities in the second half. The first part of this pattern was initiated by heavy industrialization which created millions of manufacturing jobs in the large urban areas of the eastern United States. These jobs brought a flow of workers from rural areas, particularly in the South, who joined with the huge influx of European immigrants to swell the populations of virtually every city.

After World War II, however, the trend slowly began to reverse itself. The post-war baby boom made the cities more crowded than ever, and a vibrant economy coupled with a vastly modernized transportation system gave many people the means to escape the **crime** and chaos of the cities, as well as the growing racial diversity of neighborhoods and public schools. This so-called white flight created vast landscapes of suburbs outside the city limits. Initially, these suburbs were, essentially, bedroom communities for people who still worked in the city. Eventually, however, many corporations followed the middle class out of the cities in search of better educated, more highly skilled workers, and often cut their tax rates significantly in doing so.

Inevitably, retail stores and entertainment outlets followed the money, and edge cities were born. Many suburbanites saw no reason to return to the city at all; all of their necessities and conveniences had made the transition to the sprawling expanses of parking lots, shopping malls, and office parks which formed the suburban landscape. Expressways and service roads allowed easy access to these features.

In his book *Edge Cities: Life on the New Frontier*, Joel Garreau identified and named the phenomenon and contended that, contrary to the thinking of many sociologists, edge cities were not merely a sign of racial tensions and technology run rampant. They were actually a more natural way for humans to live than the packed high-rises and subway trains of the first part of the twentieth century. In any case, the communications revolution and agricultural decline of the 1980s and 1990s point toward a continuing spread of edge cities across the once rural vastness of the United States.

EDUCATION AND DEVELOPMENT

The processes by which a **society** educates and develops its members have been a focus of study for sociologists virtually since the inception of the discipline. Among the studies of education undertaken by early sociologists, those of Émile Durkheim stand out for many reasons. First, his was the first sociologically-based study of the systems and processes by which education integrates its members into society. Second, as a result of his work, formal recognition of the function of education as a primary factor in establishing an individual's **role** within society was established. And finally, Durkheim formally stated the moral basis for social involvement in the education process. Through his writing he established the concept that if the powers of society are not employed in providing direction through education, individuals may waste their talent and engage in behavior that is actually harmful to both themselves and society.

Durkheim's study and writing was specific in its direction and focus, concentrating on the processes in which society engages in educating its members and on the broad social necessity of society's involvement in those processes. Thinking that the importance of socially directed education could not be overemphasized, he stated: ''society can survive only if there exists among its members a sufficient degree of homogeneity; education perpetuates and reinforces this homogeneity by fixing in the mind of the child, from the beginning, the essential similarities that social life demands.'' It is important to note, though, that Durkheim did not feel that it was the purpose of education to assure that all members of a society thought the same way, or valued equally the same goals or social function. For Durkheim valued diversity: ''without a certain diversity all co-operation would be impossible; education ensures the persistence of this necessary diversity by being itself diversified and specialized.'' Clearly Durkheim was concerned that it be understood that the individual within society who participates in its processes of education benefits through that participation.

The term *pédagogie,* first used in a sociological context by Durkheim in his 1904 article *''Pédagogie et sociologie''*, has become synonymous with any study, sociological or not, of childhood education. Of the various articles and essays Durkheim published between 1904 and 1916, the majority dealt with issues of the education processes involving children, or pédagogie, and the links between education and the underlying moral doctrines embraced by society. Fundamental to Durkheim's pédagogie, and at odds with most other educators in France as well as England, was his premise that most failures in the processes of education occurred as a result institutions' failure to provide any theory or systematic training which teachers might use in their work. In fact, Durkheim felt that theoretical foundations and systematic training were so important it is estimated that between one-third and two-thirds of his lecturing time was devoted to the subjects. And, while today he is remembered mostly as one of the pioneers of sociology, in his time he was regarded primarily as an educationalist.

Durkheim's work concentrated on the broad social importance and general social and moral processes of education, always emphasizing the paramount importance of proper theoretical foundations and systematic training. Later sociologists have contributed extensively to a broader and more critical sociological study of education and its relationship to social development. Most of those, including **Samuel Bowles** and Herbert Gintis, Theodore Schultz, Michael Miles, Daniel Bell, **Pierre Bourdieu**, and Aaron Cicourel and John Kitsuse, have concentrated on the development of broad social theory designed to explain the significant social forces and ideologies that underlie the institutional processes which guide public education.

Among later American sociologists who have expanded Durkheim's original pedagogical approach to education, Samuel Bowles and Herbert Gintis assessed the processes that underlie American education. Published in 1976, at a time when American education was being carefully reassessed by those within the political and education systems, their book *Schooling in Capitalist America* never made direct reference to Durkheim's work. It did, however, describe at great length, and ultimately condemn, the processes that have driven American education in the twentieth century. Bowles and Gintis embraced as fundamental truth Durkheim's ideas that underlying theory and systematic training are essential to successfully implementing of educational processes. They stated unequivocally that in America the theory and system underlying public education has been based on preserving the economic interests of the minority upper class to the detriment of most U.S. students. From their perspective, this institutionalized inequality assures that the hierarchy desired by the upper economic classes will be maintained, with power and authority vested in them. The lower economic classes, conversely, will be educated by the system to a level that is appropriate to the needs of employers. In other words, education serves the profitability needs of employers first. The economic needs of the students who become workers will then be served by the **employment** system at a level appropriate to the education provided them by the employer-controlled education system. While sociologists differ, all find at least some common theoretical ground, centering on the fact that issues of economics, manifested in varying ways, play a significant role in the **structure** and function of education and social development.

EDUCATION AND MOBILITY

A main motivation behind research in **social stratification** is the attempt to understand **social mobility**, or an individual's occupational attainment relative to the person's parents. In more **traditional societies** inheritance is the main mechanism for people to obtain their occupation. For example, in caste-based societies birth into a specific caste dictates occupation. In medieval societies most children inherited their jobs through aristocratic titles and land given to them by their parents, through peasant ties to a manor or to an urban craft or trading business handed down from father to son. In these societies little social mobility occurred: most people had the same job as their parents. In modern industrial societies most

forms of direct inheritance have disappeared. Caste and title inheritance systems have been abolished, and except for small business owners the majority of workers are unable to directly pass their jobs on to their children. Research on social stratification in modern industrial societies, and in particular studies of social mobility, thus investigates what different qualities of people lead them into different jobs than their parents. The main finding from this body of research is that the most important quality that helps individuals succeed in the economy is the amount of education they have.

Knowing that education is the most crucial asset in modern social mobility, two different research topics become crucial. The first is understanding the conditions under which this effect might vary. Are there different types of countries where education matters less or perhaps where other features of individuals might be more important than education? For example, are there societies where racial, ethnic, or caste differences remain important, perhaps even more important than education, in explaining who is able to get better jobs than their parents held? Is education less important in state socialist countries, where the labor market is radically different from that in capitalist countries? Generally, studies have found that while there is some degree of difference in the effect of education across countries, the main finding remains that education is the most important determinant of mobility in modern industrial societies.

The second research focus that emerges from the finding of the overall importance of education in mobility is on attempting to understand who is more likely to advance in the educational system and how this is related to the **status** of the **family** into which people are born. This idea has been labeled the theory of "indirect inheritance" because it posits that people are able to pass on their social status to their children, but only indirectly by making sure they succeed in the educational system. A cursory look at the educational system of the United States would initially seem to indicate that this is unlikely to be the case. Parental status was of course very important in the nineteenth and early twentieth centuries when little if any school attendance was required, and the children of lower class and farming families assumed work responsibilities quite early in life. Later in the twentieth century, as the educational system expanded in response to the government mandate to attend through high school and the number of colleges and college students greatly increased following the baby boom, coming from a privileged background would appear to matter less.

More detailed research has shown, however, that there is a crucial element of indirect inheritance in the United States in terms of educational transitions rather than average number of years of education. These transitions, such as obtaining a high school or college diploma, are important for guaranteeing a high status job and a high **quality of life**. Researchers have found that students from upper- and middle-class backgrounds are more likely to get these degrees than those from working and lower-class families. Research has shown this to be the case in all industrial countries, both western democracies and state socialist countries in Eastern Europe, where the educational system had undergone an expansion similar to that

More education leads to higher income

Median income by educational attainment and sex of year-round, full-time workers 15 years old and older, 1998

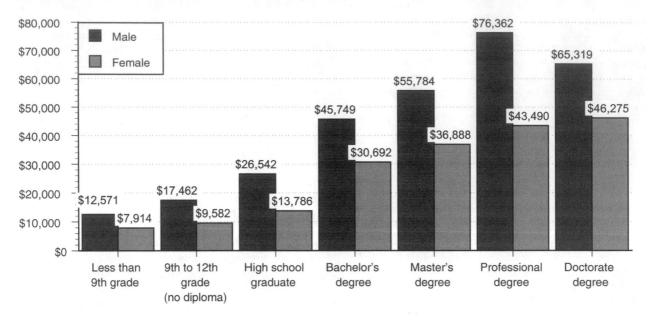

Source: U.S. Census Bureau

which occurred in the United States. This finding was especially surprising in Eastern Europe given the explicit policy of promoting educational attainment among children of farmers and blue collar workers. These findings indicate that in industrial societies parents from the middle and upper classes make sure that their children attend school and achieve a high education, and only when there is additional space left over in schools are the children of the lower classes likely to advance.

See also Social Mobility

EDUCATIONAL ORGANIZATION

The U.S. educational system, a social **institution**, is organized in such a way that schooling can take place within individual states, counties, and in some cases individual communities. The term schooling is different from the term education in an important way. Education refers to the social institution in which knowledge is conveyed to members of **society**. Schooling is the actual formal instruction given by certified teachers.

The United States provides free education for all children from kindergarten (age 5) through 12th grade. The public, however, does fund the schools indirectly through federal, state, and local taxes. Local taxes supply most of the funds, followed by state funds, and finally funds from the federal **government**. The organization of school funding generates debate. Funding for schools on the local level comes mostly from property taxes. A potential problem lies in discrepancies between wealthy and poor city areas. Reliance on local property taxes causes one school to have more than adequate funding and another school to be seriously underfunded. These discrepancies may contribute to discrepancies in academic achievement which in turn limits job opportunities.

School system goals are considered when implementing organizational plans. But those goals are sometimes different from the community's goals and an individual school's goals. Each **community** may have different goals as well. A rural farming community may want the schools to provide instruction in agriculture and training on farming machinery while a suburban community may want the school to provide college preparatory courses or dual enrollment classes for college credit. These goals are met separately through a system of **organization**.

The organization of the educational system within all public schools, while differing in some ways between states and communities, has the same basic **structure**, a **bureaucracy**, perhaps the most efficient way to manage large schools. Bureaucracies have a hierarchy of offices, **rules** and regulations, impersonality, set criteria for hiring, and formal written **communication** (vast amounts of files).

From top to bottom, the hierarchy of **authority** in the school system is school boards, superintendents, principals, teachers, staff, and students. There are many rules, procedures, and regulations within the schools: school starts and ends at specified times and students must adhere to many rules regarding behavior, dress, and academics. Teachers and administrators must also adhere to rules and procedures set by superintendents and school boards. Rules are enforced both formally and informally. Relations between members in the hierarchy of authority are also formalized. For example, teachers are expected to maintain a strictly professional relationship with students. Some schools require that students and staff must wear identification badges at all times. These badges are used to gain access to the school and pay for hot lunches and other functions. Schools employ standardized testing to gain knowledge of how students are achieving academically compared to students at other schools. Much of what happens within a school is formalized and documented, and guided by procedure. While the bureaucratization of the school system has met with opposition, it seems to work well and provide useful information regarding the quality of the educational system.

EGALITARIANISM

Egalitarianism is derived from the French word "égalité" literally meaning "equality". Initially, it referred to the equality of all men and made no allowances for the class system of nobles and peasants which held sway throughout Europe until recent centuries. In the Declaration of Independence, the founders of the United States held it "self-evident: that all men were created equal." This concept was not original to them, but the success of the American Revolution initiated sweeping **social change** in the Americas and Europe. The unwillingness of the founders to consider the equality of African Americans and women diluted the scope of the movement, and European imperialism in Africa and Asia was widening its reach; nevertheless, the importance of the eighth century American revolutionaries in establishing today's understanding of **human rights** cannot be overstated.

In France, revolutionaries who had closely studied the American success, took egalitarianism more literally. The French system had been more oppressive of the peasant classes so, perhaps, it is not surprising that the uprising took a more radical tone against the former ruling nobles. French egalitarianism was closely related to **socialism** and sought, not just freedom for the populace, but reparations for a history of tyranny by the wealthy landowners. This aspect of the revolution failed, with Napoleon Bonaparte forming a military dictatorship and, eventually, proclaiming himself emperor. Even so, one more step had been taken in undermining the once widely accepted belief in the divine right of monarchs or the nearly divine status of European elites. The next two centuries were a constant, and largely successful, struggle of the working classes to gain an equal voice in politics. Racial and gender equality were particularly long in coming, but by the end of the twentieth-century U.S. laws recognized no differences in terms of basic rights among the races or sexes.

At the turn of the millennium, some aspects of egalitarianism have formed the basis of international law. In theory, at least, individuals are born with equality and can only lose this status through the commission of crimes against **society**. Many organizations, official and unofficial, now exist to keep watch over international human rights. More controversial are the questions of whether equality should be applied absolutely to **property** or opportunity. In these concepts are the roots of socialism which would necessarily infringe on the rights of some to equalize circumstances for all. While socialized medicine and **affirmative action** are forms of egalitarianism that have been implemented in democratic countries, it remains for **government** policy in the twenty-first century to determine a balance between egalitarian programs and individual liberty.

EGO

According to Freud, *ego* refers to one of three parts of the mind, sometimes referred to as the self, also known as the "I" (as opposed to the 'me'). The term is used primarily in psychoanalytic theory, **psychology**, and **social psychology**. The other two parts of the mind are the *id* (instincts, natural desires and impulses, unsocialized) and the *superego* (conscience, demands of external social life and environment, socialized). The ego supposedly resolves conflicts between the other two, competing parts of the mind. It controls the impulses experienced by the **id** that may not be socially acceptable in a given situation, thus applying the knowledge gained and experienced by the **superego**.

The concept of the three parts of the mind, developed by Sigmund Freud, was his attempt to explain how the human mind and 'being' work. It was laid out in his 1923 publication *The Ego and the Id*. Freud believed that humans are born with only the id (instinctual, biological impulses). Thus, the human infant is controlled completely by its reactions to these biological impulses and physical sensations. It does not yet understand these sensations because it has not learned how these impulses are interpreted in **society**. He felt that infants are ruled by the 'pleasure principle,' the main goal of which is to avoid pain. As the child grows, it learns to separate physical sensations from potential responses. It learns that not all physical impulses need to be acted on immediately (i.e. it learns control and restraint, as necessitated by society). It also learns that there are various potential responses to every physical and mental stimulus. This learning leads to an ability to take in more complex intellectual ideas such as imagining, thinking, and planning. With this ability, the child can learn and internalize the rules and regulations of the world into which it is born (through socialization). This process is how a child develops a superego (conscience), which is controlled by the 'reality principle' and governs a human's interactions with others. The controls placed on the id by the superego come from **socialization**.

According to Freud, the function of the ego is to create an acceptable balance between the conflicting needs of the id and the superego; it is to find socially acceptable ways to satisfy the urges of the id. Because both types of urges must be satisfied (to satisfy biological impulses and to conform to society's demands), the ego develops different ways to accommodate them both. There are three ways people learn to accommodate these conflicting impulses: delaying gratification of biological urges until the social situation is appropriate (e.g. waiting to urinate in a bathroom rather than in public); diverting the biological urges to a different outlet (e.g. participating in sports to release **aggression** rather than fighting with others); or repressing the urges altogether (e.g. choosing not to hit a child in anger). Some psychologists claim that too much repression of the id's impulses can lead to psychosis and neurosis.

The ego is not a static aspect of one's mind. It is a process and changes over the course of one's lifetime. It is the part of the mind that internalizes and incorporates **morality** into the human existence. It provides consistency in one's actions and reactions to external stimuli. It relates experiences in the past to present and future situations. It is the part of the mind that remembers, evaluates, and plans a course of action in response to the surrounding environment. In addition to enacting the conscious knowledge gained through socialization, the ego also has preconscious functions. It controls memory, decision-making, conscious thought, voluntary physical motions (talking, walking), and physical perceptions (sight, touch, hearing).

Some modern-day social psychologists reject Freud's conceptualization of the ego. They claim that the ego is really the 'self' (i.e. what one thinks of oneself, what one **values**, and the things with which one identifies). This is different from Freud's conception because he did not think that the ego is an independent part of the mind; rather, he believed that it is dependent on interaction with the id for its energy. But other theorists believe that the ego has its own energy source, that it is a process in and of itself, not dependent on the id for energy.

Some researchers contend that 'ego strength' is an important component of **mental health**. This is the ability to distinguish when to give in to social pressures and when to give in to biological urges. Those with a strong ego are supposedly self-aware, well-organized, can manage several tasks or projects at once, can easily make decisions, and can balance the conflicting needs of their instincts and their social environment. Those with a 'weak ego' tend to be more like children. They are unable to control their biological urges, they are indecisive and disorganized, and the distinction between their internal and external realities is not always clear. In contrast to Freud's usage, in common terminology, ego is often also used to refer to personal characteristics such as selfishness, self-interest, **individualism**, inflated self-esteem, arrogance, or narcissism.

ELECTORAL SOCIOLOGY

The sociological study of **voting behavior**, or electoral sociology, addresses the issue of voter choice, including the manner in which voters obtain, process, and act upon political information. The modern study of voting behavior began to develop in the United States in the final years of the nineteenth century. Two differing methodological approaches were instituted that reflected varying theoretical understanding regarding motivational and decision-making factors that result in specific voting behaviors.

The first electoral research **methodology** was aggregate data analysis, which used tallied returns from actual elections, organized them into predetermined sections, such as wards and counties, and then compared voting patterns with census data from those particular geographical areas. Sociologists used extensive mapping of the information from voting and **census** records as their main interpretative tool. From these demographical details, sociologists drew conclusions about particular areas. For a simplified example, if the census count reveals that Catholics are the majority population in a particular area, and if the vote count shows a majority of people in that area voted for the Democratic candidate, then the researcher could draw the conclusion that Catholics tend to vote Democratic. In this manner, sociologists studied the relevance of social indicators such as class, religion, **language**, and region to voting behavior.

Although the approach was later expanded upon and improved by sociologist Franklin Giddins of Columbia University and one of his students, Stuart Rice, the introduction of modern **survey research** beginning in the 1930s greatly diminished the use of aggregate data analysis in social research. Although aggregate data analysis is no longer the preferred method of analyzing voting behavior, it does continue to play an important role in understanding long-term sociohistorical voting patterns and remains in use in areas where funding does not allow for more expensive survey-based study.

Analysis of survey data, the second early approach to electoral sociology, conducts research based on polling voters on past or future voting intentions. In the 1920s, polls based on future votes (straw polls) became a popular activity among newspapers and journals. The commercial uses of social **surveys** for creating marketing strategies spurred the development of **public opinion** research along with voter preference studies during the 1940s. It continued to be the most influential method of electoral study through the remainder of the twentieth century.

While public opinion research was flourishing, survey-based voting research was being formulated as an academic endeavor. Two studies, based on the presidential elections of 1940 and 1948, set the precedent for future research and contemporary theories of voting behavior. Paul F. Lazarsfeld, a sociologist at Columbia University, led the surveys with the goal of relating voters' presuppositions to candidate choice and tracing changes in opinion through the course of the election. The Columbia University team selected Erie County, Ohio, in 1940, and Elmira, New York, in 1948 in which to conduct their research. Participants were interviewed between four and seven times prior to and after the election.

The Erie County study, which was later expounded upon by the Elmira study, produced several important theories of voting behavior. First, individuals usually vote as they have in the past, which often reflects the voting behavior of significant **family** members. Second, membership in social and economic groups greatly influences voter preference. Specifically, lower income, urban, and Catholic voters tend to be Democrats, whereas higher income, rural, and Protestant voters tend to be Republicans. Third, change is usually precipitated by cross-pressures, when different influences provide conflicting choices. Finally, Lazarsfeld defined a "two-step flow" of information. Namely, voters seldom have extensive political knowledge but instead look to people of influence as the source of their information and opinion.

In the 1950s the Columbia School approach to electoral sociology was replaced by the work at the University of Michigan. Led by Angus Campbell, the Michigan research team conducted their first survey in 1948, followed by two major studies in 1952 and 1956. The basis of the study was vastly different from Lazarsfeld's surveys. First, the survey used a national sample rather than a limited geographical area. Second, only two interviews were conducted, one prior to and another following the election. Third, using this format, the research team focused on the psychological factors that affect voting behavior, thus drawing new conclusions regarding factors involved in voter choice.

Rejecting Lazarsfeld's emphasis on social group identity, the Michigan team concluded that the primary factor in determining voter choice was the long-term "psychological identification" the voter feels for one of the two major political parties, regardless of actual party membership. In fact, voters' opinions of candidates are formulated by filtering their perceptions of the candidates through their perceptions of the associated political party. Noting the high **correlation** between party identification between children and their parents, the researchers suggested that the development of partisanship begins in childhood.

The Michigan study revealed that voters had very little, if any, measurable amount of knowledge of political issues. Also, the research suggested that even if the voter possesses knowledge of the issues, the information seldom affects the voter's candidate choice. According to Campbell, the psychological process of viewing both issues and candidates through the lenses of party affiliation has the largest impact on voter selection. The Michigan analysis became the dominant understanding of voter analysis, but it came under scrutiny during the 1970s and 1980s as party identification appeared to wane and high-profile issues, such as the Civil Rights Movement, the Vietnam War, and Watergate, produced a more informed public.

Emerging by the 1980s, a new model called rational choice was developed. Unlike the Michigan school of thought that associated party identification with psychological attachment, rational choice proponents suggested partisanship is linked to the stance on issues of both the candidate and the political party. In its pure form, rational choice requires a well-informed, highly motivated voting public. However, numerous adaptations of rational choice have appeared to account for voters' lack of knowledge of issues. Morris P. Fiorina proposed the concept of retrospective voting. Although voters may not be knowledgeable of current political issues and a certain candidate or party's stance on it, they look to how that candidate or party has responded in the past to policy decisions. Based on retrospective knowledge, voters choose a candidate and party that best match their interests and concerns.

Electoral sociology continues to be dominated by social survey methodology as a means to understand voting behavior.

Often used in conjunction with the prediction of elections, the mostly widely used approach continues to be innumerable variations of the Michigan model. Conclusions are based almost exclusively on quantitative data, although some sociologists continue to search for innovative methods of incorporating more qualitative analysis into the study of voting behavior.

See also Voting Behavior

ELITISM

Elitism can refer to the idea that elites are desirable or to the belief that they are inevitable. The class system that ruled much of the world for most of recorded history has been replaced, gradually, by more egalitarian systems which express the belief that people are created equal and should not be granted elite **status** simply by way of the **family** or class into which they are born. On the other hand, many people favor the wealth, prestige, and power that, theoretically, follows hard work and sacrifice. Such "self-made" elites have earned the right to hold places of power and to establish the social **values** for those around them. Meanwhile, their high status serves to motivate others to achieve similar places in **society**.

True egalitarians, however, see such a system as another version of class-ordered social **structure**. Those who earn the wealth create a set of rules for functioning in society, which favors their own group. Their children start life with **money**, education, and an understanding of the system that the less wealthy, less educated do not have. This stratification creates roles from which it is difficult to escape, even in a free society.

The resentment caused by elites sometimes takes subconscious forms. A less fortunate group may be contemptuous of the wealthy even as they are trying to attain similar wealth, for instance. Likewise, education is highly valued by almost everyone and yet the academic elite are scoffed at as soft and lazy people who spend their time thinking and theorizing rather than living and experiencing; even so, few people will trust a physician or attorney who has not spent the requisite time studying and thinking about his professional role.

Public sentiment regarding elites tends to shift with the fortunes of the day. Difficult economic conditions create bitterness towards those who continue to live well; racial strife causes the oppressed to focus on real and perceived privilege of the **race** which holds the power. To this end, the economic boom at the turn of the millennium seems to have ushered in a different attitude about wealth. The stock market, casinos and lotteries, professional sports, the entertainment industry, the **Internet**, and countless other developments have unleashed a phenomenon of overnight rags to riches stories: the class the French elite have sneered at, the *nouveau riches*. This phenomenon and its saturation in the media have blurred the distinctions between economic classes more than ever. Meanwhile, a philosophy of bottom-line thinking in the marketplace has elevated the **culture** of the masses at the expense of more refined or esoteric tastes. For better and for worse the culture and values of the rich and powerful and the poor and disenfranchised are virtually indistinguishable. New elites are bound to rise; race, religion, and education continue to be divisive factors. But the tide of globalism, propelled by a truly mass media, appears to be sweeping aside many of the differences which have historically identified the haves from the have-nots.

EMERSON, RICHARD MARC (?-1982)
American sociologist

Richard M. Emerson influenced the study of social **structure** by introducing the theory of social exchange which broke new ground in three areas. First, Emerson's paradigm focused on the **interaction** and relationship between individuals rather than their individual actions. In so doing, he circumvented the limitations of **behaviorism** and **utilitarianism**, thus allowing a fuller perspective of social structure. Second, social **exchange theory** emphasizes resource availability, power, and dependence as primary dynamics within a relationship. Doing so allows the researcher to ask the question, "why," about relationships rather than merely "what kind." Third, by creating a theory that focused on the interplay between two interacting parties, Emerson provided a means to address social structure at both the micro and macro levels. If relationships, not actors, are key, then the theory can be equally applied to person-person, person-group, and group-group relations.

Emerson first outlined his original concept of social relationships in "Power-Dependence Relations," which appeared in the February 1962 issue of the *American Sociological Review.* Over the next twenty years, he continued to develop and expand his understanding of social relations. He contributed "Exchange Theory, Part II: Exchange Relations and Networks" to *Sociological Theories in Progress, Volume II* (1972) and "Social Exchange Theory" to *Social Psychology: Sociological Perspectives* (1981). He also published major articles in sociological journals, including "Power, Equity, and Commitment in Exchange Networks" (with Karen Cook, 1978) in *American Sociological Review* and "The Distribution of Power in Exchange Networks: Theory and Experimental Results" (with Cook, Mary Gillmore, and Toshio Yamagishi, posthumously, 1983) in *American Journal of Sociology.*

Emerson begins by identifying distinct types of social relations that are qualitatively unique, such as monopolies, **coalitions**, and markets. Not only are relations organized in different manners, they also differ in the type and amount of resources exchanged, such as **money**, friendship, and status. Given this network structure, Emerson argues that power and dependence are the primary dynamics that define the relationship. He devised a formal equation to denote this interaction: "The dependence of actor A upon actor B is (1) directly proportional to A's *motivational investment* in goals mediated by B, and (2) inversely proportional to the *availability* of those goals to A outside the A-B relation." In defining power, he states: "The power of actor A over actor B is the amount of resistance on the part of B which can be potentially overcome by A." In other words, when B has means to fulfill stated needs outside the relationship, B's dependence and A's power will be low. However, if B has a keen interest in resources that can only be provided by A, then B's dependence increases and A's power increases. Thus A's power over B is equal to B's dependence on A.

With power and dependence the defining characteristics of social relations, the potential for imbalance is constantly present. Imbalance in relationships occurs when one party has unequal access to or power to control resources; balance occurs when both parties have equal access to resources. Emerson argues that relationships tend to seek balance, which can be achieved through change that alters the power balance by remixing dependency variables. He offers four methods of balancing operations: (1) if B's desire for the resources offered by A is reduced; (2) if B finds other sources to fill the needs previously filled by A; (3) if A's desire for the resources offered by B is increased; and (4) if A can find no other sources to obtain the resources offered by B. He concludes that the greater the level of shared interdependence, the more cohesive the relationship and the more conflict it can endure without dissolving.

Imperative to understanding social exchange theory is the distinction between potential power and actual use of power. The relationship is determined by actual use, not potential use, of power. Even though A may have significant power over B, the relationship is altered only insofar as A employs this power to enact change. Certain social restraints can act upon A to limit the amount of potential power actually used, including friendship or commitment and organizational structure. External **authority** structures can also impede the use of power, acting as a third party in a triadic relationship with the two interacting participants.

Emerson was teaching at the University of Cincinnati in the early 1960s when he first introduced social exchange theory. He later found his academic home at the University of Washington, where he remained until his death on December 23, 1982, due to complications from surgery. At the time of his death, he was working on "Toward a Theory of Value in Social Exchange," a chapter that appears in its unfinished form in *Social Exchange Theory* (1987), a compilation edited by Cook and dedicated to Emerson.

EMPIRICAL SOCIOLOGY

Empirical sociology, in general, refers to any form of sociological study that places primary or exclusive emphasis on the collection of data. More specifically, the term refers to a specific philosophical approach within the field of sociology. By applying a scientific **methodology**, empirical sociological study attempts to guarantee objective discovery of knowledge based on verifiable facts of evidence. In this epistemological model, observation and objectivity take precedence over theory and interpretation. Such a paradigm stands in opposition to the other broadly defined epistemological method known as formalism, or **relativism**, in which theory and interpretation self-sufficiently attempt to define the methodological paradigm.

Scientific research involves both the subject (i.e., researcher) and the object of study. Whereas in a formalist approach the subject actively operates to interpret this object of study, in the practice of empirical sociology, the object is the ultimate focus and the subject plays a passive role as impartial observer. According to Castells and Ipola in their contribution on epistemological practice to *Critical Sociology* (1979), "The basis of this model is the 'evidence theory', according to which scientific activity consists of first gathering and then analyzing supposedly 'objective' information which pre-dates the actual activity (and prejudices) of the researcher."

Empirical **epistemology** assumes the existence of a concrete world, independent of the human mind, that can be known through systematic observation and study. With this assumption, empiricists conclude that scientific methods are the most reliable and rational means to obtain knowledge. Sociology has always had a broad, eclectic array of methodological and theoretical epistemologies; however, the empirical approach dominated the philosophy of science from the beginning of the twentieth century through the 1960s. In the second half of the twentieth century, strict empirical methodology came under increasing attack, and other theories, namely relativism, took the lead in contemporary sociological study.

Not only did empirical sociology come under fire from dissenting sociologists, but the field of sociology itself was continuing an ongoing battle to gain acceptance as a recognized scientific discipline. As late as the 1990s, sociology was still often considered a lesser science. In the introduction to his book *Analytical Sociology: Its Logical Foundations and Relevance to Theory and Empirical Research* (1994), Joseph R. Pearce admitted that sociology's "status as a scientific discipline remains in question despite the vast accumulation of social facts, tested empirical relationships, and numerous attempts at construction of systematic theory." For the scientific community, empirical study in a sociological setting failed to provide adequate explanation of the significant number of variables within the statistical models it produced. For example, multiple variants acting independently within the studies create complex environments from which quantitative **data** must be collected. Other issues, such as data collection methods, inadequate **measurement**, and use of inappropriate samples, can also lead to unexplained variance.

The problem with empirical research stems from the variables that are inherent in the observation itself. Unlike other fields of science in which the relationship is between subject (i.e., researcher) and object (mathematical equation, particle behavior, etc.), in sociology the relationship is an act of observation between subject and subject. Because the responses to be measured are more social than physical, potential unknown variance exists in the subject of study and in the observer. **Surveys**, questionnaires, and measurement standards all contain unexplained assumptions regarding **language** and intent that must be interpreted by the subject of study and reinterpreted by the observer. Franklin H. Giddens, a pioneer for sociology at the beginning of the twentieth century, referred to this dualism as a "double hermeneutic."

Ray Pawson identified four primary objections leveled against empirical epistemology by sociologists who adhere to relativism in *A Measure for Measure: A Manifesto for Empirical Sociology* (1989). First, sociological measurement is rendered obsolete by changes in cultural meanings. Because sociological studies deal with dynamic social and cultural interactions, these relationships are in constant flux. Thus, inherent in the nature of the subject of study is constant movement of meaning, language, perception, and interpretation. Second, relativists contend that measurement scales used in empirical research are arbitrarily chosen. Third, similar to the criticism received from the scientific community, relativists note that meanings must be created and imposed on the observation by the observer. They argue that it is simply impossible for the researcher to come to the study value-free or politically neutral. Finally, because all observation begins from a presupposed theory, measurement is selective. Subsequently, in an attempt to limit evidence to prove or disprove a theory, empirical studies and surveys ignore or purposefully omit data of significant value to theory and understanding.

The empirical methodology accounts for the difficult issue of its attempt to create objective, generalized statements of knowledge drawn from observation and quantitative study of the social world, a markedly subjective phenomenon through variable control. Strict **standardization** in observation, survey, and measurement is used in a highly controlled setting that attempts to account for all variables. According to Pearson, "Therefore, the meaning of a concept is objectified by strict **operationalization**, while the interpretation of observed empirical relationships is objectified by computation of quantitative statistical comparisons.... Interpretation of the findings is viewed as an objective, logical extension of the quantitatively established and test empirical associations."

Although few sociologists today pledge unwavering support to pure empirical methodology, empirical sociological study continues (e.g., survey studies, voting pattern analysis, racial and gender-based data collection, etc.). However, new paradigms are emerging. After the sharp reactionary turn toward formalism beginning in the 1960s, contemporary sociological epistemology turned its attention to the process of synthesizing the best of **empiricism** and relativism to create a philosophy of science that accounts for both quantitative and qualitative issues present in sociological research.

EMPIRICISM

Empiricism is, along with **realism**, **positivism** and others, a methodological and epistemological doctrine in the social sciences. The problems of epistemology (the concern with the knowability of the social world) and **methodology** (the way to gather that knowledge) have been answered by a number of stances, one of which is the empiricist position. Based to some extent on Émile Durkheim's early statements on methodology, empiricism maintains that the only basis of a science of **society** is careful observation of the empirical world and only observable facets of the social world are valid for social theories and for social explanation. Theories that postulate unverifiable underlying causes or processes, as Pierre Bourdieu's theories of habitus and field, which claims an underlying but unseen mental structure that patterns every day behavior, are rejected. Although the term "empiricism" is sometimes used in a pejorative sense to denote work that is not theoretically sophisticated, much important development of the discipline of sociology has been accomplished by empiricist scholars.

Empiricism does not actually represent a unified school of social thought but, rather, a variety of doctrines based on this fundamental stance. The Chicago school ethnographies, for instance, from the 1920s onward, represent a type of empiricist approach of sociological research into urban problems. Robert Park, who was a journalist before joining the Chicago faculty, influenced a generation of scholars with his writings that emphasized the importance of understanding the social worlds of the city through observational methods. **Symbolic interactionism** is another empiricist approach to **sociology**, a descendant of **the Chicago school**. Herbert Blumer's *Symbolic Interactionism, Perspective and Method* (1969) develops a series of methodological proposals for a scientific study of **interaction** in society. For Blumer, all steps of scientific inquiry, from the development of concepts to the testing of propositions, ought to be done in a manner consistent with a methodological stance, with the goal of accurately representing the empirical world. Another empiricist approach, **ethnomethodology**, developed by **Harold Garfinkel** in the 1940s, sought to capture and understand human interactions and the way these help people make sense of their social world. Though few scholars today would call themselves empiricists, the empiricist caution against theorizing divorced from social research remains an important corrective.

EMPLOYMENT

Employment is a transaction in which the worker receives compensation for work performed. U.S. labor trends examine the variations in employment patterns compiled from **data** on hours worked and occupation by gender and race. This information is classified according to a system developed by the Department of Labor (DOL) almost fifty years ago, when the goods producing sector dominated our domestic economy. Although temporary help workers were added to this classification in the 1960s, employment often continues to be discussed as either full-time (35 or more hours per week) or part-time (less than 35 hours per week).

Employment is often analyzed in relation to the occupational structure. Occupations are categorized according to the required tasks to be performed and the level of **skill** needed to accomplish designated responsibilities. Changes in employment can best be understood by examining occupational changes within the context of the economy, since production and new technology alter demand for particular levels of skill and education. Both the U. S. Census Bureau, which provides data on changing patterns of work by industry, and the Bureau of Labor Statistics (BLS) under the DOL, which reports on a variety of employment issues such as employment earnings, **unemployment**, and labor trends, are excellent reference

sources. Employment participation is calculated from data on employed and unemployed persons (i.e., those actively seeking employment). According to the BLS (1999), the civilian workforce totals over 139 million (46 percent female, 54 percent male). While data also indicate that the percentage of women and minorities has increased in managerial and professional occupations, most women continue to be employed in lower paying positions in retail, clerical, childcare, nursing, and social service occupations.

Employment trends are generally evaluated based on the overall earnings of workers and the degree of job growth (i.e., the number of jobs created annually). One unexpected result of the new global economy has been a lowering of the unemployment rate to 4.5 percent(1998-1999), the lowest in almost thirty years. The relative earnings of female and black male workers continue to climb, although respective gaps remain at about 76 percent of white male earnings. Recent reports also indicate wage earnings over the past three years have improved about two percent above inflation for all workers.

U.S. educational attainment is increasing, a factor contributing to wage differences and a major factor in upgrading the occupational structure. According to the DOL, in 1948, workers with a high school diploma worked more than sixty percent of the total available employment hours. By 1997, this decreased to ten percent. Technology has increased the demand for more technically skilled and knowledge-based workers, particularly in high growth industries. Yet, technology also has reduced the employment options of many workers and further polarized the workforce. Computer-based technologies have eliminated many manual and supervisory tasks, thus displacing thousands of lower skilled and middle management workers. As skills from previous economic stages depreciate, so too does compensation. While some wage increases may be the function of a tight labor market, the Bureau of Labor Statistics (BLS) indicates that occupations requiring a bachelor's degree are growing at nearly twice the rate of average job increases. Today, college graduates earn on the average 71 percent more than high school graduates. Recent **government** action, such as minimum wage increases, has attempted to decrease the escalating wage gap based on polarized employment opportunities.

The DOL recently reported that between 1993 and 1999, twenty million new jobs were created. Yet, much of this employment growth refers to the creation of part-time or nontraditional employment arrangements to replace recently downsized full-time jobs. Major organizational restructuring during the 1980s and 1990s reduced the number of traditional full-time jobs and introduced various flexible employment arrangements including outsourcing, telecommuting, and self-employment and contracted services. This restructuring coincided with growing international **competition**, which required employers to quickly shift their production to meet demand. It also required dissolving employment relationships with workers whose skills are no longer necessary and attracting new workers on a less permanent basis. This shift explains, for example, how the fastest growing and highest paid occupations in computer industries also have the highest turnover and unemployment rates.

Employment Projections, by Occupation: 1996 and 2006

[In thousands (3,146 represents 3,146,000), **except percent**. Estimates based on the Current Employment Statistics estimates and the Occupational Employment Statistics estimates. See source for methodological assumptions]

Occupation	Employment		Change		Education and training category
	1996	2006	Number	Percent	
LARGEST JOB GROWTH					
Cashiers	3,146	3,677	530	17	Short-term on-the-job training
Systems analysts	506	1,025	520	103	Bachelor's degree
					Work experience plus bachelor's or higher
General managers and top executives	3,210	3,677	467	15	degree
Registered nurses	1,971	2,382	411	21	Associate's degree
Salespersons, retail	4,072	4,481	408	10	Short-term on-the-job training
Truck drivers light and heavy	2,719	3,123	404	15	Short-term on-the-job training
Home health aides	495	873	378	76	Short-term on-the-job training
Teacher aides and educational assistants	981	1,352	370	38	Short-term on-the-job training
Nursing aides, orderlies, and attendants	1,312	1,645	333	25	Short-term on-the-job training
Receptionists and information clerks	1,074	1,392	318	30	Short-term on-the-job training
Teachers, secondary school	1,406	1,718	312	22	Bachelor's degree
Child care workers	830	1,129	299	36	Short-term on-the-job training
Clerical supervisors and managers	1,369	1,630	262	19	Work experience in a related occupation
Database administrators, computer support specialists [1]	212	461	249	118	Bachelor's degree
Marketing and sales worker supervisors	2,316	2,562	246	11	Work experience in a related occupation
Maintenance repairers, general utility	1,362	1,608	246	18	Long-term on-the-job training
Food counter, fountain, and related workers	1,720	1,963	243	14	Short-term on-the-job training
Teachers, special education	407	648	241	59	Bachelor's degree
Computer engineers	216	451	235	109	Bachelor's degree
Food preparation workers	1,253	1,487	234	19	Short-term on-the-job training
Hand packers and packagers	986	1,208	222	23	Short-term on-the-job training
Guards	955	1,175	221	23	Short-term on-the-job training
General office clerks	3,111	3,326	215	7	Short-term on-the-job training
Waiters and waitresses	1,957	2,163	206	11	Short-term on-the-job training
Social workers	585	772	188	32	Bachelor's degree
Adjustment clerks	401	584	183	46	Short-term on-the-job training
Cooks, short order and fast food	804	978	174	22	Short-term on-the-job training
Personal and home care aides	202	374	171	85	Short-term on-the-job training
Food service and lodging managers	589	757	168	28	Work experience in a related occupation
Medical assistants	225	391	166	74	Moderate-term on-the-job training
FASTEST GROWING					
Database administrators, computer support specialists [1]	212	461	249	118	Bachelor's degree
Computer engineers	216	451	235	109	Bachelor's degree
Systems analysts	506	1,025	520	103	Bachelor's degree
Personal and home care aides	202	374	171	85	Short-term on-the-job training
Physical and corrective therapy assistants and aides	84	151	66	79	Moderate-term on-the-job training
Home health aides	495	873	378	76	Short-term on-the-job training
Medical assistants	225	391	166	74	Moderate-term on-the-job training
Desktop publishing specialists	30	53	22	74	Long-term on-the-job training
Physical therapists	115	196	81	71	Bachelor's degree
Occupational therapy assistants and aides	16	26	11	69	Moderate-term on-the-job training
Paralegals	113	189	76	68	Associate's degree
Occupational therapists	57	95	38	66	Bachelor's degree
Teachers, special education	407	648	241	59	Bachelor's degree
Human services workers	178	276	98	55	Moderate-term on-the-job training
Data processing equipment repairers	80	121	42	52	Postsecondary vocational training
Medical records technicians	87	132	44	51	Associate's degree
Speech-language pathologists and audiologists	87	131	44	51	Master's degree
Dental hygienists	133	197	64	48	Associate's degree
Amusement and recreation attendants	288	426	138	48	Short-term on-the-job training
Physician assistants	64	93	30	47	Bachelor's degree
Respiratory therapists	82	119	37	46	Associate's degree
Adjustment clerks	401	584	183	46	Short-term on-the-job training
					Work experience plus bachelor's or higher
Engineering, science, and computer systems managers	343	498	155	45	degree
Emergency medical technicians	150	217	67	45	Postsecondary vocational training
Manicurists	43	62	19	45	Postsecondary vocational training
Bill and account collectors	269	381	112	42	Short-term on-the-job training
Residential counselors	180	254	74	41	Bachelor's degree
Instructors and coaches, sports and physical training	303	427	123	41	Moderate-term on-the-job training
Dental assistants	202	278	77	38	Moderate-term on-the-job training
Securities and financial services sales workers	263	363	100	38	Bachelor's degree

[1] All other computer specialists.

Source: U.S. Bureau of Labor Statistics, *Monthly Labor Review*, November 1997.

Emerging employment arrangements collectively represent a more ''flexible'' alternative to the traditional DOL classification, and some economists and social scientists argue that future employment will be less tied to specific occupations and correlate more with the demand for specific skill sets. Clearly for many workers, the employment relationship has become an organization-specific agreement whose duration is correlated directly to fluctuations in the market.

ENCULTURATION

Enculturation, an anthropological term coined by J.M. Herskovits in 1943 and popularized by **Margaret Mead**, is "the process of learning a culture in all its uniqueness and particularity." It is analogous to the sociological term "socialization." It refers to the life-long process of learning all the material and non-material components of one's **culture** (physical artifacts and **values**, attitudes, beliefs, customs, etc.). People are not born knowing about their culture; it must be taught to them. It is through enculturation that culture is generationally transmitted and people develop a competence in their own culture and are able to navigate in it on a day-to-day basis. The things learned in the process of enculturation become the roadmap for living out one's life in a given culture. People who are not well enculturated are not able to make sense of the world in which they live. Enculturation unifies groups of people by providing them with common experiences, beliefs, customs, values, **norms**, etc. Some researchers say enculturation is the learning process that takes place in childhood, and acculturation takes place after that.

People are enculturated in many ways: life-long **socialization** in the family and through education, religion, and other social institutions; being told directly what to do and what not to do; and watching others and learning indirectly what to do and not to do. Much enculturation takes place through language, both verbal and written. One can also be enculturated into a new or different **group** or social **institution**. Being enculturated into a social arena such as academia means being able to learn and use the appropriate terminology correctly, being able to identify and answer pertinent questions, and being able to perform and present valid and reliable research.

Through enculturation we also learn what and how to think about other people—those like us and those unlike us—as well as about ourselves, in both positive and negative ways. In some cultures, women are not allowed to own **property** or vote, so both men and women in those countries internalize the idea that women are not equal to men, are not as worthy as men. In the United States, everyone is allowed to vote and own property, so we internalize the idea that all people are created equal.

ENGELS, FRIEDRICH (1820-1895)

German revolutionary, social theorist, and author

The German revolutionist and social theorist Friedrich Engels (1820–1895) cofounded with **Karl Marx** modern **socialism**. Friedrich Engels was born on November 28, 1820, in Barmen, Rhenish Prussia, a small industrial town. He was the oldest of the six children of Friedrich and Elisabeth Franziska Mauritia Engels. The senior Engels, a textile manufacturer, was a Christian Pietist and religious fanatic. After attending elementary school, young Friedrich attended the gymnasium in nearby Elberfeld for three years. Although he became learned, he had no further formal schooling.

Under pressure from his tyrannical father, Friedrich became a business apprentice, but he left business at the age of twenty, in rebellion against both his joyless home and the "penny-pinching" world of commerce. After this Engels was a lifelong enemy of organized religion and of **capitalism**.

While doing his one-year compulsory military service (artillery) in Berlin, Engels came into contact with radical young Hegelians and embraced their ideas, particularly the materialist philosophy of Ludwig Feuerbach. In 1842 Engels went to Manchester, England, to work in the office of Engels and Ermens, a spinning factory in which his father was a partner. In Manchester, the manufacturing center of the world's foremost capitalist country, Engels observed capitalism's operations—and its distressing effects on the workers—first hand. He also studied the leading economic writers, among them Smith, Ricardo, and Owen in English, and Say, Fourier, and Proudhon in French. He left Manchester in August 1844.

On his way back to Germany, Engels stopped in Paris, where he met Karl Marx for a second time. On this occasion a lifelong intellectual rapport was established. Finding they shared the same opinions, Marx and Engels decided to collaborate on their writing.

Engels spent the next five years in Germany, Belgium, and France, writing and participating in revolutionary activities. After the defeat of the revolution, he escaped to Switzerland. In October 1849, using the sea route via Genoa, he sailed to England, which became his permanent home.

In November 1850, unable to make a living as a writer in London and anxious to help support the penniless Marx, Engels reluctantly returned to his father's business in Manchester. In 1864, after his father's death, he became a partner in the firm, and by early 1869 he felt that he had enough capital to support himself and to provide Marx with a regular annuity of £350. On July 1, 1869, Engels sold his share of the business to his partner.

In September 1870 Engels moved to London, settling near the home of Marx, whom he saw daily. He worked hard, doing the things he loved: writing, maintaining a voluminous correspondence with radicals everywhere, and—after Marx's death in 1883—laboring over the latter's notes and manuscripts, bringing out volumes two and three of *Das Kapital* in 1885 and 1894, respectively. Engels died of cancer on August 5, 1895.

Engels had a brilliant mind and was quick, sharp, and unerring in his judgments. A successful businessman, he also had a grasp of virtually every branch of the natural sciences, biology, chemistry, botany, and physics. He was a widely respected specialist on military affairs. He mastered numerous languages, including all the Slavic ones, on which he planned to write a comparative grammar. He also knew Gothic, Old Nordic, and Old Saxon, studied Arabic, and in three weeks learned Persian, which he said was "mere child's play." His English, both spoken and written, was impeccable.

Engels apparently never married. He loved, and lived with successively, two Irish sisters, Mary (who died in 1863) and Lydia (Lizzy) Burns (1827–1878). After he moved to London, he referred to Lizzy as his wife. The Burns sisters, ardent Irish patriots, stirred in Engels a deep sympathy for the Irish cause.

Engels published hundreds of articles, a number of prefaces (mostly to Marx's works), and about half a dozen books during his lifetime. His first important book, written when he was 24, was *The Condition of the Working Class in England in 1844,* based on observations made when he lived in Manchester. His next publication was the *Manifesto of the Communist Party* (*Communist Manifesto*), which he wrote in collaboration with Marx between December 1847 and January 1848.

In 1870 Engels published *The Peasant War in Germany,.* In 1878 he published perhaps his most important book *Herr Eugen Dühring's Revolution in Science,* known in an English translation as *Anti-Dühring* (1959). This work ranks, together with Marx's *Das Kapital,* as the most comprehensive study of socialist (Marxist) theory.

Engels's *Development of Socialism from Utopia to Science* was published in German in 1882 and in English, under the title *Socialism, Utopian and Scientific,* in 1892. In 1884 he brought out *The Origins of the Family, Private Property and the State,* an indispensable work for understanding Marxist political theory. His last work, published in 1888, was *Ludwig Feuerbach and the End of Classical German Philosophy.* Two works by Engels were published posthumously: *Germany: Revolution and Counter-Revolution* (German, 1896; English, 1933) and *Dialectics of Nature,* which appeared in English in 1964.

His work was not an imitation of Marx but constituted a consistent philosophy at which both men had arrived independently and shared in common. Engels refined the concept of dialectical **materialism**. He stressed that the materialist conception takes into consideration the whole cultural process, including tradition, religion, and **ideology**, which goes through constant historical evolution. Each stage of development, containing also what Engels called "thought material," builds upon the totality of previous developments. Thus every man is a product both of his own time and of the past. Similarly, he elaborated his view of the state, which he regarded as "nothing less than a machine for the oppression of one class by another," as evolving, through class struggles, into the "dictatorship of the proletariat."

ENVIRONMENTAL IMPACT ASSESSMENT

The process of environmental impact assessment (EIA) was first developed in the United States in 1969, through the passage of the National Environmental Policy Act (NEPA). The Council on Environmental Quality (CEQ), created by NEPA, was given the authority to create enforceable federal regulations in 1977. NEPA requires federal agencies to submit an environmental impact statement (EIS) for any federal government-related action, such as a construction or development project, that may have adverse impacts on the surrounding biophysical environment or human **community**. The EIS describes what negative impacts are likely to result from the project and what if anything can be done to prevent or mitigate them, including abandoning the project altogether. NEPA often affects projects at other levels of the **government** and in the private sector as well, since many of their activities are federally regulated through other environmental legislation.

Friedrich Engels

Richard Morgan described the EIA process as "the most important, and most widely used, tool for the protection and management of the environment." NEPA has allowed environmentalists within government agencies to force changes in how their bureaucracies work and has also given outside environmental groups the ability to sue agencies or companies whom they feel have filed inadequate or inaccurate EISs. It has also been an important aid in environmental decision-making: John Glasson wrote that "the central and ultimate role of EIA" is "to achieve sustainable development," which the 1987 Brundtland Report defined as "development which meets the needs of the present generation without compromising the ability of future generations to meet their own needs." This kind of development seeks to maintain a community's **quality of life** and access to natural resources while avoiding environmental damage.

Morgan suggested that "A sociologist might define EIA as a process of informing local communities about changes in their circumstances, and in their immediate environment, and therefore allowing those people to participate in the decision-making process more effectively." The CEQ's guidelines clearly instruct anyone preparing an EIS to make every effort to allow public comment on the proposed action: "NEPA procedures must insure that environmental information is available to public officials and citizens before decisions are made and before actions are taken.... Accurate scientific analysis, expert agency comments, and public scrutiny are essential to implementing NEPA." The guidelines also require a "scoping" procedure, which is an "early and open process for determining the scope of issues to be addressed and for identifying the significant issues related to a proposed action,'' and insist that reports are to be ''written in plain language''and contain a ''non-technical summary'' that is easily accessible to the lay reader.

Because EISs are intended to combine information about economic, social, and environmental issues, the CEQ's guidelines mandate that ''Environmental impact statements shall be prepared using an interdisciplinary approach which will insure the integrated use of the natural and social sciences and the environmental design arts.'' Social scientists often refer to doing ''social (or socioeconomic) impact assessments,'' or SIAs, which focus on how the social structures and institutions of a community may be changed by a development project. For example, development may cause rapid population growth, bring cultural **values** into question, overwhelm an area's **social services**, or rearrange power relations among groups of business owners, politicians, and activist groups. Additionally, an executive order from President Clinton in 1994 required that environmental justice issues be considered in the EIA process, through taking into consideration any disproportionately negative impacts on minority and low-income communities.

This need for interdisciplinary information-gathering means that creating a thorough EIA can be difficult. International government studies in the mid–1990s found a great need for EIA education among its practitioners, who often leave important components out of their reports and fail to follow regulations. The EIA process has also been criticized by environmentalists as being too developer-centered; those who carry out EIAs before undertaking their own projects are unlikely to predict serious environmental problems. There are also a variety of technical and conceptual difficulties that EIA practitioners must deal with, such as properly narrowing the scope of the study, finding the best ways to ensure public input, and determining accurate baseline environmental data. Even so, the concept of environmental impact assessment has caught on worldwide and is being used in a variety of ways to try to balance economic development with environmental concerns.

ENVIRONMENTAL SOCIOLOGY

Environmental sociology is the study of the intricate relationship between natural environmental and human societies. When in harmony, this relationship is symbiotic. When not in harmony, negative consequences occur for either or both systems. The current condition of environmental degradation, from high levels of industrial development and consumption, is seen as a negative imbalance between human action and the natural environment. The natural sciences may be well equipped to explain the physical abuses of the planet, but the reasons why our planet is in a state of degradation are best described by social sciences.

The work of rural sociologists, William Catton and Riley Dunlap, is generally considered to mark the emergence of environmental sociology. They argue that all previous sociological perspectives contained a fundamental, underlying flaw—anthropocentrism. According to anthropocentric ideology, humans have central importance in the universe. The human community's relatedness to the natural environment was not entirely ignored prior to Catton and Dunlap, but classical human **ecology** is substantially different from Catton and Dunlap's new human ecology. **Robert Park** and Ernest Burgess developed the field of human ecology at the University of Chicago in the 1920s emphasizing the spatial organization of human populations in relation to economic and technological bases. This precursor to environmental sociology accentuated the relevance of the environment for organized social life, but the importance of societal-environmental relations was underemphasized. Catton and Dunlap's analytical framework derives from Otis Duncan's ''ecological complex'' which stems from an effort to apply insights from general ecology to sociology. Duncan's work integrates the interdependence of population, organization, environment, and technology. Catton and Dunlap, unlike Duncan, emphasize the natural environment as an important factor that may influence or be influenced by human behavior. Catton and Dunlap's new human ecology also contends that, instead of tending toward equilibrium with the natural environment, modern societies tend to exhibit social dynamics that exacerbate environmental degradation and resource depletion.

Some sociologists argue that many founders of sociology were interested in the relationship between human societies and the natural environment, but only when environmental degradation became a social problem did the relationship get serious consideration. For example, Émile Durkheim's *The Division of Labor in Society* has been hailed as especially important to the development of environmental sociology it emphasized how social complexity develops from population growth and density. Thus, the finiteness of natural resources is sociologically significant in that it threatens competition and conflict. Influential sociologist Allan Schnaiberg established the current theoretical basis for environmental sociology. His perspective, derived from mainstream **political economy**, focuses on the ''societal-environmental dialectic'' and the treadmill of production, a **model** that shows capital-intensive technology investment, profitability, and **employment** and income generation as connected. The treadmill is structured by the nature of **competition** between owners and the profitability and predictability of high-energy mass production. The treadmill finds its sustenance in the commitment of organized labor and the state to generate employment and income.

It is important to distinguish the classical way in which sociologists have used the term ''environment'' and the distinctive way in which the term is used by environmental sociologists. Within mainstream sociology, the term ''environment'' refers to social and cultural influences upon behavior. Sociologists have, for example, made use of the term ''environment'' when speaking of such concepts as the influence of the **family** environment or the learning environment in assessing the educational experiences of young children. Catton and Dunlap disentangled the social and cultural meaning of the word ''environment'' from the physical and biological meaning of the word.

Catton and Dunlap make a strong case for an environmental sociology when they note that our species is having an unprecedented impact on the global ecosystem which may lead to serious consequences for the quality of human and nonhuman life. Environmental sociological research is unique because it departs from the traditional (Durkheimian) insistence that social facts can be explained only by other social facts. Catton and Dunlap asserted that the acceptance of environmental variables as meaningful for sociological investigation makes the field of inquiry distinguishable. One major area of research in environmental sociology has been the study of environmental concern. Here, the goal of the environmental sociologist is to examine the attitudes and behaviors of humans in relation to the natural environment and the ways in which **society** is structured to contribute to environmental degradation. Measurement scales have been developed to determine the types of individuals that adhere to certain environmental values and attitudes. In the early 1970s, the Human Exemptionalism Paradigm (HEP) and the Dominant Social Paradigm (DSP) were used to explain human relationships with the environment. These paradigms posited humans in the center of the environmental world and dominant over nature. The New Environmental Paradigm (NEP) was developed in the late 1970s by sociologists Riley Dunlap and Kent Van Liere as environmental issues came to the forefront of public policy. The NEP scale was intended to measure the pro-environment shift toward stewardship in the study of environmental beliefs. It is particularly helpful in identifying general perceptions of the environment according to demographic variables (e.g., **race**, age, gender, education, income). Environmental sociologists have also used their skills in quantitative and qualitative research to study such areas as natural and technological disasters (e.g., Love Canal, Three Mile Island), environmental racism, environmental movements, and **social control**.

EPIDEMICS

Epidemics are outbreaks of **disease** that affect an unusually large number of people. Some illnesses, the flu, for instance, may normally attack a certain percentage of the population in a given area. When the number of cases rises significantly above that percentage, an epidemic exists. An epidemic involving an entire continent or the whole world is called a pandemic.

Epidemics begin with the transmission of disease from one person to another, through the air, as with nose droplets; whooping cough is an example. It may spread from polluted water, as with typhoid fever, or bites from infected animals, as with rabies. Disease is also spread through personal contact, for example, malaria.

Examples of epidemics through the centuries are the bubonic plague, polio, and AIDS. In the fourteenth century, plague broke out in China and spread to Europe. The disease, called the Black Death for the spots it produces on the skin, was carried by infected rodents and fleas, causing fever, swelling of the lymph glands, and death. The plague spread rapidly

Epidemics are outbreaks of disease that affect an unusually large number of people, such as the small pox virus *(National Museum of Natural History, Smithsonian Institution).*

until, within five years, one-third of Europe's population had died—some 25 million people. Bubonic plague disappeared in the 1600s.

Equally feared in its time was infantile paralysis, or polio. This virus, which attacks the nervous system, not only caused thousands of deaths in the 1940s and 1950s, but left thousands more unable to walk, sit up, or even breathe unaided. In the United States, there were some 33,000 cases of polio in 1950. In 1995, Dr. Jonas Salk announced his vaccine against polio. His "killed" virus, which immunizes without infecting the patient, virtually eliminated polio within a few years. The long-term effects of the disease, however, still plague many polio surivivors.

The pandemic of the twenty-first century is AIDS, acquired immune deficiency syndrome. There is no cure for this sexually or blood-transmitted disease caused by HIV (human immunodeficiency virus) which attacks the immune system. Although all countries battle this illness, Africa has been hardest hit. Some 25 million Africans carry the virus. Most will die within eight years. Health experts call AIDS "Africa's worst social catastrophe since slavery" and the "most serious infectious disease threat in recorded human history." Various medical research programs have been implemented to search for cures and vaccines to help relieve the world population of its newest epidemic.

EPISTEMOLOGY

Epistemology is the theory of knowledge which centers on understanding how we develop or acquire knowledge. Originating with the development of scientific thought during the **Age of Enlightenment**, epistemology is distinguished by two conflicting schools of thought, rationalism and **empiricism**. Rationalism, often associated with René Descartes and his famous quotation, "I think, therefore I am," dictates that knowledge is gained through the use of logic. Thinking about the world in a logical or rational order will reveal the underlying laws of the world. Empiricism, which gained attention with the work of **David Hume**, stipulates the use of observation of things which can be perceived by the senses. Only in observing the world can the underlying laws governing it be revealed.

Immanuel Kant is widely credited with bridging the gap between these two competing ideas. He suggested that knowledge could not be obtained by simply observing the external world but rather needed to be assessed through the prism of human intuition. **Rationality** needed to be applied to the empirical world in order to understand the moral principles by which people should live. By this thinking, reason exists *a priori*, that is, independent from experience, but experience provides the boundaries within which reason can be used to understand the world.

Within **sociology**, epistemology is connected to the methods of inquiry used to obtain knowledge. For example, survey methods use an empirical epistemology as they necessitate the collection and analysis of observable **data** (even though rationality is necessary to interpret the data). Empiricism dominates contemporary sociological studies, and purely theoretical work comprises a small part of sociology publications.

Epistemology constitutes the central debate within the sociology of knowledge, which is the study of the social character of knowledge. Recent epistemological debates center on the situated character of knowledge and knowledge claims. With the development of social constructionism and constructivism, many researchers in the **sociology of knowledge** have critically examined how knowledge claims are made and the epistemological assumptions that make scientific knowledge appear absolute. This work has considered the connection between power and knowledge; basically, that knowledge reflects the power of the people who have the power to create it.

Radical re-examinations of knowledge claims, particularly those that focus on scientific practice, have been criticized for being so relativistic as to make epistemology useless. Post-structuralist discussions on epistemology have suggested that, because theories cannot be separated from the language used to describe them, theories are more representative of **discourse** than the events or phenomena they claim to describe. This approach to knowledge has not proven very useful for most social scientists, who depend upon some basis for epistemology in order to conduct their studies.

EQUALITY OF OPPORTUNITY

Equality of opportunity implies that everyone has equal chances to achieve the same ends. If equality of opportunity is a reality then an analysis of class and achievement should reveal that class origins do not effect social achievements. Therefore, there should be no intergenerational **poverty** or wealth, instead poverty and wealth should be more randomly distributed amongst the population.

The philosophy behind equality of opportunity is that all persons should have equal access to achieve desired ends based upon merit and personal talent. Thus, **society** would have an open and competitive stratification system that allowed mobility based upon merit and talent, not ascribed statuses such as race. This access would then provide the yardstick by which to measure the justness of inequality. Therefore, if all persons have equal access to opportunities, then whatever stratification develops within that system is justly unequal.

Critics argue that this standard of equality is problematic because it assumes that all persons begin with the same **life chances** and ability to use opportunities. It is argued that some persons acquire more cultural capital throughout their lives such that they can more easily gain access to opportunities and more easily take advantage of them as they arise. This critique emphasizes that some individuals enter the competitive environment with more advantages than others leading to an unjustified belief in equality of opportunity. Take, for example, the differences in opportunities that arise given the ability to go to either a public or private educational facility. Public educational environments provide different tools to take as advantages of opportunities than do private ones such that certain individuals become better equipped to find **employment**, further their education, and achieve credentials. This particular example then raises the question: is equality of opportunity a reality or a myth?

The concept of equality of opportunity is used in sociological research on **capitalism**, class, **competition**, cultural deprivation, **democracy**, status, life chances, and stratification. For each of these areas of study this conceptual tool is used to advance particular causal models and theories about the social structure. For example, extensive evidence presented by social scientists shows the impact that parents' social class position has on their children's life chances and available opportunities. Several items are documented to have an overt effect from parental class position: health, education, employment, and criminal behavior.

In sum, equality of opportunity is the notion that if a competitive social system is in place based upon merit and talent then inequalities are legitimate. However, critiques recognize that a competitive social system does not put all individuals on equal footing to acquire the same desired ends; rather, ascriptive variables have an effect.

ERIKSON, ERIK HOMBURGER (1902-1994)

American psychoanalyst and educator

Erik Homburger Erikson (1902–1994) was a German-born American psychoanalyst and educator whose studies have perhaps contributed most to the understanding of the young. On June 15, 1902, Erik Erikson was born in Frankfurt am Main, Germany, of Danish parents. His widowed mother subsequently married the pediatrician Theodore Homburger. Erikson first studied painting in Germany and Italy. Later, he joined Peter Blos and Dorothy Burlingham, Anna Freud's colleague, in the development of a small children's school in Vienna. This led to his training analysis by Anna Freud and immersion in theoretical seminars and in clinical work. Having also acquired a Montessori diploma, he graduated from the Vienna Psychoanalytic Institute in 1933.

In 1930, he had married Canadian-born Joan Mowat Serson, who was vitally interested in education, as well as arts and crafts, and deeply shared his interest in writing. The development of their three children, Kai, Jon, and Sue, as well as Erikson's work in Anna Freud's school, may have contributed much to his eventual thinking about the "epigenetic schema" of development and the vocabulary of health, in which he described the contributions of successive psychosexual stages to **ego** strengths, such as trust and **autonomy**, initiative and industry, and **identity** and intimacy.

Following Hitler's accession to power, the Eriksons went to the United States, where he began private practice and a sequence of research appointments at Harvard Medical School (1934–1935), Yale School of Medicine (1936–1939), University of California at Berkeley (1939–1951), and Austen Riggs Center, Stockbridge, Massachusetts (1951–1960); he was visiting professor at the University of Pittsburgh School of Medicine (1951–1960). One of his later appointments was as professor of human development and lecturer in psychiatry at Harvard University. At intervals he took time off for work abroad, such as travel to India in connection with his intensive study of Gandhi.

Always free from the provincialism typical of thinkers with more static and limited backgrounds, Erikson's thinking pushed toward an understanding of the ways in which the drives dominant in successive psychoanalytically defined life stages are shaped by **interaction** with the persistent needs and solutions typical of a given **culture**. These formulations were supported by field observations made with the collaboration of anthropologists, and also by observations of children's play.

Erikson's extension of the classical Freudian psychoanalytic concept of development was published in *Childhood and*

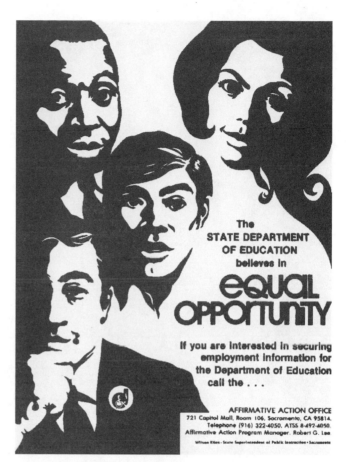

Equality of opportunity implies that everyone has equal chances to achieve the same ends and that an individual's background will not adversely affect these chances.

Society (1950). The book startled some orthodox Freudians, who viewed development as dominated solely by the sequential emergence of successively potent drives modified or exaggerated primarily by their intimate—depriving, indulging, or punishing—interactions with the parents. Erikson's broader concept of dynamics of inner-outer interactions provided inspiration, challenge, and insight to the spectrum of American social sciences concerned with child development.

Erikson's concern at Austen Riggs Center was focused on the troubled years of late **adolescence** and early **adulthood**. He emphasized the universal process of resolution of identity conflicts during this developmental phase in a profound study of the youthful Martin Luther, *Young Man Luther* (1958); in a monograph *Identity and the Life Cycle* (1959); and in a volume which he edited, *Youth: Change and Challenge* (1963). His Harvard teaching and response to students' concerns with **values** led to two collections of essays: *Insight and Responsibility* (1964) and *Identity, Youth and Crisis* (1967). The latter is a prophetic reformulation of the relation of the concepts of ego and self, and recognition of issues of nobility and cowardice, **love** and hate, and greatness and pettiness, which he sees as transcending the traditional normative issues of "adjustment to society." His contribution to understanding the prob-

Erik Erikson *(Archive Photos, Inc.)*

lem of identity in youth at times when personal change intersects with historical change has led scores of scholars to research exploring this area. In 1969 Erikson published *Gandhi's Truth*. This book focuses on the evolution of a passionate commitment in maturity to a humane goal and on the inner dynamic precursors of Gandhi's nonviolent strategy to reach this goal.

The sources of Erikson's fresh, subtle, and multimodal awareness are many: His artist's temperament and perceptiveness contribute both to sensory richness and to sensitivity to nuances of personality and behavior. His deeply satisfying family life and wide-ranging friendships, with people such as Lawrence K. Frank, **Margaret Mead**, A. L. Kroeber, and Gardner Murphy, support a sense of health as a potential for the development of human beings struggling with conflicts exacerbated by the pressures of a given life stage. His freedom from premature commitment to an academic discipline with rigid canons of concept formation released him for original formulations as well as new adaptations and implications of classical **psychoanalysis**. Erikson's shrewd "the Emperor has no clothes" type of realism and uninhibited daring in probing new areas of experience seem to draw on a never-suppressed child's penetrating curiosity. His love of life in nature and in people of all ages and many different cultures underlies the

predominantly warm and vital quality of his thinking and writing. This has evoked the resonance of students of many disciplines whom he has influenced more than any analyst since Freud.

Whereas Freud lived and worked at a time when the mentally ill were beginning to be understood and universal inner conflict needed to be understood more deeply, Erikson was maturing in a period when the fate of the Western world was threatened by violence and denigration of values—a time when health, "virtue," and strength and their origins needed to be asserted and understood. His later books anticipated the demands of youthful protesters who repudiated the falseness of politics and the **materialism** of the economic world and who called for sincerity, **peace**, love, and humane values.

Erikson died in 1994; however, his words live on—even those not familiar with his work may share his passion in language. Along with his numerous theories and plethora of information, Erikson also left educators the sound advice, "Do not mistake a child for his symptom."

ERROR (STATISTICAL ERROR)

Error (also called statistical error) refers to the known amount of imprecision in the methods researchers use in gathering and analyzing data. Despite the connotation of the word, error, statistical errors are not mistakes but merely imprecisions that are inherent within the processes of **data** collection and analysis. Error is an integral part of **inferential statistics**, in which conclusions about some population are drawn on the basis of results found within a sample drawn from that population. Given the laws of probability, researchers are able to determine and control the amount of error they are willing to accept in drawing such conclusions about the population. Thus, in inferential statistics or hypothesis testing, there is always the possibility of imprecision and an incorrect conclusion. However, the amount of error can be quantified by the researcher.

There are two types of error that accompany the use of inferential statistical techniques. Both involve the decision of whether to reject the null hypothesis, which states that there is no difference between groups or that there is no relationship between two variables. **Type I (alpha) error** occurs when a true null hypothesis is rejected. When Type I error is committed, the researcher concludes that there is a significant difference or relationship when none exists in the population to which the sample results are being generalized. **Type II (beta) error** occurs when the researcher fails to reject a false null hypothesis, thereby concluding that there is no significant difference or relationship when in fact one does exist in the population.

Type I and Type II error are inversely related, such that the amount of one increases as the other decreases. Generally, social science researchers want to reduce the amount of Type I error, and this is done by setting the level of significance (or alpha level) low. By setting the alpha low, the researcher establishes a known and relatively low risk of concluding that results are significant when in reality they are not.

Both Type I and II errors result from **sampling error** and measurement error. In order to reduce the risk of statistical error, researchers thus attempt to draw large **probability** samples that are representative of the population and to employ measures that are both valid and reliable. These procedures aid in reducing the imprecision and increasing the researcher's confidence in the conclusion drawn from the sample data.

See also Type I (Alpha) Error; Type II (Beta) Error

ESSENTIALISM

Essentialism applies to the group of theories making the claim that scientific truth is discovered by determining the underlying or essential nature of things and that things can be defined and explained by their core essence. In defining a thing, one is describing its essential nature. In sociology, essentialism is used to describe theories that claim humans have essential natures and that human action can be explained by these essential natures. For example, essentialism has been used to explain why men have exceeded women in the workforce with regards to promotions and salaries. Women's essential nature makes them better suited for the home, and men's essential nature makes them better suited for endeavors outside of the home, or in the public sphere. In his 1969 book *Conjectures and Refutations,* Karl Popper stated that essentialism supports scientists' ability to verify the truth of a scientific theory and that scientists can discover this truth by uncovering the underlying essence of the social phenomenon being described.

The current usage of essentialism is usually negative, as most sociologists acknowledge that human action is the product of many factors and cannot be explained by the essence of the individual. (In fact, most sociologists would likely not agree that individuals have such an essence, in any sociological way.) Essentialism is also sometimes used pejoratively to describe theories that explain human behavior by attributing it to membership in a particular social group, especially if that social group is viewed as marginal or oppressed.

ETHICS IN SOCIAL RESEARCH

Studying human behavior creates a number of ethical considerations and ethical dilemmas for social science researchers. Social scientists have responsibilities to their respective disciplines and to their subjects. For this reason most major professional associations, such as the American Sociological Association, have established formal guidelines for conducting research. Despite these guidelines, researchers must still make difficult decisions about important ethical issues when they conduct their research.

The first issue centers on professional integrity. Researchers must provide accurate **data** and openly acknowledge any potential biases. The outright forging of data is obviously unethical; unfortunately, several cases of data forgery have been uncovered. Social science researchers have certain biases that may affect the choice of research topics and the results of that research. It is the researchers' responsibility to openly admit to any **bias** that they may have and who is funding their research.

A second set of ethical issues concerns the use of human subjects in research. When researchers recruit subjects, they should not coerce them into participating. **Coercion** can take many forms, including excessive payments, undue use of **authority**, threats about the consequences of not participating, and excessive **persuasion**. Payment to participate may be considered coercion if too much is given to subjects. Fair time payment is acceptable, but anything more may be considered coercion. Coercion can also occur if researchers unduly use their authority, for example, when professors use their students as subjects.

Researchers disagree about the use of deception in recruiting subjects. Those who object to deceiving subjects contend that deception erodes personal liberties, betrays trust, gives researchers a bad reputation, and is often unnecessary. Despite these objections, though, numerous investigators view deception as appropriate. They believe deception is acceptable if the subjects' anonymity is maintained. Researchers who approve of deception argue that overt techniques may not provide accurate data, especially when illegal behavior or the wrongdoing of those in power is being studied. In general, most researchers agree that deception is only justified in rare cases, that open methods should be used if at all possible, and if covert methods are used, researchers should make sure their subjects remain anonymous.

Researchers should take every precaution not to harm their subjects. If care is not taken, researchers may harm their subjects physically, psychologically, and/or by invading their privacy. While physical harm is rare in social science research, it still occurs. For example, a study on the effects of competition using twelve year old boys at a summer camp had to be stopped when the boys exploded into a fist fight. Psychological harm can come to subjects if they are deceived about the nature of the study. For example, many researchers believe that Stanley Milgram's infamous study on obedience caused significant psychological harm to his subjects because he made them believe that they were administering severe electric shocks to other participants.

Sometimes the information that researchers gather can be damaging to people's private lives. Unwarranted intrusion upon a person's privacy (e.g. eavesdropping, wiretapping), public disclosure of embarrassing information, and false publicity (e.g. impersonation and forgery) can have dramatically negative impacts on subjects' personal lives. It is, therefore, necessary for researchers to make every attempt to ensure confidentiality and anonymity. Researchers must take precautions to protect confidentiality which can be done by not obtaining names in the first place, removing any identifying marks from data, storing data in a safe place, and using pseudonyms in the report.

The need to protect the rights of subjects in social research led to the use of informed consent. By signing an informed consent form, subjects acknowledge that they are participating in the study free from any element of fraud, deceit, duress, or similarly unfair inducement or manipulation. The main criticism of informed consent is that it provides more protection for researchers than it does for subjects. By signing consent forms, subjects take on responsibility for their own safety. If subjects do not fully understand the study or the long-term consequences of it, the informed consent may be impractical. Also, if people sign forms, a written record of names exists that must be protected which creates another ethical questions about how to protect the data. The situational, subjective nature of ethics ensures that disagreement and debate over research techniques will continue. It is necessary for researchers to be keenly aware of the consequences of their research.

ETHNICITY

Ethnicity, derived from the Greek word *ethnos* meaning "people" or "nation," refers to people who identify with one another on the basis of a shared **culture** and background. People may share a sense of belonging with one another based on national origin, religious affiliation, physical characteristics, and cultural distinctiveness. Shared history, distinctive foods, dress, family names, **language**, music, customs, religion, and national origin may bind people together into an ethnic group.

For example, Jews are considered an ethnic group. Not only do Jews share the same religious beliefs, but they also share a common history, customs, and often times even family names. Mongoloid Jews in China, blue-eyed blonde Jews in Sweden, and dark-skinned Ethiopian Jews are bound by a common background and culture into an ethnic group.

The idea of an ethnic group, however, is relatively new. The term first surfaced in standard English dictionaries in the 1960s as increased world migration and globalization heightened contact among different peoples. Immigration to the United States, for example, created a heterogeneous **society** of varied nationalities, religions, and cultures. By the 1970s, displaying ethnicity became popular in American multicultural society. Slogans, such as 'Kiss me, I'm Irish,'' ''I'm Polish and Proud,'' and ''Black Power,'' became increasingly popular at this time as Americans flaunted their often newfound ethnic differences.

However, relations between ethnic groups have rarely been benign. With increased contact due to global migration, technological advances, and economic globalization, ethnic **interaction** has been marked by several patterns of intergroup relations. At the positive extreme lies assimilation and **pluralism**. Assimilation refers to the absorption of a minority ethnic group into larger society. Examples include immigrant Greeks and Italians to the United States who have successfully adapted to mainstream American culture. Pluralism, on the other hand, refers to complete racial and ethnic variation in a society, a hallmark of **multiculturalism**. Switzerland, which is made up of three distinct groups living in harmony, is a prime example of pluralism. Germans, French, and Italians live together within Swiss national borders while successfully retaining their different cultural backgrounds.

The other extreme, however, is characterized by intergroup conflict, such as **genocide** and ethnic cleansing. Genocide refers to instances in which one group attempts to destroy an other. Examples include Nazi Germany and the extermination of the Jews during World War II, as well as the decimation of Native Americans by Anglo and European settlers during colonization. Modern-day horrors of ethnic cleansing, a term which emerged in 1992, was implemented by Serbians attempting to eliminate Croats and Muslims from their population. In 1994, Hutu militia in the African nation of Rwanda massacred approximately half a million of the nation's ethnic minority, the Tutsis. Ethnically motivated violence has periodically occurred all over the world.

Even in multiethnic societies, such as Canada, the United States, and Australia, ethnic group relations have been marked by **prejudice** and discrimination, unequal access to education, as well as inequity in income and employment. This unequal allocation of resources has created a system of ethnic stratification, in which some groups are more advantaged. In addition to this hierarchy, ethnic communities have long clashed with one another even beyond discriminatory practices in the form of riots, violence, and war. Examples include the massacre of Muslims and Hindus during India's partition of 1947, bloodshed between Catholics and Protestants in Northern Ireland, and the violent clash of Korean Americans and African Americans during the 1992 riots in Los Angeles.

Sociologists in the last half of the twentieth century have looked at ethnicity, **identity**, and intergroup relations. American sociologists Robert Park and **Milton Gordon** focused their work on ethnic relations and the sequence of stages that would lead to full assimilation. Park proposed four steps to assimilation that could be applied to any minority ethnic group in any society, not just the United States. Even though Park's theories proved to be incomplete and only applicable to European immigrant groups, his work provided the foundation for later sociologists, such as Milton Gordon, who developed additional theories on assimilation.

Beyond interethnic relations, sociologists have also explored ethnic identity. Sociologist Herbert Gans examined ethnic identity and coined the phrase 'symbolic ethnicity' to describe the accentuated and voluntary expression of ethnic identity among third- and fourth-generation Americans. Sociologists, in recent years, have also examined the impact of ethnic mixing and intermarriage, as well as the consequences on ethnic identity. Work by Richard Alba, Mary Waters, and Stanley Lieberson on white Americans looks at the choice in ethnic identity of those of multiple ethnic backgrounds. Like Gans, they see ethnicity increasingly as a matter of choice in multiethnic societies.

See also Multiculturalism

ETHNOGRAPHY

Ethnography refers to a style of sociological research based on direct and close observation of subjects, usually for an extended period of time. Ethnographers usually live or spend time with the subjects in their environment and participate in most or all of their activities. Ethnographers in sociology have contributed to most of the discipline's areas, including important studies of work, **race** relations, associational life, **social movements**, subcultures.

The term "ethnography" literally refers to the description of **culture** and traces its origin as a formal method to anthropologists like Margaret Mead, who studied distant and traditional cultures. In sociology, however, the origins of ethnography have to do with concerns with urban problems in industrial **society**.

Until the 1910s, **sociology** was divided into two approaches: abstract theorizing about the bases of **progress** and social development and social survey studies. Sociologists associated with the University of Chicago from the 1920s onward developed a distinctive style of sociological research on urban problems inspired as much by anthropology as by journalism. W. I. Thomas' five volume study *The Polish Peasant in Europe and America* (1918) pioneered the use of personal affects as letters and a concern for the subject's **definition of the situation**. **Robert Park**, who was a journalist before joining the Chicago faculty, influenced a generation of scholars with his emphasis on the importance of understanding the social worlds of the city through observational methods.

Important works of **the Chicago school** scholars followed this lead, including Nels Anderson's *The Hobo* (1923), which presented observation and **life histories** of various hoboes. Louis Wirth's research into urbanism as a way of life culminated in the publication of *The Ghetto* (1927). Paul G. Cresey's *The Taxi Dance-Hall* (1932) was concerned with the world of dance-halls in Chicago as a self-contained milieu.

Beginning with the advances that have made survey studies easier and more precise since the 1930s, ethnographic studies have not occupied a central stage in sociology since the days of the Chicago school. Nonetheless, ethnographers have continued to produce many important studies that enrich the discipline. Drake and Cayton's *Black Metropolis* (1945) on the exclusion of black populations in Chicago continues to inspire sociological research. Irving Goffman's *The Presentation of Self in Everyday Life* (1959) described the many strategies persons use to manage impressions about themselves and has influenced a generation of scholars.

ETHNOMETHODOLOGY

Ethnomethodology is a tradition of theory and empirical research in sociology inspired largely by the works of **Harold Garfinkel** (1917-). Garfinkel's book *Studies in Ethnomethodology* (1967) announced the presence of ethnomethodological research within **sociology** and generated a great deal of attention particularly among micro-sociologists and social psychologists. Based on the phenomenological sociology of Alfred Schutz (1899-1959), ethnomethodology emerged largely in response to the tendency of mid-twentieth century sociologists to treat social actors as the dupes of social structures and organizations. Instead, ethnomethodology focused on individual agency, and the practices and interpretations with which actors created a sense of their social world.

Ethnomethodology is generally defined as the study of the "folk methods" used in everyday, ordinary **interaction**. It endeavors to explore the common-sense knowledge and sense-making practices that individuals use in order to create the world of the taken-for-granted. The approach of ethnomethodological research typically differs from that of more traditional sociological investigations. Whereas traditional sociology might study the causes or consequences of a social phenomenon, ethnomethodology explores the socially embedded, tacit assumptions that make it possible for individuals to understand mundane events. For example, while sociologists typically study the role of gender as an important **variable** in social life, ethnomethodologists ask how it is that individuals understand and accomplish gender. They do not accept gender as a social given but instead explore the ordinary, taken-for-granted, common-sense assumptions that social actors make in creating a personal and collective understanding of gender. For ethnomethodologists, gender is not merely a biological **fact** that is embodied within an individual; it is something that is accomplished by social actors in the course of everyday life. In fact, one of Garfinkel's most famous early studies was on Agnes, a pre-operative, male-to-female transsexual and the social practices she used in her accomplishment of the female gender.

In order to discover the mundane, taken-for-granted assumptions made by actors in their everyday life, ethnomethodologists have traditionally employed, what Garfinkel refers to as, breaching experiments. These social norm violating experiments are developed to unearth the hidden assumptions embedded within social reality and to illuminate the folk methods which actors use in constructing their social world. Some of Garfinkel's most famous breaching experiments include: riding in elevators facing the back wall, marking on the grid-lines and not in the empty spaces in a game of tic-tac-toe, and pretending to be a boarder in one's own home. These experiments are designed to illustrate the minute and mundane accomplishments by which individuals order their social reality and sustain a sense of normalcy in everyday life. As a result of performing these experiments, ethnomethodology is not interested in determining what is normal or what is deviant; it instead seeks to investigate the assumptions and practices by which actors produce a sense of normality in everyday life.

More recent studies in ethnomethodology have focused on the analysis of conversation. The goal of conversation analysis is to investigate the taken-for-granted assumptions that are embedded within everyday conversations. The analytical focus in these conversation studies is not necessarily on what a conversation might mean to the participants instead on the way in which the conversation is structured and ordered. Much conversation analysis relies upon audio recordings of conversations which are analyzed in minute detail. In doing this, conversation analysts focus on who does the talking and for how long, the patterns of interruption in the conversation, and how actors support one another in keeping the flow of the conversation going. Often what conversation analysis reveals is that much of what is communicated in even mundane conversations is implicit and not directly expressed. This point is illustrated by what ethnomethodologists refer to as the "et cetera principle" and is exemplified by conversations that include the question, You know what I mean? More recently ethnomethodologists have expanded the investigative framework of conversation analysis and have begun to study non-verbal behavior ethnomethodologically through the use of video recordings of interactions.

While ethnomethodology has certainly illuminated the sociological importance of exploring ordinary social encounters, it remains marginalized within contemporary sociology. It has been criticized for its inability to deal theoretically with macro-level sociological concerns like social **structure** and issues of power. More recently ethnomethodology has been criticized for abandoning its phenomenological roots and emphasizing the study of recorded conversations over the analysis of interaction as it occurs in context. Despite these shortcomings, ethnomethodology remains an important contribution to the discipline of sociology.

EUGENICS

Eugenics, the scientific project of improving the human race through the study of heredity and control of human reproduction, can be traced to nineteenth-century ideas, particularly Darwinism. The term eugenics, from the Greek root meaning ''good in birth,'' was coined in 1883 by Sir Francis Galton, an English scientist. During the 1900s, the eugenics movement spread throughout Western Europe and the United States.

The eugenics movement in the United States unfolded in three stages. From 1870 to 1905, the primary concern of the movement was restricting reproduction of the ''unfit'' or ''dangerous classes'' of feebleminded, criminals, insane, epileptics, drunkards, and paupers while promoting procreation among the ''fit'' classes. Attempts to restrict or prohibit reproduction through means such as involuntary sterilization and institutionalization were considered negative eugenics. Positive eugenics employed methods such as education and tax incentives to encourage those with supposedly superior genes to procreate.

During the second stage of the movement, from 1905 to 1930, eugenicists increasingly directed their efforts toward blacks and immigrants. Campaigns emerged advocating immigration restrictions, custodial care, **marriage** restrictions, and sterilization of ''defectives.'' Sterilization was thought to be more cost-effective than permanent institutionalization, and Indiana was the first state to adopt a mandatory sterilization law in 1907. In 1927, the U.S. Supreme Court, in *Buck v. Bell*, upheld a Virginia statute claiming that sterilization fell within the power of the state. In addition to the restrictive methods mentioned above, the eugenics movement favored the legalization of contraception which led to an eventual alliance with Margaret Sanger and leaders of the birth control movement. This second stage of the movement marked the height of eugenics in the United States in which the study and teaching of eugenics by disciplines such as **psychology**, **sociology**, and biology flourished in universities around the country.

After 1930, new scientific evidence emerged that suggested that heredity and genetics were more complicated than proposed by eugenicists and that environment and heredity interacted to produce traits such as **intelligence**, character, and physique. At this time, the eugenics movement began to disintegrate in part due to the discovery of the use of sterilization and **euthanasia** in Nazi Germany to eliminate thousands of insane, feebleminded, and deformed patients, as well as millions of Jews, gypsies, and others in the name of racial purity. These events led many in the United States to question the rationale and motives of the eugenics movement.

Proponents of eugenics argued that social reforms were unnecessary because problems such as **poverty** and **crime** could not be attributed to the social system but rather resided in the genes of the ''unfit.'' Eugenics is no longer an active movement in the United States, yet its underlying assumptions are still evident in what has been called the ''new'' scientific racism, illustrated in works such as *The Bell Curve: Intelligence and Class Structure in American Life*. Another arena in which eugenic undertones can be seen is the pressure placed on women to abort fetuses that have been determined, through genetic screening, to be deformed or ''defective'' in some way.

EUPHORIA

Euphoria derives from the Greek word *euphoros*, *eu* which means good or well and the term *pherein*, implying to bear. Although the term is commonly used to refer to a personal state of satisfaction or drug-induced high, in sociology euphoria refers to the overall well-being of a **society**. The term ''social euphoria'' was coined by A. R. Radcliffe-Brown in his article ''Primitive Law'' in the *Encyclopedia of the Social Sciences*, 1933. Radcliffe-Brown contrasted social euphoria with social dyseuphoria, which is created when a person ''offends some strong and definite moral sentiment.'' On the other hand, social euphoria is the result of a penal sanction against the offender that supports ''the collective feeling of moral indignation.'' It is interesting to note that the penalty accrued by the offender is not for the benefit of the offender nor specifically for the person or persons offended. Instead, the euphoria of society as a whole is taken into account. ''Its ultimate function [the penal sanction] is to maintian the moral sentiment in question at the requisite degree of strength in the individuals who constitute the community.'' Penalties of offenders and offences themselves, then, are directly related to the moral feelings of the whole society and function only as they serve the euphoria of that society.

Radcliffe-Brown's conception of social harmony as an integrated social-system in his description of social euphoria makes evident the influence of Émile Durkheim. Both thought that social institutions could be studied like any scientific object. The job of the anthropologist was to describe the anatomy of interdependent social institutions—what called Radcliffe-Brown called social structure—and to define the functioning of all parts in relation to the whole. The aim of such analysis is to account for what holds a functioning society together. The fulfillment of the penal codes, then, could be seen as having a function in a causal relationship with social euphoria.

EUROPEAN STUDIES

European studies is an academic discipline that addresses the historical, cultural, social, political, economic, and literary aspects of the countries within Europe. The nature of the field of European studies can be defined using three different paradigms. First, European studies can be viewed as a comprehensive endeavor that provides a structure for teaching and research. Second, the field can be defined as functioning as a support mechanism for discipline-based studies. Finally, European studies is sometimes understood as the coordination and distribution point for interdisciplinary cooperation. Depending upon the paradigm employed, the focus of study may shift, sometimes placing higher importance on area-based studies, **theory**, or particular disciplines. This large area of interest and multiple approaches, combined with the diverse and dynamic makeup of the region, provides students of European studies with a wide array of opportunities for research as well as a number of issues that prove problematic.

Much of how European studies was done in the past had to be re-examined after the tumultuous events of the last 11 years of the twentieth century. From the fall of the Berlin Wall in 1989 and the dissolution of the Soviet Union in 1991 to the numerous redrawing of borders and rise in ethnic and religious **nationalism**, the face and nature of the European **community** changed significantly. As a result, political boundaries, once inaccessible, began to open, Cold War **ideology** was called into question, and increased access offered scholars a wealth of new research material.

A significant challenge raised by the transformation of the European landscape is how to define the geographic borders of European studies. In ''The Current State of European Studies in North America and of Scholarly Publishing in Western Europe'' (*The Journal of Academic Librarianship,* May 1998), Richard Hacken writes, ''There was a time when North Americans had a very definite idea about where the eastern fringe of Western Civilization ended, and that fringe was one that started unraveling at about Eastern Europe. For several decades before 1989, there were black-and-white notions about **Communism** versus the 'Free World,' with a line of demarcation that could be distinguished and measured down to the millimeter at the Iron Curtain.'' Prior to 1989, European studies aligned its borders with Western Europe. In the twenty-first century, those boundaries will likely be pushed farther and farther to the east.

As the nature of the European community has changed recently, so has the nature of European studies, which has dually widened and narrowed its focus. As never before the academic community is communicating on an international level. With the opening of once restricted borders and the worldwide access allowed by new, inexpensive electronic communications, scholars from all parts of the world are linking up via travel and the **Internet**. On one hand, this expansion has been accompanied by an increase in the broad-based study of the region, particularly on the creation of the European Union and the European Common Market. On the other, research focused narrowly has also become a trend in European studies scholarship. In ''The New Challenges Facing European Studies'' (*PS,* March 1994), Kenton W. Worcester and Sidney Tarrow find reason for concern, suggesting that general knowledge of Europe is declining. Once dominated by European-born or trained scholars, today's emphasis on particularism produces an imbalance in fields of knowledge for the European studies student. According to Worcester and Tarrow, the growing interest in European studies, combined with a lack of general empirical knowledge ''can lead to uninformed, overly specialized, or U.S.-based research. In the context of a changing Europe, two dangers are especially apparent: overly applied research projects designed to take advantage of rapidly changing situations and Western European specialists extending their analyses to Eastern Europe without sufficient recognition of its differences.''

European studies, similar to most area studies, is a multidisciplinary endeavor, incorporating all the fields of the social sciences, including political science, history, **language**, economics, and anthropology. The interplay between academic departments, specific roles and authority held by each can prove problematic for the field of European studies. Also, European studies centers face the threat of reduction in their funding as universities continue to look for ways to cut expenses in the face of the increasing cost of education. Because interdisciplinary programs tend to be more likely than traditional, self-contained departments to face budgetary reductions, European studies programs face the challenge of proving the field's credibility and importance. Despite concerns over its future, the field of European studies continues to consistently draw students. Along with anthropology, political science is the most popular area of focus, particularly **political economy** and political institutions.

EUTHANASIA

Euthanasia is a term derived from the Greek, meaning ''the good death.'' It has also been interpreted as ''mercy killing'' which is actually a form of euthanasia, termed ''active,'' implying a deliberate intervention to end a patient's life when the patient is terminally ill or in unbearable pain. There are, however, other forms of euthanasia. Passive euthanasia indicates withholding treatment that keeps patients alive, allowing them to die. Assisted **suicide**, recently made prominent through Dr. Jack Kevorkian, occurs when friends, **family** members, physicians, or others, comply with patients' wishes for assistance in ending their lives. Active euthanasia is illegal, and the right to assisted suicide is strongly debated. Passive euthanasia, however, has long been accepted by **society** and employed by physicians.

Medical technology has made it possible to maintain or prolong life almost indefinitely through machines which keep the heart beating, the blood circulating, and the lungs functioning, even when there is little or no hope of recovery. These technological advances have given rise to the need to consider the social and ethical implications of such treatment which is generally futile, as well as very expensive. The strong Ameri-

Jack Kevorkian (right), an advocate of legalized euthanasia, appears at a press conference with his former attorney Geoffrey Feiger *(Archive Photos, Inc.)*.

can value of personal autonomy and fear of being involuntarily subjected to a long period of pain and incapacity have generally influenced the tacit acceptance of passive euthanasia and public support of assisted suicide. However, public controversy over the right to die has made euthanasia a legal issue as well. The most prominent legal cases involving euthanasia centered on Karen Quinlan and Nancy Cruzan, both of whom were removed from life support after extended court cases brought by their families against the state.

The Cruzan case produced a decision by the Supreme Court stating that a right-to-die exists if individuals have previously stated that they would not want to continue living in their present conditions with no hope of recovery. Also growing out of these controversies were *advance directives,* such as the living will, the durable power of attorney for health care, and the Patient Self-Determination Act (PSDA). These directives have given patients more power to make their own decisions about death and dying. Physicians have traditionally been trained to save life, however, and have strongly resisted the idea of allowing patients to die. They often may disregard advance directives and provide care against patients' wishes.

Although sociologists have generally shown little interest in bioethical issues, euthanasia and related subjects provide fertile ground for social science research and insight. Some early pre-bioethical work done in the 1950s, 1960s, and 1970s in the social sciences related to death and dying. Renee Fox cited a small group of empirical studies investigating the social context of terminal illness and the ''dying trajectory'' in the modern American hospital. These first-hand inquiries investigated the effect of the social organization of the hospital on care of terminal illness and dying and on how the social **organization** was affected by them.

Sociologist Duane Matcha recently noted that the implications of end-of -life decisions are particularly important and pertinent to medical sociology. Research is needed, for example, on the impact of end-of-life decision-making on physician-patient relationships, the changing role of the physician, cost of **health care**, on cross-cultural **values** and acceptance or rejection of euthanasia, and on the uses and role of medical technology. Family dynamics are also a little-understood part of a family member's choice to die. Medical sociologist Renee Fox in 1989 invited sociologists to be more active in the area of **bioethics**. Such issues, said Fox, reach far beyond the medical field and include beliefs, values, **norms**, cultural traditions, and the collective conscience. Thus, they require sociological contributions and expertise in understanding the processes and outcomes involved in social, political, and economic questions generated by science and technology.

Since the mid-1990s, sociologists have begun to show more interest in euthanasia. Studies and research have focused on related attitudes, opinions, beliefs, religion, the elderly, and problems of legal regulation. With the projected expansion of medical technology in the twenty-first century and the accompanying **social problems** and impact, it may be expected that sociological interest and research on euthanasia and other bioethical issues should increase and expand accordingly.

See also Death and Dying

EVALUATION RESEARCH

Evaluation research, sometimes referred to as program evaluation, is conducted to appraise the utility of an implemented program or policy. In other words, did the program or policy work? Results of evaluation research studies can be used to improve programs, justify programs, or show cause to cut funding to ineffective programs. Evaluation research is normally sponsored research, so the researcher is paid by an agency. Evaluation research is used by many of the scientific disciplines such as **sociology**, criminal justice, business, and medicine. Topics of evaluation research can range from determining whether a government-funded health insurance plan alleviated health problems among the poor to examining whether bootcamps lower juvenile recidivism rates. Evaluation research is a type of **applied research** given that results are used to answer a very specific question, are often used to influence **social policy**, and provide remedies for social problems.

Evaluation research became popular in the United States in the 1950s due to the implementation of many federally funded social programs that addressed urban development, housing, education, rehabilitation, drug treatment, occupational training, and **health care**. Government accountability demanded that such programs be evaluated to ascertain whether the programs led to real social improvements. Rudimentary evaluation research, however, was seen as early as the 1600s, during which time Thomas Hobbes and his colleagues used numeric measures to identify causes and remedies for social ills of the day.

Contemporary examples of controversial evaluation research are the numerous evaluation studies of the Drug Abuse Resistance Education Program (DARE). The DARE program was implemented in schools throughout the United States and is a police-taught program that incorporates a myriad of drug related issues from drug use and misuse to media influences on drug use. Several evaluations of the program have been completed by criminologists, and common to all are results indicating the program has no effect on participant drug use. Studies do suggest however, that the DARE program may change attitudes toward drugs among participants. Although evaluation research in this case does not provide evidence to support the program's goals, the unexpected changes in participant attitudes toward drugs coupled with great improvements in police-juvenile relations are probably some reasons why this program has remained in schools.

The process for conducting evaluation research is similar to that of any research study. The first step, the planning phase, involves identification of the program's goals, the framework to achieve those goals, and the required resources. Often this phase is the most difficult, as goals of the program may not be clear or may not be easily measurable. For example, the goal of an education program may state: This program is intended to offer students a broad-base education encouraging insightful and creative thinking. How does one measure creativity and insightfulness? The **methodology** of the evaluation must address the goals. Specification of all variables is the next step followed by specification of the methodology. The research process continues with emphasis on dissemination of results.

An evaluation researcher may encounter several possible difficulties. First, priorities of the sponsor may change, leading to changes in designated resources for the program. Second, interests of stakeholders in the evaluation of the program may change. Third, organizations which implemented programs may shift their focus to another area and no longer see evaluation of an existing program as valuable. Fourth, it may be considerably difficult to implement an evaluation design for some programs, for example, programs that target social problems of transient populations. The researcher is also likely to encounter ethical issues in evaluation research because of the nature of the outcomes. Further, the evaluation researcher plays a series of roles that may cause conflict. Examples of these roles are: the evaluator as internal evaluator, the evaluator as program advocates, the evaluator as whistle-blower, and the evaluator as gatekeeper.

There are two basic types of evaluation research. The first type, *formation research,* is ongoing research of a program or policy designed to monitor its success or failure. The second type, *summative research,* is conducted at the conclusion of a program or policy and assesses outcomes. The research can be conducted using many different methodologies ranging from field research to experiments. Evaluators can be internal (sponsored by the **organization** that has implemented the policy or program) or external. Examples of agencies needing evaluation research are education, health care, criminal justice, private businesses and government.

EVANS-PRITCHARD, SIR EDWARD EVAN (1902-1973)
English social anthropologist

In 1930, Edward Evans-Pritchard, then a lecturer in anthropology at Oxford University and the London School of Economics, set off for the marshes of the Upper Nile in the Sudan, at that time a colony jointly administered by Egypt and Great Britain. His goal was to live among and study the Nuer, a pastoral people who spoke a Nilotic language. Greeted by the Nuer with suspicion and hostility—the colonial government had just launched a punitive expedition against them—Evans-Pritchard slowly gained their confidence.

Evans-Pritchard focused on the Nuer's religious practices. Unlike previous anthropologists who tended to focus almost exclusively on kinship relations, he examined the more complicated connections between social **structure** and religion. In his books *The Nuer: A Description of the Modes of Livelihood and Political Institutions of a Nilotic People* (1940), *Kinship and Marriage among the Nuer* (1951), and *Nuer Religion* (1956), Evans-Pritchard helped pioneer the argument that religious rites and thinking among so-called primitive peoples were connected in their larger view of the world and that **ritual** was a means by which they set social goals and resolved social conflict. With these theories, Evans-Pritchard helped invent social anthropology, a new sub-discipline developed by a small group of British anthropologists who focused on how primitive peoples organized themselves politically.

Evans-Pritchard was born in Sussex in 1902, his father a Welsh-speaking Church of England clergyman. He attended Winchester College from 1916 to 1921 and Exeter College, Oxford for three years after that. A bohemian and nonconformist, he socialized with a like-minded set which included celebrated novelist Anthony Powell, who described the young Evans-Pritchard as "grave, withdrawn, somewhat exotic of dress." Influenced by Edward Tylor and James Frazer—whose work focused on the infinite variety of social forms among different peoples—Evans-Pritchard opted for anthropology as his profession. And as a Welsh Celt, he was drawn to ancient peoples who maintained their customs in the face of a dominant **culture**.

With no professor at Oxford experienced in field research, Evans-Pritchard moved to the London School of Economics, where he studied under famed anthropologist Bronislav Malinowski, with whom he had a stormy relationship. From 1926 to 1930, he periodically lived among and studied the Azande people of southern Sudan, before moving on to the Nuer. His books on the Azande include *Witchcraft, Oracles, and Magic among the Azande* (1937), *The Azande* (1971), and *Man and Woman among the Azande* (1974, posthumous). Commissioned an officer during World War II, he fought against the Italians, who then occupied Ethiopia. After the war, he became a professor of social anthropology at Oxford.

From the late 1940s through 1960s, Evans-Pritchard eschewed fieldwork for teaching. At the same time, he devoted himself to strengthening the study of social anthropology within academia, conducting a course of lectures on the subject for the BBC, which were published in 1951 as *Social Anthropology*. He served as president of the Royal Anthropological Institute from 1949 to 1951 and first life president of the Association of Social Anthropologists of the British Commonwealth in 1956. Evans-Pritchard died suddenly at his home in Oxford in 1973.

EVENT HISTORY ANALYSIS

Event history analysis is a statistical technique relatively new to sociology that improves upon previous methods of **data** analysis in allowing researchers to explicitly incorporate time into the analysis of social transitions. This is an important development because many theories explored through quantitative research make explicit statements about the process of social events. This point is true for theories at both the individual level of analysis and the macro-level study of collectivities. Other techniques of data analysis were unable to adequately examine these issues. The previous standard method for examining **social change** was to use repeated cross-sectional data, which consists of data from more than one point in time for many different individuals. More recently researchers used time series data that measured the same individuals at different points in time and tried to control for the **correlation** of variables across the observations in time in order to explore how these factors influenced social change. Event history analysis is much better at modeling social transitions than either of these methods because the effect of time is built directly into the analysis.

This technique is also known as survival analysis, a term originally used in medical fields by researchers studying the conditions which led to varying times of death among people with similar diseases or conditions. For example, doctors might want to know if a certain new treatment will enable patients with AIDS to live longer. At the same time other factors such as lifestyle, diet, or family history will contribute to longevity and will thus make the effect of the treatment difficult to isolate. In order to conduct this test researchers need to control for these other factors and examine how the survival rate changes among people who differ only in terms of receiving the treatment. Survival analysis enables them to do this. Within survival analysis researchers can examine how long different participants will live by explicitly modeling the hazard rate or compare whether certain types of individuals live longer than others, which is known as proportional hazards modeling.

In **sociology**, event history analysis most often focuses on social outcomes rather than medical ones. In general sociologists have studied transitions that are quite common in the population but tend to happen at different times for different types of people. For example, one common application is the study of the influences on the timing of **marriage** or the first child's birth. Again, the basic principal is that different attributes of individuals are associated with how long it takes for them to change **status**, in these examples from single to married or from childless to being a parent, and there are many different potential effects that need to be isolated. For example, both education and job status will affect how long it takes an individual to marry. In particular, women and men with more education or higher job status will on average marry later. However, education and job status are themselves related, since people with higher levels of education are more likely to be in high status jobs. In order to understand if both truly affect marriage timing, it is important to control for each in assessing when people marry. Two additional positive qualities of event history analysis are the ability to handle censored data and changes in the values of independent variables. For example, in examining marriage rates in a representative sample of people, many younger respondents might not get married until after the study ends, and they might get more education as the study progresses. Event history analysis is able to handle these potential analytical problems.

Many other areas of sociology use this type of analysis. For example, at the individual level, researchers have examined what qualities of couples and their marriages affect how long it takes a marriage to end in divorce. Others have studied economic outcomes, such as timing of first job, who is more likely to become unemployed during a recession, and who among the unemployed is likely to get a new job quickly. Examples at the level of collectivities include research on the features of businesses that make them more likely to go bankrupt or merge with other businesses, the qualities of states within the United States that result in early implementation of certain policies, and which types of colonies are more likely to achieve independence first.

EVIL

Evil can be defined either in the context of human beings or nature. Human evil is considered by philosophers to be the suffering that is caused by wrong moral choices. Natural evil is associated with the suffering caused by natural disasters such as floods, storms, and earthquakes. Most frequently, however, the term "evil" is used with respect to a lack of human morality and the inability or unwillingness to make correct ethical decisions.

The concept of evil is most widely discussed in religious contexts. Various religions attempt to explain the existence of evil in the world in different ways. For example, the ancient Greeks considered natural disasters and other natural evils to be caused by wars between the gods, deities that attempted to create **justice** in the world, but were limited by their humanlike nature. The tenets of **Buddhism** hold that life is suffering (the first Noble Truth) and the way to redeem oneself from suffering is to follow the Eightfold Path, or incorporate a series of virtues into one's being so that human suffering may cease through selflessness. Zoroastrianism, an ancient Persian religion, argued that the forces of good and evil are separate and relatively equal. The world which humans inhabit is controlled by these two opposing forces and there is no all-powerful god.

Christian discussions of evil generally focus on what is perceived as the problem of evil. Most Western religions claim that God is omnipotent, that he can do anything that is logically possible, omniscient, that he can know everything, and that he is perfectly good. This creates a paradox. If God can do anything and knows everything and is perfectly good, the world he has created should also be perfectly good. For many, this is the main argument presented against traditional theistic religions. In response, Christian philosophers have attempted to account for the existence of evil in the world that is consistent with this view of God. One possible argument is that evil does not really exist, but human limitations make the world appear to contain evil. Another is that evil is necessary for the good of the greater whole; we would not know to appreciate the good without the dichotomy of good and evil. Thomas Aquinas, in opposition to these two views, presented evil as the deprivation of good. Here, he differs from the Zoroastrian philosophers in that evil has no existence of its own; instead it is the lack of being, or the lack of God. This argument can be extended to plausibly account for the problem of evil in the world. God created the possibility for evil by creating a contingent world, but he did not in fact create evil in the world since evil does not itself have existence. A variety of related arguments proposed from medieval times to the present continue to impact this significant theological and philosophical debate.

EVOLUTIONARY SOCIOLOGY

The evolutionary perspective arose in **sociology** prior to Charles Darwin's theory of natural selection during the mid-nineteenth century. Still, however, evolutionary sociology in its more contemporary forms largely uses the Darwinian framework. Darwin's theory followed a three-step path. First, within the biological world, certain random genetic differences appear among offspring. Second, natural selection dictates that certain variants improved the offspring's chance to survive and reproduce. And finally, the inheritance of the variant traits by future generations of offspring assists in preserving the species.

Sociologists adopted the evolutionary perspective in their approach to the study of societies. The analogy between societies and organic life had already been made popular during the late eighteenth and early nineteenth century. According to the popular theory, which supported the conservatism of the time, societies maintain organic equilibrium based on the idea that both individuals and social classes rely on the survival of the whole for their own survival. C. H. Saint-Simon expanded this idea to include the theory that societies necessarily evolved from lower to higher stages. Auguste Comte, in turn, adopted Saint-Simon's evolutionary assumptions and developed his own evolutionary sociology. According to Comte in *The Positive Philosophy*, societies move through the three stages of primitive, intermediary, and scientific. Passage from one stage to the next was based on the development of human knowledge, **culture**, and **society**, with accompanying progressive changes in theology, metaphysics, and positive reasoning. Using organismic imagery, Comte proposed that humanity consisted of various parts that interrelated to create a unified whole. Societal evolution, which presupposed the inevitability of unilateral **progress**, was marked by increasing specialization and improved **adaptation**.

Unlike Darwin's biological **evolutionary theory**, which depended on unplanned variations in offspring, nineteenth-century social evolutionists, like Comte, understood change to be an inevitable and orderly progression through specific stages. Accepting these basic assumptions, sociologists differed on the description, timing, and number of the stages. Whereas Comte proposed a movement from theological (primitive) to metaphysical (intermediary) to positivistic reasoning (scientific), numerous other models, which used both organismic and non-organismic foundations, also existed. Lewis H. Morgan suggested in *Ancient Society* (1877) the three stages of savagery, barbarism, and civilization. In *The German Ideology* (1947; first published 1846), Karl Marx and **Friedrich Engels** formed their theory of production based on the stages of tribalism, slavery, **feudalism**, **capitalism**, and **communism**. Herbert Spencer worked from the level of complexity, with societies moving from simple to complex. French sociologist Émile Durkheim outlined progress on the basis of **division of labor** within society.

Although each theory of social evolution varied greatly in the determinants and outcomes of stage development, all were bound by the common thread of belief in the unilateral, unavoidable progress toward improved social formations. Unlike the social perspectives that were built upon the life-cycle model, which theorized that societies moved through cycles from infancy to old age and death, social evolutionary theory did not involve the concept of a presupposed end to societies. They did, however, accept the notion that societies, like biological life forms, pass through predetermined, set stages that cannot be skipped or bypassed. Within this perspective, Darwin's emphasis on random variations within the evolutionary process is omitted. In this manner, evolutionary sociology of the nineteenth century may better be described as theories of progress rather than theories of evolution.

The social evolutionary perspective lost popularity early in the twentieth century. However, a second wave of interest in social evolution was sparked later in the century by an emergence of neo-evolutionary theory. This model, based on a functionalist approach, follows more closely in the path suggested by Darwin's physiological **model** in the sense that societal change and development seems also based on adaptability to the environment, including both the natural world and other societies. This new attempt to integrate evolutionary ideas and **social change** is built on a more complex multilinear theory that acknowledges numerous variations in the development of societies. Nonetheless, most social evolutionists of the twentieth century identify certain social developments as almost always occurring, including the trend of societies to move from smaller to larger, simpler to more complex, rural to urban, and low technology to higher technology. Differing from earlier social evolutionists, twentieth-century theorists believed that not all change is considered progress.

In the 1970s, **Talcott Parsons** outlined his evolutionary theory in *The Evolution of Societies* (1977). For Parsons, societal evolution is based on the growth in the ability of a society to control the environment, or "generalized adaptive capacity." Evolutionary change occurs in spurts, or breakthroughs, each of which solves a particular environmental problem. According to Jackson Toby, in his introduction to Parsons' *The Evolution of Societies,* Parsons did not argue for social progress "which must be judged in terms of the **values** of the observer, but of social evolution, which is a matter of whether generalized adaptive capacity has increased or not. Thus, in the course of explicating an early breakthrough, Parsons began to differentiate his theory of societal evolution from the nineteenth-century theories that failed to distinguish between scientific and valuational questions."

Working within the framework of primitive, intermediate, and modern social stages, one of the early breakthroughs is the development of a system of **social stratification**. According to Parsons, a society whose organizational structure is based on kinship has limited means to allocate resources because no member has a sufficiently broad base of power to provide **leadership** to the society as a whole. Parsons suggested that social evolution is not inevitable. Societies can stagnate at particular points. However, if evolution is to occur, he argued that certain social traits must form. For example, Parsons linked the development of written **language** with the passage from primitive to intermediate society. Other necessary breakthroughs for the advancement of evolution include the institutionalization of the authority of office, the development of a market economy, democratic polity, and a generalized legal order.

Parsons found company in a renewed interest in evolutionary social theory in the work of sociologists **Gerhard Lenski** and Jean Lenski, who developed an evolutionary perspective in *Human Societies: An Introduction to Macrosociology* (1982), which tracks societies in terms of transitions from hunting-and-gathering, horticultural, agrarian, and industrial economic structures. Psychologist Donald Campbell, who addressed the issue of sociobiology at the 1975 meeting of the American Psychological Association, is another example of a contemporary supporter of evolutionary theory. Despite these attempts, evolutionary sociology remains at the fringes of the social sciences as contemporary sociologists prefer to focus on the present context of society rather than long-term developments and trends.

EVOLUTIONARY THEORY

Evolution suggests the unfolding of phenomena. In **sociology** evolutionary theory traditionally holds that **social change** conforms to laws of progress. Though today evolution is commonly connected with **Charles Darwin**, evolutionary theory as a social **paradigm** predates him. In the seventeenth century Auguste Comte, considered by many to be the father of sociology, proclaimed that society evolves through three stages of history and development. At the first and most primitive stage, theological systems are at the core of human knowledge. According to Comte **society** reaches the second stage when non-

theological metaphysics and **philosophy** supplant theological **authority**. The third and final stage of social evolution is realized when society cultivates tools of scientific rationality and management. Comte, writing at the dawn of industrialization, found much evidence in this theory. Those nations developing industrial infrastructures and converting to political **democracy** were becoming powers on the globe. Sociologists who followed Comte developed on the assumption of evolutionary progress coinciding with technological development. Similarly, Karl Marx and Fredrich Engels based their theory of revolution in an evolutionary schema. They believed historical evolution was leading to utopian **socialism** where the working classes would collectively own the means of production. Generally, these sociologists viewed modern society as marching up a stairway of evolution toward **utopia**.

Other social philosophers anchored their understanding of social evolution in biological analogies. Émile Durkheim developed a **model** of society evolving from a simple state of mechanical solidarity to a complex state of organic solidarity. Simple societies lack specialization or division in labor. Members are similar to each other, and individuality is not cultivated. These societies are more unstable and prone to be influenced by change. But modernization leads society to evolve into a state of specialization, individuality, and systemic interdependence. Such societies are like biological organisms with interdependent parts working together to ensure survival. Durkheim, while using a biological analogy, focused his study on the changes in norms, ethics, and behavior in societies due to evolution.

A different variant of evolutionary theory emerged when Charles Darwin published his *Origin of Species* (1859). Darwin held that species survival depends on **adaptation**; species that do not adapt to their environment become extinct. From this general principle he reasoned that the continued existence of any species is not certain. Herbert Spencer, a British social philosopher, applied this concept of adaptation to societies. By comparing advanced industrial nations with traditional tribal groups, Spencer declared adaptive evolution to be the law of social **progress**. His scheme suggested that social groups develop specialized roles to contend with changes in their environment. These specialized roles, carried out by specialized persons, lead to social differentiation, elaboration, and higher degrees of complexity. Similar to Durkhiem, Spencer reasoned that with more division of labor and individual responsibility, social systems are more capable of responding to further changes. But unlike Durkheim, Spencer argued that evolutionary progress occurs only through pressure and adaptation. In fact, it was Spencer, not Darwin, who proclaimed that evolutionary progress yields the survival of the fittest.

In the latter years of the nineteenth century, primarily based on Spencer's books, **Social Darwinism** became an influential school of thought, both in Europe and the United States. The concept appeared to be a reasonable scheme for understanding the fast rate of social change. Founding figures in American sociology, such as **Albion Small**, Franklin Giddings, William Graham Sumner, and **Lester Frank Ward**, adopted some version of Social Darwinism to their views on societal growth. Strict interpretation of natural selection ultimately legitimized colonial expansion and the development of **eugenics** during this period. However, less pessimistic versions of evolutionary theory directed attempts to channel the laws of adaptation in order produce further progress. Lester Frank Ward and Albion Small believed that sociology would prove to be the discipline that could conquer the evolutionary laws of nature and curtail human misery.

Evolutionary theory has fallen out of favor among sociologists today. The carnage of worldwide wars between 1914 and 1950 cast doubt assumptions that evolutionary progress coincides with technological development. For in these wars the most advanced nations were also the most destructive. Germany, a nation that led the scientific world in 1900, carried out **genocide** on the Jewish race. Similarly, the United States, a global leader in industry, developed and used nuclear weaponry. Yet variants of the perspective live on today. Bio-Sociology is an effort to situate human **socialization** in evolutionary terms.

EXCHANGE THEORY

Exchange theory is based on the idea that all human behavior is a product of a cost and benefits analysis. Exchange theory can be traced back to the works of economist **Adam Smith** and Utilitarian philosophers Jeremy Bentham and **John Stuart Mill**. These theorists believed human beings constantly pursue material benefits or happiness. The way people do this is by rationally considering all alternatives, calculating the costs of a given pursuit, and weighing these costs against the potential benefits. People then act in a way that will provide the maximum payoff. That is, humans are motivated solely by self-interest, which they define in terms of pleasure and pain. **Utilitarianism** began to fade in the late 1800s.

Then Utilitarianism reappeared in the 1950s with the works of George Homans and **Peter Blau**. Taking the basic utilitarian assumptions along with ideas borrowed from psychological **behaviorism**, they produced a sociological theory of human behavior which came to be known as exchange theory. Perhaps the more influential was **George Homans** whose work was in reaction against structural-functionalism, especially that espoused by **Talcott Parsons**. Homans believed that **sociology** needed to move away from large, abstract concepts of the social system to study the "elementary" behavior of individuals interacting in groups. Elementary behavior is the face-to-face contact between individuals. Homans was interested in explaining elementary social behavior form. To do this he borrowed ideas from behavioral **psychology** and elementary economics to develop several general propositions of social behavior.

The first three propositions state that the more often a particular behavior is rewarded, the more likely that behavior will be repeated (success proposition). The opposite is also true. If a particular behavior is punished or not rewarded when it is expected to be, the less frequently this behavior will be repeated (aggression/approval proposition). Also, the more

similar an activity is to one that has been reinforced in the past, the more likely that behavior will be repeated (stimulus proposition). Homans suggested that the frequency at which people are given rewards affects the value of that reward. When people are satiated with a particular reward, the reward becomes less valuable to them; when they are deprived of the reward it becomes much more desirable (deprivation/satiation proposition). Finally, Homans' rationality proposition states that individuals make rational decisions about their behavior. They make their decisions based on the value they give to the reward expected from that behavior and on the **probability** that they will receive that reward. In mathematical terms, action is the product of value and probability. People will act in a way that results in the largest value for Action. For example, if a woman places a high Value, say 100, on dating a famous man, but the Probability of his dating her is small (.10) then this yields an Action score of 10. If she places a lower Value (50) on dating a man who is less famous, but the Probability of his dating her is higher (.5), then this **correlation** would yield an Action score of 25. Based on Homans' **rationality** proposition, the woman would be more likely to try to date the less famous person because the product of the value times probability is greater.

In sum, social exchange theory focuses on the relationships between individuals or groups and is based on the assumption that costs and rewards motivate all human behavior. Every human action is seen as having some cost, and, thus, if carried out, it must have a reward. On the other hand, if an action is costly but unrewarded in some way, the individual will not likely repeat it. Homans believed that these psychologically-based propositions made explaining patterns of human **organization** possible. Following the tradition laid down by Homans and Blau, many new theorists, including James Coleman, Linda Molm, and John Thibaut and Harold Kelley, have expanded the theory considerably. This line of reasoning has had a significant impact on sociological thinking and research and has been used to explain human behavior ranging from courtship and dating rituals to **group** membership.

EXISTENTIAL SOCIOLOGY

Existential sociology is an approach to the study of human beings and their social existence that attempts to account for the complex, changing, and emotive nature of human life. According to Andrea Fontana's introductory remarks in *The Existential Self in Society* (Fontana and Joseph A. Kotarba, editors; 1984), "Existential sociology is the sociology that attempts to study human beings in their natural setting—the everyday world in which they live—and to examine as many possible of the complex facets of the human experience.... Thus, existential sociology looks at formal behavior, informal behavior, rational elements, irrational elements, genetic dispositions, psychological traits, and social **rules**; in short, it opens its inquiry to anything that forms the context of human action."

Existential sociologists operate under certain presuppositions that inextricably link the individual self with **society**. Existential sociologists affirm the presence of one self; however, the self is known to others only as part of a social existence. "I" is only "I" as it is a part of "We." The struggle for the individual is to affirm the dependence on the social world (We), and yet to as stand uniquely different from it (I). Therefore, existential sociology theory begins with the assumption that humans necessarily participate in the social and natural world as part of a "We." In other words, human beings are fundamentally situational, or existential. Although human beings are constrained to a certain extent by their place, or situation, in the world, they are also free to make choices about what they will do and what they will become ("I"). Human beings thus are both constrained (situational) and free (transsituational). This inherent conflict in the nature of human experience leads to alienation. Nonetheless, human beings are thrown into the world and can exist only as part of a **social order**. Therefore, the goal of existential sociology is to analyze and comprehend the entirety of human experience through introspection and rational observation, continually aware that the knowner cannot be completely separated from what is sought to be known, in order to draw conclusions regarding the manner in which the existential self is manifested in and shaped by society.

Existential sociology approaches the study of human experience in a fundamentally different manner than classic sociology. When sociology emerged as a separate discipline from **philosophy** during the last part of the nineteenth century and began to flourish in the beginning decades of the twentieth century, the field was dominated by the desire to prove sociology deserving of scientific credibility. As a result, sociology assumed the theoretical and methodological assumptions of the natural sciences; namely, the pursuit of objective knowledge. The goal was to create a social theory that could be verified objectively. In order to accomplish this task, all social knowledge must be rendered into objective statements, which are products of the impartial, detached examination of externally visible social phenomena.

As sociological theories evolved, other perspectives were introduced, including structural **functionalism** and symbolic **interaction**; however, Jack D. Douglas and John M. Johnson argue in *Existential Sociology* (1977) that all classically based sociological theories are founded upon the same basic misconception. They write: "All the traditional social science conceptions of man and society agree in seeing the individual as caused by something, though their conceptions of cause and how to infer it vary. Man and his actions are the dependent variables. Each theory recognizes the existence of other causes and may even accept them as in some undetermined way important; but each theory is fundamentally monocausal." Contrarily, existential sociology acknowledges human existence as a multi-faceted, dynamic, and unpredictable endeavor dominated by emotions. Life experiences are largely shaped and experienced through feelings. Thus, rational thought can only be fully assessed when it is fused with the feelings that drive it.

Rejecting classic sociological approaches as inadequately equipped to comprehend the full extent of human and social reality, existential sociology emerged in the second half of the twentieth century. Like its philosophical counterpart, existen-

tial sociology strives to eliminate the misconstrued division between subjective and objective knowledge. As defined in the *Dictionary of Cultural and Critical Studies* (edited by Michael Payne; 1998), existentialism affirms that "there is no question of one's being alienated from the world for we have recaptured the primacy of a world that is suffused with human **values**, that is, the concrete everyday world essential to human survival and action, which is not made flat by neutral disinterest, but one highlighted and given shape by human concerns."

Although it is distinguished by its **methodology**, sociological existentialism has its roots in the tradition of philosophical existentialism. Søren Kierkegaard is commonly credited with the development of existential thought during the nineteenth century. Seeking meaning beyond the detached principles, Kierkegaard looked to life-as-it-is-lived. Even more directly impacting existential sociology as an empirical discipline is the work of Wilhelm Dilthey and Edmund Husserl, albeit indirectly, through his student **Alfred Schutz**. Dilthey provided the idea of *Verstehen,* or a concept of coming to know human beings through empathy. Although Dilthey applied his idea to history, his formulation acknowledges the existential **need** to experience the whole gamut of feelings and sensations associated with human action.

Husserl wished to apply a more scientifically precise methodology to Dilthey's empathetic understanding by focusing on the presocial consciousness through a process of "stepping back" from involvement in everyday life. This philosophical attempt at achieving pure consciousness became known as phenomenology. Schutz, in turn, applied his mentor's phenomenological approach to the social sciences. Selecting certain aspects of Husserl's methodology, Schutz began with the sensory perceptions encountered in everyday life and developed a framework for the examination of human interaction, thus offering existential sociology a concept of individual action and social interaction.

Philosophers **Martin Heidegger** and Maurice Merleau-Ponty also contributed to the development of existential sociology. Heidegger's *dasein* (being-in-the-world) and Merleau-Ponty's *être-au-monde* (being-within-the-world) offered a vision of an individual united self, which stood in contrast to the dominant dualistic understanding of the separation between the objective and subjective world, or body and soul. Although it finds roots in existential philosophy, existential sociologists distance themselves from philosophy's emphasis on theory. Whereas philosophy is ultimately thinking about thinking, with the intent to formulate theories of knowledge, existential sociology concentrates on the common social experiences of everyday life. Theory plays second fiddle to observation of concrete social situation.

EXPECTATION STATES THEORY

Expectation States Theory was developed in the mid-1960s as an attempt to explain power and prestige structures within interactions. This theoretical tradition has come to incorporate an array of social-psychological principles based on the symbolic interaction paradigm. The theory attempts to describe the mechanisms in interactions that determine performance and legitimacy. At its core is the premise that expectations of the performance and behavior of others and the self will determine how an interaction is going to unfold. Therefore, variables such as class, **race**, and gender affect the **status** rankings within an interaction and affect expectations for that interaction. Expectation States Theory takes a radical approach to the study of social factors by examining the situational and interaction processes that occur rather than focusing on the individual or the structural elements. Joseph Berger and Morris Zelditch, Jr. are prominent theorists who have developed this theory, which attempts to explain why some individuals are disadvantaged in interactions.

Expectation States Theory begins with the observation that in goal-oriented interactions participants, will look for a way to anticipate the likely usefulness of their own and others' suggestions and behaviors. The main tenants of this approach are that first interactants develop performance expectations during interactions with others based upon status characteristics they perceive. These performance expectations then direct participants' perceptions of what they and others are going to contribute to the interaction at hand and the perceived success of those contributions. Furthermore, these expectations are based upon information available to participants concerning other members' external status characteristics. An external status characteristic is then defined as an attribute that varies from individual to individual and is in some fashion associated with widely held beliefs concerning the value of that attribute. In other words, the attribute is given greater or lesser value relative to other attributes. In addition, some individuals and not others hold the attribute, which varies in esteem. Thus, variables like race, class, and gender affect performance expectations within interactions.

Expectations States Theory postulates that these external status characteristics have considerable influence on the performance expectations that arise for members of an interaction. These performance expectations in and of themselves are said to have the ability to govern behaviors, mannerisms, and reward distributions making status characteristics powerful determinants of interactional outcomes. Therefore, the primary feature of an expectation states approach to understanding interaction is analyzing the attributes used to determine performance expectations and how the societal beliefs associated with these attributes affect the performance expectations.

Beliefs cause interactants to expect that those with more socially valued status characteristics will also have higher status in interactional settings. In addition, it is argued that the **legitimacy** framework is created in the interaction by this same process. In other words, individuals with higher status characteristics will in general be perceived as having the right to certain claims or to be legitimated within the interaction.

In sum, according to the theory the behavioral status order is determined by the order of performance expectations that interactants develop for one another. The theory asserts that people form these performance expectations on the basis of information available to them about one another's external

status characteristics, reward levels, specific abilities, and behavior in the situation. Thus, any varying attribute in our society that is a status characteristic affects performance expectations and, therefore, affects behaviors and rewards in the interaction.

EXPERIMENTAL GROUP

In a classic experimental design, subjects are divided into two groups, a **control group** and an experimental **group**. These two groups are necessary in order to determine what effects on the **dependent variable** are due explicitly to the **independent variable** and what effects are due merely to spontaneous happenings that cannot be controlled by the researcher(s). The purpose of the experimental group is to receive the experimental stimulus. The control group and the experimental group are assumed to be identical along all dimensions that could be relevant to the research.

If an experiment is being conducted on the effect of watching cartoons on instances of violent behavior among children five years of age, the experimental group will contain children who are exposed to cartoons and the control group will contain children who are not. After being exposed to the experimental stimulus, the amount of violent behavior among subjects in the experimental group is compared to the amount of violent behavior among subjects in the control group. Any differences between the two groups become attributed to the experimental stimulus. If there are no differences between the experimental group and the control group in terms of violent behavior after the experimental group has been exposed to the independent **variable**, cartoons, then it can be concluded that cartoons have no effect on violent behavior.

EXPERIMENTATION

The term, experimentation, refers to the manipulation of an independent variable and the subsequent **measurement** of a **dependent variable**. Furthermore, experimenters randomly assign participants to either a treatment group or control group. On the one hand, treatment groups are presented with the actual manipulation of the **independent variable** or treatment. On the other hand, control groups are given some sort of false manipulation or placebo. The control group serves as a standard by which to compare the treatment group. Since proper random assignment assures that respondents are essentially similar across these groups, experimenters assume that any differences accounted for in the measurement of the dependent **variable** are the result of the treatment.

The main criticism regarding experimentation concerns the artificiality of the laboratory setting. It is argued that laboratory settings are too artificial; consequently, experiments offer little insight about how people act in more ''natural'' settings. Experimenters argue that this criticism is invalid because specific findings need not necessarily be replicated in a natural setting. That is, theoretical scope conditions specify the circumstances under which an experiment's findings may be supported.

The role that experimentation plays in sociological social psychology is a crucial one. Moreover, experimentation offers many advantages pertaining to constructing, empirical testing, and modifying **theory**. Experimenters maintain that these goals are requisite for any legitimate social science; it is their dedication to these goals that indicates the importance of experimentation.

EXPLANATORY RESEARCH

While social scientific research have many purposes, the three most common are exploration, description, and explanation. When research is exploratory, the purpose is to find out about a topic that remains unexamined. It lays the groundwork for other types of research. Descriptive research is used to portray certain aspects of situations, events, or populations. A popular example of research with a descriptive intent is the U.S. Census. Descriptive research can provide a precise picture of patterns and their changes over time, but it cannot answer questions which begin with why or how. These questions are addressed by explanatory research which intends to understand the process behind what we see. For example, say that from the descriptive work of the census we see that black women have lower average income than white women do. As curious researchers, we may wonder why this is. We might construct a study with the purpose of explaining the disparity in income between black and white women. Through explanatory research, we might find that white women have higher average education levels than black women which explains why white women earn larger incomes. Perhaps we find no differences in education. Now we might explain the differences we see by **discrimination** faced in the labor market.

Explanation can be of two types. *Nomothetic* explanation attempts to explain a set of situations or events. The above example of white and black women's income differences is an instance of nomothetic explanation because we are trying to understand why the disparity exists by looking at the entire U.S. population. If, on the other hand, we were interested in studying just one business and understanding why income differences exist between workers at a particular business on the basis of **race**, we would use *idiographic* explanation. This type of explanation takes a single case or instance of something and attempts to fully understand a process in that specific context. The scope of our study would be limited just to the business where we conducted the research. Exploratory research delineates what should be studied, descriptive research describes what is being studied, and explanatory research explains the processes behind what we observe. Ultimately, while these three purposes of research can be considered separate, they are often used in combination with one another.

EXTENDED FAMILY

An extended family characterizes a family **structure** that extends beyond the nuclear family in terms of other relations and/or generations. This means that beyond parents and their children, there may in addition be some combination of the parents', parents' siblings, children's spouses, children, children's in-laws, and grandchildren. There are a wide variety of extended families. The form of extended families varies historically and cross-culturally. The conventional extended family is defined as a family unit consisting of several generations all living in the same **household**. Such an extended family includes daily contact and economic interdependence. Such a social unit is also labeled a *consanguine* family or *joint* family. While these other terms are often used interchangeably, they have varying emphases. A consanguine family is an extended family defined by blood ties rather than marital ties, in which the two spouses have at least one ancestor in common. It is generally assumed that, with industrialization and modernization, the rate of these consanguineous unions declines. A joint family describes large families, such as combinations of nuclear families. An example of this type of **family** is the large families in India in which at least two brothers, with their own wives and children, live in the same household together. In joint families, the resources are often pooled.

Extended families can vary extensively in terms of size. A stem family is the smallest variety of extended family. Common in Japan and Ireland, a *stem* family includes two families in consecutive generations that are joined by economic and blood ties for example, families who share a household with one spouse's parents. In most cultures where this type of family is common, the parents live with the eldest son and his family. A stem family serves to maintain the family estate, yet the estate belongs to the eldest child rather than having the resources pooled as in the joint family.

More recently, the definition of extended family has loosened so as not to require that the family members reside in the same home and have a strictly interdependent style of living. Now extended family refers to having contact and providing and receiving assistance with kin beyond the nuclear family, such as parents, children, and other more distant relative such as grandparents, uncles, aunts, and/or cousins. This is commonly referred to as the *modified extended family*. Contrary to popular notions of the family in modern industrialized societies, the typical family form is not the isolated nuclear family. Rather it is variations on the extended family. The nuclear family is still autonomous in a modified-extended family structure, but it is not isolated. Instead, the nuclear family maintains close ties with other nuclear families. This network of families shares goods, resources, and assists each other in a variety of capacities.

Regardless of the particular family members that comprise the extended family and regardless of the size of the family unit, contact with relatives outside the nuclear family unit serves in both a functional and psychologically-rewarding capacity. One benefit that has particularly grown in importance as more women with children enter the workforce is easing the burden of childcare. Other relatives, such as grandparents, can be large influences in terms of care, affection, and **socialization** which helps relieve the parents from sole responsibility. While helping parents, this arrangement also has emotional rewards for the grandparents and their grandchildren. Having extended family networks also helps in term of both emotional and financial crises. Having a number of family members share costs and resources serves as a safety net for those individuals in times of need. Maintaining close relationships with relatives also serves as a source of identification. It is through these extended family networks that ideologies and value systems are effectively transmitted from generation to generation.

EXTERNAL VALIDITY

Based on the idea of generalizing, external **validity** is the degree to which conclusions drawn from the sample population of a study hold true for populations not directly observed in the study. External validity is the extent to which the results of a study can be applied, extended, or transferred to other people, places, or times. Threats to external validity revolve around the presence of any unique characteristics of the study. That is, if the sample population studied, or the place or time in which the study was conducted proves to be non-representative of the general population or wrought with unusual circumstance, the generalizability of the conclusions are limited. Ways to minimize these limitations include careful adherence to random sampling techniques and, if possible, conducting studies in a variety of locations at different times. An example of external validity would be the appropriateness of transferring personality conclusions made about a random sample population of national social workers to the national population of social workers. These same personality conclusions, however, would not be true, and therefore externally valid, if applied to the population of social worker clients because the two populations are unique from one another.

The conventional extended family is defined as a family unit consisting of several generations all living in the same household *(Corbis Corporation [Bellevue]).*

F

FACE VALIDITY

Face **validity** is the degree to which a research instrument *appears* to measure what it is intended to measure, according to the researcher using it. This type of validity is established though the subjective examination of measure be it a survey instrument, procedure, or intervention. Face validity does not consider whether an instrument actually measures what it is designed to measure; rather, it simply assesses the superficial appearance of accurate **measurement**. An example of face validity would be a researcher who attempts to measure the political knowledge of college students by administering a survey that asks such questions as what is a veto and what are pork barrel projects. However, a researcher who attempts to measure the political knowledge of college students by administering a survey that asks such questions as how do you administer CPR to an infant, is using a research instrument that does not have face validity.

There are a number of weaknesses in relying on face validity as a form of measurement assessment. For instance, the limited surface evaluation preformed to establish face validity is non-systematic and, therefore, not reproducible. As such, it is not rigorous in assessing what a study is attempting to investigate, let alone actually investigating. As a result, face validity is generally viewed as providing a less than accurate appraisal of the empirical reality of a measure. Yet, it is important always to conduct at least a surface inspection for the face validity of a measure to catch any mistakes before they are implemented and return invalid **data**.

FACT

A fact is a statement provable by objective and empirical means. It is the state of things in reality, or in truth. The term ''fact'' has sociological significance in its relation to value statments, or assertions about ethics, aesthetics, or any area which relies on subjective, not objective, analysis. Hume and the logical positivists of the twentieth century are seen as the key proponents of the difference between these two kinds of statements. They argued that value statements cannot be proven logically by factual statements and, thus, at least to some extent, have no empirical meaning.

Although **Max Weber** accepted this distinction, other sociologists have refused. This distinction threatens the field of social science because sociologists study human behaviors in **society** that are not always analyzable through objective facts. Although sociologists primarily use the scientific method to verify their assertions, the extent of their empirical **data** is limited and the facts of their research are often the subjective assertions of individuals. Instead of accepting the distinction between fact and value, many sociologists claim that it is irrational to deny that both facts and theories contribute to one's values. Thus, although the **values** we have may not be logically deducible from the facts we know, facts and empirical theories inform our values, giving them meaning.

Theories themselves, however, may also be questioned as to the extent that they rely on fact. What a certain social theorist might consider a fact, may be considered by another to be theory-laden, or dependent upon a certain theoretical framework for looking at the world. For example, one person may assert: it is a fact that all men are created equal. Another may counter that this statement is not a purely empirical statement, but laden with the individual's presuppositions regarding human beings. Even the assertion of empirical or scientific facts has been questioned, the basis of phenomenologists who argue that all statements are guided by presuppositions and that there are no facts, only statements of value that rely to greater and lesser extents on empirical data. Contention, therefore, exists over the relationship between facts and theories or interpretations of theories based on fact. Thus, many generalizations are debated. Most social scientists tend to agree that some social facts are packed full of theoretical assumptions.

FACTOR ANALYSIS

Factor analysis is a statistical technique used to reduce the number of variables in an equation or to estimate the effect of unmeasured, underlying variables. Quite frequently these latent variables are more interesting to social scientists, than answering specific survey questions.

Factor analysis was developed in the early part of the twentieth century by psychiatrists interested in **intelligence** testing. Respondents answered a battery of questions, and the psychiatrists attempted to find patterns of similar responses to questions, attempting to identify and measure underlying causes. Factor analysis is currently used primarily in **sociology** by those researchers in the areas closest to **psychology**, although sociologists throughout the discipline employ this technique.

Factor analysis can be used to explore latent variables in two ways. Testing whether certain unmeasured variables are present is referred to as confirmatory factor analysis. More often, however, factor analysis is done without any guiding principles predicting the number of factors to be extracted or what they might represent theoretically. This is called exploratory factor analysis.

For example, one might look at a survey of youths that asked respondents a number of questions about their participation in violent crime and vandalism. One could then attempt to extract one or more factors that may represent some unmeasured cause of some or all of the variables. There might, for instance, be one factor that is highly associated with property crime, while another factor, completely un-correlated with the first, is associated with violent crime. Alternately, one might find that there is only one, or even no, factor that can be extracted from the **data**, suggesting that there may be no common underlying cause for the delinquent acts.

The computation of factor analysis is normally done from a correlation matrix of the measured variables. The factor with the most explanatory power is extracted first; the rest in descending order of explanatory power. The eigenvalue of the factor is the amount of variance it explains among the original variables. The total amount of variance explained by all the factors extracted from a **model** is called the communality.

Unlike many other types of statistical analysis, factor analysis does not have dependent or independent variables; none of the measured variables in equation is theorized to cause any of the others. However, the factors that are extracted can be used as independent variables in other equations. Thus, factor analysis can be helpful in reducing the number of variables in an equation.

Although some conventions exist, the number of factors extracted is not limited by the mathematical technique of factor extraction, only by the number of variables in the model. Some have critiqued factor analysis on these grounds, as factors can be extracted with little or no theoretical support. Sociologists performing factor analysis commonly use the computer program LISREL, developed by Swedish psychometrician Karl Joreskog.

FAD

A fad is a temporary fashion, mannerism, or activity. The term is most often applied when a certain **group** becomes enthusiastically caught up in that fashion or activity. The word's origin is unknown, but the term has been in use since the early nineteenth century, if not longer.

Many people reserve the term "fad" for silly amusements, but the effects of fads can be staggering economically and culturally. In the seventeenth century, tulips were such a craze in Holland that a blight on the crop nearly wrecked the economy. For another example, eighteenth-century Europeans mad for beaver hats helped drive a fur trade that was instrumental in exploring and opening America's West. In the marketing revolution of the late twentieth century, it seemed that a new fad was required each year: millions of people "just had to have" Cabbage Patch Dolls one year and Beanie Babies products shortly after. This pattern fits neatly with a definition in John Naisbitt's book *Megatrends*, which stated that a fad is generated from the top down, whereas a trend—usually seen as a cultural movement of more lasting significance—is generated from the bottom up.

Fads can actually be dangerous to individuals when promoted by trusted professionals in cases like fad diets or even fad diagnoses in medicine and psychology. Often the momentum of the fad outpaces research into possible negative side-effects or outright ineffectiveness. Despite the public contempt when fads reach a certain point of over-exposure, human beings remain able to be swept up all over again when the next "new thing" comes along.

FALSE CONSCIOUSNESS

Karl Marx (1818-1883) introduced the concept of false consciousness as one way the class system is perpetuated. Marx's analyses focused on capitalism as an economic system with social consequences. In particular, he was interested in the class system which **capitalism** creates and perpetuates. For Marx, however, it is impossible to understand false consciousness without first understanding the way capitalism produces **alienation**.

The transition from an agrarian economy to a capitalist economy co-occurred with industrialization. Technological advances increased the rate of production. Much work, which up to that time had been home-based, moved into factories. Marx believed factory work alienates workers in three ways. First, workers are alienated from their work because they do not create a product from start to finish; they control only small segments of the production process and what they produce is not their own, but belongs to the owner of the factory. Second, workers are alienated from themselves because they are unable to develop mentally or physically due to the monotony of factory work. Third, workers are alienated from each other; they cannot work collectively to improve their conditions.

Under capitalism, a class system develops in which individuals divide into two groups. All workers in a capitalist sys-

The hula hoop fad had a staggering economical and cultural affect on U.S. society.

tem form a class of people which Marx called the "proletariat." Marx called the owners of the means of production the "bourgeoisie." For Marx, in the capitalist system, the bourgeoisie exploit the proletariat. Alienating the proletariat from the products of their labor, from themselves, and from other workers helps this exploitation through which owners are able to extract wealth from the workers' labor. The more hours the proletariat works and the more produced per hour, the greater bourgeois' wealth becomes.

False consciousness is Marx's label for those members of the proletariat who adhere to the **ideology** of the elite and, therefore, are unaware of the exploitative situation of which they are a part. It is in the interest of the **bourgeoisie** to have the proletariat blindly accept their situation. In this way, work hours, rate of pay, and speed of production can all be manipulated to the benefit of the bourgeoisie and the detriment of the proletariat. For individuals in the proletariat to have false consciousness, they must be unaware of their interests as a class. Marx believed it is in the interest of the proletariat to recognize their exploitation and unite to fight against it. As a **group**, they have the power to demand changes that individuals cannot. Instead, with false consciousness, they accept their subordinate and oppressed status. Marx envisioned that over time, the pro-

letariat would become aware of its fate as a class and would be united by class consciousness. Once this happened, revolution would occur, capitalism would be overthrown, and a community rid of false consciousness and oppression would develop.

FAMILY

The family is, according to sociologist William J. Goode, "the only social **institution** other than religion which is *formally* developed in all societies." Family has been traditionally defined by sociologists as a **group** of people who are related by either blood (consanguineous tie) or **marriage** (affinal tie) and who live together in the same **household**. Families are expected to have emotional closeness, with family members loving, respecting, and caring for one another. Families are held together not only by these emotional ties but also by functions, or purposes to fulfill within the larger society. Commonly noted family functions include reproduction and the care of children, as well as the transmission of social **norms** or ideals of proper behavior.

Expectations of family functioning in turn affect family form. A predominant form of family living in the United States is the nuclear family, a small unit consisting of a married couple and their children. This form became more common as industrialization provided greater **employment** opportunities outside of the home and the family no longer had to provide most of its own goods and services. The **extended family** form, where several generations live in the same household or very near to one another, is much less common now and has been replaced by the kin family network. In this form, nuclear families maintain connections with others within the same extended family system without living in the same household or following a central family **authority**.

Who counts as family and what is an appropriate basis for family varies by location. For example, in some cultures **love** is considered a necessary prerequisite for marriage, while in others love is not a critical aspect in mate selection. In some families, close friends or godparents may be considered as part of the family. The everyday reality of who is defined as family by family members themselves is an aspect of the family experience often overlooked by researchers. Feminist sociologists have suggested that traditional social research contributes to a confining and inadequate picture of family life by narrowly defining family members and family forms. In response, some feminist researchers have advocated new methods of family research. For example, Irene Levin has asked people to list who they consider family and then to map how close they feel to these people; this method of "mapping" family realities was designed to give greater understanding of people's emotional and private experience of family.

The concept of family also has an ideological function. Some family forms are considered more acceptable in a given **society** while others are seen as problematic or are not officially recognized as family at all. Family policy is directly affected by the definition of family. As a result, those who fall outside of the traditional definition of family may face discrimination. For example, gay men and lesbians are usually not granted the same partnership benefits as heterosexual couples (married or no) and are not permitted to adopt children in many states. Other family relationships that fall outside of the traditional nuclear family form are also subject to stigma, such as the parent/child dyadic family formed when a woman chooses to have a child outside of marriage.

See also Sociology of the Family

FAMILY AND RELIGION

Religion and the **family** are two social institutions that complement one another in many ways. Family celebrations and death rituals are governed by religion. Religion also plays a part in courting rituals, marital contracts, marital sexual relations, baptisms, male-female roles within the family, and parent-child relationships. Since they are frequently included in many rituals and celebrations, members of the **church** clergy also become part of the family.

Religion plays a role in the dating and mate selection process. Each of the three major religions in the Unites States

(**Judaism**, Catholicism, and Protestantism) have opposed interfaith marriages in the past. An interfaith marriage occurs when the husband and wife do not share the same religion. Some religions encourage their young members to date by setting up dating services and singles programs. Mormon church leaders tell their adolescents to date only within their religion. Some Jewish parents arrange marriages for their children as a way to sustain their Jewish **identity** and culture. The Roman Catholic Church requires interfaith couples to sign an premarital agreement stating that they will raise their children as Catholics.

Traditionally, religion dictated marital law in many ways. Religious law determined who would marry, whether or not they would use birth control, and whether or not they were allowed to **divorce**. Religion also mandated the roles and behaviors of married couples. Couples traditionally followed these rules and recommendations faithfully in their **marriage**. Today, religion still plays a large role in the marriage process for many people across the country and around the world, but many couples in the United States have opted to change or modify some of the rituals to fit their current beliefs and today's changing **society**.

There is a considerable body of research which investigates whether religion plays a role in keeping marriages together. Studies show that people who never attend religious services, or who identify themselves as "non-religious" have a divorce rate that is three times higher than those who attend religious services weekly. In keeping with this trend, couples who share the same religious faith tend to divorce less often than interfaith couples. In the United States today, more than sixty percent of marriages are between individuals of the same religious background. Though religious homogeny remains important, it has declined during the twentieth century. Protestants, Catholics, and Jews are integrated in schools, neighborhoods, and in the workplace, making interfaith matches more common and more accepted.

Religion also plays a part in the disciplinary style of parents. Many parents make use of corporal punishment a means to control and correct their child's behavior. The practice of corporal punishment, the use of physical force, or spanking, to correct a child's behavior, has its roots in religion. Many religions provide a framework for how children should be punished for their misconduct. Research illustrates that the frequency of spanking is higher in families where parents hold conservative religious views than in families who do not.

The family is the primary agent of religious **socialization** in children. Researchers have found that the family plays a central role in the transmission of religious beliefs. Acquiring religion generally follows a pattern. When they are young, the children of a family adopt the religion of their parents. As children reach the teenage years, many evaluate the religious beliefs of their family and compare them with other types of beliefs. The children then make the decision of whether they will continue with the beliefs of their parents or break away and adopt new or different beliefs. Parents are integral in this decision making process and in many close knit families this evaluation of religious beliefs can become a family process.

FAMILY LAW

Family law deals with the ways in which family groups are created, ordered, and dissolved. Primary issues in family law are **marriage**, separation, and divorce, legitimacy, child custody and support, alimony, and **adoption**, as well as questions of parentage associated with such reproductive technologies as artificial insemination and surrogate parenting.

Throughout history, family law has been closely connected to property law and laws of succession. This connection probably originated with the property issues that arose when a woman left her family of origin to become a member of her husband's family. Questions of who is a legal spouse and who a legitimate heir are also related to matters of **property** law. Since the social hierarchies on which many cultures have been structured were reinforced by marriage and property laws, family law has often been used to promote the interests of the dominant class. Revolutionary movements have often focused, therefore, on changing family law. The socialist revolutions in Russia and China, for example, rewrote traditional family laws that supported quasi-feudal regimes. Similarly, Japan's introduction of the Meiji code in 1898 led to the emergence of a new social **structure**.

In many cultures, family law has been governed by canon or religious law. English family law, for example, was under the jurisdiction of ecclesiastical courts until 1857, when the Matrimonial Causes Act was passed. In the United States, however, family law developed as an entirely secular entity. American law considers marriage to be a civil contract, not a religious sacrament. Though the clergy frequently perform marriages, their **authority** to do so is vested in them not by the **church** but by the state.

Because the U.S. Constitution does not give the federal **government** power to regulate domestic matters, family law in the United States is the province of individual states. Nevertheless, state rulings in family law matters must not violate individual rights guaranteed by the Constitution.

In general, family law in the United States has sought to minimize interference with family dynamics. Until the twentieth century, for example, almost every state recognized the validity of "common law marriages." Before the Civil War, the issuance of marriage licenses was seen more as a means of registering, rather than restricting, marriage. Yet by the late nineteenth century, marriage laws had become a means of **social control**. Age, degree of relationship, eugenic concerns, and **race** became legal impediments to marriage. **Divorce**, too, was strictly regulated. But within marriages, spouses were generally free from legal scrutiny. So entrenched was the principle of nonintervention that even spouses who wished to do so could not seek legal resolution of marital disputes. At the same time, parents were generally protected from state interference in child-rearing behavior. The U.S. Supreme Court reiterated this principle as late as 1944, in *Prince v. Massachusetts,* when it stated "the custody, care, and nurture of the child reside first in the parents, whose primary function and freedom include preparation for obligations the state can neither supply nor hinder... It is in recognition of this that [earlier] decisions have respected the private realm of family life which the state cannot enter."

During the late twentieth century, marriage and divorce laws in the United States were liberalized. Most notably, in 1967 the U.S. Supreme Court, in *Loving v. Virginia,* struck down as unconstitutional all laws prohibiting interracial marriages. Age and mental ability requirements were also eased. In addition, divorce laws were restructured; by the mid-1980s, every state had instituted "no-fault" divorce laws.

Regulation of dynamics within marriages has also occurred. Most states have abolished spousal immunity, and many now recognize marital rape as a crime. Parental behavior, too, has been subject to legal scrutiny. In cases of extreme abuse, courts have permanently removed children from parents' custody.

It is likely that the scope of family law will continue to widen, as complex **social problems** influence family structure. Population growth, for example, which has already led China to establish **family size** limits, may cause further state regulation of fertility. New reproductive technologies will raise legal questions regarding family relationships. Increasing global migration and **urbanization** are also expected to affect traditional structures of family law.

FAMILY PLANNING

Family Planning is a broad term that encompasses all types of birth control programs and organizations promoting birth control or population control. While some family planning programs focus on improving health and increasing women's control over reproduction, other programs focus on reducing birth rates. In the United States in 1873, it was illegal under the Comstock laws to use or distribute contraception or information about contraception. Throughout the late 1800s and the first half of the 1900s, three separate movements work to repeal these laws: neo-Malthusians, interested in population control; birth controllers, interested in providing women with the means to control their own reproduction; and eugenicists, interested in selective breeding. It was not until 1936 that the U.S. Court of Appeals ruled that medical prescription of contraception, for the purpose of saving a life or "promoting well-being," was not prohibited under the Comstock laws. More than twenty years after this ruling, contraception became widely available.

Margaret Sanger, one of the leaders of the birth control movement, worked particularly among poor, working class, and immigrant women to provide information and contraception. She was arrested in 1914 when the post office banned issues of her magazine *The Woman Rebel* and again in 1916 after opening the first birth control clinic in Brooklyn, New York. Sanger founded the American Birth Control league in 1921, which joined with other groups in 1939 to become the Birth Control Federation of America and eventually Planned Parenthood Federation of America (PPFA) in 1942. Sanger's original defense of birth control focused on the emancipation of women, claiming that liberating women's sexuality was essential to gaining freedom and equal participation in **society** for women. After World War I, Sanger's rhetoric linked birth control less with feminist ideals and more with **eugenics**.

In the 1930s, the eugenics movement turned its attention to the southern black population, proposing government programs aimed at reducing the black birthrate. Blacks had divided views on the topic of birth control. black women supported the establishment of family planning clinics in black communities. In the 1930s, W. E. B. Du Bois and the National Association for the Advancement of Colored People (NAACP) advocated family planning in order to "uplift the race." However, black nationalists, like Marcus Garvey and others in the black community, resisted the eugenic aims of family planning programs seeking to reduce the black birthrate. They advocated purposefully increasing the population to build political power by strength in numbers.

In the years after World War II, the diverse groups of population control advocates, birth control advocates, and eugenicists formed loose alliances within a larger population movement. Resisting opposition by the Catholic Church, they focused their efforts primarily on global population control. The birth controllers organized around PPFA. The term "family planning" was first used by PPFA to replace the term birth control and redirect the focus from women and their sexuality to the more politically safe focus of families and children. Those interested in population control were divided into two camps. The more conservative Population Council, founded in 1952 by John D. Rockefeller III, focused on scientific research and gradual policy change. The more radical wing was led by Hugh Moore who saw overpopulation as a national and global crisis and who linked overpopulation to the spread of communism. Unable to work effectively with either PPFA or the Population Council, Moore formed the Population Crisis Committee in 1963. Yet another faction of population control advocates centered their arguments on environmental conservation.

In the late 1950s, leaders of the population movement began campaigning for new contraceptive methods. This action sparked what some have referred to as the "contraceptive revolution" in the latter part of the twentieth century. The first birth control pill was approved by the Food and Drug Administration in 1960. However, it was not until 1965 that the Supreme Court established the right of married couples to obtain contraception, in *Griswold v. Connecticut.* This right was extended to single adults in 1972 in *Eisenstadt v. Baird.* and to minors in 1977 in *Carey v. Population Services International.*

Moving from a focus on international population control during the 1960s and 1970s, the country turned its attention to domestic family planning policy, hoping to control **poverty**, rising welfare costs, and out-of-wedlock births. In 1971, Title X of the Public Health Services Act provided for federal funding for family planning services and educational programs, as well as for biomedical and behavioral research in reproduction and contraceptive development. In the 1970s, with the fight for and eventual legalization of abortion, family planning rhetoric shifted from population control to women's rights. After years of struggling, with mixed success, to repeal abortion laws on the state level, abortion supporters celebrated the Supreme Court's 1973 decision in *Roe v. Wade* establishing women's rights to abortion at the federal level.

Today, advocates of population control have seen the birthrate decrease dramatically in most parts of the world, and advocates of women's reproductive rights have also seen many victories. Yet, while some people may see family planning as a success story, abuses surrounding the reproductive rights of women in the United States and around the globe continue. Poor women and minority women in this country have suffered from unnecessary and involuntary sterilization and continue to be "guinea pigs" for trials of new forms of contraception, as is the case currently with the implantable Noraplant, of which little is known about its long-term side effects. Global family planning efforts have also frequently led to testing of new products or unloading unsafe products on women in developing countries.

Limitations have been placed on women's access to abortion, particularly poor women, as Title X public funding does not pay for abortion and the 1977 Hyde Amendment prohibits **Medicaid** funds from being used for abortion. Young women have also been affected by laws requiring parental consent for minors in some states. Further, the "global gag rule" currently prohibits international family planning services from using U.S. funds to counsel women about or to provide them with access to medical abortion.

FAMILY ROLES

Family roles are positions within the family, such as parent, wife/husband, or son/daughter, that describe relations between family members and include expectations for proper behavior. All roles, including family roles, are produced through social **interaction** and are formed in relation to a companion or paired **role**. For instance, one cannot be a parent without the existence of the corresponding role of child or a wife without the existence of a husband.

One of the most famous models of roles in the family is Talcott Parsons and Robert Bales' description of instrumental and expressive roles. According to Parsons and Bales, the husband/father is the head of the **household** and is responsible for performing instrumental functions, such as earning a living and providing economic support for the family. The expressive role is performed by the wife/mother; she is responsible for the comfort and emotional well-being of other family members. This traditional model of family roles assumes a nuclear family of two biological parents and their children.

Family role expectations are strongly linked to gender role expectations. Despite greater public understanding of gender equality, researchers assert, gendered expectations that husbands will earn most of the family income while wives will do the majority of housework and **child care** persist. Feminist social psychologists have explored how **norms** of gender equality can coexist with family role expectations that support gender inequality in the home. Psychologist Caroline Dryden interviewed married couples and discovered that both husbands and wives have tactics that they use to support or excuse gender inequality in their performance of the husband or wife role. Women referred to traditional **gender norms** in excusing working husbands from housework responsibility, blamed themselves for husbands' lack of participation, and compared their husbands favorably to other women's husbands (i.e. Max may not do a great deal of housework, but he does much more than Sue's husband Sam). Husbands tended to use verbal techniques that minimized their responsibilities in the home. They described wives as "put-upon" through their own inability to say no to the demands of others, suggested that wives are over-worked because they have not organized their workday, blamed wives for not accepting their help with housework, and portrayed wives as lucky because they had the chance to stay home and do housework rather than support a family financial-ly. These husbands also reinforced traditional gendered divi-sion of family roles by portraying themselves as too overloaded to help at home, clever at home repair and there-fore fully participating in household labor, or better than most husbands at helping with family labor.

Although family sociologists have suggested that men's housework participation has increased in recent years, the evi-dence supporting this assertion is not conclusive. Reporting **bias**, or the tendency for research participants to answer ques-tions based on what they believe the researcher wants to hear or what the 'correct' response is rather than on the truth, has likely led men to over-report or exaggerate the amount of housework they do. As a result of greater expectations for wives and mothers, it is commonly understood that these roles have the potential to cause more **stress**, especially when women perceive unfairness in the distribution of household re-sponsibility. Children's perceptions of their parents' proper role behavior, or what constitutes a 'good' mother or father, illustrates the existence of greater demands on wives and mothers. Fathers are more likely to be praised for playing with children, making time for children, and 'helping' the mother with housework. In contrast, women are praised for helping behavior and for providing emotional support despite the fact that they spend more time with children and perform more housework. Sociologists Melissa Milkie, Robin Simon, and Brian Powell suggest that children's reporting differences stem from societal expectations that mothers are supposed to perform the majority of childcare and housework and, there-fore, do not receive praise for doing what is already expected.

Family roles are only one set of roles that people hold. Other roles may compete with family roles and cause people to experience stress when conflict occurs between role respon-sibilities. For example, a parent may need to stay home with a sick child but may have an important meeting to attend at work. Sociologists studying the balance between work and family roles, have concluded that both men and women experi-ence strain as a result of competing demands of these roles. Much less attention has been given to the family roles that children hold.

FAMILY SIZE

Family size refers to the number of persons related by either birth, marriage, or **adoption** that live together. Family size is influenced both by social **norms** and objective living condi-tions. One determinant of family size is the presence of **extend-

Family role expectations are strongly linked to gender role expectations *(Corbis Corporation [Bellevue]).*

ed family** and the number of generations living together in a **household**. Another major determinant of family size involves decisions about having children. First, people need to decide whether to have them. If children are desired, an individual or couple must decide how many children to have. Extensive de-bates surround issues related both to preventing child birth and increases in family size (e.g., contraception, abortion) as well as promoting child birth, thus expanding the size of a family (e.g., fertility procedures, adoption, surrogate parenting).

In the past, family farms were the main source of subsis-tence, and large families served an economic purpose. Chil-dren were valued assets. They contributed to the necessary labor on the farm and around the house and were expected to be a source of security in their parents' old age. It was common for families to have a number of children and having only one or two children was considered odd and an issue of **community** concern. Industrialization brought workers away from the fam-ily farms and into the factories. With production no longer based in the home, the need for a large number of children was diminished. With simultaneous developments in contracep-tion, children were becoming an issue of choice instead of a response to need. Social norms changed as well. The current norm regarding family size is to have two or three children. Having fewer, just one or no children, is becoming increasing-ly socially acceptable and having more than three is considered too many. Historically, children have at times been feared and others simply ignored. There is no doubt in today's climate and with transformed social norms that children put enormous demands on parents, both in terms of emotional needs and financial costs. Children are considered the responsibility of parents later into life and the rise in college attendance makes schooling a major expense for most families.

Clearly, family size has varied historically. Large variations can be found in the presence and number of children, only one of many factors affecting family size. The birth rate, which measures the number of children born per 1000 members of the population, has varied widely just over the past century. In 1910, the birthrate was 30.1. This rate decreased dramatically to 18.7 from the time of the Depression (1929-1935). By 1955, the birthrate had rebounded to 25.0. At this point a steady decrease began until the birthrate reached a low of 14.6 in the mid-1970s, but by the start of the 1990s, it was up to 16.7. Family size also varies cross-culturally. Other nations that place more emphasis on production in the home still maintain large average family size. **Culture** also plays a large part in terms of social norms. Just in the United States, marked differences in average family size can be found between different races and ethnicities. For example, on average Hispanic families have the largest families, while African Americans have the next largest, and whites have the smallest. The varying the emphasis on the importance of extended family in different cultures can explain much of this disparity.

While there is disagreement about predictions of trends in the birthrate and average family size, several factors suggest that we might expect a decrease. Not only are there improved methods of contraception, various sterilization procedures, availability of safe abortions, but we also see a trend towards delaying **marriage** and delaying first births, as well as an increased belief that childlessness is an acceptable option.

While extensively studied as a **dependent variable**, family size is also studied as an **independent variable**. The number of people in a **group** undoubtedly influences that group, both in terms of the amount of **interaction** that occurs and the types of behavior displayed. Certain family sizes are conducive to certain patterns of life. For example, the larger the family the more pull there is on resources, whether this be interpersonal resources (e.g., attention, frequency of **communication**, time for discipline, etc.) or economic resources (educational objects, entertainment, access to extracurricular activities, etc.). Ultimately, the consequences associated with certain family sizes tend to vary according to other important factors, such as religion, social class, and educational levels.

FAMILY VIOLENCE

The **family**, a primary social **group** among primates, encompasses individuals bound by heredity, **marriage**, and intimacy. In the ideal family intimate family relations are characterized by mutual respect, caring and **love**, but in many families intimacy is marred by physical and sexual violence. In the United States, any violent act perpetrated by a family member against another family member is an example of family violence. In *Understanding Social Problems*, Mooney, Knox, and Schacht summarize the research on family violence. According to their study women and children are the most likely victims of family violence although a recent national survey on family violence indicates that parents and siblings are increasingly reporting that they have been assaulted by a family member.

It is difficult to assess exactly how many families are affected by family violence which includes physical, emotional, and sexual abuse against spouses, children, and the elderly. Family violence is perhaps one of the most underreported crimes because victims tend to feel powerless and are often dependent on their perpetrators. It is difficult for children to report violence suffered at the hands of their primary caretaker. It is difficult for women to escape the psychological and physical abuse perpetrated by their lovers. Additionally, the elderly who may be dependent on their adult children for support are often immobile and ostracized.

Marital violence or spousal abuse is estimated to affect approximately fifty percent of wives at some point in their marriages according to a survey conducted by the National League of Cities. Research reported by Mooney, Knox, and Schacht (1997) indicates that women are ten times more likely than men to experience spousal abuse. Additionally, non-married, cohabiting couples are also at risk of experiencing emotional, physical and sexual abuse at the hands of their partners. Several factors increase the risk of marital violence. First, males with non-egalitarian or traditional **values** are more likely to use violence as a means of resolving problems. Second, research has shown that economic hardship, sexual inequality in decision-making, and an incongruence in educational and professional achievement of partners contribute to the risk of marital or couples violence.

Similarly, **poverty** is highly correlated with incidents of child abuse. Children living with parents who are young, poor, and single are at the greatest risk of severe physical abuse. Additionally, women and children living in violent homes are more likely to fall victim to poverty when they attempt to leave. Neglect is the most common form of child abuse. Sullivan reports that ninety percent of convicted abusers are men with a history of being abused themselves as children. Parents with difficult children, developmentally delayed children, or unwanted children are at a greater risk of being abusive.

In recent times, the issue of elderly abuse has received mainstream attention. Four to ten percent of the elderly are abused physically, psychologically, or financially according to research reported by Mooney, Knox, and Schacht (1997). The elderly are at risk of exploitation and/or neglect by their caretakers who tend to be their spouses or adult children. The burden of caring for an elderly spouse or parent can place the caretaker and the receiver at risk for hostility, frustration, and financial hardship. These factors contribute to risk of abuse in families with dependent elderly.

The only way to resolve the issue of family violence is to confront it with three levels of abuse prevention. Primary prevention strategies involve creating educational programs that inform the general population about the consequences of family violence and how to get help for victims and perpetrators. The secondary level of prevention involves targeting families who are at high risk of experiencing family violence. Secondary prevention programs include economic support groups and home visiting programs for single and young parents. The third level of prevention targets victims. Women's shelters, counseling programs, and family preservation programs are services available to families with a history of abuse and neglect.

FANON, FRANTZ (1925-1961)
Algerian political theorist, author, and revolutionary

The Algerian political theorist Frantz Fanon (1925–1961) analyzed the nature of racism and **colonialism** and developed a theory of violent anticolonialist struggle. Frantz Fanon was born in the French colony of Martinique. He volunteered for the French army during World War II, and then, after being released from military service, he went to France, where he studied medicine and psychiatry from 1945 to 1950. In 1953 he was appointed head of the psychiatric department of a government hospital in Algeria, then a French territory. As a black man searching for his own **identity** in a white colonial **culture**, he experienced racism; as a psychiatrist, he studied the dynamics of racism and its effects on the individual.

In his first book *Black Skin, White Masks* (1952), Fanon examined the social and psychological processes by which the white colonizers alienated the black natives from any indigenous black culture; he showed that blacks were made to feel inferior because of their color and thus strove to emulate white culture and **society**. Fanon hoped that the old myths of superiority would be abandoned so that a real equality and integration could be achieved.

Alienated from the dominant French culture, except for that represented by such radicals as the philosopher **Jean-Paul Sartre**, Fanon deeply identified with Algeria's revolutionary struggle for independence. He had secretly aided the rebels from 1954 to 1956, when he resigned from the hospital post to openly work for the Algerian revolutionaries' National Liberation Front (FLN) in Tunis. He worked on the revolutionaries' newspaper, becoming one of the leading ideologists of the revolution, and developed a theory of anticolonial struggle in the "third world."

Using Marxist, psychoanalytic, and sociological analysis, Fanon summed up his views in *The Wretched of the Earth* (1961), arguing that only a thorough, truly socialist revolution carried out by the oppressed peasantry (the wretched of the earth) could bring **justice** to the colonized. He believed that the revolution could only be carried out by violent armed conflict; only revolutionary violence could completely break the psychological and physical shackles of a racist colonialism. Violence would regenerate and unite the population by a "collective catharsis;" out of this violence a new, humane man would arise and create a new culture. Through all this Fanon stressed the need to reject Europe and its culture and accomplish the revolution alone.

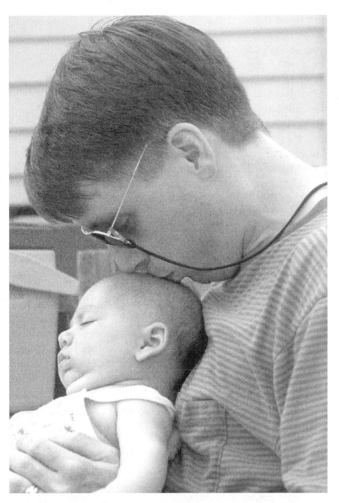

With renewed cultural awareness of fathers in recent years, being a father is defined less by biological criteria and more by social criteria *(Field Mark Publications)*.

Fanon, the antiracist and revolutionary **prophet**, never saw the end result of the process he described: full independence of his adopted Algeria. In 1960 he served as ambassador to Ghana for the Algerian provisional government, but it was soon discovered that he had leukemia. After treatment in the Soviet Union, he went to the United States to seek further treatment but died there in 1961.

FATHERHOOD

Fatherhood, like most social roles, varies across times and cultures. Dramatic changes can be documented in the United States in just the past couple centuries. Most notable of these transitions accompanied industrialization. This period of time, and the social and economic changes that took place during it, had an enormous influence on the **institution** of the **family**. Instead of production being located in the home, workers now left the home for the factory, bringing about a conception of work and home as two totally distinct spheres of life. Being employed outside the home, men saw their roles in the family transformed. Fathers no longer played a primary role in childcare and domestic responsibilities. Instead, the role of father came to be limited to providing economically for the family, to being the breadwinner.

Beyond being the primary breadwinner, however, fathers do have other purposes in the family, and these have become increasingly recognized. Children with fathers who are actively involved are much better off on a variety of indicators. For example, research on the effect of **divorce** and mother-headed single-parent families on children's development show many negative effects, such as increased rates of dropping out of high school and increased rates of teen pregnancy. In contrast, children with fathers who remain involved after divorce have better grades, **higher education** levels, stronger work ethics, more stable jobs, higher incomes, closer friendships, more stable marriages, fewer premarital births, stronger moral consciences, better health, and higher levels of life satisfaction.

Unfortunately, in general, men face several constraints including the stress of being employed, being limited to socially acceptable expressions of emotions, being more susceptible to heart attack and **suicide**, and as a consequence having a shorter life span. Fathers, in particular, also face several biases because of the traditional **gender roles** and the assumptions about parenting that are built into these roles. For example, **society** tends to equate what a man does for work with who he is as a person. From early socialization, boys are taught that their place in the **labor force** is the most important defining aspect of their **identity**. Work serves as confirmation of their **masculinity** and success. Men are also disadvantaged in custody battles. Divorced fathers are typically regarded as uninvolved with their children and career-focused and usually end up with a custody settlement that allows them to see their children less than 25 percent of the year. The assumption that women are naturally better parents than men feeds this discrimination. Increased attention has begun to be devoted to this issue of fathers' rights and equality for men inside the home, and increasingly courts are becoming more gender-neutral when making custody decisions.

While the role of fathers has been given increased importance, how fathers parent tends to be more complex than how mothers parent. There is wide variation in how men fill the role of father depending on economic factors, institutional practices, **employment** opportunities, and the quality of the relationship the father has with his spouse or partner. It is also important to keep in mind that fathering is affected by other characteristics and factors affecting where men are in the overall social **structure**. The way men father can be influenced by **race**, social class, sexual orientation, religion, marital status, and a host of other factors that shape who men are and how they approach certain social roles.

With renewed cultural awareness of fathers in recent years, being a father is defined less by biological criteria and more by social criteria. The rise in technology that minimizes the role of men in terms of reproduction (e.g. artificial insemination, **adoption**, etc.) may have contributed to this new emphasis. A fatherhood movement evolved out of a reaction to popular notions that a father was largely unnecessary in the lives of children. Groups for men such as the Promise Keepers have also emphasized the importance of fathers and have encouraged men to embrace this role and commit themselves to their children. We can see contemporary perspectives of fatherhood placing much more emphasis on the place of fathers in children's lives and in the family in general.

FEMININITY

Femininity refers to those aspects of gender typically associated with the female sex. Femininity is a label used to describe people, behaviors, or personality characteristics. It is a socially created and socially imposed framework that is juxtaposed with **masculinity**; there is an assumption that they are mutually exclusive, opposites on a continuum. **Society** often assumes that someone who is biologically female will and should display certain physical, emotional, and attitudinal (i.e., feminine) characteristics.

In 1935 **Margaret Mead** was one of the first researchers to challenge the idea that biological sex and gender were innately linked in her study *Sex and Temperament in Three Primitive Societies*. She found no universal differences in traits and temperaments between the sexes, indicating that all human beings possess both feminine and masculine characteristics and that the expression of these characteristics is culturally defined. Thus, sociologists study femininity as a social construction that is created and reinforced through individual social interactions and gender inequality in the **structure** of society. This inequality is a result of different gender expectations, and to a lesser extent, **gender socialization**.

Femininity is tied to one's gender **identity**. As an identity peg, femininity is closely connected to social structure and expectations. It is part of the internalized messages about what it means to be a woman or a man in society. Because there are two separate **gender roles** in Western **culture** (women and men), we assume that we must choose between feminine and masculine traits. Research, however, has shown that all humans possess and display both feminine and masculine characteristics. In the 1970s, another theoretical gender category, androgyny, was developed. Some theorists see androgyny as a combination of masculine and feminine traits.

Femininity is also closely linked to gender-role expectations. There are needs in all human relationships, and current gender roles implicate women (assumed to be feminine) as the ones to do the emotional work and men (assumed to be masculine) to do the rational work. Today, there are many characteristics we consider feminine. Some characteristics that can be construed as negative include traits such as being passive, dependent, physically weak or vulnerable, compliant, childlike, gullible, or soft-spoken. But other characteristics—communicative, cooperative, nurturing, maternal, sweet, sensitive, loyal, and conscientious—can be construed as positive. In addition, some of these characteristics, including empathy, compassion, understanding, and emotion rather than **rationality**, can be read as positive or negative, depending on the situation.

Femininity and feminine characteristics have traditionally been socially defined as less valuable and desirable than masculinity and masculine characteristics. This is a central principle of the patriarchal structure and **ideology** in culture, and globally there is a structural and individual subordination of feminine to masculine. According to theorists, one of the defining aspects of femininity in terms of subordination is compliance, with a focus on meeting the needs, desires, and interests of masculine beings. This is often considered one of the major characteristics of femininity—sacrificing one's own needs for the needs of others. This accommodation of the needs and desires of others was called "emphasized femininity" by R. W. Connell in 1997. Counter to this, there is also a rejection of compliance that comes when women in particular refuse to subordinate their needs and desires to the needs and desires of others. Connected to this is the common perception that to be feminine, women need to be sexually available and desirable to men. This is problematic for feminist scholars because it can lead to violence against women and others who possess feminine characteristics, such as children.

Femininity as an ideology does not necessarily correspond to the characteristics or experiences of individual women. As a social group, women suffer from institutional subordination and the denigration of feminine characteristics. But as individuals, women can both benefit from and enjoy possessing and displaying feminine characteristics.

Researchers have found that society is pervaded by many more social messages about the appropriate characteristics of femininity (women) than about masculinity (men). These messages emphasize that women are subjected to more narrow conceptions of how they need to be and act in society than are men, and illustrate how the structural and social nature of femininity impacts on and affects individuals.

See also Gender Roles

FEMINISM

Feminism is both the belief that women should be treated equally to men as well as a political movement that works to gain rights and privileges for women. Feminism attempts to explain and eradicate the **domination**, oppression, and subordination of women. It is a perspective that helps women and men better understand those forces at work in **society** that create and perpetuate inequality. Feminists want women to have equal access to and representation in jobs, education, politics, and **health care**. The objective of the feminist movement is equality of rights, social **status**, and individual and **group** power. It is not the goal of feminists to take power away from men, instead, feminists seek to create a system in which women have the same amount of power as men. Although many people think feminists are women, many men also consider themselves feminists.

Feminist beliefs have existed throughout history. One of the first feminist publications was *A Vindication of the Rights of Women* (1792) by **Mary Wollstonecraft**. She called for better and increased education for girls and women, claiming that the

Feminists such as Gloria Steinem attempted to explain and eradicate the domination, oppression, and subordination of women *(AP/Wide World Photos, Inc.).*

oppression of women and their subordinate position in society would not change until women were educated at the same level as men.

The three major types of feminism are liberal, radical, and socialist. Liberal feminists believe that women's inequality is due to lack of equal opportunity. They do not challenge the conventional **role** of women as primary caretakers in the private sphere, but focus on gaining equality in the public sphere, such as under the law, in politics, and in the economy. They believe that equality will come from equal opportunity. Liberal feminists advocate for change from within the system by focusing on changing individual women as well as the systems of inequality.

In contrast, radical feminists believe that women's inequality results from **patriarchy** (the structural dominance of men over women). They focus on the need to change the conventional roles of women in society and on the nature of **culture** as dominated by a male point of view. This perspective dates back to Simone de Beauvoir's 1952 book *The Second Sex*. Radical feminists advocate change from outside the system. They view the "personal as political," and have introduced the idea of gender **identity** politics.

Socialist/Marxist feminists, the third type of feminists, claim that women experience a dual oppression. Women experience patriarchal oppression in the home and capitalist oppression at work. Socialist/Marxist feminists believe that gender inequality will exist until both patriarchy and capitalism are abolished.

There have been two major waves of feminism in Western society. The first wave, in the late 1800s and early 1900s, focused on achieving the right to vote for women, or suffrage, and access to birth control. This wave was dominated by liberal feminist thinking. In 1920, the United States adopted the Nineteenth Amendment, granting women the right to vote. Some of the more famous women during the movement to this point were Charlotte Perkins Gilman, Susan B. Anthony, and Margaret Sanger.

After 1920, there was a decline in activism in the women's movement because the two major objectives had been achieved. But in the mid-1900s, many women began moving into the work force, changing the economy. In the 1960s a second wave of feminism emerged to become what most people today think of as "feminism." Radical feminists who focused on the political and identity aspects of women's oppression dominated this new wave of feminism. During the 1960s and 1970s, feminists forced issues relating specifically to women onto the national political agenda. Many laws were changed, giving more protections and rights to women, including the legal right to abortion and stronger rape laws.

In 1966, the **National Organization for Women (NOW)**, a national symbol of the movement, was created. NOW's central effort was proposing the Equal Right Amendment, to guarantee equal protection for women under the U.S. Constitution. It was brought to Congress in 1984 but was defeated. It has been proposed again, but has never been adopted. Many feminists consider this one of the largest remaining barriers to women's equality in the United States.

Over time, feminism has been criticized for contributing to increased social problems such as more **divorce**, rising **crime** rates, and the demise of the conventional American **family**. Research has negated this claim. The national movement has also been blamed for focusing mainly on issues pertinent to white, educated, middle-class women, ignoring the issues affecting minority and poor women. This claim was accurate, and led to a splintering of the movement, with separate groups addressing particular constituencies. Out of this emerged the concept of black feminism. Black theorists claim that black and other minority women suffer from interlocking systems of oppression—gender, class, and **race** or **ethnicity**. Their goal is to have the voices of these women heard within the context of historical and social conditions.

After the mid-1970s, the visibly active and political contingent of the feminist movement became smaller. Many assumed that these newer laws now ensured women's rights. In the 1980s, there was also a media-fueled "backlash" against feminism. The word took on a negative connotation and many people distanced themselves from the label or identity of feminist.

On the tail of this backlash, a new brand of feminism emerged in the mid-1990s—third wave feminism. This feminism is "non-feminism" and is defined by the phrase "I'm not a feminist, but..." People in this wave tend to take women's equality for granted, yet live the principles of sexual equality in their everyday lives. Unlike the second wave, this wave is characterized by a lack of cohesive and identifiable political action. There are many feminist organizations and groups in the United States today, but they often work in isolation, not always acting as part of a larger movement as was seen in the 1960s and 1970s.

FEMINIZATION OF POVERTY

The Feminization of Poverty refers to the fact that the majority of people living in poverty globally are women and children. Single mothers and their children constitute almost forty percent of the people under the poverty line in the United States with higher numbers in less industrialized countries. This demographic trend is a shift from the 1960s and 1970s, when many of the poor were members of two-parent households. This trend has been used to scapegoat, stereotype, and stigmatize single-parent households, particularly those headed by females.

The prevalence of poor women, sociologists explain, is the result of inequality, sexism, and the lower **status** of women, especially in terms of political and economic power, both individually and institutionally, not weaknesses in individual character. The social forces that create and perpetuate poverty include the lower status of women in relation to men (gender stratification) and the limited access women have to political and economic positions of power. As a result, women are concentrated in female-dominated **professions**, usually at the lower end of the pay scale where they earn less **money** than men, even for the same jobs with the same skills.

The current economic system in the United States relies on an available pool of low-paid, low-skill women workers, but an **ideology** that perpetuates myths about the individualistic causes of poverty helps maintain the oppressed status of women in all societies by blaming them for their own status as poor. In the United States, about one-third of all female-headed families live in poverty. They are five times more likely than two-parent households to be poor. This occurs because women bear more responsibility for the care and financial support of children after **divorce** or desertion; many men do not pay **child support** or alimony after divorce; and childcare is unavailable or expensive.

Some politicians blame single mothers for many of the social problems in the United States today: increased **crime** rates, low educational achievement, drug or alcohol abuse, and the breakdown of the **family**. Proponents of this viewpoint claim that welfare and **social support** programs designed to help alleviate poverty are creating more **social problems**, including welfare dependency, lack of a work ethic, and more teenage pregnancies. However, research contradicts this claim. States with the lowest welfare benefits have the highest rates of teenage pregnancy.

FERGUSON, ADAM (1723-1816)
Scottish philosopher, historian, and chaplain

The Scottish philosopher, moralist, and historian Adam Ferguson (1723–1816) produced a number of notable works concerning the nature of **society**. He is regarded as one of the founders of modern **sociology**. Adam Ferguson was born in Logierat, Perthshire. In 1739 he went to the University of St. Andrews, where he received his master of arts degree in 1742. Determined on a clerical career, he began to study divinity at St. Andrews, continuing these studies in Edinburgh. In 1745 he became first deputy chaplain and later chaplain of the Black Watch Regiment, but in 1754 he left the regiment and abandoned the ministry.

In 1757 Ferguson replaced **David Hume** as librarian to the Advocates Library in Edinburgh. In 1759 he became professor of natural philosophy at the University of Edinburgh and in 1764 was appointed to the coveted chair of "pneumatics [mental philosophy] and moral philosophy." Ferguson held this post until 1785 and retired from university life soon after. For the rest of his remarkably long life, however, he remained active as a writer, traveler, and speaker, amassing a considerable contemporary reputation for his *Essay on the History of Civil Society* (1767) and *Principles of Moral and Political Science* (1792). In 1793, on a trip to Germany, he was elected an honorary member of the Berlin Academy of Sciences.

Ferguson's importance as a thinker rests on his recognition of the important role played by society in shaping human **values**. He particularly rejected any notion of a "state of nature" in which men lived as individuals before society was established. Being a social animal, man was conditioned by necessity, habit, **language**, and familial or societal guidance. Societies as a whole, Ferguson asserted, are dynamic, following a pattern of change from "savagery" to "barbarism" to "civilization." Like individuals, they learn from and build upon the past. Different societies may, however, reflect particular characteristics based on factors such as geography or climate.

As any society becomes civilized, Ferguson suggested, it becomes more prone to conflict. Commerce breeds economic **competition**, and the state system breeds **war**. Although some benefits do result from conflict—industrial growth, scientific, and esthetic advances—Ferguson stressed that, when the **division of labor** results in economic class stratification and when warfare becomes the province of the professional military, a society faces decay and despotism and conflict is then no longer present. It should be noted that Ferguson was one of the first thinkers to point to conflict as a positive factor in human development and to argue that such conflict is more pronounced in civilized societies than in primitive ones.

FERTILITY DETERMINANTS

Fertility determinants are those variables that can be used to explain differences in fertility (the number of children that

women have). According to researchers at the Population Council (New York), four broad and sometimes overlapping perspectives are central to research on this topic. First is the *microdemographic* or sociobiological perspective, in which the immediate or proximate determinants of fertility are identified and measured. A second perspective emphasizes *fertility decision-making*—the process by which couples decide how many children to have. The third perspective deals with the *environment of fertility*—the economic, social, and institutional factors that help shape fertility desires and outcomes. Finally, an emphasis on *family planning policies and programs* shows how public and quasi-public agencies influence fertility, both directly and indirectly.

The *proximate determinants of fertility*, also called *intermediate variables*, are those biological and behavioral factors that most directly influence fertility—the mechanisms through which environmental, economic, social, and institutional factors operate. In 1956, demographers **Kingsley Davis** and Judith Blake identified eleven proximate determinants that operate at three different stages in the fertility process: intercourse, conception, and gestation. The proximate determinants that influence exposure to intercourse (*intercourse variables*) include age at entry into sexual union, permanent celibacy, and the proportion of the reproductive period spent after or between unions. *Conception variables* influence the chance of conception once intercourse has taken place. These variables include natural fecundity or infecundity, the use or non-use of contraception; and voluntary exposure to conditions or processes which alter fecundity—sterilization, for example. The last set of proximate determinants, *gestation variables*, are those factors which influence the chance of gestation and successful parturition once conception has taken place. The gestation variables include fetal mortality from involuntary causes (miscarriage) and fetal mortality from voluntary causes (induced abortion). More recently, demographer John Bongaarts identified four proximate determinants responsible for most of the variation in fertility observed throughout the world. These included: (1) proportion of women married; (2) contraceptive use; (3) induced abortion; and (4) duration of post-partum non-susceptibility to conception (mainly due to breastfeeding).

The *supply-demand framework* has been used to investigate the ways in which social and economic variables influence fertility and its proximate determinants. According to economics professor Richard Easterlin, three key factors in fertility decision-making exist: the demand for children (the number of children a couple would have if fertility control had no social or economic costs), the supply of children (the number of children a couple would have if they made no deliberate attempt to limit family size), and the costs of fertility regulation (economic, social, or psychic costs associated with obtaining and using birth control). These three factors play a critical role as the mechanisms through which broader socioeconomic and environmental factors influence fertility. The determinants of fertility (demand, supply, and cost) include variables such as female education, employment, religious **norms**, and cultural beliefs. Demographers Rodolfo A. Bulatao and Ronald D. Lee group these determinants into three main categories:

(1) the institutions, economic conditions, cultural norms, and physical environment of the **society** in which the couple lives; (2) the socioeconomic characteristics of the couple themselves; and (3) their reproductive history (nuptuality, childbearing experiences, etc.).

The economic approach to understanding variation in fertility tends to focus on *fertility decision-making*. This kind of investigation is based on the assumption that men and women make rational fertility decisions after explicitly or implicitly assessing the costs and benefits involved. Each couple can be expected to choose a **family size** which optimizes the psychic rewards of consumption. The economic approach (neo-classical household economics) generally treats children as time-intensive variables, leading researchers to focus on the ways in which women allocate their time between competing alternatives, such as childbearing and work. Demographers John Cleland and Christopher C.B. Wilson note that this emphasis on the value of women's time and labor has reinforced the notion that the social status and economic **autonomy** of women may be important mediating factors between economic modernization and fertility decline. Both macro- and micro-level studies have shown an inverse relationship between fertility and such structural variables as female education and **employment**. At the individual level, women with jobs and higher levels of education tend to have fewer children than others; at the societal level, the expansion of women's opportunities may reduce the attractiveness of childbearing relative to the other options available.

Unlike most economists, social structural theorists have emphasized the *environment of fertility*—the importance of regional and cultural determinants (rather than individual—and couple-specific factors)—in explaining variation in fertility levels. For example, researchers studying the European fertility decline found that non-socioeconomic determinants, such as religion, **language**, **ethnicity**, and region, appeared to exert a major influence on the timing of fertility decline. Institutional determinants (including local administrative **organization** and **structure**) may also have an important impact on fertility.

Last, **family planning** policies and programs have been effective in helping couples achieve their desired fertility levels. Most often, this support results in fertility decline. The effectiveness of a particular family planning program, however, depends upon the level of socioeconomic development in the community. Family planning strategies may, therefore, work best when designed in concert with other development efforts.

FESTINGER, LEON (1919-1989)
American psychologist and educator

Leon Festinger's work on cognitive dissonance is one of the landmark achievements in American **psychology**. First developed in *A Theory of Cognitive Dissonance* (1957), the theory explained how people were capable of believing one thing despite evidence to the contrary. Festinger argued that, above all else, people sought to maintain consistency in their worldview,

their **ideology**, their belief systems, and their attitudes. When facts or evidence come along that disturb that consistent worldview, a state of cognitive dissonance sets in. Cognitive dissonance, Festinger wrote, is a motivational state which contains within it a set of mechanisms—or triggers—that bring consistency back to a person's thinking, even if it means distorting or ignoring facts and reality.

Writing in the ideological rigid Cold War climate of the 1950s, at a time when the pressure for social **conformity** was an increasingly recognized problem in American life, Festinger tried to explain how people tried to fit in socially even to the extent of denying their own feelings. Specifically, he looked at the ways in which people become members of social groupings, especially those groups that required a stressful initiation, such as large corporations or social clubs. Once in, the person will continue to believe that membership in the **group** is satisfying even if that proves not to be the case. That is to say, if the group requires behavior and beliefs contrary to those of the person who sought membership, that person will deny the contradiction. In other words, the person will gradually subsume his own belief systems and come to accept those of the group.

Festinger was born to Jewish immigrant parents in Manhattan in 1919 and, like many of his generation, received his bachelor's degree from the City College of New York. He then went on to earn a master's degree and Ph.D. in psychology at the Iowa State University, the latter received in 1942. His first teaching position was at the University of Rochester from 1943 to 1945. For the next three years, Festinger served as associate professor at the Massachusetts Institute of Technology (MIT) before moving on for another three years as associate professor in psychology at the University of Michigan. From 1955 to 1968, he was a professor at Stanford University and then moved on to the New School for Social Research (now New School University) in New York City. There, he held the Else and Hans Staudinger Professor of Psychology chair from 1968 until his death in 1989. Festinger was also a fellow of the American Psychological Association and a member of the American Academy of Arts and Sciences and the National Academy of Sciences.

Throughout his professional career, Festinger continued to develop and refine his theory of cognitive dissonance, publishing *Conflict, Decision and Dissonance* in 1964. His other major work was *The Human Legacy*, published in 1983.

FEUDALISM

Feudalism is a political system in which land ownership determines authority in a given region. The owner, or lord, apportions land to vassals in exchange for their loyalty and service in military action as well as other duties regarding the upkeep and defense of the lord's domain. Various versions of this system developed around the world, notably in Japan, but feudalism as it is known today came out of the Roman Empire. Isolated freemen sought the protection, unavailable from the distant emperor, of more powerful local landowners. When

Roman lands were eventually overrun by Germanic tribes, feudalism replaced the empire as the governing system of Europe until the end of the medieval period, a time distinguished by weak, even powerless rulers.

In order to protect themselves and their **property** from invading hordes from Asia, Europe's large land holders developed feudalism to consolidate the interests of previously independent farmers. They granted land to knights who pledged an oath of fealty and aided them in defense against invaders. The knights became vassals upon acquiring their land, at which time they gained a certain amount of say in the affairs of the fiefdom, as their collective land was known. The original holder was still lord, but the vassals acted as a counsel of advisers and lawmakers. The power of these counsels varied greatly from place to place and was often controlled by the **church**, depending on the lord's religious affiliation. Eventually, this system grew into a vast hierarchy as land was subdivided again and again, forming smaller fiefs.

Because the lord and vassal titles were passed on from generation to generation, feudalism created a class system that became firmly entrenched in Europe during the Middle Ages (a term applied, variously, from the eighth to fifteenth centuries A.D.). The feudal system was gradually eroded by strengthening monarchies of Europe. As they became powerful enough to assert their authority over larger **territory**, the lords were simultaneously weakened. The Church supported the divine rights of the royal families to all land within their kingdoms forcing the lords to pledge loyalty to a still higher power in order to keep their land. Peasant rebellion and the gradual move from agriculture to manufacturing played a part, as well, and the power began to shift to cities after the twelfth century. Even so, much of feudalism survives in the legal code and in local politics. It helped to create a sense of **community** which was greatly influential in the ideological trend from tribalism and sectarianism toward national sovereignty and citizenship around much of the globe.

FEUERBACH, LUDWIG ANDREAS (1804-1872)

German philosopher

Ludwig Feuerbach was born on July 28, 1804, in Landshut, Bavaria, the fourth son of Paul Johann Anselm, a distinguished jurist, criminologist, and champion of **liberalism**, and Wilhelmina Tr''ster Feuerbach. Feuerbach's father, a temperamental and demanding man, ruled the family with stern authority, closely monitoring his children's education at all times. Feuerbach attended primary school in Munich and, in 1817, entered the Ansbach Gymnasium, completing his secondary education in 1822. The next year he enrolled at Heidelberg University to study theology where, in a course on speculative theology, he first became introduced to the philosophy of **Georg Wilhelm Friedrich Hegel**, whose thought heavily influenced Feuerbach throughout his lifetime. He was so taken with Hegel's ideas that within a year he transferred to the University of Berlin to study directly under the philosopher.

Leon Festinger *(AP/Wide World Photos, Inc.)*

At Berlin, Feuerbach studied under theologian Friedrich Schleiermacher and Hegel, soon abandoning his religious studies in favor of philosophy because he could no longer reconcile faith and reason. In 1825, he finally persuaded his father to allow him to transfer to the Philosophy Department. However, when the government discontinued the civil servant stipends to Feuerbach and his brothers, he was forced to transfer to the less expensive University of Erlangen. Nonetheless, financial hardship ultimately forced him to withdraw and return to Ansbach, where he composed his dissertation *Reason: Its Unity, Universality, and Infinity* (1828). Upon its submission to the Philosophy Department at Erlangen, Feuerbach was awarded his doctorate and offered a position on the faculty as a lecturer on the history of modern philosophy.

In 1830, Feuerbach's brief academic career ended by the publication of *Thoughts on Death and Immortality*, in which he denied the Christian idea of personal immortality. The topic of religion dominated his philosophical writings throughout his lifetime, and this publication was his first open assault on what he considered to be a subjective, self-deifying system of egotism. According to Feuerbach, the belief in personal immortality implied the infinite, and thus divine, nature of human beings. Therefore, to believe in the afterlife is equivalent to atheism because if humans are divine, then God cannot be. To avow one's own immortality is necessarily to disavow God's.

Even though *Thoughts on Death and Immortality*, which was considered heresy and politically threatening to the establishment, was published anonymously, Feuerbach was soon identified as the author. The repercussions were severe; in 1832 Feuerbach lost his position at Erlangen, and despite his academic friends' best attempts to appeal on his behalf, he never secured another academic position. He retreated into private life and wrote a series of three books on the history of philosophy. He married Berta Löw in 1837, and the couple moved to Löw's family estate near Bruckberg, where they lived modestly from proceeds of a porcelain factory Löw had inherited along with the profits from Feuerbach's writings. During his time at Bruckberg, Feuerbach wrote three more major works: *The Essence of Christianity* (1841), *The Essence of Religion* (1845), and *Lectures on the Essence of Christianity* (1848). *The Essence of Christianity*, which was hugely successful, had a lasting and important impact on **Karl Marx** and Frederick Engels and was heralded by humanists in both Europe and the United States.

In his philosophy, Feuerbach maintained a Hegelian perspective which became more and more focused on human beings' intrinsic relationship to nature and the dependence for meaning on the senses, rather than pure reason. In so doing he offered the negative of Hegel's ideas. Whereas Hegel argued that creation was the objectification of God as a means by which God comes to self-consciousness, Feuerbach suggested that the idea of God results in humanity's self-consciousness of its own essential nature. A human being (''I'') comes to self-consciousness over against something other than itself (''not I''). Hegel considered the ''not I'' to be the divine (''Thou''). For Feuerbach, the ''not I'' was both other humans and nature, thus allowing humanity to become aware of its unity within the species (thereby making way for **communication**, relationships, and **love**) and its uniqueness in contrast to its natural environment.

After the porcelain factory went bankrupt in 1859, Feuerbach and his wife moved to a more modest dwelling in Rechenberg, near Munich. Feuerbach was supported by a pension collected from his admirers that sustained the couple for the next ten years. He continued to write but failed to produce any works of sustained importance. In 1870 he suffered a stroke that left him incapacitated. Once again his admirers and supporters came to his aid and offered financial support to allow him to obtain proper medical care. Nonetheless, he grew increasingly weaker and died in Nuremberg, on September 13, 1872.

FICHTE, JOHANN GOTTLIEB (1762-1814)

German philosopher

Johann Gottlieb Fichte, son of Christian and Johanna Dorothea Schurich Fichte, was born in the small town of Rammenau near Bischofswerda in Saxony on May 19, 1762. He received financial sponsorship to attend the foundation school of Schulpforta, near Naumberg, from 1774 to 1780, where he was deeply influenced by the writings of Gotthold Ephraim Lessing and Baruch Spinoza. Honoring his mother's desires for him to become a minister, Fichte entered Jena in 1780 to study theology. After a year, he enrolled at Leipzig, where he remained until 1784 when financial difficulties forced him to withdraw. He took work as a family tutor, a job for which he was not particularly well suited due to his volatile and temperamental nature. He tutored first in Zurich and then Warsaw and Danzig. While in Zurich he met Johanna Maria Rahn, whom he married in 1793. They had one son, Immanuel Hermann.

In the late 1780s, Fichte studied extensively the ideas of Immanuel Kant. In a letter written in 1790, he described his joy at discovering Kant's philosophy of transcendental **idealism**: ''I have been living in a new world since reading [Kant's] *Critique of Practical Reason.* Propositions which I thought could never be overturned have been overturned for me. Things have been proven to me which I thought could never be proven.'' In 1791 Fichte sent Kant a manuscript in which he employed the Kantian principle of the primacy of practical reason to argue for the place of religious belief in philosophical thought. Because faith exists in the moral law, faith also necessarily exists in God, Fichte asserted, because God is revealed as the embodiment of moral reason. Kant passed the manuscript on to his publishers, and it appeared in 1792 as *Attempt at a Critique of All Revelation.* Widely read, the book generated considerable public attention and fame for Fichte. In 1793 Fichte was offered a chair at Jena. In his six years there, Fichte produced the basis of his philosophical epistemology, developing his key concepts in *Science of Knowledge* (1794). He expanded on the implications of his science of knowledge, or *Wissenschaftslehre*, in *Science of Rights* (1796-1797) and *The Science of Ethics as Based on the Science of Knowledge* (1798).

Fichte used Kantian transcendental idealism as the basis on which to formulate his **epistemology**. Before reading Kant's work, Fichte had struggled to reconcile the concepts of reason and freedom. Deeply influenced by the claims to the sovereignty of reason by philosophers Christian von Wolff and Spinoza, Fichte felt himself trapped into accepting Wolff's **determinism** or Spinoza's naturalistic pantheism. In either case, human freedom was sacrificed to the domination of reason; humanity's path was ultimately predetermined with no room for free, moral acts. Kant believed that reason, when treated with dogmatic allegiance, became unreasonable. Alternatively, Kant suggested that practical reason was, in fact, self-limiting, thus making room for morality and religion. This understanding gave Fichte the bridge between freedom and reason he had been looking for. In other words, Kant gave him a way both to affirm reason and to attest to humanity's freedom to act morally.

Although a loyal Kantian, Fichte did find room for improvement in his mentor's philosophy. Fichte attempted to develop a systematic presentation of Kant's ideas, supplementing his mentor's thought with that of his own. Essentially, he systematized Kantian **phenomenology** by linking Kant's theoretical and practical philosophy, subjects that Kant always treated separately. The result was Fichte's theory of *Wissenschaftslehre,* in which he posits that the development of a systematic philosophical treatment of consciousness must necessarily begin from a single, self-evident first principle. Considering two choices, Fichte rejects the materialist's reality of things-in-themselves and claims the freely self-positing ''I'' as the first principle of his transcendental idealism.

In developing this reflective mode of self-consciousness, Fichte outlined three processes. First, the pure I posits itself: It exists only insofar as it continues the activity of self-positing, which Fichte calls the ''thesis.'' Second, to be aware of itself, the I must necessarily have certain limitations, as Fichte explains, ''Consciousness works through reflection, and reflection is only through limitation.'' Thus the I must posit something other than itself, a non-I. This self-negation is termed the "antithesis." Finally, the thesis (positing) and antithesis (negating) must be reconciled as the "synthesis," in which the I limits the non-I, and the non-I limits the I. This synthesis involves two principles. First, the I posits itself in a reflective activity with the non-I, and second, the I posits the non-I in a reflective activity with the I. The first principle forms the foundation for Fichte's theoretical philosophy, and the second is the basis for his practical philosophy. In this way, Fichte creates an inseparable bond between "knowing" and "willing," or reason and moral action.

Fichte's tenure at Jena ended abruptly in 1799 after he was accused of atheism. When he offered to teach a class on Sundays, an anonymously written pamphlet accusing him of being a heretic and atheist began to circulate. He was a gifted and enthralling teacher but was often abrasive and brash; thus, he did not help his own cause during the ensuing "Atheist Controversy." After an inquiry that Fichte handled poorly, he offered his resignation and in 1799 left Jena for Berlin.

Over the next several years, Fichte lectured and wrote extensively. His publications, primarily drawn from his lectures, included *The Characteristics of the Present Age* (1806), *On the Nature of the Scholar, and Its Manifestations* (1806), and *The Way Towards the Blessed Life; or The Doctrine of Religion,* (1806). Fichte received wide fame in 1808 when he published *Addresses to the German Nation,* a publication based on a popular series of lectures given between December 1808 and March 1809. In the wake of Napoleon's triumph over Prussia in Jena and Auerstadt, Fichte revived German nationalism with a call for the renewal and moral regeneration of the German State. In 1810 Fichte was appointed dean of the Philosophy Department at the newly constituted University of Berlin, the first modern university. The next year he became the school's first rector.

Fichte continued to revise his *Wissenschaftslehre* throughout his lifetime, evidenced by numerous unpublished revisions discovered after his death. His early work influenced Hegel, who adopted Fichte's methodology of thesis, antithesis, and synthesis. Achieving fame as a popular lecturer and writer on the matters of political and social importance, his contribution to transcendental idealism earned him a place at the table with the time's most important philosophers. In December 1813, Fichte's wife contracted typhus from wounded soldiers whom she had attended in the hospital. Fichte became infected from his wife and died two months later, on January 29, 1814. He was buried next to Hegel in the cemetery of the Dorotheenkirche.

FIELD RESEARCH METHODS

Field research methods involve the first-hand examination of social subjects in their natural environment. Rather than allowing them to conduct research in a laboratory setting or through the use of impersonal survey instruments, field research methods take social scientists directly into "the field," the actual environment in which everyday action takes place. Also referred to as qualitative **ethnography**, field research includes a variety of observational and interviewing techniques.

The development of sociological field research methods took place primarily during the late 1940s and 1950s at the University of Chicago. Sociologists, such as W. I. Thomas, **Robert Park**, and Howard Becker, brought great recognition to the use of field research methods within the field of **sociology**. These researchers employed techniques that examined everyday experiences of human subjects, in order to sociologically interpret these experiences. Field researchers from **the Chicago School** of sociology thus developed a type of social scientific inquiry that arose as an alternative to more commonly employed quantitative statistical analyses.

The type of data collected in the context of field research differs from the statistical data produced in quantitative research. Data gathered from observational research takes the form of "field notes," a researcher's notes on what he or she actually sees taking place in the field. Data gathered in the context of **interview** research consists primarily of the subject's own words, thus reflecting the subject's interpretations of what is going on in his or her environment.

Oftentimes field researchers employ a combination of observational and interviewing techniques to produce a more well- rounded analysis of subjects' everyday experiences. Because field research studies involve the analysis of words and behavioral observations, findings drawn from this type of research do not consist of conclusive statements about numbers and statistics, as in the case of quantitative data analysis. Rather, the conclusions drawn from qualitative data analysis present assertions about overriding themes and ideas of the research.

Observational field research consists of two main techniques. In *passive observation* researchers simply enter the site they wish to study and record the activities and behaviors of subjects. The field notes produced during passive observation are later analyzed and interpreted. In *participant observation* researchers not only observe the activities of their subjects but also participate in those activities. While passive observation is thought to provide an objective or detached analysis of social action, participant observation enables field researchers to gain a subjective or "insider" understanding of social action from the actors' perspective.

Interview research can take various forms as well. Field researchers often employ informal interviewing techniques in the context of their observational analyses. During the process of either passive or participant observation, researchers often supplement their observations with informal questions which allows researchers to immediately clarify any questions they may have about what is observed. Such clarifications enhance researchers' later efforts to interpret what they have observed in the field. Rather than simply relying on one perspective— the researcher's—the use of informal interviewing in the field allows researchers to incorporate the subjects' own interpretations of their behaviors and activities.

Many researchers choose to supplement their observational field research with more formal, in-depth interviewing.

In these cases, researchers construct an interview guide, which consists of a structured list of questions that are asked of every subject. The data produced from in-depth interviewing consists of the subjects' exact words, which are typically tape-recorded and later transcribed. Like informal interviewing, formal interviews provide the benefit of enhancing researchers' observational activities, providing additional data from which to draw research conclusions.

While many researchers employ qualitative in-depth interviews to supplement observational field research, others utilize formal interviews as the primary method of investigation in a field research study. Oftentimes these researchers use observation methods as secondary, supplemental techniques for producing data. For example, interview researchers often take field notes about subjects' appearance, demeanor, or immediate environment in an effort to enhance transcription data.

While the major journals of sociology still publish few qualitative studies, journals such as *Qualitative Sociology* provide an arena for the dissemination of field research. These disciplinary circumstances reveal the traditional division between quantitative and qualitative research within sociology. However, more and more social scientists are coming to understand the value of using both quantitative and qualitative methods in their investigation of social phenomena.

FIELD THEORY

Field theory, refers to the theory of fields advanced by Pierre Bourdieu in several of his works, most notably *Outline of a Theory of Practice* (1984). Field refers to a specific social setting where actors compete over **status** and specific tangible and intangible goods. As part of his sociological project of developing a scientific practice that both avoided the objectivist pitfalls of **structuralism** and the existentially-oriented subjectivism, Bourdieu has systematically developed a theoretical apparatus that attempts to account for the reproduction of structures, like class domination, as well as for the improvisation of actors within those structures. The mediating concepts, like habitus and field, accomplish this task. Bordieu developed this approach through a long series of studies, from early research in Algeria, in *Algeria 1960* (1979) to more recent works on class **domination**, *Distinction* (1984), and politics, *Language and Symbolic Power* (1991).

Bourdieu's theory of practice seeks to understand the reproduction of structures of domination and, more specifically, class domination. Actors themselves tend to reproduce structures of domination in their thinking by the way they **structure** their preferences and the way they understand the world. Persons within dominated groups inherit these mental structures, which tend to render their social world as legitimated but also structure the way they perceive possible choices. This mental structure, called habitus in this framework, is one of the person's markers of social origin because it structures the way the person will understand future experiences. The other marker is the kind and quantity of social competences a person inherits, here referred to as a kind of capital. A person's attributes and status are marked according to the kinds of capitals—economic, cultural, social—that person possesses.

The concept of field is the third, and in some ways most important, concept of Bourdieu's **sociology**. Whereas capital and habitus account for the reproduction of structures of domination, field accounts for social change and for the improvisation of actors. Field refers to the set of objective relationships between actors competing over a specific capital. As such, the modern social world is composed of many different kinds of fields, the field of politics, the field of art, the intellectual field and so on, where persons compete for status and power by becoming competent in that field. Each field has its own logic of what counts within it. In the intellectual field, education counts more than wealth, for instance. Though relatively few scholars have taken on Bourdieu's approach entirely, the concept of field has been extremely influential in the sociology of **culture** and in political sociology.

FIRST NATIONS (ABORIGINAL CANADIANS)

The First Nations of Canada refer to the collective tribes of native, or aboriginal people, that reside in the seven provinces of Canada. The First Nations people are recognized by the Canadian Constitution as one of the nations that founded Canada, along with the English and French. However, until developments that took place at the Canadian First Ministers Conference on Aboriginal Rights in 1983–1987, First Nations members had no actual input into the country's constitution. Historically, other events served to silence the collective voice of First Nations members. The Canadian Indian Act of 1927 made it illegal for First Nations members to form **political organizations**. They were also forbidden to speak their native language or to practice their traditional religion. Religious rituals that were banned included the Potlatch ceremony, a practice that many of the tribes across Canada had in common.

First Nations peoples attempted to form a unified, political presence first after World War I (1914–1918). They formed the League of Nations, as well as the League of Indians in Canada. However, these faced resistance from the ruling Canadian government. Canadian tribes again attempted to form a national lobby group in the late 1940s (The North American Brotherhood), but it was again suppressed by the ruling government. As technology advanced rapidly after World War II (1939–1945), native Canadians realized that they would need to work hard to match the level of political expertise already established Canadian political institutions. The First Nations continued to attempt to form a unified and effective political presence. Among the challenges they faced were creating a single voice for the many tribes across the nation. The Assembly of First Nations was created in the 1980s and it included all tribal leaders. Public awareness of the issues that First Nations people faced reached a peak in the late 1980s. At this time, the Canadian government failed to recognize that First Nations had the right to self governance. However, the heightened publicity around the meetings that took place made more of the general public aware of First Nations issues such as poverty, education, living conditions, and **health care**.

The Assembly of Nations continues to act as a political and lobbying force and is involved with issues that impact Canadian native tribes. In the late 1990s the Canadian government formally apologized to the Assembly of First Nations for brutal treatment of native children in residential schools. The Canadian government also agreed to return land to the First Nations indigenous people. At the end of the 1990s, the Canadian government considered settling remaining land claims and recognizing the right to self governance for Canadian First Nations.

FISHER, RONALD AYLMER (1890-1962)
English statistician and geneticist

A statistician who injected fresh ideas into quantitative biological experiments and a pioneer in the theory of genetics, Ronald Aylmer Fisher is the author of *Statistical Methods for Research Workers* (1925). This ''bible'' of applied statistics, which remained in print for fifty years, is considered so difficult to read that a colleague once remarked, ''no student should attempt to read it unless he had read it before.''

Fisher, a surviving twin and the youngest of seven children, was born in the London suburb of East Finchley, England, on February 17, 1890. He was a precocious child. Supposedly, when he was about three years old, he questioned the process of successively dividing the number 2. He finally decided, on his own, that ''half of a sixteenth must be thirty-toof.''

During his school years at Stanmore Park and Harrow, Fisher developed the habit of seeing complex geometrical problems in his mind. His poor eyesight prevented him from reading or writing under artificial light. So he learned to listen to lectures without taking notes and to solve problems by visualizing them. He earned a scholarship to Cambridge in 1909, studying mathematics and theoretical physics with interests in biometry and genetics. Before graduating in 1912, he published his first paper, detailing the fitting of frequency curves. Fisher worked at various jobs after Cambridge until he joined the Mercantile and General Investment Company in London (1913–1915) and then became a public school teacher (1915–1919). During this period, he published a paper on statistics and two on **eugenics**, the science of using selective mating to improve the human race. Convinced that lower socioeconomic classes were less talented than his own privileged class, he grew concerned because the former were producing children at a greater rate than the latter. That may have influenced the decision of Fisher and his wife, Ruth Eileen Guinness, whom he married in 1917, to have eight children. The couple later separated.

Although he was apparently ineffective as a teacher, Fisher enjoyed a reputation as a brilliant mathematician, even if he could not explain his ideas to others, and he received two promising job offers in 1919. One was at Galton Laboratory in University College, London, to work with statistician Karl Pearson, with whom Fisher later developed a lifelong feud. Instead, Fisher joined the Rothamsted Experimental Station, north of London. His first task was to analyze some sixty-six years of statistical **data**, which he did over the next 14 years

The First Nations refer to the collective tribes of native or aboriginal people that reside in the seven provinces of Canada *(Corbis Corporation [Bellevue]).*

as well as analyze the station's plant breeding experiments. In plant experiments, Fisher tried to find ways to produce more and better data with less time and effort, a study which led to his theory of randomization. Inaccurate data often resulted from inadvertently biased material selection in experiments. Fisher said that all material units in an experiment must be randomly selected samples from the entire population they are intended to represent. That would lighten the effects of variability in experimental materials.

Fisher's work with plant-breeding experiments led to the publication of *The Genetical Theory of Natural Selection* (1930). Pursuing his interest in genetics by breeding small animals even in his own home, Fisher concluded that Charles Darwin's natural selection model for evolutionary change was superior to genetic mutation.

In 1933, Fisher left Rothamsted for University College, where he occupied the Galton Chair of Eugenics for ten years. He established a blood-typing department in 1935 and also published *Design of Experiments*, another statistical landmark. Keenly interested in human genetics, Fisher held alarmist views about the future of humankind. Regarded as an authentic genius even by his dissenters, to whom he was invariably hostile, Fisher nonetheless was seen by many as quirkish and reactionary and a master of the unbarbed phrase.

Fisher returned to Cambridge in 1943 as Balfour Professor of Genetics until his formal retirement in 1957. President of the Royal Society (1952–1954), Fisher was knighted in 1952. In the late 1950s, he published several articles on his theory of a cause-and-effect relationship between smoking and cancer. In all, he wrote some three hundred papers and seven books during his career. In 1959, Fisher moved to Adelaide, Australia, where he became a statistical researcher for the Commonwealth Scientific and Industrial Research Organization, a group founded by several former students. He died there on July 19, 1962.

Ronald A. Fisher *(The Library of Congress)*

FIXATION

Sigmund Freud theorized that the developmental stages of infancy and early childhood chart our lives in ways that are difficult to change. He believed that most adult neuroses could be attributed to a fixation developed during one of these stages of early life. Freud was especially concerned about how these stages were related to sexual development in later life, and in this he was, and continues to be, quite controversial. In his time, it was considered by many to be outlandish that an infant sucking on her mother's breast was experiencing sexual gratification, yet Freud classified it as such and composed a theory of psychosexual development.

Freud's theory of psychosexual development suggests that children pass through several stages in their earliest years. These stages are the oral stage, the anal stage, the phallic stage, the latency stage, and genital stage. During each stage, children learn to gratify themselves (Freud would say sexually) via distinct patterns of behavior. During the oral stage, for instance, children learn that the highest level of physical gratification occurs through oral stimulation. (They feed by sucking, they routinely place objects in their mouths, etc.) It was

Freud's view that during any one of these stages a person could become fixated—that is, they could be so gratified or, on the other hand, so unfulfilled, that they are marked for life by this fixation. Someone who has a fixation at the oral stage of development, for instance, might suck his or her thumb, eat or drink excessively, chew pencils, or smoke cigarettes. Adults fixated during this period of development are also thought to be inclined toward clinging, dependent relationships. Those fixated during the anal phase of psychosexual development are typically thought of as being overly controlling and obsessed with neatness or cleanliness.

Freud also considered **regression** closely linked to fixation. In his famous *Introductory Lectures on Psycho-Analysis,* he spoke of human development as a journey into new territory, much like an early migration of primitive peoples into new territory. He states that as people migrated into new, unexplored territory, certain members of the party might stop along the way at a place that offered them the prospect of a good life. These stopping points would be analogous to the fixations people develop in early life, attaching themselves to a period of safety and security before the entire journey of life is fully accomplished.

FOCUS GROUPS

The term "focus group" refers to a unit used in qualitative research in which **data** are collected through group interaction on a topic or "focus" determined by a researcher, who typically serves as moderator. The emphasis in focus groups, as opposed to other qualitative methodologies, is upon the effect of group interaction upon participants' responses. Similar to many other qualitative strategies, the goal of such research is not to acquire large amounts of generalizable data from a cross-section of the population; usually the group sizes are much too small. Instead, sampling methods for focus groups are most effective if they are geared toward the study's theoretical objectives. The intimate nature of focus groups provides their greatest advantages; both the ability to produce concentrated amounts of data on the research topic and the reliance upon group interaction are benefits that come from this type of research.

Group **interview** methodologies, used as early as Bogardus's work (1926), were often used in applied settings during the wartime era to examine such topics as propaganda effectiveness. They gained popularity through the work of market researchers, an arena where they are still commonly used. As a research tool, focus groups are highly versatile and can be used in a variety of capacities. They can be utilized as a principal or sole method of gathering data, they can be used as a supplementary source in which some other method is used primarily, or they can be used as one of several techniques in a multi-method study (in which there is no primary data-gathering method).

Merton, Fiske, and Kendall (1990) suggested that an effective focus group interview has four criteria: to cover the largest possible range of relevant topics; to provide data that are as specific as possible; to encourage interaction that examines the feelings of the interviewees; and to take into account the context used by participants in their discussion. In applying these criteria, Morgan (1997) offered several practical suggestions. He argued that a group of six to ten homogenous (i.e., by sex or age group) participants compose a group, that three to five groups are used in a project, and that a relatively high reliance is placed on structured moderator involvement. Morgan suggested that a purposive sample of strangers be used in a focus group. Given that the aim of focus groups is to induce comfortable interaction among participants, this seems counterintuitive. However, he argued that a main goal of focus groups is to examine the underlying assumptions inherent in a specific social situation; these assumptions would naturally go unspoken if they were commonly acknowledged, thus members who are unfamiliar with one another would best serve the purposes of the research.

FOLKLORE AND TRADITION

Folklore is an important part of tradition. In general terms, folklore comprises part of the **culture**, customs, and beliefs of a **society**, based on popular tradition and handed down generally by the spoken word or by demonstration. In some instances, the term, folklore, is restricted to oral tradition only to separate it from the written literature. Folklore may include music and dance and various art forms. Stories, sea chanteys, ancient rituals, folk dances, and even barn decorating with hex signs may be passed from generation to generation, from Appalachian grandmother to grandson, from an elderly blues singer in Harlem to a rapt audience, from a long forgotten explanation to the present rules for stacking hay in Kansas.

Serious studies of folklore began in the early nineteenth century. The aim of these so-called folklorists was to trace these quaint customs to their origins, depicting a kind of mental history of humankind. The appearance of the Grimm Brothers' first two collections of fairy tales in 1812 and 1815 was a great inspiration to folklorists everywhere. Inspired scholars worldwide began to record oral and written traditions. These included national ballads and plays, arts and crafts, and even riddles and proverbs. In time, all this material needed to be classified. The historical-geographical method of classification, devised by Kaarle Krohn and other Finnish scholars, was in popular use during the first half of the twentieth century. With this research method, every variation on a tale, for instance, was classified regarding time and place in order to reconstruct the original form. Although the first studies into folklore were interested in rural peasants or sought out those apart from mainstream society, by the mid-twentieth century research had also expanded into the **cities**, where it was recognized that customs and characteristic arts had long existed. Emphasis began to shift from long ago to the present, delving more into the meaning and function of a particular **custom** for current society.

Folktales, a major portion of folklore, can be divided into four general types: legends, myths, fairy tales, and ballads.

Legends claim to be eye witness accounts of history, such as the tale of "Rip Van Winkle" by Washington Irving. The "Pied Piper of Hamelin" is another popular legend, as are the tall tales of the American South and West, featuring Paul Bunyan and other colorful characters. *Myths* are often viewed as sacred truths, although the genres overlap. Greek tales of heroes and monsters are generally regarded as myths. *Fairy tales* are fiction, though they may harbor many themes of myths and legends. They abound in all countries and include such favorites as "Sleeping Beauty," "Rumpelstiltskin," and "Hansel and Gretel." *Ballads* have been studied extensively in the United States. They include songs of the chain gang and the western cowboy, sea chanteys such as "Blow the Man Down," the classic American narrative tale of Frankie and Johnny, and countless unforgettable Negro spirituals.

Often neglected in the study of folklore are the elements of so-called nonliterary folklore—superstition, folk drama, and children's games. The saying, "If your nose itches, you're going to kiss a fool," is an example of superstitions that have become part of folklore. Although it is generally difficult or impossible to ascertain the origins of these sayings, in some cases, such as "when frogs croak, winter's beginning," they may simply stem from some keen nature observations over the years. Folk dramas generally reinforce ancient myths, although they are not necessarily connected with them. Children's games and rhymes often reflect the line of oral transmission, such as Jack Sprat who could eat no fat or Little Jack Horner who found his way to goodness through a plum.

Research into folklore continues today with folklorists all over the world able to share **data** and findings. A rich source of information in the United Sates is the American Folklore Society, which has published the *Journal of American Folklore* since 1888. It contains excellent collections as well as analyses and theories of beliefs, myths, and tales. The society holds annual meetings as well. For the amateur folklorist, courses are taught at many American colleges and universities. Numerous magazines on the subject are published yearly, including the *Southern Folklore Quarterly*, New York Folklore Quarterly, *and the Journal of Popular Culture*. There is no national archive for folklore, but the Smithsonian Institution in Washington, D.C., has added a section on festivals and performances to its long outstanding interest in native Americans.

FOLKWAYS

Folkways are the general customs and accepted behaviors of a group, society, or common people. These customs are **norms** regarding commonplace behavior and are designed to facilitate comfortable living in a **society**. Folkways are typically mentioned as the companion to **mores**, which are seen as the more important and vital norms of a society without which the **group** would cease to function. These terms were developed by **William Graham Sumner** (1840-1910) in 1906 as part of a classification scheme for designating which habits developed as a result of living within a given society and which were morally necessary for survival within that society.

Folkways are established through trial and error. Behavior is attempted and either accepted or rejected by society's

Folklore comprises part of the culture, customs, and beliefs of a society, and may include music, dance, and various art forms *(AP/Wide World Photos, Inc.)*.

members. If a behavior is acceptable, it is deemed appropriate and may be repeated without fear of **sanction**. If the behavior is rejected the individual performing the behavior is subject to sanctions or punishment from other members of the group. Folkways are only mildly enforced and sanctions for the violation are typically not severe. For example, chewing with one's mouth closed at dinner or wearing proper attire to a wedding ceremony are norms that, when followed, make the occasion seem commonplace and unremarkable. However, when these folkways are violated, others could become uncomfortable with the situation and may act to rectify the violation. The appropriate sanctions in response to the violation will take a fairly mild form, such as ridicule, laughter, or requests from peers to cease the behavior. An individual is not likely to face arrest for chewing with his/her mouth open or wearing a baseball uniform to a formal occasion.

Sumner further reasoned that individuals follow these folkways despite the lack of threatening sanctions because of four aspects of **conformity** established within a society. First, as people are socialized or indoctrinated into the society, they are repeatedly told the correct way to do things; this conditioning serves to plant the seeds of conformity. As a result of this indoctrination, people begin to behave habitually in certain ways. Assuming the initial behavior supports the prescribed norms the folkway should be reinforced. Third is the knowledge that other society members are expecting a certain behavior, conforming to the folkways becomes the practical way of behaving which allows daily life to continue uninterrupted. Finally, and closely associated with the third aspect of conformity, is our need for approval from fellow members of society. By following the prescribed behaviors, we are doing the "right thing" and will be rewarded by those closest to us.

Although intended by Sumner to indicate only the informal or customary norms of society, some have redefined folkways to indicate the totality of norms held by a group. Under this definition, the formal, moral, or law-based norms, traditionally the separate category of mores, become a specific subcategory of folkways. In most cases, however, mores and folkways are still mentioned as mutually exclusive categories representing different levels of normative behavior.

See also Norms

FORMAL SOCIOLOGY

The concept of formal sociology was developed in the late nineteenth century by the German sociologist **Georg Simmel**. On the one hand, Simmel sought to defend the possibility of sociology as a science against those who would deny any social reality outside of or in addition to individuals, thus depriving sociology of any object to investigate. On the other hand, Simmel sought to avoid an all-encompassing conception of **society** which would deprive sociology of its own distinctive object or field of investigation. The solution to this dilemma, according to Simmel, is to focus neither on individuals nor on society, but rather on **interaction** between individuals. "One should properly speak," Simmel insisted, "not of society, but of sociation."

Formal sociology thus begins with social ties or transactions; it places importance on the nature of the social tie rather than what the tie connects. The task of formal or "pure" sociology is to investigate these patterns of sociation, which can be analytically distinguished from the content of social life. Simmel recognized that any concrete interaction among individuals "always arises on the basis of certain drives or for the sake of certain purposes." However, formal sociology "abstracts the mere element of sociation" from the content of social life. Simmel provided the following as examples of social forms abstracted from particular contents: "superiority and subordination, competition, **division of labor**, formation of parties, representation, [and] inner solidarity coupled with exclusiveness toward the outside." Conversely, content is defined as "everything present in the individuals... in the form of drive, interest, purpose, inclination, psychic state, [and] movement.... Sociation thus is the form (realized in innumerable, different ways) in which individuals grow together into units that satisfy their interests." There is no tight link between form and content: the same form may allow the realization of various interests, or the same interest may be realized in different forms. However, history remains important in formal sociology for heuristic purposes, as a source of examples.

Formal sociology rests on the assumption that examination of the abstract forms of sociation can lead to new insights. Some of the best examples of these kinds of insights can be found in Simmel's own work. For instance, Simmel showed how the emergence of overlapping **group** affiliations leads to individuation. Overlapping group affiliations can also help to explain how more general social categories (such as wage laborer) arise from a multiplicity of more specific categories (such as trades). Other insights can be gleaned from a formal analysis of dyads and triads. Simmel pointed out that the withdrawal of any one member threatens the existence of a dyad, unlike larger groups. As a result, the dyad does not transcend its members and "does not attain that super-personal life which the individual feels to be independent of himself." This, Simmel suggested, is the "structural reason" (his expression) why intimacy and individuality tends to be greater within dyads and why the individual members of dyads are less likely to lose their sense of personal responsibility for the group's actions. Similarly, Simmel argued that the group-forming or mediating functions and the strategic advantages of third parties are to be explained by the triad itself as a form or pattern of interaction, not by the individuals who compose it or their aims and interests.

While most sociologists have eschewed the restriction of social inquiry to form alone, Simmel's formal sociology has had a significant impact. Erving Goffman's work, for example, continued to investigate the consequences and constraints of social forms. Goffman examined techniques of impression management while leaving aside "the specific content of any activity presented by the individual participant, or the role it plays in the interdependent activities of an on-going social system." Goffman assumed that the techniques of impression management and the "contingencies associated with the employment of these techniques... are quite general; they seem to occur everywhere in social life, providing a clear-cut dimension for formal sociological analysis." More generally, close attention to the consequences and constraints of different forms of sociation is characteristic of a variety of approaches within contemporary sociology. These include approaches as diverse as the structural sociology of **Peter Blau**; the figurational sociology of Norbert Elias, which views dancing or game-playing as the most appropriate models for understanding social life; and contemporary network analysis, as exemplified by the work of Mark Granovetter and Ronald Burt.

FOSTER CARE

Foster care denotes a situation in which an individual is cared for outside the parental home, in an individual **family**, **group** setting, or other children's **institution**. Although many youngsters may spend their entire childhood in foster care, this situation is not intended to be permanent. It is estimated that one in twenty American children will at some time need the special help offered by foster care, even for a short period. Foster care services come under the heading of child welfare, which is concerned with the well being of children and problems of child-rearing, such as abuse, neglect, abandonment, and teenage pregnancy.

Foster care has a long worldwide history. Ancient Jewish custom put relatives in charge of orphaned minor children. The Catholic Church in Europe placed abandoned youngsters in facilities as early as the fourth century. Elizabethan Poor Laws, passed in 1601 during the reign of England's Elizabeth I, placed dependent minors in so-called poorhouses, or created an indenture system whereby they worked for their keep. The New York Children's Aid Society was established in 1853; however, nationwide laws to determine standards for care did not exist, and children were often poorly treated. Public agencies and religious groups set up orphanages, but it was not until 1909 in a White House Conference on Children that care was directed toward the individual child. The Children's Bureau was established, now part of the Department of Health and Human Services, heading federal programs dealing with foster care. Numerous child welfare agencies now exist at various federal, state, and voluntary levels.

Today there are more than 130,000 licensed foster families in the United States. These families are supervised by child

There are currently more than 130,000 licensed foster families in the United States *(AP/Wide World Photos, Inc.)*.

Michel Foucault *(Corbis Corporation [Bellevue])*

welfare agencies and paid for the basic needs of the child in their care. Some families spend their entire lives caring for foster children, and some eventually adopt them. Some offer only emergency care, for example, a few nights or weeks of shelter for a homeless teenager. Social workers conduct home studies of foster families before they are allowed to care for children.

FOUCAULT, MICHEL (1926-)
French philosopher, teacher, and writer

Michel Foucault is remembered as a thinker who tried to show that the basic ideas which people normally believe to be permanent truths about human nature and **society** actually change throughout the course of history. He regularly tested long-held assumptions, especially about mental illness, prisons, police, insurance, care of the mentally ill, sexuality, gay rights, welfare, and the effects of power.

Born in Poitiers, France, Foucault studied **philosophy** and psychology at the elite École Normale Superieure in Paris. During the 1960s, he served as head of the philosophy departments at the University of Clermont-Ferrand and the Universi-

ty of Vincennes. In 1970, he was elected to the highest academic post in France, the College de France, where he took the title, Professor of the History of Systems of Thought. During the 1970s and 1980s his international reputation grew as he lectured around the world.

German philosophers Frederick Nietzsche and **Martin Heidegger** were major influences on Foucault's thought, as were philosophies from ancient and medieval times. Foucault explored the shifting patterns of power within a society and the ways in which power at various levels affects individuals. He investigated how beliefs which society hold to be absolutely true in one era—for example, the idea that homosexuals are mentally ill—are proven false later and replaced by other beliefs held to be absolutely true. Foucault also studied how everyday practices, including sexuality, help shape identity, and he argued that each way of understanding has advantages and disadvantages.

In his early period, Foucault traced how, in the Western world, madness, which was once thought to be divinely inspired, came to be thought of as mental illness. He attempted to expose the creative force of madness that Western societies have traditionally repressed. In the last years of his life, Foucault questioned whether imprisonment is a more humane punishment than torture. He also traced the way in which people in Western societies have come to understand themselves as sexual beings, and he related how moral and ethical beliefs affect sexuality.

Charles Fourier *(The Library of Congress)*

A large part of Foucault's later years also were spent showing that Western society has developed a new kind of power called bio-power: a system of control that traditional concepts of **authority** are unable to understand and criticize. Rather than being repressive, this new power enhances life. Foucault encouraged people to resist the **welfare state** by developing individual ethics with which they can turn their lives into what others can respect and admire.

Foucault's major works include: *Mental Illness and Personality* (1954); *History of Madness in the Classical Age* (1961); *The Birth of the Clinic* (1963); *The Order of Things* (1966); and *The Archaeology of Knowledge* (1969). His later works dealing with sexuality and religion, as well as modern thought, include: *Discipline and Punish* (1975); *History of Sexuality* (1976); *The Confessions of the Flesh* (unpublished); *The Use of Pleasure* (1984), and *The Care of the Self* (1984).

FOURIER, CHARLES (1772-1837)
French social theorist

His reconstruction of **society** came to be known as Fourierism. Born François Charles Marie Fourier in Besancon, France, on April 7, 1772, Fourier was the ultimate **prophet** of a utopian society, so utopian that "sea water could be turned into lemonade" and human beings had remarkable powers to change their world. He departed almost entirely from established insti-

tutions and philosophies, rejecting the society in which he lived. Partly because of his lofty ideals and partly because he coupled them to a strange "theory of universal analogy," scholars have had a difficult time in accepting Fourier's theories.

As a child, Fourier was educated at a local Jesuit high school and was then apprenticed to various businesses. When the French Revolution began, Fourier, then living in Lyons, sided with the counter-revolutionaries. He was drafted into the army in 1794 but was discharged for ill health two years later. For years, Fourier lived in relative poverty in Lyons or Paris, working at odd jobs, extolling the virtues of his reconstruction of society, and waiting in vain for someone to finance his theories. In 1812, he inherited money from his mother's estate and was able to spend his time refining his views.

Fourier first aired his theories while working in Lyon. His article, "Universal Harmony," was published in the *Bulletin de Lyon*, 1803. His major work *The Social Destiny of Man, Or the Theory of the Four Movements* appeared in 1808. From then until his death in 1937, Fourier expounded on "Fourierism" in numerous pamphlets and books, among them *Treatise on Domestic and Agricultural Association,* 1822, and *False Industry, Divided, Disgusting, and Lying, and its Antidote,* 1835–36.

Fourier's reconstruction of society was based on associations of producers known as phalanges (or phalanxes). The phalange was a cooperative agricultural community with the responsibility for the welfare of each person in it. Individual members of the phalange would be rewarded according to the phalange's total productivity. Fourier believed that the phalange system would distribute wealth more equitably than **capitalism**, and in that he foreshadowed the theories of Karl Marx.

To Fourier, these concepts were not merely ideas he had constructed but actual laws that existed to govern society, much as Isaac Newton had discovered laws of physical motion. Fourier argued that a natural order existed, evolving in eight ascending periods. In the highest stage, called harmony, human emotions could be expressed freely. To reach that stage, society would best be divided into phalanges. The phalange was the ideal **community** for human society because, Fourier claimed, humans had twelve passions. These passions could be divided into 810 characters. The ideal phalange would contain 1,620 people, which meant endless combinations of characters. If the phalange were properly run, the passions of every individual would be fulfilled. Fourier added great detail to life in the phalange, including daily routines, designs of dwellings, nursery furniture, workers' uniforms, order in the community, and so on. A harmony on earth, Fourier reasoned, would extend to a kind of cosmic harmony.

To many, Fourier's ideas seemed bizarre, his writings often rambling and eccentric. In fact, some of his critics called him insane. Yet, over the years he captured a faithful group of supporters all over Europe and abroad. His followers learned to select those ideas that were deemed useful. This qualified acceptance led to the phalange concept being tried out in France, where Fourierism became a significant socialist sect in the 1840s but failed by the end of the decade. In the

United States, Fourierism was introduced by Albert Brisbane, a wealthy New Yorker who discovered Fourier while traveling in France. Brisbane studied under him for two years and returned home to try out his mentor's ideas, which Brisbane then called Associationism. A number of communities were launched but were unsuccessful, such as Brook Farm in Massachusetts (1841–46) and the North American Phalanx, Red Bank, New Jersey.

Fourier died on October 10, 1837. Although his work has never been widely read, an interest in his psychological writings, most notably his analysis of **love** and repression, emerged after World War II. Today, these theories, according to some scholars, mark Fourier as a precursor of Freud.

FRAZIER, EDWARD FRANKLIN (1894–1962)

American sociologist

Edward Franklin Frazier (1894–1962), one of America's leading sociologists, specialized in studies of black people in North and South America and in Africa. On September 24, 1894, E. Franklin Frazier was born in Baltimore, Maryland. He earned his bachelor of arts degree *cum laude* at Howard University in 1916. From 1916 to 1918 Frazier taught in secondary schools in Alabama, Virginia, and Maryland. In 1919 he began graduate studies at Clark University, Worcester, Massachusetts, receiving a master of arts degree in **sociology** in 1920. As a research fellow at the New York School of Social Work (1920–1921), Frazier studied longshoremen in New York City. In 1921–1922 he studied folk high schools in Denmark. From 1922 to 1924 Frazier was an instructor in sociology at Morehouse College, serving also as director of the Atlanta School of Social Work (1922–1927). He married Marie E. Brown in 1922.

Frazier's essay ''The Pathology of Race Prejudice'' in *Forum* (June 1927) drew an analogy between race **prejudice** and insanity. As a result, Frazier had to leave Atlanta to avoid a white lynch mob. From 1927 to 1929 he pursued advanced study at the University of Chicago, receiving his doctorate in sociology in 1931 for *The Negro Family in Chicago* (1932). From 1929 to 1934 he worked under Charles S. Johnson, an outstanding African American sociologist, at Fisk University. Frazier returned to Howard University in 1934 as head of the department of sociology. In 1959 he became professor emeritus in the department of sociology and the African studies program.

From 1944 to 1951 Frazier served as part-time instructor at New York School of Social Work, Columbia University, and from 1957 to 1962 lectured at the School of Advanced International Studies, Johns Hopkins University. Frazier also served as visiting professor at several other colleges and universities. In 1948 Frazier served as president of the American Sociological Society, and he was chief of the Division of the Applied Social Sciences, Department of Social Sciences, United Nations Educational, Scientific, and Cultural Organization, in 1951–1953. Frazier published 8 books, 18 chapters in books, and at least 89 articles. His most significant work was on the African American **family**. In *The Negro Family in Chicago, The Free Negro Family* (1932), and *The Negro Family in the United States* (1939) Frazier offered pioneering interpretations of the character, history, and **influence** of the black family. His concept of the black **matriarchy**, despite recent challenges and new approaches, dominates work on the black family.

Frazier also offered candid, often polemical, analyses of the role of the black middle class, as in *Black Bourgeoisie* (1957). *The Negro in the United States* (1949; rev. ed. 1957) and *Race and Culture Contacts in the Modern World* (1957; rev. ed. 1965) contain Frazier's analysis of the black experience throughout the world.

Frazier's death on May 17, 1962, prevented completion of his study of the black **church**. Only an outline of his views, *The Negro Church in America* (1961), was published. G. Franklin Edwards, a colleague and friend, described Frazier as ''a tough-minded intellectual'' and ''a fine exponent of the best tradition in American sociology and scholarship.''

FREE WILL

The concept of free will involves the assertion that human beings have the ability to choose between two or more genuine alternatives in determining their actions, which are not completely controlled by such external factors as genetic makeup, environment, past history, or upbringing. In *The Significance of Free Will* (1996), Robert Kane defines free will as ''the power of agents to be the ultimate creators (or originators) and sustainers of their own ends or purposes.'' Whereas structural-functionist sociological approaches yield nothing to free will by claiming that all social action is caused, other paradigms, such as **phenomenology** and symbolic interactionism, incorporate an understanding of free choice as a means of understanding the purpose, motive, and meaning of social actions.

The implications of free will have been deliberated for centuries, focusing primarily on the issue of moral responsibility. If human beings possess the will to choose their course of action, they can be said to be morally responsible. However, if free will is a farce and all human action is determined, then there is no room for the concept of moral responsibility. How can human beings be held accountable for actions over which they have no control? True responsibility lies with the true cause. Only if humans being can cause, determine, or originate actions can they be deserving of either praise or blame.

Ultimately, the question of free will became reduced to a basic argument among philosophers between free will and **determinism**. Do people have the free will to cause action, or is every action linked to a cause over which they have no control? Coming under attack from determinist theories, the concept of free has long been a contemporary philosophical challenge. Fate, divine intervention, and prophecy created the puzzle that the ancient thinkers attempted to solve. If fate, a divine being, or prophetic utterance determined history, how could it be said that humans have free will?

With the dawn of modern science, the laws of cause and effect were cited to deny the possibility of free human initiative. In "Do We Have Free Will?" appearing in *Free Inquiry* (Spring 1998), Lewis Vaughn and Theodore Schick, Jr. explain: "According to casual determinism, this something, this cause or causes, in turn must have been due to other causes (like certain brain states), and these causes must have been due to still others, and so on. Indeed, there must have been a whole succession of causes extending indefinitely into the past-stretching back before you were even born." Therefore, human action is the "result of causes over which you had no control whatsoever."

The question of human initiative has long been debated within Western religions. Augustine used the concept of free will to reconcile the concurrent existence of **evil** and God. Evil, posited Aristotle, is the result of disobeying God. Human beings freely choose the path of disobedience; therefore, God does not cause evil, humans do. But then the question arises: How can humans freely choose if God created them and had foreknowledge of their actions. How can free will be reconciled with the omnipotent nature of God? Thomas Aquinas, along with other Western theologians such as Martin Luther, John Calvin, and Jonathan Edwards, resolved the dilemma by denying the existence of free will, suggesting instead that all action is predetermined by God.

Indeterminism was posited as a response to the scientific determinism first proposed by the Stoics, who believed the world was ordered by the physical motion of atoms. Epicurean philosophers, in an attempt to find room for freedom of the will, posited the some atoms by chance "swerve." The indeterminism theory would arise again in the late twentieth century after universal scientific determinism came under questions when quantum theory proposed that such activities as quantum jumps in atoms and radioactive decay were not subject to deterministic laws, but could only be judged by statistical analysis. If nature is not bound by pure cause and effect, then neither are human beings. However, the argument fails to hold up under scrutiny. If erratic chance causes variation of action, then human beings are not free to choose, but simply dependent upon the happenings of chance rather than predetermined causes.

Psychology has also offered a formidable challenge to the concept of free will. Behavioral approaches to human action suggest that all effects (or actions) are determined by causes. Psychoanalytic theory further suggests that those causes exist even if they are unknown to the actor because they emerge from the subconscious. Sidney Callahan writes in "Free Will" appearing in *Commonweal* (19 June 1998) that "behaviorists confidently claimed that if you knew both the genetic endowment of an organism and its complete environmental history, you could predict its behavior. In a universe viewed as a giant machine, everything must follow unchangeable scientific laws."

In the contemporary debate over free will, some theorists remain adamantly deterministic and others are staunch supporters of free will as the expense of any deterministic understanding. A third choice has also emerged as the dominant choice of modern philosophers: compatibilism. Namely, compatibilist theory suggests that determinism and free will are not

René Descartes was one of the first European philosophers to propose the concept of human free will *(The Library of Congress)*.

in conflict. Causality does not preclude the ability to choose freely, nor does free will assume that physical and social factors do not influence choices.

FREIRE, PAULO (1921-1997)
Brazilian philosopher and professor

The Brazilian philosopher Paulo Freire (1921–1997) developed theories that have been used, principally in Third World countries, to bring literacy to the poor and to transform the field of education. Paulo Freire was born on the northeastern coast of Brazil in the city of Recife in 1921. Raised by his mother who was a devout Catholic and his father who was a middle-class businessman, Freire's early years paralleled those of the Great Depression. Outward symbols, such as his father always wearing a tie and having a German-made piano in their home, pointed to the family's middle-class heritage but stood in contrast to their actual conditions of **poverty**. Reflecting on their situation, Freire noted, "We shared the hunger, but not the class." After completing secondary school and with gradual improvement in his family's financial situation, he was able to enter Recife University, preparing to become a teacher of Portuguese.

The 15 years following World War II proved to be instrumental in giving direction to his later life. He had previously married a fellow teacher, Elza, in 1944. In addition to their shared careers in teaching, they worked together with middle-class friends in the Catholic Action Movement. This work became unsettling as they struggled with the contradictions between the Christian faith and their friends' lifestyles. In particular they faced strong resistance when suggesting that servants should be dealt with as human beings. Later they decided to work solely with "the people," the large population of the poor in Brazil.

A second experience that gave focus to Freire's later life came when he worked as a labor lawyer for the poor and involved a discussion with workers about the theories of **Jean Piaget**, a prominent psychologist. Evidently Freire's comments were not comprehended by one of the workers, who noted, "You talk from a background of food, comfort, and rest. The reality is that we have one room, no food, and have to make love in front of the children." Through such experiences and further study, Freire began to realize that the poor had a different sense of reality and that to communicate with them he had to use their syntax of meanings. This recognition served as a basis for his doctoral dissertation in 1959 at Recife University, where he later became professor of history and philosophy of education.

In 1962 the mayor of Recife appointed Freire as head of an adult literacy program for the city. In his first experiement, Freire taught 300 adults to read and write in 45 days. This program was so successful that during the following year the President of Brazil appointed him to lead the National Literacy Program. This program was on its way to becoming similarly successful, with expected enrollments to exceed two million students in 1964. Under Brazil's constitution, however, illiterates were not allowed to vote. The *O Globe*, an influential conservative newspaper, claimed that Freire's method for developing literacy was stirring up the people, causing them to want to change **society**, and formenting subversion. As a consequence of a military overthrow of the government in 1964, Freire was jailed for seventy days, then exiled briefly to Bolivia and then to Chile for five years.

Freire met with opposition from some Chilian citizens who viewed him as a threat to their society. However, the director of a nationwide program for reducing **illiteracy** employed him to work in the Chilian Agrarian Reform Corporation. This provided him the opportunity over the next few years to become more involved in research and to write three books, the most noted of which is *Pedagogy of the Oppressed* (1970). In 1969 he accepted an invitation to be a visiting professor at Harvard. He quickly found a large audience of growing support in America primarily through the appearance in English of his publications. He left Harvard in 1970 to join the Office of Education at the World Council of Churches in Geneva. In this office his work over the next decade was marked by efforts to increase literacy and liberty in Third World countries through educational programs. Of particular note were his efforts to rethink and apply his theories in the West African country of Guinea-Bissau.

In 1979 Freire's exile status was lifted, allowing him to return home to Brazil where he became secretary of education in Sao Paulo. During the decade of the 1980s he published widely in the areas of education, politics, and literacy. In these writings he developed themes discussed previously and he continued to rethink their practical application to new situations.

Freire believed that poor peoples of the world are dominated and victims of those who possess political power. What the poor need is liberation, an education giving them a critical consciousness, investing them with an agency for changing, and throwing off the oppressive structures of their society. Such an education would not conform and mold people to fit into the roles expected by society, but it would prepare them to realize their own values and reality, reflect and study critically their world, and move into action to transform it. When working with illiterate adults, Freire proposed the selection of words used by the poor in their everyday lives expressing their longings, frustrations, and hopes. From this list of words a shorter list is developed of possibly 16–17 words that contain the basic sounds and syllables of the language. These words are broken down (decoded) into syllables; afterwards, the learners form new words by making different combinations of syllables. In relatively a short period of time (a few days) they are usually writing simple letters to each other. During their studies a second and deeper level of analysis is occurring simultaneously. That is, the teacher using the very same words helps the students also to decode their cultural and social world. This deeper level of activity leads learners to greater awareness of the oppressive forces in their lives and to the realization of their power to transform them.

Freire wrote 25 books which were translated into 35 languages and was an honorary professor of 28 universities around the world. He maintained that he never would have been arrested or criticized had he stuck to teaching ABCs. He fell into disfavor, he said, because of his theory that illiteracy, not any religious reason, made people poor. He maintained his claim, "Education is freedom." After his death of a heart attack in Sao Paulo, Brazil, on May 2, 1997, there was a three-day mourning in the state of Pernambuco.

FRENCH SCHOOL OF SOCIOLOGY

The origins of **sociology** as a unique science in the late nineteenth century are generally traced back to France, with much of the credit given to philosopher, professor, and sociologist Émile Durkheim (1858-1917). At that time, social theory was dominated by "methodological individualism," the belief that all social phenomena should be reduced to individual psychological or biological phenomena in order to be explained. Durkheim therefore had to explain and justify his emphasis on "collective consciousness" and "collective representations."

Through his teaching (notably at the University of Bordeaux, where he became France's first professor of sociology), Durkheim helped to legitimize the application of natural science methods to social science. He had been influenced early in his career by two of his teachers at Paris' École Normale. From classicist Numa Denis Fustel de Coulanges, Durkheim had learned the importance of religion in the formation of social institutions and discovered that the sacred could be studied rationally and objectively. Philosopher Émile Boutroux had convinced him that atomism, the reduction of phenomena to their smallest constituent parts, was a fallacious methodological procedure and that each science must explain phenomena in terms of its own specific principles. Durkheim also was blessed with the company of many exceptional fellow students who certainly influenced his future work, including the socialist Jean Jaurès, philosopher Henri Bergson, psychologist Pierre Janet, historian Camille Julian, and geographer Lucien Gallois.

Durkheim's philosophy was expounded in such landmark works as *The Division of Labor in Society* (1893), *The Rules of Sociological Method* (1895), *Suicide* (1897), and *The Elementary Forms of Religious Life* (1912). Durkheim also established the *Année Sociologique,* the first French social science journal. In *The Rules of Sociological Method*, Durkheim perhaps best summarized his philosophy: ''Comparative sociology is not a particular branch of sociology; it is sociology itself, in so far as it ceases to be purely descriptive and aspires to account for facts.'' Sociology thus was a social science that synthesized all others.

However, Durkheim's work never was fully welcomed in French academic circles. He often antagonized his fellow professors by urging them to apply his philosophy and the principles of natural science to other disciplines, such as history and law. During his lifetime Durkheim was severely criticized for claiming that social facts were irreducible, that they had a reality of their own. His ideas, however, are now accepted as the common foundations for empirical work in sociology. His concept of the collective consciousness, renamed ''culture,'' has become part of the theoretical foundations of modern ethnography. His voice was one of the most powerful in breaking the hold of Enlightenment ideas of **individualism** on modern social sciences.

While Durkheim is considered by many to be the founder of modern sociology, other Frenchmen of the nineteenth century played an important role in establishing France as a pioneer in this discipline. **Auguste Comte** (1798-1857) is credited with coining the term ''sociology.'' In his key works *Cours de Philosophie Positive* and *Système de Politique Positive*, Comte developed the school of thought known as positivism. A social reformer, Comte saw sociology as a means to achieve a **society** in which harmony prevailed. He focused on examining the evolution of the human mind through what he believed were specific laws. While his work helped to shape sociology as a science, it has dwindled in significance.

One of the key developments in the tradition of quantification in social research was *statistique morale* (roughly translated as ''political arithmetic''), which aimed to use **descriptive statistics** in public policy and administration. Belgian **Adolphe Quetelet** is the best known of this school of thought, but Frenchman Andr' de Guerry de Champneuf, who served as director of the Department of Criminal Justice in the French Ministry of Justice from 1821 to 1835, also was central to its development. Jean Baptiste Fourier and Andr' de Chabrol de Crousol conducted statistical studies published during the 1820s. Regarding public health research, French physician Parent-Duch*f*telet collected and analyzed **data** on the recruitment and social origin of prostitutes, published in 1834.

The work of Frédéric Le Play led to development of a second branch of empirical research in nineteenth century France. Le Play, who also advocated for conservative reform of French society, was noted for his empirical observation of contemporary social life, such as family budgets. However, Le Play's work faded in importance as Durkheim's grew, hindered by his growing focus on social reform, and eventually had little impact on the growth of French sociology. His followers who founded the journal *Science Sociale* split into two distinct groups, those interested in research **methodology** and those involved in social reform. The Le Play school never became totally rooted in French universities, which also helps to explain its decline.

Despite the fact that many early French sociologists (e.g., Durkheim, Comte, and Le Play) were intellectuals, their work had difficulty being fully accepted by the academic community. Academic sociology in France was closely associated with anthropology, with the latter dominating. However, Durkheim and his later followers did manage to establish academic credentials for some branches of sociological thought, notably the **sociology of education**, law, religion, and economy. Quantitative sociology remained largely outside of the university system, instead becoming centered in separate institutes with ties to the French education system. Well into the second half of the twentieth century, growth of quantitative sociology in France was not as dynamic as was growth in the field of ethnological research in sociology and anthropology.

FREQUENCY DISTRIBUTION

A frequency distribution is a descriptive tool used in univariate analyses, or analyses of a single **variable**. A ''frequency'' is simply the number of times something occurs. A ''frequency distribution'' is a list of each of a variable's attributes and their corresponding frequency of occurrence.

For instance, we could conduct a survey and ask the question, ''Are you (1) male, or (2) female?'' The variable is sex, and its attributes are ''male'' and ''female.'' Respondents would answer by either circling ''(1)'' for male, or ''(2)'' for female. The frequencies would be the number of times that ''(1)'' was chosen and the number of times that ''(2)'' was chosen. A frequency distribution would display these results in a tabular format.

Frequency tables produced by statistical computer software often present not only the frequency of each variable's attributes but also the n (the total number surveyed), missing (the number of respondents who chose not to answer that particular question), the total percent (calculated with the total number surveyed), the valid percent (calculated with the total number who responded to that variable), and the cumulative percent (the total up to and including each attribute).

Sigmund Freud *(The Library of Congress)*

FREUD, SIGMUND (1856-1939)
Austrian psychologist, author, and
*   psychoanalyst*

The work of Sigmund Freud, the Austrian founder of **psychoanalysis**, marked the beginning of a modern **psychology** by providing the first systematic explanation of the inner mental forces determining human behavior. Early on Sigmund Freud distinguished himself as a histologist, neuropathologist, and clinical neurologist, and in his later life he was acclaimed as a talented writer and essayist. However, his fame is based on his work in expanding man's knowledge of himself through clinical research and corresponding development of theories to explain new **data**. He laid the foundations for modern understanding of unconscious mental processes (processes excluded from awareness), neurosis (a type of mental disorder), the sexual life of infants, and the interpretation of dreams. Under his guidance, psychoanalysis became the dominant modern theory of human psychology and a major tool of research, as well as an important method of psychiatric treatment which currently has thousands of practitioners all over the world. The application of psychoanalytic thinking to the studies of history, anthropology, religion, art, **sociology**, and education has greatly changed these fields.

Sigmund Freud was born on May 6, 1856, in Freiberg, Moravia (now Czechoslovakia), the first child of his twice-widowed father's third marriage. His mother, Amalia Nathanson, was 19 years old when she married Jacob Freud, aged 39. Sigmund's two stepbrothers from his father's first marriage were approximately the same age as his mother, and his older stepbrother's son, Sigmund's nephew, was his earliest playmate. Thus, the boy grew up in an unusual family structure, his mother halfway in age between himself and his father. When he was four, the family moved to Vienna, where he lived until a year before his death.

Freud enrolled in medical school initially attracted to the laboratory and the scientific side of medicine rather than clinical practice. He spent seven instead of the usual five years acquiring his doctorate. For the next few years Freud pursued his laboratory work, but several factors shifted his interest. Opportunities for advancement in academic medicine were rare at best, and his Jewish background was a decided disadvantage. More important, he fell in love and wanted to marry, but the stipends available to a young scientist could not support a wife and family. He married Martha Bernays in 1887. Of their six children, a daughter, Anna, became one of her father's most famous followers.

Psychiatry at this time was static and descriptive. The psychological meaning of behavior was not itself considered important; behavior was only a set of symptoms to be studied in order to understand the structures of the brain. Freud's later work revolutionized this attitude.

In his residency spent partly in France, Freud first became interested in hysteria and Charcot's demonstration of its psychological origins. Thus, in fact, Freud's development of a psychoanalytic approach to mental disorders was rooted in nineteenth-century neurology rather than in the psychiatry of the era.

Freud returned to Vienna, established himself in the private practice of neurology, and married. He soon devoted his efforts to the treatment of hysterical patients with the help of hypnosis. Freud demonstrated that hysterical symptoms could consistently be traced to highly emotional experiences which had been "repressed," that is, excluded from conscious memory. Together with Breuer he published *Studies on Hysteria* (1895). At the age of 39 Freud first used the term "psychoanalysis," and his major lifework was well under way.

At about this time Freud began his own self-analysis, which he pursued primarily by analyzing his **dreams**. As he proceeded, his personality changed. He developed a greater inner security while his at times impulsive emotional responses decreased. A major scientific result was *The Interpretation of Dreams* (1901).

Freud explored the **influence** of unconscious mental processes on virtually every aspect of human behavior: slips of the tongue and simple errors of memory. He recognized that predominant among the unconscious forces which lead to neuroses are the sexual desires of early childhood that have been excluded from conscious awareness, yet have preserved their dynamic force within the personality. He described his highly controversial views concerning infantile sexuality in *Three Essays on the Theory of Sexuality* (1905), a work which initially met violent protest but was gradually accepted.

After 1902 Freud gathered a small group of interested people on Wednesday evenings for presentation of psychoanalytic papers and discussion. This was the beginning of the psychoanalytic movement. Swiss psychiatrists Eugen Bleuler and Carl Jung formed a study group in Zurich in 1907, and the first International Psychoanalytic Congress was held in Salzburg in 1908.

At the same time Freud faced a major scientific reversal. He first thought that his neurotic patients had actually experienced sexual seductions in childhood, but he then realized that his patients were usually describing childhood fantasies (wishes) rather than actual events. He retracted his earlier statement on infantile sexuality, yet demonstrated his scientific genius when he rejected neither the data nor the theory but reformulated both. He now saw that the universal sexual fantasies of children were scientifically far more important than an occasional actual seduction by an adult. Several of Freud's closest colleagues broke with him and established splinter groups of their own, some of which continue to this day, of these Jung, Alfred Adler, Otto Rank, and Wilhelm Reich are the best known.

In 1923 Freud developed a cancerous growth in his mouth that led to his death 16 years and 33 operations later. In spite of this, these were years of great scientific productivity. In March 1938 Austria was occupied by German troops and Freud and his family were put under house arrest. Through the combined efforts of Marie Bonaparte, Princess of Greece, British psychoanalyst Ernest Jones, and W. C. Bullitt, the American ambassador to France (who obtained assistance from President Franklin D. Roosevelt), the Freuds were permitted to leave Austria in June. Freud spent his last year in London, undergoing surgery. He died on September 23, 1939. The influence of his discoveries on the science and culture of the twentieth century is incalculable.

FROMM, ERICH (1900-1980)
German psychoanalyst, psychologist, philosopher, and author

Erich Fromm (1900–1980) achieved international fame for his writings and lectures in the fields of **psychoanalysis, psychology**, and social philosophy. He wrote extensively on a variety of topics ranging from **sociology**, anthropology, and ethics to religion, politics, and mythology.

Erich Fromm was born in Frankfurt am Main, Germany, on March 23, 1900, and died in Muralto, Switzerland, on March 18, 1980. He grew up in a devout Jewish family, but abandoned religious orthodoxy early in life when he became convinced that religion was a source of division of the human race. His academic career was impressive. He studied at the Universities of Frankfurt and Munich and received his Ph.D. from the University of Heidelberg. Later, he obtained psychoanalytic training at the prestigious Psychoanalytic Institute of Berlin under the leadership of such prominent Freudian analysts as Hanns Sachs and Theodor Reik. After pursuing a brief career as a psychoanalyst he left Nazi Germany in 1934 and

Erich Fromm *(The Library of Congress)*

settled permanently in the United States. Fromm taught in various universities such as Bennington College, Columbia, Yale, New School for Social Research, Michigan State, and the Universidad Autónoma de México. In 1962 he became professor of psychiatry at New York University.

Fromm wrote more than twenty books. Some of them became popular bestsellers: *Escape from Freedom* (1942); *Man for Himself* (1947); *Psychoanalysis and Religion* (1950); *The Forgotten Language* (1951); *The Sane Society* (1955); *The Art of Loving* (1956); *Marx's Concept of Man* (1961); *Beyond the Chains of Illusion: My Encounter with Marx and Freud* (1962); *The Dogma of Christ, and Other Essays on Religion, Psychology and Culture* (1963); *Zen Buddhism and Psychoanalysis* (1960); *The Life and Work of Sigmund Freud* (1963); *The Heart of Man* (1964); *Social Character in a Mexican Village* (1970); *The Revolution of Hope* (1968); *The Crisis of Psychoanalysis* (1970); and *The Anatomy of Human Destructiveness* (1973).

A sincere and profound humanism permeates all of Fromm's writings. He was genuinely concerned with the reality of human existence and the full unfolding of man's potentialities. He searched for the essence of man, the meaning of life, and the nature of individual **alienation** in the modern technological world. Deeply moved by the destruction and the suffering caused by two world wars, Fromm wrote extensively on the threats of technology and the insanity of the arms race. Faith in the future of man and the unity of humanity was the base of his humanistic vision.

Freud and Marx were the most decisive influences on Fromm's thinking. Originally Freudian in his intellectual orientation and clinical practice, he gradually grew more distant from Freudian therapeutic principles and later became a major critic of Freud. Along with Karen Horney, Harry Sullivan, and Karl Jung, Fromm was considered a Freudian revisionist and the founder of the neo-Freudian school. He rejected Freud's libido theory, the Oedipus complex, and the instincts of life and death as universally constant in the human species. Instead, he insisted on cultural variations and the influence of the larger context of history and social conditions upon the character of the individual. The concept of the unconscious and the dynamic conception of character were considered to be Freud's major achievements. The task of analytical social psychology, Fromm wrote, is that of understanding unconscious human behavior as the effect of the socio-economic structure of **society** on basic human psychic drives. Likewise, the character of the individual is rooted in the libidinal structure of society, understood as a combination of basic human drives and social forces. In the last analysis, Fromm rejected Freudian theory as authoritarian, repressive, and culturally narrow, enabling the individual to overcome the conflict between society and personal gratification and accept bourgeois norms.

In contrast, Fromm's admiration for Marx was complete. He considered Marx a sincere humanist who sought an end to human alienation and the full development of the individual as the precondition for the full development of society (*Marx's Concept of Man*). Marx's emphasis on the socio-economic base of society as a major determinant of human behavior was accepted as a given by Fromm. Marxism, though, needed to be completed by a dynamic and critical psychology—that is, a psychology which explained the evolution of psychic forces in terms of an interaction between man's needs and the socio-historical reality in which he lives (*The Crisis of Psychoanalysis*). Fromm never renounced his project of merging psycho-analysis and Marxism. This was his major work as a member of the Frankfurt school (The Institute for Social Research), a school committed to critical theory, a critique of the repressive character of bourgeois society. Psychological theory, he wrote, can demonstrate that the economic base of a society produces the social character, and that the social character produces ideas and ideologies which fit it and are nourished by it. Ideas, once created, also influence the social character and, indirectly, the socio-economic structure of society (*Socialist Humanism*).

In his popular book *Escape from Freedom* Fromm analyzed the existential condition of man. The source of man's aggressiveness, the human instinct of destructiveness, neurosis, sadism, and masochism were not viewed as sexually derived behavior, but as attempts to overcome alienation and powerlessness. His notion of freedom, in contrast to Freud and the critical theorists of the Frankfurt school, had a more positive connotation. It was not a matter of attaining "freedom from" the repressive character of the technological society, as **Herbert Marcuse**, for instance, held, but "freedom to" develop the creative powers of man. In *Man for Himself* Fromm focussed on the problem of neurosis, characterizing it as the moral problem of a repressive society, as the failure of man to achieve maturity and an integrated personality. Man's capacity for freedom and **love**, he noted, are dependent upon socio-economic conditions, but are rarely found in societies where the drive of destructiveness prevails.

In the *Sane Society* he attempted to psychologize society and **culture** and showed that psychoanalytic principles can be successfully applied to the solution of social and cultural problems. In a society becoming increasingly insane, he wrote, only a concern for ethics can restore sanity. Each person needs to develop high ethical standards in order to rejuvenate society and to arrest the process of robotization of the human being. Technological domination is destructive of human personality. Man's need to destroy, for Fromm, stemmed from an "unlived life," that is, the frustration of the life instinct. Love becomes the only answer to human problems (*The Art of Loving*). He advocated a "socialist humanism" which in theory and practice is committed to the full development of man within the context of a socio-economic system that, by its **rationality** and abundance, harmonizes the development of the individual and society (*Socialist Humanism*).

In contrast to the pessimistic and deterministic conclusions of Freudian theory and the nihilistic implications of **critical theory**, Fromm functioned as a voice of conscience. He maintained that true happiness could be achieved and that a happiness-oriented therapy, through empathy, was the most successful one. He severely criticized established psychoanalysis for contributing to the dehumanization of man (*The Crisis of Psychoanalysis*). Also, consistent with his philosophy of love and **peace**, Fromm fought against nuclear weapons and helped organize a "sane society" movement to stop the insanity of the arms race.

His influence on humanistic psychology was enormous. Many later social analysts were inspired by Fromm's writings. An example would be the work of Christopher Laschon the *Culture of Narcissism*, which continued in the United States Fromm's effort to psychoanalyze culture and society in a neo-Freudian and Marxist tradition.

FUNCTIONALISM

Functionalism is one of the major sociological paradigms. The term "paradigm" refers to a framework or **model** for understanding the social world. The functionalist perspective is characterized by a set of assumptions that differentiate functionalism from other sociological paradigms. Functionalist sociologists are guided by these basic assumptions in their analyses of **society** and in the formation of functionalist **sociological theory**.

First, the functionalist **paradigm** holds that society is characterized by order and stability. Conflict is viewed as **abnormal** and to be avoided. Second, the functionalist perspective maintains a consensus exists regarding society's **norms** and **values**. In other words, all members of society agree about the importance and necessity of existing norms and values. Third, functionalists assert that society has many integrated parts. Each element of society functions in relation to other societal parts. Change in one element of society prompts a corresponding change in all other social domains.

Functionalism, developed during the late eighteenth and nineteenth centuries, is primarily associated with the thinking and writings of **Auguste Comte** and Émile Durkheim. Comte, who actually coined the term "sociology," made functionalism one of the earliest sociological perspectives. Theorizing during the period of the French Revolution, Comte defined **sociology** as the scientific study of the social world.

While Comte may have named the field of sociology, Durkheim is considered responsible for the origins of modern sociology. One of Durkheim's major contributions was his proposition that sociology was the study of *social facts*, which supersede individuals in society. Though Durkheim did not deny the importance of individuals' experiences in the analysis of the social world, he argued that the study of the individual should be confined to the fields of **psychology** and biology. According to Durkheim, sociology is the scientific study of social facts, which are manners of acting, thinking, and feeling external to individuals.

Robert Merton, a more contemporary functionalist, asserts that the maintenance of **social order** is accomplished by the particular functions of each element of society. *Manifest functions* are the intended functions of integrated societal elements, while *latent functions* are unintended and often unrecognized. According to the functionalist perspective, the most important elements of society are *social institutions*. Institutions are designed to fulfill the fundamental needs of society, which include maintenance of social order and preservation of society's agreed upon norms and values. Some examples of major institutions found in every society around the world are the **family**, religion, economy, education, and the state. Each of these institutions is designed to carry out certain manifest functions. For example, the family is designed to contribute new members to society, as well as socialize those new members in the context of commonly held norms and values. Social institutions may also perform some latent or unintended functions. For instance, families affected by domestic violence may inadvertently socialize children to lead violent lives.

Because functionalist analyses hold that institutions function in an integrated manner, change in one **institution** necessarily prompts corresponding change in other institutions. For example, changes in the economic structure of societies tend to affect the **structure** of families. The historical transformation of the U.S. economy provides evidence for the interdependence of these social institutions. Prior to the **Industrial Revolution**, larger families ensured that there were enough people to maintain agricultural economic production. As the U.S. economy transformed from an agricultural to a goods-producing and service economy, however, families became smaller. Children no longer were a necessity in **household** economy and eventually became more often an economic liability.

The practice of functionalist sociological analysis and the development of functionalist social theory have significant social implications. First, because society is perceived as stable and harmonious, while conflict is avoided at all costs, **social change** appears unlikely to occur. The assumption that social norms and values are agreed upon by all members constrains possibilities for social change as well. If no conflict exists regarding these norms and values, they are likely to remain fixed. Finally, although functionalism allows for some social change, it assumes that such change will affect every element of society. Thus it is impossible for change in any one arena of society to occur without subsequent change occurring in all other social domains.

FUTUROLOGY

Futurology is the act of predicting or forecasting the future. In sociology, futurology is not a separate field of study, but an aspect of various social science which attempt to forecast future sociological conditions. Daniel Bell distinguished the separate activities of social science made predictions. First, speculation with a base in an academic knowledge of the area exists in the social sciences. Second, sociologists extrapolate, or extend current trends into the future, expecting the future to in many ways resemble the present phenomena. Third, theoretical models can be used. In this case, the sociologists works within a given framework and expects the future to match predictions consistent with that framework. Fourth, sociologist attempt to predict certain events that will happen in the future, such as a change in a particular demographic statistic.

Karl Popper distinguished between predictions of science and prophesy. Prophecy exists not only within the context of religion, but also can be derived from certain theories, such as Marxism or **evolutionary theory**. Scientific prediction, on the other hand, always makes use of universal conditional statements (those that can be stated in the form of "If a, then b"). Such exact prediction rarely occurs in the social sciences due to the variety of variables that are necessary components of every prediction. Hence, social predictions usually subsist within theoretical predictions.

G

GALBRAITH, JOHN KENNETH (1908-)
American scholar and economist

John Kenneth Galbraith was a leading scholar of the American Institutionalist school and arguably the most famous economist in the post-World War II world. His views were a stinging indictment of the modern materialistic **society** that championed personal achievement and material well-being over public interest and needs. In spite of these views, he served as an advisor in both the American and Canadian governments from the 1930s onward.

Galbraith was born October 15, 1908, in southern Ontario, Canada, to a farming family of Scotch ancestry. He studied agricultural economics at the Ontario Agricultural College (then part of the University of Toronto; later University of Guelph) and graduated with distinction in 1931. He studied agricultural economics at the University of California, receiving his Ph.D. in 1934. In this year he also began his long, though frequently interrupted, tenure at Harvard University. Galbraith's academic career frequently gave way to public service. He worked in the Department of Agriculture during the New Deal and in the Office of Price Administration and Civilian Supply during World War II.

After the war in Europe, Galbraith worked with the Office of Strategic Services directing research on the effectiveness of the Allies' strategic bombing of Germany. He was a speechwriter in the presidential campaign of Adlai Stevenson and then chaired the Democratic Advisory Council during Dwight D. Eisenhower's administration. He campaigned for President John F. Kennedy, and after Kennedy's victory he was named U.S. ambassador to India in the early 1960s. An outspoken critic of U.S. involvement in Vietnam, he campaigned on behalf of presidential hopefuls Eugene McCarthy (1968) and George McGovern (1972). Later he worked in the campaigns of Morris Udall (1976) and Edward Kennedy (1980).

Galbraith's major intellectual contributions lie in the trilogy *The Affluent Society* (1958), *The New Industrial State* (1967), and *Economics and the Public Purpose* (1973). Along the way he published over twenty other books, including two novels, a co-authored book on Indian painting, memoirs, travelogues, political tracts, and several books on economic and intellectual history.

Another important work is Galbraith's *American Capitalism: The Concept of Countervailing Power* (1952) which asserts that growth of economic power in one economic sector tends to induce countervailing power from those who must bargain with the powerful. This book solidified Galbraith's position as a continuing spokesperson for the New Deal perspective in economics. Galbraith coupled the new economics of John Maynard Keynes with the New Deal corporatist view, as did other Institutionalists of the time.

The Affluent Society examined the continuing urgency that affluent societies attach to higher consumption and production. It argued that the outmoded mentality of more-is-better impeded the further economic **progress**. Advertising and related salesmanship activities create artificially high demand for commodities produced by private businesses and lead to a concomitant neglect of public sector goods and services that would contribute far more to the **quality of life**.

Galbraith's breakthrough as a best-selling author came with *The Affluent Society* for which he was honored with the American Economic Association's prestigious presidency. The book also influenced both the Great Society program and the rise of the American "counterculture" in the 1960s.

In *The New Industrial State* Galbraith expanded his analysis of the role of power in economic life. A central concept here is the *revised sequence*. The conventional wisdom in economic thought portrays economic life as a set of competitive markets governed ultimately by the decisions of sovereign consumers. In this original sequence, the control of the production process flows from consumers of commodities to the organizations that produce those commodities. In the revised sequence, this flow is reversed and businesses exercise control over consumers by advertising and related salesmanship activities.

John Kenneth Galbraith *(The Library of Congress)*

The New Industrial State filled a very pressing need in the late 1960s. The conventional theory of monopoly power in economic life maintains that the monopolist will attempt to restrict supply in order to maintain price above its competitive level. The social cost of this monopoly power is a decrease in both allocative efficiency and the equity of income distribution. This conventional economic analysis of the role of monopoly power did not adequately address popular concerns about the large corporation in the late 1960s. The growing concern focused on the role of the corporation in politics, the damage done to the natural environment by an unmitigated commitment to economic growth, and the perversion of advertising and other pecuniary aspects of culture.

Economics and the Public Purpose, the last work in his major trilogy, Galbraith continued his characteristic insistence on the role of power in economic life and the inability of conventional economic thought to deal adequately with this power. Conventional economic thought serves to hide the power **structure** that actually governs the American economy. Thus, economists fail to come to grips with this governing structure and its untoward effects on the quality of life. Galbraith employed what he called "the test of anxiety" in this attack on conventional economics. He argued that any system of economic ideas should be evaluated by the test of anxiety—that is, by its ability to relate to popular concern about the economic system and to resolve or allay this anxiety.

After years served in both the American and Canadian governments, Galbraith returned to scholarly activity, extensive travel, and writing, using Harvard University as his home base. In January 1997 Galbraith, in a lecture at the University of Toronto, again espoused his views that governments should create jobs by direct intervention in the economy. Although he represented the obscure Institutionalist school of economic thought, he nonetheless continued to convey his message that "there must be, most of all an effective safety net [of] individual and family support for those who live on the lower edges of the system."

GALLUP, GEORGE HORACE (1901-1984)
American public opinion statistician

Born on November 18, 1901, in the small community of Jefferson, Iowa, George Horace Gallup was the son of George Henry (a farmer) and Nettie (Davenport) Gallup. He attended the University of Iowa, earning his bachelor's degree in 1923. During his second year of undergraduate studies, his family suffered financial setbacks, forcing Gallup to seek funding from scholarships and a part-time job running a towel concession stand at the university swimming pool. During his junior year, he became the editor of the campus newspaper *The Daily Iowan* and, as the only newspaper in town, he widened its scope, increased its off-campus audience, and began running advertisements for community businesses.

Upon graduating from his undergraduate studies, Gallup remained at the University of Iowa as an instructor in journalism. At the same time, he began his graduate studies in **psychology**. He married Ophelia Smith Miller on December 27, 1925; they had three children: Alec Miller, George H. III, and Julia Gallup Laughlin. Gallup received his master's degree in 1925 and his doctorate in 1928. What would become a lifelong involvement, Gallup first published ideas on the issue of **public opinion** in his thesis: *A New Technique for Objective Methods for Measuring Reader Interest in Newspapers.* The next year he left the University of Iowa to become the head of the Department of Journalism at Drake University in Des Moines, Iowa, where he remained until 1931. During the 1931–1932 school year, Gallup taught journalism and advertising at Northwestern University in Evanston, Illinois.

In 1932 Gallup moved to New York City to join the Young & Rubicam Advertising Agency as the director of research, and he concurrently taught journalism at Columbia University. He gave up his professorship in 1937 upon being named vice-president of Young & Rubicam, a position he held until 1947. At the same time, Gallup continued to develop his theory and methodology of public polling. In 1935 he founded and served as director of the American Institute of Public Opinion, located in New York City and Princeton, New Jersey. In 1939, he founded and served as president of the Audience Research Institute. The Gallup Organization came into existence in 1958, and Gallup held the positions of chief operating officer and chairman of the board. He remained with all three organizations from their inception until his death in 1984.

Gallup first put his polling methods to the test during his time in Iowa, conducting reader-interest **surveys** for several newspapers, including the *Des Moines Register & Tribune*, the *Cleveland Plain Dealer*, and the *St. Louis Post-Dispatch*. By applying his polling concepts to elections, in 1934 Gallup accurately predicted that the Democrats would increase their numbers in Congress. The next year, Gallup touted his new "scientific" method of polling by guaranteeing the newspapers that he would predict the 1936 presidential election more accurately than the esteemed *Literary Digest*, which had previously correctly called the victories of Herbert Hoover and Franklin D. Roosevelt in 1928 and 1932, respectively. The outcome was the turning point for Gallup, who, unlike the *Literary Digest*, correctly picked Roosevelt as the winner.

Although the 1936 election is often considered the beginning point for modern scientific polling, Gallup's prediction was almost seven percentage points off. He responded to these results by advocating for even more advancements and improvements in the scientific methods he advocated. He also used the failure of the *Literary Digest* to his favor, claiming that the "Lesson of 1936" was the need for scientific sampling methods. Taking partial credit for the more accurate predictions of the 1936 election offered by other "scientific" pollsters, Gallup wrote in his 1940 book *The Pulse of Democracy* (co-authored with Saul F. Rae): "The surprising accuracy of the results obtained by these new polls in 1936, bearing in mind that it was the fist real test of scientific sampling in a national election, bears witness to the cogency of the criticism of the *Digest* poll, and to the underlying soundness of the alternative methods which were put to the test." Promising even better things to come, Gallup preached the benefits of the transition "from a glorified kind of fortune telling into a practical way of learning what the nation thinks."

During the 1940s Gallup rose to fame as the country's most influential surveyor of public opinion. Accurately predicting the presidential election results of 1940 and 1944, Gallup appeared on the cover of *Time* magazine, which named him the "Babe Ruth of the polling profession." Then, in 1948, disaster struck. The polling industry predicted that Thomas Dewey would defeat Harry Truman in the bid for the presidency by between five and fifteen percentage points. Gallup's own polling predicted that Truman would receive 44.5 percent of the popular vote and thus lose to Dewey. When Truman won 49.9 percent of the vote, thus securing his victory over Dewey, the scientific pollster came under attack. At first, the obviously upset Gallup blamed the election, not the polls, by suggesting bribes and rigged ballots had changed the election outcome. Soon, however, Gallup acknowledged the polling errors and, in his famous rhetorical style, turned the disaster into an opportunity for learning and improvement.

Adjusting his polling methods, Gallup gradually replaced quota sampling, which required that a specific number of respondents have certain characteristics. The interviewers selected the participants based on the quotas, but **bias** selection by the interviewers and quotas that inaccurately reflected the voting population led to skewed results. Along with expanding his use of **probability** sampling, Gallup also addressed the issues of how to screen out non-voters, how to conduct polls up to election day, and how to account for undecided voters. The changes in methods were such that the 1948 election was the only presidential contest that Gallup predicted incorrectly during his lifetime.

Although Gallup admitted that predicting elections was of little social value, he defended the practice as a means to demonstrate the accuracy of polling to the nation. As he developed the public opinion survey methodology, the manufacturing industry took notice, and soon the widespread use of public polls fueled the advertising agendas of all major businesses marketing products. Gallup had hopes for the continued prog-

George Gallup *(The Library of Congress)*

ress of polling as a means to convey the public's wishes to the **government**, who would use polls as the people's mandate. Ultimately, he dreamed of a future where public policy would be dictated by public referendum. Gallup died of a heart attack in Tschingel, Switzerland, on July 26, 1984. In his absence, the Gallup Organization, which employs more than three thousand and operates in over twenty countries, continues to lead the world as the surveyor of people's opinions.

GALTON, SIR FRANCIS (1822-1911)
English scientist

Born on February 16, 1822, in Birmingham, England, Francis Galton was the youngest of nine children of Samuel Tertius, a banker, and Frances Anne Violetta Galton. At the age of 16, Galton enrolled at Trinity College, Cambridge, to study medicine and mathematics. He spent the summer of 1840 exploring Constantinople, Athens, Venice, and Milan. Upon his return to school, he focused his attention fully on medicine but quickly grew disillusioned. When his father died in October 1844, he inherited a substantial amount of money, allowing him to abandon his medical studies.

In October 1845, Galton left England to travel around the Middle East and Africa for a year. He ventured down the

Sir Francis Galton *(The Library of Congress)*

fication of fingerprints for individual identification, a system left basically unchanged to this day, and the invention of a machine that made composite pictures, a precursor to the modern computerized method of removing noise from photographs.

Galton is best remembered for the work he did in his latter years on the topic of heredity, found primarily in *Natural Inheritance* (1889). Between 1888 and 1894, Galton gathered measurements on over 7,500 individuals ranging in age from 12 to 80 to study the role of inheritance in abilities. Focusing keenly on **measurement**, he contributed most importantly to the formulation of the theories of **regression** and **correlation**, the basis of biometry, which is the statistical analysis of biological phenomena. He noted that children of individuals who deviated from the norm of the general population also deviated from the norm in the same direction but to a lesser extent. If the parent deviated by x, then the offspring would deviate in the same manner as kx ($0 < k < 1$), with the k being the regression coefficient. Correlation marks the degree of relationship between two individuals of separate generations. Heredity influence is measured on a graduated scale in which parents contribute one-quarter each, grandparents contribute one-sixteenth each, and so on.

A cousin of **Charles Darwin**, Galton wholeheartedly supported Darwin's theory of evolution. Although Galton did not agree with Darwin on every matter, his admiration for his cousin was unwavering. In the analysis of his study of heredity, Galton created the science of **eugenics**, which he defined as the science of improving the inherited abilities of the population by giving what he considered the suitable races the best chance of survival. To this end, he proposed the need for a state eugenics record office, in which extensive genealogical work on families would be stored. Families would be rated as (a) gifted, (b) capable, (c) average, or (d) degenerate. Women from categories (a) and (b) would be given incentives to marry and produce children. On the other end of the scale, those deemed to be feeble-minded, repeat criminal offenders, or mentally ill should be prevented from creating offspring. In short, Galton proposed replacing Darwin's natural selection with a type of controlled artificial selection. His major works on eugenics were *Hereditary Genius* (1869) and *English Men of Science: Their Nature and Nurture* (1874).

In 1901, Galton founded the journal *Biometrika* to support his scientific interests, and in 1903, he opened the Eugenics Laboratory in the University of London. He spent his last years in ill health and died on January 17, 1911. Maligned by some observers of his lifetime achievements for his blatant racist format, others defend him as a product of his time who made considerable contributions to science.

Nile on a barge, rode horses, oxen, and camels, and took copious notes and measurements everywhere he went before returning in November 1846. In 1850 he planned a trip in conjunction with the Royal Geographical Society to South Africa. From this journey, Galton produced two travel books. The first book, *The Narrative of an Explorer in Tropical South Africa* (1853), a classic travel narrative, was written from an imperialist British perspective and focused on exciting adventures of the heroic explorer. Galton's second travel book, *The Art of Travel; or Shifts and Contrivances Available in Wild Countries* (1855), is a handbook of practical advice for the traveler. Galton received acclaim for his explorations, earning the Geographical Society's Gold Medal in 1856.

Having satisfied his travel urges, Galton turned his attention to other endeavors. He undertook a wide range of studies, made numerous discoveries, and designed various **inventions**. For example, his study of meteorology led to the publication of *Meteorographica* (1863) in which the anticyclone was explained for the first time. (Air circulates clockwise around a center of high barometric in the northern hemisphere whereas it circulates counterclockwise in the southern hemisphere.) He developed a high frequency whistle to study the hearing of zoo animals, a device cleverly planted in his cane that he could unobtrusively activate from the handle. Perhaps two of his most lasting inventions were the classi-

GAME THEORY AND STRATEGIC INTERACTION

Game theory and strategic **interaction** are related perspectives used by some sociologists to predict the behavior of rational actors. Both game theory and strategic interaction use the rational choice perspective, which assumes that actors seek to maximize outcomes based on rational thought processes. Game theory is a theory of social action based on systems of interdependency and reward structures. Actors are assumed to act intentionally, and behaviors are dependent on the actions and perceived reactions of other actors. Game theory assumes interactions between at least two actors, whether individuals or organizations. This perspective is most used in social psychology applications.

The strategic interaction perspective is often used in the study of collective behavior. According to Olsen, collective behavior presents a *social dilemma* in that individual rational actions will lead to outcomes that are collectively irrational. At the heart of this issue is the *free-rider problem* which assumes that rational actors will not engage in **collective behavior** to achieve a collective good if they think that others will shoulder alone the costs of the action. Much rational choice perspective on collective behavior seeks to address the apparent overabundance of **collective action** by using aspects of strategic interaction.

Strategic interaction in moderate-sized groups can overcome the free rider problem by mutual reciprocity; that is, each actor's cooperation is based on the cooperation of other actors. This rational, mutual cooperation can result in collective action when each actor has a positive expectation of other actors' behavior. In game theory, this type of strategic interaction is known as tit-for-tat, or TFT. In the TFT strategy, actors begin by cooperating and then engage in reciprocal cooperation with other actors. The threat of defection, or non-cooperation, acts as an incentive to cooperate for all actors.

Game theory hypothesizes many social dilemmas and attempts to predict outcomes based on rational behavior. The prisoner's dilemma is the most commonly used example of a social dilemma in game theory. The dilemma involves the hypothesis of two potential prisoners given the options to confess or not confess. If one confesses and the other does not, the non-confessor will spend twenty years as a prisoner and the confessor is set free. If both confess, each will spend five years in prison. If neither confesses, each will spend three years in prison. Although the collective outcome would be maximized by both potential prisoners not confessing, a rational actor will choose to confess, because the final outcome will involve a lower amount of years in prison no matter the decision of the other potential prisoner. (If his partner does not confess, he will be free if he confesses, as opposed to receiving three years in prison. If his partner does confess, he will spend five years in prison if he also confesses, as opposed to twenty years if he does not.) In the prisoner's dilemma, **group** outcomes are less desirable because actors tend to act according to self-interest rather than cooperatively, even in situations in which full cooperation would increase payoffs for the collectivity. The essential problem in the prisoner's dilemma is trust between actors who must fully cooperate to maximize payoff, or outcomes, and who are penalized when others defect.

One criticism of the rational choice/strategic interaction perspective is that it insists on the ability of actors to successfully complete logic problems which are well beyond the abilities of most people. Individuals are assumed to attempt to

Mohandas Gandhi *(Corbis Corporation [Bellevue])*

maximize the **probability** of success, although there is evidence that most people have a limited understanding of the computational processes necessary to make that prediction. Other criticisms suggest that emotional or altruistic responses may provide the basis for some behaviors.

GANDHI, MOHANDAS KARAMCHAND (1869-1948)
Indian religious leader, reformer, and lawyer

Mohandas Karamchand Gandhi was an revolutionary spiritual leader who used his **influence** for political and social reform. Although he held no governmental office, he was the prime mover in the struggle for India's independence. Gandhi was born on October 2, 1869, in Porbandar, a seacoast town north of Bombay. His wealthy family was of the Vaisya, or merchant, caste. He was the fourth child of Karamchand Gandhi, prime minister to the raja of three small city-states. Mohandas was married at thirteen by parental arrangement to a girl his own age, Kasturbai.

Leaving his wife, Gandhi went to England to study in 1888. In England he studied law but never completely adjusted to English lifestyle. He passed the bar on June 10, 1891, and sailed for Bombay. He attempted unsuccessfully to practice law in Rajkot and Bombay, then for a brief period served as lawyer for the prince of Porbandar.

In 1893 Gandhi represented a Moslem firm in Pretoria, capital of Transvaal in the Union of South Africa. A train incident in which he was asked by a white man to leave first-class seating led Gandhi to his work eradicating race **prejudice**, a cause that kept him in South Africa until 1914. Shortly after the train incident he called his first meeting of Indians in Pretoria and attacked racial **discrimination**.

Gandhi decided to buy a farm in Natal and return to a simpler life. He began to fast and in 1906 he became celibate after having fathered four sons. He also began to live a life of voluntary **poverty**. During this period Gandhi developed the concept of soul force, what he called "a quiet and irresistible pursuit of truth." Truth was Gandhi's chief concern, as reflected in the subtitle of his *Autobiography: The Story of My Experiments with Truth*. Truth for Gandhi was a principle which had to be discovered experimentally in each situation. Gandhi also felt the means necessarily shaped the ends.

In 1907 Gandhi urged all Indians in South Africa to defy a law requiring their registration and fingerprinting. He read Thoreau's essay "Civil Disobedience," which left a deep impression on him. He was influenced also by his correspondence with Leo Tolstoy in 1909–1910 and by John Ruskin's *Unto This Last*. By this time Gandhi had abandoned Western dress for Indian garb.

By the time he returned to India in 1915 Gandhi had become known as "Mahatmaji." Gandhi knew how to reach the masses and insisted on their resistance and spiritual regeneration. He spoke of a new, free Indian individual. He said India's shackles were self-made. Gandhi urged Indians to spin their own clothing rather than buy British goods. Spinning would create **employment** during the many annual idle months for millions of Indian peasants. He cherished the ideal of economic independence and identified industrialization with **materialism**.

In 1921 the Congress party again voted for a nonviolent disobedience campaign against the British whom Ghandi believed rendered India helpless. In 1922 Gandhi was tried and sentenced to six years in prison, but he was released two years later for an emergency appendectomy.

One form of passive resistance was the fast which Gandhi used increasingly. He undertook a 21-day fast to bring the Moslem and Hindu communities together. He also fasted in a strike of mill workers in Ahmedabad. Gandhi also developed the protest march. Countering British tax on salt for Indians, Gandhi's famous 24-day "salt march" to the sea led to a nationwide movement in illegal salt production and sale.

But Gandhi was not opposed to compromise. In 1931 he negotiated with Lord Irwin, a pact whereby civil disobedience was to be canceled, prisoners released, salt manufacture permitted on the coast, and Congress would attend the Second Round Table Conference in London.

Gandhi espoused improving the **status** of "untouchables," who Gandhi called children of God. On September 20, 1932, Gandhi began a fast to the death for these people, opposing a British plan for a separate electorate for them. Following the marriage of one of Gandhi's sons to a woman of another caste, Gandhi came to approve only intercaste marriages.

Gandhi devoted the years 1934 through 1939 to promotion of spinning, basic education, and Hindi as the national **language**. During these years Gandhi worked closely with Jawaharlal Nehru in the Congress Working Committee whom he designated as his successor.

England's entry into World War II brought mandated India's immediate involvement. Gandhi, in August 1942, proposed noncooperation, and Congress passed the "Quit India" resolution. Gandhi, Nehru, and other Congress leaders were imprisoned, sparking violence throughout India. When the British attempted to place the blame on Gandhi, he fasted three weeks in jail. He contracted malaria in prison and was released on May 6, 1944.

When Gandhi emerged from prison, he sought to avert creation of a separate Moslem state of Pakistan. Civil unrest regarding this matter resulted in Jinnah declaring August 16 "Direct Action Day," which initiated killings that left 5,000 dead and 15,000 wounded in Calcutta alone. Violence spread through country. Aggrieved, Gandhi went to Bengal, saying, "I am not going to leave Bengal until the last embers of trouble are stamped out," but while he was in Calcutta 4,500 more were killed in Bihar. Gandhi, now 77, warned that he would fast to death. Either Hindus and Moslems would learn to live together or he would die. The situation there calmed, but rioting continued elsewhere.

In March 1947 the last viceroy, Lord Mountbatten, arrived in India charged with taking Britain out of India by June 1948. Gandhi, despairing because his nation was not responding to his plea for **peace** and brotherhood, refused to participate in the independence celebrations on August 15, 1947. On September 1, 1947, after a Hindu mob broke into the home where he was staying in Calcutta, Gandhi began to fast which led to Hindu and Moslem leaders promising no more killings.

On January 13, 1948, Gandhi began his last fast in Delhi, praying for Indian unity. On January 30, as he was attending prayers, he was shot and killed by Nathuram Godse, a 35-year old editor of a Hindu Mahasabha extremist weekly in Poona.

GANS, HERBERT (1927-)
German sociologist

Herbert Gans was born May 7, 1927, in Cologne, Germany. He immigrated to the United States in 1940 and became a naturalized citizen in 1945. From 1945 to 1946, he served in the U.S. Army. In 1957, Gans received his doctorate from the University of Pennsylvania. He married Louise Gruner on March 19, 1967.

Throughout his career, Gans has worked for the Chicago Housing Authority as an assistant planner, the University of Pennsylvania Institute for Urban Studies as a professor of city planning and development, and he has been are search associate for the Center for Urban Education, New York City. Gans has as also been a professor of sociology at Columbia University and a professor of sociology and planning at the Massachusetts Institute of Technology, Cambridge.

Gans is known for his participant-observer sociological studies in which he immerses himself in the life of the **community** under consideration. Commentator John Goldthorpe finds that Gans's studies often expose social myths. *The Urban Villagers: Groups and Class in the Life of Italian-Americans,* Gans's study of Boston's West End, is, Goldthorpe feels, "in effect an excellent piece debunking the whole idea of the happy urban peasant. *The Levittowners: Ways of Life and Politics in a New Surburban Community,* attacks the myth of the suburb, which holds, according to Goldthorpe's summary, that suburbanites are anxious, bored, cultureless social climbers without communal roots. Gans's discovery, remarks Goldthorpe, that "most of the charges made against suburbia simply do not stick.... There are no good reasons for believing that the residents of Levittown are any more conformist, insecure, anxious, status-conscious, bored, etc. than otherwise comparable Americans who are not suburbanites."

Gans continues to contradict common social beliefs in *Popular Culture and High Culture,* in which, remarks Richard Todd, the author argues that "American **culture** includes several levels of taste—Gans calls them 'taste cultures'—and that any one of them is as good as any other, because each serves the needs and wants of a particular public." Gans also opposes policies which would urge that these "taste cultures" be improved and, as Christopher Lehmann-Haupt summarizes, "instead encourages 'more cultural pluralism' by means of 'subcultural programming' (or cultural programs that would appeal to groups that are now excluded by mass culture, like the poor, the old, and the ethnic)."

In *Middle American Individualism: The Future of Liberal Democracy,* Gans looks at the political and social viewpoints of the middle and working classes. He finds that these people are more interested in the well-being of their immediate circles—which Gans dubs "microsocieties"—than of **society** as a whole, but contends that this does not mean they are selfish. They want "an egalitarian, humane **welfare state** that takes care of their needs—low taxes, full employment—as well as the needs of the poor," summarizes Alex Raksin in the *Los Angeles Times Book Review.* Middle Americans' lack of interest in politics, Gans asserts, is the fault of politicians; he recommends that elected officials add staff members to reach out to disinterested or under-represented constituencies.

Gans turns his attention to the people at the bottom of the socioeconomic ladder in *The War Against the Poor: The Underclass and Anti-poverty Policy.* He asserts that many of the terms used to describe the poor— including the term "underclass"—help the rest of society maintain its detachment from the poor. These labels, according to Gans, also facilitate blaming the poor for their condition and interfere with anti-poverty efforts. "Labels may only be words," Gans writes, "but they are judgmental or normative words, which can steer institutions and individuals to punitive action." He calls not only for an end to such labeling, but also for numerous economic reforms aimed at combating **poverty**. Among the latter is a shorter work week, designed to increase the number of available jobs.

GARFINKEL, HAROLD (1917-)
American sociologist

Harold Garfinkel became known as the founder of **ethnomethodology** with his 1976 publication *Studies in Ethnomethodology.* The term "ethnomethodology" occurred to Garfinkel while he was writing up a study of jury deliberations. He observed that the jurors were preoccupied with a variety of methodological matters, such as the distinction between **fact** and opinion. The jurors worked with these distinctions methodically incoherently organized ways, counting upon one another's abilities to use them and make sense of them. Garfinkel recognized that these distinctions were made by reference to common-sense considerations. Thus, he defined ethnomethodology as the study of common-sense knowledge and the range of procedures and considerations by means of which the ordinary members of **society** make sense of, find their way about in, and act on the circumstances in which they find themselves. Ethnomethodology, translated as *members' methods* or *folk methods,* refers to the methods that ordinary people use to make sense of their everyday social world. Garfinkel recognized the **influence** of American sociologist **Talcott Parsons**, Austrian-born sociologist **Alfred Schutz**, and phenomenological philosophers Aron Gurwitsch and Edmund Husserl on his work in the development of ethnomethodology.

Born in 1917 in Newark, New Jersey, Harold Garfinkel became a doctoral student at Harvard University in 1946 and completed his Ph.D. in 1952. Early in his career, Garfinkel spent two years teaching at Ohio State and conducting research at the University of Chicago where he developed the framework for ethnomethodology. Garfinkel spent the bulk of his career at the University of California at Los Angeles (UCLA) where he was professor emeritus at the close of the twentieth century. As a result of his leadership, UCLA is considered a training center for ethnomethodologists.

There are three major concepts associated with ethnomethodology: reflexivity, accounts, and indexicality. *Reflexivity* refers to the process by which groups create social reality via thoughts and actions. Ethnomethodologists reject the idea that order comes from **conformity** to **norms** and argue that order is the social actors' awareness of options and their ability to anticipate how others are going to react in social situations. Hence, human **interaction** is reflexive in that humans interpret cues, gestures, words, and other information from one another in order to sustain reality. By *accounts* and/or accounting, ethnomethodologists mean ways in which social actors interpret or reflect upon social situations and offer an account of the situation to others. This accounting helps to explain **social order**. *Indexicality* refers to the context-specific meaning of social situations. Ethnomethodologists argue that all social behavior must be interpreted within the context of biography, intention, setting, time, etc. Other terms associated with ethnomethodology include etcetera principle, natural language, and conversation analysis.

Garfinkel became well known for his use of *breeching experiments.* In breeching experiments, researchers violate normal codes of behavior and observe the reaction of the sub-

Two homosexual men at gay pride rally in Manhattan, New York
(Corbis Corporation [Bellevue]).

jects as they attempt to reestablish order or make sense of the situation. Garfinkel's student sused breeching experiments to illustrate the basic principles of ethnomethodology. An example is the boarder assignment in which students imagined that theywere boarders or guests in their own homes and acted in ways congruent with this **identity**. Family members were often perplexed by such behavior and expressed emotions which ranged from shock to anger. They often tried to make sense of the situation and reestablish order by demanding explanations for such strange behavior. According to ethnomethodologists, these reactions illustrate the importance of individuals acting according to the common-sense principles of how they are supposed to act. In another breeching experiment, students were asked to engage in conversations in which they insisted that others clarify their common-sense remarks. For example, when asked, "How are you?" and given the reply, "I'm tired," students would insist that subjects specify their meaning of the word "tired." Subjects became frustrated and made attempts to restore order. These experiments have become know as "garfinkeling" and reveal that in ordinary, everyday situations, people assume that others share the same expectations. When asked, "How are you?" we expect a particular response, such as "Fine." When these expectations are violated, there is confusion. Attempts to restore order to the situation reveal something about how the structure of everyday life is produced and maintained.

GAY AND LESBIAN STUDIES

Sociologists have long been interested in gays, lesbians, bisexuals, and other people with same-sex romantic or erotic desires. However, prior to the 1960s, widespread **homophobia** convinced most of them that such desires were extremely rare,

and confined to prisoners, criminals, and the mentally ill; thus, there was no "gay and lesbian studies" as such, merely accounts of how these disreputable individuals managed to locate each other in sleazy underground "scenes" and hide their stigma from the outside world. Social **deviance** theorists such as **Peter Berger** and **Erving Goffman** frequently used stereotypes of gay and lesbian people to represent "deviants."

In the 1960s and 1970s, several widespread and multifaceted **social movements** transformed gay and lesbian self-identity from social outcast to cultural minority, from a few individuals skulking in bars to a people with a history, a **culture**, and a destiny. The number and variety of gay and lesbian social institutions increased dramatically; suddenly there were gay bookstores, community centers, business and professional organizations, churches, sports clubs, radio/TV programs, and college courses. Gradually mainstream academic, medical, religious, and legal institutions began to acknowledge that at least some gay and lesbian people might not be so "deviant" after all.

The first gay and lesbian studies appeared during this period, as William O. Murray, Esther Newton, Deborah Wolf, and others examined gay-defined neighborhoods, kinship networks, and cultural institutions. Studies of "coming out" and stigma management in a presumably hostile world were still popular, but a new generation of gay scholars, such as Barry Adam and Jonathan Katz, increasingly criticized the inevitability of this stigma and hostility, instead theorizing that anti-gay **prejudice** had its roots in gender and class oppression.

The conservative backlash of the 1980s, coupled with the devastating effects of the AIDS epidemic among gay men, decreased interest in large-scale studies of the gay community. However, a remarkable interest existed in smaller, more intimate groups of gay and lesbian people in both expected and unexpected locations, from New York City to small towns in North Dakota; ethnic and cultural minorities, teenagers and college students, activists and academics, suburbanites, older persons, church members and pagans, parents and couples were all represented. Analyses expanded from mere stigma management to political participation, belief systems, relationship dynamics, sexual practices, and especially the impact of AIDS. This period saw the establishment of gay and lesbian studies as a legitimate academic discipline, drawing from several fields of the social sciences and humanities, with courses, concentrations, and majors available at dozens of universities.

During the 1990s, queer **theory** shot into prominence in literary and **cultural studies** and, under the tutelage of Steven Seidman and others, entered the field of **sociology**, where it found a home alongside debates concerning **identity** politics. Briefly, queer theory maintains that the heterosexual/homosexual dichotomy is not a biological or cultural necessity but the product of a hegemonic **ideology** that constrains and compels individual desire; there are no gay or straight people (or even, according to Judith Butler, male or female people), merely people who have been forced to adhere to fragile, contingent, and ultimately oppressive identities. The **model** of gay and lesbian people as a cultural minority, with a distinct history and destiny, is therefore nonsense, actually presenting the experiences of white, urban, middle-class gay men as universal, and, complicit with the privileging of hegemonic **heterosexuality**, it can only contribute to the marginalization of same-sex desire. When this privilege declines and gay and lesbian identities are no longer stigmatized, no one will bother using the terms gay, lesbian, or straight to describe their relationships or their lives. Traditional theorists disagree, noting that in relatively benign, non-oppressive cultural climates, the strength of gay and lesbian identification tends to increase rather than decrease.

Queer theory can obviously have a deleterious effect on community organizing, since it posits no community to organize. Gay and lesbian studies is currently embroiled in sometimes harsh debates between traditional theorists, who maintain that gay and lesbian people and heterosexuals are uniquely different, with different cultural and even physiological traits that must be recognized and celebrated, and queer theorists, who maintain that they differ only insofaras they are forced into inauthentic, mutually exclusive categories of identity. Recent studies seem to suggest that sociological interest in queer theory is declining somewhat, as the cultural minority model achieves prominence in legal and political rhetoric and in popular opinion.

See also Bisexuality; Homosexuality

GEMEINSCHAFT AND GESELLSCHAFT

These German terms are taken from Ferdinand Tönnies 1887 book entitled, appropriately enough, *Gemeinschaft and Gesellschaft*. Translated usually as **community** and **society** respectively, this distinction is part of Tönnies' answer to one of the main questions **sociology** asks: What holds society together? This distinction serves to communicate the difference between the sort of relationships found in social groups. Simple societies, those in which relationships are built around kinship and guild, are examples of *gemeinschaft*. These relationships are more emotional and affective. They are face-to-face and generally exist in smaller, more homogeneous groups. On the other hand, complex societies are characterized by relationships built around **rationality** and calculation. They are impersonal and based on specialization and heterogeneity more than similarity. Tönnies called this type of society a *gesellschaft*. His work attempts to do more than merely describe these two types of relationships.

Tönnies' larger project, similar to the work of **Max Weber**, was an attempt to explain the process of European modernization. He described modernization as the progressive loss of gemeinschaft. The simple groupings of pre-modern Europe characterized by intimacy and sameness gave way, through a process of industrialization and **rationalization**, to complex societies. Of course, both types of relationships exist in the modern world. Intimate relationships indicative of gemeinschaft groupings do not disappear after industrialization. Rather, society as a whole is characterized by more impersonal relationships like those in a gesellschaft, while within the society one can still find smaller subgroups that function

as a gemeinschaft. For instance, families and some religious traditions attempt to provide a sense of community and belonging for members. In that sense, they function as a gemeinschaft within a gesellschaft, a community within a society. The Amish settlements of Pennsylvania and Ohio are often cited examples of a present-day gemeinschaft. Other sociologists have offered similar analyses. Most notably, Émile Durkheim in his 1893 work *The Division of Labor in Society* proposed the concepts of **mechanical and organic solidarity** to describe what holds society together. Although Durkheim's work has over shadowed Tönnies', the distinction is similar.

GENDER INCLUSIVE LANGUAGE

Gender Inclusive Language is language that avoids gender attribution by using ''neutral'' words rather than masculine-associated or feminine-associated words. Some linguists and other language theorists maintain that language is already neutral, claiming that words perceived as negative are not always intended as such. Others assert that the English language makes use of gender-biased words that causes social groups, such as women, to feel derogated, minimized, or ignored.

Language is a symbolic cultural element, a way to communicate and to share common understandings of things and experiences in life. The meanings of things and the words applied to them are socially constructed. Language is a way of creating social **structure** because it allows the communication of **values** and ideas between people. It is also a means of power and control, thus, language which makes use of gender-specific words may cause social groups, such as women, to feel oppressed.

Language is socially created, so it is one of the most obvious areas in which one can see the subordinate or dominant social position of a group, such as women. Widespread derogatory, insulting, or non-inclusive language can indicate a **group** is oppressed. There are many ways that gendered language creates, reflects, and helps perpetuate the structural oppression of women. Some words used to refer to women are derivations or extensions of words used to refer to men. The words actor/actress or mister/mistress may indicate that the masculine version is more important and the feminine version is simply an addition or an afterthought. Other titles are intended to indicate a woman's sexual or marital availability (Miss vs. Mrs.), assuming that **marriage** is the expected norm for women. This does not hold true for men, however, as ''Mr.'' is applied to both married and unmarried men. Words used to describe women or their actions often have connotations that are negative, demeaning, or belittling. The word ''mistress'' implies a woman is ''bad,'' using words such as ''kitten'' or ''doll'' suggests a woman who is dependent or a plaything, and the word ''girl,'' when used to refer to an adult woman, indicates the woman is perceived as a child, not as a responsible adult.

In the workplace, many job titles indicate that men are expected to fulfill the position (policeman, repairman, fireman). When a woman is in a traditionally male-dominated profession, her gender is often pointed out (female lawyer, female doctor). These words imply that women in certain professions are anomalies or exceptions to the rule.

Not only does the English language favor men, it is sometimes overtly hostile to women. The primary example is how it derogates them sexually. There are about 220 words or phrases for sexually promiscuous women, but only about 22 for men. There are words for women that can be sexual in nature (madam, mistress), and words whose parallel for men are indicative of power and superiority (master, lord). Also, there are many insults leveled at men that reference femaleness and derogate feminine characteristics, for example, sissy, or acting or throwing like a girl.

Unlike other forms of institutionalized oppression or inequality, language cannot be legislated. It needs to change in day-to-day life, in personal interactions, and in media usage. Professional language is one of the areas in which language has been changing. People have started using gender-neutral terms to refer to certain positions (officer, not policeman) and using "person" as a suffix rather than "man" (repairperson, not repairman). Some efforts at creating a gender inclusive language have also been made in religion. These efforts have centered on stopping the use of "he" to refer to all human beings and on demanding that words referring to God be gender-neutral or include female imagery. Most resistance has come from religions that will not ordain women or maintain a physical separation of women and men during religious rituals. Other attempts at creating gender inclusive language have focused on co-opting already existing words and altering their meanings in day-to-day usage. For example, words such as "girl" and "chick" that used to have derogatory connotations are now used as terms of endearment or empowerment. Gender inclusive language creates a neutral language that attempts to treat all social groups as equals.

GENDER NORMS

Gender **Norms** are the accepted, expected, and prohibited behaviors and beliefs in a given **society** based on gender and sex. Norms are the guidelines people are directly or indirectly pressured to follow in their interactions with others. They guide, control, or regulate how to act and what to expect of other people. There are different norms for women and men and, in many societies, these norms are mutually exclusive. Some behaviors are more acceptable or expected for one gender than for another. Boys, for example, are encouraged not to cry while girls are taught not to be too aggressive.

Some sociologists believe these differences are due to biological forces, but others argue that gender norms are learned through **socialization** as individuals and through social institutions. Norms are not innate, but they are historically-specific, situational, and culturally-specific. Although every **culture** has different norms for women and men, these norms are not the same among all cultures. Gender norms are created in, taught by, and reinforced by the social institutions in a given society; norms are affected by these institutions at the same time that they affect institutions.

First, gender norms change over time. Although each society has different norms for women than there are for men, these norms are not static. In Western societies the most evident change over time has been in the norms for women; these have become less rigid with women becoming progressively less constricted in their activities. In the United States, however, some expectations have remained consistent. Males are still expected to be masculine: strong (physically and emotionally), competent, rational, independent, and be able to provide. Females are still expected to be feminine: cooperative, compliant, emotional, dependent, empathetic, and nurturing caregivers.

Gender norms are also situational. There are some behaviors that are acceptable in one situation but not in another. Men are allowed to cry at funerals but not upon losing a poker game. There are also gender norms that are associated with certain positions, independent of the person holding the position. Nurses, for example, are expected to be kind and nurturing, whether they are female or male.

Finally, gender norms are culturally-specific. If they were innate, everyone around the world would act the same gender-wise. But this is not the case. Different cultures have different expectations for women and men. Individuals who do not conform to the accepted and expected gender norms in a particular culture are socially condemned, informally, by their social groups, or formally, by law. This can cause problems when one does not understand the gender norms in an unfamiliar culture. In Islamic countries, for example, women are not allowed to wear shorts in public but it is commonplace in the United States.

Moreover, some norms are followed more strictly than others, and some are more seriously sanctioned than others. **Folkways** are norms customary to a society but not strictly enforced. Women are expected to want children, and are criticized when they do not. **Mores** are norms that are more important to a culture and breaking one of them is grounds for public denunciation. For example, men get arrested for sexual assault. This difference in norms is linked to the distinction between ideal and real norms. Ideal norms are the standards we are supposed to follow and real norms are the way we actually live our lives. They can overlap to some degree, but ideal norms are usually more rigid and extreme than real norms.

A primary concern about gender norms for scholars is that those characteristics attributed to or associated with men are more highly valued and sought-after than those associated with women. Norms for **masculinity** and **femininity** have historically been considered mutually exclusive. But recent research shows that we all have both masculine and feminine characteristics. Women, in particular, have challenged the norms expected of them. They are now fulfilling roles that have historically been considered exclusively male. Research shows that in the United States the gender-typed restrictions on boys are more severe than they are on girls, which means that boys are more severely criticized for violating gender norms than are girls. Researchers explain this as evidence of the higher social value placed on masculine characteristics than on feminine ones. It remains acceptable for women to be like men, but unacceptable for men to be like women.

See also Gender Roles; Norms

GENDER ROLES

Gender Roles are those positions, statuses, activities, and behaviors that are designated by **society** as appropriate for one's sex. Roles are expected or prohibited behaviors that correlate with a given social **status** and are evident at the individual and institutional levels. Women and men have traditionally been expected to act and think different; they have different roles to perform. The term "gender roles" reflects the social aspects of behavior and challenges the idea that gendered behavior is innately tied to biological sex. Instead, such explanations attempt to determine to what extent social constructions of gender behavior determine gender roles.

The term "role" can be limiting because it implies that something is rigidly defined, but gender roles are culturally and historically specific, changing over time. Although certain gender roles have remained somewhat consistent over time (women as primary caretakers for children), many have changed. Gender roles can change for individual or institutional reasons. Individuals can have experiences that cause them to change their ideas about appropriate or desired gender roles. For example, a girl may be told she cannot play sports because sports are for boys, but she plays anyway. A social **institution** may also change, causing adjustments in other areas of society, such as economic changes that may force a stay-at-home mother to take a job to support her family.

There are also cross-cultural differences in gender roles. In some cultures, women must stay home and take care of their children; in others, they work outside the home and are financially independent. In some societies, women are not allowed to vote or to own **property**, while in others, women have suffrage and hold the same job positions as men. The historical and cultural specificity of gender roles shows us that they are socially created, not biologically determined.

Ultimately, the two components of gender roles are that which is expected of one by others and that which one expects of oneself. Thus, gender roles are connected to gender **identity**, or to those things that one is taught about what is appropriate and affect how one sees oneself as a gendered being. Sometimes there may be gendered expectations one does not want to fulfill. In these cases, there can be internal or external conflict which can be resolved by either conforming to the appropriate gender **role** or challenging the roles at the individual or structural level.

GENDER SOCIALIZATION

Gender **Socialization** is the process through which one learns appropriate or expected behavior and attitudes for one's gender. In general, one is taught that women and men do and

should act differently. These ideas are based on stereotypes; men are taught they should be masculine and women are taught they should be feminine. Gender socialization deeply affects a person's self-concept and **identity** as a gendered being. This process is studied extensively in sociology, psychology, and social **psychology**.

Gender socialization is a life-long process. One is continually exposed to a variety of ideas and situations in which one sees or thinks differently about our own gender and the gender of others. The messages one receives about gender, beginning in childhood, either reinforce or contradict each other, creating a constantly shifting idea about what gender is and how it affects personal identity. Gender socialization begins when a newborn is assigned the biological label of female or male. Gender and sex, although not the same, are connected and affect each other. Thus, the sex label we receive at birth will play a large part in determining our gender socialization.

Gender is an organizing principle in all societies, learned at the individual level and through social institutions. Although gender socialization is found in every **culture**, it is culturally-specific; there are no universal norms of gender socialization. Socialization is connected to the social institutions of a given culture, therefore, it will also reflect the **norms** evident in those institutions. Social institutions are those parts of **society** that show us how to act in different areas of social life. Historically, the social institutions that have most directly affected our gender socialization are the family, the media, peer groups, religion, education, law and **justice**, and politics.

Gender socialization begins in the **family** because these are the people with whom most people have the most contact at a young age. Most research on gender socialization, therefore, has concerned interactions in the family. It is through the family that we learn the jobs, behaviors, and attitudes we are supposed to do or have as women or men in the larger society.

Today, however, the media is also considered a primary socializing agent because of the extent to which people are exposed to different forms of media, including **television**, movies, magazines, and newspapers. Through the media, women and men receive gender-based images of how they should look, how they should act, how they should interact with others, and what they should own. Often, these gendered images are based on unrealistic and unattainable gender stereotypes. Their prevalence, however, leads people to act as if such ideals must be part of their own social gender identity. For example, images of overly-thin female models used in many fashion magazines have been linked to a rise in anorexia and bulimia in teenage girls trying to attain the unattainable.

The toy and clothing industries have also been identified as important agents of gender socialization. Certain clothes and toys are marketed as appropriate for either girls or boys. Dolls and pastel (particularly pink) clothing are marketed to girls and toy guns and primary colored (especially blue) clothing are marketed to boys. Although pink and blue are not biologically-determined gender colors, these stereotypes are so prevalent that they inform the social identity of boys and girls.

In the United States, particularly in recent years, **gender norms** and gender socialization have changed, especially for women. These changes are more evident in the middle class than in any other economic **group** possibly because this is the group that relies most heavily on two-incomes. Much social change can be attributed to changes in the economy. Traditionally, women were taught to be passive and dependent, and men were taught to be providers. But with the move toward a more competitive and high-pressure economy, women are now being socialized in more traditionally masculine ways that encourages them to be more independent and self-sufficient, while men are being taught to be more cooperative and emotional. This demonstrates the sociological belief that gender socialization creates and perpetuates a large part of our personal and social identities.

See also Gender Roles

GENDER STRATIFICATION

Gender Stratification is a form of **social stratification** in which people are hierarchically ranked in a **society** based on gender. It is one of the organizing components of all societies and is based on gender inequality, a system of oppression in which men are socially dominant and women are socially subordinate. In a system of gender stratification, women experience institutional inequality and a lack of access to privileges and resources. This system results from the belief that biological males are inherently masculine and biological females are inherently feminine with males superior to females.

Stratified gender systems are evidenced at both the structural and cultural levels. At the structural level a stratification system based on gender is created and maintained and at the cultural level an **ideology** exists that men's activities are more valuable than women's activities. Institutionally and individually, men are ranked above women of the same **race** and class. The activities men participate in are more highly valued and rewarded than the activities of women, even when these activities are similar. For example, male lawyers tend to earn more **money** than female lawyers in the same position. This ideology both creates and perpetuates a devaluation of women.

Across cultures different kinds and levels of gender stratification exist. Some cultures subordinate women more than others. In cultures where there is a high level of gender stratification, women have little power and few, if any, legal rights. Some of the common global disadvantages of gender stratification for women as a **group** include lack of access to education, political representation, and reproductive rights (birth control or abortion); discrimination and harassment in the workplace; lower standards of **health care**; and a "second shift" of work. One of the most dangerous results of gender stratification for women has been a sexual double standard. Men tend to have more sexual autonomy and be criticized less for sexual promiscuity. Women's sexuality is still strictly controlled in many cultures, and women continue to be the victims of much sexual violence, from rape to genital mutilation.

Gender has not always been studied as an independent component of stratification; researchers previously assumed gender was a reflection of class stratification. Now, however, gender is considered a major determinant of global stratification. Theorists continue to study how and why systems of gender stratification are created and perpetuated, and continue to explore the interconnections between gender and other components of stratification such as class, race, ethnicity, and sexual orientation.

See also Social Stratification

GENDER STUDIES

Gender Studies is a multidisciplinary approach to studying gender. It considers the nature of gender, its social construction, why and how gender is important in different cultures, and the ramifications of gender at the institutional and individual levels. Gender studies is related to, but different from, **women's studies**, which focuses on changing androcentric (male-biased) social institutions, particularly academia, to incorporate the contributions and experiences of women. Gender studies looks at the problematic nature of gender as a theoretical and methodological **concept**.

Much gender research is being done on the intersection of gender roles and identities and the gendered nature of social institutions. This research, which looks at gender both in terms of the individual and social institutions, examines why individuals or groups do and do not conform to conventional gender roles or expectations. Gender studies also explores how gender is interconnected with **race**, class, and sexual orientation, and examines how these systems of oppression affect the **life chances** people have and life choices they make as a result.

The major challenge in gender studies is how to define the components being studied. Conventional androcentric scholarship divides gender into the two mutually exclusive categories of feminine (women) and masculine (men). Studying the institutional and individual creation and perpetuation of gender within the framework of these two mutually exclusive and static categories ignores the process of gender, making it difficult to identify and define gender in research. Gender theorists challenge this traditional assumption about the mutual exclusivity of feminine and masculine and work to develop conceptualizations of gender as a social construction which is neither static nor categorical.

Some gender theorists theorize about a **society** with little or no gender differentiation. This is a purely hypothetical exercise because all societies are structured, to some extent, by gender divisions. Such attempts, however, challenge the assumption that every society needs to be structured around gender as well as the idea that gender and sex are innately connected variables.

See also Men's Studies; Women's Studies

GENDERED DIVISION OF LABOR

The Gendered Division of Labor (GDOL) is how a **society** divides labor along the lines of gender. Women and men tend to do different kinds of work in every society. Different tasks, jobs, and careers are considered appropriate for women and men both at the individual and institutional levels. Historically, this division has been based on the assumption that women and men are biologically programmed to do different kinds of work. Sociologists, however, see the GDOL as socially constructed. The current GDOL in the United States gives men more status and power and disadvantages women financially and politically. It is a structural way of maintaining women's subordination.

In the United States the GDOL is based in the ideology of separate spheres, public and private, that originated during the **Industrial Revolution**. Traditionally, the private sphere has been associated with women and the public sphere has been associated with men. During and after the Industrial Revolution, and with the rise of **capitalism**, more men moved into the paid **labor force** (the public sphere), where they received **money** for their labor and became more highly valued in the capitalist society. But household activities (the private sphere) was, and still is, unpaid labor; it is devalued as are the people who do this work. The private sphere entails domestic and family-oriented work inside the home for no pay, as well as the physical and emotional caretaking of others. The public sphere includes the labor force and work outside the home for pay, and usually entails intellectual or rational pursuits. Women, however, have never experienced the clear division between the public and private spheres as have men. For women, home has always also included work, and the labor force has always included emotional caretaking.

There are both individual and institutional ramifications of the GDOL for women and these two levels are inextricably linked. Today, the majority of adult women work outside the home, and they comprise almost half of the labor force. But they are also still responsible for sixty-five to eighty percent of domestic work (cleaning, cooking, shopping, childcare), even if they work full-time outside the home. This inequality leads to what theorist Arlie Hochschild termed the "second shift," the idea that women work a full day in the workforce but return home to another full-time job caring for the family, with little help from male partners.

Throughout the economy women and men are concentrated in different areas. Women's jobs and careers tend to be lower paid and of lower **status** than those of men. **Professions** deemed appropriate for women usually entail the same work women do in their home and family life. Women are concentrated in professions that require emotional labor, such as teachers, nurses, and receptionists while men are concentrated in professions requiring physical or intellectual labor, such as in construction, or as doctors, or politicians. When women do work in male-dominated fields, they usually make less money and have fewer opportunities for advancement (termed the **glass ceiling** effect). If women come to dominate a field previously dominated by men, the status and pay scale of that profession falls over time. An important impact on women's potential advancement in the labor force is their responsibility for their children. This can lead to interruptions in women's careers and can inhibit their ability to advance professionally.

The inferior status of women in the paid labor force can also lead to problems such as **sexual harassment** or being unable to break through the "old boy's network" (the network of contacts maintained by business men).

There are several perspectives on the GDOL. Functionalists claim that it is a necessary part of society, maintaining that we need gendered labor distinctions for the proper functioning of families and society. Human capital theorists claim that the work people do is their own choice, determined by the amount of human and **cultural capital** they accumulate and the supply and demand in a society. Thus, women and men are doing the work they choose to do and the GDOL is a result of conscious choices, not institutional gender inequality. Conflict and feminist theorists believe that the GDOL is negative and is primarily the result of male dominance in the family and the workplace. According to conflict and feminist theorists, the male-biased GDOL is a result of **patriarchy** and capitalism, both of which they believe must be abolished.

See also Comparable Worth; Dual Labor Market; Labor Force

GENDERED IDENTITY

Gendered **Identity** is one's sense of self as female or male (biological sex) and as a woman or man (gender). It is the internalization of social messages of society's expectations as to how to act as masculine or feminine beings. Gendered identity is both categorical, centering on the awareness of oneself as biologically female or male, and variable, or influenced by social expectations and the degree to which one is feminine or masculine.

Sociologists and social psychologists contend that gendered identity, like other identities, is a process, not a static achievement; it can, and often does, change over time. The sociological study of gendered identity focuses on the meanings we ascribe to ourselves. Psychologists, on the other hand, see gendered identity as a fairly stable part of our personality.

Gendered identity is not purely a result of personal choice. It is also influenced by culturally-specific **gender roles**, **norms**, and socialization. The **culture** into which we are born will contribute to determining how we see ourselves as women or men because each culture has its own conceptions of gender. How we see ourselves and how we choose to act is affected by the things we learn and are taught as appropriate, or not, for our gender in our culture. Those messages that are incorporated within the self or attributed to causes outside the self affect personal gendered identity. Research has shown that women tend to develop relational gender identities, rooted in relationships with and emotional connections to others, while men tend to develop individualistic gender identities, rooted in a sense of uniqueness or separation from others.

Our gendered identity is something we usually take for granted because gender **socialization** starts at birth. The formation of gendered identity begins when we are labeled as female or male and start to learn the social expectations that correlate with these labels. Because gendered identity can change over time, we can display different gendered behaviors at different times or in different situations. We can also question or alter how we see ourselves as gendered beings over the course of our lives because there are changing cultural expectations for women and men that are not consistent across **race**, class, sexual orientation, or religious affiliation.

See also Gender Roles

GENEALOGY

Genealogy, a critical component of kinship theory, is a significant study in kinship-based societies. Genealogy studies the origins of families based on records of events in the lives of individuals and their ancestors.

Often, people research their ancestors out of curiosity, but may use genealogical research to establish a right to **property** or to identify parents or children who have left the **family** through **divorce** or **adoption**. Researchers, some of whom may be professional genealogical agents or genealogists, create a record of the births, deaths, and marriages of all individuals in a family by researching vital records kept by government departments, churches, libraries, official archival repositories, or other locations. Researchers may use a full range of documentary evidence, including **census** records, land records, probate records, **church** records, family letters, Bibles, newspaper clippings, obituaries, and printed family histories. From these records, researchers prepare lineage charts and family histories.

There are several arenas that support genealogical research. There are national genealogical societies, state libraries, and archives. The Family History Library of the Genealogical Society of the Church of Jesus Christ of Latter-day Saints is the largest genealogical library. Located in Salt Lake City, Utah, the library houses microfilm records of government and church record repositories as well as collections of other genealogical libraries.

GENERALIZED BELIEF

A generalized belief is a proposition or a part of a proposition that supposedly reflects some part of collective reality. Sometimes known as a stereotype, and often considered common knowledge among certain groups, whether or not they are true, generalized beliefs are an interpretation of what people as a **group** have seen and experienced and how they anticipate future events.

People hold generalized beliefs about people or objects. Generalized beliefs are the attribution of certain characteristics to people solely due to their membership in a particular group or to something because it is an example of a certain occurrence or object. These beliefs can apply to certain groups based on what people see as demographic facts or concepts of them as a group or class of people, whether or not the belief is accurate (e.g., all black men are criminals), or they can focus on social institutions or professions (e.g., all lawyers are greedy, corporations do not care about consumer safety).

Generalized beliefs are necessary for **social movements** and collective action. They can be used as justification for **discrimination** or even violence against certain people. In these cases, some generalized beliefs can be justification for group action that will result in a relief of anxiety or tension, whether or not this action is productive in the long run or not (i.e., the belief in Los Angeles that the police department was racist resulted in riots). Thus, generalized beliefs are sometimes identified with **public opinion**.

Generalized belief systems are hard to change because they are usually seen as **fact**, not belief. They can persist even in the face of contradictory evidence because people ignore new evidence, interpret the new evidence so that it is harmless or coincides with the original belief, or recognize the new information as inconsistent, but maintain the original belief nonetheless. These reactions are in part because generalized beliefs give people answers to their questions or relieve **stress** in uncomfortable situations. A generalized belief can provide a source of the strain and a course of action to take to relieve the strain (e.g., because all black men are criminals, we need to put them all in jail). People also cling to their generalized beliefs because they support their world view and their place in that world. If their generalized beliefs are challenged, then their sense of **identity** is also challenged.

See also Stereotype

GENERALIZED OTHER

The generalized other is a **concept** developed by American sociologist George Herbert Mead (1863-1931) in his classic work *Mind, Self, and Society* (1934). Mead defined the generalized other as a ''community of attitudes,'' an abstract set of cultural **norms** and **values** which serves as a reference point from which individuals evaluate their identities and guide their behavior. The generalized other is an important component in Mead's theory of the social self. Mead argued that the development of the self occurs in three stages. First, in the play stage children learn to take the role of one significant individual at a time. Later, in the game stage children develop the ability to take simultaneously the roles of many individuals. Finally, in the stage of the generalized other children are able to take the role of an abstract, cultural community of attitudes. For Mead, it is the process of developing the ability to take the role of the generalized other that marks the final stage in the development of the social self.

Upon reaching this stage individuals internalize the **culture** of their society and are able to guide their self-evaluations and behavior in terms of general societal standards. The internalization of a set of abstract cultural norms and values provides the means of social coordination among the members of a social **group**. In this way, Mead's conception of the generalized other provides a theoretical link between the self, social **interaction**, and more large-scale societal processes.

Mead's notion of the generalized other has also been seen as an important theory of **social control**. Here, the forces of social **coercion** are not understood as merely external to individuals but, instead, as the result of internalized social pressures. Thus, individuals, through the internalization of the generalized, cultural standards of their **society**, are able to self-monitor their own behavior and act as their own self-sanctioning force.

More recently, Mead's conception of the generalized other has been augmented by **reference group** theory. This theoretical approach modifies Mead's theory by arguing that individuals in large, complex, and modern societies do not necessarily share the same generalized other as a social reference point. Instead, such individuals may utilize a wide array of social groups in assessing their identities and coordinating their social behavior. Thus, sociologists hope to understand how individuals in complex societies can collectively produce such a wide array of behaviors, often marked by heterogeneity and contradiction.

GENERATION GAP

The generation gap is a culturally-produced phenomenon, involving adolescents and their parents, which indicates the differences between one generation and the next. The generation gap is thought to be culturally produced because at one point in the past people went directly from childhood to adulthood, and there was no generation gap. A generation gap occurs when social changes, such as technological developments, turn the child into the expert and leave the parent to be the student. These changes make it difficult for the parent to connect with and direct the adolescent, thus creating a gap.

Currently in the United States five generations exist, each having its own view of **society** based upon that generation's upbringing and the social atmosphere of its adolescent years. The first, the G.I. Generation (born 1901–1924) raised during the Great Depression and World War II, are known for being high achievers. The Silent Generation (born 1925–1942) was raised during a relatively peaceful period in U.S. history. They invented organizations such as the Peace Corps which helped them to identify as a generation. The Silent Generation is known for being cautious. The Boomer Generation (born 1943–1960) was a generation of change, and they are known for having high self-esteem and being self-indulgent. Next, Generation X (born 1961–1981) were the first "latchkey" kids who had to learn at an early age to fend for themselves due to both parents or a single parent working outside the home. This generation is thought of as self-concerned. The Millennial Generation (born 1982–2003) has parents who are concerned with such dangers as drugs, teen pregnancy, AIDS, and media-induced violence. Parents and politicians are said to be taking renewed interest in the raising of this generation.

GENOCIDE

Genocide is the systematic, intentional attempt by an authority to kill *en masse* the members of a socially defined category. The word "genocide" was coined by scholar and Polish refu-

Six million Jews were exterminated during World War II in the most extreme episode of genocide on record *(United States Holocaust Memorial Museum)*.

gee Raphaël Lemkin in 1944, to describe the Jewish Holocaust during World War II, as well as the mass murder of other groups by the Hitler regime. Six million Jews and fourteen million others were exterminated in the most extreme episode of genocide on record. In 1948, genocide became a construct in international law with the passage of the United Nations Convention on the Prevention and Punishment of the Crime of Genocide. However, the Genocide Convention, as it is known, has been frequently criticized for excluding political victim groups from legal protection and for not offering any mechanism for the prosecution of perpetrators.

Although the word genocide is relatively new, the practice is ancient. The Roman army leveled the city of Carthage in 146 BC, leaving few survivors. In addition to the Holocaust, there were several other cases of genocide during the twentieth century, a few of which are well-known. In 1915, the Turkish Ittihada regime eliminated much of the ethnic Armenian population, which was seen as a threat to the burgeoning Turkish **nationalism**. In Cambodia (Kampuchea) during the mid-1970s, the Khmer Rouge executed over one million people, mostly city-dwellers, in an attempt to erase any trace of Western culture. More recently, the 1990s have witnessed further genocides. In Rwanda, over 800,000 Hutus were killed by the Tutsi government, military, and loyalists, partially in retribution of the 1972 genocide of the Tutsi in Burundi. In the former Yugoslavia, Serbian intellectuals recreated Serbian ethnic identity and spread anti-Muslim rhetoric, eventually leading the Yugoslav army in the genocide of Muslims in Srebrenica and other **cities**.

Sociologists and other social scientists engaged in comparative genocide studies seek to draw parallels among many instances of genocide to find common threads of **causality**. For instance, the political scientist Barbara Harff, comparing a dozen cases of genocide in the twentieth century, has found that genocide is more likely in states that have experienced dramatic structural change or sharp internal cleavages than in states with stable social structures. According to **Irving Louis Horowitz**, a sociologist, societies which are permissive and tolerant are extremely unlikely to be genocidal, whereas repressive regimes have a higher likelihood of being or becoming genocidal. The late sociologist Leo Kuper emphasized the ideological aspects of genocide, explaining that such large-scale murder is only possible after the dehumanization and vilification of the victim **group**.

GENTRIFICATION

Gentrification is the return of wealthy families or businesses to impoverished city neighborhoods. This occurrence sometimes results from specific campaign of tax or other incentives but more often results from basic economics in which urban **property** values sink to a point where the land becomes a desirable commodity once again.

These "gentry" are typically young, white, and white collar. They may have been raised in the suburbs but work in the city; thus, the move allows them easier access to their jobs and also to urban entertainment and services, such as museums, art galleries, and restaurants.

The presence of these new families and businesses generally begins to drive the prices up once more which leads to further revitalization of the area. At the same time that an apparently positive transformation is taking place, however, poorer residents may no longer be able to afford to stay in their own homes with the increased living costs and property taxes. Likewise, many of the small businesses favored by the working class may be replaced by more expensive "upscale" boutiques and gourmet shops. Even more troubling is the incidence of campaigns to clean up the streets in which the newly arrived wealthy actively seek to remove existing residents because of their perceived negative impact on the neighborhood. Gentrification often provides an apparent success story for government officials who want to prove they have rescued a blighted city, but most studies find that the problems of the urban poor require more complex and long-term solutions.

From the point of view of many of the poor and working class, however, gentrification is merely a cosmetic effect, an apparent success story for government officials to point to as an example of their efforts to rescue a blighted city. Most studies find that the problem of revitalizing a city without exacerbating the plight of the urban poor requires a more complex and far-reaching solution.

GEOPOLITICS

First used in 1917 by the Swedish scholar Rudolf Kjellen, the term Geopolitics describes a field of study that seeks to explain world political developments in terms of geographic space. Geopolitics describes the progress of a state's territorial expansion and sets up a relationship between geographic space and foreign policy that is studied by geographers, historians and political scientists. The main theory underlying geopolitics proposes that natural boundaries and access to waterways are

critical to the survival of a nation. As a result, nations struggle to possess geographical territories with strong natural boundaries and waterway access in order to survive. Kjellen claimed that a state would exhibit organic growth and behave like a biological organism, following the same kinds of evolutionary patterns. This same theory had been advocated by Friedrich Ratzel in the late 1800's.

In addition to Kjellen's writings, the theories of Halford Mackinder also helped to shape geopolitical study. In 1919, Mackinder formed a theory that described the patterns of world power in terms of geographic control. According to this theory, continental Eurasia was central to world power, and the ruling power of Eurasia would ultimately dominate world power. In Germany, Karl Haushofer used geopolitical theory to support the country's expansionist policies in the first half of the twentieth century. Haushofer founded the Institute of Geopolitics in Munich in 1922 and his theories were ultimately used to support the expansion of the Nazi rule in Germany.

The theoretical concepts of geopolitics continue to be debated. Scholars question whether geopolitical factors can be altered. They also seek to address the nature of the relationship between geopolitics and political behavior: whether geopolitics is one factor in political behavior, or whether political behavior is determined by geopolitics. By seeking to define power relationships and the implications of geography on those relationships, geopolitics plays a role in military strategy, defense, and foreign policy.

GERMAN SOCIOLOGY

By the turn of the twentieth century, **sociology** had become an exciting intellectual endeavor in France, Germany, England, and the United States, with new movements having different theorists as their leaders. Whereas the development of sociology in France was united under the work of Émile Durkheim, in Germany, sociology from the start was heterogeneous. Of the diverse paradigms that emerged, those of **Karl Marx**, **Max Weber**, and George Simmel had the longest lasting impact. During the period prior to World War II, numerous other thinkers contributed to the growth of German sociology, including Ferdinand Tönnies, Werner Sombart, Alfred Vierkandt, Franz Oppenheimer, Alfred Weber, Roberto Michels, Leopard von Wiese, and Hermann Kantorowicz. Influenced in theory by Marx, Weber, and Simmel, the path of German sociology as an academic discipline was also shaped to a large extent by the political context of the time.

Although Simmel and Weber began carving out their sociological foundations during the late nineteenth and early twentieth century, sociology was still considered a subfield of **philosophy**, economics, or law. Even though social theory found favor with a large audience in the educated middle class, sociology as an independent discipline did not initially receive academic support. In the 1920s and early 1930s significant growth for sociology as an academic discipline occurred. Over forty professorships were established, eight sociology journals were founded, and two research institutes were formed, the

Forschungsinstitut für Sozial- and Verwaltungswissenschaften at the University of Cologne and the Institut für Sozialforschung in Frankfurt. By the 1930s, all major universities offered courses in sociology.

As sociology spread across Germany during the 1920s, no unifying paradigms emerged. George Ritzer argued in *Classical Sociological Theory* (1992) that a major split developed between Marx and his followers, known as left Hegelians based on Marx's reliance on Hegel's theory, and those following the philosophical tradition of **Immanuel Kant**, namely Weber and Simmel. Even among Marxist followers, numerous interpretations emerged so that German sociology developed into a complex interplay of conflicting paradigms. The main centers of sociological work were in Frankfurt, Cologne, Berlin, and Leipzig.

Although Marx did not consider himself a sociologist, his work influenced social theory to the extent that he must be included in any discussion of German sociology. Marx was trained in, and greatly influenced by, the philosophy of Hegel. Hegel's **dialectic** construct by which the world is understood as a dynamic process of interaction, conflict, and synthesis was an important feature of Marx's theory. However, Marx rejected Hegel's emphasis on the conscious mind, arguing instead that the dialectical nature of the world is apparent in the actual physical activities of people. Marx argued that modern problems can be traced to very real sources, namely **capitalism**, and the only way to overcome injustice was to overturn the unjust structures. Building on and revising Hegel's theory, Marx created his own distinct approach, which can be referred to as dialectical **materialism**.

Weber, who died unexpectedly in 1920, did not exert his full influence on German sociological thought until after *Economy and Society* was published posthumously. By the mid-1920s Weber's work was more readily available, and he became known as one of the greatest sociologists of the German tradition. Rejecting Marxist economic **determinism**, Weber believed economics was only one aspect of social life. Focusing on the process of rationalization, Weber attempted to discover what actions and structures assisted in the development of **rationalization**. Although Marx was largely ignored until the 1970s, Weber was highly regarded in Germany and the United States by the 1930s.

Simmel, co-founder with Weber of the German Sociological Society in 1910, differed from both Marx and Weber in several ways. First, Simmel influenced American sociology long before he was widely accepted in his own country. Second, whereas Marx and Weber both looked at the whole **structure** of the social system, Simmel was more interested in sociology at the micro-level. He studied the interaction between individuals, arguing that he could identify specific forms of interaction and types of interactants that would describe basic social interplay. He published much of his theory in short essays on narrow topics such as **poverty**, the miser, and the stranger. In so doing, he became much more widely read than either Weber or Marx, which helped to increase his popularity in the United States, especially at the University of Chicago and among the social interactionists.

With the introduction of national **socialism**, German sociology, as both an intellectual and academic endeavor, ceased to exist. Because they were Marxists or social democrats, many sociologists were forced to emigrate or withdraw from public life. Those who did not leave or withdraw from public life altered their course subjects to noncontroversial topics. Most sociological scholars of merit fled Germany and, from 1933 to 1945, German sociology existed only insofar as German-born sociologists continued their work in foreign countries. It can be argued that German sociology was rescued from oblivion by American sociology. Talcott Parsons' *Structure of Social Action* (1937), a study based on the Weberian theory of the differences between democratic and totalitarian society, introduced Weber to a new generation of sociologists and ignited an interest in social theory. American sociology influenced the return of sociology to Germany at the end of the war by establishing a new focus on empirical study. The American **influence** was sustained by emerging young German sociologists who, during the 1950s and 1960s, were trained almost exclusively in the United States or England.

From the 1960s to the mid–1970s, German sociology expanded quickly. The first degree in sociology was offered at Frankfurt in the mid–1950s; by 1983, 43 universities had established sociology programs. In 1960, there were 1,086 sociology students; in 1981, there were 21,705. In the 1950s, only 50 sociology staff positions existed, including 19 full professorships; by 1981, that number had risen to 1,290, with 400 professorships. Although the sharp increase of students and faculty in sociology reflects an overall growth of the population of German universities, based on the percentage of growth, only **political science** was more popular than sociology.

The post war years of German sociology were also marked by the discipline's attempt to understand and account for the rise of the Nazi regime. Theories of confrontation and hostility between individuality and society arose, and theorists such as Ralf Dahrendorf, who had been imprisoned as an adolescent by the Nazis, argued for the dissolution of the value-neutral approach to the social sciences. This critical assessment was advocated by Jürgen Habermas, who became the world's leading critical sociologist during the 1970s. A debate was sparked within the sociological **community** and inflamed by the student protests against academia in general, regarding the role and responsibility of sociology in society. The interplay between the historical, empirical, and philosophical traditions continues to shape German sociology.

See also Marx, Karl; Simmel, Georg; Weber, Max

GERONTOLOGY

The term ''gerontology'' is derived from the Greek word *geron*, meaning ''an old person,'' indicating the study of aging and the elderly. Gerontologists study how people change as they grow older and explore the different ways in which societies around the world view the aging process which includes physical, psychological, and social. Physically, the **aging** process is noted throughout the life span. As our bodies age our skin wrinkles, and we may experience hair loss and graying, a decrease in muscular and tissue elasticity, shrinkage of the disks in the spinal column, an increased susceptibility to heart disease, and some loss of kidney function. Other physiological elements experienced through the aging process include changes in the senses. With age, vision may become impaired, and the ability to hear may lessen. Some older individuals may lose some degree of their sense of touch, taste, and smell.

Some of the physiological changes are associated to the development of psychological issues. As people lose some of their physical senses, their ability to adapt psychologically may be hindered. For example, an aged individual who is losing their hearing ability may be hindered in their ability to interact socially. Without adequately addressing the issue of hearing loss, the aging individual may begin to feel isolated, lonely, frustrated, and misunderstood, all of which affects psychological well-being. The ability or inability to adapt to the changes that accompany physical illnesses and diseases can also affect the psychological well-being of the aging individual. Other factors also affect psychological state: **retirement**, death of spouse, friends, loss of independence. With changes come the need for **adaptation**. With hindered ability to adapt to changes come psychological impacts for the aged.

Social changes are associated with the physiological and psychological changes an older person faces. Reproductive changes, noted outward physical changes bring societal expectations or attitudes. The impact of various social factors associated with aging can be examined by comparing different groups in **society** and their **life expectancy** or the average number of years one is expected to live. Life expectancy is clearly shaped by numerous social factors such as gender, **race**, and social class. Women live longer on the average than men. The average life expectancy of minorities are lower than that of whites. The life expectancy of both men and women who are poor is considerably lower than that of middle and upper classes.

Gerontology also examines stereotypes and myths of the aged and aging and the impact they have. Gerontology examines age **norms**, or societal expectations for the aged. The field of gerontology examines social **structure** of societies and cultural differences across the globe. For example, in some cultures, aging brings on increased social **status** associated with the societal beliefs of increased wisdom. In other societies, the aged are seen as less productive and youth is revered, adversely affecting the status of the aged.

GHETTO

The term ''ghetto'' is used to describe an urban area occupied by a segregated **group**. Originally ghettos referred to Jewish settlements in pre-war European cities, such as Warsaw, Poland. The term, however, has expanded to residential segregation along any dimensions. Portions of the inner-urban areas in the United States are also referred to as ghettos. Most commonly, the basis of segregation is religion, **race**, or **ethnicity**. Ghettos are typically deprived areas. The term, while not intrinsically negative, has taken on a derogatory meaning, implying a large group of impoverished and under-educated minority individuals in a destitute and crime-ridden area.

William Julius Wilson, in his 1996 book *When Work Disappears*, laid out the macro-economic processes that aided the creation of African American ghettos in urban United States. With industrialization, in the early and mid-1800s, cities in the North exploded. In urban areas industry flourished and large masses of people migrated to the city for jobs. At this time the United States saw an enormous migration particularly of African Americans from the South to the North. In the mid- and late-1900s, industry began to move out of the cities and into the suburbs. Whites and middle-class blacks had the monetary resources to leave and follow the jobs, but lower-class blacks could not. The lack of jobs left those in greater financial **need** in the cities, poor and jobless. The intersections of race and class end up trapping predominantly minorities in these areas.

More recently, Massey and Denton, in their 1993 book *American Apartheid*, explored the historical process that led to the construction of urban ghettos, as well as segregation in the suburbs. Instead of looking at the role of **employment** as Wilson did, they concentrated on processes in the housing market. Racial segregation is shown to be a slow but intentional process, maintained both through formal and informal mechanisms. For example, banks and other lending agencies highlighted areas on city maps that had high concentrations of minority residents. These highlighted areas were considered high risk and were denied any loans for buying and keeping homes, a formal process known as ''redlining.'' The lack of **money** being filtered into these areas, while white areas of the city were simultaneously receiving funds, produced areas that were desperately in need. A declining spiral of resources began. Without money coming into the neighborhood, property values declined, funding for schools declined, residences deteriorated, and crime flourished. **Redlining** could not have produced such stark racial segregation by itself, however. Research has also found considerable ''steering,'' in which realty agencies advertise specific properties to white families and other properties to minority families. Sometimes, neighborhood associations would implement ''restrictive covenants,'' in which homeowners signed contracts stating they would not sell their property to black families. Realty agencies also attempted to use fear as a mechanism to shape the racial make-up of neighborhoods. If a minority **family** moved into a predominantly white neighborhood, realty agents would instill fear into current white homeowners. They would stress the risk that the neighborhood would soon have a large minority population and that this would mean a decline in **quality of life**. Through these fear tactics, they could often encourage homeowners to sell their homes for less than they were worth in order to move quickly to another area. Agents could then advertise these properties to minority families for increased prices. This process, known as ''blockbusting,'' resulted in huge profits for the realtors. Large numbers of white families fleeing neighborhoods when black families moved in, resulting in quick racial turnover, is known as ''white-flight.''

While Wilson and Massey and Denton produced two key works examining the creation of the ghetto, research on the ghetto is far more extensive than just exploring the factors that contributed to their rise. Research also focuses on the implications ghetto life has for the individuals who live there. This work focuses on a host of aspects such as quality of education, employment patterns, criminal behavior, welfare dependence, family structures, and cultural beliefs and attitudes. Research also looks at the more macro effects that ghettos have on **society** in general, such as the role of the ghetto in a city's economy and the role the ghetto plays in sustaining racial and class inequalities. Other research concentrates on public policy strategies for correcting the problems associated with ghetto life. Both Wilson and Massey and Denton critiqued and proposed public policy suggestions in their research.

See also Segregation and Desegregation

GIDDENS, ANTHONY (1938-)
English sociologist

Despite his renown as Britain's greatest sociologist since Herbert Spencer, Anthony Giddens' contribution to social **theory** is widely debated. Some argue that his thinking has been too eclectic, eschewing grand theoretical constructs for a collection of ideas with little more than descriptive value. Indeed, his career over the years has shifted from interpretations of classical social theory and the debunking of **functionalism** and **positivism** to the elaboration of structuration theory, a set of ideas that attempts to bridge the gap between agency and **structure**.

Others, however, point to his very work of structuration as a major theoretical contribution to sociological thinking. In his book *New Rules of Sociological Method* (1976), Giddens argued that agency produces structure and that structure is constituted of **rules** and resources by which that self-same agency is recreated. That is to say, Giddens wrote that the **epistemology** of sociological research was a "double hermeneutic" in which theory offered an explanation for the phenomena of everyday life and everyday life provided a means by which theory could be understood. In other words, the two acted in a dialectical relationship to each other.

Giddens was born in London in 1938 and received his bachelor's degree from Hull University. He went on to earn his master's degree and his Ph.D. from the same institution in 1970 and 1974, respectively. While receiving his doctorate, he lectured in sociology at the University of Leicester, Simon Fraser University (British Columbia), and the University of California at Los Angeles. In the late 1960s, Giddens took up a post as lecturer at Cambridge University. In 1985, he was appointed a professor of sociology at Cambridge, where he lectured for 12 years. Since 1997, he has served as director of the London School of Economics.

Early on in his academic career, Giddens was widely respected for his work in interpreting the ideas of classic social theorists like Émile Durkheim, **Max Weber**, and **Karl Marx**. At the same time, he turned away from the functionalism and positivism inherent in these thinkers' work. In the 1970s and 1980s, Giddens focused on structuration theory in *New Rules*

The term ghetto has taken on a derogatory meaning, implying a large group of impoverished and undereducated minority individuals in a destitute and crime-ridden area *(AP/Wide World Photos, Inc.).*

of Sociological Method and *The Constitution of Society* (1984). Throughout these years, he maintained that his work was ontologically- rather than epistemologically-oriented. That is to say, he argued that he was primarily theorizing about the way social life operated and not the way it should be studied.

In the late 1980s and early 1990s, Giddens shifted his work somewhat to emphasize cultural theory. In *The Consequences of Modernity* (1990) and *Modernity and Self-Identity* (1991), he rejected the idea that post-modernism represents a meaningful shift away from modernism, as was being argued by many French and American theorists. Post-modernism, he says, is really little more than the extension—via the forces of globalization—of modernism itself. In fact, he goes on to argue, post-modernism is actually "de-traditionalization," or the destruction of the last remnants of pre-modernist behavior, beliefs, and ideas.

Giddens also argues in this vein that the modernist self—in its latest incarnation that others interpret as post-modernist—has moved beyond all tradition and is in a state of near-constant re-invention and reinterpretation, an idea that critics say contradicts his overall notion that there is little new in post-modernism. This whole process by which tradition is annihilated and the self is constantly reinvented is both troubling and exciting to people, according to Giddens. In the political realm, Giddens believes that the contradictory forces at work within the modernist self negate older notions of left and right, blurring ideologies that were once in opposition to each other. Given this thinking, it is not surprising that Giddens has recently become something of a favorite among the New Labour politicians around Prime Minister Tony Blair.

GIDDINGS, FRANKLIN (1855-1931)
American sociologist

Although his ideas seem archaic today and he is no longer widely read, Franklin Giddings remains one of the pioneers of sociological thought and a founder of the discipline of **sociology** in the United States. Indeed, he is widely seen as the key figure responsible for transforming sociology from a minor branch of **philosophy** into an independent field of social science research. His late nineteenth- and early twentieth-century work, which emphasized quantification, empirical studies, and behavioralism, laid the groundwork for the neo-positivism championed by a later generation of U.S. sociologists.

Giddings was born in Sherman, Connecticut, in 1855 and spent his early adult life working as a reporter in Springfield, Massachusetts, where he published articles and columns on the very un-journalistic topics of social science theory and practice. In 1888, he was appointed a professor of politics at Bryn Mawr College in Pennsylvania, filling the position vacated by future U.S. President Woodrow Wilson. After six years at Bryn Mawr, Giddings was hired as a professor of sociology at Columbia University, where he remained for the rest of his career, retiring in 1928, three years before his death.

Giddings' works—including the early *Principles of Sociology* (1896) and *Elements of Sociology* (1898) and the later *Studies in the Theory of Human Society* (1922) and *The Scientific Study of Human Society* (1924)—were heavily influenced by two British thinkers: the eighteenth-century political economist **Adam Smith** and the nineteenth-century philosopher **Herbert Spencer**. From Smith, he borrowed the idea of "sympathy," that is, the morally-based reactions that members of a given **society** share. As Giddings interpreted Smith, this shared consciousness, along with the interaction of individuals responding to a common set of events around them, created social homogeneity and social harmony. While Giddings never went so far as to say so, his theory explained what later sociologists called the "herd instinct."

From Spencer, Giddings appropriated ideas about evolution. Like Spencer, he took Darwin's theories about evolution in the natural world and applied them to human society where he believed they offered useful insights into history and social development. Moreover, Giddings also ventured into new areas of sociological thought. Always a strong proponent of using psychological theory in his sociological work, he believed that **evolutionary theory** was also key to understanding the development of individual, **group**, and social psychology.

Over the years, Giddings enhanced the rigorous research behind his published work, enthusiastically embracing **empiricism** and emphasizing pragmatic uses for sociological study. In this, he is considered one of the key figures in the development of neo-positivism as the dominant approach of many twentieth-century American philosophers and sociologists. Giddings died in Scarsdale, New York, in 1931.

GILLIGAN, CAROL (1936-   )
American developmental pscychologist

In 1982 Harvard University psychologist Carol Gilligan published her book *In a Different Voice* and startled a country trying to understand male and female differences. In the early 1980s the prevailing approach to **sex differences** was to ignore them. Differences implied inequality. But Gilligan's ten years of research convinced her that men and women really were different. They differed in the way they thought, in their sense of values and **morality**, and in the way they connected with other people. According to Carol Gilligan, "The spirit in which I wrote the book was to raise questions." Her research questioned traditional psychological concepts of human development that had always been drawn on a male **model**.

Carol Gilligan was an associate professor in the Graduate School of Education at Harvard University where she taught adolescent and moral development. Forty-five years old at the time of the publication of her research, she was the wife of a psychiatrist and the mother of three sons. She completed her Ph.D. at Harvard between the birth of her first and second sons, and spent years in what she called women's "kitchen world." As a graduate student in psychology, Gilligan noticed that most theories of human psychological development were based on studies of boys and men. She set out to develop a theory based on the experiences of girls and women. Gilligan "wanted to ask men to listen to women's voices—and to say to women that if men hadn't listened in the past, it wasn't simply a matter of being narrow-minded or biased. They simply didn't know what to do with these voices. They did not fit."

In 1975 when she was listening to pregnant women considering abortion, Gilligan first heard "the different voice." After researching these "voices" of girls and women, she defined two orientations or systems of moral values. The highest moral value for women was not **justice**, as it was for men, but care. "Morality for a woman was being responsible to oneself and others; as opposed to doing one's duty, fulfilling one's obligations," she said. Men resolved questions of right or wrong by looking at a broad ruling. Women questioned what was the responsible thing to do, not what was the right thing to do. In the past, the responses of girls to stories of moral choice were often considered wrong. The connection between this past research and the self-effacement typical of girls from puberty on up also interested Gilligan. She concluded that something happened to girls when they were about twelve. The confident eleven-year-old who offered an opinion on a moral dilemma would hold out for her point of view, but the fifteen-year-old would yield. Gilligan suspected that the older girls began to realize that bringing in their own **values** would make trouble in a world where male values were considered the norm. So the girls started waiting and watching for other people to give them their cues as to what their values should be. For Gilligan, a crucial question for the future was: "How do we get females not to abandon what they know at eleven?"

Before Gilligan published her studies, researchers sometimes dropped women from their samples because the women's different responses complicated the research. The publication of her landmark work made it much harder for researchers to equate "human" with male or to see female experience as simply an aberration. Gilligan hoped she had pointed the way for other researchers to continue her research. She put women on the map of human development and hoped her ideas about the differences between the sexes would change the way men and women understood themselves. For Gilligan, to label the different voice a female voice was too limiting. "I want to call it a human voice," she said, "both to emphasize for women that they're in touch with the human condition—this is a real contribution to human thought—and to get rid of the phrase, 'as a woman and as a person.'"

GINTIS, HERBERT MALENA (1940-)
American economist

Herbert Gintis was born February 11, 1940, in Philadelphia, Pennsylvania, to parents Gerson (furniture retailer) and Shirley (Malena) Gintis. He married Marci Susan Greisler, an artist, on August 26, 1961; they have one son, Daniel Moses. Gintis earned his bachelor's degree in 1961 from the University of Pennsylvania. In the same year he began graduate school at Harvard University, completing his master's degree in 1962 and his doctorate in 1969. Gintis entered Harvard intending to study mathematics; however, he was deeply influenced by the events of the 1960s, including the anti-war movement, the counter-culture movement, and the Civil Rights Movement. Subsequently he abandoned his mathematical dissertation to pursue economics, a field he believed was better able to address issues that interested him.

With his course now set on economics, Gintis began being a critic of traditional economic **theory**, as he explains in his autobiographical contribution in *A Biographical Dictionary of Dissenting Economists*: "As a graduate student, I came to believe that there were three great issues in **political economy** that could not be put right by traditional economics: inequality and **discrimination**, **alienation** and overly materialistic cultural values, and the unaccountability of economic power." Gintis examined these issues in his dissertation, "Alienation and Inequality," and numerous scholarly articles written during the early 1970s. Upon receiving his Ph.D., Gintis remained at Harvard as a faculty member until 1974, at which time he moved to the University of Massachusetts at Amherst with several colleagues to create a graduate program based on radical economics, an effort to reformulate Marxian political economic theory. Gintis served as an associate professor of economics until 1979 when he was promoted to professor, the position he holds currently.

Gintis began a lifelong collaboration with fellow economist Samuel Bowles in 1975 with the publication of *Schooling in Capitalist America*. Gintis and Bowles addressed issues of inequality and alienation within the school system, arguing that schools did not foster equality or encourage personal development. Their premise was that schools produced individuals who best suited a capitalist society's needs; namely, submissive and nonassertive workers who would conform to the inequality of the economic system. Over the next ten years, Gintis continued to work with Bowles to critique and revise Marxist economic theory in order to make it relevant to contemporary society. The culmination of their study was the 1985 publication of *Democracy and Capitalism: Property, Theory, and the Contradictions of Modern Social Theory,* in which Gintis and Bowles outlined the shortfalls of both traditional Marxism and traditional **capitalism**. They wrote: "Neither the Jeffersonian universalization of individual **property** nor the Marxian collectivization of private property is acceptable. What is needed is the displacement of property rights by democratic personal rights." Gintis and Bowles proposed a new paradigm, not a rehashing of either the traditional left or traditional right. The success of their endeavor has been a matter of much debate among economic scholars.

During the late 1980s and 1990s, Gintis turned his attention to consumer goods and international financial markets, editing two major works on the subject: *Markets and Democracy: Participation, Accountability, and Efficiency* (with Bowles and Bo Gustafsson, 1993) and *Macroeconomics in the Conservative Era* (with Gerald A. Epstein, 1995). In 1999, Gintis and Bowles revisited their political economic theory in *Recasting Egalitarianism: New Rules for Markets, States, and Communities*. Gintis's most recent publication *Game Theory Evolving* (2000) is an advanced undergraduate/graduate text on game theory. According to Gintis, game theory **methodology** allows empirical study of many complex phenomena. In his introduction, Gintis stated, "By allowing us to specify rigorously the conditions of social **interaction** (player characteristics, rules, informational assumptions, payoffs), [game theory's] predictions can be tested, and the results be replicated in different laboratory settings. For this reason, experimental economics has become increasingly influential in affecting research priorities."

Gintis is a member of the American Economic Association, the Union for Radical Political Economists, and Amnesty International. He also heads a large interdisciplinary research project with Robert Boyd, an anthropologist from the University of California-Los Angeles, entitled the Network on Norms and Preferences. The study is an attempt to modify traditional economic theory through the use of experimental economics, game theory, neuroscience, and evolutionary biology and **psychology**.

GLASS CEILING

The glass ceiling is the subtle **discrimination** which prevents women and male minorities from advancing past a certain position within white male-dominated companies. The term is usually associated with management positions in large corporations in which frequent, highly competitive promotions are used as a major incentive to employees. These companies may not outwardly favor white males in their hiring practices yet, consciously or not, consistently fail to award the highest positions to their female or minority male employees. This form of discrimination is difficult to detect and to contest because

In 1990 U.S. Labor Secretary Elizabeth Dole announced a "glass ceiling initiative" designed to include more minorities in top management positions *(Corbis Corporation [Bellevue])*.

simple statistics may fail to prove its existence; it is based on often highly subjective judgments regarding employee performance.

There have been attempts by the U.S. government to deal with this problem. For example, in 1990 Labor Secretary Elizabeth Dole announced a "glass ceiling initiative" designed to include more women and male minorities in top management positions. However, even if successful programs are implemented, it will always be difficult to reconcile perception with the actual scope since, by definition, the glass ceiling is "invisible". With regards to women the problem is even more complex because many people accept the belief that certain jobs are gender-specific.

GLAZER, NATHAN (1923-)

American sociologist

Nathan Glazer was born in New York City on February 25, 1923, the youngest of seven children. According to his autobiographical contribution to *Authors of Their Own Lives* (1990), his parents, Louis (a tailor) and Tillie (Zacharevich) Glazer, reared their children in an environment of Jewish eclecticism: "socialist, but not too socialist; Orthodox, but not too Orthodox, friendly to Palestine, but not a Zionist; Yiddish-speaking, but not a Yaiddishist." Glazer married Ruth Slotkin on September 26, 1943. They had three children, Sarah, Sophie, and Elizabeth, before divorcing in 1958. Glazer's second marriage was to Sulochana Raghavan, a researcher, on October 5, 1963.

In 1940, Glazer entered City College of New York as a history major. During his time there, Glazer joined the student Zionist organization and soon became the editor of its na-

tional newspaper *Avukah Student Action.* Just past twenty, Glazer was deeply affected by this experience. It offered him the opportunity to associate with the intellectual left who regarded social science as the premiere science of socialist thought, and those relationships in turn provided him with the impetus to pursue sociology. Thus, after brief delves into economics and public administration, he settled on **sociology** and graduated in January, 1944.

In 1942, he began studies at the University of Pennsylvania, earning a master's degree in the spring of 1944. Although he received a fellowship to study for his doctorate in anthropology at the University of Pennsylvania, he turned it down, fearing that no jobs would be forthcoming. Instead, he worked on his Ph.D. sporadically at Columbia University, spending most of the next two decades as a "wandering semiacademic grantsman, collecting small grants to write one book after another." Working primarily as an editor, instructor, and writer, by the time he completed the requirements for his Ph.D. in 1962, he was already a well-respected intellectual figure.

After turning down the fellowship, Glazer returned to New York where he took a job on the staff of the *Contemporary,* a publication of the American Jewish Committee. He remained with the magazine until 1953, when he left to become an editorial advisor for the newly formed Anchor Books. Glazer left Anchor Books in 1957 and spent the next five years moving about, working as an instructor of sociology, a writer, and an editorial adviser for Random House Publishing. His teaching sojourn included stints at the University of California-Berkeley (1957-58); Bennington College, Bennington, Vermont (1958-1959); and Smith College, Northampton, Massachusetts (1959-1960). After spending a year in Japan, funded by a grant from the Ford Foundation, Glazer joined the Housing and Home Finance Agency (later renamed Department of Housing and Urban Development) in 1962 as an expert in urban sociology. Although he held great interest in this work, Glazer was invited to join the University of California-Berkeley as a permanent faculty member in the department of sociology. In 1969 he ended his nomadic intellectual life, becoming a professor of education and social **structure** at Harvard University, where he remains currently.

Known primarily for his work in race relations and urban study, Glazer published several influential books that shaped the course of academic and political **discourse**. Although his first two books *The Lonely Crowd* (1950) and *Faces in the Crowd* (1952) both written with David Riesman, were widely read, he gained further prominence with the publication of *Beyond the Melting Pot* (1963), a collaboration with Daniel P. Moynihan. Based on a study of ethnic and cultural **identity** of people in New York City, Glazer concluded that the popular melting-pot U.S. image was misleading because ethnic groups maintained distinct and dynamic identities. Despite this evidence, Glazer maintained that assimilation is still the goal of American **culture**.

GLOBALIZATION AND GLOBAL SYSTEMS ANALYSIS

Globalization refers to the economic, social, and cultural interpenetration of nations, and its origins are most properly traced to European colonial expansion in the sixteenth century. Sociologists explored the impacts of this uneven process on populations in different parts of the world-system. World-systems analysis is one of the dominant paradigms, an outgrowth of dependency **theory**, which it essentially replaced in the sociology of development. Recent changes in the world economy, like the rise of export-processing zones and the mobility of capital, called into question the usefulness of dependency theory, which tended to posit static relationships between First and Third World nations.

     World-systems theory, first advanced by **Immanuel Wallerstein** (1974), focuses on the impacts of globalization on all countries. This kind of analysis, for example, points to the interrelationship of changes in industry throughout the global economic system. Analyses of global patterns, like the migration between industrializing and industrial nations or the flight of industry from Europe and North America, are typical of concerns of world-systems analysis. Wallerstein's framework pointed to the original expansion of European colonial powers in the sixteenth century as the beginning of the world-system of relations between nations. Core nations, in this framework, tend to have advanced economic and military capacity and increase their advantage by exploiting relations with peripheral nations. In the first period of the world-system, core nations were the colonial powers and the periphery was made up of their colonial holdings. In the modern period, core nations are the industrialized powers, while peripheral nations are the less developed countries. Semiperipheral nations are those nations that exhibit characteristics of both core and periphery. A key element of the framework is that nations may change status in this system by possessing certain comparative advantages. Much early work in world-systems theory was carried out in the Fernand Braudel Center of the State University of New York by Immanuel Wallerstein himself and his students.

     World-systems analysis has been extremely influential in various areas of sociology. Scholars interested in global patterns of **urbanization**, for instance, use world-systems theory. Alejandro Portes, Anthony King, John Walton, and Janet Abu-Lughod have sought to understand the features of the global system of **cities**. Saskia Sassen (1991) has written on the ''Global City'', the common features cities such as Tokyo, London, and New York have by virtue of occupying structurally similar positions in the world economy. Global cities are characterized by the central functions they fulfill in the world economy, like providing the coordination of financial operations. They also have certain other common features like high inequality and an almost exclusive reliance on the service economy in the urban system. Sassen, along with other scholars, has studied the process of mobility of persons and capital across the global system. This new scholarship has come to encompass changes in industrialized nations. Scholars of race relations, like William Julius Wilson, have begun, for instance, to pay attention to global trends as determining urban fates.

William Godwin *(The Library of Congress)*

     World-systems theory has been criticized for being inattentive to local outcomes and local conditions and for not taking gender or **culture** into its framework. Recent analyses of globalization tend incorporate local issues, as well as gender and culture. Analyses like Arjun Appadurai's (1997) and Aiwa Ong's (1997) *Flexible Citizenship* are examples of the new scholarship on globalization.

GODWIN, WILLIAM (1756-1836)
English philosopher, novelist, essayist, historian, and biographer

William Godwin was a controversial British thinker and philosopher whose radical and anarchistic beliefs reflected the idea that all monarchies were ''unavoidably corrupt'' and that no person should have power over another. He objected to most social institutions, including **marriage** and the accumulation of private **property**, and believed that **society** could solve its problems only through rational discussion and reason.

     Godwin was born to John Godwin and Ann Hull Godwin. As a child, he was precocious, and he had read Bunyan's work *Pilgrim's Progress* by the time he was five. At eleven, Godwin studied under Reverend Samuel Newton, a member of a strict **sect** of Calvinists who taught that men are depraved and that reason was the only basis for action. Godwin then went to Hoxton Academy until 1778, where he studied under Alexander Kippis. Upon leaving Hoxton, Godwin served as a candidate minister in Christchurch, Ware, and Stowmarket. Ultimately failing at the ministry, he began a career as a writer in 1782 on the recommendation of Joseph Fawcett, a poet and preacher. Godwin's thought was a product of his constant reading, both during school and after he completed his studies. He was influenced by Jonathan Swift and of the French philosophers of the 1700s, called the *philosophes*.

His writing career began with a biography of William Pitt in 1783, and a novel *Damon and Delia* (1784). Godwin's major work *An Enquiry Concerning Political Justice, and its Influence on General Virtue and Happiness* (1793) was steeped in ancient historians, philosophers such as **John Locke** and Joseph Priestly, and Jonathan Swift. This extensive work expresses the theoretical basis for Godwin's philosophy and later writing. In it, Godwin explores man's social nature, his relationship with **government**, and individual rights. It seeks to define the appropriate scope of the government and considers the problem of **crime** and punishment. In the radical vein, he speaks against the rights to own private property and marriage. In this work, Godwin puts forth his belief in man's ability to become perfect and his idea that government is a barrier to happiness and reform comes as the result of reason.

Godwin was writing at a time marked by hot political debate and agitation for reform, and he was highly respected by other intellectuals. *An Enquiry Concerning Political Justice* marked Godwin's literary peak, after which he wrote an extremely successful novel entitled *Things as They Are; or, the Adventures of Caleb Williams*. In spite of his open condemnation of social institutions, in 1796 Godwin married **Mary Wollstonecraft**, author of *A Vindication of the Rights of Woman* and an early feminist. She died as a result of giving birth to their daughter, Mary (ultimately the author of *Frankenstein*), in 1797. After publishing a controversially revealing biography of his wife, Godwin turned to writing essays and another novel.

After 1797, Godwin's radical thought was roundly criticized when the country took a conservative turn. Throughout the early 1800s, the political climate did not provide Godwin a forum for his views. He wrote a life of Chaucer that was well accepted and also children's literature for a new publishing venture, the Juvenile Library, under the assumed names of Edward Baldwin and Theophilus Marcliffe. In the later years of his life, Godwin wrote on the political and religious developments during the Civil War in England in *Mandeville*. He also wrote *History of the Commonwealth of England*, a four volume work that is noted as the first scholarly history of the nation written from the republican point of view. Though his ideas fell out of fashion, Godwin's own thought in turn influenced such English Romantics of the early 1800s as Percy Bysshe Shelley. He also influenced the socialists and the labor movement and is recognized as one of the first outspoken proponents of radical philosophical anarchism.

GOFFMAN, ERVING (1922-1982)
Canadian American sociologist

Despite an academic career teaching at the more prestigious universities of North America, as well as an impressive output of scholarly sociological research, Erving Goffman was perhaps best known for his perceptive and popularly-read observations on everyday life—what Goffman himself called "micro-sociology." Much of his early work focused on human interactions within the context of small institutions, as was the case with *Asylums: Essays on the Social Situation of Mental Patients and Other Inmates* (1961), perhaps his most widely-read book. In that work, Goffman argued that mental institutions do not seek to totally transform people after they are committed—that is, achieve a kind of "cultural victory"—but rather they strive to keep patients' aware of both the world inside and outside the institution, so as to create a kind of "strategic leverage" over them.

Erving Goffman was born in Alberta, Canada, in 1922, the son of Jewish immigrants from Russia. He attended the University of Toronto and received his bachelor's degree in 1945. He did his graduate work at the University of Chicago, earning his Ph.D. in sociology in 1953. From 1952 to 1954, he lectured at the university before accepting a position as visiting scientist at the National Institute of Mental Health in Bethesda, Maryland, where he worked until 1957. From 1958 to 1968, Goffman taught at the University of California at Berkeley, moving up from assistant to full professor. In 1968, he accepted the position of Benjamin Franklin Professor of Anthropology and Sociology at the University of Pennsylvania, where he remained until his death in 1982. Over the course of his career, Goffman received numerous accolades, including a nomination for a National Book Critics Circle Award for *Forms of Talk* in 1981.

As his studies on mental patients and mental institutions indicates, Goffman was especially interested in finding out how individual **identity** is shaped in **abnormal** places and situations. In this work, he concluded that the self is not defined solely in relation to the **rules** and order of the institution but also to the interstices in institutions, the gaps where the institution did not and could not maintain total control of the patient's life.

In the early 1970s, Goffman turned his attention to the ways in which people interpret experience. In *Frames of Analysis* (1974), he argued that people experience events through multiple frames that can involve ethical, aesthetic, and other values. By the late 1970s—and especially in his book *Gender Advertisements* (1979)—Goffman had turned his attention to advertising and its effects on how individual identity is shaped, especially in regard to gender. After examining display advertising in magazines, Goffman concluded that it has an important role in how we define the concepts of "masculine" and "feminine" both for ourselves and others. Specifically, he argued that advertising tended to subordinate women to men in the life situations depicted. Although widely read and respected, Goffman is not without his critics who argue that his emphasis on micro-sociology distorts the workings of institutions by depicting a kind of timeless and unchanging world of interactions between dominant and passive groups.

GORDON, MILTON MYRON (1918-)

American sociologist

Milton M. Gordon was born in Mardiner, Maine, on October 3, 1918. He completed his undergraduate studies at Bowdoin College in 1939 and received his master's and doctorate degrees in sociology from Columbia University in 1940 and 1950, respectively. From 1946-1950, concurrent with his graduate studies, he served as an instructor of sociology at the University of Pennsylvania. He taught at Drew University from 1950-1953 and at Haverford College from 1953-1957. After spending two academic years as a visiting associate professor at Wellesley College, he became a professor of sociology at the University of Massachusetts at Amherst, where he stayed the remainder of his teaching career. He was awarded the status of professor emeritus in 1986.

Gordon, who wrote numerous books and scholarly articles on the issues of **ethnicity**, assimilation, and **social stratification**, published his first major work *Social Class in American Sociology* in 1958, an analysis of research conducted on the problems caused by classes and class **structure** in the United States. At the time, social stratification theory was relatively new. Because the predominant U.S. **ideology** maintained that social **progress** had done away with a hierarchical social structure, sociologists tended to acknowledge the historically important role of **caste and class** but failed to develop a modern social stratification **theory**.

With *Social Class in American Sociology,* Gordon pioneered a new theory aimed at accounting for the complexity and fluidity of social stratification. According to Howard E. Jensen in the editor's note to the book, this new **concept** views class structure as "consisting of an informal hierarchy of groups with illy defined and highly permeable boundaries, obliquely recognized and spontaneously functioning in the dynamics of social interaction rather than directly perceived and expressed and officially maintained by various institutionalized rituals and procedures." Gordon's assessment is aimed at devising a **methodology** that will address the complexity of social status. He concludes that economic and occupational factors are the primary determinants of status order, but he insists that for a complete picture to be drawn other interactions must be acknowledged: "The empirically determined relationship of these social-status levels, or social classes, to the other stratification structures of economic power and politico-community power, to occupational categories, to group life, to cultural attributes, and to the structure of ethnic group relations constitute the full outlines of the social class system."

In 1964 Gordon published *Assimilation in American Life: The Role of Race, Religion, and National Origins,* which outlined his landmark theory of social stratification and assimilation in the United States. He later added to this assessment in *Human Nature, Class, and Ethnicity* (1978). In developing a concept of "group life," Gordon presupposes the unbalanced nature of American social structure. Anglo-Americans make up the core **society**, and other groups will either assimilate by conforming to the dominant **culture** or create methods to maintain a separate social or ethnic **identity**. Believing the

impact of social structure was not widely appreciated by social scientists, he wrote in *Assimilation in American Life:* "There is a distinct tendency to confine consideration of **cultural pluralism** to the issue of cultural differences in behavior and to slight or ignore pertinent issues of social structure and their relationship to communal group life." Thus his intent was to create a typology that would assist in the study of group life at the macro level.

Gordon suggests that there are seven possible dimensions or types of assimilation. (1)Cultural or behavior assimilation is indicated by a change in cultural patterns to mirror the core society, such as **language** and traditions. (2)Structural assimilation is defined as "large-scale entrance into cliques, clubs, and institutions of host society, on **primary group** level." (3)Marital assimilation is denoted by widespread intermarriage. (4)Identification assimilation occurs when people of a minority ethnicity feel more bonded to the dominant culture rather than their culture of origin. (5)Attitude receptional and (6)behavior receptional assimilation refer to the absence of **prejudice** and discrimination, respectively. Finally, (7)civic assimilation occurs when there is an absence of value and power conflict.

Gordon's framework for the dimensions of ethnic assimilation provided concepts on which much empirical sociological study has been based. Even though most researchers selected only one or two types of assimilation to study, Gordon gave clarity and direction to a developing field. In *The Scope of Sociology* (1988) he addressed issues of human nature and the state of **race** and ethnic relations and compared societies created by U.S. **capitalism** and Soviet **socialism**.

GOVERNMENT

Government is a formal organization that shapes political actions. Although governments occasionally exert their power over the members of a **society** through force and physical **domination**, typically to maintain control of a society the government in place must be accepted and, at least to some extent, supported by those over which it rules.

Governments are studied as one of the major social institutions (sometimes subsumed under the label of political institutions). Governments provide protection for the members of the society from outside invasion as well as internal injustice, provide a means of **social control** by reducing the possibility of **crime** and disorder, serve as a primary channel of conflict resolution among society members, and install and enforce laws which set a normative basis for behavior for the society. Government is strongly tied to the other social institutions within a society and maintains even stronger relationships with the military and **economic institutions**.

The style of government in place in a society relies on the established political system, the **attitude** of the state toward the **leadership**, and the attitudes of the masses regarding leadership styles. Four ideal types of government have been highlighted through the study of political systems: monarchy, democracy, authoritarianism, and **totalitarianism**. In practice, however, the lines between the styles often blur and recombine into hybrids that work effectively for the societies represented.

Monarchies are political systems in which a single family rules across several generations due to the fact that political power passes through the family bloodlines. Monarchies have traditionally existed in societies with somewhat limited possibility for **social mobility** as the position of the royal family, and often of the entire social **structure**, is thought to be divinely ordained. In modern societies, some monarchies have retained the traditional model of full and complete ruling power over their subjects and governing bodies, while others have retained a figurehead position while allowing elected leaders to provide the political leadership of the society.

Democracy is a political system in which power is exercised by the members of the society who participate in the decision-making process which is carried out through direct, free elections, indirectly by way of a representative democracy (electing of leaders who then make the key decisions while representing the positions of their constituency), or some combination of the two. The two most prevalent forms of democracy tend to appear in capitalist and socialist societies. Capitalist forms of democracy provide a free-market economy through which individuals within the society can act in their own self-interest and thereby maximize their own power and resources through action. In this way capitalism claims a more complete form of democracy in that individuals are encouraged to exercise their freedom and become as successful as they wish. However, the result of this freedom is often severe **social inequality** due to discrepant distribution of opportunities and resources. Socialist democracy also claims to be a superior form of democracy that it eliminates the inequality present in capitalist forms. This is often accomplished, however, at the expense of personal freedom. Socialist forms of democracy typically attempt to assure the equality of all people in their society with the use of many government programs. However, because the government is so active in such societies it may often become highly oppressive and limiting to individual freedoms.

Authoritarian governments have established political systems which refuse any popular participation in the government, opting instead to value the preservation of the government over the **social organization** and political actions of the members with that society. Often in authoritarian societies the governments have established rigid regulations and **law enforcement** within the society to assure individuals conform to the standards. Although the enforcement is rigid the government typically does not attempt to regulate all aspects of social life.

Totalitarian political systems extensively regulate all aspects of society members' lives through political action, physical **coercion**, or constant monitoring. Totalitarian systems of government have become more prevalent in modern times due to the development of technology that permits the easy monitoring of large numbers of people without constant physical occupation. Totalitarian systems often engage in rigid training and **socialization** of the members of their society to assure the full acceptance, commitment, and support of government actions.

GRAUNT, JOHN (1620-1674)
English statistician

Although he considered himself a haberdasher, John Graunt is better known as the founder of **demography**, the statistical study of human populations. With no formal training in mathematics, Graunt's work added immeasurably to human knowledge and his method of record keeping, an unknown technique more than three hundred years ago, contains lessons to be followed today. His work influenced another noted pioneer in this field, Sir **William Petty**, as well as Edmond Halley, English astronomer and "discoverer" of the comet named for him.

Born in London, England, on April 24, 1620, to Henry, a draper, and Mary Graunt, John was the eldest in a large family, and he eventually took over his father's business, as "haberdasher of small wares," a profession he continued for most of his life. His business and home, however, were destroyed in the London fire of 1666. A prosperous merchant, Graunt was a respected London citizen, holding various ward offices in the city and elected to the common council for two years. He was also a captain and later a major in a military band for several years.

While conducting his business, Graunt could not help but notice the mounting death toll in the city from the plague years, and he became curious about the offhand way records were kept by city officials covering deaths from the plague and other causes. This interest resulted in a short pamphlet to which Gaunt gave the long title of *Natural and Political Observations mentioned in a following Index, and made upon the Bills of Mortality... With reference to the Government, Religion, Trade, Growth, Ayre, diseases, and the several Changes of the said City.* This work, published in 1662 and generally called *Observations,* is given credit for beginning the idea that vital statistics, such as christenings and burials, could be used not only to keep records but to construct life tables for the entire population. Four editions of the pamphlet were eventually published, the third (1665) by the Royal Society, of which Graunt was a charter member.

Observations was Graunt's only scientific work, but it set a standard for record keeping that exists today. These are some of the lessons he left to modern-day epidemiologists: (1) be brief, (2) be clear, (3) test all theories before publishing them (for example, Graunt used five different ways to arrive at an estimation of the population of London), (4) invite criticism, (5) be willing to revise the **data** if necessary, and (6) do not be overly concerned with including data that is "only" statistically significant, which may result in important data being overlooked. In the 1620s, of course, Graunt had no interest in, nor knowledge of, "statistical significance testing."

In addition to his standards of record keeping, Graunt added to the store of human knowledge. He was the first to note the occurrence of more male than female births, but that because the male death rate was higher, the population count among the sexes was about equal. He refuted the theory that plagues are spread by contagion and showed statistically that, contrary to popular opinion, plague **epidemics** do not occur necessarily when a new monarch takes the throne. He was the first to estimate London's population and to show that the city's rapid growth was mainly the result of immigration. He offered first-time trends for many diseases. He classified death rates according to cause, including overpopulation, observing that death rates in the cities were higher than in rural areas. Perhaps Graunt's most important contribution was the introduction of his life tables. By using only two rates of survivorship—living to ages 6 and 76—he predicted the **life expectancy** of the population year by year and the percentage of persons who would live to each successive age. His colleague William Petty later was able to use these death rates in estimates of the economic losses that such deaths exact upon a community. Graunt is recognized today as having laid the foundations of the science of statistics. Graunt died in poverty on April 18, 1674.

GREAT SOCIETY, THE

The Great Society was the label that U.S. President Lyndon B. Johnson adopted to describe the program of sweeping social reforms he envisioned as his main agenda for Congress in 1965. Johnson called for the country to create a Great Society in his State of the Union address on January 4, 1965—his first after being elected in his own right. In his speech, Johnson reiterated his commitment to a "war on poverty," which was initiated in 1964 with the passage of the Economic Opportunity Act and which Johnson envisioned as the means for building a society "where the meaning of man's life matches the marvels of man's labor." The president hoped to achieve his goals through massive social welfare legislation, including federal support for education, an expanded Social Security Program that included medical benefits for the elderly, and legal protection for citizens disenfranchised by restrictive state registration laws. With the Democratic Party in control of the legislature after landslide victories in 1964, Johnson had little difficulty persuading Congress to pass what became one of the most extensive legislative programs in U.S. history.

Though the Great Society program included a wide range of reforms, education was a central component of Johnson's agenda. He urged federal support for public schools and persuaded Congress in 1965 to pass the Elementary and Secondary Education Act, which authorized grants for improvements in curricula, teaching materials and training, and educational research. Head Start, a program targeting underprivileged children of preschool age, was created under the auspices of the Economic Opportunity Act. Other landmarks of the War on Poverty were the 1965 Medicare Bill, which amended the Social Security Act to finance the cost of medical care for the elderly; the Job Corps, a youth employment training program established in 1965; Volunteers in Service to America (VISTA), a domestic version of the Peace Corps; the Model Cities Program, established in 1966 to rehabilitate **ghetto** neighborhoods; and a billion-dollar appropriation to begin economic redevelopment in impoverished Appalachia. The Great Society program also included urban renewal and beautification projects throughout the country, as well as conservation projects.

U.S. President Lyndon B. Johnson coined the term "Great Society" to describe his programs of social reforms in 1965 *(AP/Wide World Photos, Inc.)*.

The Great Society program was the national government's chief response to the harsh conditions affecting millions of African Americans who had migrated from the rural South to northern urban centers after World War II. This massive demographic shift had contributed to the growth of ghettos, segregated urban areas where residents faced chronic **unemployment**, decaying housing, inferior schools, high **crime** levels, and poor **social services**. Yet the War on Poverty's success in improving economic opportunity inadvertently worsened inner city conditions. Critics have pointed out that inner-city programs were organized without a real understanding of the complex conditions affecting ghettos. Anti-poverty programs, meant to attract investment and improve economic opportunities in ghetto areas, instead exacerbated middle-class flight from inner cities. This dynamic, in the view of many analysts, made inner cities habitable only by a chronically unemployed and unemployable "underclass."

The Johnson administration also favored community action programs rather than large-scale interventions for inner cities. This approach, innovative at the time, essentially made the community itself responsible for identifying solutions to its own problems. Though **community action** achieved significant success in developing and empowering community **leadership**, its approach was often experimental; among creative but unsuccessful strategies was a 1967 Chicago initiative that hired gang members to run a job-training program. The plan failed when members were charged with various crimes, including murder, drug trafficking, and conspiring with Libya to plan terrorist activities in the United States. Community action, in general, did not adopt cohesive strategies and lacked the resources to respond with changes when programs did not achieve desired results.

Despite the Great Society's efforts in inner cities, the program lacked an overall strategy for ghetto improvement and failed to eradicate entrenched poverty and racism. Yet the program had many successes, particularly in increasing employment and incomes for African Americans. In 1959, 55 percent of African Americans lived in poverty; by 1969, the percentage dropped to 32. Michael K. Brown and Steven P. Erie estimated in 1981 that the Great Society created more than two million new government jobs, many of which went to African Americans. Between 1960 and 1976, the black middle class tripled in size, and employment of African Americans in public social-welfare programs increased by 850,000. Medicare, too, was considered an important achievement. It is one of the few programs that remained intact, however, after subsequent government administrations eliminated Great Society programs.

GREELEY, ANDREW M. (1928-)
American priest, author, and novelist

An American Catholic priest, Andrew M. Greeley (born 1928) wrote sociological studies of American religion and of **ethnicity**, popular presentations of the Catholic faith, and a number of novels. Andrew M. Greeley was born in Oak Park, Illinois, February 5, 1928. From an early age he determined to become a priest, attending a seminary high school and college. He received an A.B. from St. Mary of the Lake Seminary in Chicago in 1950, an S.T.B. in 1952, and an S.T.L. in 1954, when he was ordained. From 1954 to 1964 he served as an assistant pastor at Christ the King parish in Chicago, during which time he studied sociology at the University of Chicago, receiving a Ph.D. in 1962. His dissertation dealt with the influence of religion on the career plans of 1961 college graduates.

Sociology, an interest in Catholic education, and a ministry to Catholic youth dominated Greeley's early career and writings. From 1961 to 1968 he was a program director at the National Opinion Research Center in Chicago, and in 1973 he became the director of the Center for the Study of American Pluralism. He taught sociology at the University of Chicago from 1963 to 1972, and beginning in 1978 he taught intermittently at the University of Arizona.

Greeley's first writings included such titles as *The Church and the Suburbs* (1959) and *Religion and Career* (1963), works in which he put **empirical sociology** to use. At the same time, he was drawing on his ministerial work with young Catholics in books such as *Strangers in the House* (1961), which described the problems of Catholic teenagers. In the late 1960s he did several studies of Catholic education, concluding that the religious impact of parochial schooling seemed negligible. He was also intent on explaining the Christian faith to lay people, producing readable books such as *The Jesus Myth* (1971) and *The Moses Myth* (1971). In 1972 he published the results of a two year study of American priests,

reporting widespread dissatisfaction. Although this work had been underwritten by the American Catholic bishops, they repudiated its findings, leading Greeley to comment: "Honesty compels me to say that I believe the present leadership in the **church** to be morally, intellectually, and religiously bankrupt." A significant aspect of Greeley's profile after 1972 was alienation from the American Catholic bishops.

Joining his interest in sociology to a strong sense of his Irish-Catholic heritage, Greeley ventured into the area of ethnicity in 1974, studying the impact of ethnic background and lamenting the assimilation of Irish-Catholics to American Protestant models. In his assessments of American Catholic faith after the Second Vatican Council (1962–1965), he focused on the 1968 encyclical of Pope Paul IV that reaffirmed the ban on artificial birth control. In Greeley's view, this encyclical greatly lowered the credibility of church leaders in the eyes of American Catholics and accounted for a significant drop in church attendance. Another reason for the drop was Vatican II's shift from a God of law to a God of love, who might be presumed to look more to the heart than such externals as attendance at Sunday Mass.

Greeley had always written for newspapers and magazines, as well as giving radio and television interviews, but he advanced the popular thrust of his work in 1979 with reports on the elections of Popes John Paul I and John Paul II, for which he traveled to Rome. In 1981 he launched what proved to be a hugely successful career as a novelist with *The Cardinal Sins,* a potboiler depicting the sordid, all-too-human inside of clerical and upper-class Chicago Catholic **culture**. After that beginning he poured forth a stream of best-sellers (*Thy Brother's Wife* [1982], *Ascent into Hell* [1984], *Virgin and Martyr* [1985], *The Final Planet* [1987], and *Angel Fire* [1988]). From the handsome royalties these novels earned, Greeley endowed a chair at the University of Chicago Divinity School in memory of his parents.

Few literary critics spoke well of Greeley's novels, but obviously they struck a chord in the lay population. Readers of newspapers, secular and Catholic, were familiar with Greeley's syndicated columns and occasional pieces, which were remarkable for their cantankerous ability to spotlight troubling issues (for example, **homosexuality** among the Catholic clergy). Greeley had a great gift for clear prose and a courageous desire to speak frankly about the actual experience of faith, both personal and social. He continued to draw on data of the National Opinion Research Institute to illuminate religious, ethnic, educational, and other trends in American culture. His own theological positions were moderate to slightly conservative, but he championed a reworking of the Church's attitudes toward sexuality and made a strong case for the importance of the religious imagination (so as to express theology through stories). Steadily he urged the Church to attend to the findings of empirical social science, so as to make its ministry more realistic and credible. His feuds with the late Cardinal Cody, and with many other personages with whom he disagreed, enlivened church life in Chicago and intrigued readers of his columns.

Living independently, and wealthy because of his royalties, Andrew Greeley went his own way, making a unique contribution to American church life. His books number over one hundred and he was one of the most quoted American Catholic priests, appearing in *TV Guide* and on numerous talk shows. In fact, few American Catholics have had a greater popular impact. Slowly, serious students of current American Catholic culture are beginning to account Greeley an influence worthy of scholarly investigation.

GREEN MOVEMENT

The environmental or "green" movement consists of a wide variety of organizations with differing philosophies and strategies. Social theorists often refer to it as a "new social movement" due to its frequent emphasis on lifestyle and cultural issues, but many organizations also use more traditional tactics aimed at producing legislative changes. While some researchers have stated that the movement's diversity has made it largely ineffective in creating social change, others claim that its diversity is actually a source of strength. Survey research by Riley Dunlap and others has shown that environmental values and objectives are increasingly accepted across **race**, class, and gender lines, though this support does not always translate into activism.

Robert J. Brulle has identified several discourses used in the environmental movement in the United States. In the mid to late nineteenth century, environmental organizations focused on discourses of "conservationism," which stresses the need to maintain the availability of natural resources for economic purposes, and "preservationism," which seeks to conserve nature for its inherent beauty and spiritual value. The formation of the American Forestry Association was based on the former approach, while the latter inspired Thoreau's Walden, and the formation of the Sierra Club and The Nature Conservancy. A third kind of **discourse**, "ecocentrism," became more widespread in the 1960s. It stresses the connection between human health and the health of **ecosystems** as a whole, and inspired Rachel Carson's *Silent Spring* and the formation of the Environmental Defense Fund, the Natural Resources Defense Council, and the Friends of the Earth.

The political **ecology** discourse developed during the 1970s and 1980s, and focuses on social structures, particularly **capitalism** and industrialism, as sources of environmental damage and human health problems. It has branched in several directions. Social ecology stresses the connections between human domination of nature and of other humans. A major proponent of this approach is the Green Party, which was officially created in Germany in 1980 and began organizing in the United States a few years later. The party seeks to elect environmentalists to public office at all levels of government, and its "Ten Key Values" stress decentralization, social **justice**, **feminism**, nonviolence and diversity. The Environmental Justice (EJ) Movement and the People of Color Environmental Movement focus on the ways in which women, minorities, and the poor and working classes are disproportionately affected by toxic waste dumps and other pollution in their communities. The Citizens' Clearinghouse for Toxic Waste serves to

Greenpeace is well known for its attention-grabbing, media-oriented tactics, such as hanging enormous protest banners *(Corbis Corporation [Bellevue])*.

connect and inform communities fighting similar battles, and Robert Bullard's Dumping in Dixie and Andrew Szasz' Ecopopulism provide important overviews of this branch of the green movement.

Ecofeminists take a similar approach to environmental issues, focusing on the ways in which the associations of "women" with "nature" in a male-dominated society have legitimated both the subjugation of women and instrumentalist, destructive attitudes towards the environment. Ecofeminism has political, economic, and spiritual/religious components, and has inspired a wide variety of writings and activist strategies. Finally, the "deep ecology" discourse stresses ideas of the interconnectedness of all life and the inherent, intrinsic worth of all living things, human and nonhuman. Deep ecologists generally believe that all species have a right to a natural, unthreatened existence. Earth First!, which has been particularly active in anti-logging protests in the Pacific Northwest, is perhaps the best known deep ecology-based organization.

These organizations and others have adopted a variety of strategies for effecting **social change**. The Nature Conservancy focuses on buying land in order to preserve endangered ecosystems. Greenpeace is well known for its attention-grabbing, media-oriented tactics, such as confronting whaling and nuclear testing vessels at sea and hanging enormous protest banners. Earth First! has engaged in acts of "monkey-wrenching," targeted vandalism against logging companies. The Sierra Club, the Environmental Defense Fund, and others have largely focused on more traditional lobbying and legal efforts. Other organizations, such as EarthSave, stress personal lifestyle changes such as adopting a vegetarian diet, recycling, reducing consumption, and having smaller families. Events, such as the annual Earth Day, which began in 1970, have served to increase public awareness of environmental problems. Assessments of the effectiveness of these combined strategies vary. While many researchers point to the passage of environmental legislation, the creation of environmental government agencies, and increased public support for environmental goals as proof of the movement's success so far, others point out that resource depletion, toxic contamination, global warming, and lax enforcement of environmental regulations are ongoing problems, some of which are becoming increasingly severe.

GREEN, RAYNA DIANE (1942-)
American educator, folklorist, and author

"I write mainly to set the record straight about Indians," said Rayna Diane Green, educator, folklorist, and Cherokee Native American. She added that she will also "write about anything that interests me, regardless of the subject—Indians, women, food, science. Green was born in Dallas, Texas, on July 18, 1942, to Floyd Franklin and Ann Naomi Burns. She was educated at Southern Methodist University where she received a B.A. in 1963 and an M.A. in 1966. She later earned a Ph.D. from Indiana University in Bloomington.

In 1971, Green began her teaching career at the University of Arkansas in Fayetteville. Although an assistant professor of English, she also taught folklore, a long-held interest. In popular usage, the term "folklore" is generally restricted to oral literature tradition, but in the academic discipline, it refers to all oral or handed-down tradition—literature, **culture**, customs. Green continued her interest in folklore when she joined the faculty at the University of Massachusetts at Amherst in 1972. She left Amherst in 1975 for the Smithsonian Institution in Washington, D.C., where she spent a year as folklorist and program coordinator for the Festival of American Folklore.

Focusing more on her roots, Green spent the next four years as director of the project on Native American science of the American Association for the Advancement of Science in Washington, D.C. From there, she joined the faculty of Dartmouth College, in Hanover, New Hampshire, as associate professor of **Native American Studies** and director of the Native American Science Resource Center (1980-1983). She became acting director of the American Indian Program in 1983. Today, she is the director of the American Indian Program, National Museum of American History at the Smithsonian.

"As a Native American, I feel a great responsibility getting the record straight about Indians," Green said, "but I feel a similar responsibility toward the truth whenever it's found." Green has written a number of books on Native American traditional culture, science, medicine, technology, folklore, and women. Her works include: *The Social Impact Assessment of Rapid Resource Development on Native Peoples* (1982), *Native American Women: A Contextual Bibliography* (1983), and *That's What She Said: A Collection of Poetry and Fiction by Contemporary Native American Women* (1984). Her articles on Native Americans have appeared in *Ms* and other publications. In addition to film and television work on scripts, she has written novels featuring Ramona Sixkiller, a Native American detective.

In 1999, Indian University Press published *The British Museum Encyclopedia of Native North America* by Green and Melanie Fernandez of the Ontario Arts Council. Intended for academic and public libraries, it was called "a very interesting departure from what one expects in encyclopedias devoted to Native Americans." Topics include arts and literature, invention, self-government, and notable personalities. It emphasizes cultural relevance among the selected Native American groups and focuses on the rich diversity that marks all ethnic people.

A resident of Washington, D.C., Rayna Green is a member of the North American Indian Women' Association, American Folklore Society, American Anthropological Association, American Indian Historical Society, and is a Fellow of the Society for Applied Anthropology.

GROUNDED THEORY

The origins of grounded **theory** lie in the expansion of quantitative research after World War II. Changes in both large-scale data collection procedures and the technologies used for analyzing such data increased the **status** and volume of quantitative research. As a result of an unprecedented enthusiasm for technology and value-free science within the **society** at large, American sociology shifted its emphasis from theory development towards procedures of theory testing, or verification, which were based on methodologies imported from the physical sciences.

The new emphasis threatened the position of qualitative **sociology**, with its more open ended method of inquiry and its reliance on the insights and choices of the individual researcher. Qualitative sociologists responded in several ways. The more intransigent argued that qualitative research could reach many areas, both substantive and formal, which were impossible to analyze through quantitative research. Others retreated to Paul Lazarsfeld's position that qualitative research was uniquely useful for theoretical exploration but it could not generate or test theory. A third response, grounded theory, took issue with verification itself.

Barney Glaser and Anselm Strauss, the founders of grounded theory, criticized the popularity of "verification rhetoric," arguing that the tightly-defined procedures necessary for rigorous verification work against the creative and open-minded interactions with the field which are the true strength of qualitative methodology. Using inductive reasoning, scientific **validity** could be achieved instead by carefully building up theories from the field itself.

Instead of starting with deductive theory building, then testing hypotheses, researchers using grounded theory enter the field with a simple question couched in lay terms. They then use induction from observations to build the conceptual apparatus, only moving into comparisons with previous research in the later stages of the process. As researchers cycle between data collection, coding, and analysis, initially scattered hypotheses gradually come together. First, categories and their properties emerge, then the relations between them are carefully examined, leading eventually to a fully integrated theoretical structure.

Grounded theory as a comprehensive framework has had limited appeal within sociology, as most qualitative sociologists continue to believe that it is impossible, even undesirable, to leave behind theory when undertaking field research. However, the methodological procedures suggested by the advocates of grounded theory have proved invaluable to many sociologists, and the method has found great support in the fields of medicine, nursing, education and business.

GROUP

The group in sociological terms is an association of individuals who are related to one another according to similarities of an attribute or set of attributes that constitute group membership. Individuals are bound to society by their group memberships. Group membership may be elective or definitional. Groups in which membership is based on objective criteria (primary groups) are considered to form the framework upon which subjective memberships are secondary, hence the designation secondary groups. Some groups have voluntary membership; others have requirements for inclusion. Primary groups are usually composed of individuals bound by ties of kinship. Individuals tend to be most tightly bound to their primary groups. According to this scheme, membership in primary groups tends to be definitional, or inherent: an individual is necessarily a member of a racial, **family**, citizenship or ethnic group according to inherited attributes.

An individual may have any number of **secondary group** memberships, including clubs, organizations, and churches. Multiple memberships may be a source of conflict for an individual or may strengthen the individual's bonds to society. Individuals are typically members of many secondary groups simultaneously, and membership in some groups may overlap. **Georg Simmel** articulated the interconnectedness of human relations in his essay ''The Web of Group Affiliations,'' which became the basis of **network theory**.

Group membership was one of the basis for early understanding of collective action, known as identity-based action. Members of a group share an identity and are assumed to be predisposed to act collectively based on that membership. An example of simultaneous, overlapping (or even nested) group memberships might be those groups to which a factory supervisor belongs. This worker might belong to an occupational group, a union, a supervisory group and an employee group.

An individual's attributes are not transparent within a group. Indeed, these attributes may serve to set an individual apart from the group or may suggest membership in still another group based on those qualities. An individual is also distinguished from other group members by the patterns of participation in other groups which may be unique to the individual.

GROUP DYNAMICS

Group dynamics refer to the way groups affect individuals' actions and interactions. A social group is defined as two or more people who interact and identify with one another. There are many types of social groups, and each is characterized by some common bond felt by its members. This common bond can stem from **values** and beliefs, **race**, religion, and even clothing style and musical preferences. Each group that an individual is a part of affects them in many ways.

Set patterns dictate how people interact with one other when in groups, whether they be small or large groups. For example, in most social gatherings or parties guests trickle in one by one. One conversation is shared by all the guests until more than six people enter the room. As the seventh and eighth person enter, the shared conversation breaks up and conversations are started in smaller groups. It becomes difficult to sustain a single topic of conversation in a large group.

In large social groups very little intimate **interaction** takes place. Intimacy is achieved more readily through groups that only have two or three members, called dyads and triad. Larger groups with their lack of intimacy allow each member a certain level of anonymity. Individuals in a large group tend to do things that they would not normally do when alone or with a small group. This idea is clear and familiar in the form of peer pressure.

Several behavioral experiments have been done to gauge to what extent individuals are affected by group pressure. Soloman Asch (1955) performed experiments to gauge whether individuals would or would not choose to conform to a group. He created an experiment where between six and eight people were seated around a table. All but one of these individuals were instructed to choose a blatantly wrong answer to a very simple question. The one individual left had to choose either the right answer or choose the wrong answer to conform with the group. Asch's experiments found that about one-third of all people in the studies chose an answer that they knew was wrong just to conform to the group. The conclusions drawn from this and other experiments show that individuals are profoundly influenced by groups. This information is used by researchers and sociologists to better understand human behavior.

GROUP LIFE

Social groups are collectives of socially-related individuals who interact interact with each other and are of particular interest to sociologists. Group life is a concept that involves two parts, primary groups and secondary groups. **Charles Horton Cooley** developed this group classification system in 1909 as he began to evaluate the organic link between the self and society.

Cooley's emphasis on the wholeness of social life led him to focus on analyzing groups that he viewed as providing the necessary integration of the individual with his **society**. This theoretical perspective originated from Cooley's insight that we imagine how we look to others and after taking that perception into account develop some self-feeling from it which forms our behaviors. According to Cooley this reflective process is the mechanism by which the self is constructed. Furthermore, Cooley argued that this processes of reflection was learned in primary groups.

A **primary group** is defined as a small group characterized by intimate face-to-face **interaction** and cooperation although there may be competition within it. In addition, this type of group is generally unified, operating according to its own **norms**. The **family**, groups of friends, and work groups are examples of primary groups becauseit is through an individual's involvement in such groups that he or she develops his or her nature and ideas. In these relations, people are supposedly functioning, as the relationship itself is the ends rather than a means to ends. Thus, instrumentality is not characteristic of these groups. The primary group provides the environment that fosters in the individual an ability to put oneself into the position of others, drawing the individual out of egotistic isolation.

A **secondary group** is larger than a primary group where members tend not to interact with every other member of the group.Although not as intimate as primary groups, these groups serve the purpose of **status** identification and provide a means to some end. This type of group would encompass, for example, trade union where there is a system of norms and a shared work experience. Primary groups are those groups that teach individuals the **rules** of social life while secondary groups tend to have means-to-ends relationships where status is the predominant characteristic.

GROUP MARRIAGE

Group marriage, as it was defined in early anthropological literature, described three or more individuals that, according to cultural traditions, were considered married. Joseph Kohler, for example, observed different forms of group marriage among Australian aborigines and American Indians in his 1897 treatise *On the Prehistory of Marriage.* Types of group marriage he and others observed included one husband with multiple wives (*polygyny,*) and one wife with multiple husbands (*polyandry*). The term commonly used today is *polygamy* which encompasses both types. By the 1950s, the sociological definition of *group marriage* evolved into four or more participants, at least two of whom were female and two male.

In spite of some mention in sociological literature, group marriage as a topic of study was virtually ignored until the 1970s. In 1973, Joan and Larry Constantine published the results of their three-year study of group marriages in the United States in *Group Marriage: A Study of Contemporary Multilateral Marriage.* In this work they introduced the term *multilateral marriage*, the purpose of which was to enlarge the concept of group marriage to include three or more partners of any gender combination. They specified that each individual must have a primary relationship (*pair-bond*) with at least two other members of the group to be considered multilateral (unlike polygamy). In addition, multilateral marriages were intended to be egalitarian; ideally, all partners had equal **status**, regardless of sex, which was also untrue for **polygamy.**

Cultural changes that took place in **American society** during the 1960s helped create impetus for wider experimenta-

tion in alternate marriage and family forms. These factors included liberalized divorce laws, birth control innovations, **cultural pluralism**, and dissatisfaction with traditional monogamous marriage. Among the sample of group marriages studied, small groups of three or four members were the most common, of the longest duration, and the most stable. In 1972, James Ramey published a paper on his theory of the evolutionary model of marriage. According to Ramey, group marriage was innovative rather than deviant. As humans are drawn to increasingly complicated problem solving, so too are they drawn to the complex, intimate, and challenging nature of group marriage. Participants of group marriage tended to be highly educated and formerly married. Motivations for involvement included personal growth, sexual variety, **community**, and socioeconomic advantages. Other sociologists published on the subject (e.g., R.D. Kilgo, E.D. Macklin, S. Salsberg, L.D. Strong), but interest seemed to wane by the 1980s.

GROUP SIZE

Group size refers to the number of individuals in a group. A social group is defined as two or more people who interact and identify with one another. Examples are groups of friends, families, members of church congregations, or couples. **Georg Simmel** was the first to discuss group size in a sociological context. He studied the smallest group sizes, naming them the dyad and the triad.

A dyad is a social group that consists of two individuals. A dyad is usually a **love** affair, a close friendship, or a **marriage**. Dyads are the most unstable of all group sizes. If one member of the group decides to withdraw, then the group collapses. As a result, each member must work to keep the group together. Dyads tend to be more intimate and intense. In a group this size, each individual has the other's full attention when conversing or otherwise interacting. **Society** places emphasis on some dyads and may even attach laws to them. A married couple is an example of a dyad that society regulates and enforces through laws.

A triad is a social group that consists of three individuals. These groups are less intense and more stable than the dyad. In a triad if one individual loses interest and withdraws, the group can still continue. Triads are also more stable because there is a mediator for disagreements or arguments between two of the group members. The mediator helps keep the group together. One common characteristic of many triads is the tendency for two members to form a coalition. Many times two members of the triad feel a stronger bond and may leave the third individual out of the group's interactions. This phenomenon is popularly known as becoming the "third wheel" of the group.

Groups larger than two or three individuals become increasingly more stable. Larger groups can withstand the loss of several group members and still function well. As groups grow larger they become more formal and are subject to **rules** and guidelines that govern their actions. In large groups more interactions take place between individuals, but these interactions are much less personal. Personal **interaction** is difficult unless the larger group is broken down into smaller groups.

Group size is also considered a significant factor in studying group dynamics. How individuals act and react in certain situations often depends on group size. Group size affects **leadership**, decision making, and conformity in many different ways.

GUMPLOWICZ, LUDWIG (1838-1909)
Polish sociologist and political theorist

The so-called Austrian school of sociologists, of which Ludwig Gumplowicz was the most prominent, consisted of influential apostles of Social Darwinism. Gumplowicz saw **sociology** as the study of groups in conflict. He applied Darwin's theories of ''survival of the fittest'' and the ''struggle for existence'' to a system called **conflict theory**, which exerted great influence in social, political, and legal studies.

Gumplowicz, born March 9, 1838, in Krakow, now in Poland, was the son of well-to-do Polish Jews. He studied at the universities of Krakow and Vienna, Austria, deciding upon journalism as his career. As a young man, he became a supporter of the Polish national movement, but after its collapse, he rejected politics and turned to the academic life. In 1875, he became a professor of public law at the University of Graz, Austria, remaining there until shortly before his death on August 19, 1909. On that day, Gumplowicz, stricken with cancer, and his invalid wife of many years committed **suicide** together. His major works were written in German, including *The Outlines of Sociology* (1885).

Gumplowicz is known mainly for his disbelief in the permanence of social progress and for his assertion that the state originates through inevitable conflict, not through cooperation or divine inspiration. The individual, he said, never functions as such, only as a member of a **group**. It is the group's influence that determines the individual's behavior. Therefore, history and social change are products of social groups. Gumplowicz called this tendency for humans to form groups and develop a sense of unity, ''syngenism.'' At first, there is conflict among races, which, according to Gumplowicz, are primitive groups. One primitive group wins, dominates the other, and forms a state consisting of winners and losers. Wars take places between states and the whole process begins again on a grander scale. Eventually, a division of labor system is formed within a state, which produces social classes. These classes engage in conflict. The laws that result in a state are determined by these class struggles, not by some sense of abstract justice. Higher civilizations are created through warfare. The defeated warriors are not killed, but forced to work for the victors. This leads to class distinctions since the winners gain prosperity, which produces **culture**. The victors now also have time for leisure, producing the appearance of an upper class, those who live their lives from the work of others. From this **leisure** class, Gumplowicz claimed, as did Aristotle, springs **civilization**, art, science, and literature. Societies, he said, cannot be stopped from inevitable collapse through welfare programs or social planning.

The primitive groups, or races, defined in Gumplowicz's theory existed at the dawn of history when humankind split into various groups depending upon physical type, language, religion, and social patterns. During tribal raids, women of the weaker tribe were captured and brought into the victors' camp. Gumplowicz believed this practice to be the start of the original family. Just as the winning warrior exercised rights over those he captured, so these wars also led to the institution of private **property**.

Although Gumplowicz laid out only the general concept of how states originate, his followers went into greater detail, dividing state formation into various stages. In the first stage, the aggressors are merely content to kill and enslave. In the second stage, they realize it is more beneficial for the losers to live and work. This stage allows the birth of the state. In the third stage, the work of the enslaved allows leisure time for the victors. In the fourth stage, the victors settle permanently in the **territory** occupied by the enslaved instead of merely visiting to collect taxes. In the fifth stage, the victors become arbitrators for disputes among the conquered, and in the sixth stage, winners and losers join, not as aliens, but upper and lesser classes to form the state.

Gumplowicz saw each primitive group alien and barely human. It was, therefore, not morally **evil** to destroy the enemy. It is this belief and his work entitled *Race Struggle* that some scholars see—ironically, since Gumplowicz was Jewish—as having an important influence of the development of Adolf Hitler and his Nazi theories.

GUN CONTROL

Gun control is one of the most divisive issues in American politics and is consistently an issue during presidential elections. This debate hinges on interpretation of the Second Amendment: ''A well-regulated Militia being necessary to the security of a free State, the right of the people to keep and bear Arms shall not be infringed.'' At the most basic level, those opposed to gun control interpret the Second Amendment as pertaining to the rights of individuals, whereas those in favor see it as preserving a group right.

The first federal restrictions on gun ownership followed a 1933 assassination attempt on President Franklin Delano Roosevelt; the National Firearms Act of 1934 imposed a $200 tax on machine guns and sawed-off shotguns. In fact, most gun control laws are passed in the wake of some act of gun-related violence; the Gun Control Act of 1968 was a response to the assassinations of President John F. Kennedy and Reverend Martin Luther King. The 1968 act, which imposed minor safety restrictions on firearm imports in order to raise prices, set the tone for future laws through its loopholes; no similar standards were created for gun manufacturers in the United States, and the domestic gun industry flourished by selling ''junk guns,'' such as the inexpensive Saturday Night Special.

The assassination attempt on President Ronald Reagan in 1981 was perpetrated by John Hinckley, who was inspired by the film *Taxi Driver* in his attempt to win the favor of actress Jodi Foster. President Reagan was not seriously injured, but his press secretary, James Brady, was shot in the head and

James Brady, one-time press secretary to former President Ronald Reagan, speaks in favor of gun control legislation at the 1996 Democratic National Convention *(Corbis Corporation [Bellevue])*.

and injuring twenty-one others before killing themselves. For some Americans, this event was seen as further proof of the need for stricter gun laws, while other Americans blamed certain alternative rock musicians and violent video games; no new legislation has been passed by the federal government, although some states have passed legislation.

In other countries, response to violent firearm events has been swift and without mercy. After a man opened fire on a kindergarten class in Scotland, Britain passed a ban on ownership of all handguns. Australian officials banned pump-action shotgun and military style rifles, instated a gun registration program and a program for private gun owners to sell their arms to the government, following the death of 35 people in Tasmania at the hands of a single gunman. Canada, with its own share of tragedies, requires universal gun licensing and registration.

One way that states are trying to fight gun traffic is by bringing lawsuits against the gun manufacturers, usually at the city level. The charges are that the gun industry makes unsafe products, resisting inexpensive safety measures like child-proof trigger locks, and are negligent in distributing and marketing their products. For example, Chicago accused gun manufacturers of flooding markets with weak gun laws with their product, in full knowledge that the excess will end up in cities with harsher laws. These lawsuits, modelled on lawsuits against the tobacco industry, were brought as a way to circumvent legislators prejudiced by dealings with the gun control lobby.

GUTTMAN, LOUIS (1916-1987)
American sociologist

The Guttman scale analysis, devised in the 1940s as a technique to measure and analyze **public opinion**, is the work of Louis Guttman, sociologist and educator. Born in Brooklyn, New York, on February 10, 1916, to a Russian immigrant family, Guttman was the third of five children. The Guttmans moved to Minneapolis, Minnesota, when Louis was still a young boy. Although chemistry and mathematics were subjects of early interest to him, his three degrees earned at the University of Minnesota—B.A. 1936, M.A. 1939, Ph.D. 1942—were all in sociology with expertise in social and psychological **measurement**. He had sufficient course work for a major in psychology as well.

Guttman taught at Cornell University (1941–1950), Ithaca, New York, and during World War II (1941–45), he served as an expert consultant in the Research Branch of the War Department. His work involved assessing the morale and spirit of the U.S. Army. The four-volume *The American Soldier*, which he co-authored, resulted from that work. In 1943, Guttman married Ruth Halpern. The couple, who would have three children, Adi, Nurit, and Daphne, moved to Israel in 1947, supported by a postdoctoral fellowship from the **Social Science Research Council**. Guttman established the Israel Institute of Applied Social Research, acting as its scientific director for 40 years. The institute, which was modeled after the U.S. Re-

sustained severe injuries, from which he was unable to completely recover. Sarah Brady, his wife, founded the lobbying organization Handgun Control, Inc., and both Bradys spent time lobbying and testifying; their efforts found fruition in the Brady Handgun Act of 1993, which mandates a background check and a five-day waiting period for purchasing firearms. The Brady Act also had an unanticipated consequence: the law does not cover flea markets or gun shows, which quickly became popular venues for gun buyers and sellers. The Act went through Congress for a long time prior to passage, as a result of objections by the National Rifle Association (NRA), which has an extensive lobbying arm and regularly contributes to the campaigns of political candidates at all levels of government; in addition to pressure from the NRA, federal lawmakers felt pressure from their pro-gun constituents to cast the "right" vote.

The late 1980s and the 1990s saw the rise of gun violence in schools; children brought guns to schools and opened fire on their teachers and classmates with increasing frequency, culminating in the 1998 "Columbine Massacre" in Littleton, Colorado. Two students laced the school with bombs and opened fire on their classmates at lunch time, killing thirteen

search Branch, was charged with conducting **surveys** on morale and other aspects of Israeli society. Issued before the Six-Day War between Arabs and Israelis in June 1967, his "Continuing Survey of Social Problems," which was copublished with the Israeli Institute and Hebrew University, remained for more than twenty years a rich data source of attitudes in Israel. In addition, Guttman taught at Hebrew University, Jerusalem (1955–1987), and was at various times a visiting professor at Harvard University, Massachusetts Institute of Technology, Michigan State University, the University of Michigan, the University of Minnesota, and the University of Texas, Austin. Guttman died on October 25, 1987, while visiting in Minneapolis, where he had returned to lecture and to receive treatments for cancer. Among his many awards are: the Rothschild Prize for Social Science (1963), the Israel Prize in the Social Sciences (1978), the Educational Testing Service Award for Distinguished Service to Measurement (1984), and the Helen Dinerman Award from the World Association of Public Opinion Research (1988).

While he was at the University of Chicago on a postdoctoral fellowship, Guttman became interested in **factor analysis**, which tries to identify an unspecified number of dimensions characterizing a set of variables. His many innovations in the social sciences, including such topics as the mathematics of reliability theory and the **theory** and practice of factor analysis, reflect his assertion that clarity and integrity should be integral parts of scientific inquiry. His oft-quoted remark on this subject was: "Throwing away items on the basis of item analysis is like throwing away evidence that the world is round." Much of Guttman's career was devoted to social and psychological measurements and to developing methods that would address such issues.

Guttman's major contribution to the field of social science is known as Guttman scaling, cumulative scaling, or scalogram analysis. The purpose is to establish a one-dimensional continuum on which to measure a concept; in other words, to predict item responses perfectly knowing only the respondent's total score. The first step is to define a focus for the scale, e.g., attitudes of American citizens toward legal immigration from Asia. From that, a set of items—80 to 100—are developed to reflect that focus, e.g., I would feel comfortable if an Asian immigrant moved onto my block. Next, a group of judges rate the statements—yes or no—according to how favorable they are to the original focus. A table, or matrix, is set up showing answers of all respondents. In general, the nearly cumulative scale that results will show that if a respondent, e.g., agreed with item 7, he or she would almost always agree with item 2, and so on. From this, the final scale elements are selected and respondents are asked to check the items with which they agree. Each element has a value. Totalling the elements of each respondent should indicate how he or she feels about legal immigration from Asia.

H

HABERMAS, JÜRGEN (1929-)
German philosopher and sociologist

The German philosopher and sociologist Jürgen Habermas challenged social science by suggesting that human beings are capable of rationality and under some conditions are able to communicate with one another successfully; the barriers preventing the exercise of reason and mutual understanding can be identified, comprehended, and reduced.

Jürgen Habermas was born in Düsseldorf, Germany, on June 18, 1929. At the end of World War II, he was repulsed by the Germans' "collectively realized inhumanity," which characterized, he believed, their lack of response to the revelations in the Nürenberg trials about the Nazi death machine. His own very different shock and horror constituted "that first rupture, which still gapes."

Entering the University of Bonn in 1946, he began to speculate about the meaning of such concepts as reason, freedom, and **justice**, in part by reading Hegel, Marx, and the Hungarian Georg Lukács. Habermas obtained his Ph.D. in 1954. Shortly thereafter he moved to the University of Frankfurt where, until 1959, he served as assistant to Professor **Theodor Adorno**, who was associated with the Institute for Social Research. The Frankfurt Institute breached traditional boundaries that separate literary criticism, philosophy, psychoanalysis, and social science and attempted to understand critically the various elements comprising modern **society**. In time Habermas would become the successor to the school's tradition.

Even before he came to Frankfurt, Habermas began publishing criticism and social commentary on a wide range of topics. As he developed more powerful ideas, and as these ideas appeared in books rather than scattered among many periodicals, his impact became widespread. His overall goal was to construct a social **theory** that could effect the emancipation of people from arbitrary social constraint.

As assistant to Adorno, Habermas collaborated in a survey of Frankfurt University students which resulted in the book *Student and Politics*. He returned to this subject when he analyzed the student movement of the late 1960s. He supported academic reform and opposed militant student behavior.

Habermas' early theoretical works examined broad changes in the way Western **civilization** treats political ideals. For example, in *Theory and Practice* (1962) he traced the change from the study of Platonic ideas to the study of effective means for manipulating citizens, as exemplified by modern social science. In *Strukturwandlung der öffentlichkeit* (1962) he examined changes in concepts of the public and the private spheres. He considered the differences between natural science research and social science research and reviewed the methods on which historical, sociological, and linguistic work was based. This work was the first which reflected his lifelong preoccupation with the ways in which social scientists study human behavior. He emphasized the importance of **language**. "What raises us out of nature," he stated, "is the only thing whose nature we can know: language. Through its structure, autonomy and responsibility are posited for us."

Contemporary society and its transformation by science and technology were his continuing concern. In the early 1970s he examined the ideological roles **science and technology** play (*Toward a Rational Society,* 1971) and studied the social and cultural contradictions in modern societies in which the **legitimacy** of political systems has been increasingly challenged (*Legitimation Crisis,* 1973).

Habermas spent most of his work life as a professor in a university setting. However, between 1971 and 1983 he directed the Max Planck Institute for Social Research in Starnberg, near Munich. His theoretical perspective included evolutionary anthropology, linguistic theory, and theories of Piaget and Kohlberg.

Habermas was often at the center of controversy. In the early 1980s, when he was still directing the Max Planck Institute, he was too controversial for the University of Munich to appoint as an adjunct professor. Still, he received many prizes, awards, and honors. He served as Theodore Heuss Professor at the New School for Social Research in New York, which awarded him an honorary degree, as did Cambridge University.

Habermas continued to involve himself in political questions of the day. In the late 1970s, when the German government was suspending civil liberties in an effort to stop terrorism, he feared that threats to democratic institutions and a possible witch hunt of left-wing intellectuals. He sent a circular letter to fifty German critics, writers, and social scientists and asked them to contribute to a book that would express the diversity of concerns about the spiritual situation of the age (*Observations on "The Spiritual Situation of the Age,"* 1979).

In 1981 Habermas published what he called his "magnum opus," *The Theory of Communicative Action.* Here he brought together previous work and developed the concept of **rationality**; he constructed a concept of society that integrated what he called "the lifeworld paradigm" with a system paradigm; and he elaborated a **critical theory** of modernity.

When Habermas left the Max Planck Institute in 1983 he returned once again to the University of Frankfurt as professor of philosophy. He was married and had three children.

Called the "leading social thinker in Germany today," Habermas was compared to Hegel and Marx. Certainly Habermas had close intellectual ties to Marx; however, he objected to the Marxian reduction of history and **culture** to mere economic processes, and humanized Marxian **dialectic** through his introduction of his theory of knowledge.

With Hegel, Habermas shared the belief in the power of reason and discourse to establish social truths, but he placed greater emphasis on the individual's ability to reason and the social group's ability to reach a consensus of opinion on **values** and social **norms** of behavior.

After *Theory of Social Action,* (1981), Habermas published *The Critique of Functionalist Reason* (1984.) In both volumes he sought to integrate the individual's life experience with his total social context, the "system paradigm." He also took to task the views of several historic and contemporary social thinkers.

Habermas published *Between Facts and Norms: Contributions to a Discourse Theory of Law and Democracy*(1996) and in 1999, he released *A Berlin Republic: Writings on Germany* on events in Germany after 1989.

HARRIS, MARVIN (1927-)

American anthropologist

Marvin Harris was born August 18, 1927, in Brooklyn, New York. He was the primary force behind the development of the theoretical perspective *cultural materialism.* Harris was trained as an anthropologist, completing his Ph.D. at Columbia University during the early 1950s. Harris continued to teach at Columbia until 1980, serving as Chair of the Anthropology Department for a period of time. Since 1981 he has held the position of Graduate Research Professor of Anthropology at University of Florida.

Although Harris's scholarly activities lie within the field of anthropology, his work in cultural anthropology has been

a great resource for various sociologists conducting cross-cultural and comparative research. Utilizing a historical and global perspective, Harris has investigated ways in which material conditions give rise to numerous cultural forms. This approach, dubbed cultural materialism, arose as a synthesis of three other theoretical perspectives: historical materialism, cultural **ecology**, and **evolutionary theory**. Historical **materialism** examines historical **social change** as inextricably intertwined with the material economic conditions of social life. Cultural ecology focuses upon the ways in which the physical environment influences demographic and cultural patterns. Evolutionary theory places human cultural forms within an evolutionary framework, drawing conclusions about the adaptive functions of various cultural patterns.

As a result of his anthropological research Harris has produced 16 books and numerous articles. In 1968 Harris published what has been called his most scholarly work *The Rise of Anthropological Theory.* In this volume Harris outlined the history of anthropological **theory** from 1750 to the present. This work also provided an analysis of the origins of cultural materialism, as well as a systematic presentation of the basic postulates of this theoretical tradition.

Cows, Pigs, Wars, and Witches: The Riddles of Culture, published in 1974, provided a cultural materialist analysis of phenomena Harris referred to as "cultural riddles." Highlighting the evolutionary component of **cultural materialism**, Harris demonstrated how certain "riddles of culture" evolved as adaptations to culturally and historically specific material conditions. For example, Harris explained the traditional Hindu sanctification of the cow, and the subsequent ban on eating it, in cultural materialist terms. He also explored the cultural significance of the Jewish-Moslem abomination of the pig, explaining the phenomenon as an adaptive response to the material conditions of Jewish and Moslem life throughout history.

In 1977, Harris's *Cannibals and Kings: The Origins of Cultures* provided a more systematic presentation of his evolutionary approach to **culture** and **society**. Harris outlined a precise theoretical model of social evolution, applying it to the last ten thousand years of human existence. In *Cannibals and Kings* Harris identified the historical processes of population growth, ecological depletion, and technological change as the primary forces behind the evolution of all major cultural forms.

When *Cultural Materialism: The Struggle for a Science of Culture* was published in 1979, Harris introduced his most complete delineation of the cultural materialist perspective to date. In addition to his more systematic presentation of the basic principles of cultural materialism, this work also contained many illuminating critiques of other major anthropological theoretical perspectives.

In 1981, Harris produced a short volume entitled *America Now: The Anthropology of a Changing Culture,* which provided a cultural materialist analysis of significant transitions in American culture since World War II. Four years later Harris published *Good to Eat: Riddles of Food and Culture,* This work was devoted to an examination of food taboos and dietary patterns throughout history and around the world. Utilizing a cultural materialist framework, Harris explained how the material circumstances of everyday life have historically influenced nutritional practices in a variety of cultural settings.

One of Harris's most recent and influential publications *Our Kind: Who We Are, Where We Came From, and Where We Are Going,* a collection of essays published in 1990, focused specifically upon the origin and evolution of human beings. In *Our Kind* Harris explained how humans evolved from lower primates. Harris also asserted that the human acquisition of the ability to speak was integral to the historical development of the variety of diverse cultures throughout the world.

Although Harris's efforts at book publication have slowed in recent years, he still makes significant contributions to the field of anthropology. Publishing articles and writing book reviews in response to recent publications in the field, Harris has continued throughout the 1990s to share his ideas about human cultures. However, Harris's most influential contribution to the field has been his systematic elucidation and application of the cultural materialist theory.

HATE CRIMES

Hate crimes, also referred to as "bias crimes," are generally those in which the perpetrator chooses a victim specifically because of the victim's perceived or actual **status** as a member of a particular **group**. Property belonging to a group or group member may also be targeted. The exact legal definition of a hate crime, however, varies considerably. While most states in the United States have passed anti-hate-crimes legislation of some sort over the last two decades, some of these laws cover only the "classic" cases of **race, ethnicity**, national origin, and religion, while others cover a broader spectrum, including sexual orientation, gender, age, disability, and even political affiliation. Additionally, some states and municipalities provide special training for **law enforcement** and/or have created special bureaus within law enforcement agencies to deal with hate crimes. The federal government, particularly the FBI, has also become involved in investigating and passing legislation against hate crimes. However, classifying, punishing, and collecting data on hate crimes has proven difficult and controversial for a number of reasons.

According to Elizabeth Cramer (1999), the Hate Crimes Statistics Act, passed in 1990, "requires the Federal Bureau of Investigation to collect statistics on hate crimes on the basis of race, religion, ethnicity, sexual orientation, and disability and to publish an annual summary of these statistics." These data have shown increasing incidences of hate crimes over the last ten years. However, the **data** are incomplete, since the FBI collects its data from local and state law enforcement agencies that may or may not keep separate track of such crimes and may or may not include all of the federally-enumerated statutes in their own hate crimes legislation. It is also possible that, much like rape statistics, what looks like an increase in incidences may actually reflect more and better reporting. Likewise, several advocacy groups that maintain statistics on the prevalence of hate crimes also report persistent increases, but they too may be working with differing definitions of hate crimes and incomplete data. Some of these groups have reported increases in the 1980s and early 1990s and decreases in the late 1990s. Frederick M. Lawrence (1999) wrote: "These trends are difficult to interpret. There is evidence that bias crimes, even if less numerous, have grown more violent...from racially motivated property crimes...to personal crimes such as assault, threat, and harassment" as well as murder. Researchers have consistently found that the perpetrators of hate crimes tend to be white men in their late teens and early twenties who are unacquainted their victims, acting alone, or (more commonly)acting in a group.

Hate crimes laws themselves have been the subject of much debate. Currently, the most common approach to hate crimes legislation is "penalty enhancement," or an increase in the sentence for a perpetrator who, according to Valerie Jenness (1995), "'intentionally selects his or her victim because of their race, religion, sexual orientation, etc." This approach is used at the federal level as well. Jacobs and Potter wrote that "The federal **Violent Crime** Control and Law Enforcement Act of 1994...mandated a revision of the U.S. sentencing guidelines to provide an enhancement for hate crimes of three offense levels above the base level for the underlying offense." While this approach has been less controversial than others which sought to create entirely new laws aimed at bias-motivated crimes, it is not without its detractors.

Opponents of such legislation insist that since crimes such as vandalism, assault, and murder, are already illegal, existing laws simply need to be better enforced. Raising penalties for some offenses, they argue, sends the message that some people have more right to protection from crime than others. Supporters of hate crimes legislation, however, state that hate crimes are in fact worse than the underlying "parallel" crimes alone. Several researchers note that hate crimes are more likely to be violent and cause serious injury. Additionally, Lawrence argued that "the very nature of bias motivation, when directed against minority victims, triggers the history and social context of **prejudice** and prejudicial violence against the victim and his group...There is a more widespread impact on the 'target community'...and an even broader-based harm to the general society."

Another issue surrounding the implementation of hate crimes laws is the difficulty of distinguishing "hate crimes" from "hate *speech*," which is protected under the First Amendment. Since the concept of "speech" is not limited solely to verbalizations, the two are not easily separated. Jacobs and Potter posed the question: "Those who believe hate crimes laws to be unconstitutional argue that... recriminalization or sentence enhancement for the same offense when it is motivated by prejudice amounts to extra punishment for **values**, thoughts, and opinions which the government deems abhorrent...is that not equivalent to punishment for 'improper thinking'?" But Lawrence, who believes such laws are constitutional, makes a distinction not only between speech and action but also between speech coupled with the *intention* to cause harm to the victim (which may be criminalized) and speech uttered with no such intention (which is protected).

Hate Crimes—Number of Incidents, Offenses, Victims, and Offenders, by Bias Motivation: 1997

[The FBI collected statistics on hate crimes from 11,211 law enforcement agencies representing over 223 million inhabitants in 1997. Hate crime offenses cover incidents motivated by race, religion, sexual orientation, ethnicity/national origin, and disability]

Bias motivation	Incidents	Offenses	Victims [1]	Known offenders [2]
Total bias motivations	8,049	9,861	10,255	8,474
Race, total	4,710	5,898	6,084	5,444
Anti-White	993	1,267	1,293	1,520
Anti-Black	3,120	3,838	3,951	3,301
Anti-American Indian/Alaskan native	36	44	46	45
Anti-Asian/Pacific Islander	347	437	466	351
Anti-multiracial group	214	312	328	227
Ethnicity/national origin, total	836	1,083	1,132	906
Anti-Hispanic	491	636	649	614
Anti-other ethnicity/national origin	345	447	483	292
Religion, total	1,385	1,483	1,586	792
Anti-Jewish	1,087	1,159	1,247	598
Anti-Catholic	31	32	32	16
Anti-Protestant	53	59	61	19
Anti-Islamic	28	31	32	22
Anti-other religious group	159	173	184	120
Anti-multireligious group	24	26	27	11
Anti-atheism/agnosticism/etc	3	3	3	6
Sexual orientation, total	1,102	1,375	1,401	1,315
Anti-male homosexual	760	912	927	1,032
Anti-female homosexual	188	229	236	158
Anti-homosexual	133	210	214	103
Anti-heterosexual	12	14	14	14
Anti-bisexual	9	10	10	8
Disability, total	12	12	12	14
Anti-physical	9	9	9	11
Anti-mental	3	3	3	3
Multiple bias	4	10	40	3

[1] The term "victim" may refer to a person, business, institution, or a society as a whole. [2] The term "known offender" does not imply that the identity of the suspect is known, but only that an attribute of the suspect is identified which distinguishes him/her from an unknown offender.

Source: U.S. Federal Bureau of Investigation, *Hate Crime Statistics,* annual; and <http://www.fbi.gov/ucr/hc97all.pdf> (accessed 30 March 1999).

Some researchers have taken a "social constructionist" approach to the issue, emphasizing the symbolic nature of hate crimes legislation rather than its efficacy or constitutionality. They suggest that we must examine how society's views of contemporary hate crimes and hate crime victims are changing. Jenness stated: "The law has played a major role in defining hate crimes as a social problem. Indeed, it is only through the adoption of legislation that hate crimes became a meaningful term and the victimization associated with the problem of hate crimes was rendered apparent and clearly defined." This approach helps explain why the "classic" hate crimes are more likely to be included in legislation than crimes such as "gay-bashing;" unlike race or religion, many lawmakers and their constituents do not consider **homosexuality** a legitimate minority status deserving of protection. Including gender in hate crimes legislation also remains controversial, largely because violence against women and the laws criminalizing it are considered more widespread and acknowledged.

HATE GROUPS

Hate groups in the United States are difficult to track and monitor. The growth of hate-based web sites, especially those aimed at children, has been a great cause of concern in recent years. Researchers have pointed out that many of these sites are put up by isolated individuals who are not necessarily connected to each other or to any larger organization. The Southern Poverty Law Center counted 305 hate sites on the **Internet** in early 2000, a notable increase from the 254 sites in 1999. However, the organization counted 457 active hate groups in the United States in 1999, down from 537 the year before. SPLC only counts those organizations which "engage in racist behavior such as crimes, marches, rallies, speeches, leafleting, or publishing literature—more than merely putting up Web sites." They attribute the drop in groups to consolidation of smaller groups into larger ones over the past few years. Another anti-hate-groups organization, HateWatch.org, counts a site if it "advocates violence against or unreasonable hostility toward a person or **group** based on **race**, religion, ethnicity, gender, sexual orientation or disability." The Simon Wiesenthal Center lists over 2,000 such sites; in marked contrast, they point out, to the single hate site in existence when the Oklahoma City Federal Building was bombed in 1995.

Hate groups have developed a variety of targets over the last ten years. In addition to racial and ethnic minorities, Jews, and immigrants, some groups also direct their rhetoric at the government, abortion providers, and gays and lesbians. The development of the "militia movement," which forms armed groups of local citizens to defend their **community** against any future government invasions, received much publicity after the Oklahoma City explosion. Researchers have explored its ties to extreme anti-abortion activists and to more traditional racist organizations like the Ku Klux Klan. The "Christian Identity" movement, most notably the World Church of the Creator, has also become more prominent as its Internet presence has increased and its leaders have been arrested for violence against African Americans. Identity adherents believe that white Christians are God's chosen people, and all others are subhuman "mud people." Many researchers also include African-American separatist groups, particularly the Nation of Islam led by Louis Farrakhan, on their lists of hate groups. The Anti-Defamation League states that "Farrakhan has often disparaged Jews and whites, delivering hate-saturated rhetoric to thousands of enthralled listeners."

Many hate groups have softened their rhetoric in recent years in an attempt to look more mainstream and respectable. Mitch Berbrier, discussing this change in tactics, wrote: "The general strategy of this package—this New Racist discourse— is to sound moderate and reasonable, set a positive tone of pride and love rather than hate and violence, and avoid any blatant references to racial superiority or inferiority. The goal is to attract a different 'element' into the white supremacist fold." David Duke, who left the Ku Klux Klan to form the National Association for the Advancement of White People (NAAWP) in 1980, is a key case in point. Duke was elected to the state legislature of Louisiana from a predominantly white suburb of New Orleans in 1989 and came within two percentage points of winning the race for governor in 1991. Another notable example, the Council of Conservative Citizens, formed in 1989, has its roots in the Citizens Council of America, which was formed to combat school desegregation in the 1950s and 1960s. The CofCC counts dozens of politicians among its membership, many of them southerners. Sen. Trent Lott (R-MS), Rep. Bob Barr (R-GA), and Mississippi Governor Kirk Fordice have all been featured speakers at the group's annual meetings. The CofCC's stated goal is "to conserve the traditional heritage, **culture**, and way of life that Euro-Americans have practiced since the inception of this country." Their web site decries the "genocide" against white people and refers to Dr. Martin Luther King as a "communist."

Both the violent and the softened forms of rhetoric can be considered reactions to the increasing ethnic and racial di-

Hate groups in the United States like the Ku Klux Klan have historically targeted minorities *(AP/Wide World Photos, Inc.)*.

versity of the United States and the increasing acceptance of **multiculturalism** that has sometimes accompanied it. While some hate groups continue to use blatant white supremacist rhetoric, others use an approach Berbrier referred to as "Kultural Pluralism," combining "Cultural Pluralism and traditional racism to present a view of white racial activism and racism as the ordinary (non-deviant) behavior routinely expected of normal people who are simply conscious and proud of their cultural heritage and ethnic roots."

HAWTHORNE EFFECT

The Hawthorne effect describes subject reactivity to researchers. Behavior exhibited by subjects is not due to any treatment variable in the study but is instead a reaction to being included in a research study. The term was coined by Elton Mayo (1966) after conducting productivity research in the Hawthorne plant of Western Electric Company near Chicago during the 1920s and 1930s. The initial stages of the study were conducted by managers of the Hawthorne plant in an attempt to ascertain whether different levels of lighting would affect productivity levels among women working in the Relay Rooms. The **research hypothesis** proposed a **positive association** between light intensity and productivity. One room was used as a control where lighting levels were kept constant. In the experimental room, the lighting level was varied, sometimes lower and sometimes brighter. Instead of finding that increased lighting led to increased productivity, productivity increased dramatically regardless of the light intensity. Even when the lights were dimmed substantially, productivity increased. Further, productivity increased among the control group.

Mayo and a team of researchers were called in to further investigate these unexpected findings. They set up other experiments in the plant, observing the women's productivity under various conditions, such as changes in the rate of pay, in work break periods, in length of work days, and in whether the company provided refreshments. No matter how the conditions of work were changed, productivity always *increased*. In a pseudo replication of these experiments, men who worked in the Bank Wiring Room were observed by Mayo and his team. This group was treated as a control, so no condition changes were made, and productivity was expected to be maintained. However, among the men, productivity *decreased*. Mayo concluded that the men were wary of the researchers and were concerned that higher productivity may result in loss of jobs or raised expectations from management. Like the women, the men reacted to the researchers presence rather than to the conditions of the experiment. The Hawthorne studies are thus better known for their findings on subject reactivity than productivity.

The Hawthorne effect can be viewed as a spurious relationship, since conditions of the study had no bearing on the change in productivity. The results of the study were not due to the **independent variable**, but a spurious variable. Aside from experiments, the Hawthorne effect is most likely to occur in field research, when the researcher is a participant, a participant observer, or an observer as participant. In these situations, the researcher identifies him or herself as a researcher and runs the risk that subjects may behave unnaturally. In field research and experiments, it is particularly important to monitor the Hawthorn effect, as its presence can threaten the validity of the study in two ways. First, because results of the study are due to a spurious variable—the presence of a researcher—results are not attributable to the independent variables, which threatens internal validity. Second, results of the study may not be generalizable which threatens external **validity**.

If subjects are studied for a long time, the Hawthorn effect may be diminished because the novelty of being observed wears off. If, for example, studies at the Hawthorn plant had continued, productivity may have decreased with decreasing lighting levels because workers would have become comfortable with the research process.

The Hawthorne effect also illustrates the ethical conflict surrounding informed consent. Ideally, a researcher should provide enough information to subjects about a study so that subjects can make an informed decision as to participation. However, this level of information can lead to unnatural behavior on the part of subjects. Not informing the subjects that they are being studied or not providing information about the purpose of the research or failing to inform the subjects of the identity of the researchers may greatly diminish the risk of the Hawthorne effect, but these omissions clearly violate ethical standards in sociological research.

HEALTH AND ILLNESS BEHAVIOR

Health and illness behavior refers to the way people perceive their physical well-being and the well-being of others. The concept also refers to how people behave when they or others

are ill. While some perceptions and behaviors are the result of individual psychological make-up, social scientists have learned that **society** and **culture** shape health and illness behavior. Culture affects our personal view of illness, our understanding of illness, how we perceive the availability of help for illness, and to what extent our illness affects the lives of our family, friends and others. Sickness is an accepted role in U.S. society, bringing attention, sympathy, and a release from performance expectation. How we respond when we or others are in the sick role is, to a great extent, dictated by the culture in which we live; worldwide, much diversity of attitudes exists. People assess how healthy they are based much more on their ability to perform social activities and fulfill social roles than actual health indicators, such as blood pressure, heart rate, cholesterol levels, etc. Teenagers who engage in school activities, exercise, and participate in sports judge themselves to be healthier than those who do not.

Studies have shown that people learn how to keep themselves healthy from their culture, families, peer groups, education, and exposure to mass media. For example, various behaviors, detrimental to health begin, in adolescence (smoking, drinking, illegal drug use, etc.). Young people who have close relationships with their families, are involved with school activities, and attend religious services are less likely to be involved in these behaviors than teens whose primary orientation is toward peers.

People are more likely to continue to engage in healthy behavior when it is reinforced by their cultural **group** than when the behavior arises only from conscious motivation. It is difficult to quit smoking, for example, when the only inhibiting factor is personal willpower. But when those actions are reinforced by societal pressure, which is increasingly causing smoking to be considered unacceptable behavior, people are much more successful in quitting.

An individual's illness is not simply a personal or family matter: In U.S. society, it is a public issue. People who are ill may spend extended periods away from employment, which may affect a company's productivity. They often lose income as a result of their inability to work, and so they collect public money in the form of insurance or disability entitlements. They may use the legal system to sue as a result of injury or illness and, of course, they use health care resources. Studies of illness behavior show how important it is to go beyond listening to initial complaints and narrow definition of the medical problem and examine the cultural factors that affect behavior and perception of the illness. The greater understanding medical professionals have of health and illness behavior, the more likely people are to receive the kind of care they **need**.

HEALTH AND THE LIFE COURSE

The term *life course* refers to a method of examining how individuals develop and go through changes within a social and cultural context. Health and the **life course** refers to how aspects of society and **culture**, such as shared life experiences, attitudes and behaviors, affect age-related transitions of a group of people, particularly a generation or a socio-economic group. Changes that take place in **society** also can alter the life course, or transitions, of individuals affected by them, thereby causing different generations to experience different life courses.

For example, current improvements in **health care** for the elderly may make it possible for people to live much longer and with less illness in the future than they do today. People will be in the elderly phase of their life for more years than generations past because their lives have been extended. But instead of experiencing long illnesses before they die, as many elderly do today, the next generation of seniors will be sick for a short period and will enjoy good health for most of their later years. The fact that a whole generation of seniors will remain healthier and more active for a much longer period will have wide-ranging implications for almost every aspect of society. Another example related to how socio-economic **status** can affect a group's health and life course. Income, educational level, and **race** strongly determine what level of disability individuals will experience in old age. Studies show that people in lower classes with less education die earlier and are at risk from more **disease** and injury than their wealthier, more educated peers.

The life course approach should not be confused with the life span perspective. The latter focuses on an individual's transitions and examines personality, cognition, emotional development, and other individual traits. In the life span perspective, these changes result from individual development, and those developments are universal, or are shared by all, no matter what their culture or society. Typically, life span changes are linked with chronological age and do not refer to what is happening in society. In contrast, the life course perspective focuses on transitions when the *social persona* undergoes change. It examines age-related transitions that are created by and recognized by society and shared by a specific group of people.

HEALTH CARE

Health care has traditionally been associated with medical care. It is generally discussed in conjunction with numerous other areas, such as health care legislation, health care policy, health care system, health care costs, and health care delivery. The concept of health care has thus often been used as an adjective or as synonymous with medical care. In fact, it is a broad, complex concept, subject to human perception, cultural norms, values and beliefs, and social resources, structures, and conventions.

The World Health Organization defines health not only as the absence of **disease** but as a state of complete physical, mental, and social well-being. The definition of health also depends upon human perception. People perceive themselves to be healthy or well, often in terms of whether they can function and engage in desired activities. The task of health care, then, might be said to be the elimination of a major source of unhap-piness, i.e. disease or disability, by restoring optimal functioning, as culturally or individually perceived, to the individual. In the broadest sense, this task would also encompasses sources of psychological or emotional distress and negative social conditions which affect well-being.

Early health care was based on addressing the culturally perceived sources of disease and illness conditions. Since illness and death were often ascribed to supernatural causes, treatments or health care often took the form of magic or **ritual** to dispose of evil spirits and restore health. Little was known about the human body, and therapies were also derived from observations of cause and effect, through trial and error. Herbal remedies were applied, depending upon local availability, and other treatments were based upon theories and beliefs of the times. Blood letting and purging, for example, were once thought to cleanse the body of bad blood and other harmful fluids.

With the Greek physician Hippocrates, around 400 B.C., an attempt was made to formulate principles of health care based upon rational thought. Those principles included the professionalization of physicians and their promise to work only for the good of the patient, never intentionally doing harm, and keeping information shared in the doctor-patient relationship confidential. The physician's knowledge used in care of the sick was to be gained from logic, observation, and an understanding of the natural sciences. Superstition and magical attributions were rejected.

Although some associations were made between various behaviors and ill health, such as overindulgence of food and drink, little or no attention was given to many social and environmental factors that we now associate with ill health, such as **poverty**, pollution, and **stress**. As Engel noted, the human body came to be seen simply as a machine, vulnerable to breakdown through disease, and in need of repair by the physician.

With the advent of the germ **theory** in the mid-1800s and the subsequent development of medical technology, health care in the West thus became oriented to the curative **model**; diseases were classified patients were diagnosed and treated, and it was hoped that health was restored. Health care was based on the scientific medical model whereby the disease, and not the patient, became the central focus of concern. This model has essentially endured to the present day.

By the 1950s, sociologists had already begun to recognize the social factors involved in health, illness, and health care. In 1951, Talcott Parsons published *The Social System,* a work that recognized a role for sociologists in addressing the behavioral aspects of the sick role. Illness was viewed as **deviance**, and medicine was prescribed by the physician, who by diagnosis and labeling became an agent of social control. Health care was still viewed as physician-dominated, but the field of medicine and health care was clearly recognized as relevant to sociological research. Health care, however, has continued to change, and the role of sociology including its relationship to related **social problems** and policy has grown and changed as well.

Several factors are responsible for the changes in health care. Rising health care costs, the growing emphasis on prevention of illness with the shift from acute to chronic illnesses, longer **life expectancy** with emphasis on **quality of life**, the entry of large corporate chains into the medical field, changing structure of medical practice from private to group organization, the rise of consumerism and the resulting view of health care as a commodity, the growth of technology and increasing numbers of individuals without health insurance, all have greatly affected how and what kind of health care is delivered. **Sociology** is uniquely equipped to tackle the types of human and social problems that have resulted.

A major problem has been the growing inadequacy of the medical model to address the of the patient population's health care needs. The trend has been away from the purely biological model of health care, toward inclusion of other facets of patients as persons. Well-being, after all, includes the psychological, emotional, spiritual, and social spheres as well as the biological. As professionals address those needs, the concept of health care has broadened to include all manner of consumer goods and services, including nutrition, exercise, mental and physical therapy, and alternative or complementary forms of medicine and therapy. Part of the health care crisis, argued Will Wright, derives from the continued denial by medicine of the social dimensions of individual health. Martha Loustaunau and Elisa Sobo argued that the social dimension also includes factors of cultural diversity which are also very much a part of individuals and their perceptions of health, illness, and health care. It seems clear that sociology will have an increasingly important role in understanding and resolving the present health care crisis, which involves pressing social, cultural, economic, and political issues that are inextricably connected to health care and health care delivery.

HEALTH CARE SYSTEMS

Health care systems are generally institutionalized means of responding to illness and disability. Since the definition of "health care" is quite broad, the systems that organize it are also socially and culturally variable. The definition of health care is culturally relative, in that each culture defines the nature of health, or what is considered "normal," and illness, or what is deviant from the norm. In one society, for example, certain types of unusual behavior may be defined as "mental illness" and treated, while in other cultures, the same behaviors are viewed as "special" or even divinely inspired. What requires care and the type of care required in one society may be defined quite differently in another society.

For those behaviors or conditions defined as illness, or conditions requiring care or treatment of some sort, systems are developed. Although systems can vary considerably, a number of elements common to most health care systems can be identified. Roemer defined health care systems as "the combination of resources, organization, financing, and management that culminate in the delivery of health services to the population."

Field identified five ideal types of health systems organization. In the *anomic model* in the United States, health care

is viewed as an item of personal consumption with strong provider control and private ownership of facilities. The physician is a solo entrepreneur, and the representative professional association is extremely powerful with regard to control and policy-making. Also characteristic of the United States in the twentieth century, another form, *pluralistic*, is similar to the anomic model, except that there is a mixture of public and private control. The physician may also be engaged in group or other forms of organizational practice. Under the *Insurance/ Social Security* model, health care is considered an insured/ guaranteed consumer good or service with more involvement and control from the public sector. Sweden and Canada fall into this model. The *National Health Service* model, characteristic of Great Britain, views health care as a state supported consumer good or service. The control and ownership of facilities are mostly public. Finally, the *socialized* model, found in Eastern Europe and the twentieth century Soviet Union, treats health care as a completely state-provided public service. Ownership is entirely public, and the physician is a state employee. Professional organizations present in the other models are weak or do not exist.

Roemer also discussed five basic components as central to all health-care systems. The *Production of Resources* included the manpower, facilities, commodities such as drugs and medical equipment, and knowledge. *Management* encompassed planning, administration, regulation and legislation, in the public or private spheres. The *Delivery of Services* was composed of primary care, or preventive services, primary care involving treatment, tertiary care at the clinic level, and care of special disorders and populations, for example psychological services, women's services, or cancer care. *Organization of Programs* included both public and private structures, such as Ministries of Health at all levels, voluntary and other public agencies, health-related enterprises and the private market. These elements rested upon *Economic Support* which covered various sources such as personal household or payment by consumer, charity, voluntary insurance, Social Security, governmental revenue, and foreign aid. The particular form or mixture of these components depends upon the particular country or society in which the system operates.

Health systems analysis has not been of particular interest to sociologists until relatively recently. Essentially a part of what was termed the *Sociology of Medicine* by Robert Straus in 1957, it implied the use of sociological research in the medical field for studying the basic issues of **social stratification**, power and **influence**, social organization, socialization, and a broader context of social **values**. With growing complexity in the organization of health care delivery, sociologists have become more interested in such systemic features as, for example, the organization of medical practice which includes solo versus group practice, and most recently, physicians as employees of Health Maintenance Organizations (HMOs) and the managed care system.

Other areas of sociological interest are regulation of medicine by governmental entities versus professionally internal or organizational bodies and the relative advantages and disadvantages of for-profit versus public facilities. As the health care system in the United States involves both types and corporate incursion into the medical field continues, this area becomes a vitally important area for research.

New areas of health systems research have opened up with the growth of medical technology. Questions of how technology is used, such as in keeping people alive who have little or no hope of recovery, in caring for those citizens who cannot afford the high costs, and in caring for a rapidly aging population all comprise issues of **social policy** which can greatly benefit from sociological research and input. Sociologically, as well as anthropologically, the use of the concept of systems allows researchers to better analyze and understand, and compare and contrast the perceptions and approaches to illness and **disease**. Such analysis also leads to better understanding of the society in general, its political, economic and social structures, its **norms**, values, beliefs, and behaviors. In the United States, this analysis is particularly relevant to **medical sociology** due to certain trends. These include but are not limited to the rising cost of services, the growing diversity of the population, exclusion of some groups to access to care, public dissatisfaction with the present medical care system, growth of alternative medicine and care, and the role of the public and private sectors in administration of the system.

HEALTH POLICY ANALYSIS

Health policy analysis studies governmental policy regarding health care, including all aspects of the legislative, executive, and judicial branches of government that deal with the pursuit of health, the organization and employment of **health care** professionals, and the administration of health care services. In addition, the social context in which health policy agendas are formed contribute to the character of health policy. According to Jennie Jacobs Kronenfeld in *The Changing Federal Role in U.S. Health Care Policy* (1997), "A nation's health policy is part of its general overall social policy. As a result, health policy formulation is influenced by the variety and array of social and economic factors that impact **social policy** development. The nature and history of existing institutions, the general climate of opinion, ritualized methods for dealing with social conflict, attitudes and behavioral characteristics of key political actors, and the general goals and values of **society** all play a role in the formulation of social policy."

Predominantly an interdisciplinary endeavor, analysis of health policy employs the tools of numerous fields within the social sciences, including anthropology, economics, **political science**, and **sociology**, as well as drawing heavily from the applied disciplines of public health, public administration, and public policy. Depending on the goals of the researcher, the focus of study and **methodology** employed can vary greatly. Broadly defined, subjects of analysis span a continuum from social issues to medical issues. At one end of the continuum, researchers attend to social and behavioral characteristics that affect health and their relationship to health care policy. At the opposite end, researchers begin by analyzing the affects of current health policy on social and behavior health. Consequently,

the possibilities for study are immense. The array of social, political, legislative, and judicial influences on policy, along with the impact of **public opinion**, the media, and interest groups and the role of the insurance companies, makes the formulation of a comprehensive assessment of health policy a seemingly insurmountable task. Thus, most research is conducted within a limited, more manageable specialized field of study.

From 1930 to 1980, the U.S. federal government became increasingly involved in establishing health care policies. In 1965, in response to a critical shortage of access to health care, **Medicaid** was enacted, a program funded jointly at the federal and state levels to provide health care to low-income Americans. During Ronald Reagan's tenure as president, he moved to reduce the rapidly increasing budget for Medicaid by pushing through legislation that limited access. As a result, cost was reduced, but the number of uninsured women and children in particular rose dramatically. This caused a backlash that instigated new legislation, which once again expanded Medicaid eligibility and benefits. From the 1980s through the end of the century, health care remained in the spotlight of public policy and partisan politics. According to the Health Policy Tracking Service's (HPTS) report *Major State Health Care Policies* (1997), in 1997 the United States spent 14.2 percent of the gross domestic product on health care. Also, reporting on the activity of the fifty states' legislative sessions, HTPS noted that during 1997 over 25,000 pieces of legislation—almost one of every five billed introduced—were health care-related.

Most research in the field being conducted by governmental organizations. Federal agencies include the National Center for Health Statistics, the Health Care Financing Administration, the Agency for Health Care Policy and Research, and the National Institute on Aging. The largest professional associations are the Association for Health Services Research and the Foundation for Health Services Research. Private foundations and think tanks, such as the Brookings Institute, the Urban Institute, and the National Bureau of Economic Research also contribute to health policy analysis. In addition, health policy and health research centers and institutes exist at over thirty U.S. universities. Analysis of health policy can also be found in numerous journals such as *Health Affairs, Health Care Financing Review, New England Journal of Medicine,* and *Journal of Health Politics, Policy and Law.*

President Clinton's failed attempt to enact comprehensive health care reform in the early 1990s, coupled with a significant rise in health care expense, the development of new, often expensive, medical breakthroughs, the expansion of the role of state governments along with public and private organizations, and a tremendous increase in the numbers of Americans seeking services produced a dynamic environment of public policy analysis. As a result, the discipline of health policy analysis has flourished. With health care costs rising, the population aging, and a consistent outcry by the public for better quality of care and delivery, it appears that the health policy analysis will continue to sustain the attention of the social sciences.

HEALTH PROMOTION

Health promotion from a conceptional point of view is identified by six primary orientations: physical functioning, **mental health**, social well-being, role functioning, general health perceptions, and symptoms. Snehendu Kar defines health promotion as individual and societal actions that advance well-being and the prevention of health risks by achieving and maintaining optimal levels of the behavioral, societal, environmental, and biomedical determinants of health. A global perspective from the World Health Organization takes an inclusive approach by defining health as a state of complete physical, social, and mental well-being.

From the Greek **civilization** to the present-day advent of technology and the ability to eradicate infectious diseases, health promotion has thrived by Western medicine. Marc Lalonde from Canada (in the l970s) is responsible for current interest in health promotion, and he questioned the relationship between one's health and the caliber as well as volume of medical care received. According to Lalonde, **disease** and death are the result of (1) inadequacies in the health care system, (2) behavioral factors or unhealthy life-styles, (3) environmental hazards, and (4) human biological factors. Also influential in health promotion, available at most North American universities, in the 1970s were the psychology courses that were a most powerful health group interested in behavior modifications, and changes in people.

The sociological aspect of health promotion is concerned with analyzing the phenomenon as a characteristic of the much wider set of socio-economic and cultural processes associated with late Modernism. In the process of modernism, Duane Matcha in his 1999 *Medical Sociology* relates that one of the most significant developments in medical sociology was the creation of the health belief model (HBM). Perceived susceptibility, seriousness, benefits, and barriers in addition to a triggering mechanism that elicits a response are the HBM major components. John Raeburn and I. Rootman explain that, while a vague goal of positive health would probably better be called prevention, health promotion goals are best characterized within a quality-of-life (QOL) context as issues of people-centered health promotion or self-care, positivity, and spirituality and spiritual health. Whether health promotion is people-centered or self-care oriented, one model shows that as a means of health education, prevention, or protection a concern for healthy living has become a preoccupation for many people.

We see QOL as being the result of identifiable determinants, divided into environmental and personal categories. Environmental determinants involve wider-system factors—such as family, neighborhood to community; personal determinants are those associated with the attributes of individuals, biological and psychological. Calling attention to the many aspects of health is regarded as beneficial and informative; yet, in reality, we are being reminded that even societal efforts to empower individuals to control their health may inadvertently create the conditions that limit such opportunity—individuals empowered to think as health consumers are being told by health promoters what their health needs are. Many health promotion programs are designed to prevent disease, which includes nutrition, exercise, or other primary preventative measures. Secondary preventive measures include immunizations against communicable diseases or other life-threatening diseases.

When parents believe in health promotion, such as good nutrition and exercise, they teach and practice beneficial habits for the well-being of the family. Many families promote by establishing specific health patterns that may emphasize, for example, sports, exercise, or nutrition, and educate younger generations to also participate in similar patterns. Self-care provides empowerment and motivation for the individual who developes independence from formal service providers and self-reliance regarding illness and health behavior. So to speak, self-care is not a new concept, and since the earliest civilization, Gregory Weiss and Lynne Lonnquist maintain that people have taken personal measures to protect their safety and well-being and to deal with illness.

As a preventative measure for good health, many organizations or institutions have designed programs that inform the public or specific persons with specific problems about information that will benefit that person or persons. Preventative measures are for diabetes, heart problems, cancer, and many other focused subjects. According to the American Dietetic Association, current interest in health promotion in the United States involves disease prevention and the problem of obesity. Health promotion is also of global interest and, in some instances, becomes political, such as cultural **imperialism**. The Olympics is a monumental example of health promotion. There are other health organizations that boost health promotion for a better **quality of life**. For example, the American Association for Retired Person (AARP) in the United States has specific interest in the well being of the older adult population.

HEGEL, GEORG WILHELM FRIEDRICH (1770-1831)

German philosopher and educator

The German philosopher and educator Georg Wilhelm Friedrich Hegel took all knowledge as his domain and made original contributions to the understanding of history, law, logic, art, religion, and **philosophy**. Living in a time of geniuses and revolutions, Hegel claimed his own work to be not so much a revolution as the consummation of human development.

Hegel was born in Stuttgart on August 27, 1770, the son of an official serving the Duke of Württemberg. Urged by his Pietist father to enter the clergy, he registered in the Tübingen Lutheran seminary in 1788. A fair student, Hegel generally preferred the conviviality of cafés and country walks to scholarly **asceticism**. His love of wine and company, his passion for the secular writings of Jean Jacques Rousseau, and his interest in practical political matters prevailed over the stern demands of a religious calling. Nevertheless, he studied philosophy for two years and theology for three, completing his theological examination in 1793.

At the seminary Hegel read deeply in German poetry and Greek literature, in the company of Friedrich Hölderlin, the poet, and Schelling, who was to reach early eminence as a philosopher of romanticism. The three friends professed ardent sympathy with the French Revolution and took for their motto ''Freedom and Reason.''

Hegel was a private tutor in Berne where he learned about the Bernese political situation. His first published work, in 1798, consisted of notes and his translation of and exiled lawyer's letters criticizing the city's oligarchy.

In 1797 Hegel became a private tutor in Frankfurt. His employer owned a fine library and allowed him time to be with friends, especially Hölderlin. Most importantly, he had time to write. Among his many concerns were the ''conditions of profit and property'' in England, the history of **Christianity**, love, the Prussian penal code, and theology.

Hegel's father died in January 1799, leaving a legacy that enabled Hegel to leave tutoring and prepare seriously for an academic career. In 1801 he lived with Schelling, already a professor, at the great University of Jena. There he worked fervently; he wrote a detailed, critical study of the Constitution of the German Empire and completed his first published book *The Difference between Fichte's and Schelling's Systems of Philosophy* (1801). Challenging the popular view that Fichte and Schelling were master and disciple, Hegel brought out their obscured but basic differences. Recognizing that their philosophies were irreconcilable, Hegel resolved to work out a complete system that would account for the common aim and many differences of previous philosophies. Hegel's would have to be the system of all philosophy.

In 1801 Hegel also submitted a Latin dissertation on the orbits of the planets and consequently was granted the right to teach in any German university (the *venia legendi*). He began to give lectures at Jena and eventually became one of the better-known lecturers. In addition to teaching and writing, Hegel worked with Schelling to found and edit the *Kritisches Journal der Philosophie* (1802–1803), to which he contributed several articles and reviews.

While at Jena the idea of a wholly reconciling philosophy was gestating in Hegel's mind. It came to fruition in 1806 as the dense but exciting work *Phänomenologie des Geistes* (*Phenomenology of Spirit*), which compares the dialectical stages of historical development with the individual's growth with regard to a concept that Hegel called Spirit. The entire book was written in haste and was completed on October 13, the very day Napoleon and his troops occupied Jena. Later, Hegel saw a parallel between Napoleon as an individual and the historical context he occupied.

Since the university was in disarray and his own financial situation desperate, Hegel arranged to become editor of the *Bamberger Zeitung*. He held this position for a year, and on November 15, 1808, thanks once again to Niethammer, he was appointed headmaster of the gymnasium, or secondary school, at Nuremberg. For eight years Hegel taught philosophy and occasionally Greek literature and calculus. In 1811 Hegel married Marie von Tucher. He had one son previously and two sons, Karl and Immanuel, by her. While at Nuremberg, Hegel completed his second major work, *Wissenschaft der Logik* (*Science of Logic*). This difficult book presents the science of thought, purified of all reference to experience, to acts, or to facts of nature.

In 1816 Hegel was called to the University of Heidelberg. He published *The Encyclopedia of the Philosophical Sciences in Outline* (1817), a summary of his system later revised considerably in 1827 and again in 1830. The book began with a section on logic, followed by ''the philosophy of nature'' and ''the philosophy of spirit,'' and concluded with the self-knowledge (or freedom) vouchsafed only to philosophy. Since philosophy includes every kind of knowledge, true freedom is not separation but the most complete relatedness. In 1817 Hegel was granted a professorship at Berlin.

By this time Hegel's enthusiasm for the French Revolution had waned, and he published his major political work. Here he insisted, ''Whatever happens, every individual is a child of his time; so philosophy too is its own time apprehended in thought.'' Published in 1821, the book as translated by T. M. Knox is entitled *Hegel's Philosophy of Right*, 1952).

Hegel did not write a book about his ideas concerning ''absolute Spirit,'' which develops through three kinds of activity: art, religion, and philosophy. But students, after his death, compiled and published their lecture notes. Hegel studied history as the development of human freedom, rather than as a series of events.

Hegel became rector of the university in 1830. The next year he wrote a critical study of the situation in England, *On the English Reform Bill*. For the fall semester of 1831, he announced two lecture courses. He gave his first lectures on November 10; on November 14 Hegel succumbed to cholera, then epidemic in Europe.

Hegel's influence on subsequent generations is incalculable. Perhaps, the history of European thought since Hegel has been a series of revolts against his ideas. Many who are sympathetic to his achievement regard his legacy as the ''crisis of philosophy'' which so preoccupies philosophers a century later.

HEGEMONY

The concept of hegemony in **sociology** addresses core and crucial questions about power—its longevity, who controls it, and how it is exercised. The concept is most closely associated with the early twentieth century Italian Communist Party leader and Marxist theorist Antonio Gramsci, who originally and most fully developed the idea. In contrast with the most popular understanding of hegemony as **domination**, Gramsci defines the term as ''leadership'' in his major work, the collected essays entitled *The Prison Notebooks*. For Gramsci, domination means rule through the exercise of physical force, or the threat thereof, whereas hegemony essentially means rule by spontaneous consent. Unlike reasoned consent, spontaneous consent is given more quickly, freely, and with less thought, questioning, and discussion.

As a twentieth century Marxist, Gramsci sought to understand the persistence of capitalist power but found traditional Marxist **theory** wanting in its strict emphasis on economic factors as the basis for power. In the narrowest Marxist ''base-superstructure'' **model**, the economic base (i.e., the means of production and their ownership by a given social class at a given period in history) more or less directly determines the superstructure, composed of everything not strictly materially productive, including religious, **family**, state, and artistic institutions. Although Gramsci maintained that the base ultimately shapes the superstructure, he afforded much more room and significance to superstructural institutions, particularly those of civil **society**, such as families, churches, schools, labor unions, and political parties.

Gramsci argued that any social **group** which seeks to maintain power in the long-term needs more than control over the military or the economic means of production; a ruling group needs to win the moral and intellectual consent of the great majority of citizens. Whereas the state is the most salient instrument of domination, the institutions of civil society are the primary instruments of hegemony. A ruling class exercises hegemony through these institutions not by force but essentially through **language**. By communicating in the course of their normal everyday lives the particular common sense meanings or "articulations" which the ruling class attaches to words, ideas, images, and behavior, the countless lay intellectuals of civil society—such as parents, priests, teachers, counselors, club leaders and politicians—intentionally or unintentionally reinforce ruling class hegemony.

However, ruling class hegemony is never complete or permanent. Moreover, hegemony itself is never eliminated, but any particular hegemony operating at any particular time and place may be overthrown in the perpetual struggle between competing class articulations. Given the importance of everyday articulations to perpetuating hegemony, Gramsci stressed the role of intellectuals in perpetuating or overthrowing the existing class hegemony. Any person who can recognize hegemony and perpetuate or undermine it can be an intellectual, according to Gramsci. To overcome capitalist class hegemony, intellectuals who speak to and for the working class must tirelessly "pull the wool" from workers' eyes, revealing capitalist hegemony and articulating an alternative common sense which speaks to the exploitation and emancipation of the working class.

Gramsci's concept of hegemony has stimulated sociologists and others to develop more subtle and sophisticated understandings of power, especially as power operates in advanced capitalist societies. The concept has been applied and extended particularly in studies of power, class, **culture** and/or social movements, including, among others, John Gaventa's *Power and Powerlessness* (1980), Chantal Mouffe and Ernesto Laclau's *Hegemony and Socialist Strategy* (1984), James Scott's *Domination and the Arts of Resistance* (1990). Influenced in part by Gramsci, Gaventa explored the nature of capitalist hegemony in contemporary Appalachian mining towns, arguing that hegemony influences not only what gets considered as common sense but also the needs of the exploited. In their own book, Mouffe and Laclau argued that capitalist hegemony is no longer strictly class-centered in contemporary societies, and hence the terrains of struggle have multiplied to include sexual, consumer, student, racial, and environmental politics, among others. Scott, for his part, suggested that hege-

mony restricts action far more than thought among the most exploited. Scott found that peasants and workers may and often do share subversive thoughts in private but typically do not act on those thoughts for fear of violent reprisal.

HEIDEGGER, MARTIN (1889-1976)
German philosopher

German philosopher Martin Heidegger (1889–1976) has become widely regarded as the most original twentieth century philosopher. Recent interpretations of his philosophy closely associate him with existentialism (despite his repudiation of such interpretations) and, controversially, with National Socialist (Nazi) politics.

Martin Heidegger was born in Messkirch, a small town in Baden in southwest Germany, on September 26, 1889. His father was a verger in the local Catholic church and he received a pious upbringing. After graduation from the local gymnasium, he entered the Jesuit novitiate; later, he studied Catholic theology at the University of Freiburg. The markedly philosophical cast of medieval theology helped attract Heidegger to philosophy, and he finished his education in that subject. In 1914 he presented a doctoral thesis entitled "The Theory of Judgment in Psychologism," which showed the strong influence of Edmund Husserl's writings. A year later he was admitted to the faculty of Freiburg as a lecturer. His habilitation thesis was on a work of medieval logic, then thought to be by John Duns Scotus.

In 1916 Husserl was called to Freiburg as professor of philosophy, and when Heidegger returned from brief military service in World War I (spent in part at a meteorological station), he sought out the teacher whose works he had admired. In the following years Heidegger became an academic assistant for Husserl and edited the latter's manuscripts for *The Phenomenology of Internal Time-Consciousness*.

Heidegger began a professorship in Marburg in 1923. Among his colleagues there were Rudolf Bultmann and Paul Tillich, theologians whose own work was profoundly shaped by discussions with Heidegger and by the publication in 1927 of his major work *Being and Time*. In the autumn of 1928 Heidegger was recalled to Freiburg to take Husserl's chair, singled out by Husserl as his only qualified successor. Though Heidegger had been, in effect, designated as the leader of the developing phenomenological movement, it soon became clear that his own philosophical aims differed radically from those of Husserl.

In *Being and Time* Heidegger had made it plain that he was fundamentally interested in one great question, about the meaning of Being. Later, in the *Introduction to Metaphysics* (1935) he accepted G.W. von Leibniz's formulation: "Why should there be any being at all and not rather nothing?" But the bulk of *Being and Time* has to do with a fundamental analysis of human existence. Heidegger regarded this as only a preparation for ontology, arguing that it is characteristic of the human being (*Dasein*) to raise the question of Being (*Sein*). The promised second half of *Being and Time,* which was to provide the new ontology, did not appear.

His analysis introduced a number of concepts that later received wide currency in existential philosophy: for example, "human finitude," "nothingness" "being-in-the-world," "being-unto-death," and "authenticity." When these ideas were picked up and developed by French philosophers during and after World War II, Heidegger explicitly repudiated the designation of his views as existentialist in a *Letter on Humanism* (1949). Nevertheless, his reputation and considerable influence stem from *Being and Time* "a work that, though almost unreadable, was immediately felt to be of prime importance."

After 1930, Heidegger turned to a more historical approach, presenting man's understanding of the "nature of being" in different epochs (especially in Ancient Greece) leading up to the 20th century, which he found to be deeply flawed in large part because it was technologically overboard. But his works did not become easier to understand because of the historical turn. His articles and short books were Delphic in their obscurity and mystical in tone. (Contemporary mainstream British and American academic philosophers who read Heidegger "tend to divide into two camps: those who believe his writings are largely gibberish and those who believe they are entirely gibberish.") Heidegger laments man's forgetfulness of Being. But it seems that Being now hides itself from man. "We come too late for the gods and too early for Being." The true calling of the philosopher, shared only with the poet, is to "watch for Being" and, in rare moments, "to name the Holy" or "speak Being."

Beginning in the 1920s Heidegger lived in a primitive ski hut high on an isolated mountain in the Black Forest. He did not know how to drive a car. Dressing in the Swabian peasant costume of his family, he and his wife lived a simple, ascetic life close to nature, from which, with the help of his favorite poet, Friedrich Hölderlin, Heidegger attempted to learn the secret of Being.

Shortly after the electoral triumph of the National Socialist party in 1933, Heidegger began an association with the Nazis which is the subject of much contemporary controversy. The leaders of the Third Reich were determined to enforce **conformity** on all the institutions of Germany and immediately began to pressure the universities. The rector at Freiburg resigned, and in April 1933, shortly after Hitler was elected Chancellor, Heidegger was unanimously elected rector by the teaching faculty. Heidegger later claimed that the faculty "hoped that my reputation as a professor would help to preserve the faculty from political enslavement." But in his inaugural address and particularly in addresses to students in July and November of that year, Heidegger went far beyond what would have been required of any rector under the regime. In these speeches he rejected the concept of academic freedom as "implying uncommittedness in thought and act," and he urged students to make an "identification with the New Order." In his declaration to students on November 3, 1933, Heidegger said, "Doctrine and 'ideas' shall no longer govern your existence. The Führer himself, and only he, is the current and future reality of Germany, and his word is your law." Despite the strength of these statements, Heidegger left his posi-

Martin Heidegger *(AP/Wide World Photos, Inc.)*

tion as rector within a year, but he continued to see a unique destiny for German **culture**. Philosophy, he said, can be written only in Greek or German, and Germany to him was still entrusted with the fate of European culture, a nation caught in great pincers between two powers, Russia and America, which share "the same dreary technological frenzy, the same unrestricted organization of the average man."

Until the late 1980s most Heideggerians viewed his encounters with Nazism as an error of enthusiasm or philosophical misunderstanding or both and it was not much of an issue. But in 1987 Victor Farías published *Heidegger and Nazism* (in French); the book "dropped like a bomb on the quiet chapel where Heidegger's disciples were gathered, and blew the place to bits." The story Heidegger had offered after the war that he supported the Nazis briefly and only to protect the university was overwhelmed by evidence of Heidegger's deep and long-lasting commitment to National Socialism, his blatant anti-Semitism, and his blackballing of colleagues for holding pacifist convictions, associating with Jews, or being "unfavorably disposed" toward the Nazi regime.

Heidegger was by no means the only German philosopher who held such views, but he was the most important, by far, and the only one who "saw himself as one of the greatest thinkers in the history of the West." After the war, a "de-Nazification" committee of Heidegger's peers at the university, many of them favorably disposed to him, were unconvinced by his claims of "intellectual resistance" to Nazism and removed him from his job, denying him emeritus status, and providing him with a pension. Heidegger himself finally admitted that his lectures after he left the rectorship were anything but tough attacks on Nazism. Otherwise, after the war, he maintained "an almost hermetic silence" about the Holocaust. For some, this was "Heidegger's crime:" he was a thinker and writer who believed such people should be "the guardian of the memory of forgetting," but who "lent to extermination not his hand and not even his thought but his silence and non-thought . . . he 'forgot' the extermination." Heidegger spent his last twenty years writing, publishing, and guest- lecturing at various places. He died in Freiburg in 1976.

HERDER, JOHANN GOTTFRIED VON (1744-1803)

German theologian and philosopher

Born into a religious family in East Prussia, Johann Gottfried von Herder became an innovator in the **philosophy** of history and **culture** and a leading figure of the Sturm and Drang literary movement. His father was a schoolmaster in the town of Mohrongen, where he was born on August 25, 1744. He was able to obtain a university education, in the capital city of Konigsberg, through a surgeon in the then occupying Russian army who offered to be the young man's patron. Herder decided on a medical career but changed his mind when he fainted at every operation he attended. Changing to theology, during this period, Herder came into contact with **Immanuel Kant**, founder of critical philosophy, and Johann Georg Hamann, a prominent critic of the Enlightenment, a European intellectual movement of the seventeenth and eighteenth centuries.

In 1764, Herder went to Riga to teach and preach. He remained there until 1769, during which time he wrote many essays and reviews. His first published work was *Fragments concerning Recent German Literature* (1767), followed by *Critical Forests, or Reflections on the Science and Art of the Beautiful* (1769). After Riga, Herder embarked upon a sea voyage to Nantes and during this time, he seems to have undergone a profound change. He saw himself as a groundless person without a safe haven, and it became his aim to uncover the future from insights he had gained from the past.

Herder traveled throughout Europe during the following years, settling for a time in Paris, where he met writers Denis Diderot and Jean d'Alembert, and in Strasbourg, where he formed a lifelong friendship with Goethe. With Goethe's inter-

vention in 1776, Herder was permanently appointed to the post of superintendent of the Lutheran clergy at Weimar, where he died on December 18, 1803.

Herder wrote prolifically during his years at Weimar, including collections of folk literature, translations, and poetry. In his later works, he tried to demonstrate that nature and history obey a uniform set of laws. Herder's works incorporate elements of historicism, the view that there are no general patterns in human **progress** and that each historical epoch holds its own place and has its particular character and culture. Herder was pessimistic about the perfectibility of **human nature**. He felt that humans play out their destiny in proportion to the power that results from **interaction** among persons, institutions, and environment. Progress can be found in the species rather than in the individual. In this way, humanity does progress despite the individuals who compose it.

Also at Weimer, Herder completed a transition within himself to classicism, with a special interest in poetry. He saw poetry as a way of coming to terms with reality. "A poet is the creator of the nation around him," he said. Herder felt that poetry appeared in its greatest purity in the uncivilized periods of every nation. Therefore, he was greatly interested in retrieving ancient German folk songs.

Throughout the nineteenth century, Herder enjoyed a reputation as a philosopher of history. His reputation in the field of socio-politics was less lasting, partly due to his negative feelings about such concepts as "state" and "sovereignty" and partly because Germany in the eighteenth century was not a rich source of political fervor. There were no political parties, few poltical clubs, and a barely existing free press. Herder concluded at one point that "political reform has to come from below," since he came to believe it would never come from German **leadership**. In the end, Herder decided that if battles were to be waged, they would be waged with his pen.

The Sturm and Drang (Storm and Stress) literary movement in the late eighteenth century, in which Herder was a leading player, exalted nature and feeling and sought to overthrow rationalism. This movement is closely associated with Johann Wolfgang von Goethe, who was inspired by Herder's ideas and, through him, became interested in Gothic architecture, Shakespeare, and German folk songs. Although Goethe went on to produce great works in classical literature, the movement soon exhausted itself. In later years, disagreements led to an estrangement between Herder and Goethe, which resulted in Herder's bitterness toward the whole German classical movement in poetry and philosophy.

HERMENEUTICS

The term, hermeneutics, derives from "Hermes," the messenger-god of Zeus. The word comes from the Greek verb *hermeneuo* meaning "to interpret" and the Greek noun *hermeneutika* meaning "message analysis". It refers to understanding an action or situation in the broader context of intentions, causes, meanings, implications. Hermeneutics bridges theories of social sciences and the "exact" sciences through emphasis on interpretation albeit interpretation of statistics, social phenomena, or literature.

Hermeneutics originated as interpretation of Biblical texts. The "father of hermeneutic philosophy" is Fredrich Daniel Ernst Schleirermacher (1768-1834) who believed in an individual connection with God that did not involve dogma. Schleirermacher believed that understanding Scripture required acknowledging that some of it was written figuratively so that contemporary people could understand it then, thus connection the meaning of Scripture to the individual reading it.

Wilhelm Dilthey (1833-1911) took Hermeneutics beyond Scriptures to a method of inquiry for the social sciences. Personal experience is the bridge for understanding something from past to present, from beginning to end. To understand something requires knowing how it is being interpreted and the event's significance to the receiver. Thus, meaning is not inherent within a message; it is an individual experience. How is "truth" determined and defined? Hermeneutics seeks to recount accurately the meanings that participants give as well as how they interpret ambiguity in a social context. Researchers need to find out meanings from all the interviewees and not just infer the meanings on their behalf. Dilthey was a major influence on **Max Weber** in his development of the concept of *Verstehen*, sympathetic understanding.

Martin Heidegger (1889-1976) and his student Hans-Georg Gadamer rejected the psychological foundations and instead focused on Hermeneutics' utility for the study of linguistic phenomena such as translation. It became the basis for deconstruction which unearths interpretations that build the structure of a text. They also developed the concept of the hermeneutic circle which later provided a foundation for therapy. This application seeks to understand the client through interactive understanding of the client and dialogue with the client. Instead of seeing **communication** as linear, this interpretation is circular in its focus on the dialogue as it loops between therapist and client.

The code focuses on the moving context. Analogies have been made between hermeneutic application and a football game or the stock market index or a good book. Curiosity draws the perceiver into the adventure of determining the implications of each shift but ultimately one has to know how it winds up to understand the beginning or the course of events. The act of interpreting the intentions and significance is an individual adventure.

HETEROGAMY

Heterogamy describes the phenomenon of individuals marrying someone of a different social **status** or with different social characteristics than themselves which is closely related to the concept of exogamy, or the practice of marrying outside of one's **group**. It has been argued that heterogamy makes cultural distinctions less pronounced in future generations of children because children of heterogamous marriages are less likely to identify with a single cultural group. Another argument suggests that heterogamous marriages promote increased intimacy between individuals in different groups and thus may promote more positive attitudes held by individuals toward groups different than their own.

Johann Gottfried von Herder

Some have argued that mixed marriages threaten internal group cohesion and thus "third parties" have a vested interest in preventing heterogamous pairings, most frequently accomplished through group identification and group sanctions. The stronger the sense of group identification, the more likely members will marry homogamously, or within the group. The most interested parties are the ones most likely to invoke sanctions: the **family**, the church, and the state. Although families in the West may not arrange marriages, they do participating matchmaking activities. When "appropriate" pairing does not occur, they may withdraw financiaces or emotional support from the family member. The **church** has an interest in having its members marry one another because doing so potentially increases members. Thus, the church may invoke sanctions such as excommunication when members marry outsiders. The state can provide legal sanctions for intermarriage as it did through antimiscegenation laws prohibiting racial intermarriage up until 1967 when the Supreme Court in *Loving v. Virginia* struck down these laws. In the United States, the law currently prohibits same sex marriages.

HETEROSEXUALITY

Heterosexuality is a type of sexual orientation in which sexual attraction and/or **sexual behavior** is directed primarily or exclusively towards persons of a different sex, or the identifica-

Heterosexuality is a type of sexual orientation in which sexual attraction is directed primarily or exclusively towards persons of a different sex *(Corbis Corporation [Bellevue]).*

tion with this type of sexual orientation. Heterosexuality assumes a binary gender system (e.g. people must be either male or female), as it refers to sexual relationships between women and men. While same-sex and different-sex sexual behavior and attraction have existed throughout human history, the concept of a person having a heterosexual orientation is somewhat new. For example, male citizens in ancient Greece were not considered to have a particular sexual orientation, but instead engaged in sexual relations based on their social standing (with more socially powerful men initiating sexual relations with less powerful boys, women, or slaves). Sexual relationships between men were considered normative for all men and adolescent boys, although this did not replace male-female sexual relations that served the purpose of procreation.

Early scientific research on sexuality reproduced theological or religious classifications of sex, focusing on ''normal'' versus ''deviant'' sexual acts within a moral framework of sin. One of the better known of these scientists was **Sigmund Freud**, who supported the belief that only heterosexuality was normal (and even within heterosexuality, many unhealthy de-

viations existed). Havelock Ellis was one of the first sexuality researchers to question homosexuality as a perversion, as well as other sexual behaviors that heterosexual people sometimes engage in (such as masturbation). He is known for proposing that sexual orientation is a congenital condition; therefore, heterosexual people are born that way and it is not something they learn or choose to be.

Since **homosexuality** was removed from the Diagnostic and Statistical Manual of Mental Disorders (the psychiatric guide for determining what constitutes mental illness) in 1987, attaching models of pathology to sexual orientation is largely eschewed by social scientists. Today, the belief that heterosexuality is better than homosexuality or is the only appropriate form of sexual behavior is referred to as heterosexism. The essentialist **theory** of heterosexuality is that it is a biological orientation to feel sexual attraction towards people of a different sex that is either genetically predisposed and/or affected by hormone levels in utero. Here, sexuality is unchanging over time and only marginally affected by social forces, and people are born either heterosexual or another type of sexual orientation (usually homosexual or sometimes bisexual). Although some essentialist definitions of heterosexuality allow for it to be affected by life events (such as the theory that sexual molestation experiences in childhood might change a person's sexual orientation from heterosexual to homosexual), sexuality is still viewed within this theoretical framework as a largely immutable characteristic of a person.

Other researchers have called into question the binary system of sexual orientation. Alfred Kinsey produced a seven-point scale measuring a continuum of same-sex and different-sex behaviors (ranging from exclusively different-sex to exclusively same-sex behaviors). Kinsey also found that people's sexual behavior did not always correspond with how they identified their sexual orientation. He believed, therefore, that labeling a person heterosexual or homosexual was not very meaningful.

Feminist theories of heterosexuality assert that it is greatly impacted by social forces and circumstances and is connected to systems of stratification. Adrienne Rich theorized that heterosexuality is compulsory, meaning that people (Rich focuses on women and girls) are taught the ''art'' of heterosexuality through romance novels and other popular media outlets, in school health classes, life course expectations, and through the practice of traditional rituals such as bridal showers and weddings. Rich believed that making heterosexuality compulsory served to maintain a gendered hierarchy in which women have a lower status than men do. Other feminist theorists have also connected heterosexuality with male power and **patriarchy**, and some have even suggested that women are inherently subordinated when engaged in sexual relationships with men.

Postmodern and queer theories of sexuality fracture the notion of sexual orientation altogether, dismissing the very notion that heterosexuality exists. These theories suggest that human sexuality is better thought of in terms of omni-sexuality or meta-sexuality. However, most current research in sexuality recognizes the importance of heterosexuality as an **identity** that has meaning to the people who adopt it. Whether it is an actual biological orientation or accurately reflects sexual behaviors or desires is not as important as the social meaning it has as an identity. Because being heterosexual places a person in a particular position within a hierarchy based on sexuality, it is a useful category for understanding stratification within various arenas (such as work or the **family**), and it provides a comparison group with other sexual identities.

See also Bisexuality; Heterosexuality

HIERARCHICAL LINEAR MODELS

Hierarchical linear models (HLM), or hierarchical models, represent one of a variety of multilevel statistical techniques that permit the investigation of social causation at different **levels of analysis**. HLM stands for a set of causal relationships between variables as well as a software program used to model those relationships, primarily in educational statistics. Multilevel statistical techniques such as HLM are also known as variance component models, random coefficient models, variable and changing coefficient models, and slopes-as-outcomes models, depending on the domain of study. In addition, statistical techniques associated with biostatistics, education and psychometric research traditions have now begun to incorporate multilevel models into latent growth curve, and structural equation, analyses. Other multilevel statistical techniques and programs are: VARCL, Mln, and BMDP5-V.

Multilevel models, like HLM, are non-trivial generalized versions of linear **regression**, according to Kreft and Leeuw, 1998. The basic principle of hierarchical models involves a nested **data** structure. In a nested data structure, variables are measured and analyzed at several levels. Students in schools, employees in firms, occupations in a sector, neighborhoods in cities, and repeated measures over time in longitudinal series are all examples of nested data structures. Hierarchical models overcome the limitations of designs that emphasize one level at the expense of another. For instance, researchers might be interested in how school classroom size influences student test scores, or voucher programs enhance extracurricular reading. Questions such as these **need** not be limited to addressing differences (i.e., variance) simply between students or between schools. Prior to development of hierarchical models, analysis at one level precluded a deeper understanding of complex social relationships.

The key innovation of the HLM modeling strategy rests on the premise that researchers can and should analyze data at all levels of the data structure. HLM proponents argue that researchers need to create multilevel models in order to correct for attenuation associated with unilevel designs. For instance, regression analysis, the workhorse of sociological methods treats contextual effects in a summary fashion or ignores within- (i.e., individual-) level variation. While analysis of covariance (ANCOVA) is one method for handling variability within and between contexts, because it corrects for individual-level differences, it falls short of treating the relationship between covariates and outcomes as a unique function of each separate context.

Hierarchical models, on the other hand, are designed to take fully into account individual and contextual variation. In a regression framework, the way in which multilevel variation is modeled depends on transforming regression coefficients from the first level of analysis into outcomes at the next level-(s). This ''slope-as-outcomes'' design derives from a simple and comprehensible linear equation: $y_{ij} = a_j + b_j x_{ij} + e_{ij}$, where y is a response variable, x an explanatory variable, a_j is the intercept, b_j is the slope and e_{ij} is the error term. Here, the subscript i refers to the first level (e.g., individuals) and the subscript j refers to the next level (e.g., context). To calculate the intercept and slope for the context, the following formula is used: $a_j = c_0 + c_1 z_1$ and $b_j = d_0 + d_1 z_1$, where c and d are the second level macro intercepts (c_0, d_0) and slopes, respectively, and z_1 is the contextual variable.

In addition to research focusing on contextual effects, one of the most interesting applications of nested designs is the use of multilevel models with longitudinal data. In longitudinal designs, a multilevel model contains the nesting of repeatedly observed phenomena within clusters of other higher-level phenomena. For example, developmental trajectories of adolescent risk behavior may be viewed as a function of life-course development, and social structural factors such as school, neighborhood, and region. The first level of the equation is represented by a person's growth pattern over time. Individuals are, in effect, nested within time and influenced by explanatory variables of interest at that level. The results of these analyses, (i.e., the individual responses, y_{ij}) are then modeled as the outcome variable for the contextual part of the equation which incorporates school, neighborhood, and region.

While hierarchical models address many problematic features of multiple sources of variation, they are nonetheless subject to some drawbacks associated with linear regression. Thus, caution must be exercised when interpreting the complex interactions that are modeled with hierarchical designs. Kreft and Leeuw (1998) provide an excellent discussion of the strengths and weaknesses of various types of hierarchical models.

HIERARCHY OF NEEDS

Hierarchy of Needs is a schema comprised of five interrelated levels where the most primitive and basic needs must be satisfied first before needs higher on the scale become relevant motivational concerns. Proposed by the American psychologist Abram Maslow, hierarchy of needs is deep-rooted in the humanistic **psychology**, a movement that began in opposition to psychoanalysis and **behaviorism** during the twentieth century. Maslow's hierarchy of human needs and his theory of self-actualization made him one of the leading architects of the humanistic psychology, and like most humanistic psychologist, he believed man—as an individua—should be recognized and treated as a unique being by social scientists. According to Maslow, the hierarchy of human needs has essentially two sets of biological needs—deficiency or basic needs and growth or

The hierarchy of needs theory was developed by U.S. psychologist Abraham Maslow *(Corbis Corporation [Bellevue]).*

for our own accomplishments, independence, and competence. Maslow maintained that to thoroughly satisfy the esteem need we should develop a combination of both self-esteem motives rather than pursue only fame, importance, and appreciation from others.

When the preconditions necessary for satisfaction of the basic needs are adequately gratified, individuals are free to explore cognitive understanding and self-actualization. People seeking self-actualization examine not only themselves but also the workings of their environment. They go beyond deficiency needs and search for their unique potentialities. However, Maslow maintained that for most people basic needs remain partially dissatisfied. Therefore, he believed that less than one percent of the population actually accomplish self-actualization; those that do are typically middle-aged or older and are free from neurosis. While Maslow believed in the validity of his hierarchy of needs, he recognized that there might be exceptions to the hierarchical arrangement. For example, ambitious individuals may posses a drive to succeed that is more powerful than any other need.

meta needs. He viewed deficiency (basic) needs as more critical than growth (meta) needs and, therefore, arranged them in a hierarchical order.

At the base of Maslow's hierarchy of needs, are physiological drives, the most powerful of the deficiency (basic) needs, followed by the drive for safety, belongingness and **love**, and esteem. Physiological needs include, but are not limited to, hunger, thirst, and sex. Individuals deprived of a physiological **need**, will increasingly focus more and more attention on their deficiency and less on other needs.

Safety needs such as **structure**, law, protection, security, and freedom from fear and anxiety are the deficiency needs that surface once physiological needs are relatively well satisfied. A child's safety need may be obvious compared to an adult's safety need which is often more subtle and more difficult to detect. For example, a child may require only a positive environment filled with constant reinforcement to satisfy safety needs while an adult may require a stable **society** with safe neighborhoods and a secure job.

Once physiological and safety drives are regularly satisfied, needs for belongingness and love appear. Maslow maintained all humans want acceptance from others and have a motivational drive to feel wanted once the lower level, more powerful needs of the hierarchy are satisfied. The need to belong may be fulfilled through relationships with family and friends or through memberships in organizations and other groups. As early as the late 1950s Maslow argued that increased **urbanization** due to great mobility leads to greater personal loneliness and **alienation** because of depersonalization and the breakdown of the traditional family. Maslow divided love into two sets: D-Love (deficiency-love) and B-Love (being-love). He used the term D-Love to describe selfish individuals concerned primarily with seeking love from others. Once D-Love is sufficiently gratified people are capable of B-Love or loving others.

The last basic need to emerge is the esteem drive. Maslow also divided esteem needs into two sets: (1) esteem based on the evaluations of others and (2) esteem based on respect

HIGHER EDUCATION

Higher education refers to education beyond the secondry, or high school, level. Undergraduate education includes both four year (e.g., colleges and universities) and two-year (e.g., junior college and **community** colleges) institutions. Post-undergraduate education includes law and medical schools as well as master and doctoral degree programs.

In the United States, up until the 1940s, only affluent people sought higher education degrees. After World War II, the number of young people attaining higher education skyrocketed, partially due to returning veterans whose higher education was partially subsidized by the federal government. The proportion of people between the ages of 18 and 20 who were attending higher education doubled from the pre-war time. Students from a variety of economic backgrounds now attend college, something that had only been done by the affluent within **society**.

Over the last decades, many two-year college and community colleges have been established to meet the needs of students from less affluent backgrounds. Although more people are attending college than in the past, the higher education system within the United States is still stratified. The top of the U.S. education hierarchy is considered to be elite private universities and colleges followed by four-year state universities and colleges. Two-year and community colleges are at the bottom rungs of the educational hierarchy. While the above hierarchy does gloss over much diversity, schools at the top of the hierarchy stress **career** development and have top resources and faculty. Schools at the bottom hierarchy stress job-training skills and have fewer resources.

Sociologists have been very concerned with patterns of enrollment across types of higher education institutions. Students at schools at the top of the hierarchy tend to come from more affluent backgrounds, while students at the lower rungs of the hierarchy tend to come from less affluent backgrounds. In addition, minority students are over-represented at colleges at the bottom of the hierarchy.

Sociologists are concerned with every aspect of the higher education experience, including curriculum, interpersonal relationships including dating, and student **protest movements**. Many sociologists have focused on the socialization processes within higher education. For example, Randall Collins, a sociologist, theorizes that college students do not necessarily learn the requisite skills for **professions** in college but rather higher education prepares students for middle-class lifestyles and **culture**. Also, Dorothy Holland and Margaret Eisenhart, both anthropologists, found that the **socialization** of female students centers on a school peer culture of romance and attractiveness.

HINDUISM

Hinduism is the third largest of the world's religions and one of the most ancient. It incorporates a wide range of practices and beliefs which vary by region, class, and education, among other factors. Like other religious groups, Hindus can now be found all over the world, but because it is not generally a proselytizing **belief system** it has not spread in any major way to cultures outside the Indian subcontinent where it originated.

The religion, or way of life as some would have it, has seen a gradual evolution for some four thousand years since the time that Aryan invaders from the north merged their beliefs with those of the indigenous cultures they conquered. It has no founder and no single historical document recording the **progress** of a chosen people; instead it has descended from a loose collection of spiritual teachings by many authors which seek to understand the mystery of life. These scriptures, the *Vedas*, were passed down by word of mouth. Of these, the most treasured are the *Upanishads* which focus on the powerful experience and truth of God.

Since the earliest days, practices have been very different from the highly developed civilizations of the river valleys to the isolated mountain regions of India. The religion has been greatly influenced by **Islam**, Christianity, Buddhism, and other beliefs of central Asia. Unlike members of those faiths which emerged from **Judaism**, Hindus do not profess to possess the one true way. Their understanding of God is not of an individual being to whom one may communicate but the source of all things; the goal is to become one with God. When this unity is achieved there is no differentiation between God, also referred to as Brahman the creator, and the Self. The inability to identify the individual ''self'' with the unified ''Self'' is seen as the cause of a man's torment. Other distinguishing characteristics include the idea that all life is, in essence, a single entity which takes on various forms based on *karma*. From this idea comes the belief in reincarnation or the transmigration of souls: that individuals are reborn over and over as higher or lower forms of life based on the way they lived their lives.

The many ways in which a person may manifest his spirituality have been greatly influenced by *gurus*, the teachers

This ornate mask of the Hindu god Siva is displayed on special religious occasions *(Corbis Corporation [Bellevue])*.

who have discovered different methods for achieving enlightenment. Their methods are called *yogas* which range from strenuous physical movement to quiet meditation. They are designed to fit the different natures of the student; no one way suits everyone. The goal of these different practices is to remove oneself from the false desires of transient things and achieve oneness with the eternal part of oneself. Yoga has been a part of the religion for thousands of years but became widely known to Westerners in the 1960s as the counterculture movement embraced many aspects of Eastern religions. One of the most common yogas involves the chanting of *mantras*, words, phrases, or merely sounds which a guru gives to a student to bring him into closer touch with a particular deity. The most famous mantra is probably the ubiquitous *om*.

The practice associated with Hinduism that is most difficult for Westerners to understand or accept is the caste system. This is a social **structure** in which all people are organized into groups which represent their place in society. Originally the castes were rather broad, and movement between them could be achieved through wisdom and enlightenment. Over time, however, it became a hereditary system from which one could not escape. Untouchables were considered beneath the system entirely and could not even enter the temples. In the twentieth century Mahatma Gandhi and others denounced the system, and it was outlawed in India in 1950; nevertheless, it is still strongly embedded in the **culture** today.

Hinduism has given rise to other sects. One such **sect** is the Hare Krishna movement which believes that God was incarnated in human form as Krishna. They are devoted to thinking about Krishna at all times and worship through the chanting of the mantra "Hare Krishna." The Jain sect believes in a strict code of non-violence toward all living things. They are vegetarians and will not move about in the dark lest they cause unintentional injury to a small animal, even an insect.

HISPANIC AMERICAN STUDIES

The study of Hispanic Americans, or *Latinos*, is vital to understanding the cultural and ethnic make up of the United States. Between 1965 and 1992, close to nine million non-Europeans came to the United States, and the number of Hispanic Americans increased by sixty percent. According to the Census Bureau, by 2050, the percentage of Latinos in the United States will almost triple, while the white population will drop from 76 to 53 percent. Such a large portion of the population will continue to **influence** America's culture and future.

"Hispanic" is a term used by the U.S. State Department to describe any person of Latin American, Caribbean, and Spanish origin. The largest groups of Hispanic Americans are Mexicans, Puerto Ricans, and Cubans. But the term also includes the descendants of Spaniards who first arrived on this continent in the seventeenth century, first-generation immigrants from El Salvador and native Peruvians. This broad category "Hispanic" encompasses many ethnic groups, including Native Americans, Arabians, and persons of a mixed heritage, each with a unique history and **culture**. Many Hispanics prefer the term Latino, short for *latino americano* (Latin American) to reflect the wide range of their diversity.

One of the first groups of Latinos to demand studies programs on the college level were Mexican Americans, or *Chicanos*. In the 1960s, Chicano students throughout California petitioned and protested for Chicano Studies programs. They wanted better opportunities for Chicano students, a curriculum that was less Eurocentric, and more Chicano professors. At the same time, African American and **Women's Studies** were gaining ground in much the same way throughout academia. This grassroots effort to include and empower a minority **group** in academia and assist Latino students and communities hoped to legitimize research in Hispanic American issues, advocate for Latino student services, record the contributions of Latinos to American culture, and develop a curriculum of interdisciplinary studies. First seen as untraditional and illegitimate, Hispanic American studies has become a legitimate, established field of study and research.

Like many ethnic studies, Hispanic American studies are designed to explore and understand a minority culture. Traditionally, academics have reflected European **philosophy**, literature, history, and politics, leaving out other ethnic groups. Hispanic American studies reflect the philosophy, literature, history, **language**, and social sciences related to Latinos. Such programs are interdisciplinary, meaning they cross different academic departments. For example, a Hispanic American studies program might offer courses on contemporary Hispanic American authors, Hispanic American folklore, migrant worker conditions, Hispanic American figures in history, or a history of the Americas. The focus is not on one discipline, such as history or **political science**, but on an ethnic group and their contribution to American culture.

Issues specific to Hispanic American studies include the diversity within the Latino population, maintenance of language and culture within the greater American population, government representation, a long-standing presence in the Americas, a history of **discrimination**, and cultural contributions. Hispanic American studies programs delve into the unique histories of Cuban Americans, Puerto Rican Americans, Mexican Americans, etc. Each population group emigrated to the United States at different points in history for different reasons. Despite differences among these populations, there is also a common bond of language and culture. Many college courses address the issue of assimilating Latinos into American culture, and the struggle to maintain a minority language and heritage. Government representation is still an issue for Latinos, and the Hispanic vote is a valuable one in states such as Florida, California, Texas, and New Mexico.

A clear advantage of any type of multicultural study is teaching students to understand, expect, and acknowledge differing viewpoints. For example, courses on pre-Colombian Mexico give students a native perspective of Columbus' landing and the impact of the arrival of Europeans on this continent rather than the European perspective of exploration. Such a course may also demonstrate that history is incomplete and one-sided until multiple perspectives of the same event are studied. Acknowledging different perspectives also encourages students to question what they have learned and what they are considered cultural givens, which fosters independent thinking.

Students are taught to understand and appreciate Latino culture rather than accept stereotypes. Many Hispanic American studies courses address images such as the snoozing Latino under a sombrero to demonstrate the creation and perpetuation of cultural stereotypes. Or they may catalog Latino leaders in the United States and their contributions to the fields of entertainment, politics, and science. Civil rights struggles and racism play a part in Hispanic American studies, too, for they are an important part of history not just for Latinos, but for all Americans.

Students of Hispanic American and multicultural studies learn to value cultures other than their own by identifying myths in their education, thinking, and culture. Through such studies, minority groups gain a place in history and respect for their contributions to American culture. One goal of Multicultural Studies is to **foster care** and understanding for other ethnic groups so that all facets of our diverse society—Caucasian, African American, Latino, Asian American, Native American, etc.—can be represented, respected, and empowered in a truly democratic way. Studying Latinos and their culture is one step towards this goal.

HISTOGRAM

A histogram is a graphic representation of **data** that shows the frequency distribution of a quantitative **variable**. The height of each bar along the vertical, or y-axis represents the number of observations in each category indicated on the x-axis, or horizontal scale. The researcher can combine observations into as many or as few categories as needed to best represent the data. Designing meaningful intervals is left to the discretion of the researcher, who should keep in mind that using too few categories results in the loss of useful information, while using too many categories may obscure important relationships that would be obvious if fewer intervals were chosen. The number of categories chosen should be appropriate to the size of the data set.

A histogram that represents categorical data (nominal or ordinal data) instead of interval data is called a bar graph. Each bar represents a named or ordered category within the data rather than a range or interval. The bar graph represents these categories in terms of their relative frequencies.

The advantage of the histogram is that it quickly conveys information about the distribution of data within meaningful categories. Using a histogram can convey information more easily, more accurately, and in less space than a written description, with the added benefit that the reader is less likely to become confused by descriptions of complicated numeric data. Most statistical software packages or spreadsheet programs can assist in designing and customizing these graphs with colors and labels to highlight important information and will automatically assign appropriate intervals to the data.

HISTORICAL SOCIOLOGY

Historical **sociology** is any sociology focusing on the study of past societies or using historical sources. It pays particular attention to culturally, geographically, and temporally located facts. Although historical sociology, which arose in the late nineteenth century, fell out of favor for a long period, it has regained respect as the result of some major studies performed by researchers in the United States and Britain.

One difficulty with historical sociology is that the two disciplines it approaches perform research in different ways. Historical research emphasizes the cultural context of events and the people's actions within a broad range of human **culture**, and it relies mostly on verifiable facts to construct a picture of what was happening at a given time. When examining events that occurred in early periods of the human record, historians use the companion disciplines of archaeology and cultural anthropology to gain perspective or insight where the historical record is weak. Historians also rely heavily on secondary research sources to gain information.

In contrast, sociological research stresses theories as a way to describe culture. Because sociology relies heavily on quantifiable research—information that can be strictly measured and verified—most of its research is limited to issues affecting societies after they begin to modernize or industrialize. Many methods sociologists use to gather information, including **surveys**, interviews, observations, questionnaires, and various forms of **experimentation**, do not apply to historians. And unlike historians, sociologists rarely use archival searches to gain information. Oriented toward **theory**, sociologists are likely to choose research topics that are generated by concepts rather than facts. Sociologists tend to be more willing than historians to make comparisons across cultural boundaries and to make generalizations that relate either to a number of cases or to phenomena that seem universal.

Historical sociology attempts to develop new theories which are capable of providing more convincing, comprehensive explanations for historical patterns and structures. It concentrates more on the experiences people lived rather than the transformations of institutions. To test their theories, historical sociologists use deductive reasoning (attempting to locate evidence that supports or refutes their theories), case comparisons (looking at similarities and differences between equal entities), and case illustrations (comparing several cases to a single theory or **concept**).

Four research areas that produce respected historical sociology studies are capitalist expansion, the growth of national states and systems of states, collective action, and sociology of religious development. Studies of capitalist expansion examine topics such as the emergence and consequences of the Industrial Revolution, the rise of the working class, population growth, and the developmental operations of the modern world system.

Studies of the growth of national states and systems of states examine political topics such as revolutions, state bureaucratization, the democratization of politics, and the **interaction** of nations in the international arena. For example, **case studies** of revolutions in England, France, the United States, China, Japan, and India attempted to understand the role of the landed upper classes and peasants in the middle-class revolutions leading to capitalist democracy, the aborted middle-class revolutions leading to fascism, and the peasant revolutions leading to **communism**.

An area of growing interest to historical sociologists is the emergence and development of historically significant religious traditions, such as the analysis of early **Christianity** as a social movement. Other researchers are looking at various hunting and gathering societies in an effort to connect religion and magic to social **structure**. Perhaps, future historical sociological studies will push beyond the bounds of examining the workings of modern institutions and begin looking more closely at cultural development. Areas which seem ripe for this kind of research involve preindustrialized and third-world countries.

HISTORICAL-COMPARATIVE RESEARCH

Historical-comparative research is the term frequently used to describe research that is based on historical **data**. These data sources may be primary (obtained through original documents) or secondary (written histories produced by historians). The major issue in historical-comparative research is determining what the practical value of materials are for evidence. Researchers need to establish the authenticity of the documents, to identify and understand authors' motives, to determine the degree of completion, as well as to interpret the documents meanings.

Some social scientists, like Goldthorpe, are opposed to historical-comparative research particularly when using secondary data which means one is merely interpreting interpretations. An equally troubling problem is that research based on historical data is limited in the questions that it seeks to address. The researcher is constrained by the data available. Moreover, scholars argue that comparative history is not composed of a single homogeneous logic. According to Theda Skocpol, there are three distinct views of comparative history: macro causal analysis, parallel demonstration of **theory**, and the contrast of context. On the other hand, Charles Tilly claims that there are four fundamental varieties of comparisons: individualizing, universalizing, variation finding, and encompassing.

HOBBES, THOMAS (1588-1679)
English philosopher and political theorist

The English philosopher and political theorist Thomas Hobbes (1588–1679) was one of the central figures of British **empiricism**. His major work, ''Leviathan,'' published in 1651, expressed his principle of **materialism** and his concept of a **social contract** forming the basis of **society**. Born prematurely on April 5, 1588, when his mother heard of the impending invasion of the Spanish Armada, Thomas Hobbes later reported that ''my mother gave birth to twins, myself and fear.'' His father was the vicar of Westport near Malmesbury in Gloucestershire. He abandoned his family to escape punishment for fighting with another clergyman ''at the church door.'' Thereafter Thomas was raised and educated by an uncle. At local schools he became a proficient classicist, translating a Greek tragedy into Latin iambics by the time he was 14. From 1603 to 1608 he studied at Magdalen College, Oxford, where he was bored by the prevailing philosophy of Aristotelianism.

The twenty-year-old future philosopher became a tutor to the Cavendish family. This virtually lifelong association with the successive earls of Devonshire provided him with an extensive private library, foreign travel, and introductions to influential people. Hobbes, however, was slow in developing his thought; his first work a translation of Thucydides's *History of the Peloponnesian Wars*, did not appear until 1629. Thucydides held that knowledge of the past was useful for determining correct action, and Hobbes said that he offered the translation during a period of civil unrest as a reminder that the ancients believed **democracy** to be the least effective form of **government**.

According to his own estimate the crucial intellectual event of Hobbes's life occurred when he was forty. While waiting for a friend he wandered into a library and chanced to find a copy of Euclid's geometry. Opening the book, he read a random proposition and exclaimed, ''By God that is impossible!'' Fascinated by the interconnections between axioms, postulates, and premises, he adopted the ideal of demonstrating certainty by way of deductive reasoning. His interest in mathematics is reflected in his second work *A Short Treatise on First Principles,* which presents a mechanical interpretation of sensation, as well as in his brief stint as mathematics tutor to Charles II. His generally royalist sympathy as expressed in *The Elements of Law* (1640) caused Hobbes to leave England during the ''Long Parliament.'' This was the first of many trips back and forth between England and the Continent during periods of civil strife since he was, in his own words, ''the first of all that fled.'' For the rest of his long life Hobbes traveled extensively and published prolifically. In France he met René Descartes and the anti-Cartesian Pierre Gassendi. In 1640 he wrote one of the sets of objections to Descartes's *Meditations*.

Although born into the Elizabethan Age, Hobbes outlived all of the major seventeenth-century thinkers. He became a sort of English institution and continued writing, offering new translations of Homer in his eighties because he had ''nothing else to do.'' When he was past ninety, he became embroiled in controversies with the Royal Society. He invited friends to suggest appropriate epitaphs and favored one that read ''this is the true philosopher's stone.'' He died on December 4, 1679, at the age of 91.

The diverse intellectual currents of the seventeenth century, which are generically called modern classical **philosophy**, began with a unanimous repudiation of the authorities of the past, especially Aristotle and the scholastic tradition. Descartes, who founded the rationalist tradition, and his contemporary Sir Francis Bacon, who is considered the originator of modern empiricism, both sought new methodologies for achieving scientific knowledge and a systematic conception of reality. Hobbes knew both of these thinkers, and his system encompassed the advantages of both rationalism and empiricism. As a logician, he believed too strongly in the power of deductive reasoning from definitions to share Bacon's exclusive enthusiasm for inductive generalizations from experience. Yet Hobbes was a more consistent empiricist and nominalist, and his attacks on the misuse of **language** exceed even those of Bacon. And unlike Descartes, Hobbes viewed reason as summation of consequences rather than an innate, originative source of new knowledge.

Psychology, as the mechanics of knowing, rather than **epistemology** is the source of Hobbes's singularity. He was fascinated by the problem of sense perception, and he extended Galileo's mechanical physics into an explanation of human cognition. The origin of all thought is sensation which consists of mental images produced by the pressure of motion of external objects. Thus Hobbes anticipates later thought by distinguishing between the external object and the internal image. These sense images are extended by the power of memory and imagination. Understanding and reason, which distinguish men from other animals, consist entirely in the ability to use speech.

Speech is the power to transform images into words or names. Words serve as the marks of remembrance, signification, conception, or self-expression. For example, to speak of a cause-and-effect relation is merely to impose names and define their connection. When two names are so joined that the definition of one contains the other, then the proposition is true. The implications of Hobbes's analysis are quite modern. First, there is an implicit distinction between objects and their appearance to man's senses. Consequently knowledge is **discourse** about appearances. Universals are merely names understood as class concepts, and they have no real **status**, for everything which appears "is individual and singular." Since "true and false are attributes of speech and not of things," scientific and philosophic thinking consists in using names correctly. Reason is calculation or "reckoning the consequences of general laws agreed upon for either marking or signifying." The power of the mind is the capacity to reduce consequences to general laws or theorems either by deducing consequences from principles or by inductively reasoning from particular perceptions to general principles. The privilege of mind is subject to unfortunate abuse because, in Hobbes's pithy phrase, men turn from summarizing the consequences of things "into a reckoning of the consequences of appellations," that is, using faulty definitions, inventing terms which stand for nothing, and assuming that universals are real.

The material and mechanical **model** of nature offered Hobbes a consistent analogy. Man is a conditioned part of nature and reason is neither an innate faculty nor the summation of random experience but is acquired through slow cultivation and industry. Science is the cumulative knowledge of syllogistic reasoning which gradually reveals the dependence of one **fact** upon another. Such knowledge is conditionally valid and enables the mind to move progressively from abstract and simple to more particular and complex sciences: geometry, mechanics, physics, morals (the nature of mind and desire), politics.

Hobbes explains the connection between nature, man, and society through the law of inertia. A moving object continues to move until impeded by another force, and "trains of imagination" or speculation are abated only by logical demonstrations. So also man's liberty or desire to do what he wants is checked only by an equal and opposite need for security. A society or commonwealth "is but an artificial man" invented by man, and to understand polity one should merely read himself as part of nature.

Such a reading is cold comfort because presocial life is characterized by Hobbes, in a famous quotation, as "solitary, poor, nasty, brutish and short," found in *The Leviathon*. The equality of human desire is matched by an economy of natural satisfactions. Men are addicted to power because its acquisition is the only guarantee of living well. Such men live in "a state of perpetual war" driven by competition and desire for the same goods. The important consequence of this view is man's natural right and liberty to seek self-preservation by any means. In this state of nature there is no value above self-interest because where there is no common, coercive power there is no law and no **justice**. But there is a second and derivative law of nature that men may surrender or transfer their individual will to the state. This "social contract" binds the

Thomas Hobbes *(The Library of Congress)*

individual to treat others as he expects to be treated by them. Only a constituted civil power commands sufficient force to compel everyone to fulfill this original compact by which men exchange liberty for security.

In Hobbes's view the sovereign power of a commonwealth is absolute and not subject to the laws and obligations of citizens. Obedience remains as long as the sovereign fulfills the social compact by protecting the rights of the individual. Consequently rebellion is unjust, by definition, but should the cause of revolution prevail, a new absolute sovereignty is created.

HOLLINGSHEAD, AUGUST (1907-1980)
American educator and author

A sociologist who is best known for his studies concerning mental health, August Hollingshead spent most of his career as an educator and author. He was born in Lyman, Wyoming, on April 15, 1907, the son of William Thomas, a stock breeder, and Daisy Rollins Hollingshead. He left home for undergraduate work at the University of California, Berkeley, where he received a bachelor's degree in 1931. In November of that year, he married Carol E. Dempsey and the couple later had two daughters, Anne and Ellen. Hollingshead continued his studies at Berkeley, earning a master's degree in 1933.

After he received a PhD from the University of Nebraska in 1935, Hollingshead began his career as an instructor in sociology at the University of Iowa in Iowa City. From there, he joined the faculty of the University of Alabama, 1935-1936, and then went to Indiana University in Bloomington from 1936 to 1947 where he attained the rank of associate professor of sociology. During that period, Hollingshead's teaching career was interrupted by World War II. He joined the U.S. Army Air Force, serving from 1943 to 1945. After receiving a General Commendation, he left the service with the rank of first lieutenant.

Hollingshead's first postwar teaching position was at Yale University in 1947. He was promoted to professor of sociology in 1952 and named Sumner Professor of Sociology, 1963. By 1959, he was chairman of the department, a position he held until 1965. He was also a visiting summer professor at the University of Southern California, 1946-1951, and visiting professor at the University of Chicago, 1948, and the University of London, 1957-1958. From 1960 to 1969, Hollingshead was a consultant to the Surgeon General of the United States. He also became a member of the research board, the National Association for Retarded Children in 1960.

While pursuing his teaching work, Hollingshead began his career as an author in 1938 with his first title *Personnel of Human Ecology.* Many of his books and articles concern **mental health**, such as *Social Class and Mental Illness,* coauthor Fredrick C. Redlich, 1958; *Social Psychiatry,* 1968; *The Mentally Ill and the Right to Treatment,* 1971; *Human Group in Patient Care,* with Dr. Raymond S. Duff, which is the study of medical and surgical patients in a New England medical center; and perhaps his best-known work *Sickness and Society,* which he also co-authored with Duff.

The book by Hollingshead and Redlich concerning social class and mental illness dismayed some of their colleagues because it took a serious, objective look at their profession. Yet, in time, it had a positive impact on the field. In *Sickness and Society,* 1968, Hollingshead and Duff strove for the same objective look and positive impact in their plea for better medical care. The book urges attention on the relationship between the care that hospital patients, both medical and surgical receive and the social environment in which that care is rendered. To find out whether patients receive optimal care in the hospital system and whether the system itself enhances or hinders such care, the authors concentrated on a single illness experience for a patient from the time he or she was admitted to the hospital, returned home, or died. Key to such a study is the definition of a hospital's effective social environment, which includes, besides the patient's immediate family, such members of a kinship group as friends, neighbors, and work colleagues. These individuals, who interact with each other on the patient's behalf, operate within a framework of role expectations, according to the authors. The expectations depend upon the person's relationship to the patient as well as on age and sex. One person may play out one or more role expectations regarding the patient. Other aspects of the effective environment include the patient's health status and abilities, the physical surroundings, and such opportunities or limitations as may be imposed by social status.

Hollingshead was a **Social Science Research Council** postdoctoral fellow, 1941-1942; a senior Fulbright scholar, United Kingdom, 1957-1958; and received the McKeever Award of the American Sociological Association. He was also a vice president of the American Sociological Association, 1957, president of the Eastern Sociological Association, 1959, and president of the American Association of University Professors, 1947-1950.

HOMANS, GEORGE CASPAR (1910-1989)
American sociologist

George Caspar Homans, an American sociologist, was a leading theorist in developing testable hypotheses and explanations about fundamental social processes in small groups. He was born August 11, 1910, in Boston, Massachusetts, the eldest child of Robert Homans, a lawyer and a fellow of Harvard Corporation, and of Abigail Adams Homans, a descendant of President John Adams. He married Nancy Parshall Cooper in 1941, and they had two children, Elizabeth Susan and Peter Homans graduated from Harvard University in English literature in 1932. Although he came from a long line of lawyers Homans chose to become a junior fellow in sociology at Harvard, 1934 to 1939, and then as professor of sociology when he was invited.

Homans taught at Harvard from 1939 to 1941, served four years as a naval officer during World War II, and then returned to Harvard where he was a faculty member from 1946 until 1970, when he retired. Homans was a fellow at the Center for Advanced Studies in the Behavioral Sciences, president of the American Sociological Association, and a member of the National Academy of Sciences.

English Villagers of the Thirteenth Century (1941) investigates two kinds of field systems (open and non-open); two settlement patterns (villages surrounded by farm lands and houses dispersed on individual family holdings); and two kinds of inheritance patterns (one in which the eldest son obtained all the family land and the other where all sons received an equal share). He discovered a high statistical **correlation** between these institutions: the open field system was associated with the village settlement pattern and inheritance by the eldest son. He later discovered that the two systems had different units of local government, different names for those units, differences in the peasant holdings, and different social classes among the peasants.

Of Homans' books, the *Human Group* (1950) was the most popular, used by two generations of sociologists in courses on small groups and **sociological theory**. He composed it by hand at his summer house in Quebec, where he wrote easily, quickly, and with considerable charm. As an exercise in general theory, he showed how three classes of variables (interaction, sentiments, and activities) are mutually related in the behavior of group members (the internal system) but also in the relationship of the group to its physical and social environment (the external system). He presented accounts of five concrete field studies of groups by other investigators and showed how the **data** are appropriately classified under each of the variables in both the internal and external system and how the variables and systems relate to each other. An example of his proposition is: the more frequently two persons in a group interact, the more apt they are to like one another.

Homans always believed in the folk adage that **human nature** is the same the world over and, hence, felt cross cultural generalizations should reflect that unity. For example, he was always fascinated by R. Firth's ethnography of Tikopia (in the Solomon Islands), a **society** where married couples lived with the husband's family and where the husband was given jural authority over his children. Homans liked to contrast this society and its relational patterns with that of the Trobrianders (off New Guinea). Here married couples lived with the wife's family; her brothers were vested with the jural authority over the children. Homans recognized that both societies, although their cultures were obviously different, evidenced the same behavioral generalization, namely that close and warm relations tend to occur on the side of the family away from the man who holds jural authority over the children. This explanation provided an alternative to Freud's theory of the Oedipus complex, which explained the strained relations between boys and their fathers as the result of unconscious competition for the sexual favors of the mother.

Homans observed that a theory is an explanation by a ''covering law.'' What sociologists try to explain are empirical propositions relating variables to one another, and Homans concluded that such generalizations are explained when they can be deduced under the specified conditions of their occurrence from more general propositions (covering laws). Homans further decided that for sociology the first approximation of covering laws were the reinforcement propositions of behavioral **psychology**, specifically those of his friends and colleagues B. F. Skinner and Richard Herrnstein (see *The Nature of Social Science,* 1967). Sociologists now tend to accept Homans' definition of theory but hesitate to accept his suggestions for covering laws.

Many feel Homans' best book was *Social Behavior: Its Elementary Forms* (1961, 1974), in which he described and explained small group behavior as an emergent social system of rewards, using as the explanatory logic Herrnstein's positive reinforcement propositions.

For sociology, perhaps the most important contribution in *Elementary Forms* was Homans' theory of stratification, which was stated in a series of scattered propositions and definitions. These included the following: The more valuable to other members of a group are the activities a person emits to them, the higher is the **status** they give him in return. The higher a person's status in a group, the greater his power is apt to be. The more group members a person is regularly able to influence, the greater is his power. The value of what a member receives by way of (monetary) rewards should be proportional to his status in the group. Distributive injustice occurs to the extent that the monetary rewards members receive are disproportional to their relative status in the group. The greater the distributive injustice in a group, the lower the productivity

In the United States, no formidable national movement has emerged to combat homelessness *(Archive Photos, Inc.).*

and morale of its members. Homans' theory seemed to be an alternative to the Marxist formulation that stratification—that is, differences in monetary rewards—was the root cause of all social problems.

Homans retired from Harvard University in 1980 to his home in Cambridge, from which he continued to write texts elucidating his social theories. He also published *The Witch Hazel, Poems of a Lifetime,* the year before his death. He died May 29, 1989, of congestive heart disease.

HOMELESSNESS

Homelessness is the lack of residential shelter or the prevalence of that lack within a population. Homelessness has conventionally been conceived of as distinct from indigence. Homeless persons were seen as somewhat adventurous drifters who lived rough lives. However, they were also sometimes glamorized as free-wheeling hobos and often as men of middle-age or older. Having been redefined as a social and political problem, having attracted sociological attention, and having been subjected to a range of **measurement** and observation modalities, homelessness is now understood to include a range of profiles, dynamics, causes, and degrees. For example, the homeless population can now be differentiated as including acute crisis cases, episodic homelessness, and the habitual street homeless.

As a social problem, homelessness is addressed by both public and private service providers, most visibly by churches. Homeless persons now have access to a wide ranges of services, from counseling and training to shelters and medical assistance. Shelters range in a number of factors, including the provision of ancillary services, but primarily in the number of beds available. (Far more are typically available during the winter, though also often fewer in the spring or fall than in summer.) Shelters also vary in whether they are short-term emergency refuges or intermediate-term transitional facilities, though either type typically focuses on victims of domestic violence rather than those already homeless.

Homelessness has also become a political problem and has attracted a vast array of social movement organizations and political activity. The United States experienced particular growth in these activities during the 1980s, as did homelessness itself. Hundreds of protests targeted government agencies, elected officials, police departments, and service providers. The homeless also began to organize, running bakeries and newspapers as well as waging political protest themselves. While the early half of the decade saw attention devoted to famine in Africa, the latter half focused on housing, food, and medical care for the poor and transient at home. By the 1990s, the web of funding and care provisions had expanded greatly, and empirical counts and studies of the homeless population began to flourish.

No strong national movement has emerged to combat homelessness. Perhaps this is appropriate, as the problem is typically understood as a local phenomenon. Although blame of individuals has somewhat subsided, both service provision and problems related to homelessness (such as perceived blight in some tourist areas) remain largely local. Nonetheless, homelessness is increasingly understood as a structural aspect of **society**, both varying with non-local factors and persistent despite individual and local efforts. Homelessness was probably exacerbated by the **structure** and **culture** of crack cocaine usage, as well as by local and regional shifts in **employment**, changes in government services and financial support (including the end of AFDC), declining **marriage** rates and rising **divorce** rates, and the **gentrification** of skid row areas which formerly offered both shelter and a veil to conceal a growing problem. Homelessness certainly increased between 1975 and 1990. However, one must wonder how much of the fourfold increase in homelessness purported to have occurred between 1980 and 1995 is due to expansion of the definition of the term. The initial influx of transients to the streets followed from the deinstitutionalization of **mental health** patients throughout the 1970s.

Even at the individual level and thanks to recent funding for empirical research, homelessness is much better understood than it has been. As a consequence of accumulated findings, earlier conceptions of homelessness have been contested or adjusted, giving way to recognition of variation in lifestyles, degrees of isolation and kinds of social ties, and degrees of mobility and patterns of migration. Homelessness can now be understood by these variations. In particular, although there has been some conflict about the migrant status of homeless persons, the homeless population is now recognized to include many who are temporarily homeless and many others who remain homeless in the same area for a long period. Indeed, the most recent research indicates that, at least in the United States during the 1980s and 1990s, most homeless persons are long-term residents of the same area. Further, there is evidence of demographic, psychological, and sociological differences associated with variations in mobility: The mobile homeless are younger, more affluent, better educated, typically unmarried,

and with more ties to both homeless persons and others. However, mobility can both exacerbate psychological problems and complicate efforts to provide services.

The measurement and assessment of homelessness has evolved along with changing conceptualization. Homelessness has been operationalized by both frequency and mobility, as well as by expectations for future mobility. Regardless of selected definition, and in part due to conflicts about the appropriateness of various methodologies, homelessness is often believed to be undercounted. Multi-method approaches are warranted, as any particular study design may encounter intrinsic weaknesses: Telephone **surveys** seeking quota sampling of the formerly homeless are able to observe only those who have been temporarily homeless and, therefore, miss the many persons whose longer-term lack of shelter is now recognized. Point-in-time surveys of shelters and other service providers, including both targeted telephone surveys and on-site bed counts, miss seasonal fluctuations as well as those many homeless persons who refuse to use shelter services and instead sleep in a vehicle, on the street, or along river beds or valley floors. Projecting annualized incidence or period prevalence from point-in-time **data** also risks the effects of seasonal variations in both homelessness and service availability. At best, censuses of homelessness are exploratory descriptions, based on samples. Census takers should, therefore, feel less burdened by statistical rigor and more free to explore qualitative measures and to generate grounded theory about homelessness.

HOMOGAMY

Homogamy describes the tendency for people to marry people with similar social statuses and social characteristics. This concept is closely related to the concept of endogamy in which members of a group are required or expected to marry people inside the group. Homogamy is influenced by individual level, group level, and structural level factors. At the individual level, people may prefer others with similar resources, **values**, and tastes. At the group level, third parties, such as the **family**, the church, or the state, may have an interest in influencing the marriage choices. At the structural level, the constraints of the "marriage market," such as **group size**, geography, and the social makeup of neighborhoods, schools, and workplaces influence homogamy. In terms of group size, members of larger groups are much more likely to marry within their group than members of smaller groups. Groups that have a large concentration in a specific geographic area, such as Asian Americans in California, are also more likely to form homogamous marriages. Finally, neighborhoods, schools, and workplaces influence rates of homogamy because they are often places where potential mates meet, and they are often socially segregated. Marriages in the United States tend to be between partners who have similar racial and ethnic backgrounds, religious backgrounds, socioeconomic backgrounds, and similar levels of education. Most people also tend to marry those who are similar to themselves in terms of age, weight, and appearance.

HOMOPHOBIA

Homophobia is an ideological position and internalized fear based on the belief that to be gay or lesbian is inherently wrong. In its most vituperative form, people who are homophobic blame gay and lesbian people for various real and perceived social ill, from urban decay to sex on TV, and warn that homosexuals are plotting to destroy the human **race**. From this position, **prejudice**, discrimination, and even violent assault are seen as justified, even laudable. More subdued forms of homophobia maintain that gay and lesbian people are deficient: immature, shallow, unstable, irresponsible. Deprived of the joy, wonder, and transforming power of heterosexual **love**, homosexuals should be pitied, perhaps avoided but not hated. Heterosexism, perhaps the most pernicious and insidious form of homophobia, oppresses gay and lesbian people by its tacit and eclipsing assumption that sex between men and women is the only form sexuality takes. The various types of homophobia are theoretically but not practically separable. Informal homophobic behaviors such as incivility, **discrimination**, ridicule, and harassment combine with heterosexist exclusion and avoidance to transform gay and lesbian people from citizens to strangers, from kin to criminals.

Prior to the 1960s, homophobia was rarely questioned, and sociologists such as **Erving Goffman** confined their research to how one practiced identity management in response to anti-gay or lesbian stigma. During the 1970s and 1980s, when changes in social climate made more blatant expressions of homophobia unpopular, scholars began exploring such everyday practices as anti-gay jokes, name-calling, and insults, especially among teenagers and college students. Sociological antecedents of homophobia were identified: homophobic individuals are usually male, young, under-educated, religious fundamentalist, and politically and sexually conservative; they are unlikely to be conscious of knowing any gay people and, like the **culture** they inhabit, they tend to attribute homosexuality to a willful deviation from normalcy.

During the 1990s, research shifted from homophobic individuals to the social, political, and **economic institutions** that foster and presumably benefit from homophobic and heterosexist ideologies. Several scholars have theorized that the public/private dichotomy engendered by late **capitalism**, with a public sphere informed by male-male camaraderie and a private sphere reserved for heterosexual love and intimacy, can be maintained only through the devaluation or erasure of same-sex desire. Thus, homophobia becomes a tool of heterosexist, political, and economic oppression.

HOMOSEXUALITY

The term "homosexuality" can be a subjective or objective evaluation of sexual activities, affective attachment, and/or self-concept. Rather than a noun that labels an entire **identity**, the term "homosexuality" is properly used as a descriptive adjective. It is not solely the choice of sexual behavior outside of a social context. Some people may occasionally engage in

Two homosexual men embrace at the 1998 Gay Pride Parade in San Francisco, California *(Archive Photos, Inc.)*.

sexual activity with a member of the same sex, which would not designate an exclusive homosexual orientation. A preference for a same-sex partner does not necessarily emerge with the onset of dating; moreover, those with a homosexual orientation frequently establish heterosexual relationships prior to recognizing a same-sex erotic attraction. In fact, years may pass before individuals recognize and identify their preference.

The predominant way homosexuality, and sexuality in general, is ordered is the Kinsey Scale. According to Alfred Kinsey, sexual orientations can be placed on a seven-point continuum that he devised. A score of three on this scale would indicate an equally homosexual and heterosexual orientation, or perfect **bisexuality**, while a seven on this scale would indicate exclusive homosexuality.

There are several competing psychological and biological theories regarding the origin of homosexuality, such as those that relate to parenting patterns, life experiences, genetic variations, hormonal variations, and individual psychological attributes. Some evidence suggests that a difference in the size of the anterior hypothalamus which affects **sexual behavior**. No direct causal linkage between hypothalamus size and homosexual behaviors exist per se; according to a study of cadavers by Simon LeVay, however, the anterior hypothalamus in homosexual-oriented subjects was less than half the size of the heterosexuals examined. There is also some indication that genetic factors influence homosexuality. Also, a linkage may exist between adult homosexuality and gender nonconformity in childhood. Thus while evidence suggests a biological propensity toward one's adult sexual orientation, most researchers agree that sexual orientation is an intricate web of psychosocial and biological considerations.

Attitudes regarding homosexuality vary from consent to damnation cross-culturally. In current **American society**, the dominant view of homosexuality is negative. Judeo-Christian history has been mostly anti-homosexual. In this tradition, sexual relations were held as a sacred activity for procreation only. Because homosexuality could not result in impregnation, it was not allowed.

Throughout the nineteenth century, the notion that homosexuals were sinners shifted to the idea that they were ill. Medical and psychological professionals performed severe treatments in order to "cure" homosexuality. Recently, however, the American Psychological Association deleted homosexuality from its diagnostic groupings of mental disorders. Homosexuality is no longer considered an illness within the medical **community**.

See also Bisexuality

HORKHEIMER, MAX (1895-1973)
German philosopher and social psychologist

Max Horkheimer is best known as one of the leading members of the Frankfurt school, and one of the leading proponents of what he called "critical theory." Born near Stuttgart, Germany, the son of a wealthy Jewish industrialist, Horkheimer attended University of Frankfurt, where he completed his doctoral dissertation, a study of German philosopher Immanuel Kant's *Critique of Judgement*. In 1930, Horkheimer became the director of the Institute for Social Research in Frankfurt, marking a turning point both for Horkheimer and the Institute. Prior to his tenure as director, Horkheimer was relatively unknown, and the Institute itself did not deviate much from traditional Marxist **theory** and research. However, the rise of Joseph Stalin's brutal dictatorship in the Soviet Union and of Nazism in Germany deeply affected Horkheimer and the Institute, prompting them to move from Frankfurt to New York City in 1935 to escape Nazi oppression.

In 1937, Horkheimer published the first of his two best known works, "Traditional and Critical Theory." In this essay, Horkheimer argued that "traditional theory," understood as heretofore existing social science scholarship, has been obsessed with the accumulation of facts in specialized, isolated fields of study. Such an obsession has tended to serve

far more than question, let alone challenge the existing **social order**, Horkheimer contended. In contrast, Horkheimer proposed a "critical theory" which would break traditional theory's separation of knowledge and action, and **values** and research. Like Karl Marx, Horkheimer earlier on believed that theory and knowledge could and should change **society** by helping those oppressed to identify and emancipate themselves from their oppression.

During his earlier years as head of the Institute, Horkheimer shared many traditional concerns of Marxist scholars, including critiquing the bourgeois myth of individual **autonomy** and studying the historical development of bourgeois society. However, Horkheimer and his Frankfurt School colleagues integrated the thought of scholars such as **Max Weber**, **Immanuel Kant**, Georg W.F. Hegel, and **Sigmund Freud** to extend Marxist inquiry far beyond its traditional concern with economic production relations to consider the influence of capitalism on personality, **family**, art, and mass **culture**, among other areas.

Faced with the horrors of Nazi fascism in Europe, the insidious growth of capitalist mass culture in the United States, and the turn of working class revolution into totalitarian dictatorship in the Soviet Union, Horkheimer grew gradually more pessimistic about the prospect for emancipation from oppression and authoritarian power. Correspondingly, his analysis moved farther from Marx, and his stress on class conflict and class emancipation, toward Weber, and his belief that **bureaucracy** would increasingly dominate social life and constrain human freedom in modern societies. In his best known work *Dialectic of Enlightenment* (1944), Horkheimer and his Frankfurt School colleague **Theodor Adorno** argued that while the Enlightenment promised freedom and progress through reason and knowledge, reason and knowledge have instead become instruments of **domination**, enabling more efficient and extensive control not only over the natural environment, but also human beings. In this and subsequent work (e.g., *Eclipse of Reason* [1947] and *Critique of Instrumental Reason* [1967]), Horkheimer stresses how "instrumental reason"—the principle and methods by which means, such as factories or consumer goods, are calculatingly designed to efficiently meet certain ends, usually greater profit or control—has come to dominate not only the work lives of modern people, but also their leisure lives through the mass consumption of commodities. In contrast with art, mass culture's commodities only confirm the existing social order, rather than "negating" it, that is, suggesting emancipating alternatives to instrumental order. Since his death in 1973, Horkheimer and his Frankfurt School colleagues' critical theory was revised most saliently by social theorist Jürgen Habermas, but also Axel Honneth, Albrecht Wellmer and Claus Offe.

HOROWITZ, IRVING LOUIS (1929-)
American educator and author

"Sociology has fallen into a 'dismal abyss' and may soon go the way of phrenology," declared Irving Louis Horowitz in

1994 while a professor of sociology at Rutgers University in New Brunswick, New Jersey. He feared that the discipline had grown far from its roots of objectivity in studying problems that concern the human condition. Horowitz was born in New York City on September 25, 1929, to Louis and Esther Tepper Horowitz. He was educated at the College of the City of New York (now city College of the City University of New York, or CUNY), B.S.S., 1951; Columbia University, New York City, M.A., 1952; and the University of Buenos Aires, Argentina, Ph.D., 1957. In 1950, he married Ruth Narowlansky; they were divorced in 1963. He married Mary Ellen Curtis in 1979 with whom he has two children, Carl and David.

From the beginning of his career as an assistant professor of social theory at the University of Buenos Aires, 1956-58, Horowitz spent the next forty-plus years at various academic institutions nationwide and abroad including posts in India, Tokyo, Mexico, and Canada. In addition to his teaching positions, he was an advisory staff member of the Latin American Research Center, 1964-1970; consultant to the International Education Division, Ford Foundation, 1959-1960; a member of the advisory board of the Institute for Scientific Information, 1969-1973; consulting editor for Oxford University Press, 1974-1969, and for Aldine-Atherton Publishers, 1969-1972; the founding president of Transaction Society; an external board member of the Radio Marti and Television Marti Programs of the U.S. Information Agency, beginning in 1985; chair of the board of the Hubert Humphrey Center, Ben Gurion University, Israel, 1990-92; and has served as an external board member of the **methodology** section of the research division, U.S. General Accounting Office.

The author of more than twenty-five books and editor of numerous other titles, Horowitz has analyzed such diverse topics as the influence of Sun Myung Moon and the Unification Church on American politics, the future of book publishing, and politics in Cuba. In 1978, Horowitz edited a work on Moon entitled *Science, Sin, and Scholarship: The Politics of Reverend Moon and the Unification Church*. It describes how Moon has infiltrated power groups in America from the federal government to universities. In *Communicating Ideas: The Crisis of Publishing in a Post-Industrial Society,* the author looked at the future of the publishing world in an age of rapid technological development and advancement. In *The Conscience of Worms and the Cowardice of Lions: Cuban Politics and Culture in an American Context* (1993), Horowitz paid tribute to Cubans and Cuban-American scholars for keeping alive the spirit of antitotalitarianism. He also spoke convincingly of the major influence Castro has had on U.S. scholarship.

In 1990, he published his autobiography, what he called a "sociological biography" rather than one that is intellectual of intimate. This was *Daydreams and Nightmares: Reflections on a Harlem Childhood,*, for which he received the National Jewish Book Award. It is an unromanticized look at growing up as the son of Russian-Jewish immigrants in the streets of predominantly black Harlem, New York City, in the 1930s. He wrote of a father who was abusive to his children, the streets where numbers-running and ticket-scalping not only provided

cases for youngsters, but taught them to survive, and of the tense relations between blacks and Jews. It throws light on the intertwining of **race**, **ethnicity**, religion, social class, and age. According to a reviewer, it is a "unique, child's eye view of Harlem... with surprisingly frank glimpses into Jewish family life in that context, but with many of the sharp edges reasoned away."

Throughout his academic career, Horowitz received many awards, including a special citation from the Carnegie Endowment for International Peace, 1957, for *Idea of War and Peace in Contemporary Philosophy;*; recognition by *Time* as the Man of the Year in Behavioral Science, 1970; the Centennial medallion from St. Peters College, Jersey City, New Jersey, 1971, for outstanding contribution to a humanistic social science; and a presidential outstanding achievement award, 1985, from Rutgers University. He is a member of the Carnegie Council, American Association of Publishers, American Political Science Association, American Association for the Advancement of Science, and past president (1961-1962) of the New York State Sociological Society.

HOUSEHOLD

The U. S. **Census** defines a household as a group of one or more persons living and eating together in a residence with its own access to the outside or to a common hallway. Generally, households are subdivided into two categories: family and non-family households. Two or more persons living together who are connected by birth, **marriage**, or **adoption** characterizes the former and the latter describes single person households and those with two or more persons who are non-related.

Since the first census in 1790, household size has steadily declined. This trend is a function of several factors, including lower fertility rates and fewer economically dependent household members (i.e., servants, apprentices). Also significant is the recent increase in non-family households, which grew from 19% of all households in 1970 to 30% in 1996. Such households are made up of elderly individuals living alone, people sharing living space for economic reasons, cohabiting couples, adults who are delaying or forgoing marriage and those who are between marriages.

Often in sociological analyses, the term household is preferable to family, as the latter often implies a nuclear structure of a married couple with children. Given the fact that over half of modern households do not fit this description, the idea of household structure is often more clarifying. The "common cooking-pot" definition of households uses as its criterion those individuals who aggregate and share their economic resources, as evidenced by the fact that they regularly take their meals together. However, this definition has its share of problems as well, as it is inadequate to describe student housing, institutions, and accommodations for the elderly.

HULL HOUSE

Hull House was the earliest and most well-known of the American settlement houses. **Jane Addams**, the well-educated

Hull House was the earliest and most well-known of U.S. settlement houses *(AP/Wide World Photos, Inc.)*.

communities. Hull House combined research and action in a unique way. Addams explicitly rejected the Victorian model of charity in favor of one of mutual education. The settlement House workers would interact with their poor neighbors to mutual benefit, and each would gain from learning from the other within the context of real-life conditions. This model of education was a practical application of the theories of Addams' friend John Dewey, based at the University of Chicago.

By choosing to live deep in the heart of the "wicked city" and by rejecting charity in favor of **organization**, the settlement house workers helped to promote the idea of poverty as a social ill rather than an individual failing. They organized several ethnic clubs, women's suffrage groups, and various activities for elderly women. The women's shirtmakers and cloakmakers unions were founded and based at Hull House. Jane Addams served as an arbitrator in the Pullman union disputes of 1894, where she advocated that the two sides should meet face-to-face in direct but nonviolent confrontation.

The Hull House workers researched and worked to solve many social problems, including tuberculosis, typhoid, housing, cocaine use, child labor, sweatshops, truancy, the lack of public bathhouses, and inadequate garbage collection. Many researchers went on to hold influential positions in government and non-profit organizations. Julia Lathrop became the first director of the United States Children's Bureau. Grace Abbott, another Hull House resident, was the first superintendent of the League for the Protection of Immigrants.

Hull House quickly grew, incorporating a boys club, theater, meeting rooms, employment agency, lunchroom, museum of work, library, apartments for working women with children, and a kindergarten. The organization became an international model for hands-on social reform. Visitors, such as W. E. B. DuBois, **George Herbert Mead**, and the Canadian Prime Minister William McKenzie King, came to observe the various programs.

Addams, Julia Lathrop, Grace Abbott, Florence Kelly, Sophonisba Breckinridge and the other Hull House workers gave impetus to the new field of social work, training many women who would become the first social workers of the coming welfare state. Yet as **social work** became institutionalized, the voluntarist spirit of Hull House was increasingly disparaged in favor of a medical model which emphasized casework rather than social reform. Hull House and the other settlement houses were gradually replaced by local government bureaucracies, and by the 1920s and 1930s, few social workers lived in the neighborhoods that they served. Hull House itself lasted on into the 1960s, when it was torn down to make way for the University of Illinois at Chicago.

The longest-lasting and most influential account of Hull House and the settlement movement has been Allen Davis's *Spearheads for Reform (1967)*, which saw the settlement houses as a vital instrument of progressivism. In contrast, Howard Jacob Karger of the **social control** school criticized the settlement houses as *The Sentinels of Order* (1987), an attempt by elites to control the lawless behavior of the poor. Other recent accounts have been more charitable, as feminist historians have recognized the unique combination of research, activism,

founder and first director of the House, was from an elite New England family. Forced to give up on her plans for medical school by chronic back pain, Addams spent her early twenties traveling in Europe. She was unhappy with the restrictions of the traditional Grand Tour and sought opportunities to visit the parts of foreign cities which were neglected by tourists. She was particularly impressed by Toynbee Hall, the first British settlement house, which had been founded in East London in 1884. When she returned to the United States, Addams approached her friend Ellen Gates Starr, with a view to establishing a similar project in Chicago. Like Addams, Starr was heavily influenced by the progressive movement and readily agreed to join her time, **money**, and talents to those of Addams.

The women who joined the settlement house movement were inspired by the idea of living and working for social **justice** with other women. Many of them came from the families of eminent (male) social reformers and philanthropists, who believed in women's education. Yet while their education had given them a burning desire for social reform, their talents and energies were frustrated. The extreme difficulty of entering the male dominated **professions** restricted most female would-be organizers and reformers to traditional Victorian acts of charity.

In 1889, Addams and Starr took over a mansion on Chicago's West Side, in an area of recent immigrants that had become known for its **poverty**, dirt and corruption. The neighborhoods surrounding the House included Italian, Bohemian, Polish, African American, Jewish, Russian and Greek

social work, and feminist sisterhood that Hull House represented. Still others have begun to question whether Hull House was in **fact** representative of the settlement house movement as a whole. The work of Ruth Hutchinson Crocker and of Elizabeth Lasch-Quinn explores differences between the progressive spirit of Hull House and the work of the more religious and anti-union settlement houses founded in less cosmopolitan cities.

HUMAN CAPITAL

Human capital refers to a set of assets that can be transferred into economic gain. Particular assets can be acquired in a number of ways, one of which is through formal education. The skills and information learned through schooling are valued in the labor market. The more formal education individuals complete, the more valued they are in the labor market. Being valued more, workers should be able to expect higher wages or larger salaries. Acquiring skills through experience is another form of human capital. Individuals with a certain number of years in the workforce possess a certain amount of skills; it can be assumed that the greater the number of years of experience a person has, the more skills that person will also have, and the more valuable they are. Often occupations offer on-the-job training that is specific to the job. Completing this training increases human capital because an employee with these skills is more qualified for the position. Ultimately any accumulation of knowledge or ability that enables an individual to enhance or develop specific competencies raises their value in the labor market and represents an increase in human capital.

For those researchers who adopt a human capital **theory** approach, human capital is central to determining labor market processes, such as the type of work individuals acquire and the levels of pay they earn. Through this theory, inequalities in income, such as those found to exist between women and men or minorities and whites, are attributed to differential investments in human capital. This theory with its emphasis on human capital as a set of economic assets has been criticized for taking a perspective of the labor market that is too rational. Those opposed to human capital theory do not dispute that a portion of the differential in earnings is due to the skills possessed. Yet a large portion of earning differentials goes unexplained in a model that relies solely on individuals' productivity levels. Remaining variance must then be attributed to the labor market's imperfect structure and functioning. **Discrimination** is one commonly cited aspect of the imperfect labor market that hurts arguments relying on human capital. Much research shows that when comparing individuals with similar levels of human capital, differences in income between certain groups, whether by **race**, gender, age, or some other dimension, are still found.

HUMAN NATURE

The concept, human nature, gives people a sense of shared meaning and experience; therefore, it works both to the advantage of the individual and the advantage of the species as a whole. Human nature is sometimes considered to be synonymous with the notion of instinct which has persisted without empirical evidence for at least 2,500 years when the ancient Greeks first made a reference to it. Instinct is a way to direct action, complete tasks, and view people's progressive lives as continuous creations.

Some academics suggest that patterns of human nature assist people in making choices about the future and dealing with habitual situations. Human nature acts as a guide in an indeterminate world and allows people to sympathize with others. However, the idea of human nature is contradictory. It implies a set of instinctive traits passed down from one generation to the next that influence social action and reaction. The reality is that human nature is probably both learned and instinctive. The debate in **sociology** over the idea of human nature deals with whether it actually exists and with how these basic human characteristics act and react with each other. Some social and political theorists have emphasized the preponderance of acts of cruelty which characterize the bulk of human existence. They think that malice stems from a biological component. Other theorists stress the positive side of human nature by citing the numerous acts of **altruism** and teamwork that occur in **society**.

Max Weber wrote about human nature as a culmination of human adventure and memory. He did not believe that human nature was instinctive. Many recent social theorists have rejected the idea of human nature altogether. By contrast, social psychologists view human nature as the "motivations for mastery and understanding that direct man's thinking." We need to secure stability and stability enables human beings to strive for higher expectations. High hopes help us expand our hopes and dreams.

The concept of human nature obscures the fact that often times individuals have little control over their environment, providing us instead with the illusion that we have a certain nature regardless of environmental influences. John MacMurray suggested that because people are always dissatisfied and never adapt to their environment completely, the stages of human development become clear only after the relationship between that person and their adaption to the environment becomes apparent. Hadley Cantril speaks of "basic functional uniformities" that we must employ in daily living.

Human nature is the way people live their lives. We seek pleasure and avoid pain; perhaps this not only keeps us alive but is our primary focus in day to day living. Humans desire security to protect their gains and assure their foothold in the larger scheme of life. They crave order to use as a premonition of what the possible outcome of certain events might be. People also want their dreams to correspond to their actual lives as they make their journey through the years but daily existence is often difficult to manipulate. Ultimately, the notion of human nature provides us with alternatives and a sense of being on steady ground.

The 1963 March on Washington united many demonstrators in their efforts to achieve civil rights legislation.

HUMAN RELATIONS SCHOOL

Developed in the late 1930s, the human relations school is a school of thought that emphasizes the importance of *informal* activities such as workplace **norms**, **communication**, and supervisory skills in enhancing worker productivity. Its founding father is generally believed to be Elton Mayo. This school originated out of the failure of Hawthorne experiments, undertaken at the Western Electric Company plant in Cicero, Illinois, under the leadership of the industrial psychologist, Elton Mayo. The experiments were intended to uncover the role of financial incentives and improved work environments, such as enhanced lighting, in engendering increased worker productivity. The conclusions of the study were surprising. The researchers discovered that in the relay assembly test room, productivity increased regardless of changes in the lighting conditions. In the bank wiring room, on the other hand, financial incentives to increase productivity failed to result in increased productivity because of an informal norm among workers that discouraged members from working either too fast or too slow. These two studies debunked the ideas that improved work environments and financial rewards were crucial to worker productivity. The results suggested instead that employees' sense of importance to management as well as workplace norms were equally important contributors to worker productivity.

HUMAN RIGHTS

Human rights are expectations that individuals may reasonably place on **society** to meet their basic needs. Human rights apply to everyone, regardless of citizenship or any other social **status**. Such rights are also conceived of as universal in terms of time and space, being the same for everyone throughout history and throughout the world.

There are two main types of human rights: positive and negative. A positive right is a right *to* something, such as adequate food, religious **identity**, physical safety, and free expres-

sion. A negative right is a right to be free *from* something, such as torture or unlawful imprisonment.

The seventeenth and eighteenth century political philosophers, among the most notable being **John Locke**, are often credited with first developing the concept of universal human rights based on the equality of all people. Furthermore, human rights have a moral component, that is, such rights are culturally constructed as being "good" and "just". With the French and American Revolutions, during the late eighteenth century, human rights became an institutionalized part of international **discourse**. The French *Declaration of the Rights of Man and of the Citizen*, signed in 1789, is an early example of universal rights being incorporated into a state's constitution.

The protection and promotion of human rights is one of the founding principles of the United Nations. The Universal Declaration of Human Rights, a 1948 UN General Assembly resolution, defines education as the key to this protection and promotion. However, some human rights activists have often criticized the Universal Declaration for not specifically protecting the rights of ethnic minority groups and other identity-based collectivities. Additionally, the Universal Declaration and other international human rights instruments generally make it the responsibility of each state to protect the rights of all persons within its borders, citizen or otherwise. This stance is particularly problematic when it is the state that is violating the rights of its population.

International non-governmental human rights organizations have been instrumental in monitoring and disseminating information about human rights abuses. Some organizations are limited in scope, such as Amnesty International, which focuses on preventing torture, illegal imprisonments, and executions. Other organizations, like the International Society for Human Rights, seek to protect human rights in general.

A key debate among sociologists concerns the function of human rights in relationship to the social **structure**. Marxists challenge the idea that rights are actually liberating. In this view, human rights **ideology** is espoused by the wealthy capitalist classes as a disguise for their economic, political, and social **domination**. Others argue that human rights are a direct challenge to state sovereignty and, therefore, help to increase equality by limiting the consolidation of power.

HUMAN-CENTERED TECHNOLOGY

Human-centered technology is an approach to technology design and work organization that strives to improve the skills and abilities of users by according equal priority to human and organizational issues as well as technical design requirements. Also referred to in manufacturing as anthropocentric production systems, this approach is in direct contrast to the technical design philosophy, which is based on the engineering assumption that humans are a source of uncertainty and error in production, and are to be eventually replaced by computer-integrated systems in the so-called unmanned factory of the future. In its ideal-typical form, human-centered technology incorporates design criteria that allow a unity of conception and execution, skill enhancement (particularly the recognition of tacit skills), and a measure of worker control over work processes and technology through participative systems design.

Human-centered technology was at first linked with the work-humanization initiatives of the 1960s and 1970s, such as the Volvo group technology experiments, job enrichment, and job enlargement programs, and the sociotechnical systems approach. More recently, human-centered technology is seen as a crucial feature of new production systems based on flexible specialization. The theory of flexible specialization assumes an emerging post-Fordist manufacturing strategy in which multiskilled and functionality flexible craft workers supplants the Tayloristic work patterns of mass production. According to the theory of flexible specialization, human-centered technology is both more efficient in management terms, and more humanitarian and democratic in terms of management-worker relations: a nonzero sum worker-management relationship. Although an important corrective to the simplistic logic of deskilling implied by labor process theory, critics of human-centered approaches to technology cast doubt on the extent to which they are realized in practice and point to the negative consequences found in **case studies**, such as increased levels of **stress** and work intensification. Furthermore, critics of flexible specialization question the extent of genuine worker participation, and point to the increase in peripheral workers on part-time or temporary contracts who support core workers enjoying greater job security and better conditions of work.

HUME, DAVID (1711-1776)
Scottish philosopher

The Scottish philosopher David Hume developed the concept of "mitigated skepticism," which remains a viable alternative to the systems of rationalism, empiricism, and **idealism**. Hume raised relevant issues and arguments that remain central to contemporary thought, but his philosophical writings went unnoticed during his lifetime. The considerable fame he achieved derived from his work as an essayist and historian.

Hume was born on April 26, 1711, near Edinburgh. A second son, he was not entitled to a large inheritance, and he failed careers in law and business because of his "aversion to everything but the pursuits of Philosophy and general learning." Until he was past forty, Hume was employed only twice.

The first two volumes of his major philosophic work *A Treatise of Human Nature* were published in 1739 and the third appeared in the following year. Book I of the *Treatise* was recast as *An Enquiry Concerning Human Understanding* and published in 1748. The third volume slightly revised appeared in 1751 as *An Enquiry concerning the Principles of Morals*. The second volume of the *Treatise* was republished as Part II of *Four Dissertations* in 1757. Hume's other important work, the controversial *Dialogues concerning Natural Religion*, complete by the mid–1750s, was published posthumously.

During his lifetime Hume's reputation derived from the publication of his *Political Discourses* (1751) and six volume

David Hume *(The Library of Congress)*

History of England (1754–1762). When he went to France in 1763 as secretary to the English ambassador, Hume discovered that he was a literary celebrity. He retired to Edinburgh in 1769 and died there on August 25, 1776.

Skepticism is concerned with the truthfulness of human perceptions and ideas. Hume was the first thinker to point out the disastrous implications of the representative theory of perception. Hume suggested that a position of complete skepticism is neither serious nor useful. Academic skepticism states that one can never know the truth or falsity of any statement (except, of course, this one). It is, however, a self-refuting theory and is confounded by life itself because "we make inferences on the basis of our impressions whether they be true or false, real or imaginary." Hume, therefore, advanced what he called "mitigated skepticism." This approach attempts to limit philosophical inquiries to topics that are adapted to the capacities of human intelligence. It thus excludes all metaphysical questions concerning the origin of either mind or object as being incapable of demonstration.

Even though an ultimate explanation of the subject or object of knowledge is impossible, Hume provided a description of how man senses and understands. He emphasized the utility of knowledge as opposed to its correctness and suggested that experience begins with feeling rather than thought. He used the term ''perception'' in its traditional sense—that is, whatever can be present to the mind from the senses, passions, thought, or reflection. Nonetheless he distinguished between impressions which are felt and ideas which are thought. In this he stressed the difference between feeling a toothache and thinking about such a pain.

Hume distinguished the various mental operations in a descriptive psychology, or ''mental geography.'' For example, impressions are described as vivacious and lively, whereas ideas are less vivid and, in fact, derived from original impressions. This thesis leads to the conclusion that ''we can never think of any thing which we have not seen without us or felt in our own minds.'' Hume stressed that the criterion for judging ideas is to remove every philosophical ambiguity by identifying the impression from which a supposed idea is derived. If there is no corresponding impression, the idea may be dismissed as meaningless. This assumption that all ideas are reducible, in principle, to some impression is central to Hume's **empiricism**.

Hume accepted the Cartesian doctrine of the distinct idea—conceivability subject only to the principle of contradiction—as both the unit of reasoning and the criterion of truth. But the doctrine of the distinct idea means that every noncontradictory idea expresses an *a priori* logical possibility. And the speculative freedom of the imagination to conceive opposites without contradiction makes it impossible to demonstrate any matter of fact or existence. For Hume, since truth is posterior to fact, the ideas of reason only express what the mind thinks about reality. On the level of ideas, Hume believed that the meaning of ideas is more important than their truth. What separates meaningful propositions from mere concepts is the subjective impression of belief.

Belief, or the vivacity with which the mind conceives certain ideas and associations, results from the reciprocal relationship between experience and imagination. The cumulative experience of the past and present—for example, the relational factors of constancy, conjunction, and resemblance—gives a bias to the imagination. But it is man's imaginative anticipations of the future that give meaning to his experience.

The most celebrated example of this argument is Hume's analysis of the causal relation. Every statement which points beyond what is immediately available to the senses and memory rests on an assumption and/or extension of the cause and effect relation. For example, we may note that certain events occur in sequence and we may assume that the first causes the second, as lightning causes thunder, or one moving billiard ball causes another to move when the make contact. But even if the first always is followed by the second we cannot assume **causality**. It is not necessary that the sun will rise tomorrow because it has always risen in the past. The future cannot be deduced from the past; it remains logically possible that the sun will not rise tomorrow, that the next billiard ball

we hit will not cause another one to move, or that the next lightning bolt will not bring about a roll of thunder. Thus, there is no justifiable knowledge of causal connections in nature, although this is not a denial that there are real causes. Man's supposed knowledge results from repeated associations of the supposed cause and effect, to the point where imagination makes its customary transition from one object to its usual attendant and presumes a causal relationship. This is considered Hume's critique of induction. Causality cannot be determined by **deductive logic**, relying instead of the uniformity of nature, and the tendency that today will be like tomorrow. While Hume does not deny that inductions are necessary for humans to live normally, he argues that they cannot be adequately justified.

Because of his skeptical **attitude** toward the truths of reason Hume attempted to base his moral theory on the certainty of feeling—''Reason is, and ought only to be, the slave of the passions.'' While this is often taken to be an amoralist attitude, Hume emphasized that reason can only tell us how to accomplish moral actions. It cannot determine what moral actions are. For this, we must rely on our emotions, both strong and weak. A change in moral character, then, cannot be accomplished by reason, but can and should be transformed by the passions. In this, Hume followed the ''moral sense'' school and, especially, the thought of Francis Hutcheson. Moreover, Hume anticipated Jeremy Bentham's utilitarianism, a debt which the latter acknowledged.

HUNTER-GATHERER

''Hunter-gatherer'' is a term that refers to a kind of primitive tribal way of life. In the strict definition of the term, the primitive group subsists in the wild on food obtained by hunting and foraging. The hunting-gathering lifestyle is thought to be the predecessor of agriculture in human history. According to Bruce Smith (National Museum of Natural History, Washington, D.C.), the transition between hunter-gatherer and agricultural lifestyles is still poorly understood, though Smith estimates that the transition in Mesoamerica took place over a 6,500 year period. (Mesoamerica extended south and east from central Mexico and included portions of Guatemala, Belize, Honduras, and Nicaragua.)

Hunter-gatherer groups still exist today. One theory of Richard B. Lee and Irven DeVore (anthropologists, Harvard University) in *Man the Hunter* (1968) proposed that hunter-gatherer lifestyles had been the exclusive lifestyle of 99 percent of the population over the last 2 million years. The scientists that study modern hunter-gatherer groups once held the general theory that modern day hunter-gathers existed as ''living fossils,'' untouched by modern influences in **society**. That assessment has changed. Thomas N. Headland studied the Agta hunter-gatherers of the Philippines in the 1960s and heard a mother singing a religious song from the United States to her child. In a *Current Anthropology* article (February 1989) Headland (and co-author Lawrence A. Reid) proposed that hunter-gatherer groups had actually interacted with outside influences (such as neighboring and state societies) for several thousand years. Headland's proposition represented a general shift in thinking about hunter-gatherers among anthropologists.

In the 1990s, archeologist Smith unearthed a finding that suggested that the Americas made the transition from hunting and gathering to agriculture earlier in history than previously supposed. Smith analyzed squash seeds (discovered in a Mexican cave) and dispelled a previous theory that the inhabitants of the Americas transitioned into agriculture 5,000 to 3,500 years ago. The analysis showed that agriculture in the Americas could have begun as long as 8,000 to 10,000 years ago.

I

IBD-KHALDUN, ABDEL RAHMAN (1332-1406)

African scholar, teacher, political advisor, and political activist

Abdel Rahman Ibd-Khaldun (1332–1406) was a scholar, teacher, political advisor and activist in north Africa and southern Europe in the late fourteenth century. Ibd-Khaldun was among the earliest scholars to focus his work on social and historical factors and the interaction of the two. Ibd-Khaldun was born in Tunis to an educated family and was schooled in mathematics, history and religious studies and later became quite active politically serving various leaders in his homeland as well as in Spain, Morocco, and Algeria as an ambassador and scholar. During this time, Ibd-Khaldun was imprisoned for several years for questioning the divinity of social and state leaders. After more than twenty years in political life, Ibd-Khaldun devoted himself to a more focused study of historical and social questions which eventually led him to a position as lecturer at Al-Azhar Mosque in Cairo. His lectures grew in popularity and focused on the importance of recognizing social thought and linking this early **sociology** with historical observation. Ibd-Khaldun also was among the first to study the interrelation of what would later be termed social institutions and to compare then modern **society** with primitive social organizations.

Ibd-Khaldun was among the first to formalize sociological questions and to recognize the link between historical time frame and construction of society. Although his work did not ''pave the way'' for the advent of the discipline of sociology, which is typically traced to Comte in the mid–1800s, it does demonstrate that sociological thought and study did take place outside of a strictly western setting and far before the enlightenment. Ibd-Khaldun's accurate place in the history of sociology is likely in company of scholars like the Scottish moralist philosophers as early evidence of sociological style analysis taking place prior to the formalization of the discipline.

ID

The id, a term coined by **Sigmund Freud** (1856-1939), represents irrational pleasure-seeking impulses, human desires, and instincts (*thanatos* and *eros*) which are inherited from prehuman ancestors. According to Freud, the id plays a central role in the formation of the personality, (**ego**). For example, children are born with demands to be cared for but are all else beyond their own demands. Over time children learn that their needs will not be immediately gratified. Further, they learn that they must face the reality that others have expectations which they must fulfill in order to obtain gratification. For example, they learn wait to be fed at certain times. Children internalize these expectations to varying degrees. The internalized expectations form a superego (conscience). The id constantly struggles with the conscience, and the ego represents the resolution of the struggles.

Freud emphasized **stages of development** that infants and children pass through. These include the oral (sucking, biting, swallowing), anal (expelling and retaining feces), phallic (self-gratification), latency (identification with like sexed parent), and genital (sexual gratification with others). At each stage the relative control of the id (desires) and **superego** (moral and ethical side) have unique outcomes and potential pitfalls. For example, during the oral stage the id wants immediate satisfaction. If the conscience (superego) is too strong, then the person might become fixated in this stage and the conscious personality (ego) will be a person who is cold and unexpressive. If the superego is too weak, then the outcome will be an oral personality who loves to talk, eat, chew fingernails, smoke—anything using the mouth. Toilet training marks the challenge in the anal stage. If the superego (conscience) is too powerful, then the outcome is an anal personality, which is stingy and demands total control and order. An extremely anal personality might have trouble tossing clothes into a laundry hamper without folding them first. If the superego is too weak and the id wins out then the person is messy and leaves piles of things everywhere. Fortunately, most people do not suffer from **fixation** or **regression** in these stages. Most individuals pass through the five stages in the "normal" range of human activity.

IDEAL TYPE

Ideal type is an analytical construct developed in the early twentieth century by **Max Weber**. It is a conceptual representation of an intangible social phenomenon. Weber developed this concept as a tool for his comparative-historical method of social analysis. This method enabled an investigation of underlying causes for phenomena such as **capitalism** and the rapid spread of rationalization.

Weber's investigation of what caused capitalism to emerge exemplified this method. Weber examined the similarities, differences, and contexts of capitalist systems in several countries to understand the forces likely to lead to the emergence of capitalism. However, Weber needed an archetypal model of capitalism to which he could compare real life examples. This model was his ideal type.

Weber's ideal types are representations not found in reality. They are abstract embodiments of conceptual definitions. In other words, they are bridges between a precise conceptualization of a social phenomenon and the actual examples of that phenomenon, which tend to vary widely in real life. The term "ideal" implies that the type is constructed logically and contains all typical characteristics of the construct.

The ideal type is not limited to sociological literature, but can be found in everyday conversation. If two people were discussing problems with their town's public library, they would both necessarily have an idea of an "ideal" public library, or what they believe a public library is supposed to be. Weber's contribution lies in the refinement and operationalization of the concept and in his application of it in developing the comparative-historical method.

The ideal type is used as a conceptual anchor in sociological literature. Often, real examples are used as ideal types. In the 1830s, Harriet Martineau, a British political economist whose writings presaged the development of sociological method, traveled to the United States to compare the "morals and manners" of Americans to the ideal type of democracies embodied in the Declaration of Independence. More recently, Sherry Turkle, a psychologist and sociologist at the Massachusetts Institute of Technology, used the learning styles of two particular children to represent the ideal types of "soft" and "hard" mastery of computers. In her book *The Second Self*, Turkle compared other students' style of mastery to those of these children.

IDEALISM

Idealism refers to a metaphysical theory that considers the world, as perceived by human beings, to consists only of ideas. Idealism contrasts with empiricism, a world view claiming that the world is separate from the sense impressions upon the mind. Plato is often considered a proponent of idealism. While the perfect world of forms requires the premise that ideas have a real existence, Plato's ideas remained separate from human minds, forming an alternate, though perfect world. **George Berkeley** is considered the first idealist proper, in this philosophical sense. For Berkeley, a thing or quality has reality only if it is perceived, and what is perceived is a sensation. There is no separate thing in the world that has this quality, there is only our idea, or perception, of it.

Incorporating both idealist and empiricist thought, **Immanuel Kant** introduced an alternate notion of transcendental idealism. For Kant, human beings bring certain ideas about the world to their experience of it. These ideas, contained in the transcendental unity of apperception, made experience of the world coherent. Unlike Berkeley, however, Kant argued that the phenomenal world exists independent of human minds.

The term "idealism" also has a less prominent use in the field of **sociology** where it refers to the doctrine mandating explanation of social phenomena by the subjective intention of individuals. This is particularly the case in such theoretical frameworks as **rational choice theory** which studies society as the result of the intentions of individual and interacting social actors. As subjects of sociological study, individuals are considered to be fairly knowledgeable about their social situation and intend certain consequences by their actions. Such frameworks, then, emphasize on individual intentionality over the general social **structure**.

IDENTITY

Identity is an important central concern of **sociology**, especially within the subfield of social **psychology**. The work of sociologists C. H. Cooley, George Herbert Mead, and Irving Goffman is central to the study of identity. While not all social psychologists agree on its exact nature or definition, identity is generally agreed to be a social construct that refers to how the individual is perceived and labeled by the self and by **society**. The nature of the construct may be determined by group memberships, categories, social roles, physical attributes, or behaviors that determine the structural position of an individual in the social world. Identity is the most public aspect of the self and forms the basis by which the individual relates to society.

The study of identity is a primary focus in **social psychology** and the related fields sociology, psychology, clinical psychology, cultural anthropology, and **political science**. But each field approaches the study of identity differently. Sociologists and social psychologists tend to focus on the process of identity formation and identity display and the consequences for social relationships. Identity may be studied from micro (individual) or macro (societal) perspectives. Some theories use identity to link micro and macro processes. Much work in this field has attempted to define the content and meaning of identity and to use identity as a basis for understanding social behavior and social structure.

The social interactionist perspective which dominates macro approaches considers the importance of identity in interpersonal relations. General interactionist orientations consider variously the situational display and maintenance of identity; the social-structural consequences of **role** relationships; and the cultural/historical construction of identity. A second orientation that focuses on the micro-level, intrapersonal dynamics of identity is more concerned with the cognitive processes that affect the individual's behavior.

Identity formation, maintenance, and affectation constitute a negotiated process that occurs both within the self and between the individual and society. Foote argued that identification was a basis for a theory of motivation. An individual has multiple identities which are active agents in giving meaning to behavior. This idea drives identity theory, a central concept of which identity theory is that behavior choices are made available and actualized through identity processes. Identity theory, as further developed by Stryker, considers the self to be composed of a hierarchical ordering of identities. The individual is more or less likely to activate an identity in a given situation depending on the nature of the ties that bind the individual to others based on that identity. The identity that is most salient and, therefore, most likely to be adopted is the one that most strongly binds the individual to others.

The importance of identity for the individual within society is central to studies of **social stratification**, which consider structural differences based on gender, racial, class, ethnic, or other categorical divisions. These studies often focus on the implications of socially constructed identity for self-evaluation and self-efficacy.

Postmodern theory focuses on the rise of **individualism** and the consequences of greater choice for the relationship of the individual to society. Identity, in postmodern theory, is ever-changing and lacks substance and permanence. The implications for the individual's relationship to society are severe, and the subject of intense debates.

IDENTITY CRISIS

Identity crisis is a term coined by psychoanalyst Erik Erikson (1964) to describe the crisis that happens in one's self when there are conflicting or confusing identities or senses of self. It can be a state in which one feels torn about what one wants and needs, to the extent that the individual questions their entire identity and asks "who am I?" It can be a state in which one decides that the identity she has assumed is not one that she wants to continue to assume, and decides to change the nature and content of her life. Erikson felt that the identity was a **concept** on the border of **sociology** and **psychology** because it is both something that is created by the self and something given to the individual by her **culture**.

Erikson identified eight distinct periods of personality development: oral, anal, phallic, latency, genital, young **adulthood**, adulthood, maturity. He claimed that in each stage, the individual would undergo an identity crisis that would either lead to healthy or unhealthy adjustment. The eight stages also corresponded to the actual conflicts that would occur within the individual: trust vs. mistrust (infant); autonomy vs. doubt

(ages 2–3); initiative vs. guilt (ages 4–5); industry vs. inferiority (ages 6–7); identity vs. **role** confusion (ages 12–18); intimacy vs. isolation (young adult); generativity vs. self-absorption (middle age); integrity vs. despair (age 60 on). He saw the first four stages as the most important because those who are unable to resolve those conflicts tend to have problems as adults because they have not learned trust, autonomy, initiative, or industry, crucial components to successfully living in **society**.

Erikson felt that the most dramatic of the crises would occur during adolescence, when teenagers are seeking an adult identity. The crisis occurs because the individual is not yet an adult, but has not yet completely left childhood behind. They are subject to a confusing and complex combination of physical and emotional changes, increased sex drive, and increased social responsibilities. Thus, adolescents "try on" different identities and are prone to go to extremes, seeing what boundaries are solid and which can be bent in their intimate relationships, particularly with their parents. At this point, adolescents often look to their peers for emotional and behavioral guidance. This can result in the cult-like or lemming behavior evident in many groups of teenagers. Because they are unsure of themselves as individuals, they will follow the crowd, which provides a sense of safety and anonymity.

For adolescents, identity crises can be particularly problematic in the arena of sexuality. There are physical urges that are part of one's identity as an emerging sexual being, but social constraints are placed on the acceptability of certain actions, whether it be because of content (in the case of homosexuality or **bisexuality**) or of timing (being considered too young for sexual activity).

Recent research has also focused on the conflicts becoming more prevalent for educated middle- and upper-class women in industrialized countries. There are competing expectations and demands on their time and energy, which often lead to crises of identity. Many women found themselves fulfilling particular roles (i.e., get married and have children), yet would feel personally unfulfilled, being torn between what was expected of them and what they wanted. They would then question the importance or the content of several, if not all, of their social identities. Another syndrome that is associated with identity crisis is the mid-life crisis, a time in which a middle-aged person (research has focused on men) decides to change his entire life.

IDEOLOGY

The word "ideology" is usually defined in **sociology** in any one of the following three ways: a coherent body of ideas about any given subject; a worldview or way of thinking, conscious or not, characteristic of a particular social **group**; and/or, a conscious and systematically organized program of political ideas designed to explain and simplify complex social phenomena and to mobilize people politically.

The term was first used in **philosophy** in the late 1700s by Destutt de Tracy to mean the study of ideas. However, ideology soon developed a negative denotation as distorted or false ideas. **Karl Marx**, for instance, advanced the popular conception of ideology as "false consciousness," as misleading ideas based on illusions rather than scientific fact. Marx argued that false consciousness plagues those members of the working class who fail to see their common exploitation at the hands of capitalist employers, and their power to overcome that exploitation as a consciously organized class. Likewise negatively, sociologist Edward Shils argued that ideology is a more explicit and systematized type of **belief system** which is relatively closed to and sharply contrasted with opposing views, demands full agreement from its adherents, and seeks to revolutionize or separate from an existing **social order**. Shils thus associates ideology with politically radical groups and cults.

Some have argued that ideology is not limited to extremists, and indeed, that more or less conscious systems of belief which mask or distort the truth are common to all social groups, however large or small. In his best known work *Ideology and Utopia* (1929), sociologist Karl Mannheim argued for a **sociology of knowledge** which unmasks the deceptions of human interest groups, yet in the process he casts doubt on the possibility of developing an objective knowledge of **society** clearly distinguished from ideology. More recently, the philosopher **Michel Foucault**, widely read by sociologists, has gone farther in rejecting the familiar distinction between truth and ideology, arguing that all forms of knowledge privilege some ideas and "facts" over others and that this has important consequences for the exercise of legitimate power.

ILLEGITIMACY

Illegitimacy is the term used to describe the **status** of a child born out of legal wedlock. In popular use before the 1960s, this term is no longer widely used because it implies that children born out of wedlock are of inferior social status. In recent decades, there has been a greater social acceptance of out-of-wedlock births, partly due to the large and rapid increase in the number of children being born out of wedlock, in all age groups, and in most social groups.

Malinowski (1930) coined the phrase "the principle of legitimacy." According to him, childbearing within **marriage** allowed for the assignation of **fatherhood** and gave women and their children social and economic support. Sociologist K. Davis later expanded this concept by saying that marriage also connected children to a wide network of adults who would assist in their growth process. Until the 1960s, marriage was the accepted and expected norm for most people and was the social institution allowing child-bearing and parenthood. The arguments for the necessity for parenthood within marriage survived until this point, when sociologists and anthropologists began discovering cross-cultural information showing a wide variety of **norms** in childbearing and marriage patterns around the world. Goode and others argued that the norm of legitimacy was only valuable in situations or societies where wealth and/or **property** were at stake, and assigning paternity was an economic factor.

Since the 1960s, the nuclear unit of the family has become just one of many family forms, and there are many fewer

social sanctions regarding or stigma associated with premarital or out-of-wedlock births. Research shows that the majority of the population is now accepting of single parenthood. This is attributed in part to declining marriage rates among many groups, high **divorce** rates, and the increase in out-of-wedlock births to white, middle-, and upper-class women.

Research has shown that illegitimacy has never been uncommon in Western societies. The biggest change has been in the social stigma surrounding it. The only period in U.S. history when there were low rates of out-of-wedlock births was the 1940s, and this was primarily among whites. Although there are currently high and increasing rates of out-of-wedlock births in most social categories, the most prevalent are women in their teens and early twenties and black women. In 1988, over one-quarter of all U.S. births were out-of-wedlock; almost two-thirds of births to teenagers, almost one-third of births to women ages 20-24, and over ninety percent of births to teenage black women were out-of-wedlock births.

Due to the increase in out-of-wedlock births, much research has focused on the social and individual causes and consequences of illegitimacy. Some research blames the single mothers (although this type has become less prevalent and less popular), while other research focuses on the social repercussions.

Some of the most obvious risks of out-of-wedlock births are economic. Nonmarital childbearing greatly increases a woman's risk of being in poverty and going on welfare, and has even been connected to extended welfare dependency among some groups (primarily young and minority women). This is partly because women in general are less-well-off financially than are men, and many men do not fulfill their financial obligations to their biological children. Thus, women and their families take on the majority of the financial burden of raising the children. Out-of-wedlock childbearing also decreases the possibilities for educational attainment for both mothers and their children, which decreases future success possibilities. But most research also shows that it is not possible to separate the effects of **poverty** from the effects of single parenthood and, thus, is it not accurate to blame single parenthood for social problems. The effects of poverty tend to be limited access to **health care**, education, and social connections (**community**) that will help ensure success in life.

On the other hand, some researchers have shown that in some situations and environments, single-parent households are healthier and more stable than are two-parent ones. This is due to the increase in spousal and child abuse and to the high rates of divorce. Children are shown to be happier and healthier in environments where there is stability and safety, not fighting or physical or emotional abuse.

Because of the increase in single parenthood, there have been policy changes regarding funding and custody issues. Recent legislation has imposed severe penalties for men who do not fulfill their financial obligations to their biological children and many are arguing for increased funding to assist single mothers.

ILLITERACY

Illiteracy has been defined in the past as an individual's inability to read, write and make simple calculations necessary to function within society. With current technological growth and the emergence of computers and the Internet in **society** and the workforce, the definition of literacy has had to change to meet the requirements of a changing society. These changes are reflected in a recent definition of literacy used by the Workforce Investment Act of 1998: "an individual's ability to read, write, and speak in English, compute and solve problems at levels of proficiency necessary to function on the job, in the **family** of the individual, and in society."

In the past literacy was measured in terms of standard grade levels on a K-12 scale. In order to encompass recent changes and developments, another method was needed for measuring literacy. The most detailed study ever compiled on literacy was the National Adult Literacy Study (NALS) done in 1992 by the National Center for Education Statistics (NCES). This study measured literacy in three different dimensions: prose literacy, which refers to sentences and passages that define, describe, or inform (i.e. newspaper articles); document literacy, which refers to structured prose that is represented in an arranged order for the purpose of obtaining information (i.e. table of contents or graphs); and quantitative literacy, which refers to visual displays such as graphs and charts or other numerical **data** which may appear in prose or document form (i.e. arithmetic operation). In these three areas, each were given five levels of difficulty, level one was the lowest and level five was the highest people were tested and scored based on their level of performance.

The NALS found that there is a connection between literacy levels and quality of life. People who scored in the lower two levels are likely to make less than half the amount of **money** as people who scored in the three higher levels. People who score in the lower levels is more likely to use food stamps, live in **poverty**, and work fewer weeks during the year than people scoring in the higher levels. Those in the lower groups is less likely to have voted in the past five years and less likely to report having earned interest on a savings or bank account. But there are exceptions: there are people within the level one category who have a professional or managerial position and people in the higher level living in poverty.

IMPERIALISM

Imperialism is a foreign policy of economic **domination** and inevitable underdevelopment of another **territory**. It is achieved by seizing political control of a territory through military means for the purpose of acquiring raw material easily and inexpensively. Imperialism involves one government appropriating another.

In the actual process of imperialism the colony plays two roles: it supplies natural resources and buys the finished product. Peasant workers in colonies extract natural resources, like minerals, oil, cocoa, from the land, which are then sold cheaply. These raw materials are refined and made into products and merchandise the sale of which requires a market—the colony; loyal colonies provide imperialist industries with a market in which to sell their products. Furthermore, the rate of sale is determined by the industry. This process has two consequences: it leaves the colony almost exclusively reliant on the selling of raw materials for national subsistence, and it leaves the multinational industries in a lucrative position and in complete control of the process.

In social science, imperialism has generated shrewd deliberation. Economist and author of *Imperialism: A Study,* J. A. Hobson contended that while imperialism is bad business policy, non-lucrative on the national level, it served the interest of certain industries and professional classes. Additionally, imperialism was a way of staying on top of rival imperial powers.

Marxists, on the other hand, argued that imperialism was an unavoidable phase in **capitalism**. Vladimir Ilyich Lenin, author of *The Highest Stage of Capitalism* argued that imperialism was an inevitable and essential feature of modern finance capitalism. More specifically, he stated that national capitalism would eventually evolve into a global monopolistic force that would require the creation of new markets. In the early nineteenth century, Marx prophesied that the industrial middle class in imperial nations would be driven to establish a world market; that the need to constantly expand the market for products would chase the **bourgeoisie** across the globe. Moreover, for Marxists, the term imperialism and **colonialism** are synonymous; they evolve concurrently with the same goal in mind: political subordination for economic domination.

Meanwhile, D. K. Fieldhouse, in *Colonialism 1870-1945,* contended that the terms, imperialism and colonialism, are distinct and unique. Particularly, he suggested that imperialism caused colonialism. From Fieldhouse's perspective, imperialism is "the tendency of one society or state to control another, by whatever means and for whatever purpose," while colonization refers to how immigrants establish territories in the images they left behind. Fieldhouse posited that imperialism was shaped by at least five metropolis needs: 1) the need to establish naval and military bases, 2) the need to protect areas that are nationally important from rival powers, 3) the need to support European settlers, 4) the need to dictate diplomacy, and 5) the primal urge for unlimited territorial acquisitions. Further, Fieldhouse asserted, imperialism and colonization were not calculated or intended; in fact, they were "largely unplanned, and as it turns out, transit phase[s] in the evolving relationship between more and less developed parts of the world in the century after 1870."

In extreme contrast to the Leninist-Marxist perspective is the position of J.A. Schumpeter in *Imperialism as Social Atavism,* who argued that capitalism, by nature, is anti-imperialist and that economic and political expansion into foreign territory is not inherent in or necessary to capitalistic evolution. Murray Green, in *Schumpeter's Imperialism—A Critical Note,* offered important criticisms to Schumpeter's contentions. Green charged that Schumpeter "develops a very specialized definition of imperialism.... He also set up a very specialized definition of capitalism, which he then showed to be inconsistent with his definition of imperialism, thereby *proving* that capitalism is anti-imperialist.'' Last, in *Bases of a New National Imperialism*, C. J. Hayes maintained that new imperialism was a nationalist phenomenon. He asserted that individual capitalists promoted imperialism and profited from it. It has also been argued that the imperialist impulse is a moral calling to civilize native populations, a naïve notion that is often a point of criticism of European imperialism.

INCEST

Incest is sexual abuse between nuclear **family** members, between a parent and child or between siblings. It involves fondling, vaginal penetration, or oral, genital, or anal intercourse. It is often difficult to evaluate the damage because of its hidden, **taboo** nature.

     Historically, incest was permitted within some royal circles, for example, the royal families of ancient Egypt, Hawaii, and the Inca of Peru. By contrast, countries such as China and India have stringent prohibitions which may outlaw marriage between distant relatives, like sixth cousins. In the United States almost thirty states have laws that prohibit **marriage** between first cousins. In fact, all societies control **sexual behavior** through the institutions of the **family and religion**. Regulations governing marriage in general control sexual behavior and define the traits of acceptable sexual partners.

     Traditionally, kinship systems protect or insure the maintenance and continuance of family systems. Although kinship systems vary widely across societies, some universal taboos exist. The incest taboo is a cultural universal but what constitutes incest varies across cultures. Generally speaking, family members must choose to marry into alternative kinship systems. This principle ensures a wider gene pool and allows for economic and social unity among various members of **society**.

     Although incest occurs across social classes, it is more likely to occur at or below the **poverty** line. Any child can be a victim of incest, but a female is more likely to be victimized than a male and the most likely perpetrator of an incestuous relationship is the biological father. However, there is an increased risk for adolescent women with their step-fathers.

     Incest is more common between step-fathers and step-daughters because step-fathers may not feel the biological barrier that exists between a biological father and daughter. The step-father and step-daughter relationship do not experience the same bonding process that generally occurs among biological relatives. A Freudian explanation is that a step-daughter who feels betrayed by her mother's **remarriage** might unintentionally compete for the attention of her step-father.

     An analysis of adults who committed incest revealed some inconsistencies in their reasoning. People who commit incest nearly unanimously believe that they performed acts of **love**, yet they recognize they could not stop even when their victims told them to stop. Many defined their behavior as appropriate and fair; some described the experience as ''mutual

romantic love.'' Often times incest grew out of family play situation such as watching television, bedtime reading, backrubs, or wrestling. More than fifty percent of the perpetrators believed their victims enjoyed the abuse.

     The victims' experience contrasted with those of their perpetrators. Many blamed themselves and felt confused because of the non-verbal interactions that occur during abuse. The victims were left to fend for themselves emotionally. Some consequences of early childhood sexual abuse are sexual dysfunction, depression, suicidal tendencies, teenage pregnancy, **prostitution**, and homelessness.

INCOME DISTRIBUTION IN THE UNITED STATES

Beyond looking at the average income for members of a **society**, social scientists often look at how that income is distributed. Income inequality is one of the main indicators in describing how fairly the benefits of society are distributed. This disparity can be looked at either by comparing the distribution differences by things like **race**, gender, education level or occupation, or more broadly by looking at the overall trend in distribution.

     Generally speaking, the income distribution of the United States became more equal during the years after World War II, peaking in the late 1960s, but becoming more unequal in the 1970s and 1980s, increasing in inequality only slightly in the 1990s. The share of income received by the top fifth of families increased from 40.5% in 1968 to 47.2% in 1997, while that of the lowest fifth fell from 5.6% to 4.2%. Of the top 5%, the shift is even more dramatic, increasing from 15.6%, to 21.7% over that same period, meaning that most of the shift in wealth went to this small group of very wealthy households.

     In comparative perspective, the United States ranks as one of the more unequal developed nations in terms of income distribution. Many other nations have not experience the increase in inequality that the United States has had over the past thirty years. Although international **data** are often not easily available and not entirely comparable, some conclusions can be drawn. For example, during the 1980s, the **ratio** of the highest-paid full-time employees to the lowest was 50% higher in the United States than the next nearest country. Among all workers, the annual rate of increase in this measure of inequality was growing at nearly twice the rate of other countries.

     Income inequality among racial groups has also persisted, with white and Asian **American families** holding a substantial income advantage over African American and Latino families. Additionally, differences within racial and ethnic groups have increased over the last thirty years in levels of inequality, particularly among Latinos. While income differences between men and women have generally decreased over the last generation, inequalities still remain. Much of this is related to barriers to women's participation in the paid workforce, although stratification still persists among those working full time outside the home. In 1997 full-time working women

Money Income of Households—Percent Distribution, by Income Level, Race, and Hispanic Origin, in Constant (1997) Dollars: 1970 to 1997

[Constant dollars based on CPI-U-X1 deflator. Households as of **March** of **following year.** Based on Current Population Survey]

Year	Number of house-holds (1,000)	Percent distribution							Median income (dollars)
		Under $10,000	$10,000-$14,999	$15,000-$24,999	$25,000-$34,999	$35,000-$49,999	$50,000-$74,999	$75,000 and over	
ALL HOUSEHOLDS [1]									
1970	64,778	13.4	7.5	15.1	16.1	21.1	17.7	9.0	33,942
1975	72,867	12.6	8.7	15.9	15.3	19.4	18.3	9.9	33,699
1980	82,368	12.4	8.2	15.8	14.0	19.2	18.4	12.0	34,538
1985	88,458	12.3	8.2	15.1	14.1	17.9	17.9	14.4	35,229
1990	94,312	11.6	7.9	14.8	13.8	17.7	18.2	16.0	36,770
1995	99,627	11.4	8.4	15.3	14.0	16.7	17.7	16.5	35,887
1996	101,018	11.5	8.4	15.1	13.6	16.1	18.2	17.1	36,306
1997	102,528	11.0	8.1	14.9	13.3	16.3	18.1	18.4	37,005
WHITE									
1970	57,575	12.2	7.0	14.5	16.1	21.8	18.6	9.7	35,353
1975	64,392	11.2	8.2	15.6	15.2	20.0	19.3	10.6	35,241
1980	71,872	10.8	7.7	15.4	14.1	19.7	19.4	12.8	36,437
1985	76,576	10.7	7.8	14.8	14.1	18.4	18.8	15.5	37,154
1990	80,968	9.8	7.5	14.6	14.0	18.1	19.1	17.0	38,352
1995	84,511	9.8	8.0	15.1	14.0	17.0	18.5	17.7	37,667
1996	85,059	9.8	8.0	14.9	13.7	16.4	19.0	18.1	38,014
1997	86,106	9.5	7.8	14.6	13.2	16.5	18.8	19.7	38,972
BLACK									
1970	6,180	24.3	12.2	20.9	15.8	14.5	9.2	3.0	21,518
1975	7,489	24.6	13.5	18.8	15.9	14.3	9.8	3.2	21,156
1980	8,847	25.3	12.8	19.2	13.3	14.7	10.5	4.2	20,992
1985	9,797	25.2	11.9	18.3	13.6	14.1	11.1	5.6	22,105
1990	10,671	25.8	11.3	16.5	13.0	15.0	11.5	6.9	22,934
1995	11,577	22.8	11.3	18.0	14.3	14.6	11.9	7.2	23,583
1996	12,109	22.6	11.5	17.6	13.9	14.1	12.6	7.8	24,021
1997	12,474	21.4	10.5	17.9	14.2	14.9	13.1	7.9	25,050
HISPANIC [2]									
1975	2,948	16.5	11.2	21.8	17.2	18.7	10.8	3.8	25,317
1980	3,906	16.1	10.5	20.2	16.5	17.1	13.6	6.0	26,622
1985	5,213	17.3	12.1	18.6	15.3	16.9	12.7	7.1	26,051
1990	6,220	16.2	11.5	18.5	15.7	17.1	12.9	8.1	27,421
1995	7,939	18.8	11.9	21.0	15.2	14.1	12.1	6.9	24,075
1996	8,225	16.7	12.0	20.8	14.9	15.0	12.5	8.1	25,477
1997	8,590	16.8	10.7	19.7	15.0	16.6	12.2	9.1	26,628

[1] Includes other races not shown separately. [2] Persons of Hispanic origin may be of any race. Income data for Hispanic origin households are not available prior to 1972.

still earned only 74 cents for each dollar of men of the same education level. Stratification among different levels of education is an area that has shown one of the greatest levels of increase over the last thirty years. The **median** income for an individual with a college education is almost double that of an individual with a high school diploma; in 1963, the college advantage was only 33%. In constant dollars, the income of the college educated has increased, while those with a high school diploma or less has actually decreased.

The most common measure of inequality is the Gini index, developed by Italian economist Corrado Gini in 1912. **Values** for a Gini coefficient range from 0, when every family or household has the same income, to 1, where one family or household has all of the income. The Gini coefficient for the United States in 1997 was .412, while in 1965 it was .356.

While a Gini coefficient does provide an overall picture of a distribution, it does not distinguish between shifts at the top and at the bottom, and it is heavily weighted towards shifts in the middle. Other measures commonly used include the Theil Entropy Index, Atkinson's Measure, and the ratio of the earnings of the top 10% to those in the bottom 10%.

The most reliable data on inequality trends in the United States comes from the Census Bureau, which has been studying the distribution of income only since 1947. Data from before the first half of the twentieth century is usually gathered from examinations of old tax returns, but only the very wealthy were required to pay income taxes, and that data starts only in the 1920's. Sociologists looking back further usually attempt to sample such data as wills and other probate documents, but the evidence is incomplete at best and often is better at suggesting wealth inequality than income inequality.

The sociological examination of income inequality roughly parallels the development of measurable data. While reformers have long decried the concentration of wealth in America, particularly during the Progressive Era, rigorous scientific examination of the field began in the post World War II period, most significantly with the work of Simon Kuznets. His prediction, referred to as the Kuznets' curve, was that as societies became more advanced and industrial inequality would increase, until a certain stage of development was reached. After that, inequality would begin to reverse and decrease. Inequality in the United States, however, has not followed this pattern for the last thirty years.

Sociologists and other social scientists have posited a number of explanations for the recent rise in inequality, looking primarily at structural changes in the United States and global economy, along with government policies that also served to exacerbate the trend. One central structural component which many authors have cited is the trend toward a service economy, where high-wage, manufacturing jobs are being shifted overseas, while service economy jobs grow. These jobs generally pay low wages but high wages for a small number of technically skilled positions. Additionally, union membership, a traditional way to enter the middle-class, has decreased. Others have pointed to shifts away from a progressive income tax in the s and attacks on welfare in the 1990s, which increased post-tax and transfer income. Finally, others have looked at the U.S. government's monetary policies that tend to favor the lenders (those at the top end of the income distribution) over borrowers.

Examining income inequality is important for social scientists for a number of reasons. First, it is a measure of other kinds of inequalities in a society, as **health care** and other **quality of life** determinants are generally being distributed in a similar manner. Second, the income structure of a society reveals much about the other institutions in the society, particularly to what extent a government exacerbates or ameliorates existing inequalities. Finally, income inequality impacts many other aspects of society, shaping everything from housing patterns to politics to race relations.

INDEPENDENT VARIABLE

The independent **variable** predicts change in another variable. In quantitative research, attributes of a variable are assigned numerical values. For instance, a researcher may gather information via a survey on the **race** of respondents and assign a value to each racial category in the **data**. Then, statistical analyses can determine if another variable is correlated with race. It can predict whether change from one category of race to another throughout the sample, produces consistent change in some other **dependent variable**.

Imagine a grid with race on the horizontal axis and income on the vertical axis. Race is measured using three categories numbered 1 through 3 (1=Black, 2=White, 3=All Others), and income is measured in $10,000 increments. If we plot each respondent's score on both race and income, then fit the dots on the graph with a line that represents the least overall distance from each dot to that line, the result is something called a **regression** line. Following this line from one racial category to the next, we can estimate the relationship between the independent and dependent variables. It tells us what happens to respondents' income when we move from one racial category to another. In other words, it represents the change in income (the dependent variable) that is due to race (the independent variable). Given the pattern estimated by the **regression line**, we can predict individuals' income based on their race.

A word of caution: the independent variable is often referred to as the "causal" variable, but this term can be misleading. On the one hand, several different types of causal relationships exist, and on the other hand, two variables can be correlated but not causally related. One variable can produce change in another but not cause that change. For instance, we may notice that fire damage increases whenever more fire trucks appear at the same location. Although we can predict fire damage (the dependent variable) by the number of fire trucks at the scene (the independent variable), one important causal variable is missing: the fire itself. We can predict fire damage with fire trucks, but they do not cause the damage.

INDIGENOUS PEOPLES

Indigenous peoples are those who originated in and continue to live in a particular environment or location. Indigenous peoples live in many places around the world; the Penans of Borneo, Malaysia, are an example of indigenous people, as are aboriginal people of Australia and the Native Americans of North America. In 1999 there were an estimated 300 million indigenous peoples worldwide.

Indigenous peoples faced various pressures as the world becomes more populated and competition for land and resources is pursued, in some cases, by non-indigenous populations. Some indigenous peoples have suffered from attempts to make them assimilate into non-indigenous **society** and have been at risk for losing their own cultural **identity**. Indigenous cultures face their own challenges as they attempt to keep their traditions. Often, they must also deal with the impediments of **poverty**, poor living conditions, and environmental destruction.

In 1999 the World Health Organization (WHO) met with indigenous representatives to discuss issues of concern to indigenous populations, including deteriorating health conditions among their populations and environmental issues. WHO noted that indigenous peoples have a **life expectancy** of ten to twenty years less than the average for the rest of the world population. Indigenous infants are 1.5 to 3 times more likely to die than infants in the general population. Health issues among indigenous peoples can be aggravated by malnutrition, communicable diseases, and inadequate **health care** opportunities. Indigenous peoples are also at risk for mental illness and problems of drug or alcohol abuse, according to WHO, since these populations are often forced to coexist in a world with values very different then those of their tradition. Indigenous peoples also face environmental pressures that often involve natural resources in the locale of these populations. The Penans of Malaysia, for example, faced pressure from loggers in the 1990s. Penans considered the forests essential to their tribal life and defended the resource nonviolently, going as far as putting up barriers to stop loggers. Penans have also faced the pressure of cultural assimilation, and some tribal groups have converted to **Christianity**. The numbers of Penans dwindled from 15,000 in the 1970s to about 500 at the beginning of the 1990s. One Penan member said of his continued efforts to block logging: "If we die, we die in the forest. There is no other place for us to go." Many indigenous groups struggle with land management issues today. At the 1999 meeting between WHO and indigenous representatives, a Cree leader advocated for more control over **health care systems** and natural resource management at the local level.

In 1984 the Center for World Indigenous Studies was formed by indigenous activists and leaders from around the world. The center serves as an information clearinghouse for resources on indigenous nations.

INDIVIDUALISM

Individualism has taken on a variety of different meanings within and beyond **sociology**. Methodological individualism, generally associated with the work of **Max Weber** and Karl Popper, is the notion that sociological explanations must ultimately refer to individual persons and their reasons and motives. From this point of view, explanations that rely on concepts such as capitalism, bureaucracy, the state, or **society** are at best incomplete; such abstract concepts must be thought of as a kind of shorthand that ultimately refer to individual persons.

More generally, individualism refers to a variety of doctrines that stress the individual's self-consciousness, **autonomy** and self-determination, self-interest, and/or creative self-expression. What all of these perspectives share is the primacy they grant to the individual, who is often seen as existing prior to and in opposition to society. In contrast, sociologists have generally sought to show how the individual and individualism are social products. For some sociologists, this means examining individualism as the product of historical and structural

Indigenous peoples, such as this Papua New Guinean man, are those who originated and continue to live in a particular environment or location *(Corbis Corporation [Bellevue])*.

changes at the macrolevel. **Karl Marx**, for example, saw individualism as a product of modern civil society, the historical result of the dissolution of **feudalism** and the development of new productive forces. "Human beings become individuals only through the process of history," Marx concluded, and "exchange itself is a chief means of this individuation." Yet capitalist development gives rise to a distorted and alienated form of individuality, according to Marx, in which "the various forms of social connectedness" confront the individual as an alien and hostile force. In contrast, he sees socialism as allowing for a more genuine flourishing of individuality.

Émile Durkheim also saw individualism as a social product: "Collective life did not arise from individual life; on the contrary, it is the latter that emerged from the former." Like Marx, Durkheim saw individualism as a modern phenomenon, but he traced it to the increasing division of labor in society and the growing complexity and interdependence that result. Also like Marx, Durkheim distinguished between a distorted and a more genuine form of individualism. The former gives primacy to individual self-interest, whereas the latter involves "the glorification not of the self but of the individual in general." The sacredness of the individual thus serves to check and constrain self-interest in important ways.

Georg Simmel and Alexis de Tocqueville provided similar accounts of individualism as a modern product of historical and structural changes. For Simmel, individuality emerges as the result of a shift from concentric group affiliations to intersecting or overlapping group affiliations. Because no one stands at precisely the same intersection of group affiliations as others, individuals become increasingly unique. Tocqueville conceptualized this shift in terms of a transition from aristocracy to democracy. "Aristocracy had made a chain of all the members of the community," he noted, but "democracy breaks that chain and severs every link of it." As a result, each member of the community tends "to draw apart with his family and friends, so that after he has thus formed a little circle of his own, he willingly leaves society at large to itself." While Simmel shared the ambivalence of Marx and Durkheim to individualism, Tocqueville laid greater stress on its negative implications, particularly the threat it poses to political liberty. More recent investigations of individualism in American life by Robert Bellah and others have underscored Tocqueville's concerns.

Other sociologists have sought to understand individualism as the product of microlevel face-to-face interaction rather than structural changes at the macrolevel. Erving Goffman, for instance, while sharing Durkheim's notion of the sacredness of the individual, suggested that such sacredness is enacted by the performance of seemingly trivial rituals such as respecting the personal space of others or conveying appropriate salutations, compliments, and apologies. The individual self, Goffman concluded, is a "dramatic effect"; its possessor "merely provide[s] the peg on which something of a collaborative manufacture will be hung for a time." Similarly, George Herbert Mead suggested that the individual self is "something which has a development; it is not initially there at birth but arises in the process of social experience and activity." For Mead, individual self-consciousness can only emerge when one is able to take the role of the other and see oneself from this perspective. Language, in his view, is the essential means through which this is accomplished.

Inductive Logic

Inductive logic makes generalizations from particular circumstances. Conducting inductive research involves generating a theory from data gathered in a particular setting. Information gathered through qualitative methods is more suitable to inductive logic because it allows the researcher to gather detailed information about a single phenomenon.

For example, a researcher may be interested in developing a theory as to what motivates thieves to steal. Generating

a theory requires detailed information about a group of subjects in a single setting. The researcher may decide to interview 15 to 20 thieves incarcerated in a local prison. The interviews would have to be conducted in a very unstructured manner in order to ascertain as much detail as possible. Then, when all of the interviews were complete and the information was transcribed, the researcher could begin to analyze the data.

Moving from particular reasoning to general reasoning requires careful examination of data. The researcher's job is to identify general themes in the data and to construct a theory from the information gathered that could be used perhaps to explain motivation for other types of crime. The information gathered by inductive research is intrinsically useful. It provides rich and detailed information about a specific phenomenon. Additionally, once the data from several similar inductive studies have been analyzed and a general theory has been constructed, then the theory can be tested deductively in subsequent studies.

Industrial Revolution

The Industrial Revolution refers to the period between the mid-eighteenth and mid-nineteenth centuries during which western Europe, and later the United States, changed from an agrarian, handicraft economic system to an industrial system based on mechanical manufacturing. The Industrial Revolution began in England in 1760 and was largely confined there until about 1830, after which Britain eased its restrictions on the export of machinery and skilled labor, leading to the rapid growth of industrialization in Belgium and France. By 1848, these countries had become industrial powers. Industrialization did not take hold in Germany, however, until 1870, after which the country quickly grew to outstrip Britain in steel production and to become the world leader in chemical industries. Countries in southern and eastern Europe were similarly slow to industrialize. In the United States, the Industrial Revolution began in the early 1800s with the founding of textile mills in Lowell, Massachusetts.

The Industrial Revolution, which is usually dated from 1760 to 1850, featured massive technological, economic, and social changes. Among these were the use of new basic materials for manufacture, particularly iron and steel; the use of new power sources, including coal, steam, electricity, and petroleum; new machine technologies, including the invention of the spinning jenny and the power loom, capable of mass production; the introduction of the factory system, which regulated and specialized labor; new transportation and communication systems, including railroads, steamships, automobiles, airplanes, telegraph, and radio; and the application of scientific principles to industry.

Several economic and social developments have been associated with the rapid growth of industrialization. Agricultural improvements, the use of new food crops such as the potato, and a temporary reduction in epidemic disease contributed to substantial population growth, with the populations of major European countries increasing 50 to 100 percent between 1750 and 1800. Old systems of inheritance could no longer accommodate this unprecedented growth in population. Peasants and artisans were forced to seek new types of paid labor, and merchants and landlords sought ways to support large numbers of surviving children. As a result, increased commercialization occurred in many areas. Domestic manufacturing, especially of textiles, soared, and urban craft work began to shift toward export. A basic social division between owners and workers quickly developed and established conditions leading to oligarchic control of the means of production as industrialism grew. Expanding production led to the beginning of consumerism, as rural workers used wages to buy commercially-produced goods such as clothing and urban middle-class families used discretionary income to buy luxury goods such as books.

The Industrial Revolution led to radical and often abrupt social changes. Though economic opportunity was generally expanded, the Industrial Revolution displaced many categories of workers, particularly handloom weavers. Many resisted mechanization of their crafts; the Luddite movement (1811-1813) incited bands of displaced workers to riot and destroy textile machinery in the areas around Nottingham, Yorkshire, Lancashire, Derbyshire, and Leicestershire. The Luddites were brutally suppressed by the Liverpool government; many members were hanged or exported after a mass trial at York in 1813. In addition to threatening traditional jobs, the Industrial Revolution created conditions that made laborers vulnerable to changing economic cycles. As rural jobs declined and populations continued to increase, workers streamed into cities to find employment. Within a few decades, manufacturing centers such as Manchester expanded from small villages to major cities, with populations in the hundreds of thousands. Rapid urban growth created many problems; insufficient housing and lack of sanitation created crowding, slum conditions, and health hazards. The factories to which new laborers came profoundly altered the conditions of production. Under the domestic manufacturing system, workers produced goods at home during self-controlled hours. The factory system, however, regulated labor at a central site and during particular hours. It also controlled the worker's time during the workday and led to increased specialization of tasks, conditions which many workers resented and which **Karl Marx**, in *Das Kapital* (1867), later associated with **alienation** of labor. In addition, factories exposed workers to many dangers from heavy machinery, and contributed, especially by burning vast amounts of soft coal, to widespread pollution and its attendant public health problems.

The factory system, however, significantly increased productivity. Efficient mass production made goods, especially cotton clothing and household items, affordable to large numbers of consumers and helped create new domestic and overseas markets. To distribute larger amounts of manufactured goods, commercial patterns changed. Shops increased in number and size, often replacing itinerant peddlers in small towns and villages, and in 1830, the first modern department store opened in Paris. Large-scale transportation projects, including canals railways, facilitated the efficient movement of

The Industrial Revolution took shape in the United States with the founding of textile mills in Lowell, Massachusetts, in the early 1800s (Corbis Corporation [Bellevue]).

both raw materials and finished products, further streamlining distribution of goods to distant markets. Rapid industrialization also required the accumulation of substantial capital to pay for new machines, facilities, and production methods. Though most firms remained relatively small, the need to raise money through partnerships, bank loans, or joint-stock ventures led to an expansion of the business unit.

Despite the massive social and economic upheavals that resulted from the Industrial Revolution, some relatively traditional economic sectors survived and even prospered. Urban growth, though extreme, had not entirely depopulated rural areas; by 1850, half of the British population lived in urban areas, and cities employed as many craft producers as factory workers. New demands for housing construction and food production provided expanded opportunities for workers in those fields. At the same time, industrialization produced new tools, such as scythes and seed drills for planting, that increased production in agriculture and some trades. New economic sectors, however, saw the most significant expansion.

By the late nineteenth and twentieth centuries, much of Europe and the United States were heavily industrialized, leading to a new period of economic and technological expansion that included electric power, chemicals and synthetic products, telecommunications, and automation. Some analysts refer to this development as the second Industrial Revolution.

INDUSTRIAL SOCIOLOGY

The roots of industrial **sociology** can be traced back to the writings of **Karl Marx** which explain the concept that all social **structure** and interaction are based ultimately on economic issues and the class structure that developed through economic forces, provided the framework for the expansion of what has become known as industrial sociology. While many sociologists have expanded upon theory founded on economic processes, **Thorstein Veblen** (1857–1929) contributed most directly to what has become known within the discipline as industrial sociology. Veblen departed from some doctrines of classical economic theory developed by Marx, dissecting those doctrines in light of how **society** had actually evolved. According to Veblen, society had become what it was not due only to forces as simple and easily understood as an economically-based classed system such as Marx had envisioned. Instead, Veblen visualized society as having evolved through continuous processes of adaptation. As industrial society developed, new means of **adaptation** had become available, and would continue to become available and society would continually utilize the new economic means to accomplish the desired economic ends or results.

Marx had based much of his economic theory on the precept that there were finite limits to the capabilities of production. The limitations Marx envisioned arose through exhaustion of natural resources, as well as technological limitations that would simply preclude further industrial development and progress. Veblen, on the other hand, based his new industrial theory on the concept that human evolution involved, above all, virtually inexhaustible invention of new and ever more effective technologies. Those technologies would allow society to adapt to its changing environment. As envisioned by Veblen, as society exhausts one resource, technological advances assure the ability of society to successfully substitute other resources in its place.

Such successful adaptation and exploitation would obviously affect the habits, customs, and thought processes within society, thus encouraging gradual changes in the institutions and social overall structure. The institutions that fulfilled the needs of the evolving society would dominate. Those that no longer served critical needs would gradually wither away. And all of the change, adaptation, and evolution envisioned by Veblen would be based on technological development.

Expanding on his notions of industrial evolution, Veblen applied his theory to modern capitalist society, in the process utilizing some of Marx's notions of class structure. Veblen reasoned that for this industrially structured social system to advance, social thought and process would ultimately be divided into two factions based on an individual's position within the social structure. The first faction would consist of those involved in the development and management of money resources. That faction would develop social thoughts and processes that were somewhat primitive in nature, focusing more on the survival of the economic system and processes than on the rational and logical care of the individuals within the society. The second faction would actually be employed and physically involved in the industrial process. As a result of their closer involvement in the industrial process, Veblen theorized they would be inclined to think in terms he considered to be more rational. And, in the rapidly industrializing and technologically evolving society, their thought processes would ultimately prevail, issues of **rationality** and pragmatism outweighing those of economic survival in mechanically structured and orderly modern industrial society. Explained simply, Veblen viewed the first faction as predators. It was his belief that the rational and organized thought processes of the second faction, which were based on modern industrial technology and progress, would ultimately prevail over the predatory beliefs of the first faction.

In the course of the industrial and technological advancement Veblen envisioned there would be numerous stages of evolution. Veblen viewed the early twentieth century's world's changing social structure as evolutionary and thus as evidence of the validity of his theory. He readily identified the western industrial powers, such as Germany, England and the United States, as societies crucial to the industrial evolutionary process. Caught up in the ongoing transition from agrarian to industrial **domination**, those societies provided sound examples of the industrial evolutionary process. Looking further abroad, though, Veblen identified non-industrialized societies, such as Japan at the turn of the century, as being excellent prospects of proof of the validity of his theory. Japan, emerging from a feudal social structure and entering the company of industrialized western nations, would provide an easily observed society as it proceeded through his evolutionary stages of industrial social development.

Today, many sociologists view Veblen's industrial evolutionary stages as simplistic. But his fundamental concept of industrial sociology, that of continuous and virtually inexhaustible industrial and technological advancement coupled with some of Marx' economic theory, exerts strong influence among contemporary social scientists. Many social scientists may no longer focus specifically on industrialized powers such as Germany, England, the United States, or Japan. Instead, their attention may be directed toward societies emerging industrially in Africa, Asia, and South America. Veblen's fundamental concepts of industrial sociology provide social scientists with a sound basis for study as well as the development of **social policy** intended to promote stable and progressive industrial development.

INFANT AND CHILD MORTALITY

The infant mortality rate is the number of deaths of infants under age one per 1,000 live births in a given year. The crude death rate is recorded as the number of deaths per 1,000 in a population. The child mortality rate is an age-specific calculation of the crude death rate. Infant mortality rates in industrialized nations can be as low as five per 1,000. In many developing countries; however, the number can rise higher than 180 deaths per 1,000. Infant and child mortality rates can be calculated for different racial and ethnic groups, people of different social classes, and across different populations and societies. This information can help researchers make generalizations about **quality of life** and survival of members of particular populations, classes, or ethnicities.

The infant mortality rate in the United States is about 6 per 1,000. These rates, however, vary greatly by **race**. African Americans have an infant mortality that is more than twice the rate for Caucasian Americans with 14 per 1,000. African Americans in the United States also have a **poverty** rate that is two and a half times that of Caucasian Americans. Other

Infant Deaths and Infant Mortality Rates, by Cause of Death: 1990 to 1997

[Excludes deaths of nonresidents of the United States. Deaths classified according to ninth revision of *International Classification of Diseases*]

Cause of death	Number			Percent distribution			Infant mortality rate [1]		
	1990	1995	1997	1990	1995	1997	1990	1995	1997
Total....................	38,351	29,583	27,692	100	100	97	9.2	7.6	7.1
Congenital anomalies................	8,239	6,554	6,063	21	22	21	2.0	1.7	1.6
Disorders relating to short gestation and unspecified low birth weight.......	4,013	3,933	3,727	10	13	13	1.0	1.0	1.0
Sudden infant death syndrome.........	5,417	3,397	2,705	14	11	9	1.3	0.9	0.7
Respiratory distress syndrome.........	2,850	1,454	1,262	7	5	4	0.7	0.4	0.3
Newborn affected by maternal complications of pregnancy..........	1,655	1,309	1,242	4	4	4	0.4	0.3	0.3
Newborn affected by complications of placenta, cord, and membranes.......	975	962	927	3	3	3	0.2	(NA)	0.2
Accidents and adverse effects..........	930	787	753	2	3	3	0.2	(NA)	0.2
Infections specific to the perinatal period..	875	788	756	2	3	3	0.2	(NA)	0.2
Pneumonia and influenza.............	634	492	397	2	2	1	0.2	(NA)	0.1
Intrauterine hypoxia and birth asphyxia...	762	475	456	2	2	2	0.2	(NA)	0.1
All other causes....................	12,001	9,432	9,404	31	32	33	2.9	(NA)	2.4

NA Not available.   [1] Deaths of infants under 1 year old per 1,000 live births.

Source of Tables 133-135: U.S. National Center for Health Statistics, *Vital Statistics of the United States*, annual; *National Vital Statistics Reports (NVSR)* (formerly *Monthly Vital Statistics Report);* and unpublished data.

countries show similar statistics. Frequently one racial or ethnic **group** holds a higher infant and child mortality rate. The reason for this fact becomes clear when incomes of the different racial groups are compared. Among groups with higher rates, the common factor is poverty rather than race. Stated another way, income level is a better predictor of infant and child mortality rates than race.

Poverty can affect mortality rates in children and infants in many ways. Lack of prenatal care is the most prominent cause of high infant and child mortality rates, but other factors contribute. Using drugs during pregnancy, drinking, smoking, and poor maternal diet are other causes of higher infant mortality. Generally, individuals who do not get adequate prenatal care are from poorer families. These individuals may not be as educated about the dangers of smoking, drinking, and using other drugs during pregnancy. These individuals have less access to medical care and may not know what foods to eat to keep the fetus healthy.

Child mortality and, more specifically, infant mortality rates are good indicators of a population's health, as well as the effectiveness of social welfare and health care systems. Infant mortality rates can indicate the level of prenatal care, childbirth procedures, and maternal and postnatal care. Infant mortality is linked to the absence or lack of access to these supports. The poor and people of certain races and ethnicities tend to have less access to health facilities and, thus, have a higher infant mortality rate. Consequently, poorer, underdeveloped nations have higher mortality rates. Per 1,000 live births, the average infant mortality rate for less developed countries is 66; the child mortality (under five years old) rate stands at 38. In

the more developed countries the infant mortality rate is 11, and the child mortality rate is 2.

In India and China, infant and child mortality rates are affected by cultural biases against female children. Male children are a commodity while female children are considered a liability. At the time of their daughters' marriages, parents of the bride must pay a dowry to the groom's family. The bride is then sent to live with her new husband's family. When sons marry, they bring their brides into the **household**, and the family receives money from the new wife's dowry. Moreover, females cannot perform certain religious rites and cannot possess **property**. If property is left to the daughter, when she marries, the property is taken over by her husband's family. Because of these and other social **rules**, male children are favored over female children, and female infant and child mortality rates are higher than that of male children. In these societies, infant and child deaths are directly or indirectly attributed to the parents. Parents may kill female children, choose abortion if the sex is determined prenatally, deny females or starve them. In these countries the mortality rate is linked to poverty and to sex **discrimination**. While infant and child mortality rates remain fairly high in poorer, underdeveloped countries, through greater education and improved health practices, these rates have steadily fallen in the United States.

INFERENTIAL STATISTICS

Inferential statistics use laws of **probability** to make inferences about a population based on information gleaned from a sample. Such statistics are particularly useful given the unlikely occurrence that a researcher has access to an entire population. The population is the larger group of interest from which a sample is drawn. For example, if we wanted to study education levels among women incarcerated in state prisons, all female state prisoners comprise the population. Studying all the women would be time consuming and expensive. Instead, the researcher could randomly choose a sample of one hundred women from this group and use inferential statistics to suggest results to the entire population. There are always some differences between the characteristics of a sample and the characteristics of a population simply because of natural variation, referred to as **sampling error** which is always estimated in inferential statistics.

An important part of inferential statistics is the estimation of population parameters from sample statistics. In doing this, the researcher should state how confident he or she is that the parameter will fall close to the statistic. Confidence is expressed as a confidence interval or a range of values within which the parameter is expected to lie. Confidence criteria are fixed and are based on the **normal distribution**. When calculating a mean for a sample, the researcher can always be 68 percent confident that the population **mean** will fall between -1 and +1 standard errors from the sample mean. If a researcher wants to be more confident in his or her results, the interval widens. Ninety-five percent confidence requires that the population mean will lie between -1.96 and +1.96 standard errors from the sample mean, and 99 percentconfidence widens the interval further to between -2.58 and +2.58 standard errors from the sample mean.

The most basic inferential statistics are based on the normal distribution and involve calculation of z scores. Scores are first converted to z scores and then are compared to the normal distribution. A researcher then uses confidence intervals to provide a range of the sample statistics within which he or she can be confident that the population parameter will fall. This confidence is stated along with the possible margin of error. Other inferential statistics are t- tests, ANOVA, Chi-square, F-tests, and **regression** analysis.

INFLUENCE

Influence is an aspect of social **psychology** that centers on the ability of one individual (the source) to affect a change in the behavior, beliefs, attitudes, or opinions of another individual (the target), or to convince the target to perform an act that, under normal circumstances, the target would typically not perform. Various types of influence are present in daily life in the forms of media advertisement, social activism, and through the words of local and national opinion leaders.

Two general types of influence permeate social situations, open or blatant influence and closed or manipulative influence. Open influence involves attempts to alter an individuals' behavior or beliefs in which the targets are very much aware that they are being enticed by the source. Open influence typically involves the source attempting to use of

some form of power over the target. The power can take the form of a message from a trustworthy source (a famous athlete endorsing a brand of athletic shoes), threats and promises from the source designed to offer punishment and/or reward for a change in the target's behavior, or from directives and orders from the source to the target. Also, if the source is aware that the target has some level of knowledge or involvement with the topic of the attempted influence, the source may choose to incorporate discussion of topical information in the message. In this situation, the open influence is not based on power over the target but on knowledge held by the source, which the target may be interested to know. Here trustworthy sources may also be used but threats and directives are ineffective.

Manipulative influence eschews the directness of open influence in favor of a more covert approach in which the attempt to modify the target's behavior or attitudes is disguised as some other form of social **interaction** designed to activate other emotional responses toward the source which will in turn increase the influence the source holds over the target. Among the more common of these tactics are to ingratiate (flatter), altercast (cause guilt), and manage appearances (attract). Manipulative influence, though more common in everyday interactions than open influence, often goes unnoticed or misidentified.

INFORMAL ECONOMY

Informal economic activity is referred to by many familiar terms including "moonlighting," "working off the books," "fiddly work," and "working for cash." The informal economy refers to the production and distribution of licit goods and services outside the state- regulated economy (e.g., the formal economy). Informal modes of production and distribution circumvent state regulation including taxation, licensing, zoning ordinances, immigration status of employees, etc. Informal economic activity is, in a sense, hidden economic productivity within a country because it is usually not counted in government ledgers. Employment within the informal economy is not subject to the regulations of state. Informal work arrangements tend to be temporary, and the workers are often paid in cash. Informal workers usually do not receive the benefits available in the formal economy to employees, including paid-sick leave, maternity leave, or vacation time.

The informal economy includes a wide range of activities and products. A moonlighting electrician may do a job for a neighbor and request to be paid in cash. A farmer may sell surplus vegetables alongside the road for pocket money. Recent immigrants may work "under the table" for a business because they lack proper state required documentation to work in the formal economy. A woman may sew garments at home for a subcontractor. All of these activities involve compensated productive activity that occurs outside the regulated, or formal, economy.

The concept of the informal economy first gained attention in the early 1970s. Researchers at the International Labor Office and Keith Hart, a sociologist, studied the developing economies of several African countries, including Ghana and Kenya. The studies revealed that many entrepreneurial activities occurring within the developing countries fell outside the boundaries of the state-sanctioned economy. The studies discovered that a lot of waged work within Ghana and other developing nations occurred outside state-sanctioned businesses and firms. The International Labor Office and Hart theorized that this economic activity occurring outside the formal economy was not simply a leftover of pre-modern modes of production that would disappear as economic development progresses, but that the informal economy was a vital and productive sector that had been overlooked by both government agencies and theories of development. The concept of the informal economy quickly gained attention. Today, many international agencies recognize and examine the informal economic activities of developing nations. In the early 1980s, Louis and Patricia Ferman, sociologists, were the first to extend this concept to advanced economies by examining the informal activity among the urban poor in the United States.

Researchers, including sociologists and economists, have found that informal economy activities are vital parts of all economic systems. The informal economy is a universal phenomenon existing under every economic and political system. The informal economy is not marginal to the production of a country or region, but rather the formal economy and the informal economy are mutually reinforcing. A formal business may rely on informal subcontracts and homework for production. An unemployed worker from the informal economy may turn to informal economy as a way to survive financially between jobs.

Since the concept gained prominence in the early 1970s, many theorists have debated over what activities constitute the informal economy. Sociologists Manuel Castells and Alejandro Portes developed a concise and influential definition. Following their definition, the informal economy includes the production and distribution of licit goods and services outside formalized regulatory structures (e.g., employment regulation, taxation, etc.). Most definitions of the informal economy distinguish informal activity from other types of productive work that also fall outside the formal economy. Unlike the informal economy, the criminal economy includes the production and distribution of illicit products (e.g., crack cocaine) and services (e.g., prostitution). The household economy includes unremunerated work within the household that is necessary for the survival of the household including childcare, cleaning, and food gathering. The communal economy includes work outside employment that occurs as part of **community** or neighborly activities (e.g., barn raisings or volunteer work for the local church).

Research on the informal economy is important because it examines the productive efforts of many groups, including women, the unemployed, and new immigrant groups, that would otherwise be overlooked. Feminists have long pointed out that policy makers and researchers have largely overlooked women's productive efforts in both the domestic and informal economies. Emphasis on the informal economy is a way to consider and highlight productive efforts that would otherwise remain invisible if only regulated forms of production and employment are considered.

INFORMAL ORGANIZATION

The term "informal organization" refers to the informal practices in which members of an **organization** engage to supplement, reorient, or subvert the practices in a formal organization. An informal organization is found within the confines of a formal organization, and there is a constant interplay between the formal organization and the informal organizations within it. Whereas a formal organization consists of a system of clearly-defined achieved statuses and formal titles based on predetermined criteria, an informal organization consists of ascribed statuses, emotion, feelings, **values**, and people's interpersonal relationships, based on personal characteristics and undefined criteria. An informal organization is the basis of cohesion within a formal organization, and without this system, a formal organization is not navigable.

Research has shown that the **rules** or interactions of an informal organization are often more powerful than those of the formal organization. It is through the communication networks of the informal organization that most information is transmitted. Thus, one important aspect of an informal organization is access to and control of information. Those who have or control information have the most power in both informal and formal organizational systems.

Informal organizations can serve several positive purposes within the formal organization: create an "esprit de corps" or increased cohesiveness between members of the organization; increase productivity; allow for personal or unique contributions in a closed system; create a personal atmosphere in an otherwise impersonal environment; reduce the boredom and monotony in a rigid, formal system; or create a sense of **egalitarianism** in a hierarchical system. They can, however, also have negative consequences: undermining of authority of formal system which can lead to an overall breakdown of the organization or system; creating of in-groups and out-groups that leads to tension and conflict between or exclusion of certain members of the organization; or creating an uncontrolled informal hierarchical system that is destructive to individuals.

Some informal organizations are as large and complex as the Mafia. They are not organized politically but are organized around family connections and money. The organization is dependent on personal relationships and interactions, and can appear nepotistic. However, other informal organizations can be as small and as simple as the relationships between workers in a small deli. Larger informal organizations can offer a threat to the broader system in which it operates, whereas small ones can add to the productivity and cohesiveness of the larger system.

INFORMATION SOCIETY

The information **society** is a theoretical construct representing a stage of societal development where the growing use of computer technology and digital telecommunications (hereafter referred to collectively as information technology) has become central in shaping development and social change. The concept entered sociological **discourse** in the United States during the 1970s and became most prominent in the 1980s as **information technology** began to proliferate at a global level. Central to the construct is the notion that developed nations are undergoing a period of social transition to information societies. A number of different interpretations of the information society construct vary on the key dimensions of **social change** underlying the social transition, and the implications of these changes. However, at a broad level, one dimension of social change common to all these interpretations was that the growing development and use of information technology was becoming central in shaping development and social change within developed nations.

Another dimension of change specified by some advocates of the concept was the shift from an industrial economy driven by the manufacture of goods to one based on information and knowledge industries as the focal point of economic growth. This dimension was based on several studies indicating that an increasing percentage of Gross National Product in the U.S. economy was accounted for by industries engaged in the production, processing, or selling of information-related goods and services, and the informational activities of both government and private sector bureaucracies. A third dimension of change was a shift of the **labor force** into occupations primarily engaged in the production, processing and distribution of information and knowledge. This aspect was based on studies of **employment** in the U.S. economy which indicated a declining proportion of the labor force employed in occupations engaged in the manufacture of goods and an increasing proportion of the labor force employed in occupations concerned with information and knowledge production, processing, or transfer.

A fourth dimension of social change was the growing importance of information technology in transforming work and other social activities. Applications of information technologies have been developed for labor processes across all sectors of the economy. These applications have the potential of transforming labor processes, either through the replacement of human labor or through necessitating the development of new, advanced skills by affected workers. Some advocates of the information society construct presented visions that were utopian in nature. They contended that information technology had to potential to free humans from the drudgery of many menial and subsistence jobs. Through being able to access on-line education and databases, workers could continually up-grade their skills, re-educate themselves, and heighten their self-potential. True participatory **democracy** could be attained by wiring all homes with digital technology and allowing citizens to participate on-line in the political process. New types of on-line communities could be created as humans increasingly interact and establish relationships via information technology.

Advocates of Marxist **theory** assailed these ideas as being obviated of concern with the underlying social relations of the economy. While information and knowledge-intensive industries may provide the key sources of economic growth and the majority of the labor force may be engaged in the pro-

duction and distribution of knowledge and information, these changes are occurring within the context of capitalist market economies and are influenced by the dynamics of capitalist development. In effect, advocates of the information society failed to distinguish between changes in the forces of production (the shift to production based on information technology) and the social relations of production (**capitalism**). Therefore, the rapid development of information technology was driven by the desire of the capitalist class to develop new avenues for the accumulation of wealth and by the need to increase labor productivity and gain greater control over the working class through the application of information technology to labor processes. Two primary critical perspectives of the information society were developed. On the one hand, it was contended that the growing use and importance of information technology only represented an extension of industrial capitalism. Like earlier production technologies, the key role of information technology would be to increase labor productivity through the further automation and deskilling of labor processes. The second perspective was that the set of changes collectively labeled the information society represented a new stage of capitalism, where information technology had the potential of initiating major changes in the processes and dynamics of a capitalist market economy.

INFORMATION TECHNOLOGY

Information technology is dedicated to the creation, discovery, distribution, and interpretation of information. Information technology includes developments such as computers and the **Internet**, as well as the myriad of applications for these developments that allow instant **communication** of information and automated methods for finding, sorting, and analyzing information. While defining information technology is fairly straightforward, assessing its impact and role in **society** is considerably more involved.

Societies seek more efficient ways to process information. At the present time, information technology is expanding at unprecedented rates, and an increasing number of people are required to dedicate their work to information related activities in organizations throughout society. Information technology has changed the lives of individuals as well. Cell phones, E-mail, and the Internet have made communication faster and more efficient, though perhaps less personal.

While the historical impact of modern information technology has yet to be determined, many feel that the recent and rapid advances in information technology are nothing short of revolutionary. Some argue that the substantial change in the cost, availability, and quality of information brought about by recent technology advances have profoundly affected our society and economy. In modernized societies, information technology has proliferated to become an increasingly large proportion of the economy. In pre-modern societies, most of the population works to produce food. In industrial societies, technological advances increase productivity, and most people work to produce goods. Post-industrial societies emphasize services as the dominant commodity. Information technology has brought about a new type of socioeconomic era in which the majority of society works to provide information services, an **information society**.

In an information society, several types of activities regarding information occur. First, information creation requires obtaining facts and **data** and organizing them into a meaningful collection. Information distribution requires effort and equipment that convey information where it is needed. Information processing and analysis transform information to maximize its usefulness for specific situations. Information storage ensures that information will continue to be available, while information retrieval activities make it easier to find relevant information in the future.

Unlike other economic activities, information activities are not confined to a specific sector of the economy. Information activities are useful and relevant in the production, distribution, and consumption of all types of goods and services. Sometimes, information activity is indistinguishable from the production of goods and services. Someone who builds a computer is both producing a good and creating a tool to perform information activities. Someone who creates and maintains a web site may be providing a service while also distributing, storing, or retrieving information.

While some dispute that information technology is fundamentally changing society, most agree that information technology is having a significant impact on many organizations. Organizational employees often need to have skills related to the use and implementation of informational technology. Many organizations use web sites and the Internet for marketing, communication, advertising, sales, and other functions. The structure of organizations has also been influenced by information technology. With the implementation of information technology to increase the efficiency of communication, organizations can be more flexible and less centralized.

Information technology has had an impact on individuals' lives. With recent developments such as the home computer and widespread Internet access, ordinary citizens now have direct and instantaneous access to huge volumes of information. With the amount of information readily available, citizens of the information society must learn the skills to locate, obtain, process, use, and evaluate information. Because of the rapidly growing need for information related skills, educational efforts and institutions have had to make significant changes to remain effective in their goals, just one example of how developments in educational technology have spread throughout society.

Advances in information technology and the dawn of the information society have revised the basis for social class division. In industrial societies, those that control the means of production are poised to become the dominant class. In an information society, those that control the distribution of and access to information have the most influence and power.

Information technology has changed the nature of the **community**. Once geographically determined, communities today may consist of people from diverse areas of the world who have never even seen each other. E-mail and Internet chat

Information technology includes such developments as computers that allow instant communication of information and automated methods for finding, sorting, and analyzing it *(Corbis Corporation [Bellevue])*.

rooms can facilitate communities based on shared interests and ideas rather than physical proximity. However, the anonymity that information technology can provide creates opportunities for deception.

Information technology is important to **sociology** and sociologists. Its recent development that has had an undeniable effect on society, within organizations, and on the way people interact. While information technology has always been a part of human society, it has recently become an increasingly powerful force that is qualitatively changing many elements of society. The rapid development of information technology currently shows no sign of abating and information technology may have an even greater societal impact in the future.

INSTITUTE OF SOCIAL RESEARCH (FRANKFURT SCHOOL OF CRITICAL THEORY)

The Institute of Social Research, also known as the Frankfurt School of **critical theory**, was founded in 1923 in Frankfurt, Germany, by Felix Weil, a political scientist strongly committed to Marxist analysis of **society**. The institute was founded in order to revitalize and reinterpret Marxism as well as to lay the foundation for a critique of both **capitalism** and fascism. The institute moved from Germany in 1934 with the rise to power of Adolph Hitler and the Nazi Party, relocating itself in New York at Columbia University. After the fall of Hitler and the end of World War II, the institute returned to Frankfurt where it remained until 1969 when it was disbanded.

While many scholars and intellectuals are often associated with the Frankfurt School, its central and most influential figures have been: Max Horkheimer, **Theodor Adorno**, **Herbert Marcuse**, **Erich Fromm**, Walter Benjamin, Leo Lowenthal, Fredrick Pollack, and Karl Wittfogel. The individual works of these scholars covers a broad intellectual territory, and at least seven central themes emerge from their collective works: first, a revivification of the Marxist analysis of the exploitative dynamics of capitalism in a context of twentieth-century capitalism; second, the development of a critical theory that can be directly applied to cultural forms of **domination**, **ideology**, and propaganda; third, the search for both a theory and a method that can be directed towards the cultivation of reason and the emancipation of human beings from the dehumanizing influences of modern bureaucratic rationality; fourth, the investigation of human liberation in a context of the rise of politically totalitarian and fascist regimes (including the United States); fifth, a synthesis of the works of both Marx and **Sigmund Freud** which integrates theories of class-based oppression under capitalism with its effects on the repression of libidinal impulses; sixth, in the absence of the revolutionary force of the proletariat, the search for the source of a critical consciousness; and seventh, the critique of both technology and science (especially sociological positivism) as facilitating systems of cultural and intellectual domination.

Despite the consistency with which these themes appear, the Frankfurt School cannot be said to have developed a completely unified perspective. The most influential ideas to have emerged from the institute are not collective statements but are instead the prominent works of its individual members. Arguably the most significant work, Horkheimer and Adorno's collaborative piece *The Dialectic of Enlightenment* (1947) analyzes the "culture industry," that aspect of capitalism reflected in its self-conscious attempts to ideologically indoctrinate a consumer society. Adorno's influential, co-authored work *The Authoritarian Personality* (1950) studies **prejudice** and **discrimination**. In addition, the collective works of Marcuse, especially his *One Dimensional Man* (1964) which analyzes the missing negative element in dialectical criticism, have been received as an inspirational source of social criticism by counter-cultural movements. Finally, Benjamin's essay "The Work of Art in the Age of Mechanical Reproduction" (1955) has become the foundational text for the examining advertising and other forms of mass-cultural production in modern societies.

In contemporary **sociology** many ideas of the Frankfurt School have fallen into disuse. With the collapse of fascist regimes and the fall of Soviet Communism, the focus on the expansion of the Marxist project has been largely replaced by the postmodern emphasis on **multiculturalism** and postcolonial studies. However, the Frankfurt School of critical theory endures in the contemporary works of Douglas Kellner, Andrew Feenberg, and most notably Jürgen Habermas. These authors' works reflect the search for an emancipatory project, in the spirit of the Frankfurt School. Kellner emphasizes human emancipation in conditions of mass-mediated and **internet communication** systems, Feenberg focuses on the technological domination and complexity of modern societies, and Habermas explores the colonization of human communication and consciousness by the rationality of bureaucratic social systems. While interest in the Frankfurt School has waned since the 1970s, it remains an important source of inspiration for sociologists working within the traditions of critical theory.

INSTITUTION

All societies are made up of institutions, which are large-scale social structures designed to fulfill certain fundamental societal needs. Talcott Parsons identified the most basic needs of all societies. Parsons stated that societies must be able to organize the activities of their members in order to prevent chaos, strive to protect their members from internal or external threats such as **crime** and invasion, and replace members lost either through death or emigration. Societies must also be able to transmit the knowledge necessary for individuals to function properly within their **society**, motivate both new and present members to fulfill responsibilities and obligations proscribed by their **culture**, and provide formalized ways through which social conflict may be resolved.

Sociologists have identified five basic institutions that function to fulfill society's most fundamental needs: the **family**, religion, the economy, education, and the state. The more effective the institutions are at meeting society's various social needs, the more orderly that society is. Although no one institution is capable of fulfilling every social need, each institution has been constructed to meet a number of fundamental needs at once.

While the family's most basic function is to replace lost members, it also organizes the activities of new societal members, influencing their participation in other social institutions. For instance, when parents or other family members teach children the importance of church or school attendance, they encourage participation in the institutions of religion and education. Emphasizing the importance of paid work socializes societal members to play a role in the economy. Furthermore, teaching children and other family members about the significance of voting encourages their participation in the institution of the state.

Another example of a single institution meeting a number of social needs is the state, or the government. The state establishes police forces, which are designed to protect societal members from the internal threat of crime. The state's military forces protect society from external invasion. The state encourages societal members to fulfill their social responsibilities through the establishment of formal laws, while the governmental court system provides a mechanism for resolving social conflict. In a similar fashion, each of the other basic social institutions attempts to address and fulfill society's various fundamental needs. According to Parsons, the maintenance of social harmony and stability is vitally dependent upon the integrated functioning of all social institutions.

INTELLIGENCE

Intelligence is formally defined as the ability to learn, understand, and deal with new instances related to the application of knowledge, abstract thought, and the manipulation of situations. However, the definition of the term only establishes the basis for the controversy that has surrounded the study and application of intelligence and related topics such as the measurement and testing.

In 1904, Alfred Binet (1857–1911) developed a test to measure the intelligence of mentally handicapped children in hopes of determining the children's mental age. Binet believed intelligence to be an innate ability to learn that was negligibly affected by social factors. Binet's attempts to establish an intelligence quotient (IQ) were further developed and applied as a means of determining the ability of any individual to learn, master, and retain knowledge. The typical IQ test provides a **ratio** of the scores attained by an individual relative to a score of 100 which is believed to be the average. The use of IQ tests has raised considerable controversy within **sociology** based primarily on claims that intelligence may not be a solely genetic predisposition but rather a learned characteristic that may be highly affected by environmental factors. Parallel claims regarding possible cultural **bias** in the tests have thrown the use of "scientific" measures of intelligence into question.

As early IQ tests were developed with the belief that intelligence was an inborn characteristic, no consideration was given to the potential biasing of results by the inclusion of questions that may place racial, ethnic, gender, and class minorities at a disadvantage. Similarly, claims have been made that IQ tests do not measure innate intelligence but rather knowledge deemed important by the middle socio-economic classes of dominant **culture**. If this is indeed the case, then the exams do not measure intelligence but knowledge of the dominant culture. However, if intelligence is indeed solely a genetically based, in-born trait, then differences in intelligence scores between racial/ethnic minorities and white-ethnic groups, men and women, and across social classes can be attributed only to the superior intellect of the dominant groups: these patterns could subsequently be used to explain the positioning of each group in the stratification of **society**.

As the basis for intelligence has yet to be determined (and may never be), the debate surrounding what is and is not an appropriate measure of intelligence will continue with research generated to support both sides. In 1994, an elaborate work by Richard Herrnstein and Charles Murray called *The Bell Curve* reinvigorated the debate surrounding intelligence testing. Herrnstein and Murray found, through what they claimed to be highly rigorous testing, that a vast majority of intelligence differences between white subjects and subjects of varying racial and ethnic minorities were hereditary. These difference, therefore, were minimally affected by education, socio-economic differences, **socialization**, or other environmental factors. Upon further review, the work was roundly criticized for its methodologies and its results were questioned, although often not to the level of notoriety afforded the initial findings.

Another theory of intelligence developed by Howard Gardner attempted to elucidate the discussion of intelligence by taking a radically different path. Gardner saw intelligence as the ability to resolve, create, and locate problems which lays the groundwork for acquiring knowledge. Rather than diving into the continuing argument concerning the basis of intelligence, Gardner avoided this issue and instead focused on the application of various abilities across individuals. Seeing no need to further reify a concept which he believed to be poten-

tially little more than a label for some phenomena which may not even exist, Gardner wrote of six intelligences that parallel the unique abilities in which any given individual might show proficiency. The six intelligences, outlined his the work *Frames of Mind,* included linguistic, musical, logical-mathematical, spatial, bodily-kinesthetic, and personal. Gardner hesitated to refer to his constructs as "intelligences" (at the risk of further promoting the idea of a preestablished mental state) but did so, while continuing the **stress** that these processes and abilities are continuous with one another, with no single type dominating any other. Furthermore his work maintained that the search of an intelligence was useless as these features existed only as scientific constructs and not as verifiable entities. In this way, Gardner attempted to further the use of intelligence by minimizing its importance and maximizing its potential applications. Gardner's work has been met with marginal acceptance; it has spawned further research on emotional intelligence and has been applied in areas as diverse as setting elementary school curricula and the selecting of medical school applicants.

INTELLIGENCIA

The intelligencia (also spelled intelligentsia) is a stratum of society first identified by the sociologist **Karl Mannheim** (1893–1947). Interested in the **sociology** of knowledge, Mannheim believed that all knowledge and facts are biased because of learners' subjective interpretation and perspectives. Mannheim argued that sociologists and other scholars should work to consider perspectives other than their own in an effort to recognize their own biases.

Though he believed that complete objectivity was impossible, Mannheim asserted that some people could approach this objectivity by a careful process of studying and understanding diverse perspectives. He called these people the intelligencia. Though Mannheim viewed the intelligencia as an important class of people and considered them to have a superior perspective on knowledge, he did not believe that this group of intellectuals should comprise a superior social class. Mannheim felt that the intelligencia should represent other groups and classes in **society** but not mar their objectivity by becoming a part of any class or group, including the ruling class. Mannheim asserted that the task of the intelligencia was to promote the diversity of perspectives in society to increase tolerance, diversity, and freedom.

INTENTIONALITY

Intentionality refers to the **attitude** with which an action or behavior is done. An intentional action is done voluntarily and with a purpose. It is very closely linked to meaning. It refers to the notion that an action or emotion is about, for, or of something. In other words, an intentional action is deliberate and it has a specific motive. For example, given one act, a person may insult someone else either intentionally or by accident with the same action. The difference is in what the actor meant by the action. By the same token, one is seldom insulted by a child's words even when the same words would be extremely rude from another adult. That is because the child does not intend or mean the same thing as the adult even though each may use the same words. The difference is of a symbolic interpretive variety rather than a clear grammatical one. Each individual could interpret it differently.

The field of **ethnomethodology** emphasizes that intentionality does not consist only of purpose, it also involves the actor's tacit knowledge related to the action. Tacit knowledge is knowledge that the actor may not be able to express, but factors into his intentions, according the ethnomethodologists. Anthony Giddens formulated the distinction that was later adopted by ethnomethodology. Practical knowledge or practical consciousness is ''what any social actor knows,'' but does not have the ability to express. Discursive consciousness ''what actors are able to say, or give verbal expression to, about social conditions, including especially the conditions of their own action'' (Giddens 1984). For Giddens, however, discursive knowledge is not a suffficient analysis of human action. The practical consciousness plays a key role in determining action and actors may intentionally act according to both their discursive and practical knowledge of a social situation or relationship. Moreover, practical knowledge is necessary for competent action in the social world.

Intentionality remains a key concept in moral and legal issues. For example, the determination of intentionality for the action of murder drastically increases the charge and consequent penalty. Whether or not a person intended to do what he did do is a difficult determination, but has become a necessary one in making moral decisions.

INTERCULTURAL MARRIAGE

Intercultural **marriage** refers to the marital union of two people from distinct cultural groups, ethnic groups, and/or nationalities. While contact between people of similar backgrounds remains the norm, recent world trends have increased the contact between people of different cultural backgrounds. Since the mid-twentieth century, increased technology, economic globalization, and world migration have worked to bring diverse cultures together.

In the United States in particular following World War II, intercultural and international marriage increased dramatically. This trend, however, received little attention by scholars until the mid-1970s. At the turn of the century, when immigration to the United States was at its height, intercultural marriage was common among various European ethnic groups. In addition, **data** published since 1945 by the U.S. Immigration and Nationalization Service show that the average yearly immigration of European and non-European foreign spouses married to U.S. citizens has increased with each decade, almost four times as much from the 1940s to the 1980s.

Early research on intercultural marriage primarily looked at cross-national marriage, concentrating on colonial

Intercultural marriage refers to the marital union of two people from distinct cultural groups, ethnic groups, and/or nationalities *(Archive Photos, Inc.).*

and war bride marriages. For instance, many studies examined U.S. soldiers and their Asian or European war brides, as well as British soldiers and the native women they married in colonial India. Many researchers characterized these couples as socially isolated: men cut off from their families and women from nations traumatized by war. Research on cross-cultural marriage caused by recent international migration has mostly explored social and cultural adjustments of partners engaged in a marriage involving a Western and a non-Western spouse. Both partners tend to be from similarly advantaged and highly educated backgrounds, and many have had at least some contact with other cultures before marrying their spouses. Intercultural marriage between distinct ethnic groups in the United States has been explored by prominent sociologists such as Richard Alba, Milton Gordon, Andrew Greeley, and Stanley Lieberson. They looked at issues such as intermarriage rates and assimilation, as well as interfaith, interracial, and interethnic marriage within the United States.

Scholarly research in intercultural marriage may give us additional insight and understanding into the immigration process, intergroup relations, and minority group assimilation. Rates of intercultural marriage may be a unique indicator of current racial and ethnic relations. Further, with the astronomical increase in intermarriages worldwide, additional research on the families and children may aid us in understanding the

•

These firearm lobbyists—an important political interest group—confer with a U.S. House State, Veterans, and Military Affairs Committee member (AP/Wide World Photos, Inc.).

effects on children of multiple ethnic backgrounds, ethnic **identity** and **socialization**, as well as the intercultural family's influence on larger **society**.

INTEREST GROUP

Important entities in American politics, interest groups are collectivities of individuals who mobilize around an organized issue or cause that is of great concern to that group in order to influence public policy. These individuals practice what is known as contentious politics, in that they seek a change in the normative order. While many groups mobilize for change, interest groups are usually defined as those that work within the dominant political paradigm, having routinized stable ties with a **government** or government agency. These groups use traditional political tactics such as lobbying elected officials and promoting legislation. In contrast, social movement organizations (SMOs) are those collectives that engage in the politics of disruption beyond the realm of traditional political action such as voting. It may be difficult at times to distinguish SMOs and interest groups since their tactics can overlap.

Institutionalized interest groups usually have identifiable leaders, tactics, and goals, and theorists commonly do not distinguish between the interest group and the representative **organization**. Laborers, environmentalists, women, and farm workers are all examples of interest groups. Some organizations that represent their interests are the AFL-CIO, the Sierra Club, the National Organization for Women (NOW), and the United Farm Workers (UFW), respectively.

Mancur Olsen noted that the "free rider problem" may prevent groups from acting in their interests in the absence of coercion or selective incentives. When the achievements of an interest group would benefit every member of the group equally (a collective good), regardless of an individual's contribution, many individuals will prefer to let others bear the cost of the action so that they may benefit. Rational actors will become "free riders." Olsen predicted that only in the presence of **selective incentives** would individuals agree to bear the cost of a collective good. Olsen's theory has since driven much research and theory of **collective action**.

INTERGENERATIONAL RELATIONS

Intergenerational relations have been affected by social and demographic changes that have precipitated alterations in the obligations and influence experienced among generational levels. Three historical changes can be identified as contributing to the makeup of contemporary intergenerational relations. First, demographic changes reflect an increased lifespan, resulting in older adults constituting the fastest growing age group. Basically, more people are living significantly longer lives. Second, expectations for middle age have changed, particularly for women. With women's mainstream entrance into the workforce, the traditional roles and responsibilities as primary caretaker have been stretched and challenged. Despite sometimes their conflicting demands, eighty to ninety percent of the time women still tend to be the main providers of hands-on assistance to elderly parents. Third, with increased economic security and the support of governmental assistance such as social security, the elderly have become more financially independent from their grown children. At the same time, grown children are less financially dependent on family businesses or wealth. As a result, family ties are based less on financial need and more on emotional commitment.

Scientific interest in and analysis of relations among the generations did not develop until the nineteenth century. Early sociological influences on intergenerational studies arose out of the positivist tradition, including August Comte (1798–1857), Jean-Louis Giraud/Soulavie (1753–1813), John Stuart Mill (1806–1873), and Ottokar Lorenz (1832–1907). These social scientists were among the first to analyze what influences and forms intergenerational **interaction**. Although their theories dealt with a wide variety of social aspects of generational differences and similarities, a unified theory of generations did not appear until the middle of the twentieth century, particularly in the work of **Karl Mannheim**.

Approaching intergenerational relations from a macrosociological perspective, Mannheim developed his understanding around the idea of **cohort** analysis. While he used the term, generation, contemporary sociologists have adopted the term, cohort. According to Mannheim, all individuals are born into a specific historical context. Those born at a similar time share the same life-shaping sociopolitical events as they are growing up. Consequently, cohorts, based on their common location within history, tend to exhibit similar characteristics and thought patterns. Like other socioeconomic conditions, position within a cohort defines viable choices available to an individual. Because experiences and values may differ among cohort groups, conflicts may arise between generations. Mannheim acknowledges that conflicts can also develop within a cohort, creating subgroups with a single cohort, which he calls generational units. Nonetheless, he maintains that cohort factors play a significant role in defining generational identity.

Much research on intergenerational relations has focused on the problems that arise between generations. Contrary to popular tradition, which views the past as a time of sublime interconnectedness among intergenerational families, early American households were primarily based on the nuclear family unit. Although elders were afforded more respect and high prestige in **society**, research indicates an ongoing tension across history between personal concerns and family obligations. In his contribution "Research Perspectives on Intergenerational Interaction" to *Aging Parents* (1979; edited by Pauline K. Ragan), Vern L. Bengtson suggested four common problems that arise from contemporary intergenerational interaction: role transition, **autonomy** or dependency, equitable exchange, and continuity verses disruption.

First, role transition occurs as an individual ages and expectations change. Major life events, such as children leaving the home, retirement, or the death of a spouse, require new roles to be taken on. Whereas some of the results of these changes may be enthusiastically anticipated, such as parents having more time and money to spend on themselves after the last child leaves the home, other changes can cause tremendous **stress** and depression, such as being widowed. Second, the balancing levels of autonomy and dependency can cause conflicts between generations. Teenage children are notorious for their desire for independence, and parents are often torn between the desire to see their children grow up and the fear that their children lack the ability to handle their new autonomy with responsibility. Elder adults often fear the loss of their own autonomy as their dependence on their adult children increases. Third, by equitable exchange, Bengtson referred to the balance between giving and receiving among the generations. Most often reflected in the relationship between adult children and their parents, equitable exchanges addresses questions of give and take. What can I leave my children? Fourth, in modern society, numerous circumstances can cause disruption and threaten family continuity. Bengtson listed four: geographic mobility, **divorce**, changes in life-style adopted by younger generations, and death. In each case, major changes in family structure and relations must be negotiated and resolved for family continuity to remain intact.

As the number of elder adults continues to grow, intergenerational relations will remain a topic of considerable discussion as social sciences attempt to resolve issues of elder care, intergenerational interdependence and independence, and the many social, political, and economic factors that affect multiple levels of generations.

INTERGENERATIONAL RESOURCE TRANSFERS

Intergenerational resource transfers take different forms, follow different directions, and exist at different levels of a **soci-**ety. Demographers study intergenerational resource transfers in terms of the impact on fertility; economists to determine flows of wealth; and sociologists to examine family dynamics.

Intergenerational resource transfers involve the flow of capital from one generation to another, whether from parents to their children or through programs like Social Security. When the capital goes to a younger generation, the flow is said to be downward, whereas flows to parents or grandparents are upward; in describing the flow of public funds, the government takes the place of the "middle" or working-age generation and directs capital either to children or the elderly.

The currency used within these transfers encompasses both the intangible and monetary. Transfers can be physical gifts, services rendered, advice, money, or even the promise of future financial gain; interfamily transfers can take any of these forms, while public transfers are generally direct transfers of capital, such as food stamps for families on Temporary Assistance for Needy Families (TANF, which replaced the more extensive and better-known Aid for Dependent Children, AFDC, as a result of the Welfare Reform and Personal Responsibility Act of 1996), or more removed transfers in the form of federal funding for health and education programs.

The traditions of a society determine the direction of intergenerational resource transfers on the micro level. If children normally provide for their parents, people can maximize the value of their position by having many children; this upward flow is evidenced in China, where male children are valued because care of their parents is traditionally their responsibility, which is one factor behind the massive population growth that led to the passing of the one-child policy. Small farm owners can benefit from having multiple children, whose labor is less expensive than hired workers from outside of the family; similar forces were at work during the **Industrial Revolution**, when children worked at factories alongside their parents and contributed their wages to the **family**. (During times of high infant mortality having many children insured that some would survive.) At the same time, if resources flow downwards, fewer children are the less costly route. If adolescents remain with their parents for eighteen years in a society, having one or two offspring keeps family resources from being spread too thinly, both during their childhood and after the death of the parents, if the parents wish to leave a bequest.

Samuel Preston, in his 1984 presidential address to the Population Association of America, raised an alarm that the net flow of wealth in the United States is upward, particularly in the public sector, to the detriment of the country's children. His speech ignited a robust debate since his conclusions were based on a number of factors, including: increased age of mothers at first births; anti-poverty programs directed at the elderly; the strength of senior citizens in the electorate; downward trends in fertility; the growth of the elderly population as a result of increased **life expectancy**; the tendency of voters to look towards securing their futures and those of their parents. Preston's speech shaped the way sociologists looked at intergenerational resource transfers at the end of the twentieth century.

INTERGROUP AND INTERORGANIZATIONAL RELATIONS

Intergroup and interorganizational relations refer to the experiences people have within and between different groups and formal organizations. Groups and organizations interact with one another just as individuals do. **Interaction** within groups, associations, collectives, and organizations is a ubiquitous part of social life. From birth until death, humans interact with one another in differing sized collectivities. Thus, social groups and organizations form the contemporary context for all human social interaction.

Groups are possessed of definitive place and **structure**. Organizations are established and built with definite goals and possess a physicality as displayed in physical settings, buildings, machines, and tools used by those individuals within the **organization**. Organizations are more formal than are social groups. While individual social life takes place within groups and organizations, the spontaneous and creative impulses of individuals are channeled into the **rules**, policies, and structure of formal collectives that makes organizational life stable and predictable. For example, a worker in a larger corporation does not act on his or her own ideas alone but follows the policies of the corporation if they desire to maintain their **employment**. Individual variation that might be part of a less formal social **group**, such as an after school club, is limited in larger, more formal organizations. Therefore, determining and explaining human behavior does not simply depend upon individual characteristics or assumptions of **free will**. How an individual interacts with others and how that interaction takes place within and between groups and organizations determines the shape of social life. Thus, the larger scale of social groups and organizations shapes the nature of everyday individual life. The interaction between groups and organizations create the necessary coordination of activities, resources, and planning that produces the current arrangement of modern social life.

At the level of everyday social interaction, some sociological researchers have focused on how the social relations within groups and organizations shape an individual's sense of self and other people. What makes a person see another person as a friend, colleague, or an enemy? Part of the answer is the natures of our interactions within groups and organizations that color our interactions with one another. Social life is a web of interactions that takes place with other people. The nature of social relations depends on the type of organization, the organization of the entity, the definitions placed on it, and the size of the group.

The research of nineteenth century German sociologist, Georg Simmel noted that the size of the group influenced how members of the group interacted with one another. A two-person group, or dyad, allowed for communication of ideas and feelings directly from one person to another. Add a third person, forming a triad, and suddenly the group dynamic changes as **coalitions** of two individuals against the remaining person become possible. As more individuals are added to the group, the need for greater coordination leads to the rise of **authority**, **leadership**, and formal organization. Thus, the size of a group shapes how people treat and respond to one another.

The type of group also shapes the social relations within it. People act differently in a church or school than they do at home. The context of the situation—the where, when, what, and ideas associated with the space—mold the interaction of people. Individuals act differently in public than in private groups because of the feelings of differing groups evaluating their actions.

At a larger level of social life, other sociological researchers have examined the influence of groups and organizations on each other. While organizations are not alive in a conventional sense, they do engage in action consistent with their strategies to reach goals. Organizations emulate influential and successful organizational practices. For example, over time the less dominant organizations in a field or industry emulate the dominant organizations in an effort to partake in their success. Just as individuals consider the consequences of their behavior, so do groups and organizations.

The more formal the group or organization, the more constrained the social interaction between people. Individuals act the most freely in small, informal groups that are not connected to larger, more formal processes. However, as the context changes to become larger and more organized, people's behavior becomes more constrained according to rules of behavior, processes, and policies established by increasingly larger organizations. Individual spontaneity becomes limited by the formal organization. Organizational behavior is also dependent upon the activities of other organizations. Therefore, intergroup and interorganizational relations are shaped by individuals, groups, and organizational interactions and experiences.

See also Group; Interaction; Organization

INTERNAL COLONIALISM

Internal **colonialism** is a concept used to describe exploitative relations occurring between a dominant **group** and one or more subordinate groups residing within a single **society**. The term is an adaptation of the more traditional colonialism **model**, which examines international relations of exploitation whereby powerful nations exert political, economic, and cultural dominance over weaker nations. The internal colonialism model originated among Marxists such as Vladimir Lenin and Antonio Gramsci in their analysis of the capitalist exploitation of workers. More recently, however, the term has been employed in the examination of historical processes of racial and ethnic subordination as well.

Many American social scientists have utilized the internal colonialism model in the investigation of racial and ethnic oppression within the United States. These analyses have focused primarily upon the historical experiences of Native Americans, African Americans, and Mexican Americans. It is argued that the historically discriminatory and exploitative practices of European populations led to the internal colonization of these racial and ethnic minority groups. Through the conquest of Native Americans, the enslavement of African Americans, and the forcible annexation of Mexican **territory**,

European Americans effectively subordinated the political, economic, and cultural interests of Native American, African American, and Mexican American populations.

Many social scientists have recently utilized the internal colonialism model in examining the more contemporary experiences of African Americans. While the political, economic, and cultural exploitation of blacks began during the American era of slavery, exploitative relations between dominant white European Americans and African Americans did not cease with **abolition**. It is argued that because the U.S. government, the economy, and mainstream American culture continue to be dominated by white American influence and interests, the political, economic, and cultural subjugation of African Americans persists to the present day.

The internal colonialism model has not been limited to the examination of dominant/subordinate relations in the United States, however. Other contemporary analyses have employed the internal colonialism model in the examination of exploitative relations among opposing ethnic groups in Latin America and Europe as well. While some critics of internal colonialism assert that particular applications of this model stray too far from traditional interpretations of the concept of colonialism, supporters of the concept take little issue with such discrepancies. Advocates of the internal colonialism model maintain that the utility of the model lies in its ability to reveal the common experiences of exploited and oppressed groups around the world.

INTERNAL MIGRATION

No universally accepted definition of *internal migration* exists, although the term is frequently used to refer to movement between the administrative units within a nation. The distinction between internal and **international migration** is, therefore, a political one. In most countries, individuals are free to move within the nation without government regulation or intervention. Consequently, there is no need for passports or visas. While it is true that some totalitarian regimes (e.g., China and the Soviet Union) have controlled or otherwise limited internal mobility, these limitations have generally been less restrictive than those governing movement across national boundaries. Like international migration, internal migration is defined as a permanent (long-term) change in residence, with an implied disruption of previous social and economic relations. Internal migration is often associated with a new place of **employment**, for instance, or with the establishment of friendships within a new neighborhood. Internal migrants are referred to as *outmigrants* from the perspective of the origin **community** and as *inmigrants* from the perspective of the destination community.

Internal migration does not involve the crossing of national boundaries. To measure migration rates and flows, we must therefore specify the political, administrative, or other geospatial units over which internal mobility is measured. These geospatial units are often states, counties, metropolitan areas, linguistic regions, or economic development districts. At the county scale, for instance, mobility across county

boundaries is counted as internal migration while mobility *within* a single county is not. At the state level, only migration between states is counted as internal migration. The United Nations has recommended that each nation define a *geographical scale*—a geospatial unit that can be used to determine when individuals have entered a new cultural, political, or economic environment—at which internal migration will be measured.

Movement within a single geospatial unit is often referred to as *residential mobility* rather than migration. Similarly, the United States **Census** makes a distinction between *movers* (those who move within a single county) and *internal migrants* (those who move across county lines). This distinction is not always meaningful, however, since relocation from one county to another need not coincide with a change in social or economic environment. For example, someone who lives near a county boundary and moves a short distance to a neighboring county will be considered a migrant, while someone who moves a great distance across a large county will be counted as a mover.

Some nations, such as Sweden and the Netherlands, maintain continuous population registers. In this record-keeping system, an information card is made out at birth for each individual, and all subsequent vital events (marriage, **divorce**, change of residence, and death) are entered on the card. This system provides an excellent source of **data** for demographers, who are then able to compile data on inmigration and outmigration for any desired period. In the United States, however, information on internal migration is gathered from national censuses and **surveys**. Questions such as "Where were you born?" or "Where did you live X years ago?" are used to obtain information on internal mobility. Based on these questions, internal migrants can be identified as individuals whose area of residence at the time of the survey differs from their area of residence at a particular time in the past. This method of data collection is not entirely accurate, as multiple migrations between the two periods will be counted only as a single migration from the area where the person resided a certain number of years ago to the area where he resided at the time of the survey.

Studies of internal migration frequently focus on four types of mobility: rural-rural, rural-urban, urban-urban, and urban-rural. These distinctions are of special importance in many developing countries, where rural and urban environments may be dramatically different. Geographer Wilbur Zelinsky and demographer Ronald Skeldon maintained that different patterns of mobility are associated with the various stages of the **demographic transition**. In pre-transition societies, there are fluctuating levels of mobility. As economic development progresses, rural-urban migration becomes the predominant type. Later, in advanced societies, inter-urban moves predominate, and migration rates may decline as various forms of **communication** and short-term mobility serve as substitutes for internal migration.

Rural-urban migration has been the dominant type in developing countries over the past few decades. According to economist Michael P. Todaro, individuals move from rural to urban areas in response to rational economic considerations such as expected urban-rural wage differentials (this has been referred to as the "Todaro hypothesis"). This rural-urban migration brings a surplus of labor to the urban centers of developing countries and increases the economic disparity between rural and urban areas. The Todaro hypothesis has been subject to a number of critiques but remains influential.

Internal migration patterns in the industrialized nations have also been the subject of close scrutiny. For much of the twentieth century, major U.S. migration flows brought migrants to the industrial **cities** of the northeastern and north central states. This pattern shifted dramatically, however, in the later decades of the century; in recent decades, the Northeast has been losing population to the Sunbelt.

In the 1970s an unexpected demographic phenomenon occurred in the United States (and in many other developed countries) when the nonmetropolitan population was found to be increasing at a faster rate than the metropolitan population. Although the turnaround in growth rates reversed itself by 1980, today some large central cities in the United States are losing population while the nearby suburbs are flourishing. Violent **crime** and urban **unemployment** continue to promote city-to-suburb mobility while discouraging suburb-to-city moves.

INTERNAL VALIDITY

Internal **validity**, like other types of validity, is an assessment of how well an instrument measures what it is intended to measure. Specifically, internal validity assesses whether the conclusions derived from a research study accurately reflect the results of an experiment or the implementation of a **measurement** instrument. In other words, a research study with high internal validity produces results that are not biased by factors outside the study. For example, a study assessing people's opinions on capital punishment conducted over a time period that included a highly publicized execution would decrease the internal validity of the study because responses would be highly influenced by this event and would likely be different than responses given at another time. While there is no way of completely assuring the internal validity of a study or experiment, it is possible to minimize the factors that threaten internal validity.

The example above shows how history (or current events) is a threat to internal validity. Maturation is another threat to internal validity. People change over time, both short-term and long-term. In the short term, people become tired, bored or frustrated, while in the long term they grow older and wiser. An experiment begun while subjects are fresh and energetic may lose internal validity as their changing attitudes compete with the experimental stimulus as an influence on results and responses.

Testing and instrumentation can threaten internal validity. Testing or surveying people gets them to focus on the intended measurement topics. Therefore, responses at the end of a test or the responses obtained by a follow-up test may have reduced internal validity because people's subsequent consideration of the issue may be an external factor influencing results. Also, inconsistencies or problems with instrumentation can introduce biases that threaten internal validity.

Internal validity can also be threatened by a phenomenon known as regression to the **mean**. Generally, extreme cases tend to change and become less extreme. This statistical tendency can influence results, particularly in follow-up or comparison studies. In studies conducted over time, attrition is another problem that can negatively affect internal validity. People leave ongoing experiments for a variety of reasons, which can add additional **bias** to results.

INTERNATIONAL MIGRATION

International migration is mobility across national boundaries with the intention of a long-term or permanent relocation (change of residence). International migrants are referred to as *emigrants* from the perspective of the nation they have left and as *immigrants* from the perspective of the receiving nation. (The corresponding processes are *emigration* and *immigration*.) Unlike other key demographic concepts such as fertility and mortality, the definition of migration lacks clarity due to its temporal dimension. Tourists, for example, are not usually considered international migrants. To maintain consistency in terminology and to facilitate international comparisons, the United Nations has adopted the demographic concept of a "long-term immigrant": Any person—regardless of citizenship or legal immigration status—who remains in his or her new country for more than twelve months.

International migration may be either voluntary or involuntary. Individuals who migrate across international borders can be further classified as one or more of the following: legal immigrants, illegal (or undocumented) immigrants, refugees (including asylees), and slaves. Legal immigrants have official legal and political approval to migrate, whereas illegal (or undocumented) immigrants do not. A refugee is someone who has fled or been expelled from his or her homeland because of natural catastrophe, **war**, military occupation, or religious, ethnic or political persecution. An *asylee* is a refugee who already resides in the country in which he or she is seeking protection and immunity from extradition.

The push-pull framework is commonly used to explain international migration. *Push factors*—origin characteristics that encourage emigration—include conditions such as **unemployment** or underemployment, low wages, war, and political and religious persecution. *Pull factors*—destination characteristics that encourage immigration—may include **employment** opportunities, family reunification, religious freedom, and better living conditions. In recent years, social scientists, such as **sociology** professor Douglas Massey, have developed sophisticated theoretical models to account more fully for the factors that create and sustain international migration flows. Among the potential causes of international migration are wage differentials between sending and receiving countries (neoclassical economic **theory**), efforts to diversify a family's income (new

Rate of immigration
Legal immigrants admitted as a percentage of the total population, 1820-1998

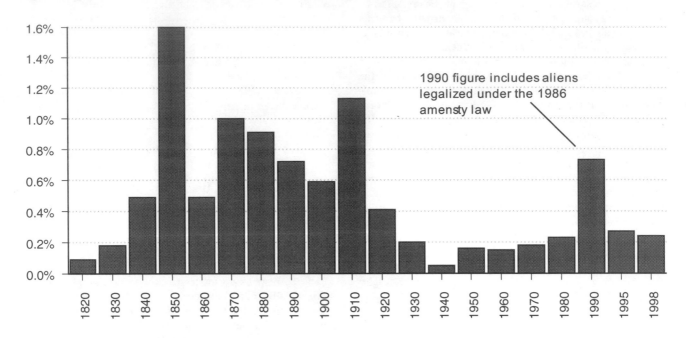

Source: U.S. Census Bureau and Immigration and Naturalization Service

economics of migration), labor demands and recruitment efforts (segmented labor market theory), and capitalist market penetration (world **systems theory**). Moreover, long-term immigration may result in the establishment of social and economic relationships that reinforce and sustain existing patterns of migration. Family and friendship networks promote migration (**network theory**), institutions develop in support of transnational movement (institutional theory), and each act of migration changes the context and likelihood of subsequent migration decisions (cumulative causation).

According to Douglas Massey, the modern history of international migration can be divided into four periods: (1) the mercantilist period; (2) the industrial period; (3) the period of limited immigration; and (4) the post-industrial era. From 1500 to 1800 (the mercantilist era), immigration flows were conditioned by the patterns of colonization and economic growth that occurred as a result of mercantile **capitalism**. During this era the population of Europe grew rapidly, and millions of Europeans left for North and South America, eastern and southern Africa, Australia and Asia to take advantage of expanding economic opportunities. The migrations of this era included not only voluntary migrants, but also slaves (approximately 11 million Africans) who were employed largely as domestic servants and agricultural workers in the colonies.

The second phase of international migration (the industrial period) began early in the nineteenth century and

stemmed from the economic development of Europe and the spread of industrialism to former European colonies in the New World. Between 1800 and 1925 approximately fifty million people left Europe (primarily Britain, Italy, Norway, Portugal, Spain and Sweden) in search of better economic opportunities in the Americas and Oceania (mainly Argentina, Australia, Canada, New Zealand and the United States).

The period of limited migration began with the outbreak of World War I and lasted for nearly four decades. When the war ended and immigration resumed, many nations (especially the United States) introduced quotas to suppress immigration. Economic depression and World War II further reduced immigration during the 1930s and 1940s.

The period of postindustrial migration began during the 1970s and represented a significant shift from earlier patterns. Specifically, the supply of immigrants shifted from Europe to the developing world, and the range of both receiving and sending countries diversified. While the United States continues to attract a large number of immigrants, the new arrivals now often come from Latin America and Asia. Many countries in northern and western Europe (including Germany, France, Belgium, Switzerland, and the Netherlands) have also experienced sizable net inflows. The petroleum-exporting countries of the Middle East have attracted many immigrants as well, chiefly from south and east Asia. By the 1980s several rapidly industrializing nations in Asia (Japan, South Korea, Hong Kong, Taiwan, Malaysia, and Thailand) were importing labor from nearby Asian countries.

According to Philip Martin, a professor of agricultural economics, and Jonas Widgren, director of the International Center for Policy Development in Vienna, Austria, in the mid-1990s approximately 125 million people—about two percent of the world's population—lived outside their countries of birth or citizenship. According to the United States Committee for Refugees, there were approximately 13.5 million refugees (a decline from the early 1990s) at the end of 1998. Most refugees are concentrated in developing countries.

International migration has economic and social consequences for both sending and receiving regions. In many developing nations, remittances from family members abroad are an important source of household income. At the same time, immigration policies that give preference to highly-educated professionals may attract the most economically valuable migrants to countries such as the United States, thereby contributing to the "brain drain" in India, Great Britain, and other nations.

Recent research has focused considerable attention on the labor-market impact of immigration. The *displacement hypothesis* asserts that immigrants displace native workers by doing the same jobs for lower wages. In contrast, the *interdependency or complementary skills hypothesis* suggests that immigrants take those jobs that the native **labor force** will not accept. Most current studies show that immigrants have only a modest impact on the wages of natives. The fiscal impact of immigration is another recent concern. While this impact varies with the type of migrants (refugees or legal immigrants, for example), studies in the United States suggest that immigrants represent a net cost to state and local governments but a net fiscal gain at the federal level.

INTERNET

The Internet is a network interface connection that uses technology to allow computers and electronically smart equipment such as telephones and cable wired televisions to interact globally online. The Internet has become a powerful medium that enables access to information within seconds. It also enables businesses to conduct electronic commerce without concern for the physical location of users. Just as almost every household has a telephone in the United States, it would seem likely that each household will also have a computer or Internet connection at home, on the job, and on their person.

The Internet protocol is a technology based medium that initially allowed companies to create systems for electronic mail, file transfers, and access to remote distribution locations. By the mid-1990s, the Internet had contributed to the expansion of the international market through electronic transactions, had reduced decision-making time through increased access to information, and eliminated many distribution channeling costs of production. The rapid growth of electronic business on the Internet affected the U.S. domestic economy.

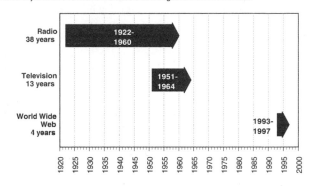

Internet's rate of growth

Number of years before various communications technologies reached 50 million users

Source: "The Emerging Digital Economy," April 1998, Department of Commerce

As the Census Bureau (1999) notes, the **unemployment** rate is the lowest in thirty years and the prosperity of the economy is reflected in the stock market, the increase in new construction, and a higher **standard of living** for most Americans. Many government officials attribute these changes to the successful positioning of the United States in the world economy. Electronic offerings include music, books, groceries and banking, pharmaceuticals, vacations, and stocks. Internet advertising and links are an important aspect of conducting business today.

The social changes as a result of the Internet are continuing to affect people's everyday lives. The Internet offers individuals with disabilities greater access to information, **employment**, resources, and social interaction. Educational research indicates that the Internet provides wider access to information, allowing for better decision-making and learning, and the exposure to culturally varied issues and experiences. In addition, the growth of electronic business, Internet access and computer-mediated technology has also affected the occupational structure as many low skilled and middle management jobs are eliminated particularly in manufacturing, while demand is increasing in the personal service and information services sector. The Internet is an important factor in the globalization of the workforce, as highly industrialized countries such as the United States have increased their demand for workers with excellent computer skills. Internet companies also have challenged the traditional way of doing business. Companies such as IBM have moved their personal computer sales to online transactions, and many web-based retailers have reduced costs by cutting sales personnel and the need for a sales room.

The growth of electronic business, however, has also created public concern about online sales of alcohol to minors, prescription drug sales with little direct doctor interface, questionable stock sales, auctions of stolen property, and the potential for credit card fraud. Computer **crime** from hackers and stalkers also has grown as a result of the Internet. Computer viruses have threatened to affect the operating systems of many organizations including corporations and federal agencies. The government is beginning to design legislation relating to the Internet, and these efforts will increase as more issues regarding the safety and security become apparent. For example, in 1998, the Children's Online Privacy Act required web operators to post their privacy policies and to provide details on how information on children will be used and to identify who has access to that information. Social scientists have also voiced their concern about the emerging inequality regarding access to computers and are particularly concerned since many low-income families lag in the ability to develop technical skills. Nevertheless, the extraordinary stock performance of many Internet companies suggests that while these issues will require solutions, they will not detract from the increasing use of Internet.

Internet2 is a consortium effort between universities, funded by the federal government, to create an even faster network than the current Internet. Computer technology and the Internet have permanently changed scientific research as advances in DNA and biotechnology continue. In the social sciences, more research is conducted online, while questionnaires can be distributed through listservs or E-mails. In addition, many universities are using the Internet for interactive classroom discussions, long-distance learning, and teaching students bibliographic research and web searches. Electronic archives, online retrieval, and computer technology to develop graphic displays and innovative and interactive websites allow the individual or the **organization** to communicate globally. As this technology becomes more prevalent, the influence of Internet in the academic world will become obvious as libraries move to online texts and retrieval systems.

INTERPERSONAL ATTRACTION

Interpersonal attraction is the starting point of most relationships, whether romantic or platonic, a point probably well-understood by the general public. However, most people do not realize that interpersonal attraction processes are socially patterned. That is, attraction to others is not random, but rather the product of societal arrangements. In making interpersonal attraction the focus of a rigorous, scientific examination, sociologists point out that attraction to others is patterned and influenced by the larger society. Thus, the sociological perspective on interpersonal attraction is more empirical and reliable than is 'common sense knowledge' about what attracts one person to another.

The sociological study of interpersonal attraction is rooted in the sub-field of social **psychology**. Social psychologists' work on interpersonal attraction centers upon the identification of the various social factors that influence attraction to others. Social psychologists have identified seven factors influencing interpersonal attraction, and they point out that these factors often interact with one another to produce an overall sense of attraction to another person.

First, social psychologists find that proximity, or nearness in physical space, positively influences interpersonal at-

traction. Being physically close to someone else permits more opportunities for **interaction**. Those who are nearer to us appear more available and, in turn, more attractive as potential partners for interaction than do those who are far away. Being near to someone else increases the **probability** of contact; hence, interaction is less costly in terms of effort expended. Because proximity acts to decrease the costs of interacting with someone else, there are greater opportunities for attraction to develop.

Familiarity also tends to increase interpersonal attraction. Social psychological research indicates that repeated exposure to some stimulus (including another person) that is initially perceived as positive or neutral often leads to the development of an increased positive **attitude** toward the stimulus. This tendency is called the mere exposure effect, as identified by Robert Zajonc. Shared activities tend to increase interpersonal attraction as well. Participating the same activity serves as a basis for forming an interpersonal relationship. The shared endeavor also provides a focus for the interaction, as the common bond facilitates the initial contact and conversation between two people.

Similarity in attitudes also increases interpersonal attraction and liking. Research suggests that the higher the correspondence of attitudes held by two people, the greater is their attraction to one another, and the longer the relationship tends to last. Social psychologists argue that people who hold congruent attitudes and beliefs experience the world similarly, and this shared sameness leads to greater understanding and more effective communication. Furthermore, interacting with someone having similar attitudes is rewarding, as it validates one's attitude and thus reaffirms that one's beliefs are "correct".

In addition, there are **norms** within any **society** that dictate what kinds of people are appropriate targets of attraction. Interpersonal attraction in **American society** is influenced by the norm of homophily, or the tendency for people to associate with others who are like themselves in terms of social characteristics, such as **race**, age, social class, and religion. According to this norm, friends and romantic partners should be of similar social backgrounds. The norm of homophily clearly influences marriage partner selection, as people with similar social characteristics marry more often than would be expected by chance. This norm further demonstrates that attraction is not a purely individual choice, but one that is influenced by the society in which we live.

Similarity, both in attitudes and in social characteristics, is a very good predictor of the degree of attraction between people. However, differences can also lead to interpersonal attraction, through **role** compatibility. Role compatibility refers to the fit between people's characteristics or behaviors, where each person can fulfill some need in the other person. For instance, a person who feels the role of provider is important is likely to attract someone who wants to be provided for. While most research suggests that similarity increases attraction, role compatibility explains the comparatively rarer situation in which opposites attract.

Finally, attraction is based in part on physical appearance. Social psychological research indicates that looks do indeed matter, and ideally, we prefer the company of attractive others because their beauty reflects positively on us. However, in reality, there is evidence that we tend to acquire partners whose degree of physical attractiveness is similar to our own. Identified by Ellen Berscheid, this tendency is called the matching hypothesis. This concept further reinforces that even physical attraction to another is influenced by the larger society.

INTERPERSONAL CONFLICT RESOLUTION

Interpersonal conflict resolution is a process that attempts to resolve conflict, or disagreement between two parties, using mediation. A neutral third party, or mediator, facilitates resolution of the conflict in a way that will benefit all involved in the dispute. The process differs from the tradition U.S. legal system in several ways. According to Stewart Levine, author of *Getting to Resolution*, traditional courtroom resolution of disputes rewards one party only—there is a winner and a loser. In Interpersonal Conflict Resolution, "a fair outcome from everyone's perspective leads to resolution," according to Levine. Interpersonal Conflict Resolution is less costly and time consuming than traditional legal approaches to dispute.

Accordingly, the mindset of a mediator differs from that of a courtroom lawyer. The mediator generally regards conflict as an opportunity for all rather than a situation that can ultimately only benefit one side. According to Levine, the correct approach to Interpersonal Conflict Resolution includes: the belief that there is adequate resources for everyone, an openness to creative solutions, the **adoption** of a long term timeframe for the implementation of collaboration that is part of the solution, and respect for people's feelings so that all viewpoints can be aired.

Interpersonal Conflict Resolution has been used to resolve disputes in the workplace, and may involve hiring consultants who specialize in the process. The process could include an assessment of the situation, and mediation proceedings. Supervisors may also be trained to carry out mediation processes.

Good conflict resolution abilities may improve the odds of a marriage succeeding, according to 1994 research by **family** therapists. The research showed that between forty and sixty percent of marriages will fail but that ability to handle conflict was the single most important aspect of a successful marriage. In 2000, a *Time* article reported on conflict resolution techniques used in U.S. schools. Children were taught how to manage their anger and resolve their conflict constructively. **Role** playing and puppetry were some of the ways in which children learned interpersonal conflict resolution skills.

INTERPERSONAL POWER

Interpersonal power is what enables one person to control the behavior of another, usually without voluntary cooperation and often with coercion of some kind. It is the ability to get others to do either socially acceptable or unacceptable things. One person's power over another is the result of the superior position that person holds in a social relationship. Personal power also exists when one person has something someone else requires, and which cannot be obtained anywhere else. It is also the power to resist change. Interpersonal power is based on knowledge, position, and the ability to take autonomous action. It can be a formal or legal superiority (an employer's power over an employee) or it can be informal and based solely on interactions (a husband's power over his wife). It is usually seen at the individual level, although it is in part a result of structural and institutional power. Interpersonal power is different from interpersonal **influence** because it implies some form of **coercion**. One of the most important components of power is perception—if you are perceived as powerful, then you are powerful.

The word power can often have negative connotations, although it exists at all levels of social life, from individual to institutional interactions. This is because power can indicate that one or several people are being coerced, dominated, or manipulated. The components of power are: the bases of power, the means of power, the strength of power, the amount of power, the scope of power, and the domain of power. There is, however, much disagreement about which of these constitute power, to what degree, and how they interact. Another major question is how much compliance exists in interpersonal relations and how much coercion is involved in the use of interpersonal power.

There are several types of interpersonal power. Expert power is based on one person's perception of another's competence, knowledge, or expertise. Referent power is based on one person's liking for another and that person's ability to make one feel approved of or accepted. Reward power is based on one person's ability to provide the things someone desires or to remove the things the person does not want. Legitimate power is based on the internalization of social **norms** or **values** and is rooted in one's feeling of obligation or responsibility. Information power is a leader's ability to influence behavior by creating feelings of independence based on sharing information and expertise with followers. Interpersonal power can manifest itself in any or all of these forms.

There are certain social characteristics that tend to confer or result in more interpersonal power than others. These characteristics are being white, male, heterosexual, educated, and of high **socioeconomic status**. People with these characteristics tend to have superior institutional and structural power, which translates both directly and indirectly to individual and institutional interactions.

Much research on interpersonal power has been done using gender and race as key variables. Both have been shown to be instrumental in both individual—and institutional—level interactions. Gender has also been shown to be particularly important in intimate relationships and family dynamics. Most studies show that whites have more interpersonal power than do minorities and that men have more interpersonal power than do women. This is a result of the cultural, political, institutional, and economic forces benefiting and supporting their superior power in general.

Extensive research has studied the many ways men's superior interpersonal power is manifested in day-to-day life. Men appear to have superior interpersonal power in the family, particularly in regard to the division of labor. Women are still primarily responsible for the majority of care work, both in and out of the home. Whether or not they work outside the home, women still do the large majority of housework (Hocschild, 1989). In conversation, men interrupt and overlap more than and women support and nurture the flow of talk. Men still hold the majority of power positions in the economy and politics and women are the majority of victims of relationship and sexual violence.

INTERPRETIVE SOCIOLOGY

In its broadest definition, all sociological study is interpretive insofar as it analyzes concrete situations upon which certain assumptions bear. However, in a more limited sense, interpretive **sociology** refers to the theoretical perspective based on the understanding that social action is defined by the meaning placed upon it by social actors. Thus, interpretive sociological study emphasizes the need to understand or interpret actors' meanings. Social reality is defined as pre-interpreted and can only be delineated by the result of actors' beliefs about their own acts and their interpretation of others' acts.

Modern sociology tends to be divided between empirical and interpretive understandings of sociological **epistemology**. **Empirical sociology**, also called "mainstream" sociology, relies on scientific **methodology** to create formal standards by which quantitative analysis of social processes and structures can be measured against a formalized **sociological theory**. This approach, supported by logical **positivism**, focuses on macrostructural relationships in terms of social and historical concepts that allow for the formulation of objectively acquired social laws. By contrast, interpretive sociology is a relativist method of inquiry that denies the positivist idea that social life is dictated by objective social and cultural structures that are external to, and independent from, individual actors. Meaning is not an object reality that needs to be discovered; rather, it is created by social action and emerges from social processes. Although many blendings of theoretical positions exist, the history of interpretive sociology began with **Max Weber** and is foundational in sociological theories of **symbolic interactionism**, social **phenomenology**, and ethnomethodology.

Max Weber's theory is considered the precursor to modern interpretive sociology. Unlike previous work, Weber's analysis focused on individual actors rather than social structures. **Lewis Coser** explained Weber's premise in *Masters of Sociological Thought* (1971; expanded edition, 1977): "Weber's primary focus was on the subjective meaning that human actors attach to their actions in their mutual orientations within specific social-historical contexts. Behavior devoid of such meaning, Weber argued, falls outside the purview of sociology." Weber suggested that social phenomenon could be accurately interpreted by a process of *Verstehen,* or sympathetic understanding.

Despite his focus on individual action, Weber did not claim a pure relativist position. Charles A. Pressler and Fabio B. Dasilva, in *Sociology and Interpretation: From Weber to Habermas*, wrote: "The sociohistorical sciences are to use a form of interpretation adequate to their object of study, and such a position is legitimate if the intent of the procedure is not immediate 'understanding,' as an act of intuition, but rather the formulation of interpretive hypotheses open to empirical verification and causal explanation." By claiming that meaning is assigned by individual actors and that this meaning can be interpreted and formulated in a way that could come under objective, empirical scrutiny, Weber attempted to work in the theoretical and methodological ground between the pure relativist and pure positivist position.

Symbolic interactionism, first introduced by **Herbert Blumer** in the late 1930s, stood in stark contrast to the functionalist emphasis on determining the role of social structures. Symbolic interactionism rests on the premise that meaning is not found in objective reality; rather, no meaning is possible outside the assignment of meaning by human understanding. Blumer argued that human behavior could not be reduced to a combination of psychological factors, such as stimuli, motivation, and attitudes. Neither could it be defined by a conglomeration of social traits, such as **status**, social roles, **norms**, and values. In both cases, the individual is treated as a passive participant through which social forces act, but by which no true action is possible. Blumer outlined his theory in three points: (1) "human beings act toward things based on the meaning that the things have for them;" (2) "the meaning of such things is derived from, or arises out of, the social **interaction** that one has with one's fellows;" and (3) "these meanings are handled in, and modified through an interpretive process used by the person in dealing with the things he encounters." Eminent sociologists of the symbolic interactionism school of thought include **George Herbert Mead**, Charles Cooley, Howard S. Becker, and **Erving Goffman**.

Social phenomenology, a form of **idealism**, takes meaning as the central focus of sociological study. The external world is only meaningful through human experience of phenomena, namely, all things humans perceive consciously. Meaningless sensory **data** is assigned meaning by the individual's conscious act. Ian Craib wrote in *Modern Social Theory: From Parsons to Habermas* (1984), "[The sociologist] is only interested in the world insofar as it is meaningful and must therefore understand how we make it meaningful. This is achieved through setting aside what we normally assume we know and tracing the process of coming to know it." **Alfred Schutz** was the first major proponent of social phenomenology, outlining his ideas in his classic work *The Phenomenology of the Social World* (1932). The clearest presentation of contemporary social phenomenological theory can be found in **Peter Berger** and Thomas Luckmann's widely read *The Social Construction of Reality* (1967).

The term "ethnomethodology," as coined by **Harold Garfinkel**, literally means "people's method." Drawing from social phenomenology and the linguistic philosophy of Ludwig Wittgenstein, ethnomethodological study emphasizes the everyday, ordinary experiences of people and the manner in which their actions and conversation make sense to them. Its primary focus is the study of the methods by which individuals create, revise, and maintain a consistent sense of social reality. Completely rejecting any notion of cultural, structural, or behavioral **determinism**, it emphasizes people's common sense knowledge and social competence.

Garfinkel believed that individuals are rational beings who have the ability to categorize and define language and actions in such a way that social order is created. He called this process "indexing" and "reflexivity." As individuals converse, meaning is both understood and created. Garfinkel attempted to prove his theory by conducting studies that upset the taken-for-granted knowledge that people use to communicate and relate sensibly. For example, he would send his students out to barter for goods at a department store, conduct conversations in which they offered constant interruptions, and go to their family home and act like boarders. In each case, chaos was the result; thus Garfinkel argued that a basis of common knowledge and expectations governs much of everyday life.

Much interpretive sociological theory was produced as a polemic against the predominant structuralist view of sociology during the twentieth century. Although extreme forms of interpretive sociology, such as ethnomethodology, were highly popular during the 1970s, contemporary sociological theory tends to attempt a blend between interpretive and empirical sociology, keeping the best of both schools. Nonetheless, the field of sociology continues to debate the role of the interpretive process in sociological analysis.

INTERVENING VARIABLE

The intervening **variable**, a mediating variable that helps to explain some phenomenon, is the variable through which an **independent variable** works to affect change in a **dependent variable**. For illustration, with regard to the relationship between sex and violence, males are three to four times more likely to commit acts of violence than are females. But does a person's sex cause violence? While some may posit a genetic link between sex and violence, sociologists would argue that differences between males and females in the way that they are socialized lead to different levels of violence by sex.

Boys are given toy guns and soldiers and are encouraged to play games that emphasize physical dominance over others. Girls are taught to be more physically subdued. They are encouraged to play with dolls and take on care-giving roles. Theoretically, given these differences in the ways in which boys and girls are socialized even within the same families, it is no wonder that boys typically grow up to act more violently than girls.

Speaking in a variable language, sex is the main independent variable, socialization is the intervening variable, and violent behavior is the dependent variable. Sex affects change in the likelihood of violent behavior, but only through **socialization**. If girls and boys were similarly socialized, then they would express similar levels of violence. A relatively new statistical technique, called structural equation modeling, helps researchers to identify intervening variables, and to test the relationships between them and the independent and dependent variables.

INTERVIEW

An interview is a method of social research, a question/answer session between at least one researcher and one or more subjects. Interviews are conducted many different ways in social research and for several different reasons. Primarily, the purpose of interviewing is to garner detailed information from an individual about a specific topic. Interviews can be conducted via the telephone, face-to-face, or in a computer accessed chatroom.

Two interview types are structured and unstructured. These interview types should be thought of ends of a continuum. At the one end of the spectrum are structured interviews, in which the researcher may be present only to answer respondent questions while the respondent answers questions prepared in a survey format. Sometimes, the researcher asks the questions and records the answers for the respondent. Structured interviews generate quantifiable information for statistical analyses.

The less structured the interview is, the more qualitative the information generated. In a less structured interview, the researcher may follow a script of open-ended questions, Answers to the questions are recorded and later transcribed for qualitative analysis. Several gradations of this type of interview are possible. In some instances, the script is strictly followed; no deviation from the intended inquiry occurs. In less structured formats, the researcher may follow general guidelines of inquiry but welcome deviation from the main topic.

The type of interview chosen depends on the type of information sought and on the purpose of inquiry. Highly structured interviews generate more quantitative **data**, and loosely structured interviews garner more qualitative information. When the goal of the research is an ideographic explanation of some phenomenon—detailed information about a single topic—then a few loosely structured interviews are best. If, however, the goal is to generate a nomothetic explanation of something—a precisely defined area of inquiry that can be applied to several similar situations—then a structured interview is necessary.

INVENTIONS

Inventions occur when various items or ideas which already exist within a **culture** or **society** are combined in a different way to create a new item or idea which previously did not exist. Inventions, along with discovery (the uncovering of a previously existing aspect of society or culture), are viewed as forms of innovation within a culture which can serve as a means of societal change.

The term invention is typically associated with aspects of the material culture such as the automobile, **television**, or

Inventions, such as Alexander Graham Bell's telephone, are viewed as forms of innovation within a culture that can serve as a means of societal change *(United States National Aeronautics and Space Administration)*.

personal computer, each of which was constructed using previously existing materials, combined to serve an entirely new purpose. However inventions can also be made in the realm of the non-material culture, injecting new combinations of ideas and beliefs into a society. Innovations in political ideologies (**socialism**, democracy), religious belief systems (Protestantism, American Catholicism), and language each would constitute a combination of previously existing ideas into a new usage.

Sociologically, inventions are important because they contribute to change within a culture. Both discovery and invention, along with cultural diffusion, serve as primary means of changing the standards and normative behaviors within a society, forcing both intended and unintended alterations in social life. For example, the invention of the automobile allowed for relatively rapid, cost effective travel while simultaneously decreasing the use of public transportation and increasing the amount of traffic and road usage. Also, the proliferation of the automobile led to increased levels of individuality and eventually became a **symbol** of **status** and success in American society.

IRON LAW OF OLIGARCHY

The "iron law of oligarchy" was developed by German political sociologist Robert Michels in his classic book *Political Parties*, first published in 1911. Oligarchy means rule by the few, an elite, in any given **organization** or **society**. In his book, based on an intensive study of the German Social Democratic Party, then the largest socialist party in the world, Michels forcefully argued that **democracy** is impossible and oligarchy eventually, if not immediately, reigns in modern, large-scale organizations, including those organizations which ideologically support democracy. Michels iron law of oligarchy is one of the very best known contributions to elite theory, which includes the work of classical theorists like Gaetano Mosca and **Vilfredo Pareto** (both of whom influenced Michels' thinking) and more contemporary sociological scholars like **C. Wright Mills** and G. William Domhoff.

Michels based his iron law of oligarchy on several tendencies he remarked in organizational behavior. First, given the pulls of work, **family**, and leisure pursuits, most rank and file members in all kinds of organizations, from political parties and labor unions to professional and **leisure** groups, tend to participate far less and defer authority to organizational leaders. Second, the growing complexity of decision-making in modern, large-scale organizations, driven in part by an ever more complicated and specialized **division of labor**, makes educated, trained and/or specialized **leadership** all the more indispensable. Third, the leadership, in part as a function of its relative isolation from the rank and file membership, develops its own distinct perspectives and interests, notably including an interest in maintaining its leadership privilege. All of these common factors, Michels argued, contribute to the tendency toward a stable leadership which may oppose the elites of competing organizations (e.g., competing political parties) in order to maintain its own membership's support but which treats opposition within the organization as a threat to the unity of the organization. Hence, Michels rejected the contention that an organization's leadership, however distinguished from the membership, can still effectively represent the rank and file members' will.

Michels' iron law of oligarchy squarely challenges democratic and socialist theory which advocates participatory **social organization** in modern societies. In response to that challenge, some Marxists, including Sidney Hook and Nicolai Bukharin, distinguish economic and administrative power and argue that if education and administrative training are brought fully to the masses of citizens, in accord with socialist plans, it becomes far more difficult for a stable administrative elite to develop in any given organization. However, the Russian revolutionary and organizational theorist Vladimir Illich Lenin independently prescribed and organized what Michels theorized, an elite of revolutionaries to effectively lead the Russian masses to revolution. Most organizational case studies and **surveys** that have accumulated partly in response to Michels' iron law of oligarchy for the most part support his basic assertions.

Michels' iron law of oligarchy has had a large impact on organizational and **political sociology**. **Max Weber** was a close friend of Michels and freely admitted that Michels' theory influenced his own famed analysis of the nature and consequences of **bureaucracy**. The iron law of oligarchy has also influenced elite democratic scholars like Seymour Martin Lipset and Joseph Schumpeter. In contrast with participatory or "radical" democratic scholars and in accordance with Michels' iron law, elite democrats argue that the substantial and continuous participation of citizens in complex, modern mass democracies is impossible. However, departing from Michels, elite democratic scholars contend that most elites who run political parties and interest groups can and often do represent their membership and, moreover, that competition between diverse political organizations helps maintain their basic democratic **accountability** to their members and the mass of modern citizens.

ISLAM

Islam, one of the world's great monotheistic religions, was founded (or restored) by the **Prophet** Muhammad (570-632 CE), who lived in Mecca and Medina on the Arabian Peninsula. Islam means "submission," and Muslims are those who express their submission to God by following the five pillars of Islam: *shahada*, formally witnessing the unity of God; *salat*, formally praying five times daily; *zakat*, providing for the poor; *saram*, fasting during the month of **Ramadan**; and *hajj*, completeing a pilgrimage to the holy city of Mecca. Shortly after the death of Muhammad, early Muslims, inspired by missionary zeal, stormed out to restore the world to God. By 652, they had conquered Egypt, Libya, Syria, Mesopotamia, and Persia. By 752, Islam extended from France to China and from Afghanistan to Ethiopia. No religion has ever spread so quickly.

During the next eight centuries, Muslims were the world's leaders in artistic and scientific achievement. In Spain, philosophers translated Plato and Aristotle; in India, they invented algebra. Universities prospered. Muslim traders and missionaries sailed up the Nile to its source and around South Asia to present-day Indonesia. A fifteenth-century geographer and historian, Ibn Khaldun, is often called the father of scientific **sociology** for his grand theory, which accounted for the rise and fall of civilizations based upon conflicts between urban and pastoral subcultures.

The golden age of Islam was informed by a distinctive superstructure, *umma*, a **community** which recognizes no difference between secular and sacred; thus, the rights and obligations of citizens and believers are identical. Umma is the ideal human **society**, based upon the unchanging, universal laws of God as expounded in the Qur'an and Hadith (short accounts of Muhammad's oral teachings). Certainly *sunna*, regulations concerning the details of religious observation, **morality**, ethics, and legal and legislative matters could vary from place to place, and a class of professional scholars, the *ulama*, was necessary to offer legal/theological opinions and moderate disputes, but in the end it was presumed that Muslims around the world were united by a single faith, a single law, and a single polity.

Islam was founded by the prophet Muhammad (570—632 CE).

In the twelfth century, Mongols burst from Central Asia to carve their own empires from Islamic dominions. Turks, British, French, Italians, and Russians followed, making umma increasingly fragmented and problematic. In the twentieth century, nation-states replaced the colonial powers, and Muslim leaders found themselves facing modernization, with its increasingly pervasive expectations concerning gender, sexuality, education, economics, and religious pluralism. Modernization, together with the expansion of Muslim communities into Europe, North America, and other regions where they are a small and sometimes oppressed minority, makes the conflation of divine and secular seem increasingly unfeasible.

The late twentieth-century Muslim response to modernization, globalization, and Westernization has varied. While decrying capitalist economic polity and Western mass media as colonial intrusions, many Muslim sociologists despair of ever again finding true solidarity in the umma. At the same time, folk beliefs, mysticism, and syncretic faiths such as the Nation of Islam have become increasingly popular, and the well-publicized resurgence of Islamic fundamentalism has had a profound effect on the social structures and political economies of countries from Algeria to Pakistan.

Today there are 950 million Muslims in the world, including most of the people in the Middle East, North Africa, and Indonesia, and significant minorities in Europe, sub-Saharan Africa, and North America. New converts are submitting to God daily in such unlikely places as Paris, Moscow, Tokyo, and Buenos Aires. The two main branches of Islam, Sunni and Shi'a, arose during a dispute over the succession of Muhammad, but currently they express many more distinctions in theology, religious observance, and social custom. Sunni predominates in most Muslim communities, while Shi'a, generally more conservative and hierarchical, is common primarily in Iran, parts of Turkey and Iraq, and among immigrant populations elsewhere.

The first mosque in North America was constructed in 1934 by a group of immigrants in Cedar Rapids, Iowa. However, within the last few decades, the political and social upheavals in the Middle East have multiplied the number of political and religious refugees, and an aggressive program of proselytization has produced many American converts, especially among African-Americans. There are now about six million Muslims in the United States.

Max Weber and Émile Durkheim produced extended studies of other religions but barely discussed Islam. Their successors have likewise expended very little energy on Islam, certainly much less than anthropologists or political scientists, and they have often produced poorly theorized, simplistic, and even stereotypic portrayals. Only within the last two decades have some sociologists, both Muslim and non-Muslim, begun to investigate the depth and complexity of Islamic life. Among the most important topics of study are Islamic fundamentalism, the lives of converts, the roles of women in traditional and modern Islamic societies, religious minorities in predominantly Muslim countries, anti-Muslim prejudice, and the **socialization** of Muslim immigrants.

J

JAMES, WILLIAM (1842-1910)
American psychologist and philosopher

William James was born January 11, 1842, in New York City, and died at his home in Chocorua, New Hampshire, on August 26, 1910. His family's wealth made travel and adventure a major part of his lifestyle while he was growing up. His education, therefore, came from tutors and private schools. He and his father, theologian Henry James, Sr., were very close. His father supported anything that William James wanted to do. However, his formal schooling was irregular and intermittent owing in part to the accidents of residence, and in part to his father's scrupulous regard for the genius of his children and his desire that they should develop from within rather than be molded from without. In consequence, James was impulsive in his studies. He began his higher education studying art under William Morris Hunt making a major change of course to study chemistry in 1861 at Lawrence Scientific School at Harvard. He then changed course again and decided to study medicine in 1864 at Harvard Medical School. He received his Medical Degree in 1869 but did not have much respect for the medical profession at the time of his studies at Harvard.

In the fall of 1872, James was appointed instructor in physiology in Harvard College where he taught courses in the biological sciences, a field closely related to both **philosophy** and **psychology** at the time, for the next ten years. He married Alice Howe Gibbens on July 10, 1878. Together they had five children: Henry, William, Herman (who died in one year after birth from pneumonia), Margaret Mary, and Alexander Robert.

William James published his most impressive work *The Principles of Psychology* in 1890 after 12 years of research. This was his defining work that lives on almost a century after his death due to its in-depth research on the discipline of psychology. Today this work is considered the definitive work of nineteenth-century psychology due to its comprehensive research. James himself realized, though, that the book would be outdated soon after its publication due to the research into a field that was, at the time, becoming newly recognized as a science. One idea put forth in this work, "stream of consciousness," describes the human thought process as flowing like a river of ever-changing thoughts, even while dreaming. This thought process never takes the same path twice.

James' ideas were controversial in both the fields of psychology and philosophy. James believed that the medical profession should not rule out such hard to understand events as supernatural healing and psychic phenomena simply because there is no scientific evidence. He wanted to change the field of philosophy to encompass everyday life and personal experience. He considered philosophy until that point to be nothing more than biographies of past philosophers.

Between 1879 and 1897, James intermittently published articles that were collected in *The Will to Believe*. The radical empiricism that had been anticipated in the *Principles* was formally announced in the preface of this volume. The most significant article, "The Sentiment of Rationality," dealt with "the purely theoretical of logical impulse,"—comprising the "passion for simplification" and the opposing passion for making distinctions. The remaining chapters undertook the psychological project of discussing "practical and emotional motives" and the "soundness of different philosophies." But the titular essay, "The Will to Believe," took the more advanced position that philosophies might *legitimately* be adopted from such motives.

The Varities of Religious Experience, 1902, encompassed another collection of essays. This work approached religion empirically and examined the validity of religious knowledge. James contended that religious beliefs must be fruitful, and mist be in agreement with man's moral and esthetic demands. The religious hypothesis has, in other words, two types of proof, the proof by immediate experience and the proof by life. He sought to define and systematize a metaphysics that would offer a satisfactory conception of reality.

James' major work in philosophy, *Pragmatism*, was published in 1907. His philosophy was based on individuality.

William James *(The Library of Congress)*

He denied that there could ever be absolute truth. The doctrine that truth of ideas is relative to the interests which generate them implies nothing whatsoever regarding the character of these interests. Hence, James' pragmatism did not emphasize worldly success, but the human interpretation of reality and the role of subjective interests in an individual' interpretation. The most common charge brought against him, however, was that of skeptical subjectivism.

Although suffering from intermittent periods of ill-health, James continued to devote himself to teaching, lecturing, reading, and writing. Other significant works include *Some Problems in Philosophy*, a compilation of lectures given as a visiting professor at Stanford University, *Essays in Radical Empiricism*, 1912, a series of articles in which James was prepared to take reality for what it appeared to be, and *Talks to Teachers on Psychology: and to Students on Some of Life's Ideals*, a collection of lectures that popularized his ideas, emphasizing the unique experience of each individual and providing a foundation for the newer discipline of educational psychology.

JANOWITZ, MORRIS (1919-1988)
American sociologist

Morris Janowitz is best remembered perhaps as the preeminent sociologist of the military. But his work went beyond analyses of the **institution** itself to examine patriotism, **nationalism**, and the balance between citizens' individual rights and their obligations to the **community**. In two early works—*The Professional Soldier* (1946) and *Sociology and the Military Establishment* (1959)—Janowitz argued that as industrial societies evolve and their institutional structures grow more complex and enveloping, **democracy** becomes more difficult to maintain.

Janowitz was born in Paterson, New Jersey, in 1919 and received his bachelor's degree in economics from New York University in 1941. For the first two years after graduation, he served as a propaganda analyst for the Department of **Justice** in Washington before joining the army and serving through the end of World War II. From 1948 to 1951, he served as an assistant professor of **sociology** at the University of Chicago, where he also earned his Ph.D. in 1948. From 1951 through 1961, he worked on the sociology faculty at the University of Michigan, before returning to the University of Chicago as a professor of sociology. From 1972 on, he served as the Lawrence A. Kimpton Distinguished Service Professor.

Janowitz was also been a frequent government advisor, beginning with his service on President Truman's Commission on Civil Rights in 1947. In 1962, he founded the Inter-University Seminar on Armed Forces and Society, where he served as chair until 1981. In 1986, he was appointed to occupy the S.L.A. Marshall Chair at the United States Army Research Institute for Behavioral and Social Sciences.

In his work on the subject of patriotism—including, most notably, *The Last Half-Century: Societal Change and Politics in America* (1978) and *The Reconstruction of Patriotism* (1983)—Janowitz argued forcefully that modern **American society** had placed individual rights far ahead of civic obligations. Moreover, he said that those institutions which could best inculcate **values** like civic-mindedness and patriotism—specifically, public schools and the military—were often failing to do so. This situation, he asserted, was a byproduct of the civil rights and antiwar movements of the 1960s and 1970s, which questioned people's commitment to national institutions while ridiculing the idea of patriotism. For Janowitz, these movements were seen largely in negative terms, with his focus being on how they destroyed a sense of social commitment among those who participated in them.

Critics of Janowitz's arguments claim that, while he claimed not to want to promote ''old-fashioned, blind, mechanical nationalism,'' this effect is exactly what he achieves in his work. Then, too, they say that he failed to distinguish between civic consciousness and nationalism. For example, Janowitz's critics say, both the civil rights and antiwar movements were intensely concerned with and promoted a strong commitment to civic institutions, even if this devotion came about in ways that moved people away from unquestioned loyalty to those same institutions.

Although most of his life's work involved research on patriotism and nationalism, Janowitz also wrote about such diverse themes as general sociological theory, political and **urban sociology**, and **race** and **ethnicity**. In 1950, he co-authored with Brunn Bettelheim an early and critical work on racial relations entitled *The Dynamics of Prejudices*.

JIM CROW LAWS

Jim Crow Laws refer to segregation laws common in the American South from 1883 to 1954 that permitted various forms of **discrimination** against African Americans. Following the Civil War and the **abolition** of slavery, the relationship of owner and **property** that characterized **race** relations between whites and blacks changed. Many whites still believed blacks were inferior. Following Emancipation, many blacks were still poor and often indebted to whites under the system of sharecropping. During Reconstruction (1865–1896), northern lawmakers attempted to regulate relations between blacks and whites and leverage the political power of the North. The Civil Rights Act of 1875, which made discrimination in public accommodations illegal, was one effort to ameliorate race relations.

However, in 1883, the U.S. Supreme Court overturned the Civil Rights Act of 1875, laying the groundwork for the institution of Jim Crow laws. The Court's *Plessy v. Ferguson* ruling provided further basis for segregation. Homer Plessy purchased a first-class train ticket for intrastate travel and was convicted of violating a Louisiana statute because he refused to accept seating in the coach designated for blacks. Plessy's lawyer made an argument based upon the Thirteenth and Fourteenth Amendments, but the Supreme Court ruled that "separate but equal" facilities were constitutional. Following this decision, states were free to mandate "separate but equal" restrooms, parks, transportation, schools and other public facilities. Throughout the South, "colored only" and "white only" signs were commonplace. Separate schools designated for blacks generally failed to provide equal access to educational resources and other black facilities were substandard.

Many segregation laws prohibited interracial **marriage**, carved out residential areas by race, and limited African American access to political power. Poll taxes, for example, which required citizens to pay fees in order to vote, discriminated against those with little money. Grandfather clauses, which made certain voting rights contingent upon the status of one's ancestors, could prevent descendants of slaves from participating in governmental elections.

For decades, this system of segregation perpetuated inequity and the disadvantages which African Americans had suffered in slavery. In 1954, in the landmark *Brown v. Board of Education* ruling, the U.S. Supreme Court proclaimed that school segregation based on race was unconstitutional. The Civil Rights Act of 1964, which was signed into law by President Lyndon B. Johnson, reclaimed some anti-discriminatory provisions overturned in the late 1800s. The Act made discrimination in public accommodations illegal and also outlawed discrimination in **employment** based on race, color, religion, sex, or national origin. The Equal Employment Op-

Jim Crow Laws permitted discrimination against African Americans in most Southern states through the mid-1960s *(AP/Wide World Photos, Inc.).*

portunity Commission, a governmental agency created to oversee and administer fair labor practices, was also established in 1964. In addition, the Civil Rights Act gave the government the right to penalize agencies with discriminatory practices by withholding funding. Over a century after Emancipation, legislation finally ended the Jim Crow Laws.

See also Discrimination; Segregation and Desegregation

JOHNSON, VIRGINIA ESHELMAN (1925-   )
American psychologist and sex therapist

Virginia Eshelman. Johnson is a researcher in human sexuality. With her then-husband, Dr. **William Howell Masters**, she co-wrote *Human Sexual Response* in 1966. In collaboration with Masters, Johnson pioneered the study of human sexuality under laboratory conditions. She and Masters published the results of their study as a book entitled *Human Sexual Response* in 1966, causing an immediate sensation. As part of her work at the Reproductive Biology Research Foundation in St. Louis and later at the Masters and Johnson Institute, she counseled many clients and taught sex therapy to many professional practitioners.

Johnson was born on February 11, 1925, in Springfield, Missouri, to Hershel Eshelman, a farmer, and Edna (Evans) Eshelman. The elder of two children, she began school in Palo Alto, California, where her family had moved in 1930. When they returned to Missouri three years later, she was ahead of her school peers and skipped several grades. She studied piano and voice and read extensively. She entered Drury College in Springfield in 1941. After her freshman year, she was hired to work in the state insurance office, a job she held for four years. Her mother, a republican state committeewoman, introduced her to many elected officials, and Johnson often sang for them at meetings. These performances led to a job as a country music singer for radio station KWTO in Springfield, where her stage name was Virginia Gibson. She studied at the University of Missouri and later at the Kansas City Conservatory of Music. In 1947, she became a business writer for the St. Louis *Daily Record*. She also worked briefly on the marketing staff of KMOX- TV, leaving that position in 1951.

In the early 1940s Johnson married a Missouri politician, but the marriage lasted only two days. Her second marriage (to an attorney many years her senior) also ended in divorce. On June 13, 1950, she married George V. Johnson, an engineering student and leader of a dance band. She sang with the band until the birth of her two children, Scott Forstall and Lisa Evans. In 1956, the Johnsons divorced.

In 1956, contemplating a return to college for a degree in sociology, Johnson applied for a job at the Washington University **employment** office. William Howell Masters, associate professor of clinical obstetrics and gynecology, had requested an assistant to interview volunteers for a research project. He personally chose Johnson, who fitted the need for an outgoing, intelligent, mature woman who was preferably a mother.

Gathering scientific **data** by means of electroencephalography, electrocardiography, and the use of color monitors, Masters and Johnson measured and analyzed 694 volunteers. They were careful to protect the privacy of their subjects, who were photographed in various modes of sexual stimulation. In addition to a description of the four stages of sexual arousal, other valuable information was gained from the photographs, including evidence of the failure of some contraceptives, the discovery of a vaginal secretion in some women that prevents conception, and the observation that sexual enjoyment need not decrease with age. In 1964, Masters and Johnson founded the non-profit Reproductive Biology Research Foundation in St. Louis and began treating couples for sexual problems. Originally listed as a research associate, Johnson became assistant director of the Foundation in 1969 and co-director in 1973.

In 1966, Masters and Johnson released their book *Human Sexual Response,* in which they detailed the results of their studies. Although the book was written in dry, clinical terms and intended for medical professionals, its titillating subject matter made it front-page news and a runaway best seller, with over 300,000 volumes distributed by 1970. While some reviewers accused the team of dehumanizing and scientizing sex, overall professional and critical response was positive.

At Johnson's suggestion, the two researchers went on the lecture circuit to discuss their findings. Their book and their public appearances heightened public interest in sex therapy and a long list of clients developed. Couples referred to

their clinic would spend two weeks in intensive therapy and have periodic follow-ups for five years. In a second book *Human Sexual Inadequacy* published in 1970, Masters and Johnson discuss the possibility that sex problems are more cultural than physiological or psychological. In 1975, they wrote *The Pleasure Bond: A New Look at Sexuality and Commitment,* which differs from previous volumes in that it was written for the average reader. This book describes total commitment and fidelity to the partner as the basis for an enduring sexual bond. To expand counseling, Masters and Johnson trained dual-sex therapy teams and conducted regular workshops for college teachers, marriage counselors, and other professionals.

After the release of this second book, Masters divorced his first wife and married Johnson on January 7, 1971, in Fayetteville, Arkansas. They continued their work at the Reproductive Biology Research Foundation, and in 1973 founded the Masters and Johnson Institute. Johnson was co-director of the institute, running the everyday business, and Masters concentrated on scientific work. Johnson, who never received a college degree, was widely recognized along with Masters for her contributions to human sexuality research. Together they received several awards, including the Sex Education and Therapists Award in 1978 and Biomedical Research Award of the World Sexology Association in 1979.

Their book *Homosexuality in Perspective* documents their research on gay and lesbian sexual practice and homosexual sexual problems and their work with ''gender-confused'' individuals who sought a ''cure'' for their **homosexuality**. One of their most controversial conclusions from their ten year study of eighty-four men and women was their conviction that homosexuality is primarily not physical, emotional, or genetic, but a learned behavior. Some reviewers hailed the team's claims of success in ''converting'' homosexuals. Others, however, observed that the handpicked individuals who participated in the study were not a representative sample; moreover, they challenged the team's assumption that heterosexual performance alone was an accurate indicator of a changed sexual preference.

In 1988, Masters and Johnson, along with Robert Kolodny, published *Crisis: Heterosexual Behavior in the Age of AIDS.* The book, commented Stephen Fried ''was politically incorrect in the extreme'': it predicted a large-scale outbreak of the virus in the heterosexual **community** and, in a chapter meant to document how little was known of the AIDS virus, suggested that it might be possible to catch it from a toilet seat. Several prominent members of the medical community questioned the study, and many accused the authors of sowing hysteria. Adverse publicity hurt the team, who were distressed because they felt the medical community had turned against them.

The board of the institute was quietly dissolved and Johnson went into semi-retirement. In 1992, after 21 years of marriage, Masters and Johnson filed for divorce because of differences about goals relating to work and retirement. Following the divorce, Johnson took most of the institute's records with her and is continuing her work independently.

JUDAISM

Judaism, perhaps the first of the world's monotheistic religions, is the religion of ancient Palestinian farmers and shepherds who heard the ancient Shema, which states: "Hear, O Israel! The Lord our God is One!" Buffeted about by Egypt, Assyria, Persia, and Rome, the Jews (so called from their origin in the Roman province of Judea) settled in every corner of the Old World, as far south as Ethiopia and as far east as China; more recently they have settled in such remote places as Iceland and Toga.

During the Middle Ages, two distinct branches of Judaism emerged. The Sephardim of Greece, Italy, and the Middle East spoke a modified form of Spanish called Ladino, while the Ashkenazim of Germany, Eastern Europe, and Russia spoke a modified form of German called Yiddish. The two differed so widely in their beliefs, worship traditions, costume, and diet that they sometimes did not even recognize each other as fellow Jews.

Early sociologists were extremely interested in the social, political, and cultural structures of Jewish life, both ancient and modern; **Sigmund Freud**, Émile Durkheim, and **Karl Marx** discussed Judaism in detail, though not always with sensitivity or even tolerance. Weber coined the frequently-excoriated term, pariah people, to refer to the marginalization and exclusion of Jewish persons from mainstream European **culture** and theorized that the stability of Jewish communities over the centuries resulted, to a great extent, from the boundary maintenance required by this outsider status.

More recently, scholars have suggested that Jewish communities depend not upon external marginalization but upon the observance of *halakha* (**rules**, rituals and social practices) delineated in the Bible, Talmud, and various commentaries, which dictate how individuals in every station of life (husband/wife, parent/child, teacher/student) should conduct themselves in relation to their own and other social roles, as well as in relation as to outsiders and to God. The most important halakha are the *mitzvot* (blessed acts such as charity and study of the Torah) which bring joy to the **community** and also coincidentally increase group solidarity.

The vision of Jews as a separate people, distinct ethnically and culturally as well as by religious belief, may have helped ensure Jewish survival through the centuries, but it has also been used as an excuse for non-Jews to practice antisemitic **prejudice, discrimination**, and brutal acts of violence, up to and including the Holocaust, the destruction of six million Jews and the entire civilization of Jewish Europe during World War II. While the Holocaust has been extensively studied, most sociologists are more interested in the depth and extent of everyday antisemitic prejudice, which seems remarkably insidious and can exist even in areas where the Jewish population is minimal.

There are four major branches of contemporary Judaism: Orthodox, which attempts to maintain the tradition of Jews as a separate ethnic and cultural group, with distinctive costume, diet, and social structures; Reform, which attempts to maintain Judaism as a religious faith, requiring few if any distinctive cultural practices (kosher laws are optional, for instance); Conservative and Reconstructionist Judaism which are compromises between the other two. Of course, the branches cannot be reduced to a simple debate over religion and culture (that is, whether one is Jewish or practices Judaism).

Drawn by the promise of religious freedom in the New World, a small group of Sephardic Jews settled in New Amsterdam in 1653; however, the flood of Jewish immigration in the late 1800's came mostly from Germany, Poland, and Russia, so American Judaism became more or less synonymous with Ashkenazim. Never more than three percent of the total population, the Jewish community has had a profound effect on **American society**, immeasurably enriching philosophy, literature, science, and the fine arts. Today seven million Americans consider themselves Jewish, but only about half maintain membership in synagogues; the others may be members of other religions, atheists, or simply uninterested in their faith. Levels of observance have been declining steadily for the last century, for which scholars often blame Jewish assimilation into the mainstream of American culture. At best a shift from an essentially religious to an essentially secular Judaism, assimilation is also theorized as an inauthentic co-option of the Protestant Christian state-church dichotomy, and even as a serious threat to Jewish **identity** itself.

There are about 17.6 million Jews in the rest of the world, including large minorities in Russia, the Middle East, South Africa, and South America. The 1948 creation of the modern nation of Israel, the world's only officially Jewish state and the site of massive immigration of Jews around the world, sparked a flurry of interest among sociologists. Among the chief objects of study are the growth of an essentially Western culture in a Middle Eastern setting, the impact of Orthodoxy on Israeli politics, the role of ethnic and religious minorities, and the distinctive kibbutzim models of communal living. Other sociologists have researched sectarian impulses in modern Judaism, intermarriage, and conversion; they have produced many portrayals of specialized groups, such as Hasidic and other sects, Zionist youth movements, Jewish intellectuals, women, and gay men and lesbians.

JUNG, CARL GUSTAV (1875-1961)
Swiss psychologist and psychiatrist

The Swiss psychologist and psychiatrist Carl Gustav Jung (1875–1961) was a founder of modern depth **psychology**. Carl Jung was born on July 26, 1875, in Kesswil, the son of a Protestant clergyman. When he was four, the family moved to Basel. As he grew older, his keen interest in biology, zoology, paleontology, philosophy, and the history of religion made the choice of a career quite difficult. However, he finally decided on medicine, which he studied at the University of Basel (1895–1900). He received his medical degree from the University of Zurich in 1902. Later he studied psychology in Paris. In 1903 Jung married Emma Rauschenbach, his loyal companion and scientific collaborator until her death in 1955. The couple had five children. They lived in Küsnacht on the Lake of Zurich, where Jung died on June 6, 1961.

Carl Jung *(The Library of Congress)*

Jung began his professional career in 1900 as an assistant to Eugen Bleuler at the psychiatric clinic of the University of Zurich. During these years of his internship, Jung, with a few associates, worked out the so-called association experiment. This is a method of testing used to reveal affectively significant groups of ideas in the unconscious region of the psyche. They usually have a disturbing **influence**, promoting anxieties and unadapted emotions which are not under the control of the person concerned. Jung coined the term ''complexes'' for their designation.

When Jung read Sigmund Freud's *Interpretation of Dreams,* he found his own ideas and observations to be essentially confirmed and furthered. He sent his publication *Studies in Word Association* (1904) to Freud, and this was the beginning of their collaboration and friendship, which lasted from 1907 to 1913. Jung was eager to explore the secrets of the unconscious psyche expressed by dreaming, fantasies, myths, fairy tales, superstition, and occultism. But Freud had already worked out his theories about the underlying cause of every psychoneurosis and also his doctrine that all the expressions of the unconscious are hidden wish fulfillments. Jung felt more and more that these theories were scientific presumptions which did not do full justice to the rich expressions of unconscious psychic life. For him the unconscious not only is a disturbing factor causing psychic illnesses but also is fundamentally the seed of man's creativeness and the roots of human consciousness. With such ideas Jung came increasingly into conflict with Freud, who regarded Jung's ideas as unscientific. Jung accused Freud of dogmatism; Freud and his followers reproached Jung for mysticism.

His break with Freud caused Jung much distress. Thrown back upon himself, he began a deepened self-analysis in order to gain all the integrity and firmness for his own quest into the dark labyrinth of the unconscious psyche. During the years from 1913 to 1921 Jung published only three important papers: ''Two Essays on Analytical Psychology'' (1916, 1917) and ''Psychological Types'' (1921). The ''Two Essays'' provided the basic ideas from which his later work sprang. He described his research on psychological typology (extro- and introversion, thinking, feeling, sensation, and intuition as psychic functions) and expressed the idea that it is the ''personal equation'' which, often unconsciously but in accordance with one's own typology, influences the approach of an individual toward the outer and inner world. Especially in psychology, it is impossible for an observer to be completely objective, because his observation depends on subjective, personal presuppositions. This insight made Jung suspicious of any dogmatism.

Next to his typology, Jung's main contribution was his discovery that man's fantasy life, like the instincts, has a certain structure. There must be imperceptible energetic centers in the unconscious which regulate instinctual behavior and spontaneous imagination. Thus emerge the dominants of the collective unconscious, or the **archetypes**. Spontaneous **dreams** exist which show an astonishing resemblance to ancient mythological or fairy-tale motifs that are usually unknown to the dreamer. To Jung this meant that archetypal manifestations belong to man in all ages; they are the expression of man's basic psychic nature. Modern civilized man has built a rational superstructure and repressed his dependence on his archetypal nature—hence the feeling of self-estrangement, which is the cause of many neurotic sufferings.

In order to study archetypal patterns and processes, Jung visited so-called primitive tribes. He lived among the Pueblo Indians of New Mexico and Arizona in 1924–1925 and among the inhabitants of Mt. Elgon in Kenya during 1925–1926. He later visited Egypt and India. To Jung, the religious symbols and **phenomenology** of **Buddhism** and **Hinduism** and the teachings of Zen Buddhism and **Confucianism** all expressed differentiated experiences on the way to man's inner world, a world which was neglected by Western civilization. Jung also searched for traditions in Western **culture** which compensated for its one-sided extroverted development toward rationalism and technology. He found these traditions in Gnosticism, Christian mysticism, and, above all, alchemy. For Jung, the weird alchemical texts were astonishing symbolic expressions for the human experience of the processes in the unconscious. Some of his major works are deep and lucid psychological interpretations of alchemical writings, showing their living significance for understanding dreams and the hidden motifs of neurotic and mental disorders.

Of prime importance to Jung was the biography of the stages of inner development and of the maturation of the personality, which he termed the "process of individuation." He described a strong impulse from the unconscious to guide the individual toward its specific, most complete uniqueness. This achievement is a lifelong task of trial and error and of confronting and integrating contents of the unconscious. It consists in an ever-increasing self-knowledge and in "becoming what you are." But individuation also includes social responsibility, which is a great step on the way to self-realization.

Jung lived for his explorations, his writings, and his psychological practice, which he had to give up in 1944 due to a severe heart attack. His academic appointments during the course of his career included the professorship of medical psychology at the University of Basel and the titular professorship of **philosophy** from 1933 until 1942 on the faculty of philosophical and political sciences of the Federal Institute of Technology in Zurich. In 1948 he founded the C. G. Jung Institute in Zurich. Honorary doctorates were conferred on him by many important universities all over the world.

JUSTICE

Justice is a social obligation as well as a description of appropriate social conduct. The concept of justice and, in particular, social justice, has a wide variety of meanings. Justice is fundamental to ethical theory and political **philosophy**. It is an overarching idea that has prominence in the fields of philosophy, political science, **social policy**, religion, psychology, and the law.

The term, justice, is usually divided into formal or procedural justice and material substantive justice. Justice is often associated with issues of equity (impartiality) and equality. Both areas deal with due process, impartiality, and the distribution of justice; however, procedural justice focuses on how justice is distributed in **society**, and substantive justice focuses on the individual and individual freedoms. Procedural justice is thought to benefit the individual even if justice is not equally distributed. Our system of justice emphasizes equal outcomes. This theory resembles former political theories that adopt a notion that a rising tide floats all boats.

Another problem with the issue of justice is that the principles are often obscure and difficult to apply from a theoretical perspective to a practical application. For example, procedural justice might deal with an issue such as equal opportunity but describing what criteria to employ in considering people as equal remains difficult. The treatment of criminals is another murky area. American justice is supposed to believe in rehabilitation, but our focus is often on retribution. The American justice system's emphasis is on punishing those who commit illegal activities, on getting even. Restorative justice policies focus on awarding the victim some form of compensation.

Within the United States especially there is a call for justice to be fair since justice is viewed as an essential part of a legitimate government, and many cultures believe that socie-

ties should be instilled with principals of justice. Social justice often causes dispute. The problem is that different political ideologies tend to favor different justice principles. The idea that justice is blind refers to the ideal that decisions of justice are made impartially. The study of justice in **sociology**, however, directs attentions to the areas of stratification, welfare, **family**, and education, all of which influence decisions.

JUVENILE CRIME

Juvenile **crime** is defined as **measurement** of the behavior that is committed by someone under the legal age of adulthood that violates a state's penal code. Sociologists use two different types of statistics to measure juvenile crime, official and unofficial **crime statistics**. Official crime statistics are those based on aggregate records of offenders and offenses processed by the formal **justice** and corrections systems. The most widely known and used of these is the Uniform Crime Reports (UCR), which utilizes **data** from virtually all (approximately 96 percent in 1997) United States police agencies. The two most commonly utilized statistics from these data are the delinquency rate (number of offenses per 100,000 juveniles) and the percent change statistic (ratio of amount of change between two specific time periods).

Sociologists also often use unofficial crime statistics, which are produced by people and agencies outside the formal criminal justice system. These studies attempt to measure hidden delinquency (crime that goes unreported) by using victimization **surveys** and self-reporting crime surveys, which ask people questions about the number of crimes committed against them or that they themselves have committed. Obviously, each of these methods carries certain advantages and disadvantages. Official crime statistics are highly accurate in reporting arrests and convictions, but are limited to only these numbers. Conversely, any studies that ask people to report victimization or criminal activity suffer from social desirability problems, low response rates, memory errors and respondents' fear of being identified.

When sociologists examine juvenile crime in the United States, they see several interesting trends emerge. Most notable is the recent reduction in overall crime: between 1993 and 1997, **violent crime** among juveniles declined six percent and property crime decreased by three and a half percent. This fact seems particularly surprising in light of the rash of school shootings and the mass media's emphasis upon **gun control**. Within this overall trend, however, certain stark demographic differences still present themselves. One significant demographic shift is **sex differences**. The proportion of female juveniles committing crimes is on the rise. Although girls still commit fewer crimes than boys do, female arrests for violent crimes between 1988 and 1997 increased by just over one hundred percent, more than double the increase in male arrests. In addition, female drug use and gang participation have been steadily increasing in the past decade. There are large racial discrepancies in juvenile crime as well. In 1997, the **ratio** of African American arrests to those of White juveniles was 4:1

Juvenile Arrests for Selected Offenses: 1980 to 1997

[**169,439 represents 169,439,000.** Juveniles are persons between the ages 10-17]

Offense	1980	1985	1990	1991	1992	1993	1994	1995	1996	1997
Number of contributing agencies . .	8,178	11,263	10,765	10,148	11,058	10,277	10,693	10,037	10,026	9,471
Population covered (1,000)	169,439	206,269	204,543	189,962	217,754	213,705	208,035	206,762	195,805	194,925
NUMBER										
Violent crime, total.	77,220	75,077	97,103	95,677	118,358	122,434	125,141	123,131	104,455	99,342
Murder.	1,475	1,384	2,661	2,626	3,025	3,473	3,114	2,812	2,184	1,873
Forcible rape.	3,668	5,073	4,971	4,766	5,451	5,490	4,873	4,556	4,228	4,102
Robbery.	38,529	31,833	34,944	35,632	42,639	44,598	47,046	47,240	39,788	36,059
Aggravated assault	33,548	36,787	54,527	52,653	67,243	68,873	70,108	68,523	58,255	57,308
Weapon law violations	21,203	27,035	33,123	37,575	49,903	54,414	52,278	46,506	40,145	39,001
Drug abuse, total	86,685	78,660	66,300	58,603	73,232	90,618	124,931	149,236	148,783	154,540
Sale and manufacturing	13,004	14,846	24,575	22,929	25,331	27,635	32,746	34,077	32,558	30,642
Heroin/cocaine.	1,318	2,851	17,511	16,915	17,881	18,716	20,327	19,187	17,465	15,778
Marijuana	8,876	8,646	4,372	3,579	4,853	6,144	8,812	10,682	11,489	11,168
Synthetic narcotics	465	414	346	570	663	455	465	701	614	671
Dangerous nonnarcotic drugs .	2,345	2,935	2,346	1,865	1,934	2,320	3,142	3,507	2,990	3,025
Possession.	73,681	63,814	41,725	35,674	47,901	62,983	92,185	115,159	116,225	123,898
Heroin/cocaine.	2,614	7,809	15,194	13,747	16,855	17,726	21,004	21,253	17,560	18,104
Marijuana	64,465	50,582	20,940	16,490	25,004	37,915	61,003	82,015	87,712	93,579
Synthetic narcotics	1,524	1,085	1,155	885	897	1,008	1,227	2,047	1,713	1,987
Dangerous nonnarcotic drugs .	5,078	4,338	4,436	4,552	5,145	6,334	8,951	9,844	9,240	10,228

Source: U.S. Federal Bureau of Investigation, *Crime in the United States*, annual.

for violent crime and 2:1 for property crime, a statistic that owes largely to higher rates of gang participation.

See also Juvenile Delinquency

JUVENILE DELINQUENCY

Juvenile delinquency refers to any activity by persons classified as ''juveniles'' given their age, that violates a criminal law or other legal code. The term first appeared in 1899 when the first U.S. juvenile court was established in the state of Illinois. In addition to the legal definition of delinquency, there are two other types of delinquency definitions: status offense definitions and sociological definitions.

Criminal definitions of juvenile delinquency hinge on the offender's age. If an offender was thirty-six years old at the time he or she committed a criminal offense, that person would be termed a criminal. A person of twelve who commits the very same act is termed a juvenile delinquent. Age is also the pivotal factor in status offenses, a class of delinquent acts committed by offenders that are criminal violations simply because of the offender's age or status. For example, the purchase of alcohol by a fifteen-year-old is a status offense. The offender's age makes the action an infraction of the law. The age of juveniles varies from state to state; for example, in states such as New York, Connecticut and North Carolina, a juvenile is age sixteen and under, while in the majority of states and in all federal districts, a juvenile is age eighteen and under.

Sociological definitions of juvenile delinquency also depend on age and are largely focused on whether there is an infraction of the criminal law. Therefore, deviant actions by juveniles that violate social **norms** but not legal codes are not considered delinquent. In the United States, sociological explanations of delinquency were developed parallel to the establishment of juvenile institutions. These definitions factor in social influences, such as **family**, environment, social class, and relationships with peers and authority figures.

During the period of social adjustment following industrialization, juvenile institutions aimed at alleviating problems of the poor were established in the United States. In New York City, Boston, and Philadelphia, ''Houses of Refuge'' were used to educate and train troubled and poor youth and to separate juveniles from negative influences found in adult criminal institutions. Troubled and poor youth were the first juvenile delinquents of the Unites States. The rationale for such innovations was based on **positivism**, or a belief that one's social environment influenced behavior rather than one's own free will. If the social environment could be ''fixed,'' behavior would improve.

The intention of early juvenile courts was to provide an informal forum where the juvenile could be helped and treated rather than punished. A juvenile delinquent was thus perceived as different from a criminal, as the nature of delinquency was far less grievous than criminal offenses. Today's juvenile courts are also less formal than their adult counterparts. Juvenile delinquents are taken into custody and petitioned rather than arrested and indicted. They receive dispositions and may be committed rather than sentenced and incarcerated.

For many years, juvenile courts in the United States acted in accordance with the principle *parens patriae*, or the state as parent, which meant that when a juvenile committed any act that society had deemed delinquent, the courts could step in and institutionalize the juvenile. The belief was that the state was acting in the best interests of juveniles since their parents appeared to be incapable or unwilling to properly care for these children. The remnants of this **philosophy** can be seen in today's court system as juvenile delinquents are sometimes referred to as PINS (persons in need of supervision), CHINS (children in need of supervision), or JINS (juveniles in need of supervision).

Compared to other social sciences, **sociology** has arguably contributed the most to the study of juvenile delinquency; its most influential perspectives are on social learning, **social control**, labeling, conflict, social disorganization, and strain and feminist theories. These areas of study have been evaluated, criticized, and reformulated, resulting in various perspectives that attempt to explain why juveniles violate social norms.

The most important social control **theory** and one of the landmark theories of juvenile delinquency is Travis Hirschi's (1969) social bonding theory. Hirschi cites delinquency as resulting from a weakening of an individual's bond to **society**. The weakness of the bond does not cause delinquency but rather allows for delinquency. The bond comprises attachment, commitment, involvement, and beliefs. Attachment refers to how much the individual cares about what others think. If what others think matters a great deal, the person is less likely to be involved in delinquency. The second element, commitment, refers to the amount of time and level of commitment an individual gives to pursuing conventional interests and goals. The stronger the commitment, the less likely one is to become involved in delinquency, since conventional goals are at risk. Involvement, "engrossment in conventional activities," (Hirschi, p. 22) leaves little time and energy for delinquency. Finally, belief refers to the **probability** that once an individual is socialized into a common belief system, involvement in a delinquent **belief system** becomes unlikely. Hirschi's was the first theory of juvenile delinquency to be successfully applied across socioeconomic groups, groups of different ethnicities and both genders.

The extent of juvenile delinquency in the United States can be ascertained through official statistics or unofficial measures. Many agencies, such as the FBI, juvenile courts, juvenile agencies and juvenile detention facilities, keep records of the characteristics of juvenile offenders, their offenses, and their victims. Official statistics, such as the FBI Uniform **Crime** reports, may not be accurate given that these statistics are based on arrest rates and do not include any estimate of the dark figure of crime. Two examples of widely recognized unofficial measures of juvenile delinquency are the National Youth Survey and Monitoring the Future Survey. These **surveys** address respondents' experiences with crime, their attitudes toward it, and a variety of factors addressing behavior and other social issues.

The Office of Juvenile Justice and Delinquency Prevention (OJJDP), which is under the Department of Justice umbrella, publishes a National Report on juvenile offenders and victims each year. The statistics used to compile this report come from a variety of sources including official statistics and victimization reports. The most recent edition of this report concurs with current notions that the rate of serious, violent crimes committed by juveniles have decreased compared to twenty years ago. Further, violent juvenile offenders are geographically concentrated: more than 25% of juvenile murderers in 1997 came from only eight counties in the United States.

K

KANT, IMMANUEL (1724-1804)
German philosopher

The major works of the German philosopher Immanuel Kant analyze speculative and moral reason and the faculty of human judgement. Kant exerted influence on the intellectual movements of the nineteenth and twentieth centuries. The fourth of nine children of Johann Georg and Anna Regina Kant, Immanuel Kant was born in Königsberg on April 22, 1724. In 1740 Kant entered the University of Königsberg where he became interested in **philosophy**, mathematics, and the natural sciences. Kant accepted the rationalism of Leibniz and Wolff and the natural philosophy of Newton until he read the works of David Hume.

Impoverished by the death of his father in 1746, Kant became a private tutor for seven years. He published several papers dealing with scientific questions, the most important of which was "General Natural History and Theory of the Heavens" (1755). Here Kant postulated the the solar system originated from the gravitational interaction of atoms. This theory anticipated Laplace's hypothesis (1796).

Kant spent the next 15 years (1755–1770) as a nonsalaried lecturer whose fees were derived entirely from the students who attended his lectures. In order to live he lectured between 26 and 28 hours a week on metaphysics, logic, mathematics, physics, and physical geography. Despite this enormous teaching burden, Kant continued to publish papers. He finally achieved a professorship at Königsberg in 1770.

Kant produced *Critique of Pure Reason* (1781; second edition 1787), one of the most important and difficult books in Western thought which attempts to resolve the contradictions inherent in perception and conception as explained by the rationalists and empiricists.

Kant was the first thinker to posit the problem of pure reason correctly by isolating a third order of judgment. The fundamental propositions of mathematics, science, and metaphysics are *synthetic a priori*, and *Critique of Pure Reason* explores how understanding and reason can be known apart from experience. The solution to this problem is Kant's "Copernican Revolution." He bridged the widening gap between rationalism (Descartes, Leibniz, Spinoza) and empricism (Hobbes, Locke, Hume) in modern philosophy.

Unlike later idealists, Kant does not say that the mind creates objects but only the conditions under which objects are perceived and understood. These, for Kant, are the *synthetic a priori* truths that guide our experience. The attempt to preserve a realist orientation led Kant to distinguish between the appearances of things (*phenomena*), as conditioned by the subjective forms of intuition, and the categories of the understanding and things-in-themselves (*noumena*). In brief, mathematics and science are true because they are derived from the ways in which the mind conditions its percepts and concepts and metaphysics is an illusion because it claims to tell us about things as they really are.

The first critique attempts to reconcile the conflict between rationalism and **empiricism** over the role of experience. Kant's ingenuity is to suggest that both parties are correct but one-sided. The problem of the transcendental esthetic can be seen in the term "a priori intuition." That is, what does the mind tell us about experience prior to having experience? Kant argues that if one eliminates the content of any possible intuition, space and time remain as the *a priori* forms, or ways, in which the mind can perceive. Thus, for Kant, space and time are "transcendentally ideal" and "empirically real" as conditions of experience and objective, constitutive principles of intuition. Also necesary for experience is the *trascendental unity of apperception*, that one consciousness has experiences, thus unifying our perceptions. Here, Kant offers a solution to Hume's claim that there is no reason for connected experiences to be causally related. In effect, Kant simply says that cause and effect is a necessity for experience, positing it in the noumena, even though it cannot be justified in the phenomenal world.

Kant believed science is knowing and metaphysics is false, speculative thinking. Knowing is confirmed by experi-

Immanuel Kant *(The Library of Congress)*

ence as above, but the categories can be extended beyond space and time, and they, then, function as ideas of pure reason. Since metaphysics claims to speak about things as they are rather than as they appear, such pure thinking must justify itself without appeal to experience. But that is just the difficulty when one asks questions about the unconditioned reality of the self, world, or God. It is not that reason is incapable of producing arguments, but rather that there are equally valid arguments that contradict one another, and experience is unable to resolve these ''antinomies,'' or seeming contradictions.

In 1783 Kant restated the main outlines of his first critique in a brief, analytic form in the *Prolegomena to Any Future Metaphysics*. In 1785 he presented an early view of the practical aspects of reason in *Fundamental Principles of the Metaphysic of Morals*. In 1788 he published the *Critique of Practical Reason*.

While theoretical reason is concerned with cognition, practical reason is concerned with will, or self-determination. There is only one human reason, but after it decides what it can know, it must determine how it shall act. Thus the freedom of the will, which is only a speculative possibility for pure reason, becomes the practical necessity of determining how one shall lead his life. And the fundamental, rational principle of a free morality is some universal and necessary law to which a man commits himself. This principle is called by Kant the ''Categorical Imperative,'' which states that a man should obligate himself to act so that any one of his actions could be made into a universal law binding all mankind.

In 1790 Kant completed his third critique, which attempts to draw these conflicting tensions together. In pure reason the mind produces constitutive principles of *phenomena,* and in practical reason the mind produces regulative principles of noumenal reality. The *Critique of Judgment* attempts to connect the concepts of nature with the concepts of freedom.

Although Kant continued writing until shortly before his death, the ''critical works'' are the source of his influence. Only a life of extraordinary self-discipline enabled him to accomplish his task. He attributed his longevity to a fixed daily routine, consisting of meditation, study, lecturing, socializing with friends over dinner, and taking a long mid-afternoon walk. In old age, Kant became totally blind and died on February 12, 1804.

KING, JR., MARTIN LUTHER (1929-1968)
American civil rights activist and minister

Nobel Prize winner Rev. Martin Luther King, Jr. originated the nonviolence strategy within the activist civil rights movement. King was born on January 15, 1929, in Atlanta, Georgia. Following graduation from Morehouse College in 1948, King entered Crozer Theological Seminary, having been ordained the previous year. He graduated from Crozer in 1951 and received his doctorate in theology from Boston University in 1955.

In Boston, King met Coretta Scott, whom he married on June 18, 1953. They had four children. King became minister of Dexter Avenue Baptist Church in Montgomery, Alabama, in 1954, and became active with the National Association for the Advancement of Colored People (NAACP) and the Alabama Council on Human Relations.

In December 1955, Rosa Parks, a black woman, was arrested for violating a segregated seating ordinance on a public bus in Montgomery, thus initiating a series of protests which ultimately led to the boycott the segregated city buses and the formation of Montgomery Improvement Association (MIA). The boycott lasted over a year, until the bus company capitulated. Segregated seating was discontinued, and some African Americans were employed as bus drivers.U.S. Supreme Court affirmed that the bus segregation laws of Montgomery as unconstitutional.

In January 1957 approximately sixty black ministers in Atlanta formed the Southern Christian Leadership Conference

Dr. Martin Luther King, Jr. *(New York Amsterdam News)*

(SCLC). A few months later King met Vice President Richard Nixon, and a year later King and three other black civil rights leaders were received by President Dwight Eisenhower. However, neither meeting resulted in any concrete relief for African Americans.

In February 1958 the SCLC resolved to double the number of southern black voters. King traveled constantly, speaking for **justice**, and he and his wife visited India at the invitation of Prime Minister Nehru. King had long been interested in Mahatma Gandhi's practice of nonviolence. Yet when they returned to the United States, the civil rights struggle had intensified.

In 1960 King became minister of his father's church in Atlanta. The sit-in movement began in Greensboro, North Carolina, by African American students protesting segregation at lunch counters in city stores. King urged the young people to continue using nonviolent means. The Student Nonviolent Coordinating Committee (SNCC) emerged, and for a time the SNCC worked closely with the SCLC.

By August sit-ins had succeeded in ending segregation at lunch counters in 27 southern cities. SCLC delegates resolved to focus nonviolent campaigns against all segregated public transportation, waiting rooms, and schools; to increase emphasis on voter registration; and to use economic boycotts to gain fair **employment** and benefits.

The Congress of Racial Equality (CORE), SCLC, and SNCC joined in a coalition. A Freedom Ride Coordinating Committee was formed with King as chairman. The idea was to "put the sit-ins on the road" by having pairs of black and white volunteers board interstate buses traveling through the South to test compliance with a new federal law. Finally, nonsegregation laws were followed in buses engaged in interstate transportation and in their terminals.

In an ambitious voter education program in Albany and the surrounding area, SNCC and SCLC members were harassed by whites. Churches were bombed, and local black citizens were threatened and sometimes attacked. King's nonviolent crusade responded with **prayer** vigils. The 1964

Federal Civil Rights Act finally desegregated public facilities in Albany.

In May 1962 King took on the Birmingham, Alabama, campaign. In early 1963 King made a speaking tour, recruiting volunteers and obtaining money for bail bonds. The SCLC's campaign continually met harassment from Birmingham police. Finally, a period of truce was established, and negotiations began with the city power structure. Though an agreement was reached, the Ku Klux Klan bombed the home of King's brother and the motel where SCLC members were headquartered.

On August 27, 1963, over 250,000 black and white citizens assembled in Washington, D.C., for a mass civil rights rally, where King delivered his famous "Let Freedom Ring" address. That same year he was featured as *Time* magazine's "Man of the Year."

The next year King and his followers moved into St. Augustine, Florida, where after weeks of nonviolent demonstrations and violent counterattacks, a biracial committee was set up to move St. Augustine toward desegregation. A few weeks later the 1964 Civil Rights Bill was signed by President Lyndon Johnson.

In September 1964 King received an honorary doctorate from the Evangelical Theological College in Berlin. Back in the United States, King endorsed Lyndon Johnson's presidential candidacy. That December, King received the Nobel Peace Prize.

In 1965 the SCLC concentrated its efforts in Alabama. The prime target was Selma. King announced a march from Selma to Montgomery to demonstrate the black people's determination to vote. But Governor George Wallace refused to permit it. But the march continued. Twenty-five thousand met in Montgomery for the march to the capital to present a petition to Wallace.

In 1967 King began speaking directly against the Vietnam War, and he also announced that the Poor People's March would converge in Washington in April. Following the February rally, King toured key cities to see firsthand the plight of the poor. Meanwhile, in Memphis, black sanitation workers were striking, and protests generalized to grievances ranging from police brutality to intolerable school conditions. In March, Memphis demonstrations ended in a riot. In Memphis on April 3, King addressed a rally; speaking of threats on his life, he urged followers to continue the nonviolent struggle no matter what happened to him. The next evening, as he stood on an outside balcony at the Lorraine Hotel, King was assassinated. In December 1999, a four-acre site near the Lincoln Memorial in Washington, D.C., was approved as the location for a monument to King. The site is near the place where King delivered his "I have a dream" speech in 1963. The monument will be the first to honor an individual black American in the National Mall area.

King was a prolific writer. Among his most important works are *Stride toward Freedom* (1958), *Strength to Love* (1963), *Why We Can't Wait* (1964), *Where Do We Go from Here* (1967), and *The Trumpet of Conscience* (1968). Collections of his writings include *A Martin Luther King Treasury* (1964) and *I Have a Dream* (1968).

KINSHIP SYSTEMS AND FAMILY TYPES

Kinship systems and **family** groupings are institutionalized mechanisms for ordering specific types of social relationships. Although the social scientific analysis of kinship systems and family types originated within the discipline of anthropology, sociological analyses of these social formations have contributed a great deal to the understanding of kinship and family arrangements. While not all kinship and family arrangements fit neatly within traditional anthropological and sociological kinship and family **typologies**, existing models for classifying kinship systems and family types are useful in the examination of a diverse array of kinship and family forms. Many contemporary researchers, however, have moved beyond existing typologies in an effort to further illuminate the cultural, historical, and societal variation characteristic of kinship and family systems.

Traditional analyses of kinship systems have highlighted the various instrumental and emotive functions that such systems fulfill for particular social groups. Kinship systems function first and foremost as a symbolic bounding mechanism for classifying those individuals that are to be considered kin. Furthermore, these symbolic boundaries of kinship function to delineate bloodlines, which determine patterns of **property** ownership and inheritance. *Unilineal* kinship traces descent through one bloodline, either the father's (*patrilineal descent*) or the mother's (*matrilineal descent*). *Bilateral* kinship traces descent through both the father and the mother's bloodline.

Kinship systems may also function as a mechanism for determining residential patterns. In *patrilocal* kinship groups a newly married couple goes to live with the husband's family. In *matrilocal* societies newlyweds move in with the wife's family. In a *bilocal* system, couples may live with or near either of the two families, while couples who live on their own, away from both families, exhibit a *neolocal* residence pattern. In addition, the countless emotional functions that kinship systems fulfill for their members are accomplished by such activities as keeping in touch with kin **group** members, gift giving, and the formation of lasting affectionate bonds.

According to the traditional anthropological and sociological literature on kinship and family patterns, individual families exist as the primary building blocks for larger kinship systems. In this context, families are constructed through **marriage** and procreation or **adoption**. Family structure has been most commonly dichotomized as either nuclear or extended, and families, like kinship networks, are characterized as fulfilling specific instrumental and emotive functions for family members. One most basic and universal function of the family is the **socialization** of young children.

While marriage and family formation do not always occur simultaneously, existing marriage typologies are instructive in the examination of cross-cultural and historical diversity in family forms. *Monogamy* is defined as a marital union formed between one man and one woman. *Polygamy* involves marital arrangements in which one individual forms marriage alliances with two or more members of the opposite sex. Anthropological research has indicated that the majority of human societies, both historically and cross-culturally, have practiced some form of **polygamy**. Polygyny, in which one man is married to two or more women, has historically been the most common form of polygamy. By contrast, *polyandry,* which involves a marriage between one woman and two or more men, has been quite rare. Another uncommon form of polygamy is known as *group marriage*, which involves the union of two or more men and two or more women.

Nuclear and *extended* families are the most common family typologies employed within traditional anthropological and sociological literature. Nuclear families, the smallest family form, typically consist of two parents and one or more children. Extended families, whose members commonly live in close proximity to one another, include a more vast arrangement of kin, including grandparents, aunts and uncles, and cousins. This dichotomous analysis of nuclear and extended families is misleading, however, because few families, cross-culturally or throughout history, have existed as entirely nuclear or entirely extended.

While the preceding examination of traditional kinship and family typologies is by no means obsolete within contemporary kinship and family research, its explanatory potential may be limited in the context of many contemporary kinship and family arrangements. For example, **divorce, remarriage,** and the increase in never married individuals and couples (with or without children) has had an enormous impact upon kinship and family arrangements. Single-parent families and blended families or stepfamilies constructed through remarriage are steadily increasing. Furthermore, life-long singlehood is becoming more common in contemporary societies. While singlehood has rarely been associated with family life in the kinship and family literature, the majority of single people still maintain ties with **extended family** members, as well as with members of their nuclear family of origin. Furthermore, many never married individuals and couples are forming families that were traditionally restricted primarily to marital relationships. Because social **norms** and **values** have been changing at a rapid pace within recent decades, particularly within Western societies, childbirth and adoption are no longer exclusively confined within the bounds of marriage.

Kinship and family arrangements among gay, lesbian, and bisexual individuals and communities have become increasingly more common in contemporary times as well. While gay, lesbian, and bisexual men and women have indeed formed families through the traditional means of procreation and adoption, the construction of fictive kin arrangements has been prevalent among gay, lesbian, and bisexual communities as well. Moreover, the prejudicial belief that gay, lesbian, and bisexual men and women are somehow rejecting their nuclear and extended families of origin negates the continued significance of these families, which do not automatically disappear from the lives of those who are gay, lesbian or bisexual. And although gay and lesbian couples are still denied legal marital status virtually everywhere around the world, such unions are officially recognized and protected in a few societies. Furthermore, many gay and lesbian couples have still entered into committed marital unions with one another, despite the lack

of legal recognition of such marriages. While the steady increase in family diversity may not have rendered existing anthropological and sociological kinship system and family typologies obsolete, such diversity necessitates the academic acknowledgement and analysis of these alternative kinship and family arrangements.

KOHLBERG, LAWRENCE (1927-1987)
American psychologist and educator

Born in Bronxville, New York, on October 25, 1927, Lawrence Kohlberg grew up in the well-to-do **community**, but was more interested in world events than in academics. After World War II, he became second engineer on an old freighter that helped to smuggle Jewish refugees past the British blockage of Palestine in the late 1940s. He returned to what became the nation of Israel in 1969 to study the **morality** of young people in that country's collective settlements.

Ready to pursue his education, Kohlberg enrolled at the University of Chicago. His scores on the admissions tests were so high that he was excused from most of the required courses and earned his bachelor's degree in one year, 1948. He began study for his doctorate degree, which he earned at Chicago in 1958. Kohlberg's career started at Yale University, as an assistant professor of **psychology**, 1956-1961. In 1955, he married Lucille Stigberg, and the couple had two sons, David and Steven. Kohlberg spent a year at the Center for Advanced Study of Behavioral Science, 1961-1962, and then joined the staff of the University of Chicago as assistant, then associate professor of psychology and human development, 1962-1967. He spent the next ten years at Harvard University, as a professor of education and **social psychology**.

While studying for his doctorate degree, Kohlberg became fascinated with the theories of **moral development** in children and adolescents proposed by Swiss psychologist **Jean Piaget** (1896-1980). For his doctoral dissertation, Kohlberg set six stages of moral development in children, in contrast to Piaget's two stages. Kohlberg interviewed 72 boys in Chicago concerning whether a man with no money is morally right or wrong for stealing drugs that would benefit his desperately ill wife. He concluded that in stage one, most children say the man is wrong because it is wrong to steal. By stage two, the child realizes that here is more than one way of doing things. By stage six, the child has grown to the point of understanding that to work for a moral or just society, it is sometimes necessary and valid to disobey existing laws. This concept of the child as a ''moral philosopher'' was at odds with earlier psychological views of morality. Kohlberg was often criticized, for example, by Harvard Graduate School of Education professor **Carol Gilligan**. She disagreed with his decision only to study male's moral development and, in her 1982 book *In a Different World,*, Gilligan cited the case of an 11-year-old girl who was the question about the morality of stealing to aid an ill person. The girl answered, ''It depends.'' Later, however, Kohlberg and Gilligan held many discussions on the subject of adolescent reasoning and co-author a paper.

The psychoanalytic explanation for morality in children is that it is a concept imposed on them by adults. Behaviorists claim that it is based only on avoiding such bad feelings as guilt. Kohlberg, however, believed that children are their own moral agents or moral philosophers. They are moved to become so through many emotions, such as **love** or respect.

While doing cultural work in the Central American nation of Belize in 1971, Kohlberg contracted a parasitic infection. For the next 16 years, he was in constant pain, which brought on debilitating physical and mental problems. Nonetheless, in 1974, he became interested in the concept of cluster schools—a school within a school—in Massachusetts. In these cluster, or "just," schools, moral discussions would be conducted. A number of such schools formed in Massachusetts and New York with Kohlberg's help. Just schools were also started in a women's prison in Connecticut; in a program for dropouts in a high school in Bronx, New York; and one in a high school in France. However, most did not last long after Kohlberg's death. With no solution for his ailment, Kohlberg increasingly tried nontraditional remedies to little avail. On January 19, 1987, after leaving a treatment session at a local hospital on Cape Cod, Massachusetts, he reportedly walked into the Atlantic Ocean and committed suicide.

Kohlberg is the author of *The Philosophy of Moral Development*, 1981. He also contributed articles to professional journals and texts, such as "The Just Community School: The Theory and the Cambridge Cluster School Experiment," with E. Wasserman and N. Richardson, 1975, for Harvard University Center for Moral Education.

KROEBER, ALFRED LOUIS (1876-1960)
American anthropologist

An authority on the **culture** of native American tribes, Alfred Kroeber was known among colleagues as the "man who shaped the science of anthropology." His most noted publication is the massive textbook *Anthropology*, considered the most authoritative work in the field.

Kroeber was born in Hoboken, New Jersey, June 11, 1876, the son of Florence, a dealer in clocks, and Johanna Mueller Kroeber. As a youth, Kroeber began to collect natural history specimens. He was educated at Columbia University in New York City, earning an B.A. in 1896, an M.A. in 1897, and a Ph.D. in 1901. While at Columbia, he came under the influence of noted German-American anthropologist **Franz Boas**. During his tenure (1899–1942), Boas developed one of the foremost departments of anthropology in the United States. Choosing anthropology as his life's work, Kroeber made collecting trips during summer breaks, sponsored by the American Museum of Natural History, to native American sites in the Great Plains area.

In the summer of 1900, Kroeber was named curator at the California Academy of Sciences, San Francisco. He left in 1901 to begin his career as an instructor at the University of California, Berkeley, in the museum and Department of Anthropology, newly formed under the patronage of Phoebe Apperson Hearst. Joining museum research with university instruction was a common pattern at the turn of the century.

Between 1903 and 1931, this dual pattern meant university instruction at Berkeley and museum research carried out in San Francisco.

In 1906, Kroeber married Henriette Rothschild, who died in 1913. In 1908, he became curator of the San Francisco museum, but gradually, teaching began to occupy more and more of his time at Berkeley. In 1926, he married Theodora Kracaw Brown, a psychologist, and the couple raised Clifton and Theodore, Kroeber's stepsons, as well as another son and daughter, Karl and Ursula. In all, Kroeber spent 45 years at Berkeley, becoming professor of anthropology in 1919, a post he held until 1946 when he was named professor emeritus. He kept that title until he died in Paris of a heart attack on October 5, 1960, returning home from a conference in Vienna, Austria, on anthropological linguistics. He was 84 years old.

In addition to the demands of his teaching career, Kroeber was curator of Berkeley's anthropological museum, 1908–1925, and its director, 1925–1946. He took part in Columbia University's anthropological expeditions in New Mexico, 1915–1920; Mexico, 1924, 1930; and Peru, 1925, 1926, 1942. Beginning in 1925, he became a research associate at the Chicago Natural History Museum and was a visiting professor at Harvard, 1947–1948; at Columbia University, 1948–1952; at Brandeis University, 1954; and at Yale University, 1955–1956. Kroeber was also a fellow of the Center for Advanced Study in the Behavioral Sciences, Palo Alto, California, 1955–1956.

As influenced by Boas, Kroeber tried to salvage the remnants of pre-contact cultures. Some of his extensive work involved the Yurok and Mojave tribes of California. He collected tools, unfinished objects such as a bow, and unusual items such as a shell that was used to cover the thumb when making string. He tried to avoid collecting objects made for sale. "The requirements of our museum make it most desirable," he said, "that we should obtain old pieces that have seen use." Some critics sight Kroeber's inattention to documentation, but others point out that for Kroeber, the artifact was not the goal. Rather, artifacts were only one part of the approach to learning about native culture. Everything—photographs, sound recordings, writings—were artifacts as well.

Kroeber is the author of numerous articles and books, most to do with his observations. His writings on his California collections include: *Basket Designs of the Mission Indians of California,* 1905, republished in 1964 as *Basket Designs of the Indians of Northwestern California;Handbook of the Indians of California* ; and *Yurok Narratives.* For his outstanding work in anthropology, in 1945, Kroeber received the Huxley Medal, the highest award from the Royal Anthropological Institute of Great Britain, as well as the Viking Medal of the American Anthropological Association. After retirement, he was honored with a building on the Berkeley campus to house the departments of art and anthropology named Kroeber Hall.

KUHN, MANFORD H. (1911-1963)

Manford H. Kuhn (1911–1963) was the founder of the Iowa School of **Symbolic Interactionism**. The other major school of thought was the Chicago school, associated with **Herbert Blumer**. Both schools emerged from the writings and teachings of **George Herbert Mead**.

Some main concepts in symbolic interactionism are self, self-concept, self **theory**, **Identity**, **role** taking, **role theory**, **status**, and social construction of reality. Kuhn's greatest contribution to social **psychology** was his development of the concept of a core self and his coining of the term, self theory, for his brand of symbolic interactionism. His underlying theoretical assumption was that every person has stable components of their self that are unchanging from situation to situation. Whereas Blumer saw behavior as situational, emergent, and nondeterministic, Kuhn believed that it was determined by pre-existing variables having to do with static and measurable aspects of the self in combination with social, historical, and developmental conditions. He understood the self as an object, and as both a cause and a consequence of behavior. He felt that the self was important because it revealed people's conceptions of their own identity, which would in turn reveal their behavior patterns. He felt that a person's plan of action in response to a particular question or situation was indicative of a person's total behavior pattern and attitude toward that particular object or situation.

Kuhn's work emphasized structural as opposed to processual conceptions of self and **society**. He believed that social **structure** consists of networks, statuses, and associated roles. He emphasized both the individual and social nature of role-taking in day-to-day life. Although he saw this social structure as being created, maintained, and changed through social **interaction**, he also saw this social structure as constraining individual and **group** behavior. So he saw the self as a mediating force between social structure and individual or group behavior. Kuhn also highlighted the importance of roles, and he assimilated role theory and **reference group** theory into his conceptualization of the core self.

Because Kuhn took a structural approach to **social psychology**, he advocated survey methods, objective measures, and quantitative analysis of self-concept. He believed in the stability of the self, so he felt that it could be measured through conventional scientific **research methods**. Kuhn believed in clear, concise definitions of what he was measuring as well as in the possibility of scientific objectivity. He thus believed that he could develop and test specific hypotheses about **human nature** and behavior. He advocated using traditional scientific methods and paradigms until they were proven ineffective. This position distinguished him from other symbolic interactionists such as Blumer, who advocated developing less conventional research methods, methods that would allow theory to emerge from **data**, rather than imposing theory on the data.

It was out of this structural perspective and the belief that the self is a stable entity that Kuhn and Thomas McPartland developed the Twenty Statements Test (TST) in 1954 to measure **self-concept**. They developed this test with the assumption that they could develop a standardized way to identify and measure self-attitudes. In this test, people were asked to respond to the question "Who Am I?" or "I Am..." with up to twenty different responses. The goal of this test was to uncover the components of an individual's core self. The test's analytic assumption is that the response patterns to the question could reveal the structure of self because people see themselves as an object in ways that closely mirrors their self structure. Through this test, which has been used widely by researchers in social psychology and psychology, Kuhn made the concept of the self more concrete by using quantitative methods.

Kuhn published on a variety of subjects, but his most influential and well-known publications dealt with his conceptualization of the self and how to measure it. The two most often cited works are: "An Empirical Investigation of Self-Attitudes", which appeared in the *American Sociological Review* in 1954 and was co-authored with McPartland and "Major Trends in Symbolic Interaction Theory in the Past Twenty-Five Years", which appeared posthumously in *Sociological Quarterly* in 1964.

KUHN, THOMAS SAMUEL (1922-1996)
American historian and philosopher

Thomas Samuel Kuhn was an American historian and philosopher of science. He found that basic ideas about how nature should be studied were dogmatically accepted in normal science, then increasingly questioned, and overthrown during scientific revolutions. Born in Cincinnati, Ohio, in 1922, Thomas Kuhn was trained as a physicist but became an educator after receiving his Ph.D. in physics from Harvard in 1949. He taught the history of science at Harvard, University of California/Berkeley, Princeton, and Massachusetts Institute of Technology (MIT). He was a member or director of many professional organizations and received many awards.

Kuhn was best known for debunking the common belief that science develops by the accumulation of individual discoveries. In the summer of 1947 something happened that shattered the image of science he had received as a physicist. He was asked to interrupt his doctorate physics project to lecture on the origins of Newton's physics. Predecessors of Newton such as Galileo and Descartes were raised within the Aristotelian scientific tradition. Yet Kuhn was shocked to find in Aristotle's physics precious little with which a Newtonian could agree or of which he could even make sense. He asked himself how Aristotle, so brilliant on other topics, could be so confused about motion and why his views on motion were taken so seriously by later generations. One hot summer day while reading Aristotle, Kuhn had a brainstorm. "Suddenly the fragments in my head sorted themselves out in a new way, and fell into place together." He realized that he had been misreading Aristotle by assuming a Newtonian point of view. Taught that science progresses cumulatively, he had sought to find what Aristotle contributed to Newton's mechanics. This effort was wrong-headed because the two men had basically different ways of approaching the study of motion.

For example, Aristotle's interest in change in general led him to regard motion as a change of state, whereas Newton's interest in elementary particles, thought to be in continuous motion, led him to regard motion as a state. That continuous motion requires explanation by appeal to some force keeping it in motion was taken as obvious by Aristotle. But Newton thought that continued motion at a certain speed needed no explanation in terms of forces. Newton invoked the gravitational force to explain acceleration and advanced a law that an object in motion remains in motion unless acted upon by an external force.

This discovery turned Kuhn's interest from physics to the history of physics and eventually to the bearing of the history of science on the philosophy of science. His working hypothesis that reading a historical text requires sensitivity to changes in meaning provided new insight into the work of such physicists as Boyle, Lavoisier, Dalton, Boltzmann, and Plank. This hypothesis was a generalization of his finding that Aristotle and Newton worked on different research projects with different starting points which eventuated in different meanings for basic terms such as ''motion'' or ''force.'' Most people probably think that science has exhibited a steady accumulation of knowledge. But Kuhn's study of the history of physics showed this belief to be false because different research traditions have different basic views.

Especially striking to Kuhn was the fact that scientists rarely argued explicitly about these basic research decisions. Scientific theories were popularly viewed as based entirely on inferences from observational evidence. But no amount of experimental testing can dictate these decisions because by their nature they are logically prior to testing. What, if not observations, explains the consensus of a **community** of scientists within the same tradition at a given time? Kuhn boldly conjectured that they must share common commitments, not based on observation or logic alone, in which these matters are implicitly settled. Most scientific practice is a complex mopping-up operation, based on group commitments, which extends the implications of the most recent theoretical breakthrough. Here, at last, was the concept for which Kuhn had been searching: the concept of normal science takes for granted a **paradigm**, the locus of shared commitments.

In 1962 Kuhn published his landmark book on scientific revolutions, which was eventually translated into sixteen languages and sold over a million copies. He coined the term ''paradigm'' to refer to accepted achievements such as Newton's *Principia* which contain examples of good scientific practice. These examples include law, **theory**, application, and instrumentation. They function as models for further work. The result is a coherent research tradition. In his postscript to the second edition, Kuhn pointed out two senses of paradigm used in his book. In the narrow sense, it is one or more achievement wherein scientists find examples of the kind of work they wish to emulate, called ''exemplars.'' In the broad sense it is the shared body of preconceptions controlling the expectations of scientists, called a ''disciplinary matrix.'' Persistent use of exemplars as models gives rise to a disciplinary matrix that determines the problems selected for study and the sorts of answers acceptable to the scientific community.

Using the paradigm concept, Kuhn developed a theory of scientific change. A tradition is pre-scientific if it has no paradigm. A scientific tradition typically passes through a sequence of normal science-crisis-revolution-new normal science. Normal science is puzzle-solving governed by a paradigm accepted uncritically. Difficulties are brushed aside and blamed on the failure of the scientist to extend the paradigm properly. A crisis begins when scientists view these difficulties as stemming from their paradigm, not themselves. If the crisis is not resolved, a revolution sets in, but the old paradigm is not given up until it can be replaced by a new one. Then new normal science begins and the cycle is repeated. Just when to accept a new paradigm and when to stick to the old one is a matter not subject to proof, although good reasons can be adduced for both options. Scientific **rationality** is not found in rules of scientific method but in the collective judgment of the scientific community. We must give up the notion that science progresses cumulatively toward the truth about reality; after a revolution it merely replaces one way of seeing the world with another.

Kuhn died June 17, 1996, at his home in Cambridge, Massachusetts. Kuhn transformed the image of science by emphasizing that it is both a social and rational process. His theory has profound implications for any area of knowledge, since scientific knowledge is generally taken as the benchmark to which other forms of knowledge are compared. Moreover, the terminology of ''paradigm'' and ''paradigm shifts'' has been incorporated into the study of knowledge into other fields of study.

KURTOSIS

Stemming from the Greek word *kurtos* meaning curvature, kurtosis is a measure that expresses how closely a distribution resembles a normal bell curve distribution. A single measure of kurtosis describes both the height of a distribution and the length or ''fatness'' of its tails as compared to a bell curve. The kurtosis of a **normal distribution** is three. Measured against this standard, a distribution is described as having a kurtosis value that is either less than three, equal to three, or greater than three.

A kurtosis value less than three indicates a fairly uniform distribution of observations or **data** on either side of the **mean** stretching to the tails, which results in a fat midrange and short thin tails. This type of distribution, known as *platykurtic*, is distinguished by a low peak and a wide, flat elevation. A distribution with a kurtosis value equal to three is called *mesokurtic*. This type of distribution resembles a standard bell curve in which there is a natural balance between a tapering elevation and the tails. A distribution with a kurtosis value greater than three is called *leptokurtic*. In this type of distribution, observations cluster around the mean and in the tails as outliers with few in the regions in between. A leptokurtic distribution is characterized by a sharp peak spanning only a few values and long, fat tails. It is important to consider the kurtosis of a distribution when using tests which are sensitive to normality assumptions. When these assumptions are platykurtic and leptokurtic data can often be transformed, through Log techniques for example, to reduce the effects of the violations.

L

LABELING THEORY

Sociologists, especially those specializing in **criminology**, have long attempted to explain why individuals commit deviant and criminal acts. Labeling theory provides a unique approach to this research, one that is distinct from other prominent theories. Instead of examining why people participate in deviance, labeling theorists focus on how and why certain people come to be defined as deviant and what happens after they are defined as such. According to labeling **theory**, **deviance** is best understood not by analyzing the act itself, but by noting the societal reaction to the individual perpetrating the act.

The basic proposition of labeling theory is that the formation of an individual's **identity** is a reflection of others' definitions of him or her. People who are labeled as deviant are likely to take on a deviant identity and engage in more, rather than less, deviant behavior than if they had not been labeled. Labels become attached through the process of society's reaction to and attempts to prevent deviant behavior. Ironically, the unintended consequence of labeling is that the person becomes exactly what the sanctioning process wanted to prevent.

The labeling process is not presented as automatic as many critics claim. Rather, a person's **self-concept** is formed through an interactive process where labeled persons try to manage how others view them. In some cases, individuals are successful in preventing the label. Often, however, individuals assigned a deviant label have a difficult time resisting the label when it is applied by formal agents of **society**, such as police, courts, and government officials, because individuals have little power to resist labels given by those in authority.

Labeling theory is best exemplified in the works of sociologists Frank Tannenbaum, Edwin Lemert, Howard Becker, William Chambliss, and Edwin Schur. While all of these theorists differ on minor points and emphasize different aspects of the labeling process, they still share many of the previously mentioned beliefs about the nature of deviance. One of the earliest formulations of labeling theory is attributed to Frank Tan-

nenbaum in 1938. In addition to describing the process by which people are labeled deviant, he introduced the concept of "dramatization of evil." This occurs when a person who has been publicly defined as deviant begins to associate more with others defined as deviant and less with non-deviants. This change leads to the adoption of a deviant identity, and a deviant career develops. He also notes that a "tag" is given to a child when he or she is caught in delinquent behavior. People then react to the tag and not to the child. Thus, the process of tagging criminals actually helps create delinquency and criminality.

Edwin Lemert explained this process using the concepts of primary and secondary deviance. **Primary deviance** refers to an initial act that violates some societal norm and/or criminal law. When caught in the act of primary deviance, individuals are typically punished through formal and informal means, and this punishment attaches a deviant label. **Secondary deviance** is deviant behavior that is created by societal reactions and by stigmatizing labels. After individuals are labeled, they often internalize the label and begin to think of themselves in the same manner. Then, as they accept the deviant label, they often continue acting in the same manner that caused them to receive the label in the first instance.

Labeling theory is criticized on several grounds. First, many think that it is overly deterministic and denies individual responsibility. Some have interpreted the theory as implying that an individual's actual behavior is unimportant and that all that is important is the application of deviant labels by society. Second, it ignores the fact that some acts are universally regarded as intrinsically "wrong." Labeling theorists tend to concentrate on public order crimes but then generalize to all forms of deviance, such as murder and rape, where labeling theory may be less appropriate. Finally, this approach does not adequately explain the causes of the initial deviant act. Despite these criticisms, labeling theory has added a great deal to the understanding of deviance and **crime** by calling into question the unintended consequences of formal and informal punishment.

LABOR FORCE

The labor force is currently undergoing a complex, and historically significant transformation during this global, computer-mediated stage of economic development. Many factors such as increased workplace flexibility, technological innovation, and the globalization of capital (profit) are shaping the demand for specific **skill** sets. The continuing entry of women into the labor market, the rise in educational attainment, the demographic composition of the labor force, and alternative **employment** relationships are also critical variables in this transformation.

According to the Department of Labor (DOL) 1999 report, there are over 139 million civilian workers in the labor force, 46 percent of whom are females. The high employment rate, as measured by the lowest **unemployment** rate in 30 years of 4.5 percent, has been attributed to the dominant position of the United States in the global market. Approximately, 70 percent of the workforce is concentrated in white-collar work, which includes managers, professionals, and even low level administrative, sales, and service occupations. In the past, changes in labor force demand have correlated with domestic shifts in occupations within particular industries. Since the mid-1990s, globalization of the workforce has increased demand for specific skill sets and knowledge based education, particularly in highly industrialized countries, suggesting skills rather than occupation experience will correlate to future employability.

Middle-aged workers born between 1948 and 1962, known as the baby boomers, represent the largest age **cohort** in the labor force. These workers are also the most vulnerable to economic changes due to their existing skill sets and compensation histories. In addition, computer technology has displaced or deskilled many responsibilities of middle managers and tasks of lower skilled workers. According to the DOL (1986) over 750,000 managers and professionals were terminated or displaced in the mid-1980s as many organizations became "lean and mean". The result was high unemployment rates, particularly for white males who previously dominated those positions.

Restructuring in the 1990s involved more sophisticated human resource planning that often included retaining a core group of employees, and several nontraditional options such as utilizing outsourced, leased, temporary help workers for specific tasks, functions, or projects, as well as an in-house supply of part-time workers. Although definitional debates have produced differing estimates of nontraditional workers, there is agreement that this trend is most likely to affect women, the young, and workers over the age of 55. Examples of employment flexibility can range from innovative scheduling arrangements to new employment relationships such as short-term contract employment, outsourcing, telecommuting, and self-employment.

While the educational attainment of the labor force has continued to increase since 1980, continuing inequality of opportunity and access has created a polarity between low and highly skilled workers. In the past thirty years, the average ed-ucational level of workers has risen from 10 to 13 years, while the educational attainment of female college graduates continues to exceed the number of male undergraduates. According to the Census Bureau, many ethnic groups, particularly Hispanics, lag in wage gains as they remain at the lowest stratum of educational attainment. While workers with a high school diploma once dominated the workforce, by 1998 their share of total employment hours dwindled to ten percent. During the same time, the total percent of male workers with a college degree increased from 7 percent to 25 percent, while female workers made even greater strides with an increase from 4 percent to 24 percent. Many immigrants continue to enter the labor market, most securing employment at the low end.

Wage inequity continues to exist, particularly for ethnic groups. Women and black males have increased their wages to 76 percent of white males, although much of this progress is due to the stabilization of male wages. Black females earn about 91 percent of black males, while Hispanic females earn about 80 percent of Hispanic males. Much of the disparity in female wages relates to their high concentration in the lowest paying jobs (e.g., childcare, teaching, clerical), while two-thirds of men are in the higher paying occupations (e.g., managers, professionals, operators).

Access to education and training will be critical factors for the labor force of the future, particularly for ethnic workers. Income differentials between low skilled and educated workers indicate polarization is underway. Inter-organizational mobility also has increased and it is now estimated that workers will change jobs between seven and ten times during their lifetimes. Employment insecurity has become a major characteristic of new employment arrangements, as increased mobility and changing terms of employment will shift many responsibilities such as training and education to the worker.

LABOR MOVEMENTS AND UNIONS

Labor unions are organized collectivities of workers formed to pursue the group's collective interests. Through collective bargaining, labor unions negotiate with management primarily in order to address problems associated with **social inequality**. Labor unions focus on improving working conditions and negotiating for higher compensation. Labor unions are democratic membership organizations that operate as interest groups within the political sphere.

Research on labor movements within the field of **sociology** usually falls into one of two broad categories: the development of labor unions or the socioeconomic and political impact of the labor movement. The study of the labor movement is also the study of class, **ideology**, organizations, **collective action**, industrialization, and stratification. No one theory of labor movements can account for all aspects of unionism and its social impacts.

Fundamental to the labor movement is the belief that the interests of workers are in conflict with the interests of employers. Through collective bargaining and the threat of strikes, workers are more able to leverage their interests with employers than if they pursued their interests individually. Currently, union membership in the United States stands at more than fifteen million, the strength of labor unions ebbs and flows. In 1945, 36 percent of all workers were unionized. Since World War II, the percentage of unionized workers has steadily fallen from this all-time high. Public perceptions about unions have also changed dramatically: unionism was equated with Communism in the 1930s and at other times has enjoyed much more favorable public opinion.

Unlike European countries, the United States has no working-class political party closely tied to unions. The failure to develop a strong labor political party has often been attributed to the lack of a coherent working class identity among blue collar workers. Union ideology is fairly diverse, from the conservative "business unionism" of the larger organizations like the AFL-CIO to the radically Socialist **philosophy** of some smaller unions. The conservatism of some unions reflects the ethnic and racial diversity within the working class in the United States, which prevents much coordinated identity-based action.

One question in the study of unions and labor movements concerns when and under what conditions labor movements form. The study of **group** predispositions to unionize may include the economy, worker ideology, socioeconomic and demographic macro-level factors. The micro-level perspective of individual predisposition to unionize focuses on individual decision-making and personal attitudes. Other research focuses on the mechanisms through which labor unions effect change. These efforts consider labor's successes in pursuing political action such as legislation or the impact of labor union activities on workers' socioeconomic positions.

LANGUAGE

Language enables humans to categorize the world and human experience into an organized system of meaningful symbols. People use these symbols to communicate with each other and to share the ideas of a **culture**. All societies have a **communication** system based on a spoken language, and most have that language contained in written form. Many argue that language is one of the factors that distinguish human beings from other social animals. Although research findings indicate that some animals, such as monkeys and dolphins, have successfully learned some language and human methods of communication, no animal has been able to transfer that knowledge to other animals without the medium of a human being.

While the majority of the world views language in terms of its verbal and written capabilities, language can also be comprised of gestures and nonverbal communications. Sign language, for example, designates nonverbal symbols to represent the context of written and verbal communications. The development of computers also has produced programming machines that allow computers to communicate with one another or with a human interface. Basic, Fortran, and Cobol are examples of computer languages which fall under the rubric of computer science.

Members of a labor union conduct a sit-down strike in the early twentieth century *(Corbis Corporation [Bellevue])*.

Language is the primary mechanism through which culture is translated. It is through language that an individual becomes socialized into the customs, rules, and practices of a **society** and its institutions. Language is also embedded with the traditions and cultural heritage of its people. In fact, the popularity of words and phrases often capture the historically specific symbolism of our cultural heritage. Usage by subsequent generations of speakers perpetuates the specific meaning of those word and phrases, even when the symbolism has lost its original meaning in our everyday communications. In addition, words especially reflect what a culture deems worthy or valuable. American English includes a great deal of technical language and this extensive technical vocabulary refelcts the country's value of **progress**.

Linguistics is the study of the role of language in society. Sociolinguistics investigates attitudes among populations about language, the origins and variations of language, and the relationship and social context of language to social interactions within society. How some people in the United States feel about Spanish speaking residents and the controversial debates about the posting of public signs or directions in Spanish is one example of the attitudes about language. The main argument on one side of the debate is that people who immigrate to America should learn and use the language of their new country. On the other side of the debate, it is argued that, in order to maintain a connection to their cultural roots, immigrants should continue to use their native language. The origins of language can best be explained by looking at countries in Africa formerly colonialized by European nations such as, for the purpose of this example, France. Today, many African countries have unique dialects that are often interlaced with French words and phrases, a native tongue, and some English. Social context refers to the common symbolism and style embedded in social interactions and language. For example, age and gender may be factors shaping the social context of interactions for many people and they may also be the source of different interpretations of the acceptable manner by which to introduce or greet another. Some may be comfortable greeting a person informally using their first name, while others may prefer being addressed formally, and expect the use of a title such as ''Mrs.'' or ''Ms.'' and the person's last name. **Sociolinguistics** also examines the changing social, political and cultural context of language in relation to gender, color/race, class, religion and other factors. For example, prior to 1970, many words in the English language were male gendered and used as representations of males and females. By the 1990s, words such as ''chairman'' became ''chairperson'', and ''humanity'' is often substituted for earlier references to ''mankind''.

Another area of study examines language as **discourse**, in which the text of language is viewed as an object of study and its boundaries and power relations are analyzed. Discourse is thus often viewed as the academic discussion of how objects of analysis are shaped within an institutional context. Examining the emergence of discourse requires understanding the socio-cultural forces shaping the historical recording and transcription of language. The notion of ''reconceptualization'' in discourse is derived from the writings of Foucault and post-structuralist **theory** which states that people and documents are formed both within and outside an institutional life, and must be included in an analysis. Another significant aspect of discourse relates to the process of meaning. Post-structuralist theory argues that meaning is never fixed, but is contained in discursive articulations that embody power and power relations to become dominant aspects of everyday thinking and shape our notions of the ''truth''.

LATENT FUNCTION

Latent functions can be defined as the goals and consequences of social action which are not openly acknowledged and may not be realized or intended by the participants in a social system but which nevertheless result from that system. The term was first used by American sociologist Robert K. Merton to describe the unintentional positive effects of an action on a social **structure**, although common usage of the concept also includes negative effects. Latent functions are complemented by manifest functions, which are the intentional goals and consequences of social actions and institutions.

For example, while the manifest functions of the **higher education** system are to provide students with an education and to train them to perform a particular job when they graduate, the higher education system also has many latent functions. Many people who attend college meet and begin dating their future spouses at college. Attending college also allows many people to postpone entering the work force, thereby helping to increase **employment** opportunities for other members of **society** and reduce **unemployment** rates. Another potential latent function of the higher education system is to provide a sense of identity and camaraderie among those associated with certain colleges or groups within colleges through alumni associations, athletics, fraternities and sororities, and other groups.

Merton contrasted latent functions with latent dysfunctions, which are unintentional negative effects of an action on a social structure. A university's decision to raise tuition may be intended to increase revenue and to diversify the student body (the **manifest function**). However if the tuition increase is too much, it may have the latent **dysfunction** of driving students away, and thus decreasing revenue and perhaps denying access to some of the very students the university is seeking to attract.

The distinction between manifest and latent functions has been criticized by some sociologists for being too vague and inconsistent in use. In some instances Merton used manifest and latent to indicate intention. The manifest function is intended, whereas the latent function is unintended. However, Merton also used the same terms to indicate the depth of intention. Manifest functions describe the surface level intentions, while latent functions describe the underlying intentions. An application fee for renting an apartment has the manifest function of offsetting the costs of processing and verifying the information on the application. It also potentially has the latent function of circumventing **discrimination** laws by discouraging or preventing people of lower socioeconomic classes from applying for an apartment in the complex because they may not be able to pay high application fees.

LATIN AMERICAN STUDIES

The study of Latin American **culture** is relevant for many reasons. First, Latin America reflects the early globalization and colonization of the Spanish-speaking world. Second, Latin America reflects a large range of peoples, including Native Americans, Africans, Middle Easterners, Asians, and a mixture of many of these races. Third, the history of Latin America is closely tied to our own. From colonization to independence, we have similar experiences. Furthermore, for the last one hundred years, the United States has had a political and economic interest in Latin American. The mineral and agricultural resources alone in Latin America demand our attention. Understanding Latin American culture helps us understand a mix of cultures and our own culture and history, while it prepares us for a future of globalization.

Along with African and Asian studies, Latin American studies grew out of the strong American presence in the Third World. These programs focused on U.S. and Third World relations, training specialists to uphold and maintain American interests in Third World countries. Following the 1960s, however, these programs became more critical of the United States and more sympathetic towards Latin American, African, and Asian Third World nations. In Latin American studies programs, the term ''Latin America'' refers to Caribbean nations, Mexico, Latin America, and South America.

Like many ethnic studies, Latin American studies is designed to explore and understand another culture. Traditionally, academics have reflected Western European **philosophy**, literature, history, and politics, leaving out other ethnic groups. As mentioned earlier, Latin America has traditionally been left out of academic study except when discussed in relationship to imperialism. Latin American studies explores the philosophy, literature, history, language, and social sciences related to the people of Latin America, bringing their perspectives into academia. Such programs are interdisciplinary, meaning they cross different academic departments. For example, a Latin American Studies program might offer courses in contemporary Peruvian playwrights, the influence of the Panama Canal on Latin American economies, the relationship between Spain and Latin America, or the political climate of Latin America. The focus is not on one discipline, such as history or **political science**, but on an ethnic **group** and their contribution to history and culture.

Latin American studies includes a foreign language and often a chance to study abroad. Because Latin American studies are interdisciplinary, students can concentrate on history, literature, current events, politics, women's issues, etc. within the Latin American Studies program.

The **colonialism** of Latin America was key to early globalization. Although Columbus' dreams of a shortcut to the East were not realized, trade between the East and Europe was made easier by Latin America. Direct trade between Acapulco and Manila brought the spices and riches of Asia that much closer to Europeans. In addition, the sugar trade between the Caribbean and Europe required pricing and other regulations that led the way for the international trade regulations in practice today.

Unlike the "melting pot" idea of cultures in the United States, Latin America has enjoyed a mixture of cultures. The meeting of **Christianity** and Native religions did not override the beliefs of the Natives, as Catholic missionaries hoped, but led to a mixture of Christian belief and Native practices. In addition, due to the unique growth during the nineteenth century, many languages are spoken and written in Latin America, such as Welsh, German, Japanese, French and English.

The history of Latin America is one of colonization but also revolution. The revolutions of this region reflect its culture: through revolution, a people express who they are, what they find important, and where they are headed. This relationship among history, culture, and **identity** is key to learning about Latin Americans and may unlock some truths about Northern Americans, too.

A clear advantage of any type of multicultural study is teaching students to understand, expect, and acknowledge differing viewpoints. For example, courses on pre-Colombian Mexico give students a native perspective of Columbus' landing and the impact of the arrival of Europeans on this continent rather than the European perspective of exploration. Such a course may also demonstrate that history is incomplete and one-sided until you address multiple perspectives of the same event. Acknowledging different perspectives also encourages students to question what they have learned and what they consider cultural givens, which fosters independent thinking.

Students are taught to understand and appreciate Latin American culture rather than accept stereotypes. Many Latin American studies courses address images such as migrant workers and guerilla warfare to demonstrate the creation and perpetuation of cultural stereotypes. Or they may catalog Latin American leaders and their contributions to the fields of art, politics, and science.

Students of Latin American studies learn to value cultures other than their own by identifying myths in their education, thinking, and culture. Latin American Studies programs prepare teachers for the diverse population they will meet in the classroom, and bilingual teachers are especially valuable as the *Latino* population in the United States grows. The world continues to get smaller, and geographic boundaries are blurring. A global workplace will soon be a reality. In order to succeed in business, communications, government service, research, and teaching, cultural boundaries need to be understood and overcome. One of the best ways to do that is to delve into another culture and people, as is accomplished through Latin American studies.

See also Hispanic American Studies

LAW AND LEGAL SYSTEMS

It is not possible to consider the sociological perspective of a society's law and its legal system without simultaneously considering the role deviance performs as a part that **society**. As part of **deviance theory**, it is assumed that within all societies the activities of a society's members are governed by established **norms**, which are socially acceptable behaviors. Those norms are the basis for the formal and informal **rules** for social **interaction** in which the members commonly and normally engage. As a part of deviance theory, norms are divided into three categories: **mores**, customs, and **folkways**. Of the three studied by sociologists as they consider a society's law and legal system, the mors are of the greatest interest.

Customs and folkways are typically norms that are associated with informal social behavior that does not threaten the stability and security of a society. An individual violation of a **custom** or folkway, while not pleasing to the members of a society, is generally not severely punished. However, the norms that are considered mores are so important to the stability and security of the society they are generally codified, or written into specific codes or statutes which comprise the laws of a society. The society's governing agencies, such as the United States Congress or the individual State legislatures, establish these formal laws recognizing the importance of the most important mores. Specific examples of mores that have been codified are the statutory prohibitions against murder, robbery, or assault. In fact, statutes have been enacted that codify the mores governing many behaviors and interactions that commonly take place between members of a society. Included would be what society considers appropriate and normal behavior concerning sexual relationships, business practices between individuals and corporations, and financial transactions that occur as part of the ongoing daily activities. It is, then, those codified mores that comprise the law of any society. And, as a part of and an extension of that law, the legal system of a society is charged with enforcing the laws that have been enacted.

From the sociological perspective the norms of a society, whether mores, customs, or folkways, are considered social constructions. In other words, as a social construction, a norm represents an expectation of acceptable behavior that is created by the society. But norms are not omnipresent. They are structured and constructed by individual societies to meet the social needs of their members. But among the shared social needs of most societies is the need for order and stability. Order and stability may be achieved and maintained through the social construction and common acceptance of the norms that have been codified into laws.

The legal system, the socially recognized **structure** charged with interpreting and enforcing the laws, is the formal organization society turns to when the codified mores are violated. Customs and folkways are commonly enacted through relatively simple private social sanctions. Such sanctions may include actions as simple as removing offenders from guest lists of popular parties or gatherings. Or, in the event the infraction takes place within a family, it may even involve the exclusion of a family member from activities in which the entire family would normally engage. In such cases the rest of society, those outside of the offender's immediate family or social **group**, may be totally unaware an offense has been committed and that actions have been taken to unofficially punish the offender.

When a mores, that has been codified into law is violated, however, it becomes the concern of the entire society. Special members of society, typically **law enforcement** officers such as members of a police force, are empowered by the society to apprehend the offender. And, if the offender is considered a threat to the order and stability of the society, those police officers are empowered to detain and isolate the offender in a special and secure facility, such as a jail. Then, other members of the legal system who represent the interests of the society, those designated as prosecutors, are required to prove that the person who has been apprehended did, in fact, violate the codified more. In America that process typically involves a formal legal trial. In some trials the evidence of violation is presented by the prosecutors and is heard and acted upon by a formal group of individuals known as a jury. In other trials, the evidence is heard and a decision of innocence or guilt is made by only one person known as a judge. But, in both types of trials, a judge is in charge of assuring that both the interests of the society and those of the individual charged with violating the law, are properly protected through the use of socially acceptable processes and procedures.

The intent of the laws and the legal system governing acceptable behavior within any society are typically neither less nor more complicated than the mores of the society. But the processes required for enacting and enforcing the laws become extremely complex within many societies. The complexity of the processes is generally related directly to the society's level of economic development. The greater the economic development, the more complex the laws and the legal system tend to be. Such complexity is, in fact, a direct part of the continued development of a society, giving rise to the institutional bureaucracies are an important and powerful part of the American social structure.

LAW AND SOCIETY

Most people view the law as the sanctioning body within **society**, equating the law with the restraint of criminal behavior. However, the law is much broader than this conception, as both a method for recourse and constraint. The study of law and society is concerned with the social context and social implications of the law. A sociological lens on the law points to the role that the law plays in defining relationships, determining explicit **rules** of conduct, and coming to an understanding of the consequences for failing to abide by those legal rules. In addition, law is viewed as a mechanism by which **social solidarity** and cohesion are established and as an explicit method by which power may be legitimized.

A sociological analysis of the law allows us to specify the social norms or rules for a given society. Émile Durkheim attempted to explain this very process of explicating social **norms** and creating social solidarity in *The Division of Labor in Society*. According to Durkheim, law provides a mechanism by which persons in a collectivity, or society, can make visible the **collective conscience**, the group's shared values and ideas. For Durkheim law makes visible this index of social solidarity. In other words, law allows societal members to have a **structure** of order that brings about cohesion among them, as they share the same standards by which to judge social conduct.

Max Weber also saw the law as an essential component in any society. In *The Theory of Social and Economic Organization* Weber argued that the law was a method for an **authority** to claim its legitimacy. In particular, Weber was concerned with the role that a rational-legal authority had in modern society. Investigating Western development, Weber determined that the rational-legal component was becoming a prominent form of authority. Weber defined rational-legal authority as that which is based upon rational grounds and anchored by impersonal rules. The law then, as he saw it, had the ability to directly influence distributions of power, economics, and resources. From this perspective the law structures relations within society by legitimizing authority. In other words, the law is a symptom of the rationalizing of modern society.

Karl Marx also discussed the role of law in society. For Marx, the law was a method for the **bourgeoisie**, or those persons who owned the means of production, to produce an environment in which the workers were powerless to overcome class stratification. According to Marx, because the bourgeoisie are the owners of the means of production they are in a position to determine the laws. Therefore, laws are a mechanism by which the ruling class can maintain its position in the hierarchical structure because it can provide sanctions that perpetuate the status quo and restrict proletariat access to social change. For example, property laws benefit the bourgeoisie by solidifying its position in relations to those who do not own property. In other words, Marx argued that the law is epiphenomenal, or a derivative of the economic relations in society.

These three sociological theorists attempted to demonstrate the significant role the law plays in the realm of sociological studies and more broadly within society. Many sociologists, philosophers, and psychologists have acknowledged the importance of understanding the influence of law on individuals, groups, organizations, and society. The importance of the law in society can be better understood, for example, by discussing the definition of a **family**, how that definition has developed over time, what the definition provides for in terms of conduct and responsibilities, and how that definition provides avenues for sanctioning persons within the relationship. The definition of the family and the responsibilities of its members have changed over time and have led to one part of our legal system, family court. These are the kinds of issues and components that make the law an influential structure within a social system.

To see how law defines relationships, consider the relationship of husband and wife. The law defines the criteria that must be met in order for two people to enter into this relationship. In fact, law is specific in its definition: a husband is a married man, one who has a lawful wife living; a wife is a married woman, one who has a lawful husband living. Thus, the law organizes how this relationship may occur and what qualifications people must meet in order to enter into it. Law sets up the explicit criteria for entering into legally recognized relationships such as the marital union.

Law shapes our understanding of the appropriate conduct for a relationship given its legal definition. In other words, the legal process of defining the relationship clarifies what is appropriate and legitimate conduct for persons within that relationship. As the law permits a man and woman to marry in order to be husband and wife, it also sets the rules of conduct in that relationship and provides recourse and sanctioning based upon its definition of that relationship. In other words, the law is embedded in this social relationship.

Law has extended its influence into all arenas of social life, from birth and defining fetal rights to death and determining when that occurs. The law is ubiquitous: no person, **organization**, or relationship remains untouched by it. Some of the most intimate details of social life are intertwined with the legal. Marital, parental, and **employment** relationships are all affected by legal codes. The point is that the law intrudes upon social life in ways that people generally take for granted. The law is a resource that can be exercised just as money can be used to access certain resources. The law, when employed, provides individuals with the ability to invoke legal codes for assistance or recourse when conduct is not within predetermined legal limits. For sociologists there is much to explain about why some have more access to the law than others and the consequences of this social inequity.

LAW ENFORCEMENT

As the most visible part of the criminal **justice** system, law enforcement agencies, more commonly referred to as police agencies, have a unique role within North **American society**. There are several unique features of government-mandated local police forces. First, police are authorized to use force, including deadly force, to enforce compliance with local, state, and federal laws. Second, police may legally detain individuals and remove them from society via arrest. Third, police are given discretion to enforce existing laws and to maintain public order. Finally, police must perform many duties, including law enforcement, restoration of order after traffic accidents and other emergencies, and provision of emergency assistance to those who are ill, injured, or need drug treatment.

Many historical figures and developments have influenced the state of modern police agencies. Most researchers locate the starting point for formal policing in mid-eighteenth century England. In the 1740s, Henry Fielding organized a small **group** of paid constables to enforce local laws. This group later became known as the Bow Street Runners. In 1829, Sir Robert Peel initiated passage of the Metropolitan Police Act, which created a broader police force—one that had several units and was responsible for law enforcement throughout London. These new forces quickly spread, and by the 1840s, the large majority of English towns had local police forces mandated by the national government.

Policing in the United States developed in a similar manner. As in England, early policing was done by small groups of constables in small jurisdictions. Initially in northeastern states such as New York, Pennsylvania, and Massachusetts, many local governments created full-time local police departments and, over time, a large number of cities nationwide developed local law enforcement agencies. Once they became more formalized in the 1850s, most local departments were intricately tied to local governments. Police chiefs and officers reported to local government officials and were expected to carry out their wishes.

With the creation of a government-directed, organized police force came the possibility of corruption. Many early studies of police agencies document high degrees of corruption in municipal police departments nationwide. Because they were tied to the political system, police were often guilty of ignoring the illegal acts of politicians and their associates, of committing illegal acts themselves, and of targeting enemies of politicians for arrests and harassment. This style of policing was common throughout the latter part of the nineteenth century and the early part of the twentieth century.

American policing then entered a professional policing phase in the 1920s and 1930s. Reformers such as August Vollmer argued that police forces should be more professional and scientific in their approach to **crime** control. He suggested that policing had become corrupted by political controls and social networks which guaranteed that only those closely tied to government leaders could be police officers. The professional policing movement called for a militaristic, hierarchical, politically neutral police force dedicated to law enforcement and order.

The professional policing movement advanced to another level with the advent of the automobile. Police agencies began the use of motorized, random patrols to answer calls for service. Citizens subsequently had less interaction with police and typically only saw them in emergency situations. This lack of interaction led many citizens to feel alienated by police, especially as police became more resistant to **community** input in policing matters. This problem was even more pronounced for poor individuals and racial minorities who often complained of being unfairly targeted by police. In fact, two government-sponsored studies in the late 1960s concluded that the aggressive, militaristic style of many police departments exacerbated urban unrest during the civil rights battles of the 1960s.

In an attempt to become less corrupted by political and community influences, police had perhaps gone to the other extreme by becoming overly aggressive and insulated from local residents and community leaders. Even after the Law Enforcement Assistance Administration was created in 1968 to provide better training and educational opportunities for officers, police departments largely continued the aggressive, detached tactics of the professional policing movement.

Since the early 1980s, the dominant trend in law enforcement is known as community policing. Community policing, as a response to the perceived punitive and reactive nature of professional policing, is based on the premise that crime control is best accomplished as a joint venture between police and community residents. Examples of community policing strategies include foot and bicycle patrols, assignment of officers to specific neighborhoods, police substations, and officer-organized neighborhood meetings. The philosophy is that police must work with residents to maintain order and control crime, and that more cohesive communities will be better able to resist crime.

According to recent **surveys**, approximately 85 percent of police agencies nationwide report using community policing strategies. Despite the ubiquitous nature of community policing, results from empirical studies are mixed, and it is unclear whether the strategies are effective in reducing crime and stimulating community cohesion. Numerous studies also indicate that many police departments have failed to make major changes in departmental organization and officer tactics since the community policing movement began. Nevertheless, as we enter the twenty-first century, community policing is still the dominant force in policing and appears to be a long-lasting strategy, though perhaps more in rhetoric than in reality.

LAWRENCE-LIGHTFOOT, SARA
(1944-)
American educator, sociologist, and writer

A sociologist and professor of education at Harvard University and the second African American woman in that university's history to become a permanent faculty member, Sara Lawrence-Lightfoot has received many prizes for her work, which deals with **race**, class, American schools, and the education of minorities.

Lawrence-Lightfoot's book *I've Known Rivers: Lives of Loss and Liberation* about the black middle class, was selected as a Book-of-the-Month Club main choice. Her book Balm in Gilead chronicles her own mother's life. Among other awards, Lawrence-Lightfoot won Harvard University's George Ledlie Prize for her research.

Lawrence-Lightfoot is ''a pioneer of what she calls human archeology.'' In her book *I've Known Rivers*, she uses interviews with six black professionals to explore both the individual experience and social experience it implies.

Lawrence-Lightfoot lives in Boston and has two children—a daughter, Tolani, and a son, Martin—but she spent her teenage years in Pomona, New York. Her parents were leftists and pacifists who encouraged her to read black writers and understand her own, so-called counterculture curriculum. Lawrence-Lightfoot attended Swarthmore College, the Bank Street College of Education in New York, and Harvard University where she attained a doctorate in the sociology of education.

In *Beyond Bias: Perspectives on Classrooms,* with Jean V. Carew, (1979) and in another work, she focused on the positive aspects of six schools in the United States, public, suburban, and private alike. Through interviews with teachers and studying the schools' unusual programs for students, she identified the institutions' strengths.

Lawrence-Lightfoot received a MacArthur Award, enabling her to write her fourth book *Balm in Gilead: Journey of a Healer* (1988), which chronicles the life of her mother, Margaret Morgan Lawrence, who battled through **discrimination** to achieve a professional life as a Harlem child psychiatrist.

Lawrence-Lightfoot's *I've Known Rivers,* the title of which comes from a poem by Langston Hughes, focuses on six middle-aged members of the black middle class, three men and three women, and provides in-depth interviews with each about their lives and families. She selected these individuals, she said during an interview in *Publishers Weekly,* ''not because they are famous, but because they are known in their particular communities and fields as being very good at what they do.... I very much wanted people from different walks of life, from different geographical origins and different social class backgrounds. I wanted to chart different journeys.'' The journeys many of these black Americans took were from indigence to privilege.

According to Karen De Witt in the *New York Times,* ''Dr. Lawrence-Lightfoot asked her subjects to talk about their lives, to describe the seminal experience—the relations with family and friends, with spouses and siblings and with work—that have brought them to middle age. Each person's story touches on historical milestones: the Civil Rights era, the Vietnam War, the Clarence Thomas-Anita Hill hearings, the Rodney King trial.'' The book received mixed reviews.

Lawrence-Lightfoot wrote *I've Known Rivers* in part as a reaction to the late Professor E. Franklin Frazier's *Black Bourgeoisie,* after being exposed to Frazier's book about the black middle class as a Harvard graduate student in sociology and previously as a teenager during Sunday dinners when she listened to her family and their middle-class intellectual black friends—among them the psychologist Kenneth Clark—discussing the book. She came to consider Frazier's book to be short sighted.

Broadly, it contended that when middle-class blacks are absorbed into mainstream white **society** they deliberately leave their roots behind, becoming estranged from the black **community** as a whole. This contention, Lawrence-Lightfoot believed, did not seem to apply to her family or herself. In the *New York Times* she said, "I want to challenge caricatures and stereotypes and those typical static categories used in the social sciences."

Over the years, Lawrence-Lightfoot has developed a rich and broad philosophy about her role as a teacher and teaching itself. As she told Moyers, "In our schools, students are mostly trained to get to the answer quickly. Part of teaching is helping students learn how to tolerate ambiguity, consider possibilities, and ask questions that are unanswerable.... In some sense you have to see yourself reflected in the eyes of those you teach—or at least see your destiny reflected in them.... When teachers can't imagine themselves in their students, when there is no reflection back and forth, then there can be pernicious, discriminatory behavior on the part of the teacher, which is often expressed quite passively. This happens in a lot of schools where kids are very poor or predominantly minority or speak another language."

Concerning the improvement of our country's schools, an issue that has gained public attention in the 1990s, Lawrence-Lightfoot said to Moyers, "There are all kinds of suggestions for school reform that I absolutely agree with. We need to build schools smaller. We need to give teachers much more of a say in developing curriculum and in seeing themselves as major educational actors in the school and the community. We have to find ways of engaging parents or caretakers in the work of the school and building bridges between families and schools."

Aside from writing books, teaching, and doing research, Lawrence-Lightfoot gives lectures and has served on professional committees and national boards, among them the National Academy of Education, the Boston Globe, and the John D. and Catherine T. MacArthur Foundation. She also has been a fellow at Radcliffe College's Bunting Institute and at the Center for Advanced Study in the Behavioral Sciences at Stanford University, and has received many honorary doctoral degrees.

LAZARSFELD, PAUL FELIX (1901-1976)
Austrian sociologist

Paul F. Lazarsfeld combined his interests in mathematics, psychology, and **sociology** to become one of the most influential and innovative forces in quantitative social analysis during the twentieth century. He pioneered a broad range of methodological advancements noted for their quantitative and qualitative mixture of **data** analysis. Applying his research to the areas of mass **communication**, **public opinion**, **voting behavior**, and popular culture, Lazarsfeld combined the study of social units and individuals through the use of survey analysis and panel analysis with the goal of empirically determining the causation of action.

Lazarsfeld was born on February 13, 1901, in Vienna, Austria, to parents Robert and Sofie (Munk) Lazarsfeld. After receiving his doctorate degree in mathematics from the University of Vienna in 1924, he remained to serve as an instructor

in mathematics for the next five years. In 1929 he turned his attention to social psychology, accepting a position as an instructor at the Psychological Institute of the University of Vienna and serving as the director of the Division of Applied Psychology. In 1931 he conducted a study of Marienthal, a small industrial town near Vienna with a high **unemployment** rate. Published in 1933 as *Marienthal: The Sociography of an Unemployed Community*, the study gives insight to Lazarsfeld's ability to combine quantitative and qualitative approaches. For example, he measured the walking speed of unemployed men, using the rate at which the village women traveled as a base line. From this, the study showed that over half of the unemployed men walked at a rate of less than two miles an hour whereas fewer than a quarter of the women did. In a typical trip across the village, only nine percent of the women made three or more stops compared to almost sixty percent of the men. By careful assessment of social conditions, **life histories**, family budgets, spending habits, and daily routines, Lazarsfeld transformed qualitative data into quantitative analysis.

In 1933 Lazarsfeld traveled to the United States on a grant from the Rockefeller Foundation to study psychology. After beginning as an instructor of psychology at the Psychological Institute, in 1937 he accepted a position as director of the Rockefeller Foundation's Office of Radio Research and led studies on the influence of radio on **society**. In 1940 Lazarsfeld moved to New York City, joined the Sociology Department at Columbia University, and established himself as the director of the newly formed Columbia Bureau of Applied Social Research, which would become the prototype for social research institutes. In the 1940s he published several books concerning his radio studies, including *Radio and the Printed Page: An Introduction to the Study of Radio and Its Role in the Communication of Ideas* (1940), *Radio Research, 1941* (1941; with Frank Stanton), and *Radio Research, 1942-43* (1944).

By the mid-1940s, Lazarsfeld had begun to focus on voting patterns and behavior. He conducted two early landmark studies of presidential elections in 1940 and 1948. His conclusions on voting decisions were published as *The People's Choice: How a Voter Makes Up His Mind in a Presidential Campaign* (with Bernard Berelson and Hazel Gaudet; 1944) and *Voting: A Study of Opinion Formation in a Presidential Campaign* (1954). In an attempt to connect preexisting attitudes and expectations with voting behavior and monitor changing opinions throughout the course of an election season, Lazarsfeld located his studies in Erie County, Ohio, and Elmira, New York, in 1940 and 1948, respectively. Interviewing the same people up to seven times in the Erie study and up to four times in the Elmira study, Lazarsfeld created the survey method of panel analysis. Although electoral research would abandon Lazarsfeld's interest in a particular locale in favor of nationwide **surveys**, the panel design became standard practice in sophisticated voting studies.

Several important findings resulted from the two studies. First, Lazarsfeld found that people tended to vote as they, and their families, had voted in the past. Voting opinions are connected to influences found in membership in various social groups. More specifically, people with lower incomes, urbanites, and Catholics tended to vote for Democratic candidates, and people with substantial incomes, those living in rural areas, and Protestants were more apt to vote for the Republican ticket. Third, change is more likely to occur when cross pressures are present and when different group affiliations provide conflicting attitudes and opinions. Finally, Lazarsfeld developed the understanding of a "two-step flow of information." According to this theory, people are not highly influenced by the media but rather look to opinion leaders for advice and information. Not necessarily knowledgeable of the issues or candidates personally, the voters turn to respected members of similar social groups who stay updated on current affairs and relay both information and opinion to the voter.

Lazarsfeld gave up his duties as director of the Bureau of Applied Social Research in 1950 to chair Columbia University's sociology department. He was named Quetelet Professor of Social Science in 1963, a position he held until 1969. From 1970 until his death in 1976 he was a distinguished professor at the University of Pittsburgh. Throughout his career as a researcher and scholar, Lazarsfeld continued to expand his focus and widen his interests as reflected in the array of his published works, such as *Continuities in Social Research* (1950), *Personal Influence: The Part Played by People in the Flow of Mass Communications* (1955; with Elihu Katz), *Mathematical Thinking in the Social Sciences* (1954), *The Academic Mind: Social Scientists in a Time of Crisis* (1958; with Wagner Thielens, Jr.), *Organizing Educational Research* (1964; with Sam D. Sieber), and *Latent Structure Analysis* (1968; with Neil W. Henry).

On the force of his powerful personality, Lazarsfeld created new, sometimes controversial directions in applied social research. Criticized by some sociologists such as **C. Wright Mills** for reducing all qualitative data into mere numbers and statistics, he was admired by others who thought his work offered new and challenging directions in the social sciences. In the introduction to *The Varied Sociology of Paul F. Lazarsfeld* (1982; edited by Patricia Kendall), James S. Coleman, who calls Lazarsfeld the founder of modern mathematical sociology, writes: "Paul Lazarsfeld was one of those rare sociologists who shaped the direction of the discipline for the succeeding generation. It is this that gives the key to the fascination that Lazarsfeld's life and work holds for many sociologists, for they know... that had it not been for Lazarsfeld, they might have been pursuing quite different directions in sociology, and pursuing them in a different manner."

LE PLAY, PIERRE GUILLAUME FRÉDÉRIC (1806-1882)
French sociologist and economist

Considered the pioneer of the social-survey research method, Pierre Guilliame Frédéric Le Play was born on April 11, 1806, at La Rivière, Saint-Sauveur (Calvados). From 1818 to 1822 he studied the classics at the CollŠge du Havre where he earned his undergraduate degree. After spending a year work-

ing as an engineer, he went to Paris to study at the College Saint-Louis, the École polytechnique, and the École des mines. During his academic period, Le Play showed intense interest in the study of social conditions. In 1829, while on a walking tour of the forests and mines of Hartz, he lived with a mining family. From this experience, he wrote his first case study of family budgets, a methodology he adhered to in his later studies. The next year he was severely injured in an explosion at the school's chemical lab. Initially not expected to live, he spent a year recovering. During his convalescence, Le Play spent much time contemplating, writing later, "During this time, the blood spilled in the [French] Revolution of July, 1830, flowed under my window, and I vowed to give the rest of my life to the re-establishment of social peace in my country."

Supported financially through the 1830s by his official duties at École des mines, Le Play graduated from the school with honors in 1840 and accepted a position as professor in metallurgy. His work allowed him to travel extensively across Europe where he not only studied the conditions and operations of the mining industry but also took copious notes on the living conditions of the miners and their families. By 1848, Le Play's interest in sociological study was beginning to outweigh his interest in metallurgy, and he gave up his teaching position to devote himself to the study of social conditions, although he did continue to work as a consulting engineer until 1954.

In 1855 Le Play completed his first important manuscript, published as *Les ouvriers européens* (European Workers). It was a six-volume compilation of monographs describing the moral life and living conditions of 36 families Le Play had studied during his travels from 1829 to 1855. The study was based on the carefully detailed examination of each family's budget, which was laid out in an exact formula, thus becoming one of the first sociological comparative studies. Le Play's premise was that a certain family structure is linked to a certain social structure. By comparing the budget information of both impoverished and prosperous families, Le Play was able to draw conclusions about the factors surrounding social decline and social improvement. Although difficult to read because of the intricately detailed budget information, the instant success of the book was due to Le Play's insights found in explanatory notes that accompanied each budget entry.

His new fame and rapidly growing base of followers allowed Le Play to form the Société Internationale des Études Pratiques d'Économie Sociale in 1856 as a means to promote his theories of social reform. Throughout the remainder of his life, Le Play wrote profusely. In 1864, at the request of Napoleon III, Le Play published *La Réforme sociale en France* (Social Reform in France), which dealt with a variety of social issues including religion, **poverty**, family groups, and government and was based heavily on the research found in *Les ouvriers europ'ens*. During the 1870s, he published books that expanded his theories of the organization of work and family and social reform, in addition to a two-volume study of the English system of education and legislation, which Le Play believed to be superior to France's system.

The foundation of Le Play's social **philosophy** relied heavily on his Christian beliefs. He affirmed the traditional

Christian **values** of duty and obedience to **authority**. Rejecting the socialist idea of communal ownership of **property**, Le Play believed that **society** is best formed under private ownership. Standing against the predominant individualistic **liberalism** spawned by the French Revolution, he called upon employers to cooperate with workers and the wealthy to attend to the poor as a matter of moral obligation. To this end, in 1871 he began forming local groups called Unions for Social Peace, which served to propagate his reform ideas and abide by the principles outlined in *La Réforme sociale en France* on such issues as wages, family structure, and industrial reform.

By examining seven elements of social structure (family, **mores**, religion, government, individual property, property of the ruling classes, and community property), Le Play defined a society as simple or complicated. A simple or a complicated society can be further defined as prosperous or suffering. Ultimately, Le Play believed that the family was the defining social unit that both determined and reflected the health of a society. He categorized families into three types: patriarchal, famille-souche, and unstable.

Patriarchal families are found predominantly in simple-prosperous societies. The preservation of the family unit has the highest priority, which is reflected in the importance of tradition, faith, and family unity and stability. Children tend to grow up, marry, and settle close to the homestead. On the other hand, unstable families, usually found in complicated-suffering societies, offer no long-term commitment to maintaining cohesive family units. Self-preservation is primary and seen as a personal, not a family, obligation. Children, once grown, are expected to leave the home and provide for themselves with little or no support from the homestead.

Famille-souche represents families that combine some characteristics of both patriarchal and unstable families. In French, "souche" usually refers to grapevines, thus conjuring the image of a family that is both rooted and expanding. Found in complicated-prosperous societies, this family unit maintains a homestead, but children are free to go beyond the childhood home to live and work. The immediate family continues to act as the vine, maintaining traditions and offering help in times of need. Thus the famille-souche is a paradigm that promotes stability and also allows for change.

Le Play acquired numerous admirers and followers during his lifetime, including many influential government leaders of Europe. Although his death on April 5, 1882, received little attention, his impact on sociological study and social reform continued for years. Philippe Périer writes in "Le Play and his Followers," appearing in the *International Social Science Journal* (September 1998): "Le Play's pioneer work in applying the principles and methods of scientific research to social facts was fully appreciated in learned circles, and the publication of *Les ouvriers européens* may be regarded as a landmark in the history of science."

LEADERSHIP

In any group of people, there are those who step forward to organize people and events to achieve a specific result. In orga-

nized activities, leaders can be designated and, in informal contexts, such as a party, they may emerge naturally. What makes certain people into leaders is open to debate. Thus leadership seems to be comprised of a cluster of traits, a few inborn but most of them acquired or at least developed by contact with the environment. Leadership has also been defined as a mentality, as opposed to aptitude, the assumption being that mentalities can be acquired. Leaders can be "idea generators" or "social facilitators." Leaders have their own leadership style, and that style may not transfer from one situation to another.

Child psychologists who study girls, and particularly educators and parents advocating equal-opportunity education for girls, have remarked that girls with leadership potential often have to struggle with various prejudices, which also include the notion that leadership is a "male" characteristic. In a study of 304 fourth-, fifth-, and six-graders enrolled in 16 Girl Scout troops, psychologist Cynthia A. Edwards found that in an all-female group, leaders consistently display characteristic qualities such as organizational skills and independent thinking. Significantly, election to leadership posts was based on perceived managerial skills, while "feminine" qualities, such as empathic behavior, were generally not taken into account. However, in examining the research on mixed (male-female) groups, Edwards has found studies that show "that the presence of male group members, even in the minority, suppresses the verbal expression and leadership behavior of female group members." The fact that leadership behavior can be suppressed would seem to strengthen the argument that leadership is, indeed, a learned behavior.

A study by psychologists T. Sharpe, M. Brown, and K. Crider measured the effects of consistent positive reinforcement, favoring skills such as leadership, sportsmanship, and conflict resolution, on two urban elementary physical education classes. The researchers found that the focus on positive skills caused a significant increase in leadership and conflict-resolution behavior. These results seem to support the idea, discussed by Maynard, that leadership behavior can be non-competitive (different individuals exercising leadership in different areas) and also conducive to group cohesion.

LEARNING THEORIES

Groups tend to operate under a unique process wherein they engage in particular behaviors that represent some predefined social role. These social roles are enacted within a set of predetermined social boundaries. Thus, interactions in groups occur through these social roles that elicit certain behaviors within a set of "acceptables" for that group. The question of most import for the social scientist is, then, what is the mechanism by which a person comes to learn the role and the acceptables in an **interaction**? In other words, how does the individual learn to behave in a certain manner? Learning theories are a specific attempt to answer these questions.

Learning occurs when behavior or responses change as unexpected consequences or reinforcements/punishments occur following an elicited behavior. Thus, learning occurs when **unanticipated consequences** arise after a response or behavior has been performed. Individuals tend to learn primarily through operant **conditioning**; essentially behavior is shaped by its consequences. A behavior is strengthened through rewards and avoidance of punishment, or it is weakened by aversive stimuli and/or the loss of rewards. Individuals can also learn through interactions with others where various definitions about behaviors serve as discriminative stimuli so that behaviors can be defined as "good" or "bad" leading to the likelihood of an individual engaging in that behavior. Learning theories tend to have the following causal order. Definitions of situations, roles, and the like are formed, and behaviors are carried out. Attached to these behaviors are reinforcements or punishments which provide feedback that a behavior is either acceptable or that a behavior must be changed. Behavior is, thus, either maintained or modified given the consequence after previous enactment of it. In addition, learning theories may or may not allow for learning to occur by observing others' behavior, also known as cognitive learning.

B.F. Skinner and Albert Bandura are the most prominent figures associated with learning theories. Skinner in the 1950s developed the operant behavioral model of learning, which emphasized reinforcements as the mechanism by which a behavior was maintained or changed. Bandura, beginning in 1977, on the other hand, developed what is known as cognitive learning **theory** that incorporated the use of thoughts and images into the learning process outlined by Skinner. These two models of learning are the primary foundation upon which contemporary learning theories have been built.

Learning theories are used to explain behaviors ranging from **crime** and deviance to **conformity**. These theories attempt to describe, predict, and explain behaviors through analysis of experience and conditioning of a given individual or group. Thus, behavior is viewed as a response to cues in an individuals' environment. For example, individuals learn specific table manners given their place in the social **structure**. Eating a seven-course meal requires different behavioral skills versus eating a hamburger at a fast food restaurant. These behaviors and cultural prescriptions for behavior are assumed to be acquired through a process of learning during interaction with others. This assumption leads theories based on learning to predict behavior patterns as related to an individual's **culture**, associations, and conditioning. In terms of probabilities, learning theories predict that there is an increase in a given behavior being elicited if the environment surrounding that individual would stimulate such a response as normative.

LEAST SQUARES REGRESSION LINE

The least squares **regression** line is the best-fitting line in a linear regression **model**. This line is the best prediction for a value of response variable y based on a fixed value of explanatory variable x for the **data** being studied. When a scatterplot of the data suggests a linear relationship between x and y, it is possible to draw any number of lines that closely approxi-

mate that relationship. The distance between each plotted case and the line is the residual. When the case is plotted above the line, the residual value is positive; when it falls below the line, the residual value is negative. The sum of all residual values is zero. The line that returns the lowest value for the sum of the squared residuals (also called the sum of squared errors, or SSE), obtained by the formula $(Y-\hat{Y})^2$, is the best-fitting line. This is known as the least squares method.

Using the least squares method, we produce a prediction equation with the form $(\hat{Y}) = a+bX$, where a is the constant, or Y-intercept, and b is the slope of the line. This linear function predicts a value of y for fixed values of X. There may be more terms (usually $X^1, X^2,..., X^n$) when additional variables are introduced in the model. The values for the constant and slope for the least squares **regression line** are easily obtained using statistical software packages.

See also Regression Line

LEGISLATION OF MORALITY

The legislation of **morality** is the idea that the law can and should be used to impose ideas about what is and is not moral in a given society. According to this way of thinking, the law is not based in an objective reality, but emotional reactions about the supposed morality or immorality of certain actions. Thus, people use the law to exert power over others who disagree with them, based in their own sense of morality, or right and wrong.

The history of this concept originated with Émile Durkheim, who rejected the idea that certain actions were inherently **evil** or wrong and that they were condemned because they were harmful to the group as a whole. He saw **crime** and **deviance** as socially constructed. He felt that societal reactions to actions were not based in rationality, but on emotions, characterized by moral condemnation and outrage. This outrage was based in the collective conscience of **society** or of a group of people in society, and was a form of social control that would reinforce and maintain the group's collective norms and **values**, even if those **norms** and values were not held by the majority of the population, but only by the people in power.

Karl Marx and **Friedrich Engels** expanded Durkheim's concept by considering why certain things became considered wrong or evil, and eventually illegal, not why people broke laws in the first place. They felt that the legal system was an instrument of **social control** and was a source of both legitimation and justification for social and legal sanctions (punishments). They differed from their predecessor in that they considered the law a form of class consciousness, while Durkheim saw it as a form of social consciousness.

Recent investigations into legislation of morality, particularly in the United States, have focused on moral panics (AIDS, abortion), moral entrepreneurs (pro-life movement, **gun control** advocates), and victimless crimes (drug use, prostitution). This research examines morally charged topics and looks at the effects both the media and **social movements** have in the development of ideas about and laws pertaining to these issues.

Some researchers have put forth the idea that legislation may not be the result of certain moral crusades, but in fact the instigating factor of such crusades (Taylor 1982). They claim that changes in the legal system that do not take into account changes in other social institutions can create a situation in which people's options will be limited and they will have no recourse but to break the laws.

Some researchers claim that moral panics are a normal, continuous, predictable part of modern popular **culture** (Cohen 1972). They see moral campaigns as organized by people who feel there are differences in the moral and ideological quilt of society. They are usually people associated with social institutions that have historically been associated with the control and determination of morality, such as religious organizations, political parties, and community organizations.

All areas of life that have been legislated in a moral way have a similar pattern of development. They begin as critical issues for a small portion of the population. This segment slowly begins to gain support by lobbying local or national legislatures and by spreading their opinions through mass communication channels (newspapers, **television**, radio) and through grassroots organizing efforts. Once the movement has gained momentum, there are often changes in both local and national laws. There is usually also an opposition movement that grows in conjunction with the original moral movement, arguing that the issue is a personal one and should not be addressed by legislation, or that the argument the original group is making is not the moral one. The issue of abortion is an illustrative example of this dynamic. Both sides of the debate claim that they are morally right, that they are using the correct and moral argument.

Recent research has shown that modern moral panics in the United States are centered to a great deal around women's increased autonomy and participation in the workforce, the increasing diversity in sexual expression, and the changing nature of the **family** structure in the United States. This has resulted in people directly or indirectly lobbying for legislation to prevent these patterns from spreading. Most sociologists, however, claim that these developments are simply a matter of natural changes in the social fabric of our country due to broad social and institutional changes and must be treated and studied as such.

LEGITIMACY

Legitimacy is defined by **Max Weber** as the "inner justification" upon which obedience to **authority** rests. A legitimate political order is one that is recognized as right and just. Implicit in the concept is the assumption that political order cannot be established and maintained through coercion alone but requires a certain degree of mass loyalty from those who are subject to it. In this respect, the concept is similar to the Marxist notion of hegemony, developed by Antonio Gramsci, and to Émile Durkheim's argument that an anomic **division of labor** (one lacking moral regulation) is inherently unstable and conflict ridden.

Weber distinguished three forms of legitimation. *Traditional* legitimacy rests on "the authority of the 'eternal yester-

day.'" It is an unreflective form of legitimation in which the political order is merely taken for granted, "sanctified through the unimaginably ancient and habitual orientation to conform." **Custom** serves as a source of legitimacy but also constrains traditional leaders in important ways. Weber contrasted this form of legitimacy to its modern *legal-rational* form, which rests on a "belief in the validity of legal statute and functional 'competence' based on rationally created rules." Legal-rational legitimacy is unique in that obedience is owed to an impersonal set of **rules** rather than to an individual. Opposed to both of these is *charismatic* legitimacy, which rests on "the absolutely personal devotion and personal confidence in revelation, heroism, or other qualities of individual leadership." **Charisma** is a dynamic and disruptive force in Weber's political sociology; it provides little structure for the political system aside from the communion between leader and disciples. However, the death of the charismatic leader always results in the **routinization** of charisma and a return to either traditional or legal-rational authority. Weber stressed that these three forms of legitimation are ideal types and that any concrete historical political order typically rests on some combination or mixture of the three.

The concept of legitimacy has continued to be a subject of debate within sociology since Weber's time. It is not clear, for example, whether the concept can be applied to prestate societies or whether it should be restricted exclusively to political orders. There is also disagreement concerning the relation between legitimation and class conflicts as well as the existence and nature of legitimation problems in advanced capitalist societies. Jürgen Habermas's attempt to resolve these questions has been particularly influential. Habermas further elaborated the concept of legitimacy by suggesting that new and different levels of justification are required in the course of social evolution. Each level requires not only new reasons for obedience, but new kinds of reasons. In early civilizations, rulers derived their legitimacy from myth. Later, legitimacy had to be tied to the "unifying principles" of "philosophically formed world views." Finally, in modern societies, "since ultimate grounds can no longer be made plausible, the formal conditions of justification themselves obtain legitimating force.... Only the rules and communicative presuppositions that make it possible to distinguish an accord or agreement among free and equals from a contingent or forced consensus have legitimating force today." Habermas concluded that legitimacy claims can only be evaluated intersubjectively from the viewpoint of the participant, not from the neutral viewpoint of the social-scientific observer. Where charisma served as the dynamic and disruptive force in Weber's **political sociology**, the concept of systemic contradictions plays this role for Habermas. In Habermas's view, the legitimacy of the modern state depends upon its capacity to minimize the dysfunctional side effects of capitalist economies. This act is accomplished by the provision of money, leisure time, and security. The legitimacy of the state is jeopardized if the demand for such primary goods exceeds the state's capacity to provide them or if new and different needs and expectations arise that cannot be satisfied in this way.

LEGITIMATE AUTHORITY

Since **Max Weber**, sociologists have posited the existence of something called "'legitimacy'' that motivates people to accept authority without needing to be forced into compliance. **Legitimacy** is the people's belief that the governing **authority** is the best available and will act in their best interest. Weber posited the existence of three types of legitimate authority: charismatic, traditional, and rational-legal. Charismatic authority is based on the people's belief that their leader has some sort of access to superior insight or supernatural power. Although the oldest form of authority, it is represented by such modern leaders as Vladimer Lenin and Martin Luther King Jr. As these examples suggest, charismatic authority generally functions as a revolutionary force in **society**. Charismatic authority depends on close proximity between the **leadership** and the movement's rank and file. It is the hardest type of authority to pass from one person to another, but rituals are often developed such as the laying on of hands in certain religious traditions that are meant to transfer charismatic authority. Traditional authority is based on habit and appears natural to those that accept it; they cannot imagine social life organized in any other fashion. Whereas charismatic authority looks forward to some sort of **utopia** ushered in by the leader, traditional authority often looks backward to some sacred state of affairs that existed years earlier. Traditional authority, represented best by medieval feudalism or tribal societies, is passed on by kinship and **marriage**. Rational-legal authority is based on the rule of law. That law is written down so anyone can look it up and, therefore, hold authority figures accountable. Unlike in the other two forms of legitimate authority, obedience is not owed to a person under rational-legal authority. It is owed instead to impersonal principles that apply to everyone, even the leaders. Since this type of authority is invested in offices instead of persons, transfers of power are smooth and predictable. Every democratic election represents a chance for a transfer of rational-legal authority. The out-going office holder loses the power of the office as soon as the newcomer takes over. Although rational-legal authority is indicative of the modern era, charismatic and traditional appeals for legitimacy can still be made. Indeed, candidates trying to win election, who are themselves manifestations of rational-legal authority, often depend either on a certain measure of **charisma** or appeals to tradition to attract voters.

See also Legitimacy

LEISURE

Leisure can be defined as free time. It is time not spent at work or maintaining one's **household**. Leisure activities are diverse and include rest, hobbies, and recreation. The **sociology** of leisure has emphasized two separate aspects. Some sociologists stress the freedom of the individual during leisure time in comparison to time spent at work or domestic chores; others stress the constraints **society** places on leisure time, either through consumerism or **capitalism**, and thus contend that the use of the terms "free time" and "leisure" is somewhat illusory.

At the end of the nineteenth century, **Thorstein Veblen** published*The Theory of the Leisure Class*. Veblen, an economist, was the first to look at work and human relationships in terms of consumption rather than production. Veblen did not equate leisure and pleasure; instead, he saw leisure as a conduit for **status** displays. **Property** is the measure of success, and self-esteem is tied to property, in what Veblen called a competitive society. If a man is to keep the esteem of his neighbors and his self-esteem, he has to have the things others in his circle own, which traps all involved in a cycle of procurement; in other words, Veblen gave life to the idea and the term "conspicuous consumption" which describes an ethic anathema to the Protestant work ethic described by **Max Weber**, even though they lived during the same period and, presumably, studied groups of people typical to the era.

Conspicuous leisure arrives hand-in-hand with conspicuous consumption for the leisure, or upper, class. According to Veblen,, the leisure class, because they cannot always be in the public eye, must prove that they have adequate **money** not to work when no one is looking. He cited various cultural trends which reflect this attitude: the Victorian obsession with pale skin when people who worked had darker skin; members of the leisure class would learn multiple languages simply to show them off; and, one of his most well-known examples, long fingernails as evidence of not working with one's hands.

A desire for more than personal displays of leisure led, according to Veblen, to vicarious leisure. The **family** is the primary vehicle for vicarious leisure, but servants are also a reflection of leisure status, in their number and in their dress; liveried servants, for example, dress up not to enhance their own status but to enhance that of their master. A butler who arrives at the door in clean, expensive clothes and, especially, clean gloves, is evidence that his master can afford not only his own leisure, but that of others. Such a butler does not have multiple household duties because the master is able to pay others to perform these tasks and keep one person waiting to answer his door.

"Keeping up with the Jones's" was once confined to the leisure classes, but Veblen noticed that the competition had spread throughout the social structure, as each class tried to emulate the class directly above it. In addition o feeling it necessary to emulate the leisure class, lower classes began to strive for the appearance of leisure. To offer a contemporary example, dark, not pale, skin is a sign of leisure, as most people work inside. People who work all day often tan themselves in booths, giving the appearance of leisure. Fake fingernails are also evidence of conspicuous leisure, an appearance which, paradoxically, takes one's "free time" to effect. Furthermore, although those at the bottom of society were better-off than their predecessors, they felt as if they were poorer because the standard of comparison had changed; this concept later became known as "relative deprivation." Veblen believed that the key to human economic activity is the desire to excel over one's neighbors.

Developing out of **industrial sociology** in the 1950s, some theorists within the sociology of leisure claimed that leisure had replaced work as a central interest. Such a society can be called a *leisure society*, one in which work is gradually losing its place as a central focus. The leisure society, then, is generally correlated with a decrease in paid hours of work that leaves people more time to focus on leisure activities. Whether or not the leisure society is an adequate description of the social system of the twentieth and twenty-first centuries, however, remains a point of contention. The actual number of hours worked in the past in comparison to the present is still debated and there is also evidence to support the argument that leisure was a focus of past social systems and preindustrial societies.

Typical leisure activities of the late twentieth century were increasingly influenced by technological advances, providing consumers an outlet for their time and their money. Many of the time-saving advances employed outside industry were and are directed toward easing the daily duties of the homemaker. Washing machines and dryers replaced a time-consuming and tedious process, as did dishwashers, vacuums, electric stoves, food processors, and other appliances; innovations surrounding home appliances had their heyday in the 1950s, and did their job so well that being a homemaker no longer took an entire day. Betty Friedan, in her groundbreaking book *The Feminine Mystique,* detailed the results of all of this increased leisure for middle-class women: bored, frustrated, over-educated housewives longed to give up their "free time" for demanding jobs in the outside world. Friedan's book helped spark the second wave of the women's movement; these were the perfect people to work on a political movement, as they had the time, money, and education to dedicate themselves to a cause.

Advances in entertainment give consumers an outlet for their time and their money. In addition to watching **television** or seeing a film at a theater, people can watch films at home on video cassette recorders or digital video discs; chat with someone on the other side of the world over the Internet; listen to compact discs on a home, personal, or car stereo; use video cameras to make their own films; play video games by themselves or against others over a network; or create web pages to reflect their interests, desires, and political leanings. Of course, more traditional activities, such as reading a book, are available, but even this has been moved forward with the invention of the electronic book.

Several time-use studies conducted in the 1990s revealed that Americans feel as if they have less leisure time than their predecessors. But hour-by-hour analyses reveal that they actually enjoy more free time, most of which is used up by large amounts of television viewing. However, with so many additional options for filling leisure hours, this perception seems to be a symptom of relative deprivation.

LENSKI, JR., GERHARD EMMANUEL (1924-)

American sociologist

Gerhard Lenski was born on August 13, 1924, in Washington, D.C., to parents Gerhard Emmanuel, Sr. and Christine (Umhau) Lenski. He served in the U.S. Army Air Force from

Several studies conducted in the 1990s revealed that Americans feel as if they have less leisure time than their predecessors *(Field Mark Publications).*

1943 to 1945, earning the rank of sergeant. Attending Yale University, he earned his B.A. in 1947 and his Ph.D. in **sociology** in 1950. Upon graduation, he accepted a position first as an instructor and later as an associate professor at the University of Michigan. In 1963 he moved to Chapel Hill, North Carolina, to become a professor of sociology at the University of North Carolina, chairing the Department of Sociology from 1969 to 1972. During his ten-year tenure at the University of North Carolina, he held a concurrent position as a research professor in the Institute for Research in Social Science. When he retired in 1973, he was named professor emeritus. Lenski married Jean Virginia Capplemann in 1948; they had four children.

Lenski's professional endeavors outside the classroom included serving as an associate editor for the journal *Social Forces,* beginning in 1963, and as a consultant for McGraw-Hill Book Company (1963-1970). His published works include *The Religious Factor* (1961), *Power and Privilege* (1966; with Jean Lenski), *Human Societies: An Introduction to Macrosociology* (1970; with Jean Lenski). His most influential work was completed in *Human Societies,* which was republished in 1974, 1978, 1982, 1987, and 1991 and continues to appear regularly on the reading list of college sociology classes.

The Religious Factor is based on a 1958 survey study that included personal interviews with 656 people in Detroit regarding their religious and communal involvement, attitudes, and behavior. Lenski's goal was to discover the impact of religion on secular life, including politics, economics, and family life in the urban setting. In *Power and Privilege* Lenski sets out a system of social stratification based on "the distributive process in human societies—the process by which scarce **values** are distributed." In other words, "Who gets what and why?" Basing his theory on the distributive systems, he divides societies into the categories of hunting and gathering, simple horticultural, advanced horticultural, agrarian, and industrial.

Lenski begins *Human Societies* by offering a definition of **society** that includes five characteristics. First, a society is territorially distinct, and second, it is made up of a single species of animal. Third, an **organizational structure** exists by which members of the society interact on a consistent and regular basis. Fourth, as a form of organization, a society subsists on a relatively high degree of interdependence among its members. In other words, members depend on other members to fulfill different roles and functions to provide for the needs of the entire society. Finally, a society maintains independence from outside regulation or control of any significance. Ultimately, Lenski suggests that a society exists "to the degree that a territorially bounded population of animals of a single species maintains ties of association and interdependence and enjoys autonomy."

Offering an evolutionary understanding of the function of society, Lenski proposes that societies did not always exist. They were, in fact, a development in the evolutionary process of the attempt to survive. As societies appeared and proved to be beneficial to survival, they spread widely. Just as characteristics determined survival, such as speed, **intelligence**, and strength, the development of an organized society became an asset in the struggle to survive. Thus Lenski suggests that "the societal form of organization is a mode of **adaptation** whereby certain types of organisms have increased their chances of surviving and multiplying." On this premise, Lenski constructs a **model** of social development that is dependent on the understanding of human society as part of the biological world and its influences.

Arguing that universal statements can be made that encompass the experience of all of the biotic world, Lenski offers eight relevant universals that define the condition of all living organisms. First, all organisms require food, water, and air. Second, because of this **need**, all living things necessarily interact with, or are dependent on, one another to maintain sustenance. Third, all living things can reproduce at a rate that exceeds the available food supply. Fourth, because living things reproduce at this higher rate, the food supply is continually short. Fifth, with a less than adequate amount of food, competition for it exists. Sixth, although not the norm, in large populations production of genetic variations can be expected. Seventh, due to the competition for sustenance and the fact that differences exist between and among species, certain species will be more suited for survival. Thus a process of natural se-

lection occurs. Lenski lists numerous characteristics such as fecundity, strength and offensive weapons, defensive armament, speed, and social organization. Finally, variation and natural selection bring about organic and behavioral evolution, which is nonrandom and progresses in the direction of the desirable traits of survival.

LEVELS OF ANALYSIS

Three levels of analysis are employed in the social sciences: univariate, bivariate and multivariate analyses. **Univariate analysis** involves the examination of a single **variable**. Conducting univariate analysis gives the researcher descriptive information about a variable that helps researchers to locate errors in the **data** and to identify trends in the population from which the data were gathered. Information generated from univariate analysis includes the frequency of the distribution of cases over the attributes of a variable, measures of central tendency, and **measures of dispersion**.

Bivariate analysis refers to the examination of the effect of one variable on another. Only two variables are involved in this type of analysis. It is predictive, in that it estimates the extent to which change in one variable predicts change in another. The association between two variables can be one of **correlation** or causation. **Measures of association** include eta, gamma, lambda, Pearson's r, Kendall's tau, Spearman's rho, and chi^2, among other measures.

Multivariate analysis refers to the examination of the effects of many independent variables on one or more dependent variables. Examples include multiple **regression**, **path analysis**, discriminant analysis, logistic regression, and structural equation modeling. The level at which the independent and dependent variables are measured and the purpose of the research determine which statistical procedure will be used. Common to most multivariate statistical procedures used in the social sciences is the goal of measuring the extent to which one variable produces change in another while controlling for the effects of other variables.

For example, let us assume that a researcher wants to test the theory that people who receive more formal education earn higher salaries. A survey is distributed to the general population in which respondents are asked what level of education they have received and what their current salary is. Education is measured in years attended school, and salary is measured in whole dollars. Both variables then are measured at the interval level so regression analysis would be used to analyze the association among them.

However, what if we find that people who receive more years of education do earn higher salaries? Would this finding support the hypothesis? It would not exactly. We have ignored other, very important causal variables. What else might explain differences in salary? How about age, sex, **race**, and occupation? All of these factors are related in some way to the **dependent variable**. Older people are more likely to have been in the work place for a longer time and earned tenure and promotions resulting in higher pay. In spite of the narrowing wage gap between men and women, women on average still earn 75 cents on the dollar compared to men. Also, racial minorities have lower access to **higher education** than whites which results in lower wages. Certainly, a person's occupation may determine level of pay, regardless of educational attainment. All of these independent variables in some way influence the dependent variable.

If we could take the effect of age on education and salary out of the relationship between education and salary, we would have a clearer picture of the impact that education really has on salary. Additionally, if we could remove the effects that each of the independent variables has on each other and on the dependent variable, then we would have a true measure of the extent to which someone's education predicts salary. That is exactly what is accomplished by multivariate analysis. We are able to assess the extent to which the main independent variable predicts the dependent variable while controlling for the effects of all of the independent variables on the dependent variable. Since causation in the social sciences is almost always attributable to multiple sources, multivariate analyses most often used in social research.

LÉVI-STRAUSS, CLAUDE GUSTAVE (1908-)
Belgian anthropologist

The French social anthropologist Claude Gustave Lévi-Strauss became a leading scholar in the structural approach to social anthropology. Claude Lévi-Strauss was born on November 28, 1908, in Brussels, Belgium, of a cultured Jewish family. He grew up in France, attended a lycée in Paris, and studied **philosophy** at the Sorbonne, University of Paris. After holding several provincial teaching posts, he became interested in anthropology and accepted an appointment as professor of **sociology** at São Paulo University, Brazil (1935–1939), which enabled him to do field research among Brazil's Indian tribes.

Lévi-Strauss returned to wartime France and served in the army (1939–1941). He taught in New York City at the New School for Social Research and at the École Libre des Hautes Études (1942–1945). He was also cultural attaché in the French embassy (1946–1947).

Back in France, Lévi-Strauss was associate director of the Musée de l'Homme, director of the École Pratique des Hautes Études, and editor of *Man: Review of French Anthropology*. From 1960 he was professor of social anthropology, professor of comparative religions of nonliterate people, and director of the Laboratory of Social Anthropology at the College of France.

Lévi-Strauss's fame began with his book *Tristes Tropiques* (*A World on the Wane*, 1961). It is partly biographical, partly a philosophical reflection on travel, and mainly a systematic account of four primitive South American Indian tribes. In this and his next influential book *The Savage Mind* (1966), he expressed his belief that in their potential all men are intellectually equal. Instead of primitive man's being frozen in his **culture**, he wrote, "A primitive people is not a back-

ward or retarded people; indeed it may possess a genius for invention or action that leaves the achievements of civilized peoples far behind."

Citing examples, Lévi-Strauss argued that primitive man's conceptual mental structures, though of a different order from those of advanced man, are just as rich, utilitarian, theoretical, complex, and scientific. There is no primitive mind or modern mind but "mind-as-such," in which is locked a structural way of thinking that brings order out of chaos and enables man to develop social systems to suit his needs. Man's mental structures and ways of achieving order are derived as much from primitive magic as from Western science, as much from primitive myth as from Western literature, and as much from primitive **totemism** as from Western **morality** and religion.

Lévi-Strauss's thesis, which excited world attention, is that if social scientists can understand man's mental structures, they can then build a study of man which is as scientific as the laws of gravity. If order exists anywhere, says Lévi-Strauss as a structuralist, then order exists everywhere, even in the brain.

Lévi-Strauss's search for the common denominator of human thought derives from structural linguistics, a twentieth-century science which set out to uncover the possible relationships between the origins of human speech and the origins of culture. He goes beyond **language** in adding as concepts for **social order** such activities as music, art, **ritual**, myth, religion, literature, cooking, tatooing, intermarriage, the kinship system, and the barter of goods and services. He sees each as another related way by which a **society** maintains itself. Man's mental structures in bringing order out of chaos, no matter how divergent his patterns may seem in old and new cultures, may derive from a common mental code.

The work of Lévi-Strauss seeks to stimulate thinking and research on breaking the mystery of this code. His popularity rests on his belief that there are no superior cultures, that man acts according to a logical structure in his brain, and that once the code of this logical **structure** can be discovered, the human sciences can be as scientific as the natural sciences.

Lévi-Strauss was awarded the Wenner-Gren Foundation's Viking Fund Medal for 1966 and the Erasmus Prize in 1975. He has been awarded several honorary doctorate degrees from prestigious institutions such as Oxford, Yale, Harvard, and Columbia. He has also held several academic memberships including the National Academy of Sciences, the American Academy and Institute of Arts and Letters, the American Academy of Arts and Sciences, and the American Philosophical Society.

LIBERALISM

Liberalism traces its roots to the Renaissance, the Protestant Reformation, and the Enlightenment. **Anthony Giddens** wrote that "the left—and most liberals—were for modernization, a break with the past, promising a more equal and humane social order." Originally, that meant support for democracy and the newly emerging capitalist economic system and an end to the old monarchies, the dominance of the Catholic Church, and the longstanding feudal system. Liberals were concerned with protecting individual rights and liberties, such as the right to vote, to own **property**, and to freedom of speech, thought, association, etc. They felt that **government** should exist to prevent harm to citizens but not to enforce traditions or allegiance to any church or hierarchy. Liberals embraced the changes brought about by modernization, including secularization, industrialization, and the development of rational thought and scientific inquiry. These ideas were highly influential in the eighteenth century, and inspired the Declaration of Independence, the U.S. Constitution, and the French Revolution.

As industrialization continued, however, vast inequalities emerged in capitalist societies, monopolies grew, and workers were increasingly exploited by their employers. Many workplace regulations that exist today in the United States did not exist before the Progressive Era of the late 1800s through the 1920s. Activists at that time fought for minimum wage laws, a forty-hour work week, worker safety regulations, anti-child-labor ordinances, and the right to unionize. The economic boom of the 1920s made the country's inequalities even more apparent, and when the Great Depression of the 1930s hit, the term "liberal" began to be used to describe those who believed the government should intervene in economic matters. While liberals generally support the maintenance of a capitalist economy, they also believe that it is the government's responsibility to help those who are disadvantaged. George McGovern insisted that "liberalism has saved American **capitalism** from the excesses of the right and left since the 1930s.... [It] is the 'middle way' between the right-wing glorification of the free market and the left-wing advocacy of full-scale government ownership and direction." Today some government social programs that were created during the 1930s New Deal, such as social security, are largely taken for granted by Americans of all political persuasions.

Liberalism in the United States peaked in the 1960s, when the government began numerous other social programs intended to end the **discrimination** and poverty that still existed despite post-war affluence. The Civil Rights movement resulted in the anti-discrimination measures of the Civil Rights Act of 1964, and the federal "war on poverty" consisted of efforts to construct public housing for those with low incomes, provide **health care** for the poor, create a welfare system that could serve as a "safety net" for families that fell on hard times, and desegregate public school systems. James Tobin described this approach as "specific **egalitarianism**...the view that certain commodities should be distributed equally, or at least less unequally than the ability to pay for them." Many of these programs have come under fire in recent years from conservative politicians who insist that they have done more harm than good. Some public housing units, said to encourage **crime** and drug use, have been torn down. The welfare system was markedly changed in 1996 by the institution of strict time limits and work requirements for recipients, in an effort to discourage "welfare dependency."

On cultural issues, contemporary liberals have continued to support the individual rights and liberties that inspired their forebears, along with social responsibility. Wilson Carey McWilliams pointed out that "liberals incline to see most communities and social relationships in terms of their utility to the individuals they comprise, and hence properly redefined or abandoned in response to changes in one's life stage or historical developments." They generally welcome changes that give people more lifestyle options, believe in freedom from government interference in personal decisions (such as those surrounding sexuality, relationships, birth control, and abortion) and have worked to include homosexuals in civil rights legislation. Liberals have also been concerned with church-state separation issues and have fought to keep mandatory **prayer** out of public schools and to ensure that the theory of evolution remains a part of high school science curriculums. Liberals also tend to support environmental regulations aimed at protecting wildlife habitats and public health, as well as government subsidies that support mass transportation and research on alternative energy sources rather than benefitting the petrochemical and highway industries.

LIFE CHANCES

Life chances, a term coined by **Max Weber** in the early 1900s, describes disparities among social classes. More specifically, life chances is a term basically for estimating an individual's ability to obtain access to what is needed or wanted in **society**. In the marketplace, life chances translates into purchasing capabilities and insulation from others.

According to sociologists, the more affluent members of a society (the rich) typically have better life chances compared to the less affluent (the poor) because they have greater access to society's limited or scarce resources. Resources are anything valued by the society and are considered scarce when they are unequally distributed among social groupings. These resources may include, but are not limited to, such things as high-quality nutrition and health care, safe neighborhoods, quality education, and a vast array of other goods and services.

Life chances are reflections of the socioeconomic make-up of a society and are often tangled with ascribed characteristics such as **race** and gender. Because members are born with these characteristics, they have virtually no control over them. Moreover, in almost every society, human attributes such as race and gender are used to the advantage of some and the disadvantage of others. Therefore, ascribed characteristics often influence life chances because they are repeatedly the focus for **prejudice** and **discrimination**.

Though not necessarily an indication of individual worth, life chances are also routinely associated with achieved characteristics such as marital status, income, occupation, and education. For example, the higher level of education achieved typically results in higher occupational status. Ascribed characteristics influence life chances mainly by shaping access to certain achieved characteristics.

LIFE COURSE

The life course approach is both a theoretical and a methodological strategy for understanding individual development and change over time. Although its roots can be traced to the 1920s, the life course approach did not gain ascendancy in **sociology** until the early 1990s. The approach is currently used in general sociological studies and especially in the related field of **criminology**.

The origin of life course work in sociology is typically located in the 1920s with the work of University of Chicago sociologists such as Ernest Burgess, **Robert Park**, and W. I. Thomas. These researchers were interested in understanding the development of individual lives and their relationship to historical context. In fact, Thomas's *The Polish Peasant in Europe and America* provides an insightful analysis of the effects of immigration on a **group** of individuals over time.

The life course approach was used only infrequently by sociologists for the next several decades, being used mostly by developmental psychologists, demographers, and economists. It was not until the 1990s and the work of sociologist Glen Elder that the approach became widely accepted. Elder describes the life course as the interconnectedness of trajectories and transitions within individual lives. Trajectories are long-term pathways such as work, marriage, education, and **family**. Embedded within these general trajectories are specific transitions. Transitions are short-term pathways such as getting a job, getting divorced, completing a degree, or having children. For most individuals, each trajectory will consist of a large number of transitions. For example, under the trajectory of work, a person may make a transition to a new job, to being fired or laid off, or to a higher- or lower-paying job. Researchers have documented how individuals tend to progress along reasonably similar trajectories and experience similar transitions within them.

Perhaps the most important contribution of Elder to life course theory is the recognition of how the age at which transitions occur, their timing, and their meaning will vary widely and will affect individual lives differently. For example, a transition to **unemployment** will likely affect a young adult with a college degree much differently than it will affect an older, uneducated person. In *Children of the Great Depression*, Elder observed how differently individuals in their early teens during the late 1920s and early 1930s were affected by the major economic decline versus those in early **adulthood** at the time. In this instance, individuals as few as five years apart in age were affected in dramatically different ways by economic collapse.

The theoretical point is that even though most individuals go through the same life cycles and have similar experiences, the timing and sequencing of these events will affect them differently. In fact, some transitions may be significant enough, either positively or negatively, that they serve as "turning points" for individuals' lives. For example, a transition to having children may cause a person to become more responsible and focused, while loss of a job or **divorce** may cause major distress and eventual alcohol or drug abuse.

The life course approach also entails a distinct **methodology**. Cross-sectional studies have been most common in sociology and related fields where a sample of people are studied at one point in time. However, because a life course approach is geared toward studying individual change and development over time, researchers must use longitudinal studies in which samples of individuals are initially interviewed and then re-interviewed at regular intervals over time. The high cost of longitudinal studieshas limited their use until recently when there has there been adequate funding for and interest in these types of studies.

The life course approach continues to be a useful tool for theory and research in many of the social sciences, particularly in the field of criminology. Currently, researchers are studying the developmental patterns of offenders over time, including the ways they are initiated into **crime**, persist in crime, and desist from crime. They also study how many life events such as marriage and **employment** may serve as turning points away from criminal activity.

LIFE EXPECTANCY

The chances of dying are widely variable and largely depend on factors that are outside an individual's control. Since everyone dies the majority die in later life, it can be concluded that age is one of the major uncontrollable factors related to death. Sex is also a factor. Both in infancy and in the post-retirement years, men tend to die at a more rapid rate than women in all industrialized societies. Because of these factors, it is difficult to compare death rates across societies or across time.

More specifically, if one country has seven deaths per thousand people annually and its neighbor has ten deaths per thousand people, it would be easy to assume that the first country is a healthier place to live. It could be concluded that the first country has more advanced medical technology, more adequate nutrition, or a healthier living environment than its neighbor. It is equally possible, however, that the country with the higher death rate simply has an older population. It is also possible that this country, like many oil producing countries in the Middle East, experiences massive migration of male workers. Having an older or more male population can push up death rates, even for advanced countries with excellent living conditions. Thus, if sociologists want to use death as an approximate measure of changes in health conditions or compare deaths from country to country, they must compare death rates for each age group and both sexes.

To simplify this comparison, sociologists use the conept of the expectation of life at birth, usually referred to as "life expectancy." Calculating life expectancy is rather complex, but it can generally be thought of as the average number of years a person born in a particular **society** can expect to live. The earliest tool for calculating life expectancy—the life table—dates back to early Western **civilization**. Computers able to deal with large number matrices have rendered life tables somewhat as a tool for life expectancy calculation. Most life expectancies are now calculated using advanced statistical analysis which is much more complex but also more accurate. Sociologists studying **demographic methods**, however, continue to be taught how to calculate life tables as an aid in understanding complexities of the life expectancy concept.

Most scientists agree that the maximum life expectancy for an entire population is about 85 years; certain subgroups—

Expectation of Life at Birth, 1970 to 1997, and Projections, 1995 to 2010

[**In years.** Excludes deaths of nonresidents of the United States]

Year	Total			White			Black and other			Black		
	Total	Male	Female	Total	Male	Female	Total	Male	Female	Total	Male	Female
1970	70.8	67.1	74.7	71.7	68.0	75.6	65.3	61.3	69.4	64.1	60.0	68.3
1975	72.6	68.8	76.6	73.4	69.5	77.3	68.0	63.7	72.4	66.8	62.4	71.3
1980	73.7	70.0	77.4	74.4	70.7	78.1	69.5	65.3	73.6	68.1	63.8	72.5
1982	74.5	70.8	78.1	75.1	71.5	78.7	70.9	66.8	74.9	69.4	65.1	73.6
1983	74.6	71.0	78.1	75.2	71.6	78.7	70.9	67.0	74.7	69.4	65.2	73.5
1984	74.7	71.1	78.2	75.3	71.8	78.7	71.1	67.2	74.9	69.5	65.3	73.6
1985	74.7	71.1	78.2	75.3	71.8	78.7	71.0	67.0	74.8	69.3	65.0	73.4
1986	74.7	71.2	78.2	75.4	71.9	78.8	70.9	66.8	74.9	69.1	64.8	73.4
1987	74.9	71.4	78.3	75.6	72.1	78.9	71.0	66.9	75.0	69.1	64.7	73.4
1988	74.9	71.4	78.3	75.6	72.2	78.9	70.8	66.7	74.8	68.9	64.4	73.2
1989	75.1	71.7	78.5	75.9	72.5	79.2	70.9	66.7	74.9	68.8	64.3	73.3
1990	75.4	71.8	78.8	76.1	72.7	79.4	71.2	67.0	75.2	69.1	64.5	73.6
1991	75.5	72.0	78.9	76.3	72.9	79.6	71.5	67.3	75.5	69.3	64.6	73.8
1992	75.8	72.3	79.1	76.5	73.2	79.8	71.8	67.7	75.7	69.6	65.0	73.9
1993	75.5	72.2	78.8	76.3	73.1	79.5	71.5	67.3	75.5	69.2	64.6	73.7
1994	75.7	72.3	79.0	76.4	73.2	79.6	71.7	67.5	75.8	69.6	64.9	74.1
1995	75.8	72.5	78.9	76.5	73.4	79.6	71.9	67.9	75.7	69.6	65.2	73.9
1996	76.1	73.0	79.0	76.8	73.8	79.6	72.6	68.9	76.1	70.3	66.1	74.2
1997	76.5	73.6	79.2	77.1	74.3	73.9	(NA)	(NA)	(NA)	71.2	67.3	74.7
Projections: [1] 1995 ..	75.9	72.5	79.3	76.9	73.6	80.1	(NA)	(NA)	(NA)	69.7	64.8	74.5
2000 ..	76.4	73.0	79.7	77.4	74.2	80.5	(NA)	(NA)	(NA)	69.7	64.6	74.7
2005 ..	76.9	73.5	80.2	77.9	74.7	81.0	(NA)	(NA)	(NA)	69.9	64.5	75.0
2010 ..	77.4	74.1	80.6	78.6	75.5	81.6	(NA)	(NA)	(NA)	70.4	65.1	75.5

NA Not available. [1] Based on middle mortality assumptions; for details, see source. Source: U.S. Census Bureau, *Current Population Reports*, P25-1130.

Source: Except as noted, U.S. National Center for Health Statistics, *Vital Statistics of the United States,* annual, and *National Vital Statistics Reports (NVSR)* (formerly *Monthly Vital Statistics Reports*).

like women in the United States—come close to reaching that maximum although entire populations do not. The life expectancy in most developed countries today is usually in the mid-seventies. On the other hand, since life expectancies are calculated based on the death rates of previous generations, it is impossible to determine how closely today's life expectancy figures will accurately reflect a society's actual mortality. Because of advances in medicine, it is generally accepted that life expectancies underestimate actual life chances by several years.

Life expectancy is different from life span, since life span deals with the biological capacity of a single individual. Many sociologists expect that humans, under optimal conditions, can live to be about 120 years old. Thus, maximum life span is 120. Life expectancy, however, takes the entire population into account. The fact that some individuals will die in infancy and others will die in their teen and young adult years lowers the life expectancy for the entire population. Consequently, while many Americans can expect to live into their early eighties and beyond, the life expectancy for the U.S. tends to hover around 76 years, and many scientists have concluded that even advancements in the treatment of cancer or

heart **disease** will only raise life expectancy by two or three years.

See also Birth and Death Rates

LIFE HISTORIES

Many sociologists engaged in what is known as qualitative studies of society seek an understanding of sociological process that approaches what Max Weber referred to as *verstehen.* Mastering social knowledge at a level comparable to Weber's envisioned *verstehen* requires an understanding so thorough and complete that the knowledge becomes nearly intuitive in nature. Within such gathered knowledge there must be complete revelation of even the most minute details of the social action studied, with few or no social processes left undiscovered and thus not studied.

In direct response to the need for such comprehensive study, the life history method of sociological study was developed. Explained simply, the life history requires the researcher to observe first hand, whenever possible, the progress of the lives of those involved in the segment of **society** being studied. Therefore, to a large extent, the life history form of study is

Weberian in nature, the developing history of the individual member of society, his circumstances and surroundings being important to an understanding of the activities and problems of both the individual and the greater society. The significance of the individual roles being played or to be played, and those played by institutional forces in the course of developing life history studies should not be underestimated. Both individual and institutional actions and responses vary within any society. Processes observed in some societies, or segments of a particular society, might fall within normal parameters for the group under study. Conversely, similar processes might be considered intolerable and unacceptable in other societies or even within other segments of the society under study.

Because life history work requires the entry into and study of a social setting at a random time, with an objective of discovering aspects of social process as they present themselves for observation, it is difficult to discern in advance what specific sociologically significant **data** might emerge from such life histories. It is clear, though, that in undertaking life history studies, the researcher expects the work will yield an understanding of the social interactions in progress and thus yield representations of lives lived in certain ways. Generally limited in length by restrictions of time and research funding, the life histories touch on the lives of those observed and on the lives of those close to those actually being studied. But based on the knowledge obtained in the life history work, broader future study could emerge. With broader study the researcher might develop data relevant to the general society of which the study was a part. Therefore, the potential for far reaching impact of a life history on the larger society cannot be underestimated.

In fact, one of the most compelling reasons for selection of the life history method is the fact that through life history work there is opportunity for open ended exploration of the sociological experience of each participant. Through such open ended exploration even more pathways may be discovered for future exploration and study of a larger segment of the society. The life history technique, with its inherent opportunity for this open ended exploration, provides what many consider to be the best method for gathering such broad data which might then direct further inquiry.

Finally, the life history method also presents opportunity to utilize a professionally recognized framework through which data gathered can be presented in a format that is readable and coherent to not only those within *academ,* but to the general public as well. C. Wright Mills, in his great work *The Sociological Imagination* repeatedly reminds us of the importance of the aforementioned. He further reminds us of the necessity of social scientists to lead, rather than follow, to help rather than hinder the process of understanding society. There is, in effect, an obligation for the social scientist to lead the way, providing society and the general public with knowledge, reason and guidance not otherwise readily obtainable: "...ordinary men, when they are in trouble or when they sense that they are up against issues, cannot get clear targets for thought and for action; they cannot determine what it is that imperils what they vaguely discern as theirs." (Mills 169-170)

Life history work, most commonly written up and presented in a style criticized as being somewhat literary by some sociologists, provides such a bridge for greater understanding between social scientists and the public to which their life's work is directed and dedicated.

LIFESTYLES AND HEALTH

Lifestyles and health are closely related in that the way individuals choose or are forced to live can have a decided impact on their health and well-being. Health lifestyles were defined by Abel as "patterns of health-related behavior, **values**, and attitudes adapted by groups of individuals in response to their social, cultural, and economic environment." Individuals' health lifestyles are, therefore, determined by behavioral choices and options, which may, in turn, be limited by their *life chances.* **Life chances** are determined through a combination of variables, including socio-economic **status**, educational level, age, gender, **race**, and ethnicity. Profession or occupation, physical environment, **disabilities**, and access to preventive **health care** may also affect people's health status.

The World Health Organization (WHO) noted that during the nineteenth century, health was improved through *engineering methods*, which included safe water supplies, sewage systems, and improvement of diet through advances in agriculture. The first sixty years of the twentieth century was termed the *medical era*, during which infectious **disease** was attacked with vaccinations and antibiotics. The WHO suggests that we are entering a *postmedical era* in which environmental and social or behavioral factors not directly treatable by medicine are largely responsible for health status. Non-medical factors thus become primary in addressing many problems of health and illness.

To emphasize the growing importance of lifestyle, it was noted by Hamburg that "half of the mortality from the ten leading causes of death in the United States is strongly influenced by lifestyle." He included factors of smoking, obesity, lack of exercise, substance abuse, reckless driving, nonadherence to medication regimens, and lack of coping mechanisms or maladaptive response to **stress** and social pressure.

In addition, major patterns of disease have changed from acute or infectious disease to chronic illnesses which are long term and require management and cooperation by both physician and patient, and which cannot be cured. Such problems as cancer, heart disease, diabetes, and arthritis require behavioral changes on the part of the patient. Other diseases significantly associated with styles of living include smoking-induced lung cancer and autoimmune deficiency syndrome (AIDS). The implication is that the individual must take responsibility for maintaining an optimum level of health through habits, behavioral change, and lifestyles that promote good health.

Early research on the connection of health to lifestyle was conducted in California in the mid-1960s by Bellock and Breslow. A ten-year follow-up identified some major "good health habits." In 1979, the Surgeon General's Report on

Health Promotion and Disease Prevention listed Health Objectives for the Nation. Modification of detrimental behaviors was identified as a major source of health improvement. By pursuing a healthy way of life, an individual attempted to produce good health based upon motivation, effort, and capabilities. The mass media have strongly promoted this pursuit in advertising and selling everything from vitamins and exercise equipment to courses in stress reduction and diet pills.

The concept of lifestyles has long been relevant to sociologists. Max Weber's views on lifestyles, expressed in his *Economy and Society* in 1922, proposed that a person's status, or prestige, and power, as well as access to the means of production, helped to determine a person's social rank. Weber noted that lifestyles are based not upon what a person produces but on what he or she consumes. Consumption, in turn, is limited by life chances, which are shaped and determined by one's social circumstances.

While the upper and middle classes have more resources to direct toward healthy lifestyles, many components of health lifestyles have spread across social classes. Weber's work suggested that the aim of pursuing health for all classes is consumption. However, Cockerham noted that people pursued or "consumed" health for different purposes, depending upon their social class. For example, good health allows people to work harder and longer or to be more vital and able to enjoy life.

While early work addressed the **role** of social distribution of wealth, status, and power, Nettleton and Bunton have noted criticisms that the concept of healthy lifestyle has now focused primarily on modifying behavior. Consequently, health education in targeting high risk groups and "blaming the victim" may promote stigma and **discrimination** at the expense of collective social action to change negative economic, social, and political lifestyle factors over which individuals have no control.

LIKERT, RENSIS (1903-)
American educator

Rensis Likert is well known in the field of conflict management. He was born in Cheyenne, Wyoming, on August 5, 1903, the son of George Herbert, an engineer, and Cornelia Zonne Likert. In 1926, he graduated from the University of Michigan, Ann Arbor. Two years later he married Jane Gibson, an editor and consultant. The couple had two children, Elizabeth and Patricia.

Likert continued his studies at Columbia University in New York City, earning a Ph.D. in 1932. By that time he had begun his teaching career as an instructor at New York University, New York City, becoming an assistant professor in 1935. Likert spent a year on the faculty of Sarah Lawrence College in Bronxville, New York, 1935-36, before being named head of the Division of Program **Surveys**, Bureau of Agricultural Economics in the U.S. Department of Agriculture, Washington, D.C. Also during that period, he was research director for Life Insurance Agency Management Association, 1935-39,

and director of the Morale Division of the U.S. Strategic Bombing Survey, 1944-46, during World War II. He returned to the University of Michigan in 1946 and remained there until 1970 as professor of **psychology** and **sociology**. Likert was named professor emeritus in 1971. During his tenure at Michigan, he also served as director of the **Survey Research** Center, 1946-48, and in the Institute for Social Research, 1948-70, becoming director emeritus in 1971.That year, Likert also formed his own company, Rensis Likert Associates, in Ann Arbor. It was concerned with management styles and systems in conjunction with survey research.

In addition to his teaching career, Likert contributed to numerous publications, including the *Internatinal Encyclopedia of Neurology, Psychiatry, Psychoanalysis, and Psychology*. He is the author of six books, most dealing with management, such as *Morale and Agency Management,* 4 volumes, with J.M. Willits, 1940-41, and *The Human Organization: Its Management and Value*, 1967. With his wife, he wrote *New Ways of Managing Conflict*, published by McGraw-Hill in 1976. Intended for laypersons seeking to resolve most types of conflicts, the book applies research **data** concerning organizations and their effectiveness to the management of conflict.

Likert was a fellow and board of directors member of the American Psychological Association, past president of the American Statistical Association, and a member of the national Academy of Public Administration. In 1955, he received the Paul D. Converse Award from the University of Illinois; in 1962, the James A. Hamilton Award and awards from the Organization Development Council and the McKinsey Foundation for his book *New Patterns of Management;* in 1968, a human relations award from the **Society** for the Advancement of Management and a professional achievement award from the American Board of examiners of Professional Psychologists; and outstanding achievement awards from the **American Society** for Training and Development (1969) and the American Association for **Public Opinion** Research (1973).

LIKERT SCALE

The Likert scale is a technique used for the **measurement** of attitudes, developed by **Rensis Likert** in 1932 as a means of emphasizing simplicity and clarity in acquiring opinions toward certain values or ideas. The method is broad enough to be used for a wide range of attitudinal variables. Used often on questionnaires, Likert Scales generally measure respondents' level of agreement with certain statements, such as "The United States government should ban abortion." Responses use a scale with five categories, a common range being Strongly Agree, Agree, Neutral, Disagree, Strongly Disagree. Responses are given consecutive numerical values (either during the construction of the survey or during the coding stage) so that they can be summated with other responses to create an **attitude** scale. Thus, a numerical **mean** may indicate overall attitudes toward a single topic that is measured by a series of related variables.

Reacting to previous survey methods in which researchers acted as raters or judges after **data** were gathered to evaluate interviewees' responses, Likert developed this technique as a means of attaining high specificity among respondents' attitudes. He devised the method to measure what he called ''Judgement of Value'' rather than ''Judgement of Fact'' and to ensure that every question may be structured such that the respondent is allowed to choose from two clearly opposed alternatives.

Demonstrating great forethought in terms of future methodological issues regarding the procedure, Likert listed several suggestions in his original article for the use of this type of attitude measurement. Response categories should each involve a single attitude **variable** and be listed in a consecutive order such that the **model** response is approximately in the middle of possible responses. Further, to ensure **reliability**, a series of statements measuring the same attitude should be devised in such a way that a strong inclination toward one side would mean that a respondent answered half the questions with ''Strongly Agree'' and the other half with ''Strongly Disagree.''

Nan Lin (1976) suggested the following procedure when gathering Likert data: 1) the construction/selection of positive and negative statements with five response categories; 2) collection of responses; 3) computation of total score across all related statements; 4) examination of consistency (by comparing responses to related statements); 5) elimination of inconsistent statements; 6) compilation of final statements; and 7) recomputation of the final score. Used in several disciplines (e.g. **psychology**, **sociology**, political science, communications), this method is particularly easy to understand and use for a wide variety of respondents.

LINE GRAPH

A line graph is a graphic representation of the distribution of cases across some **variable**. This kind of graph is used to display differences among the variable's categories. Line graphs (also called frequency polygons) are used with interval-ratio, continuous variables as a means of visually presenting **descriptive statistics**, such as the frequency or percentage of cases falling within each variable category. Because they are used to show the distribution of interval-ratio level, continuous variables, line graphs are often used to showcase trends over time.

In a line graph, intervals spanning variable categories are placed on the horizontal x-axis, with a mark on the axis designating the interval's midpoint. The frequency or percentage of cases is displayed on the vertical y-axis. A dot is placed at the corresponding number or percentage of cases in the categories contained within each of the intervals. Once all of the dots have been marked, straight lines are drawn between adjacent dots to produce a comprehensive line that summarizes the entire distribution of cases for some variable.

A line graph is an alternative to a **histogram**, since both types of graphs are used to display the same kinds of **data**. In many instances, line graphs and histograms can thus be used interchangeably. There are situations, however, where line graphs are preferable to histograms. For instance, researchers can construct line graphs that show a variable's distribution across two or more different samples or populations. This task can be accomplished using a line graph because it is possible for several lines to be displayed simultaneously, thereby permitting an easy comparison of the groups. However, histograms are unsuited to visually represent the distribution of more than one group, as the bars do not allow multiple groups' distributions to be displayed simply and efficiently.

Line graphs can also be used to compare a single group in terms of two or more different variables (measured in the same units). Furthermore, unlike histograms, line graphs are useful in displaying the distribution of some trait during two or more time periods. These types of graphs, which include multiple lines representing multiple groups or time periods, are called complex line graphs. In contrast, graphs which only display the distribution of some variable for a single group are called simple line graphs.

See also Histogram

LIPSET, SEYMOUR MARTIN (1922-)
American sociologist and political scientist

Seymour Martin Lipset is primarily known as a student of democracy. Although much of his work focuses on the United States, he also studies democracy in its many manifestations around the globe. Lipset often makes comparisons between **government** systems, and he has a special interest in analyzing the differences between **democracy** in its Canadian and U.S. forms. Lipset has frequently argued that because the United States was born of revolution, its governing forms and its attitudes about democracy are profoundly different from its northern neighbor, even though both countries have had remarkably similar histories following their initial formation. Methodologically both a sociologist and a political scientist, he uses theories developed in a variety of fields while, at the same time, infusing into his work a strong admixture of historical **empiricism**.

Lipset's career has been remarkably prolific. Born in New York City in 1922, he received his bachelor's degree from the City College of New York in 1943 and his Ph.D. from Columbia University in 1949. He has also received numerous honorary degrees, including LLDs from universities in the United States, Latin America, Israel, and Europe. While earning his Ph.D. in sociology, Lipset lectured at the University of Toronto. After receiving his degree, he went on to teach for three years at the University of California at Berkeley, before heading back to Columbia University as an assistant professor of sociology from 1950 to 1956. For the next decade, he was back at Berkeley as a professor of **sociology**, before accepting the position of George Markham Professor of Government and Sociology at Harvard University, which he held from 1965 to 1975. After that, he became a professor of **political science** and sociology at Stanford University, where he served until 1992. Since 1990, he has also held the Hazel Chair of Public Policy at George Mason University. Lipset has also held numerous

Poverty rate for children higher than for adults
Poverty rate by age group, 1960-1998

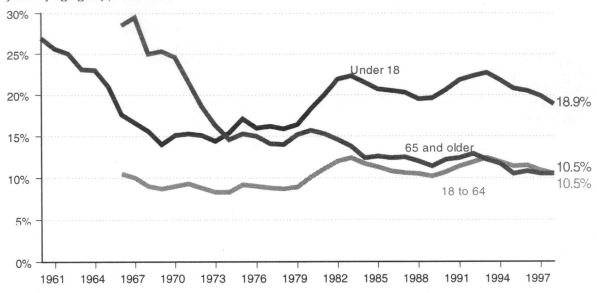

Source: "Poverty in the United States: 1998," September 1999, U.S. Census Bureau

A line graph is a graphic representation of the distribution of cases across some variable. It is used to display differences among the variable's categories over time. (© *Data Copyrighted by Source. © Graphics Copyrighted by Public Agenda 2000. No reproduction/distribution without permission.*)

positions at research foundations. He has been a fellow or visiting scholar at Hebrew University (Israel), the Russell Sage Foundation, the Woodrow Wilson Center (Princeton University), the Hoover Institute (Stanford University), and the Progressive Policy Institute, the latter two positions he currently holds.

In his political writings, Lipset owes a great debt to John Stuart Mill and his theory of countervailing powers within democracies. At the same time, Lipset shares Max Weber's concern that modern bureaucracies and the sheer complexity of modern states can produce a citizenry unaware of and uninterested in the role they must play in maintaining a functioning democracy. While Lipset agrees with Marx that class divisions can erode the civil **society**, he believes that democracy in its existing form—that is, allied with capitalist economic relations—can and should survive. Thus, while Marx expected to see class divisions intensify until eliminated by revolution, Lipset believes they should be managed so as to both avoid revolution and limit their destructive tendencies. The key to maintaining bourgeois democracy—to use Marxist terms—is economic growth, according to Lipset. As long as enough members of society believe that they and their children can expect a more abundant future, the divisions between classes can provide a healthy dynamism, rather than a destructive force for violence and revolution.

Examining democracy in its various manifestations through American history—as well as in its many forms around the contemporary world—Lipset argues that this form of government rests on a subtle interplay of forces, with those pushing for **conformity** and those setting the stage for disintegration existing in a carefully maintained balance. If a state moves too far in one direction or the other, he says, democracy is likely to fail. Lipset also sees a usefulness in the sharp disagreements among citizens over important issues, so long as those disagreements are counter-balanced by others. For example, it is healthy for American democracy, he says, that there are both fiscally-conservative Republicans who support social libertarianism and economically-liberal Democrats who tend toward conservative positions on social issues. These crisscrossing political cleavages, he argues, maintain both healthy debate and insure that alliances remain fluid, thereby avoiding widespread zealotry and intransigence.

The evidence for why this system works can be found in U.S. history, Lipset concludes, beginning with America's break with Great Britain which balanced strong, centralized **leadership** with the centrifugal forces of revolution. More generally, the revolution and subsequent American history has involved a playing out of the antagonistic forces of **equality of opportunity** and an acceptance of the inequality of condition. That is to say, Americans have effectively balanced a strong and fair rule of law with a capitalistic system that abundantly rewards aggressive achievers.

LOCKE, JOHN (1632-1704)
English philosopher and political

The English philosopher and political theorist John Locke began the empiricist tradition and thus initiated the greatest age of British philosophy. He attempted to center **philosophy** on an analysis of the extent and capabilities of the human mind.

John Locke was born on August 29, 1632, in Wrington, in Somerset, where his mother's family resided. She died during his infancy, and Locke was raised by his father, a small-town attorney. John was tutored at home because of his delicate health. He then went to Christ Church, Oxford, where in 1658 he was elected senior student and taught Greek and moral philosophy. He changed his subject to medicine and received a license to practice. Here Locke met Robert Boyle, the distinguished scientist and one of the founders of the Royal Society, and, under Boyle's direction, took up study of natural science. Finally, in 1668, Locke was made a fellow of the Royal **Society**.

Locke met Lord Ashley, first Earl of Shaftesbury, and later lord chancellor of England, and their lifelong association drew Locke into political affairs. He attended Shaftesbury as physician and adviser, and in this latter capacity Locke drafted *The Fundamental Constitutions of Carolina* and served as secretary to the Board of Trade. Locke wrote most of his important writings in Holland where he lived with the exiled Shaftsbury. Locke died in Essex on October 28, 1704.

None of Locke's major writings were published until he was nearly sixty. In 1690 he brought out his major works: *Two Treatises* and the *Essay Concerning Human Understanding*. But the four books of the *Essay* were the culmination of twenty years of intellectual labor.

The intention of Locke's *Essay* was positive in that Locke wished to establish the dependence of all human knowledge upon everyday experience or sensation. The alternative theory of innate ideas he vigorously attacked. Although it is not historically certain whether anyone seriously maintained such a doctrine, Locke's general criticism lends indirect support to an experiential view of knowledge. Innatism can be understood in a naive way to mean that there are ideas of which we are fully conscious at birth or which are universally acknowledged, so that the mind possesses a disposition to think in terms of certain ideas. The first position is refuted by observation of children, and the second by the fact that there are no acknowledged universal ideas to which everyone agrees. The sophisticated version falls into contradiction by maintaining that we are conscious of an unconscious disposition.

Having refuted the *a priori*, or nonexperiential, account of knowledge, Locke devoted the first two books of the *Essay* to developing a deceptively simple empirical theory of knowledge. Knowing originates in external and internal sources of sensation and reflection. The objects or ideas present to con-

John Locke

sciousness are divided into simple and complex. Simple ideas are primitive sense **data**, which the mind passively receives and cannot alter, delivered by one sense (seeing blue), by several senses (eating an orange as a synthesis of taste, touch, and smell), by reflection (hunger), or by a combination of sensation and reflection (pleasure and pain). The objective orientation of simple ideas follows from the fact that we cannot add or subtract from their appearance or conception in the mind. In relation to simple ideas, at least, the mind is passive, a "blank" or "white" tablet upon which sensations are impressed. Complex ideas are formed by actively combining, comparing, or abstracting simple ideas to yield "modes, substances, and relations." Modes are class concepts or ideas that do not exist independently, such as beauty.

Locke was faced with an acute dilemma. If the immediate object of knowledge is an idea, then man possesses only a derivative knowledge of the physical world. To know the real world adequately requires a complex idea which expresses the relation between the qualities that we perceive subjectively and the unperceived existent. The substance which unites the common perceived qualities of figure, bulk, and color into this one existing brown table is, in Locke's terms, an "I don't know what." His honesty almost brought Locke to a modern relational definition of substance instead of the traditional notion of a thing characterized by its properties. But the conclusion drawn in the *Essay* is that knowledge is relational; that is, it consists in the perception "of the agreement or disagreement among ideas."

The third book of the *Essay* deals with words, and it is a pioneer contribution to the philosophy of **language**. Locke is a consistent nominalist in that for him language is an arbitrary convention and words are things which "stand for nothing but the ideas in the mind of the man that has them." Each man's understanding can be confirmed by other minds insofar as they share the same linguistic conventions, although one of the singular abuses of language results from the fact that we learn names or words before understanding their use. The purpose of Locke's analysis is to account for generalization, abstraction, and universals in terms of language. The final section of the *Essay* deals with the extent, types, and divisions of knowledge. This work seems to have been written earlier than the others, and many of its conclusions are qualified by preceding material.

In this view the actual extent of man's knowledge is less than his ideas because he does not know the real connections between simple ideas, or primary and secondary qualities. Also, an intuitive knowledge of existence is limited to the self, and the only demonstrable existence is that of God as an eternal, omnipotent being. With the exception of the self and God, all knowledge of existing things is dependent upon sensation, whose cognitive status is "a little bit better than probability." The **poverty** of real knowledge is compensated to some extent by human judgment, which presumes things to be true without actually perceiving the connections. And, according to Locke's commonsense attitude, the severe restrictions placed upon knowledge merely reflect that man's mental capacity is suitable for his nature and condition.

LONG TERM CARE

As life expectancies rise, concern about funding and availability of long term care increases in salience; the population of the United States may be living longer, but for some that can mean spending more time disabled or chronically ill. Dealing with a loved one who requires long term care takes its toll both financially and emotionally, whether that individual is cared for at home, or resides in a nursing or assisted living facility.

Candidates for long term care are those individuals who have difficulty performing activities of daily living (ADLs). These include bathing, dressing, and feeding oneself, continence, toileting, and transferring (moving from one seat in a room to another); the actions considered as ADLs can differ by study or agency, but an inability to perform these six activities are considered "triggers" for qualifying for benefits from the state or private insurance.

There are several options for providing someone with everyday health care over long periods of time. Care can be provided in the home, either by home health aides, private nurses, or by relatives; this can take place in the patient's original home or in the home of children or other relatives. Another option is **nursing homes**, which provide full-scale medical and residential care. Assisted living facilities allow people who have some difficulties with ADLs to live more independently than in a nursing facility but with twenty-four hour access to medical care and other types of aid. Adult day care facilities, which began cropping up in the late 1990s, allow relatives who

have taken responsibility for the care of an elderly person to continue working; in a similar vein is respite care, which offers the primary caregiver "time off" from a draining task.

The baby boomer generation is the first in which a large proportion are in the position of caring for parents and children at the same point in their **life course**. Daughters are more likely to take on the care of elderly parents than are sons, which can be difficult both physically and financially for female-headed households. Women, whose **life expectancy** exceeds that of men, are also more likely to need long term care, yet they are the least able to afford it; women save less money for **retirement** than men do, which is partly a function of income disparities, and can also result from taking time off of work to raise children (or care for elderly parents). Women make up the majority of the elderly population living in **poverty**. And as families become scattered across the country, elderly parents can be isolated from relatives who could care for them at home.

Long term care is extremely expensive, especially within the confines of a care facility; in 1995, the cost of a year in a nursing facility averaged $41,000. **Medicare**, the primary source of health insurance for most elderly, does not pay for long term care, leaving people to rely on **Medicaid**, but only after they have spent all of their assets. Medicaid, however, cannot afford to provide care to the entire generation of baby boomers. Government policymakers and independent think-tanks have begun to urge people to buy long term care insurance if they can afford to do so, which has a two-fold purpose: it leaves Medicaid funding for the truly indigent and prevents the impoverishment of an individual family in the process of receiving government aid. Insurers offering long term care policies can refuse to insure someone on past or present health history; for this reason, buying a long term care policy is best done before problems arise, when rates are lower, and rejection is less likely. Although the elderly are the primary consumers of long term care, people with physical **disabilities** or slow-healing injuries are also candidates, as are individuals with a chronic illness such as AIDS.

LONGITUDINAL RESEARCH

When designing a study, the researcher(s) must decide over what period of time and at how many points the observations will be made. Cross-sectional research involves observations at one point in time. Most studies, whether exploratory or descriptive, are cross-sectional. Most explanatory studies are cross-sectional as well, but such studies face a fundamental limitation. Singular observations, observations at one point in time, make determining causality difficult. Measuring variables only once does not allow a researcher to understand which variables cause which effects. Associations can be delineated, but **causality** can only be established when a time order can be determined so that researchers can be certain which **independent variable** precedes which dependent **variable**.

As opposed to **cross-sectional research**, longitudinal research uses observations over an extended period of time. This allows researchers to draw conclusions regarding causes and effects. There are three types of longitudinal research. Trend studies examine a specific aspect of a population over time. For example, every ten years the **census** collects information on characteristics such as income, education, and **race**. Looking at the changes over time for any or all of these characteristics of the population constitutes a trend study. A second type of longitudinal is the **cohort** study. Instead of following a particular characteristic over time, cohort studies follow individuals who are similar along a specific dimension. Most commonly, this dimension is age, but it can also be based on some other grouping such as year of college graduation or time of **marriage**. For example, researchers might follow attitudes about the environment over time among persons who graduated at the time of the Exxon oil spill. The third type of longitudinal study is the panel study. While neither the trend nor the cohort study requires the same sample for each observation, the **panel study** follows the exact same set of individuals over time. In other words, a new sample could be selected for each point of observation in either the trend or the cohort study. This is possible because changes in the particular individuals are not the focus. A panel study is focused on changes in the individuals, however, and therefore requires the same sample for each observation. The trend study is centered on an issue or characteristic, the cohort study is centered on groups of similar individuals, and the panel study is centered on a specific set of individuals. For example, researchers might study attitudes toward parents among a sample of adolescents over time. Because the emphasis in this type of study is on changes among individuals, it is important to take the multiple observations using the very same individuals.

LOOKING-GLASS SELF

The looking-glass self is a celebrated concept developed by early twentieth-century sociologist **Charles Horton Cooley** (1864-1926). It is used to express the idea that individual self-conceptions are intimately linked with social interaction and **society** in general. By using the metaphor of the looking-glass, Cooley suggested that the emergence and development of an individual's self-conception is the consequence of the reflective appraisals of others. In this way, the world of social interaction is understood as a mirror from which individuals derive their ideas about who they are as social objects. Cooley described the looking-glass self as being composed of three fundamental elements. First, individuals in the course of interaction imagine themselves as they most likely appear to relevant others in the situation. Second, individuals reflect upon these imagined judgments made by others and develop a sense of themselves as a social object. Finally, these reflective appraisals result in a set of self-conceptions and self-feelings such as pride, embarrassment, or shame. As these self-feelings and self-conceptions accumulate over time, individuals come to develop a more or less stable sense of their social self.

The significance of Cooley's idea of the looking glass self lies in its conceptualization of the self as both imaginative

The term "love" refers to kinds of emotional, often affectionate, ties between people who are connected in various ways *(Corbis Corporation [Bellevue])*.

and the product of a social process. Individuals develop self-conceptions by internalizing the appraisals of others and by imagining how others are imagining them. It is this social process of sympathetic and imaginative reflection that Cooley argues drives the development of the social self. Simply put, the notion of the looking glass self describes the process through which individuals come to conceptualize themselves in the same way that they imagine that others imagine them.

Cooley's conceptualization of the looking glass self has been widely influential in the development of contemporary sociological approaches to self, self-conception, and **identity**. It influenced George Herbert Mead's famous theory of the self and the tradition of symbolic interaction that later emerged from Mead's work. Mead was aware of Cooley's theory of the looking-glass self and his notion of the "me" provides a direct parallel to the idea looking-glass self.

See also Self-Concept

LOVE

The term "love" refers to kinds of emotional, often affectionate, ties between people who are connected in various ways. Customarily, people think of parental love of offspring as the starting place for ties which individuals attempt to replicate, improve, or develop through their lifetimes. Thus, as individuals develop in healthy ways, they tend to connect with loving feelings to siblings and **extended family** members, and gradually as they enter the world, they may feel love for neighbors, others in groups to which they belong, and, finally, with chosen sexual partners, life companions, and spouses.

For **sociology**, love remains an elusive concept, as it is difficult, if not impossible, to quantify scientifically. Its elusiveness likely accounts for the predominance of poetry and spiritual writings on the subject with respect to the relative lack of scientific and quantitative research. Moreover, definitions of love vary greatly. Some believe it to be a way of behaving, others consider it to be an enduring feeling or emotion, and still others represent love as an **attitude** toward another person. Furthermore, one's concept of love may also vary according to the relationship of which it is attributed: for example, brother-sister, parent-child, husband-wife, boyfriend-girlfriend, friend-friend, etc.

Regardless of the type of relationship to which love is attached, most sociologists consider love to be learned through cultural experience. We first form our sentiments regarding love through our experience with our parents. These relationships generally reflect the cultural of which the parents and child are a part. In response to the love the child experiences with his parents, the child also learns to love. Conceptions of love vary cross-culturally and historically, but individuals tend to experience love according to the culture in which they are raised.

In contemporary times, the notion of love primarily concerns the narrower notion of romantic love. In the Western world, many people relate to one of the five dimensions of romantic love that are depicted through literature, media, and cultural attitudes. These aspects consist of the following dimensions: unrealistic expectations of the loved one, the notions of one true love, love at first sight, the idea that love conquers all, and the allowance for an individual's indulgence of personal emotions at the other's expense. In many respects romantic love is a Western idea. Westerners marry for love but historically in the United States and most of the world today kin and economic and status conditions are still factors that effect considerations of **marriage**. Many cultures, particularly those in the East, believe that love develops after marriage. In America, on the other hand, love is thought to be the foundation of every marital union. **Society** promotes the idea of love as a condition for sexual exclusivity and marriage without love is thought to be reprehensible. Wealthy cultures are more likely to indulge in the idea of romantic love as well as cultures that the value the concept of **individualism** over the community.

This enduring quest for romantic love, termed the romantic love complex, has affected members of **American society** in a psychological way. Americans tend to believe that love should cross cultural barriers; people are expected to fall in love with those who differ from them and their ability to transgress such barriers is sighted as proof of the power of love. In reality, however, people tend to be attracted to and fall in love with people who are relatively similar to them in age, **race**, socio–economic status, and appearance. Here, the issue is raised regarding whether people tend to deny themselves ro-

mantic love, securing instead a relatively stable relationship based on perceived similarities between individuals, or whether romantic love is a powerful figment of the American imagination that could be more quantitatively explained by theories of **interpersonal attraction** and mate-selection.

The relationship between sexual impulses and romantic love is also elusive. In many relationships, both sexual and romantic fidelity are promised to and maintained with the same person. An array of cases exist, however, which do not connect these two acts. Many persons have sex before marriage, have sex with multiple people whom they do not love, or have sex with a person while married and romantically attached to another. It is difficult, then, to firmly connect sexuality with love.

The complexity of romantic love also raises issues for gay couples. Indeed, a gay couple engages in sexual activity, but a general societal consensus regarding the nature of love in homosexual relationships has yet to be reached. Moreover, ''marriage'' is not a possibility for gay couples, although there is a legal union that takes place in Vermont. Several other states provide gay and lesbian couples with legal benefits although they do not allow them to formally wed. It still remains to be determined whether love between gay couples should be considered romantic love, in the way the term is normally used to refer to love between a man and a woman, or if a new form of love will surface with respect to this relationship.

Love is a difficult concept to operationalize, or develop quantitative research hypotheses for, and, therefore, there are not many studies or a tremendous amount of literature that addresses this issue. We do know that the concept of love is not as free as we think it is. Although we choose our partners there are certainly cultural an societal expectations that play into that choice. How free are we to choose? Interestingly, the studies of Arlien Hochschild show that women are more likely to be deliberate in their love for a man and that men tend to fall in love more quickly and suffer more emotional stress at the termination of a relationship. A possible explanation for this phenomenon is that women have more to lose, both socially and economically, by entering into a serious relationship and so show more prudence in their choices.

Besides sexuality, other physical attributes are often associated with love. A rapid heart beat, accelerated breathing, sweating, etc., are generally considered indications of the arousal that eventually grows into a love response. This process, from physical excitement to love, may be partially conditioned by cultural **norms** and expectations. Because society associates these physical reactions with love, the individual does so as well. From this point, individuals may participate in other rituals associated with love in their **culture**. In the United States, these include dating, displays of affection, gifts, loyalty, and meeting the **family** and friend's of one's partner. If the love is maintained, engagement and marriage may follow.

M

MacIver, Robert Morrison (1882-1970)

Scottish American sociologist and educator

A leading theorist of the interaction between **individualism** and social organization, Robert MacIver was born April 17, 1882, in the small town of Stornoway on the island of Lewis, most northerly of the Outer Hebrides, Scotland. His father, Donald, came from a long line of farming country people; his mother, Christina Morrison, was from town and, as Morrison himself said in his autobiography, was "more sophisticated, less tradition-bound." His parents sent him away at the age of 16 to the University of Edinburgh and Oxford University for his classical education. His teaching career began in 1907 when he accepted a post as lecturer in **political science** and **sociology** at Aberdeen University. In 1915, he journeyed to Canada and the University of Toronto where he was first a professor and then head of the department of political science. MacIver earned a PhD from Edinburgh in 1917. He remained at Toronto until 1927, during which time he wrote a number of books and articles, among them *Elements of Social Science* (1921). During this period, he was also vice chairman of the Canadian War Labor Board (1917–1919).

MacIver left Toronto for Barnard College, part of Columbia University in New York City, in 1927, where he chaired the Department of Economics and Sociology for two years. From 1929 to 1950, he was Lieber professor of political philosophy and sociology at Columbia. During this period, he was also director of research for the Jewish Defense Agencies, the Assault on Academic Freedom, the United Nations, and the **Juvenile Delinquency** Evaluation Project for New York City. He ended his academic career by serving as president and then chancellor of the New School for Social Research in New York City (1963–1966).

MacIver believed that societies evolve from strongly communal states to those in which the functions of the individual and affiliations of the group are extremely specialized. A political philosopher with a broad range of interests, he saw the state as a social **institution** interdependent with the prevailing class system and with other institutions. These ideas are expressed in two early works: *Community: A Sociological Study* (1917) and *The Modern State* (1926). His *Society: Its Structure and Changes* (1931), which came out in several editions and won him an honorary degree from Harvard University (1936), expressed his view of **society** as a network of interests that are expressed in groups and in institutions. In 1942, his book on *Social Causation* viewed **social change** as a complex process, a key aspect of which is the shared evaluation of cultural and technical innovations. His 1947 work *The Web of Government,* which won the Woodrow Wilson Prize, analyzed the two forms of interest in promoting social change—goals or means and techniques. Among the many accolades given to MacIver by his contemporaries and critics, a major compliment is that his writings on sociological matters are "clear, artistic, and literate."

Of his many contributions to **political sociology**, MacIver is perhaps most noted for four major concepts. (1) He classified social interests, in particular the distinction between like and common interests, demonstrating the value of analyzing the implications to society of these various interests. (2) He distinguishes between **community**, the matrix of social organization, and society. The state is viewed as an association of and within the community. This distinction allows for a framework that permits a better understanding of the multigroup society. (3) MacIver valued the social evolution concept, tracing a pattern of social change from primitive to evolved and diverse. (4) MacIver stressed a basic harmony—although imperfect—that exists between society and individuality.

In addition to sociological concerns, MacIver was aware of pressing public issues. He saw the dangers threatening modern society, for instance, warning about effects of racial **prejudice** and **discrimination** in *The More Perfect Union* (1949). Other concerns led to *Freedom in Our Time* (1955), about the importance of academic freedom in a workable society, and *The Nations and the United Nations* (1959). An investigation of juvenile delinquency programs in New York City was the subject of *The Prevention and Control of Delinquency* (1966). MacIver's last works were his autobiography*As a Tale That is Told*(1968) and *Politics and Society* (1969). He died in New York City on June 15, 1970.

MACROSOCIOLOGY

Macrosociology involves the sociological analysis of large-scale social structures that are designed to coordinate broad patterns of economic, political, and cultural relationships forged throughout the social world. The primary macro social structures examined within the context of macrosociological analysis include world systems, societies, and institutions. A world system is an international network organized primarily around the exchange of goods and services. Societies, which are located within the world system, are organized and self-governing cooperatives of people that typically share a common **territory**. Institutions, which are found within particular societies, are large-scale social structures designed to fulfill the fundamental needs of individuals and groups living within any given **society**.

The most encompassing level of macrosociological analysis examines the operation of world systems. A world system is made up of the economic, political, and cultural relationships forged among nations throughout the world. While world systems are constructed primarily in relation to the economic exchange of goods and services, political and cultural concerns also shape the relationships. Nations located within a world system are typically stratified on the basis of economic and political power. Furthermore, cultural diffusion, which involves the sharing or appropriation of cultural **norms** and **values** from one nation or society to another, is a common occurrence.

According to **Immanuel Wallerstein**, the macrosociologist responsible for developing world-systems **theory**, the current world system is divided into three major economic categories: the core, the semi-periphery, and the periphery. In the context of a global exchange of goods and services, the location of a nation within any one of these economic categories is determined by its particular role in producing the world's goods and services. Production within core nations relies heavily upon technology derived from machinery rather than manual labor. The human labor that does take place in core nations is highly paid (at least in relation to wages in the semi-periphery and periphery) and typically requires a high level of **skill**. Although most core nations are much wealthier than semi-peripheral and peripheral nations, not all those who live in core nations are wealthy. Currently some of the major core nations include the United States, Great Britain, Japan, and Germany.

Semi-peripheral and peripheral nations differ from core nations in that they rely more upon cheap human labor than technologically complex machinery. While semi-peripheral nations depend upon a combination of machinery and human labor, peripheral nations typically depend primarily upon low-skilled, low-wage manual work. Although semi-peripheral nations are poorer than core nations, and peripheral nations tend to be the poorest of all, not all those who live in the semi-periphery and periphery are poor. The coexistence of wealth and poverty that is characteristic of core nation inhabitants is also found among those who live in semi-peripheral and peripheral nations. Countries such as India, Egypt, and South Africa reside in the semi-periphery, while Bangladesh, Sri Lanka, and Zaire have been identified as peripheral nations.

The second level of macrosociological analysis involves the examination of societies, which are large-scale social structures consisting of a self-governing body of residents who share a common territory and are typically committed to the survival of all societal members. While both societies and nations are located within the broader world system, societies and nations are not necessarily one in the same. Although many nations house only one society, in many other cases two or more societies may coexist within the same nation. In the United States, for example, many Native American tribes, although physically located within the national boundaries of America, continue to function as self-governing societies. As another example illustrates, prior to the breakup of Yugoslavia, the Serbs, Muslims, and Croatians existed as separate societies within one nation. Perhaps the most important difference between societies and nations relates to globally recognized geographical boundaries. While officially established nations are always geographically bounded, this is the case only for those societies residing alone in a particular nation.

The third major level of macrosociological analysis involves the examination of social institutions. Institutions are large-scale social structures that are designed to fulfill the most fundamental needs of a society. Macrosociologists have identified five major institutions that are found in every society around the world: the **family**, religion, the economy, education, and the state. Although global conditions of economic, political, and cultural diversity yield a great deal of societal variation in the basic institutions, each **institution** functions to fulfill certain specific and fundamental social needs regardless of the society in which it is found.

Talcott Parsons identified the most basic social needs as follows: First, societies must organize the activities of their members in order to prevent chaos, a need that every institution works toward fulfilling. Second, societies must strive to protect their members from internal or external threats such as **crime** and invasion. The state accomplishes this through the establishment of police forces and the military. Third, societies must be able to replace members lost either through death or emigration. The institutions of family and the state function to meet this need. The family replaces lost members through sexual reproduction, as does the state through the establishment of immigration policies.

Fourth, societies must transmit the knowledge necessary for individuals to function properly within their society, a need met by all five institutions. Fifth, societies must motivate both new and present members to fulfill responsibilities and obligations proscribed by their **culture**, another basic need addressed in some manner by each institution. Sixth, societies must provide formalized ways through which social conflict may be resolved, a need conventionally addressed by institutionalized state **court systems**. World systems, societies, and institutions are interrelated social structures that organize patterns of economic, political, and cultural relations on a truly global scale. Macrosociology provides the social scientific framework within which these macro social structures may be most fully understood.

MAINE, SIR HENRY JAMES SUMNER (1822-1888)

English historian and anthropologist

Born on August 15, 1822, Henry Maine received his schooling at Christ's Hospital and Pembroke College, Cambridge. He received his degree in 1844 and the following year was appointed junior tutor at Trinity College, Cambridge, which position he held until appointed regius professor of civil law at Cambridge in 1847. In 1850 he was called to the bar and two years later accepted appointment as first reader in Roman law and jurisprudence at the Inns of Court. He steadily gained in reputation as a philosopher of law and a brilliant legal antiquary until, with the publication of his first work *Ancient Law* (1861), he emerged on the Victorian scene as a leading scholar-intellectual.

Maine was a legal member of the Council in India (1863–1869) and served for a time as vice-chancellor of the University of Calcutta. He formulated a general scheme for the codification of Indian law and organized the legislative department of the Indian government. He was corpus professor of jurisprudence at Oxford from 1869 until 1877, when he assumed the mastership of Trinity Hall, Cambridge.

Maine continued to write extensively on the theme that the history of law illustrated a course of development which he did not entirely approve. He contended that the whole idea that material improvement was linked with political **democracy** was a mistaken conception of some of his contemporaries. Unlike the historical-anthropological school, which thought of liberty as having originated in primitive communes, Maine believed that the legal relationships of most primitive societies were based upon long-established historical customs deriving from the patriarchal family system. Under such a system, land and goods were held in common by all members of the family and individual private property was unknown. Gradually the family was absorbed in the larger tribal unit and then, with the passage of time and the growth of trade, evolved into an urbanized, economically sophisticated **society**.

Meanwhile, **property** holding in common gave way to property holding in severalty, so that men, in a famous Maine phrase, moved "from status to contract" in their legal relations. Common ownership in the family-organized society was thus transformed into private ownership in an individual-organized society and, by implication, a larger measure of political freedom became possible.

Some critics have seen Maine as an antagonist of late Victorian mass democracy and a defender of laissez-faire eco-

Sir Henry Maine *(The Library of Congress)*

nomic **individualism**. Others have regarded him as a brilliant innovator in the fields of anthropology and comparative history. He has also been defined as an evolutionary determinist, although he explicitly rejected the belief that "human society went everywhere through the same series of changes." Maine was not a systematic thinker and could not always perceive some of his own intellectual contradictions. Undoubtedly his major contribution lay in the interest he stimulated and the arguments he raised among his contemporaries.

Maine's most important works (in addition to *Ancient Law*) were *Village Communities* (1871), *Early History of Institutions* (1876), *Dissertations on Early Law and Custom* (1883), *Popular Government* (1885), and *International Law* (1888). He died on February 3, 1888, in Cannes, France.

MAISTRE, JOSEPH DE (1753-1821)

French political philosopher

One of the chief opponents of the Enlightenment (from the French "siecle de lumières, "or Age of the Enlightened) was Joseph de Maistre, French political philosopher and diplomat. The Enlightenment was a European intellectual movement during the seventeenth and eighteenth centuries that celebrated reason, the power by which humans improve their condition.

Joseph de Maistre *(Corbis Corporation [Bellevue])*

This synthesis of ideas concerning God, reason, nature, and humans led to revolutionary developments in **philosophy**, art, and politics.

Maistre was born at Chambery, Savoy, then in the French-speaking area of Sardinia, Italy, but now part of France, on April 1, 1753. His family had served the state for generations, his father being a civil servant and former president of the senate. After being educated by Jesuits and then at the royal college in Chambery, Maistre went to Turin to study law. In 1787, he followed in his father's footsteps and became a member of the Savoy senate. When his father died two years later, Maistre inherited the family estate, his father's title of count, and all responsibilities. But that was also the year the French Revolution began. Napoleon and his revolutionary army invaded Savoy in 1792, prompting Maistre to leave his family—Francoise-Marguerite de Moraud, whom he had married in 1786, and their three children—for refuge and lifelong exile in Switzerland and Italy.

After being named regent of the island of Sardinia, Maistre was appointed Sardinian ambassador to Russia in 1802, beginning a 14-year sojourn at the Russian court of St. Petersburg. Although he was often lonely and without funds, Maistre nonetheless enjoyed the diplomatic **society** at the Russian court, which included cordial terms with Czar Alexander. Finally, in 1815, Maistre was joined in Russia by his wife and two daughters.

Probably hoping to restore the Bourbons to the throne, Maistre requested an interview with Napoleon Bonaparte. He was refused. His attempt to see Louis XVIII to become the exiled king's ambassador in Russia was also refused. Maistre left

Russia with his family on May 27, 1817, and saw Paris for the first time that June. This time, however, he did meet Louis XVIII, who reportedly gave the exile a rather cool reception. The reason might have been Maistre's political opinions expressed in his *The Essay on the Generative Principle of Political Constitutions*, 1814. The king regarded himself as a constitutional monarch, not an absolute ruler, as Maistre had indicated. Also while in Paris, Maistre tried to get support for the publication of his major work *Du pape* (On the Pope, 1819). It was published in December 1819. Maistre returned to Sardinia, where he died in Turin on February 26, 1821.

Joseph de Maistre was convinced of the absolute rule of sovereign and pope and the need for Christian supremacy. He was against the liberal beliefs of and the scientific progress advocated by such philosophers as Voltaire, Rousseau, and Bacon. In particular, he disagreed with Rousseau and the social contract, stating that people cannot give themselves a body or rights through a **social contract**. The right must exist in the political tradition of a people; otherwise, the written document simply will not be followed or will be followed in such a way as to make the rights meaningless. In his first major work *Considerations on France* (1796), he emphasized this theme, stating that "paper" constitutions can never and will never establish the rights of a people.

Maistre wrote numerous works stating his views, filling 13 volumes while in exile in Russia, mainly arguing against the Enlightenment and the French Revolution. Perhaps his best, although unfinished, work written in Russia is *Les Soirées de St. Petersbourg* in which he acclaimed the public executioner as guardian of social order. It contains his analysis of the French Revolution and his belief that the Church should be not only the spiritual ruler of the world but its indirect temporal ruler as well. He wanted the monarchy restored in France, held in check by councils named by electors, whom the king would appoint. If such measures failed, the authority of the pope would be brought into play. Maistre believed the pope to be divinely instituted to judge human affairs. All human institutions, Maistre claimed, were the work of God operating through secondary causes.

MALINOWSKI, BRONISLAW KASPER (1884-1942)

English anthropologist and author

Born April 7, 1884, in Krakow, Poland, British anthropologist and author Bronislaw Malinowski, who earned a doctorate in mathematics and physics from the University of Krakow, is widely acknowledged as the father of the functional school of anthropology, which stresses the importance of scientific method over abstract **theory**. He is best known for stressing the importance of ethnography, or detailed participant observation, in anthropology. His use of a detailed ethnographic diary is notable is this regard.

Malinowski became noted for his fieldwork on the Trobriand Islands off the northeast coast of New Guinea, where he lived among primitive island inhabitants from 1914 to

1918. From his research he published a series of monographs, including *The Sexual Life of Savages in North-Western Melanesia: An Ethnographic Account of Courtship, Marriage, and Family Life Among the Natives of the Trobriand Islands, British New Guinea* (1929).

Malinowski was a professor of social anthropology at the University of London from 1927 to 1942 and a Phi Beta Kappa lecturer at Harvard University in 1936, as well as a visiting professor at Yale University beginning in 1939. Together with **A. Radcliffe-Brown**, he defined British structural-functionalist anthropology while teaching at the London School of Economics. His concentration on the functional needs of a sociocultural system did not prevent him from attempting to put psychoanalytic theories into practice in many of his works.

Malinowski received an honorary doctorate from Harvard in 1936 and was a member of the Polish Academy of Science and the Royal Academy of Science of the Netherlands. His numerous scholarly works include: *The Family Among the Australian Aborigines: A Sociological Study* (1913), *Argonauts of the Western Pacific* (1922), *Crime and Custom in Savage Society* (1926), *Sex and Repression in Savage Society* (1927), *Freedom and Civilization* (1944), and posthumously *Magic, Science, and Religion, and Other Essays* (1948) and *Sex, Culture, and Myth* (1962). Malinowski died on May 16, 1942.

MALTHUS, THOMAS ROBERT (1766-1834)

English political economist

Thomas Robert Malthus was born at his family's country home in Wotton, Surrey, on February 13, 1766. He was raised in a wealthy family, the sixth child of seven born to Daniel and Henrietta Malthus. His father, an eccentric liberal landowner who enjoyed studying **philosophy** and botany and maintained friendships with both **Jean-Jacques Rousseau** and **David Hume**, educated Malthus at home until the age of ten. In 1782, after six years of study at Claverton Rectory near Bath, Malthus, then sixteen years old, was sent by his father to study under radical Unitarian Gilbert Wakefield. Two years later, he enrolled at Jesus College, Cambridge, and received his undergraduate degree in 1788. Despite a serious speech defect due to a cleft palate and harelip, Malthus earned awards for his declamations in Latin and English.

After being ordained by the Church of England, Malthus accepted an appointment as curate at Okewood in Surrey in 1789. He became a nonresident fellow of Jesus College in 1793, a position he acquiesced in 1804 when he married his cousin, Harriet Eckersall, with whom he had three children. In 1805 he became Professor of History and **Political Economy** at the East India Company College in Haileybury. He was also appointed rector of Walesby in Lancashire, a nonresident position he held the remainder of his life.

Malthus maintained a close relationship to his father until his father's death in 1800, and although often in disagreement, they corresponded regularly on a wide range of issues during Malthus's time away at school. Upon his graduation, Malthus returned to live with his parents, and the spirited debates between he and his father continued with new zeal. After one particular discussion in which Malthus's father praised and defended the perfectibility of humanity as espoused by utopian thinker **William Godwin**, Malthus was compelled to respond in detail. This written rejection of Godwin's optimistic understanding of human progress towards a utopian **society** resulted in Malthus's seminal work *An Essay on the Principle of Population*. At his father's urging, Malthus first published the work in 1798; he would revise it numerous times before his death in 1834.

In *An Essay on the Principle of Population*, Malthus attacked the optimistic social vision that prevailed at the time, replacing utopian **idealism** with a starkly contrasting, dismal vision of the future. According to Malthus, whereas the population increased geometrically (1, 2, 4, 8, 16, 32, 64, 128, 256, 512, etc.), food supply increased arithmetically (1, 2, 3, 4, 5, 6, 7, 8, 9, 10). Left unchecked, the population would quickly expand well beyond available resources, thus resulting in misery and poverty for the masses. The overwhelming success of the book placed Malthus in the public limelight, and the well-written exposition of his population theory crushed utopian visions so completely that economics soon became known as "the dismal science."

Malthus did recognize certain checks that could at least retard the growth of the chasm between population and resources. He stated, "By that law of our nature which makes food necessary to the life of man, the effects of these two unequal powers must be kept equal. This implies a strong and constantly operating check on population from the difficulty of subsistence. This difficulty must fall somewhere and must necessarily be severely felt by a large portion of mankind." Actual population growth could be slowed by both "preventive" and "positive" checks. Preventive checks, which affect all social classes, include delay of **marriage**, sexual intercourse that did not result in procreation, such as **homosexuality** and use of contraception, and abortion. Positive checks, which fell mostly upon the poor, include famine, disease, **war**, and infanticide. Short-term increases in food supply could suspend suffering temporarily, but ultimately no human effort could save the masses from misery. In a later edition, Malthus modified his population checks by including "moral restraint," which is defined as postponed marriage and celibacy and offers some hope that the masses could be taught this restraint through education.

The **social policy** implications that Malthus drew from his population theory are found primarily in his call to abolish the Poor Laws, a national assistance program for the needy. According to Malthus, this benevolence was misplaced because it destroyed an important preventive check on population. He argued that if offered assistance, men would be more inclined to marry and have children that they could not support, thus placing more demand on the limited food supply and in turn causing even greater suffering. Malthus also believed that the Poor Laws encouraged laziness and idleness, and provided a "strong and immediate check to productive industry." At the time of his writing, England was dealing with high food prices and an increasing number of poor seeking assistance. The middle and upper classes were primed to hear Malthus's message to the poor: "They are themselves the cause of their own poverty; that the means of redress are in their own hands, and in the hands of no other persons whatever; that the society in which they live, and the government which presides over it, are totally without power in this respect."

Malthus continued to revise and expand *An Essay on the Principle of Population*, producing new editions in 1803, 1806, 1807, 1809, 1817, and 1826. His vast influence over the social reform of his time resulted in passage of the New Poor Law in 1834. Although it did not end all public support, by denying assistance to all able-bodied men, the new law was founded on the Malthusian principle that each man is solely responsible for his own family. Later in his career Malthus turned more attention to economical issues such as wealth, money supply, and measure of value, rent, and wages. A persuasive writer, he produced numerous other books and pamphlets on these subjects for a wide audience in hopes of influencing social policy. The most important work of his later years was published in 1820 as *Principles of Political Economy Considered with a View to their Practical Application*.

Malthus died at Bath on December 29, 1834, just four months after the passage of the New Poor Law. Although his influence as a political economist had waned by the time of his death, his work as a population theorist continued to influence thinkers, including **Charles Darwin**, for years to come. Contrarily, Malthus was constantly faced with staunch opposition to his ideas. Godwin, whose utopian vision first inspired Malthus to write, called him "a dark and terrible genius that is ever at hand to blast all the hopes of mankind." For better or worse, clearly Malthusian ideals helped form the social culture of his lifetime and well beyond.

MANDEVILLE, BERNARD (1670-1733)
Dutch physician, philosopher, and satirist

Dutch-born Bernard Mandeville followed in his father's footsteps when he completed his medical degree in 1691 at the University of Leyden. He had a modest medical practice and is best known for his satirical social commentaries, notably *The Fable of Bees, Or Private Vices, Public Benefits*.

Little is known of Mandeville's private life. He was born in Rotterdam in 1670 and baptized there in November of that year. Although he entered the University of Leyden with the intention of becoming a physician, he enrolled initially as a student of philosophy. Upon completing his medical studies, he decided to specialize in nervous disorders, like his father's.

Mandeville traveled to England not long after completing his studies to learn the English language better. He decided to stay, adopting the contemporary attitude that English **society** was the most advanced in Europe. He married Ruth Elizabeth Laurence on February 1, 1669 and was the father of Michael and Penelope.

Some Fables After the Easie and Familiar Manner of Monsieur de la Fontaine was Mandeville's first publication in

English. Printed anonymously in 1703, it contained two original fables written in verse and adaptations of 27 of Fontaine's fables. The reissue of this work, titled *Aesop Dress'd: Or, a Collection of Fables Writ in Familiar Verse*, was published in 1704 under Mandeville's name. In 1705, *The Grumbling Hive: Or, Knaves Turn'd Honest* was published. This work became the basis for *The Fable of Bees* but at the time did not arouse much response.

Mandeville's first English publication in prose appeared in 1709. *The Virgin Unmask'd: Or, Female Dialogues Betwixt an Elderly Maiden Lady, and Her Niece* was also the first of many texts written as a dialogue. Subsequent publications included *A Treatise of the Hypochondriack and Hysterick Passions* (1711), *Wishes to a Godson, With Other Miscellany Poems* (1712), and *Free Thoughts on Religion, the Church, and Natural Happiness* (1720).

The first issue of *The Fable of Bees, Or Private Vices, Public Benefits* appeared in 1714, and included the original *The Grumbling Hive*, twenty essays explaining or remarking on the verse and an essay titled "Enquiry into the Origins of Moral Virtue." In this essay, Mandeville declared that morals are not inherent in humans but are imposed on mankind by those in **authority**. He argued that as self-denial became equal to moral superiority, a moral code was imposed. This essay offended readers and met with criticism, but nothing like the attention Mandeville received upon the reissue of *The Fable of Bees* in 1723. This version contained more remarks on the fable and two new essays: "A Search into the Nature of Society" and "An Essay on Charity and Charity-Schools." The response was immediate and hostile: the book was denounced throughout England and presented before the Grand Jury of Middlesex as a public nuisance.

These new essays expanded Mandeville's theory on the origin of morality. He claimed that morals were an invention defined and imposed by society. In "An Essay on Charity and Charity-Schools," Mandeville argued that people are charitable to impress their peers, not to help others, and that acting out of pity is a means of removing oneself from unpleasant realities. He viewed morals not as ideals but as tools used to keep society together. Like Thomas Hobbes, he believed that societies formed not out of companionship, but a desire for comfort and security.

Also like Hobbes, Mandeville was seen as a corrupter of religion and society. At a time when any criticism against **human nature** was resented, Mandeville was hated by many and referred to as "ManDevil." Equal to Jonathan Swift in his satirical wit, Mandeville created much greater public outrage and hostility. It was not merely his theories that outraged the public but also his stinging description and unscholarly language. He further generated hostility with the 1724 publication of *The Fable of Bees*, which included a "Vindication of the Book," a courteous explanation that his writings were intended to entertain an intelligent audience and were not meant to offend. Subsequent publications of *The Fable of Bees*, however, leave one wondering if Mandeville did not enjoy his notoriety. It was reissued again in 1728, and his final publications *An Enquiry into the Origin of Honour, and the Usefulness of*

Christianity in War and *A Letter to Dion* (both 1732) are considered additions to *The Fable of Bees.* To this day, Mandeville is recognized as influential in philosophy, economic thought, and psychological theory. Moreover, his writings remain just as entertaining, engaging, and comic as he intended them to be centuries ago.

MANIFEST FUNCTION

Manifest functions can be defined as the goals and consequences of social action which are openly intended and acknowledged by the members of a social system. The term was first used by American sociologist Robert K. Merton to describe those actions intended to improve the condition of the social structure. Manifest functions are complemented by latent functions, which are the unintentional goals and consequences of social actions and institutions.

Social institutions have a variety of manifest functions. Universities, for example, may intend to teach and train students to perform a particular job or type of job when they graduate. They also seek to provide students with rounded educations and to expose them to different ideas, disciplines, and people with whom they might otherwise have little or no contact by requiring them to take a variety of courses unrelated to their fields of interest. The legal system also has a number of manifest functions: laws, for example, are intended to create safety and security within **society**. They also clearly delineate behaviors which are unacceptable and prescribe punishments or treatments for offenders of those laws. These are the stated goals as to why the various social institutions exist.

These institutions also have latent functions, however. Institutions of **higher education** reduce the number of adults actively seeking employment at a given time and provide cheap labor to employers through internships and practicums; the legal system provides jobs (for guards, judges, law enforcement officers, probation officers, contractors to construct prisons, etc.) as well as an inexpensive **labor force** (such as those sentenced to perform community service by cleaning roadways or performing volunteer work).

The distinction between manifest and latent functions has been criticized by some sociologists for being too vague and inconsistent in use. In some instances Merton used manifest and latent to indicate intention. The manifest function is intended, whereas the **latent function** is unintended. However Merton also used the same terms to indicate the depth of intention. Manifest functions describe the surface level intentions, while latent functions describe the underlying intentions. An application fee for joining an organization or renting an apartment has the manifest function of offsetting the costs of processing and verifying the information on the application. It also potentially has the latent function of circumventing **discrimination** laws by discouraging or preventing people of lower socioeconomic classes from applying for the organization or apartment because they may not be able to afford to pay high application fees.

MANNHEIM, KARL (1893-1947)
Hungarian sociologist and educator

The Hungarian-born sociologist and educator Karl Mannheim (1893–1947) explored the role of the intellectual in political and social reconstruction. He also wrote on the **sociology** of knowledge. Karl Mannheim was born on March 27, 1893, in Budapest to a German mother and a Jewish middle-class Hungarian father. He attended a humanistic school in Budapest and did further study in **philosophy** (particularly **epistemology**), languages, and the social sciences at the universities of Budapest, Berlin, Paris, Freiburg, and Heidelberg (1920). His doctoral dissertation in 1922 was *The Structural Analysis of Knowledge.* In 1921 he married Juliska Lang.

Mannheim was a lecturer in sociology at the University of Heidelberg (1926–1930) and then became professor of sociology and head of the department at the University of Frankfurt. The Nazi government forced his dismissal in 1933. He moved to England, where he became a lecturer in sociology at the London School of Economics (1933–1945). He was also lecturer in the sociology of education (1941–1944) and then professor of education and sociology (1944–1947) at the Institute of Education of the University of London. He died in London on January 9, 1947.

Mannheim's early writings dealt with the leadership role of intellectual elites in maintaining freedom. This concern reflected his study of Max Weber, Max Scheler, and **Karl Marx**. Mannheim's most important early book *Ideology and Utopia* (1929 in German, 1936 in English) introduced the **sociology of knowledge** as a new field of study in the social sciences. Antipathy to the Nazi movement in Germany deepened his interest in democratic dynamics. His writings increasingly focused on the political, social, and moral problems involved in the survival of **democracy** and freedom. He saw interdependence as the characteristic feature of the modern era and viewed education and planning as essential for improving **society**. This concern is expressed in *Man and Society in an Age of Reconstruction* (1940), in which he weighed the political strengths and weaknesses of intellectual elites. His *Diagnosis of Our Time* (1943) explored ways to reestablish rational means of social organization. In *Freedom, Power, and Democratic Planning* (1950), published after his death, he continued his concern about the intellectual as leader in a planned society.

In his last years Mannheim made the problem of planning and education his principal concern. As editor of the *International Library of Sociology and Social Reconstruction*, he stimulated thought and publications in sociology, education, and planning. He sought democratic ways to achieve consensus in a **mass society**, believing that studies in the sociology of education could help achieve this consensus.

Mannheim was a successful and inspiring teacher with a contagious passion for his subject. He was articulate and provocative, had a Socratic tolerance for opposition and a lively sense of humor, and was nonpartisan in sociological controversies. Although he did not create a sector school, he influenced many students and colleagues.

Herbert Marcuse *(Corbis Corporation [Bellevue])*

MARCUSE, HERBERT (1898-1979)
German American political philosopher

A leading philosopher of the New Left and follower of **Karl Marx**, Herbert Marcuse became popular among student leftist radicals in the latter half of the twentieth century, especially after rebellions at New York City's Columbia University, the Sorbonne in Paris, and in West Berlin (1968). Despite his student following, he disapproved of campus demonstrations. He said, "I still consider the American university an oasis of free speech.... Any student movement should try to protect this citadel...[but] try to radicalize the departments within the university." Marcuse's writings reflect a discontent with modern **society** and the necessity of revolution, based on Marxist theories.

Herbert Marcuse was born in Berlin, Germany, on July 19, 1898, and in 1922 earned a PhD from Freiburg University, where he joined the Social Democratic Party. Fleeing the coming of the Nazis, he emigrated to the United States in 1934. He taught at Columbia University, joined the Institute of Social Research in New York City, and became a U.S. citizen.

In 1941, his *Reason and Revolution* was published, studying the philosophy of German-born **Georg Wilhelm Friedrich Hegel** and fascist interpretations of his theories. In the twentieth century, the idea developed among some scholars that Hegel's theories showed a direct line to the development of Hitler. Marcuse wrote the book to dispute that theory and to argue that, instead, Hegel was a revolutionary.

During World War II, Marcuse worked for the American government as an intelligence analyst for the U.S. Army. At war's end, he headed the Central European Section of the Office of Intelligence Research until he returned to teaching duties in 1951. In 1955, he married Inge S. Werner. Marcuse taught at Columbia; Harvard University; Brandeis University (1954–1965); and the University of California at San Diego (1965–1976). After his retirement, he held the title of honorary emeritus professor of **philosophy** until his death on July 29, 1979.

Outside academic circles, Marcuse was virtually unknown until the 1960s. Then in 1964, *One-Dimensional Man* was published. Students and young radicals of the time embraced it. Marcuse argued that modern technological society was inherently repressive. Workers had become so traumatized by the products of their own labor that they were now in a "state of anesthesia," which could be changed only by those outside the system— intellectuals, minorities, and students. That work, Marcuse's best known, has been called by some the single most influential publication of radical social theory of the 1960s. In 1965, he published a controversial essay, "Repressive Tolerance," in which he said that the United States is a repressive country because dissent is not heard and alternatives to the established views are not considered. Therefore, it is proper to disrupt or obstruct those who speak for the establishment.

With Marcuse's popularity in some circles came unrest. After student revolts, a campaign was started to fire him from his teaching position in California. He reportedly received a threat from the Ku Klux Klan. For his loss of hope in the working class, the Maoist Progressive Labor Party attacked Marcuse as a CIA agent because of his World War II duties. Added to that, in 1969, Pope Paul objected to Marcuse's views on sex. This stemmed from his 1955 publication *Eros and Civilization* in which Marcuse argued for greater tolerance of eroticism, claiming that tolerance toward sexuality would bring society a more satisfactory life. Because of this publication, some consider Marcuse to be a philosopher of the "sexual revolution."

Marcuse wrote extensively on the **culture** of Nazi Germany. He said Naziism was "becoming the executive organ of the imperialist economic interests." He argued that Nazi culture rested on "abolition of highly sanctioned taboos." When the system encouraged extramarital relations or ended discrimination toward unwed mothers or out-of-wedlock children, this led to more repression, not more liberty, because the new sexual release merely reinforced the Nazi system.

After World War II, Marcuse's hopes for a radical transformation to the left in West Germany were disappointed. As the decade of the 1960s and student rebellions faded into the early 1970s with its decline of social unrest, so Marcuse faded in popularity. He continued to write, however, publishing *Counterrevolution and Revolt* and *Studies in Critical Philosophy* in 1972.

MARGINALITY

The concept of marginality refers to the condition of groups living 'on the edge' of societies, deprived of the benefits and resources available to the rest of the population. Definitions vary according to the kind of resource that the marginalized are thought to lack, so that marginality has been defined as economic, political, institutional, or cultural, or combinations of the above.

Modernization theory, popular in the 1950s and 1960s, considered economic marginality to be related to cultural backwardness, and therefore the use of this term by modernization theorists contained this double meaning. During the late 1960s and 1970s, most sociologists of development turned away from the modernization school in favor of **dependency theory** and world-systems analysis. Marginality lost its cultural connotations, now referring purely to the condition of people excluded from the economic or political reward system of the society, particularly stigmatized ethnic minorities and/or the very poor.

The concept of marginality followed a similar trajectory in urban sociology. Since the late 1960s, studies of urban marginality have focused on mechanisms of exclusion rather than on the **values** or behaviors of the poor. (Meanwhile, those exploring the cultural basis of marginalization have instead used the concept of the ''underclass.'')

The **informal economy**, always large in the **cities** of the Third World and the newly industrializing countries, has returned to the cities of Western Europe and the United States in the late twentieth century. ''Sweatshops,'' casual day labor, and illegal restaurant work account for millions of ''shadow'' workers in these countries. Informal workers tend to exemplify multiple kinds of marginality. The illicit basis of their work deprives them of protective legislation, unions, benefits, pensions, or any kind of legal recourse against their employers. Many are also recent immigrants and are, therefore, poorly integrated into mainstream educational, cultural, or political institutions.

One major cause of urban marginalization is racial and ethnic discrimination. Of the advanced industrialized countries, the United States has the highest rate of residential segregation, due largely to the extremely high concentration of African Americans in specific neighborhoods. While the economic, educational, and political power of some African Americans has improved greatly since the civil rights movement, both residential and educational segregation remain very high. Other racial and ethnic minorities, especially Latinos, also suffer from systematic social and economic inequalities and often lead highly segregated lives. The decline of the manufacturing sector of the U.S. economy has disproportionately affected African Americans and Latinos, and male joblessness in some African American communities has reached eighty percent.

MARITAL ADJUSTMENT

Marital adjustment is the way married people, individually or together, adjust to being married. It is considered one of the most important factors in determining marital stability and longevity. Marriages that are well-adjusted are expected to last longer than those that are not well-adjusted. There is little agreement, theoretically or methodologically, regarding what marital adjustment is, how to study it, or its specific effects.

Marital adjustment is one of the most popular topics in the sociology and **psychology** of the **family**. It is assumed to be closely related to martial success and longevity, two of the most extensively studied components of marriage. However, research results have been contradictory, depending on the definition of terms and the **methodology** used. This concept has been termed marital satisfaction, marital happiness, and marital quality in different studies. All agree that it is a subjective evaluation of a **marriage** that is made by the people involved, but there are differing opinions on how it can be quantified and measured by objective research.

There are components of marital adjustment upon which most researchers agree: cohesion; agreement; affection; tension; and happiness or satisfaction. Marital cohesion is the level to which both partners are committed to a marriage and their relationship, and includes sharing common interests and activities. Marital agreement is the degree to which partners agree on such issues as child-rearing, political or religious affiliations, and beliefs about gender roles. Marital affection is the level of physicality wanted, needed, and achieved between two partners. Marital tension is the amount of tension that remains unresolved in a relationship. Finally, marital happiness or satisfaction is considered the most important component of marital adjustment. All these components fall on a continuum and the level needed for successful marital adjustment varies between couples. Symbolic interactionists, for example, claim that people will be well-adjusted in their marriages if they look around themselves and, in comparison to others, feel happy and adjusted.

One of the biggest critiques of research on marital adjustment is that its components are not always studied as subjective concepts. Some researchers assume they know what successful marital adjustment is and, thus, project these beliefs onto their research participants. This does not allow for the participants themselves to judge what they personally find to be successful adjustment. Thus, some researchers emphasize that measurements of marital adjustment and marital quality should be based on the evaluations of the people involved, rather than on objective measurements of specific components determined by the researcher.

One of the continuing debates in research is whether marital adjustment and satisfaction are theoretically similar or different concepts. Marital satisfaction is often considered a static outcome of marital adjustment, which is seen as more of a dynamic process (Spanier and Cole, 1976). Many researchers focus on the fact that there is often a female satisfaction and a male satisfaction in marriages and that the level of these different satisfactions do not always coincide. It has been shown that married men are generally much more satisfied with their relationships than are married women.

One of the goals of research on marital adjustment is to predict the potential for success of specific couples or groups with similar demographic characteristics. Robert Lewis and Graham Spanier identified three components attributed to predicting marital quality. The first is satisfaction with lifestyle, which includes according to Michael Fendrich: material resources; the presence of children (which has been shown to decrease marital adjustment and satisfaction, particularly for women); and satisfaction with work status (a woman's work status has both a detrimental and instrumental effect on her husband's satisfaction with their lifestyle). Disagreements regarding these aspects of life tend to lead to low levels of marital adjustment. Second is rewards from partner interactions: amount of time spent together; level of communication; and amount of positive reinforcement received from each other. Third is the level of personal and social resources. The more alike partners are demographically and the more they share a social network, the more adjusted they are likely to be.

Ultimately, the research has been unable to predict whether or not marital adjustment leads to marital longevity. In some cases it does, and in others it does not. But there is agreement on the fact that it is an important component to both satisfaction and longevity. One of the limits of this research is that it has focused almost exclusively on heterosexual unions, ignoring the dynamics in same-sex partnerships.

MARRIAGE

Marriage is many things: a legal contract, a religious union, the beginning of a new generation, and a rite of passage. Sometimes, it is all of these at once. It is a commitment between husband and wife, **family** and family, and the couple and the state. Historically, marriage was neither a legal contract nor a religious union in many European countries. The Catholic Church assumed jurisdiction over marriage during the Middle Ages, and although some marriages occurred outside the church, they were not considered valid. In the United States in the nineteenth century, marriage became a civil union; however, a religious marriage ceremony is still very common. Eighty percent of couples are married by a religious leader performing a sacrament, which ensures the approval of their religious **community** and the **government**. Twenty percent of couples are married by a judge or **justice** of the **peace**.

In most societies it is understood that people get married to have children. Marriage offers a stable living arrangement for a new family and signals that the bride and groom have entered **adulthood**. Marriage is considered a permanent bond and, in some cultures, cannot be broken. This stability makes marriage most suitable for raising children. In some cultures, being unable to conceive a child is automatic grounds for **divorce**; in others, a marriage begins with conception.

The reason for marrying given most often in the United States is love. This is a relatively new concept, however, is still not a reason for marriage in some cultures. In Colonial America, for example, marriages were arranged between families to secure their economic status. Other reasons include economic

security, a need for a new living arrangement, or a feeling that a long-standing relationship should logically move onto marriage.

Arranged marriages are common throughout the world: for girls, they are arranged in 44 percent of cultures; for boys, marriages are arranged in 17 percent. These arranged unions ensure a family will maintain its political and social status. The bride and groom often have a voice in the arrangement, but some elope to avoid an undesirable arranged marriage.

In the United States, marriage is generally considered a legal contract between a man and a woman. Most states require a license to marry, that couples be a certain age, that people entering into marriage are not currently married, that they are not related, and that they are married by a representative of the state in front of witnesses. Other states require blood tests, premarital counseling, or a waiting period between the purchase date of the license and the marriage ceremony.

The main types of marriage include **monogamy, polygamy**, group marriage, and common-law marriage. Monogamy, marriage between a man and a woman, is the only legal type of marriage in the United States. Polygamy is a marriage in which someone has more than one spouse, but in most cases involves a husband with multiple wives. This is the preferred type of marriage in seventy-five percent of the world's cultures. However, only very wealthy men have multiple wives.

Group marriage describes a group of men and women who live together and consider themselves married. Group marriages were popular in the United States in the 1970s and were usually made up of two couples who lived together. Common-law marriage occurs when a man and woman who are old enough to marry and legally able to marry agree to live together as husband and wife. Such marriages are recognized in 12 states and the District of Columbia.

Through marriage, a man and woman undergo emotional and social changes. For example, newly married couples are considered adults and are expected to create their own home and family. A ceremony marks this passage from youth to adulthood and from child to parent. Ceremonies involve family and friends to indicate their support for the couple. Because the families of the couple usually pay for the ceremony, the occasion symbolizes their investment in the couple and their hope for a new generation of the family. Ceremonies are a demonstration of wealth or social status as well, often reflecting the property exchanged between families, such as a bride price or dowry.

For the most part, ceremonies include religious **ritual**, oaths, dance, music, food, and gift exchange. However, in some cultures, couples simply start living together to indicate they are married. Marriage is a rite of passage, one of very few in the United States, and often ceremonies include religious aspects of **prayer** and worship. Generally, vows promise commitment and loyalty. Religious ceremonies include vows that reflect religious beliefs. A common aspect of the marriage ceremony is costume. A change in appearance indicates the bride and groom's new status as husband and wife. An exchange of rings or other jewelry also serves this purpose.

The wedding ceremony varies throughout the world, and even within the United States they are as different as the couples who marry. There are many traditional events that make up the ceremony in this country, but couples often pick and choose which events to include in their wedding. Such traditions include a bridal shower, which helps the bride establish her new home; a bachelor party, considered the groom's final rowdy outing before becoming a husband; the exchange of rings, symbolizing a never-ending commitment; and a white wedding gown and veil, indicating purity. A formal wedding involves more traditions and is usually followed by a reception and meal for the guests. Music and cutting the wedding cake are also often part of the reception. Informal weddings take place in a more casual setting with fewer guests and less formal clothing. Wedding ceremonies among ethnic groups in the United States often reflect both American **culture** and the couple's ancestry.

The marriage rate is on rise, yet so is the number of unmarried adults. The number of people who delay marriage and the number who get divorced are increasing. As more and more couples file for divorce or undergo therapy to solve marital strain, researchers are trying to find a good measure of a successful marriage. Stability is not the best measure, and it has been found that marital problems such as arguments do not indicate a poor marriage.

The image of marriage is changing to reflect changes in the family and in **society**. Both men and women tend to wait until their mid- to late-twenties to marry. Likewise, as more couples divorce, many families are made up of single parents or stepparents and stepchildren. Traditionally, wives kept the home and raised the children while husbands earned a living. More families see both the husband and wife working, reflecting changes within marriage and more opportunities for women. As marriage changes, the ceremonies do to. Many couples chose to leave out traditional aspects of weddings or to hold an informal ceremony.

MARRIAGE AND DIVORCE RATES

The **divorce** rate compares the presence of divorce in different cultures and is often used to measure social **stress** in **society**. By this definition, the population of the United States is under increased stress and has little interest or respect for **marriage**. There are, however, several factors contributing to the divorce rate, which do not make it an accurate measure for society as a whole. For example, divorce is less costly than it used to be and does not have the stigma it once did. Changes in divorce laws have also made divorces easier to obtain. Furthermore, because the divorce process is easier, marriages that in that past would have ended in abandonment or legal separation now end in divorce. In other words, an increase in divorces does not necessarily mean that more marriages are failing. It may mean that more marriages are ending in divorce than by other means.

Other factors affecting the marriage and divorce rate include who is marrying and who is not marrying. According to the U.S. Census Bureau, people wait longer before their first marriage. As of 1996, women marrying for the first time were

the average age of 24.8 and men were age 27.1 on the average. A significant increase in the average marrying age occurred between 1975 and 1995. The increase from 1955 to 1975 was only one year; in the following twenty-year period, the increase was three years. In addition, the **ratio** of adults in their late twenties and early thirties who had never married increased greatly from 1970 to 1996. The percentage of 25- to 29-year-old women who had never married rose from 11 percent to 38 percent from 1970 to 1996. The ratio of never-married women age 30 to 34 also increased from 6 to 21 percent. In the same time period, men in their late twenties who had never been married rose significantly from 19 to 52 percent. Men age 30 to 34 who had never married rose from 9 percent to 30 percent.

Despite a significant increase in the number of married people since 1970, the number of unmarried people (meaning either divorced, widowed, or never married) has grown much faster. The proportion of married adults, therefore, has actually decreased from 72 percent in 1970 to 60 percent in 1996. In 1970, 28 percent of the adult population was unmarried; in 1996, 40 percent of adults were unmarried. In other words, more adults are delaying marriage or divorcing, so that the division of married and unmarried adults is closing in on an even split.

Although divorcees make up a small portion of adults (9.5 percent compared to 23.3 percent never married), divorced is the fastest-growing marital status. The divorced population has more than quadrupled from 1970 to 1996, growing from 3 percent to nearly 10 percent of adults in 25 years. The number of adults never married more than doubled from 1970 to 1996 and make up 59 percent of the unmarried population, followed by divorcees at 24 percent and widows/widowers at 18 percent.

Divorce and marriage rates differ among racial groups in the United States. The decrease in the ratio of married African-American adults has been the most drastic, for example. Forty-two percent of African-American adults were married in 1996, down from 64 percent in 1970. The decrease was also large among Hispanics, dropping from 72 percent to 58 percent in the same time period. Among whites, the percentage fell only 10 percent, from 73 to 63 percent. The ratio of adults that have never been married increased among all three racial groups from 1970 to 1996. Among whites, the ratio rose from 16 to 21 percent, and among Hispanics, it rose from 19 to 30 percent. In 1996, 39 percent of African-American adults had never married, a significant increase from 21 percent in 1970.

As the proportion of married and unmarried persons changes in our country, the make up of families and households will also change. For example, when adults divorce, children are affected. More children live with only one parent now than in the past. The picture of a **family** is no longer a young couple with children but includes images of single-parent families or divorced couples with joint custody. Likewise, as divorces increase and people delay marriage, the number of adults living alone increases, changing the makeup of households and living arrangements.

Marriage and divorce rates have both increased in the United States in the last thirty years. The proportion of unmar-

Marriages and Divorces: 1970 to 1997

Year	Marriages [1]						Divorces and annulments		
	Rate per 1,000 population						Rate per 1,000 population		
					Unmarried women				
	Number (1,000)	Total	Men, 15 yrs. old and over [2]	Women, 15 yrs. old and over [2]	15 yrs. old and over	15 to 44 yrs. old	Number (1,000)	Total [2]	Married women, 15 yrs. old and over
1970	2,159	10.6	31.1	28.4	76.5	140.2	708	3.5	14.9
1975	2,153	10.0	27.9	25.6	66.9	118.5	1,036	4.8	20.3
1980	2,390	10.6	28.5	26.1	61.4	102.6	1,189	5.2	22.6
1984	2,477	10.5	28.0	25.8	59.5	99.0	1,169	5.0	21.5
1985	2,413	10.1	27.0	24.9	57.0	94.9	1,190	5.0	21.7
1986	2,407	10.0	26.6	24.5	56.2	93.9	1,178	4.9	21.2
1987	2,403	9.9	26.3	24.3	55.7	92.4	1,166	4.8	20.8
1988	2,396	9.8	26.0	24.0	54.6	91.0	1,167	4.8	20.7
1989	2,403	9.7	25.8	23.9	54.2	91.2	1,157	4.7	20.4
1990	2,443	9.8	26.0	24.1	54.5	91.3	1,182	4.7	20.9
1991	2,371	9.4	(NA)	(NA)	54.2	86.8	1,189	4.7	20.9
1992	2,362	9.3	(NA)	(NA)	53.3	88.2	1,215	4.8	21.2
1993	2,334	9.0	(NA)	(NA)	52.3	86.8	1,187	4.6	20.5
1994	2,362	9.1	(NA)	(NA)	51.5	84.0	1,191	4.6	20.5
1995	2,336	8.9	(NA)	(NA)	50.8	83.0	1,169	4.4	19.8
1996	2,344	8.8	(NA)	(NA)	49.7	81.5	1,150	4.3	19.5
1997	2,384	8.9	(NA)	(NA)	(NA)	(NA)	1,163	4.3	(NA)

NA Not available.   [1] Beginning 1980, includes nonlicensed marriages registered in California.   [2] Rates for 1981-88 are revised and may differ from rates published previously.

ried adults has increased due to more divorces and a delay in first marriages. As we study marriage and divorce rates, what is most important is the effect these changes have on our perception of the family, the rearing of children, and **adulthood**. The marriage and divorce rates indicate not just a change in marriage but a change in the make up of family and adult life.

MARTINEAU, HARRIET (1802-1874)
English writer and sociologist

Harriet Martineau (1802–1874), the "founding mother of sociology", was the daughter of an English textile manufacturer who lost his business during a depression in 1825 and died in 1826. Martineau supported herself, her mother, a crippled sister, and alcoholic brother by writing. Her publications include thousands of articles and many books.

Martineau was painfully aware of the discrepancies in opportunities for males and females. For example, she was not given the education afforded her brothers. In 1823 she published her first article *On Female Education* for the *Unitarian Journal* which began her career as an outspoken critic of injustices against women, slaves, children, mentally ill, the poor, and prostitutes. She studied stratification in Europe and the United States and advocated protective legislation, equal rights, and education including medical education for women. Her other credits included a popular thirty-four book series published 1832–1834 *Illustrations of Political Economy,* a scholarly *History of England*, and a study of major world religions called *Eastern Life*.

Included in Martineau's many contributions to **sociology** is her translation of Auguste Comte's *Les Cours de Philosophie Positive* from French to English. This four-volume set outlined the theoretical foundation for sociology. Her condensation was so clear that the normally reticent Comte had her version translated back to French, substituting it for his own in the Positivist Library. Comte's admonition that **society** should be studied objectively led Martineau to write the first book of social research **methodology** *How to Observe Manners and Morals* (1838). In this text she advocated development of theoretical framework, research questions, objectivity, and representative sampling.

Martineau was vilified in her time and subsequently ignored by many historians because of her blunt exposure of inequality. In contrast to de Tocqueville's 1835 *Democracy in America,* Martineau's book *Society in America* published in 1837, was incisively critical of America's failure to realize the full potential of citizen empowerment in **democracy**. In the chapter "The Political Non-existence of Women," she argues that women were indulged instead of treated equally, bolstering her claim that they were treated like slaves. She felt that the system of slavery in the South led to inherent social decay because the power of white males as property owners often led to potential harems composed of all slave women over the age of fifteen. The owner could father slave children then sell them for profit while his unsuspecting wife served merely as "an ornament in her husband's house." Planters' wives were kept from intellectual pursuits by lack of exposure to appropriate conversation, men choosing instead to patronize women and ignore that intellectual capabilities. In the meantime, horrible atrocities occurred on the plantations (such as the burning alive of four male slaves) during Martineau's thirteen-month tour of America. She also wrote that American women were trained "to consider **marriage** the sole object in life," but in marriage they were expected to be subservient and dependent. In religion they were "expected to be pious but not educated in philosophy, politics, or morals so as to prevent anything more than passive participation."

Martineau is identified with the American Transcendentalist movement despite her English roots. In the United States, she was associated with Transcendentalists Ralph Waldo Emerson and Margaret Fuller and in England with utilitarian **Jeremy Bentham**. Study of her contributions continues through Martineau societies in England and in the United States.

MARX, KARL (1818-1883)
German philosopher and economist

The German philosopher, radical economist, and revolutionary leader Karl Marx founded modern scientific **socialism**. His basic ideas—known as Marxism—form the foundation of socialist and communist movements. Marx spent most of his life in exile, antagonizing Prussian, French, and Belgium governments. He settled in London, where he spent the rest of his life in dire **poverty** and relative obscurity. His reputation began to spread only after the emergence of the socialist parties in Europe, especially in Germany and France, in the 1870s and 1880s. From then on, Marx's theories continued to be hotly debated in the growing labor and socialist movements everywhere, including Czarist Russia.

By the end of the nineteenth and beginning of the twentieth century, socialist parties had mostly accepted Marxism, particularly the idea of the class struggle and the establishment of a socialist **society**. Lenin, a lifelong disciple of Marx, organized the Soviet Union as a proletarian dictatorship based on Marx's **philosophy**

Marx was born in Trier, Rhenish Prussia, on May 5, 1818, the son of Heinrich Marx, a lawyer, and Henriette Presburg Marx, a Dutchwoman, both descendants of rabbis. Karl later became an atheist; he coined the aphorism, "Religion is the opium of the people," a cardinal principle in modern **communism**. At school, Karl became proficient in French and Latin; later years he taught himself other languages, so that as a mature scholar he could also read Spanish, Italian, Dutch, Scandinavian, Russian, and English.

In Berlin, Marx joined the Young Hegelians, who met frequently to debate. Marx spent more than four years in Berlin, completing his studies there in March 1841. The University of Jena awarded him the degree of doctor of philosophy on the strength of his abstruse and learned dissertation. In Paris, about 1842, Marx first came in contact with the working class, gave up philosophy as a life goal, and began to study economics.

In Brussels in 1848 he founded the German Workers' Party and was active in the Communist League, for whom he

Karl Marx *(The Library of Congress)*

and **Friedrich Engels** wrote *Manifesto of the Communist Party* (known as the *Communist Manifesto*)(1848). Expelled by the Belgian **government** Marx moved back to Cologne, where he was editor of the *Neue Rheinische Zeitung* for less than a year, until paper was suppressed and he was exiled again. He finally settled in London, where he lived as a stateless exile (Britain denied him citizenship, and Prussia refused to renaturalize him). In London, Marx's sole means of support was journalism, but it paid wretchedly. Marx was literally saved from starvation by the continuous financial support of Engels.

A man of immense learning and sharp intellectual power, Marx, often impatient and irascible, antagonized people by his sardonic wit, bluntness, and dogmatism, which bordered on arrogance. His enemies were legion. Yet despite his deserved reputation as a hard and disagreeable person, he had a soft spot for children. Marx was married to his childhood sweetheart, Jenny von Westphalen, who died of cancer on December 2, 1881, at the age of 67. For Marx it was a blow from which he never recovered. The Marxes had seven children, four of whom died in infancy or childhood. Of the three surviving daughters, two were suicides.

Marx spent most of his working time in the British Museum, doing research. He was a most conscientious scholar. In preparation for *Das Kapital,* he read virtually every available work in economic and financial **theory** and practice in the major languages of Europe.

Marx's excessive smoking, wine drinking, and consumption of heavily spiced foods may have contributed to his illnesses. In the last two decades of his life he was tormented by a mounting succession of ailments. He died in his armchair in London on March 14, 1883, just before his sixty-fifth birthday. He is buried in London's Highgate Cemetery.

Marx's writings fall into two general categories, the polemical-philosophical and the economic-political. The first reflected his Hegelian-idealistic period; the second, his revolutionary-political interests. Marx wrote hundreds of articles, brochures, and reports but only five books were published during his lifetime. His worldwide reputation rests on *Critique of Political Economy* and, more particularly, *Das Kapital* (Capital).

A fourth volume of *Das Kapital* was brought together by Karl Kautsky after Engels's death. It was based on Marx's notes and materials from *Critique of Political Economy* and was published in three parts, under the title *Theories of Surplus Value*.

Marx is best understood if one studies his theory of history and politics. The central idea in Marx's thought is the materialistic conception of history which involves two notions: that the economic system at any given time determines the prevailing ideas; and that history is an ongoing process regulated—predetermined—by the **economic institutions** which evolve in regular stages.

To Marx, **capitalism** is the last stage of historical development before communism. The proletariat, produced by capitalism, is the last historical class. The two are fated to be in conflict—the class struggle which Marx proclaimed so eloquently in the *Communist Manifesto*—until the proletariat is inevitably victorious and establishes a transitional order, or the proletarian dictatorship, a political system which Marx did not elaborate or explain. The proletarian dictatorship, in turn, evolves into communism, or the classless society, the final stage of historical development, when there are no classes, no exploitation, and no inequalities. This Marxist interpretation of history, with its final utopian-apocalyptic vision, has been criticized in the noncommunist world as historically inaccurate, scientifically untenable, and logically absurd. Nevertheless, Marx's message of an earthly paradise has provided millions with hope and new meaning of life. From this point of view, one may agree with the Austrian economist Joseph A. Schumpeter that "Marxism is a religion" and Marx is its "prophet."

MARXIST SOCIOLOGY

Marxist Sociology does not refer to a single unified body of scholarship or **theory** within sociology but rather to work by various scholars who were inspired by the writings of **Karl Marx** and later Marxist thinkers. Unlike Europe or Latin America, the United States has not had an independent tradition of Marxist political groups or Marxist public figures, so Marxist sociology in the United States does not refer to any political position or advocacy of any political group. Despite the fact that Karl Marx is considered one of the first sociological thinkers, an explicitly Marxist sociology developed relatively late within the discipline, only fully developing in the 1960s and 1970s.

Scholars in the Marxist tradition are usually influenced by the Marxist concept of class and class analysis and, less often, by a Marxist theory of history and historical change. A Marxist conception of class defines classes in terms of their relationship to means of production; societies are divided into persons who own and those who do not own the means of production. Later Marxist sociologists added to this definition, but a fundamental axiom is that classes have fundamentally opposing interests which causes a split in modern **society**. A Marxist conception of history and historical change sees conflict as a basic cause of **social change** and understands historical epochs in terms of their economic organization of production. Within these broad parameters Marxist sociologists have made important contributions to the understanding of class and class conflict, the study of the state, to the sociology of development, the study of **culture** and **ideology**, and the study of work, among other areas. Marxist scholarship in the United States essentially developed in the 1960s in the period after McCarthyism. Earlier scholarship, like that of W.E.B. Dubois, was certainly influenced by Marxist ideas but did not explicitly incorporate Marxist ideas.

A number of scholars working on questions related to the sociology of development, and in particular with **dependency theory** were directly influenced by Marxist ideas. Prevailing wisdom and scholarship in the form of modernization theory advocated greater sustained involvement of industrialized nations in the form of investment and cultural exchange with Third World nations, dependency theorists generally tended to see this relationship as a continuation of imperialist domination. Whereas Marx himself did not write about underdevelopment, these scholars offered a re-reading of the ideas of later Marxist thinkers, like V.I. Lenin and N. Bukharin, arguing that the current period represented a further stage of imperialist exploitation. These scholars looked instead to alternative models of development, as present in the apparent successes of socialist experiments like those in Cuba and in Tanzania. Dependency scholars argued that because of the external ties of Third World nations that made them dependent on industrialized nations for capital, advanced technology, and expertise, these nations would remain in a state of underdevelopment, or stunted economic and social growth marked by **poverty**, continued dependence on international finance, and an export-oriented economy based on cash crops or basic manufactured goods. Largely associated with scholars like Paul Baran, Sweezy, Andre Gunther Frank, the journal *Monthly Review*, in New York City, did much to disseminate their approach.

Another important area within sociology influenced by Marxist ideas was the study of the state. Some of Marx's own writings on the state suggested that it reflected the interests of the capitalist class. Lenin's analysis in *State and Revolution* (1907) went further, arguing that democratic proceduralism within capitalist society produced little more than a "smoke-mirror" that hid the state's true, repressive, functioning in the interests of the capitalist class. While mainstream scholarship until then tended to view **democracy** in industrialized countries as the expression of the interests of competing groups within the polity, Marxist scholars pointed to the ways in which the state tended to reflect the interests of elites and to reproduce the conditions necessary for the accumulation of capital. A number of important debates about the form and functioning of the state took place with no ultimate agreement among scholars, but the legacy of this scholarship is still important within **political sociology**. Scholars like Nikos Poulantzas, Claus Offe, Goran Thernborn, Fred Block are associated with the debate on the nature of the state in capitalist society.

Marxist sociologists have also been influenced in the study of culture by the ideas of Marxist thinkers like Antonio Gramsci, **Louis Althusser**, and the scholars of the Frankfurt School. Sociologists have studied the ways in which culture reflects the ideology of ruling classes and of the capitalist system itself. Particularly, scholars have tried to explain the apparent lack of revolutionary activity and consciousness within industrial nations. The Birmingham School of **Cultural Studies** and scholars like Stuart Hall have attempted to understand the making of common sense that reflects these ideological features as well as the ways in which working class persons reappropriate and resist this common sense.

One notable recent development within Marxist sociology has been the development of Analytical Marxism, as espoused by Jon Elster, John Roemer, Gerald Cohen, and Erik Wright, among others. Developed as a self-conscious attempt at theoretical renewal within the Marxist tradition, analytical Marxism focuses on concepts and theoretical formulations, rigorous empirical testing, and methodological **individualism**. Here, concepts of class, exploitation, and the elements of a Marxist theory of history have been precisely reformulated. The concept of class, for instance, as reformulated by Wright in *Classes* (1985), develops a framework that includes owners, workers, and a number of intermediary categories, like managers and self-employed persons, that fall between the two groups.

MASCULINITY

Three decades ago, social science began being criticized for being largely a male domain. Established by men, the discipline until recently was predominantly male. For this reason, decisions on what to study, who to study, and how to interpret results were influenced by a male perspective and male bias. The area of **gender studies** arose as a response to this slant, an attempt to include female experience and knowledge in order to balance the foundation of understanding in the disciplines. Today, gender is central to social science.

Despite this historical **bias**, little is known about manhood and masculinity. None of the work amassed by male researchers actually focuses on the male experience. In fact, the male bias in research assumes man to be universal, representative of all individuals in a population, a non-gendered being. Gender studies have explored the problems here. While the Women's Movement helped make people more gender conscious, one consequence was that gender research was stereotyped to be solely about and for women. However, both men and women have gender. More recently, gender research has extended to men; only this time the focus is on *as men*.

When people think about gender, they often think about a continuum with masculinity on one extreme and **femininity** on the other. Masculinity is a set of characteristics that are associated with maleness while femininity is a set of characteristics that are associated with femaleness. Beyond this definition are several specific approaches to masculinity. Masculinity can be theorized and analyzed at several levels. Some researchers focus on masculinity as existing within males, properties of males that serve as the motivation for masculine-typed actions. Another approach to masculinity is to see it as a set of expectations outside of males, a set of socially designated traits, attitudes, and behaviors prescribed for those individuals who are biologically male. From this perspective, masculinity does not characterize the individual, rather it characterizes what the individual does, the action in which an individual engages. The expectations within a particular interactional context determine how masculinity is acted. A structural approach asserts that masculinity is determined by the social **structure** of **society**, so differences in class and **race** can also affect what is masculine within a particular context. Another approach sees masculinity as embedded within social institutions, for example, work. Joan Acker is well known for her thesis that work is organized through a masculine lens. Hours and job requirements are often created with the assumption that workers are male. After becoming a lawyer, a person may wait about ten years to become partner in a law firm. If a woman were to go right through her education to become a lawyer and start a **career**, these ten most intensive years would coincide with prime child-bearing years. Another example is rainmaking. In occupations where a worker must generate business to get ahead, men are benefited by the masculine **culture** that characterizes such rainmaking, such as golf, drinking, and patronizing strip clubs. Another example of a masculinized **institution** is sports.

There are several other aspects of masculinity to understand. First, it is important to note that the historical context shapes masculinity whether it is conceived of as something internal to individuals, external to individuals, or some combination of both. Masculinity, much like femininity, varies and transforms over time. Masculinity is continually created and recreated through structural changes in institutions, such as work, economy, politics, the family, and culture, and these changes have both social and psychological impacts. The historical context must be taken into account in order to understand masculinity. Another important point is that masculinity varies as it interacts with other dimensions of difference among individuals, such as social class, occupation, race, sexual orientation, religion, and other qualities. Masculinity of an upper class white male may vary drastically from masculinity of lower-class minority males.

See also Gender Roles; Gendered Identity

MASS MEDIA RESEARCH

Mass media research in **sociology** includes investigations into the social effects of print, visual images, recorded music, telecommunications, the internet, film, and other mediated forms of **communication**. Early twentieth-century studies were primarily concerned with the role of mass media in creating social communities and disseminating propaganda and consequently shaping public opinion. Since these studies, however, the research on mass media effects has greatly expanded, probably as a result of the media's diversity and extensiveness. Most contemporary research has focused upon the role of media, primarily television, in shaping the attitudes, cognitions, behaviors, and interpersonal relationships of individuals.

Several different traditions of mass media research exist, each with specific emphases and assumptions. The earliest of these models of media research were those which assumed a *direct effects model* of media **influence**, or what has been called a "hypodermic needle" **model** of media effects. These models produced in the 1940s and 1950s were really more sensationalistic models of mass media research suggesting that media served as a direct means of brainwashing individuals through simple stimulus-response, effectively reducing their critical and self-reflexive capacities and injecting new information below cognitive awareness.

Direct effects models, however, have been criticized by those who argue that the media have *limited effects*. These models are most typically represented by the "uses and gratification" research that is premised upon the notion that individuals do not accept media messages without resistance. Individuals encounter media with a complex set of predisposed attitudes and **values**. Individuals use their prior cognitions, attitudes, and experiences in evaluating media messages and are not merely passive consumers of mediated information.

The uses and gratifications approach, however, has also been significantly challenged by a series of media effects models which are directed towards an examination of the *socialization effects* of mass media. Here, a tradition of research based upon social learning theory examines the importance of mediated portrayals of social activity and their ability to create modeling behaviors in others. This research has been based upon experimental investigations of mediated violence and its function in role modeling violent behavior.

The **socialization** research, however, while demonstrating that the media does have some effects on modeling behavior has been widely criticized for its inability to generalize its results beyond the laboratory setting. Thus, other investigations into media have moved away from such experimental research and have redirected attention to media content. This tradition of *mass media content analysis* seeks to explore the biases embedded in the media and its ability to set political and social agendas. Empirical studies in this tradition have explored the way in which media framing devices are constructed to caricature or eliminate minority groups and opinions. In addition, **content analysis** examines advertising to investigate the mechanisms behind the persuasive or subliminal nature of advertising content.

The inability of much mass media research to generalize to real world situations has resulted in the tradition of *audience studies*. These studies have been directed towards an examination of audiences in the everyday context of their media exposure and engagement. One striking result of this research is the revelation that while individuals may spend on average four hours a day in front of the **television**, for example, they are not necessarily watching the television with any degree of intimacy or interest. The central insight of these audience studies is that individuals do not just simply experience mass media in a social vacuum, but instead they experience mass media in a social context. Individuals may also be eating, exercising, napping, or talking, and often may be engaged in multiple forms of mass media simultaneously.

Finally, *cultivation effects* models have been developed which argue that heavy media consumers, primarily of television, cultivate an entire world-view from their media viewing. This world-view, the cultivation approach suggests, comes to supplant the real. This process, called *mainstreaming,* suggests that the real power of the media is in its ability to saturate the symbolic environment of everyday life with mediated symbols, such that they are taken for reality itself. Additionally, when these mainstreamed media symbols are reinforced by real world experience, the real world and the mediated world may *resonate* in such a way that the "reality" of the mediated world is reinforced.

MASS SOCIETY

According to the **model** of mass **society**, modernization is seen as leading to two important consequences. On the one hand, individuals are detached from social groups, leading to social fragmentation, atomization, isolation, alienation, and anxiety. On the other hand, this process of social atomization renders individuals increasingly susceptible and vulnerable to manipulation by elites. Both of these notions can be traced back to the work of Alexis de Tocqueville, who saw modernization as a leveling process that obliterated the social bonds of aristocratic societies and led individuals to withdraw from public affairs. This pattern made individuals vulnerable, Tocqueville suggested, to a new kind of "tutelary" despotism. However, while Tocqueville is an important precursor, theories of mass society were most influential in the years just prior to and following World War II. The twin notions of atomization and manipulation at the heart of mass society theories can be found in the work of a wide variety of authors from this period, including Hannah Arendt, the various members of the Frankfurt School, William Kornhauser, C. Wright Mills, and David Riesman.

The influence of mass society theories at this time can be attributed in part to an effort to understand the various forms of totalitarianism<fascism in Italy, Nazism in Germany, and Stalinism in the Soviet Union<then posing a challenge to liberal democracies. Author Hannah Arendt, for example, concluded that totalitarian movements required unconditional loyalty which, in turn, was only possible from isolated individuals with no other ties. Such individuals became available due to the breakdown of the class system and class society. In her view, this breakdown fostered feelings of superfluity, a sense of homelessness, and a lack of concern for self-preservation, all of which made isolated individuals susceptible to totalitarian manipulation.

However, the line separating **totalitarianism** from mass **democracy** was sometimes obscured by mass society theories. **Max Horkheimer**, for example, emphasized new forms of **domination** embodied in mass media and mass culture that were not confined to totalitarian societies. Similarly, C. Wright Mills did not characterize postwar America as a totalitarian society, but he saw it as one in which power tended to become concentrated in the hands of business, military, and political elites as each of these institutional domains became enlarged and centralized. Like Horkheimer, Mills also stressed the concentration and centralization of the mass media, which he saw as strengthening the hold of the **power elite**. This concentration of power went hand in hand with the transformation of postwar America into a ''mass-like society'' that bore ''little resemblance to the image of a society in which **voluntary associations** and classic publics hold the keys to power.'' While the ''top of the American system of power'' was ''unified'' and ''powerful,'' the bottom remained ''fragmented'' and ''impotent.''

Kornhauser, among others, was more careful to distinguish mass from totalitarian societies, although he clearly saw a close kinship between the two. Individuals are atomized in both kinds of society, according to Kornhauser, but elite competition in the latter provides non-elites some degree of access and influence. Because access is direct and unrestrained, elites are unable to exercise strong, decisive, independent **leadership**. The combination of atomized masses and accessible elites generates what Kornhauser called ''mass behavior'': individuals focus on objects and events that are remote from their personal experiences and daily lives, they respond to these objects in a direct and unmediated way, they alternate between apathy and extremism, and they are available for mobilization into mass movements that may potentially become totalitarian. Mass behavior is, in turn, supported by the weakness or absence of intermediary groups, the isolation of personal relations, and the centralization of national relations. Cultural standards in mass societies become uniform and fluid, and a self-estranged personality type comes to predominate, both of which foster manipulation.

The popularity of mass society theories waned in part as a consequence of the ''new social movements'' of the 1960s and 1970s, such as those in civil rights, antiwar, feminist, and environmentalist groups. On the one hand, these movements belied the assumption of an apathetic and manipulated mass of isolated individuals incapable of concerted resistance to a unified power elite. On the other hand, these movements could not easily be assimilated to the model of totalitarian and mass movements, which were viewed as efforts to overcome self-alienation or anxiety rather than as rational political action.

MASTER STATUS

The concept of master status was introduced by Everett Hughes in 1945 as part of his work on **race** and **ethnicity**. Master status is the single, defining characteristic by which an individual is best known by those around him/her. Hughes

Author Hannah Arendt concluded that totalitarian movements required unconditional loyalty which, in turn, was only possible from isolated individuals with no other ties *(Corbis Corporation [Bellevue])*.

believed that individuals occupied many statuses, identities, and social positions in their lives. Some of these statuses were ascribed, meaning individuals had no choice regarding their placements into a category or **identity** (i.e. racial group, sex, physical handicap), and others were achieved, meaning that individuals had to reach some achievement to be awarded this status (i.e. occupation, club member). To any individual, each status would hold a different level of importance. Hughes was more interested in studying the way other people perceived an individual's master status than how the individual perceived it in him/herself. Hughes believed that a master status was powerful enough, in most cases, to minimize all of the other statuses held by an individual.

Hughes believed the master status could be either an achieved status (i.e. physician, lawyer, athlete) or an **ascribed status** (i.e. African-American, woman, handicapped person), but it was likely to be a characteristic that is readily available and knowable about the person. Due to the availability of many ascribed characteristics in making immediate judgements, the ascribed features tend to serve more often as an individual's master status. Individuals have little control over what their statuses are because they are perceptions made by others.

The master status can immediately establish expectations about individuals and their behavior which may affect the

Virginia Johnson and Dr. William Masters *(Corbis Corporation [Bellevue])*

perception of their performance in other areas. For example, many female physicians are typically treated as nurses in hospital settings. Hughes would explain this by pointing out that the physician's master status is that of "woman" not "physician" and that she is working in a situation where most women serve in a less prestigious capacity than physician. In this way the individual's ascribed master status can hinder performance in an achieved setting as many would assume that a woman working in the **health care** field is likely to be a nurse.

MASTERS, WILLIAM HOWELL (1915-)

American psychologist, obstetrician, and gynecologist

William Howell Masters was the first to study the anatomy and physiology of human sexuality in the laboratory, and the publication of the reports on his findings created much interest and criticism. Since then, he and his colleague, Virginia Johnson, have become well-known as researchers and therapists in the field of human sexuality, and together they have established the Reproduction Biology Center and later the Masters and Johnson Institute in St. Louis, Missouri.

Masters was born on December 27, 1915, in Cleveland, Ohio, to Francis Wynne and Estabrooks (Taylor) Masters. He attended public school in Kansas City through the eighth grade and then went to the Lawrenceville School in Lawrenceville, New Jersey. In 1938 he received a B.S. degree from Hamilton College, where he divided his time between science courses and sports such as baseball, football, and basketball. He was also active in campus debate. He entered the University of Rochester School of Medicine and started working in the laboratory of Dr. George Corner, who was comparing and studying the reproductive tracts of animals and humans.

During his junior year in medical school, Masters became interested in sexuality because it was the last scientifically unexplored physiological function. After briefly serving in the navy, he received his M.D. degree in 1943. Masters became interested in the work of Dr. Alfred Kinsey, a University

of Indiana zoology professor who had interviewed thousands of men and women about their sexual experiences. Choosing a field that would help him prepare himself for human sexuality research, Masters became an intern and later a resident in obstetrics and gynecology at St. Louis Hospital and Barnes Hospital in St. Louis. He also did an internship in pathology at the Washington University School of Medicine. In 1947 he joined the faculty at Washington and advanced from instructor to associate professor of clinical obstetrics and gynecology. Masters conducted research in the field and contributed dozens of papers to scientific journals. One of his areas of interest was hormone treatment and replacement in post-menopausal women.

By 1954 Masters decided that he was ready to undertake research on the physiology of sex. He was concerned that the medical profession had too little information on sexuality to understand clients' problems. Kinsey had depended on case histories, interviews, and secondhand **data**. Masters took the next step, which was to study human sexual stimulation using measuring technology in a laboratory situation.

Masters launched his project at Washington University, assisted by a grant from the United States Institute of Health. At first he recruited prostitutes for study, but found them unsuitable for his studies of "normal" sexuality. In 1956 he hired **Virginia Eshelman Johnson**, a sociology student, to help in the interviewing and screening of volunteers. The study was conducted over an eleven-year period with 382 women and 312 men participating. Subjects ranged in age from eighteen to eighty-nine and were paid for their time. Masters found a four-phased cycle relating to male and female sexual responses. To measure physiological changes, he used electroencephalographs, electrocardiographs, color cinematography, and biochemical studies.

Masters was very cautious and meticulous about protecting the identity of his volunteers. In 1959 he sent some results to medical journals, but continued to work in relative secrecy. After the content of the studies leaked out, the team had difficulty procuring grant money, so in 1964 Masters became director of the Reproductive Biology Foundation, a nonprofit group, to obtain private funds.

In 1966 Masters and Johnson published *Human Sexual Response*. In this book, the researchers used highly technical terminology and had their publisher, Little, Brown and Co., promote the book only to medical professionals and journals. Nevertheless, the book became a popular sensation and the team embarked on a speaking and lecture tour, winning immediate fame. As early as 1959 Masters and Johnson had begun counseling couples as a dual-sex team. Believing that partners would be more comfortable talking with a same-sex therapist, the team began working with couples' sexual problems. In their second book *Human Sexual Inadequacy* (1970), they discuss problems such as impotence.

Masters divorced his first wife, Elisabeth Ellis, not long after the publication of *Human Sexual Inadequacy* and married Johnson on January 1, 1971, in Fayetteville, Arkansas. In 1973 they became codirectors of the Masters and Johnson Institute. In 1979 Masters and Johnson studied and described the sexual responses of homosexuals and lesbians in *Homosexuality in Perspective*. They also claimed to be able to change the sexual preferences of homosexuals who wanted to change. Masters also maintained a biochemistry lab and continued to receive fees from a gynecology practice. He retired from practice in 1975 at the age of sixty. In 1981 Masters and Johnson sold their lab and moved to another location in St. Louis. At this time they had a staff of 25 and a long list of therapy clients.

Further controversy over their work developed when in 1988 Masters and Johnson coauthored a book with an associate, Dr. Robert Kolodny. The book *Crisis: Heterosexual Behavior in the Age of AIDS* predicted an epidemic of AIDS among the heterosexual population. Some members of the medical **community** severely condemned the study, and C. Everett Koop, then surgeon general of the United States, called Masters and Johnson irresponsible. Perhaps as a result of the negative publicity, the number of clients seeking sex therapy at the institute decreased. In early 1992, Bill Walters, acting director of the institute, announced that Masters and Johnson were divorcing after 21 years of marriage—conflict in their ideas about retirement was cited as the reason for the breakup. Masters vowed he would never retire and continued speaking and lecturing at the institute, in addition to working on another book. The divorce ended their work together at the clinic.

For his pioneering efforts in making human sexuality a subject of scientific study, Masters received the Paul H. Hoch Award from the American Psychopathic Association in 1971, the Sex Information and Education Council of the United States (SIECUS) award in 1972, and three other prestigious awards. He belonged to the American Association for the Advancement of Science (AAAS), the American Fertility Society, and several other medical associations.

MATE SELECTION THEORIES

The process of choosing a mate is not necessarily left to chance. There are several patterns that people follow when selecting mates. There are several factors that affect who a person courts and eventually marries. Even today, with a **divorce** rate of fifty percent, most people are still surprisingly devoted to the institution of **marriage**.

People tend to choose a mate that has similar personal and social characteristics. This practice of selection is called **homogamy**. People tend to choose a mate that is of the same **race**, social class, religion, and **family** background. Though marriages that are heterogamous (selecting a mate of dissimilar social characteristics) do occur, the overwhelming trend is toward homogamy. For example, interracial marriages account for only three percent of all marriages.

One theory of mate selection is the **exchange theory**. This theory is popular in explaining interactions between individuals. It asserts that individuals enter into a relationship that holds maximum benefits and minimum costs for them. In each relationship a process of exchange occurs; one commodity to be exchanged is power. People hold sets of rewards to offer their partners. Previously, men were the ones who offered so-

cial status, money (economic support), power, and protection. Women offered physical attractiveness, and the ability to create a home. Today, however, the range of rewards for both sexes are different. Women may seek partners who are caring, sensitive, and willing to share **household** responsibilities. Men in turn may seek mates who are assertive, independent, and creative. Thus, people choose mates to maximize their rewards. When the costs of a relationship begin to outweigh the rewards, the relationship is likely to end.

The filter theory of mate selection posits that the pool of potential mates is vast, but individuals go through a filtering process that reduces this pool significantly until only a few eligible individuals are left. The pool is reduced on the basis of propinquity (geographical proximity), social class, race, **ethnicity**, religion, physical attractiveness, age, family and friends. Once individuals filter out many people, they are left with a small group from which to select partners.

Another theory of mate selection is the stimulus-value-role theory (SVR). According to this pattern, during the mate selection process, couples pass through three stages. In the stimulus stage, individuals are attracted to each other by some stimulus (physical attractiveness, social status, reputation). This stimulus is such that it moves the relationship beyond the boundaries of friendship. The value stage transpires as the couple compares their value or belief systems regarding such issues as religion or politics. The last stage couples pass through is the role stage in which couples decide what roles they will take on as partners, mother, father, lover, confidant, housekeeper, friend. These roles must be agreed upon in order for the relationship to continue. If the three stages are successfully completed, the couple may consider marriage.

Though there are several different theories describing how individuals select mates, sociologists often choose one theory with which to work. Sociologists then collect **data** to seek patterns in mate selection. The data are interpreted and mate selection theories are used to explain the patterns found.

MATERIALISM

While the term "materialism" is used popularly to refer to an emphasis on the ownership of material possessions, in **sociology** it refers to a theory of social organization and material production developed by Karl Marx and **Friedrich Engels**. Materialism explains social **structure** as resulting from the way in which material production takes place. Through the division of labor and control of capital, particular groupings or classes are formed. Because people in different classes have different interests, antagonism between classes occurs. Thus, the basic feature of materialism is the subordination and **domination** that occurs between classes, as more powerful classes attempt to exploit less powerful classes. In this way, materialism is not only a theory of economics but also of group relations.

Marx theorized that in the process of social interactions that occur between people in their everyday lives (and in particular as they perform work to maintain their livelihood), they enter in specific relations with other people that are somewhat autonomous from their individual control. These "relations of production," as Marx called them, coincide with a particular point in the development of material production and the power hierarchy that results. The aggregate of these relations of production result in the social organization by which resources are allocated. A key point to the theory of materialism is that the material position a person has in **society** that determines his or her consciousness, and not the other way round. In this way, materialism runs contrary to idealist theory proffered by Hegel.

Marx and Engels also applied materialism to the development of historical periods, called historical materialism. Historical materialism emphasizes the importance of social institutions that were previously thought to have little effect on social hierarchy, such as the **family**, religion, and legal institutions. Marx and Engels argued that these institutions contributed to the maintenance of the system of domination exists in a given period of history. This system of domination, then, is only overthrown through social conflict, resulting in revolution and a change in the social system. Because of this process of conflict and change, historical materialism is referred to as dialectical.

Materialism was unique in that it required the consideration of sensual experiences and human agency in the development of social structure and historical change. While it has been criticized for being too economically deterministic, Marx and Engels did attempt to expand what was defined as economic to include all types of productive activity (such as the contribution of the family to the capitalist system). Contemporary Marxists and neo-Marxists have tried to respond to the economic deterministic criticism by examining the relationship of **culture** to the formation of classes and class consciousness (see the work of Raymond Williams for examples).

MATING GRADIENT

The mating gradient (also called **marriage** gradient) is based on the idea that men prefer younger women and those with lower education and occupational status, while women date older men with higher age, income, and education. There are two explanations for this pattern. One is that men prefer this arrangement because it reinforces traditional patterns of **patriarchy**, and women prefer it because it provides economic security while they raise children. A second explanation is that although they are different, each partner has power. The woman can garner power in the relationship because of her youth and/or beauty while man possesses economic power. Basically, the *social capital* each brings to the relationship enhances the happiness and social status for the other. One outcome of this cultural trend is a *marriage squeeze* in that high status women have difficulty finding men with higher status because they are competing with lower status women for relatively fewer men in **higher education** and occupational categories. Similarly, low status men have difficulty finding women with less social status.

The utility of the marriage gradient **theory** is debated on several points. One criticism is cultural **bias**. The tendency for

men to marry younger women has been a trend in the United States but not in France where older women are preferred. Secondly, women in higher status positions are not necessarily looking for a higher status male. Many of these women are not married by preference and choose to focus on a **career** instead of marriage. A third criticism is that statistics do not consistently back up this theory. There appears to be statistically significant trends in some age groups for women to marry younger men.

Betty Yorburg identified *marriage gradient reversal*. She argued that postindustrial societies offer more career opportunities for women. As women are able to enter **professions**, the need to obtain one's financial security and social status from a husband is less important. Yorburg's prediction is that there is potential for an increase in marriages between wealthier, more educated, older career women and men in lower status positions.

MATRIARCHY

Matriarchy is social organization in which females are dominant. In this **society**, women rule over men by matrilineal and matrilocal arrangements. In a matrilineal arrangement, namesake, lineage, **property**, and marital controls are owned by women and passed down through female **family** members. In a matrilocal arrangement, newly married couples reside in the bride's parents' home. The benefit here is that another young person is brought into the family to help out in the home and to bring in additional income.

Today there are no documented cultures or societies that employ a matriarchial arrangement, nor has there ever been such a society. But individual women have held great power, wealth, and control over men. Women have served as queens, political leaders, and heads of individual families or kin groups. In much of the world, however, women are not leaders or hold political positions in the same numbers as men.

Some anthropologists and ethnographers believe there have been matriarchial societies. For example, in the Iroquois tribe, residing in northeastern North America, women controlled the production and distribution of food. They also headed households and occupied important political offices. Women had the right to veto declarations of **war** and the right to present conflict resolution proposals. Though men did occupy the most powerful political positions, women had the right to select and remove them. Researchers differ in their opinions about whether this is a true matriarchy, but it remains an alternate example to a patriarchal society.

MATRIX OF DOMINATION

The matrix of **domination** rests on the fact that each individual is characterized by many socio-psychological-economic variables. Many of these have different *social weight* (or *social capital*) in interactions. Although the most widely recognized of these are socio-economic status (SES). **race**, **ethnicity**, sex, and sexual orientation, one could also add physical or **mental health**, attractiveness, rural/urban/suburban residence, age, and religion.

Different *social weight stratification* for each dimension makes each of these characteristics a basis for discrimination. Any combination of these intensifies the obstacles to overcome. An individual who holds minority status in several categories is more oppressed than someone who is a minority in only one. For example, a well-educated black male from a wealthy **family** has more opportunities than a poor, uneducated, rural gay black male.

Patricia Hill Collins used the matrix of domination to describe different opportunities available to individuals based on their social class, race, and gender. This technique provides an analytical tool for linking intensity of discrepancies in opportunity in our **culture** with underlying structure of discrimination based on class, race, sex. For example, race affects educational, occupational, and social opportunities. However, social class and sex can also pose limitations or opportunities for obtaining a good education. Overall, these opportunities are affected by all three variables (race, sex, class). An upper class individual has a wider range of opportunity regardless of race or sex. A lower class individual has fewer opportunities, and these are magnified by inequality based on race or sex.

There are several implications here. First, people have different views of the system and different analysis of opportunity based on differential opportunity as explained by the stand point **theory**. Second, race, class, and sex are created both by the social structure (opportunities, expectations, patterns in **society**) and by interaction of the person with the social structures. Opportunity begets expectations of opportunity. Lack of opportunity begets lower expectations for future opportunities. People experience opportunity or oppression depending on their position in the system. Third, within class, race, and sex, stratifications of power are linked to reinforce the existing systems of stratification. Little incentive exists for those in privileged positions to reach out in meaningful ways because to do so may result in a loss of power.

MEAD, GEORGE HERBERT (1863-1931)
American philosopher

The American philosopher and social psychologist George Herbert Mead (1863–1931) offered a naturalistic account of the origin of the self and explained **language**, conception, perception, and thinking in terms of social behavior. George Herbert Mead was born on February 27, 1863, in South Hadley, Massachusetts. He graduated from Oberlin College in 1883 and attended Harvard University in 1887 and 1888. While studying in Leipzig and Berlin (1888–1891), he was influenced by the physiological psychologist Wilhelm Wundt. Mead taught at the University of Michigan (1891–1893) and the University of Chicago (1894–1931). He died in Chicago on April 26, 1931.

The notion of ''gesture,'' which Mead took from Wundt, is basic to Mead's behavioristic **psychology** and to all

George Herbert Mead *(The Library of Congress)*

of his philosophic thinking. If the behavior of one animal evokes a response in another that is useful in completing a more inclusive act, it is called a gesture, and the behavior of the participants of the act is social.

In *Mind, Self and Society*, Mead shows that human beings are distinguished from all other animals in that an individual can by his gestures (words, that is, language gestures) evoke in himself the same response that he evokes in another and can respond to his own behavior (words) as do other members of the **community**. This means that the human individual can look at his own behavior from the point of view of the other; or he can take the role of the other and, thus, be an object to himself. When the child can view its own behavior from the perspective of another, it is a self or it has a self. Selves emerge in children out of social behavior with other members of the group who, with the child, are participants in social action. The meaning of a gesture is the response it evokes; a language gesture has the same meaning to the speaker as it does to the one to whom it is addressed. When a gesture (or significant **symbol**) has common meaning, it is universal in that the response it evokes is the same for each member of the community. One perceives an object, such as a tree, only in relation to behavior or to responses evoked by what is seen, heard, or smelled. The lumberman ''sees'' the tree in terms of lumber, and his responses are organized accordingly.

It is only because symbols have common meaning that men can think or reason. Thinking is a conversation of the self, the individual, with the other, or with what Mead calls the **generalized other**. Individuals have minds, therefore, because they can take the **attitude** of others (take the role of, or enter into the perspective of, others) and can thus anticipate the response that others will make to their gestures. The individual member of **society**, through thinking, can propose new ways of acting which can be shared and tested by other members of the community.

The physiological basis for thinking and for basic distinctions between man and lower animals is the hand. Not only can men move physical objects from place to place, but they can also dissect objects and reassemble them in various ways. Thinking has to do with the manipulatory phase of social action.

In Mead's last work *The Philosophy of the Present,* he shows that the same basic principle used in creative, or reflective, thinking, resulting in acts of adjustment between the individual and its environment, applies also to every kind of adjustment in the process of evolution. The adjustments that new planets make to the system from which they emerged (and vice versa), as well as adjustments made by lower animals to their respective environments (and the environments to them), take place in accordance with the same principle applied in reflective thinking. This is the principle of sociality, and it requires that the newly arisen entity, the emergent, be in two or more different systems at once, even as reflective thinking requires that the individual be in both his own perspective and in the perspective of the other.

Through the principle of sociality Mead not only accounts for the process of adjustment, and thus strengthens his position as a process philosopher, but he also develops a system of **philosophy** based on the act of adjustment as a unit of existence. His system explains how emergence, novelty, creativity, thinking, **communication**, and continuous adjustment are interrelated and why each is a phase of the natural process of adjustment.

MEAD, MARGARET (1901-1978)

American anthropologist

The American anthropologist Margaret Mead (1901–1978) developed the field of **culture** and personality research and was a dominant influence in introducing the concept of culture into education, medicine, and public policy. Margaret Mead was born in Philadelphia, Pennsylvania, on December 16, 1901. She grew up there in a liberal intellectual atmosphere. Her father, Edward Sherwood Mead, was a professor in the Wharton School of Finance and Commerce and the founder of the University of Pennsylvania's evening school and extension program. Her mother, Emily Fogg Mead, was a sociologist and an early advocate of woman's rights.

In 1919 Mead entered DePauw University but transferred after a year to Barnard College, where she majored in **psychology**. In her senior year she had a course in anthropology with **Franz Boas** which she later described as the most influential event in her life, since it was then that she decided to become an anthropologist. She graduated from Barnard in 1923. In the same year she married Luther Cressman and entered the anthropology department of Columbia University.

The Columbia department at this time consisted of Boas, who taught everything, and **Ruth Benedict**, his only assistant. The catastrophe of World War I and the dislocations that followed it had had their impact on the developing discipline of anthropology. Anthropologists began to ask how their knowledge of the nature of humankind might be used to illuminate contemporary problems. At the same time the influence of **Sigmund Freud** was beginning to be felt in all the behavioral sciences. The atmosphere in the Columbia department was charged with intellectual excitement, and whole new perspectives for anthropology were opening up.

Mead completed her studies in 1925 and set off for a year's fieldwork in Samoa in the face of opposition from older colleagues worried about sending a young woman alone to a Pacific island. Her problem was to study the life of adolescent girls. She learned the native language (one of seven she eventually mastered) and lived in a Samoan household as "one of the girls." She found that young Samoan girls experience none of the tensions American and European adolescents suffer from, and she demonstrated the kind of social arrangements that make this easy transition to **adulthood** possible.

On returning from the field Mead became assistant curator of ethnology at the American Museum of Natural History, where she remained, eventually becoming curator and, in 1969, curator emeritus. Her mandate in going to the museum was "to make Americans understand cultural anthropology as well as they understood archaeology."

When Mead wrote *Coming of Age in Samoa* (1928), her publisher, concerned that the book fell into no conventional category, asked for a chapter on what the work's significance would be for Americans. The result was the final chapter, "Education for Choice," which set the basic theme for much of her lifework.

In 1928, after completing a technical monograph *The Social Organization of Manuá,* Mead left for New Guinea, this time with Reo Fortune, an anthropologist from New Zealand whom she had married that year. Her project was the study of the thought of young children, testing some of the then current theories. Her study of children's thought in its sociocultural context is described in *Growing Up in New Guinea* (1930). She later returned to the village of Peri, where this study was made, after 25 years, when the children she had known in 1929 were leaders of a **community** going through the difficulties of transition to modern life. She described this transition, with flashbacks to the earlier days, in *New Lives for Old* (1956).

Mead's interest in psychiatry had turned her attention to the problem of the cultural context of schizophrenia, and with this in mind she went to Bali, a **society** where trance and other forms of dissociation are culturally sanctioned. She was now married to Gregory Bateson, a British anthropologist whom she had met in New Guinea. The Balinese study was especially noteworthy for development of new field techniques. The extensive use of film made it possible to record and analyze significant minutiae of behavior that escape the pencil-and-paper ethnographer. Of the 38,000 photographs which Mead and Bateson brought back, 759 were selected for *Balinese Character* (1942), a joint study with Bateson. This publication marks a major innovation in the recording and presentation of ethnological **data** and may prove in the long run to be one of her most significant contributions to the science of anthropology.

Largely through the work of Ruth Benedict and Margaret Mead, the relevance of anthropology to problems of public policy was recognized to a degree, though somewhat belatedly. When World War II brought the United States into contact with allies, enemies, and peoples just emerging from **colonialism**, the need to understand many lifestyles became apparent. Mead conducted a nationwide study of American food habits prior to the introduction of rationing. Later she was sent to England to try to explain to the British the habits of the American soldiers who were suddenly thrust among them. After the war she worked as director of Research in Contemporary Cultures, a cross-cultural, trans-disciplinary project applying the insights and some of the methods of anthropology to the study of complex modern cultures. An overall view of the methods and some of the insights gained is contained in *The Study of Cultures at a Distance* (1953).

For the theoretical basis of her work in the field of culture and personality Margaret Mead drew heavily on psychology, especially learning **theory** and psychoanalysis. In return she contributed significantly to the development of psychoanalytic theory by emphasizing the importance of culture in personality development. She served on many national and international committees for mental health and was instrumental in introducing the study of culture into training programs for physicians and social workers.

In the 1960s Mead became deeply concerned with the unrest among the young. Her close contact with students gave her special insight into the unmet needs of youth—for better education, for **autonomy**, for an effective voice in decisions that affect their lives in a world which adults seem no longer able to control. Some of her views on these problems are set forth in *Culture and Commitment* (1970). Her thoughts on human survival under the threats of war, overpopulation, and degradation of the environment are contained in *A Way of Seeing* (1970).

Ever since Margaret Mead taught a class of young working women in 1926, she became deeply involved in education, both in the universities and in interpreting the lessons of anthropology to the general public. She joined the anthropology department at Columbia University in 1947 and also taught at Fordham University and the Universities of Cincinnati and Topeka. She also lectured to people across America and Europe. Mead died in 1978 and was posthumously awarded the Presidential Medal of Freedom.

Margaret Mead was a dominant force in developing the field of culture and personality and the related field of national character research. Stated briefly, her theoretical position is based on the assumption that an individual matures within a cultural context which includes an ideological system, the ex-

Margaret Meade

pectations of others, and techniques of **socialization** which condition not only outward responses but also inner psychic structure. Mead was criticized by certain other social scientists on methodological and conceptual grounds. She was criticized for neglecting quantitative methods in favor of depth analysis and for what has been called ''anecdotal'' handling of data. On the theoretical side she was accused of applying concepts of individual psychology to the analysis of social process while ignoring historical and economic factors. But since her concern lay with predicting the behavior of individuals within a given social context and not with the origin of institutions, the criticism is irrelevant.

There is no question that Mead was one of the leading American intellectuals of the twentieth century. Through her best-selling books, her public lecturing, and her popular column in *Redbook* magazine, Mead popularized anthropology in the United States. She also provided American women with a role model, encouraging them to pursue professional careers previously closed to women while at the same time championing their roles as mothers.

MEAN

The mean is one of three **measures of central tendency** used in univariate analysis. Univariate analyses produce summary statistics for individual variables. Measures of central tendency indicate the area around which cases cluster.

The mean is a mathematical term that refers to the average of some set of numbers. When ''mean'' appears unspecified, (i.e. ''mean''), it is meant as the arithmetic mean. Other means include the geometric and harmonic means, which are not typically used in sociological analysis.

The mean is calculated by summing a set of numbers, then dividing by the number of cases summed ($\Sigma x_i / n$: where Σ indicates to sum, x_i indicates the values of each case, and n is the total number of cases). It is typically symbolized as

"X-bar." For example, the **variable**, "age" represents age in years. For simplicity, let us calculate the mean of only four cases. To calculate the mean age of respondents whose ages are, 12, 18, 25, and 16, we add the ages together (12 + 18 + 25 + 16 = 71), and then divide the total by 4 (the number of cases): 71/4 = 17.75. The arithmetic mean of these four cases on the variable "age" is 17.75, or about eighteen years of age.

When we calculate a mean from multiple cases with the same scores or from a frequency table produced by statistical computer software, the process is simple. For each case score, we multiply the case score by the frequency of occurrence, then add those products together and divide by the total number of cases. For example, referring to the previous example, let us say that there are 10 people who are 12 years old, 5 who are 18, 15 who are 25, and 10 who are 16. Calculation of the mean would be as follows: X-bar = (10 x 12) + (5 x 18) + (15 x 25) + (10 x 16) / 40 ("40" comes from summing the number of cases: 10 + 5 + 15 + 10), X-bar = 120 + 90 + 375 + 160 / 40, X-bar = 18.63, or about 19 years of age.

Meaningful Sociology

Meaningful **sociology** refers to any form of sociology premised on the assumption (a) that social actors above all inhabit a universe of social meanings; (b) that social action is meaningful action; and (c) that social occurrences must be explained primarily as the outcome of actors's meanings, that is, the beliefs, motives, purposes, reasons, etc. that lead to actions. The term is commonly applied to German sociologist Max Weber's action theory but can equally apply to related approaches such as **symbolic interactionism**.

Measurement

Measurement is intentional and purposeful observation used to assess the world. In **sociology**, social measurement is indispensable. While people observe the social world around them, using sociology to attain a scientific understanding of human social existence requires measurement. Social measurement allows the classification, comparison, and assessment of a variety of elements in **society**. To ensure that measurements are accurate and useful, social scientists employ specific methods and evaluate their results based on specific criteria.

Sometimes measurement is relatively easy and straightforward. For example, counting the number of people in a certain place or setting can unambiguously measure population or attendance. Many times, however, social researchers need to measure factors that are less tangible and more abstract. Trying to assess the presence or strength of patriotism, religiosity, prejudice, social class, or **anomie** requires more carefully designed measurement techniques. Because terms such as these are abstract concepts rather than concrete objects, it is impossible define and measure these concepts in a way that will accurately reflect each individual's understanding of them.

Research to understand and improve society often relies on measuring abstract concepts. To maximize measurement

effectiveness in these cases, researchers use the process of conceptualization to arrive at a specific definition of the term that is to be measured. If the **concept** is something that is not constant but differs from case to case, it is called a **variable** (if the concept does not vary, further measurement becomes unimportant). Once a variable has been conceptualized, other variables must be created that can concretely measure the conceptual variable. This process is called operationalization. Through **operationalization**, indicators are derived to measure the conceptual variable. For example, a researcher trying to measure religiosity might conceptualize this term as consisting of an individual's active participation in formalized religious ceremonies. The measurement of religiosity could be operationalized by measuring the indicator variable of church attendance.

In the process of operationalization, the social scientist must determine what type of measurement can be obtained. Some observations allow classification into two or more categories. These observations are referred to as categorical or nominal **data**. Classification of a person's sex is an example of a nominal variable. Other observations allow cases to be ranked (referred to as ordinal data). Measuring someone's level of support for a new program or policy as high, medium or low would result in ordinal data. Finally, interval or ratio data allow ranking on a consistent numerical scale. Measuring household income in dollars allows the precise observation at one-dollar intervals necessary for interval or **ratio** data. Researchers must determine the most appropriate type of measurement for each variable that is operationalized. The type of measurement for each variable affects what types of evaluation and analysis will be available when the measurement is complete.

After conceptualization and operationalization, researchers gather data through the use of a measurement instrument, a set of techniques and procedures designed to minimize error. A measurement instrument can consist of structured observation, **content analysis**, **surveys**, and other defined and developed measurement techniques. Sometimes multiple instruments are combined in a process called triangulation which allows observations to be crosschecked and confirmed.

Once a measurement instrument has been implemented, the obtained measurements must be evaluated. Two general criteria used to evaluate measurements are reliability and **validity**. **Reliability** refers to the consistency of results obtained from multiple implementations of the measurement instrument. A reliable instrument will generate consistent results. While an instrument may generate consistent results, reliability does not ensure that the instrument accurately measures what it is intended to measure. A test designed to predict success in school may yield consistent score distributions, but the scores could be unrelated to school success. Thus, a measurement instrument must have validity as well as reliability.

Validity describes how accurately a measurement describes reality. Because measurements are often the only ways to describe reality, validity must sometimes be ascertained through indirect means. For example, face and content validity are determined by examining the items on the instrument to make sure concepts have been operationalized correctly and that all the items are relevant to the concept in question. Construct validity assures that the measurement instrument yields results that are meaningful in a larger context. **Internal validity** assures that items correlate with other items used to assess the same concept, and **external validity** assures that the results obtained by the instrument resemble the results of other measurements.

Once the results of a measurement instrument have been evaluated and deemed suitable, the results must be analyzed. Translating observations into measurement allows the use of mathematics and statistics to explain, explore, predict, and evaluate the social world. Statistics can describe a population, explore relationships among variables, explain correlations and try to determine causation, or evaluate the impact of a program or experimental condition.

Measurement is an invaluable tool for social scientists, though it has some limitations. Measurement can allow detailed analysis and inference about some the elusive concepts that are essential to understanding society. However, researchers must remember that these concepts, no matter how well they are operationalized, can only be measured indirectly through indicator variables. Researchers must take great care to maximize the reliability and validity of measurement instruments to obtain the measurements used to understand, explain, and predict forces in society.

MEASURES OF ASSOCIATION

Measures of association are statistics that indicate how two or more variables are related to, or vary with, each other. These relationships are described in terms of strength or magnitude and direction. If an independent variable increases, the direction of a measure of association will describe how the **dependent variable** is affected. For example, consider alcohol abuse as an **independent variable** and domestic violence as a dependent variable. As alcohol abuse increases, we would expect to see an increase in domestic violence. Such a relationship would be quantified by a positive measure of association—as one **variable** increases so does the other. If we were to consider education level and domestic violence, the measure of association would most likely be negative, indicating that an increase in one variable (education) results in a decrease in the other (domestic violence). This negative association is sometimes referred to as an inverse relationship. Interpretation of the strength of a relationship depends on the type of statistic used. Examples of statistics of association are correlations and regression.

Before measures of association are calculated, it is conventional practice to calculate **measures of central tendency** and dispersion, which describe the shape of the distribution. After this, researchers often examine a scatterplot of variables. Scatterplots serve as an initial indicator of association. From a plot of two variables, three observations can be ascertained. First, the plot gives an indication of linearity—whether the variables are related to each other in a straight line pattern.

Second, outlying or deviant cases can be identified. Identification of such cases is important given that they may inflate or reduce measures of association. Third, an indication of direction of the association between the variables can be gained from the direction and slope of a line that best fits the **data**.

Measures of association have their own class of hypotheses known as association or relationship hypotheses. Such hypotheses state expected relationships between variables and are tested using various statistics of association. An example **null hypothesis** may state that there is no relationship between an independent and dependent variable, while a **research hypothesis** may state that there is a relationship between an independent and dependent variable. In some instances, it is appropriate for these hypotheses to be directional. For example, consider the variables delinquency and delinquent peers and assume simple linear **regression** as the measure of association. The research hypothesis may state that there is a positive relationship between delinquent peers and delinquency, while the null would state that there is either a negative association or no association between the two variables.

The most commonly used measures of association are correlations. There are a number of different **correlation** statistics, such as Pearson's product moment correlation, Spearman's rank order correlation, Kendall's tau, and Goodman and Kruskal's gamma. A researcher must decide which of these measures are appropriate given characteristics of the data being analyzed. All the above correlation statistics are **descriptive statistics** given that they describe relationships between variables. Chi-square is also a type of correlation and is unique in that it is also used as an inferential statistic.

Another way to analyze relationships between variables, regression expresses a relationship in an equation to see how much change in a dependent variable is associated with a one-unit change in an independent variable. As with correlations, different types of regression can be used with different types of data. The most commonly employed regression method is ordinary least squares (OLS) regression or linear regression. This type of regression finds a line that best fits the data—in graphic terms, a line that can be drawn on a scatterplot that cuts through most of the data points, or is close to most of the data points. The regression equation is calculated using means and so is affected by outlying cases. Outliers in regression can be easily identified by plotting residual values.

An additional measure of association used in both correlation and regression is the coefficient of determination, or r^2. This statistic conveys the amount of variance in the dependent variable that is explained by the independent variable or variables. When this amount is low, the researcher should be alert to possible extraneous variables. Coefficients of determination, correlation, and regression are all statistics that help the researcher define how variables are related to each other. Identifying relationships between variables helps the researcher refine research, answer research questions, and pose future research questions.

See also Variable

MEASURES OF CENTRAL TENDENCY

Measures of central tendency is a statistical term which refers to the several ways available to determine a statistical average, midpoint, or center score of a distribution of values or scores. The three most commonly used measures of central tendency are the **mean**, or arithmetical average; the median, or exact middle case of a set of scores; and mode, or the most frequently occurring value. The measures that may be accurately used are determined by the level of **measurement** of the **data** in use.

The mean is the most common measure of central tendency and what is most commonly referred to as an average. To obtain the mean simply sum all the values in a data set and divide by the number of cases in that set. A mean should only be calculated for data that are either interval or ratio level data. At this level of data, values have a true numeric meaning, and their addition and division provide meaningful and interpretable answers (i.e. age, income). Mean values can be altered by the existence of outliers, defined as cases with extremely high or low values that can artificially raise or lower the mean. For example, the presence of a seventy-seven year old student in a small freshman **sociology** course could make it appear that the average age of the students is twenty-one when it is actually closer to eighteen.

The **median** is the exact middle case, or the midpoint, of a distribution of cases. To locate the median value of a set, arrange all the values in the set from highest to lowest, or vice versa, and locate the case that falls midway between the extreme points. Median can be used with either interval/ratio or with ordinal level data. With ordinal level data values have an order to them but no set distance between each value as with interval/ratio (i.e. clothing sizes or military rankings). Since there are no set distances it is impractical to calculate a mean for this type of data. Use of the median value is less precise than the mean but issues with outlier values are eliminated when used with interval/ratio data.

The mode is the value that occurs most frequently within a data set. The mode can be found using frequency tables or by simply counting the occurrence of each value. Mode is effective with any level of measurement but is the only measure of central tendency available for use with nominal level data, categorical data in which numbers have no numerical significance and are used only for purposes of classification (i.e. 1= male, 2= female; 1= Christian 2= Muslim, 3= Jewish, 4= Other). With nominal level data finding a mean or median value would be useless as an arithmetical average would be interpretable and due to the fact that the values have no natural order. A midpoint would also explain little of the data. These measures of central tendency are useful tools when applied correctly with the appropriate level of measurement. Mean is the most powerful, mode the least, but each provides vital information about the data.

MEASURES OF DEVIATION

A common measure in statistical analysis is the **mean**, or average. This measure, which is calculated by adding the sum of the **values** for each case and dividing by the number of cases, gives an overall view of the variable under study. However, a single number is inadequate for describing the variation from the mean of individual cases. For this, we employ measures of deviation.

The most commonly used measure of deviation is the standard deviation. Deviation is the difference between the value of the observation and the mean. By summing the square of the deviation divided by the number of cases minus one (for samples) we obtain the variance, which approximates the average of the squared distances from the sample mean. The standard deviation is obtained by taking the square root of the variance.

The standard deviation is a statistic that describes the sample, and by comparing the standard deviation, or standardized distance, of any single case to the standard deviation of the sample we can make inferences about that case. For example, we may conclude that a case that falls more than 3 standard deviations from the mean should be considered an outlier. Probability estimates are based on the **probability** of a case falling within a certain number of standard deviations from the mean.

The standard deviation and variance are measures of deviation about the mean. Other measures of deviation, such as the Pearson statistic and the likelihood **ratio**, are other measures of deviation that do not apply to the mean. The Pearson statistic and likelihood ratio are chi-squared goodness-of-fit statistics that summarize the discrepancies between the **model** being tested and the complete model. In general, measures of deviation standardize the absolute value of residuals, the difference between a case and the mean, in order to summarize the **data** and enable comparison across models.

MEASURES OF DISPERSION

Measures of dispersion are aspects of statistical analysis that deal with the amount of variation from the typical or average case among an aggregate of cases. Measures of dispersion are vital in social research which typically deals with general group patterns and not merely with average cases. Measures of central tendency, or averages, although important in social research, are unable to provide information other than the typical or normal case. This information must be paired with measures of dispersion in order to provide a precise picture of the set and the amount of heterogeneity or variety contained within the **data**. Among the most common measures of dispersion are the index of qualitative variation, range, standard deviation, and variance.

The index of qualitative variation, sometimes called IQV, is a basic measure of dispersion that is typically used with nominal or categorical data. The IQV is a **ratio** comparing the amount of observed variation in a set of scores to the amount of variation that is possible in that same set. In this way categorical data can be shown to be more, less, or equally heterogenous than a typical or average group. The IQV can be used with more complex data, but other measures of dispersion can often provide more detailed information about the distribution of a set of scores.

Range, another basic measure of dispersion, is the distance between the extreme upper and lower values of a set of scores. This measure is easily calculated by subtracting the lowest value of the set from the highest value. The range is effective in giving an indication of the dispersion of the data; however, because only the highest and lowest values are used in the calculation, the range is subject to contamination from outlying scores. For example, if only one student, scoring twenty-five percent on that exam, fails an exam in a class of one hundred students, the range of scores on the exam would indicate a fairly diverse groups of scores, when in fact only one student did poorly. Therefore, the primary weakness of the range is the lack of information it provides about the data between the highest and lowest scores.

Standard deviation, the most commonly used measure of dispersion, uses a **normal distribution** to summarize information about the homogeneity or heterogeneity of the data by indicating how many cases fall within a set distance from the central point. In a normal distribution sixty-eight percent of the cases will be contained with the first standard deviation away from the central point, ninety-five percent of the cases with the second deviation and 99.7 percent within three deviations. Using this formula, the amount of clustering can be determined by indicating how many cases fall within each deviation. If most cases are contained within the first deviation, most cases are clustered close to the central point, and the set includes little dispersion. If most cases are spread among the second and the third deviations, then many cases are divergent from the central point, and the data set includes many diverse scores. Variance, the squared value of a standard deviation, is difficult to interpret and has little use when used with **descriptive statistics**, yet it is very important in the measures of dispersion using inferential statistics, correlation, and **regression** techniques.

MECHANICAL AND ORGANIC SOLIDARITY

Mechanical and organic solidarity are the distinctions made by Émile Durkheim (1858–1917) in his work *The Division of Labor in Society* to describe the degree to which those who participate in a social system identify with and support that system. Each describes a different type of **society**, and each type has distinctive characteristics and consequences for its members.

Mechanical solidarity occurs most often in less advanced societies and is based on similarities among individuals: shared experiences, common values, similar **professions**, etc. For example, in an agricultural society each member of that society is likely to take part in the raising and harvesting of crops and livestock, provide for most of their own families' needs, have a similar family **structure**, and share a common set of religious beliefs and practices. As a result the members of the society see themselves as part of a group to which they can relate. This type of society forms a strong collective consciousness (i.e. **group** mind or group consciousness) based on

these similarities. The function of each person in the group is similar to that of all of the others, so if someone leaves the society, that person's absence is not greatly felt by the society; her or his roles can easily be replaced by another member.

Durkheim contrasted mechanical solidarity with what he called "organic solidarity". Organic solidarity is found in a more developed society and is based on the **division of labor** in those societies. Individuals are much more diverse and specialized in their roles and experiences. People in these societies depend on each other to a great degree in their everyday lives because a high level of specialization has developed which makes it impossible for people to survive on their own. Whereas a **family** in a society with mechanical solidarity could basically be self-sufficient, those in societies with organic forms of solidarity require many others to fill roles they cannot for their daily survival. For example, they purchase food at grocery stores which has been grown by one group, perhaps prepared by another, packaged by another, transported by another, stocked by another, and sold by yet another.

In this form of society, the role of the collective consciousness has been overtaken by that of the individual consciousness, and this type of society is based on the differences of its members. Each role within society is important to that society and any loss is felt; therefore societies with organic solidarity have higher levels of interdependence and interconnectedness than societies where mechanical solidarity is prevalent.

MEDIAN

The median is one of three **measures of central tendency** used in univariate analyses which produce summary statistics for individual variables. Measures of central tendency indicate the area in which cases cluster.

The median is a mathematical term that refers to the middle score for a set of ranked numbers. If there is an odd number of scores, then the median is simply the middle score. For example, if for the **variable**, "income," there are five responses; $10,000, $15,000, $22,000, $40,000, and $60,000, the median would be $22,000 because it is the middle score in the series of ranked scores on income. If there is an even number of scores, then an average of the two middle scores is considered the median.

When we estimate the median from multiple cases with the same scores, or from a frequency table produced by statistical computer software, the process is simple. Using the example above, let us say that there are 5 cases of $10,000, 4 cases of $15,000, 12 cases of $22,000, 2 cases of $40,000 and 8 cases of $60,000. First, we calculate the "n", or the number of cases. There are thirty-one cases. We estimate the halfway point, which would be the sixteenth case; therefore there are fifteen cases that appear on either side of the sixteenth case. There are 5 cases of $10,000, and 4 cases of $15,000, which together equal 9. There are 12 cases of $22,000, which added to the previous cases equal 21, so the sixteenth case is in the category of $22,000 in the ranked series of incomes. Therefore, the median income in this particular series of scores for income is $22,000.

Medicaid—Selected Characteristics of Persons Covered: 1990 to 1997

[In thousands, except percent (24,160 represents 24,160,000). Represents number of persons as of March of following year who were enrolled at any time in year shown. Person did not have to receive medical care paid for by medicaid in order to be counted]

Poverty status	1990	1995	1997							
			Total [1]	White	Black	His-panic [2]	Under 18 years old	18-44 years old	45-64 years old	65 years and over
Persons covered, total	24,160	31,621	28,707	19,460	7,703	5,898	14,434	8,097	3,276	2,901
Below poverty level	15,175	16,900	15,386	9,521	4,940	3,744	8,550	4,356	1,520	958
Above poverty level	8,985	14,721	13,321	9,939	2,763	2,154	5,884	3,741	1,756	1,943
Percent of population covered	9.7	12.0	10.7	8.8	22.4	19.3	20.3	7.8	6.3	9.0
Below poverty level	45.2	46.4	43.2	39.0	54.2	45.1	60.6	32.4	32.8	28.4
Above poverty level	4.2	6.5	5.7	5.0	10.9	9.6	10.3	3.9	3.4	6.8

[1] Includes other races not shown separately.   [2] Persons of Hispanic origin may be of any race.

Source: U.S. Census Bureau, *Current Population Reports*, P60-201, earlier reports; and unpublished data.

MEDICAID

Medicaid, Title XIX of the Social Security Act, was created in 1965 as part of President Lyndon Johnson's Great Society plan to improve education and **health care**, and eliminate **poverty**. Under the plan, each state develops its own health care program for the poor within specified federal guidelines. The state and federal governments then share program funding.

Medicaid provides all medically necessary services for those persons living below the poverty line, and to pregnant women and children under the age of six who may be somewhat above that line. It may also be used to supplement Medicare coverage for low-income elderly patients. In 1997 about 33% of all children under six and all adults above 85 years of age received at least some Medicaid.

Because of the flexibility allowed to each state, there are major differences, nationally, in coverage. In some places, Medicaid may require deductibles or co-payments of some of its recipients. Soaring costs for medical care caused Medicaid expenditures to more than triple in the ten years from 1987 to 1996—an increase much greater than the inflation rate—and Medicaid is now the largest program run by the state and federal governments to assist low-income families and individuals.

MEDICAL SOCIOLOGY

Medical **Sociology** is a sub-field within sociology that examines the social **organization** of medicine and the impact of social activity and circumstances on health and illness. Medical sociologists investigate (among other things) the social functions of health institutions and organizations, the types of social behavior that distinguish **health care** professionals and consumers, and identifies the consequences of particular social behaviors on physical and **mental health**. Delineation exists in the field between the application of sociological concepts to medicine, the sociological study of health and illness, and the sociological study of medicine and health care as a profession. The latter two are the predominant interests within the sociology of medicine, as the first is generally considered to be more a part of the medical than sociological arena.

Early sociological theorists saw their work as being in opposition to medicine, which was providing biological (and thus competing) explanations for human behavior. As medicine became a more significant social institution, it began to capture the attention of sociologists. Medical professionals have also paid more attention to the contributions of sociology to their profession as they have increasingly recognized the role of social life in physical and mental health.

Medical sociology is now one of the largest specialties within the profession. The term itself first appeared in an article by Charles McIntire in 1894 (''The Importance of the Study of Medical Sociology''), but medical sociology has its true origins in the United States following World War II, when federal funding for sociomedical research increased significantly. The creation of the national Institute of Mental Health (under the National Institutes of Health, or NIH) spurred this growth, as it was one of the first NIH institutes to sponsor joint medical and social research.

Because of the importance of federal funding to the field, there has been pressure to direct much of the work towards findings that can be applied to medical practice and health care policy. Thus, medical sociologists often are marginalized from their more theoretically-oriented colleagues. However, theoretical work in the area began quite early with the publication of Talcott Parson's *The Social System* in 1951, which laid out Parson's functionalist **model** for **society**, and also included what he called the ''sick role.'' Parson's believed that the role of the patient-doctor relationship was different from other roles in a capitalist **structure** and served a unique function in his model. Many later theorists have asserted that Parson's sick role was the single greatest contributor to the theory of the sociology of medicine.

Theoretical traditions from other areas of sociology have made contributions to medical sociology. Followers of **functionalism**, which was popular in the early development of medical sociology, were influenced by *The Student Physician*, authored by Merton and his colleagues in 1957. Then in 1961, Howard Becker examined the **socialization** process of medical school students using **symbolic interactionism** in *Boys in White*. The introduction of symbolic interactionism into medical sociology resulted in a clash between these two schools of thought. Symbolic interactionism gained popularity for explaining micro-level processes, and was used to develop labeling theory, which was used heavily in the sociology of mental health and mental illness. In fact, some of medical sociology's greatest impacts in the field of medicine have been in understanding the role of social life in mental health and illness. The publication of *Being Mentally Ill* (1966) by Thomas Scheff solidified the use of labeling theory to examine mental illness from a sociological perspective.

By the late 1970s the use of symbolic interactionism declined with the increased used of complex quantitative analytic techniques that were better at describing macro-level phenomena. Macro-level analysis was (and probably still is) more appealing to federal funding agencies, which have been important institutions in the continued growth of medical sociology. Epidemiology, or the study of incidence and spread of **disease**, gained importance during this time.

Also during this time, **feminism** influenced sociology, and studies on gender differences in health and illness were increasing. Studies on the social stratification of health and illness were influenced by theories in feminism, social inequality, and **urban sociology**, and examined health differences by gender as well as by **race**, **ethnicity**, and class. Studies by Bruce and Barbara Dohrenwend (gender differences in psychiatric disorders), Catherine Ross and John Mirowsky (gender, race, and class differences), and Mervyn Susser (health care for the poor) were part of a movement in medical sociology towards greater recognition of social position and **culture** on health-related lifestyle and access to and attitudes toward health care and health care providers. This work has only gained in importance as behavior-related illnesses such as cancer and heart disease have become the leading causes of death for men and women, and of significant portion of health care expenditures.

Current issues in medical sociology continue in the tradition of examining the effects of **social stratification** on health and illness. Increased funding in AIDS research has extended the importance of sociology in medicine, in studying the social factors related to both HIV infection and compliance with the taxing pharmaceutical treatment for the disease. The changing organization of health care (particularly the growth of health management organizations, or HMOs) has resulted in renewed interest in the study of the health care profession.

MEDICAL-INDUSTRIAL COMPLEX

The medical-industrial complex refers to the explosive growth and penetration of profit- making corporations into medical services. The concept was discussed by Arnold S. Relman, editor of the *New England Journal of Medicine*, and physician Stanley Wohl in the early 1980s, in the same sense as the *military industrial complex*, signifying the extensive growth of industries in and around a particular social **institution** with a resulting **structure** of economic interdependence and consolidation of control. Corporations have become giant health care providers, and medical care has become a competitive, lucrative corporate endeavor, driven like other industries by profit and profitability.

Traditionally, medical care in the United States was delivered through a system of *fee-for-service*. Physicians went to medical school then opened offices for the private practice of their skills. Costs for care and treatment were paid out-of-pocket by clients to physicians, dentists, hospitals, and other professional **health care** providers. World War II, however, set in motion profound changes which changed the way health care was conceptualized and delivered. Primary contributors to the changing system included tremendous growth in technology and pharmaceuticals, a change in the major causes of death and **disease**, the burgeoning population and increasing life expectancy, and increasing **urbanization**, all resulting in exploding costs for care.

Obviously, this system worked for those who could afford to pay, but those who could not had to seek medical care through state and county facilities. In the 1950s and 1960s, the federal and state governments began to finance care for the poor and disadvantaged with such programs as **Medicare** and Medicaid. Both private and government insurance companies thus became *third party payers*, and regulations with accompanying paperwork proliferated.

By the mid-1960s, large-scale organizations began to emerge to deliver care in a different format. Health Maintenance Organizations (HMOs) were organized and encouraged group practice and pre-paid health plans. Corporate entities were already supplying many services required by health care professionals. Medical supply companies, hospital construction, laboratories, and insurance companies offered corporate entities an entree into the field and led to increasing control and *corporatization*. Sociologists Weiss and Lonnquist described corporatization as the increasing amount of corporate control of medicine through such practices as utilization and quality review and incentive payment structures. Other developments which enhanced corporate control were specialization and increasingly complex medical technologies.

Private, individually-owned hospitals and **nursing homes** had previously existed, but they were generally operated only as small scale enterprises. As costs escalated, it became more and more difficult for government to pay for these public programs. Paul Starr described the corporate transformation of American medicine as beginning in earnest in the 1960s with corporate chains purchasing hospitals, nursing homes, and other facilities. Public financing made health care an attractive investment for large scale corporate conglomerates. Acquisitions, mergers, and diversifications also brought in many additional services, such as emergency-care centers, substance abuse centers, medical offices and buildings, hospital restaurants and food services, and home health care services. Non-profit organizations also were forced to compete through consolidation and **adoption** of new management techniques. By the 1980s, health care had become big business, as corporations recognized the profit potentials within the medical field.

Of particular interest to sociologists are the social consequences of the corporate incursion into the medical field. Some major issues include changing roles and relationships of doctors and patients, loss of professional dominance for physicians, and the growth of consumerism. Various studies in **medical sociology** have indicated that medicine no longer has exclusive control over either the content or the context of its work.

Another area for sociological research involves the conflict of interest that often arises between the profit motive and the needs of the patient. Starr has noted that as corporate chains attempt to attract the paying patients with private health insurance and locate primarily in attractive areas and up-scale neighborhoods, the poor are excluded and must rely on shrinking and financially-strained government programs. As Stanley Wohl observed, the system requires both management and capital, but unlike other corporate enterprises, if **society** recognizes a right to health care, the trick will be to find the balance of public and private services and financing that will ensure equity of care for all citizens.

See also Health Care Systems

MEDICALIZATION

Medicalization refers to the process of providing a social or natural phenomenon with a medical designation and a medically based solution. Conditions such as pregnancy and menopause, sexuality, **drug abuse**, dying, and social deviance have been deemed illnesses that can be treated with medicine and/or scientific technology. According to the medical **model**, illness occurs when the body is inflicted with a **disease** that causes the body to malfunction. The process of medicalization turns conditions other than diseases into illnesses through the use of medical terminology.

The sociological model of illness extends the medical model by incorporating social structural and social psychological components. Sociologists contend that illness is not only biologically produced by microorganisms, but it is socially constructed through the process of labeling physiological and non-physiological conditions as abnormal.

The process of medicalization or labeling certain conditions as illnesses is a popular Western tradition according to Conrad and Schneider (1980), sociologists who have studied the medicalization process extensively. As the practice of treating disease has moved from the hands of lay healers who acquired their skills through experience to the hands of medical professionals trained in elite educational institutions, the use of medical designations has increased. Medical professionals diagnose and treat conditions such as mental illness, alcoholism, and sexual **deviance** with prescription drugs and modern medical techniques. The days of women bearing children in the comfort of their own home are all but gone. Pregnancy, like death, is perceived to be a condition requiring medical treatment which can only be administered by a licensed or certified medical practitioner.

So, what is the function of medicalization? Conrad and Schneider (1980) presented a critical analysis of the medicalization of deviance in *Deviance and Medicalization: From Badness to Sickness*. According to the authors, four primary explanations justify giving non-medical conditions a medical designation. First, Western cultures extraordinary faith in science and technology contributes to the medicalization process. Societies that rely heavily on science to solve problems are more likely to use science as a means of solving non-scientific problems. A recent example of this trend is the questionable use of medication to treat childhood hyperactivity and attention problems and the use of prescription medicines to treat alcoholism and cigarette addictions.

Second, medicalization has grown out of the credibility and autonomy of U.S. medical professionals. Physicians dominate the practice of healing through the use of medicine; therefore, when a medical doctor says a particular condition requires medical treatment **society** tends to agree. The dominance of physicians is closely connected to the third explanation. The practice of medicine is highly profitable. The more ailments and conditions that receive a medical designation, the more money hospitals, medical practitioners, insurance providers, and pharmaceutical companies are able to make. Therefore, the process of medicalization is spurred on by the nature of **capitalism**.

Last, medicalization serves as an explanation or justification for treating conditions that are socially unacceptable and in need of **social control**. Medicalization allows for the treatment of non-normative behavior that majority view as harmful or undesirable by the majority. Freund and McGuire's research, in *Health, Illness, and the Social Body* indicates that **homosexuality**, schizophrenia, and menopause are conditions that have been medicalized as a means of social control. The medical designations given to physiological and non-physiological conditions that are not necessarily brought about by disease is a sociological process with structural and psychological components. Structurally, the process of medicalization impacts how illness is defined and how society manages illness. Psychologically, the labeling process influences the self-image of labeled individuals and how they deal with their illnesses.

MEDICARE

Established in 1965 as Title XVIII of the Social Security Act, Medicare is a government sponsored medical insurance program that primarily serves the elderly. It is automatically pro-

Growing number of Medicare beneficiaries
Millions of Hospital Insurance and/or Supplementary Medical Insurance enrollees, 1966-2017

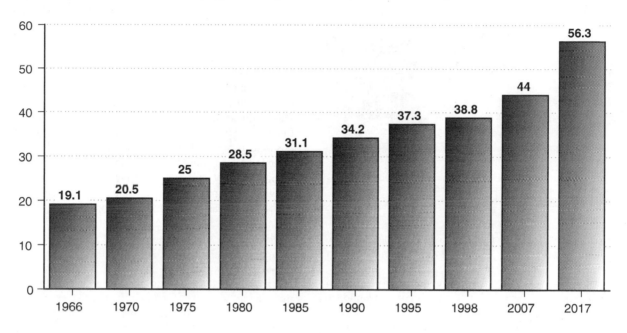

NOTE: Numbers for 2007 and 2017 are projections

Source: "Medicare Chart Book 1998," Health Care Financing Administration; "Medicare Enrollment Trends: 1966-1998," June 30, 1999, Health Care Financing Administration

vided to Social Security beneficiaries and to a relatively small number of people with **disabilities**. Persons not automatically eligible may also choose to enroll by paying premiums as in private insurance plans.

The program is financed by working Americans through mandatory payroll deduction; employee and employer split the premiums equally. This arrangement is identical to Social Security in that people are essentially paying into a trust fund that will insure their future **health care**. The benefits, divided into Hospital Insurance and Supplemental Medical Insurance, provide for physician and home nursing care and are used annually, in varying degrees, by over 85% of all enrollees which includes about 95% of all U.S. elderly. In the 1990s it became possible to be part of a Health Maintenance Organization while on Medicare. HMOs often provide services, such as eye and dental care, that would not normally be covered by Medicare.

The Department of Health and Human Services is responsible for the operation of the program. **Medicaid**, a similarly named federal program, is actually run much differently and is designed to serve the poor. At times, however, there is crossover between the two plans.

MEN'S STUDIES

Men's studies is a relatively new research sub-field within the sociology of gender which focuses on the way men's gender affects their social life and social position. It is usually conceptualized as complimentary to women's studies, in that they both attempt to draw out the unique aspects of gender from the gender-neutral human assumed in previous research. Men's Studies is rooted in the politics of the pro-feminist men's movement, which supports the basic tenets of **feminism** and embraces the goal of eliminating men's privilege over women. It has also been influenced by the gay liberation movement, which has in part called for a redefinition of appropriate **masculinity**.

In his 1987 article, "A Case for Men's Studies," Harry Brod defined the field generally as the "study of masculinities and male experiences in their own right as specific and varying social, cultural, and historical formations." Brod argues (as do others before him) that earlier research has treated men's experience as universal, thus making invisible the experiences of women as well as men's experiences that are specifically male. Men's studies is designed to study men as a gender, not as a gender-neutral, universal manifestation of humanity. Rather

Sociologists contend that abnormal behavior be evaluated not so much by its effect on the individual as by society's response to the behavior *(Custom Medical Stock Photo, Inc.)*.

than using men as the referent group to which women are compared, men and masculinity are treated as problematic gender concepts.

Men's studies is not a tightly-organized collection of work with a specific origin, and its legitimacy in academic **sociology** is still scrutinized within some circles. It grew rapidly in the late 1970s through the 1980s, developing alongside **women's studies** as an increasingly valid area of scholarship. Significant contributions have been made to men's studies by Michael Kimmel (masculinity and **identity**), Michael Messner (masculinity and sport), Tim Beneke (men's perspective of rape), R.W. Connell (masculinity and sexuality), and Harry Brod (masculinity through history).

Resistance to men's studies programs in sociology departments has come from two fronts. From mainstream sociology, critics have argued that men's studies, along with women's studies, are trivial areas of research that provide negligible contributions to the whole of sociological knowledge. From feminist sociology, critics contend that all areas of inquiry that do not specifically study women are really studies of men, and thus anything that is not women's studies is in fact men's studies. Proponents of men's studies respond to the latter criticism by pointing out that, while research that does not explicitly center on women is in fact research on men, this research treats men's gender as natural rather than problematic. As for the former criticism, the sociology of gender is one of the largest fields of study in the profession, and as a sub-field with the study of gender, men's studies will likely continue to grow in importance.

See also Gender Studies; Women's Studies

MENTAL HEALTH

Sociologists expect societies to include diverse groups of people. But while diversity is anticipated, it is also expected that the **society** will display patterns of behaviors that sociologists

consider to be normal for the society. Those behaviors are identified as **norms**. Behaving in accordance with the norms, the populace will interact as they go about their family, social and business experiences. Mental health becomes an interest of sociologists when individuals within a society fail to behave in ways that are considered normal or when they violate the society's norms for behavior.

In his late nineteenth-century study *Le Suicide*, Émile Durkheim became the first social scientist to scientifically study an abnormal social action, the act of committing **suicide**. Organizing his research around statistical procedures, Durkheim considered the **probability** of an individual committing suicide based on the individual's identification with various aspects of social **organization** that help build social norms. Included among those norm building agencies were the suicide victim's family **structure**, involvement in religion, business activities, and participation in political processes. In essence, it was not the act of suicide itself an act considered by most to be one of an individual in a state of poor mental health that Durkheim as a sociologist studied. It was the individual's incomplete social organization, specifically one lacking adequate norms (a condition describe by Durkheim as *anomie*), that Durkheim felt led to or might even have helped to predict the suicide.

Most of us have encountered people whose behavior we considered to be unusual, **abnormal**, or the result of a state of poor mental health. The sociological perspective requires that such unusual behavior be evaluated or judged not so much by its effect on the individual as by society's response to the behavior. The processes whereby society and the individual respond to each other contribute to the social structure of interest to sociologists. The value society places on mental health may be judged by how much money the society is willing to expend in sociological studies aimed at identifying and evaluating mental health needs. The expenditure of funds for such processes helps create and maintain what is called our mental **health care** system.

In his *Asylums* (1959), American sociologist Erving Goffman carefully examined the workings of our mental health care system. He analyzed the social processes in which patients confined to formal institutions engage as they construct new, but workable, social orders. Unfortunately, that study, considered by some to be critical of the system, was misinterpreted and was used to restructure and reduce the size of the system. For example, despite the fact that at least twenty million people, and perhaps in excess of thirty million, actually need some form of mental health care, the National Advisory Mental Health Council reported in 1996 that $245 per U.S. citizen was spent on mental illness, a decrease of one percent in funding since 1986.

Society's perception of poor mental health as a social problem is essential to understanding the sociological perspective of mental health. Due to their large numbers within society, mental health issues are statistically important. But despite their statistical importance, government and corporate America have turned their attention from mental health issues. Many medical insurance plans provide few benefits for mental health care. And, as stated, funding for mental health research and facilities is decreasing. Part of the work of sociologists is to familiarize the public with the dangers of social problems that may result from the declining importance that society places on mental health issues.

Sociologists have been able to measure some of the economic costs which results from poor mental health. Suicide, an act related to mental health, was estimated by the U.S. surgeon general in 1999 to have an indirect cost to the economy of $9.3 billion per year, or $233,337 per suicide. While poor mental health culminating in suicide may be an extreme example of the costs of society failing to deal with mental health issues, the point is that mental health problems are an expensive social problem that receive inadequate attention and support. One task of sociologists is to provide understandable and accurate information to the government and the public to assure that future funding decisions for mental health issues are made in the best interests of the society.

MENTAL ILLNESSES AND DISORDERS

Mental illnesses and disorders are serious problems for both the afflicted people and those around them. Several studies indicate the rate of mental illness has increased sevenfold since the end of World War II. A 1993 update of the Epidemiologic Catchment Area survey reported that approximately 22.1 percent of Americans had some kind of psychiatric disorder during that year and that 32 percent were at risk for serious mental illness at some point in their lives.

Mental illness takes two forms. Mental **disease** is commonly associated with mental illness that is organic in nature and results from chemical excess, deficiency, or imbalance. Mental disorder, or mental illness is induced by lived experience. While treatment of mental illness and disorder is the domain of psychiatrists and psychologists, issues surrounding mental illness and disorders are also partly the domain of sociologists because of their impact on the **society** in which afflicted individuals function and interact.

For the past fifty years, those sociologists ascribing to the theory known as **Symbolic Interactionism** have been most actively involved in studying the impact of mental disorders on the larger **social order**. The interactionist perspective differs from the perspective of most psychiatrists and sociologists who for the past one hundred years have based their theory and methods on Sigmund Freud. Simply stated, Freud theorized that most mental disorders arise from early interaction between a child and his or her parents. Interactionists maintain that mental disorder emerges from other factors as well. Included among these are failed or inadequate communications between individuals and society, failure of individuals to operate within what are considered social norms with that failure triggering ongoing and escalating negative social responses, and the reciprocal processes by which society labels individuals and the responses of individuals to those labels.

The interactionist theories of **deviance** and labeling help explain the sociological perspective on mental illness and dis-

order. As developed by Howard Becker, Edward Lemert, John Kitsuse, Martin Weinberg, and many others, theories of deviance generally maintain that ongoing internal conflict experienced by an individual who cannot conform to society's expectations (also known as **norms**) leads to displayed symptoms commonly associate with mental disorder. When the symptoms become too obvious or too objectionable to the general society, the individual is perceived to be mentally ill. Sociologists who develop **labeling theory**, postulate that in a similar process, society affixes labels, or names, to both the behavior of individuals, and to the individuals themselves, when they are perceived to be acting outside norms. The individual's response to being labeled, and society's response to the individual's initial reaction to having been labeled set off a series of interactions, driving the individual and society apart. The hypothesis here is the constant, mostly unsatisfactory interaction between the individual and society produces the behavior that is identified as symptomatic of mental disorder.

Other sociologists have contributed to the sociological study of mental disorder, particularly **Erving Goffman** and Thomas Scheff have contributed to public awareness. Their contributions have directly shaped public policy and **government** funding directed at the treatment of mental disorder. In his 1961 book, Asylums: Essays on the *Social Situation of Mental Patients and Other Inmates*, Goffman depicted the social processes in which sufferers of mental disorders engage. In Asylums he traced the patients' progress from diagnosis to commitment to mental institutions. Then he explored the secondary social systems such patients develop while incarcerated in asylums. Thomas Scheff, in his 1961 *Being Mentally Ill* similarly traced the life of the mental patient, exploring processes of being labeled ''mentally ill'', the deviance related to the labeling process, and the institutional organization and medical and psychological processes involved in maintaining the mentally ill. Unfortunately, these works were grossly misinterpreted by important politicians.

Legislators, first in California and then throughout the United States, used these works to justify drastically altering and disassembling important parts of the system. While critical of the existing system, both sociologists had clearly identified in their initial and subsequent works the methods by which society might contribute to the improved treatment and through which society would, in the long term, be better served. Unfortunately, due mostly to financial considerations, the legislators chose to disassemble much of the old structure without implementing recommendations, the result being even worse conditions for individuals suffering mental disorders, and greater problems for the society the sociologists intended to help.

MERITOCRACY

Michael Young was the first to use the term meritocracy in his 1958 book *The Rise of the Meritocracy, 1870-2033*. Here, meritocracy referred to a form of **government** by those considered to be the highest achievers in terms of **intelligence** and effort. Young's work projects to the year 2033 and anticipates the extreme consequences of a meritocratic system in which **equality of opportunity** is implemented and social strata develop accordingly. His predictions serve as a warning that such a system institutionalizes inequality as much as a system based on some ascribed characteristic. A meritocracy has come to be understood as a social system in which rewards are distributed on the basis of achieved characteristics such as ability and effort, rather than ascribed characteristics such as **race**, gender, age, or any other inherited advantage. In such a system only those who achieve **status** through merit (e.g., ability or effort) are deserving. Those who achieve status through means other than these (e.g., inheritance) are not meritorious and do not deserve their advantages. Interestingly, social scientists have yet to agree on reliable measures of merit. Part of the reason is that the educational system, accepted as representing the ideals of equality of opportunity, often reproduces the inequalities found in **society** on the basis of ascribed characteristics such as race, gender, and social class.

MERTON, ROBERT K. (1910-)
American sociologist

Robert K. Merton was a sociologist, educator, and internationally regarded academic statesman for **sociology** in contemporary research and social policy. He was also a leading interpreter of responsible functional analysis, of major social factors in scientific development, and of underlying and unanticipated strains in modern society. He is considered the founder of the sociology of science.

Born in Philadelphia on July 5, 1910, Robert Merton was educated at Temple University and received his doctorate from Harvard University in 1936. After being attracted to sociology by George E. Simpson, he studied with or was profoundly influenced by such thinkers as George Sarton, Pitirim Sorokin, Talcott Parsons, and L. J. Henderson. An instructorship at Harvard was followed by a professorship at Tulane University. From 1941 until his **retirement** in 1978 he was one of the key figures in the development of the Department of Sociology at Columbia University and in received national and international recognition for his contributions to sociological analysis.

As a consequence, Merton held a number of important positions, among them associate director of the Bureau of Applied Social Research at Columbia University, trustee of the Center for Advanced Study in the Behavioral Sciences at Stanford University (1952–1975), and president of the American Sociological Association (1957). He received several prestigious awards: one for distinguished scholarship in the humanities from the American Council of Learned Societies (1962); the Commonwealth Award for Distinguished Service to Sociology (1970); a MacArthur Prize Fellowship (1983); and the first Who's Who in America Achievement Award in the field of social science and **social policy** (1984). In 1985 Columbia University honored him with the Doctor of Letters degree.

Though Merton studied a considerable range of social situations and social categories or groups, his basic and endur-

ing contributions to sociological analysis consist of three complementary themes. First, human behavior can best be understood as embedded in social structures (groups, organizations, social classes, communities, nations) which simultaneously present opportunities and constraints to their members. Second, in varying degrees individuals confront differing clues and ambiguities in social demands, and thus humans develop mixed or ambivalent **values** and motives in their responses to others. Consequently, sociologists cannot focus on either formal, official patterns (**rules**, laws, etc.) or the special features of individuals to understand the course and variations in important social structures. Third, because of this pervasive complexity in social experience, normal or "routine" social behavior typically generates multiple consequences, some predictable and desirable, but others largely unanticipated and even contrary to the intentions of many persons. On the whole, then, Merton advocated careful and yet imaginative study of social phenomena and cautioned against superficial, "common sense" investigations and slavish dependence on any technique of probing human social participation.

More specifically, Merton combined study of actual (or historically significant) social organizations and groups with a focus on some limited but crucial and recurring problem in social structures—the so-called "middle range" problems and related explanations. One such focus was social specialization and related issues of differences in responsibilities, types and complexity of social contacts, and cultural interests. Merton distinguished "local" versus "cosmopolitan" types of leaders and showed how such differences underscored meaningful differences in influence. Similarly, Merton connected different levels of **status** with availability of different forms of personal influence ("reference groups") and linked the process of changing one's status—social mobility—with the selection of new reference groups ("anticipatory socialization") in the cases of soldiers, voters, and some nonconformists.

Another cardinal issue was **socialization**, the process of acquiring and sustaining legitimate roles in given social organizations. In this respect Merton studied medical students, intellectuals, scientists, bureaucrats, and various professionals. He and his associates gave much attention to the conflict between ideal goals and personal status concerns, and even to the "normal" inconsistency between accepted **norms** in academic training and the realities of "on-the-job" training of scientists and professionals.

Much of Merton's continuing sociological concern, however, centered on the twin sociological problems of social regulation and social deviation—each type of phenomenon necessarily **conditioning** the other. Merton inferentially demonstrated the basic fragility of such normal forms of social regulation as formal **leadership**, dominant cultural values, and professional standards. Furthermore, he pointed to such basic patterns as the variable consequences in behavior of imposing demanding objectives without providing suitable means; the fact that people often estimate their social opportunities and limitations not in objective terms, but in comparison with some desired level or with a self-selected "new" reference group (the source of the term "relative deprivation"); and the special and virtually unshakable advantage of persons in favored social positions (the "Matthew Effect"), which dissipates attempts at equalization and implicitly undermines the legitimacy of those in positions of responsibility.

After the mid–1960s Merton immersed himself in the sociology of science, the study of major cultural and organizational factors in the work of scientists (principally in the physical and biological sciences). This involved careful analysis of the careers of Nobel laureates, the processes of competition among scientists, the connection between publication and scientific investigation, and the problematic nature of discovery and acceptance in the sacred realm of science. However, Merton also demonstrated his intellectual versatility in a delightful spoof of scholarship in his *On the Shoulders of Giants*. In retrospect, his entire intellectual career was notable for the flexibility with which he combined theoretical formulations, useful **typologies** and classifications, empirical investigations, and a concern for the practical implications of sociological work in modern society.

His major works include *Social Theory and Social Structure* (1949), and *The Sociology of Science* (1973). His collection of essays, *On Social Structure and Science,* was reprinted in 1996. In the introduction, the editor of the collection, Piotr Sztompka, wrote that Merton's work had "opened up fruitful areas of inquiry along lines that he and generations of others would pursue for decades."

METATHEORY

Metatheory, also known as axiomatic **theory**, is the study of the underlying structure of **sociological theory** as well as the study of the use and applicability of sociological theory. Many have written in the area of metatheory, both in classical and modern theory, under a sociological banner and among the most familiar of the studies of sociological theory is the work of George Ritzer outlined in the 1991 book *Metatheorizing in Sociology*. Ritzer has outlined three varieties of metatheorizing: metatheory as understanding, metatheory as development, and metatheory as perspective creation. The point of differentiation among these types of metatheorizing is that each is typically undertaken with a different end point in mind. Ritzer intended these varieties to serve as ideal types while recognizing that most metatheoretical work could fit in multiple categories.

Metatheorizing with the intention of developing a more complete understanding of sociological theory is concerned with the studies of theories, theorists, theoretical perspectives and the social contexts which have given rise to the theories. The understanding form of metatheory is composed of four basic subtypes, the internal-intellectual, the internal social, the external-intellectual, and the external-social, all of which involve study of theory to attain a deeper understanding. The internal-intellectual subtype deals with attempts to highlight major cognitive paradigms and develop the metatheoretical tools with which to analyze and develop sociological theory.

Robert K. Merton *(Archive Photos, Inc.)*

The internal-social, concerned with the social factors of theory, focuses on the history of the predominant perspectives in the discipline and with the study of the career patterns and affiliations of the theorists themselves. External-intellectual aspects of metatheory embrace multi-disciplinary approaches and consider the impact of theories from other academic discipliners for sociological theory. Finally, the external-social approach deals with the effect that **society** has on shaping the theoretical approaches that come from it's members.

Metatheorizing as a means of theory development studies existing sociological theory with the intention of developing new or revised theories. Ritzer points out that most of the metatheory in **sociology** fits this type as much of the classical theories in sociology were formulated using combinations of existing work and writing to contradict or respond to established perspectives.

The third variety involves using metatheory as a source for creating sociological perspectives that encompass several existing theories. In this way, metatheory is a integrative force in sociology in that it attempts to pull together similar theoretical ideas into a coherent whole under a single banner such as "neofunctionalism" or "postmodernism". This type of metatheory attempts to compare theories relationally to determine the most accurate positioning in the theoretical landscape.

Although the amount and scope of metatheoretical work has increased over the last decade, this style of analysis is not without criticism. The more consistent criticisms of metatheoretical work involve claims that it is actually counterproductive to the theoretical process. Some have claimed that metatheory has stagnated at the point of general categorization of social theories and no longer serves any creative purpose, instead only serving to raise interesting, but ultimately unproductive and useless work. Also metatheory is criticized for focusing only on the critique of existing theory while failing to provide any unique theoretical ideas.

METHODOLOGY

Methodology refers to the set of rules and principles that guides the investigation of a research topic. To study various social phenomena, researchers must decide on the exact way in which they will gather information about a topic or how they will test existing theories or propositions about a topic. Researchers typically begin the research process by choosing a topic and formulating a specific research question. Next, they choose a methodology to identify how they will attempt to answer the research question. When researchers select a methodology, they move from conceptual thought to actual investigation of a topic.

Researchers generally choose either quantitative or qualitative research techniques to conduct their studies. Quantitative techniques are rooted in the principles of **objectivism** and **positivism**. The goal is that findings will emerge from the research process without **bias** from researchers' **values** and ideologies. **Quantitative research techniques** are detached, data-centered, and descriptive in nature. The most common quantitative techniques are surveys, analysis of existing **data**, secondary data analysis, and experiments.

Qualitative research techniques, by contrast, are individual- and group-centered in nature. Qualitative research is rooted in the principles of subjectivism and interactionism. The goal of qualitative research is an in-depth understanding of individuals' attitudes and behaviors, what **Max Weber** referred to as verstehen. The most common qualitative techniques are in-depth interviews, participant observation, focus groups, **content analysis**, and life history analysis.

Once researchers choose a research strategy and gather data, they then use either quantitative or qualitative methods to analyze the data. Researchers using quantitative techniques will use both univariate and multivariate statistical methods to analyze their data. These analyses allow researchers to determine trends and patterns in the data, relationships between variables, and differences among the individuals and groups under study.

Researchers using qualitative techniques will use more subjective methods to analyze their data. They will attempt to develop themes and highlight commonalties in their interviews with or observations of their subjects. The goal is a more in-depth understanding of the meaning that individuals and groups give to their attitudes and behaviors.

Ideally, a good research project will incorporate both quantitative and qualitative **research methods**. For example, researchers often conduct mail or telephone **surveys** and supplement with in-depth interviews or focus groups. Whatever the topic of study, it is important for researchers to be specific and systematic in the methodology used for the study.

METROPOLITAN STATISTICAL AREA

The metropolitan statistical area is a geographical area comprised of an urban center and surrounding area with a large population. The U.S. Census Bureau defines a metropolitan statistical area as consisting of a county or counties containing a city with a population of fifty thousand or more people. When an agglomeration of counties contain a single metropolitan statistical area or when a significant amount of commuting occurs between different metropolitan statistical areas, that area is referred to as a consolidated metropolitan statistical area.

The term is a functional definition for demographers studying population distribution as a way to delineate metropolitan and non-metropolitan areas. It is also used by urban sociologists to define the boundaries of the particular urban environment they wish to study. As the U.S. population has urbanized, using city governmental limits to determine the area of study is not a very useful **operationalization** because city life often extends beyond those boundaries (for example, as people commute from suburban residential areas to metropolitan employment areas). Metropolitan statistical areas take into account the extension of urban social relations beyond the borders of city limits, and the U.S. Census Bureau includes them in the **data** they collect for the decennial census as well as other **surveys** they conduct.

MEXICAN STUDIES

The study of Mexican **culture** is relevant for many reasons. First, Mexico reflects the early globalization and colonization of the Spanish-speaking world. Second, Mexico reflects a large range of peoples, including Native Americans, Europeans, Asians, and a mixture of many of these races. Thirdly, the history of Mexico is closely tied to our own. From colonization to independence, we have similar experiences. Understanding Mexican culture helps us understand our own culture and history.

One of the first groups of *Latinos* to demand studies programs on the college level were Mexican Americans, or *Chicanos*. In the 1960s, Chicano students throughout California petitioned and protested for Chicano studies programs. They wanted better opportunities for Chicano students, a curriculum that was less Eurocentric, and more *Chicano* professors. At the same time, African-American and **Women's Studies** were gaining ground in much the same way throughout academia. This grassroots effort to include and empower a minority group in academia and assist Latino students has become a legitimate, established field of study and research that includes Mexican studies.

Like many ethnic studies, Mexican studies is designed to explore and understand a minority culture. Traditionally, academics have reflected European philosophy, literature, history, and politics, leaving out other ethnic groups. Mexican studies reflect the **philosophy**, literature, history, language, and social sciences related to Mexicans. Such programs are interdisciplinary, meaning they cross different academic departments. For example, a Mexican studies program might offer courses on contemporary Mexican authors, Mexican folklore, migrant worker conditions, Mexican figures in history, or a history of the Americas. The focus is not on one discipline, such as history or political science, but on an ethnic group and their contribution to history and culture.

A clear advantage of any type of multicultural study is teaching students to understand, expect, and acknowledge differing viewpoints. For example, courses on pre-Colombian Mexico give students a native perspective of Columbus' landing and the impact of the arrival of Europeans on this continent rather than the European perspective of exploration. Such a course may also demonstrate that history is incomplete and one-sided until multiple perspectives of the same event are explored. Acknowledging different perspectives also encourages students to question what they have learned and what they have considered cultural givens, which fosters independent thinking.

Students are taught to understand and appreciate Mexican culture rather than accept stereotypes. Many Mexican studies courses address images such as the snoozing Latino under a sombrero to demonstrate the creation and perpetuation of cultural stereotypes. Or they may catalog Mexican leaders and their contributions to the fields of entertainment, politics, and science.

Students of Mexican studies learn to value cultures other than their own by identifying myths in their education, thinking, and culture. Mexican studies programs prepare teachers for the diverse population they will meet in the classroom, and bilingual teachers are especially valuable as the Latino population in the United States grows. The world continues to get smaller and geographic boundaries are blurring. A global workplace will soon be a reality. In order to succeed in business, communications, government service, research, and teaching, cultural boundaries need to be understood and defeated. One of the best ways to do that is to delve into another culture and people, as is accomplished through Mexican studies.

MICHELS, ROBERT (1876-1936)
German sociologist

The German sociologist Robert Michels (1876–1936) wrote on the political behavior of intellectual elites and on the problem of power and its abuse. Robert Michels was born on January 9, 1876, in Cologne. He studied in England, at the Sorbonne in Paris, and at universities in Munich, Leipzig (1897), Halle (1898), and Turin.

While teaching at the University of Marburg, Michels became a Socialist. He was active in the radical wing of the German Social Democratic party and attended its party congresses in 1903, 1904, and 1905. Although he left the party in 1907, government opposition to his activities limited his academic career in Germany. He went to the University of Turin, Italy, where he taught economics, **political science**, and **sociology** until 1914, when he became professor of economics at the University of Basel, Switzerland, a post he held until 1926. He spent his last years in Italy as professor of economics and the history of doctrines at the University of Perugia and occasionally lectured in Rome, where he died on May 3, 1936.

Michels's involvement in German revolutionary causes gave him insights into trade unions, party congresses, demagogues, and the role of the intellectual in politics. His widely translated book *Political Parties* (German ed. 1911; English ed. 1949) is an analysis of pre-war socialism in Germany, with examples also drawn from political protest movements in France, Italy, England, and the United States. In this and other writings he developed the hypothesis that organizations formed to promote democratic values inevitably develop a strong oligarchic tendency. His view on the nature of **leadership** was that, despite the original commitment to **democracy**, the demands of the **organization** compel the leader to rely on a **bureaucracy** of paid professional staff and to centralize **authority**. This process causes displacement of the original democratic goals by a conservative tendency to retain power at all costs as well as an unwillingness to have that power challenged by free elections. Michels called this theory the "iron law of oligarchy." He is criticized for failing to define "oligarchy," which some of his adherents have equated with the term "ruling class."

Michels compared working-class societies in Germany, Italy, and France and wrote about the political **culture** of Italy. He analyzed the Tripolitan War of 1911–1912 in terms of the suffering it caused and the impact of war propaganda. Italian **imperialism**, he believed, resulted from demographic pressure and from the social and cultural loss caused by overseas migration. His writings in the 1920s and 1930s dealt with **nationalism**, Italian socialism and fascism, elites and **social mobility**, the role of intellectuals, and the history of the social sciences. He often returned to the problem of oligarchy and democracy. Some critics describe him as a disappointed democrat whose disillusionment led him toward adopting elitism and made him comfortable with Italian fascism.

MILITARY SOCIOLOGY

Military **sociology** is primarily concerned with the ideologies, structures, policies, actions, and interpersonal relationships that constitute the armed forces and how these interact with civilian **society**. Aspects of the military generally spotlighted are organization, profession, disorganization, and civil-military relations. Although sociologists who specialize in military sociology tend to be prolific writers, the subfield is considered very small compared to the size and importance of the military institution. Reasons for this often cited include the liberal attitudes and pacifist beliefs of many sociologists and the semi-closed nature of military organizations. Theoretical and methodological approaches to American military sociology most often employed include structural functionalism, **conflict theory** (including **social stratification**), ethnomethodology, comparative **macrosociology**, and social **identity** theory.

Early social theorists, such as **Herbert Spencer**, Jacques Novicow, and Saint-Simon, contemplated the changing role of the armed forces in the modern world and often criticized the institution as outdated and imperialist. They generally predicted that industrialization would eliminate the need for warfare entirely. However, the unprecedented devastation and loss of life that occurred during World Wars I and II sharpened the interest of sociologists and other social scientists as they realized that the incidence and impact of warfare was increasing rather than disappearing. It was not until after WWII, when the *American Journal of Sociology* published a special issue on the military in 1946, that study of the military gained legitimacy as a subfield of sociology in the United States. Most early empirical studies were commissioned by bureaucratic organizations in response to the needs of the military to address problems of mobilization, morale, motivation, and adjustment. Once such study, conducted by **Samuel A. Stouffer** and colleagues for the Army Research Branch, surveyed attitudes and behavioral patterns of enlisted men in the early 1940s. The results, published in 1949 as *The American Soldier*, were influential in shaping an applied approach to military sociology. A great deal of military research was then and still is done by private corporations or military agencies, which are usually headed by interdisciplinary teams. Many of these studies were and are used for purposes internal to military organizations and remain unpublished.

Of the published sociological studies, a few stand out in breadth and influence. In 1957, Samuel P. Huntington published *The Soldier and the State,* which was hailed as the first major treatment of civil-military relations. Huntington, using a structuralist **model**, conceptualized the military as a profession that focused on the management of violence. Morris Janowitz enlarged on this idea with the publication of *The Professional Soldier* in 1960. He, like Huntington, concentrated on the military's shift from a fraternalistic, institutional environment to an individualistic, occupational one. Morris viewed his study as a group biography in an organizational setting, and the military organization as a creation of contemporary society. In addition to numerous journal articles and other publications, Janowitz wrote *Military Institutions and Coercion in the Developing Nations* (1977). In this work he used comparative analysis to examine the interplay between military forces and societal political processes and the relation of paramilitary agencies and police forces to the central armed forces of nation-states in Africa, Asia, Latin America, and the Middle East. The main focus of Janowitz's body of work was the analysis and impact of change on military organizations and military life.

Following the Vietnam War, a change from the draft to an All-Volunteer Force (AVF) in 1973 prompted a flurry of sociological attention. As after World War II, applied sociological approaches helped identify and solve personnel problems. Theoretical work on the changing role of the American military was also increasing. Charles C. Moskos' work incorporated a more pluralistic perspective and called for role expansion and redefinition of the military profession following the Vietnam War. He viewed the transition from conscription to the AVF as a clash of America's fundamental **values**, namely patriotism and obligation versus monetary incentives. Moskos, in *Peace Soldiers* (1976) and David Segal, in *Recruiting for Uncle Sam* (1989), examined the expansion of the role of the soldier to include disaster relief and peacekeeping missions, in addition to traditional combat missions. Along with his wife Mady, David Segal's work included the changing **structure** of families in military life and the work-family interface.

The advent of the AVF also resulted in increased attention to race, class, and gender issues in the military. Sue E. Berryman addressed the issues of **race** and class by challenging the perception of the military as an extension of the **welfare state**. In her 1988 publication *Who Serves? The Persistent Myth of the Underclass Army*, she found that most recruits came from middle to lower-middle class families and that they were highly educated when compared to their peer group. Berryman conceived of military service as opportunity for the otherwise disenfranchised (especially minorities) to secure legitimate careers. Mady Wechsler Segal, with her husband David R. Segal, studied the role of women in combat, women and career development in military institutions, and the problem of **sexual harassment**. The increased participation of female soldiers in the Persian Gulf War stimulated additional analysis. In *Camouflage Isn't Only for Combat* (1998), Melissa S. Herbert conceptualized the military as a gendered institution and examined how women dealt with a military environment that encouraged masculinity yet penalized those who were perceived either too 'masculine' or too 'feminine.' In addition to contemporary concerns, race and gender were also being reexamined historically. For example, in *To Serve My Country, to Serve My Race* (1996), sociologist Brenda L. Moore performed case studies of African American women who served in WWII. Other contemporary issues in military sociology include a focus on the nature of the armed forces in a post-Cold War world, the expanding role of the military in Eastern Europe and developing countries, and the downsizing of the armed forces in industrialized countries.

MILL, JAMES (1773-1836)
Scottish economist, journalist, philosopher, reformer, and historian

James Mill was born in Scotland in 1773 to a shoemaker. It was his mother's goal that Mill rise above his social **status**. Through her social connections, he met Sir John Stuart, who became a mentor and benefactor to young Mill, housing him and helping finance Mill's education at the University of Edinburgh. Mill first studied **philosophy** at the university and was especially interested in Greek philosophy. In 1798, he graduated as a licensed preacher but had little success in this career. He took up tutoring instead soon after.

In 1802, Mill traveled to London with John Stuart and began working as a journalist for the *Anti-Jacobin Review.* The following year he began working for the *Literary Journal.* In 1805, he married Harriet Burrow and began writing for the *St. James Chronicle.* A year later, his son John Stuart Mill was born, followed by eight other children.

Throughout the next few years, Mill slowly moved from a devoted, conservative Christian to an agnostic liberal reformer. One key influence during this period and indeed throughout his life was meeting **Jeremy Bentham** in 1808. Mill and Bentham, a leading Utilitarian of the times, soon became close friends and spent every evening together. Utilitarians thought that happiness should be sought after and that pain and suffering should be minimized not just for individuals but for the whole of **society**. Mill adopted Utilitarian principles and became a disciple of Bentham. Also in 1808, Mill wrote his first article for the *Edinburgh Review,* addressing social issues such as economics, law and religion, freedom of the press, and education. These issues were pressing to many English thinkers of the time, as corruption infiltrated the government, the Church, and the press. Education was inadequate, and the government was seen as undemocratic. Mill, Bentham, and other Utilitarians saw their social ideas as a program of reform and were interested in changing what they considered to be the sorry state of government and society. Mill assisted Bentham with his works *Table of the Springs of Action* and *Chrestomathia.*

Mill began writing a series of articles for *Encyclopedia Britannica* in 1814 and would continue writing them for the next nine years. These articles were a chance to lay out his theories on subjects such as education, government, and liberty of the press. At this time Mill turned to his original interest in philosophy. In fact, these articles were key in making **Utilitarianism** a philosophy rather than a method of reform. Mill sought to influence thinking men of England and the general public with his theories. He succeeded: the articles were so popular among young philosophers that they were reprinted as a series and adopted as a bible for radicals of the time.

In 1819, Mill published *History of British India,* to which he had devoted 12 years of work. The success of this publication earned him a job at India House as an assistant in the area of India correspondence. Despite his work as a journalist, this is the first salaried position Mill held. It was a substantial enough salary that he could fully devote his free time to develop his philosophy.

The result of his dedication was his first philosophical treatise *Analysis of the Phenomenon of the Human Mind* published in 1829. This treatise laid out the psychological basis for Utilitarianism and the concept that sensation and stimuli control the thinking and actions that we classify as the concepts of belief, imagination, judgement, will, etc. Although the theory of associationism was first laid out by Aristotle, Mill's work is still regarded as an important description of associationism and human behavior. Other publications include *Elements of a Political Economy* (1820), articles for the radical quarterly the *Westminster Review* (1823-1826), which he and Bentham formed, and articles for the *London Review* (1825-

John Stuart Mill *(The Library of Congress)*

1836). These articles, published anonymously due to his position at India House, include subjects that continued to be important to Mill: education, the Church, and the government. "On the Ballot," "Aristocracy," "Formation of Opinions," and "Law Reform" are especially significant and point to Mill's goal of practical reform and his concern with the immediate problems of England. In 1835, Mill published *Fragment of Mackintosh,* in which he explained that **morality** is based on utility. Just as Mill's own philosophical beliefs developed from **conservatism** to radical Utilitarianism, he helped move Utilitarian thought from a practical idea of legal reform to political creed and finally to a philosophy. This was his contribution to British philosophy.

MILL, JOHN STUART (1806-1873)
English reformer, philosopher, and politician

Son of philosopher and reformer **James Mill**, John Stuart Mill began his career as a philosopher at a young age. He helped edit many of his father's and Jeremy Bentham's works and helped educate his sisters. The oldest of nine children, Mill was born in North London in 1806. Educated at home by his father and Bentham, Mill learned Greek, French, and Latin at a young age and was encouraged by his father to argue every idea presented to him. He did just that when he began to argue against the Utilitarian ideas his father promoted.

In 1823, Mill was hired by his father's employer, the East India Company, as a junior clerk. He worked there for thirty-five years, working his way up into management. Meanwhile, he wrote essays for *The Examiner* and *The Westminster Review*. These early essays reflected the ideas held by James Mill and **Jeremy Bentham** and were radical, reformist, and Utilitarian. From 1865 to 1868, Mill was a Member of Parliament, where he argued for women's legal and social equality, for Irish independence, and a national security system. Mill died of consumption in 1873 having gained respect as an important intellectual.

In 1831, Mill met Harriet Taylor, a married woman, an intellectual, and the person Mill said was the inspiration for his work. Their twenty-year friendship and, after Taylor was widowed in 1849, their consequent marriage in 1851 was one of the great love relationships of the nineteenth century. Inexperienced himself in sexual matters, Mill later credited Taylor with having helped him to see how oppressed women were in Victorian **society** and in marriage.

In 1826 after a serious mental breakdown, Mill re-evaluated his Utilitarian education. He turned to William Wordsworth's poetry, and its emphasis on feeling redirected Mill's thinking toward issues of oppression and social injustice. While James Mill, Jeremy Bentham, and **Robert Owen** believed that character could be shaped by outside forces, they did not address the possibility that a persons could change by their own desire or initiative. Mill believed individuals deserve absolute freedom to develop as they choose. Mill explored the idea of **custom** and by pointing out evidence that customs are culturally and temporally defined, he made the case that custom is not innate but rather consists of those behaviors which a society is conditioned toward and individuals are led to expect. The customs of a certain place and time shape individuals from birth, artificially encouraging certain traits while discouraging others. Thus, as people mature, they are forced into certain roles and patterns of behavior which over time are assumed to be natural. While it is understandable that within a certain society prevalent patterns would seem ''natural,'' it is nonetheless the case that normative behavior is acquired and not inborn. Without using the word, Mill was explaining social **conditioning**. As a young man, Mill participated in disseminating information about birth control, and as a member of the House of Commons, he was the first man to speak in Parliament on behalf of women's rights.

In his essay *On Liberty* (1859), Mill explained the tyranny of the majority and how important men of genius and idiosyncrasy are for guiding less enlightened and more conforming others. The rule of the majority, Mill believed, threatened individual liberty. Similarly, conformity works against the development of natural, inborn talents. Since individuals cannot know what they are suited for unless they are free to experiment, absolute freedom ought to be available for every person. In a society in which perfect equality of opportunity and rights is the case for all, individuals will develop as they are so inclined and the society will benefit from their contributions. Any oppression of a group denies the whole society of the contributions from that group's members. *On the Subjection of Women* (1869) explores specifically gender-linked oppressive social patterns. Here Mill made the startling analogy of marriage to slavery, continuing the argument begun by **Mary Wollstonecraft**, in her *The Rights of Woman*, that the goal of marriage ought to be complete equality and friendship and yet as long as husbands have absolute control of wives, friendship is not possible.

A gentleman and a scholar, Mill was first and foremost a moral thinker. He envisioned a world of equality and freedom in which individuals could choose their paths of development and the rest of society would be enriched by their contributions. Living in accord with his precepts, he signed a prenuptial agreement with Harriet Taylor, pledging never to exercise his legal rights as her husband. Though married to Mill, Taylor retained possession and control of her estate, an act on Mill's part of conspicuous fairness and equality in a time when custom and law defined all a bride's **property** as the possession upon marriage of her husband.

In later life, Mill moved from a laissez-faire economic **theory** toward socialism as he realized that **government** must take a more active role in guaranteeing the interests of all of its citizens. The greatest sadness of Mill's later years was the unexpected death of his wife in 1858. He took a house in Avignon, France, in order to be near her grave and divided his time between there and London. He won election to the house of Commons in 1865, although he refused to campaign. He died on May 8, 1873.

MILLS, C. WRIGHT (1916-1962)
American sociologist and political polemicist

American sociologist and political polemicist C. Wright Mills (1916–1962) argued that the academic elite has a moral duty to lead the way to a better society by actively indoctrinating the masses with **values**. On August 28, 1916, C. Wright Mills was born in Waco, Texas. He received his bachelor's and master's degrees from the University of Texas and his doctorate from the University of Wisconsin in 1941. Subsequently, he taught **sociology** at the University of Maryland and Columbia University and during his academic career received a Guggenheim fellowship and a Fulbright grant. At his death, Mills was professor of sociology at Columbia.

Mills has been described as a ''volcanic eminence'' in the academic world and as ''one of the most controversial figures in American social science.'' He considered himself, and was so considered by his colleagues, as a rebel against the ''academic establishment.'' Mills was probably influenced very much in his rebellious **attitude** by the treatment his doctoral mentor, Edward Allsworth Ross, had received at Stanford. Ross was fired from Stanford in 1900, largely, it is thought, because he urged immigration laws against bringing Chinese coolies into America to work on railroad building. (Stanford was funded primarily by monies from a railroad which employed such labor.) The firing of Ross spurred the movement for academic freedom in the United States under the leadership of E. R. A. Seligman of Columbia University. Ross then went on to Wisconsin, where, together with John R. Gillin, he built up one of the broadest sociology departments in the nation and where Mills was one of his early doctoral students.

Mills emerged as an acid critic of the so-called military-industrial complex and was one of the earliest leaders of the New Left political movement of the 1960s. Against the overwhelming number of academic studies, Mills insisted—and this is the central thesis of virtually all of his works—that there is a concentration of political power in the hands of a small group of military and business leaders which he termed the "power elite." Essentially, what he proposed was a cure for this immoral situation is that this power be transferred to an academic elite, a group of social scientists who think as Mills did.

As to how the power is to be transferred, Mills was not too clear, as he died before he was able to complete a final synthesis of his thought. In general, he maintained that the academic elite already wields the power but that it is subservient to a corrupt military-industrial complex which it unthinkingly serves simply because it is the going system, the establishment. The task, then, is to convert the academic elite through moral suasion or a kind of "theological preaching," as one sympathetic critic has commented. A major reason why the academic elite unwittingly serves this complex is the elite's behavioral approach, its commitment to value-free social science. In the past, conservatives have attacked the academic **intelligencia** on the same grounds, that it has been immoral not to inculcate moral values.

Now Mills and the New Left made the same criticism, although in the interest of rather different moral values. Mills and his followers argued that the so-called value-free commitment to analyze "what is," that is, the existing system, automatically buttresses that system and—since the system is wrong—is thus immoral. In a sense, then, as one commentator has observed, what Mills's program amounts to is: "Intellectuals of the world, unite!"

Mills's analysis of political influence has received a much more favorable response. Mills, like a number of earlier writers, as far back as Plato and as recent as Walter Lippmann, perceptively pointed out that eminence in one field is quickly transformed into political influence, especially in a **democracy**, where **public opinion** is so crucial. Thus, movie stars, sports stars, and famous doctors use their fame to secure elections or political followings. However, there is no rational basis for this, since competence is related to function. If one functions as a film actor or doctor, that does not mean that he has political wisdom. Mills thus advocated his social science elite to replace such corrupt manifestations of the existing system, thereby calling into question many of the fundamental assumptions of democracy. He advocated a **community** of social scientists, similar to Plato's philosopher-kings, throughout the world, but especially in the United States, and this elite would wield power through knowledge.

MODEL

A model tends to function in much the same way that analogies and metaphors do. A model is any representation of one abstract concept by another. The representation, through conceptualization and explanation, approximates and/or offers a more simplified version of reality. Sociologists commonly utilize models for both theory building and statistical analysis.

The term model is often deemed synonymous with theory. That is, models are typically theory driven. In fact, models and theories alike seek to simplify reality through conceptualizations that facilitate explanations. For example, in **sociology**, **rational choice theory** is considered to be a simplified model of reality. In short, rational choice theory posits that human behavior may be explained by individuals' rational thought processes. So, through the conceptualization of rational thought processes, human behavior may be explained.

Models are also very important for statistical analyses. In statistical regression, for instance, models take the form of linear equations. These equations estimate or model the relationship between the given variables. Moreover, linear **regression** models predict the value of a given **variable** Y, knowing X. Since the true relationship between the given variables is rarely ever known, statistical models are important tools for sociologists.

MODERNIZATION THEORY

Modernization **theory**, a body of scholarship within **sociology** that originated in North America in the 1950s, was concerned with **social change** and industrialization in Third World societies. Since the post-World War II period newly-independent nations in Asia and Africa and older republics in Latin America were not developing substantial industrial growth, sociologists began to explore the preconditions for such social change. Modernization theory makes up some of the earliest work in the field of **sociology of development** and was strongly influenced by the **functionalism** of **Talcott Parsons** as well as by the political context of the Cold War.

The fundamental tenet of modernization theory is that all societies follow the basic same path of gradual social change toward modernization. W. W. Rostow's (1960) book on **stages of development** argued, for instance, that less developed nations were undergoing a process of social change similar to that of European countries prior to the **Industrial Revolution**. Many of these nations had yet to reach the take-off stage, where industrialization, urbanization, and cultural change would transform them. Presumably, preconditions for this transition required greater contact with the cultural **values** and economic expertise of industrialized countries. Like work influenced by functionalism, modernization theory posited that social change would occur at a single pace throughout all of society's systems: its economic production, its cultural values, its **social order**, and its political system.

Taking the capitalist transformation of Europe as a **model**, these scholars posited that as nations urbanized and develop industrial capacities, they would also adopt modern and meritocratic social systems, rational cultural orientations, and democratic political institutions. Early works on the European transition to **capitalism** within a functionalist perspective were especially influential. Neil Smelser's *Social Change and the Industrial Revolution*(1959) developed a seven-step model of increasing structural differentiation and emphasized the interplay between new ideas and economic innovation as driving forces in social change.

Moreover, Weber's *Protestant Ethic and the Spirit of Capitalism*, posited that **rationalization** was both a prerequisite and an outcome of modernization. Modernization scholars, therefore, developed schemes, like Hoselitz' (1960), that differentiated the ideal characteristics of traditional and modern societies. Modern societies were differentiated, democratic, universalistic, and meritocratic. **Traditional societies** were undifferentiated, authoritarian, particularistic, and based rewards on ascriptive characteristics. Scholars, like Bellah (1957), studied the impact of Western values on traditional societies. Other scholars dealt with the apparent co-existence of these dual ways of life in Third World societies. Oscar Lewis (1963) studied how slum dwellers in Third World cities maintained value-systems that were not conducive to integration into modern social relations; their "culture of poverty" prevented them from becoming modern.

Modernization scholarship has been strongly criticized since its inception, most notably by scholars associated with **Marxist sociology** and with dependency theory. Scholars like **C. Wright Mills** (1959) criticized modernization theory and functionalism more generally for being inherently conservative. Others criticized modernization theory as providing justification for U.S. foreign policy (Cardoso and Faletto, 1979). A branch of the sociology of development critical of modernization theory grew out of criticisms of the theory's failings. Beginning with Baran's (1953) *Political Economy of Growth*, dependency scholars questioned the idea that there would be one path for all nations. Instead, these scholars argued that current relations between industrialized nations and less developed countries would tend to maintain their underdevelopment. Other scholars, like Frank (1969) and Cardoso and Faletto (1979), also questioned the causal order and model of social change of modernization arguments. It was argued that an empirical examination of Third World societies would reveal that modern values, institutions, and economic relations did not change in concert. Taylor (1979) and Quijano (1977) strongly questioned the **dualism** of traditional and modern that modernization theorists proposed.

Modernization theory ceased to be influential in development sociology by the 1970s, but some of its concepts, like the irrevocable chasm between traditional and modern worldviews, have been occasionally revived in reference to the Islamic world by scholars like Huntington (1996) who predicted a "clash of civilizations" between the modern West and Islamic traditional societies. Other scholars, like Putam (1993) drew some inspiration from Modernization ideas about the importance of values in promoting economic development.

MONEY

One of the earliest sociological discussions of money can be found in Karl Marx's 1844 manuscripts. In opposition to

Hegel, who saw the realization of human personality in private **property**, Marx looked upon money as the alienated self of its possessor. First, money transforms qualitative differences into quantitative differences and substitutes interchangeability for individual uniqueness. Second—and here Marx anticipated Max Weber's discussion of the spirit of capitalism—the saving of money is only possible on the basis of deferred satisfaction and enjoyment. "The less you are, the less you express your life," Marx concluded, "the more you have, the greater is your alienated life and the greater is the saving of your alienated being." Finally, human capacities are determined by money rather than wealth by human capacities. "What I am and can do," Marx suggested, "is therefore, not at all determined by my individuality. I am ugly, but I can buy the most beautiful woman for myself.... I am lame, but money provides me with twenty-four legs."

Georg Simmel's discussion of money is more ambivalent. On the one hand, he shared many of Marx's concerns about the alienating effects of money. In his view, monetization has a leveling effect on social life, rendering it impersonal and "colourless." The mediation of social interaction through money spreads egoism and rational calculation, changes the pace of life, and distances human beings from other persons, from objects, and from nature. On the other hand, if people in modern societies are able to "secure an island of subjectivity," it is because "money relieves us to an ever-increasing extent of direct contact with things, while at the same time making it infinitely easier for us to dominate them and select from them what we require."

The pessimism of these earlier sociological studies of money was tempered by **Talcott Parsons**, who emphasized the integrating and enabling functions of money in modern societies. Parsons divided social systems into four analytically distinct and functionally specialized subsystems: the economy, the polity, the societal **community**, and the fiduciary system. Each subsystem, Parsons suggested, produces resources necessary for the other subsystems and receives in return the resources for its own functioning. These interchanges may involve real entities such as goods and labor, but exchanges that are symbolically mediated through money allow more flexibility. Parsons suggested that money is an instance of a more general phenomenon and that there are other symbolic media that are like money in their capacity to allow flexible market-like exchanges between subsystems. These include power, which Parsons defined as the generalized capacity to bind and direct others on behalf of collective goals and influence, which is the generalized capacity to persuade; and generalized value-commitments. Parsons suggested that these other symbolic media share many of the same features as money. In addition to being symbolic, they can be used to acquire a variety of goods, they are not committed to particular uses, and they are subject to inflation and deflation depending on how confident people are that they are backed by the real capacities they symbolize.

While Jürgen Habermas borrowed much from Parsons, he reincorporated many of the earlier concerns of Marx and Simmel. Like Parsons, Habermas also saw money (and power)

as symbolic steering media that help to integrate complex, modern societies. These steering media "stabilize nonintended interconnections of actions by way of functionally intermeshing action consequences." Money and power, therefore, ease the burden on actors who must otherwise coordinate all of their actions through **language** and mutual understanding. However, Habermas argued, integration through language remains necessary in some areas of social life, such as cultural reproduction and **socialization**. Money and power become harmful and destructive when they undermine and supplant integration through language in these areas, a process that Habermas calls the "colonization of the lifeworld."

More recent studies in the **sociology** of money have questioned many earlier assumptions. Viviana Zelizer, for example, has challenged the notions that money is interchangeable, impersonal, substitutes instrumental calculation for ties of **social solidarity**, or leads to cultural disenchantment. Through a careful examination of domestic, gift, and charitable money, she showed how money embodies cultural meanings and is subject to social influences and constraints, how people "earmark" monies for specific purposes, and how the appropriate uses of the "multiple monies" thereby created have been challenged and contested over time.

Contemporary sociologists have emphasized the integrating and enabling functions of money in modern societies *(Archive Photos, Inc.)*.

MONOGAMY

Monogamy is the practice of being married to only one person at a time. It is the most common form of **marriage** in the world, by far, and in many places is the only accepted form. In most cultures **divorce** or death of a spouse are acceptable preconditions for **remarriage**; in fact, some people divorce and remarry many times, a process called "serial monogamy."

Along with legal prohibition and societal disapproval of **polygamy**, economics is another factor in the predominance of monogamy worldwide. Having more than one spouse requires greater wealth and has historically been reserved for kings and queens. Some famous stories of polygamy occur in the Bible. King Solomon and Jacob had multiple wives, but modern adherents to Judeo-Christian faiths reject the practice, by and large.

In the United States monogamy has been the only legal form of marriage except for a few decades when polygamy was practiced by Mormon church members. Public opinion was opposed to the idea, however, and the Mormons moved west to avoid persecution. Divorce has become much more common in the United States in the last fifty years, but although people remarry more often, marriage itself continues to be defined as monogamous.

MONOTHEISM

The word monotheism is derived from the Greek words *monos*, meaning "only," and *theos*, meaning "god". Thus, monotheism refers to any religion which asserts only one god exists separate from the world. A monotheistic religion be-

lieves in a personal god, one that is directly involved in man's physical and temporal world while remaining distinct from it. **Judaism**, **Islam**, and Christianity are monotheistic religions. **Christianity** bridged a gap between pantheism (that is, the belief in many gods) and monotheism. The trinity, or god in three persons, presented an image that pantheists were accustomed to envisioning while also continuing Judaic monotheism by asserting that this god with three aspects was one. Ancient Greeks and Romans were polytheistic. They worshipped a **community** of gods (imagined more as superhumans) who formed a pantheon. Within this world of gods, one god was supreme. Zeus, a dominating god, was known as "president of the immortals" in Greek mythology. Greeks and Romans envisioned these immortals as having human-like emotions and conflicts. For example, these gods could be self-seeking, mean-spirited, and competitive. It took the Jews to develop an image of deity that was characterized in moral terms and who gave a divine ethical code to humans.

Archaeologists and archaeological anthropologists have determined that prehistoric peoples believed in a female god, a progenitor of the world. Thousands of tiny goddess statues have been found that suggest the earliest belief systems imagined god as a full-bodied female and that this connection occurred because females were to able to bleed without injury, that these periodic bleedings were somehow connected to lunar cycles, and that they were able replicate the **race** by giving birth. The connection of female reproductive cycle with a heavenly body may have initiated belief in gods who inhabit the sky. It may be correct to say that **indigenous peoples** who live close the earth tend to be polytheistic because they invest natural phenomena with spiritual or divine essence, whereas the industrialized West has mainly embraced the monotheistic Judeo-Christian traditions.

Other systems exist besides polytheism and monotheism. Henotheism concentrates on one god but includes appreciation for other gods. Henotheism can also be the worship of one god that is identified by different names at different times. For example, Vedic Indians call their god Indra, Mitra, or Varuna. Pantheism is another way of thinking about a supreme being. In this system, god is imagined as a part of the universe. Pantheism asserts that god permeates the created world. By contrast, deism envisions a single god as separate from the physical universe, not a part of it. Moreover, monism shares the monotheistic tenet of one god, but asserts that this unity encompasses the physical as well as the spritual and lacks monotheism's emphasis on the personal nature of God.

MONTAGU, ASHLEY (1905-1999)
English anthropologist

A wide-ranging intellect whose more than sixty books—including several non-fiction bestsellers—covered a vast array of topics, Ashley Montagu was an intellectual maverick often shunned by the academic community for his unorthodox ideas. Although an anthropologist by training, he nevertheless wrote about such diverse subjects as human anatomy, **marriage**, crying, swearing, and prehistoric man. Despite the eclecticism of his interests, Montagu maintained that there was a common theme to all of his work. "[My] major interest," he told an interviewer, "is the relation of cultural factors to the physical and behavioral evolution of man."

Ashley Montagu was born Israel Ehrenburg in the working-class East End section of London in 1905. Although claiming at times that his father was a successful stockbroker in London's financial district, Montagu was in fact the son of Jewish immigrants from Russia and Poland and his father was a tailor of modest means. In 1925, he graduated from the University of London, with perhaps that institution's first ever bachelor's degree awarded in physical anthropology. After studying briefly at the University of Florence in the late 1920s, he earned his Ph.D. from Columbia University in 1937, studying under the pioneering anthropologist of the day, **Franz Boas**.

Montagu began his career as a museum researcher and curator, working at the British Museum of Natural History and the Wellcome Historical Medical Museum from 1926 to 1930. His teaching career began at New York University, where he served as assistant professor of anatomy from 1931 to 1938. For eleven years after that, he worked as an associate professor of anatomy at Hahnemann Medical College and Hospital in Philadelphia. From 1949 to 1955, he served as chair of the anthropology department at Rutgers University. Over the course of his career, Montagu lectured at a number of universities in the United States, including the New School for Social Research (now New School University), the University of Delaware, the University of California at Santa Barbara, and Princeton University. Yet for all of his extraordinary output of books, he never achieved tenure anywhere, a discrepancy some say was due to his unorthodox ideas, especially those concerning the equality of the races and sexes.

Indeed, in scholarly circles, Montagu was best-known for his iconoclastic approaches to **race** and gender. Race, he argued in *Man's Most Dangerous Myth* (1942), was neither a legitimate category by which to understand humankind nor did it offer any real clues to a person's innate character or **intelligence**. In *The Idea of Race* (1965), he took this notion further, denouncing virtually all accepted social and biological ideas about race then prevalent in the academic community. His work on gender issues was, if anything, even more controversial. In perhaps his best-known book *The Natural Superiority of Women* (1953), Montagu put forward the idea expressed in the title, arguing that males were in fact physically, intellectually, creatively, and financially less capable than females. Yet his emphasis on the fact that women were superior because they possessed two X chromosomes contradicted his work on race, where he maintained that genetics were far less important than environment in shaping human potential.

Montagu's controversial ideas, his accessible writing style, and his demeanor as the quintessential eccentric professor made him a popular academic figure in the media. He was a regular guest on "The Tonight Show" with Johnny Carson and other **television** talk shows. He died at the age of 94 in 1999.

MONTESQUIEU BARON DE (1689-1755)
French philosopher, jurist, and satirist

The French jurist, satirist, and political and social philosopher Charles Louis de Secondat, Baron de Montesquieu (1689–1755), was the first of the great French men of letters associated with the Enlightenment. In order to understand the Baron de Montesquieu, one must look back to the age of Louis XIV. During his long reign, Louis XIV had attempted to assert the absolute authority of the Crown over all aspects of French life and to make France supreme in Europe. Although the Grand Monarch achieved success in many of his endeavors, both his attempt to impose cultural and religious unity and his unsuccessful wars provoked sharp reactions that continued throughout the eighteenth century. It is within this milieu that Montesquieu must be understood.

Charles Louis de Secondat was born on January 18, 1689, at the castle of La Brède near Bordeaux. His father, Jacques de Secondat, was a soldier with a long noble ancestry, and his mother, Marie Françoise de Pesnel, who died when Charles Louis was seven, was an heiress who eventually brought the barony of La Brède to the Secondat family. As was customary, the young Montesquieu spent the early years of his life among the peasants in the village of La Brède. The influence of this period remained with Charles Louis, showing itself in his deep attachment to the soil and in his rustic Gascon accent.

In 1700 Charles Louis was sent to the Oratorian Collège de Juilly, at Meaux, where he received a progressive education. Returning to Bordeaux in 1705 to study law, he was admitted to practice before the Bordeaux Parlement in 1708. The next five years were spent in Paris, continuing his studies. During this period he developed an intense dislike for the style of life of the capital, which he later expressed in his *Persian Let-*

ters. In 1715 he married Jeanne de Lartigue, a Protestant, who brought him a large dowry. He was also elected to the Academy of Bordeaux. The following year, on the death of his uncle, Jean Baptiste, he inherited the barony of Montesquieu and the presidency of the Bordeaux Parlement.

Montesquieu had no great enthusiasm for law as a profession. He was much more interested in the spirit that lay behind law, that is, the meaning, development, and variations of established laws and their relationship to customs and history. It is from this interest that his greatest work, *The Spirit of the Laws,* developed. To free himself in order to continue his scholarly interests, Montesquieu took little concern in the routine of the Bordeaux Parlement and eventually sold his office as president in 1721.

Montesquieu's early works were concerned with what would now be termed biological investigations. From these studies emerged Montesquieu's interest in the effect of environment on men. During this same period Montesquieu devoted a good deal of time to reading highly popular travel literature, including the newly translated *Arabian Nights* and Morana's *Spy of the Great Mogul in the Courts of the Christian Prince*. The combination of this reading and Montesquieu's own critical attitude toward contemporary manners led him to write the first of his great works, *The Persian Letters*.

The Persian Letters (1721) sparkled with wit and satirical irony, but hidden beneath its deft irreverence was a fierce and bitingly critical view of European **civilization** and manners. The work takes the form of letters to families and friends at home from three Persians traveling in Europe. Their letters are commentaries on what they see in the West. Montesquieu endowed his travelers with the foreign, commonsense understanding necessary to effectively criticize European (French) customs and institutions, yet he also gave to his Persians the foibles and weaknesses necessary to make his readers recognize in them their own weaknesses. All facets of European life were criticized. Louis XIV was "a great magician"; the Pope "an old idol worshiped out of habit"; great nobles achieved their status by sitting on chairs and possessing ancestors, debts, and pensions. Beneath the wit was the message that **society** endures only on the basis of virtue and justice, which is rooted in the necessity of human cooperation and tolerance.

Although the *Letters* was published anonymously, it was quickly recognized as the work of Montesquieu and won for him the acclaim of the public and the displeasure of the regent, Cardinal André Fleury, who held up Montesquieu's induction into the French Academy until 1728. In the same year Montesquieu began the first of his extensive tours of Europe, which brought him from Italy to Holland to England (in the last country he was elected to the Royal Society). After his return to Bordeaux in 1731, Montesquieu began his study of the history of Rome. By 1734 he had finished his *Considerations on the Causes of the Grandeur of Rome and Its Decline*. Though less well received than *The Persian Letters* —Voltaire referred to it as less a book than an ingenious table of contents—the work was less a history than an attempt to get behind history to the general secular causes of events.

According to Montesquieu, Rome achieved greatness because of the martial virtues of its citizens and the flexibility

Baron de Montesquieu *(The Library of Congress)*

of its institutions, which could be modified to correct political and social abuses. Rome's failure to maintain these characteristics once it acquired an empire marked the beginning of its decline. The development of imperial despotism, epicurean tastes, and the rejection of commerce only hastened the decline of Roman grandeur. Montesquieu's history may not have been scientific in the modern sense, but despite the criticism leveled against it, it was his search for general causal factors that helped to lay the basis for the **secularization** of historical studies.

Fourteen years after his study of Rome, Montesquieu brought his search for the general laws active in society and history to its completion in his greatest work. Published in 1748, *The Spirit of the Laws* was not an analysis of law but an investigation of the environmental and social relationships that lie behind the laws of civilized society. Combining the traditions of customary law with those of the modern theories of natural law, Montesquieu redefined law as "the necessary relationships which derive from the nature of things." Laws, and their most basic political expression, government, thus became a relative relationship between a people's physical environment and their social needs and traditions. Although the basic substance of laws—"reason in action"—remained generally the same under all circumstances, their concrete expression varies according to time and place. Laws "must be adapted to each peoples."

Montesquieu's work was an attempt to study the process of adaptation. Thus, the diversity of laws was viewed as natural and desirable. The best legislator was one who pragmatically adjusted law to the physical and social conditions confronting him. Within this framework Montesquieu defined the basic types of **government**, identified the dominant virtues associated with each, and stated his most widely known concept of the balance of powers as the best means of establishing and preserving liberty.

An aspect of *The Spirit of the Laws* that has often been overlooked by its commentators is its role in the controversy over the legal rights of the autonomous groups in France following the death of Louis XIV. The last five books are an analysis of medieval French history, designed to prove that, to protect the liberties of the nation and the inviolability of the law, autonomous judicial bodies—the *parlements* of France— possessed independent or "intermediary" powers to thwart the natural despotic tendencies of an absolute monarchy. This aspect of the work helped to lay the basis of the eighteenth-century movement for constitutionalism, which culminated in the Revolution of 1789. In this sense, Montesquieu's most fundamental thesis may be viewed as an attempt to indicate the necessity of judicial review. *The Spirit of the Laws* was immediately acclaimed as one of the great works of French literature. Following the completion of his work, Montesquieu, who was going blind, went into semi-retirement at La Brède. He died on February 10, 1755, during a trip to Paris.

MORAL DEVELOPMENT

Moral development can be described as the process of incorporating a set of **values** that governs behavior in a manner that promotes human welfare and cooperation. Psychologists have employed numerous standards to critique a person's moral aptitude, including criteria based on cognitive evaluation (moral judgment), emotional attunement (empathy and caring), and the internalization of social **norms** (habits). Considerable debate exists among social scientists regarding the nature of **morality** and moral development. Theorists can be divided into two basic camps: relativists and universalists. While relativists look to environmental and cultural factors, universalists believe that a standard set of moral principles exists that transcends cultural issues.

The relativist standpoint is best represented by Albert Bandura in *Social Learning Theory* (1977). This theory of social learning focuses on environmental stimulation, such as reinforcement, punishment, and observational learning, as the impetus for developing moral aptitude. Morality is linked to the values of the local **community** and **society**, which determines both acceptable and unacceptable social behavior. According to Bandura, children are affected by a variety of behavior models, and norms are internalized based on the pattern of reinforcement and punishment for compliance and noncompliance, respectively.

Although social learning theory has generated serious discussion among theorists, the contemporary study of moral development has been dominated by the universalistic approach of **Lawrence Kohlberg** and his cognitive-developmental theory, which was first introduced by **Jean Piaget** in *The Moral Development of the Child* (1932). Focusing on the maturation of a child's moral judgment as the gauge for moral development, Piaget suggested that the process was characterized by three progressive stages: amoral (little understanding of **rules**), heteronomous (rules are followed because they are dictated by **authority** figures), and autonomous (personalized acceptance of rules as a means to a organized society).

Piaget offered four defining characteristics of the three cognitive stages of moral development. First, a qualitative difference exists between each stage. As individuals **progress** through the stages, they may come to the same conclusion regarding a moral dilemma, but the processes by which they arrive at their decisions will be different depending on the stage level. Second, the sequence of the stages is invariable. Although the pace of progression through the stages will vary, all individuals master the first stage before moving to the second, and the stages must be completed sequentially. Third, each individual possesses an underlying cognitive structure that denotes an organized framework for processing information. Thus stage level is not determined by isolated responses to stimuli but is indicative of the cognitive process as a whole. Finally, the stages are structured hierarchically. The amoral stage is most primitive, the heteronomous stage is more advanced, and the autonomous stage is cognitively supreme.

Building on Piaget's work, Kohlberg first introduced his cognitive-developmental theory in "Stage and Sequence: The Cognitive-Developmental Approach to Socialization," which appeared in *Handbook of Socialization and Theory* (1969). Kohlberg suggested a more complex scheme and offered a fuller description of the process that, unlike Piaget's analysis, accounted for moral development into **adulthood**. Kohlberg postulated that moral development occurred in six stages, with two stages at each of three levels: preconventional, conventional, and postconventional. Like Piaget' system, Kohlberg's stages are sequential and hierarchical, and both theorists considered moral development as a completely rational activity. The progression of moral judgment mirrored the progress of intellectual development.

In the first stage of the preconventional level, moral understanding is dictated by punishment and obedience. A child makes decisions based on an attempt to avoid punishment. The second stage in the preconventional level is called instrumental. The child acts on self-interest but begins to comprehend reciprocity; the child may share one toy in order to gain access to another child's toy.

At the beginning of the conventional level, moral judgment in the third stage is determined by a good boy/good girl understanding. A child can comprehend what behavior is expected and will gain approval and acts accordingly. The fourth stage is considered the law and order stage. Moral codes become a personally accepted part of the **social order**; therefore, moral behavior is a reward in itself as one fulfills a moral duty to abide by social rules.

At the final, postconventional level, the fifth stage is characterized by an understanding of **social contract**. Moral decisions are based on a combination of internalized values and a sense of moral responsibility. Social rules are seen as serving a utilitarian function of creating a system of social order. By the time an individual reaches the sixth and final stage of moral development, all moral judgment has been sufficiently internalized so that all moral behavior is founded on universal ethical principles, which stem solely from the individual's own conscience.

Since Kohlberg introduced his cognitive-developmental theory, the majority of discussion on moral development has either been a variation of, or a reaction against, Kohlberg's theory. Numerous criticisms have been leveled against Kohlberg and his followers. First, critics suggest that the cognitive-developmental model is biased in both cultural and gender perspectives. According to dissenting social scientists, the Kantian framework of Kohlberg's theory that holds reason as supreme is heavily weighted to Western thought as the purest thought form, and his universalistic laws of stage development do not account accurately for other cultural situations. Challenging Kohlberg on the issue of gender bias, **Carol Gilligan** in *In a Different Voice: Psychological Theory and Women's Development* (1982) argued that the cognitive-developmental theory is more descriptive of males than females and pointed to Kohlberg's early research that used male-only sample groups for testing. Gilligan offered an alternative **model** that accounts for moral reflection from two different foundational perspectives: justice and caring. She argued that women tend to operate from the caring model, whereas men operate from the justice model.

Another major argument lodged against Kohlberg is his presumption that moral judgment is intricately linked to moral behavior. Knowing the difference between right and wrong and acting on that knowledge appropriately is a more complex process that engages the whole individual and must account for the impact of the both personal self-identity and the surrounding social environment, argue Kohlberg's critics. Relying completely on the cognitive development of moral judgment, Kohlberg ignores the impact of emotions and passions as indicative of moral sensitivity, motivation, and character. In an outright rejection of Kohlberg's premise that moral reasoning is essential to moral behavior, Martin L. Hoffmann argues that moral action arises from the development of empathy, which is the main motivation for pro-social behavior. Hoffmann suggests that although moral reasoning may be involved, it is not necessarily a determining factor in moral activity.

Despite the theoretical and methodological criticisms against Kohlberg's cognitive-development theory, an alternative theory has yet to replace it as a generally accepted formula for moral development. Work on the horizon in the field suggests a turn toward a more comprehensive understanding that incorporates the cognitive, emotional, and social elements of human development of moral standards in a manner that correlates specifically to moral behavior.

MORALITY

Morals are conceptions of right and wrong. Ethics is the value system within which judgments or behaviors are practiced with reference to morals. Morality is the state or character of ethical conduct and is typically a subject of **philosophy**. **Sociology** engages morality in three ways: in discussions about sociology's role, in the ethics of sociological practice, and as a subject of sociological study.

The first sociology, begun and named by August Comte, was conceived during discussions of a science of morality. Comte's religion of humanity concerned the conditions impeding **social order** and the steps needed to protect or restore it. Comte conceived of sociology as a science of advancing harmony. Sociologists, in particular, have since questioned the existence of universal norms, and a search for objective morality was ceded, appropriately, to philosophy. Belief in a transcendent origin of moral principles and attempts to discern such principles from science have given way to the idea that absolutes are constructed in a functional or even utilitarian fashion. The principles themselves are no less significant or impactful for having been socially constructed, indeed, construction imbues them with social life and **status**. The construction may, as E. O. Wilson contended, have a biological origin which would enable scientific exploration for identifying moral codes and better construct consensus. Sociologists, in contrast, seek a social origin of morals. **Karl Marx**, for example, placed morality under his critique of capitalist superstructure. Marx also critiqued the role of intellectuals and questioned whether ethical arrangements could be achieved through science rather than practice.

Rather than as a tool for achieving morality, science is seen by some as an opposing force. Reactions to Comte involved debates about Max Weber's value-free sociology and the need to distinguish sociological study of values from conduct which implements or prefers **values**. Weber distinguished value reference from value judgment. Scientific facts can support, though never validate, ethical values. Further, we in part want research to be guided by morality. Concerns about science acting contrary to morality, or in accord with an unacceptable morality, have brought morals to bear upon scientific practice. Early experiments raised ethical questions about the propriety of relationships between sociologists and their subjects. But ethical dilemmas of sociology are more extensive and more subtle than the moral issues raised by code of ethics.

Because the results of social science may raise contentious issues and have political impact, the need for reliability and clarity is high. Ethical behavior in sociology (as in any science) thus also includes sharing of results, clarity of records, and disclosure of results contrary to expectations. These needs, such as of protecting confidentiality and preventing harm, are balanced with needs for observation and understanding. As a result, sociology, like science generally, has its own ethics, its own morality. Research ethics include guidelines for sociological practice as well, the application of sociology to addressing **social problems**: Results ought not be selective or otherwise biased, should not be inferred beyond the population studied, and should not be construed as implying a moral judgment.

Morality is not only a guide, but an aspect of social life worthy of study in itself. Right and wrong entail variable social facts. Early studies of morality conceived of it in the abstract, addressing its presence or absence, weakness or strength, prerequisites and impediments. But in a remarkable twist on early discussions of sociology and morality, the sociological study of morality has become thoroughly scientific. That the presence and meaning of morality are contingent has been carried to a propositional state by Donald Black. The strategy extends from work in the tradition of Émile Durkheim, who emphasized social life as an enunciation of morality, an expression and reinforcement of widespread psychological states, and a source for moral order.

Rather than focusing on the fundamental distinctions of what is right and what is wrong, a Durkeheimian approach observes transgressions whenever there is a sanction. Moral life, from this perspective, is understood as the distribution of expressions of grievance not by individual behavior but by responses to it. Moral order, according to M. P. Baumgartner, is the patterns of those responses which constitute the behavioral framework of right and wrong. Morality shifts and is distributed according to social structure, and Black's **model** accounts for this distribution and behavior. Morality is no longer understood as something fundamental but as something useful, not as something persistent and enduring but as a characteristic of the case, including the relative social locations of adversaries and the social distances between them. Black casts his explanatory strategy as an epistemological revolution in sociology in general, in particular, that revolution changes how morality is observed and measured because it reconceives the way in which morality is understood.

MORES

Mores (pronounced more-AYS) are the **norms** of **society** that have been deemed highly necessary for the survival of a society and of those living in it. These norms are designed to embody the most important principles held by society members. The term ''mores'' is often paired with ''folkways,'' the general customs and **rules** of daily behavior within a given society. Both terms were established by **William Graham Sumner** (1840-1910) when he created a classification scheme to designate which habits were established as a result of living in a given society (**folkways**) and which were moral imperatives for survival within that society (mores).

Mores refer to morally-based rules of behaving that most members of society believe are necessary to maintain an appropriate standard of decency within their unit. These rules surpass mere suggestions for appropriate behavior given by folkways. The violation of mores is typically met with fear, outrage, moral indignation, and severe sanctions including monetary fine, imprisonment, and in some cases, death. Common mores in **American society** inhibit cannibalism, incest, and the unjustified taking of a human life. While in some cases the violations can be justified and thereby overlooked (i.e. murder in self-defense, consuming human flesh to avoid starvation), these rules are vital for the continuity of society, and breaking them will nearly always bring on punishment.

Often mores derive from the same moral codes and beliefs as enforceable laws; therefore, overlap occurs commonly between mores and legal codes. While according to Sumner, mores and laws (defined as norms which are established and maintained by **authority** figures) are not synonymous, mores are quite often officially codified into laws. However, most laws do not constitute mores. For example, refusing to pay income tax to the U.S. Government, while a **crime** punishable by severe sanctions (i.e. large monetary fine, imprisonment), would not be considered violation of a more.

Finally, mores, like folkways, are culturally based. Each **culture** and society will its own value system by which to judge what is and is not considered a violation of these rules. For example, in the United States the practice of bigamy (having multiple spouses) violates a more regarding **monogamy** and would be met with considerable scorn and punishment by the society at large. However, in most societies, bigamy is an accepted practice. Therefore, any discussion of norms requires an understanding of the cultures involved and the purpose served by its mores.

See also Norms

MORGAN, LEWIS HENRY (1818-1881)
American anthropologist and ethnologist

An attorney by profession, Lewis Henry Morgan became an anthropologist and ethnologist, noted for his comprehensive theory of social revolution. He was born near Aurora, New York, on November 21, 1818, and graduated from Union College in Schenectady in 1840. He read for the law and opened an office in Rochester in 1844. Although Morgan concentrated on his law duties, he also became interested in the Iroquois people of western New York State. This interest grew into a lifelong championship of native Americans against white oppressors. Morgan began an exhaustive study of the Iroquois Confederation, especially the Seneca tribe, which adopted him in 1846. He surveyed their history, social organizations, and material **culture**, culminating in his 1851 publication *League of the Ho-de-no-sau-nee, or Iroquois.* It is considered to be one of the earliest objective ethnographic works.

Between his law practice and investments, Morgan accumulated a small fortune. In 1856, he attended a meeting of the American Association for the Advancement of Science. (In 1879, he would be elected president of the organization, the first anthropologist so honored.) After that meeting, Morgan decided to follow his anthropological interests in a scientific way. He had noted in his studies that the Seneca had a very different way of designating relatives than did white civilizations. The Seneca placed relatives such as uncles, cousins, nephews into a direct line that classified these kin as fathers, brothers, etc. Whereas white civilizations showed distinctions in the line of descent, the Seneca did not. In 1858, Morgan traveled to Michigan on a business trip. There he discovered that the Ojibwa tribe classified their kin in a manner very similar to the Seneca. If this system was characteristic of native

Americans, might it not hold true for all tribal civilizations? If the system was used for tribes in Asia, for instance, might not the Asiatic origin of native Americans be proven?

Thus began a far-flung investigation of kinship terms used by various peoples. Morgan began by sending questionnaires to likely informants. Evidence that he was on the right track came from as far as India. From 1859 to 1862, Morgan undertook four field trips in his quest to gather information on classification terms and other aspects of culture. His travels took him up the Missouri River to western Montana. Finally, in 1871, the results of his pioneer investigation produced *Systems of Consanguinity and Affinity of the Human Family,* an influential work that inaugurated the modern anthropological study of kinship systems as a basic principle of **organization** in most tribal societies. Morgan showed how widespread this classification system was in both the Old and New Worlds. It remains his most lasting contribution to the field.

Despite the importance of his pioneer work, many anthropologists today disagree with Morgan's conclusions. Morgan believed that this kinship classification system resulted from a "period of promiscuity" when it was not possible to distinguish father from uncle or son from nephew, for instance. Although marriage rules were later adopted, the old terminology remained in use and later still, according to Morgan, as societies became more civilized, distinctions were made between one's own immediate family and other relatives. However, anthropologists generally do not agree that a "period of promiscuity" existed in the development of the family.

From the kinship study, Morgan developed a theory of cultural evolution expressed in his most famous work *Ancient Society, or Researches in the Lines of Human progress from Savagery through Barbarism to Civilization* (1877), the first major scientific account of civilization's origin and evolution. Morgan stated that the three stages in human cultural evolution—savagery, barbarism, and civilization—resulted mainly from changes in the production of food. Savagery, Morgan's term for the hunting-and-gathering stage, was preagricultural. Barbarism was a period of settled agriculture and the making of pottery. The more advanced stage was **civilization**, an urban **society** with more advanced agriculture and marked by the invention of writing.

Lewis Morgan, who died in Rochester, New York, on December 17, 1881, believed that human evolution is essentially a single development from savagery to civilization and his emphasis on material factors in evolution caught the attention of **Karl Marx** and **Friedrich Engels**, who viewed Morgan's work as complementing their own. *Ancient Society* is viewed by Marxists as a classic work.

MOTHERHOOD

Motherhood is an historically and culturally variable status. Broadly defined, mothering involves caring for and nurturing others. Some theories of motherhood rely on biological arguments, claiming that women's mothering capacities are rooted in their genetic makeup.

In the United States, expectations of mothering have varied depending on prevailing economic conditions. When

Some theories of motherhood rely on biological arguments claiming that women's maternal capacities are rooted in their genetic makeup (*Field Mark Publications*).

women's labor is required outside the home, as was true during World War II, the importance of the mother-child bond is downplayed. On the other hand, when women are not needed in the paid workforce, motherhood and the mother-child bond is idealized.

Sociologist and psychoanalyst, Nancy Chodorow, in *The Reproduction of Mothering,* used pyschoanalytic **theory** to suggest that because women are the primary caretakers of children, they develop strong emotional bonds with their daughters, yet the bonds between mothers and sons are eventually severed in order to resolve the Oedipus Complex. Boys distance themselves from their mothers and thus form strong **ego** boundaries as part of the process of developing masculine identities. Girls do not develop these boundaries and thus are able to reproduce the mother-child bond with their own children.

Adrienne Rich, a feminist poet and essayist, made an important sociological distinction between motherhood as experience and as **institution**. The experience of motherhood can be a powerful one, connecting women to their bodies, their reproductive capabilities, and their children. Yet, the institution of motherhood with all its related expectations leads to oppressive conditions for women.

Patricia Hill Collins asserted that traditional scholarship on motherhood has focused on white, middle-class motherhood and does not adequately address the institution and experience of black motherhood. She articulated a tradition of bloodmothers and othermothers in African American communities in which the boundaries distinguishing biological mothers and other women are ambiguous. In such communities a network of bloodmothers and othermothers (grandmothers, sisters, aunts, cousins, and friends) shares responsibility for children. This responsibility includes temporary and long term child-care arrangements that, when necessary, can turn into informal **adoption**.

In addressing white, middle-class feminist theorizing about motherhood, Collins argued that it has assumed survival and material comforts for children and thus focused on psychological aspects of mothering. Women of color, because of various oppressions in the United States that lead to high poverty rates, high infant mortality rates, and environmental racism, have had to focus on fighting for the physical survival of their children and their communities.

MULTICULTURALISM

Multiculturalism is the acknowledgement, acceptance, and promotion of **cultural pluralism** within a diverse **society**. Culturally diverse societies may also be marked by a desire for cultural unity. For example, in the United States popular and political wisdom historically called for new immigrant groups to assimilate. This assimilation process involves the abandonment of an individual's native **culture** and language and the **adoption** of the dominant group's culture. Immigrants to the United States were expected and often wanted to adopt the English language and ''American'' culture (e.g. European history, middle-class lifestyles, Christian religion) as their own. Multiculturalism is the celebration of cultural diversity within a society; all cultures are valued and promoted.

Multiculturalism affects many aspects of social life including the workplace, entertainment, and the political arena. Much research in sociology and education and debate in the public sphere have focused on multiculturalism in one institution—education. Multicultural education incorporates many different cultures, languages, and histories into a school's curriculum. Multicultural education exists at every level of education including elementary, high school, and college. For example, instead of a school only offering European history, schools include African, Latino, Native American, and Asian histories. The school's curriculum may try to mirror the ethnic diversity of the student body. Some systems have special programs such as an African American history month or a special assembly on Native American cultures or the experiences and contributions of women. Other school systems may strive for a more inclusive curriculum throughout all academic subjects.

In addition, some schools offer core classes in languages to meet the needs of students from various ethnic backgrounds. These education promote cultural diversity, improve academic performance of minority students, instill ethnic pride and improve interethnic and interracial relations in the school and in the wider community.

Many social scientists are interested in improved interethnic and interracial relations. Social scientists have found that brief interventions can alter a student's racial attitudes. Curriculum interventions, such as reading a positive story about another ethic **group**, can help to develop more positive racial attitudes and tolerance. Although not all studies have had consistent findings, this area of social science research does point to the power of curricular and teaching methods in conveying positive racial attitudes.

Multicultural education is opposed by many within the fields of education and politics, as well as from many in the general public. These critics feel for children to succeed in the ''real world'' they need to share the language (e.g. English) and cultural standards of middle class America. Opponents feel that schools should stress a core curriculum, basic skills, and achievement. Some critics assert that emphasis on cultural diversity actually promotes segregation.

The multicultural perspective sees knowledge as reflecting the experiences, needs, and history of the politically dominant group. As a form of social activism, multicultural education challenges this knowledge production monopoly. Proponents feel that to be truly egalitarian all lifestyles and experiences must be valued and expressed.

MULTIPLE INDICATOR MODELS

Multiple indicator models, also known as structural equation models (SEM), are used in research that relies on non-experimental **data**. Areas as diverse as biology, education, and the social sciences have adopted structural equation models. Structural equation modeling is a composite multivariate technique encompassing several analytic procedures: multiple **regression**, path analysis, exploratory and confirmatory **factor analysis**, reciprocal causation, models with time-dependent data, and covariance **structure** models. Elements common to different varieties of structural equation models include latent and manifest variables, **measurement** error structures, reciprocal causation, simultaneity, and interdependence.

Use of structural equation models became popular in the social sciences with the release of Jöreskog and Sörbom's LISREL program in the 1970s. Several current popular computer software packages for running SEMs are Amos, EQS, Liscomp, LISREL, and Mplus. Most computer packages assume a minimum of mathematical training. They rely on path diagrams to translate substantive hypotheses into statistical models. Most beginning students quickly become familiar with multiple regression and path analytic applications. Recently, hierarchical models have been incorporated into the structural equation framework and vice versa. Referred to as second generation structural equation models, latent growth curve analysis, second-order factor analytic models, and SEMs with categorical data are expanding the uses of structural equation models.

SEMs are helpful to researchers when issues such as measurement fallibility, correlated error, and directionality of relationships between variables are of substantive interest. The most basic application of structural equation models involves multiple regression or **path analysis** between two or more latent (unobserved) variables, each measured by several (observed) variables. The steps in this application are as follows.

Theoretical relationships are translated into a mathematically oriented diagram of the relationships between the latent constructs and between the latent constructs and the observed variables. Unlike multiple regression, structural equation models permit assessment of the measurement properties of the latent variables. In effect, this means that in structural equation models, measurement error is explicitly modeled. Simultaneous equations are developed in the form of hypotheses about expected relationships. Data are organized in the form of covariance or **correlation** matrices. The covariances in these matrices become the primary analytic units. The program then estimates the parameters and reports a number of statistics.

One favorite procedure for testing a structural equation **model** is to examine the measurement part of the model and then assess the structural or substantive relationships between the latent constructs. Typically, latent variables or **variable** constructs, which represent some unobserved phenomenon, are linked to multiple measures or indicators of that phenomenon through a series of simultaneous equations. After conducting a confirmatory factor analysis to establish the plausibility of the linkage between indicators and constructs, the structural part of the model is then examined to determine whether the substantive hypotheses are borne out. The structural model takes the form: $\eta = B\eta + \Gamma\xi + \zeta$, where η and ξ are vectors of latent dependent and independent variables, respectively, B is the matrix linking latent dependent variables, Γ is the matrix linking latent independent variables to dependent variables, and ζ is the error term.

Researchers determine the adequacy of the model using a number of goodness-of-fit indices at various stages. Goodness-of-fit indices allow researchers to determine how well the original covariance matrix is reproduced by the covariance matrix based on the model with the parameter estimates. If the hypothesized model does not reproduce the covariance matrix very well, it is said that the fit of the model is poor. Otherwise, the fit is good. Basically, the relationship between measured variables and latent constructs, including the error structure, is assessed by testing the hypothesis that the covariance matrix has a particular form which is represented by the model provided by the researcher. Researchers attempt to reproduce the variance/covariance structure. This is the key principle underlying model-fitting in structural equation modeling. The statistical underpinnings involved in reproducing the variance/covariance matrix depend on the assumption that a linear equation represents the relationship between X and Y. This assumption is equivalent to comparing the variances and covariances of the Xs and Ys. The comparison, with increasing complexity, generalizes to the relationships between the latent variables and to the relationships between the latent and observed variables. The great advantage of structural equations is the explicit modeling of the several error terms, as well as the flexibility in examining reciprocal causal flows. In addition, with recent advances, structural equation models have been shown to be effective in modeling dynamic social processes found in longitudinal data.

MULTIVARIATE ANALYSIS

Multivariate analysis is a simultaneous investigation of multiple variables. In **sociology** a multivariate analysis is one way that social scientists understand **social problems**. The cause of a social problem may be attributed to many different factors. For instance, fertility or the number of children a woman has may be the result of the age at which she begins to have children, but age may not be the sole **variable** affecting the number of children a woman has. The number of years she spends acquiring education may be another factor. Whether the woman lives in a developed country or a developing country is another important issue and, similarly, if she lives in a rural community or an urban one. Other variables to consider are **race**, class, religion, and political affiliation. Considering as many variables as possible constitutes multivariate analysis. Thus, a multivariate analysis is an extension of a univariate (a single) and bivariate (two variable) examination. In other words, a multivariate analysis permits an examination of at least three or more variables.

Sometimes multivariate statistical techniques involve an analysis of independent and dependant variables. Most commonly, multivariate statistics are used for **regression** analysis; however, the level of **measurement** of a variable, particularly a **dependent variable**, will determine what kind of statistic is more appropriate for analysis, ordinary regression or logistic regression.

MUMFORD, LEWIS (1895-1990)
American philosopher

Lewis Mumford (1895–1990), American social philosopher and architectural critic, analyzed civilizations for their capacity to nurture humane environment. He emphasized the importance of environmental planning. Lewis Mumford was born in Flushing, Long Island, New York, on October 19, 1895. He attended Stuyvesant High School until 1912. He studied evenings at the City College of New York for five years but did not receive a degree. Instead he became a student of the cities, beginning with New York City, whose libraries, theaters, and museums were his academy. Later, he wrote a series of ''Skyline'' essays for the *New Yorker* magazine which were intimate visits to buildings and quarters of the city that illustrated New Yorkers' aspirations and failures in their continuing act of building and rebuilding.

In 1915 Mumford read Patrick Geddes's essays expressing an organic view of **society** and claimed Geddes as his men-

Lewis Mumford *(The Library of Congress)*

tor in the years after 1923 when they met. In 1916 Mumford gained experience in the labor movement by serving as investigator of the dress and waist industry. Briefly in 1917 he worked for the Bureau of Standards in Pittsburgh, testing cement. He served as a radio operator in the U.S. Navy in 1918. The following year he became an editor of *Dial* magazine and then went to London in 1920 to serve as acting editor of the *Sociological Review.* Returning to New York City, he wrote *The Story of Utopias* (1922).

The English utopian planner and advocate of garden cities, Ebenezer Howard, inspired Mumford toward an active **role** in city and regional planning. He helped organize the Regional Planning Association of America (1923) and served as special investigator for the New York Housing and Regional Planning Commission, beginning in 1924. He edited the pioneering regional planning issue of *Survey Graphic* (1925) and helped edit five volumes of *The American Caravan* (1927–1936). In city planning, he advocated the conservation of "green belts," with self-contained cities supporting residence, work, markets, education, and recreation. The new cities were to be constructed on a pedestrian's scale with organic coherence among the urban functions. As a city planning consultant, he forcefully urged such ideas throughout the world.

In his writing, Mumford tried to define the American conscience: its traditions and allegiances and the forces that periodically betrayed it. Louis Sullivan is the hero of *Sticks and Stones;* Henry Hobson Richardson is the hero of *The Brown Decades* and *The South in Architecture;* both men were gargantuan talents who wedded art and technology to give a distinctively indigenous form to American architecture. In his pioneering study *Herman Melville* (1929), Mumford disclosed his tragic sense of art and life. Art, he affirmed, is man's declaration against a universe that is "inscrutable, unfathomable, malicious . . . Not tame and gentle bliss, but disaster, heroically encountered, is man's true happy ending."

In *Technics and Civilization*(1934) and *The Culture of Cities* (1938) Mumford tried to show that artifacts are instruments of a civilization's cultural and social process and to examine architecture and machines in terms of the social conditions that nurture them. His thesis was that contemporary **civilization** must undergo a moral reformation to have the **quality of life** known to many earlier societies.

Soon after World War II erupted in Europe, Mumford, convinced that Adolf Hitler had to be defeated, joined Allen White's Committee to Defend America by Aiding the Allies. In *Men Must Act* (1939) he strongly urged military preparedness in the face of fascist aggression. In 1944 he published *The Condition of Man*, the third book in a series of publications he labelled "The Renewal Series." The 1950s were very prosperous for Mumford's literary works. His early books including *Sticks and Stones,The Brown Decades,* and *The Golden Day* were all republished in 1995.

After the war Mumford worried about the ruin of cities through wholesale urban renewal, the growing dominance of highways, and the military mind's domination of foreign and nuclear policies. In *Faith for Living,* he wrote that "in a world in which violence becomes normalized as part of the daily routine, the popular mind becomes softly inured to human degeneracy." He held visiting professorships at North Carolina State College, the University of Pennsylvania, and the Massachusetts Institute of Technology. In his most searching book *The City In History* (1961), he wrote, "We need a new image of order, which shall include the organic and personal, and eventually embrace all the offices and functions of man." *The City In History* was honored the National Book Award for nonfiction in 1962. In 1964, Mumford made six twenty-eight minute films based on *The City In History.*

In his much later work *The Myth of the Machine* (1970) he looks down upon technology, labeling the megamachine as the "guilty party." Mumford died in 1990.

MYSTICISM (OTHER-WORLDLY)

According to the Greek definition, mysticism refers to the "practice of those who are initiated into the mysteries." It also refers to the process of putting oneself into a direct relationship with God, or some other divine or unifying principle in life. The meaning of "mysticism" has become broadened to include magic, the occult, or other subjects which have esoteric natures. The topic has attracted some stereotypes, including the perception that mystics are impractical and revolutionary and that they spend the majority of their time alone.

Because of its nature, mysticism is difficult to study. Relatively few psychologists have researched the topic. During the 1600s and 1700s, Henry More (British philosopher and theologian, 1614–1687) and William Law (British clergyman, 1686–1761) wrote on mysticism. **William James** (American psychologist, 1842–1910) attempted to better understand the topic but reached no conclusion that satisfied him. Henri Bergson (French philosopher, 1859–1941) looked at mysticism in a philosophical context.

Mystics generally approach their practice with one of two assumptions: God is outside one's soul (and can be reached as the soul ascends to higher levels) or God is within one's soul (and can be reached by greater introspection). One example of those who consider the God outside the soul is the Gnostics. The **Society** of Friends (often called Quakers), by contrast, believe that God is within the soul.

Mysticism's esoteric nature also makes the subject difficult to describe. To get around this problem, mystics from the Roman Catholic and Islamic traditions used language based on human **love** to describe their mysticism and its process. Using this language, such mysticism might be described in the following way: the soul is purified, leading to enlightenment and a feeling of love for God; the soul enters into a union with God; after a period of contemplation, the soul reaches perfect union with God. Before reaching final and perfect union, the soul may go through a period of dark times and desertion by God. During this time, the mystic may have visions, hear voices, or feel ecstasy. What sets mysticism apart from many religions is that the mystic regards the experience leading to unification with the soul as reality which the mystic has sensed or perceived directly.

Several variations on mystical practice are known. Quietism, established by Miguel de Molinos, a priest who lived in the 1600s, emphasized a completely passive role for the soul and the elimination of self-consciousness. Madam Guyon (French mystic, 1648-1717) claimed that she was incapable of sin, since she had rid herself of self-consciousness. Quietism was condemned by the Pope in 1687. Theosophy occupied a broader scale than mysticism and went beyond the bounds of a relationship between God and soul to describe a complete relationship between man and nature. Jakob Boehme (German mystic and theosophist, 1575–1624) developed a system of theosophy; the Theosophical Society was created in 1875. Illuminism, a third mysticism which began in the eighteenth century, blended Christian elements with other-worldly elements, such as magic, alchemy, and the invisible. Notable illuminists included Emanuel Swedenborg (Swedish mystic and scientist, 1688–1772), who claimed to be able to talk to the dead, and Alessandro Cagliostro (adventurer and charlatan, 1743–1795), who claimed he could raise spirits. Seen as a reaction to the rational philosophies of the eighteenth century, illuminism continued to influence nineteenth-century literature.

Mystical topics continued to fascinate humans to the end of the twentieth century, with interesting consequences. For example, a 1991 *Scientific American* article reported that Soviet citizens were showing a marked increase in interest in the paranormal. According to Loren Graham, a Harvard University historian, the Soviet trend also indicated a decreased respect for science, which "would not bode well for a free society." Paul Kurtz, a philosopher at State University of New York/Buffalo, found the situation particularly interesting in the Soviet Union, and suggested that these citizens—due to previous media censorship—had not developed critical thinking which might otherwise cause them to examine paranormal phenomena more skeptically.

A 1996 *New Statesman* article noted a similar trend in western **culture**, a growing popularity of the supernatural and an increasing skepticism with science. Pat Kane suggested that in order for science to be better accepted by society, science must be truthful about its shortcomings, be open to ambiguity, and recognize the influence of society and culture. Particularly in the United States, a trend emerged toward the end of the twentieth century that demonstrated the rising popularity of the Kabbalah among non-Jews. The historically well-guarded Kabbalah contained the Jewish esoteric teachings and tradition.

A mystical trend in China was particularly threatening to that country's Communist regime in the late 1990s. Falun Gong, a **group** that practiced a moving meditation exercise, had become increasing popular and was practiced in the parks every morning. The group was founded in 1992 and claimed 100 million practitioners. The Chinese government, however, banned the practice in mid-1999 and rounded up and detained participants. According to a *Time* article, the Chinese government was threatened by the fact that so many people could assemble without government security being immediately aware of it.

MYTHS AND MYTHOLOGY

The original Greek meaning of the word *mythology* was the telling of stories. Some of the oldest and well known myths are Greek and Roman, but mythology pervades all cultures and other mythologies include: Jewish, Norse, Indian, Egyptian, and Mesopotamian. Myths may consist of fables (which instruct), etiological tales (which explain), and folktales (which entertain). However, the larger role of myth may be to lend explanation to a culture's construction of time or its history. Myth differs from history in that history is based on recent, documented happenings, and myths are often located in an imagined past without time. Myths tell the stories that explain the origins of people, animals, and plants; they may incorporate magic or supernatural elements.

Cultural myths may cover many topics. Creation myths, for example, range from an earth that is formed by gods to creation which is initiated by the action of animals. Many myths have a cyclical death and rebirth theme which can also be portrayed as repeated destruction and creation. A common mythological theme describes a Golden Age which humans once attained but have since fallen away from. Many myths include

Joseph Campbell was one of the most renowned scholars of world mythology *(AP/Wide World Photos, Inc.).*

a flood, which destroys and recreates the world. Other myths describe the beginnings of fire and the connection between the dead and the living.

The analysis of myth has led some to wonder why many myths are similar. Although some have posited that myths are simply inaccurate recountings of history, Greek scholars believed myths were exlanatory in some way and attempted to see reality in the myth's poetic images. A proponent of this approach was Theagenes of Rhegium (sixth century BC). The Stoics also attempted to make myth more real by giving the gods in Greek mythology moral principles and natural inclinations. Some interpreted myths through the context of animism, a **belief system** that assumed that all human and non-human elements inhabited the world in a spiritual form. Those who studied with animism in mind saw myth as a way to close the separation between human and non-human elements. Still others considered myth to arise for the purpose of moral teaching, and only later to become accepted as literal truth.

However, the study of mythology made significant advances in the 1800s. Sir James Frazer (Scottish anthropologist, classicist, and folklorist, 1854-1941) and Edward Burnett Tylor (English anthropologist, 1832-1917) were among the first to argue that myth was not a misrepresentation of history

but a social institution. In his book *The Golden Bough* (1890), Frazer claimed that myths reuse the themes of dying and re-generating vegetation to represent the fertility of nature. Carl Jung (Swiss psychoanalyst, 1875-1961), also noting repetition in mythology, claimed that it occurs because humans tend to recreate the same mythological symbols. Mircea Eliade (Ru-manian religious scholar, 1907-1986) believed that by focus-ing on creation, myths allowed people to return again and again to creative acts of their own.

As the study of myth progressed, focus eventually turned away from attempts to find similarities. Instead, atten-tion was given to the different contexts of myth. **Sigmund Freud** (Czech psychoanalyst, 1856-1939) believed that myths, like **dreams**, symbolized repressed fear and anxiety. **Bronislaw Malinowski** (Polish anthropologist, 1884-1942) claimed that myths validate common practices and institutions. Similarly, A. R. Radcliffe-Brown studied how myth reflects a society's beliefs and attitudes. **Claude Levi-Strauss** believed that myths inherently contain contrasts and that these oppositions have a universal quality.

In the late 1990s, Stanley Krippner, Ann Mortifee, and David Feinstein (in *Futurist,* March 1998) proposed that the state of the world necessitated the adoption of a new world myth. They used the historical example of Easter Island to por-tray the world's current direction. Easter Island occupants de-pleted their natural resources, and the society degenerated into violence and cannibalism. The authors suggested that the cur-rent societal myth (which they called the ''Grand Narrative of Progress'') needs to be replaced by a myth that includes sus-tainable growth. Such a myth was proposed by Sam Keen (American philosopher). According to Keen, bringing a myth of sustainability to the earth would involve: halting population growth, focusing on economic cooperation rather than compe-tition, considering nature as sacred rather than as raw material to be used, and distributing resources fairly between the rich and the poor. Keen's myth of sustainability also involved peaceful resolution rather than **war** and a mindshift toward a **community** focus rather than an individual focus. According to Krippner et al., humanity must adopt a new myth such as Keen's in order to ''shape the future'' and to prevent extinc-tion. Keen worked closely with Joseph Campbell (American mythologist, 1904-1987), who also argued that the current world's mythology (which promoted belonging and empathy for an ''in group'' and violence and **discrimination** for an ''out group'') needed to change.